THE
PSYCHOLOGY
OF
ATTITUDES

To
Robert, Ingrid, and Ursula Eagly
and
Bernard Chaiken

THE
PSYCHOLOGY
OF
ATTITUDES

ALICE H. EAGLY

Purdue University

SHELLY CHAIKEN

New York University

HBJ

Harcourt Brace Jovanovich College Publishers

Fort Worth   Philadelphia   San Diego   New York   Orlando   Austin   San Antonio
Toronto   Montreal   London   Sydney   Tokyo

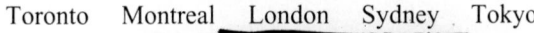

Publisher: Ted Buchholz
Acquisitions Editor: Eve Howard
Senior Project Editor: Dawn Youngblood
Production Manager: J. Montgomery Shaw
Senior Book Designer: Don Fujimoto

ISBN: 015-5-00097-7

Library of Congress Cataloging-in-Publication Number:
92-052667

Address for editorial correspondence:
301 Commerce Street, Suite 3700
Fort Worth TX 76102

Address for orders:
6277 Sea Harbor Drive
Orlando FL 32887
1-800-782-4479 outside Florida
1-800-433-0001 inside Florida

PRINTED IN THE UNITED STATES OF AMERICA

3 4 5 6 7 8 9 0 1 2   0 3 9 9 8 7 6 5 4 3 2 1

Copyright acknowledgments on page 766.

Preface

When we started writing this book, we envisioned a substantial volume that would provide review and analysis of virtually all domains of attitude theory and research that have been approached from a psychological perspective. We sketched out a plan for such a book without fully appreciating the challenges that we were posing for ourselves. The project proved to be formidable because of the richness and complexity of the work that attitude researchers have produced during the several decades during which the attitude construct has been important in psychology and throughout the social sciences. We could have reacted by becoming less ambitious and omitting certain areas or types of theory. We did not take this course because we were convinced of the value of a broader discussion of attitude theory and research. As a consequence, we have provided readers with a long book that covers a considerable range of topics, some of which encompass quite complex material.

We wrote this book with graduate students in mind as its primary audience, and also with concern for the needs of colleagues in psychology and related fields who seek an integrative overview of the research literature on attitudes. Yet we have endeavored to write clearly enough and with enough introductory detail that the book should be accessible to a wide audience. It is therefore possible that the book can be useful for undergraduates, when their background is relatively sophisticated and their motivation is especially strong.

The Psychology of Attitudes is centered on research in the field of social psychology, where the attitude construct has been preeminent since the very beginnings of systematic research. Yet research on attitudes is a shared endeavor in the social sciences, with especially important contributions from the fields of sociology, communications, political science, and marketing. Although our book considers some of the work carried out in these neighboring fields, our own disciplinary background in psychology leads us to focus on distinctively psychological issues. Nonetheless, the book should be useful to graduate students and researchers in related fields, because a very large portion of the existing literature on attitudes is in fact psychological in its focus. Much of this work can be applied in natural settings and should therefore also be interesting to practitioners, especially to those who design programs to change attitudes and behavior.

Evolving a plan for organizing such an extensive literature as that on attitudes was a major problem that we faced at the outset. One principle that immediately came to mind was organization in terms of theories, and another was organization in terms of issues and topics. We decided that neither of these schemes would serve our purposes. Instead we evolved a hybrid organization with broad topics as its most general organizing principle. Within these topics organization proceeds in part by theories and in part by research areas and issues. At its most general level, the organization consists of the following sequence of topics: the attitude concept, attitude measurement, attitude structure, the impact of attitudes on behavior, attitude change, resistance to change, and social influence. Yet, as all familiar with this field know, each of these broad areas of study encompasses a diversity of theories and many specific research questions. This diversity especially characterizes the study of attitude change. Consequently, our discussion of attitude change spans seven chapters, with an internal organization that proceeds in terms of types of theories (e.g., combinatorial models, process theories of persuasion), processes emphasized (e.g., cognitive processes, motivational processes), and phenomena examined (e.g., impact of behavior on attitudes). Within chapters, depending on the material at hand, organization proceeds in terms of theories or in terms of phenomena. This flexibility in organization is needed to accommodate the variability that exists in the manner in which work has developed. In some areas, for example, research has been formulated primarily in terms of theories (e.g., dissonance theory, attribution theory), and in other areas, attention has been directed primarily to one or more phenomena (e.g., the sleeper effect, the effects of mood on persuasion).

The book is presented in fourteen chapters. Persons relatively unfamiliar with attitude research would best read these chapters in sequence because they build on one another. For example, concepts pertaining to attitude structure, which are introduced in Chapter 3, reappear at many points during the book—for example, in Chapter 12, which includes discussion of how attitude structures can produce resistance to attitude change. Chapter 3, in turn, builds on our discussion of the attitude concept in Chapter 1 and on the consideration of attitude measurement provided in Chapter 2. Yet readers already generally familiar with the attitudes field will have little difficulty in reading single chapters. For the most part, single chapters can stand alone. To aid people who read only particular chapters, we provide a reasonable amount of cross-referencing throughout the book, so that it is easy to find closely related material that appears in other chapters.

This book does not promote a single theoretical perspective. Our own work has mainly concerned attitude change, where we of course have theoretical preferences. Nevertheless, we have tried to be even-handed in evaluating the theories that other attitude researchers have proposed. We have emphasized the contributions of the approaches more than their weaknesses and shortcomings. However, our analysis of theories and research is critical as well, because we believe that carefully considered criticism facilitates progress in scientific fields.

Writing this book has been an exciting and intellectually stimulating project for us. The work, although exhausting at times, can even be said to have exceeded our expectations as far as intellectual interest and challenge are concerned. When attempting to integrate research on various topics, we not only read new work but also reread much of the work that we had read in years past. We were very often impressed with the creativity and excellent thinking that had gone into attitude research. We experienced renewed admiration for this vital area of social scientific work, oriented to issues of utmost importance in natural settings.

Neither of us could have written this book alone. Our interaction and mutual criticism immensely improved the quality of what we wrote. One of us initially drafted each chapter, in consultation with the other. Then came the process of criticism and refinement. For some of the chapters drafted at an early point, this process continued over several years, as our understanding of the material deepened through discussion and additional thinking.

As we completed drafts of chapters, a number of colleagues read these drafts and commented on them. We are especially grateful to Mark Zanna, who read every chapter and produced for each one a substantial list of suggestions. His advice, enthusiasm, and encouragement were exceedingly helpful throughout the writing of the book. Wendy Wood, Blair Johnson, Diane Mackie, and Samuel Himmelfarb read several chapters and provided very helpful advice. Other colleagues provided comments on particular chapters. In particular, we thank Robert Abelson, John Bargh, Jerry Busemeyer, Donal Carlston, Joel Cooper, Susan Fiske, Joe Forgas, Tory Higgins, Klaus Jonas, Melvin Manis, Paul Nail, Patricia Pliner, Eliot Smith, Valerie Steffen, Wolfgang Stroebe, and James Tedeschi. In addition, the graduate students in our attitudes courses at Purdue and New York University read drafts of many of the chapters while the book was in preparation. Class discussions and informal discussion with our graduate students provided us with a great deal of useful feedback, particularly on issues of clarity and emphasis. Among these graduate students, we thank in particular Akiva Liberman and Steven Hines for their detailed comments. A seminar at the University of Tübingen also produced stimulating discussions of the issues covered in several of the chapters. We also thank those students and colleagues who merely told us that they had appreciated one or the other of the draft chapters, because their enthusiasm motivated us to carry on.

Samuel Himmelfarb wrote Chapter 2 of the book, on attitude measurement. Had we attempted to write this chapter ourselves, we certainly could not have approached the task with Sam's depth of knowledge of measurement issues. Moreover, we enjoyed the many discussions we had with him on attitude assessment as he developed his chapter and we developed the book. Sam's willingness to integrate some of the general themes of the book with his writing has allowed the chapter to fit in nicely with the rest of the book.

We thank the staff at Harcourt Brace Jovanovich for their fine work in publishing the book. In particular, we acknowledge Marcus Boggs, who was Acquisitions Editor when we signed our contract. We appreciate his support of our project and his patience as the writing of the book proceeded more slowly than we had anticipated. Eve Howard, Acquisitions Editor during the production of the book, and Catherine Townsend, Assistant Managing Editor, have been extremely helpful and very knowledgeable. Charles Naylor provided careful and thoughtful copy editing. Dawn Youngblood, Nicole Boyle, and Matt Ball also helped with the production of the book. Finally, we very much appreciate HBJ's decision to produce an advanced book at a moderate price in an attractive format.

Others who helped with the book were recruited by us for specific tasks. In particular, Stacey Lutz assisted us enormously in indexing the book. Stacey Otto and a long list of Purdue work-study students checked our references for accuracy and copied materials that we needed to study and review. Our secretaries at Purdue and New York University also provided excellent support with a variety of tasks related to producing the book.

Finally, for their abundant personal support and for their interest in our project, we thank our families, our good friends, and the graduate students with whom we have worked during the past few years. We would have been better companions to family members and friends had we not so often been working on the book. "I can't do it until the book is done," became an all-too-familiar refrain, and we thank family and friends for their patience with us. It is also true that our collaborative work with our graduate students and colleagues moved more slowly than it would have if we were not writing this book. Their consideration helped give us the peace of mind to complete this book. In addition, our universities, Purdue University and New York University, were generous in their support of our efforts. Our psychology departments offer a stimulating, collegial environment, excellent facilities, and good staff support. During the final stages of work on the book, one of us (AHE) was a visiting professor at the University of Tübingen and supported by a grant from the Deutsche Forschungsgemeinschaft. Without the excellent circumstances provided by these three universities, we would have found it much more difficult to write this book and certainly could not have maintained our research programs at the same time.

Alice H. Eagly
Shelly Chaiken

Contents

1

The Nature of Attitudes

Some people support social policies such as legalized abortion or welfare assistance for the poor, and others oppose such policies. Some people endorse ideologies such as feminism or political conservatism, whereas others disapprove of them. Some people are satisfied with their jobs, and others are not. Understanding individual differences such as these has been a longstanding interest of social psychologists, who use the concept of attitude to describe them. In the parlance of social psychology, a person who favors legalized abortion is viewed as holding a *positive attitude* toward this policy, whereas a person who is unfavorable toward legalized abortion is viewed as holding a *negative attitude* toward this policy.

Social psychologists have traditionally assumed that people's evaluations of social policies and other entities in their social environment have major consequences. Attitudes have been postulated to motivate behavior and to exert selective effects at various stages of information processing (e.g., attention, perception, retrieval). The discrepant attitudes that often characterize different subgroups of a society are believed to underlie the social conflict that political and social issues sometimes engender. Because of the importance accorded to attitudes as causes of individual phenomena such as attitude-consistent behavior and selective perception as well as of societal phenomena such as social conflict and discrimination, the concept of *attitude* has become a fundamental construct for most social scientists.

Although research on attitudes has been popular throughout the social sciences, the construct has been more central to social psychology than to any other academic discipline. Allport's (1935) assertion that "the concept of attitude is probably the most distinctive and indispensable concept in contemporary American social psychology" (p. 198) is as valid today as it was fifty years ago. Despite some fluctuations in the popularity of attitude research (see McGuire, 1986b), the attitude concept has remained in wide use in social psychology and has been the focus of extensive theoretical and empirical development since the 1920s. It is this social psychological literature on attitudes that is the principal subject matter of our book.

Definition of Attitude

The conceptual definition of attitude that we use in this book is the following: *Attitude is a psychological tendency that is expressed by evaluating a particular entity with some degree of favor or disfavor.* As we will explain in more detail, *psychological tendency* refers to a state that is internal to the person, and *evaluating* refers to all classes of evaluative responding, whether overt or covert, cognitive, affective, or behavioral.

This psychological tendency can be regarded as a type of bias that predisposes the individual toward evaluative responses that are positive or negative.

An attitude develops on the basis of evaluative responding: An individual does not have an attitude until he or she responds evaluatively to an entity on an affective, cognitive, or behavioral basis. Evaluative responding, whether it is covert or overt, can produce a psychological tendency to respond with a particular degree of evaluation when subsequently encountering the attitude object. If this tendency to respond is established, the person has formed an attitude toward the object. Moreover, a mental representation of the attitude may be stored in memory and thus can be activated by the presence of the attitude object or cues related to it.

In terms of this definition, attitude is one of many *hypothetical constructs* used by psychologists (MacCorquodale & Meehl, 1948). Like other hypothetical constructs, attitudes are not directly observable but can be inferred from observable responses. The relevant observations are responses that are elicited by (or occur in close conjunction with) certain stimuli. As a general strategy in psychology, when certain types of responses are elicited by certain classes of stimuli, psychologists infer that some mental state (e.g., mood, emotion, attitude) or disposition (e.g., personality trait) has been engaged. It is this state or disposition that is said to explain the covariation of stimuli and responses. Attitude is one of numerous implicit states or dispositions that psychologists have constructed to explain why people react in certain ways in the presence of certain stimuli. Whether psychologists use the term attitude or some other construct to account for an observed covariation between stimuli and responses depends on the conventions they have established for defining these inner states and dispositions. For this reason, it is important to discuss in more detail the type of inner state that is implied by defining attitude as an evaluative tendency.

Attitudes as Tendencies

One aspect of this inner state is inherent in our definition of attitudes as *tendencies*. In referring to an attitude as a tendency, we mean to imply that attitude is an internal state that lasts for at least a short time. As well as the term *tendency*, the term *disposition* has been used by psychologists to refer to such internal states, and, indeed, some social psychologists have used the term disposition (or predisposition) in their definitions of attitude (e.g., Ajzen, 1984; Chein, 1948; D. Davis & Ostrom, 1984). For example, Donald Campbell (1963), in a widely read discussion of the attitude construct, treated attitude as an *acquired behavioral disposition*, that is, a learned state that creates an inclination to respond in particular ways. In addition to attitude, Campbell considered concept, habit, schema, and many other constructs to be instances of acquired behavioral dispositions. However, because *disposition* is often used by psychologists and laypeople to describe personality, the term tends to connote states that endure for a relatively long period of time. Yet some attitudes are relatively temporary and changeable, especially if they are unimportant to the people who hold them (see Chapter 12). Because the term *tendency* does not necessarily imply a very long-term state, we prefer to use this term in our definition of the attitude construct, even though many attitudes, of course are quite enduring.

Despite Campbell's (1963) definition of attitudes as *acquired* and many other theorists' assumption that attitudes are learned (e.g., Allport, 1935; Doob, 1947), the idea that attitudes are learned is best not included in the definition of the attitude construct. Instead, the definition of attitude should allow for the possibility that some attitudes are unlearned insofar as they originate at least partially from some biological base. For example, McGuire (1985) has suggested that some attitudes may arise from genetic sources, and this suggestion has received some support from sociobiological research (e.g., Lumsden & Wilson, 1981) and behavior geneticists' studies of attitudes held by twins reared apart and together (e.g., Lykken, 1982; Waller, Kojetin, Bouchard, Lykken, & Tellegen, 1990). Moreover, Zajonc's (1980b, 1984; Zajonc, Murphy, & Inglehart, 1989) argument that affect can be triggered by purely sensory input without mediation by higher mental processes also supports the view that some attitudes may have an unlearned component. Even though the attitudes most widely studied by social psychologists probably are learned, it is unwise for theorists to rule out by definitional fiat attitudes that are not acquired from experience.

It should now be apparent that our definition of attitude in terms of a tendency that is expressed by evaluating an entity with some degree of favor or disfavor possesses advantages in terms of its generality. This definition readily encompasses attitudes that are learned or unlearned, enduring or changeable, and important or unimportant.

Attitudes as Evaluative

Our definition of attitude as an evaluative tendency presumes that attitude is an evaluative state that intervenes between certain classes of stimuli and certain classes of responses (see Figure 1.1). Moreover, this evaluative state is assumed to account for covariation between these stimuli and these responses. Explaining the important role of evaluation in this definition requires discussion of the classes of stimuli and responses whose covariation is ordinarily ascribed to attitudes.

We first consider the matter of responses. The responses that are regarded as attitudinal are evaluative in nature, where evaluation is defined as the imputation of some degree of goodness or badness to an entity. Because evaluation is the critical feature of attitudes, the observable responses relevant to inferring the presence of an attitude are therefore those that are regarded as revealing or expressing evaluation. Thus, evaluative responses are those that express approval or disapproval, favor or disfavor, liking or disliking, approach or avoidance, attraction or aversion, or similar reactions.

FIGURE 1.1.
Attitude as an
inferred state that
accounts for
covariation between
stimuli denoting
attitude object and
evaluative responses
to these stimuli.

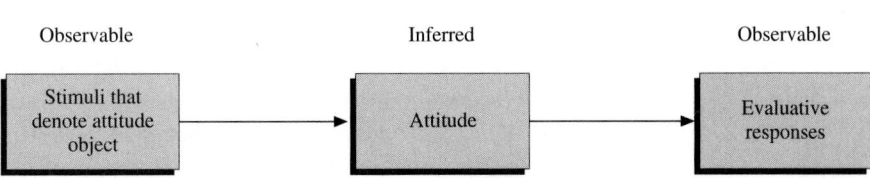

Evaluative responses and the tendencies that are presumed to underlie them are regarded as differing in *valence* or *direction*, because they can be bifurcated into positive and negative evaluations. In addition, evaluations of a given valence differ in *intensity* or *extremity*, when, for example, very positive evaluations are distinguished from moderately positive evaluations, which are, in turn, distinguished from slightly positive evaluations. Therefore, social scientists often represent the hypothetical state that they assume underlies evaluative responding as a location on a bipolar continuum or dimension that ranges from extremely positive to extremely negative and that includes a reference point of neutrality. The task of attitude measurement, which we consider in Chapter 2, is to order people in terms of this quantitative latent variable.[1]

Evaluation, the imputation of some degree of goodness or badness to an entity, can be regarded as one aspect of the ascription of meaning to entities in the environment. Although attitude researchers have been occasionally criticized for their emphasis on evaluation (McGuire, 1985), this tradition has remained very strong over the years. In the broadest sense, the utility of focusing on evaluation, in contrast to other types of meaning, can be judged by the body of research on attitudes, which is reviewed in this book. For example, to the extent that research has shown that people's behavior can be predicted from knowledge of the evaluative meaning that they assign to entities (see Chapter 4), the study of attitudes is important and properly is a major focus of social psychology.

Another testimony to the importance of evaluation is found in Charles Osgood's research on meaning (e.g., Osgood, Suci, & Tannenbaum, 1957). In numerous studies, Osgood and his colleagues had respondents rate a large number of concepts on adjectival scales, each defined by a pair of words of opposite meaning (e.g., hard-soft, weak-strong, excitable-calm, good-bad, active-passive, noisy-quiet, valuable-worthless). When people's ratings of concepts were submitted to the statistical procedure of factor analysis, three dimensions or components of meaning usually emerged and accounted for most of the variability in these ratings (see discussion of semantic differential in Chapter 2). The dimension typically accounting for the largest proportion of the total variance was labeled *evaluation* because it related very closely to ratings on scales such as good-bad and valuable-worthless. The two other dimensions that commonly emerged, but accounted for smaller proportions of variance in respondents' ratings, were labeled *potency* (relating to ratings on scales such as strong-weak and hard-soft) and *activity* (relating to ratings on scales such as active-passive and fast-slow). This research thus suggested that a large portion of the meaning that people assign to entities in their world is evaluative in nature. In fact, Osgood and his associates equated a concept's location on the evaluative dimension with attitude toward the concept (e.g., Osgood et al., 1957).

Attitude Objects

An evaluation is always made with respect to some entity or thing that is the object of the evaluation. This entity yields the stimuli that elicit the evaluative responses that are regarded as following from the attitude. In the language of social psychology, entities that are evaluated are known as *attitude objects*. Virtually anything that is discriminable can be evaluated and therefore can function as an attitude object. Some attitude objects are abstract (e.g., liberalism, secular humanism), and others are concrete (e.g., a chair, a shoe). Particular entities (e.g., my green pen) can function as attitude objects, as can classes of entities (e.g., ballpoint pens). Behaviors (e.g., playing volleyball) and classes of behaviors (e.g., participating in athletic activities) can also function as attitude objects. In general, anything that is discriminated or that becomes in some sense an object of thought can serve as an attitude object.

Although the attitude objects that could be studied are limitless, certain types of attitude objects have received a large share of the attention in research. Social scientists have most often examined attitudes toward social policies (e.g., offshore oil drilling, busing schoolchildren to achieve racial integration), ideologies (e.g., political liberalism and conservatism), and social groups, especially minorities (e.g., blacks, Hispanics). The terms *social attitudes* or *political attitudes* are somewhat loosely applied to such attitudes, which generally have implications for relations between social groups and are relevant to governmental policy as well. In addition, attitudes toward minority groups are often called *prejudice*, especially if these attitudes tend to be negative. Attitudes toward individual people, often called *liking* or *interpersonal attraction*, have also been studied a great deal. Attitude toward one's self is often termed *self-esteem* (M. Rosenberg, 1965). Attitudes toward relatively abstract goals or end states of human existence (e.g., equality, freedom, salvation) have also been of interest. These attitudes are usually termed *values*.[2] Although we do not make the conceptual distinction between values and attitudes that some theorists have made (e.g., Rokeach, 1968, 1980; M.J. Rosenberg, 1960a), we do endorse the importance of understanding the relations that exist between evaluations of more abstract and more concrete attitude objects (see Chapter 3).

An attitude object, even if it is a unique entity, is encoded from a variety of stimuli. For example, the attitude object *my brother* is in fact perceived through a variety of stimuli (his name, a picture of him, a letter from him, etc.). When the class of stimuli that denote my brother are observed to elicit responses expressing a certain degree of evaluation, it is inferred that I hold an attitude toward him described by some degree of favorability or unfavorability. In general, when observations of an individual show that a class of stimuli (those denoting a given attitude object) and a class of this individual's responses (those expressing a given degree of evaluation) covary, social scientists infer that this individual holds an attitude toward this entity.

Attitude is distinguishable from other concepts that also refer to people's implicit tendencies or dispositions because an attitude is inferred only when stimuli denoting an attitude object are observed to elicit responses expressing a given degree of evaluation. Some other concepts, such as personality traits, are considerably broader than attitude because the class of stimuli that allows observers to infer the disposition in question encompasses much more varied stimuli than those that denote a single entity. For example, because people characterized as high in the personality trait of *self-monitoring* are particularly sensitive to cues concerning the situational appropriateness of their behavior, they would respond to other people and a large variety of interpersonal events in distinctive ways (see M. Snyder, 1974, 1987). In addition, for trait-like concepts, the class of responses that is relevant to inferring the disposition is generally much broader

5

than evaluative responses. For example, behaviors relevant to self-monitoring include self-presentation, friendship choices, sexual behavior, and responsiveness to persuasive communications. Other concepts, such as mood, are broader on the stimulus side, but are primarily evaluative on the response side. For example, a depressed mood might be ascribed to people who react unfavorably (and perhaps relatively passively as well) to a variety of personal and impersonal entities. By specifying that attitude should be inferred only on the basis of evidence of evaluative responding to a circumscribed entity, social scientists give precise and distinctive meaning to the concept.

Our definition of attitude as an evaluative tendency represents consensual usage in modern social psychology. Yet, as shown by the long and interesting history of the attitude concept, this meaning evolved gradually over a number of decades (see Allport, 1935; D. T. Campbell, 1963; D. Fleming, 1967; McGuire, 1969). Gordon Allport's (1935) statement, no doubt the best known of the early definitions provided by psychologists, illustrates the more global nature of earlier definitions: "An attitude is a mental and neural state of readiness, organized through experience, exerting a directive or dynamic influence upon the individual's response to all objects and situations with which it is related" (p. 810). Although historically important, this definition does not satisfactorily distinguish an attitude from a trait, mood, habit, or other tendencies or dispositions of the individual because the key notion of evaluation is missing. Still, our definition shares an important feature with Allport's—namely, the idea that an attitude is an internal state that intervenes between stimuli and responses and affects these responses. Moreover, Allport's emphasis on an internal state (or, as we would term it, a psychological tendency) was consistent with earlier psychological conceptions of attitude (e.g., Spencer, 1862/1895; Titchener, 1910).

Attitude and Latent Processes

The treatment of attitude as a hypothetical construct or latent variable that is not directly observable raises the issue of whether attitude is merely a conceptual convenience—a construct invented by social scientists because it is a handy tool for describing a certain type of covariance between stimuli and responses. Alternatively, attitude might be meant to imply some sort of hidden mechanism or latent process that truly exists in people's minds but that cannot be observed directly, given current technology. Although the attitude concept has been used in both ways (see DeFleur & Westie, 1963), modern usage favors the latent process idea.

The latent process conceptualization implies that psychological and physiological events underlie attitudes, although the exact description of these events is a matter of continuing scientific debate. A minimal sense in which attitudes presume a latent process follows from the idea that the formation of an attitude entails the cognitive activity of assigning evaluative meaning. Zanna and Rempel (1984, 1988) regarded this cognitive activity as a type of categorization whereby an entity is assigned some degree of evaluative meaning; they defined attitude as the categorization of an entity along the evaluative dimension. However, from our point of view, attitude should not be defined as synonymous with this categorization process. Rather, attitude is more appropriately regarded as an outcome of this categorization process (or other processes). As a result of having evaluated an entity with some degree of favor or disfavor, the individual may assign evaluative meaning to the entity. The individual would then possess an attitude, which is an internal state that endures for at least a short period of time and presumably energizes and directs behavior.

The cognitive phenomena that comprise this internal state may include a mental representation of the tendency that results from having responded evaluatively to an entity. This mental representation is stored in memory and can be subsequently activated. These memorial processes are being considered by contemporary social psychologists whose interests center on the accessibility of this mental representation (e.g., Fazio, Sanbonmatsu, Powell, & Kardes, 1986). Other cognitive research pertains to the structural details of attitudes' mental representations. For example, a structural issue of current interest is the extent to which representations of attitudes are unipolar and thereby represent only one's own position or are bipolar and thereby represent opposing positions on issues (see Chapter 3). Further amplifying the latent processes underlying attitudes is psychophysiological research on the linkages of attitudes to physiological substrates (e.g., Cacioppo, Petty, & Geen, 1989; see Chapter 2).

Consideration of latent processes raises the issue of whether the abstract definition of attitude should be framed in terms of one or more of these latent processes. For example, Doob (1947) defined attitude as a learned, implicit anticipatory response and analyzed attitudes by means of Hullian learning theory constructs such as gradients of generalization and discrimination. Zanna and Rempel (1988) defined attitude in terms of the cognitive process of categorization. Currently popular is Fazio's (1986, 1989) definition of attitude as an association in memory between an attitude object and an evaluation.

From our perspective, such definitions are overly narrow because they presume a particular model of the processes that underlie attitudes. Thus, Doob's (1947) definition reflects the Hullian learning theory perspective popular in the 1940s. Not only does this definition follow from a particular understanding of the nature of learning (see Chein, 1948), but also the definition unwisely rules out the possibility that some attitudes are unlearned. Zanna and Rempel's (1988) definition illustrates the general perspective of cognitive psychology with its emphasis on categorization. Fazio's (1986) definition of attitude reflects an associative learning model that has been popular at various points in the history of psychology (see J.R. Anderson & Bower, 1973), most recently in contemporary associative network models of memory (e.g., J.R. Anderson, 1983; Bower, 1981; see Chapter 3). These and other definitions of attitude that invoke particular models of psychological process run the risk of going out of style as the focus of psychological theories evolves over the decades. Only a more general and abstract definition can endure among researchers and scholars, despite inevitable shifts in consensual opinion regarding what key processes underlie attitudes.

Definitions of attitude in terms of particular processes are sometimes thought to be more objective than more abstract definitions such as the one we advocate. This objectivity is believed to follow from aligning attitude with a specific process that can be assessed using accepted methods in psychological laboratories. Yet we view the more abstract definitions of attitude, such as our own evaluative tendency definition, as equally objective because they can also be assessed using objective indicators. By not equating attitude with a particular process, however, more abstract definitions allow attitudes to be assessed by means of a variety of indicators. These measurement issues are considered in Chapter 2.

Despite our preference for a general and abstract definition of attitude, narrower definitions are sensible within certain theoretical traditions and certainly can provide a useful guide to thinking about certain problems. For example, in terms of Fazio's (1986) definition of attitude as an object-evaluation association, the strength of this association becomes important, and strength is assessed by the latency of research subjects' evaluative responses to representations of the attitude object (see Chapter 4). Fazio's perspective suggests a theory of how attitudes guide behaviors—namely, that stronger attitudes are more likely to induce attitude-consistent behavior. Nonetheless, many other considerations are relevant to understanding the attitude-behavior relation, and the majority of these other factors cannot readily be coordinated to the association-ist conception of attitude (e.g., prior knowledge, see Chapter 4). In other domains of attitude research as well, the associationist definition would yield certain insights but fail to encompass others.

In summary, although we do not advocate defining attitude in terms of particular psychological processes, there is growing evidence of the reality of attitudes at the level of latent cognitive and physiological processes. This reality suggests that the concept of attitude is more than a mere conceptual convenience postulated to describe broad stimulus-response correlations. Indeed, scientific evidence demonstrating that latent processes underlie attitudes lends considerable plausibility to Allport's (1935) claim that an attitude is "a mental and neural state of readiness" (p. 810).

The Commonsense Concept of Attitude

In daily life, laypeople use the concept of attitude in approximately the same manner that social scientists use it. As we have explained, social scientists infer an attitude upon observation that evaluative responding is elicited by stimuli that denote a particular attitude object. Laypeople may also infer attitudes on the basis of such observations. For example, noticing that an individual sends money to organizations such as the Sierra Club, writes letters to legislative representatives supporting the regulation of industrial pollution, and circulates petitions opposing nuclear power plants and offshore oil drilling might lead observers to label this person an *environmentalist*. In this example the attitude object can be regarded as environmental preservation, an object that encompasses a number of specific social goals as well as organizations supportive of these goals. Similarly, noticing that an individual donates money to right-wing political candidates, endorses a tax code of limited progressivity, and opposes legal abortion might lead observers to label this person a *conservative*. In this example the attitude object can be regarded as political conservatism, which encompasses various social policies. Thus, in realms such as these, laypeople often infer that individuals' social attitudes account for the patterning of their evaluative behavior. Even though laypeople may spontaneously invoke the term attitude only occasionally (e.g., "she has a racist attitude"), the very common practice of using a label implying an attitudinal position (e.g., "she is racist") surely qualifies as an instance of attitudinal inference.

Occasionally the term attitude is used in the natural language in a broader sense than it is used in the social scientific literature. For example, in contemporary American slang, a person is sometimes described as "having attitude," when a trait of "pugnacity, sullen deviance, and self-confidence tipping over into arrogance" (Safire, 1990, p. 18) is implied. Similarly, when an uncooperative person is described as having a "bad attitude" or an "attitude problem," attitude has taken on personality-trait meaning, and no specific attitude object is indicated. Also, when athletes and their coaches emphasize "mental attitude" in explaining successful competition, there is no attitude object in the sense that we have defined it. Despite such exceptions, the formal definition of attitude presented in this book is consistent with most everyday usage of the term attitude as well as with the application of labels that imply attitudinal positions (e.g., "environmentalist"). This close link with the natural language is no doubt one source of the popularity and enduring appeal of attitudinal research in the social sciences. Yet social scientists have restricted the term attitude to a particular meaning and provided a formal and precise definition. Clear meaning of this sort is a great advantage because it fosters the development of measuring instruments and facilitates research.

Research on Inferences about Attitudes. In social psychology a moderate-sized research literature has accumulated concerning people's inferences about others' attitudes (see E. E. Jones, 1979; M. Ross & Fletcher, 1985). In typical experiments of this genre subjects are presented with statements of beliefs about an attitude object that were allegedly made by a target person (e.g., a student's essay containing the statement "Castro can and does attempt to take over our neighbors and convert them to communist sattelites [*sic*] by using methods of infiltration sabotage and subversion [*sic*]" Jones & Harris, 1967, p. 5). Subjects are then asked to infer this target person's attitude (i.e., toward Castro). In such research, subjects typically infer that target persons hold attitudes that are evaluatively consistent with their belief statements. Yet, these inferences are also influenced to some extent by information about the conditions under which the targets' statements were made. For example, if the target person is said to have been required to take the viewpoint expressed in the statements, subjects infer a less extreme attitude than they infer if the target is said to have made the statements of his or her own free will. In general, if situational cues convey that a target was constrained to take a particular viewpoint, perceivers are less likely to believe that the target's attitude corresponds to his or her expressed viewpoint, especially if having to advocate this position appears to have been an unforeseen consequence or in some other sense an unintended behavior (H. J. Fleming & Darley, 1989).[3] In related research on subjects' inferences concerning their *own* attitudes (e.g., Bem, 1972), people have been shown to use the evaluative implications of their own behaviors as a guide to inferring their attitudes (see Chapter 11). This research has also yielded important insights concerning the cues that people take into account in making attitudinal inferences.

Questions concerning the processes underlying attitudinal inferences are quite important in social psychology insofar as they are part of a more general interest in understanding people's causal attributions as well as their inferences about personal tendencies and dispositions (E. E. Jones & Davis, 1965; H. H. Kelley, 1967; L. Ross, 1977). In this book, attitudinal inferences are explored in some detail as aspects of persuasion and social influence (see Chapters 8, 11, and 13). These forms of attitude change require that people interpret and react to the statements that convey other people's attitudes.

In experiments on commonsensical attitudinal inferences, subjects are required to answer inquiries about attitudes. Thus, their spontaneous inferences are not examined.[4] Despite this limitation, this research is generally consistent with the claim that people commonly infer the attitudes that underlie their own and others' behavior. People may often think about themselves and others in terms of the attitudes that their public statements and overt behavior convey.

The Cognitive, Affective, and Behavioral Analysis of Attitudes

Classes of Evaluative Responses

As depicted in Figure 1.2, social scientists often have assumed that responses that express evaluation and therefore reveal people's attitudes can be or should be divided into three classes—cognition, affect, and behavior (e.g., D. Katz & Stotland, 1959; M. J. Rosenberg & Hovland, 1960). The *cognitive* category contains thoughts that people have about the attitude object. The *affective* category consists of feelings or emotions that people have in relation to the attitude object. The *behavioral* category encompasses people's actions with respect to the attitude object.

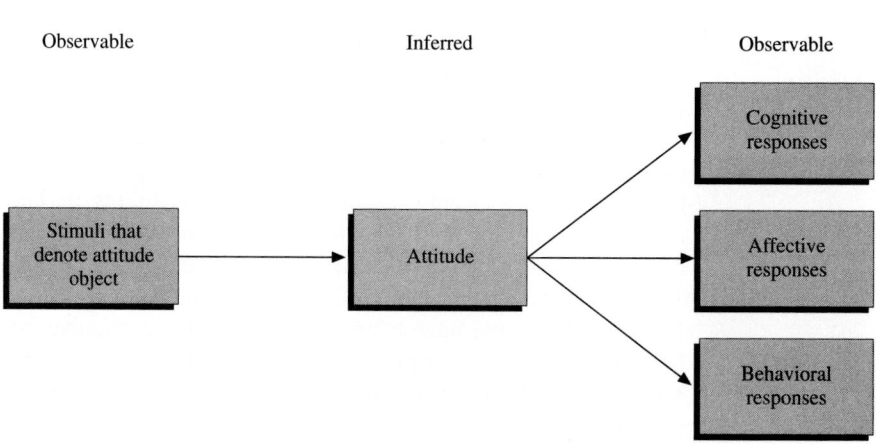

FIGURE 1.2. Attitude as an inferred state, with evaluative responses divided into three classes (cognitive, affective, and behavioral).

Evaluative responses of the cognitive type are thoughts or ideas about the attitude object. These thoughts are often conceptualized as *beliefs*, where beliefs are understood to be associations or linkages that people establish between the attitude object and various attributes (Fishbein & Ajzen, 1975). These cognitive evaluative responses include the covert responses that occur when these associations are inferred or perceived as well as the overt responses of verbally stating one's beliefs. The attributes that are associated with the attitude object express positive or negative evaluation and therefore can be located by psychologists on an evaluative continuum at any position from extremely positive to extremely negative, including the neutral point. For example, some people believe that nuclear power plants cause dangerous nuclear contamination. This belief links the attitude object with a negative attribute. Other people may believe that nuclear power plants provide cheap and abundant electricity. This belief links the attitude object with a positive attribute. Although we use the term *belief* to describe all thoughts that people have about attitude objects, evaluative responses that are cognitive in nature have sometimes been given a variety of other names, including cognitions, knowledge, opinions, information, and inferences. These terms are useful in some contexts but overlap considerably with the concept of belief that we emphasize.

A question that students raise from time to time is whether beliefs that are located at the neutral point of an evaluative dimension should be regarded as evaluative. Although a belief located at the neutral or zero point of the evaluative continuum might be considered non-evaluative by some psychologists, we prefer to regard it as expressing a degree of evaluation that happens to fall between positive and negative values. Although in theory beliefs can be truly non-evaluative in the sense that they express only other aspects of meaning (e.g., potency or activity), virtually all beliefs, including those that are heavily weighted with non-evaluative meaning, express evaluations to some degree. For example, the belief that the Purdue Boilermakers are *strong* expresses primarily potency but in addition expresses positive evaluation to some extent.

In general, people who evaluate an attitude object favorably are likely to associate it with positive attributes and unlikely to associate it with negative attributes, whereas people who evaluate an attitude object unfavorably are likely to associate it with negative attributes and unlikely to associate it with positive attributes. Formulating more exact models of this assumed relation between people's evaluations of attitude objects and their beliefs about these objects has been a focus of attitude research for a number of years. We consider this material in detail in Chapters 3 and 5.

Evaluative responses of the affective type consist of feelings, moods, emotions, and sympathetic nervous system activity that people experience in relation to attitude objects. These affective responses can also range from extremely positive to extremely negative and therefore can be located on an evaluative dimension of meaning. For example, when considering the concept of nuclear power plants, some individuals may experience a feeling or emotion of anger, and others may experience a feeling or emotion of hope and optimism. In general, people who evaluate an attitude object favorably are likely to experience positive affective reactions in conjunction with it and are unlikely to experience negative affective reactions; people who evaluate an attitude object unfavorably are likely to experience negative affective reactions and are unlikely

11

to experience positive affective reactions. We consider the importance of affective responding in various parts of this book (see Chapters 3, 9, and 10).

Social psychologists have sometimes regarded affect as isomorphic with evaluation itself and used the terms interchangeably (e.g., Fishbein & Ajzen, 1975; M. J. Rosenberg, 1960a; Zajonc & Markus, 1982). In agreement with some more recent treatments of attitude (e.g., Millar & Tesser, 1986a; Zanna & Rempel, 1984, 1988) and in recognition of the growing body of research on affect and emotion, we prefer to regard evaluation and affect as conceptually distinct. Thus, we treat evaluation as an intervening state that accounts for the covariation between classes of stimuli and the evaluative responses elicited by the stimuli, and we treat affect as one type of responding by which people may express their evaluations.

Evaluative responses of the behavioral (or conative) type consist of the overt actions that people exhibit in relation to the attitude object. Because these responses also range from extremely positive to extremely negative, they too can be located on an evaluative dimension of meaning. For example, in relation to nuclear power plants, some individuals may circulate petitions opposing their construction, and others may write letters to their legislative representatives calling for government support for their construction. In general, people who evaluate an attitude object favorably tend to engage in behaviors that foster or support it, and people who evaluate an attitude object unfavorably tend to engage in behaviors that hinder or oppose it.

Behavioral responses also can be regarded as encompassing *intentions* to act that are not necessarily expressed in overt behavior. For example, an individual may intend to circulate a petition tomorrow, but may or may not actually carry out this intention. Not surprisingly, positive evaluations are related to holding supportive intentions in relation to attitude objects, and negative evaluations to holding non-supportive intentions. More exact models of the ways that evaluations relate to behaviors and behavioral intentions are considered in detail in Chapter 4.

The division of evaluative responses into three categories has a very long history that, as McGuire (1969, 1985) has claimed, extends as far back as classical Greek and Hindu philosophers. Certainly the tradition has a long history in social psychological discussions of attitude, where the three classes of responses are sometimes referred to as the three *components* of attitudes (see D. Katz & Stotland, 1959; Krech & Crutchfield, 1948; M. J. Rosenberg & Hovland, 1960; M. B. Smith, 1947; Triandis, 1971). Given the penchant of both psychologists and philosophers to think in terms of this trinity of cognition, affect, and behavior, the distinction must be accorded a certain heuristic value. However, to be worth preserving in modern attitude theory, the distinction should have more than heuristic value. The division of evaluative responses into three components must have some discriminant validity (D. T. Campbell & Fiske, 1959). Thus, despite the positive correlations between cognition, affect, and behavior that follow from the fact that responses of all three types can be located on the common underlying dimension of evaluation, responses within each of the three categories should relate more strongly to other responses within that category than to responses in the other two categories. That is, as Ajzen (1988) also has argued, each of the three components should possess unique variance not shared with the other two. Fortunately, several empirical studies have examined these issues.

In initial studies examining the tripartite model of attitudinal responding, subjects completed a number of instruments designed to provide questionnaire measures of cognitive, affective, and behavioral responses elicited by an attitude object, and correlations within and between types of measures were examined (see reviews by Breckler, 1984a, 1984b). Studies of this type by Kothandapani (1971) and Ostrom (1969) yielded three dimensions. However, more sophisticated data analysis techniques involving structural equation analysis (see Bentler, 1980; Kenny, 1979, 1985) have subsequently been applied to these data sets by Bagozzi (1978) and Breckler (1984b), both of whom concluded that Ostrom's (1969) data weakly supported the three-dimensional model, whereas Kothandapani's (1971) data failed to support it. In addition, on the basis of analyses of questionnaire measures of attitude (excluding measures of self-reported behaviors and behavioral intentions) reported by Fishbein and Ajzen (1974), Bagozzi and Burnkrant (1979, 1985) argued for a two-dimensional model representing affect and cognition, whereas Dillon and Kumar (1985) argued that alternative models conceptually consistent with the one-component model fit these same data.

Breckler (1984a) took the view that these tests of the tripartite model were insufficient because they relied on verbal measures of responses of the three classes and presented subjects with only symbolic representations of the attitude objects (i.e., a verbal label). To correct these deficiencies Breckler had subjects respond to an attitude object (a snake) that was physically present and assessed their cognitive, affective, and behavioral responses using both verbal and nonverbal measures. Analysis of the resulting data found a three-dimensional, but not a one-dimensional, model statistically acceptable. In a second study, Breckler had subjects respond to the verbal label of "snake" and obtained only verbal self-reports of the three classes of responses. Although in this study the tripartite model was rejected because it did not sufficiently account for the systematic variability in the data, it did fit the data somewhat better than a one-dimensional model.

Given these various findings, it appears that a definitive empirical determination of the dimensionality of evaluative responses is unlikely in the near future. To date, the outcomes of statistical analyses of dimensionality appear to be affected by methods of data analysis (including the particular version of LISREL or other computer programs that investigators use to perform structural analyses) and the details of the particular models that investigators propose (see Bagozzi & Burnkrant, 1979, 1985; Dillon & Kumar, 1985). More important, Breckler's (1984a) research suggests that dimensionality may vary as a function of the direct or indirect mode of presentation of the attitude object and the verbal or nonverbal nature of the response measures. In addition, different types of attitude objects may produce different sorts of reactions, and, in this regard, Breckler's choice of an attitude object (a snake) known to provoke strongly fearful reactions in some people may have been important to insuring a multidimensional outcome in his research. These issues have yet to be explored in depth. Suffice it to say that, at the present, evidence supports the empirical separability of three classes of evaluative responses under some but certainly not all circumstances.

Because cognitive, affective, and behavioral responses are often not empirically distinguishable as three classes, the three-component terminology is overly strong and is inappropriate in its implication that the three types of responses are generally distinct, that is, distinguishable in most people most of the time (see Fishbein, 1967c; Fishbein & Ajzen, 1974). A formal three-component model will probably be rejected for many, perhaps even most, attitudes. Nonetheless, the tripartite distinction provides an important conceptual framework, one that allows psychologists to express the fact that evaluation can be manifested through responses of all three types, regardless of whether the types prove separable in appropriate statistical analyses. Use of the terms cognitive, affective, and behavioral should help researchers evolve an understanding of the conditions under which attitudes truly have varying numbers of components. In short, the tripartite terminology continues to be a convenient language for thinking about attitudinal responding. Therefore, in this book we refer to three *classes of evaluative responses* but eschew the formality of a three-component model of attitudes.

Because of our limited support of the tripartite language, we do not agree with the details of Fishbein's (e.g., 1967c) unqualified endorsement of a one-component model and rejection of a three-component model. Fishbein argued that only a unidimensional model of attitude is acceptable because all measures of attitudes, whether based on cognitive, affective, or behavioral responding, order individuals along an evaluative continuum. Fishbein's point that all measures of attitude assess evaluation is indeed valid and is in fact noncontroversial: Attitude theorists have usually regarded evaluative responses of all three types as expressing degree of evaluation. The cognitive and behavioral components of attitudes have ordinarily been thought to reflect location on a common evaluative dimension, just as the affective component has. Nevertheless, the assumption that these responses can be divided into three classes implies, as we have noted, the testable hypothesis that correlations between responses in the same class are higher than correlations between responses in different classes. Even in circumstances in which this hypothesis is supported, correlations between responses of different classes are positive because these responses are manifestations of a position on a common underlying evaluative continuum. The dimensionality of attitudinal responses thus remains an important issue for empirical and theoretical development.

Classes of Antecedents of Attitudes

Consonant with the idea that attitudinal responses can be divided into three classes is the assumption that attitudes have three different types of antecedents (see Figure 1.3). Indeed, the idea that attitudes are formed through cognitive, affective, and behavioral processes has been proposed in numerous discussions of attitudes (e.g., Breckler, 1984a; A. G. Greenwald, 1968; Insko & Schopler, 1967; Triandis, 1971; Zanna & Rempel, 1988).

The assumption that attitudes derive from a process of cognitive learning is implicit in much of the research that we review in this book and explicit in some theoretical perspectives. A cognitive learning process is assumed to occur when people gain information about the attitude object and thereby form beliefs. Information is gained by direct experience with attitude objects and by indirect experience with them. For example, one may learn directly about the attributes of a new brand of soft drink by

FIGURE 1.3.
Attitude as a
product of cognitive,
affective, and
behavioral
processes.

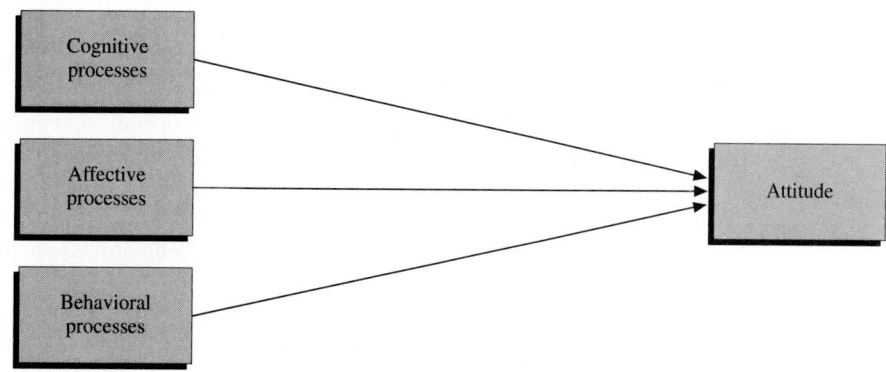

drinking it. Alternatively, one may learn indirectly by watching a television advertisement that describes the drink's taste and other qualities or by observing a friend's reaction to tasting the drink. One's attitude is assumed to derive from the favorability of the beliefs that are acquired directly or indirectly. Whether beliefs are acquired by direct or indirect experience with the attitude object is one determinant of the extent to which people's attitudes predict their behavior (see Chapter 4). In addition, the general idea that attitudes derive from the information that people gain about attitude objects, especially from indirect experience with them, is particularly important in research on persuasion (see Chapters 6, 7, and 8). In such research, message recipients are presented with information about an attitude object. To the extent that recipients accept this information, they are assumed to form new beliefs from which a new or changed attitude is derived. More formal development of the idea that attitudes stem from beliefs about attitude objects has been provided by expectancy-value and other algebraic models of the nature of attitudes (see Chapters 3 and 5).

The claim that attitudes are formed on the basis of affective or emotional experiences has appeared in different forms in the literature on attitudes (see Chapter 9). For example, in one of its earlier manifestations the assumption that attitude formation is an affective process appeared in the classical conditioning model of attitude change (e.g., A. W. Staats & Staats, 1958). From this perspective, attitude is a product of the pairing of an attitude object (conditioned stimulus) with a stimulus that elicits an affective response (unconditioned stimulus). As a result of repeated association, the attitude object comes to elicit the affective response, and an attitude is thereby formed. For example, stimuli repeatedly associated with the onset of electric shock would acquire negative evaluation via this affective process, and stimuli paired with the offset of electric shock would acquire positive evaluation (e.g., Zanna, Kiesler, & Pilkonis, 1970). In a different and more recent manifestation of the idea that affective responding

15

underlies attitudes, Zajonc (1980b, 1984) argued that "preferences" (i.e., evaluations) are based primarily on affective responses, which are often quite immediate and are not mediated by thinking about the attributes of attitude objects.

The idea that evaluations are based on behavioral responses was central in research by Bem (e.g., 1972), who argued that attitudes derive from past behavior (see Chapter 11). By this *self-perception* account of attitude formation, which we already acknowledged in our discussion of attitudinal inferences, people tend to infer attitudes that are consistent with their prior behavior. However, Bem also argued that people take into account the conditions under which they perform behaviors, with the result that they form attitudes more readily on the basis of behavior when they do not think that external forces compelled them to engage in the behavior. In addition, learning theorists have described attitudes as deriving from behavioral responses. In the stimulus-response behavior theory tradition, when overt behaviors (or covert cognitive responses) elicited by attitude objects are rewarded or punished, implicit evaluative responses occur (e.g., Doob, 1947; Hovland, Janis, & Kelley, 1953). As we noted in our discussion of Doob's definition of attitude, it is these implicit evaluative responses that learning theorists have regarded as attitudes.

Implications of the Cognitive, Affective, and Behavioral Analysis

We have asserted that attitudes are manifested in cognitive, affective, and behavioral responses and formed on the basis of cognitive, affective, and behavioral processes. This tripartite view of attitudinal responding and attitude formation raises a number of important questions.

One question is whether attitudes must have all three of these aspects, either at the point of attitude formation or at the point of attitudinal responding. Although the older three-component definitions of attitude may have implied that these three aspects must be in place in order for a true evaluative tendency to emerge, our answer to this question is a decided *no*. Attitudes can be formed primarily or exclusively on the basis of any one of the three types of processes. Individuals may, for example, learn about certain attitude objects entirely on the basis of reading. Under such circumstances of indirect experience with an attitude object, they may not engage in behaviors relevant to the attitude (except the behavior of reading) when the attitude is being formed, and the remote nature of the contact with the attitude object probably decreases the likelihood that emotional responses will be triggered by the stimuli representing the attitude object. In such instances the attitude would be formed on the basis of acquiring beliefs about the attitude object. Other attitudes may be formed primarily by affective or behavioral processes or by a mix of processes. Especially when people directly encounter attitude objects, attitude formation probably occurs by a variety of processes (see Zanna & Rempel, 1988).

It is also not universal that people respond to attitude objects by cognitive, affective, and behavioral reactions. People may hold beliefs about some attitude objects but never engage in overt behaviors with respect to them or have emotional reactions.

Other attitudes may be emotion laden or action inducing in the sense that they induce primarily affective or behavioral responses.

Another issue related to the limited tripartite idea that we have espoused is the extent to which the three classes of evaluative responses are consistent with one another. In this context, consistency means that people tend to express about the same degree of evaluation of an attitude object through responses of each of the three classes. As we explained in our discussion of the dimensionality of attitudes, very high consistency between classes of evaluative responses implies that appropriate statistical analyses of an attitudinal domain would yield a one-dimensional solution. To the extent that classes of responses display some inconsistency, a multidimensional solution would be obtained. As we have indicated, statistical analyses of attitudes have yielded solutions of varying dimensionality. Thus, responses associated with some attitudes are quite consistent across response classes, and responses associated with other attitudes are somewhat less consistent. Eiser (1987) suggested that cognitive, affective, and behavioral responses will be evaluatively consistent to the extent that all three response classes contributed to the initial formation of the attitude. Breckler and Wiggins (1989a) presented findings suggesting that cognitive and affective facets of attitudes are more consistent to the extent that attitude domains are familiar and likely to be thought about frequently (e.g., abortion, nuclear weapons). Although other research has examined such consistency issues, most of this research is somewhat limited in modern terms because of the earlier tendency to view evaluation and affect as synonymous, with the consequence that only the consistency between affect (i.e., general evaluation) and cognition was investigated (see Chapters 3, 5, and 10).

A largely unexplored issue is the extent to which the cognitive, affective, or behavioral processes by which an attitude is acquired relate to the cognitive, affective, or behavioral responses that the attitude object subsequently elicits. It is possible that some sort of matching tends to occur (Millar & Tesser, 1986a; see Chapter 4). For example, an attitude acquired via a cognitive route might tend to elicit primarily cognitive responses, one acquired via an affective route might tend to elicit primarily affective responses, and one acquired via a behavioral route might tend to elicit primarily behavioral responses. However, any strong one-to-one relationships of this sort are quite unlikely. As suggested in particular by research on the cognitive-affective interface that we discuss in Chapter 9, different classes of evaluative responses impinge on one another and exist in what might be described as a cooperative, synergistic relation. One may, for example, acquire beliefs about an attitude object, think about this knowledge, and thereby decide upon a course of action or generate an emotional response. A cognitively based attitude thus feeds back on other psychological processes and gives the attitude behavioral and affective bases. Similarly, one's initial response to another person may be emotional (e.g., sexual attraction). Yet the positive attitude produced on this basis may lead to a course of action (e.g., asking the individual to dinner) or influence perception of the person's attributes (e.g., the formation of beliefs that the individual is warm and friendly). Understanding how modes of attitude formation relate to subsequent evaluative responding is clearly very challenging, and aspects of this issue are considered at various points in this book.

————— ## Attitudes as Schemas

A useful perspective for thinking about attitudes is to regard them as one type of *schema*, which is a broader classification of cognitive structures that has been investigated quite extensively by cognitive psychologists and cognitive social psychologists. Although the exact meaning of this popular concept has varied somewhat (see Landman & Manis, 1983; Markus & Zajonc, 1985), schemas are typically said to be "cognitive structures of organized prior knowledge, abstracted from experience with specific instances" (Fiske & Linville, 1980, p. 543). Exploration of attitudes as a type of schema highlights the implications of attitudes for information processing. In applying the schema construct to the social world, social psychologists have built upon the theories and methods that cognitive psychologists developed to account for the representation and processing of nonsocial stimuli. The resulting body of knowledge on social cognition is closely related to some of the work that has traditionally been carried out by investigators of attitudes. Moreover, treating attitude as a type of schema has much in common with a considerably older tradition of regarding attitude as one type of *frame of reference* (A. L. Edwards, 1941; J. M. Levine & Murphy, 1943; M. Sherif, 1936; W. S. Watson & Hartmann, 1939). This tradition also was allied with cognitive psychology—in particular, with F. C. Bartlett's (1932) demonstrations of the influence of cultural and individual factors on remembering.

As we have noted, there is consensus that schemas are cognitive structures that represent past experience in a stimulus domain by a higher order or abstract cognitive structure. In this respect, the schema construct resembles the cognitive aspect of attitudes. Thus, experience with attitude objects is assumed to lead people to associate them with attributes or more generally to think about attitude objects. These thoughts are stored and, as we explain in greater depth in Chapter 3, can be regarded as cognitive structures that organize prior knowledge.

The assumption that attitudes have affective and behavioral aspects, in addition to cognitive, is central to the theoretical framework that we have introduced. Paralleling attitude theorists' assumptions about affect, some schema theorists (e.g., Fiske & Linville, 1980) have asserted that schemas "elicit affect as well as inference" (p. 522). However, other schema theorists (e.g., S. E. Taylor & Crocker, 1981) have preferred to limit schemas to their cognitive aspects. Paralleling attitude theorists' attention to behavioral manifestations of attitudes is schema theorists' assumption that schemas have behavioral consequences. However, despite the universality of this assumption, the impact of schemas on behavior has been explored relatively little. In contrast, the relation between attitudes and behavior has been studied extensively (see Chapter 4).

Given that the cognitive aspects of attitudes strongly resemble those of schemas and the assumptions made about the affective and behavioral manifestations of attitudes partially overlap assumptions made about schemas, it is important to emphasize the sense in which the two concepts are distinguishable. The concepts differ because the term attitude refers to evaluation, whereas the term schema has been used more broadly. Because attitude pertains to evaluation and not to all aspects of mental representations, it is possible to regard attitude as a subtype of the more general schema concept. Nonetheless, the focus of attitude researchers on evaluations will likely maintain some separation between social cognition and attitude research. Because evaluative structures are very likely to be infused with affect and to energize and direct behavior, this concentration of attitude researchers on evaluations may be advantageous with respect to some kinds of predictions, especially those regarding behavior. Cognitions not laden with good-versus-bad meaning are probably much less likely to elicit emotions or energize behavior. Thus, it is with good reason that many schema theorists have been cautious about making specific claims concerning the affective and behavioral manifestations of schemas.

The gain from thinking about attitudes as a type of schema comes from the link that is forged with existing knowledge about the impact of schemas on cognitive processing. Schemas have been held to influence all aspects of information processing (see review by Markus & Zajonc, 1985). On the input or encoding side, schemas have been shown to affect the attention given to information as well as the encoding and judgment of this information. Evidence for this impact on attention and encoding comes from a variety of studies showing that comprehension and memory for stimuli are improved if some label, category, or concept is also presented to enable people to organize the stimuli in some way (e.g., Bransford & Johnson, 1972). Presumably the label, category, or concept activates a schema, which allows people to comprehend and organize the stimuli in its terms.

On the output or decoding side of information processing, schemas are held to have a selective effect on the retention, retrieval, and organization of memory. Under some circumstances, people have better memory for stimuli that fit their schemas than for stimuli that do not fit, and under other circumstances, schema-inconsistent information is particularly memorable (see Higgins & Bargh, 1987; Stangor & McMillan, 1992). Thus, the effects of schemas on memorial processes appear to be somewhat complex. Very similar issues of selectivity in information processing have long been an interest of attitude researchers, who have claimed that attitudes influence attention to and interpretation of attitude-relevant information as well as memory for this information. These issues are considered primarily in Chapter 12.

Attitudes and Motivational Issues

The view that schemas are useful because they allow people to represent and organize the information they encounter echoes one of the important themes of attitude theorists' analyses of the functions or needs that attitudes serve for individuals. For example, in his taxonomy of four types of functions relevant to attitudes, Daniel Katz (1960; Katz & Stotland, 1959) asserted that one of the functions attitudes serve is to organize and simplify people's experience. Katz named this function the *knowledge function*. Katz's thinking about this aspect of attitudes resembles the view that schemas are needed to enable people to make sense out of their experience.

Katz (1960; Katz & Stotland, 1959) proposed three additional functions that attitudes may serve. His *adjustment* or *utilitarian* function presumed that attitudes enable people to maximize rewards in their environment and to minimize punishments. As would be expected from this function's learning-theory heritage, attitudes satisfy this function by means of a presumed tendency for people to form favorable attitudes toward stimuli associated with satisfaction of needs and unfavorable attitudes toward stimuli associated with punishment. According to Katz's *ego-defensive* function, attitudes also enable people to protect themselves from unpleasant realities. Theorizing about this function derived from psychoanalytic ideas about defense mechanisms. Finally, according to Katz's *value-expressive* function, attitudes allow people to express their personal values and self-concept. Theorizing about this function derived from ego psychology and other varieties of personality theory.

The functions proposed by Katz (and by other theorists; see M. B. Smith, Bruner, & White, 1956) presume that certain general needs or motives energize and direct attitudinal functioning. The particular needs and motives that are considered by attitude researchers at any point in time tend to derive from the type of theory that is popular in social psychology and in psychology more generally. For example, Katz's utilitarian function reflected the importance of learning theory, and his ego-defensive function reflected the impact of psychoanalytic theory. Both of these theories were much more popular in the 1950s, when Katz developed his typology, than they are now. Because cognitive theorizing has been dominant in social psychology and in psychology more generally during recent years, much current thinking about motivational issues by attitude researchers has the cognitive flavor of Katz's knowledge function. Cognitive accounts of motivation have included, in addition to the idea that people are motivated to simplify and organize stimuli, the idea that people desire to reduce inconsistencies between related cognitions. Also, as theories about the self-concept and self-presentation have become increasingly important in social psychology (e.g., A. G. Greenwald, 1980; Schlenker, 1980; Steele, 1988), principles somewhat like those which Katz included in the value-expressive function have gained adherents in some types of attitude research. Accounts of motivation emphasizing that attitudes facilitate the formation and maintenance of social relationships have also been important in attitude research (e.g., Kelman, 1958; Smith, Bruner, & White, 1956). In addition, as noted in our discussion of the attitude construct, attitudes are themselves assumed to energize and direct behavior, and thus to have motivational implications in and of themselves, quite apart from broader motives that they may serve. Consideration is given to these motivational themes in Chapter 10 and elsewhere in this book. Indeed, motivation is an increasingly important component of contemporary research on attitudes.

——— Notes ———

1. Whether people represent their own attitudes as a point on a continuum is a considerably more subtle issue that we address in Chapter 3. Here we refer only to social scientists' common practice of defining attitudes operationally as points along an evaluative continuum (see Chapter 2).

2. For example, Rokeach (1968, p. 160) defined value as "an enduring belief that a specific mode of conduct or end-state of existence is personally and socially preferable to alternative modes of conduct or end-states of existence." Evaluation is the central feature of this statement, which is thus consistent with our definition of attitude.

3. Yet the major issue in this research tradition is whether observers sufficiently take into account the situational constraints that may induce people to take attitudinal positions. According to the widely cited concept of *fundamental attribution error* (L. Ross, 1977), perceivers insufficiently weight situational constraints in their interpretations of others' behavior and overestimate the importance of personal tendencies and dispositions, which include personality traits and abilities as well as attitudes.

4. Although research by Winter and Uleman (1984) and by Winter, Uleman, and Cunniff (1985) has examined the spontaneity of people's inferences about personality traits, analogous research on attitudinal inferences has yet to be conducted.

2

The Measurement of Attitudes

SAMUEL HIMMELFARB

Attitudes are not directly observable; their existence can only be inferred from overt responses or *indicators*. Attitudes as evaluative tendencies manifest themselves in three general classes of indicators: *cognitive*, *affective*, and *behavioral*. This chapter considers how responses belonging to the three classes have been or could be used to measure attitudes.

The chapter is organized into several sections. We begin with a general discussion of basic concepts and ideas about measurement. The next section presents some of the more common ways attitude scales are constructed. Most of these scaling techniques are quite general and may be used to construct attitude measures within any of the three indicator classes. This section is followed by a discussion of attitude measures that have been linked to a particular class of indicators and that generally have not been based on formal scaling models. Finally, we discuss various ways of assessing the reliability and validity of attitude measures and some of the factors that influence reliability and validity.

Basic Concepts and Ideas

Measurement

S. S. Stevens (1946, 1951), one of the founders of modern measurement theory, defined measurement as the assignment of numbers to objects or events according to rules. Measurement, however, requires more than number assignment by some rule. Our real number system has certain properties such as order (e.g., $4 > 2$), difference (e.g., $4 - 3 = 1$), and ratio (e.g., $6/2 = 3$). The aim of measurement is to assign numbers to objects so that the properties of the numbers that are assigned reflect the relations of the objects to each other on the attribute being measured (e.g., attitude). For example, if Person A has twice as much of the relevant attribute as Person B, we would like to assign numbers to A and B that reflect that 2-to-1 relationship.

Levels of Measurement. The relations between the real numbers assigned to objects in the measurement process may or may not reflect the actual relations that exist between the objects on the attribute being measured. This fact led Stevens to the concept of *levels of measurement*, or types of scales. In *nominal scales*, the lowest level, the numbers assigned to objects reflect only *equivalence* versus *difference*. Objects that are the same on the attribute are given the same number, and objects that are

FIGURE 2.1. Two scalings that have the same ordinal properties.

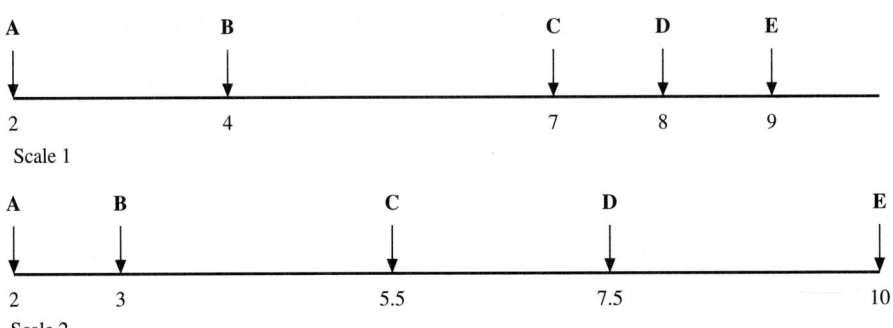

different are given different numbers. For example, different numbers are assigned to ball players to reflect the fact that they are different players. The numbers assigned stand for the players' names (hence, "nominal") and imply nothing about their relative abilities. Similarly, the coding of all males as "1" and all females as "2" would yield a nominal scale of gender that reflects only one property of the number system, equivalence or difference.

The assignment of numbers on the basis of difference versus equivalence is rarely the goal of scale construction. Yet, the categorization of stimuli into same or different classes is fundamental to scaling because we must be able to distinguish between the objects being scaled. When we can also determine whether one object has more or less of the attribute than another, an *ordinal scale* can be constructed. For example, if we can discern that Person A has a less positive attitude than Person B and that Person B has a less positive attitude than Person C, numbers can be assigned to A, B, and C that reflect this ordering. Figure 2.1 illustrates an attitudinal dimension on which five persons have been located and assigned numbers that reflect the ordered relations among their attitudes. The values assigned in Scale 1 of Figure 2.1 are arbitrary and reflect only the ordinal properties of our scale. Persons A through E could have been assigned other values as long as the numbers assigned preserved the ordinal relationship between their attitudes. Such an alternative scaling is also shown in Figure 2.1 (Scale 2). A change from one set of values to another, even the arbitrary changes implemented in Figure 2.1, is called a *monotonic transformation*, if it preserves the ordering among the objects that are assessed. The two scales shown in Figure 2.1 thus preserve the ordinal relations among the persons, but not the distances between them on the attitudinal dimension.

When we can ascertain not only the order but also the exact size of the differences between objects, an *interval scale* of measurement can be constructed. To determine

TABLE 2.1

Measured Distances Between Persons and Alternative Interval Scalings

Person	Distance between persons	Scaling 1	Scaling 2	Scaling 3
A		0	0.0	–1.0
}	2			
B		2	1.0	0.0
}	1			
C		3	1.5	0.5
}	2			
D		5	2.5	1.5
}	1			
E		6	3.0	2.0

how much Person A differs from Persons B and C, a *unit of measurement* is required. That is, we need some standard device or unit that can be used to measure the distances between A, B, and C. The size of the unit of measurement can be arbitrary, just as it is arbitrary whether height is measured in inches or centimeters, or temperature in degrees Fahrenheit or Celsius. Suppose we had such a unit and observed the differences shown in column 2 of Table 2.1. From that table, we know that Persons A and B differ by 2 units, that Persons A and C differ by 3 units, and so on. Person A could then be assigned the number 0, B the number 2, and C the number 3, and so on (see Scaling 1 in Table 2.1). Yet, it would also be possible to assign to Persons A through E the numbers indicated in Scaling 2 and Scaling 3 of Table 2.1. Scaling 2 differs from Scaling 1 only in a change of the unit of measurement from the difference of 1 between B and C to the difference of 2 between A and B. The location of the zero point on an interval scale also is arbitrary. The numbers assigned in Scaling 3 differ from those in Scaling 2 in that B instead of A was assigned the value of 0. Because the zero point and unit of measurement in an interval scale are arbitrary, any system of number assignment can be changed to another one by a *linear* transformation.[1] Scalings 1, 2, and 3 differ from each other by linear transformations but preserve the basic distance relationships between persons that are given in column 2 and from which the scalings were derived.

If objects are measured on an interval scale, it is possible to make general statements about the *differences* between objects on the scale. For example, given the numbers assigned in Scaling 1 of Table 2.1, we can say that the difference between D's attitude and C's attitude (2) is twice the difference between B's attitude and C's attitude (1). This statement is true in all three of the scalings (or in any other linear transformation of them). However, it is not possible to say that D's attitude is 2.5 times more favorable than B's attitude because this statement would not be true across different interval scalings of the attitude such as those shown in Table 2.1.[2]

Ratio scale measurement is necessary in order to make statements about the number of times one person's attitude is more favorable or less favorable than another person's attitude. To construct a ratio scale, the numbers assigned must reflect distances from a *unique origin* or *zero point*, a point that is the same for all possible scalings of the objects and independent of their units of measurement. Then statements can be made about the relative magnitudes of objects on the attribute. Because the size of the unit of measurement of a ratio scale is arbitrary, this unit can be changed without distorting the ratios of the objects to one another on the scale. A change in the unit of measurement without a change in the zero point of the scale is known as *multiplicative transformation* $(Y = bX)$. If two scalings of the same stimuli are on a common ratio scale, they should be linearly related to one another and have the same origin.

Representational Measurement. The ideal measuring instrument assigns numbers to people's attitudes (or other attributes) such that the relations among these numbers mirror aspects of the actual relations that exist among the attitudes of the people measured. When there is a correspondence between an empirical relation system and a numerical relation system, we have *representational measurement* (Dawes & Smith, 1985; Krantz, Luce, Suppes, & Tversky, 1971; Suppes & Zinnes, 1963). The importance of representational measurement is that the numbers assigned to objects allow us to deduce relationships that exist empirically between the objects on the dimension scaled. For example, if we knew that A has an attitude score of 8 and B an attitude score of 2 on a ratio scale, we would know that A is four times as favorable as B toward the attitude object. Because ratio scales of psychological attributes are quite rare, we are seldom in a position to make such statements about attitudes.

To determine whether representational measurement exists at a particular measurement level (e.g., ordinal, interval, or ratio), checks on the consistency of the number assignments should be conducted during the process of scale construction.[3] These consistency checks make use of the properties of the real number system to ascertain whether the numerical relations of the assigned scores mirror the empirical relations among the objects. For example, ordinal scales have the property not only of order, but also of *transitivity*: If B $>$ A and C $>$ B, then C $>$ A. Thus, transitivity provides a way of assessing whether a true ordinal scale has been constructed. For example, if Person D is judged to have a more positive attitude than Person C, and C a more positive attitude than Persons A and B, then D should be judged to have a more positive attitude than B or A. Intransitivities suggest that the people cannot be ordered consistently on a single dimension.

Interval scales have additional properties that can be used to check whether the scaling has met the basic requirements of an interval scale. For example, if Persons B, C, D, and E have been assigned the numbers 2, 3, 5, and 6, respectively, this implies that the difference between B and C should be judged equal to the difference between D and E. The various properties of different measurement levels are detailed in several useful discussions of measurement (e.g., A. B. Anderson, Basilevsky, & Hum, 1983; Dawes, 1972; Krantz et al., 1971; Suppes & Zinnes, 1963).

Attitude measures that lack representational measurement properties have been labeled *index measurement* (Dawes, 1972) or *nonrepresentational measurement* (Dawes & Smith, 1985). The fact that a particular scale yields "attitude scores" that are not based on representational measurement does not mean that the scale is worthless, however. The scale still may be useful in predicting scores on other variables. Yet nonrepresentational measures do not permit us to deduce the precise relations between persons from knowledge of their attitude scores or between groups of persons from knowledge of their mean attitude scores. In considering how attitude scales are commonly constructed, we will discuss how they may be checked to determine if they have representational measurement properties.

Levels of Measurement and Statistics. In calculating certain descriptive and inferential statistics in attitude research, researchers typically add and multiply the numbers that represent subjects' attitudes. For example, in calculating the mean attitude of a group of individuals, researchers add the numbers assigned to those individuals and divide by the number of individuals. A person with a score of 8 contributes twice the amount in determining the group mean that a person with a score of 4 does. Yet, if the measurement level of the scale is only ordinal, a score of 8 may only indicate that the person's attitude is more positive than that of the person whose score is 4. It would be entirely consistent with the relations that exist between people's attitudes to transform the assigned values to some other set of numbers that preserves the existing ordinal relationships. Such a transformation would yield a different mean for the group. Moreover, the relationships between the means of different groups could be quite different depending upon the nature of the ordinal transformation. Recognition of this fact led Stevens (1951) and others (e.g., Siegel, 1956) to conclude that common statistical tests that require adding values should not be performed on scales that lack interval scale properties. Ordinal scales, they argued, require statistics such as the median that do not make use of scores' values but only of their order. Such statistics are called *nonparametric*.

Stevens' dictum led to considerable debate in the 1950s and early 1960s about the appropriateness of various statistical methods and tests at different levels of measurement. The debate subsided for a while among psychologists but was renewed in papers by Borgatta and Bohrnstedt (1980), Gaito (1980), and Townsend and Ashby (1984). Critics of Stevens' position argued that the level of measurement is not a problem for statistics but for the *interpretation* of certain statistical results (e.g., N. H. Anderson, 1961; Hays, 1963; F. M. Lord, 1953). After all, it was argued, the calculator or computer does not know where the numbers came from. It is a fact that the mean of the numbers assigned to one group is higher than the mean of the numbers assigned to another group. Given a significant *t*-test for this difference, the fact that the group means differ is likely to reflect a corresponding difference in their population means. These arguments are correct as far as the numbers are concerned. However, they do not resolve the issue of whether we can conclude that the two groups differ on the underlying attribute independent of the scale-specific method of number assignment.

This issue is complex because it is bound up in different theories or paradigms of what constitutes measurement (Michell, 1986). Yet, some progress has been made toward the resolution of this forty-year-old debate. Davison and Sharma (1988, 1990) have shown that, if an observed measured variable is a continuous ordinal variable that is a monotonically increasing function of an underlying latent variable (and the standard assumptions of homogeneity of variance and normality hold), the conclusion to reject or not reject the null hypothesis of no difference between the means on the basis of a *t*-test or one-way analysis of variance on the measured variable also may be applied to the null hypothesis about the means on the latent variable. The same logic holds for tests about whether a correlation coefficient or multiple correlation coefficient is different from zero. Because it is reasonable to expect that our methods of measuring attitudes ordinarily are at least monotonically related to the true attitudes of our respondents, Davison and Sharma's findings indicate not only that the usual parametric statistical tests performed on our measured attitudes are permissible, but also that the conclusions drawn from them are likely to apply to the underlying attitudes.[4]

Reliability and Validity of Measurement

Any instrument designed to measure attitudes should be both a reliable and valid indicator of the underlying attitude. The *reliability* of a measuring instrument refers to the extent to which that instrument yields consistent scores or values over repeated observations. The *validity* of a measuring instrument refers to the extent to which that instrument measures what it claims to measure. That is, reliability is concerned with whether an instrument—regardless of what it "truly" measures—yields scores that are consistently repeatable. The validity of an attitude measure pertains to whether scores on that scale in fact indicate people's attitudes toward the object.

Errors of Measurement. All measurement is subject to some degree of error. Errors may arise from a variety of sources: The measuring instrument itself may have certain limitations that produce fluctuations; the object measured may vacillate on the attribute from one time or place to another; or, the observer or recording device may produce variability. For example, the measured weight of a person may differ from its true value and from a second or third measurement because of certain physical properties of the scale on which the person stands, because the person's weight fluctuates at different points in the day, or because the observer may read the scale from different visual perspectives and under different lighting conditions. Similarly, variability may be introduced by the electrical apparatus used to measure attitudes physiologically, attitudinal expressions may vary at different points in time, or people may misread an item or check the wrong alternative in responding to an item on a self-administered questionnaire.

Some errors fluctuate randomly; they are just as likely to cause the observed score to be higher as lower than its true value. By definition, such *random errors* have a mean of zero over repeated observations. That is, in the long run, errors in one direction will be balanced by errors in the other direction. *Systematic errors*, on the other hand, are departures from the true value that do not cancel themselves out over repeated observations. A tendency to make socially desirable responses, for example, would repeatedly lead to responses that depart from the true value only in the socially desirable direction. Random errors are the basis of a measuring instrument's un-reliability, whereas systematic errors contribute to the instrument's invalidity.

Correlation coefficients typically are used to assess reliability and validity. There are a number of different ways of obtaining an index of reliability, but the basic idea is to obtain a measure of the extent to which a set of scores on an instrument correlate with themselves on several observations (i.e., how consistent the scores are). In validity assessment, the relevant correlation is between scores on the measuring instrument and on some other variable to which the scores might reasonably be expected to be related if, in fact, the instrument measures what it claims to measure. A more detailed discussion of ways of assessing the reliability and validity of attitude measures is presented after discussion of some of the more common ways that attitudes have been measured.

Models of Measurement

There have been two traditions of measurement in psychology: psychophysical scaling and psychometric assessment. Both have influenced the ways we commonly measure attitudes.

Psychophysical scaling developed in the nineteenth century to examine the relationships between the attributes of physical stimuli and the psychological sensations that these stimuli produced. For example, researchers investigated how changes in the sound pressure of a tone related to sensed changes in loudness. To study this relationship, researchers would manipulate the tone's sound pressure and have perceivers judge how loud the tone was or how much louder it was than another tone. Psychophysical scaling involves mapping a psychological judgment dimension (e.g., loudness) onto the different physical values of a stimulus attribute (i.e., sound pressure).

The *Thurstone judgment* and *magnitude estimation* techniques of attitude measurement that we consider below have historical roots in psychophysical scaling. N. H. Anderson's functional measurement, covered in Chapter 5, fits within the psychophysical tradition as well. Given this heritage, these techniques scale *stimuli* (e.g., statements of belief, affect, or behavior) on a psychological dimension of evaluation, just as psychophysical techniques scale stimuli (e.g., tones) on a psychological dimension (e.g., loudness). However, because attitudes are attributes of persons, a second phase of scaling is used to locate *persons* on the attitude continuum. To recognize these two steps in this type of attitude measurement, these methods are referred to below as *stimulus, then person* scaling techniques. Generally, methods modeled on the psychophysical tradition aspire to some form of representational measurement.

The second measurement tradition, *psychometrics*, has its origins in the methods of mental and psychological testing. In contrast to psychophysical scaling, the attributes measured (e.g., intelligence) usually have no physical stimulus counterpart. On these tests, an individual responds to a series of items, each of which purports to assess the common underlying attribute that the test is designed to measure. Because more precise information about the attribute accumulates as the number of items increases, the sum (or average) of the scores on a number of items provides a good indication of where the person stands on the attribute. In the psychometric tradition, *persons* are located directly on the attribute based upon their total scores on a set of items. The typical multiple-choice course exam is an example of a test based on this psychometric model.

This psychometric heritage is also well represented in attitude measurement. Both *Likert's method of summated ratings* and *Osgood's semantic differential* fit within this approach. Techniques based on the psychometric model are referred to below as *person* scaling techniques. The representational measurement properties of scales derived from these person scaling techniques are generally unknown.

Guttman scaling, which we also discuss, combines aspects of both the psychophysical and psychometric heritages. As we shall see, Guttman scaling locates stimuli and persons simultaneously on the attitude continuum and in this chapter is labeled a *simultaneous stimulus and person* scaling technique. Guttman scaling yields ordinal scales with representational measurement properties.[5]

Scaling models differ in a variety of ways other than whether they scale stimuli, persons, or both. For example, the data used by a model may require judgments of order, while other models require distance or similarity judgments (Coombs, 1964; Coombs, Dawes, & Tversky, 1970; Dawes, 1972). Models also differ in whether they are designed to locate objects on a single dimension or to provide multidimensional representations. Because the most common techniques for measuring attitudes seek to locate people on a single dimension of favorability, this chapter focuses exclusively on *unidimensional* models. Readers may wish to consult other sources for discussion of multidimensional scaling (e.g., Kruskal & Wish, 1978; Schiffman, Reynolds, & Young, 1981; Shepard, Romney, & Nerlove, 1972). In the subsequent three sections we review and illustrate some of the traditional ways that researchers have constructed attitude scales by stimulus, then person scaling, by simultaneous stimulus and person scaling, and by person scaling. Most of these methods are quite general and can be applied across the three classes of indicators (cognitive, affective, behavioral). Other examples of these scaling techniques may be found in Shaw and Wright (1967), Robinson, Rusk, and Head (1968), Robinson and Shaver (1973), and Robinson, Shaver, and Wrightsman (1991).

Attitude Scale Construction: *Stimulus, Then Person Scaling*

Stimulus, then person scales require a two-step process. In the first step, stimuli (e.g., statements describing beliefs, affects, or behaviors) are judged and scaled to determine the location of each stimulus on a favorable-unfavorable dimension. For example, Table 2.2 presents some belief statements from the Attitude toward Capital Punishment Scale (R. C. Peterson & Thurstone, 1933/1970). Next to each item is a *scale value* representing the position of the item on an unfavorable (0) to favorable (11) dimension. The item scale values were derived from judges' ratings by the Thurstone method of equal-appearing intervals that is described subsequently. Once the items have been scaled, then persons (i.e., respondents whose attitudes are to be measured) are located on the same dimension by their endorsements of one or more of the scaled statements.

TABLE 2.2

Some Items and Their Scale Values from Attitude Toward Capital Punishment Scale

Scale value	Item
0.0	Capital punishment is absolutely never justified.
1.5	We can't call ourselves civilized as long as we have capital punishment.
2.4	Capital punishment cannot be regarded as a sane method of dealing with crime.
3.4	Life imprisonment is more effective than capital punishment.
3.9	I think the return of the whipping post would be more effective than capital punishment.
5.5	It doesn't make any difference to me whether we have capital punishment or not.
6.2	I think capital punishment is necessary, but I wish it were not.
7.9	Capital punishment is justified only for premeditated murder.
8.5	We must have capital punishment for some crimes.
9.1	Capital punishment should be used more often than it is.
9.6	Capital punishment is just and necessary.
11.0	Every criminal should be executed.

Note: Scale values of the items were obtained by the method of equal-appearing intervals (see text).
Source: This scale was presented by R. C. Peterson and Thurstone (1933/1970, pp. 22–23).

Thurstone Judgment Techniques

Louis L. Thurstone (1927a, 1927b), in two papers on psychophysics and what he called the *Law of Comparative Judgment*, developed a theory of judgment and choice that revolutionized psychophysics as well as psychological measurement. Many psychophysical experiments required subjects to compare a series of stimuli to some standard stimulus and to indicate which of the two was louder, brighter, or heavier. These judgments were then related to their physical stimulus dimensions and psychologically scaled in units of the physical dimension. Earlier psychophysicists saw a physical stimulus as producing a fixed sensation. In contrast, Thurstone theorized that the reaction to or judgment of a stimulus might vary slightly in a random fashion from one presentation to another and follow the shape of the normal curve. Figure 2.2 shows the psychological reactions to three different stimuli, i, j, and k. Thurstone called these distributions *discriminable dispersions*. The most typical psychological reaction, the mean, is the stimulus' *scale value*. Thurstone's great insight was that the extent to which one stimulus is judged to be greater (e.g., louder, more favorable) than another is related to the distance in their scale values on the psychological dimension (e.g., stimulus k should be judged greater than stimulus i more often than stimulus j is judged greater than stimulus i). By assuming that the distributions were

**FIGURE 2.2.
Discriminable
dispersions created
by variability in
psychological
reactions or
judgments to three
different stimuli *i*, *j*,
and *k*. The ordinate
indicates the
likelihood of a
judgment of a given
psychological value.
The means of the
respective
distributions (the
scale values of the
stimuli) are s$_i$, s$_j$,
and s$_k$.**

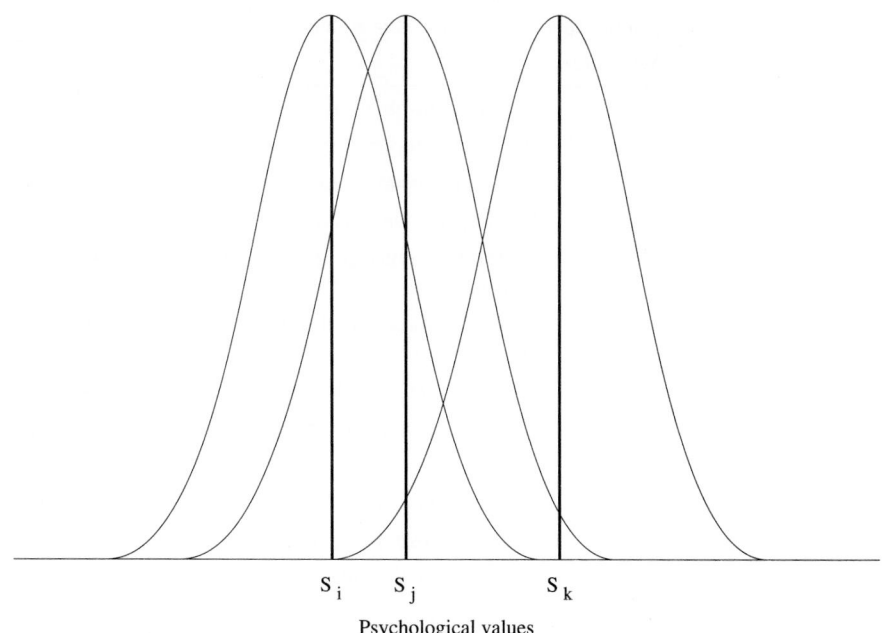

$$S_i \quad S_j \qquad S_k$$

Psychological values

normal, Thurstone was able to measure the distances between stimuli in normal curve units of the psychological dimension rather than in units of a physical scale. The theory provided a rationale for the measurement of psychological attributes that did not have an underlying physical dimension.

In 1928, Thurstone published a paper entitled, "Attitudes can be measured." In this paper he demonstrated how his theory and the methods of psychophysical scaling—especially the *method of paired comparisons*—could be extended to attitude measurement. Thurstone and his coworkers subsequently developed the methods of *equal-appearing intervals* (Thurstone & Chave, 1929) and *successive intervals* (Saffir, 1937) as additional judgment techniques for attitude measurement and as approximations to the law of comparative judgment and the method of paired comparisons. This work marked the first applications of formal scaling methods to the measurement of attitudes.

In all of the Thurstone attitude scaling methods, the process of scale construction begins with the writing and assembling of a pool of statements that express varying degrees of favorability and unfavorability toward the attitude object. The item pool should be large enough to represent as many different points as possible, including neutral points, along the favorable-unfavorable continuum. Once the pool of statements is assembled, the items are presented to a group of judges for the purpose of locating the items' positions on the evaluative dimension.

As noted, a basic assumption common to all Thurstone scaling methods is that each stimulus produces a normal distribution of judgments on the dimension of judgment (see Figure 2.2). For example, the dimension of judgment could represent the degree of favorability toward capital punishment that a belief statement is judged to express. The distribution arises from the fact that the same statement may elicit somewhat different degrees of judged favorableness in different individuals or in the same person (i.e., judge) from one occasion to another. The point of central tendency of the distribution, the mean or median (which are the same in a normal distribution) represents the item's scale value on the evaluative dimension. Below, we consider how the scale values of the items may be obtained from the methods of equal-appearing intervals, successive intervals, and paired comparisons.

Method of Equal-Appearing Intervals. In this method the judges are instructed to place each stimulus into one of a number of rating intervals (usually 11) according to how favorable or unfavorable an evaluation it expresses. For example, in the first application of this method to attitude measurement, Thurstone and Chave (1929) had 300 judges sort 130 belief statements about the church into 11 piles or intervals according to how favorable or unfavorable the item was toward the church (i.e., institutionalized religion). In some applications of the method the judges are instructed to treat all of the intervals as equal, but that instruction is not essential.[6] The method assumes that the judges, even without being told, sort the items into what appear to them to be equal intervals. As in the other Thurstone judgment techniques, judges are told not to express their own views about the attitude object or issue but to judge the favorableness or unfavorableness expressed by the item.

Scale values for the items are easily determined by the method of equal-appearing intervals. Because each interval is assumed to be equal to every other interval, the width of each interval can be arbitrarily set equal to 1. Consecutive scores (e.g., 1 to 11) can then be assigned to each of the intervals. A score can be assigned to each item equal to the value of the interval in which each judge placed the item. For example, if a judge placed the item into the fifth interval, the item would have a score of 5 based on that judgment. The scale value of an item is the median of the scores assigned to the item by all the judges.

Table 2.3 shows another set of items scaled by the method of equal-appearing intervals. The statements, which describe affective reactions, are from a scale that Breckler and Wiggins (1989b) developed to measure attitudes toward donating blood. The scale values were based on 15 judges' sortings of the items into 7 intervals ranging from very unfavorable (1) to very favorable (7) about blood donation.

TABLE 2.3

**Affect Items and Their Scale Values
from Attitudes Toward Blood Donation Scale**

Scale value	Item
3	Blood donation makes me feel *uncomfortable*.
6	Blood donation makes me feel *generous*.
2	Blood donation makes me feel *unhappy*.
1	Blood donation makes me feel *ill*.
4	Blood donation makes me feel *bored*.
5	Blood donation makes me feel *assured*.
5	Blood donation makes me feel *relaxed*.
3	Blood donation makes me feel *jittery*.
2	Blood donation makes me feel *bad*.
6	Blood donation makes me feel *useful*.
4	Blood donation makes me feel *indifferent*.
7	Blood donation makes me feel *overjoyed*.

Note: Scale values of the items were obtained by the method of equal-appearing intervals. The items were selected to represent each integer point on the 1–7 scale.
Source: This scale was presented by Breckler and Wiggins (1989b, pp. 401–404).

Measurement of Respondents' Attitudes. The scaling of items merely locates the items on the attitude dimension. The next step is to select from the pool of scaled stimuli a subset of items to be administered to the respondents whose attitudes are to be measured. Items are selected so that collectively they represent, in even gradations, the range of possible scale values from very unfavorable to very favorable toward the attitude object. As explained below, these items should meet other criteria as well (e.g., low variability in their placements by the judges). These items are presented in a random order (without their scale values) to the respondents, who are asked to indicate the items with which they agree. A respondent's attitude score is the mean or median of the scale values of the items that she or he endorses in all Thurstone methods.

Method of Successive Intervals. Research comparing the scale values obtained by the method of equal-appearing intervals and the method of paired comparisons (see below) indicated that the relationship was not perfectly linear. Stimuli tended to be bunched together more at the extremes by the method of equal-appearing intervals (see A.L. Edwards, 1957b; Guilford, 1954). The intervals at the extreme needed stretching, and the middle intervals needed contracting in order for the two methods to be perfectly related. Because Thurstone regarded the method of equal-appearing intervals as yielding only an approximation to the results obtained by the method of paired comparisons, he devised the method of successive intervals as another way of obtaining scale values for the stimuli and improving upon the method of equal-appearing intervals.[7]

TABLE 2.4

Some Behavioral Items and Their Scale Values from Social Distance Scale

Scale value	Item
0.00	I would marry this person.
11.11	I would accept this person as an intimate friend.
21.50	I would accept this person as a close kin by marriage.
29.50	I would accept this person as a roommate or I would date this person.
38.70	I would accept this person as a neighbor.
49.40	I would live in the same apartment house with this person.
52.40	I would accept this person as one of my speaking acquaintances.
63.10	I would give asylum to this person, if he were a refugee, but I would not grant him citizenship.
69.70	I would not permit this person to live in my neighborhood.
81.00	I would not permit this person's attendance of our universities.
95.00	I would exclude this person from my country.
97.20	I would be willing to participate in the lynching of this person.

Note: Scale values of the items were obtained by the method of successive intervals. By a linear transformation of the original scale values, marriage was given a scale value of 0, and the item scale values extend over a 100-point range. To use this scale to assess attitude toward a group, the wording should be modified to read "I would _____ a person of Group X."

Source: These items were presented by Triandis and Triandis (1960, Table 1, p. 111).

The method, first reported by Saffir (1937), uses the same sorting or rating procedures for judging the items as the method of equal-appearing intervals. The judges are not told to treat the intervals as equal, but it would not matter if they were. The method assumes that the intervals may not be equal and derives their widths from the judgment data. Thus, data obtained by the method of equal-appearing intervals could be scaled by the method of successive intervals.

Table 2.4 presents 12 items from a scale designed to measure attitudes toward individuals or groups on the basis of statements that describe interpersonal behavior. Triandis and Triandis (1960, 1965) scaled these and other items by the method of successive intervals on the basis of 35 undergraduates' judgments.

To appreciate the specifics of deriving scale values by this method, we must understand the logic by which the method derives the widths of the intervals and locates the items on the resulting scale. For simplicity, assume that each judge sorted a number of items into one of five intervals (categories) according to how unfavorable (1) or favorable (5) the item was toward the attitude object. For the group of judges as a whole, suppose that the proportions of judges who placed item i in the successive intervals 1 through 5 were .023, .136, .341, .433, and .067. As in the other Thurstone methods, the judgments of each item are assumed to be normally distributed around the mean, which is the item's scale value (s). Figure 2.3(a) shows the discriminable dispersion for item i. The differently shaded patterns shown on this curve demarcate the portions of the area under the curve that correspond to the proportion of times the judges placed item i in each of the intervals 1 through 5. As can be seen, because these demarcated areas vary in size, the widths of the intervals differ.

The widths of the intervals are derived from the assumption that the judgments of an item are normally distributed and from the properties of the normal curve. In a normal curve, 2.3 percent of the scores fall below a z-score of -2. Therefore, if 2.3 percent of the judges placed item i in Interval 1, the upper boundary of Interval 1 would be defined by a z-score of -2. If 13.6 percent of the judges placed item i in Interval 2, the proportion of times that item i was placed in Intervals 1 and 2 would be .159 (.023 + .136). In a normal curve, .159 of the area is below a z-score of -1. Therefore, the value of the upper boundary of Interval 2 is -1. It follows that the width of Interval 2 is 1. More generally, a z-score expresses how much any point (t) on the horizontal axis deviates from the mean (s) in units of the standard deviation (σ) of the distribution. Symbolically,

$$z = (t - s) / \sigma \qquad (2.1)$$

FIGURE 2.3.
Discriminable dispersions for stimulus i, Panel (a), and stimulus j, Panel (b), in relation to the interval boundaries and to each other, Panel (c), in the method of successive intervals. Numbers in the different shaded areas give the interval in which the item was placed, and the size of the area indicates the proportion of times the item was placed in each of the five intervals. Panel (b) assumes that none of the judges placed the item in Interval 1. Panel (c) shows both distributions placed on the same horizontal axis. The horizontal axis of each panel is measured in z-score units of the standard normal curve.

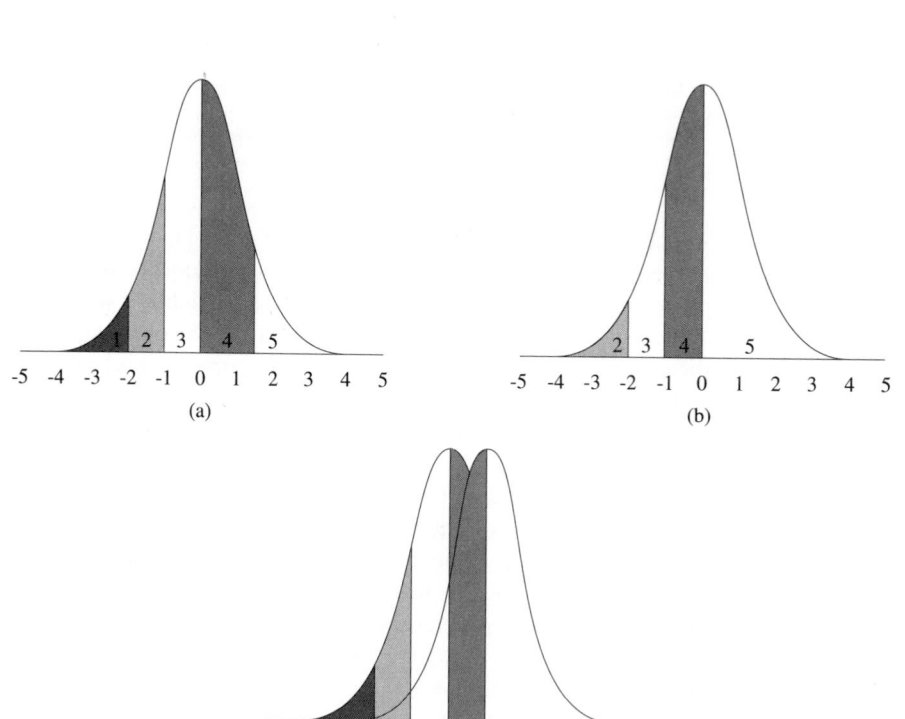

Consequently, we know that the upper boundary of Interval 1 is 2 standard deviations below item i's scale value and that the upper boundary of Interval 2 is 1 standard deviation below. Thus, given normality of the judgment distribution of an item, the proportions of judges who locate an item in each category provide estimates of the widths of the intervals and the locations of the interval boundaries relative to the item's scale value.

Figure 2.3(b) shows the normally distributed judgments for a second item, j. The area of the curve has been partitioned according to the proportion of times item j was placed by the judges in the various intervals. As was the case with item i, these proportions yield estimates of the widths of the intervals and the locations of their boundaries expressed in z-score units. Accordingly, Figure 2.3(b) shows that the upper boundary of Interval 2 is located 2 standard deviation units below the mean of the judgment distribution for item j.

In applications of the method of successive intervals, it is quite common to assume that the distributions of judgments for different items have the same standard deviation. Consequently, Figures 2.3(a) and 2.3(b) were drawn so that both distributions would have standard deviations equal to 1.[8] We know that the upper boundary of Interval 2 was -1 in units of distribution i's standard deviation and -2 in units of distribution j's standard deviation. With both item distributions having a standard deviation of 1, it follows that the scale value of item i is 1 unit below the scale value of item j. This difference is shown in Figure 2.3(c) where the two distributions can be seen on the same attitude continuum. More generally, in the method of successive intervals, the scale values of the items are determined in relation to the interval boundaries, whose locations are derived from the judgment data.

The specifics of estimating the scale values of the items and the interval boundaries follow the underlying logic outlined above. To estimate the interval boundaries and the scale values of the items we first obtain the proportion of times each item was sorted into each interval category or the categories below it in rank. These *cumulative proportions* are entered into a matrix like that shown in Table 2.5. In this matrix, the rows represent the items, and the columns represent the intervals. With the aid of a table that gives z-score values for areas (i.e., proportions) under the standardized normal curve (found in any elementary statistics book), the cumulative proportion matrix of Table 2.5 is then transformed into a matrix of z-scores (see Table 2.6). For example, the cumulative proportion of .30 in the upper left cell of Table 2.5 corresponds to the z-score of $-.52$ in the upper left cell of Table 2.6 because 30 percent of the area in a normal distribution lies below a z-score value of $-.52$. Note that in Table 2.6 the last column from Table 2.5 has been omitted because of the indeterminancy of z-scores for proportions of 1.00. Similarly, if any columns on the left of Table 2.5 contained only proportions of 0.00, these columns would have been omitted.[9]

Given the assumption that the standard deviations of the judgments are equal to 1 for all items, the difference between any two z-scores in the same row of Table 2.6 provides an estimate of the difference in the locations of the interval boundaries and

TABLE 2.5

**Proportion of Times Each of Five Items
Was Placed in Each Interval or Intervals
Below it in Rank in the
Method of Successive Intervals**

	Intervals					
Item	1	2	3	4	5	6
1	.30	.55	.75	.85	.95	1.00
2	.20	.50	.85	.90	.96	1.00
3	.20	.45	.80	.85	.95	1.00
4	.10	.20	.40	.70	.85	1.00
5	.05	.15	.30	.50	.90	1.00

TABLE 2.6

Normal Curve z-Score Values for Cumulative Proportions of Successive Intervals in Table 2.5

	Interval boundary							
Item	1	2	3	4	5	Row sum	Row mean	Scale value
1	−.52	.13	.67	1.04	1.64	2.96	.59	−.35
2	−.84	.00	1.04	1.28	1.75	3.23	.65	−.41
3	−.84	−.13	.84	1.04	1.64	2.55	.51	−.27
4	−1.28	−.84	−.25	.52	1.04	−.81	−.16	.40
5	−1.64	−1.04	−.52	.00	1.28	−1.92	−.38	.62
Sum	−5.12	−1.88	1.78	3.88	7.35		1.20	.00
Mean (Interval boundary)	−1.02	−.38	.36	.78	1.47		.24	

thus of the interval width. Each row provides a separate estimate of the differences in location of the corresponding interval boundaries and of the interval width. In addition, the difference between any two z-scores in the same column of Table 2.6 provides an estimate of the difference in the scale values of the items in the corresponding rows. For example, the difference between −.52 and −.84 in column 1 is an estimate of the difference in scale values between items 1 and 2. The difference between .13 and .00 in column 2 also is an estimate of the difference in scale values between items 1 and 2. The values in rows 1 and 2 for each of the other columns also yield estimates of the scale values of items 1 and 2.[10]

In actuality, we can avoid calculating all of these differences to estimate the interval boundaries and scale values because the mean of the differences is the same as the difference between the means. Therefore, the differences between the column means reflect the average of the estimated differences between the interval boundaries. Similarly, the differences between the row means reflect the average of the estimated differences between the item scale values.

In order to determine the final scale values of the items, a zero point needs to be set. One simple way to do this is to allow the zero point to be the mean of the assigned scale values (i.e., of the values in the "row mean" column of Table 2.6). This value is .24 in Table 2.6. The final scale values of the items are obtained by subtracting the row means from this value.[11] The locations of the category boundaries are given by the column means in the z-score matrix. When some entries in the z-score matrix are missing because the obtained proportions are extreme, a somewhat more complex procedure must be used for obtaining interval widths and scale values (see A. L. Edwards, 1957b; B. F. Green, 1954; Torgerson, 1958).

Several consistency checks on scalings by the method of successive intervals were suggested by A. L. Edwards and Thurstone (1952). For example, the assumption that the dispersion distributions are normal can be checked by plotting on normal probability paper the cumulative proportions for an item (i.e., the entries in a given row of Table 2.5) against the interval boundary values obtained from Table 2.6. The plot for each row should be approximately linear. The consistency of the scaling also can be checked by working backwards to generate the predicted cumulative proportions in each of the categories once we have determined the scale values of the items and the category boundaries. A. L. Edwards (1957b) reported average absolute discrepancies of .025 and .021 between the predicted and obtained cumulative proportions for two different scalings. Average errors of these magnitudes appear to be quite minor, but the statistical properties of this discrepancy index are unknown. To our knowledge, an overall statistical test of goodness-of-fit has not been developed.

Once the items have been scaled from judgments by the method of successive intervals, the items can be used to measure the attitudes of respondents. This procedure, by which respondents indicate the items they agree with, is the same as that described for the method of equal-appearing intervals.

Method of Paired Comparisons. The core of Thurstone's initial theoretical development concerned comparative judgments and was designed for data collected by the method of paired comparisons. In this method each stimulus is paired with every other stimulus. For each pair, judges are required to state which of the two stimuli lies above the other on the judgmental dimension. For example, a set of n belief statements about capital punishment may be paired with one another, resulting in $[n(n-1)]/2$ pairs. For each pair, judges indicate which member of the pair is more favorable toward capital punishment. For a group of judges, the proportion of times statement j is judged more favorable than statement i is obtained. The method makes use of the data on the proportion of times the judges view one item as more favorable than another to derive the distances between the items' scale values and to position the items on the attitude dimension.

The details of how the scale values are determined by the method of paired comparisons are not pursued here (see A. L. Edwards, 1957b; B. F. Green, 1954; Torgerson, 1958) because of the limited usefulness of this method for scaling a large number of attitudinal statements. This limitation stems from the requirement that judges compare each stimulus with every other stimulus. As the number of stimuli increases, the number of required pairings and judgments increases more rapidly, and the technique becomes unwieldy. For example, 10 stimuli require 45 pairings, but 20 stimuli require 190 pairings. Yet, in order to construct a scale containing a sufficient number of items located at various points along the evaluative continuum, most investigators would probably want to scale 20 to 25 attitudinal statements, at least. Because of these practical limitations, Thurstone developed the methods of equal-appearing intervals and successive intervals, which require far fewer judgments.[12]

The theory underlying the method of paired comparisons is richly developed in Thurstone's (1927a) paper on the law of comparative judgment. The paper also considers a variety of subcases that make different assumptions about the equality of the standard deviations of the item dispersions and the correlations of the judgment pairs. Many further developments are discussed in Torgerson (1958). As in the method of successive intervals, the method of paired comparisons has associated with it a way of checking the consistency of the scaling. After the scale values of the items are obtained, the formulas can be reversed to generate predicted proportions which can be compared to the obtained proportions. Yet, in contrast to the method of successive intervals, the method of paired comparisons has in addition a statistical test of goodness-of-fit of the scaling (Mosteller, 1951). Consequently, the accuracy of the scaling and the interval scale assumption can be rigorously checked. The method of paired comparisons is highly recommended for scaling stimuli when the large number of judgments required by this method is not a serious limitation.

Item Selection in the Thurstone Techniques. Using the methods of equal-appearing and successive intervals, researchers can readily scale more items than are needed on the final questionnaire to represent the range of the evaluative dimension. However, some of these items might be inappropriate because they are ambiguous or irrelevant. Following Thurstone and Chave (1929), there are two criteria for eliminating inadequate items.

One of these criteria allows researchers to detect *ambiguous items*. With an ambiguous item, some of the judges might see it as favorable toward the attitude object, and others might judge it as considerably less favorable or even as unfavorable. Highly ambiguous items would be distributed by the judges across a wide range of intervals on the evaluative continuum. Therefore, items that have a large spread should be eliminated because their judged favorableness varies considerably with different judges. Thurstone and Chave (1929) suggested the use of Q (the interquartile range) as an index of spread, but the standard deviation of the item would do as well except when the items are quite skewed (Guilford, 1954). Given two or more items of roughly the same scale value, the one with the least spread is preferred for the final scale.

The second criterion is intended to eliminate *irrelevant items*, that is, items that do not differentiate between people with different attitudes on the issue. For example, people with different attitudes toward organized religion did not respond differently to the statement *I am interested in a church that is beautiful and that emphasizes the aesthetic side of life* (Thurstone & Chave, 1929). People who are favorable to religion generally are interested in beautiful churches, but many atheists evidently are interested too. Such an item would probably not be eliminated because of ambiguity concerning its location on the scale (i.e., it definitely favors churches). Nonetheless, the item is inappropriate because it does not discriminate between people who are favorable and unfavorable toward religion.

To eliminate such items, researchers need to determine how each item relates to the attitudes of the respondents. This relation can be examined by determining the item's *operating characteristic*, which plots respondents' probability of agreement with an item as a function of their attitude scores on the entire scale. To obtain an item's operating characteristic, a large number of respondents are grouped according to their attitude scores on the scale (e.g., all those with a score of 1 are grouped together, those with a score of 2 are grouped together, and so on). Within each score group, the proportion of respondents who agreed with the item is obtained. When these proportions are plotted against their respective attitude scores, the resulting curve should resemble that shown in Figure 2.4. This figure shows an ideal operating characteristic curve for an item with a scale value of 6. As depicted in this figure, people whose attitude scores are in the middle of the distribution should agree with the item because it is close in value to their

FIGURE 2.4.
Ideal operating characteristic curve for a Thurstone scale item with a scale value of 6. The figure indicates that the probability of agreement should be highest for respondents whose attitudes are close to the item's scale value and should decrease as respondents' attitudes are less or more favorable than that expressed by the item.

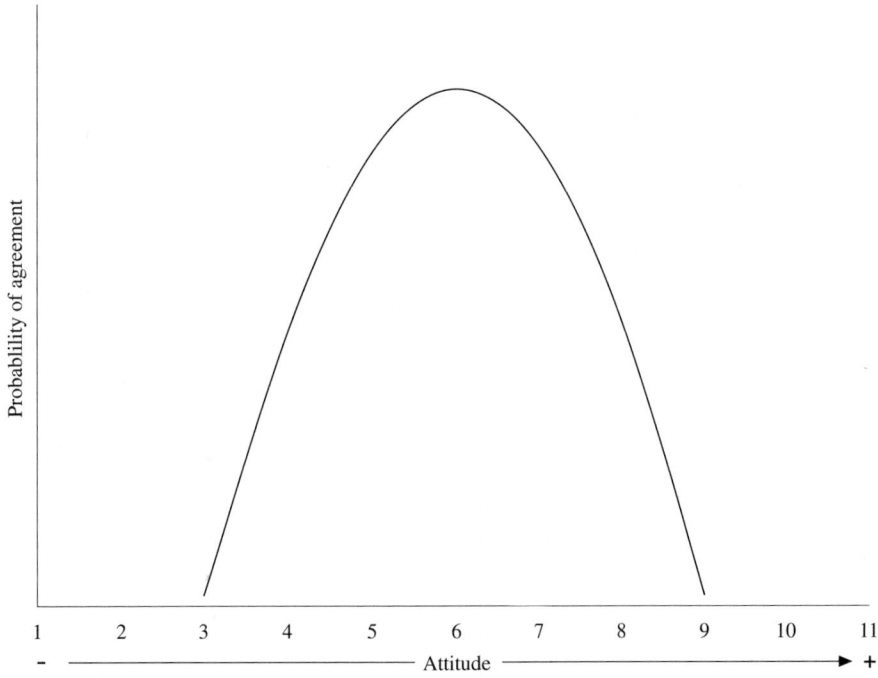

attitudes, and those whose attitudes are more extreme in either direction should be less likely to agree. In general, an item scaled by any of the Thurstone methods should have a *nonmonotonic* operating characteristic with a single maximum like that shown in Figure 2.4. The curve should peak somewhere close to the item's scale value. Yet items with extreme scale values would exhibit a monotonic operating characteristic. Items with flat or multipeaked operating characteristics should be discarded as irrelevant to the attitude dimension because they are endorsed by people whose attitudes are at various locations on the scale.

Evaluation of Thurstone Judgment Techniques. The methods of paired comparisons and successive intervals are sophisticated techniques with well established traditions in psychological scaling. Moreover, these two methods have built-in procedures for checking whether the scalings have interval scale properties. However, the method of paired comparisons is typically used only for scaling a small number of stimuli, while the most popular of the Thurstone techniques, the method of equal-appearing intervals, is based on a nontestable and unrealistic assumption that the scale intervals are in fact equal. Thus, attitude researchers have favored the weakest of these three techniques.

A major drawback to the Thurstone methods is that they tend to eliminate items at the extremes of the favorability continuum. Extreme items are generally placed by all of the judges in the same extreme interval, or all of the judges agree that the item is more favorable (unfavorable) than other items. These items are eliminated because they violate the normality assumptions of the methods. Thus, they are not eliminated because they fail to reflect an attitude, but because they do not satisfy the underlying Thurstone theory, which requires that the judgments be subject to random variation among the judges. The techniques therefore are unable to handle items that produce little or no variation in the judgments. Although few people may endorse extreme items as representative of their attitudes, in some research we would like to be able to identify individuals with very extreme attitudes. The Thurstone methods may not permit us to do so.

One key question about the Thurstone techniques for scaling attitudes is whether the scalings of attitudinal stimuli are influenced by the attitudes of the judges from whose responses the scalings are derived. Early research on scaling attitudes toward blacks (Hinckley, 1932), war and peace (Ferguson, 1935), and patriotism (Pintner & Forlano, 1937) concluded that there was little or no influence of the judges' attitudes. However, Hovland and Sherif (1952) noted a methodological problem with some of this early work and presented data that showed systematic biases due to the judges' own attitudes. Indeed, Sherif and Hovland (1961) provided a theoretical account of these judgmental biases (see Chapter 8).

Subsequent research has confirmed that judges' attitudes influence the perceived position of attitudinal statements (e.g., Eiser, 1971; Manis, 1960, 1961b; Selltiz, Edrich, & Cook, 1965; Upshaw, 1962, 1965; Zavalloni & Cook, 1965; see Chapter 12). However, Upshaw (1962, 1965, 1969) presented evidence that the judges' attitudes influence only the origin and unit of measurement of the scale. Because the origin and unit are arbitrary for interval scale measurement, Upshaw claimed that bias due to judges' attitudes does not invalidate the scaling technique. Research by Kelley,

Hovland, Schwartz, and Abelson (1955) suggests that the problem may be most serious for scalings by the method of equal-appearing intervals. They found that a scaling by the method of successive intervals showed less influence of the judges' own attitudes, and a scaling by the method of paired comparisons evidenced no influence at all. Because the method of paired comparisons forces the judges to discriminate between each item pair, that method is likely to be least susceptible to biases from the judges' attitudes.

Because all of the Thurstone techniques require a scaling of items and then of persons, they are often regarded as more tedious and cumbersome than other methods of attitude measurement. Yet all scaling techniques require pretesting and that calculations be performed to select the items for the scale. Although the calculations required for Thurstone's successive intervals and paired comparisons techniques were once regarded as time-consuming, this criticism was relevant only before the advent of modern data-processing techniques. With computers, the scale values of items can be obtained efficiently for all of the Thurstone techniques. Also, reliable scalings of items can be obtained when as few as 15 judges are used (see A. L. Edwards, 1957b, pp. 94–95).

Magnitude Estimation

Psychophysics offers a number of additional techniques that can be used to obtain scale values for attitudinal stimuli. One of the more useful methods is Stevens' *magnitude estimation* task (Stevens, 1956; Stevens & Galanter, 1957). Although Stevens (1966, 1972) and Hamblin (1974) noted the utility of this method for scaling stimuli of interest to social psychologists, the technique has received only limited attention from social scientists (e.g., W. E. Dawson, 1982; W. E. Dawson & Brinker, 1971; Lodge, 1981; Lodge & Tursky, 1982; Wegener, 1982).

In the magnitude estimation method, two stimuli are presented to judges who are required to judge the ratio of the stimuli. Typically, a judge is presented with one stimulus (i.e., attitude item) called the modulus, which is given an arbitrary numerical value, say 100. A second stimulus is provided, and the judge is required to assign a number that reflects the ratio between the two stimuli. For example, in relation to an attitudinal modulus (i.e., a belief statement) located at 100, a judge would assign a stimulus (i.e., a second belief statement) a value of 200 if he perceived it as twice as favorable as the modulus, 150 if he perceived it as one and one-half times as favorable, 50 if he perceived it as half as favorable, and so on. As in the Thurstone methods, the mean numerical judgment of each stimulus is calculated. These means are analogous to the item scale values in the Thurstone techniques. If the judges did make ratio judgments, the item means would differ from the Thurstone scale values because they would be measured on a ratio scale as opposed to the interval scale assumed by the Thurstone techniques.

Once the items have been located on the attitude dimension, the scaling of persons would generally follow the procedure used in Thurstone techniques. The respondents whose attitudes we wish to measure would be presented with the items or a subset of them and would be instructed to indicate which ones represented their position on the issue. The respondent's attitude score would be the mean or median of the scale values she or he endorsed.

Tasks other than number assignment have also been used to obtain estimates of magnitude. For example, judges may be instructed to treat the prestige of a particular occupation as equal to the brightness of a modulus light. Judges would then estimate the prestige of a second occupation by adjusting the brightness of a variable light so that the relative brightness of the two lights indicates the relative magnitudes of the prestige of the two occupations. The variable light would thus be set twice as bright as the modulus light to indicate that the second occupation has twice the prestige as the first occupation. In addition to judgments of the brightness of lights, several other response tasks have been used to obtain estimates of the magnitudes of social stimuli—namely, judgments of the strength of handgrips, the loudness of tones, and the length of lines.

One advantage of magnitude estimation techniques is that multiple modalities (e.g., brightness of lights and loudness of tones) can be used to cross-validate a scaling; that is, a scaling obtained using one modality (e.g., brightness) can be compared with a second scaling using a second modality (e.g., loudness; see W. E. Dawson, 1982).

In addition to scaling stimuli such as occupations for their prestige value, researchers have used magnitude estimation techniques to scale the favorability of adjectives associated with the response categories often used in survey research (Lodge, Cross, Tursky, & Tanenhaus, 1975). For example, ratings of the favorableness of adjectives yielded scale values of 233 for *excellent*, 107 for *good*, and 47 for *neither good nor bad*, averaged over several different policy issues. These results suggest that favorability denoted by a response of *excellent* is approximately twice that of *good*, which, in turn, is approximately twice that of *neither good nor bad*. When these adjectives are used as response categories to measure attitudes, a respondent can be assigned an attitude score equal to the scale value of the adjective that she endorsed. Research on this technique has been limited to responses to single items and has not included multi-item scales.

The magnitude estimation task is suited for the scaling of attitudinal stimuli, and the use of cross-validation techniques in this work is quite sophisticated. Yet, it is not clear whether magnitude estimation judgments yield ratio or interval scales. M. H. Birnbaum (1982) persuasively argued that magnitude estimation judgments do not have the ratio properties that Stevens claimed. Moreover, most of the work on magnitude estimation has focused on the scaling of stimuli, and only a few studies considered the subsequent step of using these scaled stimuli to scale persons' attitudes (e.g., Lodge & Tursky, 1979). Consequently, additional research is needed before the value of these techniques for attitude measurement can be assessed.

Attitude Scale Construction: *Simultaneous Stimulus and Person Scaling*

As noted earlier, Louis Guttman (1941, 1944) developed a scaling technique that simultaneously scales stimuli and persons. This technique orders stimuli and persons on a single dimension that has *cumulative* properties. In attitude measurement, this single cumulative dimension would be an evaluative dimension. To understand what is meant

TABLE 2.7a

Raw Data Matrix for Guttman Scalogram

Persons	C	E	B	D	A
	Stimuli (rods)				
2	1	1	1	1	0
4	0	1	0	1	0
3	1	1	0	1	0
6	0	0	0	0	0
5	0	1	0	0	0
1	1	1	1	1	1

TABLE 2.7b

Reordered Data Matrix for Guttman Scalogram

Persons	A	B	C	D	E	Score
	Stimuli (rods)					
1	1	1	1	1	1	5
2	0	1	1	1	1	4
3	0	0	1	1	1	3
4	0	0	0	1	1	2
5	0	0	0	0	1	1
6	0	0	0	0	0	0

by a cumulative scale and how such a scale simultaneously orders both stimuli and persons, consider a simple example of scaling along the physical dimension of length. Assume that we have five rods that vary in length between 5 and 7 feet, although the exact length of each rod is unknown. We will use these rods to create an *ordinal* scaling of the height of various persons by comparing each person's height to the length of each rod.

To construct a Guttman scale of length (or height), we begin with a matrix in which (a) the columns represent the stimuli (rods) and (b) the rows represent the persons whose heights we intend to measure (see Table 2.7a). Guttman called this matrix of stimuli by persons a *scalogram*, and his method of scaling is often referred to as *scalogram analysis*. If a person is taller than a particular rod, we place a 1 in the corresponding stimulus-person cell. If a person is not taller than a particular rod, we enter a 0 in the corresponding cell. The results of our measurements might look like those displayed in Table 2.7a. This table shows that Person 2 is taller than Rods C, E, B, and D, but not taller than Rod A. In contrast, Person 4 is taller than Rods E and D, but not taller than Rods C, B, and A.

The next step in scalogram analysis is to reorder the stimulus columns on the basis of how many 1s each column has so that the rightmost column has the most 1s, and the leftmost column has the least 1s. The person rows of the matrix also are reordered so that the top row has the most 1s (i.e., the tallest person is at the top), and the bottom row has the least 1s (i.e., the shortest person is at the bottom). Table 2.7b shows the reordered measurement matrix. Notice that the cell entries follow a pattern in which the 1s form a triangle. This triangular pattern indicates that we have successfully created a Guttman scale in which both the stimuli (rods) *and* the persons have been ordered (i.e., scaled) on a length dimension, even though we never directly compared one person to another person or one rod to another. The reason we could order both the rods and the persons is that the dimension of length has cumulative properties. Length accumulates such that the magnitude of a longer rod includes the magnitude of a shorter rod. Therefore, when we observed that Person 1 was taller than Rods A and B and that Person 2 was not taller than Rod A but was taller than B, it followed that Person 1 must have been taller than Person 2 and that Rod A must have been longer than Rod B.

In the last column of the matrix in Table 2.7b, the persons have been assigned scores that consist of the number of 1s in their respective rows of the matrix. Because of the properties of the scale, Person 2's score of 4 tells us not only that he surpassed 4 rods in height but also that he is taller than Rods B, C, D, and E. Similarly, Person 3's score of 3 tells us that she is taller than the 3 lowest-ranked rods (i.e., Rods C, D, and E). In general, a person's score tells us not only how many but also which specific rods she or he surpasses in height. Accordingly, in this example, we can reproduce the entire matrix of measurements from knowledge of the persons' scores. When a matrix is reproducible from persons' scores, the scale that has been constructed is said to be unidimensional. The reproducibility of the measurement matrix was thus regarded by Guttman as a way of testing the hypothesis that a stimulus attribute (e.g., height, attitude) is scalable on a single dimension. Indeed, *reproducibility* of the matrix from respondents' scores defines *scalability* and *unidimensionality* in Guttman scaling.

Guttman Attitude Scales. Let us now substitute attitudinal stimuli for the rods in the above example. To illustrate a Guttman attitude scale, Table 2.8 shows the items from the Bogardus (1925, 1959) Social Distance Scale, one of the earliest efforts to measure attitudes toward ethnic groups. On this scale, the items reflect how closely one would be willing to associate with members of a particular ethnic group. Bogardus found

TABLE 2.8

Bogardus' Social Distance Scale

According to my first feeling reactions I would willingly admit members of each race (as a class, and not the best I have known, nor the worst members) to one or more of the classifications under which I have placed a cross (x).

	To close kinship by marriage	To my club as a personal chum	To my street as neighbors	To employment in my occupation	To citizenship in my country	As visitors only to my country	Would exclude from my country
Armenians							
Bulgarians							
Canadians							
Czecko-Slovaks							
Danes							
Dutch							
⋮							

Source: This instrument was presented by Bogardus (1925, p. 301).

that the items formed a hierarchical ordering of social distance. That is, people who indicated their agreement to permit members of an ethnic group to become part of their family also indicated agreement to allow these persons to do things that were less intimate (e.g., be a member of their occupational group). Conversely, if they agreed to exclude members of the group from their country, they did not agree to permit these persons to be neighbors. Although the social distance scale predated Guttman scaling, the behavioral intention items that Bogardus used for this scale appear to be cumulative and fit the requirements of a Guttman scale. Therefore, it would be possible to assign scores to individuals that unambiguously indicate the social distances they were willing to permit for members of a particular group. These scores represent the individuals' attitudes toward the group. Furthermore, knowledge of an individual's score also tells us which other items he endorses and which items he does not.[13]

Properties of Guttman Scales. The ability to reproduce the individuals' patterns of agreement and disagreement to each of the items necessarily follows from the nature of the operating characteristics of the items required for a Guttman scale. As we indicated earlier in relation to the Thurstone techniques, an item's operating characteristic indicates the relationship between respondents' attitudes and the probability that they agree with an item. An ideal Guttman operating characteristic, which takes the form of a step-function, is displayed in Figure 2.5: *All* persons below a certain point on the

FIGURE 2.5.
Ideal operating characteristic curve for a positive Guttman scale item. The step function shown indicates that the probability of agreement should be zero as respondents' attitudes become more positive up to the point where the item is located. Respondents whose attitudes are equal to or more positive than that expressed by the item should all agree with the item.

47

attitudinal dimension should disagree with the item, and *all* persons above that point should agree with the item.

Unfortunately, a perfect Guttman scale is rarely obtained. Usually people's endorsements of attitude items do not form the triangular pattern of a perfect scale. To assess how common deviations from this pattern are, Guttman proposed a *coefficient of reproducibility*. This coefficient measures the extent to which the respondents' endorsements of the items can be reproduced from the triangular relationship that defines a perfect scale. The coefficient of reproducibility, R, is equal to 1 minus the proportion of responses that must be changed (i.e., *errors*) to produce a perfect scale (i.e., a perfect triangular pattern for all respondents). Guttman (1950) suggested that a coefficient of at least .90 is desirable to indicate scalability of stimuli on a single dimension.[14]

Guttman's coefficient of reproducibility has proven to be less informative than originally thought. High coefficients can sometimes be obtained from random patterns, and the value of the coefficient depends upon the proportions of respondents who endorse items. For example, Nunnally (1978) noted that a three-item Guttman scale with almost perfect reproducibility could easily be constructed by choosing one item endorsed by 10 percent of the respondents, a second endorsed by 50 percent, and a third endorsed by 90 percent, regardless of whether the items related even to the same content area. Corrections for this problem have been proposed (A. L. Edwards, 1957b; B. F. Green, 1956). Furthermore, there is disagreement about the counting of errors and the assignment of scale scores. These problems, some proposed solutions, and alternative measures of reproducibility are discussed in more detail elsewhere (Dawes & Smith, 1985; Dotson & Summers, 1970; A. L. Edwards, 1957b; McIver & Carmines, 1981).

Because a Guttman scale is an ordinal scale, a zero point is unnecessary and, at best, arbitrary. Nonetheless, Guttman (1947a) and Suchman (1950) suggested that it would be useful to distinguish between favorable and unfavorable attitudes. They further suggested that the zero point of the scale be located at the point where intensity of feeling about the issue is lowest. One way to determine this point is to ask the respondents "How strongly do you feel about this?" after eliciting their agreement or disagreement with the item. Suchman (1950) found a ∪-shaped relationship between intensity and Guttman scale scores such that people at both extremes of the scale felt more intensely about the issue. The low point of the ∪-shaped relationship—that is, a point of indifference—became the zero point of the scale.

Evaluation of Guttman Scaling. Guttman succeeded in constructing a number of attitude scales during World War II (Stouffer et al., 1950), and other scales have been constructed with the technique since then (see Robinson, Rusk, & Head, 1968; Robinson & Shaver, 1973; Robinson, Shaver, & Wrightsman, 1991; Shaw & Wright, 1967). Nonetheless, constructing a scale by Guttman's method is not an easy task. Several revisions generally are required. One problem is that the initial selection of items that may meet Guttman scaling criteria remains intuitive (A. L. Edwards, 1957b). Items often are discarded, rewritten, rescored, or otherwise manipulated in order to obtain a scale that meets satisfactory reproducibility criteria (see A. L. Edwards, 1957b;

McIver & Carmines, 1981). Scales exceeding 6 to 10 items rarely meet these criteria. Yet, since the number of items determines the number of different attitude scores that can be assigned to persons, short scales provide less discrimination between individuals' attitudes.

Some of the features of Guttman scaling are illustrated in Table 2.9, which lists 13 items used by Teske and Hazlett (1985) to construct a Guttman scale to measure attitudes toward handgun control. This scaling was based on data from a large sample of Texans who responded to an annual mail survey on crime. Respondents indicated whether they (a) strongly favor, (b) somewhat favor, (c) do not favor, or (d) have no opinion about the proposal expressed in each item. To construct a Guttman scale, Teske and Hazlett collapsed the first two alternatives into an agreement category, and the remaining two into a no agreement category.

The first nine items in Table 2.9 form a Guttman scale with a coefficient of reproducibility of .915, which far exceeds chance reproducibility. The remaining four items were eliminated from the scale because they lowered the reproducibility of the scale. In order to achieve the reported reproducibility, a step-by-step process was

TABLE 2.9

Items from a Guttman Scale of Attitudes Toward Handgun Control

1. Institute a waiting period before a handgun can be purchased, to allow for a criminal records check.

2. Require all persons to obtain a police permit before being allowed to purchase a handgun.

3. Require a license for all persons carrying a hundgun outside their homes or places of business (except for law enforcement agents).

4. Require a mandatory fine for all persons carrying a handgun outside their homes or places of business without a license.

5. Require a mandatory jail term for all persons carrying a handgun outside their homes or places of business without a license.

6. Ban the future manufacturing and sale of non-sporting-type handguns.

7. Ban the future manufacture and sale of all handguns.

8. Use public funds to buy back and destroy existing handguns on a voluntary basis.

9. Use public funds to buy back and destroy existing handguns on a mandatory basis.

Discarded items

A. A crackdown on *illegal* handgun sales.

B. Strengthen the rules for becoming a commercial handgun dealer.

C. Require a mandatory prison sentence for all persons using a handgun to commit a crime.

D. Ban the manufacturing and sale of small, cheap, and low-quality guns like the "Saturday Night Special."

Source: These items were presented by Teske and Hazlett (1985, p. 375).

followed in which an item was eliminated, the reproducibility of the remaining items recomputed to see if it met acceptable levels, another item was eliminated, the reproducibility of remaining items recomputed, and so on. One of the difficulties with this procedure is that the results may capitalize on chance variations among item frequencies. In order to be more certain that such an outcome has not occurred, the final scale should be cross-validated on a second sample to see if it again yields an acceptable level of reproducibility.

Guttman scaling is referred to as an *interlocking* technique (Dawes & Smith, 1985) because the resultant scale is a joint product of both stimuli and the persons scaled. In order to be successfully applied, the technique requires a particular relationship between the stimuli and the persons—namely, people who agree with an item also agree with items of lesser rank. To meet this requirement, successful Guttman scales often incorporate in the wording of the items certain circumstances or policies that make agreement with an item of a particular rank imply assent to the circumstances or policies described in the items of lesser rank. Thus, the items used by Teske and Hazlett are worded to have implications for one other. For example, someone who favors the most extreme item, which dictates mandatory destruction of all existing handguns, should also agree to less extreme items—for example, the item that calls for banning the future manufacture and sale of handguns. In general, the chances of creating a scale with Guttman properties are enhanced by wording the items so that acceptance of more extreme items has logical implications for acceptance of less extreme items.

Certain reactions, behaviors, and experiences occur in an orderly progression that make them amenable to Guttman scaling. For example, fear reactions in combat often progress from a pounding heart to urinating involuntarily (Stouffer et al., 1950). Sexual behavior between opposite sex college students appears to follow an orderly progression as well (Bentler, 1968a, 1968b; Podell & Perkins, 1957). So does social distance (see Table 2.8). Guttman scalings of attitudes are more likely to be successful if the items on the scale represent a clear progression from one to another. Conversely, the less they represent an orderly progression, the less responses to them are likely to be reproducible and fit Guttman's criterion of scalability.

To illustrate this issue, Guttman (1944) gave the example of a three-item scale of mathematical ability consisting of a problem on finding the area of a circle, a problem requiring the solution of a quadratic equation, and a problem in differential calculus. He noted that "there is no necessary logical reason why a person must know the area of a circle before he can know what a derivative is... The reason for a scale emerging in this case seems largely cultural. Our educational system is such that the sequence with which we learn mathematics... is first to get things such as areas of circles, then algebra, and then calculus" (p. 149). Elsewhere, he wrote that "If a population is not subjected to the same social stimuli with respect to the attitude, it might be expected that it will prove unscalable for them" (Guttman, 1947b, p. 461). In this respect, Guttman scaling can provide a useful technique for ascertaining whether stimuli have the cumulative, progressive, stepwise structure required by the scaling model.

The issue of whether a Guttman scale of a particular set of attitudinal expressions is achievable relates to yet another aspect of Guttman's theorizing. He viewed his scaling technique as more than a method of constructing ordinal scales. He saw it as a way of testing whether attitudes toward some object or issue—"content universe," as he termed it—fell on a single dimension. Unidimensionality, of course, was defined by the successful construction of a Guttman scale. Determining whether various attitudinal responses toward some object form a unidimensional ordinal scale requires a somewhat different research strategy than determining whether a set of items and a set of respondents can be made to interlock to form a Guttman scale. To investigate unidimensionality of the content universe, a large, representative sampling of attitudinal responses toward the object should be subjected to the scaling technique. Moreover, some of the tactics that researchers often use to attain a successful scaling (i.e., the discarding and rewriting of items) would no longer be appropriate, just as discarding data from an ordinary study is not appropriate to coerce the data to fit the hypothesis.

Guttman was pessimistic that people's beliefs about most attitude objects would prove to be unidimensional. Early in the development of his scaling method, he recognized that "scalable universes may be the exception rather than the rule" (Guttman, 1947b, p. 461). Therefore, Guttman devoted much of the latter part of his career to the development of partial order scalogram analysis (e.g., Shye, 1978), multidimensional scalogram analysis, and other techniques of multidimensional scaling (e.g., Guttman, 1959, 1968; Lingoes, 1963; Zvulun, 1978).

Attitude Scale Construction: *Person Scaling*

In the scaling techniques discussed thus far the persons whose attitudes we wish to measure are positioned on the evaluative dimension in relation to the locations of the stimuli they have endorsed. The locations of the stimuli were either determined as a first step (e.g., Thurstone scaling) or simultaneously with locating the persons on the dimension (Guttman scaling). In contrast, in the methods considered in this section, there is no attempt to locate the stimuli at different points on the evaluative dimension. Stimuli are classified *a priori* as either favorable or unfavorable toward the attitude object, and the locations of persons on the attitude dimension are determined by the number of stimuli with which they agree and the extent of their agreement. As indicated earlier in this chapter, these scaling methods are derivatives of the *psychometric model* tradition in which responses to items are viewed as indicators of a common latent variable.

In this section we consider two such scaling techniques: *Likert scaling* and the *semantic differential*. Like the other scaling techniques we have considered, Likert's method is a general scaling technique that may be applied to any of the three classes of attitudinal responding. In contrast, the semantic differential does not apply across all three classes of indicators. It is instead based on ratings of the attitude object on adjective scales that present generalized evaluative beliefs (e.g., good vs. bad). The semantic differential is discussed in this section because the underlying measurement model is similar to that of Likert scaling.

Likert Scaling

Rensis Likert (1932) developed his *method of summated ratings* because he believed that Thurstone's techniques were too cumbersome and time-consuming. He set out to develop a simpler method of scaling that would be at least as reliable and valid as Thurstone's method of equal-appearing intervals.

Likert's scaling technique, like Thurstone's, begins with a large pool of items that are chosen intuitively for their relevance to the attitude object. Although in most applications of the technique these items consist of statements of belief, statements about behaviors or affective reactions toward the attitude objects have been used (e.g., Fishbein & Ajzen, 1974; Kothandapani, 1971; Ostrom, 1969). Unlike Thurstone items which are written to represent a variety of points along the evaluative continuum,

TABLE 2.10

Some Items from the Short Form of the Attitudes Toward Women Scale

The statements listed below describe attitudes toward the role of women in society that different people have. There are no right or wrong answers, only opinions. You are asked to express your feeling about each statement by indicating whether you (A) agree strongly, (B) agree mildly, (C) disagree mildly, or (D) disagree strongly. Please indicate your opinion by blackening either A, B, C, or D on the answer sheet for each item.

1. Swearing and obscenity are more repulsive in the speech of a woman than of a man.
2. Women should take increasing responsibility for leadership in solving the intellectual and social problems of the day.
3. Both husband and wife should be allowed the same grounds for divorce.
4. Intoxication among women is worse than intoxication among men.
5. Under modern economic conditions with women being active outside the home, men should share in household tasks such as washing dishes and doing the laundry.
6. There should be a strict merit system in job appointment and promotion without regard to sex.
7. Women should worry less about their rights and more about becoming good wives and mothers.
8. Women earning as much as their dates should bear equally the expense when they go out together.
9. It is ridiculous for a woman to run a locomotive and for a man to darn socks.
10. Women should be encouraged not to become sexually intimate with anyone before marriage, even their fiancés.
11. The husband should not be favored by law over the wife in the disposal of family property or income.
12. The modern girl is entitled to the same freedom from regulation and control that is given to the modern boy.

Source: These items were presented by Spence, Helmreich, and Stapp (1973, pp. 219–220).

Likert items are written and selected so that agreement with the item represents either a favorable or unfavorable attitude toward the object. The degree of favorability or unfavorability is ignored. Each item is presented to respondents in a multiple-choice format such as the following: A. Strongly Disagree; B. Disagree; C. Undecided; D. Agree; E. Strongly Agree. Respondents choose the alternative that best represents their degree of agreement or disagreement with the item. Each alternative on a Likert scale receives a score from 1 to 5 depending on the respondent's degree of disagreement or agreement with it. If, as is conventional, strong agreement with favorable items receives a high score (5), the scoring is reversed for unfavorable items so that strong disagreement receives a high score (5). Sometimes items are scored −2 to +2; both the scoring direction and the number assignments are arbitrary. Additional variations on the Likert procedures include provisions of more or fewer than five alternatives of agreement and disagreement as well as omission of the neutral or undecided alternative. For example, Table 2.10 reproduces some of the items from the short form of the *Attitudes toward Women Scale* (Spence, Helmreich, & Stapp, 1973), which assesses attitudes toward equal rights for women. These items have four alternatives and no neutral alternative. Likert's technique is referred to as the method of summated ratings because the scores received on each item are summed to obtain the respondent's total score on the attitude scale.

Item Analysis. In order to establish a Likert scale, the initial pool of items must be pilot tested on a group of respondents to eliminate ambiguous and nondiscriminating items. One frequently used technique in precomputer days for assessing whether an item was properly discriminating was to select those people in the top and bottom 27 percent of the total scale score distribution and test whether there was a statistically significant difference between the two groups' mean scores on the item.[15] The preferred contemporary procedure is to examine the *item–total score correlations*, each of which correlates the respondents' scores on an item with their scores summed over all the items.[16] A good item will have a positive item–total score correlation. Generally speaking, higher correlations indicate better items. Items with low or no correlation with the total score are discarded.[17]

In a complete item analysis, the researcher also examines the operating characteristic of each item, the relation between probability of agreement with an item to attitude scores on the total scale. Because Likert scales usually have several alternatives that reflect degrees of agreement, the frequencies of responses to the various agreement alternatives would have to be combined to determine the proportion of respondents who agree with an item. A much easier and equally valid way of examining how the item operates is to plot the item scores against total scale scores. The ideal operating characteristic for a Likert scale item is a monotonic function with probability of agreement or item scores increasing with increasing favorability of attitude for favorable items. Figure 2.6 illustrates several item operating characteristic functions consistent with the ideal. The exact shape of the function will depend upon the distributions of scores on the item and the total scale and on the favorability of the item. More critical is the slope of the function: relatively flat operating characteristics suggest

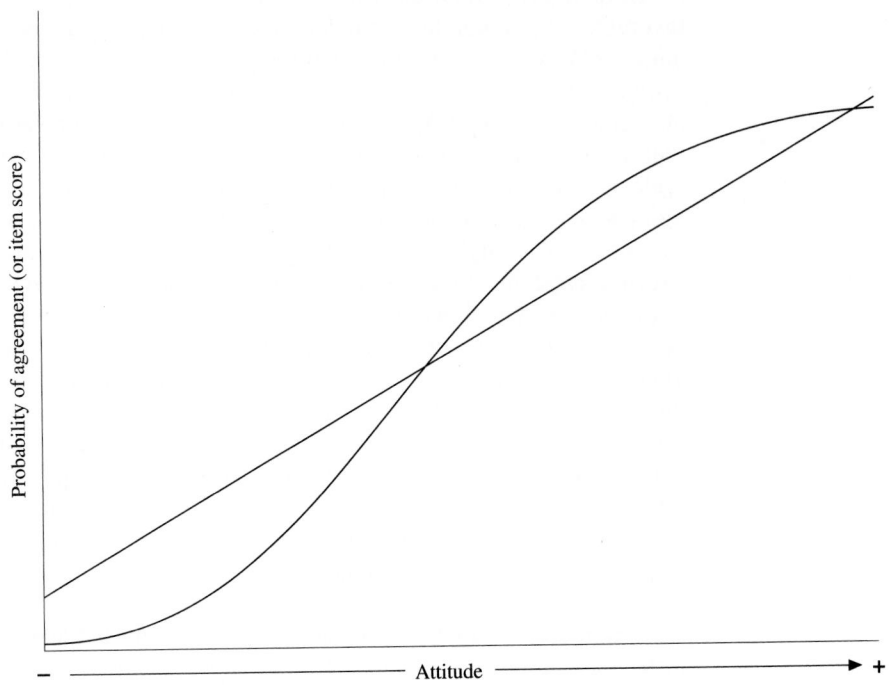

FIGURE 2.6.
Ideal operating characteristic curves for a positive Likert scale item. Probability of agreement or the degree of agreement (item score) should increase as respondents' attitudes become more positive.

that the item is ambiguous or irrelevant because it is endorsed by persons with quite different attitudes toward the object.

Because the underlying measurement assumptions of Likert scaling are similar to those of other psychometric tests (e.g., achievement tests), the same item selection criteria used to construct these other tests are valid for maximizing the discriminatory power, reliability, and validity of a Likert scale. We will consider some of these criteria, including Cronbach's (1951) alpha, later in the chapter. More extensive coverage of these criteria may be found in most books on psychometric methods (e.g., M. J. Allen & Yen, 1979; L. Crocker & Algina, 1986; Nunnally, 1978).[18]

Evaluation of Likert Scaling. Generally, Likert accomplished his goal of developing an attitude scaling method that is as reliable and valid as Thurstone's technique but less time-consuming to construct than Thurstone's successive intervals and paired comparisons techniques. However, claims about efficiency gains (Barclay & Weaver, 1962) have been negated in recent years by the widespread availability of computers and research that indicates that reliable Thurstone scalings can be obtained from a much smaller group of judges than Thurstone initially suggested. Careful pretesting of items, item analyses, and item culling are time-consuming features of good scale construction that are required by both the Likert and the Thurstone methods.

Alternative form reliabilities of Likert scales have frequently been found to be greater than those of Thurstone scales when the two methods are compared or when respondents answer Thurstone scale items that are presented in the Likert format (see Seiler & Hough, 1970). However, direct comparisons between the two methods using the same items are problematic (e.g., Likert, Roslow, & Murphy, 1934; Poppleton & Pilkington, 1963). As B. F. Green (1954) has noted, the two methods require items with different operating characteristics, so that items appropriate for one type of scale should not ordinarily be used in constructing a scale of the other type.

The main disadvantage of Likert scales is that the exact level of measurement of the resulting scale scores is unknown. Unlike the Guttman and some of the Thurstone scaling techniques, Likert scaling does not have any internal checks for its representative measurement properties. Therefore, it is difficult to say whether it yields interval or ordinal level measurement. However, recent developments in item response theory (e.g., A. Birnbaum, 1968; Rasch, 1960) appear to provide a basis for assigning metric properties to various psychological tests (Weiss & Davison, 1981). Although these innovations could be applied to attitude scaling, researchers have not taken much advantage of them (but see Reiser, 1980).

Another disadvantage of Likert scaling is that, unlike Guttman's method, there are no built-in tests of dimensionality. Although Likert scaling attempts to locate people on a single dimension of favorability, it is impossible to make statements about the underlying dimensionality of Likert scales without further statistical analysis. As a means of assessing the dimensionality of tests, investigators often employ factor analysis as an adjunct to item analysis, particularly confirmatory factor analysis.[19] Indeed, when factor analyzed, they frequently yield more than one dimension.

Semantic Differential

Osgood, Suci, and Tanenbaum's (1957) semantic differential is the most popular way of measuring attitudes in contemporary research. The semantic differential consists of a series of bipolar adjective scales, each of which is conventionally separated into seven categories, as shown in Figure 2.7. The attitude object is placed at the top of the

Americans

FIGURE 2.7.
Several semantic
differential bipolar
scales that connote
evaluative meaning.

Beautiful	___:___:___:___:___:___:___	Ugly
Bad	___:___:___:___:___:___:___	Good
Pleasant	___:___:___:___:___:___:___	Unpleasant
Dirty	___:___:___:___:___:___:___	Clean
Wise	___:___:___:___:___:___:___	Foolish

page and respondents are asked to rate this object by checking a category on each of the bipolar scales (e.g., good-bad). Typically the instructions tell the respondent to check the middle category if neither adjective describes the object better than the other or if both are irrelevant to it. Respondents are told to check further along the scale to the extent that the object is described by either of the two adjectives. These category ratings are usually scored −3 to +3. Scores on the individual bipolar scales are summed or averaged to arrive at a total attitude score for each respondent.

As noted in Chapter 1, the semantic differential was developed to measure the connotative meaning of concepts. In numerous studies, Osgood and his colleagues (1957) had a large number of people within a number of cultures rate many concepts on many bipolar adjective scales. These ratings then were factor analyzed to determine whether the interrelations among the scales could be accounted for by a smaller number of underlying dimensions or factors. These analyses generally yielded three factors, which were labeled *evaluation*, *potency*, and *activity*. The evaluative factor ordinarily accounted for the largest amount of variability among scale ratings and was identified by Osgood and his colleagues as synonymous with *attitude*. Consequently, bipolar adjective scales that load on the evaluative dimension (e.g., those shown in Figure 2.7) are used to measure attitudes in the semantic differential technique.

Item Analysis. Despite Osgood and his associates' extensive research showing that certain adjectives generally indicate evaluative meaning, such adjectives may have more specific meaning in relation to particular attitude objects and issues. For example, the adjective pair *warm-cold* generally indicates evaluative meaning in rating people, but would convey meaning that is less evaluative and more denotative in ratings of the Mojave Desert or Alaska. Such tendencies for particular scales to convey specialized meanings in the context of particular concepts were dubbed *concept-scale interactions* by Osgood and his colleagues. Because of the possibility of such interactions, it is wise to assess the extent to which individual bipolar scales in any particular investigation can, in fact, be treated as forming a common evaluative scale. As in Likert scaling, this assessment can be performed by examining item operating characteristic curves or analyzing the correlations between respondents' scores on the individual scales and their scores summed or averaged across the scales (i.e., their total scores). The ideal item operating characteristic curve would be the same as that for a Likert scale item: Increasing favorability of respondents' total scores on the set of items should be accompanied by increasing favorability on the item (see Figure 2.6). In addition, the factor structure of the bipolar scales can be analyzed more formally through factor analysis (see note 19).

Heise's (1970) review of attitude research that has used the semantic differential suggested that the intercorrelations among the various bipolar adjective scales usually are sufficiently high that four or five bipolar scales yield adequate reliability for most purposes. Generally, for a given attitude object, evaluative scores from the semantic differential correlate highly with scores produced by other attitude scaling techniques (e.g., Breckler, 1984a; Fishbein & Ajzen, 1974; Jaccard, Weber, & Lundmark, 1975; Osgood et al., 1957).

Evaluation of the Semantic Differential. Unlike the other techniques discussed in this section, the semantic differential cannot be applied across all classes of evaluative responding. Despite this limitation, the semantic differential has become the most popular method of measuring attitudes. Its popularity stems from the ease with which it permits researchers to obtain an attitudinal index. Because the semantic differential uses adjectives (i.e., beliefs) that are very general and heavily saturated with evaluative meaning, specific belief items do not have to be prepared in advance and scaled. Therefore, the bipolar scales of the semantic differential have been described as the attitude researcher's "ever-ready batteries." In contrast, the indicators of evaluation used by other techniques (e.g., Thurstone, Likert, Guttman) typically must be inferred from the person's endorsements of favorable or unfavorable beliefs, affects, or behaviors that have been selected for their relevance to a particular attitude object.

Because the semantic differential does not depend upon items specific to a particular attitude object, it has the advantage of allowing comparisons of attitudes across different attitude objects (e.g., social groups, social policies). Using the technique, a researcher might find out, for example, whether respondents are more favorable toward Republicans than Democrats or toward affirmative action in college admissions than toward affirmative action in employment. Although attempts to construct such generalized attitude scales date back to the 1930s (Remmers, 1934; Remmers & Silance, 1934), the semantic differential is the most successful "Master Scale" developed thus far.

The main disadvantage of the semantic differential is that its representational measurement properties are essentially unknown. Consequently, it is difficult to know what level of measurement is obtained or what properties the obtained attitude scores have. However, as noted in the discussion of Likert scaling, recent advances in item response theory may provide a measurement metric for scales that, like the semantic differential, are based on the psychometric tradition.

Attitude Measures Linked to Specific Indicator Classes

Within the conception of attitudes adopted in Chapter 1, virtually any response can serve as an indicator of an attitude, provided that it is reliably associated with respondents' tendencies to evaluate the attitude object. The previous section discussed methods of attitude measurement based on standard scaling techniques that, with the exception of the semantic differential, are applicable to any of the cognitive, affective, and behavioral classes of indicators. In this section we consider methods that are linked to one specific class of indicators and that are not scaled by any of the general scaling techniques we have discussed. This presentation also omits discussion of methods that, like the lost letter technique, yield an attitude measure for populations but not for individuals (see Sechrest & Belew, 1983; Webb, Campbell, Schwartz, & Sechrest, 1966; Webb, Campbell, Schwartz, Sechrest, & Grove, 1981). Projective techniques are also omitted because they have not proven to be more valid than standard questionnaires (see Kidder & Campbell, 1970, p. 369).

Cognitive Indicators

A number of techniques are based on the assumption that attitudes lead to systematic distortions in thoughts and judgments (see Chapter 12). To the extent that attitudes do exert selective effects at various stages of information processing, these systematic distortions can be used as indicators of attitudes.

One of the earliest measures of attitudes based on the assumption that attitudes bias judgments was Hammond's (1948) *error-choice method*. In this technique, respondents are presented with questions that they are to answer by selecting one of two alternatives that are provided. Although the respondents are led to believe that the questions test their factual knowledge, neither of the alternatives is actually correct. Instead, the alternatives embody either errors in opposite directions from the correct answer or opposing responses to questions that have no determinable answers. Hammond assumed that respondents' choice of one error or answer over another reflects their attitudes. For example, one of the questions Hammond used to measure attitudes toward labor versus management was the following:

The average weekly wage of the war worker in 1945 was:

a. $37
b. $57

The correct answer, $47, was not given as an alternative. Yet, forced to choose one of the two erroneous alternatives, members of businessmen's luncheon clubs were more likely to choose alternative *b*, and people working for a major labor organization were more likely to choose *a*. Hammond also found that alternatives unfavorable toward the Soviet Union were more likely to be chosen by the businessmen than by labor union workers.

Working along similar lines and with similar assumptions, Thistlethwaite (1950) investigated *distortions in logical reasoning* as indicative of prejudice and ethnocentrism. Students at northern and southern colleges were asked to judge whether a conclusion was true or false given certain premises. Both neutral and more "emotional" arguments were used. One of these presumably emotional arguments was the following:

> *Given:* If production is important, then peaceful industrial relations are desirable. If production is important, then it is a mistake to have Negroes for foremen and leaders over Whites.
>
> *Therefore:* If peaceful industrial relations are desirable, then it is a mistake to have Negroes for foremen and leaders over Whites (p. 444).

Thistlethwaite found that white students at southern colleges were more likely to make logical errors in the judged truth value of such emotional items that supported their prejudices (in comparison with more neutrally framed arguments) than were students at northern colleges.

In addition to judgments of logical conclusions, judgments of the *plausibility* of arguments have been examined as a measure of attitudes by Stuart W. Cook and his colleagues (Selltiz & Cook, 1966; Waly & Cook, 1965). Under the guise of taking a logical reasoning test that required judging arguments from a debate, students rated the effectiveness of various arguments labeled as pro-segregation or pro-integration. Presumably, subjects would rate arguments consistent with their attitudes as more effective than arguments opposed to their attitudes. Correlations between plausibility scores and self-report measures of attitude ranged from .54 to .88 for students from various colleges in these studies, with the higher values associated with students at southern colleges.

Another judgmental phenomenon that has been applied to attitude measurement is the *contrast effect*, a tendency for persons at one end of an attitudinal continuum to displace statements that are distant from their position toward the opposite end of the continuum (see C. W. Sherif & Sherif, 1967; C. W. Sherif, Sherif, & Nebergall, 1965; M. Sherif & Hovland, 1961; M. Sherif & Sherif, 1967). That is, if people are asked to sort opinion items into various categories according to how favorable or unfavorable the items are toward the attitude object, people with favorable attitudes tend to judge unfavorable items as more unfavorable than do people whose own attitudes are not as favorable. Conversely, people with unfavorable attitudes tend to judge favorable items as closer to the favorable end of the continuum. Indeed, some of the influence of judges' attitudes on their judgments of items, a topic we discussed earlier in conjunction with Thurstone scaling, takes the form of contrast effects (see also Chapters 8 and 12).

The Sherifs based their *own categories method* of assessing attitudes on this judgmental contrast effect. When subjects were told to sort opinion items into categories according to how they "belong together," those who had extreme attitudes (a) sorted the items into fewer categories than those who were less extreme and (b) placed more items into the categories at the opposite end of the attitude continuum from their own position (C. W. Sherif & Sherif, 1967). Thus, the Sherifs argued that the number of categories respondents use and their placement of a disproportionate number of items in extreme categories can serve as another measure of attitudes (see Chapters 3 and 8).

Over the years, a variety of other cognitive measures (e.g., the learning and retention of arguments) have been explored as possible mediators of attitude change, particularly in response to persuasive messages. In fact, contemporary research has identified a variety of cognitive responses that are correlated with attitudes and are potential indicators of attitudes (see Chapters 3, 4, 6, and 7). For example, the number of positive or negative thoughts obtained in the *thought-listing* procedures used to investigate the mediational role of cognitive responses in persuasion experiments might serve as an indicator of attitudes (Brock, 1967; A. G. Greenwald, 1968; Petty, Ostrom, & Brock, 1981; see Chapter 6). The sum of these self-generated cognitions might have psychometric properties similar to other summative scales (e.g., Likert scales).

Although thought listing and other cognitive responses have not been systematically investigated as attitude measures, cognitive measures of the strength and favorability of beliefs have been studied. In the expectancy-value model of attitudes, attitudes are viewed as a function of the person's beliefs or expectancies that the attitude object has certain characteristics or attributes and the values attached to these characteristics (e.g., Fishbein, 1963; Rosenberg, 1956; see Chapter 3). For example, in Fishbein's research, the expectancy or strength of association between the attitude object and a characteristic is measured on probabilistic scales (e.g., likely-unlikely, possible-impossible, etc.), and the evaluation of each characteristic is measured on semantic differential scales. The product of these two ratings is obtained for each characteristic associated with the attitude object, and these products are summed over all characteristics. The sum of these cross-products can be regarded as an index of attitude toward the object. This sum has been shown to correlate positively with a semantic differential measure of the attitude (see Chapter 5). Such summed Expectancy × Value products can be viewed as a respondent-weighted summative scoring system that fits at least informally within the psychometric measurement tradition. A number of methodological issues associated with expectancy-value techniques are discussed in Chapter 5. Finally, it is worth noting that Fishbein and Ajzen (1975) argued that all of the standard methods of measuring attitudes (i.e., Thurstone, Likert, Guttman, and semantic differential) can be regarded as deriving attitude scores from the product of a person's beliefs and the evaluations of associated characteristics or attributes.

Affective Indicators

According to the conceptualization of attitude in this book, attitudes, considered as evaluative tendencies, can be expressed in terms of affect responses (e.g., feelings, emotions) and can originate in affective experiences (see Chapter 1). Therefore, it is reasonable that social psychologists would attempt to measure attitudes through physiological responses that may be linked to emotional processes. In the following pages we briefly review and assess the status of physiological and other affective indicators of attitudes.

Galvanic Skin Response. The galvanic skin response (GSR) is a measure of skin resistance, the ability of the skin to conduct electricity. This response is under the control of the sympathetic nervous system and is related to activity of the sweat glands. Typically, GSR is measured by placing electrodes across the palm of the hand. Because sweating is often a response to stress or emotionality, strongly held attitudes may elicit sweat secretions that can be detected by a galvanometer or voltmeter.

Rankin and Campbell (1955) are generally credited with the first successful demonstration that attitudes may be related to galvanic skin responses. White male subjects had their right arms strapped to a board and GSR electrodes attached to their right palms. A set of dummy electrodes was placed on their left wrists. These subjects were given a word-association test that included words that might evoke emotional responses. The experiment was conducted by an experimenter and assistant, one of whom was black and the other white. On separate occasions, the experimenter and his assistant each made physical contact with the subject by adjusting the dummy electrodes. Rankin and Campbell found that the mean GSR was higher when the individual who made contact with the subject was black.

Porier and Lott's (1967) subsequent replication of this study failed to obtain differential GSRs to black and white experimenters but did find a correlation between the ethnocentrism scores (a measure of prejudice) of their white subjects and the degree of differential GSRs to their black and white experimenters. Westie and DeFleur (1959) and Vidulich and Krevanick (1966) presented pictures of blacks and whites in interaction and found that white subjects with negative attitudes toward blacks, as measured by standard self-report methods, exhibited higher GSRs to these pictures than did subjects with more positive attitudes toward blacks. J. B. Cooper and his colleagues obtained higher GSRs to the names of negatively valued as opposed to positively valued ethnic groups (J. B. Cooper & Siegel, 1956). They also found higher GSRs when names of negatively valued groups were inserted in complimentary statements (J. B. Cooper & Pollock, 1959; J. B. Cooper & Singer, 1956). However, the GSRs in the latter studies may reflect responses to the inconsistency or unexpectedness of the stimuli rather than attitudinal responses toward the groups.

Despite these early positive findings, there is general agreement that the galvanic skin response is inadequate as a physiological measure of attitudes in several respects (Cacioppo & Sandman, 1981; S. W. Cook & Selltiz, 1964; Mueller, 1970; Petty & Cacioppo, 1983; Shapiro & Crider, 1969). First, large GSRs can be triggered by both negative and positive emotional reactions. As a measure of attitude, therefore, the GSR lacks the important property of directionality. Second, GSR appears to reflect not only arousal, activation, or emotionality, but also the orienting response that is triggered by surprise, change, novelty, inconsistency, or by the unexpected. As such, it may not be a very good measure of an attitude, as reflected in the positive or negative affect attached to an attitude object.

Pupillary Response. The pupils of the eye dilate and constrict and therefore have the potential to yield the bidirectional indicator of attitude that is lacking in skin conductance measures. Although the relation of pupillary response to affect-arousing stimuli had been noted as early as 1920 (Löwenstein, 1920), the potential of these responses to serve as an index of attitudes was first stimulated by the work of Hess and Polt (1960), who suggested that pupil size is related to the interest value of visual stimuli. These investigators exposed male and female subjects to photographs of male and female figures as well as to other stimuli; they found that male subjects showed greater pupil dilation to a photograph of a female nude relative to a control stimulus than did female subjects. In contrast, female subjects exhibited greater dilation to photos of a partially clothed man, a mother and baby, and a baby alone than did male subjects. A subsequent study by Hess, Seltzer, and Shlien (1965) found that male homosexuals showed greater dilation to photos of men than did heterosexual men.

More critical to the potential use of pupillary response as a bidirectional indicator of attitudes is Hess's (1965) report that disliked or aversive stimuli (e.g., a photo of a shark or several emaciated concentration camp victims) initially produced pupillary dilation but with repeated exposures led to constriction. Although some subsequent research has confirmed Hess's work (e.g., Atwood & Howell, 1971; Barlow, 1969), many other studies have failed to find *both* dilation to positive stimuli and constriction to negative or disliked stimuli (e.g., B. E. Collins, Ellsworth, & Helmreich, 1967; Nunnally, Knott, Duchnowski, & Parker, 1967; Woodmansee, 1970). Reviews of this literature suggest (a) that the least reliable aspect of this research is pupillary constriction to aversive or negative stimuli, and (b) that dilation, like the GSR, may occur as part of an orienting reflex and may therefore be a better measure of attentiveness to stimuli than affect toward them (Petty & Cacioppo, 1983; Woodmansee, 1970).

Facial Electromyographic Activity. Darwin (1872) theorized that different emotions were linked to different overt facial expressions. Recent attempts to develop a bidirectional physiological measure of attitudes have centered on facial muscle contractions. In current thinking, different emotional or affective states give rise to electrical activity in different facial muscle groups even when the person's face remains relatively passive and expressionless. These covert responses are detectable by modern electromyographic (EMG) techniques (see Cacioppo & Petty, 1979c; Cacioppo, Petty, & Geen, 1989; Petty & Cacioppo, 1983).

Evidence that EMG activity can detect positive and negative emotional states was obtained in a number of studies by Schwartz and his colleagues (G.E. Schwartz, Ahern, & Brown, 1979; G.E. Schwartz, Fair, Salt, Mandel, & Klerman, 1976; Sirota & Schwartz, 1982). When subjects were told to imagine positive events, they showed more EMG activity in the zygomatic (smiling) muscles and less in the corrugator (frowning) muscles than when they imagined negative events (G.E. Schwartz et al., 1976).

Extending this work to attitudes, Cacioppo and Petty (1979a) showed that the presentation of a counterattitudinal message, which presumably evoked negative affect and thoughts, elicited less zygomatic muscular activity than a proattitudinal message. Subjects also exhibited more activity in the corrugator muscles when confronted with a counterattitudinal message compared with a proattitudinal message. This pattern of muscular activity also occurred, although more weakly, when subjects were warned about the topic and position of the message but had not yet received it.

Obviously, attitude measurement through electrophysiology has practical limitations because it requires elaborate instrumentation and respondent cooperation. Although having potential for the study of attitudes in the laboratory, research has focused, not on attitude assessment *per se*, but on the use of these techniques for inferring various cognitive mediators of attitude change in reaction to persuasive messages (see Petty & Cacioppo, 1983; and Chapter 6). Greater exploration of EMG techniques in settings in which respondents confront only questionnaire items or the name of an attitude object would be desirable.

Self-Reports of Affect. In addition to physiological measures, a number of researchers have used self-report questionnaires to measure affective reactions to attitudinal objects. Various investigators have constructed affective measures using Thurstone, Likert, and Guttman scaling techniques (Breckler, 1984a; Kothandapani, 1971; Ostrom, 1969). In addition, Breckler and Wiggins (1989a) had subjects rate their affective responses to attitude objects on the same scales that are commonly used in the semantic differential measure of attitudes (e.g., good vs. bad). Among efforts not involving standard scaling models, Nowlis's (1965) Mood Adjective Check-List (MACL) has been popular. Breckler (1984a, Experiment 1) found that scores on both positive and negative adjective lists from the MACL correlated moderately highly with his Thurstone measure of affect.

This work on self-report measures of affect appears quite promising, but more research is needed before we can assess their general value as indicators of affect. The practical advantages of self-report questionnaire measures are obvious, especially when compared to the laboratory apparatus required to measure affect physiologically. Nonetheless, self-report measures of affect no doubt share many of the biases of other self-report measures (see section below on Response Distortions).

Behavioral Indicators

Behavioral responses may also serve as indicators of evaluation (see Chapter 1). To serve as an indicator of attitude, a behavior must relate to the dimension of favorability-unfavorability toward the attitude object. Because there are other determinants of any action besides attitude toward the object, whether a person performs an act, in and of itself, cannot necessarily be regarded as a valid indicator of attitude. Whether one attends church on a given Sunday does not necessarily indicate a favorable attitude toward religion in general or toward a specific religion or church. As Fishbein and Ajzen (1974, 1975) noted, indexes of behavior aggregated over multiple acts (or repeated observations) are potentially valid measures of attitude if the various actions have in common some degree of favorableness or unfavorableness toward the attitude object (see Chapter 4). Just like a single belief, a single behavior may not provide a reliable or valid indicator of the attitude. Behavioral responses ordinarily become more indicative of an underlying attitude when aggregated across a variety of attitude-relevant behaviors.

As our discussion of formal scaling models has already shown, items describing behaviors and intentions to act have been used to construct attitude measures by the standard attitudinal scaling techniques (e.g., DeFleur & Westie, 1958; Fishbein & Ajzen, 1974; Kothandapani, 1971; Ostrom, 1969; Rosander, 1937; Triandis & Triandis, 1960, 1965; see Table 2.4). Behavioral instruments not derived from standard scaling models have also been constructed. Triandis (1964) created what he called a "behavioral differential" in which subjects rate on 9-point scales whether they would or would not engage in particular behaviors with the stimulus person. Beginning with 700 descriptions of interpersonal behaviors sampled from novels, Triandis reduced these by eliminating redundancies and low frequency behaviors to 61 socially important and diverse behaviors. Triandis had subjects indicate their willingness to engage in these 61 behaviors with respect to 34 stimulus persons who varied in race and other attributes. A factor analysis of the intercorrelations among mean ratings of the behaviors yielded five meaningful, relatively independent social distance factors. Although Triandis concluded that social distance was not unidimensional, the factors he derived can be regarded as measures of attitude because they express evaluation of social groups.

In most of the behavioral studies we have noted and in many of those discussed in Chapter 4, the investigators did not observe actual behavior but relied on respondents' self-reports of behavior or intentions to behave. These measures, therefore, can suffer from the same response distortions and biases as other indicators measured by questionnaires (see section below on Response Distortions). That such biases occur in reports of behavior and behavioral intentions is illustrated in a study by Linn (1965), in which female (presumably, white) subjects indicated on a questionnaire their willingness to pose for a photograph in which they would be portrayed as part of an interracial mixed-sex couple. These subjects indicated the acceptability of various possible uses of the photograph, ranging from display to a very limited audience (professional research sociologists) to display to a very wide audience (people who would be exposed to a nationwide campaign advocating racial integration). Four weeks later, the same subjects were confronted with a face-to-face request to pose for the photograph and to indicate the uses they were willing to permit. Although the measure of behavioral intention and the subsequent measure of actual behavior referred to the same behavior, subjects were willing to permit only a more limited display of the photograph than the level they had stated in the questionnaire, probably because social desirability pressures had biased their earlier questionnaire responses. Moreover, the questionnaire scores and these subsequent behavioral scores did not correlate significantly.

In some studies, attitude measures based on overt behaviors have been constructed by aggregating behaviors over acts (see Chapter 4). For example, Tittle and Hill (1967) constructed several behavioral indexes of student political participation in student government: A single-act measure based on documented voting in a previous student election, an index based on a count of the number of times the student had reported voting in the previous four elections, a Guttman scale of participation in eight student political activities, and a Likert scale of participation in ten activities. These indexes were significantly correlated with one another and with measures of attitude based on belief statements that were constructed by several different scaling methods.

Studies that have used indexes of aggregated behaviors typically have merely summed the number of acts that have occurred or were reported (e.g., Weigel & Newman, 1976). Yet indexes of behavioral acts that are intended to serve as measures of attitude would ideally be subjected to the item analysis procedures associated with the traditional attitudinal scaling techniques considered earlier in this chapter.

Reliability and Validity of Attitude Measures

Reliability

Earlier in this chapter, we defined the reliability of a measuring instrument as the extent to which it yields *consistent* results over repeated observations. Another way of thinking about the reliability of a measure is the extent to which it is free from *random error*. As also noted earlier, the reliability of a measure generally is assessed by determining how well scores on the measuring instrument correlate with themselves. This section explains why the correlation between two sets of observations using the same or an equivalent measure provides an estimate of the scale's reliability. We also consider how those two sets of observations may be obtained in practice.

If you suspected that your bathroom scale was somewhat unreliable, you probably would weigh yourself several times and average the weight scores that you obtained. You would probably regard that average as a good estimate of your "true" weight. To assess the unreliability of the scale, you might note how much the obtained weights fluctuated over observations. To be more rigorous, you might even compute a statistic that measured the variability in the observed weights (e.g., the standard deviation, σ). If you thought about this statistic for a moment, it might occur to you that this estimate could be specific to your "true" weight. Therefore, a more general estimate of unreliability could be obtained by sampling other people who varied considerably in their "true" weights, taking repeated observations of their weights on the scale, and computing the standard deviation over all the observations.

Without knowing it, you would have done what *classic true score theory* says one ought to do in order to assess the unreliability of a scale. In classic true score theory, each observed value, X, is viewed as a combination of true score, T, plus random error, e. Symbolically, the relationship is expressed as follows:

$$X = T + e \tag{2.2}$$

T, the true score, is assumed to be a constant for an individual within a given time frame, so Equation 2.2 indicates that the reason that X varies from one observation to the next is because of e. Classic true score theory further assumes that errors and true scores are independent of one another (i.e., they are uncorrelated) and that the expected value of the errors (i.e., their average over many observations) is zero. Therefore, for any individual the average of his or her X scores over many repeated observations is T. That is, a person's true score is the mean of his or her observed scores. Conceptualized in this way, taking the average of the values of your weight as an estimate of your "true" weight makes good sense.

Classic true score theory assumes that the errors in the observed scores of one person are independent of the errors in the observed scores of another person and that true scores are independent of error scores both within or between persons. Then, the variance of the observed scores, σ_X^2, is given by the following expression:

$$\sigma_X^2 = \sigma_T^2 + \sigma_e^2 \tag{2.3}$$

This equation states that the variation in observed scores is in part due to the fact that they are based on different individuals with differing true scores and in part due to random error. If the terms in Equation 2.3 are rearranged to express the fact that true score variance is equal to observed score variance minus error variance and both sides of the equation are divided by σ_X^2, we arrive at the following theoretical definition of reliability:

$$\text{Reliability} = \sigma_T^2/\sigma_X^2 = 1 - (\sigma_e^2/\sigma_X^2) \tag{2.4}$$

Equation 2.4 states that the reliability of a measure is the proportion of observed score variance that is true score variance. This proportion is equal to 1 minus the proportion of observed score variance that is error variance. Reliability would be equal to 1 if all of the observed score variance were due to true score variance. As the proportion of variance that is due to error increases, reliability decreases.

Suppose that instead of measuring each person repeatedly we only measured each person twice; that is, we used what is known as a *parallel measurement*. Because each person's true score, T, is constant, his or her first observed score, X, would differ from the second observed score, X', only because of random error.[20] Given the assumptions of true score theory about the independence of errors and true scores, the above equations would be applicable to X' as well. Parallel measurement is important because it can be shown that the correlation between parallel measures, $\rho_{XX'}$, yields the proportion of observed score variance that is true score variance (M. J. Allen & Yen, 1979; F. M. Lord & Novick, 1968).[21] That is, defined as the proportion of observed score variance that is true score variance, the reliability of an instrument is given by the correlation between two parallel measurements. Therefore, an estimate of the reliability of an instrument can be obtained by correlating individuals' observed scores on two parallel measures.[22]

Estimates of the correlation between parallel measures can be obtained in several ways. One obvious way is to obtain a measure of each person's attitude twice using the same scale and items. The correlation between scores obtained at Time 1 and Time 2 is known as *test-retest* reliability. Although this method of assessing reliability is straightforward, it has some serious drawbacks. If the test-retest interval is short, people may remember their previous responses and thereby produce a higher estimate of reliability than would be obtained with independent administrations of the scale. Yet, if the test-retest interval is long, differences between the two administrations might reflect changes in the underlying attitude rather than mere random error.

To circumvent the problem of choosing an appropriate interval for retesting, several other ways of estimating reliability have been devised. One such method is to develop *equivalent* or *alternative forms* of the same scale, administer both forms to the same people at the same time, and correlate the scores on the two forms. Alternative forms should have the same mean and standard deviation but differ in their items so that respondents' recall of previous responses would no longer be a problem. The reliabilities of Thurstone scales have frequently been assessed by alternative forms (e.g., Likert, 1932; Seiler & Hough, 1970; Thurstone & Chave, 1929).

Another method of determining the reliability of an attitude scale is to split the items into two parts of equal size (e.g., odd-numbered vs. even-numbered items) and correlate the scores across the two parts. However, splitting the scale into two parts results in a scale that is half as long as the original scale. Because the reliability of a test increases with the number of items on the test and conversely is reduced by decreasing the number of items, the *split-half* correlation will be lower than that of the original test. The appropriate correction for the lowered reliability correlation between halves is the *Spearman-Brown prophecy formula*, which gives the value of the reliability of a test that is N times longer than the original test. The Spearman-Brown formula is:

$$r_{XX'} = \frac{N r_{YY'}}{1 + (N-1)\, r_{YY'}} \qquad (2.5)$$

where $r_{XX'}$ = the reliability of an entire scale composed of several components or parts and $r_{YY'}$ = the reliability (correlation) of the parts. In the case of split-half reliability assessment, $r_{YY'}$ would be the correlation between the halves, $r_{XX'}$ would be the reliability of the full scale that is twice as long, and N would equal 2. More generally, Equation 2.5 could be used to determine the effect that lengthening or shortening a scale by a certain amount has on the scale's reliability.

The correlation obtained between two halves of an attitude scale depends on the items that compose the two halves. Splitting a scale by an odd-even or any other method is arbitrary and does not necessarily guarantee that the two parts are equivalent or parallel. Might not a measure based on the average of all possible splits of the items provide a better estimate of the scale's reliability? Why not split the test into many parts, intercorrelate each of the parts with the other parts, and base an estimate of reliability on the average of the correlations between all the various parts?

A measure of reliability that has these properties is Cronbach's (1951) *alpha* (α), which is given by the formula:

$$\alpha = \left[\frac{N}{N-1} \right] \left[1 - \frac{\sum \sigma_{Y_i}^2}{\sigma_X^2} \right] \qquad (2.6)$$

Alpha yields an estimate of the reliability of a composite, X, made of N parts, Y_i. In most applications, these parts are considered to be single items. In such cases, $\sigma_{Y_i}^2$ is the variance of the respondents' scores on item i, $\sum \sigma_{Y_i}^2$ is the sum of the item variances, σ_X^2 is the variance of the respondents' total scores (i.e., each respondent's item scores summed over all of the items), and N is the number of items. When the item variances are equal, the formula for alpha becomes:

$$\alpha = \frac{N \bar{r}_{ij}}{1 + (N-1) \bar{r}_{ij}} \qquad (2.7)$$

where $\bar{r}_{ij}$ is the average correlation between the N items. Equation 2.7 clearly shows the dependence of α on the intercorrelations among the items.

Alpha is the current standard statistic for assessing the reliability of a scale composed of multiple items (but see Greene & Carmines, 1980, for alternative measures). It is the most appropriate reliability measure to use for Likert and semantic differential scales because these methods assume that the items are parallel sample measures of the same attitude content domain. Alpha is not an appropriate reliability measure for Thurstone and Guttman attitude scales because in those methods the items are regarded as representative of *different* points along the evaluative continuum. The calculation of alpha is ordinarily part of the item analysis procedures discussed earlier in connection with these two attitude measurement techniques. Because alpha considers the degree to which items on a scale intercorrelate with one another, it is often referred to as a measure of *internal consistency* (or *homogeneity* or *equivalence*). Reliability measures of internal consistency (e.g., alpha, split-half reliability) are appropriately differentiated from measures of *stability* (i.e., test-retest) because the latter may include changes in true scores over time in addition to random error.

Finally, we note that a high value of alpha is often erroneously assumed to indicate that a scale has a single factor structure. Because alpha, like other measures of reliability, is a function of the number of items on the scale, high alphas can be obtained for scales with many items even when the average intercorrelation between items is only moderate. Moreover, a scale composed of several factors might still yield a high alpha. Because of this fact, investigators constructing Likert scales commonly subject their preliminary scales to factor analysis procedures, as we explained earlier in this chapter.

Validity

The validity of an attitude scale refers to the extent to which the scale truly measures the attitude it is intended to assess. Beneath the superficial simplicity of this definition lurks a problem of considerable complexity. If, like other psychological constructs, attitudes cannot be observed directly and can only be inferred from indicators or instruments designed to measure them, how can we determine whether a particular measure really measures the attitude it claims to measure?

Someone once said that "if something looks like a duck, walks like a duck, and quacks like a duck, it must be a duck." The validation of an attitude measure is much like the validation of whether something is a duck. We must determine whether the measure looks like and behaves like a measure of the presumed attitude. This sort of validation, which is known as *construct validity*, is an ongoing process that is based on theory. That is, either on the basis of specific theory or more general assumptions about attitudes, a valid measure of the underlying attitude should enter into certain relationships and not into other relationships. Thus, construct validity of a scale is determined by certain theoretically based predictions about how the scale should behave in relation to other measures of the same construct and other constructs.

The predictions underlying the construct validation of a particular scale do not necessarily require elaborate theoretical development, however. In many instances, these predictions are based on certain generally accepted ideas about the nature and functioning of attitudes. For example, we would expect that a scale designed to measure pro-abortion versus anti-abortion attitudes would yield different average scores for members of a right-to-life group compared with members of a pro-choice group. In fact, this *known groups* method of validation has frequently been used to validate and refine attitude scales. The idea that right-to-life and pro-choice groups should differ in their attitudes toward abortion is so fundamental that investigators would probably discard any scale or items designed to assess attitudes toward abortion that did not differentiate between these groups.

Another common method of assessing the validity of a scale is to see how well it correlates with alternative measures of the same attitude. Donald T. Campbell and Donald W. Fiske (1959) have termed this kind of validation *convergent validity*.

However, alternative measures of a construct may correlate with each other not only because they measure the same construct but also because they share common sources of bias or method variance (D. T. Campbell & Fiske, 1959). For example, scores on the original Fascism, Ethnocentrism, Anti-Semitism, and Anti-Negro Scales of the classic study of the authoritarian personality were highly correlated with one another as predicted by theory (Adorno, Frenkel-Brunswick, Levinson, & Sanford, 1950). However, all of the items were worded so that agreement indicated a high level of prejudice (see Chapter 12 for some illustrative items). Subsequent research suggested that these measures were correlated with each other at least in part because they all may have assessed two types of bias—namely, a tendency to agree with items (i.e., acquiescence; Couch & Keniston, 1960), and a tendency to agree with items that express socially undesirable views (A. L. Edwards, 1957a; J. B. Taylor, 1961). Thus, the high relationships observed between these scales could have reflected common sources of bias or systematic error.

The authors of the authoritarian personality study argued that a fascist personality as well as ethnocentric, anti-Semitic, and anti-Negro attitudes, although related, were different constructs. However, the very high correlations obtained between these scales called into question the assumption that the instruments really measured different concepts. It was thus possible that these measures lacked *discriminant validity*, the ability to distinguish themselves as measures of unique constructs.

More generally, Campbell and Fiske (1959) proposed that convergent validity as well as discriminant validity are essential components of construct validity. To demonstrate convergent validity, an instrument designed to measure a particular construct should correlate highly or converge with other measures of that construct. In addition, for discriminant validity, the instrument should not correlate too highly with measures of different constructs. Campbell and Fiske suggested that the convergent and discriminant validity of various measures could be examined in what they called a *multitrait-multimethod matrix*.

Table 2.11 provides a hypothetical illustration of a multitrait-multimethod matrix in which there are three different attitudes each measured by three different methods. The entries in the matrix are correlations between measures. The rs in the main diagonal represent reliabilities (e.g., alphas), which express the extent to which a measure correlates with itself. The vs in the other diagonals represent validity coefficients, which indicate the extent to which different measures of the same construct correlate or converge with each other. Campbell and Fiske argued that the magnitude of these validity coefficients should not be judged in terms of their statistical significance or in absolute terms but in relation to the reliability coefficients and the other correlation coefficients in the matrix. Judgment of the validity coefficients in relation to the reliabilities is important because the reliabilities of the various measures set an upper bound for the validity coefficients. According to classic true score theory, a measure's validity coefficient cannot be greater than the square root of its reliability coefficient (F. M. Lord & Novick, 1968).[23] The observed reliabilities of the measures in the multiattitude-multimethod matrix thus provide some indication of the magnitudes of validity coefficients that are attainable.

TABLE 2.11

Hypothetical Multiattitude-Multimethod Matrix

	Method 1			Method 2			Method 3		
	A1	*A2*	*A3*	*A1*	*A2*	*A3*	*A1*	*A2*	*A3*
Method 1									
A1	r								
A2	m	r							
A3	m	m	r						
Method 2									
A1	v	h	h	r					
A2	h	v	h	m	r				
A3	h	h	v	m	m	r			
Method 3									
A1	v	h	h	v	h	h	r		
A2	h	v	h	h	v	h	m	r	
A3	h	h	v	h	h	v	m	m	r

Note: A1, A2, and A3 are three different attitudes; r = reliability coefficient; v = validity coefficient; m = monomethod-heteroattitude coefficient; h = heteromethod-heteroattitude coefficient.

The validity coefficients in the matrix should also be examined in relation to two other sets of correlations: correlations between different attitudes measured by *different* methods (*h*s in Table 2.11) and correlations between different attitudes measured by the *same* method (*m*s in Table 2.11). In practice, neither of these sets of coefficients can necessarily be expected to be equal to zero. The magnitude of these correlations depends on how different the attitudes toward the various objects are and how different the methods are from one another. If the measures share a common source of bias (e.g., because they are all questionnaire measures or were measured by a particular kind of scale), the validity coefficients may be quite high because of the common method variance. The correlations between attitudes toward different objects assessed by either the same or different methods could also be high because the respondents do not discriminate between attitude objects and thus the measures assess the same attitude (e.g., toward minority groups in general rather than toward different groups). By specifying that the validity coefficients in the matrix must exceed both the correlations between different attitudes measured by the same methods and the correlations between different attitudes measured by different methods, Campbell and Fiske (1959) required that the measures exhibit both convergent and discriminant validity.

The multitrait-multimethod approach has been used by a number of attitude researchers to determine the convergent validity of scales constructed by various scaling techniques (e.g., Jaccard et al., 1975; Kothandapani, 1971; Ostrom, 1969). However, the approach as formulated by Campbell and Fiske did not include a way of statistically evaluating the relationships observed in the matrix. Among contemporary investigators there is general agreement that the best approach is through structural modeling and confirmatory factor analysis (Alwin, 1974; Bohrnstedt, 1983; Kenny, 1979; Marsh & Hocevar, 1988; Schmitt & Stults, 1986; Widaman, 1985; see note 19).

Another important aspect of a measure's construct validity is that it enter into relationships that are theoretically expected. A study by Hendrick and Seyfried (1974) that illustrates this point was built on the finding that people like others who are attitudinally similar (Berscheid, 1985; Byrne, 1971; see Chapter 9). In this experiment, subjects were presented with a persuasive message designed to produce attitude change and had their attitudes measured immediately thereafter. A day later they were asked to indicate their liking for two persons after seeing these persons' ostensible responses to an attitude questionnaire. One person's questionnaire responses corresponded to the attitude expressed by the subjects prior to having their attitudes changed and the other person's responses corresponded to the presumably changed attitude. The logic of Hendrick and Seyfried's test of validity was that if the subjects had truly changed their attitudes as a result of the persuasive message, they should indicate greater liking for the person who exhibited an attitude corresponding to their changed attitudes. If the change was fleeting or non-genuine, subjects should prefer the person who held an attitude corresponding to their old position. The results of the study indicated that subjects preferred the person whose attitude on the issue corresponded to their newly changed attitudes. Therefore, the study suggested that the attitude changes observed on the attitude scale were real and somewhat enduring.

Although Hendrick and Seyfried were not interested primarily in testing the validity of their scale but in demonstrating the validity of the observed changes on the scale, their experiment established the validity of their attitude measurement. Here, though, the construct validity of their scale of measurement was not established by its convergent and discriminant validity in relation to other methods of measurement but by its ability to reflect a known relationship between attitude similarity and liking.

Various expositions often mention an additional form of construct validity known as *criterion validity*. This form of validity refers to the extent to which scores on the measuring instrument are correlated with some external criterion. For example, do scores on an attitude scale predict behavior? When scores on the criterion measure are obtained within the same time frame as scores on the instrument to be validated, this form of criterion validity is known as *concurrent validity*. When scores on the criterion are obtained at a subsequent point in time, the form of criterion validity is known as *predictive validity*.

Consideration of criterion validity immediately raises the question of what should serve as a criterion for validating an attitude measure. In applied contexts the answer to this question follows from the reasons for creating the attitude measure. That is, attitude measures often are created to predict some aspect of behavior (e.g., votes for a candidate or party; employee absenteeism; purchases of a particular product). In these applied situations, validity is determined by whether the measure predicts what it was designed to predict. If it does not, then it is an invalid predictor in this practical sense. Nonetheless, the instrument itself could have reasonable validity as a measure of attitude because a failure to predict a specific behavior may arise from a variety of causes (see Chapter 4). Moreover a particular measure could be valid for predicting one criterion and not another.

When attitude measures are created primarily for the scientific purpose of understanding the processes underlying attitude change, assessment of the validity of the attitude measure may hinge on theory-relevant predictions (for example, that attitudes polarize when people are given an opportunity to think about the attitude object; see Chapter 12). As relevant theory evolves and a measure enters into more and more empirical relationships, the construct validity of the measure increases, as does the validity of the theory. Thus, the establishment of construct validity, of which criterion validity is a part, is an ongoing process.

Response Distortions

As this chapter has shown, most attitude measures rely on self-reports of beliefs, feelings, or behavior. This practice is potentially problematic because people may evade answering questions or distort their reports to protect their privacy, to avoid legal prosecution, to gain economic advantage, to obtain social approval and avoid social disapproval, and to project or protect particular identities. *Response distortions* of these and other types could produce systematic errors in attitude measurement.

Attitude researchers typically adopt several strategies to reduce response distortions. One strategy is to embed the measure of interest among items that are of little or no interest to the researcher. The use of such *filler items* is intended to disguise the researcher's interest from the respondents in order to decrease their efforts to provide answers in accordance with their perception of the researcher's or interviewer's expectations. Another strategy is to enlist respondents' cooperation by assuring them of the acceptability of all responses. Generally, they are told that there are "no right or wrong answers. The correct answer is an honest and truthful answer." Furthermore, the respondents are assured of confidentiality by the promise that no one but the research staff will ever know how each individual reacted and that all reports of the research will present the data aggregated across the respondents. In addition, respondents usually complete attitude scales under conditions of anonymity, that is, without giving their names or providing other identifying information.

Research on the efficacy of some of these strategies for reducing response distortion suggests that these strategies are, at best, only partially successful in reducing response distortion (see Bradburn, 1983; Nederhof, 1985; Schuman & Kalton, 1985; Sudman & Bradburn, 1974). Consequently, several other techniques have been developed to reduce motivated distortions.

Bogus Pipeline. The efficacy of the bogus pipeline in reducing response distortions stems from respondents' beliefs that their self-reports are subject to validation. Specifically, the bogus pipeline attempts to control response distortions by leading respondents to believe that the investigator has a foolproof procedure for detecting their true attitudes. Adapted by E. E. Jones and Sigall (1971) from a technique introduced by Gerard (1964), the bogus pipeline typically uses fake electronic apparatus and a set of electromyographic (EMG) electrodes that are attached to respondents' arms. Respondents are led to believe that this apparatus records minute muscular contractions that yield a precise assessment of their true beliefs and feelings. A meter, controlled by a confederate in an adjacent room, ostensibly provides output from the EMG machine to be viewed by the respondent. In addition, subjects are given a steering wheel connected to a pointer on a meter that allows them to rate the attitude object by turning the wheel (see Sigall & Page, 1971). The electrodes, they are told, can predict how far and in what direction they will turn the wheel. To demonstrate to the respondents that the electrodes work, the EMG output meter then predicts their responses to a number of questions. The meter actually reproduces responses that the respondents gave on another occasion that was apparently unrelated to the pipeline study. On several questions respondents may even be invited to try to "fake out" the EMG machine. After the respondents are convinced that the pipeline works, they are asked to see "how in touch they are with their true feelings" by predicting the EMG results by responding to attitude items using the steering wheel. In essence, the bogus pipeline is a fake "truth detector," but respondents are made to believe it is real. Its main premise, of course, is that respondents' motivations to distort their responses will be reduced if they are subjected to this procedure.

Tests of whether the bogus pipeline reduces response distortion have yielded controversial findings. Sigall and Page (1971) found that white subjects' stereotypes about blacks were more unfavorable and their stereotypes about Americans more favorable under bogus pipeline conditions than under standard rating scale conditions (although Schlenker, Bonoma, Hutchinson, & Burns, 1976, were unable to replicate these findings fully). Other studies have found differences in responses obtained in bogus pipeline and standard rating conditions that are in keeping with the idea that the bogus pipeline reduces social desirability or impression management concerns (Arkin, Appelman, & Burger, 1980; Gaes, Kalle, & Tedeschi, 1978; R. A. Page & Moss, 1975; Riess, Kalle, & Tedeschi, 1981; see also Ostrom, 1973). In contrast, Cherry, Byrne, and Mitchell (1976) obtained no differences between conditions and raised the possibility that the bogus pipeline may heighten conformity to the demand characteristics of the experiment (Orne, 1962) among subjects high in social desirability. However, the evidence on this point is inconclusive (Arkin & Lake, 1983; Byrne & Cherry, 1978; Gaes, Quigley-Fernandez, & Tedeschi, 1978). Also, E. E. Jones and Sigall (1971) noted that the pipeline may cause respondents to focus more on feelings and affect toward the attitude object than they ordinarily would in responding to standard assessment techniques.

The best evidence in support of the bogus pipeline as a means of reducing response distortion comes from two studies reported by Quigley-Fernandez and Tedeschi (1978). In these experiments, subjects who were waiting to participate in an experiment overheard information about the correct answers to a test given in the experiment from someone who presumably had just participated in that experiment. Later in the experiment, these subjects were questioned under either standard or bogus pipeline conditions about whether they had previously heard anything about the test. Both studies showed higher "confession" rates with bogus pipeline assessment.

Related to the bogus pipeline method are a number of studies that have obtained differences in self-reports under standard conditions compared with conditions in which the respondents are led to believe that their reports will be validated in some way (Arkin & Lake, 1983; Bauman & Dent, 1982; Evans, Hansen, & Mittelmark, 1977; P. C. Hill, Henderson, Bray, & Evans, 1981). For example, Bauman and Dent (1982) compared self-reports of smoking behavior by respondents who did or did not have prior knowledge that they would be asked subsequently to provide breath specimens that would reveal their smoking behavior. As an objective measure of smoking behavior, breath specimens from all respondents were analyzed for carbon dioxide levels. According to this test, among adolescents who had smoked recently, only 64 percent indicated under standard self-report conditions that they had smoked within the last four hours. In contrast, 86 percent of those who were aware that the objective measure would be used reported smoking within the last four hours. In another variant of the standard bogus pipeline method, Jamieson and Zanna (1983) found that subjects who expected that their attitudinal responses would be validated by a "lie detector" failed to show attitude shifts that normally occur for self-presentational purposes in anticipation of a counterattitudinal message.

Randomized Response Technique. Warner's (1965) randomized response technique (RRT), like the bogus pipeline, was designed to reduce response distortion in answering questions that are sensitive or potentially embarrassing. Unlike the bogus pipeline, it does not require the use of deception or elaborate apparatus and therefore has wider applicability. Essentially the randomized response technique attempts to eliminate refusals to answer and response distortions by guaranteeing respondents that no one can know for certain whether the answers they gave were in response to the sensitive question.

In Warner's (1965) original model of the RRT, the respondent is confronted with two questions, the sensitive question (e.g., Are you in favor of quarantining people with AIDS?) and its logical complement (e.g., Are you *not* in favor of quarantining people with AIDS?). Through the aid of a randomizing device (e.g., a die), respondents are directed to answer either Question 1, the sensitive question, or Question 2, its logical complement. For example, respondents may be instructed to roll a die and conceal its outcome from the interviewer. They may be told that, if the roll of the die results in a 1, 2, 3, or 4, they are to answer Question 1, but if the roll of the die results in a 5 or 6, they are to answer Question 2. They are told not to disclose which question they answered but merely to report the answer. Thus, a response of "Yes" can mean that the person either is or is not in favor of quarantining people with AIDS. Because only the respondents know which question was answered, complete confidentiality has been guaranteed to the respondents. Warner reasoned that this guarantee would be sufficient to eliminate refusals to answer and response distortions.

Despite lack of knowledge of which question the respondent answered, the application of elementary probability theory yields an estimate of the proportion of people in the population who favor the quarantine of people with AIDS. For example, if P is the probability that a respondent is directed to answer Question 1 and π is the proportion of people in the population who favor quarantine, then $P\pi$ is the proportion of people who would answer "Yes" to Question 1. Similarly, $(1 - P)$ is the probability that a respondent is directed to answer Question 2, and $(1 - \pi)$ is the proportion of them who would answer "Yes" because they do not favor quarantine. Assuming that all respondents answer as instructed and truthfully, the probability of a "Yes" response, τ, is given by:

$$\tau = P\pi + (1 - P)(1 - \pi) \qquad (2.8)$$

Because P is known and τ can be obtained from the data, Warner showed that Equation 2.8 can be solved for π to obtain an estimate of the proportion of people in the population who are in favor of the quarantine of people with AIDS. The sample estimate, $\hat{\pi}$, is given by:

$$\hat{\pi} = [\hat{\tau} + P - 1] / (2P - 1) \qquad (2.9)$$

when $P \neq \frac{1}{2}$ and where $\hat{\tau}$ is the obtained proportion of "Yes" responses in the sample. Thus, the randomized response technique does permit inferences about the population parameters even though the question any given respondent answered is unknown.

Despite its simplicity, the randomized response technique does have a major drawback: The randomization process introduces an additional source of random error that makes estimation of population parameters less efficient than it is for direct questioning. Consequently, much of the research on the randomized response technique since Warner's initial presentation has been concerned with the development of alternative RRT models that would make the technique more statistically efficient and, thereby, more practical. One widely used development is the unrelated question RRT (Greenberg, Abul-Ela, Simmons, & Horvitz, 1969). In this variant, the respondent is directed with probability P to answer the sensitive question and with probability $(1 - P)$ to answer a totally innocuous question (e.g., Were you born in the month of April?). Other major developments include extensions to questions involving more than two response categories (Abul-Ela, Greenberg, & Horvitz, 1967; Liu & Chow, 1976; Liu, Chow, & Mosley, 1975) and to questions requiring a quantitative or numerical response (Greenberg, Kuebler, Abernathy, & Horvitz, 1971; Himmelfarb & Edgell, 1980). This literature has been reviewed and summarized by Horvitz, Greenberg, and Abernathy (1975) and by Fox and Tracy (1986), and comprehensive bibliographies are available in Nathan (1988) and Himmelfarb and Edgell (1988).

Individuals' responses to questions obtained by various RRT models can be correlated with each other or with other variables to investigate their relationships. That is, even though respondents' answers in an RRT procedure are not always in response to the sensitive question, their respective answers can be scored and treated as individual values in standard formulas for various correlation coefficients. The obtained correlations will be attenuated relative to the true correlation between the variables, but the correlations can be corrected for this attenuation (see Fox & Tracy, 1984; Himmelfarb & Edgell, 1982; Kraemer, 1980). Statistical tests of the corrected correlation coefficients must be adjusted for the additional error introduced by an RRT procedure (Edgell, Himmelfarb, & Cira, 1986).

A number of experiments have compared responses obtained through direct questioning and an RRT procedure. Many of these studies involved questions about drug and other abuses or illegal activities. In general, higher rates of drug and alcohol use and fewer refusals to respond were reported under RRT conditions than under direct questioning (G. H. Brown & Harding, 1973; Goodstadt & Gruson, 1975; Reaser, Hartsock, & Hoehn, 1975; Zdep, Rhodes, Schwarz, & Kilkenny, 1979). Also, RRT compared with standard interview conditions produced higher rates of reported child abuse (Zdep & Rhodes, 1976) and reported abortions (I-Cheng, Chow, & Rider, 1972; Krotki & Fox, 1974). Yet, the strongest evidence for the superior validity of the RRT was obtained in a laboratory study by Shotland and Yankowski (1982), which resembled Quigley-Fernandez and Tedeschi's (1978) test of the bogus pipeline. Subjects, while waiting to participate in an experiment, overheard information about the correct answers to a test given in the experiment. When questioned in a face-to-face interview, 27 percent reported receiving this information and only 10 percent said they had used it. In the RRT condition, 64 percent confessed hearing the information, and 80 percent reported using it. Finally, attesting to the fact that social desirability does bias conventional self-reports and that the RRT reduces this distortion, Himmelfarb and Lickteig (1982) found a significant relation between the social desirability and undesirability of behaviors and attitudes and the extent to which these behaviors and attitudes are overreported and underreported on an anonymous self-administered questionnaire compared with a questionnaire completed through the use of an RRT procedure. Although more evidence is needed on the validity of the RRT, the research has supported the ability of the technique to reduce distortion in self-reports of socially undesirable behaviors.

Response Sets. In addition to motivated response distortions, a variety of more subtle response sets have been implicated as sources of invalidity in psychological measurement (Cronbach, 1946, 1950; Guilford, 1954). *Response sets* are tendencies to respond in particular ways that are not tied to the particular content of items or scales. These response tendencies have traditionally been viewed as reflecting consistent habits within individuals that vary across persons (Guilford, 1954, p. 453). It is also usually assumed that respondents are unaware of their response sets.

Response sets that have been considered particularly important in attitude measurement include tendencies to answer *yes* or to *agree* with items (acquiescence; Couch & Keniston, 1960), tendencies to give or avoid giving extreme responses, and tendencies to be cautious and noncommittal by choosing the neutral category. Although the pervasiveness of these response sets has been questioned (Rorer, 1965), strategies for minimizing them are frequently implemented by researchers. For example, to correct for acquiescence sets, researchers often include equal numbers of positively worded and negatively worded items on their scales. And to avoid noncommitment tendencies, investigators sometimes omit neutral response options (see Table 2.10), thereby forcing respondents to choose among nonneutral alternatives.

Because techniques for eliminating the effects of response sets and motivated response distortions are not always successful, attitude researchers have attempted to develop disguised, unobtrusive, or indirect measures of attitudes that do not rely on self-reports or even on verbal measures (see D. T. Campbell, 1950; Kidder & Campbell, 1970; Sechrest & Belew, 1983; Webb, Campbell, Schwartz, & Sechrest, 1966; Webb, Campbell, Schwartz, Sechrest, & Grove, 1981). Some of these instruments were considered in the earlier discussion of specific indicators of attitudes (e.g., physiological measures, Hammond's error-choice method).

Context and Other Response Effects

Survey researchers have identified a number of other factors that may bias questionnaire responses. A detailed examination of these *response effects* is beyond the scope of this chapter (see Bradburn, 1983; Schuman & Presser, 1981; Schuman & Kalton, 1985).[24] Here, we consider a subset of response effects that are particularly relevant to social psychological studies of attitudes. Because such studies are likely to use closed-ended, self-administered questionnaire measures of attitudes, interviewer effects and effects due to method of administration (e.g., face-to-face interviews versus telephone interviews) are of marginal concern. Also of marginal concern are response alternative order effects, which are minimized when attitudes are measured by questionnaires that allow respondents to review all the available alternatives. Schwarz, Strack, Hippler, and Bishop (1991) have provided an excellent discussion of how differences in administration method produce various types of response effects.

The question of whether to include a noncommittal or neutral response category in attitude assessment has been of considerable interest to survey researchers (e.g., Kalton, Roberts, & Holt, 1980; Schuman & Presser, 1981). Schuman and Presser's (1981) analysis of research on the *don't know* response category concluded that including or excluding an explicit don't know or neutral response alternative has little overall impact on estimates of the relative proportion of people who favor, versus oppose, an attitude issue. Nonetheless, Krosnick and Schuman's (1988) meta-analysis of the impact of attitude strength on response effects found that people with weaker attitudes tended to use neutral response alternatives more than did people whose attitudes were stronger (see discussions of attitude strength in Chapters 3, 4, and 12). Similar findings were obtained by Bishop (1990) in a meta-analysis of 18 telephone interview experiments.

Survey researchers have also examined a variety of response effects that reflect the order in which questions are asked. When questioned about either fictitious or unfamiliar issues, respondents frequently use the context created by earlier questions to interpret the question (see Schwarz & Strack, 1991). For example, Strack, Schwarz, and Wänke (cited in Schwarz & Strack, 1991) asked German college students about their attitudes toward an "educational contribution." For half of the students, this question was preceded by a question about the amount of tuition fees paid by students at U.S. universities. For the other half, the target question was preceded by a question about the amount the Swedish government pays college students for financial support. Attitudes were more favorable toward the "educational contribution" item when the question preceding it concerned the fees paid *to students*, rather than *by students*.

Question order effects are not limited to ambiguous questions and unknown issues. For example, Hyman and Sheatsley (1950) varied the order in which respondents were asked two questions about allowing newspaper reporters to enter foreign countries in order to report back to their own countries. One question asked whether U.S. reporters should be allowed into communist countries, and the other asked whether communist reporters should be allowed into the United States. The results indicated that respondents were *more* willing to allow communist reporters into the United States if they had first answered the question about U.S. reporters. Similarly, respondents were *less* willing to allow U.S. reporters into communist countries if they had first answered the question about communist reporters. According to Schuman and Ludwig (1983), who reported several replications of this finding, respondents' answers to the first question that was posed reflected their attitudes toward the United States and communism. Responses to the second question, however, reflected respondents' tendencies to be "even-handed." For example, if they had just endorsed the rights of U.S. reporters to enter communist countries, they presumably felt compelled to extend the same rights to communist reporters.

Feldman and Lynch (1988) have suggested a somewhat different and more general interpretation of this and other question order effects. In their view, people's responses to attitude queries reflect both constructive and memorial processes. Thus, earlier items often make salient to respondents information that they might not ordinarily consider in responding to subsequent, thematically related questions. In the Hyman and Sheatsley (1950) study, then, respondents exposed to the U.S. reporter–communist reporter order may have based their responses to the latter item on information that came to mind in responding to the U.S. reporter item, information that may not have been accessible to respondents exposed to the communist reporter–U.S. reporter order.

A more recent example of how earlier questions can bias responses to subsequent, related questions is contained in the results of the National Crime Survey (cited in Schuman & Presser, 1981). Respondents were asked to report victimization experiences. Half of the respondents answered 16 attitude items about crime prior to reporting their actual experiences, whereas these questions were omitted for the remaining respondents. Reports of victimization, especially of less serious crimes, were higher for the sample who responded to the earlier attitude items. Apparently, the attitude questions activated memories or images of victimization experiences. Another item order effect was reported by Turner and Kraus (1978). Some of their respondents were asked whether spending should be increased in 11 federal spending areas (e.g., defense, environment) and were then asked a general question about taxes (whether they paid overly high federal income taxes). Other respondents were asked about the spending areas *after* responding to this general question. Results showed that when the spending area questions came first, 14 percent fewer respondents thought income taxes were too high. The specific questions about federal spending areas presumably made respondents more aware of the many services funded by income tax revenue. As Schuman and Presser (1981) suggested, respondents may have derived their general conclusions about necessary income tax levels from the implications of the specific spending items. Such *general-specific* versus *specific-general* order effects have also been documented in other topic domains (e.g., Kalton, Collins, & Brook, 1978; Krosnick & Schuman, 1988; Schuman & Presser, 1981; Schwarz, Strack, & Mai, 1991; T. W. Smith, 1982).

Although various response effects have been demonstrated by survey researchers, the conditions under which they occur and their relation to seemingly relevant moderator variables such as attitude strength are not well understood at present (see Schuman & Kalton, 1985). Attempts to broaden our knowledge of context and other response effects are now focusing on ideas from basic research and theory in social cognition and information processing. Many of these ideas are discussed in this book (see Chapters 3 through 8). Significant conceptual contributions to this area have been made by Tourangeau and Rasinski (1988), Strack and Martin (1987), Schuman and his colleagues (e.g., Krosnick & Schuman, 1988; Schuman & Presser, 1981), and Schwarz and his colleagues (e.g., Hippler, Schwarz, & Sudman, 1987; Schwarz, Strack, Hippler, & Bishop, 1991; Schwarz & Sudman, 1992). This collaboration between survey researchers and cognitive social psychologists holds considerable promise for enriching our understanding of both basic processes in social cognition and attitudes as well as applied issues in attitude measurement (for an overview of this collaboration, see Jobe & Mingay, 1991).

Single- Versus Multiple-Item Measures

Surveys frequently measure attitudes by a single evaluative item (e.g., Do you approve of the way the President is doing his job?). The justification for using single-item measures is primarily economic: Surveys are costly, and the costs increase with the number of questions asked. As we have explained, however, there are good methodological reasons to prefer a composite score based upon a multiple-item index.

Multiple-item measures can compensate for the limitations inherent in most individual items. Any single item typically contains nuances of meaning and tone that may exert unintended influences on subjects' responses. Indeed, survey research has provided abundant evidence that slight differences in item wording can exert pronounced effects on responses. For example, in a classic study by Rugg (1941), one national sample was asked: "Do you think the United States should allow public speeches against democracy?" Another comparable sample was asked: "Do you think the United States should forbid public speeches against democracy?" Approximately 20 percent more of the respondents were willing to *not allow* such speeches than were willing to *forbid* them. This *forbid-versus-allow* effect has been replicated in several subsequent studies (Schuman & Presser, 1981). Similarly, T. W. Smith (1987) reported the results of a number of surveys that yielded systematic differences in the percentages of people indicating favorable attitudes toward the government doing more for "the poor" or "the unemployed" than for people "on welfare."

Clauses or phrases that are ostensibly irrelevant to the main issue posed in questions have also been shown to have a substantial impact on survey responses. For example,

Cantril (1940) asked one group of respondents: "Do you think the U.S. should do more than it is now doing to help England and France?" When the phrase "in their fight against Hitler" was added to the end of this question, the percentage saying *yes* increased from 13 percent to 20 percent. Similarly, support for sending U.S. troops to intervene in regional wars such as Vietnam was increased by adding the phrase "to stop a Communist takeover" (Mueller, 1973; Schuman & Presser, 1981).

Although research has documented that wording effects can occur, the extent to which minor wording differences influence survey responses is presently unknown, and a systematic understanding of when and why wording effects occur has yet to be achieved (Schuman & Kalton, 1985). Even in the absence of systematic theory about question wording, a number of principles of good question writing have been articulated (e.g., A. L. Edwards, 1957b; Payne, 1951; Sheatsley, 1983; Sudman & Bradburn, 1982).

In our discussion of various scaling techniques, we saw how poor items can be eliminated through item analysis procedures. By examining an item's operating characteristic, we can frequently tell whether the item is appropriate or not. The operating characteristic of an item relates scores on an item to attitude scores obtained over many other items (i.e., to total scores). With a single item, however, we cannot determine the item's operating characteristic nor can we correlate scores on that item with scores on other items. In essence, we lack an internal way of distinguishing between good and bad items when we only have a single item. Moreover, we have no way of estimating the reliability of the item or of estimating the magnitude of the relationships that would exist, in the absence of errors of measurement, between the variable that the item assesses and other variables.

In discussing the split-half method of assessing reliability, we noted that the correlation between the two halves is less than the reliability of the total scale. The Spearman-Brown formula was introduced to correct for this reduction. What may not have been apparent in the formula, however, is the general relationship that exists between the average reliability of items and the number of items in the scale. This relationship is shown in Figure 2.8 for several different possible item reliabilities. Although the relationship between the reliability of the total score and the number of items is one of diminishing returns, Figure 2.8 shows that the reliability of the total score always increases as the number of items increases if the average inter-item correlation remains constant. Indeed, given a particular average inter-item reliability estimate (correlation), one could determine from the Spearman-Brown formula how many items of that same reliability would be needed to boost the reliability of the total scale to any particular value. Thus, multiple-item measures have the added advantage of greater reliability.

In our discussion of validity, we noted that the validity of any measure is in part determined by the reliability of the measure. Unreliable measures of variables attenuate the relationships between the variables and, therefore, make it more difficult to observe the true relationships between variables. A reliable measure not only yields consistent scores from one observation to another, but also has greater potential for correlating highly with other variables. The value of aggregated measures for establishing strong

FIGURE 2.8. Total scale reliability as a function of the number of items in the scale and inter-item reliability values of .2, .4, .6, and .8.

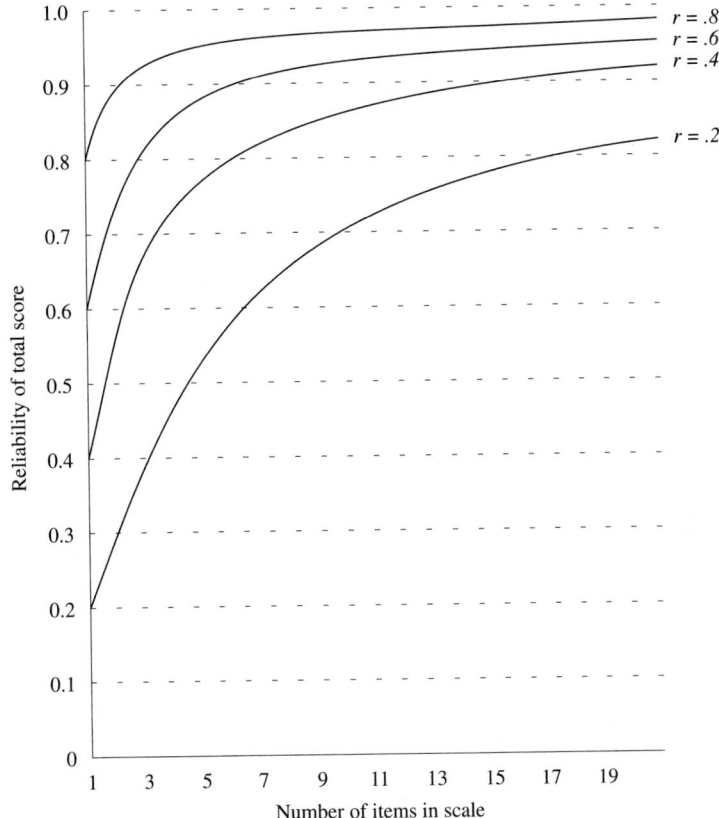

relations between variables is illustrated in Chapter 4 by Fishbein and Ajzen's (1974, 1975) research on the attitude-behavior relationship.

This chapter has emphasized attitude measurement methods based on multiple-item scales because of these well-known psychometric principles. Yet, as will become apparent in the following chapters, many successful studies of attitudes have assessed attitudes informally by one or two rating scales. These successes indicate that these single-item measures are reliable enough to detect mean differences between groups of reasonable size when variables are powerfully manipulated in carefully controlled settings. Yet, they may not be sufficiently reliable to correlate strongly with other measures, particularly hypothesized mediating variables. The reliability of our measures could be improved and, therefore, the relationships between variables enhanced with multi-item measures. Many of the other techniques discussed in this chapter should also prove useful for the development of more reliable and valid measures of attitudes.

────── **Conclusion**

Sixty years have passed since Thurstone initiated the development of formal scaling techniques of attitude measurement. Since then, a variety of both simple and mathematically complex models have been developed and applied to attitude measurement. The more popular unidimensional techniques have been summarized here.

Investigators of the 1930s, 1940s, and early 1950s were particularly interested in developing attitude measures and assessing their validity and susceptibility to bias. Such concerns continue today mainly among applied researchers. Interest in attitude measurement and related methodological issues declined in the late 1950s among most attitude researchers. By then, existing research suggested that attitude measures based on the Thurstone, Likert, Guttman, and semantic differential scaling techniques usually correlated quite well with one another, with none having any particular advantage over the others except for differences in their ease of construction. From the 1960s onward researchers became more involved with the testing of theoretical propositions related to issues of attitude formation and change.

Interest in attitude measurement may be increasing once more. This renewal of interest may be traced to several factors. First, there is increased concern about the applied relevance of attitude research. Applied researchers desire to develop scales for measuring attitudes toward a variety of contemporary issues. Because these scales are intended for general use beyond a single investigation, they are ordinarily constructed in accord with modern psychometric principles. These principles encourage multiple investigations to demonstrate that scales have sufficiently high reliability and validity to be useful for predicting and understanding the correlates of attitudes. Second, there is growing awareness that the study of relationships between theoretical variables cannot be divorced from the issue of how these variables were measured. This point was made salient in research on the attitude-behavior relation, where single-item measures of behavior contributed to the erroneous conclusion that attitudes were not related to behavior (see Chapter 4). Also, the increased use of sophisticated statistical techniques (e.g., structural equation models with latent variables; see Chapter 4) for testing mediational models of attitude change focuses concern on measurement issues.

Many of the measurement techniques considered in this chapter were imported from other areas of psychology at a time when there was little or no attitude theory. In contrast, as the chapters that follow attest, there is now an abundance of theories. A closer integration of theory and research on attitudes with the methodology of attitude measurement might prove to be quite fruitful. For example, current interest in attitude structure (see Chapter 3) might well lead to a greater emphasis on multidimensional aspects of attitude measurement and to the development of new techniques for measuring attitudes. The traditional scaling techniques described in this chapter could be adapted more fully for the assessment of attitude structure.

Particularly relevant to issues of attitude measurement is current theory on stages of information processing. Indeed, Tourangeau and Rasinski (1988) provided an excellent analysis of context effects in such terms. More generally, not all methods of assessing attitudes require that respondents engage in the same underlying processes, even when the attitude scores that are produced by various methods correlate highly with one another. Some methods require more elaborate and deeper cognitive processing, particularly when respondents must consider the implications of a large number of belief statements. Other methods, especially single-item measures, may encourage respondents to answer on the basis of a stored general evaluation of an attitude object. Moreover, certain methods may heighten respondents' self-presentational concerns or provide superficial cues that may guide their answers to attitudinal items. Obviously, these issues (e.g., depth of processing, self-presentational pressures, use of attitude-relevant cues) are of considerable interest in attitude theory and are considered throughout this book. Greater recognition of the interdependence of theory and measurement has considerable potential for the future of attitude research.

Notes

1. A linear transformation is of the form: $Y = bX + a$, where X is the original set of values, Y is the new set of values, b is the ratio of the unit of measurement of Y to the unit of measurement of X, and a is the origin or zero point—the value of Y when $X = 0$. For example, the transformation of Celsius to Fahrenheit is given by the linear equation $F = (9/5)C + 32$, where 9/5 is the ratio of the units of measurement of F and C and the 32 is the value of F when $C = 0$.

2. Measurement theorists often define different types of scales or levels of measurement by classes of *admissible scale transformations* (e.g., Krantz, Luce, Suppes, & Tversky, 1971; Suppes & Zinnes, 1963). Statements are regarded as meaningful only if they are invariant under all admissible scale transformations. In the case of an interval scale, only positive linear transformations are admissible. By that criterion, the statement that D's attitude is 2.5 times more favorable than B's is not a meaningful one because it is not invariant under all positive linear transformations (see Michell, 1986).

3. In the measurement and scaling literature these checks for consistency are often referred to as *internal consistency tests*. We have omitted the word *internal* and substituted *checks* for *tests* to avoid confusion with certain methods of estimating reliability that are frequently labeled measures of internal consistency (e.g., alpha; see subsequent discussion).

4. These statements about the Davison and Sharma (1988, 1990) findings simplify certain highly technical and important conditions that must be met before conclusions concerning measured variables apply to the underlying latent variable. Moreover, their proofs concern tests of the null hypothesis about differences between means or associations between variables. Conclusions about the size of a difference between means or the strength of an association do not apply to the underlying latent variable unless the observed variable was measured on an interval scale. Also, the results Davison and Sharma obtained for *t*-tests, one-way analyses of variance, and correlations do *not* generalize to the analysis of variance of factorial designs (see Davison & Sharma, 1990).

5. Coombs' (1950) unfolding technique also locates both stimuli and persons simultaneously on the attribute being scaled. Because this technique has received only quite limited attention within the attitudes domain, it is omitted from this chapter (see Coombs, 1950, 1964; Dawes, 1972; Dawes & Smith, 1985; McIver & Carmines, 1981).

6. It is unclear whether the instruction to sort the items into equally spaced intervals is an integral part of the method. Thurstone and Chave's (1929, p. 31) description of their instructions to their judges does not mention this instruction. The end intervals and the middle interval were labeled, but Thurstone and Chave thought any further descriptions would prevent the subjects from sorting the items into what appeared to the subjects to be equal shifts of opinion between successive piles (p. 30). However, in a subsequent paper by Thurstone (1930) that described a scale for measuring attitude toward the movies, the judges were instructed to treat the intervals as equal steps. A number of general descriptions of scaling techniques describe the method of equal-appearing intervals as including the instruction (e.g., B. F. Green, 1954; Torgerson, 1958), but others do not (e.g., A. L. Edwards, 1957b). Regardless of whether the instruction is included, it is clear that the method assumes that the interval widths are equal.

7. The method of successive intervals was apparently independently derived by Guilford (1938), who called it the "method of absolute scaling" and by Attneave (1949), who called it the "method of graded dichotomies."

8. Setting the standard deviations equal to some number is equivalent to choosing a unit of measurement. The unit of measurement is arbitrary for an interval scale.

9. Because the normal distribution extends from $-\infty$ to $+\infty$, proportions of 0.00 and 1.00 have indeterminant z values. Also, when a proportion is quite extreme (e.g., $\leq.02$ or $\geq.98$), its z-score value can vary considerably depending on the value in the third decimal place of the proportion. Reliable determination of the value in the third decimal place would require an impractically large number of judges. Therefore, B. F. Green (1954) recommended that z-score cell entries with values greater than ± 2 should also be eliminated.

10. The mathematical details for deriving the interval widths and scale values are quite simple. The z-score in any cell of Table 2.6 is the location in normal curve units of the upper boundary of that interval (column) in the distribution for that item (row). Thus, t_c, the upper boundary of interval c in the distribution of item i, has a z-score value of $z_{ci} = (t_c - s_i) / \sigma_i$. The difference between the upper boundaries in any two adjacent intervals, c and c', in the same distribution is then given by:

$$z_{ci} - z_{c'i} = [(t_c - s_i)/\sigma_i] - [(t_{c'} - s_i)/\sigma_i] \quad (2.1a)$$

Because the s_i values in the first and second terms on the right side of the equation cancel, $z_{ci} - z_{c'i} = (t_c - t_{c'})/\sigma_i$. We see, then, that the difference between z-scores in adjacent columns of the same row is proportional to the width of the interval between their boundaries. The difference between the upper boundary of interval c in any two different distributions i and j is given by a similar expression:

$$z_{ci} - z_{cj} = [(t_c - s_i)/\sigma_i] - [(t_c - s_j)/\sigma_j] \quad (2.1b)$$

If we make the usual assumption that the standard deviations of all the item distributions are equal (i.e., $\sigma_i = \sigma_j$ for all i and j), then the σs in the above equations are equal to a constant which can be set equal to 1 with no loss of generality (see note 8). Equation 2.1a then simplifies to $z_{ci} - z_{c'i} = t_c - t_{c'}$ and Equation 2.1b simplifies to $z_{ci} - z_{cj} = -s_i - (-s_j) = s_j - s_i$. We see then that the difference between the z-scores in adjacent columns in the same row provides an estimate of

the width of the interval between the two columns and that the difference between the z-scores in the same column but in different rows provides an estimate of the difference in the scale values of the items.

11. Under the assumption that the item distributions all have standard deviations equal to 1, the z-score in any cell ci is $z_{ci} = t_c - s_i$. When there are entries in each of the cells, the mean of any column c is $\bar{z}_c = t_c - \bar{s}$. By fixing the zero point of the scale at $\bar{s} = 0$, the mean of the z-scores in a column is just t_c. The mean of any row i is $\bar{z} = \bar{t} - s_i$, where $\bar{t}$ is the mean of the column means (grand mean). The scale value of the item in row i, s_i, then is just $\bar{t} - \bar{z}_i$.

12. Since Thurstone's early work, a number of procedures have been developed to reduce the labor involved in judging a large number of stimuli. For example, subsets of stimuli can be judged by subgroups of judges (see Torgerson, 1958, pp. 191–194). Nonetheless, these techniques have not been put to much use in attitude item scaling.

13. Guttman scaling is not limited to items that involve only two response categories, such as *agree* or *disagree*, but can handle multiple response categories that indicate the degree of agreement and disagreement (see Guttman, 1944, 1947a).

14. In theory no allowance is made for error, although Guttman's concept of quasi-scales and the acceptability of coefficients of reproducibility between .85 and .90 indicates some tolerance of random error in practice. *Latent structure analysis* (Lazarsfeld, 1950, 1954; Lazarsfeld & Henry, 1968), which incorporates aspects of Guttman scaling, more realistically allows for a probabilistic relationship between the latent, underlying attribute and the overt response (B. F. Green, 1954; Torgerson, 1958).

15. T. L. Kelley (1939) found that if the total scale scores are distributed normally, the selection of respondents from the upper and lower 27 percent of the distribution provides optimal discrimination. For flatter than normal distributions, the

percentage needed for optimal discrimination is larger (Cureton, 1957).

16. The item-total score correlation is calculated with the item score excluded from the total score.

17. A high negative correlation indicates that the item was scored incorrectly either because the investigator incorrectly judged its favorability or in some way mixed up the scoring of the alternatives. In either case, items that correlate negatively should have their scoring reversed.

18. It is common in the research literature to see various sorts of rating scales erroneously described as *Likert-type* scales, even scales that do not require respondents to indicate the extent of their agreement or disagreement with the content of an item about an attitude object. General rating scales should certainly not be called Likert scales. Furthermore, agree-disagree scales should not be labeled Likert scales because the term *scale* should be reserved for the *set of items* that has been chosen based on Likert scaling procedures (i.e., item analysis) and that can therefore be used as a scale to assess an attitude.

19. Factor analysis is a statistical technique that attempts to account for the intercorrelations among variables by a smaller number of underlying dimensions or factors. It examines the intercorrelations among items and attempts to find clusters of items that are highly correlated with one another but are not correlated highly with items in other clusters. These clusters are called "factors" or "dimensions."

   Confirmatory factor analysis tests hypotheses about which variables are related to or "load on" which underlying factors and how the factors themselves are related. Most confirmatory factor analysis programs incorporate a test of goodness-of-fit that assesses how well the observed relationships among the variables can be accounted for by the hypothesized model. To assess whether a set of items has a single factor structure, one would specify that all the items load on a single common factor. The fit of the single factor model could be contrasted with that provided by a multidimensional factor structure.

20. The notion of strictly parallel measures with the same means and standard deviations should be regarded as part of an idealized model that can only be approximated in reality. Similarly, the assumptions of independence of true scores and errors in classic true score theory are also an approximation to reality. Discussion of some alternative item response theories that do not make these restrictive assumptions is beyond the scope of this chapter (see Crocker & Algina, 1986; Nunnally, 1978).

21. By definition, two measures are parallel if, for each individual, they yield the same true score and differ only in their errors, that is, $X = T + e$ and $X' = T + e'$. The correlation between parallel measures, $\rho_{XX'}$, is given by the expression:

$$\rho_{XX'} = \frac{\sigma_{XX'}}{\sigma_X \sigma_{X'}}$$

where $\sigma_{XX'}$ is the covariance of measures X and X'. Because parallel measures have the same means and standard deviations, the denominator of the equation above is σ^2_X. The numerator of the equation can be rewritten as $\sigma_{(T+e)\,(T+e')}$. When the expected value of the numerator is taken and the independence assumptions of classic true score theory are invoked, the numerator becomes σ^2_T. Then:

$$\rho_{XX'} = \frac{\sigma^2_T}{\sigma^2_X}$$

which is the proportion of the observed score variance that is true score variance or the reliability of a measure.

22. An alternative to the theory of parallel measurement is domain sampling theory, which assumes that items are sampled randomly from the content domain (see Nunnally, 1978). Both theories lead to the same results and equations, given the assumptions of classic true score theory. We have chosen to explicate reliability theory in terms of parallel measurement theory because the ideas of domain sampling, while fitting attitude measures based on the psychometric model, seem less appropriate for attitude measures based on psychophysical and other models.

23. In classic true score theory, the reliability of a measure also can be shown to be equal to the square of the correlation between true and observed scores. Since a variable cannot correlate with the true score of another variable higher than it correlates with its own true score, the square root of the reliability coefficient of a measure is the upper limit for its validity coefficient.

24. Biases that may affect the proportion of people who favor an issue are of particular concern to survey researchers because they are interested in generalizing their results to some real population.

Although this issue is less troublesome to laboratory researchers, whose main interests are in finding relative differences between experimental and control conditions, response effects can affect the precision of experimental outcomes and restrict generalizability of results. Moreover, even in the laboratory, an attitude measure is rarely administered by itself. Information on other variables (e.g., manipulation checks, measures of possible mediators and moderators) is often collected along with the attitude measure. Context effects can occur between different measuring instruments as well as within a particular instrument.

3

The Structure of Attitudes and Beliefs

Psychologists have often ascribed structural properties to attitudes. One sense in which they have investigated structure is in terms of mental representations of the attitude itself and of the various classes of responses used to infer and measure attitudes. Because such structural properties describe the internal structure of attitudes, we refer to them as aspects of *intra-attitudinal structure*. We consider such properties in the first half of this chapter. For example, an assumption that some psychologists have made about intra-attitudinal structure is that people represent their own attitudes as locations along a pro-versus-con or agree-versus-disagree dimension. Yet the primary emphasis in research on the internal structure of attitudes is on just one of the classes of responses used to infer or measure attitudes—namely, the beliefs that people hold about attitude objects. For example, research has examined the extent to which these beliefs are *complex* or *simple* as well as *consistent* or *inconsistent* with evaluations of the attitude object.

The term *structure* also implies relationships between attitudes. When psychologists regard attitudes as related to one another, they consider the attributes of larger structures that link attitudes with other attitudes. In this book, we term such properties *inter-attitudinal structure* and discuss them in the second half of the chapter. For example, these larger structures may be *cognitively consistent* as defined by balance theory (Heider, 1958) or may be thematically consistent in the sense that they form an *ideology* (of political conservatism, for example).

Although some aspects of attitude structure have been studied extensively (e.g., cognitive balance), knowledge about other aspects is quite rudimentary. In fact, despite their obvious importance, some basic structural issues remained unresolved. Therefore, it is quite impossible for us to tell a coherent story that progresses smoothly from one aspect of structure to another. As we tell the story that research and theory have made available to us, we point out the many lacunae in our knowledge of intra-attitudinal and inter-attitudinal structure. We of course review in some detail the structural topics that have been researched most thoroughly.[1]

INTRA-ATTITUDINAL STRUCTURE

To begin our analysis of the internal structure of attitudes we must first return to our definition of attitude and consider its implications for structural issues. As we explained in Chapter 1, an attitude is a psychological tendency that is expressed by evaluating particular entities with some degree of favor or disfavor. Because of the simplicity of this definition, attitudes cannot have structural properties except of a relatively elementary sort when they are viewed solely at the abstract level of evaluation. More complicated structural properties come into play only when we take into account, along with evaluation, the cognitive, affective, and behavioral aspects of attitudes. We consider these more complex aspects of intra-attitudinal structure later in the chapter. First we discuss the representation of attitude structure in terms of an evaluative dimension.

Dimensional Representations of Attitude Structure

As we pointed out in the first two chapters, social scientists typically assess people's attitudes by placing them on a bipolar evaluative continuum. Techniques of attitude measurement provide methods of locating people's attitudes on such a dimension. It is quite another matter to assume that people represent their own attitudes as a point on a dimension. Only occasionally have psychologists interpreted the idea that attitudes exist on a bipolar continuum as an assumption about the psychological structure of individuals. When applied to individuals, this assumption implies that people encode, store, and retrieve attitudinally relevant information in terms of this bipolar evaluative schema.

Research Testing the Assumption That
Attitudes Have Bipolar Structure

Charles Judd and James Kulik (1980) provided one of the only empirical tests of the idea that people conceptualize their attitudes in terms of a bipolar evaluative schema. Consistent with research on the effects of schemas on information processing (see Markus & Zajonc, 1985), they reasoned that people who hold such a schema should process information that "fits" it more easily than information that fits it less well. Judd and Kulik's experimental design involved giving subjects attitude-relevant statements on three issues: women's rights (e.g., "The Equal Rights Amendment should be supported by all who believe that discrimination is wrong"); capital punishment (e.g., "Only for the very most serious crimes should capital punishment even be considered"); and majority rule in South Africa (e.g., "Majority rule would only complicate the lives of most South Africans"). To examine the ease with which subjects processed the statements Judd and Kulik assessed the *speed* with which subjects (a) indicated their agreement with the statements and (b) judged how favorable or unfavorable a position each statement took on the issue; they also examined subjects' *recall* of the statements. Treating faster response times and better recall as indexes of ease of processing, these investigators found that statements that were favorable or unfavorable were processed more easily than more neutral statements. These findings suggest that information fits an attitude schema to the extent that the information is definitely pro or con on the issue that is represented.

Interestingly, Judd and Kulik (1980) did not define the dimensional schema underlying their subjects' attitudes in terms of favorability toward the attitude object. Instead, they defined this dimension in terms of their respondents' *agreement* (or disagreement) with statements about the attitude object (see also Pratkanis, 1985, 1989). Because this definition implies that information eliciting extreme agreement or disagreement best fits the attitudinal schema, Judd and Kulik's primary aim was to show that extremity of agreement or disagreement (not extremity of favorability or unfavorability) is related to ease of processing. Indeed, they did find that statements were more easily processed to the extent that they elicited strong agreement or disagreement. However, this relation was, on the whole, no larger than that between ease of processing and subjects' judgments of favorability.

From a practical standpoint, it may usually be unimportant whether psychologists regard people as conceptualizing the attitudinal continuum in terms of favorability or agreement. Suggesting that it may not matter are findings showing that people with favorable attitudes on an issue are able to generate mainly pro statements with which they agree and con statements with which they disagree and that people with unfavorable attitudes generate mainly con statements with which they agree and pro statements with which they disagree (e.g., Feather, 1969).[2] As a consequence, agreement and favorability tend to be collinear, and a distinction between the two is unneeded. Notwithstanding this practical consideration, for people whose attitudes are moderate on a scale of favorability versus unfavorability, an agreement continuum would order beliefs differently than a favorability continuum. Specifically, people with relatively neutral attitudes would place statements they accept at the middle of a favorability continuum and statements they reject at both ends. The correlation between agreement and favorability would be near zero for such individuals. Research on relatively neutral attitudes thus may help resolve the issue of whether people define their attitudinal schemas in terms of favorability on issues or in terms of their own agreement or disagreement.

Finally, we note that the notion of "fit" between belief statements and dimensional schemas needs clarification. Judd and Kulik's (1980) findings suggested that statements at the extremes of favorability or agreement continua are more easily processed than less extreme statements and therefore can be considered to have fit the schema more closely than less extreme statements. Yet, because a dimension has a middle as well as two ends, logic suggests that *all* information located along a dimension could be regarded as fitting it. Perhaps regions of attitude dimensions containing positions that people are indifferent about or that people cannot identify as pro or con are relatively vague and unelaborated in their cognitions. If so, information would not fit middle regions of dimensions in the same sense that it would fit the clearer and more elaborated regions at the ends of dimensions.

Social Judgment Theory and the Dimensional Representation of Attitudes

The assumption that people conceptualize their attitudes in terms of a bipolar evaluative schema is a central feature of only one general theory of attitudes—namely, *social judgment theory*, which was formulated by Muzafer Sherif and Carolyn Wood Sherif (C. W. Sherif, Sherif, & Nebergall, 1965; M. Sherif & Hovland, 1961; see

TABLE 3.1

Statements Representing the Attitudinal Continuum for Attitudes Toward Legalized Abortion

A. A Constitutional Amendment guaranteeing the right to life of the unborn is absolutely necessary; legal abortion should never be available.

B. To protect the rights of the unborn baby, legal abortion should not be available.

C. To protect the right of unborn children, legal abortion should be available only if childbirth would cause the woman's death.

D. To protect the rights of the unborn children, legal abortion should require the consent of the husband (or parents, if the woman is a minor) and be performed only in case of rape or incest, thus severely limiting the number of abortions performed.

E. To protect the rights of unborn children, legal abortion should require the consent of the husband (or parents, if the woman is a minor) and be performed only if childbirth could impair the woman's health, thus somewhat limiting the number of abortions performed.

F. It is difficult to decide whether the rights of the unborn or of the woman are more important in formulating laws regarding abortion.

G. A legal abortion should be available during the first 3 months of pregnancy, but not after.

H. A legal abortion should be available during the first 6 months of pregnancy, but not after.

I. A legal abortion should be available during the first 6 months of pregnancy, but after that time only if the woman's life or health would be endangered by a birth.

J. The law should allow the woman to control her own body by permitting a legal abortion upon her request.

K. Abortion on demand and paid by the state should be guaranteed by law to any woman when she asks for it; without this protection, she is a slave to the state through compulsory pregnancy.

Source: These statements were presented by C. W. Sherif (1980, p. 26).

Chapter 8). The Sherifs maintained that people represent their attitudes in terms of a dimensional schema or internal reference scale, which was sometimes called a psychosocial scale in this tradition. To investigate this dimension, researchers' first step is to write a series of belief statements about an attitude object and order these statements along a continuum of favorability.[3] Table 3.1 shows a list of such statements prepared for a study of attitudes toward abortion (Kearney [1975], as summarized by C. W. Sherif, 1980).

Latitudes of Acceptance, Rejection, and Noncommitment. Social judgment theorists proposed that people divide the evaluative continuum into three ranges or latitudes, which are known as the *latitudes of acceptance, rejection, and noncommitment.* The latitude of acceptance is the region of the continuum containing the beliefs that a person finds acceptable, and the latitude of rejection is the region containing unacceptable beliefs. Finally, the latitude of noncommitment is the region containing those beliefs found neither acceptable nor unacceptable. These latitudes are estimated by presenting respondents with a list of belief statements on a particular issue and asking them to indicate, in separate presentations of the list, (a) the most acceptable statement, (b) all other acceptable statements, (c) the most objectionable statement, and (d) all other objectionable statements. Operationally, statements selected as acceptable or the most acceptable define the latitude of acceptance, statements selected as objectionable or the most objectionable define the latitude of rejection, and statements *not* selected for any of these categories define the latitude of noncommitment.

These operations resemble those used when attitudes are assessed on a Thurstone scale (see Chapter 2). In both methods, respondents agree or disagree with belief statements that represent varying positions along the evaluative continuum. However, absent from Thurstone operations (and present in social judgment procedures) is respondents' categorization of the beliefs that they do *not* endorse into classes of (a) objectionable beliefs and (b) beliefs that are neither acceptable or objectionable. In addition, whereas Thurstone procedures average the scale values of the endorsed beliefs to represent the respondent's attitude as a point on the evaluative dimension, social judgment research focuses on the locations of all acceptable and unacceptable beliefs. Although the Sherifs were also interested in respondents' most acceptable position, they repeatedly emphasized that attitude cannot be reduced to a point. Instead, they regarded the individual's representation of the entire dimension, as structured into latitudes, as essential to understanding attitudes.[4]

By postulating latitudes of acceptance, rejection, and noncommitment, social judgment theorists assumed that people represent the attitudinal continuum in terms of their agreement with belief statements *and* the favorability of these statements toward the attitude object. Recall that the Judd and Kulik (1980) research described in the preceding section did not resolve the issue of whether people conceptualize the dimensional schemas that represent their attitudes in terms of agreement or favorability. Social judgment researchers have it both ways, so to speak: They suggested that people define the attitudinal continuum itself in terms of favorability versus unfavorability toward the attitude object, but define the latitudes in terms of their personal agreement and disagreement with varying degrees of favorability or unfavorability. By this device, people's agreement and their perceptions of the favorability of attitudinal positions are both represented.

To illustrate their assumptions about attitude structure, social judgment researchers assessed latitudes of acceptance, rejection, and noncommitment for a number of issues. For example, C. W. Sherif and collaborators' (1965) study of attitudes toward presidential candidates in the 1960 election shows common patterns in the width and location of these latitudes. Table 3.2 lists the statements used in this research, and Figures 3.1 and 3.2 display the latitudes of a sample of college students from Washington and Oregon whose attitudes were assessed before the 1960 election. Figure 3.1 displays the latitudes of respondents who had relatively extreme attitudes concerning this election. The upper panel of the figure shows the latitudes of the respondents who chose statement A (highly pro-Republican) as most acceptable, and the lower panel shows the latitudes of the respondents who chose statement I (highly pro-Democratic). Note that the latitude of acceptance in each panel is located at the

TABLE 3.2

Statements Representing the Attitudinal Continuum for Attitudes Toward Republican and Democratic Presidential and Vice-Presidential Candidates

A. The election of the Republican presidential and vice-presidential candidates in November is absolutely essential from all angles in the country's interests.

B. On the whole the interests of the country will be served best by the election of the Republican candidates for president and vice-president in the coming election.

C. It seems that the country's interests would be better served if the presidential and vice-presidential candidates of the Republican party are elected this November.

D. Although it is hard to decide, it is probable that the country's interests may be better served if the Republican presidential and vice-presidential candidates are elected in November.

E. From the point of view of the country's interests, it is hard to decide whether it is preferable to vote for presidential and vice-presidential candidates of the Republican party or the Democratic party in November.

F. Although it is hard to decide, it is probable that the country's interests may be better served if the Democratic presidential and vice-presidential candidates are elected in November.

G. It seems that the country's interests would be better served if the presidential and vice-presidential candidates of the Democratic party are elected this November.

H. On the whole the interests of the country will be served best if the presidential and vice-presidential candidates of the Democratic party are elected this November.

I. The election of the Democratic presidential and vice-presidential candidates in November is absolutely essential from all angles in the country's interests.

Source: These statements were presented by C. W. Sherif, Sherif, and Nebergall (1965, p. 28).

preferred end of the scale, the latitude of rejection at the non-preferred end, and the latitude of noncommitment near the middle.

In contrast, Figure 3.2 displays the latitudes of respondents who had more neutral attitudes concerning the 1960 election. The upper panel of the figure shows the latitudes of the respondents who chose statement D (mildly pro-Republican) as most acceptable, and the lower panel shows the latitudes of the respondents who chose statement F (mildly pro-Democratic). Note that in these panels the latitude of rejection is located at both ends of the scale, the latitude of acceptance near the middle, and the latitude of noncommitment between the accepted and rejected statements.

Social judgment theorists made various predictions that invoked the assumption that people commonly divide the attitudinal continuum into three regions. Among these predictions is the Sherifs' claim that the width of the latitude of rejection is positively related to the importance or involvingness of attitudes—a variable we consider later in this chapter as well as in subsequent chapters (C. W. Sherif et al., 1965; Sherif & Hovland, 1961). Furthermore, these theorists proposed that (a) the widths of the latitudes and their locations on the evaluative continuum determine people's judgments of attitude-relevant messages and (b) these judgments in turn affect the attitude change that these messages induce. These claims are considered in Chapters 8 and 12.

**FIGURE 3.1.
Latitudes of
acceptance,
rejection, and
noncommitment for
the 1960
presidential
election. For
respondents
choosing an extreme
position as *most
acceptable*, each
panel represents the
percentages of
respondents who
accepted and
rejected the other
positions and who
remained
noncommitted on
them. The upper
panel shows the
respondents who
chose position A
(extremely pro-
Republican) as most
acceptable, and the
lower panel shows
those who chose
position I (extremely
pro-Democratic).
This figure was
adapted from C. W.
Sherif, Sherif, and
Nebergall (1965,
Figure 2.1a, Panels
A and I, p. 32).**

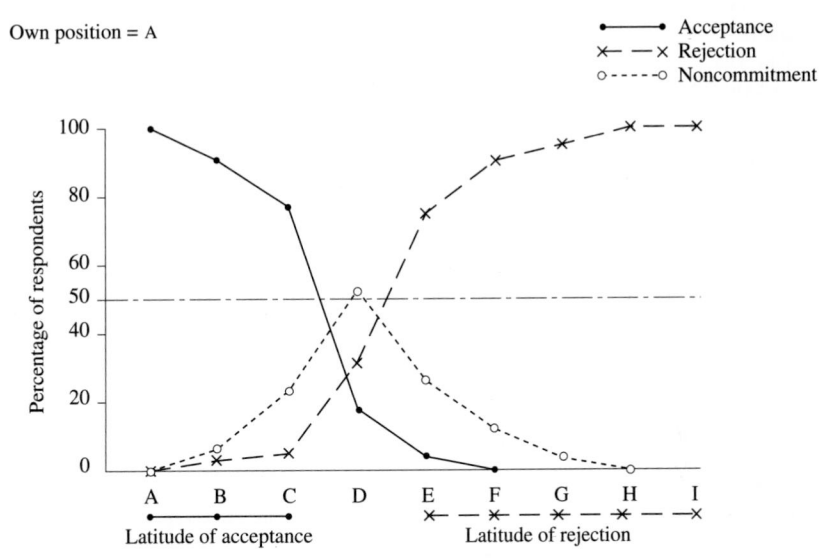

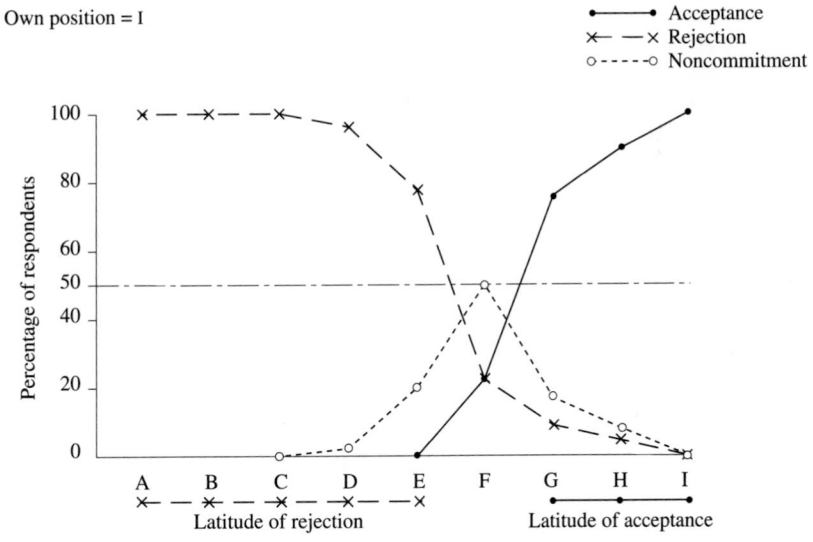

**FIGURE 3.2.
Latitudes of
acceptance,
rejection, and
noncommitment for
the 1960
presidential
election. For
respondents
choosing a moderate
position as *most
acceptable*, each
panel represents the
percentages of
respondents who
accepted and
rejected the other
positions and who
remained
noncommitted on
them. The upper
panel shows the
respondents who
chose position D
(mildly pro-
Republican) as most
acceptable, and the
lower panel shows
those who chose
position F (mildly
pro-Democratic).
This figure was
adapted from C. W.
Sherif, Sherif, and
Nebergall (1965,
Figure 2.1a, Panels
D and F, p. 35).**

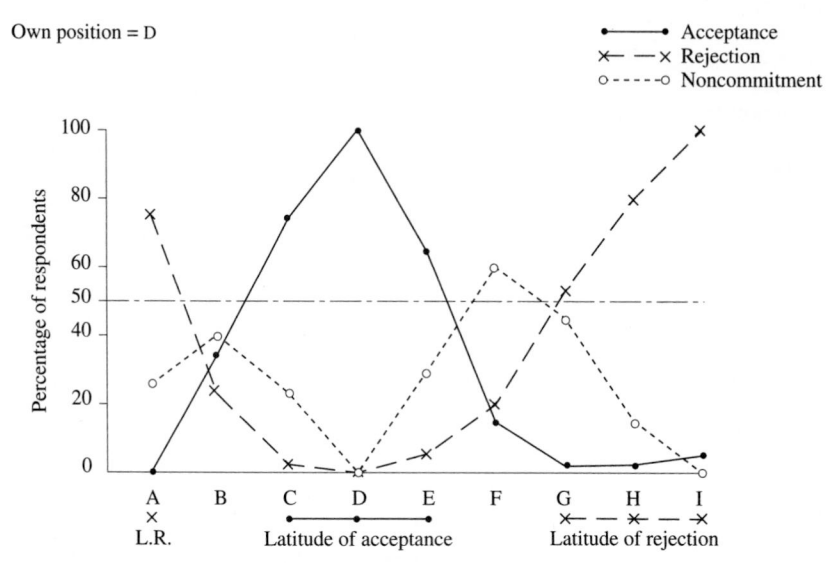

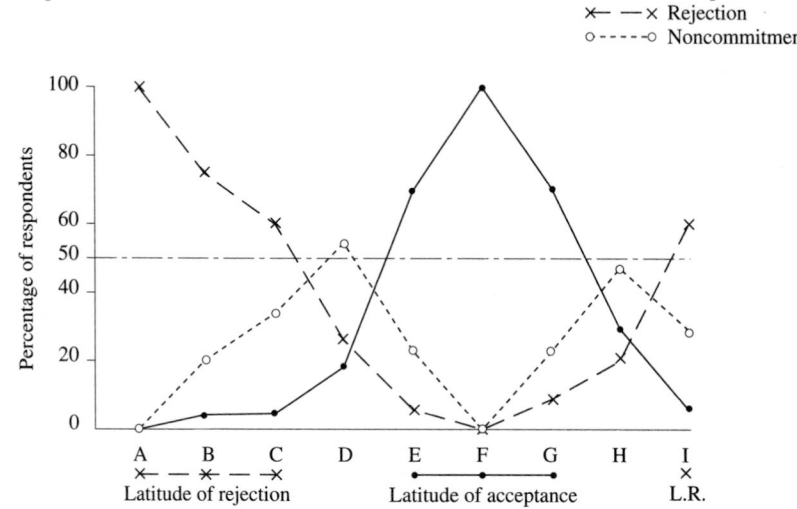

The Articulation of Attitudinal Dimensions. If readers will step back for a moment from the social judgment idea that people divide attitudinal dimensions into three latitudes, it can be appreciated that this division is one specific version of a more general structural property of attitudinal dimensions—namely, the property of *articulation*. Thus, articulation of an attribute or dimension has been defined as "the number of reliable distinctions among objects that a person makes on the attribute" (W. A. Scott, 1969, p. 263). In relation to an attitudinal dimension, articulation is greater to the extent that people can make a larger number of reliable distinctions between stimuli (i.e., belief statements, behaviors) in terms of their favorability to the attitude object.

Although social judgment theorists maintained—through their concepts of latitudes of acceptance, rejection, and noncommitment—that people categorize attitudinal stimuli into just three groups, they also regarded the articulation of the attitudinal dimension as a variable property of attitudes. Using the method that they dubbed the *own categories procedure*, the Sherifs and their colleagues investigated respondents' spontaneous groupings of attitudinal statements into categories (see C. W. Sherif et al., 1965). This method, as described in Chapter 2, requires that subjects sort statements into as many or few categories as seem necessary to put into the same pile statements that express the same stand on the issue under consideration. Their research using this sorting task particularly focused on the influence of subjects' ego-involvement in a topic, a variable that we discuss later in this chapter and more extensively in Chapter 8. These studies indicated that subjects who were highly involved in a topic used fewer categories than subjects who were relatively uninvolved; involved subjects thus had a less articulated attitudinal dimension. Moreover, involved subjects placed many statements in the category most distant from their own attitudinal position, that is, in a category identifiable as a latitude of rejection. Less involved subjects distributed their statements more evenly across their categories. The Sherifs thus initiated research on the articulation of attitudinal dimensions, but there has been little subsequent attention to this issue. The extent to which people ordinarily make fine or coarse discriminations along attitudinal dimensions surely deserves more extensive study.[5]

Research Questioning
Biopolar Dimensional Representations of Attitudes

In describing people's representations of social attitudes, social judgment researchers always placed statements expressing the views of social groups who oppose one another on an issue at the opposite poles of the attitudinal continuum (see, for example, Table 3.1). Yet there are reasons to doubt whether people routinely conceptualize attitudes in this manner. In particular, research by Kerlinger (1984) that we review in this section has raised questions about such representations of attitudes, and, as we will show, other investigators' work is relevant as well.

Kerlinger's Research. Challenging this social judgment assumption that people's attitudinal schemas are bipolar, Kerlinger (1984) argued that attitudinal domains such as liberalism and conservatism are better represented by two relatively independent dimensions because people who strongly agree with statements at one end of a conventional attitudinal continuum are often indifferent to statements at the other end. They do not oppose the beliefs of the opposite camp so much as they find them somewhat irrelevant to their own beliefs. As Kerlinger (1984) showed, people who are liberal endorse ideas such as freedom of the individual, participatory social equality, tolerance of different viewpoints, constructive social change, the rights of minorities, rational approaches to social problems, and positive government action to ameliorate social problems. In contrast, people who are conservative endorse social stability, the maintenance of religion and morality, the natural inequality of people, individualism and individual initiative, the sanctity of private property, and the importance of business and industry in the society.

Kerlinger argued that liberals are generally not opposed to the values of the conservative agenda, nor are conservatives generally opposed to the values of the liberal agenda. Instead, people who have one set of these political commitments regard the other set of commitments as somewhat unimportant and give them a low priority. In Kerlinger's treatment, political values such as freedom of the individual and the rights of minorities are termed *referents*. Referents on one's own side of the issue are regarded as *criterial*, whereas referents on the other side of the issue are not. Responses to non-criterial belief statements tend to be unpredictable and typically average to neutral ratings or slight disagreement (see Kerlinger, 1984).

In essence, Kerlinger's research has shown that social attitudes that have ordinarily been considered unidimensional and bipolar by researchers who have constructed attitude scales (see Chapter 2) often have a bidimensional and unipolar structure in the population at large. From this perspective, liberalism versus conservatism would be represented by two unipolar dimensions, one containing liberal belief statements and the other containing conservative statements. Kerlinger (1984) presented numerous factor-analytic studies of social attitudes that supported his claim that such two-dimensional structures are common. Specifically, he typically obtained a two-factor structure, with a small negative correlation between the factors.

This two-dimensional structure is obtained when data from populations of respondents are analyzed. However, as our discussion of attitude structure has already implied, it is a different matter to analyze structure at the level of individual and thereby to assume that people represent their own and others' attitudes in terms of two dimensions.[6] Individuals presumably think about social issues mainly in terms of their own values or criterial referents. For example, conservatives would tend to think about political issues in terms of values such as individualism and individual initiative, and the values of the opposing camp (i.e., non-criterial referents) would be less elaborated. Perhaps people are relatively unfamiliar with opposing values, or perhaps their relevance to the issue has been rejected by a more dynamic process that people invoke to defend their own position (see Chapter 10). At any rate, conservatives would be unlikely to think about political issues in terms of liberal concepts such as constructive social change. More generally, people who are politically conservative base their political attitudes on beliefs that are relatively non-overlapping with those that underlie liberals' attitudes.

Other Research Relevant to Dimensional Representations. Kerlinger's views are consistent with research by Kristiansen and Zanna (1988) on the values that people use to justify their attitudes. In a sample of Canadians, these researchers assessed attitudes toward the issue of abortion on demand and allowing nuclear weapons in Canada. These respondents also indicated the relevance that each of 18 values had to their attitude on each issue (e.g., values such as a world at peace, happiness, wisdom, national security, salvation). Respondents with negative and positive attitudes differed in the values that they regarded as relevant to these issues. For example, respondents who favored nuclear weapons rated national security and a comfortable life as more relevant than did respondents opposed to nuclear weapons. These antinuclear respondents selected wisdom, salvation, and true friendship as more relevant than did the pronuclear respondents (see van der Pligt & Eiser, 1984, for related findings on nuclear weapons).

Also supportive of Kerlinger's claims that liberals and conservatives base their attitudes on different beliefs is Luker's (1984) research on pro-life and pro-choice activists. Luker's study, which was based on unstructured interviews with activists, suggested that pro-life activists based their attitudes toward abortion on beliefs such as the following: The purpose of sex is procreation; parenthood is a natural and necessary function, not a social role. In contrast, pro-choice activists based their attitudes on beliefs such as the following: The purpose of sex is to foster intimacy and experience pleasure; parenthood means wanting a child and giving it one's best psychological, social, and financial resources.

These conclusions about attitudes toward abortion were supported by Tourangeau, Rasinski, and D'Andrade's (1991) hierarchical cluster analysis of college students' sorting of statements on abortion and welfare into categories based on similarity. These sorting data, when interpreted in conjunction with students' agreement with the statements, suggested that students holding contrasting views on these issues framed the issues quite differently by linking the issues to differing values and premises, especially on the welfare issue. For example, antiwelfare students believed that welfare is too widespread and has a disincentive effect that discourages poor people from seeking work; they also believed that the poor should be trying to help themselves. In contrast, prowelfare students believed that welfare provides a necessary safety net and that society has a responsibility to take care of poor people; they also believed that poverty is a consequence of the economic system and not the fault of the poor. In summary, the findings from several research projects (see also J. Scott, 1989) are consistent with Kerlinger's (1984) views that liberals and conservatives think about issues in quite different terms. Moreover, the more general point that different beliefs are salient to different groups of people has been made in other contexts—for example, by van der Pligt and Eiser (1984) in research comparing smokers' and nonsmokers' beliefs about smoking and by Kluegel and Smith (1986) in research comparing blacks' and whites' beliefs about equal opportunity and affirmative action.

Conditions Under Which Attitudinal Structures May Be Dimensional. Research by Kerlinger (1984) and the other investigators we have noted thus raises doubts about the extent to which people's knowledge structures for representing attitudes are dimensional in nature. Indeed, if people are familiar mainly with beliefs compatible with their own attitudinal position, they may not array beliefs along a dimension at all, even though they are probably aware that other people have contrasting positions. Therefore, at least in terms of people's more detailed thinking about issues, the assumption that they adopt dimensional representations of their attitudes may not be valid. However, we suggest that bipolar, unidimensional structures *may* develop under certain circumstances, especially when social conflict causes groups favoring different policies to be pitted against one another. The abortion issue provides an example of such social conflict: Activists of the pro-life and pro-choice camps do oppose one another (Luker, 1984). As a result, supporters of one of these opposed policies are unlikely to remain indifferent to the beliefs held by supporters of the other policy. To lessen the political power of the other camp, supporters are likely to become aware of the opposition's beliefs and strongly oppose them or strongly refute their relevance to the issue. Illustrating this political process are the pro-life and pro-choice statements shown in Table 3.3. These statements, widely circulated by pro-choice activist groups such as the

TABLE 3.3

Pro-Choice Activists' Statements Defining and Refuting Pro-Life Beliefs

Beliefs labeled anti-choice	*Pro-choice refutations*
Abortion is morally wrong.	Most Americans reject the absolutist position that it is always wrong to terminate a pregnancy and believe that abortion may be the morally right choice under certain circumstances.
The right of the unborn to live supersedes any right of a woman to "control her own body."	Margaret Sanger said, "No woman can call herself free who does not own and control her own body." This concept is fundamental for women.
Adoption, not abortion. There are alternatives to abortion. Abortion is never the best solution.	A woman should be able to decide for herself. Some single women do choose childbirth followed by adoption; many more choose single parenthood. For a married woman, especially one with other children, giving a baby up for adoption is virtually impossible.
Pro-life is pro-family. Pro-abortionists are anti-family. Abortion destroys the American family.	Legal abortion helps parents limit their families to the number of children they want and can afford, both financially and emotionally. Anti-abortion laws create new families, consisting of a child and her child, living at the lowest levels of society. Pro-choice is definitely pro-family.

Source: Excerpted from statements prepared by P. Rothstein and M. Williams, Westchester Coalition for Legal Abortion, 1983.

National Abortion Rights Action League, are intended to acquaint pro-choice sympathizers with pro-life views (labeled "anti-choice" in these materials) and to provide effective refutations of these views.[7]

Our speculation that partisans often develop a detailed cognitive representation of the views of the opposing camp is consistent with a classic study by E. E. Jones and Aneshansel (1956), in which prosegregation and antisegregation students at a private, Southern university were asked to learn a series of antisegregation statements (e.g., "The Negro points up the greatest disparity between the theory and our practice of democracy"). Some subjects were instructed that they should learn these statements because they would need to use them in a debate-type format later in the experiment, and other subjects were instructed merely to learn the statements. With instructions merely to learn these antisegregation statements, subjects with antisegregation attitudes learned them better than subjects with prosegregation attitudes—a finding that supports the *congeniality hypothesis* we discuss in Chapter 12. This finding is also consistent with our suggestion that, in general, people lack well-developed schemas that enable them to encode the views of people who disagree with them on issues. In contrast, when instructed to learn the antisegregation statements for use later in the experiment, the prosegregation subjects showed better learning than the antisegregation subjects. These findings suggest that when people have a reason to represent views of an opposing group, they are able to access or develop appropriate cognitive structures. To the extent that people do represent attitudinal positions opposed to their own, it is appropriate to regard them as having bipolar attitudinal schemas.

Nondimensional Representations of Attitude Structure

Contemporary Associative Network Models

Providing one of the several approaches that depart from treating attitudes as dimensional schemas, a number of psychologists have interpreted attitudes in terms of the associative network models that cognitive psychologists have popularized in their efforts to understand memory (see J. R. Anderson, 1983, 1985; J. R. Anderson & Bower, 1974; Bower, 1981; A. M. Collins & Quillian, 1969). Although this framework is relatively modern in the specific form in which it has been proposed by John Anderson and others, the approach reflects the more general tradition of associative learning models (see Anderson & Bower, 1973).

These associative network models (also called semantic or propositional network models) were proposed to understand how propositions are stored in long-term memory. For example, consider the statement, "John bought some candy because he was hungry" (see Anderson, 1985, pp. 118–121). In the network form of representation, simple propositions composed of a subject and predicate (e.g., John is hungry) are presented as nodes (or concepts) that are linked (e.g., the *John* and the *hungry* nodes are linked). Propositions, in turn, can be linked to other propositions (e.g., John bought some candy) to represent causal or other relations between propositions (e.g., that the purchase of candy was caused by the hunger). Various textbooks provide good descriptions of the details of this representational language (e.g., Anderson, 1985; Fiske & Taylor, 1991).

Although a few cognitive psychologists (e.g., Bower, 1981) have taken interest in the representation of affect and emotion in network models, they have not extended the approach to the representation of evaluation in the general and abstract sense in which we use the term in this book. However, as we noted in Chapter 1, Fazio (e.g., 1986, 1989) took this step when he defined attitude as an association between an attitude object and an evaluation. By this definition, an attitude object is a concept or node in an associative network, and so is positive or negative evaluation. A linkage between an attitude object and an evaluation is thus the form that an attitude is assumed to take within long-term memory. By this conceptualization, an attitude is a proposition stored in the same form in which other propositions are stored and presumably following the same laws of memory that other propositions follow.

The utility of this treatment of attitude will be displayed only by the application of principles of memory to attitudinal phenomena, with successful demonstrations yielding findings that would not follow from alternative frameworks. Along these lines, perhaps the most important principle held to govern the functioning of associative networks is that links between nodes are strengthened every time the linked nodes are activated. For example, if a person watching a television show on China thinks that "China is crowded," the link between *China* and *crowded* is strengthened because the *China* and *crowded* nodes are activated at the same time, and activation spreads along the link between these nodes. Due to the increased associative strength, the concept of *China* should cause one to quickly retrieve the adjective *crowded*, and the entire proposition "China is crowded" should be more quickly verified than propositions not characterized by strong associative links. Moreover, if the concept *China* is activated (or *primed*), the strongly linked concept *crowded* should be activated as well because of a process of spreading activation by which the activation of one node causes linked nodes to be activated. Conceptualizing attitudes in terms of associative networks thus suggests that activation of an attitude would lead strongly linked beliefs to come to mind. More important from Fazio's perspective, repeated activation of an evaluative response to an attitude object would strengthen the attitude-evaluation association and thereby make the attitude more accessible upon the presentation of attitude-relevant cues.[8] This assumption has led Fazio to infer associative strength from the accessibility of the attitude, which he has operationally defined in terms of the speed with which an attitude-relevant cue elicits an evaluative response. He has argued that the associative strength as indexed by accessibility has important consequences, such as the tendency to enhance the extent to which people engage in behavior consistent with attitudes (see Chapter 4).

Various advantages have been ascribed to the representation of attitudes in associative networks rather than the dimensional schemas of the social judgment tradition (see Ostrom 1987, 1988). Yet network-like approaches are not new in social psychology. As explained in the next section, Fishbein and Ajzen's (1975) interpretation of beliefs as linkages between attitude objects and attributes should be quite congenial to network theorists. Moreover, as we point out later in this chapter, the close tie between network representations of inter-attitudinal structure and the traditional balance theory representations long popular in social psychology has gone largely unrecognized. Nonetheless, the network approach, in the specific form in which it has been derived from modern cognitive psychology, has so far been applied to only a limited number of attitudinal phenomena. The basic assumption of the network approach—that memorial processes mediate attitudinal phenomena—will no doubt produce some insights that would not have been produced within the conceptual frameworks of other theories.

Classic Belief-Attitude Models

To discuss the more classic rendition of network-like models in attitude theory, we must again consider the concept of *belief* that we introduced in Chapter 1. Beliefs are extremely important in attitude theory: The assumption is common among attitude theorists that people have beliefs about attitude objects and that these beliefs are in some sense the basic building blocks of attitudes. Although in Chapter 1 we defined beliefs as the associations or linkages that people establish between the attitude object and various attributes, we have not considered the detailed nature of beliefs and their exact relation to attitudes.

Attitude theorists, especially Fishbein and Ajzen (1975), have long represented beliefs in a propositional form that links an attitude object (e.g., affirmative action in employment) to some other entity (e.g., equality of opportunity) by means of a verb expressing association or dissociation (e.g., protects; undermines) or by means of other relational terms (e.g., is inimical to). The other entities to which attitude objects are linked are as diverse as attitude objects themselves and frequently are expressed in adjectival form (e.g., inequitable, as in "Affirmative action is inequitable"). Thus, in emphasizing the propositional nature of beliefs, network theorists are in the mainstream tradition of attitude theory. The attitude object and the entities with which it is associated, traditionally interpreted as "beliefs," can be regarded as linked nodes in a propositional network.

In the analysis of beliefs, recognition must be given to the idea that the information people store about attitude objects does not necessarily take the form of propositions linking attitude objects to abstract attributes. Most of the examples that we have given so far in this book have in fact involved such relatively abstract attributes. A brand of ice cream, for example, may have excellent *flavor* but a displeasing *texture*. Yet beliefs about attitude objects may take several other forms, including images of attitude objects (a beautiful double-scoop ice cream cone) and representations of one's experiences or behavior in relation to them (the last time I went to Baskin Robbins and had a dish of pistachio nut ice cream).

Especially for attitude objects that have a physical embodiment (e.g., people, animals, plants, inanimate objects), representation may often take a visual-spatial form. For example, when thinking about George Bush, most people may be able to imagine him by bringing to mind a representation of his physical appearance—perhaps delivering a speech to a television audience or engaged in some leisure activity such as fishing or jogging. Cognitive psychologists have studied such mental images, at least in limited domains, and suggest that such images may be represented in propositional form (see J. R. Anderson, 1983, 1985). However, they have not examined the evaluative meaning contained in these images—the aspect that is relevant to the study of attitudes. Yet these images no doubt carry evaluative meaning, just as propositional beliefs do. Consider, for example, the negative evaluation expressed in a mental image of Bush that takes the form of an ugly political caricature and the positive evaluation expressed in a mental image that takes the form of a dignified and statesmanlike visage. Suggesting that mental images are prevalent, Fiske, Pratto, and Pavelchak (1983) found that, in a random sample of Pittsburgh adults, responses to a question asking respondents to "name the first few things you think of when you imagine a nuclear war" (p. 52) included concrete, visual-spatial images (e.g., blinding light, barren land, photographs of Hiroshima, finger on button, buildings on fire) as well as more abstract beliefs (e.g., it would destroy people, chaos, the loser will be gone completely). The role that concrete mental images may play as constituents of attitudes deserves closer study.

The general idea that people associate beliefs with attitude objects is a traditional emphasis of research on prejudice and stereotyping. As we noted in Chapter 1, prejudice, which is often studied in relation to minority groups, corresponds to attitude toward a social group, although the term prejudice is generally used only to describe attitudes that are negative. In contrast, a stereotype about a social group is the beliefs held about the group. Thus, a stereotype is ordinarily defined as the attributes that an individual ascribes to a social group (e.g., Ashmore & Del Boca, 1981; Krech & Crutchfield, 1948; Secord & Backman, 1964). Consistent with the idea that there is some correspondence between attitudes and the evaluative content of beliefs about attitude objects (see subsequent discussion), people who are prejudiced in relation to a group are generally thought to have a negative stereotype about group members (see Eagly & Mladinic, 1989).

Affect and Behavior
Associated with Attitude Objects

Affective reactions can also contribute to evaluations of attitude objects and thus be linked to attitudes in network-type associations. For example, if a woman experiences a warm feeling in the presence of a particular man, her affective state informs her of her reaction to him and thus contributes to her attitude toward him, as does her more abstract belief that this man is, for example, handsome or kind. Consistent with Zajonc's (1980b) views that affect and cognition are separate and partially independent systems, the impact of affect on evaluation can be direct—in other words, feelings may produce positive or negative evaluation without necessarily impacting on one's beliefs about the attitude object. Alternatively, as M. F. Kaplan (1991; Kaplan & Anderson, 1973b) has argued, affect can function as a source of information by inducing thoughts about the attitude object. For example, a woman's warm feeling about a man may cause her to think that the man is handsome and kind, and these beliefs may be the direct determinants of her evaluation.

In considering affective responses as constituents of attitudes, we think that Schwarz and Clore's (1988) distinction between moods and emotions is important. According to their analysis, moods are general positive or negative feelings that people have at a particular time (e.g., being in a good or bad mood). Moods are quite general in the sense that they do not take on a specific affective coloration (e.g., one is in a bad mood, but not in a "mad" or "jealous" mood). In contrast, emotions such as anger and jealousy are more distinctive in tone and, unlike moods, have an identifiable cause; one experiences the emotion of anger, for example, in relation to a particular person or event. Because emotions rather than moods are ascribed to particular attitude objects, it is therefore emotions that influence our evaluations of them.[9]

Behaviors also inform us about our attitudes and therefore may be part of the network of associations formed around the attitude object. In fact, beliefs that take the form of concrete representations of one's experiences with an attitude object have been examined quite extensively, primarily in terms of *script theory* (Abelson, 1976, 1981; Schank & Abelson, 1977; see also Chapter 4). For example, a person's attitude toward Japanese restaurants might be a function, not of one or more abstract attributes that are ascribed to this type of restaurant, but of the recollection that "Once in Chicago I ate in a Japanese restaurant that served small portions of raw fish and other unusual dishes that I didn't know how to eat and I felt hungry afterward." As Schank and Abelson suggested, this sort of *episodic script* may become more abstract after a person has had more experience with an attitude object. For example, the memory of the single episode at a Japanese restaurant might be stereotypically transformed into the more abstract belief that "Japanese restaurants serve food that is exotic and not very filling." Yet we do not know the extent to which such recollections of vivid personal experiences are a more common base of attitudes than are more abstract beliefs. Because the possession of a script with negative implications for the attitude object may discourage the additional experiences that would favor a more abstract representation, concrete, script-like memories of particular experiences may often accompany negative attitudes. Thus, the person whose initial exposure to a Japanese restaurant resulted in the script we noted might never eat in a Japanese restaurant again.

Repeated or habitual behaviors also inform people about their attitudes. For example, the fact that a person frequently eats Japanese food informs him about his positive attitude toward this cuisine, as his penchant for donating money to groups representing environmentalist causes informs him of his positive attitude toward environmental preservation (e.g., Bem, 1972). The important role of behavioral information as a determinant of attitudes is considered in considerable depth in Chapter 11.

Although the consequences of distinguishing between images, affective experience, representations of behavior, and more abstract beliefs as bases of attitudes are not well understood at this point, implications of some of these distinctions will be considered in subsequent chapters. For example, whether an attitude is affectively or cognitively grounded has been shown to have implications for the effectiveness of persuasive appeals (K. Edwards, 1990; Millar & Millar, 1990). Yet our general point is quite simple—images as well as affective and behavioral experience may function in the same way as more abstract attributes in conveying evaluative meaning that becomes attached to attitude objects.

The Prediction of Attitudes from Beliefs

The idea that attitudes can be associated with beliefs, affects, and behaviors in network-type attitudinal structures is surely useful, but it does not provide a detailed picture of the relation between attitudes and these other aspects of attitude structure. Many questions remain. For example, readers might ask whether the relation between attitudes and beliefs can be described more exactly. Can we successfully predict people's attitudes from the content of their beliefs? Are people's beliefs (also, affects and behaviors) about an attitude object evaluatively consistent with their overall attitude? These important questions about attitude structure have been addressed in some detail within several interrelated traditions of attitude research. First we consider two quantitative models of the relation between attitudes and beliefs: the expectancy-value model and information integration theory, both of which allow attitudes to be predicted from beliefs. Then in the subsequent section of this chapter, we consider the question of evaluative consistency between attitudes and the other classes of evaluative responses (beliefs, affects, and behaviors).

Expectancy-Value Model

The most popular framework for understanding the relation between attitudes and the evaluative meaning of beliefs is provided by the expectancy-value model. The central idea of this model is that one's attitude (understood in the abstract sense of evaluation) is a function of one's beliefs, when these beliefs are represented as the sum of the *expected values* of the attributes ascribed to the attitude object. These expected values have an expectancy and a value component. The expectancy component of each attribute's expected value is the subjective probability that the attitude object has or is characterized by the attribute, and the value component is the evaluation of the attribute. For example, if a person believes that a new film has amusing dialogue but lacks a strong story line, these attributes would be represented by the subjective probability that the film has each attribute (i.e., the high probability of amusing dialogue and the low probability of a strong story line), as well as by the evaluation of each attribute (i.e., the positive evaluations of amusing dialogue and a strong story line). To predict an attitude, the expectancy and value terms associated with each attribute are multiplied together, and these products are added. This model thus proposes that evaluation of an attitude object is a summation of the evaluations associated with the particular attributes that are ascribed to the attitude object. Hence, the expectancy-value model of attitudes can be represented as follows:

$$\text{Attitude} = \Sigma \text{ Expectancy} \times \text{Value} \qquad (3.1)$$

In using the expectancy-value principle, attitude theorists have built on a well-established tradition in psychology (see Feather, 1982). The principle has been central to several influential theories of motivation (e.g., J. W. Atkinson, 1958; Lewin, 1938; Tolman, 1958), and other well-known applications include Rotter's (1954) social learning theory, expected-value and utility models of decision making (see Abelson & Levi, 1985), and expectancy models of job satisfaction, occupational preference, and effort (T. R. Mitchell, 1974).

Early Work of the Michigan Group. The first work on an expectancy-value approach to understanding attitudes was carried out by a group of social psychologists at the University of Michigan: Helen Peak, Milton Rosenberg, and Earl Carlson. In the first published presentation of an expectancy-value theory of attitudes, Peak (1955) analyzed attitudes in terms very close to those of the expectancy-value theories of motivation that were influential in the 1950s. Reflecting the penchant of psychologists of the 1950s for using the term *affect* as we use the term *evaluation* in this book, she defined attitudes as concepts with affective properties and proposed that an attitude is determined by the individual's *attitude structure*. Structure was formulated as the *instrumentality* of the attitude object for aiding or interfering with goal attainment and the *satisfaction* derived from attaining goals. Thus, attitude was assumed to be a function of the subjective probability that the attitude object leads to good or bad consequences (i.e., instrumentality) and the evaluation of these anticipated consequences (i.e., satisfaction).

This framework was explored empirically in experiments carried out by Milton Rosenberg and Earl Carlson, two of Peak's doctoral students. Rosenberg (1953, 1956) examined students' attitudes on the issue of whether members of the Communist party should be allowed to address the public. To provide a measure of the instrumentality of this attitude, these respondents judged the extent to which having members of the Communist party address the public would lead to or block the attainment of each of 35 goals, which he termed *values* (e.g., all human beings having equal rights; people being well-educated). Subjects also estimated the amount of satisfaction or dissatisfaction they would gain from reaching each of these goals. Subjects' instrumentality and satisfaction ratings were then multiplied for each goal, and these products were summed according to the Expectancy × Value equation. Rosenberg found that these summed products related positively to a one-item self-report measure of subjects' favorability toward allowing Communists to address the public.

Carlson (1953, 1956) assessed subjects' attitudes toward abolishing housing segregation and, following the same procedures as Rosenberg (1953, 1956), obtained subjects' instrumentality and satisfaction ratings in relation to a number of values. Subjects then listed their own reasons and listened to a communicator's reasons why abolishing housing segregation would lead to the attainment of four values (e.g., maintaining property values). Three weeks later subjects again indicated their attitudes and rerated the extent to which desegregation would allow the values to be attained (i.e., instrumentality ratings) and the extent to which they would get satisfaction from attaining the values (i.e., satisfaction ratings). Among subjects who were not already extremely favorable or extremely unfavorable on the desegregation issue at the beginning of the experiment, attitudes changed toward greater approval of desegregation, and, consistent with expectancy-value theory, attitude change related positively to change in subjects' estimates of the extent to which desegregation would lead to the four goals. Carlson's experiment introduced the possibility that the expectancy-value approach might yield a useful general theory of attitude change (see Chapter 5).

Fishbein's Development of the Expectancy-Value Model. The development of the expectancy-value approach as a general framework for understanding attitudes was continued by Martin Fishbein (1961, 1963, 1967b), who proposed that attitudes are a function of (a) beliefs about the attitude object, defined as the subjective probability that the attitude object has each attribute, and (b) the evaluative aspect of these beliefs, defined as the evaluation of each attribute. Whereas in Peak, Rosenberg, and Carlson's formulation, these attributes were goals (or values), Fishbein's formulation did not limit the attributes of the attitude objects in this way. Fishbein's more general expectancy-value formulation is expressed algebraically as follows:

$$A_o = \sum_{i=1}^{n} b_i e_i \qquad (3.2)$$

where A_o is the attitude toward the object, action, or event, o; b_i is the belief i about o (expressed as the subjective probability that o has attribute i); e_i is the evaluation of attribute i; and n is the number of salient attributes. In his early work on this expectancy-value model, Fishbein (1961, 1963) showed that attitudes, as assessed by evaluative semantic differential items, were highly correlated with their summed expectancy-value products (i.e., the summed cross-products of subjects' probability and attribute evaluation ratings). As we show in Chapter 5, later tests of the relation between attitudes and summed expectancy-value products have had somewhat more heterogeneous outcomes. We also review in that chapter some of the technical and methodological discussions that have surrounded the use of expectancy-value products.

Because Fishbein's equation expresses a relation between attitudes and beliefs, it could be regarded merely as a predictive model having no implications for psychological process. However, such a narrow interpretation of this model would not acknowledge Fishbein's (e.g., 1967b, 1967c) extensive discussions of beliefs as determinants of attitudes. Although causation could go in either or both ways in the expectancy-value equation—from attitudes to beliefs or from beliefs to attitudes, Fishbein and his collaborators have focused on beliefs as causes of attitudes and thereby assumed that attitudes derive from beliefs about attitude objects. This viewpoint thus implies that people form attitudes by learning what the characteristics of attitude objects are.

The expectancy-value principle that people come to hold positive attitudes toward things that they think have good attributes and negative attitudes toward things that they think have bad attributes has a certain obviousness to it that may make the theory somewhat uninteresting when initially encountered. Yet the representation of beliefs in terms of the probabilities and evaluations associated with the attributes of attitude objects does provide a model for predicting attitudes from the information people acquire about attitude objects. The approach has some interesting implications for attitude change that we develop in Chapter 5. Also, we explore the expectancy-value approach as a model of the relation between attitudes and behavior in Chapter 4. As we shall see, for the prediction of behavior, the attitude of interest is attitude toward the behavior, and the attributes of this attitude object (i.e., of the behavior) are its perceived consequences.

Information Integration Theory

Whereas the expectancy-value approach provides one specific model of the relation between beliefs and attitudes, Norman Anderson's information integration theory (e.g., 1971, 1981a, 1981b, 1991) provides a much more general model. Similar to the expectancy-value model, Anderson's approach assumes that attitudes are formed and modified as people receive and interpret information and then integrate this information with their prior attitudes. Departing from the expectancy-value model, information integration theory does not assume that multiplying expectancies times values necessarily provides an adequate mathematical model of the relation between beliefs and attitudes. Although this broader theory is actually extremely general because it can address any type of judgment, its relevance to attitudinal judgments concerns us here.

In the information integration approach, there are two basic operations involved in forming or changing attitudes. These operations are described as the *valuation* of the incoming information and its *integration* into the current attitude. Valuation refers to the determination of the *meaning* of the information and of its *importance* or *relevance* for evaluating an attitude object. This valuation operation is represented in information integration theory in terms of the determination of two components: the *scale value* (i.e., evaluative meaning) and the *weight* (i.e., importance) of information. The scale value of information is its location on the evaluative dimension, and its weight is its importance or psychological impact in relation to the individual's judgment. For example, the scale value of a newspaper editorial on reduction of the capital gains tax is its location on a pro-versus-con scale of favorability on this issue. The weight of this information is its importance as a determinant of the newspaper reader's attitude.

Integration refers to the combining of items of information. The central assumption of the theory is that integration can be described in terms of simple algebraic models. Anderson has repeatedly emphasized that these models have an *as if* status in the sense that people are presumed to respond to stimuli as if they were following the algebraic rules given in the models. Demonstrating that people respond as if they follow a particular equation raises the question of *how* they do so, that is, what is the process that underlies such a response? The algebraic model approach addresses the issue of underlying process only to a limited extent (see Chapter 5).

We illustrate algebraic models by presenting the most popular variants—adding and averaging models. If a person receives n items of information, and the scale value of stimulus i is represented by s_i and its weight by w_i, the response to the total set could be described by the following model:

$$R = w_0s_0 + w_1s_1 + w_2s_2 + \ldots + w_ns_n \qquad (3.3)$$

In this equation w_0 and s_0 are the weight and scale value of the person's initial attitude. This equation specifies an adding model. Each item of information is added to the others, with the result that the response to the total set becomes more extreme as more items of the same sign are added together.

In contrast, averaging models assume that people respond as if they have taken an average of items of information. Response to the total set would therefore not necessarily become more extreme as the number of items of information of the same sign became greater. Averaging in a new item of the same value as the average of the prior items would not change the response at all (although adding this new item via Equation 3.3 would make the response more extreme). One way to transform Equation 3.3 into an averaging model is to require that the weights sum to one. More commonly, the averaging model is frequently shown in a form that displays a numerator that repeats Equation 3.3 and a denominator that contains the sum of the weights:

$$R = (w_0s_0 + \sum_{i=1}^{n} w_is_i) / (w_0 + \sum_{i=1}^{n} w_i) \qquad (3.4)$$

The breadth that the information integration approach possesses stems in large part from its inclusion of a variety of specific integration rules as plausible combinatorial models. Yet the integration rule that has proven to have the widest applicability is averaging, and most critical tests of averaging versus adding rules have favored averaging (e.g., N.H. Anderson, 1965a, 1968b; Gollob & Lugg, 1973; Hamilton & Huffman, 1971; Hendrick, 1968; Himmelfarb, 1973).[10] Subtractive models appear to be appropriate for judgmental problems involving ratings of differences between stimuli (e.g., determining one's degree of preference for one object over another; Shanteau & Anderson, 1969). A multiplying rule is appropriate for still other judgmental problems, such as the determination of subjective expected value (i.e., evaluation) from subjective probability and subjective value (e.g., Anderson & Shanteau, 1970), which we have discussed in relation to expectancy-value models. It might also be noted that a multiplying rule is a component of the averaging rule itself because the scale value of the information is multiplied by its weight before the resulting products are averaged.

Advantages and Disadvantages of Information Integration Approach. The flexibility of information integration theory with respect to the specific integration rule differentiates it from the expectancy-value model. Within information integration theory, the Expectancy × Value equation becomes merely a particular integration rule that adds expectancy-value cross-products across the attributes of the attitude object. Thus,

110

Anderson's theory provides a much more general set of algebraic models that encompasses the expectancy-value model as one specific instance. The generality and flexibility of the information integration approach is admirable from some perspectives, but these features can be regarded as a liability if they prevent the theory from making predictions for specific situations. We consider this issue in Chapter 5, where we discuss algebraic models in more depth and explore the utility of such models for predicting attitude change.

As a final point in relation to integration models, we note that these models are not restricted to the integration of abstract attributes about attitude objects. Consistent with our discussion of visual-spatial images as well as representations of one's own behavior, the evaluative information carried by these other forms of knowledge contributes to attitudes and presumably can be combined with the evaluative information conveyed by more abstract attributes. Moreover, M. F. Kaplan (1981, 1991; Kaplan & Anderson, 1973b) has demonstrated that algebraic models can incorporate affective information, and presumably they could be applied with equal ease to the integration of information of all types. The very general terms in which algebraic models have been formulated thus gives them considerable potential (largely untapped so far) for exploring, in quantitative terms, the contribution of affective and behavioral information to attitudes.

Questioning of Assumption that
People Form Attitudes by Aggregating Their Beliefs

Various questions have been raised about the extent to which people form (and re-form) their attitudes by taking the attributes of attitude objects into account, as is implied by quantitative models of the belief-attitude relation. The most pointed criticisms have been directed to the expectancy-value model because of Fishbein and Ajzen's (1975) greater explicitness in claiming that people derive their attitudes from their beliefs (e.g., McGuire, 1985). Indeed, Fishbein and Ajzen repeatedly asserted that people typically base their attitudinal judgments on a set of beliefs, albeit usually a relatively small set of beliefs. Their approach treats a person's attitude at a particular point in time as a function of the beliefs that are *salient* (or accessible) at that point.[11] Supporting this claim, research by van der Pligt and Eiser (1984) has shown that salient beliefs ordinarily correlate more highly with attitudes than do nonsalient beliefs, and that prediction of attitudes is not lowered by removing nonsalient beliefs from the composite score representing respondents' evaluative beliefs. Although the limiting case of the model is that only one attribute is salient, Ajzen and Fishbein (1980) suggested that a somewhat larger number of beliefs, perhaps five to nine, are more typically salient.

Direct Retrieval of Attitudes. Although people may indeed consider the attributes of an attitude object in initially evaluating it, it is more doubtful that a review of the attributes of the attitude object is necessary at later points in order to evaluate it. If the evaluation has been stored, it may subsequently be retrieved, without retrieval of the attributes that originally gave rise to the evaluation or even a subset of these attributes (N. H. Anderson & Hubert, 1963; Dreben, Fiske, & Hastie, 1979; Hastie & Park, 1986; see also Chapters 4 and 5). Quantitative theories of the belief-attitude relation do not foreclose the possibility that attitudes can be stored separately from the beliefs that support them, but clearly the emphasis of these theorists is on beliefs determining attitudes rather than on direct retrieval of abstract evaluations. Yet it seems plausible to think that in daily life direct retrieval may be the rule rather than the exception. For example, by trying out a new brand of ice cream, a person may decide that it is inferior, based on its flavor, texture, and price. When subsequently passing the ice cream section at her local supermarket, she may recall merely that the ice cream is inferior, without reviewing the attributes of the ice cream and inferring her attitude from these attributes. Indeed, consumer psychologists have shown considerable interest in the issue of whether people choose products based on their overall attitudes toward brands or their knowledge of specific product attributes (e.g., Bettman, 1981). Also, Fazio and his associates have maintained that attitudes high in associative strength are automatically activated, upon mere presentation of the attitude object (e.g., Fazio, 1986; Fazio, Sanbonmatsu, Powell, & Kardes, 1986; see Chapter 4).

Category-Based Versus Piecemeal-Based Evaluations. Susan Fiske and her colleagues provided an interesting suggestion for predicting whether evaluations of attitude objects are activated directly or inferred from beliefs about the attributes of the attitude objects (Fiske & Neuberg, 1990; Fiske & Pavelchak, 1986). Although this formulation is helpful only for understanding evaluations of attitude objects that happen to be instances of more general categories, the suggestion is well worth noting.

Working within the general framework of the associative network models that we have already discussed in this chapter, Fiske and her colleagues represented an attitude object as a *category label* (e.g., schizophrenic) within an associative network; such an attitude object is in turn linked to its attributes (e.g., confused, bizarre), which are nodes in the network. These investigators treated attitude as an *affective tag* that is attached to the category label and that represents the evaluation that has been learned from prior experience with the attributes of the attitude object.[12] The attributes that are linked with the category label also have evaluative tags associated with them, in order to represent the evaluation inherent in each attribute.

Whether people evaluate an instance of a category by directly accessing the evaluative tag associated with the category label (in our terms, by retrieving their attitude toward the category) or instead by generalizing their attitude from the tags associated with the instance's attributes (in our terms, by inferring their attitude from their beliefs about the instance) depends on the degree of fit between the instance and the category. If the fit is good, the instance can be evaluated in what Fiske and her collaborators called a *category-based mode* by directly attaching the evaluation of the category to the particular instance. For example, if a particular Spaniard seems typical of Spaniards, one's evaluation of this individual can be taken directly from one's evaluation of Spaniards as a group. If, in contrast, the particular instance fits poorly, the instance is evaluated in what these investigators called a *piecemeal-based mode* by integrating the evaluations associated with each of the instance's attributes. For example, if a particular Spaniard seems somewhat atypical (e.g., blonde and methodical), one's evaluation of this individual would be formed by aggregating the evaluations associated with the characteristics ascribed to this particular individual. Predictions based on this formulation have received empirical support (see Fiske & Neuberg, 1990; Fiske & Pavelchak, 1986; Sujan, 1985).

The Construction-by-Aspects Principle. Even the idea that attitudes are *initially formed* by summing a number of attributes of the attitude object has been questioned. For example, McGuire (1985) suggested that people may instead often consider just one salient attribute of an attitude object, presumably the most important attribute. People would multiply this attribute by its evaluation, and then form an attitude on the basis of this single attribute, if the result of this streamlined process was sufficient to allow them to make an attitudinal decision. This description of attitude formation, which McGuire labeled the *construction-by-aspects* principle, is closely related to the *elimination-by-aspects* rule of decision making proposed by Tversky (1972; Tversky & Sattath, 1979) and the *sequential processing model* proposed by Jaccard (Jaccard & Becker, 1985; Jacoby, Jaccard, Kuss, Troutman, & Mazursky, 1987). To illustrate this mode of forming attitudes and making decisions, imagine a consumer wary about the use of artificial sweeteners in food products. He may review the labels of soft drinks to determine whether these products contain such additives. Upon encountering the name of such a sweetener on a label, this consumer may form a sufficiently negative evaluation of a soft drink to eliminate it from consideration for possible purchase. Only if several brands of soft drinks remained after these eliminations would he use another attribute (e.g., price or flavor) to decide among them. Similarly, people with strong commitments to single political issues may evaluate candidates for public office solely on the basis of their positions on the one issue (e.g., reproductive rights). One or more other, less important attributes would become relevant only to the extent that more than one candidate survive this initial screening.

These ideas are consistent with descriptions of information processing that emphasize efficiency and the minimization of effort (e.g., McGuire's lazy organism, 1969; Taylor & Fiske's cognitive miser, 1978; and Chaiken's heuristic model, 1987; see Chapter 7). To understand the conditions under which people use the efficient processes described by the construction-by-aspects and related rules or the more effortful process that many researchers have assumed is implied by expectancy-value models, psychologists will have to take functional considerations into account. For example, in important areas of consumer decision making such as evaluating cars or houses for possible purchase, people are probably willing to spend time and energy to investigate the attributes of attitude objects with some thoroughness, whereas in more trivial areas such as evaluating shampoos or toothpaste for possible purchase, people probably use strategies such as construction-by-aspects that minimize the amount of information processed.

Recapitulation: Predicting Attitudes from Beliefs

To summarize this discussion of models of the relation between attitudes and beliefs we note that psychologists have had considerable success in using simple algebraic equations to model the relation between people's attitudes about an entity and the evaluative content of their beliefs about the entity. Whereas the expectancy-value equation has proven to be quite popular for expressing this belief-attitude relation, the information integration approach opens up the possibility that a variety of other specific equations might provide more adequate models of the belief-attitude relation. Despite the general success of the quantitative approach to modeling belief-attitude relations, psychologists have nonetheless questioned the extent to which people base their attitudes on beliefs about the specific attributes of attitude objects. Under many circumstances, people no doubt retrieve intact evaluations, obviating the need to consider or review their beliefs. Moreover, even when initially forming their attitudes, they may often use a minimalist approach that derives an attitude from only one or a very few beliefs.

Attitudes' Consistency with Beliefs, Affects, and Behaviors

Quantitative models of the belief-attitude relation, in regarding people as forming their attitudes by integrating the evaluative content of their beliefs, assume an overall consistency between beliefs and attitudes. Yet attitude theorists have questioned whether attitudes are necessarily consistent with the evaluative content of relevant beliefs. In considering this issue, we describe research that has treated belief-attitude consistency as a variable property of attitude structure. Subsequently we consider the consistency between attitudes and affect as well as attitudes and behavior.

Evaluative-Cognitive Consistency

The degree of consistency between one's overall evaluation of an attitude object and the evaluative content of one's beliefs about it is an important structural property of attitudes. We name this property *evaluative-cognitive consistency*, even though it was classically known as *affective-cognitive consistency*. This earlier label reflects the fact that this property was initially proposed before psychologists thought it important to distinguish between affect and evaluation (see Chapter 1). Evaluative-cognitive consistency thus pertains to the consistency between one's abstract evaluation of an attitude object and the evaluative content of one's beliefs about the object. As W. A. Scott (1969) defined this property, evaluative-cognitive consistency exists if "[attitude] objects are liked to the extent that they are seen as possessing desirable characteristics" (p. 263) and are disliked to the extent that they are seen as possessing undesirable characteristics. As explained in Chapter 1, an overarching assumption of attitude theory is that evaluations of attitude objects tend to be consistent with the evaluative

114

meaning of the attributes ascribed to them. This assumption follows from the principles (a) that people form their attitudes at least partially on the basis of learning about the attributes of attitude objects and (b) that they then ascribe to objects additional attributes that are evaluatively consistent with their existing attitudes. Amplifying this logic, the expectancy-value and information integration approaches provide explicit models of the link between beliefs and attitudes. However, thinking about attitudes and beliefs as generally correlated does not preclude regarding evaluative-cognitive consistency as a variable property that may be manifested to a greater or lesser extent, depending on circumstances and differences between individuals. The idea that evaluative-cognitive consistency is a variable property of attitude structures was first proposed by Milton Rosenberg (1956, 1960a).

Although, as we noted earlier in this chapter, research by Rosenberg (1956, 1960a, 1968b) was influential in the initial stages of expectancy-value theorizing about attitudes, he did not develop the approach as a general theory of attitudes. Instead he confined most of his work to studying the degree of consistency between attitudes and beliefs. Following the cognitive consistency theme that dominated the study of attitudes in the late 1950s and the 1960s, Rosenberg postulated that a person's evaluation of the attitude object tends to be consistent with his or her beliefs, when these beliefs are defined in terms of expectancy-value products. When there is inconsistency between an attitude and associated beliefs, the individual is motivated to reduce the inconsistency by changing either the attitude, the beliefs, or both.

As evidence for the assumption that people reduce inconsistency, Rosenberg argued that most persuasion research induces change in beliefs, which then results in a corresponding change in associated attitudes (see Chapters 6, 7, and 8). Indeed, Carlson's (1956) explicit demonstration of this point, which we already described, showed that a message altering perception of an attitude object's relation to valued goals brought about change in the attitude. Conversely, change in an attitude should bring about corresponding change in beliefs about the attitude object. In a clever demonstration of this principle, Rosenberg (1960b) used posthypnotic suggestion to alter subjects' attitudes and subsequently observed corresponding changes in their beliefs (see Chapter 10).

In summary, attitudes tend to be moderately consistent with the evaluative implications of the beliefs associated with them, but fairly wide individual differences occur in the degree to which this consistency is found. These individual differences in the degree of consistency between attitudes and beliefs have predicted attitudinal responding in several domains (see Chapters 10, 11, and 12).

Bases of Evaluative-Cognitive Inconsistency. There is more than one possible source of evaluative-cognitive inconsistency. In particular, people who are inconsistent may (a) hold beliefs whose evaluative implications are truly discrepant from their attitudes or (b) merely lack beliefs about the attitude object (and perhaps lack a definite attitude as well). Rosenberg (1968b) proposed that beliefs and attitudes are absent when he suggested that people who are inconsistent are *vacuous*. He reasoned that the inconsistency of vacuous people is more apparent than real because it stems from their uncertainty about how to respond to questionnaire measures of beliefs and attitudes. Essentially, such people lack attitudes and beliefs about an attitude object and therefore respond to questions about it in an unreliable fashion.[13] In contrast, Rosenberg believed that people who genuinely hold attitudes typically have beliefs consistent with these attitudes. In Rosenberg's (1968b, p. 84) terms, such people have a "dispositional orientation" in relation to the attitude object—in other words, have a relatively stable attitude that expresses their personal orientation toward the attitude object.

Rosenberg's thinking about vacuous attitudes reflects the multi-component view of attitudes that was common in the 1960s (see Chapter 1). Thus, he evidently believed that attitudes (which he viewed as synonymous with affect) were based on cognitions, and, to the extent that an attitude was not based on cognitions, its origin was unclear, and in fact no genuine attitude existed. He did not, as we do, view attitudes in terms of the higher order abstraction of evaluation and realize that attitudes could be based on affective, behavioral, or cognitive input. From our more modern standpoint, evaluation and cognitions could easily be inconsistent, merely because the evaluation is based primarily on affective or behavioral input, which happens to have different evaluative implications than cognitions about the attitude object's attributes. In addition, and more in line with Rosenberg's idea about vacuous attitudes, evaluations could merely appear to be inconsistent with beliefs because the individual has had little or no cognitive, affective, or behavioral input and therefore lacks an attitude altogether. Response latency data collected in studies using various types of attitudinal measures (e.g., cognitive, affective) might prove useful in evaluating these various possibilities.

Research conducted in the 1980s increased knowledge about the cognitive basis of degree of consistency between attitudes and beliefs. Contrasting with Rosenberg's ideas about inconsistency indicating vacuity or the presence of nonattitudes, this research has suggested that the beliefs of inconsistent people tend to be organized differently than those of consistent people. In such research, Chaiken and Yates (1985) found that high- and low-consistency subjects, although not differing in the amount of attitude-relevant information they possessed, differed in their handling of information discrepant from their attitudes: High-consistency subjects showed a stronger tendency to probe the implications of discrepant information by generating refutational thoughts that discredited or minimized the importance of inconsistent information. This research thus implied that consistent people may have well-organized sets of beliefs that they can deploy to analyze the implications that incoming information has for their attitudes. Suggesting more directly that high- and low-consistency people differ in the organization of their cognitions, Chaiken and Baldwin (1981) found that high-consistency subjects held beliefs that were more highly intercorrelated than those of low-consistency subjects. The higher intercorrelations are not surprising because beliefs that are highly correlated with evaluation would also be correlated with one another (see W. A. Scott, 1969). These highly intercorrelated beliefs would thus tend toward a unidimensional structure that is itself organized in terms of evaluation. However, this conclusion that differences in cognitive organization underlie differences in evaluative-cognitive consistency does not preclude inconsistency sometimes being a product of the other sources that we have mentioned (e.g., a grounding of evaluation in affective or behavioral input; absence of an attitude). These issues are currently unresolved and warrant additional research (see Chaiken, Pomerantz, & Giner-Sorolla, in press).

Consistency Between Evaluation and Other Attitudinal Responses

Evaluative-cognitive consistency can be regarded as one type of consistency between evaluation and classes of attitudinal responses. Our analysis of three classes of evaluative responses—cognitive, affective, and behavioral (see Chapter 1)—suggests that affective and behavioral responses can be more or less consistent with an overall evaluation, just as cognitive responses can.

Evaluative-Behavioral Consistency. Relevant to this point is research by Ross and his associates examining the consistency between people's attitudes and their beliefs about their own past behavior (e.g., M. Ross, 1989; M. Ross & Conway, 1986; M. Ross, McFarland, & Fletcher, 1981). These investigators have shown that people tend to reconstruct their past behavior as relatively consistent with their current attitudes. When people's attitudes change, they often alter their ideas about their past behavior so that the recalled behavior is consistent with their current attitudes. Thus, attitudes function as important cues when people recollect their behavior—people tend to believe that they have done things in the past that are consistent with their current attitudes, even when these current attitudes are newly revised. Also related to these issues of evaluative-behavioral consistency is the general question of whether attitudes cause people to behave in ways that are consistent with their attitudes, a topic that we consider in detail in Chapter 4.

Evaluative-Affective Consistency. Consistency between affect and overall evaluation has been examined less extensively, although an interesting study on reactions to political figures did examine affective reactions (e.g., anger, happiness, sadness, disgust, hope) elicited by politicians such as Reagan, Kennedy, Carter, and Bush (Abelson, Kinder, Peters, & Fiske, 1982). This research found that affective reactions to the politicians were somewhat more consistent with evaluations of them than were cognitive reactions, as indexed by the ascription of positive and negative traits and behaviors to them. This tantalizing finding suggests that evaluations of politicians may tend to be affectively grounded. In addition, Breckler and Wiggins (1989a) explored the contribution of beliefs and affects to attitudes by asking subjects to evaluate various attitude objects (e.g., blood donation, computers, admissions tests) while thinking about either their beliefs or their feelings about each issue. Although these measures would have provided only quite indirect indicators of beliefs and affects, the correlations of these measures with a single-item self-rating of attitude on a like-versus-dislike scale suggested a somewhat stronger impact of beliefs than affects for most attitude objects. Expanding the precedent set by these studies, research examining the consistency between evaluation and cognitions, affects, and behaviors would be especially informative.

The type of response (cognitive, affective, or behavioral) that produces the smallest discrepancy with evaluation may be the primary basis for the attitude.

The Structure of Beliefs:
Belief Complexity

When examining our discussion of the relation between attitudes and beliefs, readers may well have thought about the fact that beliefs themselves can have structural properties. The beliefs associated with one attitude can be structurally quite different from the beliefs associated with another attitude. Psychologists have considered in some detail the structure of beliefs, and it is to this material that we now turn. In this section of the chapter, we consider one especialy important structural property of beliefs—their complexity. Indeed, there is great variation in the extent to which people hold simple or complex beliefs. In subsequent sections, we consider the relation of beliefs to one another, in particular, their evaluative and logical consistency with one another.

Defining Belief Complexity

The complexity of beliefs associated with attitude objects is typically defined as the *dimensionality* of the beliefs that a person holds about an attitude object, that is, the number of dimensions needed to describe the space utilized by the attributes ascribed to the attitude object. This aspect of attitudinal structure has often been explored under the rubric of cognitive complexity (Bieri, 1966; Crockett, 1965) as well as related terms such as dimensionality (W. A. Scott, 1963, 1969; W. A. Scott, Osgood, & Peterson, 1979), differentiation (Zajonc, 1960b, 1968b), and integrative complexity (Schroder, 1971; Schroder, Driver, & Streufert, 1967; Tetlock, 1989). Although researchers' measurement methods differ, complexity is not ordinarily considered to be identical to the sheer number of beliefs that a person holds about an attitude object because beliefs can be quite redundant (e.g., Shelly is warm, friendly, amiable, and sociable) and therefore not require representation by more than one dimension of meaning.

There may appear to be some contradiction between defining attitude as location on an evaluative dimension and defining the complexity of cognitions about the attitude object as the dimensionality of the multi-attribute space within which attitude objects are located (e.g., Bieri, 1966; Schroder, 1971; W. A. Scott, 1969). In fact, however, there is little contradiction because the attributes considered in research on complexity are typically conceptualized without regard to evaluation and therefore at a less abstract level than general evaluative meaning. For example, one may have a positive attitude toward (i.e., evaluation of) a particular university, yet ascribe a number of more concrete attributes to the university (e.g., it is large, midwestern, oriented to science and engineering, well administered, etc.). The degree to which these attributes tap distinctive meaning dimensions determines the complexity of a person's beliefs about the university, whereas the evaluative meaning of the attributes aggregates to influence the person's overall evaluation of the university. Thus, evaluative meaning is a higher-order, more abstract inference from *all* of the attributes ascribed to an attitude object. In this regard, we note that the other models we have reviewed that treat attitudes as a function of beliefs, most notably the expectancy-value and information integration approaches, do not recognize the issue of the multidimensionality of beliefs in this sense.

The complexity of people's beliefs has been assessed in a variety of ways. The particular method chosen to assess complexity is consequential in view of numerous demonstrations that measures that are seemingly conceptually related are not highly correlated.[14] One measure that is especially popular among social psychologists was introduced by Scott (1962, 1969; Scott et al., 1979) and based on information theory concepts (see Attneave, 1959). This measure, known as Scott's *H*, is based on groupings of attributes of the attitude object according to the respondent's perception that certain of them "go together" in groups. For example, in Linville's (1982) research on cognitions about in-groups and out-groups, male undergraduates were presented with a list of 33 traits preselected (via pretesting with other subjects) to be commonly ascribed to both college-age men and men in their sixties and seventies. These respondents were instructed to sort the traits into groups representing traits that seemed to belong together. Respondents could form as many groups as they wished and were allowed to place the same trait in as many groups as they desired. Respondents performed this sorting task while thinking about men who were either college age or in their sixties and seventies.

Scott's *H* was calculated to assess complexity of respondents' beliefs about college-age and older men. This measure can be interpreted as the minimum number of independent (i.e., uncorrelated) binary dimensions needed to produce a sorting of the traits equal in complexity to that produced by the respondent. *H* is calculated by the following formula:

$$H = \log_2 n - (\Sigma n_i \log_2 n_i) / n \qquad (3.5)$$

where n = total number of traits (e.g., 33); and n_i = the number of traits that appear in a particular group combination, $n = \Sigma n_i$. As Linville (1982) explained:

> To define a *group combination*, consider a trait that is sorted into Group 1 and Group 2 but no others. This trait is said to fall into the group combination 1–2. More generally, if a person forms two groups, a given trait may fall into one of four possible group combinations: 1, 2, 1–2, or no group. The n_i in the above formula would be interpreted as follows in this example: n_1 = number of traits sorted only into Group 1; n_2 = number of traits sorted only into Group 2; n_3 = number of traits sorted only into both Group 1 and Group 2; and n_4 = number of traits not sorted into any group. (p. 199)

Belief Complexity and the Extremity of Attitudes

Whether more complex beliefs about an attitude object are associated with attitudinal extremity or moderation has been the focus of considerable research. This question is quite an important one in attitude theory because it relates a structural property of beliefs (their complexity) to the overall attitude. We describe the research on this issue in some detail because of the very interesting results that were produced—namely, that greater complexity of beliefs can be associated with attitudinal extremity *or* moderation, depending, as we will explain, on the extent to which beliefs are evaluatively redundant.

More Complex Beliefs Can Be Associated with More Moderate Attitudes. Central to understanding the relation between belief complexity and attitudinal extremity are studies by Patricia Linville in which belief complexity was defined by the dimensionality of people's beliefs about attitude objects as assessed by Scott's *H* (Linville, 1982; Linville & Jones, 1980). This work showed that the *less* complex one's set of beliefs, the *more* extreme is one's attitude in either a positive or negative direction. Linville reasoned that the greater the number of nonredundant (i.e., orthogonal or uncorrelated) attributes a person uses in thinking about an attitude object, the less likely it is that the attitude object is perceived as consistently good or consistently bad in all its aspects. This reasoning follows from the fact that location on the evaluatively positive side of an attribute dimension (e.g., warmth) is not predictive of location on the positive side of another attribute dimension (e.g., competence), if the dimensions are uncorrelated. Thus, when the evaluative meaning of a relatively large number of nonredundant attributes is aggregated, the attitude should average out to some moderate value. When one or only a few attributes are ascribed to an attitude object, evaluation tends to be more extreme because a favorable or unfavorable location on one attribute would not be balanced by other locations on the other attributes. Therefore, according to Linville, people with relatively simple belief structures should have more extreme attitudes than those with more complex structures.

Linville extended her analysis of the attitudinal implications of belief complexity by arguing that people's beliefs about out-groups (e.g., whites' schemas of blacks) are less complex than their beliefs about in-groups (e.g., whites' schemas of whites). As a consequence, members of out-groups should be evaluated more extremely than members of in-groups. For example, in Linville's (1982) study that used age as a basis of grouping, college-age subjects rated an older man described by a favorable vignette more positively than a comparable college-age man. Similarly, these subjects rated an older man described by an unfavorable vignette more negatively than a comparable college-age one.

More Complex Beliefs Can Be Associated with More Moderate or More Extreme Attitudes. Pursuing in more detail the relation between attitudinal extremity and the complexity of people's cognitions about attitude objects, Judd and Lusk (1984) obtained evidence that this relation depends on the extent to which the dimensions that underlie the beliefs are intercorrelated. As we already explained, Linville's research had operationalized the complexity of beliefs in terms of uncorrelated (i.e., orthogonal) dimensions and found that more complex beliefs were associated with more moderate attitudes. In contrast, Judd and Lusk manipulated the extent to which the dimensions were correlated—merely by instructing subjects that attributes (which were relevant to judgments of target persons' mental health) were correlated or uncorrelated. Also, in a second study Judd and Lusk explored individual differences in the correlations between attribute dimensions in students' naturally occurring belief structures pertaining to rock groups and sororities. This research suggested that to the extent dimensions are correlated rather than orthogonal, Linville's finding that complex schemas are associated with more moderate attitudes disappears and can even reverse. Evidently, when dimensions are correlated, they tend to be evaluatively redundant. For example, warmth, competence, and morality may be highly correlated in some belief structures because a "halo effect" or other factor causes one good quality to imply other good qualities. Under such circumstances, more dimensions (i.e., greater complexity) produce more extreme evaluation, as suggested by the *set size effect* (see Chapter 5) and earlier research by Tesser and Leone (1977; see Chapter 12). In contrast, with relatively orthogonal dimensions, greater complexity is associated with more moderate attitudes (i.e., Linville's finding).[15] The important mediating role of dimensions' interdependence has been confirmed in subsequent research (Lusk & Judd, 1988; Millar & Tesser, 1986b).

The Integrative Complexity of Beliefs

Other research on the complexity of beliefs ascribed to attitude objects has defined complexity in terms of the more complicated property of *integrative complexity*. This type of complexity, first investigated by Schroder and colleagues (1967) as an individual difference variable, expands the typical definition of complexity as dimensionality by simultaneously taking into account the *integration* of dimensions with one another. Whereas dimensionality or differentiation (the latter term being favored by integrative complexity researchers) refers to the number of dimensions required to describe an attribute space, integration refers to (a) the extent to which these dimensions are perceived to be linked to one another and (b) the nature of the links. These links do not take the form of the high correlations between dimensions that, as we have explained, reflect evaluative redundancy of beliefs. Instead they take the form of logical or causal bonds. In the political domain, for example, people's integration of their beliefs about an issue might refer to value conflicts or trade-offs that they realize are inherent in an issue or to their understanding of the joint or interactive impact of various influences on the issue.

In general, with low integration, the various dimensions of a belief structure are perceived simply as isolated properties of an attitude object, whereas with high integration, the dimensions are perceived to operate interactively and contingently. For example, a person's beliefs about blacks might indicate that, as a group, blacks have relatively high unemployment, low education, unstable families, and suffer from job discrimination. If these beliefs were integrated, they would be perceived as related to one another—for example, the unemployment might be perceived to result from discrimination and to cause family instability. If these beliefs were not integrated, they would be regarded merely as isolated properties of the group.

Beliefs that are integratively complex have both high dimensionality and integrative bonds between beliefs. These features of belief structures were originally assessed by means of a coding system applied to responses to a semi-projective test that presented respondents with sentence stems to complete (see Schroder et al., 1967). In research on political attitudes, both Peter Suedfeld and Philip Tetlock subsequently applied a similar coding scheme to various types of archival documents, including letters, speeches, judicial opinions, and policy statements (Suedfeld & Ramirez, 1977; Suedfeld & Rank, 1976; Suedfeld & Tetlock, 1977; see Tetlock, 1989).

Integrative Complexity and Attitudinal Extremity. Tetlock also addressed the question that Linville, Judd and Lusk, and others investigated—whether belief complexity relates to the extremity of the attitude. Specifically, he investigated the relation between integrative complexity of political beliefs and attitudinal extremity on the political continuum of liberalism versus conservatism (Tetlock, 1981a, 1983b, 1984, 1989). In examining the cognitive structures associated with differing political attitudes, this work has reintroduced an issue of long-standing interest among attitude researchers. Although the authors of the classic authoritarian personality study maintained that right-wing ideological extremists think in relatively rigid, dichotomous, and simple terms (Adorno, Frenkel-Brunswik, Levinson, & Sanford, 1950; see Chapter 12), other researchers argued that extremists on both the political left and the right view issues in rigid, dichotomous terms (Rokeach, 1960; I. A. Taylor, 1960). Tetlock found that political extremists of both the left and the right in the United States and Great Britain were less integratively complex in their reasoning than politicians closer to the middle of the political spectrum (see also de Vries & Walker, 1987). Yet Tetlock's studies found maximum integrative complexity, not at the exact location most people would regard as the middle of the political spectrum, but somewhat to the left of center.

The negative relation that Tetlock and others have demonstrated between integrative complexity and political extremity is consistent with Linville's (1982) contention that complexity fosters attitudinal moderation. This consistency between the two research programs suggests that the measure of integrative complexity used by Tetlock does not reflect correlated and evaluatively redundant dimensions. As we have explained, correlated dimensions should produce a positive relation between complexity and extremity (see also Tesser & Shaffer, 1990). Although the type of content analysis procedures used to assess integrative complexity precludes any formal determination of the extent to which respondents' beliefs are correlated, Tetlock (1983a) had judges count the number of liberal and conservative thoughts subjects wrote down on three contemporary political issues (e.g., increased American defense spending). Subjects who were integratively complex listed thoughts on both sides of the issues to a greater extent than did subjects who were simpler. These findings suggest that the beliefs that contribute to integrative complexity are not evaluatively redundant and may even be inversely correlated.

122

Integrative Complexity and Linkages to Values. Tetlock (1986, 1989) has suggested that the integrative complexity of people's beliefs about social issues reflects the linkage of these issues to their underlying values. Thus, people tend to think about an issue in an integratively complex fashion to the extent that it activates values with conflicting implications for their attitude on the issue. For example, an individual high in integrative complexity might perceive that her positive attitude toward maintaining profitable trade relations with countries that deny basic civil liberties to their citizens enhances one of her values (e.g., a comfortable and prosperous life) but diminishes another value (e.g., individual freedom).

The Structure of Beliefs:
Relations Between Beliefs

As suggested by the research we have reviewed on complexity, the beliefs that people hold about attitude objects are often linked to other beliefs in various ways. One way that we have seen that beliefs can be linked is that they imply similar degrees of evaluative meaning and therefore are evaluatively redundant. As we explain in this section, the extent of beliefs' evaluative dissimilarity (or inconsistency), a property usually known as ambivalence, is an important structural property in and of itself. In addition, as suggested by the research on integrative complexity that we have reviewed, beliefs may be linked by means other than their evaluative consistency or inconsistency, namely, via causal, logical, and other sorts of linkages. In fact, as we explain later in this section, several researchers have suggested that beliefs can be linked by inferences that allow people to deduce a belief from one or more other beliefs. We will consider in some detail this issue of the logical consistency of beliefs and discuss psychologists' modeling of the logical processes by which people derive beliefs from other beliefs.

Evaluative Inconsistency Between Beliefs: Ambivalence

In addition to examining consistency *between* evaluations and each class of attitudinal responses, social psychologists have considered evaluative consistency *within* each of these classes and sometimes across response classes. With respect to cognitions, for example, the beliefs an individual holds about an attitude object may often be evaluatively consistent with one another, that is, located at approximately the same position on the evaluative continuum. This type of consistency is inherent in the social judgment theory assumption that one's beliefs about an attitude object fall in one's latitude of acceptance, which surrounds one's most preferred position. In addition, this type of consistency may be characteristic of people who show high evaluative-cognitive consistency with respect to a particular attitude (see prior discussion). However, even if people's beliefs typically are evaluatively consistent in particular attitudinal domains, common sense suggests that sometimes people simultaneously hold evaluatively inconsistent beliefs, that is, some beliefs that express positive evaluation and other beliefs that express negative evaluation. Similarly, affective

123

responses to an attitude object (e.g., emotional reactions) can be evaluatively consistent or inconsistent with one another, and so can behavioral responses.

People holding inconsistent beliefs or harboring inconsistent emotions ("mixed feelings") have been described as *ambivalent*. In addition, emotions inconsistent with beliefs can be regarded as ambivalent—this is the "heart versus mind" conflict so prevalent in literary works. Emphasizing inconsistency in beliefs, W. A. Scott (1969) suggested that "an *ambivalent* image is one that includes both desirable and undesirable characteristics" (p. 263). As Irwin Katz (1981) has shown, the concept of ambivalence has its roots in psychoanalytic writings, where it generally refers to conflict between love and hate. Thus, a woman may find that a friend is lovable because of his good looks and charm, yet quite detestable because of his deceitfulness and unreliability. In such circumstances both cognitions and affect would probably reflect a mix of positive and negative evaluation.

To assess the ambivalence that follows from evaluatively inconsistent beliefs, K. J. Kaplan (1972) modified the semantic differential technique by separately assessing the positive and the negative attributes ascribed to an attitude object. One unipolar measure thus assessed the good attributes ascribed to the attitude object (e.g., clean, wise, healthy), and another unipolar measure assessed the bad attributes (e.g., dirty, foolish, sick). Given these separate measures of good and bad attributes, Kaplan proposed that ambivalence increases to the extent that (a) the attributes ascribed to an attitude object are more polarized and (b) the positive and negative attributes are more equal in the absolute value of the evaluative meaning that they convey (see Hass, Katz, Rizzo, Bailey, & Eisenstadt, 1991, for a related method). Other efforts to assess ambivalence have assumed that ambivalence is expressed through slower response times in responding to attitudinal inquiries (I. Katz, 1981) and positive and negative responses that are relatively uncorrelated (Abelson et al., 1982).

The Ambivalence-Amplification Hypothesis. Although sociologists and social psychologists (e.g., Simmel, 1908/1955) have speculated for many years about the effects of ambivalence on social interaction, empirically these implications have been explored only relatively recently. Most of this research has been carried out by Irwin Katz, R. Glen Hass, and their associates, who maintain that people often harbor ambivalent beliefs and feelings about stigmatized social groups such as minorities and the handicapped (see Katz, 1981; Katz & Glass, 1979; Katz, Wackenhut, & Hass, 1986). These researchers also argue that this ambivalence causes reactions to members of these groups to be more extreme than reactions to members of non-stigmatized groups (see also Gergen & Jones, 1963). This tendency for responses to become more extreme, termed *amplification*, can occur in either a favorable or an unfavorable direction, dependent on the social context. Katz's ambivalence-amplification prediction that reactions to stigmatized groups are more extreme thus resembles Linville's (1982) prediction about more extreme evaluations of out-groups than in-groups (although, as we will see, a different mechanism is implicated).

Katz and his associates have presumed that this tendency for ambivalence to produce amplification arises from the threat to the self-concept that follows from being

124

ambivalent about members of a stigmatized group. When favorable and unfavorable beliefs are simultaneously held, both classes of beliefs can threaten the self-concept. Reactions expressing one's negative beliefs about stigmatized people threaten one's self-image as humane because they contradict one's positive beliefs about the group. Similarly, reactions expressing one's positive beliefs threaten one's self-image as objective and discerning because they contradict one's negative beliefs about the group. According to Katz, the resulting threat to the self-concept produces psychological discomfort that elicits efforts to reduce the threat (see Hass, Katz, Rizzo, Bailey, & Moore, in press).

How can an individual preserve his positive self-image as humane yet still view himself as objective and discerning? Efforts often take the form of extreme reactions that would discredit or negate either the positive or the negative aspect of the ambivalent attitude. For example, a white supervisor who was critical of a black worker's performance might find her self-concept as a humane person threatened because she believes that blacks are victims of discrimination. To defend her self-regard, the supervisor might then react by being either extremely harsh toward the worker or extremely polite and friendly. An extremely unfavorable reaction would allow her to perceive this particular black person as completely unworthy and thus would discredit the positive aspects of her attitude toward blacks. This reaction would allow her to regard herself as objective and discerning, yet protect her from feeling inhumane (after all, the negative reaction would be justified because this black individual would seem really very unworthy). In contrast, an extremely favorable reaction would make salient the favorable attributes she ascribes to blacks and would discredit the negative aspect of her attitude. This reaction would allow her to regard herself as humane, yet protect her from feeling non-objective (after all, the positive reaction would be justified because this particular black individual would seem really very worthy).

Substantiating these predictions concerning reactions to minorities and stigmatized groups, Katz and his associates established that members of such groups often elicit more extreme reactions than other people do. For example, Katz, Glass, and Cohen (1973) induced white male college students to give painful or mild electric shocks to a white or black male confederate working at a learning task. These subjects rated the confederate on a questionnaire before and after the learning session. As predicted, the pre-shock ratings did not differ across the various conditions of the experiment, but the post-shock ratings showed derogation of the black confederate in the strong shock condition. Not only is such research consistent with the ambivalence-amplification hypothesis, but several of the studies carried out by Katz, Hass, and their collaborators also directly assessed ambivalence in an effort to show that it accounts for the mix of unusually favorable and unfavorable reactions that they have termed amplification effects. These studies have produced findings supportive of the mediating role of ambivalence in amplifying responses toward stigmatized others (see Hass et al., in press; Hass et al., 1991; Katz et al., 1986).

The Origins of Ambivalence in Attitudes' Linkages to Values. The sources of white Americans' ambivalence concerning black Americans have been probed in research by Katz and Hass (1988). As this research showed, whites often endorse beliefs favorable to blacks, such as "This country would be better off if it were more willing to assimilate the good things in Black culture" and "Too many Blacks still lose out on jobs and promotions because of their skin color" (p. 905). However, whites also often endorse beliefs unfavorable to blacks, such as "Many Black teenagers don't respect themselves or anyone else" and "The root cause of most of the social and economic ills of Blacks is the weakness and instability of the Black family" (p. 905). Katz and Hass argued that this ambivalence stems from the linkage of whites' racial attitudes to two contrasting values. The favorable beliefs, which generally sympathize with blacks as minority underdogs, are linked with the value of *communalism*, which expresses humanitarian and egalitarian precepts that foster concern about the community and the well-being of others. The unfavorable beliefs, which generally criticize blacks as socially deviant, are linked with the value of *individualism*, which expresses Protestant ethic precepts that foster achieving success through hard work and self-denial. Thus, associations that many whites have established between their attitude toward blacks and other, more abstract attitudes (termed values) with conflicting implications for this attitude may cause these whites to hold both favorable and unfavorable beliefs about blacks (see Kluegel & Smith, 1986, for a related analysis).

A similar interpretation of attitudes toward blacks is that white prejudice takes the form of *symbolic racism*, which is defined as a blend of negative affect toward blacks and antiblack beliefs that stem from traditional American values such as those embodied in the Protestant ethic (Kinder, 1986; Kinder & Sears, 1981; McConahay & Hough, 1976; see discussion of ideology in this chapter). Like Katz and his associates, theorists of symbolic racism have assumed that white Americans tend to be ambivalent about blacks and that American values are a source of this ambivalence (see McConahay, 1983).

Linkages of attitudes to values with conflicting implications for an issue have also been considered in Tetlock's (e.g., 1986) investigations of policy issues and in Rokeach's (1973) research on value confrontations. As we have already noted, Tetlock (1986) showed that people often relate social policy issues to values with conflicting implications for the issue. For example, the issue of whether more public parklands should be opened to mining and oil exploration in order to promote economic growth and prosperity might be related to valuing a world of beauty versus valuing a comfortable and prosperous life. With value linkages of this type, the beliefs underlying people's positions on an issue would be ambivalent. Tetlock has maintained that such ambivalence fosters complexity in people's thinking about issues (see prior discussion of complexity).

Because Tetlock's claim that integrative complexity is a product of linkages to values with opposing implications for one's attitude resembles Katz and Hass's (1988) idea that linkages to such values underlie whites' ambivalent beliefs about blacks, it is striking that these two lines of work suggest opposite effects of these value linkages. Thus, Tetlock's empirical relation between integrative complexity and political attitudes suggests that such linkages create *attitudinal moderation*, whereas Katz's ambivalence-amplification findings suggest instead *polarization*. These apparently opposed effects could perhaps be explained in terms of the differing attitudinal domains investigated in these research programs, the differing methods used to assess complexity, the differing social contexts of the research, or other factors (for discussion of related issues, see Liberman & Chaiken, 1991; Sidanius, 1988; Tesser & Shaffer, 1990).

Other Implications of Holding Ambivalent Beliefs. Ambivalence should decrease the stability of attitudes. This decline in attitudinal stability occurs because the relative accessibility of the favorable and unfavorable attributes ascribed to an attitude object would affect the attitude expressed at any one point in time. In our example of the good-looking, charming, unreliable, and deceitful friend, some social contexts (e.g., a party) might increase the accessibility of good looks and charm, whereas other contexts (e.g., working with him on a demanding task) might increase the accessibility of unreliability and deceitfulness. As Katz (1981) has also argued, such attitudes should therefore shift easily from positive to negative, depending on the context.[16] Indeed, Bargh, Chaiken, Govender, and Pratto (1992) have shown that more ambivalent attitudes are more unstable. Ambivalent attitudes should in addition be relatively poor predictors of behavior (M. Moore, 1973, 1980; see Chapter 4).

Even though holding evaluatively inconsistent beliefs may produce quite unstable expressions of attitude, a thoughtful and thorough general review of one's ambivalent beliefs should produce a relatively neutral attitude. Curiously, not a great deal is known about whether attitudinal neutrality typically stems from ambivalence or from other causes. The ascription of both good and bad attributes to an attitude object is surely one source of attitudes that are relatively neutral. In fact, following K. J. Kaplan's (1972) method of assessing ambivalence, more ambivalent respondents should have more nearly neutral attitudes, when attitudes are assessed on traditional bipolar scales. However, attitudinal neutrality could also reflect evaluatively homogeneous beliefs with mid-scale locations. In addition, attitudinal neutrality might reflect a relative absence of knowledge about the attitude object, because people with little basis for evaluating an attitude object (i.e., who have nonattitudes) may categorize it in the neutral range of evaluation (see DuBois & Burns, 1975; Klopfer & Madden, 1980). Further research on neutrality could thus shed some light on attitudinal ambivalence and related issues.

Affective and Behavioral Ambivalence. Little attention has been directed to affective and behavioral ambivalence. Yet, Abelson and his colleagues' study of reactions to politicians did examine affective ambivalence (Abelson et al., 1982). These researchers found that positive and negative affective reactions clustered separately, that is, they formed two factors that showed only a small negative correlation. These findings suggested, for example, that having good feelings about Senator Kennedy did not imply an absence of bad feelings. Although a variety of attitude objects other than important political figures might also elicit affective ambivalence (e.g., family members, one's job), this matter has not been studied. Finally, we note that psychologists have examined approach-avoidance conflicts, a form of behavioral ambivalence, for many years (e.g., N. E. Miller, 1944). Although the approach-avoidance paradigm has been generally important in psychology, it has rarely been applied to the study of attitudes (but see Kelman, 1962, for a rare exception).

Logical Relations Between Beliefs

Although we have concentrated so far on beliefs' evaluative relations with one another, beliefs can be related in other ways. Especially important to consider are logical relations between beliefs: Beliefs may follow from one another logically or may be logically inconsistent. Also, new beliefs may be formed by logical deduction from existing beliefs. Beliefs that are inferred from other beliefs are especially important to understand to the extent that attitudes are based on those beliefs that are salient at a particular point in time. Some of these salient beliefs may be inferred from other beliefs.[17]

The most popular approach to understanding these inferential links between beliefs is based on probability theory and known as the *probabilogical model*. This approach defines beliefs as subjective probability judgments (e.g., the perceived likelihood that a nuclear war will occur within the next ten years). Because this model examines the general proposition that relations among beliefs obey the laws of mathematical probability theory, it is a normative model in the sense that it specifies how beliefs *ought* to be related to one another within the individual's cognitive system and how beliefs *should* change when other, probabilistically related beliefs are formed, modified, or made salient to the individual.

McGuire's Probabilogical Model. Working within a cognitive consistency framework, McGuire (1960a, 1960b, 1960c) first proposed a probabilogical model of belief inferences that provided a quantitative definition and assessment of the logical consistency among beliefs. Formulated in the context of logical syllogisms, the McGuire model pertains to sets of syllogistically related belief propositions such as the following:

> A (Minor premise): A major nuclear war will occur within the next ten years.
>
> B (Major premise): A major nuclear war would result in violent death to at least half the earth's population.
>
> C (Conclusion): At least half the earth's population will meet violent death within the next ten years.

In relevant research, a person's beliefs in the above three propositions would be assessed in terms of subjective probabilities (i.e., the person's judgment of the probability that each proposition is true). According to the laws of formal logic and probability theory, if these beliefs manifest complete logical consistency, their relations should conform to the following equation:

$$p(C) = p(A)p(B) + p(K) \qquad (3.6)$$

In this equation, $p(A)$, $p(B)$, and $p(C)$ are the person's beliefs in the minor premise, major premise, and conclusion, respectively. The final term, $p(K)$, represents the person's belief in the conclusion as derived from "bases other than the conjunction of A and B" (McGuire, 1960a, p. 346). For our nuclear war example, $p(K)$ refers to the belief that "factors other than nuclear war are going to result in violent death to at least half the earth's population within the next ten years" (McGuire, 1960c, p. 68).

Wyer's Version of the Probabilogical Model. Wyer subsequently proposed a conditional inference model of belief inferences (Wyer, 1970, 1974b; Wyer & Goldberg, 1970; Wyer & Hartwick, 1980). Although Wyer's model was neither developed within the general framework of cognitive consistency theory nor applied exclusively to syllogistically related belief propositions, it is closely related to McGuire's (1960a, 1960b, 1960c) earlier model of cognitive structure. Conditional inferences refer to judgments concerning the validity of one proposition, given the validity of others. To the extent that conditional inference processes play a role in belief formation and change, we might expect, for example, that people's belief in the proposition, "marijuana should be legalized," might be dependent on their beliefs associated with a second proposition such as "marijuana is harmless."

According to Wyer's (1970) conditional inference model, a person's belief (assessed in probabilistic terms) in a target proposition C should be related to her beliefs associated with a second proposition A in the following manner:

$$p(C) = p(A)p(C/A) + p(A')p(C/A') \qquad (3.7)$$

In this equation $p(C)$ is a person's belief in C, $p(A)$ and $p(A')$ [where $p(A') = 1 - p(A)$] are beliefs that A is and is not true, respectively, and $p(C/A)$ and $p(C/A')$ are conditional beliefs that the target proposition C is true if A is and is not true, respectively. For the marijuana example, Equation 3.7 states that a person's belief that marijuana should be legalized [$p(C)$] should be equivalent in strength to her belief that marijuana is harmless [$p(A)$], weighted by the conditional belief that marijuana should be legalized if it is harmless [$p(C/A)$], plus her belief that marijuana is not harmless [$p(A')$], weighted by the conditional belief that marijuana should be legalized even if it is not harmless [$p(C/A')$].

Reexamination of the nuclear war example introduced earlier reveals the similarity between the Wyer and McGuire models. According to Wyer, a person's belief in the conclusion "at least half the earth's population will meet violent death within the next ten years" (C) should be a function of his beliefs and conditional beliefs associated with the *minor premise*, "A major nuclear war will occur within the next ten years" (A). In the McGuire model (Equation 3.6), belief in the *major premise*, "A major nuclear war would result in violent death to at least half the earth's population," is denoted by $p(B)$. Because belief in this major premise is essentially the person's conditional belief that the conclusion C is true *if* the minor premise A is true, the $p(B)$ term in Equation 3.6, the McGuire model, is equivalent to the $p(C/A)$ term in Equation 3.7, the Wyer model. Finally, Wyer (1970) has pointed out that the $p(K)$ term in the McGuire model—the belief that the conclusion is true on the basis of factors *other* than the conjunction of the two premises—can be denoted more precisely by the person's belief that the minor premise is *false* [i.e., $p(A')$], weighted by his conditional belief that the conclusion C is true *if* the minor premise A is not true [i.e., $p(C/A')$]. In summary, as Wyer (e.g., 1970) and McGuire (1981) themselves maintained, the two formulations of the probabilogical model are identical when McGuire's $p(B)$ is assumed to be equivalent to Wyer's $p(C/A)$ and McGuire's $p(K)$ equivalent to Wyer's $p(A')p(C/A')$.

Empirical Evidence Supporting the Probabilogical Model. When applied to relations among beliefs, considerable support has been obtained for the McGuire-Wyer probabilogical model. In relevant studies, subjects were presented with sets of belief propositions like the previous examples and then gave their own probability estimates for each term in Equation 3.7 [i.e., $p(C)$, $p(A)$, $p(A')$, $p(C/A)$, $p(C/A')$]. In such studies, predicted and observed values of $p(C)$ have generally shown at least a moderately high degree of correspondence, although errors in predicting individual subjects' beliefs have typically been greater than errors based on grouped data (e.g., Wyer, 1970; Wyer & Goldberg, 1970). A plot of the mean obtained values of $p(C)$ versus the mean predicted values from one of Wyer's experiments is shown in Figure 3.3.

To provide additional evidence that beliefs associated with the premises of a syllogism [i.e., $p(A)$, $p(A')$, $p(C/A)$, $p(C/A')$] combine functionally to affect belief in its conclusion [$p(C)$] in the manner prescribed by Equation 3.7, Wyer carried out experiments that manipulated subjects' beliefs in premises. For example, Wyer (1975) presented information to subjects that manipulated $p(A)$ and $p(C/A)$. Subjects' estimates of $p(A)$ were manipulated by telling them that people usually, versus sometimes, versus rarely have gene x. Subjects' estimates of $p(C/A)$ were manipulated by telling them that persons who have gene x usually, versus sometimes, versus rarely have attribute X. After exposure to these manipulations, subjects judged $p(C)$, the probability

FIGURE 3.3. Mean obtained versus mean predicted estimates of $p(C)$ for two sessions of an experiment and for two issue replications. Predicted estimates were based on Equation 3.7. This figure was adapted from one presented by Wyer and Goldberg (Experiment 3, 1970, Figure 5, p. 110).

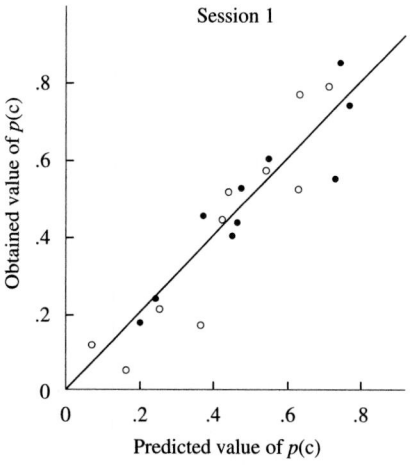
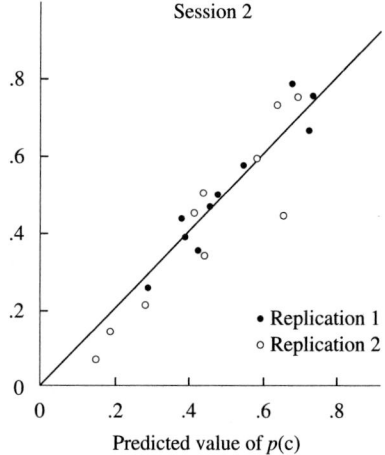

that a particular person had attribute X. In accord with the model's predictions, the findings of this study showed that subjects' judgments of $p(C)$ increased as $p(C/A)$ increased, but this increase was greater when $p(A)$ was high rather than low.

Research on the probabilogical model has yielded far more than these basic demonstrations that Equation 3.7 describes people's inferences of conclusions from premises with at least moderate accuracy. The most interesting applications of the model pertain to belief change and are thus considered in Chapter 5.[18]

Concluding Comments on Intra-Attitudinal Structure

Available and Accessible Structure

During our discussion of intra-attitudinal structure, especially knowledgeable readers may have occasionally wondered whether we meant to imply available or accessible structure when we considered complexity, ambivalence, and other characteristics of attitudinal structures (see Higgins & King, 1981; Higgins, King, & Mavin, 1982; Tulving & Pearlstone, 1966). The *availability* of a structure is its presence in memory so that it could potentially be used for processing stimulus input. The *accessibility* of a structure is its readiness to be used in information processing at a particular point in time. Unfortunately, it is very often not clear whether the methods that researchers have used to assess various structural variables measure accessible or available structure.

To illustrate the availability-accessibility distinction in relation to the complexity of the beliefs associated with an attitude, we note that the complexity of the available beliefs could well differ from that of the accessible beliefs. For example, the accessible structure could be relatively simple, but potentially much more complex if a large amount of knowledge had been stored in memory (i.e., was available). In general, the complexity of available structure generally increases as perceivers have more experience with the attitude object and thus learn about its attributes (see Schlegel & DiTecco, 1982). However, not all aspects of a complex structure would necessarily be accessible at any one point in time, because accessibility is a product of the demands of the perceiver's situation as well as a variety of other factors (see Higgins & King, 1981).

The impact that the situation has on the accessibility of structures has been shown by Tetlock's demonstrations that tendencies to be integratively complex vary with changes in political roles and in one's accountability for the consequences of one's decisions (see Tetlock, 1989). For example, occupying a policy-making role evidently encourages integrative complexity. As Tetlock's (1981b) research showed, American presidents manifested less complexity during an election campaign than after coming to power. Similarly, the judicial opinions of the United States Supreme Court justices tended to be more complex when they expressed the majority view of the court rather than a dissenting or minority opinion (Tetlock, Bernzweig, & Gallant, 1985). In laboratory studies, making subjects accountable for the consequences of their behavior (e.g., by telling them they will have to explain and justify their decisions or policy positions) promoted integratively complex reasoning (see Tetlock, 1983a; Tetlock & Kim, 1987).[19]

Tetlock's findings recall much earlier research by Zajonc (1960b) demonstrating that people activate cognitive structures that are instrumental for the task they face—a tendency that Zajonc labeled *cognitive tuning*. In Zajonc's experiment, subjects expecting to transmit information to others accessed structures that were more complex and that were composed of more highly interdependent attributes, compared with the structures accessed by subjects who expected merely to receive information (see Guerin & Innes, 1989). Such findings, which are congenial to the functional perspective that we develop more fully in Chapter 10, suggest that situational demands affect the accessibility of attitudinal structures, with more complex aspects of structure becoming more accessible when complexity would be useful in terms of the perceiver's goals. In general, the distinction between availability and accessibility should be considered more fully in an attitudinal context, along with its implications for attitudinal functioning (see Chaiken & Stangor, 1987; Tourangeau & Rasinski, 1988).

Summary

The significance of intra-attitudinal structure to the psychology of attitudes should now be apparent. In very general terms, three structural issues have been investigated continuously for several decades: (a) the dimensional representation of attitudes, (b) the relation between attitudes and beliefs, and (c) the structure of beliefs. Although some consensus has emerged on quite a few points in these three domains, some issues remain unresolved. In particular, some attitude researchers have maintained that people represent attitudes cognitively in terms of dimensional schemas that order positions on issues (including one's own position) and the beliefs that express these positions. Yet even among the researchers who have pursued the notion of such dimensional knowledge structures, there is little agreement about the exact nature of this dimension. Researchers need to clarify whether attitudinal dimensions are defined in terms of favorability or agreement (or both) and the extent to which these dimensions are articulated into discriminable regions or positions along the dimensions.

In contrast to the uncertain state of our knowledge about attitudinal dimensions, there is considerable consensus that attitudes are typically correlated with the evaluative implications of beliefs about the attitude object. In fact, we reviewed quantitative models of this relation. Yet there is also general agreement that consistency between attitudes and beliefs is a variable property of attitude structure. Thus, people's attitudes can be more or less consistent with their beliefs, and inconsistency between attitudes and beliefs can occur for a variety of reasons.

Beliefs associated with attitude objects also have important structural properties. The complexity of beliefs is one such property, and particular attention has been directed to understanding the relation between complexity and the extremity of attitudes. The beliefs by which people express their attitudes are also known to differ in the extent to which they are ambivalent (versus evaluatively consistent), and ambivalence has a number of consequences. The logical relations between beliefs have been investigated as well, primarily in terms of the probabilogical approach, which models how beliefs affect other probabilistically related beliefs.

Although many of these structural matters have been extensively investigated, other aspects have been only minimally explored—for example, little is known about the extent to which people represent opposing views as well as their own views on controversial issues or about the extent to which attitudes are commonly based on beliefs, affective reactions, or behavioral experience. Nor do we have much understanding of the consistency that may be displayed between cognitive, affective, and behavioral classes of attitudinal responding and the implications that this type of consistency may have for attitudinal responding.

INTER-ATTITUDINAL STRUCTURE

As our discussion of bonds between attitudes and values has already shown, attitudes are generally not isolated within the individual's mind but are linked to other attitudes in molar cognitive structures. Of particular interest to social psychologists are the cognitive linkages that may be formed between attitudes toward issues and attitudes toward people. These connections between attitudes develop as a product of social interaction. For example, if a person holds an attitude toward the United States' military participation in the Persian Gulf War and discusses this issue with a friend, this attitude would likely become linked, in a molar schema, with both the friend's attitude on the issue and the person's attitude toward the friend. The dynamics of this larger system of attitudes would then become important. Balance theory has provided the most popular framework for studying attitudinal schemas of this type. Alternatively, psychologists have sometimes assumed that attitudes are linked to other attitudes in thematically consistent structures known as ideologies or that attitudes' linkages to other attitudes are reflected in attitudes' importance or involvingness. We consider in turn these several traditions of investigating inter-attitudinal structure.

Balance Theory

Balance theory, originally formulated by Fritz Heider (1946, 1958), provides a symbolic language for describing the cognitive structures that represent attitudes and their relations to other attitudes.[20] The theory also provides a dynamic model of the changes that inter-attitudinal structures undergo (see Chapter 10). This formulation derived from Gestalt psychology (see below) and also drew on the writings of various philosophers (especially Hume and Spinoza) and on folk wisdom (see Weir, 1983). Heider developed this set of ideas and applied them to understand people's attitudes, as perceived in the context of their interpersonal relations. The resulting theory has been widely recognized as an especially innovative and creative contribution to social psychology.

133

Heider's Balance Model

Heider's symbolic language is a convenient aid to analyzing the knowledge structures that are comprised of sets of attitudes. The major terms of this language are *elements* and *relations* between elements. One of the elements is the *perceiver* or *reference person*, *p*, whose cognitions are described. The other two elements are usually the *other person*, *o*, and the *impersonal entity* or *thing*, *x*. Thus, the symbol *o* represents any person other than the perceiver, and the symbol *x* represents anything other than a person, including physical objects, social issues, and values and other abstractions.[21]

Two types of relations can link these elements. One of these types, the liking or *sentiment relation*, symbolized by L, corresponds to attitude, as we have defined attitude in this book. The second type of relation, known as the *unit relation*, and symbolized by U, is nonattitudinal. It represents any bond between two elements that is perceived to be based on something other than evaluation. Unit relations thus include similarity, proximity, ownership, causality, and possession. Both liking and unit relations have either a positive (L+ or U+) or negative (L− or U−) sign. Note that treating attitudes as dichotomous reduces the evaluative continuum to two values.

Heider used this symbolic language of elements and relations to analyze structures in which two elements or three elements are related to one another. A two-element structure includes only *p* and *o* or *p* and *x*, and a three-element structure generally includes *p*, *o*, and *x* (see examples in Figure 3.4). Heider proposed that two states can exist in these structures: balance and imbalance. He assumed that balance is a steady state and imbalance an unsteady state. When imbalance occurs, a structure is unstable and tends to change over time to a state of balance. To the extent that people maintain imbalanced states in their cognitions, they tend to experience tension (Heider, 1958). Heider's assumption about cognitive units gravitating toward balance had its roots in the work of Gestalt psychologists such as Köhler (1929) and Koffka (1935), who argued that cognitions tend toward simple "good figures."

Using the symbolic language of balance theory, Heider (1946) defined balanced states as follows:

FIGURE 3.4.
A balance theory representation of a two-element and three-element structure. An unbroken arrow signifies a positive relation, and a broken arrow signifies a negative relation. The direction that the arrow points indicates which element initiates the relation and which receives it (e.g., an arrow pointing from *p* to *o* represents *p*'s attitude toward *o* and an arrow pointing from *o* to *p* represents *o*'s attitude toward *p*, as perceived by *o*).

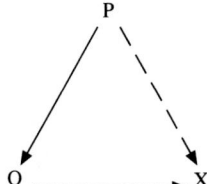

In the case of two entities [i.e., elements], a balanced state exists if the relation between them is positive (or negative) in all respects, i.e., in regard to all meanings of L and U.... In the case of three entities [i.e., elements], a balanced state exists if all three relations are positive in all respects, or if two are negative and one positive (p. 110).

Because a two-element structure with two relations would be balanced if the signs of the relations between the elements were the same, the configuration *p* likes *o* and perceives that *o* likes *p* as well as the configuration *p* likes *x*, which he owns (i.e., a positive unit relation), are examples of balanced states. Because Heider defined balance in a three-element structure by (a) three positive relations or (b) two negative relations and one positive relation, imbalance occurs with (a) three negative relations or (b) two positive relations and one negative relation. In Figure 3.5, which shows the eight possible configurations of positive and negative relations in a three-element schema composed of *p*, *o*, and *x*, the balanced triads are *a*, *b*, *c*, and *d*, and the imbalanced triads are *e*, *f*, *g*, and *h*. Triad *a*, for example, may be interpreted as *p* likes both *o* and *x* and perceives that *o* also favors *x*. This triad, as well as triad *b* in which *p* likes *o* and both *p* and *o* dislike *x*, are instances of agreement with a liked *o*. Balanced triads *c* and *d* are instances of disagreement with a disliked *o*. Imbalanced triads *e* and *f* are instances of disagreement with a liked *o*, whereas imbalanced triads *g* and *h* are instances of agreement with a disliked *o*. Describing these configurations in ordinary language, we can say that agreement with friends and disagreement with enemies are balanced, or steady states, whereas disagreement with friends and agreement with enemies are imbalanced, or unsteady states.

FIGURE 3.5. Balanced and imbalanced triads. An unbroken arrow signifies a positive relation, and a broken arrow signifies a negative relation.

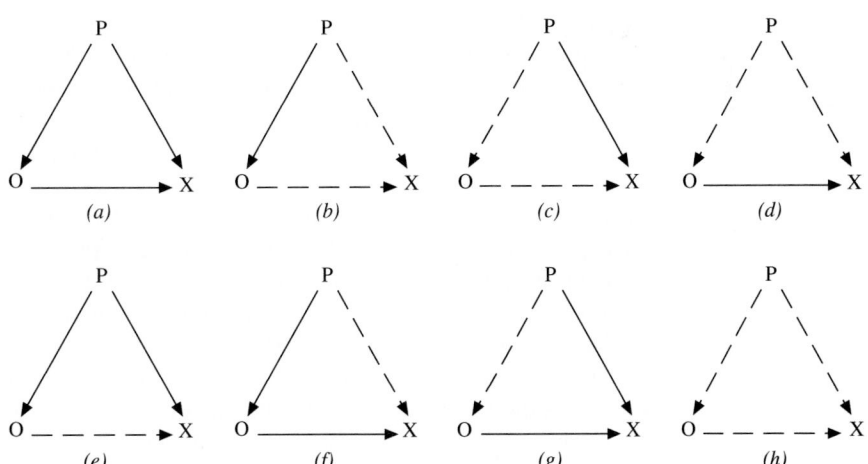

According to the theory, the four imbalanced schemas shown in Figure 3.5 should tend not to be maintained over time, but to be transformed into one of the four balanced schemas. Balance could be established in any of the imbalanced triads by (a) change in p's attitude toward o, (b) change in p's attitude toward x, or (c) change in o's attitude toward x.[22] As Heider and other balance theorists (e.g., Abelson, 1959) have pointed out, people may at times resolve imbalance by more complex reactions that involve adding new elements and relations or altering existing elements. For example, *bolstering* consists of adding several new elements that are consistent with an element that is already a component of an imbalanced structure. Using bolstering, a smoker concerned about the association of smoking with cancer might then think that smoking is relaxing, aids mental concentration, facilitates weight control, and so on. By this device, the one imbalanced structure is countered by a larger number of balanced structures (see Chapter 10).

Some Extensions of Balance Theory

Cartwright and Harary (1956) proposed an extension of balance theory based on the formal mathematical principles of the *theory of directed graphs*, which provides a symbolic language similar to the one that Heider proposed (see Cartwright & Harary, 1979; Harary, Norman, & Cartwright, 1965). This type of mathematics is useful for describing and analyzing the structural properties of systems, including cognitive structures. Among the advantages of the graph-theoretic formulation of balance theory is its derivation of a multiplicative rule for defining balance. According to this rule, a structure is balanced if the multiplicative product of the signs of its relations is positive and imbalanced if this product is negative. By this rule, balance can be determined for cognitive structures containing any number of elements—not just the two or three analyzed by Heider. A related extension of balance theory, based on matrix algebra, was proposed by Abelson and Rosenberg (Abelson & Rosenberg, 1958; M. J. Rosenberg & Abelson, 1960). In addition, Runkel and Peizer (1968) explicated the similarity of balance theory to traditional two-valued logic, and Gollob (1974) reformulated balance theory in syntactic terms that describe p-o-x triads as composed of a subject, a verb, and an object.

Several psychologists have produced versions of balance theory that yield quantitative predictions. These models modify Heider's representation of the attitudinal continuum in terms of just two values (positive and negative attitude) by treating at least some of the relations in the p-o-x triad as continuous scales. The first such effort was Osgood and Tannenbaum's (1955) congruity theory, which placed the p-o and p-x relations on continuous scales and predicted changes in p's attitude toward o and toward x. Although the quantitative predictions of this model have not proven to be particularly successful (see Zajonc, 1968b), congruity theory has interesting implications for modes of resolving inconsistency, which we discuss in Chapter 10. Wiest (1965) subsequently proposed that the three relations of the p-o-x triad be treated as three dimensions of a cube and thus as three continuous variables. This interesting approach has numerous applications (see Insko, 1984). For example, the model can be used to predict the exact value of a relation, given exact values for the other two relations (Tashakkori & Insko, 1979, 1981; Wellens & Thistlethwaite, 1971a, 1971b).[23]

Research Relevant to Balance Theory

As discussions by Heider (1958) and Insko (1981) have shown, various aspects of attitude research can be interpreted as consistent with balance theory. For example, one implication of the theory is that a person's attitude toward an issue depends on his or her attitude toward a source who provides information on the issue. The model predicts that people tend to agree with sources whom they evaluate favorably and disagree with sources whom they evaluate unfavorably. The work from the 1930s and 1940s on prestige suggestion as well as much of the later research on communicator variables in persuasion (see Eagly, 1983b) can be interpreted as supporting this prediction. Balance theory also predicts that individuals are attracted to people whom they perceive hold attitudes similar to their own. Attitudinal similarity has been repeatedly shown to enhance interpersonal attraction (see Berscheid, 1985; Byrne, 1971).

The Jordan Paradigm. Most of the explicit attempts to test balance theory have implemented some version of the research design that came to be known as the *Jordan paradigm* in honor of Jordan's (1953) seminal experiment in which subjects rated hypothetical *p-o-x* triads for their pleasantness. Jordan constructed sets of statements representing all of the eight types of triads shown in Figure 3.5—for example, "I like *o*; I dislike *x*; *o* likes *x*." The subjects were instructed to imagine themselves as the "I" in these situations and to rate them for pleasantness. The mean ratings for each of the eight triads are given in Table 3.4. When the ratings for the first four triads, which are balanced, were compared with the ratings for the second four triads, which are

TABLE 3.4

p-o-x **Triads and Jordan Paradigm Research**

Triad	Attraction	Agreement	Balance	Jordan data[a]
a	Yes	Yes	Yes	26.2
b	Yes	Yes	Yes	39.5
c	No	No	Yes	55.3
d	No	No	Yes	62.4
e	Yes	No	No	57.0
f	Yes	No	No	58.2
g	No	Yes	No	56.0
h	No	Yes	No	58.4

Note: [a]Means are on a scale ranging from 10 to 99 on which low numbers indicate greater pleasantness.

Source: These means were summarized from data presented by Jordan (1953), Table 2, p. 277).

imbalanced, the resulting difference indicated that the balanced triads were perceived as more pleasant than the imbalanced triads. However, most of this difference was due to the first and second triads. These triads, which describe agreement with a friend, were perceived as more pleasant than the remaining six, which differed little from one another.[24] This pattern of findings has been replicated by many other investigators who obtained subjects' judgments of the pleasantness, harmony, tension, expectancy, consistency, stability, or other qualities of these hypothetical triadic situations (see Insko, 1984; Zajonc, 1968b).

Zajonc's Interpretation of Jordan Paradigm Findings. From among the several interpretations that were initially offered for the distinctiveness of triads *a* and *b* (see Insko, 1984), the most influential was proposed by Robert Zajonc (1968b).[25] This interpretation followed from Zajonc's insight concerning the importance of comparing the eight triads on two bases in addition to balance versus imbalance: (a) the triads in which *p* likes *o* can be compared with those in which *p* dislikes *o* (in Table 3.4—*a, b, e,* and *f* versus *c, d, g,* and *h*), and (b) the triads in which *p* and *o* agree in their evaluation of *x* can be compared with those in which *p* and *o* disagree (in Table 3.4—*a, b, g,* and *h* versus *c, d, e,* and *f*). The first of these two additional comparisons, known as the *attraction effect*, showed that subjects rated triads with *p-o* liking more favorably than triads with *p-o* disliking. The second of the comparisons, known as the *agreement effect*, showed that subjects rated triads with agreement between *p* and *o* more favorably than triads with disagreement between them.

This partition of Jordan paradigm findings into three independent effects—preferences for balance, attraction, and agreement—suggests that the two triads indicating agreement with a friend were rated more favorably than the other six triads because of the cumulative impact of these three preferences (see Table 3.4). That is, these two triads are maximally pleasant because they manifest balance, attraction, and agreement. All other triads manifest only *one* of these three preferences—balance, attraction, or agreement. Based on these assumptions about attraction and agreement effects as well as the observation that the agreement effect in Jordan paradigm experiments tended to be somewhat stronger than the balance effect, Zajonc (1968b) concluded that the findings of these experiments were not favorable to balance theory.[26]

Insko's Interpretation of Jordan Paradigm Findings. Contrary to Zajonc's interpretation of Jordan paradigm findings, Chester Insko (1981, 1984) has shown that attraction and agreement effects need not be viewed as inconsistent with balance theory, if investigators take into account subjects' inferences from the information they are experimentally given in Jordan paradigm research. In an interesting series of experiments developing this alternative interpretation of attraction and agreement effects, Insko and his colleagues (see Insko, 1981, 1984) have argued that subjects typically interpret the situations described by *p-o-x* triads as having more relations than the three explicitly given to them by balance researchers. Once these additional relations are recognized, it is possible to explain the attraction and agreement effects on the basis of the balance principle. For example, subjects may tend to assume that they will interact with *o* in the future, even though they are not given this information. In balance theory, this assumption of future contact with *o* is represented by a unit relation between *p* and *o*, which would exist in addition to the sentiment relation between *p* and *o* that is ordinarily given to subjects in studies using the Jordan paradigm. With this addition, the complete structure would contain four relations. As shown in Figure 3.6, this four-relation structure can be decomposed, following graph theory conventions, into three component substructures or closed loops, which Insko, Songer, and McGarvey (1974) labeled *cycles*.

The first of the cycles in the four-relation structure shown in Figure 3.6 represents the attraction effect: It is balanced when there is attraction between *p* and *o*. The second cycle represents the agreement effect: It is balanced when *p* and *o* agree. The third cycle is the conventional *p-o-x* triad, which is balanced when all three relations are positive or two are negative and one positive. When the eight triads are analyzed in terms of the four-relation structure that includes the *p-o* unit relation, all three of these component cycles are balanced only for the two agreement-with-a-friend triads, which have consistently elicited the most favorable ratings in research. Each of the other six structures manifests balance in only one of the component cycles (see Figure 3.6).

Experiments testing this interpretation of Jordan paradigm data (see Insko, 1981, 1984) manipulated the perception of future contact with *o*: Some subjects were told to assume future contact, others were told to assume no future contact, and still others were told nothing about future contact. According to the analysis, attraction and agreement effects should be obtained (a) when future contact is explicitly indicated or

FIGURE 3.6.
A graph theory representation of the *p-o-x* triads assuming *p-o* contact. A solid line represents a positive relation; a dashed line, a negative relation; a curved line, a unit relation; and a straight line, a sentiment relation. An entry of 1 indicates that the cycle is balanced, and an entry of 0 indicates that the cycle is imbalanced. This figure was presented by Insko, Songer, and McGarvey (1974, Table 1, p. 56).

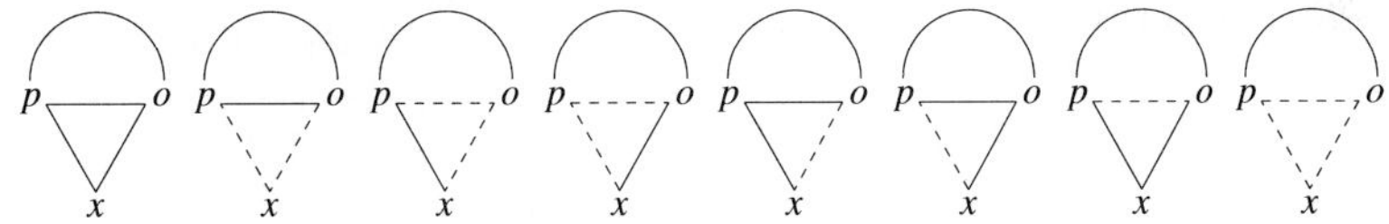

	Three–sign balance				Three–sign imbalance			
	+ + +	+ – –	– + –	– – +	+ + –	+ – +	– + +	– – –
Cycle 1	1	1	0	0	1	1	0	0
Cycle 2	1	1	0	0	0	0	1	1
Cycle 3	1	1	1	1	0	0	0	0
Sum	3	3	1	1	1	1	1	1

(b) when future contact is not mentioned (because, presumably, most subjects assume it will occur). When subjects are assured of no future contact, the *p-o* unit relation should be absent, and only the balance effect (i.e., in Cycle 3 of Figure 3.6) should be obtained. Findings were somewhat supportive of these (and other) balance theory predictions: In the no contact condition, attraction and agreement effects were smaller than they were in the conditions in which contact was explicitly indicated or not mentioned. Nevertheless, the attraction and agreement effects were not entirely eliminated in the no contact condition.

Because the assumption that subjects add an implicit unit relation to Jordan paradigm triads did not completely account for attraction and agreement effects, Insko and his associates (see Insko, 1981, 1984) have explored still other implicit relations (and elements). These other implicit components (e.g., an implicit *p-o* similarity relation) would result in additional cycles that are balanced or imbalanced. To varying degrees, the findings of this additional research have also supported the ability of balance theory to account for the attraction and agreement effects.

The approach taken by Insko and his colleagues suggests that the apparent inability of balance theory to account for Jordan paradigm findings stems, not from the theory's inadequacy, but from the excessive simplicity of social psychologists' typical applications of the theory. People's cognitions about interrelated attitudes appear to be more complex than Heider's *p-o-x* triad, and researchers' efforts to track this complexity have reinvigorated balance theory in recent years. Nevertheless, the adequacy of Insko's approach is difficult to evaluate because there are many implicit elements and relations that might be accessible, perhaps even in addition to those already investigated. Furthermore, the extent to which people take into account implicit and explicit aspects of triads may depend on a variety of characteristics of the situation and the perceiver. For example, in a Jordan paradigm experiment in which subjects rated the pleasantness of hypothetical *p-o-x* triads, Cacioppo and Petty (1981a) manipulated the amount of time subjects had to study the triads and, in a second experiment, varied the involvingness of the issue *x* (operationalized as the issue's importance and personal consequences). Greater time and higher involvement increased the tendency for the balance effect to emerge and slightly enhanced the agreement effect as well, whereas the attraction effect was unaffected by time and involvement. These interesting findings show that situational demands can affect the relative strength of the attraction, agreement, and balance effects and presumably, therefore, the accessibility of the implicit elements and relations that Insko and his colleagues have studied (see also Zajonc & Burnstein, 1965a).

Another barrier to a definitive conclusion about Insko's interpretation of Jordan paradigm research is that it is difficult to evaluate the simultaneous contributions of several implicit aspects of schemas (e.g., assumption of future contact with *o*, assumption of similarity to *o*). Although it is therefore not clear whether the proposal that people add implicit elements and relations to *p-o-x* triads *fully* accounts for the attraction and agreement effects, the supportive data that have been obtained demonstrate the importance of taking into account people's inferences from the information experimentally given in balance theory research using the Jordan or other paradigms.

Balance as a Conceptual Rule

The idea that balanced cognitions have schematic properties has been elaborated by a number of social psychologists. If balance is a type of schema or conceptual rule about how one's attitudes ordinarily mesh with others' attitudes, people should expect to agree with people they like and disagree with people they dislike. In general, information that fits this general rule or schema should be more readily learned and retained than information that does not fit it. In support of this derivation, Zajonc and Burnstein (1965a, 1965b) demonstrated that information consistent with the balance rule is more easily learned and more accurately retained than information inconsistent with this rule.

In a somewhat different test of the schematic effects of the balance rule, Cottrell (1975) had subjects attempt to classify triads into two groups based on a principle that they had to infer from the feedback (i.e., correct versus incorrect) that they obtained on each trial. Although subjects required more trials to learn to classify triads by a balance rule than by an attraction or agreement rule, it was easier for them to classify triads by the balance rule than by any other rule that, like balance, required that they take all three p-o-x relations into account.

In yet another test of the schematic effects of the balance rule, Sentis and Burnstein (1979) had subjects study scenarios describing balanced or imbalanced triads and answer questions requiring knowledge of one, two, or three of the relations in the triads. For example, one of the balanced scenarios was the following:

> Bill is a senior at a large university and has majored in Sociology. Bill is applying to several prestigious law schools and strongly opposes the graduate schools' admissions policy that is based on racial quotas. John is also a senior at the same university and he is an Urban Studies major. John is applying to these law schools also and is very much opposed to the quota system. Bill and John are friends; in fact, they like each other very much (p. 2203).

An example of a question requiring knowledge of one relation was whether Bill and John were friends. A two-relation question was whether Bill and John were friends and John disapproved of quotas, and a three-relation question was whether Bill and John were friends and both of them disapproved of quotas. For imbalanced triads, subjects' reaction times to these questions increased as the questions required that they retrieve more relations. In contrast, for balanced triads, subjects' reaction times decreased as the questions required that they retrieve more relations. The speed with which subjects were thus able to verify the three relations in balanced structures suggests that people possess a conceptual rule for balance that allows them to efficiently process information that is consistent with this rule. In general, research has supported the assumption that balance functions as a conceptual rule that people have stored and that influences information processing in the same way as other such rules (see also Hummert, Crockett, & Kemper, 1990). The idea that balance has schematic properties will be encountered again in Chapter 7's discussion of the heuristic model's liking/agreement rule.

Balance Theory and Intra-Attitudinal Structure

Fans of balance theory will no doubt be disappointed that we delayed the presentation of the theory until the second half of this chapter, thus removing the possibility of thoroughly considering the implications of the theory for intra-attitudinal issues. This decision followed from the fact that most applications of balance theory have pertained to bonds between different attitudes, not to bonds between attitudes and component beliefs or between beliefs. However, a theory as abstract as balance theory also can be applied very generally to structural issues of the intra-attitudinal kind. In fact, various of the findings we explored in our discussion of intra-attitudinal structure already have been interpreted in terms of balance theory or some close relative in the extended family of cognitive consistency theories. For example, in discussing dimensional representations of attitudes, we cited Feather's (1969) balance finding showing that people with positive attitudes generate mainly pro statements with which they agree and con statements with which they disagree, whereas people with negative attitudes generate mainly con statements with which they agree and pro statements with which they disagree. Also, in view of M. J. Rosenberg's (1960a) formulation of evaluative-cognitive consistency theory in terms quite close to those of balance theory, it is hardly surprising that many of the findings on this structural variable are compatible with balance theory (see Chapter 10). Similarly, the probabilogical model was originally proposed by McGuire (1960c) as another variant of cognitive consistency theory, and its propositions and findings could be translated into balance theory terminology. More generally, balance theory can provide an overarching framework within which to discuss a great many aspects of attitude structure.

Balance Theory Reborn Within Associative Networks

Readers familiar with cognitive psychology may notice a certain similarity between the representational language of balance theory and that of the associative network models that have been imported into social psychology from cognitive psychology (e.g., J. R. Anderson, 1983; Bower, 1981). Balance theory allows the representation of attitude objects as elements that are associated by positive or negative relations, and associative network models similarly allow the representation of attitude objects as nodes that are linked. Associative networks theory can thus be applied, not merely to issues of intra-attitudinal structure that we discussed earlier in the chapter, but also to issues of inter-attitudinal structure.

In an associative network interpretation of inter-attitudinal structure that explicitly invokes the balance principle, Judd and Krosnick (1989) represented attitudes as a positive or negative sign attached to each attitude object. Treating these valanced attitude objects as nodes in a network allows the representation of relations between attitudes—the traditional focus of balance theory. In fact, an identical representation, which also placed signs on the attitude objects themselves, was used by Abelson and Rosenberg in their variant of balance theory (Abelson & Rosenberg, 1958; M. J. Rosenberg & Abelson, 1960). In both approaches, the links between attitudes take the form of positive or negative implicational relations: A relation is positive if one attitude implies the other but negative if one attitude implies the opposite or converse of the other attitude. To give Judd and Krosnick's example, the policy of affirmative action might have a positive implicational relation to (i.e., be perceived as enhancing) the value of equality and might have a negative relation to (i.e., be perceived as diminishing) the value of freedom. The three attitude objects in this example—affirmative action, equality, and freedom—would have signs attached to them to represent p's attitude toward them. Within this system, Judd and Krosnick proposed a definition of attitudinal consistency borrowed from balance theory, that is, attitudes are consistent if the product of the signs on the attitude objects times the sign of the relation between them is positive.

Within this framework for analyzing inter-attitudinal structure, the spreading activation principle of network theories, which we introduced in our discussion of intra-attitudinal structure, has some interesting implications. For example, in a demonstration of spreading activation between attitudinal nodes, Judd, Drake, Downing, and Krosnick (1991) showed that answering attitude questions about one political issue (e.g., equal rights amendment) increased the accessibility of attitudes (operationalized by the latency of an attitudinal response) on a related issue (e.g., right to abortion) but not on an unrelated issue (e.g., nuclear weapons freeze). In addition, these investigators showed that answering questions on one attitude issue, which causes people to think about an issue and polarizes their attitudes (Tesser, 1978; see Chapter 12), resulted in more extreme responses to a related attitude issue, presumably because of spreading activation between attitudes that are linked in long-term memory.

Consistent with associative network models (e.g., J. R. Anderson, 1983) is Judd and Krosnick's (1989) suggestion that nodes (i.e., attitudes) have the property of strength as well as valence. Strength reflects the frequency with which a node has been activated in the past. The stronger two attitudinal nodes are, the greater the probability that these attitudes are brought simultaneously into awareness and the greater the probability that the attitudes are evaluatively consistent with one another via the balance definition of consistency. This strength property thus suggests a moderating condition for the balance principle—namely, that balance is more likely in relation to cognitive elements that we think about often. Indeed, Cacioppo and Petty's (1981a) Jordan paradigm experiment showed that greater time and higher involvement, which are both conditions that should increase thinking, increased the balance effect. Moreover, balance theorists have often suggested that imbalance is resolved over time and is more likely to be resolved when inconsistent elements are brought into awareness and become the object of thought (e.g., Abelson & Rosenberg, 1958).

Evaluation of Balance Theory

Although some social psychologists seem to believe that balance theory has had its day and is no longer a viable approach to understanding some of the schemas that govern the processing of attitudinal information (e.g., Abelson, 1983), to us these relatively negative verdicts appear unjustified because they fail to fully take into account the renewal of interest in the balance principle in the 1980s and the increasingly sophisticated uses of balance theory that underlie this renewal. In fact, balance theory has proven to be one of the most enduring of the theories that have been applied to attitudinal phenomena, and it has been pursued with considerable rigor. We believe, as Runkel and Peizer's (1968) logical analysis implies, that balance theory explicates a fundamental aspect of how people think. Although the balance principle can and should be incorporated into broader theoretical frameworks, the importance of the principle is unlikely to decrease. Along these lines, Judd and Krosnick's (1989) analysis is instructive because it incorporates the balance principle in a framework that also includes principles of human memory presented within network models.

Balance theory has inspired research other than studies in which people rate, learn, or otherwise react to hypothetical social situations. For example, in an innovative field study, Newcomb (1961) examined students' attitudes toward issues and toward other members of their living group and obtained many findings consistent with balance theory. In a well-executed laboratory experiment, Aronson and Cope (1968) confirmed the balance proposition that people like individuals who punish their enemies and reward their friends. In addition, political psychologists have applied balance theory to understand voters' perceptions of candidates' positions on issues. According to this research, perception of candidates' positions can be biased by the balance schema that liked candidates agree with the voters' own positions on issues whereas disliked candidates disagree (e.g., Krosnick, 1988b; Ottati, Fishbein, & Middlestadt, 1988; see Chapter 12). These studies are important because they enlarge the evidential bases of balance theory beyond the Jordan paradigm, which has been used so heavily to test the theory. Overreliance on this one type of research has left balance research vulnerable to the criticism of methodological narrowness. Moreover, Jordan paradigm experiments require that subjects imagine themselves in *p-o-x* situations and are thus vulnerable to the many criticisms of experimentation that requires subjects to play a role (e.g., Freedman, 1969; A. G. Miller, 1972).[27]

Balance theory enjoyed great popularity in the 1960s when it was understood in the relatively simple terms introduced by Heider, but by the late 1960s interest had waned. The amount of research stimulated by the theory increased again in the late 1970s and the 1980s (see Abelson, 1983). The newer elaborations of the theory have kept pace with the complexity of the findings the theory has generated. It would be unfortunate if the effort that is required to understand the newer work on balance theory were to discourage interest in it. The effort that readers must put forth to understand complex journal articles on balance theory clearly does not imply that perceivers must exert a great deal of effort to function in the ways the theory suggests. As Insko (1984) has emphasized, a complex schema containing several cycles may be learned over a period of time and may subsequently function relatively automatically, without conscious control or elaborate thinking. This view that balance principles operate by relatively heuristic processes has much in common with some of the viewpoints we consider in Chapter 7.

144

Attitudes and Ideologies

Political scientists and social psychologists interested in political attitudes have often approached issues of attitudinal consistency in terms quite different from those of the cognitive consistency theories that have long been popular in social psychology. They have assumed that, at least for some people, attitudes are components of larger structures that take the form of *ideologies* (see Kinder & Sears, 1985; McGuire, 1985). Ideologies have typically been defined as clusters or configurations of attitudes and beliefs that are interdependent or organized around a dominant societal theme such as liberalism or conservatism (Converse, 1964; Newcomb, 1950). In fact, people who hold ideologies are thought to derive their attitudes toward specific policies from the more general principles of the ideology. For example, a person holding a conservative political ideology might consult general principles of conservatism in developing a position on a specific issue such as federal supports for agriculture.

Political Attitudes and Ideologies

The extent to which the average person's attitudes are systematically linked to one another in recognizable ideologies has proven to be quite controversial. Some investigators of political attitudes have claimed that most U.S. citizens lack political ideologies and instead possess relatively unformed and unintegrated nonattitudes (Converse, 1964, 1970, 1975). Others have claimed that overarching ideologies are common (Judd, Krosnick, & Milburn, 1981; Judd & Milburn, 1980), although, according to some social scientists, these ideologies are often organized according to themes other than liberalism and conservatism (e.g., "prolabor traditionalism" or "economic moderation"; see Fleishman, 1986) and may appear even in quite individualized forms that are revealed only through detailed interviewing (Lane, 1962, 1973). Still other researchers have adopted the moderate view that, although the majority of U.S. citizens are quite willing to identify themselves ideologically in the political domain (e.g., as liberal or conservative), ideologies of this sort often do not entail the development of positions on policy issues that seemingly have ideological implications (Sears & Kinder, 1985). Instead, consistent with the research on symbolic attitudes that we discuss later in this section, for the majority of U.S. citizens political attitudes seem to be grounded in relatively vague attachments to certain groups and symbols as well as in rather general moral preferences and commitments to values.

To some degree, situational pressures may affect the extent to which people's political attitudes are consistent with one another and thus appear to be organized thematically. In support of the situational plasticity of ideology, Milburn (1987) showed that activating a liberal or conservative schema (by the instruction to "Tell me everything that comes into your mind when you think about a Liberal [Conservative]" p. 388) caused subjects' political attitudes to become more consistent with one another, although only for subjects who defined themselves by adjectives characteristic of liberals or conservatives. Thus, a politicized situational context may cause people who are identified as liberals or conservatives to think more ideologically.

There is more agreement among researchers that people with considerable expertise about political matters do possess recognizable ideologies, and research has shown that politically knowledgeable citizens and members of political elites differ from less knowledgeable citizens and members of the general public in their organization of political information (e.g., Judd & Downing, 1990; Judd & Krosnick, 1989; Tetlock, 1989). For example, Lusk and Judd (1988) examined political expertise among college students and a representative sample of American adults. Not surprisingly, they found that respondents who were generally more expert in the political realm reported a larger number of beliefs about political candidates. Moreover, experts' beliefs about political candidates were more highly intercorrelated and more evaluatively redundant than those of nonexperts. This organization of political beliefs in terms of a single evaluative dimension may reflect the kind of cognitive organization that political scientists refer to when they ascribe political ideologies to people.[28]

Also relevant to understanding political ideology are Tetlock's findings pertaining to integrative complexity and political attitudes (Tetlock, 1981a, 1983b, 1984, 1989; Tetlock, Hannum, & Micheletti, 1984). As we indicated earlier in this chapter, members of political elites vary considerably in their integrative complexity with respect to political issues, with politicians who are ideologically extreme manifesting simpler cognitive organization than politicians nearer the middle of the liberal-conservative continuum.[29] Finally, we note that political ideologies have important implications for political behavior, but a detailed review of this topic lies beyond the psychological focus of this book.

Racial Attitudes and Ideologies

The question of whether attitudes are linked to broader ideologies has also been raised in research on various specific attitudes—for example, attitudes toward capital punishment (Ellsworth & Ross, 1983), toward AIDS (Pryor, Reeder, Vinacco, & Kott, 1989), and toward abortion (Luker, 1984).[30] Yet, aside from political attitudes, racial attitudes have received the major share of attention in relation to ideology. In particular, Kinder and Sears (1981) have described a contemporary ideology about race that, as we noted earlier in this chapter, they have labeled *symbolic racism*. They defined symbolic racism as:

> a blend of antiblack affect and the kind of traditional American values embodied in
> the Protestant Ethic. Symbolic racism represents a form of resistance to change in
> the racial status quo based on moral feelings that blacks violate such traditional
> American values as individualism and self-reliance, the work ethic, obedience, and
> discipline (Kinder & Sears, 1981, p. 416).

These investigators claimed that this ideology is not based on actual experience with blacks but on "deep-seated feelings of social morality and propriety and in early-learned racial fears and stereotypes" (Kinder & Sears, 1981, p. 416). White Americans' resistance to policies that would improve the status of blacks is held to have symbolic roots in American values rather than more realistic or utilitarian origins in beliefs that pro-black policies have specific negative consequences for whites or the society more generally. Presumably symbolic racism has replaced the older, more blatant redneck racism that was prevalent in an earlier generation of Americans.

We are not the first to point out that there is some lack of clarity in this (and other) definitions of symbolic racism (see critiques by Bobo, 1983; Pettigrew, 1985; Sniderman & Tetlock, 1986b; Weigel & Howes, 1985). Nonetheless, if we assume that the term "affect" in the Kinder and Sears (1981) definition of symbolic racism refers to *evaluation* as we use the latter term in this book, their definition links whites' evaluations of blacks with certain values that whites are assumed to hold (see also McConahay & Hough, 1976). This reasoning is thus consistent with our general theme that attitudes may be embedded in a thematically organized structure. In particular, whites' racial prejudice is held to derive from the linkage of this attitude to a subset of Protestant ethic values having to do with self-reliance, discipline, and the work ethic. Consequently, whites tend to be opposed to social policies such as busing and affirmative action, which are oriented to changing the racial status quo, because they view these policies as violating a central tenet of the Protestant ethic—that success is achieved through hard work, discipline, and self-denial.

As readers may recall from our discussion of attitudinal ambivalence, the idea that racial attitudes are linked to values was confirmed in the research by I. Katz and Hass (1988). These investigators directly assessed relations between racial attitudes and values and argued in favor of linkages to *two* clusters of values. One of these clusters, *individualism*, corresponds to the Protestant ethic values emphasized in discussions of symbolic racism. The other cluster, *communalism*, which emphasizes concern about community and the well-being of others, has been neglected by theorists of symbolic racism, as has the idea that these values' conflicting implications for racial attitudes produce ambivalence on the part of white Americans.

In addition to this emphasis on the link between white racism and one cluster of values, several other aspects of the theory of symbolic racism are controversial (see Bobo, 1983; Sniderman & Tetlock, 1986a, 1986b). In particular, the claim that symbolic racism is a new ideology about race appears doubtful. Weigel and Howes's (1985) research showed that scales measuring symbolic racism were highly correlated with more traditional measures of anti-black prejudice. Moreover, their measures of anti-black prejudice were correlated with measures of prejudice toward other groups (homosexuals, the elderly) and with political conservatism and traditionalism about marital roles. The existence of this broader set of relationships is consistent with the claims of researchers who investigated *authoritarianism* in the 1940s (Adorno et al., 1950; see Chapter 12). They maintained that prejudice against out-groups is a syndrome: Prejudice toward one group tends to be correlated with prejudice toward other groups, and all types of prejudice are related to authoritarianism—a tendency to be deferent to authority and to be intolerant of deviance from traditional social norms. In this older tradition, the strength of people's prejudices toward outgroups was assumed to vary widely, and the broader ideology of authoritarianism was thought to characterize only a subset of white Americans. As we argued for political attitudes more generally, there is no doubt considerable variability in the extent to which attitudes on racially relevant topics are consistent with one another and warrant description in terms of the sort of thematic organization inherent in the concept of ideology.

Attitudes about race (and attitudes about gender as well) may also be linked to a broader ideology that many U.S. citizens may hold concerning the American stratification system. This ideology, labeled the *dominant ideology* by Kluegel and Smith (1986; see also Huber & Form, 1973), has as its major premise the idea that economic advancement follows readily from hard work. The deduction follows that people are responsible for their own economic fate and that the distribution of economic rewards is basically fair. According to Kluegel and Smith, the prevalence and durability of this ideology help explain Americans' ambivalence toward social policies such as affirmative action and busing that are designed to reduce inequality.

The Importance or Involvingness of Attitudes

Social psychologists have often assessed the linkages of attitudes to other attitudes through variables such as the *importance* or *involvingness* of attitudes. Although such variables serve primarily as motivational variables in attitude theories and therefore are discussed mainly in Chapters 7, 8, 10, and 12, they have sometimes been given a structural interpretation that we present here. Accordingly, such variables are thought to express the degree to which attitudes are embedded in a molar structure. This approach is quite different from that of balance theory, which provides an exact description of particular linkages (i.e., an attitude toward a particular x is linked to an attitude toward a particular o, etc.). The approach differs as well from the ideology tradition, which presumes thematic consistency of attitudes. In contrast, in the *involvement* approach to understanding inter-attitudinal structure, attitudes that are important or that produce involvement are assumed to be linked to other aspects of cognitive structure, but no particular bonds or content-specific themes are described or assessed.

Importance and involvement concepts were first articulated in a detailed way in the 1940s. In a discussion that had more of a motivational than cognitive emphasis, M. Sherif and Cantril (1947) treated involving attitudes as components of the "ego," or self-concept. Such attitudes "have the characteristic of belonging to *me*, as being part of *me*, as psychologically experienced" (p. 93). Similarly, Krech and Crutchfield (1948) regarded attitudes as *important* to the extent that "they are functionally related to the more central characteristics of the individual's personality structure,... and when they are based upon needs for identification with other people and groups" (p. 164). This view of attitudinal involvingness as the degree to which the attitude is linked to the self-concept was further developed in the Sherifs' writings on social judgment theory in the 1960s (C. W. Sherif et al., 1965; M. Sherif & Hovland, 1961). They suggested that ego-involving attitudes are components of a person's "self-picture—intimately felt and cherished" (C. W. Sherif et al., 1965, p. vi).[31]

Later efforts to define involvement and related constructs were formulated in more strictly cognitive terms. For example, Ostrom and Brock (1968) proposed that

> The basic feature of an ego-involved attitude is its relation to the manner in which the individual defines himself. The individual defines himself primarily in terms of that "distinct constellation of social and personal values" he has acquired. The closer the relation between his attitude and these values and the more central these related values are, the higher the degree of attitudinal involvement. (p. 375)

Ostrom and Brock thus argued that involvement increases to the extent an attitude is (a) related to more central or important values, (b) related to a larger number of values, and (c) highly relevant to these values. This idea that involving attitudes are embedded in a larger structure can be viewed in terms of W. A. Scott's (1968) conception of a more general property of attitudinal *embeddedness*, which he defined as the degree of connectedness (vs. isolation) of an attitude in relation to "other cognitive elements (for example, beliefs, values, other attitudes)" (p. 207).

The idea of cognitive linkages is the common denominator in structural interpretations of involvement: Important or involving attitudes are more extensively linked to other components of cognitive structure such as other attitudes, values, and the self-concept. Unimportant or uninvolving attitudes are structurally isolated. Indeed, there is empirical evidence, at least for the political domain, that important or central attitudes are more highly intercorrelated (Judd & Krosnick, 1982; Schuman & Presser, 1981).

Descriptions of the nature of the linkages that involving or important attitudes have to other aspects of cognitive structure have differed as a product of theorists' general frameworks. For example, M. Sherif and Cantril (1947) emphasized linkages to the ego, but regarded the ego as composed of attitudes. Ostrom and Brock (1968) emphasized the bonds of attitudes to values, but, as we explained in Chapter 1, values should be regarded as attitudes toward relatively abstract end states of existence (e.g., freedom, equality). Because attitude is the focal concept of our own analysis, we find it convenient to treat this type of attitudinal involvingness as the degree to which an attitude is linked to other attitudes in a molar cognitive structure.

Involvement, as described by the Sherifs, has been thought to impart resistance to attitude change (e.g., M. Sherif & Hovland, 1961; Ostrom & Brock, 1968). The reasoning underlying this prediction is the inertial notion that, for an attitude embedded in a larger structure, resistance occurs because the entire structure would have to change to some degree to accommodate the changed attitude (see Chapter 12). This prediction about resistance to change can be examined in an extensive research literature on involvement and persuasion (B. T. Johnson & Eagly, 1989) and in public opinion data (Krosnick, 1988a). As our discussion in Chapters 7, 8, and 12 reveals, the effects of involvement in persuasion research are quite varied, in part because in more recent years the term involvement has been used to label concepts that depart considerably from the structural embeddedness idea that we have introduced in this chapter.

In addition to involvement, attitude researchers have proposed a family of related concepts—for example, conviction, centrality, crystallization, importance, and intensity

(Abelson, 1988; Judd & Krosnick, 1982; Krosnick & Schuman, 1988; Schuman & Presser, 1981). In a general sense, these terms refer to the strength or importance of attitudes, but the terms have been given a variety of conceptual definitions and have been operationalized in a variety of ways (Petty & Krosnick, in press; Raden, 1985; see Chapters 4 and 12). Moreover, as we have indicated in this chapter, the treatment of attitudes in the associative network tradition includes the idea that links between nodes (e.g., between an attitude object and an evaluation) have the property of associative strength. The relation between associative strength and more traditional concepts of attitude importance and involvement is an area of increasing interest (see Bargh et al., 1992; Krosnick, 1989).

Concluding Comments on Inter-Attitudinal Structure

As our discussion has shown, inter-attitudinal structure has been approached from a variety of perspectives. Balance theory in its many variants has clearly received the lion's share of attention as a model of the relations between attitudes. The balance approach has shown remarkable durability and flexibility in its many applications to structural issues and thus remains a viable approach to analyzing linkages between specific attitudes.

We have considered two other approaches to inter-attitudinal structure that have also been the focus of considerable attention: the ideological organization of attitudes and the embeddedness of attitudes in a structure of related attitudes, which is thought to make attitudes involving or important. Neither the ideology nor the involvement approach provides the explicit mapping of attitudes' relations to specific other attitudes that balance theory provides, but both approaches have yielded significant insights about attitude structure. Issues of ideology are especially important in understanding the context of people's attitudes on social and political issues. The concepts of attitudinal involvement and importance are linked to a much larger set of issues about the strength of attitudes and the origins of attitude strength in cognitive or motivational factors. This is an issue that we return to at several points in this book, especially in Chapter 12.

To reiterate a theme of this chapter, we note that the structural concepts we have introduced gain validity to the extent they predict attitudinal responding. Structural concepts that have been proposed but so far have had little impact in terms of stimulating attitude research have been mentioned only briefly or omitted from our presentation altogether. For example, W. A. Scott (1969) proposed a concept of *evaluative centrality*, which he defined as the degree to which attitude objects are defined by evaluative (versus non-evaluative) attributes. This property of attitudinal structure, although potentially interesting, has received very little attention. The concepts we have emphasized do have demonstrated implications for attitude or belief change or for the prediction of behavior. Some of these predictions have been discussed in this chapter, but many others will appear in subsequent chapters.

Notes

1. Readers should note that we place in other chapters some topics that some other psychologists have considered structural. For example, McGuire (1985) regarded the relation between attitudes and behavior as a structural issue. McGuire's position on this matter is defensible because, as we indicated in Chapter 1, behaviors are one class of responses that may be related to attitudes. Just as the relation between attitudes and beliefs is traditionally considered a structural issue, the relation between attitudes and behaviors could be considered a structural issue. Similarly, the relation of attitudes to the broader goals of the person, a topic dubbed *functional* by attitude theorists (e.g., D. Katz, 1960), is structural because the embeddedness of attitudes in a molar structure of goals is the focus of research in this tradition (see Chapters 1 and 10). Because these quite diverse aspects of structure could not be considered in a single chapter, we have adopted narrower and more conventional boundaries for our discussion of attitude structure.

2. This finding as well as several others presented in our discussions of intra-attitudinal structure can be interpreted in terms of balance theory. We omit this interpretation at this point because we introduce balance theory in the second half of this chapter as a model of inter-attitudinal structure.

3. The process by which social judgment researchers have obtained this order is relatively informal, but the resulting list of belief statements usually possesses a logical order that lends it a certain face validity as representing positions along an attitudinal continuum. Because the statements lack scale values, no assumptions are made about the size of the intervals between the statements' locations along the continuum (see Chapter 2's discussion of Thurstone scaling).

4. Indeed, M. Sherif and Sherif (1967) operationally defined attitude in terms of latitudes or categories along the attitudinal dimension: "Operationally, an attitude may be defined as the individual's set of categories for evaluating a stimulus domain, which

he has estalished as he learns about that domain in interaction with other persons and which relate him to various subsets within the domain with varying degrees of positive and negative affect" (p. 115).

5. For a treatment of this issue with respect to person perception, see Linville, Salovey, and Fischer (1986).

6. In particularly interesting discussions of this point, Judd and his colleagues have argued that analyses of attitude structure computed across subjects may not provide valid indicators of the structure of individual attitudes (Judd & Krosnick, 1989; Lusk & Judd, 1988).

7. Whether the statements labeled anti-choice fairly represent the views of those opposed to abortion is an interesting issue. Consistent with research on attitudinal selectivity (see Chapter 12), these statements may be somewhat biased renditions of those views.

8. More generally in this tradition, both the frequency and the recency of past activation of a construct increase its accessibility (see Higgins, 1989a).

9. In addition, mood states can bias attitudinal judgments, and to some extent they can be attributed or misattributed to particular causes. See discussion in Chapter 10.

10. Whether an adding or averaging equation provides a more valid combinatorial rule was once regarded as a major controversy in social psychology, especially in research on forming impressions of people (see N.H. Anderson, 1974, 1981a; Fishbein & Ajzen, 1975; D.J. Schneider, Hastorf, & Ellsworth, 1979).

11. For Fishbein and Ajzen (1975), salient beliefs are those that serve as determinants of one's attitude at any given moment. These theorists also argued that, when beliefs are elicited by asking people to write down the beliefs that come to mind in

relation to a particular attitude object, the beliefs elicited first are more likely to be salient. Although they suggested that the first five to nine beliefs elicited are likely to be salient, they also suggested that at some point the respondents probably start eliciting non-salient beliefs. We have thus sometimes rendered Fishbein and Ajzen's salience concept as accessibility, a term that we believe often captures their meaning better for contemporary readers.

12. Note that these investigators (1986) followed the early tradition among attitude researchers by using the terms *affect* and *evaluation* interchangeably.

13. Rosenberg's concept of vacuous attitude is very similar to the construct of *nonattitude*, which Converse (1964, 1970, 1975) has applied to explain various phenomena in public opinion research—especially the low correlations often found between attitudes on related issues and the low consistency of attitudes over time. Although Converse regarded such findings as evidence that people often do not really have attitudes and therefore respond randomly, there are other plausible interpretations of such findings (e.g., measurement error; see T. W. Smith, 1984, and Kinder & Sears, 1985).

14. Correlations between complexity measures as well as descriptions of measures can be found in several sources (e.g., O'Keefe & Sypher, 1981; W. A. Scott, 1969; Sypher, Witt, & Sypher, 1986; Vannoy, 1965). In general, measures consist of various indices typically based on one of the following types of responses: (a) groupings of exemplars of the attitude object on the basis of those that appear to belong together or on the basis of common characteristics provided by the experimenter; (b) ratings of exemplars on adjectival scales, which are then factor analyzed; (c) descriptions of exemplars' attributes in respondents' own words, which are then counted or content analyzed in some way; and (d) descriptions of the bases of the similarities and dissimilarities between pairs of exemplars.

15. See Judd and Lusk (1984) for a presentation of these findings' consistency with N. H. Anderson's (1981a) weighted averaging model.

16. Tourangeau and Rasinski (1988) have provided a useful discussion of some of the ways that the immediate context in which attitudes are measured (e.g., question wording, content of prior questions) affect belief accessibility.

17. Beliefs can be introduced in other ways into attitudinal structures. Of course, many beliefs are immediately perceived upon mere observation of an attitude object. Such beliefs have been called *descriptive beliefs* (Fishbein & Ajzen, 1975) or *first-order beliefs* (Bem, 1970). Still other beliefs are based on accepting information provided by some source or authority. Such beliefs have been called *informational beliefs* (Fishbein & Ajzen, 1975) or *beliefs based on external authority* (Bem, 1970).

18. Models not based on probability theory have also addressed relations between beliefs. For example, such models have concerned how people infer personality traits from other personality traits, utilize multiple cues in making decisions, and form concepts based on various kinds of information. We refer readers to Fishbein and Ajzen's (1975) useful discussion of the implications that several of these frameworks have for research on the beliefs that may underlie attitudes.

19. Yet some ambiguity surrounds these findings. We do not know whether people access a less complex structure in some situations (e.g., when a politician gives a campaign speech) or whether people access the same structure that they would in other circumstances but merely decide to express their position more simply.

20. Newcomb (1953, 1959) provided another early version of balance theory. His version of this theory gave the label *strain toward symmetry* to the tendency for triadic structures to change toward balance and emphasized communicative exchanges as the common method of reducing strain. See Chapter 10 for a discussion of Newcomb's theory.

21. If two people, in addition to the perceiver, are represented in the same structure, generally the letters *o* and *q* are used to refer to them. Similarly, if two impersonal entities are represented in the same structure, generally the letters *x* and *y* are used to refer to them. Additional letters can represent even larger numbers of persons or entities.

22. Readers should keep in mind that balance theory concerns elements and relations as they are perceived by *p*. For example, a relation between *o* and *x* represents *p*'s perception of *o*'s relation to *x*, not the actual relation between these two elements. Therefore, change in *o*'s attitude toward *x* could entail actual change in this attitude, which is then perceived by *p*, or it could occur through misperception of *o*'s attitude.

23. Other approaches to quantification can be found in articles by Morrissette (1958) and Mohazab and Feger (1985).

24. Because Heider (1946) did not indicate whether the negative unit relation (e.g., the negative of belonging) should be interpreted as the absence of a positive relation (e.g., *p* is not a member of the American Psychological Association) or the opposite of a positive relation (e.g., *p* has resigned from the American Psychological Association), Jordan's (1953) experiment included unit relations of both types. Following Cartwright and Harary's (1956) suggestion, the negative unit relation subsequently came to be treated as the opposite of the positive relation. By this convention, Jordan's triads in which the negative unit relation was rendered by the absence of a positive unit relation should be removed from his data. However, the findings are not greatly changed by this refinement (see Cartwright & Harary, 1956).

25. In another interpretation, Newcomb (1968) proposed a psychological state of *nonbalance*, which is characterized by a lack of clear preference for accepting or modifying a structure. Nonbalance was held to occur principally in the presence of a negative *p-o* relation. As a consequence, balance theory predictions were expected to hold only for the four triads containing a positive *p-o* relation (in Figure 3.5 and Table 3.4, triads *a, b, e,* and *f*).

26. In general, ratings on affective scales such as pleasantness, harmony, and tension showed larger attraction and agreement effects than did ratings on more cognitive scales such as expectancy, consistency, and stability (see Insko, 1984).

27. However, other psychologists have defended role-playing as an experimental technique. See, in particular, several of the articles contained in a symposium on role-playing published in *Personality and Social Psychology Bulletin* (Hendrick, 1977).

28. In addition, Lusk and Judd (1988) reported that the more expert respondents evaluated political candidates more extremely than the less expert respondents, a finding consistent with Judd and Lusk's (1984) earlier demonstration that more complex beliefs are associated with more extreme attitudes to the extent that these beliefs are intercorrelated (see discussion of complexity in this chapter).

29. Underscoring our earlier point about the need to discover how measures of complexity relate to one another, Tetlock's (1989) findings that ideologically extreme politicians have simpler structures are not easily reconciled with Lusk and Judd's (1988) finding that experts' beliefs were more complex and their attitudes were more extreme. Yet these findings may well be consistent if we take into account that Tetlock assessed a special form of complexity (i.e., integrative complexity) and that Lusk and Judd's experts had evaluatively redundant beliefs.

30. Research on the instrumental-versus-symbolic bases of social attitudes is discussed in Chapter 10.

31. C. W. Sherif, Sherif, and Nebergall (1965) proposed that the width of the latitude of rejection is

positively related to involvement. Thus, people with involving attitudes reject a wider range of belief statements discrepant from their own attitudinal positions than do people with less involving attitudes. The Sherifs also assessed involvement through the own-categories procedure, which, as we described earlier in this chapter, requires that respondents sort belief statements into as many categories as they find appropriate. More involved people were assumed to use fewer categories.

4

The Impact of Attitudes on Behaviors

In Chapter 1 we presented the view that attitudes, tendencies to evaluate an entity with some degree of favor or disfavor, are ordinarily expressed in cognitive, affective, and behavioral responses. This perspective leads one to expect that people's attitudes are positively correlated with the evaluative implications of their overt behaviors. People who hold positive attitudes should engage in behaviors that approach, support, or enhance the attitude object, and people who hold negative attitudes should engage in behaviors that avoid, oppose, or hinder the object. Of course, no social scientist would expect uniformly high correlations between attitudes and behaviors. Neither attitudes nor overt behaviors are assessed with perfect reliability or validity (see Chapter 2), and as many researchers have noted, attitudes represent only one of several important classes of variables that guide overt behaviors. Given these limitations, positive correlations of no more than moderate magnitude are probably the best expectation that most social scientists could hold about the relation between attitudes and behaviors. Yet, starting in the 1950s, the size of these correlations became a controversial issue, and social scientists made divergent claims concerning the attitude-behavior relation.

Empirical studies suggesting weak relations between attitudes and seemingly relevant behaviors appeared from the 1930s onward (e.g., Kutner, Wilkins, & Yarrow, 1952; LaPiere, 1934). Although the earliest warnings about empirically weak relations between attitudes and behavior fell on deaf ears, in 1955 a prominent sociologist, Herbert Blumer, criticized the definition of the attitude construct and the assumption that attitudes influence behavior. Somewhat later Irwin Deutscher (1966, 1973), another sociologist, produced a more extensive critique in which he complained about the empirical weakness of demonstrated relations between attitudes and ostensibly relevant behaviors. During this period, a number of psychologists also discussed the fact that correlations between attitudes and behaviors were often low (e.g., D.T. Campbell, 1963; Festinger, 1964a; B.F. Green, 1954).

This criticism and concern escalated in the late 1960s with the publication of an article by Alan Wicker (1969). Particularly among psychologists, Wicker's article attracted much more attention than earlier papers questioning the attitude-behavior relation. Wicker maintained that there was little evidence that people possess stable, underlying attitudes that influence their overt behaviors. Much of the power of Wicker's paper stemmed from his review of empirical evidence concerning the attitude-behavior relation. This review was much more extensive than any provided by other critics. In support of his claim that attitudes are not strongly related to behaviors,

Wicker presented a review of 42 studies, most of which had been conducted in experimental laboratories. In these studies, investigators had assessed an attitude in a sample of subjects and observed an ostensibly relevant behavior. For example, many of these studies concerned whites' attitudes toward blacks or other minority groups, which were then correlated with behaviors such as white subjects' willingness to have their picture taken with a black person and widely distributed (e.g., DeFleur & Westie, 1958) or to have coffee with a black person (e.g., Rokeach & Mezei, 1966). Wicker found few studies in which the correlation between attitude and behavior was as high as .30. The average correlation appeared to be about .15. Wicker concluded that "taken as a whole, these studies suggest that it is considerably more likely that attitudes will be unrelated or only slightly related to overt behaviors than that attitudes will be closely related to actions" (p. 65).

The verdict of Wicker and other critics about the poor predictability of behavior from attitudes had very clearly taken its toll by the early 1970s. Social psychologists' readiness to accept a negative verdict about attitude-behavior research at this time of course reflects the cumulative impact of the critical literature that had collected. Yet perhaps more important is the broader intellectual context within which the critiques then fit. The period from the mid-1960s to mid-1970s in social psychology had a certain "crisis" Zeitgeist, and many aspects of the field were subjected to rather scathing criticism (see Elms, 1975). This atmosphere created a generalized readiness to accept negative assessments. Moreover, in the minds of many psychologists, the plausibility of the idea that attitudes are predictors and causes of behaviors had been lessened by the publication and widespread discussion during the late 1950s and 1960s of numerous studies demonstrating that behavior influences attitudes (e.g., Festinger & Carlsmith, 1959). Many of these studies tested Festinger's (1957) dissonance theory, which was very popular at that time and featured the influence of behavior on attitudes as one of its key hypotheses (see Chapters 10 and 11). Thinking about behavior as causing attitudes apparently made it more difficult for social psychologists to presume that the opposite causal link could be as strong or even stronger. Several factors thus conspired to produce a readiness to reject attitudes as causes of behavior, and the accepted wisdom that evolved among social psychologists was that attitudes have little impact on ostensibly related behaviors. However, from the vantage point of the 1990s, Wicker and others who challenged attitude-behavior research were led into an extreme position based on a somewhat superficial analysis of the issues surrounding attitude-behavior relations. To demonstrate why the generalization that *attitudes do not predict behavior* is an inaccurate summary of the available evidence, we review in this chapter the many lines of research that have delineated the conditions under which relatively good prediction can be achieved. We also consider efforts to understand the psychological processes that mediate the link between attitudes and behavior.

The gauntlet flung down by Wicker and other critics greatly stimulated research on the attitude-behavior relation. As we show in this chapter, understanding of how attitudes relate to behavior improved very substantially, subsequent to the critics' discouraging integration of available research. Yet it appears to us that many social scientists found the claim that attitudes do not predict behavior so memorable and discouraging that they have failed to assimilate the very large amount of new research and theory on the attitude-behavior relation that has accumulated since the late 1960s. Analysis of this material is the central purpose of this chapter.

Early Reactions to the View That Attitudes Do Not Predict Behavior

Some social scientists promptly took issue with Wicker's (1969) review of attitude-behavior research by pointing out that he based his conclusions on a narrow sample of studies that happened to be heavily weighted toward laboratory studies. Notable for their omission were more applied studies that had used the methods of survey research. Both Kelman (1974a) and Schuman and Johnson (1976) maintained that a pattern of positive and moderately strong attitude-behavior relations characterized existing survey research findings. Most strikingly, numerous studies of voting behavior had shown that attitudes toward candidates predicted voting for these candidates with considerable accuracy (e.g., A. Campbell, Converse, Miller, & Stokes, 1960). Schuman and Johnson's summary of this broader literature was the following: "far from it being difficult to obtain reliable A-B [i.e., attitude-behavior] associations, few plausible studies fail to find significant relationships. It is harder to summarize the magnitudes of these associations, but they seem to vary from small to moderate in size" (1976, p. 167).

There are many reasons to expect that attitudinal findings would differ, depending on whether the data were collected by laboratory or survey methods. Indeed, Hovland (1959) made this point in a classic paper on experimental and survey studies of attitudes. Central among the reasons for differences between laboratory and survey findings is the tendency for survey research to examine attitudes that are more important and involving and that therefore may be more influential in relation to behavior (see subsequent discussion in this chapter). In addition, as Kelman (1974a) emphasized, laboratory researchers typically assess behavior in relatively constrained situations offering few behavioral options, whereas survey researchers assess behavior in natural settings allowing considerable freedom of choice about how to behave. As others have also maintained (e.g., M. Snyder & Ickes, 1985), the strong situational constraints of many laboratory settings lower the predictability of behavior from attitudes and other individual differences.

Although impactful situational cues need not totally eliminate the effect of attitude on behavior, such cues can create barriers that discourage attitude-consistent behavior in natural settings as well as laboratories. For example, Donald Campbell (1963) argued that people who hold negative attitudes toward minorities may be reluctant to express their attitudes through public behavior because norms of tolerance and politeness are typically held in American society. More generally, he argued that social norms and other situational constraints may create differing *thresholds* for expressing attitudes and thereby produce apparent discrepancies between attitude and behavior. Campbell's analysis of the early LaPiere (1934) study in these terms is particularly apt.

In this study, which was extensively discussed by the 1950s and 1960s critics of attitude-behavior research, only one of the proprietors of a sample of 250 hotels and restaurants refused service to a visiting Chinese couple. Yet among these same proprietors who returned a mailed questionnaire, 92 percent indicated that they would not be willing to "accept members of the Chinese race as guests" (LaPiere, 1934, p. 233). A norm of tolerance or politeness may have inhibited discriminatory behavior toward the Chinese couple in face-to-face interaction, even though discriminatory attitudes were readily expressed on a questionnaire.

Although a number of analyses thus raised serious issues about Wicker (1969) and other critics' negative portrayal of the extant literature, these discussions were only a prelude to the later empirical demonstrations that the size of correlations between attitudes and behaviors is to a great extent under the investigator's own control. The magnitude of these correlations varies systematically with the characteristics of the measuring instruments used to assess attitudes and behaviors. In fact, as we will explain, much of the variation in attitude-behavior correlations can be understood in terms of elementary psychometric principles. The straightforward application of these principles allows researchers to readily create strong correlations between attitudes and behaviors, at least for the kinds of simple, non-habitual behaviors that have typically been studied in attitude-behavior research.

In view of the ease with which investigators can create high attitude-behavior correlations, they would do well to keep in mind that there is no necessary relation between the magnitude of these correlations and the efficacy of attitudes as *causes* of behavior. Strong statistical relations do not insure a causal relation, nor, for that matter, do somewhat weak statistical relations indicate that attitudes have no causal impact on behavior. Demonstrating that attitudes cause behaviors in the sense that they exert the directive or dynamic influence claimed by Allport (1935) is a considerably more subtle matter that we address later in this chapter when we consider a number of models that specify causal linkages between attitudes and behavior.

Using Multiple-Act Criteria to Increase Attitude-Behavior Correlations

The attitudes that social scientists traditionally related to behaviors concerned entities of social and political significance such as ethnic groups, nationalities, social policies, and social institutions. Such attitudes can show substantial correlations with behavior if the behavioral measure is *aggregated* across a number of specific behaviors. To understand why aggregative behavioral measures correlate moderately highly with attitudes, consider a person's attitude toward the Democratic party. One can quickly list a large number of behaviors that may be related to this attitude—for example, voting, donating money, and participating in political campaigns. Although attitude toward the Democratic party may influence these behaviors, each behavior is no doubt also determined by a variety of additional factors. For example, donating money to the Democratic party would probably also be a function of how affluent citizens are, whether they have been approached for a contribution, and whether they were in a bad mood or in a hurry at the time they were approached.

Because single behaviors are generally a function of many factors in addition to a seemingly relevant attitude toward an entity, in psychometric terms each such behavior should be considered a somewhat unreliable indicator of the attitude. As explained in Chapter 2, when a number of somewhat unreliable indicators of an attitude are summed into a composite index, the proportion of variability that is predicted by the attitude is ordinarily considerably larger in this composite index than in the single indicators making up the index. Single behaviors are analogous to single items on the scales ordinarily used to assess attitudes. Single behaviors, just like responses to single questionnaire items, are influenced by a host of arbitrary factors that are irrelevant to the attitude that is assessed. When a composite index of behaviors is formed, these irrelevant factors tend to cancel one another as long as they do not influence all of the behaviors or a sizable subset of them in the same way. Therefore, an appropriate aggregation of attitude-relevant behaviors creates a reliable behavioral measure of an attitude, just as an appropriate aggregation of responses to attitude-relevant question-naire items creates a reliable measure of an attitude. Two reliable measures of the same attitude—one based on questionnaire items and the other based on observations of behaviors—should correlate quite highly. By this logic, correlations between attitudes (i.e., as measured by questionnaire techniques) and composite indices of behaviors should be considerably stronger than correlations between attitudes and single behaviors.

Although this psychometric logic had been noted by a number of social psychologists (e.g., D. T. Campbell, 1963; Tittle & Hill, 1967), Martin Fishbein and Icek Ajzen (1974, 1975) provided its most systematic statement. As these investigators pointed out, overt behavior may be assessed by (a) single behaviors or (b) composite indices that compile behaviors over time or over various exemplars of a class of behaviors. They suggested the term *single-act criterion* for a specific behavior at a single point in time, *repeated-observation criterion* for an index based on a single behavior assessed at a number of points in time, and *multiple-act criterion* for an index based on differing behaviors combined on a single- or repeated-observation basis. According to Fishbein and Ajzen, the type of attitudes typically assessed by social scientists, which examine the evaluations people attach to quite broad concepts such as religion and political conservatism, are good predictors of appropriately constructed multiple-act criteria.

In a study testing this logic, Fishbein and Ajzen (1974) had subjects respond to five measures of attitudes toward religion (self-report on favorable vs. unfavorable scale, semantic differential, Guttman scale, Likert scale, Thurstone scale; see Chapter 2). These subjects also indicated which of 100 religious behaviors they had performed. As Table 4.1 shows, these measures of religious attitude predicted single behaviors quite poorly on the average, but they were much more highly related to a multiple-act criterion defined as the total number of different behaviors performed. This outcome is not surprising and in fact is wholly predictable by psychometric principles. As Dawes and Smith (1985) pointed out, if the average of correlations between a measured attitude and each behavior is, for example, .13, and the average intercorrelation among

TABLE 4.1

**Correlations of the Five Attitude Scales
with Single-Act and Multiple-Act Behavioral Criteria
in the Fishbein and Ajzen (1974) Study**

Attitude scale	Single-act criterion[a]	Multiple-act criterion[b]
Single favorability item	.137	.640
Semantic differential	.149	.714
Guttman	.121	.608
Likert	.141	.684
Thurstone	.131	.648

Notes: [a]This column contains the mean of the correlations between the relevant attitude scale and each of the 100 reported behaviors.
[b]This column contains the correlation between the relevant attitude scale and the sum of 100 reported behaviors.
Source: This table was adapted from one presented by Fishbein and Ajzen (1974, Table 2, p. 63).

the behaviors is .03, then the correlation between the attitude and an additive composite of 100 such behaviors is .65 (see Equation 5 in Gulliksen, 1950, p. 89).

Although Fishbein and Ajzen (1974) provided an insightful analysis, their study did not provide a stringent test of their psychometric logic because they assessed subjects' retrospective reports of behaviors in the same session in which they assessed attitudes. A desire on the part of respondents to appear consistent or a tendency to infer their attitudes from their reported behaviors (see Chapter 11) might have contributed to the relatively successful predictions that were obtained. In a demonstration of the efficacy of multiple-act criteria that avoided these difficulties, Weigel and Newman (1976) assessed attitude toward environmental preservation at one point in time and obtained unobtrusive measures of a variety of ecologically oriented behaviors several months later. As Table 4.2 shows, whereas the attitude was only weakly related to single behaviors, it was somewhat more related when behaviors were aggregated within categories of behaviors to create indices for petitioning, litter pick-up, and recycling; the attitude was most highly related when all the behaviors were aggregated into a more comprehensive multiple-act criterion.

The question of how many items are required to form a multiple-act criterion that will correlate at least moderately highly with an attitude should be answered in terms of the scaling issues that were addressed in Chapter 2. Attentive to these issues, Fishbein and Ajzen (1974) demonstrated that a multiple-act index composed of many behaviors, such as their own 100-item aggregate of reported religious behaviors, is not inevitably required to obtain relatively high correlations between social attitudes and relevant behaviors. In fact, many specific behaviors that are included in such an index because they seem as if they should be related to the attitude may be related only very weakly (or not at all) for a variety of reasons (e.g., very high or very low base rates in the sample of subjects). Such indicators contribute little or nothing to the reliability or validity of the multiple-act criterion. Fishbein and Ajzen showed how these faulty

TABLE 4.2

**Correlations Between Subjects' Environmental Attitudes and Behavioral Criteria
in the Weigel and Newman (1976) Study**

Single behaviors	r^a	Categories of behavior	r^b	Behavioral index	r^b
Sign petition on					
Offshore oil	.41**				
Nuclear power	.36*	Petitioning scale	.50**		
Auto exhaust	.39**	(0–4)			
Circulate petitions	.27				
Pick-up litter					
As individual	.34*	Litter pick-up scale	.36*		
Recruit friend	.22	(0–2)		Comprehensive	.62***
				behavioral	
Recycle during				index	
Week 1	.34*				
Week 2	.57***				
Week 3	.34*				
Week 4	.33*	Recycling scale	.39**		
Week 5	.12	(0–8)			
Week 6	.20				
Week 7	.20				
Week 8	.34*				

Notes: $N = 44$.
[a]Point-biserial correlations are reported in this column.
[b]Pearson product-moment correlations are reported in this column.
  *$p < .05$.
  **$p < .01$.
  ***$p < .001$.
  Source: This table was presented by Weigel and Newman (1976, Table 1, p. 799).

indicators of attitudes can be removed from a composite index by the application of some of the scaling models considered in Chapter 2. Applying the Likert, Thurstone, and Guttman scaling models, these researchers selected small sets of behaviors (containing as few as eight items) that met the criteria of each scaling model. These behaviors were thus analogous to the items researchers select for the attitude scales typically administered by questionnaires. These sets of scaled behaviors correlated almost as highly with respondents' religious attitudes as did the 100-item index formed by aggregating all of the assessed religious behaviors. Thus, a reliable multiple-act criterion can be produced on the basis of relatively few behaviors, if these behaviors are selected by an appropriate scaling model. If behaviors are selected informally without the use of a scaling model, a much larger set of behaviors may be needed to produce a reliable behavioral criterion.

In summary, relatively high attitude-behavior correlations can be obtained by relating a general attitude (e.g., toward religion or environmental preservation) to a reliable behavioral index of the attitude, one that has been constructed by aggregating attitude-relevant behaviors (see also Sjöberg, 1982; Werner, 1978). Although this point has been minimized by some commentators as only restating what is obvious on the basis of classic psychometric principles (e.g., Abelson, 1982; Dawes & Smith, 1985), evidently many psychologists either did not understand this aspect of psychometric theory or had difficulty applying it to the attitude-behavior issue.

A very similar debate about prediction of behavior occurred in personality psychology when it was "discovered" that personality traits do not relate strongly to single behaviors (Mischel, 1968) and subsequently shown that personality traits predict behavioral aggregates (i.e., appropriate multiple-act criteria) with considerable success (Epstein, 1979; Jaccard, 1974). The parallelism between the discussions of behavioral prediction in the attitude and the personality literatures has been analyzed in some detail (Ajzen, 1988; S. J. Sherman & Fazio, 1983). In general, it is now fairly common knowledge among social scientists that constructing an appropriate aggregative index of behaviors is one way to obtain moderately high correlations between people's behaviors and their tendencies (e.g., attitudes) or dispositions (e.g., personality traits). The practical implications of this point for attitude research can be stated as follows: Although a general attitude (e.g., attitude toward religion) is typically only a weak predictor of a single behavior (e.g., attending religious services on a particular day), such an attitude is a relatively good predictor of the general tendency to engage in behaviors relevant to the attitude object (e.g., to engage in religious behaviors).

Using Compatible Measures to Increase Attitude-Behavior Correlations

Fishbein and Ajzen considerably refined their position on attitude-behavior correlations beyond their demonstration that the types of attitudes that had typically been assessed by social scientists predict multiple-act criteria much better than they predict single-act criteria (Ajzen & Fishbein, 1977; Fishbein & Ajzen, 1975). These investigators placed this generalization within a more comprehensive understanding of relations between different kinds of attitudes and behavioral criteria. In this further analysis, they argued that attitudes and behaviors must be *compatible* (or *correspondent*) to ensure a strong relation, that is, to ensure a moderate-to-large correlation.[1] One way to think about compatibility is in terms of the generality versus specificity of the attitudes and behaviors that are related. Thus, as we explained in the preceding section, general attitudes, such as attitudes toward religion, disarmament, and affirmative action, are good predictors of similarly general behavioral criteria that are summed over appropriately chosen behaviors (i.e., multiple-act criteria). In contrast, more specific attitudes, particularly attitudes toward behaviors, tend to be good predictors of specific behaviors. More generally, Fishbein and Ajzen suggested that attitudes and behaviors should be defined at an equivalent level of specificity (or generality) in order to obtain relatively high correlations between the two.

In discussions of the attitude-behavior relation, compatibility often has been explained in the way we just described it, that is, in terms of matching the specificity (or generality) of the attitude and behavior. However, the idea was developed more precisely by Fishbein and Ajzen, and understanding the details of this more precise description is worthwhile (see Ajzen & Fishbein, 1977; Fishbein & Ajzen, 1975). They suggested that every behavior has the elements of *action*, *target*, *context*, and *time* and argued that the specificity versus generality of the attitude and behavior should be evaluated in relation to all four of these elements. By this logic, any single behavior consists of (a) a specific action or behavior, (b) performed toward a target, (c) in a context,[2] (d) at a time or occasion. For example, a car owner (a) washes (b) her car (c) in the driveway (d) on a particular afternoon in April. In attitude research, as in this example, a behavioral criterion may be very specific in the sense that it represents a particular action, target, context, and time. Alternatively, a behavioral criterion may be more general in the sense that it is aggregated over *a range* of actions, targets, contexts, and times. In fact, the behavioral criteria that researchers design vary from specific to general with respect to *each* of the four elements of behavior. Therefore, as suggested by Fishbein and Ajzen's action, target, context, and time elements, a criterion may assess (a) a single action or a range of actions, (b) toward a single target or a range of targets, (c) in a single context or a range of contexts, and (d) at a single time or a range of times.

Students often find the distinction between the terms *target* and *object* (i.e., attitude object) confusing and ask whether the target is the same as the attitude object. The answer is, in general, no. The target is the entity (e.g., thing, person) toward which a particular behavior is directed (e.g., the *car* that the owner washes in our example). As the next paragraphs clarify in more detail, an attitude object can be a target (e.g., as in attitude toward one's car), but could incorporate action, context, or time elements as well as a target (i.e., the owner's attitude toward washing her car in the driveway on Sunday afternoon). Although a behavior can be an attitude object, it cannot be a target because the target is the entity the behavior is directed toward.

Just as a behavioral criterion may be analyzed in terms of the four elements (action, target, context, and time), attitudes can also be evaluated in terms of the generality or specificity of their representation of the elements. An attitude may be defined so that the attitude object names a particular instance of each of these elements—for example, an attitude toward attending (action) a mass (target) with particular friends (context) on a particular day (time) names all four elements as components of its object. Alternatively, an attitude may name *a range* of eligible exemplars for one or more of the four elements, in the manner that attitude toward attending mass with particular friends *during the next six months* names a range of times.

Attitudes may also be defined *without reference to* action, context, or time and thereby implicitly include all exemplars of that element. In fact, the most commonly studied attitudes indicate only a target (e.g., a person, group, idea, or institution) as the object of the attitude. Attitudes of this type do not specify any particular action, context, or time. For example, attitude toward the attitude object *religion* names religion as its target, but does not specify any particular action, context, or time for the attitude. As a result, the attitude object implicitly includes all actions, contexts, or times that are perceived as relevant to religion in the population of respondents. Such attitudes, which distinguish only a target, are often called *attitudes toward objects* to distinguish them from *attitudes toward behaviors*. However, this terminology, which implies that an object (i.e., an entity that is not a behavior) can be an attitude object only muddies the conceptual waters by imparting yet another, narrower meaning to the term object. Therefore, to establish a consistent terminology, we distinguish between *attitudes toward targets* and *attitudes toward behaviors*.

In contrast to attitudes toward targets, attitudes toward behaviors (e.g., attitude toward attending church services) are evaluations of the respondent engaging in a single behavior or a set of behaviors.[3] These attitudes necessarily name an action or a range of actions as their object and typically name a target or a range of targets:

1. With respect to *action*, attitudes toward behaviors may name *a particular* action, as attitude toward my attending church services specifies the behavior of attending. Alternatively, these attitudes may imply *a range* of actions, as attitude toward my supporting church services includes a range of actions (e.g., attending church services, donating money at services, encouraging others to attend).

2. With respect to *target*, attitudes toward behaviors may name *a particular* target that is the object of the action(s), as attitude toward my attending mass specifies mass as the object of attending. Alternatively, these attitudes may imply *a range* of targets, as attitude toward my attending church functions includes a range of targets (e.g., choir practices, lectures, discussion groups, picnics, retreats). More rarely, attitudes toward behaviors may specify *no* target and thus imply all possible targets. For example, targetless attitudes toward behaviors would include attitudes toward my studying or toward my running.

Attitudes toward behaviors do not necessarily name contexts or times:

1. With respect to *context*, attitudes toward behaviors may name a particular context, as attitude toward attending synagogue services with one's family specifies a context. Alternatively, these attitudes may name *a range* of contexts (e.g., with friends or family), or specify *no* contexts and thus imply all contexts.

2. With respect to *time*, attitudes toward behaviors may name *a particular* time or occasion, as attitude toward my attending religious services on next Sunday specifies a time. Alternatively, these attitudes may name *a range* of occasions (e.g., during the coming year), or specify *no* occasions and thus imply all occasions on which the behavior (or class of behaviors) might occur.

Fishbein and Ajzen maintained that relations between attitudes and behaviors are maximally strong to the extent that their action, target, context, and time elements are assessed at the same level of generality or specificity. This matching with respect to the four elements is known as the *principle of compatibility* (Ajzen, 1988; see note 1).

Incompatibility often occurs in research because a broadly defined attitude that specifies only a very general target (e.g., attitude toward Russia) is correlated with a specific behavior that is defined in terms of a specific action, target, context, and time. In stipulating that the appropriate criterion for such an attitude is a broadly formulated multiple-act criterion that includes a range of actions, contexts, and times, the principle of compatibility resembles the familiar psychometric principle that an index (i.e., a test) becomes more reliable as the number of items that enter into it increases (e.g., Ghiselli, 1964). Yet the principle has the less obvious implication that a narrowly defined attitude such as an attitude toward a behavior is more compatible with a narrowly formulated behavioral criterion than it is with a multiple-act criterion. In fact, a *very* limited behavioral criterion is sometimes appropriate—for example, a single behavior is the compatible criterion if the attitude in question is an attitude toward a particular behavior on a particular occasion in a particular context. The compatibility principle thus applies a logical rather than a strictly psychometric analysis to suggest the conditions under which broader and narrower behavioral criteria are appropriate.

The most interesting implications of the compatibility analysis concern attitudes toward behaviors because, as we have explained, these attitudes can vary in generality with respect to all four of the elements provided by the analysis. Because attitudes toward targets specify only a target, the compatibility analysis has more limited implications for these attitudes—namely, that to maximize prediction of behavior, (a) the definition of the target should be the same for the measure of attitude and the measure of behavior, and (b) appropriate multiple-act behavioral measures that include a wide range of actions, contexts, and times should be used in research.

As stated by Ajzen and Fishbein (1977), the compatibility analysis tells researchers how to construct their attitudinal and behavioral measures to maximize prediction. However, it does not address the question of what attitude comes to the minds of the people whose behavior is predicted and exerts a causal impact on their behavior. Yet determining what attitude does come to mind may further refine the compatibility analysis. Research by C. G. Lord, Lepper, and Mackie (1984) is relevant to this issue, although it was not framed in terms of compatibility. These investigators argued that individuals may determine their attitude toward a social group, not by thinking about the group as a whole, but by imagining a prototypical group member (see also C. G. Lord, Desforges, Fein, & Lepper, 1992). As Lord and his colleagues (1984) demonstrated, behavior toward a specific group member was more consistent with attitude toward the group when this group member had characteristics that closely matched those of the prototypical group member, presumably because attitude toward the group was actually attitude toward a prototypical group member. These findings suggest that compatibility is maximized by assessing behavior toward the exact target that is cognitively accessible to the respondent. This research thus raises the important issue of the psychology underlying the compatibility analysis. Researchers can ask people questions about broader or narrower attitudes and can assess single behaviors or broader behavioral aggregates. Prediction is indeed improved by matching attitudinal and behavioral measures. However, this improved prediction is a psychometric gain that bears little necessary relation to the psychological processes underlying the prediction. Successfully addressing these psychological issues can also produce gains in prediction, as the research by Lord and colleagues suggests.

Analyzing Compatibility in Prior Attitude-Behavior Research

According to the principle of compatibility, attitude-behavior correlations are strengthened if researchers match their measures of attitude and behavior with respect to action, target, context, and time. To the extent that incompatibility occurs, these correlations should be smaller. Not surprisingly, there was considerable incompatibility in the majority of traditional attitude-behavior research, such as the studies reviewed by Wicker (1969). This lack of compatibility typically followed from researchers' practice of relating attitudes toward targets (e.g., racial attitudes) to criteria usually consisting of single behaviors. A single behavior is of course specifically defined with respect to action, target, context, and time, whereas an attitude toward a target specifies only a target. In addition to the resulting incompatibility of the action, context, and time elements, incompatibility with respect to the target was often considerable as well, because the attitude measure specified a target (e.g., Chinese) that was considerably more general than the target of the specific behavior assessed in the study (e.g., a particular Chinese couple). Because of the large amount of incompatibility in most prior research, relatively low correlations should have been obtained, according to this analysis. Indeed, Ajzen and Fishbein's (1977) review of attitude-behavior research showed that, under conditions of low compatibility, attitude-behavior correlations were generally nonsignificant.

Although the quantification that Ajzen and Fishbein (1977) used in this review stopped considerably short of the meta-analytic techniques that have more recently become available (see Cooper, 1989; Hedges & Olkin, 1985), their review is reasonably convincing in its demonstration that much of the variability in the magnitude of the attitude-behavior correlations that had been reported in research is predicted merely by taking into account the degree of compatibility between the attitudinal and behavioral measures. Representing compatibility at three levels (low, partial, and high), Ajzen and Fishbein reported a rank-order correlation of .83 between compatibility and the available attitude-behavior correlations. This strong relation attests to the point we made earlier—namely, that the magnitude of these correlations is largely a product of researchers' choice of measures of attitudes and behaviors. However, until the principle of compatibility was explicitly recognized, the level of generality (vs. specificity) at which such measures were constructed was typically arbitrary, and the importance of compatibility in accounting for the variability shown by attitude-behavior correlations went unrecognized.

Strong Attitude-Behavior Relations, Despite Incompatibility. Ajzen and Fishbein (1977) acknowledged that, despite incompatibility, sometimes attitudes toward targets are strongly related to single behaviors. They suggested that this outcome is obtained when a single-act criterion "involves an action that is little more than an evaluation of the target" (p. 891). They cited petition signing and voting as examples of such highly evaluative single-act criteria. Although such acts are predicted somewhat better by attitude toward the specific behavior (e.g., attitude toward voting for a particular candidate) than by attitude toward the target (e.g., attitude toward the candidate), attitude toward the target can be highly related to such a behavior (see Fishbein, Middlestadt, & Chung, 1986). In fact, Fishbein and Ajzen (1974) presented a method for selecting single behaviors that are maximally correlated with attitudes toward targets. To implement this method, an investigator obtains judges' ratings of the likelihood that people with positive (vs. negative) attitudes would perform each behavior. A large difference between these likelihoods suggests that a behavior will correlate strongly with the attitude, provided of course that the judges' ratings are valid. This method, although somewhat cumbersome, no doubt would improve prediction considerably over that obtained when researchers use ordinary armchair speculation to select single-act criteria.

Predicting Behaviors from Attitudes Toward Behaviors

If investigators wish to use an attitude to predict, with at least moderate precision, a single behavior or a relatively small set of behaviors (rather than a multiple-act criterion), they have the option of turning to a compatible attitude toward the behavior (or behaviors). Most clearly, response to an inquiry about *an attitude toward a specific behavior directed toward a given target in a given context at a given time* should predict the specific behavior quite well because this attitude exactly corresponds to the specific behavior. For example, students' attitudes toward attending their introductory psychology lecture in the regular lecture hall next Monday may predict attendance on that day quite well. Yet investigators ordinarily have more than good prediction as their goal and, for a variety of reasons, may not work with theories that include these very specifically defined attitudes as causes of behavior. Indeed, the observation that such attitudes predict specific behaviors has an obviousness that may reduce interest in relations of this sort. Expressing this view, Dawes and Smith (1985, p. 560) wrote, "The reductio ad absurdum occurs when the attitude question targets the behavior of interest with such specificity that the response to the former is tantamount to a behavioral intention concerning the latter."

Despite the non-surprising quality of the good prediction obtained from attitudes toward specific behaviors, the further proposal that these high correlations occur because of the causal impact that attitudes toward behaviors have on behaviors is more interesting and warrants careful evaluation. As we detail in the next section, Fishbein and Ajzen (1975) ascribed precisely such a causal role to attitudes toward behaviors; however, they did not make the more general claim that the strong statistical relations insured by following the compatibility principle reflect the psychological processes that mediate attitudes' influence on behavior. Still, they did address process in a limited way by arguing that broad attitudes influence specific behaviors only indirectly through their impact on more specific determinants of behavior, including attitudes toward behaviors. As we noted earlier, establishing compatibility of attitudinal and behavioral measures should be regarded primarily as a psychometric advantage that increases an investigator's chances of obtaining substantial attitude-behavior correlations.

Finally, a short digression may help readers to attach some intuitive meaning to the generalization that attitudes toward behaviors are better predictors of single behaviors than are attitudes toward targets. In our earlier example of behaviors related to attitude toward the Democratic party, we suggested that attitude toward the party would be only one determinant of donating money, because other variables, such as one's level of affluence, are obviously also important. If the same logic held for attitudes toward behaviors, it should not be possible to obtain relatively high correlations between these attitudes and compatible behaviors. Clearly, the same logic does *not* hold because, in forming an attitude toward donating money to the Democratic party, one would take into account considerations that become salient in the action situation, such as having money available. An individual favorable to the party would not necessarily be favorable toward personally donating money, because lack of money and other factors may lower her evaluation of this particular political behavior. Attitudes toward behaviors are thus a distinctly different class of attitudes than the attitudes toward targets traditionally studied by social scientists. The sense in which these attitudes are different is explicated in considerable detail in the next section of this chapter.

Theory of Reasoned Action

Fishbein's efforts to understand the underlying psychological processes by which attitudes might serve as causes of behavior first appeared in the published literature in the 1960s (Fishbein, 1967a). Although some attitude researchers have asserted that attention to the psychological processes underlying attitude-behavior correlations is a relatively recent development in social psychology (e.g., Zanna & Fazio, 1982), this claim is not entirely accurate. Fishbein's model, which he and Ajzen came later to call the *theory of reasoned action*, was presented well over twenty years ago and unquestionably provides a model of the psychological processes that mediate observed relations between attitudes and behavior.

Building on a theory that Dulany (1961, 1968) proposed to explain the role of awareness in verbal conditioning (see also Chapter 9), Fishbein (1967a; Fishbein & Ajzen, 1975) suggested that the proximal cause of behavior is one's *intention* to engage in the behavior. Attitudes influence behavior by their influence on intentions, which are decisions to act in a particular way. The scientific and philosophical issue of how the mental event of holding an attitude is transformed into observable action was thus resolved by interposing another psychological event, the formation of an intention, between the attitude and the behavior. Intention, a psychological construct distinct from attitude, represents the person's motivation in the sense of his or her conscious plan to exert effort to carry out a behavior.

Fishbein's introduction of the construct of intention into the debate about the attitude-behavior relation is noteworthy. In suggesting that behavior is under the control of intentions, Fishbein restricted himself to the class of behaviors that can be termed *volitional* or *voluntary*, that is, behaviors that people perform because they decide to perform them. As we discuss later in this chapter, this restriction is consequential because behaviors requiring skills, resources, or opportunities that are not necessarily available are not fully volitional. In interposing intention between attitudes and behaviors, Fishbein also chose to disallow the possibility that attitudes sometimes elicit behavior with little or no intervening thought. Such behavior might occur, for example, when hate of another racial or ethnic group elicits sudden, spontaneous violence; craving for a pleasurable state induces drug use; or liking for a product elicits the sort of behavior commonly known as impulse buying (see discussion later in chapter). Confining his model to volitional behavior, Fishbein also excluded behavior that may occur independently of attitudes because it is habitual in the sense that buckling up one's seat belt may be a well-established habit.

The class of attitudes taken into account in the theory of reasoned action is attitudes toward behaviors, not attitudes toward targets. Attitude toward the behavior enters the model as one of the determinants of intention. The other determinant of intention, called *subjective norm*, consists of a person's belief about whether significant others think that he or she should engage in the behavior. Significant others are individuals whose preferences about a person's behavior in this domain are important to him or her. Hence, behavioral intention is a linear regression function of (a) attitude toward the act (or behavior) and (b) subjective norm. The model can be stated algebraically as follows:

$$B \approx BI = w_1 A_B + w_2 SN \tag{4.1}$$

where B is the behavior, BI is the behavioral intention, A_B is the attitude toward the behavioral act, SN is the subjective norm, and w_1 and w_2 are empirical weights indicating the relative importance of the first and second terms. This equation thus indicates that behavior is a function of one's intention to engage in the behavior, which is in turn a function of both one's evaluation of personally engaging in the behavior and one's belief that significant other people think one should engage in the behavior.

Determinants of Attitudes Toward Behaviors. Attitude toward the act is itself a function of *behavioral beliefs*, which represent the perceived consequences of the act. For example, a perceived consequence of donating money to the Democratic party might be that more Democratic candidates would win in the next election. Following the expectancy-value tradition we introduced in Chapter 3, the model quantifies consequences by multiplying the subjective likelihood that a consequence will result from the behavior times the *evaluation of that consequence*. These Expectancy × Value products are then summed over the various salient consequences. This relation between attitude toward the behavior and behavioral beliefs can be expressed algebraically as follows:

$$A_B = \sum_{i=1}^{n} b_i e_i \tag{4.2}$$

169

where b_i is the behavioral belief that performing the behavior leads to some consequence i (i.e., subjective probability that the behavior has the consequence i); e_i is the evaluation of consequence i; and n is the number of salient consequences.

Table 4.3 illustrates behavioral beliefs by showing the consequences that a sample of childless married women believed would follow from having a child in the next three years. These women indicated their behavioral beliefs and evaluations of these beliefs on 7-point scales that ranged from $+3$ to -3. On these scales, higher (positive) numbers represented likely outcomes and favorable evaluations. The table compares the beliefs of women who intended and did not intend to have a child in the next three years and shows that more positive Belief × Evaluation products were associated with intending to have a child. In other words, women who intended to have a child believed that this event would have more pleasant results than women who did not intend to have a child. As we explain in Chapter 5, knowledge of people's behavioral beliefs

TABLE 4.3

Mean Beliefs, Evaluations, and Belief × Evaluation Products for Women Intending and Not Intending to Have a Child Within the Next Three Years in Fishbein's (1980) Study

	Mean belief		Mean evaluation		Mean b × e product	
	Intenders	Non-intenders	Intenders	Non-intenders	Intenders	Non-intenders
Having a child I could not afford	−1.63	1.11**	−2.06	−2.51**	3.46	−2.57**
Having a child while at a good age	2.56	1.19**	2.71	1.68**	7.13	2.95**
Too much of an emotional strain	−2.17	0.27**	−1.89	−2.24	4.86	−0.97**
A restriction on my freedom	−0.40	1.22**	−1.00	−2.00**	0.22	−3.32**
Stronger marriage	0.86	−1.57**	2.22	1.92	2.37	−3.62**
Fulfillment of my family life	1.90	−1.24**	2.40	1.70**	5.33	−1.41**
An added responsibility	2.30	2.46	1.16	−1.49**	3.57	−4.14**
Having less time for my own goals and plans	0.65	2.00**	−0.83*	−2.08**	−0.56	−5.41**

Notes: Significance levels refer to differences between the intenders and the non-intenders.
*$p < .05$
**$p < .01$
Source: This table was presented by Fishbein (1980, Table 8, pp. 108–109).

can be quite useful in designing information campaigns to persuade them to change their behavior (see Sutton, Marsh, & Matheson, 1990).

Determinants of Subjective Norms. In this model, subjective norm is itself a function of *normative beliefs*, which represent perceptions of significant others' preferences about whether one should engage in a behavior. For example, an individual might believe that his mother thinks that he should not donate money to the Democratic party and that his best friend thinks he should donate. The model quantifies these beliefs by multiplying the subjective likelihood that a particular significant other (called a referent) thinks the person should perform the behavior times the person's *motivation to comply* with that referent's expectation. These products, which are analogous to the Expectancy × Value products computed for behavioral beliefs, are then summed over the various salient referent persons. This relation between the subjective norm and normative beliefs can be expressed algebraically as follows:

$$SN = \sum_{j=1}^{r} b_j m_j \qquad (4.3)$$

where b_j is the normative belief (i.e. subjective probability) that some referent j thinks one should perform the behavior; m_j is the motivation to comply with referent j; and r is the number of relevant referents. Thus, in parallel fashion, both normative beliefs and behavioral beliefs are represented by summed Expectancy × Value products.

From some perspectives, Fishbein and Ajzen's distinction between attitude toward the behavior and subjective norm is somewhat arbitrary. As Miniard and Cohen (1981) argued, the perceived impact of one's actions on other people can generally be stated equally well in terms of (a) a behavioral belief (e.g., serving spaghetti for dinner will make my daughter happy) or (b) a normative belief (e.g., my daughter thinks that I should serve spaghetti for dinner). It is thus not surprising that there can be considerable confounding between the attitudinal and normative aspects of the model, sometimes resulting in statistical problems (i.e., multicollinearity) when the two predictors are simultaneously entered into a regression equation to predict behavioral intentions.

One solution to these problems is to represent other people's preferences for one's behavior in terms of behavioral beliefs rather than normative beliefs, that is, in terms of the perceived likelihood that others would be pleased or displeased with one's act and one's evaluation of their pleasure or displeasure. This solution would treat others' reactions (i.e., subjective norm) as a component or determinant of attitude toward the behavior (see Smetana & Adler, 1980). However, Fishbein and his colleagues have preferred to maintain separate attitudinal and normative terms for predicting behavioral intentions. In defense of their position, a classic feature of social and personality psychology is a division of the determinants of social behavior into two categories—attributes of the person and attributes of the social environment (e.g., Lewin, 1936). Maintenance of this dichotomy in the theory of reasoned action by treating attitude and perceived social norm as separate determinants of behavior allows it to address a variety of traditionally important questions concerning the attitudinal versus normative regulation of conduct.

Theory of Reasoned Action as a Model of Volitional Behavior. The causal model shown in Figure 4.1 summarizes the theory of reasoned action: (a) behavior is determined by intention to engage in the behavior, (b) intention is determined by attitude toward the behavior and subjective norm, (c) attitude is determined by behavioral beliefs and evaluation of the salient outcomes, and (d) subjective norm is determined by normative beliefs and motivation to comply with the salient referents. According to proponents of this approach, the model provides a complete theory of voluntary behavior in the sense that no other variables influence behavior, except through their impact on behavioral and normative beliefs and on the relative weight of the attitudinal and normative terms of the model. Because attitudes toward targets—the attitudes traditionally important in attitude research—do not appear in this model, readers may wonder what their role might be. Where is political

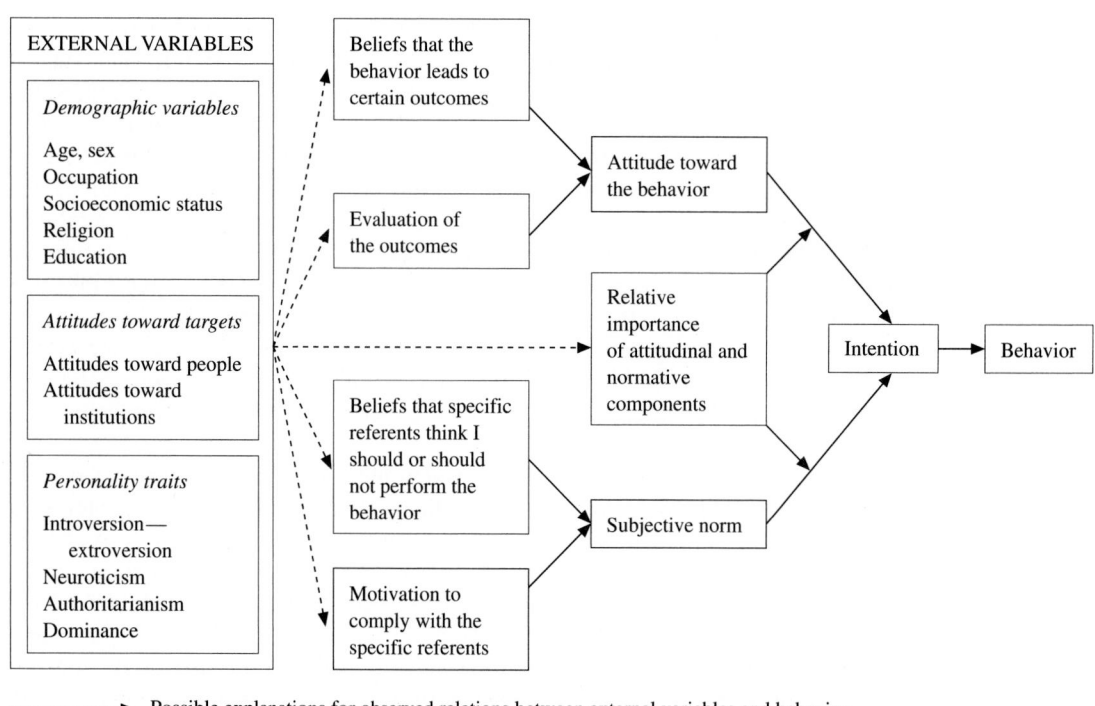

- - - - - - - - - ► Possible explanations for observed relations between external variables and behavior

———————► Stable theoretical relations linking beliefs to behavior

172

liberalism-conservatism represented, for example, when political behaviors are predicted? According to Fishbein and Ajzen (1975), such an attitude, as well as all other variables, affects behavior only through the more proximal determinants of behavior specified by the model. For example, liberal-conservative attitude would influence attitude toward voting for Bush, and this attitude toward a behavior, along with subjective norm, would influence intention to vote for Bush, which controls the voting behavior itself. By this logic, all variables not specified by the model are labeled *external variables*, as shown in Figure 4.1.

The theory has an inherent reasonableness that is nicely captured by the term *theory of reasoned action*. People are assumed to behave as they intend to behave. They intend to behave in ways that allow them to obtain favorable outcomes and that meet the expectations of others who are important to them. However, because the theory does not include the sorts of predictors that have ordinarily been regarded as important, neither laypeople nor the majority of social scientists are likely to believe that this theory has provided a complete description of the causes of behavior. For example, as applied to explain criminal behavior, the theory would suggest that people engage in criminal behavior because they intend to do so, and they intend to do so because they think that this behavior is of personal benefit and/or that important others want them to behave in this way. Theories of criminal behavior have typically examined more general characteristics of the environment (e.g., poverty) and the person (e.g., deviant identity), which are not included within the theory of reasoned action (see Short & Meier, 1981). Fishbein, Ajzen, and their associates would of course treat these and any other variables as external to their model. Yet the model provides no theory specifying these more distal variables and indicating the ways that they affect behavioral and normative beliefs. As a result, the theory does not speak to the majority of the variables that social scientists have regarded as important to behavior, except insofar as it suggests a set of determinants of behavior that may *mediate* the effects of such variables on behavior. In short, the theory of reasoned action is not a general theory of behavior. Rather, it is a theory of the immediately proximal causes of volitional behavior.

Theory of Reasoned Action as a Model of Cognitive Processes. The theory has been criticized for its presumed assumption that people necessarily engage in elaborate cogitation prior to behaving. For example, Fazio (1986, p. 236) suggested that, according to the theory of reasoned action, "When faced with a decision, people consider closely their beliefs toward the act in question and then summate those beliefs to arrive at a specific attitude toward the act." However, this criticism seems misdirected in view of Ajzen and Fishbein's (1980) clear statement that their theory does *not* assume that people scrutinize the determinants of their behavior prior to every behavioral act. Instead, the theory assumes that people *form* their intentions by thinking about their attitudes and subjective norms, *form* their attitudes by thinking about the consequences of their behavior, and *form* their subjective norms by thinking about significant others' approval or disapproval of their behavior. Once these intentions, attitudes, and subjective norms have been formed, all of them are not necessarily reviewed prior to each and every behavioral opportunity. People may retrieve only an intention, or an attitude toward a behavior and perhaps a norm, which then produce an intention in that situation. Yet in a research setting, when confronted by questionnaires probing the terms of the model, people are fully capable of retrieving the specific beliefs that underlie their attitudes and subjective norms. Although Ajzen and Fishbein's position that all of the processes of the model need not be activated for behavior to occur is entirely reasonable, their stance leaves unanswered the important question of which processes are activated and which are not, prior to behavioral acts.

Some Complexities in Applying the Theory of Reasoned Action

The Fishbein-Ajzen model is not restricted to predicting single behaviors, but can be used to predict sets of behaviors aggregated over actions, targets, contexts, and times. When applying the model to single behaviors or sets of behaviors, researchers are cautioned to employ compatible definitions of all of its terms. For example, if the behavioral criterion in a study is aggregated over a six-month period, intentions should be queried with respect to the same six-month period, and so should attitudes and subjective norms. High predictability of behavior from the model is presumed only under conditions of compatible definitions of behavior and its determinants. Although this insistence on compatibility may maximize prediction of behavior, it begs the question of the level of generality at which people formulate their intentions. Do people intend to engage in a behavior for a six-month period in a particular context, or do they merely intend to engage in the behavior? In imposing the compatibility principle on the theory of reasoned action, Fishbein and Ajzen thus allowed concerns about measurement and statistical prediction to coerce their causal model.

Fishbein and Ajzen also argued that it is often wise to implement their model in a more complex form to predict behaviors that represent a choice between two or more alternatives (Ajzen & Fishbein, 1980; Fishbein, 1980). For example, smoking reflects a choice between smoking and not smoking. Because attitude toward smoking and attitude toward not smoking can have similar valence (e.g., both negative), it would be consistent with the theory of reasoned action to find that some people with negative attitudes toward smoking nevertheless smoke, if their attitudes toward *not* smoking were even more negative. Because of such considerations, prediction of smoking behavior should be more successful if attitudes, norms, and intentions are taken into account for both of these behavioral alternatives, smoking and not smoking. Presumably people compare the relative strengths of their intentions toward each alternative and choose the behavior with the stronger intention.[4]

In general, for behaviors that are perceived as a choice between two or more alternatives, Fishbein and Ajzen recommended that their model be implemented with its terms represented by *differences* in the intentions (as well as attitudes, subjective norms, etc.) associated with each of the alternatives (see also Davidson & Morrison,

1983; Jaccard, 1981a; Jaccard & Becker, 1985; van den Putte, Hoogstraten, & Meertens, 1991). Implementing the model in this way has been shown to improve the predictability of some behaviors (see Ajzen & Fishbein, 1980; Fishbein, 1980). For a particular multi-alternative choice (use of contraceptive methods), Davidson and Morrison (1983) demonstrated the importance of assessing the differences between people's attitudes (and intentions) toward the several alternatives. Nevertheless, when there are only two mutually exclusive and exhaustive alternatives, the gain in prediction from using the difference score approach is negligible if attitude toward one of the alternatives is highly negatively correlated with attitude toward the other alternative.

When implemented with respect to choices between alternatives, the Fishbein-Ajzen model becomes very similar to subjective expected value and subjective expected utility models of decision making (see Abelson & Levi, 1985; Hastie, 1991; T. R. Mitchell & Biglan, 1971; Stevenson, Busemeyer, & Naylor, 1990). Such models have long been popular in psychology (e.g., W. Edwards, 1954) and economics (e.g., Arrow, 1951). These theories maintain that behavioral alternatives each have a value (or utility) and that each such value is the sum of the products of the likelihoods and values of the various outcomes associated with each behavioral alternative. The individual is assumed to choose the alternative with the highest overall value (or utility). Although much criticized and modified, these models represent an important tradition in the study of decision making.

Because attitude toward the behavior in the Fishbein-Ajzen model is a function of the perceived likelihoods of outcomes and their perceived value, the attitude aspect of the model resembles expected utility models. However, in contrast to decision theorists, who work directly with the likelihoods and values associated with the various outcomes, attitude theorists work mainly with attitude toward the behavior, which is thought to summarize the evaluated outcomes. Therefore, in attitude research relatively little attention is given to the complex functions by which the likelihoods and values associated with particular outcomes may multiply, summate, and relate to people's behavioral intentions (or choices).

Empirical Tests of the Theory of Reasoned Action

The theory of reasoned action has been tested in scores of studies and has generally fared well when the terms of the model were carefully operationalized. For example, the model has been applied, with considerable success, to strategy choices in Prisoner's Dilemma games (Ajzen, 1971a), blood donation (Pomazal & Jaccard, 1976), voting (Ajzen & Fishbein, 1980; Fishbein et al., 1986), church attendance (G. W. King, 1975), family planning (Crawford & Boyer, 1985; Davidson & Jaccard, 1975), eating at fast-food restaurants (Brinberg & Durand, 1983), smoking marijuana (Ajzen, Timko, & White, 1982), mothers' infant feeding practices (Manstead, Proffitt, & Smart, 1983), dental hygiene behaviors (McCaul, O'Neill, & Glasgow, 1988; Toneatto & Binik, 1987), having an abortion (Smetana & Adler, 1980), purchasing various consumer products (Brinberg & Cummings, 1983; Warshaw, 1980), and attendance at an employee training session (Fishbein & Stasson, 1990).

In several reviews of this research, Fishbein and Ajzen maintained that intentions to engage in volitional acts were usually well predicted by the combination of attitude toward the behavior and subjective norm (Ajzen, 1984; Ajzen & Fishbein, 1973, 1980; Fishbein, 1980). Indeed, Ajzen and Fishbein (1973) reported a mean R of .81, based on the 10 studies that were available to them. Sheppard, Hartwick, and Warshaw's (1988) later review applied meta-analytic techniques to a more extensive research literature that provided 87 estimates of the predictability of intention and behavior. These investigators reported a mean R of .66 for the prediction of intention from attitude and subjective norm (see also Farley, Lehmann, & Ryan, 1981). For the relation between intention and behavior, they reported a mean r of .53. Van den Putte (1991) provided a more extensive meta-analysis based on 113 articles that provided estimates of various relations in the model for 150 groups of respondents. His mean R for predicting intention from attitude and subjective norm was .68, and his mean r for predicting behavior from intention was .62. Van den Putte also reported mean correlations of (a) .53 for the relation between attitude and behavioral beliefs and (b) .53 for the relation between subjective norm and normative beliefs. In addition, he found that the relation between intention and attitude was stronger than the relation between intention and subjective norm.

Both of these meta-analyses found that the variability across studies was particularly large for the prediction of behavior from intention (see also Belk, 1985). Yet inconsistencies in the magnitude of the intention-behavior relation are not problematic for Fishbein and Ajzen, who often stated that the correlation between intention and behavior would not necessarily be high. They noted in particular that a delay between the assessment of the intention and the opportunity to engage in the behavior would reduce the intention-behavior correlation by allowing intentions to change before the behavior could occur. However, as we show later in this chapter, weak relations between intentions and behavior could also reflect the determination of behavior by processes not considered by the model.

In evaluating the magnitude of the relations found between the variables of the theory of reasoned action it is important to consider that some of the studies aggregated into the mean correlations reported in these meta-analyses involved the prediction of behaviors that are only partially under volitional control (e.g., having a child in the next three years). Because (a) the theory of reasoned action applies only to volitional behaviors and (b) intention should be a weaker predictor of behavior to the extent that behavior is not volitional, these quantitative reviews may underestimate the true strength of the relations between the terms of the model.

Finally, we note that Ajzen and Fishbein (1980) provided an excellent set of instructions for implementing the theory of reasoned action. Their 1980 book explained the model in detail, illustrated it with summaries of several specific studies, and included a sample questionnaire that gives the exact wording they recommend for items assessing the terms of their model.

Criticisms of the Theory of Reasoned Action and Proposals of Variant Models

The theory of reasoned action has been repeatedly challenged in its assumption that it provides a sufficient description of the proximal causes of behavior and that therefore other variables influence behavior only through their impact on the terms of the model. Fishbein and Ajzen's usual method of testing this claim entailed (a) correlating behavior with intention to engage in the behavior, (b) regressing intention onto attitude toward the act and subjective norm, (c) correlating attitude toward the act with behavioral beliefs, and (d) correlating subjective norm with normative beliefs (see Ajzen & Fishbein, 1980). If other variables (i.e., *external variables*) were analyzed, they were usually entered into a regression equation predicting behavioral intention or behavior, once the predictors specified by the model had already been entered. Researchers committed to the theory thus hoped to show that other variables (e.g., attitudes toward targets) failed to account for additional variability in behavioral intention or behavior, once the terms of the model were taken into account (e.g., Pomazal & Jaccard, 1976).

Perceived Moral Obligation and Self-Identity as Omissions from the Reasoned Action Model

Investigators who have challenged Fishbein and Ajzen's claim that their model is sufficient have shown that intention is determined by a larger set of variables than attitude toward the behavior and subjective norm. One such suggested addition is perceived moral obligation, which represents people's personal beliefs about right and wrong (e.g., S. H. Schwartz & Tessler, 1972). This variable reflects internalized moral rules—not perceptions of others' ideas about what one should do. Although Fishbein (1967a) had originally defined the normative variable of his model in terms of personal morality, he subsequently defined norms as beliefs about what others think one should do. To explain this shift, Fishbein and Ajzen (1975) noted that personal beliefs about what an individual thinks he or she ought to do are so confounded with behavioral intention that they do not add to prediction. However, some studies have found that prediction improved when personal moral obligation was taken into account along with attitude toward the act and subjective norm (e.g., Gorsuch & Ortberg, 1983; Pomazal & Jaccard, 1976; S. H. Schwartz & Tessler, 1972; Zuckerman & Reis, 1978; see also L. Beck & Ajzen, 1991).

Other research suggests that self-identity as well as attitudes and subjective norms can determine intentions and behaviors (see Biddle, Bank, & Slavings, 1987; Charng, Piliavin, & Callero, 1988; Granberg & Holmberg, 1990). For example, political activists may participate in protest actions because activism has become a central aspect of their self-concepts, and blood donors may give blood because being a donor has become an important part of their self-identities. Consistent with this reasoning, variables representing self-identity have been shown to account for variability in intentions and behavior over and above the variability accounted for by the theory of reasoned action. Moreover, the contribution of identity becomes greater to the extent that a behavior is repeated (Charng et al., 1988). For example, among people who have given blood several times, self-identity may regulate donation behavior to a greater extent than attitude toward donating blood does.

We could argue that moral obligation and self-identity, like subjective norm, could be subsumed under attitude toward the behavior, because guilt, self-reinforcement, and other outcomes of meeting or violating one's own standards are merely additional consequences of behaviors. Yet the improvement in prediction of behavioral intention that is sometimes achieved by adding a direct measure of moral obligation or self-identity to Equation 4.1 suggests that such consequences may not be especially salient when respondents rate behaviors on the evaluative scales used to assess attitude toward the act, even though these moral consequences impact on behavioral intentions. These questionnaire items apparently do not provide a context that makes these classes of outcomes highly accessible for respondents (see Tourangeau & Rasinski, 1988).

Whether it is important to distinguish between various classes of outcomes of behaviors is an even broader issue than implied by our discussion of the separability of attitude toward the behavior from subjective norms, perceived moral obligation, and self-identity. Looking back to our general discussion of attitudes in the prior three chapters of this book, we remind readers that attitudes, understood in the sense of general evaluations, may be products of affective and behavioral reactions to attitude objects, as well as cognitive responses. Developing this theme, some investigators have considered distinctively affective consequences of behaviors, that is, the positive and negative feelings that people anticipate will ensue from engaging in behaviors. Indeed, some evidence has been produced for the separability of cognitive (i.e., costs and benefits) and affective (i.e., negative and positive feelings) determinants of attitude or intention (Ajzen & Driver, 1991, 1992; Bagozzi, 1989; see subsequent discussion of Triandis, 1977, model). At least under some circumstances prediction may be improved by taking both of these classes of consequences into account.

Past Behavior or Habit as
Omissions from the Reasoned Action Model

The influence of past behavior on present behavior was examined in Bentler and Speckart's (1979) application of *structural equation analysis* to test the theory of reasoned action against alternative models. These methods provide explicit and statistically justified tests of the assumptions of the theory of reasoned action in competition with models that make different assumptions.[5] Specifically, Bentler and Speckart compared the Fishbein-Ajzen model (see Figure 4.2) with a model that added a direct causal path from attitude to behavior, not mediated by intention (see discussion later in chapter). They also presented a second alternative model that included, in addition to the direct link between attitude and behavior, another new independent variable, *past behavior*, which was presumed to affect subsequent behavior directly as well as indirectly through its impact on intention. This extended model is presented

FIGURE 4.2. A representation of the theory of reasoned action. This figure was adapted from one presented by Bentler and Speckart (1979, Figure 1, p. 454).

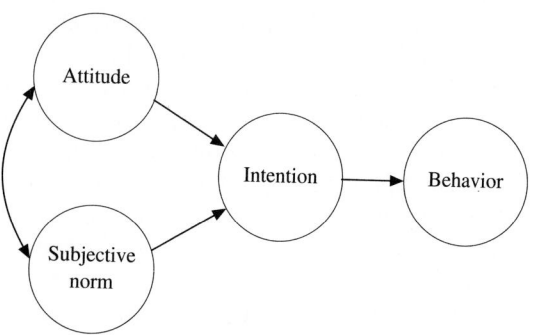

in Figure 4.3. The addition of past behavior to the model is eminently sensible from behaviorist perspectives which postulate that behavior is influenced by habit, or more generally, by various types of conditioned releasers or learned predispositions to respond that are not readily encompassed by the concepts of attitude and intention. Thus, the relation between past behavior and subsequent behavior may not be completely explicable through past behavior's impact on attitudes and intentions.

FIGURE 4.3. A representation of Bentler and Speckart's attitude-behavior model that included past behavior (Behavior I). This figure was adapted from one presented by Bentler and Speckart (1979, Figure 3, p. 455).

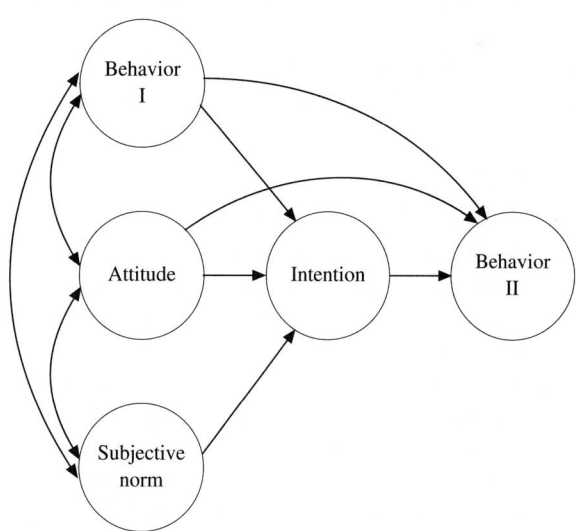

Triandis's Model. Bentler and Speckart's (1979) inclusion of past behavior in their model reactivated a theme introduced somewhat earlier when Triandis (1977, 1980) included a *habit* term in his model of the attitude-behavior relation. Triandis (1980, p. 204) defined habit conceptually as "situation-specific sequences that are or have become automatic, so that they occur without self-instruction" and defined it operationally as the number of times an act has been performed in the past. More generally, the concept of habit implies that a behavior has become so routinized through repetition that a person has ceased to make any conscious decision to act yet still behaves in the accustomed way. In Triandis's model, behavior is a joint outcome of behavioral intention and habit; to the extent that behaviors are habitual, they should be less affected by behavioral intentions.

Paralleling the Fishbein-Ajzen model, the Triandis model treated attitude toward the act and social-normative considerations as determinants of intentions. However, departing from the Fishbein-Ajzen model, Triandis separated attitude toward the act into two terms, *affect* toward the act and the *value of the perceived consequences* of the act. The perceived consequences term thus corresponds to Fishbein and Ajzen's behavioral beliefs, but the theory of reasoned action does not include Triandis's affective term, which he defined as "the particular configuration of emotions [that] becomes activated at the thought of the behavior" (Triandis, 1977, p. 16). Using multiple regression techniques, Triandis and his associates tested the model in several studies and found that, although the model fared well, it did not predict intentions and behaviors consistently better than the Fishbein-Ajzen model (e.g., Brinberg, 1979; Davidson, Jaccard, Triandis, Morales, & Diaz-Guerrero, 1976; Jaccard & Davidson, 1975; see reviews by Triandis, 1977, 1980). Although past behavior (or habit) sometimes contributed to predicting behavior, over and above behavioral intention, the overall importance of habit remained unclear.

Bentler and Speckart's Test of Their Extended Models. Pursuing the role of past behavior in predicting later behavior, Bentler and Speckart (1979) tested their extended models in a study of students' self-reported use of alcohol, marijuana, and hard drugs. They obtained estimates of past behavior, attitude, subjective norm, and intention at one point in time and then assessed self-reported behavior again two weeks later. All terms of the model shown in Figure 4.3 were defined in the compatible manner recommended by Ajzen and Fishbein (1977, 1980). Furthermore, each term was assessed by three items. This step was taken in order to estimate each term as a *latent variable*. To accomplish this estimation, Bentler and Speckart calculated a measurement model for each variable using confirmatory factor analysis. This procedure is designed to remove the effects of unreliabilities in the measured variables from the regression coefficients that estimate the relations between the terms of the model. Consequently, causal relations in the models can be estimated without contamination by unreliability in the overt, measured variables (see Bentler, 1980; Kenny, 1979). This latent variable form of causal modeling has been adopted in much of the newer research that has tested models of attitude-behavior relations.

Parameters for the Fishbein-Ajzen model and the two extended models were estimated, and appropriate comparisons between the models showed that the most complex of the models (Figure 4.3) fit the data most adequately. This outcome thus supported the addition of direct paths from attitude to behavior and from previous behavior to both intention and behavior. The finding that both attitudes and past behavior accounted for significant variability in drug consumption that was not explained by intentions called into question Fishbein and Ajzen's (e.g., 1975) claim that intention is the only immediate determinant of overt behavior. However, it should be kept in mind that Fishbein and Ajzen restricted their model to volitional behaviors, and drug consumption is no doubt not under complete volitional control (Tiffany, 1990). In addition, respondents' intentions may have been unstable over the two-week time span of the behavioral criterion, and therefore the importance of intentions could have been underestimated by the data.

Other Studies Examining Past Behavior. That the inclusion of past behavior improves prediction of behavior is consistent with studies of other behaviors that may seem relatively habitual—studying and exercise (Bentler & Speckart, 1981), students' class attendance (Fredricks & Dossett, 1983), voting for a particular political party (Echabe, Rovira, & Garate, 1988), seat belt use (Budd, North, & Spencer, 1984; Mittal, 1988; Sutton & Hallett, 1989; Wittenbraker, Gibbs, & Kahle, 1983), and blood donation (Bagozzi, 1981; Charng, Piliavin, & Callero, 1988). In these studies, multiple regression analyses showed that the prediction of behavior was improved by the addition of past behavior or self-reported habit to the Fishbein-Ajzen model or to the prediction achieved on the basis of intention.

Despite these demonstrations, the role of habit *per se* remains indeterminate in this research because of the difficulty of designing adequate measures of habit. Unfortunately, statistical associations between measures of past behavior and later behavior (controlling for the terms of the theory of reasoned action) are ambiguous because they could represent the influence of many other factors that are present on both occasions when behavior is assessed but are not taken into account by the reasoned action approach (see Ajzen, 1991). For example, self-identity or perceived moral obligation could determine behavior on both occasions. Moreover, researchers' measures of past behavior and later behavior may have shared error variance due to the use of a similar response format for the two measures. Nonetheless, the research now available suggests that quite a number of everyday behaviors are controlled only partially by intentions and *may be* controlled in part by habit. Although Ajzen and Fishbein acknowledged that extremely well learned behaviors may be habitual and therefore not controlled by intentions, they maintained that such behaviors are not particularly important because most behaviors "of social relevance" are under volitional control (Ajzen & Fishbein, 1980, p. 5). However, we have already noted important behaviors (e.g., drug use, seat belt use, class attendance) that may have strongly habitual aspects.

Scripted Behavior. Other research, especially that of Langer (e.g., 1978, 1989a, 1989b), also has drawn attention to behavior that does not follow from intentions or plans, although this research did not follow in the tradition of the regression models we have so far discussed in this chapter. Langer labeled such behavior *mindless* because it is carried out without much conscious control or attention and might therefore be considered in some sense "automatic" (see Bargh, 1989). Langer suggested that such nonvolitional behavior is under the control of *scripts* (e.g., Abelson, 1976, 1981, 1982; see Chapter 3) that are formed on the basis of repeated behavior as well as other types of learning. These scripts are schemas that contain expected sequences of behaviors used to reach certain goals (e.g., a script for driving home from work) or to behave appropriately in certain settings (e.g., a script for eating dinner in a restaurant). Distinguishing scripted behavior from habitual behavior and behavior that is normatively regulated remains problematic. The main value of the script concept may be its provision of a model of how habits and social norms may be represented cognitively.

The Reasoned Action Model's Difficulties in
Predicting Behaviors That Require Resources, Cooperation, and Skills

In a widely read article critical of the theory of reasoned action, Liska (1984) argued that the restriction of the Fishbein-Ajzen model to volitional behavior excludes, not just habitual behavior, but behavior that requires "skills, abilities, opportunities and the cooperation of others" (p. 63). The volitional restriction limits the model to actions that require only motivation on the part of the individual. According to this view, the great majority of the studies that have supported the theory of reasoned action have concerned relatively simple behaviors that do not require much in the way of resources or specialized skills. Indeed, behaviors such as voting, church attendance, and choice of strategies in Prisoner's Dilemma games have these attributes. Whereas Ajzen and Fishbein (e.g., 1980) argued that the restriction of their model to volitional behavior did not rule out many behaviors of interest to psychologists, Liska maintained that behaviors not under volitional control (or only partially under such control) are at least as interesting and important as those that are.

Fishbein and Ajzen (1975) were not unaware of the issues that Liska (1984) raised. They suggested that the need for resources or others' cooperation does not require changes in their model but merely produces changes in intentions, if these resources or cooperative behaviors are not forthcoming. For example, an individual who intends to go running with her friend tomorrow afternoon would surely change this intention if she found out that the friend was unavailable. Similarly, a person who intends to buy a house would surely change this intention if he found out that the needed mortgage would not be available to him. Thus, problems in obtaining resources and cooperation would have little effect on short-term predictions from intentions assessed immediately before an act, but they would weaken predictions from intentions assessed much in advance of behaviors. For these reasons, Fishbein and Ajzen emphasized that a measure of intention should reflect the intention that exists immediately prior to engaging in the behavior.

Problems in predicting skilled behaviors were also acknowledged by Fishbein and Ajzen (1975), who provided a solution similar to the one they suggested for behaviors requiring resources or cooperation. They suggested that the extent to which an act requires specialized skills may sometimes not be thoroughly understood by individuals before they attempt the behavior (e.g., I expect to ski the advanced trail without falling). With such lack of foresight, intentions would change after the behavior has been unsuccessfully attempted. Therefore, the intention-behavior relation would probably be stronger for subsequent acts than it was for the initial act. At least after the first attempt to engage in the behavior, intentions held immediately prior to the behavior should provide reasonably good prediction.

Because behaviors that require resources, cooperation, and skills, such as going on a camping trip, are not single behavioral acts but complex sequences of coordinated acts, the reasoned action model is problematic in its focus on predicting a particular behavior. Indeed, the proponents of the theory acknowledged the serious problems encountered in applying the model to predict a criterion that is a *goal* of a behavior or an *intended outcome* of a sequence of behaviors (Ajzen & Fishbein, 1980; Davidson & Jaccard, 1979; Fishbein, 1980). For example, losing weight is not a behavior but is an outcome of a set of behaviors having to do with expending physical energy and restricting food intake. One reason that the intention to lose weight is only weakly related to losing weight is that this intention is often not closely related to intentions to engage in the specific behaviors that bring about weight loss, such as avoidance of high-calorie foods (see Sejwacz, Ajzen, & Fishbein, 1980). Although the theory of reasoned action thus could not be properly implemented with respect to intentions to achieve a behavioral goal such as weight loss, it can be applied to predict the individual behaviors that underlie the achievement of such a goal. Indeed, this approach was suggested by Ajzen and Fishbein (1980). This point holds for a variety of behavioral outcomes, such as achieving a good grade in a course, obtaining a raise at work, and being liked by others. Predicting whether people attain such goals is thus not within the domain of the theory of reasoned action except if prediction is approached through the rather cumbersome procedure of determining people's intentions to engage in all of the behaviors that can underlie achievement of the goal. These intentions would then be aggregated into an overall prediction about goal attainment.

It is reasonable for Fishbein and Ajzen to have argued that their model presumes that the time gap between the assessment of intention and the assessment of behavior be minimum and that outcomes be distinguished from behaviors. However, as a consequence, their model largely abandoned the question of how intentions relate over broad time spans to behaviors that are complex sequences of acts and to the attainment of goals that are difficult to achieve. Social scientists are understandably interested in predicting complex behaviors and goal attainment over longer as well as shorter time periods. Very often people do not succeed in turning their intentions into the desired behaviors or outcomes, and understanding the causes of these failures is important. As Liska (1984) argued, to address this issue, we would need to understand how people gain skills, locate opportunities, and access resources. The social context of behavior would have to be examined, particularly with respect to the individual's status within the social structure and other determinants of access to resources and opportunities. People of higher status and power have more chances to turn their intentions into behavior than do those who are less favorably situated.

Expectancies versus Plans. The extent to which problems in obtaining opportunities and resources and in acquiring skills lower intention-behavior correlations may depend on whether intention is operationalized by assessing respondents' *expectancies* about performing a behavior or by their *plans* to perform the behavior. As we will explain, these problems should impact on expectancies much more than on plans. Fishbein and Ajzen (1975) framed the intention construct in terms of expectancies by defining it as personal beliefs about whether one will engage in a behavior; they referred to intentions as "people's expectancies about their own behavior in a given setting" (p. 288). Given this definition, it is not surprising that researchers testing the reasoned action model have sometimes assessed intention by asking respondents to estimate the probability of engaging in a behavior (e.g., "Are you likely to do X?"). In adopting this type of operational definition of intention, researchers departed from laypeople's common understanding of intention in terms of a conscious plan. As Warshaw and Davis (1985) noted, standard dictionary definitions suggest that intention is usually understood as "the degree to which a person has formulated conscious plans to perform or not perform some specified future behavior" (p. 214). Conforming more closely to this common understanding of intention, investigators of Fishbein and Ajzen's theory have often assessed intentions through items that ask about purposive plans (e.g., "Do you intend to do X?"). Indeed, there has been little consistency in whether intentions were assessed via questions about expectancies or plans. In fact, Ajzen and Fishbein (1980, p. 42) suggested that the two types of measures can be used interchangeably.

Other researchers have questioned this practice of equating expectancies (i.e., self-predictions of behavior) and what might be considered genuine intentions (i.e., plans to engage in behaviors). Warshaw and Davis (1985) demonstrated that people's plans to act do not predict their behavior as well as their expectations about acting. In addition, Sheppard and associates' (1988) meta-analysis, using a large sample of studies, established that the superiority of expectancies over plans is slight for predicting behaviors but substantial for predicting the attainment of goals. This superiority of expectancies over plans no doubt stems from a tendency for expectancies (but not plans) to make some allowance for anticipated deficiencies of resources, opportunities, and skills as well as for a variety of other nonvolitional factors and foreseeable changes, all of which as we have already argued, are understandably more important to predicting goal attainment than to predicting specific, volitional actions. It thus follows that Ajzen and Fishbein's (1980) position that self-predictions of one's own behavior and statements of one's purposive plans are interchangeable in research is generally valid as long as simple, volitional behaviors are predicted rather than the attainment of more remote goals (see Fishbein & Stasson, 1990). If a behavior is truly under an individual's control, he ordinarily does what he plans to do, and he predicts that he will do what he plans to do.

Questioning the Reasoned Action Model's Assumption That
Intention Necessarily Mediates the Influence of Attitude on Behavior

In discussing intentions, it is appropriate to return to Bentler and Speckart's (1979) suggestion that attitude may sometimes impact directly on behavior without mediation through intentions. Additional research has sometimes replicated Bentler and Speckart's finding of a direct influence of attitudes on behavior, without mediation by intention (e.g., Albrecht & Carpenter, 1976; Bagozzi & Warshaw, in press; Bentler & Speckart, 1981; Manstead, Proffitt, & Smart, 1983; Zuckerman & Reis, 1978) but sometimes not replicated it (e.g., Bagozzi, 1981; Fredericks & Dossett, 1983). This research should be interpreted with caution, however, because investigators have often not given sufficient consideration to the statistical power of their test procedures or to the reliability and validity of the measures that assessed the terms of the models (see Bagozzi, Baumgartner, & Yi, 1989). Some studies may not have been able to detect a relation between attitude and intention that was actually present.

Despite the ambiguity of most existing evidence of the attitude-intention relation, it seems reasonable to postulate that people may sometimes act on their attitudes in a relatively impulsive or spontaneous manner, without forming an explicit intention. Moreover, even for the simple, nonhabitual behaviors that psychologists would ordinarily consider to be volitional (and not particularly spontaneous or impulsive), the assumption that behaviors are regulated by intentions may sometimes be faulty. As Bagozzi and Yi (1989) have shown, people sometimes do not form intentions, or at the least do not formulate them clearly, because they lack the motivation or opportunity to do so (see also Bagozzi, Yi, & Baumgartner, 1990). When Bagozzi and Yi used a distraction task to restrict students' opportunity to form an intention to read some course material, their data suggested that these students' attitudes had a direct impact on behavior; the mediating role of intention was diminished. Such findings indicate that the concept of intention remains underdeveloped in the reasoned action model. Intention might, as Sternberg (1990) has suggested, be conceptualized as a continuum running from vaguely formulated thoughts about future behavior to clear-cut plans that one is going to engage in a particular behavior at a particular point in time.

Concerns about the Direction of Causation
in the Reasoned Action Model

Liska (1984) also criticized the theory of reasoned action for its emphasis on causation that flows in a single direction from *beliefs* to *attitudes and subjective norms* to *intentions* to *behavior*. This causal structure is of course an oversimplification of the links between attitudes and behaviors. In particular, behavior has been shown to influence attitudes (see Chapter 11), and such feedback effects of behavior on the model's antecedent variables are not represented.

When researchers assess both behavior and attitudes at two or more points in time, they can estimate the relative importance of the attitude-behavior and behavior-attitude relations. The majority of such efforts, which have relied on cross-lag

185

correlations and variants of structural equation modeling, provide evidence for reciprocal effects but suggest also that the effect of attitudes on behavior is stronger than the effect of behavior on attitudes (e.g., Andrews & Kandel, 1979; Bentler & Speckart, 1981; Heise, 1977; Kahle & Berman, 1979). Nonetheless, these findings support the criticism that at least part of the covariation of attitudes, intentions, and behaviors observed by Fishbein and Ajzen and their collaborators is incorrectly ascribed to a one-way attitude-to-behavior causal flow by the theory of reasoned action.

Beyond Reasoned Action: *Theory of Planned Behavior and Other Variants*

Theory of Planned Behavior

Attentive to some of the criticisms of the theory of reasoned action, Icek Ajzen proposed an alternative theory of planned behavior that substantially enlarges the Fishbein-Ajzen model (Ajzen, 1985, 1987, 1988, 1991). Although Ajzen maintained that the reasoned action model remains valid for volitional behavior, he acknowledged that it must be revised to account for behaviors that are not wholly under volitional control. Departing from a strict distinction between behaviors and behavioral outcomes (or goals), Ajzen further contended that every behavior can be regarded as a goal, even the easily executed behaviors typically investigated in attitude-behavior studies. For example, a behavior as predominantly volitional as voting in an election could be thwarted by circumstances beyond an individual's control if, for example, he finds himself extremely ill on election day. Thus, voting can be regarded as a goal or an outcome of the behavior of attempting to vote and can, at least under some circumstances, have non-volitional aspects. The goal in turn organizes a sequence of more specific behaviors that are required to attain it (e.g., putting on one's coat, driving or walking to the polling place, indicating one's preference on the ballot).

According to Ajzen (1985), the extent to which one's intentions to perform behaviors can be carried out depends in part on the amount of control one has over the behavior. Although any behavior may be blocked by uncontrollable circumstances, some behaviors, such as obtaining a large raise in salary, may ordinarily be mainly out of individuals' own control. In the theory of planned behavior, the control that people have over behaviors is treated as a continuum, with easily executed behaviors (e.g., saying "good morning" to one's spouse) at one end and behavioral goals demanding resources, opportunities, and specialized skills (e.g., becoming a senator) at the other end. For non-habitual behaviors that are easily executed by almost everyone, without special circumstances, the theory of reasoned action should prove adequate. To the extent that behaviors are more difficult to execute, one's control over the needed resources, opportunities, and skills needs to be taken into account, and Ajzen's enhanced version of the reasoned action model should provide better prediction of behavior.

In the theory of planned behavior, control is taken into account as a variable labeled *perceived behavioral control*, which is defined as one's perception of how easy or

186

FIGURE 4.4.
A representation of Ajzen's theory of planned behavior. This figure was presented by Ajzen (1991, Figure 1, p. 182).

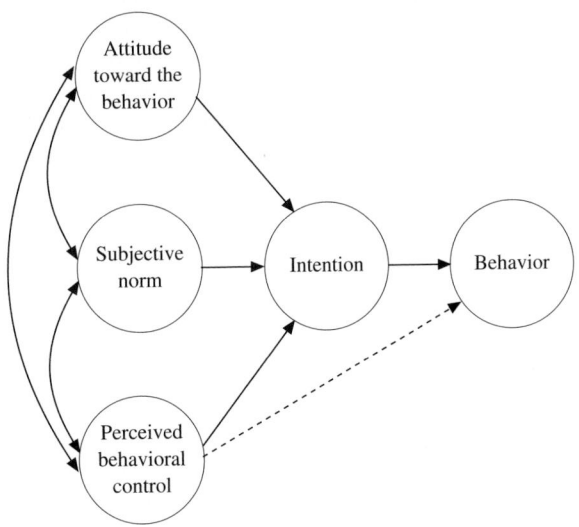

difficult it is to perform the behavior. This construct is similar to Bandura's concept of self-efficacy—"the conviction that one can successfully execute (a given) behavior" (Bandura, 1977, p. 193; see also Bandura, 1982; Bandura, Adams, & Beyer, 1977; Bandura, Adams, Hardy, & Howells, 1980; McCaul et al., 1988). Perceived behavioral control is in turn determined by *control beliefs*, which are beliefs about the likelihood that one possesses the resources and opportunities thought necessary to execute the behavior or attain the goal. Salient control beliefs thus determine perceived behavioral control in a manner analogous to the determination of attitude by behavioral beliefs and subjective norm by normative beliefs.

The role of perceived behavioral control in the theory of planned behavior is depicted in Figure 4.4. Thus, perceived control affects behavior in two ways: It influences intention to perform the behavior, and it may have a direct impact on behavior. In postulating a relation between control and intention, the theory thus assumes that people intend to engage in behaviors to the extent that they believe that they have control over them, that is, to the extent they have confidence in their ability to perform the behavior.

Concerning the direct link between control and behavior, Ajzen maintained that it is actual control, not perceived control, that is most relevant. Actual control, which encompasses factors such as availability of opportunities and resources that are prerequisites for engaging in the behavior, is distinguishable from perceived control because an individual's perceptions of control may not be entirely accurate. For example, a university student may perceive a good deal of control over attending class

187

but nevertheless be unable to attend because actual control is lessened by a completely unforeseen event such as an auto accident or a blizzard. However, because the determination of actual control by environmental events makes it very difficult to assess, Ajzen used perceived control as a proxy for actual control and argued that ordinarily people's beliefs about their degree of control are at least moderately accurate. Yet this substitution of perceived for actual control can be criticized in view of evidence that beliefs about control tend to be biased toward a somewhat exaggerated sense of personal control (see Langer, 1975; Langer & Roth, 1975). Ajzen has also suggested that perceived behavioral control may have a direct impact on behavior via the psychological route of increasing the effort that people devote to bringing a set of behaviors to a successful conclusion.

In his initial studies Ajzen tested the theory of planned behavior in relation to losing weight (Schifter & Ajzen, 1985) as well as attending college lectures and getting an "A" in a college course (Ajzen & Madden, 1986). In all cases, perceived control improved the prediction of intention over and above that achieved on the basis of attitude and subjective norm, and the prediction of intention was moderately successful on the basis of the three independent variables (Rs of .64 or higher).

In these studies, perceived control had a less consistent impact on behavior than on intention. Perceived control was especially important for predicting weight loss, and, in fact, intention predicted attainment of this behavioral goal only in interaction with perceived control (i.e., intention related positively to weight loss only for people who perceived they had a relatively high degree of control). In contrast, perceived control failed to improve prediction of class attendance, once intention was taken into account. This outcome is reasonable, because students should have a relatively high degree of actual control over their class attendance. For such behaviors, the theory of reasoned action, which omits the perceived behavioral control term, is adequate. Whether perceived control predicted attaining an "A" in a course, a behavioral goal that is surely less controllable than class attendance, depended on when control and the other predictors were assessed. When the predictors were assessed early in the semester, perceived control had no impact on grade attainment, presumably because students' beliefs about control were not very accurate at this point. When the predictors of the model were assessed near the end of the semester, perceived control did improve the prediction of grade attainment, over and above the prediction achieved on the basis of intention.

Quite a few additional studies have been carried out to test the theory of planned behavior, and Ajzen (1991) provided a review of twelve of these studies, which predicted a variety of behaviors including playing video games, performing cognitive tasks, election participation, voting choice, shoplifting, and giving a gift. The multiple correlations predicting behavior from intentions and perceived behavioral control ranged from .20 to .78, with an average of .51. The prediction of behavior was improved by adding perceived behavioral control as a predictor in most of these studies as well as in other studies that have appeared in the literature (Beale & Manstead, 1991; Borgida, Conner, & Manteufel, 1992; DeVellis, Blalock, & Sandler, 1990; Netemeyer & Burton, 1990). In most studies, intentions accounted for more variability in behavior

188

than perceived behavioral control, but control was more important in some studies. In addition, the prediction of intentions was generally improved by taking perceived behavioral control into account along with attitude toward the behavior and subjective norm; the mean R for predicting intentions was .71 in Ajzen's review. In summary, research in quite a few domains suggests that the addition of perceived control to the reasoned action model results in a more comprehensive model that applies to behaviors that require skills and resources and thus do not occur merely because people decide to act.

Despite the obvious success of the theory of planned behavior in those domains in which the reasoned action model is less appropriate, there are several aspects of the theory that warrant scrutiny. First of all, Ajzen's proposal of a causal link between perceived behavioral control and intention is worth pondering because it suggests that people intend to engage in actions or to attain goals merely because they have control over them. It is probably true that the perception of controllability or self-efficacy ordinarily increases the propensity to act, but this causal link seems less reasonable for negatively evaluated behaviors. People no doubt assume, for example, that they have control over the behaviors of shouting loudly in libraries and insulting strangers on street corners, but the mere fact of controllability would not seem to encourage people to engage in these negatively evaluated behaviors. Perhaps people take control into account *in conjunction with* their desire to engage in a behavior or attain a goal. If so, controllability would increase the likelihood of intending to engage in a behavior, to the extent that the behavior is positively evaluated. This potential interaction between attitude and perceived behavioral control has evidently not been evaluated, nor, for that matter, have other possible interactions between attitude, subjective norm, and behavioral control.[6]

A second consideration is the extent to which the theory of planned behavior provides a sufficient model of behavior by introducing just one new variable, perceived behavioral control. We have already reviewed evidence suggesting that other factors, namely, habit, perceived moral obligation, and self-identity, may predict intentions and behavior even when the terms of the reasoned action model have been taken into account. These additional variables may also predict when the terms of the planned behavior model have been taken into account, as Ajzen has shown in relation to perceived moral obligation (Beck & Ajzen, 1991). In contrast to Fishbein and Ajzen's (1975) advocacy that the theory of reasoned action is a sufficient model, Ajzen (1991) has indicated that he is open-minded on this sufficiency issue and thus remains receptive to the possibility that other variables may be needed to predict behavior under some circumstances.

Finally, the name of Ajzen's model, the theory of planned behavior, is somewhat anomalous given that the theory does not articulate the processes by which people formulate and act on plans. Presumably, to the extent that behaviors are not perceived as easily controllable, people must engage in planning as they negotiate the problems of obtaining resources, cooperation, and skills. All the theory of planned behavior does to acknowledge these processes is to introduce the behavioral control term that predicts weakened intentions for less controllable behaviors and lowered likelihoods of engaging in them. But how *do* people plan, and how does planning relate to perceived behavioral control? Perhaps as people engage in the cognitive processes of planning and identify a route for attaining a desired goal, they view their behavioral control as increasing. This issue warrants investigation in future research on planned behavior.[7]

Other Approaches to Understanding Goal-Oriented Behavior

Theory of Goal Pursuit. In another approach to predicting goal-oriented behavior, Warshaw, Sheppard, and Hartwick (1982) and Bagozzi and Warshaw (1990) modified the theory of reasoned action by proposing that goal attainment is determined by a process labeled *trying*. In this model, which they have named the *theory of goal pursuit*, trying refers to the mental and physical processes that intervene between intention to attain an outcome and actual attainment of it. Because trying encompasses the instrumental acts that must be carried out before an outcome is attained, this approach takes into account at least some aspects of the planning that allows people to reach remote goals.

In this reformulation of the reasoned action model, the behavior predicted is trying to attain a goal. Trying is a function of one's intention to try, which is, in turn, a function of both attitude toward trying to attain the goal and a normative term, in the general manner of the theory of reasoned action. Subjective norm is defined as others' expectations concerning one's trying to attain the goal. In a departure from the theory of reasoned action, attitude toward trying is separated into three components. Two of these components take success and failure into account: One component is attitude toward successful attainment of the goal, which is weighted by the perceived likelihood of success, and a second component is attitude toward unsuccessful attainment, which is weighted by the perceived likelihood of failure.[8] Attitude toward success and failure are in turn determined by Belief × Evaluation products, which detail the various expected consequences of success and failure.

In addition to these attitudes toward success and failure, this framework includes a third attitudinal component, attitude toward the processes involved in trying, which is also a function of Belief × Evaluation products. These beliefs pertain to the specific intermediate actions that are prerequisites to attaining the outcome. This component of attitude toward trying acknowledges people's expectations that achieving desired outcomes (e.g., weight loss) requires certain instrumental actions (e.g., eating low-fat foods, doing exercises), which are positively or negatively evaluated. This aspect of goal-relevant attitudes should be especially important in relation to behavioral outcomes that require considerable intermediary action, like losing weight. In general, considering perceptions of instrumental actions as well as perceptions of possible failure to attain a goal introduces aspects of planning that are neglected by the reasoned action model and its close relatives. However, the concept of trying and its elaboration in terms of three attitudinal determinants has so far received only limited empirical testing (see Bagozzi & Warshaw, 1990).

The Importance of Planning. As we have emphasized, any detailed consideration of the processes by which people plan their actions is absent from the theory of reasoned action and related models, and the theory of goal pursuit that we have just discussed considers only limited aspects of planning. Yet carrying out even mundane actions like voting for one's favorite candidate in an election often requires that one evolve a plan of some complexity. For the voting example, one must plan to set aside a brief period of time, get oneself to the polling place, and carry out the act of voting. For some individuals, voting demands a more elaborate plan because it requires the prior behavior of registering to vote. Although the execution of relatively simple behaviors does not necessarily presuppose a complex series of preparatory acts, attaining long-term goals *surely* requires planning a series of actions. Therefore, theories of behavior should consider how people conceptualize and then execute the set of actions required to engage in a consequential behavior.

Many psychologists have examined psychological processes directly relevant to planning and goal-oriented behavior (e.g., Kuhl, 1986; Kendzierski, 1990; Read & Miller, 1989; Sternberg, 1990; Wilensky, 1983). In particular, the regulation of behavior has been analyzed in terms of principles of feedback control by which people set standards for their behavior, compare their behavior with the standard, and attempt to reduce discrepancies between their behavior and the standard (e.g., G. A. Miller, Galanter, & Pribram, 1960; Powers, 1973; Scheier & Carver, 1988). People are thus regarded as setting goals and adjusting their current behavior in order to match these goals. Informational feedback from one's behavior serves as a guide to one's progress in reaching goals.

Although the theories of planning that emphasize goal setting and feedback control have not been formulated as attitudinal models, the goals these theorists emphasize can be translated into attitudinal terms. Thus, for an attitude theorist, goals are end states or outcomes toward which people hold positive attitudes. For example, a graduate student who desires to finish a term paper has a positive attitude toward this outcome, which leads him to have a positive attitude toward instrumental acts that he believes help him progress toward the goal.

Despite the general compatibility of theories of goal-oriented behavior and attitude-behavior models, different antecedents of behavior have been elaborated in the two approaches. Missing from attitude-behavior theories but present in most theories of behavioral self-regulation is the idea that goals are ordered in a hierarchy. At higher levels of such a hierarchy individuals may have very general goals (e.g., having a successful career), which are in turn related to less general goals (e.g., obtaining a Ph.D.). These less general goals are in turn related to more specific goals (e.g., successfully completing the first-year graduate curriculum), which are related to even more specific goals, sometimes in an elaborate hierarchy (e.g., earning an "A" in first-year statistics, which is related to studying for the upcoming exam, etc.). According to this general type of approach, plans often take the form of complex hierarchical structures.

As Vallacher and Wegner have shown, the type of goal that is salient (or *prepotent*) in relation to a particular action varies considerably, depending on the situational context and other factors (see Vallacher & Wegner, 1985, 1987; Wegner & Vallacher, 1986). Consider a graduate student who is solving a statistics problem for a particular assignment in a first-year statistics course. At a given moment, she may construe or identify her action concretely in terms of solving the problem or somewhat less concretely in terms of preparing for an impending exam. At a higher level of abstraction, she might identify her action as part of her effort to obtain a good grade in the course or even as part of her effort to obtain the Ph.D. or have a successful career in psychology.

This attention to the varying ways that people construe their behavior, which Vallacher and Wegner termed *action identities*, is consequential in relation to one of the issues neglected by the theories of the attitude-behavior relation that we have reviewed—namely, the level of abstraction at which people formulate their intentions and actions. Vallacher and Wegner (e.g., 1985, 1987) have proposed that people carry out actions in relation to whatever action identity is prepotent. They also maintained that people formulate this identity at higher levels of abstraction, provided that a higher level still allows for successful performance of the action. When people encounter difficulties in carrying out an action identified at a relatively high level, they are thought to revert to a lower level of abstraction. For example, a graduate student who identifies his current activities as part of reviewing for a statistics exam might become stuck on a particular problem and, as a consequence, he might at least temporarily reformulate his action identity in terms of solving this problem. These propositions, which have been tested in Vallacher and Wegner's research program, provide some useful insights into the level of abstraction of the attitudes and intentions that regulate behavior.

To the extent that people formulate their intentions at the level of broader goals, their individual goal-oriented behaviors are understood only incompletely in terms of the theory of reasoned action and related models. Such models do not represent behaviors as linked to one another in hierarchies that are structured in terms of more abstract intentions to reach goals (e.g., an intention to have a successful career). Research on goal-oriented behavior thus contributes to a view of attitudes toward behaviors as but one determinant of behavior—a determinant that becomes especially important for behaviors that are (a) volitional, (b) easily executed because they require few resources or skills, (c) not normatively regulated, and (d) not habitual.

What about Attitudes Toward Targets?

The theoretical innovations proposed by Ajzen and his colleagues, by Warshaw and Bagozzi, and by the planning theorists attempt to deal with at least some of the complexities that are not adequately resolved by Fishbein and Ajzen's (1975) view that the proximal causes of behavior can be understood in terms of attitudes toward behaviors, subjective norms, and intentions. Although these newer theories are substantially different from the reasoned action model, none of them considers in much depth the sense in which behavior may be caused by attitudes toward targets (i.e., by attitudes toward the entities to which behaviors are directed; see the earlier discussion of compatibility). Consequently, the social and political attitudes traditionally studied by social scientists have not been given any attention in this research. Because an important early impetus for studying attitudes was the belief that such attitudes do determine behaviors, we turn now to an explicit consideration of the impact that attitudes toward targets have on behavior.

Predicting Behavior from Attitudes Toward Targets

Many investigators have maintained the traditional approach of predicting behavior from attitudes toward targets (e.g., Fazio, 1989; Fazio & Zanna, 1981; Millar & Tesser, 1986a). Moreover, by most frequently using few rather than many acts to index behavior, they have chosen to forego maximizing their chances of producing high attitude-behavior correlations by following the compatibility rule. These investigators have thus continued to focus on the *general-to-specific* problem of correlating general attitudes with specific behavioral criteria. Although attitude-behavior relations are ordinarily weak under such circumstances, they are quite inconsistent in magnitude, as suggested by Fishbein and Ajzen's (1974) analysis. A desire to explain this variability is no doubt part of the implicit rationale for continuing to investigate the prediction of specific behaviors from general attitudes. Also, many social psychologists believe that, despite the possibility that attitudes toward behaviors influence behavior, attitudes toward targets nonetheless play the directive and dynamic role that Allport (1935) ascribed to them.

Consistent with our earlier argument that people do not take into account the effects that nonattitudinal variables (e.g., anticipated situational constraints) have on their behavior when they form attitudes toward targets, nonattitudinal variables generally remain substantial predictors of behavior when attitudes toward targets are used as predictors. Nonetheless, the importance of nonattitudinal variables should vary widely across behaviors and social settings, and this variation would produce inconsistency in correlations between behaviors and attitudes toward targets. Although the trade-offs between these attitudes and a large number of nonattitudinal variables would be difficult to track, scores of nonattitudinal variables should affect the magnitude of attitude-behavior relations. In other words, many nonattitudinal variables should *moderate* the attitude-behavior relation when attitudes toward targets are investigated.

Consistent with our logic, investigators of attitudes toward targets have identified numerous variables that influence attitude-behavior correlations. For example, Sivacek and Crano (1982) showed that the behavior of individuals who do not have a vested interest in an issue is less predictable from their attitude than the behavior of individuals who have a vested interest. Various personality variables, including level of moral reasoning (Rholes & Bailey, 1983) and having a *doer* self-concept (L. Z. McArthur, Kiesler, & Cook, 1969), have been shown to influence the magnitude of attitude-behavior relations. Because many of these moderating variables do not readily fit into any larger theoretical structure pertaining to attitudes and behaviors, such findings are not easily summarized and are not covered in this chapter (see reviews by Ajzen, 1988; Canary & Siebold, 1984; Ehrlich, 1969; Wicker, 1969; Zanna & Fazio, 1982). More critical in terms of the theoretical framework we have developed in this book are proposals that attitude-behavior correspondence is affected by the nature of the attitude and by the implications that the attitude is perceived to have for the behavior that is assessed. Therefore, we consider attitude-behavior findings that can be interpreted in terms of such factors. As we introduce these factors, we temporarily suspend consideration of whether attitudes toward targets have a causal role in relation to behavior—in other words, exert the directive and dynamic influence that Allport (1935) ascribed to them.

Past Behavioral Experience with the Attitude Object
As a Determinant of Attitude-Behavior Consistency

Research on past behavioral experience with the attitude object raises particularly interesting questions about how the nature of attitudes affects the size of observed correlations between attitudes and behavior. In terms of the tripartite analysis we presented in Chapter 1, behavior provides one of three types of information on which an attitude may be based. Research on direct experience raises the question of whether the information provided by one's own behavior has a distinctive impact on the attitude-behavior relation.

Typical studies in this area have shown that the attitudes of people who have had direct experience with an attitude object (i.e., with the target) correlate moderately with subsequent attitude-relevant behaviors, whereas the attitudes of people who lack direct experience correlate very weakly.[9] For example, Regan and Fazio (1977) presented subjects with five types of intellectual puzzles. The manner in which subjects formed their attitudes was manipulated by giving some subjects direct experience in working an example of each type of puzzle and giving other subjects indirect experience by only allowing them to examine previously solved examples of each type of puzzle. Subjects' ratings of each puzzle type's "interest value" served as a measure of their attitudes. Behavior was then observed in a 15-minute free play situation during which the subjects could work on any of the puzzles. The extent to which subjects played with each type of puzzle was assessed. As expected, attitude-behavior correlations were larger among direct experience subjects than among indirect experience subjects.

A conceptually similar demonstration in a field setting showed that the attitudes of students who had direct experience with a campus housing shortage (by being forced to live in temporary quarters) predicted relevant behaviors (e.g., signing a petition asking the administration to take action to alleviate the shortage) better than did the attitudes of students who had not had this direct experience (Regan & Fazio, 1977). In yet another study, students' attitudes toward participating in psychological experiments were related to their willingness to commit themselves to joining a "subject pool" (Fazio & Zanna, 1978a). This attitude-behavior correlation was larger for students who had prior experience participating in psychological experiments. In summary, in these less controlled field studies as well as laboratory experiments (see review by Fazio &

Zanna, 1981), the tendency appears robust for attitude-behavior correlations to be larger for attitudes based on behavioral experience with the attitude object than for attitudes not based on such experience (see Schlegel & DiTecco, 1982, for an exception).

Explanations for the Effect of Direct Experience on Attitude-Behavior Consistency

Clarity, Confidence, and Certainty. Russell Fazio, Mark Zanna, and their colleagues initially maintained that the impact of direct experience on attitude-behavior relations is explained by differences in the nature of attitudes that are based on direct rather than indirect experience (see Fazio & Zanna, 1981). Attitudes based on direct experience, they suggested, have greater clarity and are held with more confidence and certainty than attitudes based on indirect experience. Although these researchers operationalized clarity in terms of the width of the latitude of rejection (see Chapter 3), they did not coordinate confidence and certainty with structural properties of attitudes (instead, subjects' self-reports of their confidence or certainty served as measures of these variables). Consistent with the idea that these aspects of attitudes, which were dubbed *attitudinal qualities* by Fazio and Zanna, mediate the relation between direct experience and attitude-behavior correspondence, studies found that clarity, confidence, and certainty correlated significantly with extent of direct experience (e.g., Fazio & Zanna, 1978a, 1978b) and that attitude-behavior correspondence could be increased by bolstering subjects' confidence in their attitudes (Fazio & Zanna, 1978b). These attitudinal qualities and others (e.g., centrality, involvement, extremity) have been conceptualized either as equivalent to attitude strength or as measures of a latent construct commonly known as attitude strength (see Raden, 1985). Thus, these findings might be interpreted as indicating that stronger attitudes are more highly correlated with behavior.

Accessibility and Strength. As Fazio, Zanna, and their colleagues developed their research, they came to believe that the underlying reason why attitudes based on direct experience are more predictive of behavior is that they are more accessible from memory. According to this explanation, attitudes based on direct experience are more easily retrieved from memory than those not based on direct experience (see Fazio, Chen, McDonel, & Sherman, 1982). More specifically, the speed with which attitudes are accessed, which provides an index of *accessibility*, is regarded as consequential in relation to attitude-relevant behavior. Attitudes that are more accessible (i.e., activated quickly) are presumed to be more powerful determinants of behavior than attitudes that are less accessible (i.e., activated more slowly) because they are more likely to be activated upon exposure to the attitude object or other relevant cues.

Fazio and his colleagues have often operationalized accessibility by measuring subjects' speed of retrieving their attitudes in response to direct inquiries about their attitudes. The rationale for this operationalization is that people should be quicker to respond evaluatively to attitude-relevant cues to the extent that their attitudes are highly accessible. This idea follows from an underlying associative learning model whereby attitude is regarded as an association between the attitude object and an evaluation (see Chapters 1 and 3). Using this model, Fazio gave more precise meaning to the term *attitude strength* by conceptualizing this construct as the associative strength of the link between an attitude object and its evaluation. To the extent that this object-evaluation association is strong, the evaluation is accessed easily and quickly in response to cues conveyed by the attitude object. Associative strength is thus the underlying structural characteristic of attitudes that determines accessibility, according to Fazio. Although various measures of attitude strength (e.g., self-reported confidence, width of the latitude of rejection, attitudinal stability) might also serve to operationalize accessibility, Fazio has favored the response latency operationalization, presumably because it most closely approximates his conceptual definition of attitude strength and the idea that this construct is the antecedent of accessibility.

According to this line of reasoning, attitudinal qualities (e.g., confidence, certainty, clarity and stability) happen to be correlated with attitude strength and therefore with accessibility. These variables therefore moderate the attitude-behavior relation only because of their relation to associative strength and to its consequence, accessibility. However reasonable this claim, there is little information available concerning the relation between such characteristics and the response time measure that serves as an index of accessibility. Yet Fazio, Herr, and Olney (1984) reported a correlation of .38 ($p < .01$) between speed of response and a variable that has been interpreted as a measure of attitudinal strength—the width of the latitude of rejection, and Krosnick (1989) reported somewhat lower correlations between speed and self-reports of attitudes' importance. Indeed, such low-to-moderate correlations between presumed indicators of attitude strength are typical of attitudinal data (see Krosnick, Boninger, Chuang, & Carnot, 1991; Raden, 1985). Correlations of this magnitude suggest that the effects of attitudinal qualities on attitude-behavior correspondence may not be completely explained by their relation to accessibility. Moreover, such findings raise questions about the assumption that there is a unitary property of attitude strength that completely accounts for the ability of various aspects of attitudes to moderate the attitude-behavior relation.

Fazio has marshaled a variety of evidence for his proposal that associative strength increases accessibility and that accessibility mediates the impact of direct experience on the magnitude of attitude-behavior correlations. People whose attitudes are based on direct experience respond to inquiries about their attitudes with shorter latencies than do people whose attitudes are based on direct experience (e.g., Fazio, Chen, McDonel, & Sherman, 1982). In additional research, Fazio and his colleagues reasoned that the strength of the object-evaluation association could be manipulated directly by having subjects repeatedly express their attitudes (e.g., Fazio, Chen, McDonel, & Sherman, 1982; Powell & Fazio, 1984). Subjects whose attitudes had been (vs. had not been) strengthened in this way responded more quickly to attitudinal inquiries and behaved more consistently with their attitudes. Also, a field study that predicted voting from attitudes toward presidential candidates provided correlational evidence of the link between response latency and attitude-behavior correspondence (Fazio & Williams,

1986). In this study, naturally occurring individual differences in the speed of response to attitudinal inquiries were related to the correlation between attitudes and voting: In general, people who responded quickly when evaluating the presidential candidates voted somewhat more consistently with their attitudes than people who responded slowly.

These studies showed that direct experience and repeated expression, both of which were assumed to increase the associative strength of attitudes, were related to the speed of responding to direct inquiries about one's attitude. However, this research did not establish that manipulations of these variables increase the likelihood that attitudes are *spontaneously* activated in the presence of cues associated with the attitude object. In daily life, attitudes would very often be spontaneously activated and relatively rarely be activated in response to direct questions about one's attitude. To explore the spontaneous activation of attitudes, Fazio, Powell, and Herr (1983), again using the puzzle paradigm, first increased experimental subjects' associative strength by having them either repeatedly express their attitudes or by giving them direct experience with the puzzles. Control subjects' attitudes were not strengthened in this way. Afterward, subjects participated in an ostensibly unrelated experiment in which their attitude toward one of the puzzles (either their most or least favorite) was primed (i.e., activated) by presenting the relevant puzzle within a series of drawings. As predicted, for subjects whose attitude had been strengthened but not for control subjects, this priming manipulation influenced their subsequent evaluative rating of an ambiguous stimulus (a description of some actions by a previous subject) in the direction of the valence of their attitude toward the puzzle that had been used as a prime. In other words, for the strong attitude subjects, if a positive attitude had been primed, the ambiguous stimulus was rated more favorably than it was if a negative attitude had been primed. These findings were interpreted by Fazio and his colleagues in terms of the general principle that activating a category increases its temporary accessibility and thereby enhances the likelihood that the category is used in subsequent judgments (e.g., Higgins, 1989a; Higgins, Rholes, & Jones, 1977; Wyer & Srull, 1981).

In summary, attitudes that are repeatedly expressed or based on direct experience have a greater influence on judgment and behavior because such attitudes are presumed to have the underlying property of increased strength. Stronger attitudes are more accessible, and this greater accessibility increases the likelihood that they will be activated spontaneously in the presence of cues related to the attitude object. Once a positive or negative evaluation is activated, other judgments are assimilated to this salient evaluative category. Alternatively (and less consistent with Fazio's reasoning), both strong and weak attitudes might be activated spontaneously, but the stronger attitudes might have more impact on other judgments because of related properties of such attitudes (e.g., greater confidence and stability or lesser ambivalence).

Automatic Activation of Attitudes. Fazio (e.g., 1986) has further maintained that attitudes that are highly accessible will be automatically activated in the presence of the attitude object, that is, without any conscious, intentional cognitive processing (see Bargh, 1982, 1984, 1989; Higgins & Bargh, 1987). To demonstrate automaticity,

Fazio, Sanbonmatsu, Powell, and Kardes (1986) first either (a) selected each subject's four fastest and four slowest favorable and unfavorable attitudes, based on a preliminary task that had assessed subjects' response times in relation to various attitude objects (Experiments 1 and 2) or (b) varied the number of times subjects expressed their attitudes (Experiment 3). Both the selection of attitudes by subjects' response times and the manipulation of repeated expression presumably indexed the strength of the object-evaluation association. In a subsequent task, each attitude object (e.g., the word music, guns) was briefly presented to subjects as a prime just before they judged an evaluative adjective (e.g., appealing, repulsive) by indicating whether the adjective was *good* or *bad* in meaning. Response times for these evaluative judgments of the adjectives served as the primary dependent measure.

The logic of this design is that presentation of the attitude object as a prime activated the evaluation associated with the attitude object, and this activated evaluation then influenced the speed with which subjects could classify the target adjective as positive or negative. If the activated attitude is of the same valence as the adjective, response time should be faster. In contrast, if the activated attitude is of the opposite valence as the attitude, response time should be slower because the activated attitude would interfere with the correct response to the adjective. In Fazio et al.'s (1986) experiment, priming subjects with attitude objects for which their attitudes matched the evaluative valence of the target adjective facilitated response times with respect to the judgments, but mainly for subjects who could be assumed to have a strong object-evaluation association (because of their fast response time on the preliminary task or their prior repeated expression of their attitude).

Because this priming effect occurred when the interval between the attitude object prime and target adjective presentations was short (0.3 second) but not when it was longer (1 second), Fazio and his associates concluded that, for the subjects with strong object-evaluation associations, attitude activation had occurred automatically. The rationale for this conclusion is that people require a longer time interval (perhaps 0.7 second) to develop a more conscious expectancy or response strategy. Thus, if the attitude activation process were controlled, allowing subjects more time to retrieve their attitudes should have enhanced the strength of the priming effect. In contrast, if the process were automatic, allowing subjects more time should not have this impact. In summary, the research program carried out by Fazio and his associates has suggested that (a) the effects of direct experience on attitude-behavior correspondence are to some extent mediated by the greater accessibility of attitudes based on direct experience, (b) more accessible attitudes are more likely to influence behavior, and (c) stronger attitudes are accessed spontaneously and automatically upon mere presentation of cues related to the attitude object.

Generality of the Automaticity Effect. Research by Bargh, Chaiken, Govender, and Pratto (1992) has called into question Fazio and associates' (1986) claim that upon mere observation of an attitude object, one's attitude is activated automatically to the extent that it is highly accessible. In the study by Bargh and colleagues that replicated Fazio's automaticity paradigm, the majority of subjects' attitudes produced the automatic activation effect, not just attitudes that were highly accessible. In other studies in this series of experiments, certain theory-irrelevant features of the Fazio group's experimental paradigm were deleted. For example, in Fazio's experiments the priming task, which assessed automatic activation, occurred immediately after subjects had indicated their attitudes toward the priming stimuli. When Bargh and associates placed a two-day delay between these tasks, even subjects' weakest attitudes produced the automatic activation effect. In general, Bargh and colleagues showed that the automatic activation effect was very general and held across a very wide range of attitude objects. Indeed, their findings suggested that virtually *all* attitudes may be capable of being automatically activated, not just strong ones.

Other Explanations for the Effects of Direct Experience and Repeated Expression

Manipulations of direct experience and repeated expression may operate at least partially through aspects of attitudes (e.g., increased stability, extremity) that are not wholly a function of accessibility, although they may be correlated with it. Indeed, prior to their focus on associative strength and accessibility, Fazio and Zanna (1981) themselves argued that the effect of direct experience on attitude-behavior correspondence may be a product of factors such as certainty (see prior discussion) as well as attitude stability and amount of knowledge. Consistent with this general argument, direct experience and repeated expression subjects might be more confident or certain of the positions that they give in response to the attitude instrument, or their attitudes might be more stable or less ambivalent. Moreover, the Fazio group's individual difference measure of accessibility, response latency, may also covary with these other indicators of strong attitudes. Indeed, Bargh and colleagues (1992) found a number of such variables to be correlated with the latency of subjects' responses to attitudinal inquiries—specifically, responses were faster to the extent that attitudes were more extreme, more consistent over time, less ambivalent, and more polarized (i.e., either positive or negative evaluation predominated).

Attitude Stability as a Mediator of Direct Experience Effects. Ajzen and Fishbein (1980) argued that attitudes based on indirect experience may predict behavior poorly because they are easily changed. The idea that such attitudes may be less stable has an inherent plausibility. In particular, changes might occur when a person whose attitude is based only on indirect experience finally encounters the attitude object—for example, a person who has only read about Los Angeles might visit the city on a smoggy day in August and breathe the air. The behavioral information gained through such direct experience might change the attitude and therefore weaken correlations between the *prior attitude* and subsequent behavior (i.e., because the contemporaneous attitude, not the prior attitude, controls current behavior). In the laboratory studies we have cited, the attitudes subjects formed on the basis of indirect experience might have changed when they finally confronted the attitude object (see Steffen, 1986). For example, in the puzzle paradigm of Regan and Fazio (1977), indirect experience subjects may have changed their attitudes when they first played with the puzzles during the 15-minute free play period. Direct experience subjects should have been less affected by information obtained during the free play period because the feedback they would have obtained from their own behavior would largely have duplicated the feedback they had already gained during their prior opportunity to play with the puzzles. Although the behavior of direct and indirect experience subjects might have been equally predictable from their contemporaneous attitudes, which are not assessed in this research, subjects' prior attitudes, which were assessed, would have predicted more poorly for the indirect experience subjects because their attitudes would have changed when they finally were allowed to engage in the behavior.[10]

This idea that direct experience's effects on the attitude-behavior relation may be mediated by attitude stability was confirmed in research by Doll and Ajzen (in press) using a video game paradigm similar to Regan and Fazio's (1977) puzzle paradigm. These investigators showed that direct experience increased the temporal stability of attitudes as assessed by within-subjects correlations between the attitudes that were assessed before and after the free play period. Although Doll and Ajzen's finding that direct experience also lowered the latency of attitudinal responses is consistent with Fazio's emphasis on accessibility, correlational evidence in this research suggested that attitude stability was the primary mediator of the effects of direct experience.

Possible Mediators of the Effects of Repeated Expression. The possibility that the effects of repeated expression manipulations are not exclusively mediated by attitude accessibility also warrants examination. Repeated expression of one's attitude could readily affect the accessibility of one's *beliefs*. Alternatively, thinking about the attitude object while repeatedly expressing one's attitude could cause one's beliefs to become more evaluatively consistent with one another and with one's attitude (Tesser, 1978; see Chapter 12). These temporary differences in attitude structure may be at least partially responsible for the effects of the repeated expression manipulation on attitude-behavior correspondence. Also, Downing, Judd, and Brauer (1992) have shown that repeated expression of an attitude induces greater extremity of the attitude as well as greater accessibility (i.e., shorter response latency).

Prior Knowledge About the Attitude Object as a Determinant of Attitude-Behavior Consistency

Because, as Fazio and Zanna (1981) suggested, direct experience may convey greater information about attitude objects than indirect experience, it is relevant to mention research showing that the amount of stored information or knowledge that is available and accessible to people moderates attitude-behavior correspondence. In an experiment on attitudes toward preservation of the environment, Kallgren and Wood (1986) assessed subjects' prior knowledge about this attitude object by asking them to recall and write down their beliefs and behavioral experiences related to preservation (see Chapter 7 for further discussion of prior knowledge). Two weeks later, these subjects were contacted at home and asked to sign and circulate proenvironment petitions and to participate in a recycling project. Subjects who had written down many beliefs and behaviors behaved more consistently with their attitudes than subjects who had written down fewer beliefs and behaviors (see also Davidson, Yantis, Norwood, & Montano, 1985).

The mechanisms by which amount of information affects the correspondence between attitudes and behaviors are not yet understood. A possibility consistent with our preceding discussion is that differences in the stability of attitudes based on much (vs. little) information are critical. The less information possessed by an individual, the greater the change induced by any new piece of information; in other words, the attitude is more unstable. Because behavior is presumably under the control of the attitudes held at the time of the decision to behave, unstable attitudes are less predictive of later behavior. Of course, attitude accessibility also provides a possible explanation of the effects of amount of information (e.g., Fazio, 1986). Perhaps attitudes backed by more information are more readily accessed from memory, and, as Fazio and his associates have shown, more accessible attitudes are more highly correlated with behavior. Indeed, Kallgren and Wood (1986) framed their study in terms of accessibility.

Summary of Research on Potential Mediators of Attitude-Behavior Correspondence

The relation between attitudes toward targets and attitude-relevant behaviors is affected by a number of variables. In particular, the finding that past behavioral experience with an attitude object increases the correspondence between the attitude and behaviors proved to be especially provocative to researchers because it raised questions of why such attitudes should be more predictive of behavior. The tendency for behavioral experience to enhance several aspects of attitudes (i.e., clarity, confidence, certainty) enjoys empirical support, and there is some evidence that such attitudinal qualities moderate the attitude-behavior relation. Although it is possible that such qualities have this impact merely because they are correlates of attitude accessibility or its immediate antecedent, associative strength, other possibilities deserve consideration. As recent research has shown, accessibility, as assessed by response latency, is correlated with several other indicators of attitude strength (Bargh et al., 1992; Doll & Ajzen, in press; Downing et al., 1992). The consistency between attitudes and behaviors is also increased by prior knowledge about attitude objects, another factor that may be increased by direct experience. It is thus clear that the relations between these potential mediators and moderators of attitude-behavior correspondence need to be elucidated.

More generally, the importance that attitude-behavior research has accorded to the behavioral bases of attitudes as well as to their cognitive bases is important in terms of our tripartite analysis of attitudes, which suggests that attitudes may be grounded in behavioral experience, affective experience, and beliefs acquired from informational sources (see Chapter 1). Given the synergistic relation that we presume exists between these three classes of attitudinal experience, it is likely that an increase in one of these types of evaluative input causes the other types to increase as well. For example, while interacting behaviorally with an attitude object, one gains information about its attributes and may experience various emotions as well. As a consequence, a high level of one type of input should be correlated with high levels of the other types of input. From this perspective, one way of summarizing the research we have reviewed on the attitudinal characteristics that moderate the attitude-behavior relation is the following: Attitudes that are based on *more* input are likely to relate more strongly to attitude-relevant behaviors, whether this input is behavioral or cognitive. Thus, research on behavioral experience has shown that increased behavioral input enhances attitude-behavior correspondence, and research on prior knowledge has suggested that increased cognitive input has the same impact. Unfortunately, research on affective experience is lacking, but increased input from this source may similarly increase attitude-behavior correspondence.

The Processes by Which
Attitudes Toward Targets Affect Behavior

To return to an explicit consideration of the causal issues we addressed earlier in this chapter, we once again note that neither the theory of reasoned action nor related causal models treated attitudes toward targets as antecedents of behavior (except as one type of external variable). Yet attitudes toward targets were the predictors of behavior in virtually all of the research we have reviewed on direct experience and attitude accessibility.

To explore the causal relation between attitudes toward targets and behavior, Fazio has proposed a framework that describes some of the processes that may mediate the attitude-behavior relation (Fazio, 1986, 1989, 1990a; Fazio et al., 1983). This approach, which Fazio viewed as a spontaneous- or automatic-processing model, is summarized in Figure 4.5. In this model, the attitude-to-behavior sequence is initiated when an attitude toward a target is accessed from memory by the presentation of cues

FIGURE 4.5. A representation of Fazio's model of the effect of attitudes on behavior. This figure was presented by Fazio (1986, Figure 8.1, p. 212).

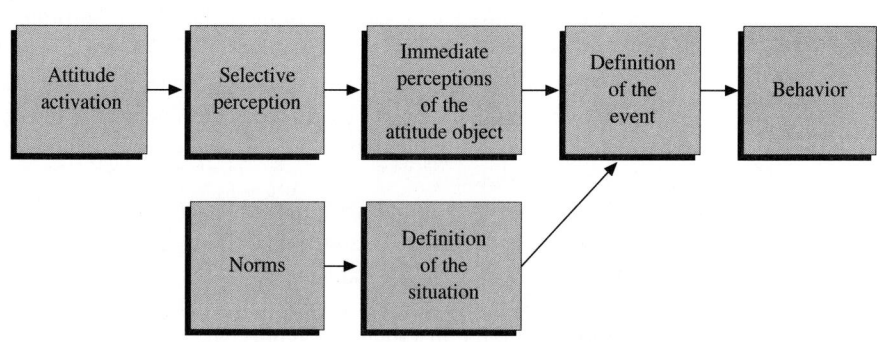

related to this attitude object. Consistent with the research by Fazio and his associates that we have already reviewed, this activation process is assumed to be automatic in the sense that it is relatively effortless and not mediated by active attention or conscious thought. This automatic activation is presumed to ensue to the extent that there is a strong association between the attitude object and the person's evaluation of the attitude object. If the object-evaluation association is weak, the automatic attitude-to-behavior sequence is assumed not to occur (see Fazio, 1986, p. 238). Although a weak attitude might be retrieved by a more effortful, reflective process, Fazio maintained that with such attitudes, behavior is often controlled by features of the attitude object that happen to be salient (see Fazio, Powell, & Williams, 1989).

After a strong attitude is accessed automatically, it is assumed to exert a selective effect on one's perception of the attitude object. Selectivity in this context implies that the qualities of the attitude object are perceived as congruent with one's attitude, possibly by means of considerable distortion of reality. Given activation of a favorable attitude, positive qualities are ascribed to the attitude object, whereas, given activation of an unfavorable attitude, negative qualities are ascribed to the attitude object. These perceptions of the attitude object "comprise at least part of the individual's definition of the event" (Fazio, 1986, p. 213). Parallel to Fishbein and Ajzen's (1975) emphasis on subjective norms, normative factors may also affect the definition of the event in Fazio's approach. The definition of the event is then held to determine behavior.

Fazio's research has addressed the selective perception step of his model. Indeed, as a general proposition, the idea that attitudes often have selective effects on perception, learning, and memory is probably true (see Chapter 12). However, Fazio's claim is more specific—namely, that attitudes have this selective effect only to the extent that they are highly accessible. To support this proposition, Fazio and Williams (1986) assessed the speed of respondents' answers to attitudinal inquiries about presidential candidate Reagan. This latency measure predicted the magnitude of the correlation between their attitude toward Reagan and the evaluative implications of their beliefs about his performance in the televised presidential debates: Respondents with shorter latencies showed a stronger relation between their attitudes and their beliefs. To provide additional evidence of the mediating role of accessibility on the attitude-belief relation, Houston and Fazio (1989) examined subjects' perceptions of articles on capital punishment in two studies. In the first study the speed of subjects' response to an inquiry about their capital punishment attitudes served as the measure of accessibility, and in the second study accessibility was manipulated by having some subjects express their attitude toward capital punishment five times and others express it once. Results showed that subjects with shorter response latencies (first study) or who had repeatedly expressed their attitudes (second study) judged the articles in a manner that was more congruent with their attitudes. Although these findings are consistent with Fazio's claim that attitudes exert a selective effect on perceptions to the extent that they are accessible, as we noted earlier, other factors that covary with response time or are influenced by repeatedly expressing one's attitude may also have contributed to these effects.

Fazio's model (e.g., 1986, 1989, 1990a) becomes less definite as it progresses toward behavior. Attitude-consistent beliefs presumably join with perceived social norms to determine the definition of the event. As we indicated earlier in this chapter, the importance of the normative regulation of behavior has been demonstrated in research conducted within the reasoned action tradition. However, according to the reasoned action model, attitudes (toward behaviors) and norms then impact on intention, which is the proximal determinant of behavior. In contrast, Fazio has argued that attitudes toward targets (acting via selective perception) and norms (acting via definition of the situation) impact not on intention but on the definition of the event. Fazio thus maintained that "once activated, the attitude biases perceptions of the object in the immediate situation, and behavior *simply follows* [italics added] from these perceptions without any necessary conscious reasoning process" (Fazio, 1986, p. 237). The definition of the event, the process presumably involved in simply following, has not been given a conceptual definition independent of the two prior processes and thus was defined as "perceptions that involve both the attitude object and the situation in which the object is encountered" (Fazio, 1986, p. 208). Moreover, the assumption that defining the event is the proximal determinant of behavior leaves unanswered many questions about the role of attitudes toward behaviors, behavioral intentions, habits, scripts, plans, and other factors as possible proximal determinants of behavior. The definition of the event merely provides a label for a set of not necessarily simple processes that link one's evaluation of and beliefs about an attitude object to one's behavior. A large gap remains between (a) mental events pertaining to attitudes and beliefs and (b) overt behaviors.

Although Fazio (1986) has described his model as an alternative to the theory of reasoned action and related models, the lack of elaboration of the proximal determinants of behavior in Fazio's framework suggests that it is inappropriate to regard the two approaches as alternatives. Because the Fazio model elaborates some of the more distal determinants of behavior, it should be regarded as a very useful *supplement* to the reasoned action model and other approaches that consider attitudes toward behaviors. Fazio has thus described the processes that may occur *prior to* the processes described in the models that focus on attitudes toward behaviors. In other words, the models that are based on attitudes toward behaviors provide descriptions of attitude-behavior processes that may intervene at the point when Fazio's model ceases to provide a description—namely, at the point when the definition-of-the-event label appears. We encourage readers to think about the models we presented earlier in the chapter as located within Fazio's definition of the event (except for these models' normative determinants of action, which parallel Fazio's treatment of norms as a separate determinant of the definition of the event).

In casting his approach as an alternative rather than a supplement to the theory of reasoned action, Fazio (1986) essentially miscasts the Fishbein-Ajzen approach as assuming that an individual "considers the attitude in a deliberate reasoning process to arrive at a behavioral decision" (p. 237). As we explained earlier in this chapter, Ajzen and Fishbein (1980) assumed merely that the attitude was initially formed on the basis of deliberative reasoning (i.e., the attitude toward the behavior was formed by thinking of the consequences of the behavior). In contrast to Fazio's interpretation of the theory of reasoned action, Fishbein and Ajzen did *not* presume that people necessarily think

204

about these consequences at each behavioral opportunity and recompute their attitudes on the spot. Yet, according to the reasoned action model, a thought of some sort must be formed or retrieved to activate behavior. At a minimum, an intention must become salient to direct behavior. Because intentions are presumably relatively conscious decisions to act, the Fishbein-Ajzen model does in this very limited sense assume a relatively conscious and deliberative process. However, more automatic processes not involving intention (but involving habit or a direct attitude-behavior link) have been introduced in expanded models proposed within the reasoned action tradition (e.g., Bentler & Speckart, 1979). Such models do allow behavior to occur in the absence of a consciously controlled reasoning process.

If readers will for the moment regard Fazio as having elaborated some of the distal determinants of behavior and Fishbein and Ajzen as having elaborated some of the proximal determinants of behavior, the compatibility of the spontaneous processing model and the theory of reasoned action is easily understood. Thus, Fazio's research has dealt with attitudes toward targets, which are distal or external to the attitudes toward behaviors that enter into the theory of reasoned action and related models. In the spirit of Fishbein and Ajzen's (e.g., 1975) external variable argument, attitudes toward targets as well as the selectively perceived attributes of these targets would affect behavior through their impact on attitudes toward behaviors (or, possibly, on subjective norms). For example, spontaneous activation of a person's negative attitude toward Michael Dukakis upon seeing his image at the beginning of a televised speech in 1988 might have induced the possibly selective but certainly congruent perception that he had not been an outstanding governor of Massachusetts. This perception could then have induced the person to conclude that four years of weak leadership would be an outcome of electing Dukakis. His attitude toward personally voting for Dukakis would then become more negative because he would believe that his vote would increase the likelihood of this negative outcome. Following this sequence of attitude-toward-target→behavioral-beliefs→attitude-toward-behavior→behavioral-intention, he would then intend to vote against Dukakis (or for Bush), and this intention would be the immediate determinant of his action. Except for his consideration of selective perception, Fazio's framework is silent concerning the links between activated attitudes toward targets and the processes that are the more proximal determinants of behavior.

In agreement with Fazio, we do find it plausible that the processes by which attitudes toward targets affect behavior are often triggered by the automatic activation of these attitudes and sometimes by a more effortful activation. In the presence of cues associated with an attitude object, one's attitude toward the target probably does come to mind *before* attitudes toward the behaviors in which one might engage in relation to that target. However, much more controversial is Fazio's (1986) proposition that with highly accessible attitudes the *entire* attitude-to-behavior process is likely to be relatively spontaneous or automatic. Instead, we suggest that whether activation of an attitude toward the target is quicker or slower or whether it occurs by a controlled or automatic process does not have any necessary implications for the controlled versus automatic nature of the processes that occur *subsequent* to this activation. If quickly accessed attitudes have different implications for later processes than more slowly accessed attitudes do, we suspect that these differences are due, not to accessibility, *per se*, but to differences in the structural properties of attitudes that are quickly or more slowly accessed. For example, more accessible attitudes may be accompanied by a more evaluatively consistent belief structure, which may provide a clearer guide for attitude-relevant behavior.

In a more recent statement that approximates our own view somewhat more closely, Fazio (1990a) acknowledged that an automatically activated attitude toward a target could elicit an attitude-to-behavior process that involves a consciously controlled, active search for the most strategically appropriate behavior. In addition, recognizing Ajzen and Fishbein's (1980) disclaimers, he retreated from his earlier description of the theory of reasoned action as necessarily presuming that deliberative thinking about the consequences of behavior precedes every behavioral act. He no longer regarded his own spontaneous processing model and the theory of reasoned action as clear alternatives, with the implication that the entire attitude-to-behavior process is either spontaneous or deliberative. Instead, he outlined a more interesting set of possibilities whereby more automatic and more deliberative processes might be intertwined. In particular, following the logic of the dual-process models of persuasion that we consider in Chapter 7 (Chaiken, Liberman, & Eagly, 1989; Petty & Cacioppo, 1986a, 1986b), Fazio argued that more deliberative processes, involving thoughtful analysis of the perceived consequences of behavioral alternatives, would likely occur only to the extent that people have the motivation to engage in such processes and the relevant opportunity or ability. Lacking motivation or opportunity, people may rely on more global attitudes that they retrieve from memory. Indeed, Sanbonmatsu and Fazio (1990) provided a demonstration of the impact of motivation and opportunity on the processes that mediate attitudes' influence on consumer decision making.

In summary, there remains uncertainty about the psychological processes that account for the influence that attitudes toward targets have on behaviors. The speed with which people respond to attitudinal inquiries moderates attitude-behavior relations in the sense that attitudes that are accessed more quickly are more highly correlated with behavior. However, it is critical to understand the structural properties of attitudes that may be correlated with accessibility and that may be at least partially responsible for its enhancement of attitude-behavior correlations (and attitude-belief correlations). Moreover, as we have suggested, possibilities abound for linking the attitude-toward-target problem with models that have specified some of the more proximal determinants of behavior.

Research on the Perceived Relevance
of Attitudes to Behavior

Research by Mark Snyder and his associates helps bridge the large gap in our knowledge about the processes that intervene between the activation of attitudes toward targets and the elicitation of attitude-relevant behavior. Snyder (1982) proposed a *relevance principle*, which holds that attitudes must be seen as relevant and appropriate guides to the behavioral choices an individual faces in order for activated attitudes to affect behavior. Thus, an activated attitude would not necessarily affect a seemingly relevant behavior if the individual does not perceive its relevance for the particular behavior. Snyder further suggested that people low in the personality variable of self-monitoring are chronically more likely to view their attitudes as relevant to the situations in which they find themselves. Therefore, as demonstrated by Snyder and Swann (1976), they behave more consistently with their attitudes than do people high in self-monitoring.[11] However, because the impact of self-monitoring on attitude-behavior consistency might be explained in terms of attitude accessibility (i.e., attitudes of lows might be more accessible; see Kardes, Sanbonmatsu, Voss, & Fazio, 1986), a situational manipulation of attitude relevance would provide more convincing evidence for the importance of this construct.

In a study by Snyder and Kendzierski (1982) that included just such a manipulation, subjects took the role of jurors in a sex discrimination case. Subjects in the attitude-relevant situation were told that their judgments in the court case had implications for the general issue of affirmative action. These instructions implied that jurors might adopt an advocacy role on affirmative action. Presumably this *relevance* manipulation not only made their affirmative action attitude accessible, but also made this attitude seem an appropriate guide to their judgment on the particular case. In another condition, which was assumed to increase only the *accessibility* of attitudes, subjects were instructed to think over, reflect upon, and privately articulate their affirmative action attitudes.

Suggesting that accessibility is not sufficient to ensure a strong attitude-behavior relation, the accessibility manipulation increased the strength of the attitude-behavior relation for subjects who were low in self-monitoring but not for those who were high in self-monitoring. Presumably the high self-monitoring subjects were not affected by the increased accessibility of their attitudes because they did not regard their attitudes as relevant to their behavior. In contrast, low self-monitoring subjects chronically perceived their attitudes as relevant to their behavior.[12]

As expected, the relevance manipulation increased attitude-behavior consistency, regardless of subjects' level of self-monitoring. Thus, given that the attitude was accessible and there were strong situational cues concerning relevance, all subjects tended to perceive the link between their attitudes and their behavior, even if they were not chronically disposed to perceive such connections.

Related research by Borgida and Campbell (1982) demonstrated that even taking both accessibility and relevance into account is not sufficient to ensure a strong attitude-behavior relation. In this research, the accessibility and relevance of some subjects' proenvironmental attitudes were increased by having them listen to a conversation in which one discussant pointed out that environmental attitudes were germane to the issue under discussion (the construction of more on-campus parking to alleviate a shortage). When the behavioral measure (signing a petition favoring more parking) was administered one day later in an ostensibly unrelated experiment, attitude-behavior correspondence was stronger for subjects who had been exposed to this accessibility-plus-relevance manipulation, but only if they did not have much personal experience in coping with the parking shortage. Borgida and Campbell argued that for those subjects with such direct behavioral experience, making their environmentalist attitude accessible and relevant created a conflict between their vested interests (i.e., being able to find a parking space) and their environmentalist attitude. Evidently, for students who regularly faced the problem of finding a parking space, this conflict was not typically resolved in favor of their positive attitude toward environmentalism.

The research by Snyder and his colleagues as well as by Borgida and Campbell (1982; see also Salancik, 1982) suggests that the retrieval from memory of an attitude toward a target is not a sufficient condition for it to influence behavior. In addition, the attitude must be regarded as having implications for the behavior. Perhaps only then does an attitude toward a target affect the attitude toward the behavior that, as Fishbein and Ajzen (1975) argued, is one of the proximal determinants of the behavior. Moreover, the activated attitude must not be overridden by other considerations such as one's vested interest in an outcome inconsistent with the behavior.

However important the relevance principle, it does not provide a complete account of the processes by which an activated attitude toward a target may affect behavior. There is still a large gap between (a) the mental events of activating an attitude and perceiving it as relevant to a behavior and (b) the attitude-relevant action. Does the activated attitude impact directly on the behavior, or does it have its impact via the more proximal determinants of action described in the theory of reasoned action (i.e., formation of an attitude toward the action and an intention to engage in it)? Although the more proximal determinants of behavior have not been examined in research on attitudes toward targets, these factors have been scrutinized in considerable detail in research on attitudes toward behaviors.

Snyder's relevance principle is particularly important in the complex situations of daily life. In fact, this very principle leads us to advocate that attitudes toward behaviors be retained in any causal model that initiates the attitude-to-behavior sequence with the activation of attitudes toward targets. Thus, if a person perceives his attitude toward a target as relevant to a behavior, this attitude should lead him to have a positive attitude toward the behavior. For example, if he perceives his positive attitude toward international cooperation as relevant to taking a foreign language course, he should form a positive attitude toward the behavior of taking such a course. Yet attitudes toward other targets (e.g., his negative attitude toward the instructional methods he knows are used in such courses) may also impinge on his attitude toward taking a language course. Laboratory situations, in contrast, are generally constructed so that (a) the particular attitude under investigation is perceived as highly relevant to the behavior that is assessed, and (b) competing attitudes are not strong determinants of behavior. In these simplified situations it is less necessary to take perceived relevance and subjects' other attitudes into account.

Investigators of attitudes need to broaden their perspectives to encompass a wider variety of daily life behaviors. Moving beyond laboratory paradigms would foster clearer recognition of the potential compatibility of the two major traditions of research on the attitude-behavior relation—investigations of attitudes toward behaviors and attitudes toward targets. The fact that these two traditions emphasize different points in the attitude-to-behavior process has gone largely unrecognized.

FIGURE 4.6. A representation of a composite attitude-behavior model.

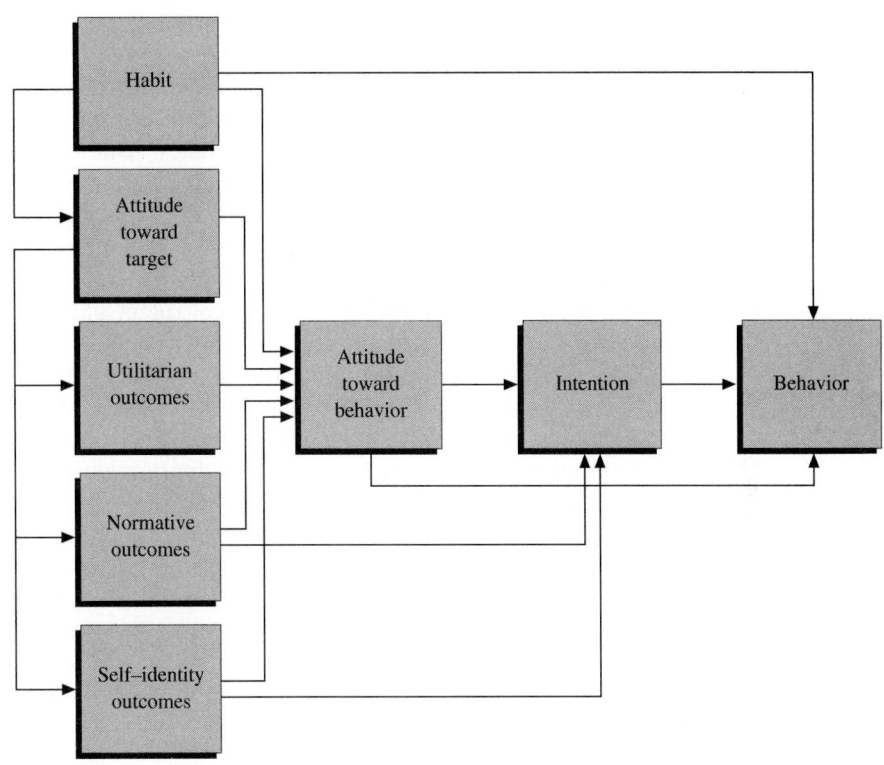

A Composite Model of the Attitude-Behavior Relation

To help readers envision the compatibility of models based on attitudes toward behaviors and those based on attitudes toward targets we provide an outline of a composite model of the attitude-behavior relation (see Figure 4.6). This approach takes both attitudes toward targets and attitudes toward behaviors into account, but at different points in a sequence of processes. In this model, behavior originates in the activation of habits, attitudes toward targets, and three classes of anticipated outcomes of behavior (utilitarian, normative, and self-identity). Habits should be understood in Triandis's (1977, 1980) terms as sequences of behavior that have become relatively automatic in the sense that they occur without self-instruction. Attitudes toward targets consist of evaluations of targets of behavior formulated at any level of abstraction. These are the social, political, interpersonal, and other attitudes that come to mind in everyday situations. Outcomes are the anticipated consequences of behavior that may come to mind if one contemplates engaging in a behavior; these outcomes are valenced in the sense that they vary in desirability. Utilitarian outcomes consist of those rewards and punishments that are anticipated to follow from engaging in the behavior. In

Fishbein and Ajzen's (1975) terms, utilitarian outcomes are behavioral beliefs. Normative outcomes pertain to the approval and disapproval that significant others are expected to express in relation to a behavior as well as self-administered rewards (pride) and punishments (guilt) that follow from internalized moral rules. When self-administered rewards and punishments relate to central aspects of the self-concept, they can be regarded as self-identity outcomes. This class of outcomes refers to affirmations or repudiations of the self-concept that are anticipated to follow from engaging in the behavior (see Biddle et al., 1987; Charng et al., 1988).

Attitudes toward targets could impact on the anticipated outcomes of behavior, as Fishbein and Ajzen (1974) suggested when they viewed attitudes toward targets as variables external to their model. Yet, more consistent with Fazio's (1986) perspective, attitudes toward targets could impact directly on attitudes toward behaviors by a more spontaneous, less deliberative route than that implied by the theory of reasoned action. If so, a behavior (asking a person to lunch) would seem attractive merely because the attitude toward the target (attitude toward the person) came to mind; there would be little or no consideration of the potential utilitarian, normative, or self-identity outcomes of this behavior. Yet, as suggested by Snyder's (1982) relevance principle, this link between attitude toward the target and attitude toward the behavior may require that the individual perceive that the behavior provides a means of expressing one's attitude toward the target.

In order to highlight that various classes of rewards and costs are relevant to behavior, we choose to define utilitarian, normative, and self-identity outcomes. These three classes of anticipated behavioral outcomes could all impact on attitude toward the behavior. Particularly in the case of normative and self-identity outcomes, more direct impact on intentions may occur as well, as assumed in the theory of reasoned action's treatment of social norms. Thus, because not all outcomes would necessarily affect attitude toward behavior, we have depicted normative and self-identity outcomes as influencing behavior by two means—through their impact on attitude toward behaviors or through their direct impact on intention.

As shown in Figure 4.6, habits can impinge directly on behavior, without mediation by other processes. Yet habits, by a self-perception process (see Chapter 11), may also influence behavior indirectly by influencing attitudes toward behaviors (e.g., I am always eating frozen yogurt, so I must like eating frozen yogurt). Of course, habits could also influence attitudes toward targets, which in turn influence attitudes toward behaviors (e.g., I am always eating quiche, so I must like quiche and therefore like eating quiche).

Just as a subjective assessment of relevance is often required to link attitudes toward targets to attitudes toward behaviors, a subjective assessment is often required to link attitudes toward behaviors with intentions. This link may be mediated by the individual's assessment of the constraints that he faces in the immediate situation. Such considerations were treated by Ajzen's (1987, 1988) concept of perceived behavioral control and other formulations that take self-efficacy into account (e.g., Bandura, 1977). Thus, an individual may form a positive attitude toward a given behavior but not intend to engage in it because he lacks the time or ability or cannot obtain the needed resources or cooperation from others.

Consistent with the research we reviewed earlier in this chapter (e.g., Bagozzi & Yi, 1989), sometimes intentions remain quite vague or are not formulated at all. In such circumstances, behavior may follow more directly from attitude toward the behavior in a more spontaneous manner. In contrast, atttitudes toward targets do *not* impact directly on behavior because behavioral choices require that an individual use some cognitive process, however rudimentary, to translate his evaluation of an entity into a choice of an overt behavior. This translation requires, at a minimum, forming a positive attitude toward some behavior (e.g., Harry loves Sally and therefore forms a positive attitude toward inviting her to a party).[13]

The link between intentions and behavior is often mediated by planning processes. Turning intentions into behaviors is not necessarily easy and may require considerable cognitive work as various routes to engaging in the behavior are evaluated. The cognitive processes that mediate this intention-behavior link are not elaborated in the theory of reasoned action and its variants.

Theories that consider planning processes do elucidate the intention-behavior linkage. According to such theories, behavior is often perceived by the individual as relevant to one or more goals. The idea that people orient their behavior to goals is not incompatible with attitudinal theories of behavior, although this theme is not emphasized in such theories. Consistent with our discussion of planning and goal-oriented behavior earlier in this chapter, attitudes toward targets could be represented in the form of goals toward which the individual has a positive attitude. Alternatively, goals might be regarded as outcomes of behavior: In the spirit of expectancy-value models, a positive attitude is formed toward a behavior to the extent that the behavior is perceived as resulting in progress toward one or more goals. In theories that consider planning processes in detail (e.g., Scheier & Carver, 1988), progress toward goals is evaluated subsequent to behavior by a matching-to-standard process. Depending on the outcome of this process, the attitude toward a behavior may be recomputed based on a revised estimate of the goal relevance of the behavior (e.g., if outlining textbook chapters did not give a student improved exam performance, she might lower her evaluation of this behavior). Alternatively, attitudes toward goals may be modified (e.g., a student might evaluate obtaining an "A" less positively or, in a sense, "give up on" this goal).

The formulation depicted in Figure 4.6 has not undergone empirical testing and is offered here as a possible integration of the existing models of the relation between attitudes and behaviors. In our view, existing models have been helpful in developing theory about attitude-behavior correspondence, but have provided piecemeal views of the role of attitudes in determining behavior. Our major purpose in presenting our composite model is to show that behavior is very plausibly determined by both attitudes toward targets and attitudes toward behaviors. Our integrative framework in addition emphasizes a point made repeatedly in this chapter—namely, that the relation between attitudes and behavior is best understood by placing attitudes in the context of other psychological factors that also determine behavior. We consider habit, norms, and self-identity to be important instances of such other psychological factors, but our list is no doubt incomplete.

Introspection about Attitudes Toward Targets as a Determinant of Attitude-Behavior Consistency

Some subtle but important elements of the processes by which attitudes toward targets influence behavior have been considered in studies of introspecting about one's attitude. In demonstrating that different types of instructions to introspect can have quite different effects on attitude-behavior correspondence, this research has made the broader point that researchers need to consider the particular aspect of attitude structure that is activated by attitude-relevant cues. As our discussion of this research will indicate, viewing attitudes only in terms of abstract evaluation is insufficient to encompass the findings in this research area. It is necessary to consider in addition the cognitive, affective, and behavioral bases of attitudes.

In research relevant to these issues, Timothy Wilson and his colleagues had subjects consider the reasons why they hold the attitude that they do immediately before they expressed their attitudes toward a given target (Wilson & Dunn, 1986; Wilson, Dunn, Bybee, Hyman, & Rotondo, 1984; Wilson, Dunn, Kraft, & Lisle, 1989). Wilson suggested that this *analyzing reasons* manipulation, through a process called *cognitivization* (Wilson et al., 1989), activates a somewhat different set of attitude-relevant cognitions than those that are normally accessible and that ordinarily guide behavior toward the target. This biased set of beliefs underlies the attitude measured in the analyzing-reasons conditions of such experiments. This attitude then relates poorly to later behavior, because behavior is guided by the aspects of the attitude that are more typically accessible and therefore are salient immediately prior to engaging in the behavior.

This hypothesis has been supported in a number of studies (see Wilson, Dunn, Kraft, & Lisle, 1989). For example, in a field setting, Wilson and Dunn (1986) had students who were waiting in a cafeteria line participate in a survey of their soft drink preferences. Just before soliciting their attitudes toward each of six drinks, some subjects were asked to give reasons why they liked or disliked each drink, while others were not. Subjects' consumption of soft drinks during the meal was then assessed. Subjects who had analyzed their reasons evidenced a lower correlation between their beverage attitudes and behavior than control subjects did, presumably because the attitudes subjects expressed after cognitivization did not match the attitudes that influenced their purchase behavior.

Subsequent research by Wilson, Kraft, and Dunn (1989) showed that analyzing reasons produced attitude change, albeit change that was temporary and inconsistent in direction across the subjects. The reasons subjects brought to mind thus induced a temporary change in their evaluation of the attitude object. This research also showed that the effects of analyzing reasons on attitude change and on attitude-behavior correspondence were confined to subjects who were not very knowledgeable about the attitude object, perhaps because their cognitions were more evaluatively inconsistent than those of more knowledgeable people. With cognitions that are evaluatively inconsistent, retrieving a biased subset is more likely to change the attitude than it would with cognitions that are evaluatively consistent and therefore redundant with one another.

On the surface, the findings of Wilson and his collaborators seemed surprising because they appeared to contradict studies demonstrating that enhancing people's awareness of their attitudes (by having them consider their attitudes or become more generally aware of themselves) increases the magnitude of attitude-behavior correlations (e.g., Carver & Scheier, 1981; M. Snyder & Swann, 1976; Wicklund, 1982). For example, Snyder and Swann (1976) had subjects participate, as mock jurors, in the same judicial decision-making task used later by Snyder and Kendzierski (1982; see earlier discussion of the relevance principle). Subjects' attitudes toward affirmative action were related to the favorability of their judicial judgments of the female plaintiff in this sex discrimination case. Some subjects were encouraged to reflect upon their attitudes by thinking about questions such as "Is it important to you that everyone be given equal opportunity in obtaining employment?" (p. 1037). Other subjects were not given this opportunity to think about their attitudes before considering the court case. The attitudes of the subjects who had been encouraged to reflect correlated more highly with their judicial judgments than did the attitudes of the subjects who had not been so encouraged. In this and other experiments, attitude-relevant thought thus *increased* attitude-behavior consistency, whereas in the research by Wilson and his colleagues, the opposite effect was obtained.

In a very interesting experiment designed to reconcile such seemingly divergent findings, Millar and Tesser (1986a) reasoned that superficially similar manipulations that induce thought about attitudes may differ in the extent to which they activate the cognitive or affective aspects of attitude structure. In addition, they reasoned that the same behavior may be determined by the cognitive or affective aspects of attitude structure, depending on the contextual features of the situation. Taking both the introspection manipulations and the context into account, Millar and Tesser argued that it is necessary to understand the conjunction of these two factors in order to predict the effects of introspection. Specifically, introspection enhances attitude-behavior correspondence only when the aspect of an attitude made salient by the introspection manipulation is the same aspect that drives the behavior in that context.

In their study, which used Regan and Fazio's (1977) puzzle paradigm, Millar and Tesser (1986a) first influenced subjects to introspect about their attitudes (i.e., toward the puzzles) from either a cognitive or an affective perspective. In addition, the context encouraged subjects to focus on either the cognitive or the affective implications of their behavior toward the puzzles (see discussion of these manipulations below). Subjects then evaluated the puzzles on a rating scale and were given a 7-minute period in which they were free to play with them. Correlations between subjects' ratings of the puzzles and the time they spent playing with each of them served as a measure of attitude-behavior correspondence.

To induce introspection that would be cognitively focused, Millar and Tesser instructed subjects to analyze their reasons for holding their attitudes about the puzzles ("analyze WHY you feel the way you do about each type of puzzle," p. 272). Instructions to analyze reasons produced relatively high attitude-behavior correlations only for subjects who in addition had been influenced to view their behavior from a cognitive (i.e., instrumental) perspective. This context was induced for the behavior by telling subjects that they would be taking a test assessing an analytic ability that would be developed by working on the puzzles. Millar and Tesser assumed that, as a consequence of this instruction, these subjects would be interested in the attributes of the puzzles and how they related to analytic ability. They were assumed to form their attitudes toward puzzle-playing behaviors with such instrumental, or extrinsic, consequences in mind.

To induce introspection that would be affectively focused, Millar and Tesser instructed other subjects to analyze how they felt about the puzzles ("analyze HOW you feel while performing each type of puzzle," p. 272). Instructions to focus on feelings produced relatively high attitude-behavior correlations only for subjects who in addition had been influenced to view their behavior from an affective (i.e., consummatory) perspective. This context was induced for the behavior by telling subjects that their puzzle playing was merely for enjoyment and did not pertain to success on an anticipated test. As a consequence of this instruction, these subjects presumably were concerned only with how the puzzles made them feel. When subjects regarded their behavior as having no purpose other than enjoyment, their behavior was presumably "affectively driven" (Millar & Tesser, 1986a, p. 270), meaning that they brought to mind the affective implications of puzzle playing when choosing among the puzzles. These subjects were assumed to form their attitudes toward puzzle-playing behaviors with such consummatory, or intrinsic, consequences in mind.

Millar and Tesser argued that their findings demonstrated that attitude-behavior consistency is enhanced to the extent that the aspect of attitude structure that underlies the expressed attitude matches the aspect that underlies the behavior. This experiment is thus relevant to the matching hypothesis that we introduced in Chapter 1 where we speculated about the consequences of matching the cognitive, affective, or behavioral bases of an attitude to the cognitive, affective, or behavioral nature of attitude-relevant responses.

Millar and Tesser's (1986a) intriguing research shows that it is useful to move beyond global notions that activated attitudes toward targets influence later behavior. Investigators can in addition take into account the structural issues that we discussed in Chapter 3. Specifically, psychologists should consider what aspect of attitude structure may be activated when an attitude is assessed (e.g., beliefs, feelings, memories of past behavior) and what aspect may be activated when people decide how to behave. For example, in Wilson's (e.g., Wilson, Dunn, Kraft, & Lisle, 1989) research, the introspection elicited by analyzing reasons probably activated subjects' beliefs about the attributes of the attitude objects (i.e., the cognitions underlying their evaluations). Wilson's subjects probably made their behavioral choice in terms of the affective aspects of their attitudes (i.e., the pleasure and good feeling that the behavior would induce). Understandably, introspection lowered the magnitude of attitude-behavior correlations in that research. In the M. Snyder and Swann (1976) research, the required introspection probably also activated the cognitive aspects of the attitude, but the behavior was also viewed in a cognitive perspective because it was not engaged in for enjoyment but was instrumental to obtaining a just decision in the

214

court case. Understandably, introspection increased the magnitude of attitude-behavior correlations in that research.

More generally, Millar and Tesser's (1986a) analysis demonstrates the value of looking at different classes of the antecedents of attitudes and different classes of attitude-relevant responses. However, in terms of our tripartite analysis (see Chapter 1) and our assumption of synergism between the three classes, there is some reason to question the generality of Millar and Tesser's findings. If input of one type tends to spill over and enhance the likelihood of input of the two other types, there may be considerable similarity in the evaluative content of various aspects of attitudes. Such similarity would lessen matching effects of the sort that Millar and Tesser obtained. Indeed, Millar and Tesser (1989) made this very point in a subsequent experiment that also used the puzzle paradigm. In this study, Millar and Tesser replicated their earlier experiment (Millar & Tesser, 1986a) and added separate assessments of the affective and cognitive aspects of attitude structure. The cognitive aspects of attitudes toward the puzzles were assessed by having subjects write down their reasons for liking or disliking each puzzle; the affective aspects were assessed by having subjects write down how each type of puzzle made them feel. These measures allowed Millar and Tesser to classify subjects according to the evaluative consistency between the affective and cognitive aspects of their attitudes. Findings revealed that the matching effects produced in the Millar and Tesser (1986a) experiment were confined to those subjects who were relatively low in affective-cognitive consistency. This outcome substantiates Millar and Tesser's interpretation of their research because the particular aspect of attitude structure that underlies an expressed attitude or a behavioral response would be irrelevant to attitude-behavior predictions if both aspects produced the same evaluation.

Limitations of Research on Attitudes Toward Targets

As readers will recall, the domain of behaviors explored in research testing the theory of reasoned action and related models has been criticized as consisting of simple, volitional behaviors that require little in the way of resources and cooperation (e.g., Liska, 1984). Yet the domain of behaviors investigated in contemporary research on attitudes toward targets is even more limited than that studied in research on attitudes toward behaviors. A much smaller set of relatively simple, volitional behaviors have been investigated in research on attitudes toward targets (e.g., playing with puzzles, voting, petition signing).

Readers should also recall our general argument that confining research to behaviors of this general type obviated the need for investigators of attitudes toward behaviors to regard people as striving for goals and thinking in terms of sequences of goal-oriented behaviors. Recognizing the seriousness of such limitations, some researchers (e.g., Ajzen, 1988, 1991) have attempted to evolve theories that are suitable for a larger set of behaviors. The challenge of predicting such behaviors has not yet been met in research on attitudes toward targets.

Conclusion

Social psychologists have made very substantial progress in understanding the relations between attitudes and behaviors. From the low point of the late 1960s, when many social scientists believed that attitudes were probably epiphenomena with little causal impact on behavior, understanding has developed to the point that investigators now have considerable knowledge of the web of relations between attitudes, behaviors, and other variables. Although Ajzen and Fishbein's (1977) ideas about the compatibility of attitudinal and behavioral measures were exceedingly important, these insights gave researchers the power to predict behavior without much understanding of the role of attitudes as directive and dynamic forces that control behavior. Yet the theory of reasoned action (Fishbein & Ajzen, 1975; Fishbein, 1980) did place attitudes in a causal role in relation to behavior. Even though the considerable limitations of the theory have spawned substantial revisions, its seminal importance cannot be underestimated. Yet the limited range of the theory of reasoned action is now fully appreciated, and the approach no longer appears viable except for relatively simple and easily executed behaviors that are under one's own control but are not strongly habitual. Moreover, in focusing on the proximal determinants of behavior, the theory did not give explicit consideration to attitudes toward targets as potential causes of behavior.

Fortunately, other researchers maintained an interest in predicting behavior from attitudes toward targets. As the compatibility principle indicates, high correlations between these attitudes and overt behaviors can be produced by aggregating behaviors to create a measure that corresponds in generality to the attitude measure. Moreover, despite the generally low magnitude of correlations between attitudes toward targets and single behaviors (or minimally aggregated behaviors), several conditions typically increase this magnitude to the moderate range—namely, direct experience with the attitude object, high accessibility of the attitude, possession of substantial information about the attitude object, and perception of an explicit link between the attitude and the behavioral choice at hand. These conditions give some important hints concerning how a model that begins with the activation of attitudes toward targets might be constructed. However, as we have indicated, research on attitudes toward targets provides a narrow base for constructing a general theory of attitude-behavior relations because this research, like the earlier research on attitude toward behaviors, has been executed almost exclusively with nonhabitual, volitional behaviors that are quite easily executed without resources or cooperation. As more recent analyses of attitudes toward behaviors have suggested, this realm of behavior, although important, probably excludes the majority of actions carried out in everyday life. In order to construct more general theories of how behavior is affected by attitudes toward targets and toward behaviors, social scientists must move beyond simple, volitional behavior and, to do this, must place attitudes within a theoretical structure that includes the major nonattitudinal determinants of behavior (e.g., habits, self-identity, norms). Understanding how people's attitudes cause them to behave is thus an essential part of the shared mission of all psychologists, which is understanding the causes of behavior.

Notes

1. The principle we discuss in this section was originally termed the "principle of correspondence" (see Ajzen & Fishbein, 1977; Fishbein & Ajzen, 1975). Unfortunately the term *correspondence* is widely used by attitude researchers in a broader sense to indicate a relatively strong relation between an attitude and a behavior (i.e., an attitude is correspondent with a behavior when the correlation between the two variables is at least moderately high). Therefore, we concur with Ajzen's (1988) substitution of the term *compatibility* for correspondence when referring to the equivalence of definitions of attitudes and behaviors.

2. Context encompasses social context (e.g., with family, friends) and physical context (i.e., locations).

3. Note that attitudes toward behaviors are attitudes toward *the respondent engaging in* a behavior or set of behaviors, not attitudes toward engaging in behavior in general. Therefore, items assessing these behaviors generally ask respondents to evaluate *my* engaging in a behavior (e.g., my attending class), not merely engaging in the behavior (e.g., attending class). That the two types of attitudes are not the same is suggested by the armchair analysis of thinking about the typical psychology professor's positive attitude toward participating in psychological experiments, which is not usually accompanied by a positive attitude toward the professor herself participating in psychological experiments.

4. It is also consistent with the theory of reasoned action to argue that the appearance of a new behavioral alternative can change an individual's intention to engage in a behavior by leading to change in his or her attitude or subjective norm in relation to this (previously available) behavior. More generally, any addition to the set of choices may cause each alternative action to be reappraised.

5. Structural or "path" analysis is a correlational technique for testing the plausibility of alternate causal models of the relations among variables.

Such models specify both the temporal nature of variables and the causal paths that are assumed to exist between variables. The plausibility of the specified paths is evaluated through a sequence of multiple regression equations in which variables in the model are predicted from all variables assumed to be causally prior. For detailed discussion of path analysis and related techniques for testing causal models in social psychological research, see Bentler (1980), Kenny (1979, 1985), Reis (1982), and Tanaka, Panter, Winborne, and Huba (1990).

6. Yet, primarily in the context of the theory of reasoned action, a number of studies have examined the interaction between attitude and subjective norm (see Grube & Morgan, 1990, for discussion). Also, a number of studies have examined whether behavioral control and intention interact in determining behavior. As already noted, Schifter and Ajzen (1985), obtained evidence for this interaction, but it has not been found in several other studies (see Ajzen, 1991).

7. For most complex behaviors carried out in an organizational or small-group context, people no doubt regard themselves as interdependent and perceive that control is shared with others. As effective planning takes place, it may be less appropriate to represent control over behaviors and outcomes in purely personal terms, in the manner of the planned behavior model. It is an understanding of interdependence and shared control that allows people to attain goals in complex social settings.

8. These success and failure terms have their roots in Kurt Lewin's work on level of aspiration. Lewin proposed that the valence (or attractiveness) of a goal is equal to the product of the valence of achieving success times the subjective probability of success, minus the product of the valence of failure times the subjective probability of failure (Lewin, Dembo, Festinger, & Sears, 1944).

9. Research on direct experience does not, however, compare the impact of behavioral information

with the impact of affective and cognitive input. In the direct experience conditions of these experiments, subjects receive other kinds of information in addition to information from their own behavior. Moreover, it is not clear what kind of input subjects receive in the control (i.e., indirect experience) conditions, although cognitive input would seem to predominate.

10. Such attitude change on the part of indirect experience subjects would not necessarily result in a change in the mean level of the final attitude, because of probable differences between subjects in the direction of the changes. Therefore, the attitudinal stability interpretation of the effects of direct experience cannot be tested by comparing mean attitudes in the direct and indirect experience conditions.

11. However, it should be noted that the behavioral measure in this study, writing an essay justifying a verdict in a court case (the essay was rated by independent judges), did not assess overt behavior in a manner typical of attitude-behavior research.

12. Alternatively, the attitudes of high and low self-monitors might be equally relevant to their behavior, but high self-monitors might be more concerned about the situational appropriateness of their behavior. Therefore, situational cues may compete with attitudes as determinants of behavior for high self-monitors.

13. The depicted model does not include Fazio's (1986) steps of *selective perception* and *immediate perceptions of the attitude object*. We regard these steps as referring to the processes by which beliefs become consistent with attitudes. As the work we discussed in Chapters 1 and 3 indicated, the evaluative content of people's beliefs about attitude objects is ordinarily at least moderately consistent with their attitudes. Achieving this consistency is in part a product of selective perception of the attributes of attitude objects (see Chapter 12). Thus, the *attitude toward target* variable in our composite model is meant to encompass the beliefs that are associated with such attitudes.

CHAPTER

5

Combinatorial Models of Attitude Formation and Change

This chapter as well as most of the material in the subsequent chapters of our book concern attitude change. The introduction of this topic signals a major shift in our focus because, until this point, we have treated attitudes as static structures. We have defined attitudes as tendencies to evaluate and have described the most common methods for assessing these tendencies. We then considered the structure of attitudes and beliefs and reviewed the multiple ways that attitudes relate to behaviors. Yet attitudes often change over time as a result of many influences, including persuasive messages received from other people and the impact of one's own attitude-relevant behavior. Psychologists have typically assumed that, to predict the extent to which attitudes will change, researchers must understand the psychological processes that underlie attitudes and their change. Therefore, theories of attitude change generally follow from assumptions that certain cognitive, affective, or motivational processes mediate such change.

As readers might expect, psychologists have analyzed attitude change from many different theoretical perspectives. To encompass this rich and varied domain, we have organized the material so that theories and research that reflect similar assumptions about psychological processes appear in the same chapter. We begin our analysis of attitude change in this chapter by considering combinatorial models, which are based on formal mathematical models. Chapters 6, 7, and 8 discuss verbally formulated models of the cognitive processes that mediate the effects of persuasive messages on attitudes. Chapter 9 considers the role of simple affective mechanisms in the formation and change of attitudes, and Chapter 10 considers the role of motivational processes. The impact of one's own behavior on attitude change is treated in Chapter 11, and resistance to change and the persistence of changed attitudes over time are examined in Chapter 12. Finally, we analyze the social context of attitude formation and change in Chapter 13.

Psychologists often use the term *attitude change* quite broadly in the sense that they treat attitude formation as well as attitude change under this rubric. Although some of the approaches that we consider, especially the simple affective mechanisms reviewed in Chapter 9, are especially tailored to explaining attitude formation, much of the research ordinarily thought to consider attitude change has used attitudes that Converse (1964, 1970, 1975) would probably label as nonattitudes. In particular, a substantial portion of the research on message-based persuasion that we review in Chapters 6, 7, and 8 has investigated attitudes that are relatively unfamiliar to research subjects and relatively unimportant to them. When investigators attempt to "change" attitudes for which their research subjects possess neither a developed structure of beliefs nor prior affective or behavioral input, the distinction between attitude formation and attitude change blurs. Although we follow tradition by using the term attitude change quite generally, at various points in this book we discuss issues that are relevant to distinguishing between formation and change.

The generic sense in which researchers often apply the term attitude change also typically does not distinguish between changing general evaluations of attitude objects and changing specific beliefs about the attributes of these attitude objects. Although some persuasive messages are designed to influence general attitudes and others to influence specific beliefs, this distinction has been unimportant to most theorists of attitude change, with the exception of some whose work we discuss in this chapter (e.g., Fishbein & Ajzen, 1975, 1981; Wyer & Hartwick, 1980).

The great amount of attention we devote to attitude change in this book reflects attitude researchers' emphasis on this topic. Because people's attitudes often seem problematic to social scientists and laypeople alike, this focus on changing attitudes is not surprising. If people's attitudes could be changed, the reasoning goes, we would have a better world—one in which prejudices are lessened, social conflict is reduced, and life-styles are more healthful. Of course, many practitioners' desires to understand attitude change stem from less altruistic motives such as a desire to induce consumers to like a particular product or a desire to persuade citizens to have a positive attitude toward particular political candidates. Although social scientists may not endorse all applications of their theories of attitude change, they do hope that these theories have wide applicability in natural settings. The extent to which this hope has become a reality is a matter that we consider in the final chapter of this book.

A major distinction between theories of attitude change is that some provide verbal descriptions of particular mechanisms or processes involved in changing attitudes, whereas others provide a mathematical description of how people combine or integrate the various cues that are available to them. For convenience, theories that primarily provide verbal descriptions of particular mechanisms involved in attitude change will be referred to as *process theories*. In these terms, the majority of attitude change theories can be considered process theories. Theories that provide primarily quantitative descriptions of the integration or combination problem will be referred to as *combinatorial theories*. We review these theories in this chapter.

The coverage of combinatorial theories of attitude formation and change in this chapter continues the quantitative theme we introduced in our discussion of the structure of attitudes and beliefs in Chapter 3. There we introduced three classes of quantitatively formulated models of attitude structure: (a) the probabilogical model, (b) expectancy-value models, and (c) algebraic models, particularly information integration theory. The probabilogical model assumes that the laws of mathematical probability describe how beliefs are related to other beliefs. Expectancy-value models adopt a specific equation that describes how attitudes are derived from beliefs about the attributes of attitude objects. Information integration theory encompasses a very wide set of algebraic equations that model how beliefs are integrated to produce evaluations. Our discussion of these models in Chapter 3 delineated their basic properties and explored their relevance to issues of attitudinal structure. However, we did not examine the considerable facility that each model has for predicting attitude and belief change. These dynamic aspects of combinatorial models are the focus of this chapter.

Probabilogical Model

The probabilogical model predicts changes in beliefs that occur when people hold certain logically related beliefs. As indicated in Chapter 3, this model defines beliefs as subjective probability judgments—for example, the perceived likelihood that humans will colonize Mars during the twenty-first century. The model examines the general proposition that the relations among beliefs obey the laws of mathematical probability theory. William McGuire (1960a, 1960b, 1960c) developed the first such model, and Robert Wyer subsequently explored a more general formulation (Wyer, 1970, 1974b; Wyer & Carlston, 1979; Wyer & Goldberg, 1970; Wyer & Hartwick, 1980).

As we explained in Chapter 3, Wyer's version of the probabilogical model predicts a person's belief in a target proposition or conclusion (C). An example of such a conclusion is the statement that *illicit drug use will decline substantially in the U.S. during the next ten years*. To express their belief in this proposition, people would estimate the probability that drug use will decline. According to Wyer's model, people's belief in this conclusion is related to their beliefs associated with a second proposition or premise (A), when these beliefs are also expressed as subjective probabilities. In our drug use example, this premise might be that *the federal government will impose the death penalty for drug trafficking*. The relation between belief in this premise and belief in the conclusion is indicated by the following equation:

$$p(C) = p(A)p(C/A) + p(A')p(C/A') \tag{5.1}$$

The terms of this equation are defined in Table 5.1.

Because the derivation of Equation 5.1 may be obscure to some readers, we show that the equation is a mathematical truism. By definition,

$$p(C) = p(AC) + p(A'C) \tag{5.2}$$

where $p(AC)$ is the probability that C occurs when A occurs and $p(A'C)$ is the probability that C occurs when A does not occur. Also, by the definition of conditional probability,

$$p(C/A) = p(AC)/p(A) \tag{5.3}$$

$$p(C/A') = p(A'C)/p(A') \tag{5.4}$$

221

TABLE 5.1

Definition of Terms in Probabilogical Model (Equation 5.1)

Symbol	Abstract definition	Example
$p(C)$	Belief in the conclusion, or subjective probability that conclusion is true.	Subjective probability that illicit drug use will decline substantially in the U.S. during the next ten years.
$p(A)$	Belief in the premise, or subjective probability that the premise is true.	Subjective probability that the federal government will impose the death penalty for drug trafficking.
$p(A')$	Belief that the premise is not true, or subjective probability that the premise is false, where $p(A') = 1 - p(A)$.	Subjective probability that the federal government will not impose the death penalty for drug trafficking.
$p(C/A)$	Conditional belief that the conclusion is true, if the premise is true; or subjective probability that the conclusion is true, given that the premise is true.	Subjective probability that illicit drug use will decline, given that the federal government imposes the death penalty for trafficking.
$p(C/A')$	Conditional belief that the conclusion is true, if the premise is false; or subjective probability that the conclusion is true, given that the premise is not true.	Subjective probability that illicit drug use will decline, given that the federal government does not impose the death penalty for trafficking.

Solving these equations for $p(AC)$ and $p(A'C)$, respectively, yields:

$$p(AC) = p(A)p(C/A) \qquad (5.5)$$

$$p(A'C) = p(A')p(C/A') \qquad (5.6)$$

The terms on the right-hand side of Equations 5.5 and 5.6 are then substituted for the $p(AC)$ and $p(A'C)$ terms, respectively, in Equation 5.2. The result is Equation 5.1, which expresses the Wyer model.

The mathematical truism expressed by Equation 5.1 happens to be psychologically interesting when we represent people's beliefs in terms of subjective probabilities. In general, the equation predicts belief in a conclusion from belief in a premise and the conditional beliefs that relate belief in the conclusion to the premise. For our drug use example, the equation states that a person's belief that illicit drug use will decline substantially in the United States during the next ten years [$p(C)$] should be equivalent in strength to his belief that the federal government will impose the death penalty for trafficking [$p(A)$], weighted by his conditional belief that drug use will decline if the death penalty is imposed [$p(C/A)$], *plus* his belief that the federal government will not impose the death penalty for trafficking [$p(A')$], weighted by his conditional belief that drug use will decline if the death penalty is not imposed [$p(C/A')$].

In this model, a premise makes a conclusion highly probable if, first of all, the premise elicits strong belief, that is, there is a high probability that the premise is true [$p(A)$] and a low probability that the premise is false [$p(A')$]. In our example, a person would think it very probable that the death penalty will be imposed and very improbable that the death penalty will not be imposed. However, a premise does not make a conclusion highly probable, even if the premise itself is highly probable, unless it is perceived to have an impact on the conclusion. In our example, believing that the death penalty very likely will be imposed wouldn't necessarily make a person believe that drug use will decline; the person would in addition have to believe that the death penalty would have some causal impact on drug use. In terms of the model, this causal impact is expressed by the individual believing it likely that drug use would decline *if* the death penalty were imposed. This relation between the premise and the conclusion is expressed by the conditional probability terms of the model, which are multiplied by the terms indicating belief in the premise itself. In summary, this model says that a premise should make a conclusion seem highly likely to the extent that the premise is both likely to be true and highly consequential in relation to the conclusion.

Wyer demonstrated the utility of the probabilogical model in studies in which subjects responded to premises and related conclusions by giving probability estimates for each term in Equation 5.1: Each subject estimated the probability of the conclusion [$p(C)$] and the probability of each of the terms pertaining to the premise [$p(A)$, $p(A')$, $p(C/A)$, $p(C/A')$], which appear on the right side of the equation. The model was tested by comparing subjects' actual estimates of the probability of the conclusion [$p(C)$] with the equation's prediction of this probability on the basis of subjects' estimates of these premise-related beliefs. As we noted in Chapter 3, the observed values of $p(C)$ and the values predicted from the equation have generally shown a moderately high degree of correspondence in studies of this type (e.g., Wyer, 1970; Wyer & Goldberg, 1970).

Implications of the Probabilogical Model for Predicting Belief Change

In addition to specifying how beliefs ought to be interrelated within the individual's cognitive system (Equation 5.1), the probabilogical model predicts how a person's belief in some conclusion should change when her belief in a probabilistically related premise undergoes revision. This application of the probabilogical model is important to understanding message-induced persuasion because communicators often try to convince message recipients of the truth of particular premises that have positive implications for the communicator's position on an issue. According to Wyer's formulation, changes in a person's belief in a conclusion, C, should be related to changes in his or her beliefs associated with a related premise, A, in the following manner (see Wyer, 1970; Wyer & Goldberg, 1970; Wyer, Carlston, & Hartwick, 1979; Wyer & Hartwick, 1980):

$$\Delta p(C) = \Delta[p(A)p(C/A) + p(A')p(C/A')] \qquad (5.7)$$

Note that this equation differs from Equation 5.1 only in the addition of the Δ symbol, which indicates change in a quantity.

Research that has examined the effect of changing subjects' belief in a premise $[p(A)]$ on change in their belief in a conclusion $[p(C)]$ has generally supported the utility of the McGuire-Wyer model for understanding belief change. Numerous studies have shown that persuasive messages that successfully change subjects' beliefs in such premises do result in significant changes in their beliefs in logically related conclusions, even though these conclusions are not, themselves, mentioned in the persuasive messages that subjects receive (Dillehay, Insko, & Smith, 1966; Holt, 1970; Holt & Watts, 1969; McGuire, 1960a, 1960b; Wyer, 1970). Important as these findings are, readers should keep in mind that earlier research established that messages tend to be even *more* persuasive if the communicator explicitly draws the conclusion for the audience rather than allows the audience to infer this conclusion on the basis of their understanding of the messages' premises (e.g., Hovland, Lumsdaine, & Sheffield, 1949; Hovland & Mandell, 1952; McKeachie, 1954; Thistlethwaite, de Haan, & Kamenetzky, 1955). Nonetheless, research testing the probabilogical model has demonstrated that messages that do not explicitly draw conclusions for recipients can, in fact, induce significant change in their beliefs.

A simplifying assumption that is often made in applying the probabilogical model to predict persuasion is that persuasive messages ordinarily induce people to change their belief in some premise (i.e., some idea or argument that is related to the position the communicator advocates) but do not change people's conditional beliefs that relate the premise to the conclusion endorsed by the communicator.[1] In our drug use example this simplification presumes that a message would change people's belief that the death penalty will be imposed for drug trafficking but would not change their belief in the relation between the death penalty and drug use. Expressed symbolically, we thus assume that persuasive messages change $p(A)$ but not $p(C/A)$ or $p(C/A')$. We also take into account that increasing belief in the premise A implies an equivalent decrease in belief that the premise is not true—in other words, $\Delta p(A') = -\Delta p(A)$ [which follows mathematically from the definition, $p(A') = 1 - p(A)$]. Given these assumptions, Equation 5.7 reduces to the following:

$$\Delta p(C) = \Delta p(A) [p(C/A) - p(C/A')] \qquad (5.8)$$

The difference between the two conditional probabilities $[p(C/A) - p(C/A')]$ can be viewed as expressing the *relevance* of an argument or premise for a conclusion because it is the difference in the probability of the conclusion given that the premise is or is not true. If this difference is large, the premise is consequential for the conclusion, whereas if this difference is small the premise's truth or falsity has little impact on the probability attached to the conclusion. In our example this relevance term is equal to the probability that drug use will decrease given that the death penalty is imposed minus the probability that drug use will decrease given that the death penalty is not imposed. If an individual perceives the death penalty as consequential for drug use, he would perceive a reduction in drug use as much more likely if the death penalty were imposed (vs. not imposed).

The model thus predicts that the extent to which belief in a conclusion changes as a function of change in belief in a premise depends on the *perceived relevance* of the premise to the conclusion, that is, on the difference between $p(C/A)$ and $p(C/A')$. In line with this expectation, Wyer (1970, p. 561) found that a persuasive communication that induced a change in subjects' belief in a premise A, such as the premise that "Governor Smith will be reelected," resulted in a large change in their belief in an unmentioned conclusion C, such as the conclusion that "state aid to education will be increased," to the extent that a large difference existed between the two conditional probabilities. The difference between the two conditional probabilities in Equation 5.8 might thus be viewed as an index of the strength of a premise in relation to a conclusion. That some persuasive messages contain premises or "arguments" that are "strong" in this or other senses is an idea that we will return to in Chapters 6 and 7, where we discuss the cognitive response and elaboration likelihood models of persuasion.

Bayes's Theorem. Worth considering in the context of the probabilogical model's treatment of belief change is the question of how change in a premise is brought about. Whereas the probabilogical model considers the effect of change in one belief (a premise) on change in another belief (a conclusion), it does not consider how new information changes belief in the premise in the first place. Bayes's theorem specifies how beliefs should change if information is used properly (that is, according to the laws of mathematical probability). The approach thus provides a normative model that prescribes how beliefs, which are called *hypotheses* in this tradition (e.g., "research on groups will become dominant in social psychology"), should change in response to the introduction of some new information called *evidence* or *datum* in this tradition (e.g., "During the past three years there has been a 50 percent increase in the number of journal articles published on groups research").

Although discussion of the Bayesian model is beyond the scope of this chapter, we note its relevance to persuasion. Persuasive messages ordinarily present not just premises (i.e., arguments) that have positive implications for conclusions, but information that is designed to increase the plausibility of the premises. Bayes's rule models how beliefs may be affected by the presentation of information that is relevant to them. A substantial psychological literature addresses this kind of information processing (see W. Edwards, Lindman, & Savage, 1963; Fischhoff & Beyth-Marom, 1983; Slovic & Lichtenstein, 1971; Stevenson, Busemeyer, & Naylor, 1990). In addition, Fishbein and Ajzen (1975) provided a helpful discussion of the implications of Bayes's theorem for persuasion.

The Socratic Effect

In addition to demonstrating that communications that change people's beliefs in one proposition can lead to change in probabilistically related but unmentioned beliefs, research stimulated by the probabilogical model showed that belief change can be produced simply by asking people to express related beliefs (e.g., Henninger & Wyer, 1976; McGuire, 1960a; Watts & Holt, 1970; Wyer, 1974b). If people merely direct their thoughts to beliefs with logical implications for one another, these beliefs become more consistent. McGuire (1960a) dubbed this phenomenon the *Socratic effect*. For example, investigators documented that logical consistency among conditionally related beliefs increased from the first administration of a questionnaire that solicited these beliefs to a second administration one week later (e.g., Henninger & Wyer, 1976; McGuire, 1960a). In these studies, logical consistency was defined by a lack of discrepancy between the beliefs subjects reported they held in conclusions and the beliefs predicted on the basis of the probabilogical model.

McGuire's (1960a, 1960c) assumption that this Socratic effect was due to a motivated process of cognitive restructuring followed from the cognitive consistency heritage of his early work in this area. Specifically, he reasoned that his questionnaire respondents were motivated by the desire to reduce logical inconsistencies among beliefs that had been made salient as a result of reporting them on the initial questionnaire (see the discussion of motivation in consistency theories in Chapter 10). Proposing an alternative interpretation of the Socratic effect, Wyer and his colleagues suggested that the reduction of inconsistency over repeated questionnaire administrations may be due to a relatively more passive cognitive process (Henninger & Wyer, 1976; Wyer & Hartwick, 1980). According to this explanation, because respondents' beliefs in premises were elicited during the first administration of a questionnaire, they became more accessible and consequently likely to influence beliefs in logically related conclusions during the second administration of the questionnaire. This interpretation suggests that the Socratic effect manifested on the second administration of the questionnaire would be especially strong if respondents had no chance to take the premises into account in estimating their beliefs in the conclusions during the first administration of the questionnaire. These circumstances could be arranged merely by having respondents indicate their belief in the conclusions *before* they indicate their belief in the premises on the first questionnaire. In contrast, prior experiments on the Socratic effect had ordered the premises and conclusions unsystematically throughout the questionnaire.

In an experiment that varied whether subjects responded first to the premises or the conclusions in the initial questionnaire, Henninger and Wyer (1976) presented various sets of premises (e.g., American factory workers are bored) and conclusions (e.g., American industry is producing substandard merchandise). They found a greater reduction in logical inconsistency over time if on the first questionnaire subjects gave their beliefs in the *conclusions* before their beliefs in the related *premises*. In contrast, if subjects indicated their beliefs in the *premises* before their beliefs in the *conclusions* on the first questionnaire, their beliefs appeared to be already relatively consistent on this first administration of the questionnaire.

226

More generally, the probabilogical model indicates that belief in a proposition can be changed merely by directing people's thoughts to a logically related belief that has positive implications for the proposition. For example, in one study (Wyer & Henninger, 1978, reported in Wyer & Hartwick, 1980), subjects were asked merely to report their beliefs in premises that had been constructed to have positive implications for logically related conclusions. These subjects' beliefs in the conclusions became significantly stronger when assessed in the second session of the experiment.

This research suggests that persuasive messages could bring about a desired change in some (mentioned or unmentioned) conclusion either by presenting individuals with unfamiliar premises with positive implications for the conclusion or merely by presenting assertions (again with positive implications for the conclusion) with which the individual already agrees. The latter technique, which merely makes existing beliefs more salient, is reminiscent of Rokeach's (1968, 1973) work showing that belief in propositions (e.g., that civil rights activities should be supported) can be increased simply by making individuals think about their existing values (e.g., equality) that have positive implications for the proposition. Indeed, the appeals for monetary donations that many people frequently receive by mail often attempt to draw readers' attention to premises with which they already agree (e.g., that higher education is important and that you are a loyal alumnus of your college). These premises presumably have positive implications for the proposition advocated in the appeal (e.g., that you should donate to your college's current fund-raising campaign).

The idea that persuasion may be, in part, a function of whatever logically related beliefs, or premises, are most salient to respondents at the time they indicate their beliefs in propositions, or conclusions, suggests that any factor that enhances the accessibility of such information may, consequently, affect persuasion. Consistent with this idea, Wyer and Hartwick (1980) maintained that persuasive argumentation that is processed more extensively should, subsequently, be easily retrieved and thus exert a greater impact on future belief judgments than argumentation that is initially processed less extensively. Wyer and Henninger (1978, cited in Wyer & Hartwick, 1980) obtained some counter-intuitive findings consistent with this general argument. These researchers hypothesized that messages containing relatively implausible premises (e.g., Edward Kennedy is a good friend of Richard Nixon) with relatively weak or unclear implications for a conclusion (e.g., Edward Kennedy made illegal contributions to Nixon's campaign fund) would be more thought provoking and thus engender more cognitive activity on the part of the subjects than messages containing relatively plausible premises (e.g., Vast oil resources lie under the frozen earth of Antarctica) with fairly strong implications for a conclusion (e.g., The settlement of Antarctica will be vastly accelerated in the next few years).

Consistent with the hypothesis that implausible statements are processed more thoroughly, subjects showed superior recall for premises and conclusions when the premises were implausible rather than plausible (see also Wyer & Hartwick, 1984). Moreover, this tendency was particularly evident when the implications of the premises for the conclusions were weak rather than strong. Most intriguing, this research found suggestive evidence of greater increase in subjects' beliefs in conclusions to the extent that they had more extensively processed the premises and their implications for the conclusions; specifically, more belief change occurred when subjects had initially been exposed to messages containing relatively implausible premises with weak implications for the conclusion rather than messages containing fairly plausible premises with strong implications for the conclusion. This finding is somewhat surprising and may not generalize to contexts in which people are motivated to counterargue implausible premises. Nonetheless, the Wyer and Henninger study does illustrate the kinds of hypotheses that follow from the assumption that factors that influence the accessibility of persuasive information exert corresponding effects on belief change.

Implications and Extensions of the Probabilogical Model

The main contribution of the McGuire-Wyer probabilogical model is the molecular analysis it provides of people's inferences about premises and logically related conclusions, which may be mentioned or unmentioned. The main idea of the model is that people align conclusions in logical fashion with premises that come to mind, when logic is defined mathematically according to principles of probability. This approach makes the important point that people take into account, not only the truth value of premises, but also the conditional relation that they perceive to exist between premises and conclusions. Although conditional inferences no doubt play an important role in persuasion, they should be regarded as only one of a variety of inference processes that have been postulated to underlie belief change and other social judgments. For example, other inference models that we consider in this book include heuristic and attributional reasoning (see Chapters 7 and 8) as well as algebraic combinatorial processes (see expectancy-value and information integration models in this chapter).

The model in the form we have presented it predicts the effects of a single premise on belief in a conclusion. Were the model confined to this application, its usefulness for predicting persuasion would be somewhat limited because message recipients often consider more than one premise in deciding whether to accept a communicator's recommended position. In particular, recipients' beliefs in conclusions may take previously acquired beliefs into account along with the information in the message. To allow for this possibility, Wyer expanded Equation 5.1 to apply to the situation in which people's belief in a conclusion follows from both a previously acquired premise and a newly presented premise (Wyer, 1976; Wyer & Hartwick, 1980). Yet even this enlarged equation would be inadequate in many practical situations because a message may induce belief in more than one premise, and people may have already acquired several relevant premises. Certainly the probabilogical model principle could be extended to consider beliefs derived from larger numbers of premises, although the model becomes somewhat unwieldy for such applications.

Another limitation is that research testing the utility of the model has focused heavily on subjects' inferences about *nonevaluative* propositions concerning the likelihood of events (e.g., whether marijuana *will* be legalized) and has less commonly examined inferences about *evaluative* propositions (e.g., whether marijuana *should* be legalized). Among the relatively few efforts to predict evaluative judgments from the model is an application to interpersonal attraction, that is, to predicting the subjective probability that a person is likable (Wyer, 1973b). In this application, the relevant premise was that a person possesses a particular trait (e.g., honesty), and the conditional beliefs were the subjective probabilities that a person is likable if he possesses and if he does not possess the trait. However, because one's liking for another may commonly represent an inference from a cluster of traits that represent the person's attributes (and possibly from affective and behavioral input as well), the model has not proven popular for predicting interpersonal attraction, or, for that matter, for predicting attitudes more generally.

Wyer and Hartwick (1980) maintained that for predicting evaluative judgments, the probabilogical model is less appropriate than the expectancy-value and other algebraic models we consider in the remainder of this chapter. Wyer and Hartwick's reservations about the utility of the probabilogical model in the evaluative domain followed from their argument that (a) in judging nonevaluative propositions (e.g., whether the Supreme Court *will* reverse the *Roe* v. *Wade* decision), people retrieve premises (e.g., that several conservative justices have been appointed to the Supreme Court) and (b) in judging evaluative propositions (e.g., whether the Supreme Court *should* reverse the *Roe* v. *Wade* decision), people retrieve consequences (e.g., that more women would die from illegal abortions). Thus, in basing its predictions on premises, or antecedent conditions, the probabilogical model may not be appropriate for predicting evaluative judgments, which are ordinarily based on consequences.

The Separate Prediction of Evaluative and Likelihood Judgments. William McGuire and Claire McGuire have recently returned to the ground of the probabilogical model and produced what might be considered from some perspectives an extension of the model, albeit a very substantial elaboration (McGuire, 1990; McGuire & McGuire, 1991). Their *dynamic theory of thought systems* makes a fundamental distinction between judgments of evaluation and judgments of likelihood and therefore predicts them separately. In their research, the McGuires investigated the thoughts evoked by "core events," some of which were societal (e.g., "there will be a constitutional amendment banning alcoholic beverages") and some of which were personal ("your becoming very disappointed in future years in your chosen field of work"). When directing their thoughts to such an event, people are assumed to think about both its likelihood and its desirability. Consistent with Wyer and Hartwick's (1980) point about the differing beliefs that are relevant to evaluative and likelihood judgments, one of the central propositions of the McGuires' theory is that considering an event's likelihood leads to thoughts that focus on the event's antecedents, the conditions that would promote it or prevent it. In contrast, considering an event's desirability focuses thought on the event's consequences, which can be pleasant or unpleasant.

In this theory, the relation between the perceived likelihood of an event and its antecedents is expressed in its *sufficient reason postulate*, which is recognizable as a restatement of the relation between premises and conclusions given by the proba-bilogical model. This postulate indicates that the perceived likelihood of an event is greater to the extent that many antecedent conditions are perceived to promote it and

229

few antecedent conditions are perceived to prevent it. The relation between the desirability of events and the pleasantness of their consequences is expressed in the model's *utility-maximizing postulate*, which maintains that desirable events are perceived to have many pleasant consequences and few unpleasant consequences. This principle is in harmony with the expectancy-value models that we consider in the next section of this chapter. The theory also assumes that the judged desirability of an event is related to the desirability of the forces that brought it about, as expressed by the model's *congruent-origins postulate*. One of the more interesting features of the McGuires' empirical tests of these postulates is that the utility-maximizing and congruent-origins postulates were more successful in predicting their subjects' evaluative judgments than the sufficient reason postulate was in predicting their likelihood judgments. The McGuires' rationale for this finding was that desirability judgments are more emotionally involving than likelihood judgments and therefore are more tightly organized according to the principles of the model.

The McGuires' work also reintroduced an assumption of William McGuire's (1960a, 1960c) early theorizing related to the probabilogical model—the idea that there is spillover between judgments of desirability and of likelihood, a feature left out in Wyer's rendition of the probabilogical model. The McGuires thus included a *wishful-thinking postulate* by which good events become likely and a *rationalization postulate* by which likely events become good. These postulates introduce a certain autistic tendency into the characterization of people's thinking. Although empirical support for these spillover propositions was weak in McGuire and McGuire's (1991) empirical work, especially for the rationalization postulate, perhaps support would be stronger if the core events presented to subjects were real rather than hypothetical. At any rate, the McGuires accounted for this limited evidence for spillover between likelihood and desirability by arguing for a tighter organization of thoughts within the desirability and the likelihood systems than across them.

This rather complex system of postulates proposed by the McGuires is admirable in placing a set of principles in a common framework and thus illuminating how the probabilogical model might fit within a larger system of people's thoughts about an event. Empirical testing of the theory has not been extensive so far, and this research has proceeded only in what might be considered a semi-quantified form, which does not take into account conditional probabilities or degrees of likelihood and desirability of antecedents and consequences. The testing of the fully quantified form of the theory should prove enlightening; the breadth and scope of the approach as well as the support already demonstrated in the McGuires' research program recommend this theory to attitude researchers.

The Utility of the Probabilogical Model as a Theory of Persuasion. The most serious limitation of the probabilogical model (as well as the McGuires' elaboration of this approach to take desirability judgments into account) is that it lacks an explicit account of how distal persuasion variables such as source, message, and contextual factors influence the terms of the model. If, for example, messages ascribed to likable communicators are more persuasive than ones ascribed to less likable communicators (e.g., Eagly & Chaiken, 1975), the probabilogical model provides no mechanism for explaining this relation, except for the very general idea that communicator likability must have affected message recipients' subjective probabilities related to the premises contained in the argumentation of the messages. Thus, although the model helps explicate some of the psychological processes that may underlie persuasion, its lack of predictive power with respect to distal persuasion variables renders it inadequate as a general theory of persuasion. Despite this limited scope of the probabilogical model, it possesses several unique and important implications for persuasion, as we have shown in our review of the research it has inspired.

Other analyses that emphasize the importance of belief retrieval for the attitudes and beliefs expressed at any one point in time, such as the recent work on context effects in attitude assessment (Schwarz & Strack, 1991; Tourangeau & Rasinski, 1988; see Chapters 2 and 3), might profit from application of the probabilogical model. Research on context effects, like research on the probabilogical model, suggests that the answers questionnaire respondents give to questions depend on the beliefs they retrieve at the moment they give their answers. Context researchers have shown that these beliefs are a function, not just of respondents' preexisting beliefs, but also of the context provided by prior questions and the wording of the target question. Following the probabilogical model, the effects of the beliefs that are retrieved on respondents' answers to questions should depend on these beliefs' conditional relations to the beliefs reflected in their answers. Although the process of forming a judgment from the information that is retrieved has not been explored in this degree of detail in work on context effects, the probabilogical model describes one possible mechanism that might underlie such effects. The model is thus worthy of careful consideration by investigators of context effects, to the extent that they are interested in quantitatively modeling the combinatorial processes that may underlie the phenomena that they have brought to the attention of attitude researchers.[2]

Expectancy-Value Model

The expectancy-value model provides a popular framework for describing how beliefs are combined to form and change attitudes. As we explained in Chapter 3, this model proposes that an attitude (interpreted as the evaluation of an attitude object) is a function of the sum of the *expected values* of the attributes ascribed to the attitude object. The *expectancy* associated with an attribute is one's subjective probability that the attitude object has the attribute, and the *value* of an attribute is one's evaluation of it. For example, if a citizen believes that a presidential candidate is intelligent, knowledgeable about foreign policy, but lacks compassion, these attributes would be represented by the subjective probability that the candidate has each attribute (i.e., a high probability of intelligence and knowledgeability about foreign policy and a low probability of compassion) as well as by the evaluation of each attribute (i.e., a positive evaluation of intelligence, knowledgeability, and compassion). To predict an attitude, the expectancy and value terms associated with each attribute are multiplied together, and these products are summed. Thus, Martin Fishbein's (1961, 1963, 1967a) version of the expectancy-value model is expressed algebraically as follows:

$$A_o = \sum_{i=1}^{n} b_i e_i \tag{5.9}$$

where A_o is the attitude toward the object, action, or event, o; b_i is the belief i about o (expressed as the subjective probability that o has attribute i); e_i is the evaluation of attribute i; and n is the number of salient attributes.

This Expectancy × Value model of attitudes is one component of Fishbein and Ajzen's (1975) theory of reasoned action, which many investigators have used to predict behavior from attitudes. As detailed in Chapter 4, when behavior is predicted by this model, the relevant attitude object is a behavior (or set of behaviors), and the attributes of this attitude object are the perceived consequences of the behavior. This attitude, in conjunction with subjective norm, determines behavioral intention in the theory of reasoned action, and behavioral intention determines behavior.

Correlational Research Relevant to Expectancy-Value Model

To test the model's assumption that attitudes are determined by the evaluative content of the beliefs a perceiver takes into account, numerous studies have correlated a measure of attitude with a measure of the summed products that represent beliefs and appear on the right side of the equation. In such studies, attitudes are assessed by relatively direct measures—namely, the semantic differential (e.g., Fishbein, 1963; A. J. Smith & Clark, 1973) or single-item self-reports of favorability toward the attitude object (e.g., Cronen & Conville, 1975a, 1975b). To assess beliefs, investigators often have respondents assign probabilities and evaluations to beliefs that pretesting has established are very commonly held by members of the respondent population. In this tradition, such beliefs are known as *modal salient beliefs*. Alternatively, beliefs about the attitude object are elicited from each individual subject, who subsequently rates each belief's value (e.g., on a good vs. bad scale) and its likelihood as a characterization of the attitude object.

Most such studies have obtained at least moderately high correlations between attitudes and beliefs (e.g., Cronen & Conville, 1975a, 1975b; Fishbein, 1963, 1965; Fishbein & Coombs, 1974; A. J. Smith & Clark, 1973), although some correlations have been relatively low (see Eagly & Mladinic, 1989; K. J. Kaplan & Fishbein, 1969). However, even relatively high correlations between attitudes and summed Expectancy × Value products do not necessarily demonstrate that beliefs determine attitudes rather than vice versa. In the weaker tests of the expectancy-value assumption that the beliefs people retrieve determine their attitudes, the sums of subjects' Expectancy × Value products for modal salient beliefs are correlated with their attitudes, as assessed by a more direct measure such as the semantic differential (e.g., Fishbein, 1963, 1965; Fishbein & Coombs, 1974). The weakness of tests based in this manner on modal salient beliefs has been shown by demonstrations that attitude can be predicted about as well from belief in attributes known to be non-salient in a population as from belief in attributes known to be salient (e.g., Hackman & Anderson, 1968; K. J. Kaplan & Fishbein, 1969). For example, A. J. Smith and Clark (1973) predicted respondents' attitudes toward blacks as successfully from their beliefs that blacks had attributes commonly ascribed to Chinese Communists as from their beliefs that blacks had attributes commonly ascribed to blacks.

The beliefs people report on a questionnaire can serve merely as indicants of their attitude in the sense that they are *determined by* their attitude (see Feldman & Lynch, 1988; K. Thomas, 1975). A person with a positive attitude may thus infer that the favorable attributes listed on a questionnaire probably describe the attitude object and that the unfavorable attributes probably do not, even though she has not previously considered whether the attitude object possesses or doesn't possess these attributes. For example, a person who has a positive attitude toward Dustin Hoffman based on admiration of his acting may not have considered whether he is friendly, kind, or politically aware. Yet if confronted by a questionnaire on which Hoffman must be judged on such attributes, this person would probably tend to rate Hoffman favorably on them because it would seem plausible that such a fine actor would have other favorable qualities. In such instances, an abstract attitude may be retrieved and, from this attitude, attitude-consistent beliefs about specific attributes may be constructed. Although the mechanisms underlying such an effect are not clear (and might reflect pressures to maintain cognitive consistency or other factors), this example should demonstrate that high correlations between attitudes and ratings of modal beliefs are as compatible with the claim that attitudes determine beliefs as they are with the claim that beliefs determine attitudes.

Relatively high attitude-belief correlations based on individual respondents' idiosyncratic reports of those beliefs that are salient for them personally provide somewhat stronger evidence that beliefs determine attitudes, because it is less likely that respondents merely inferred these beliefs from their overall evaluation of the attitude object (e.g., Cronen & Conville, 1975a, 1975b; Hackman & Anderson, 1968; Jaccard & Fishbein, 1975). However, it is still possible that questionnaire respondents, especially those with few beliefs about an attitude object, could invent beliefs on the spot when faced with the type of belief-elicitation task that expectancy-value researchers use to produce individualized measures of respondents' beliefs. These newly constructed beliefs would presumably tend to be consistent with the overall attitude.

We note in addition that *low* correlations between attitudes and the evaluative implications of the beliefs elicited from individual respondents should not be taken as evidence of the *inadequacy* of the expectancy-value model. Consistent with our analysis in Chapters 1 and 3, attitudes do not derive exclusively from beliefs that people hold about attitude objects, although cognitive input, which can be regarded as stored in the form of beliefs, is certainly an important source of evaluations under most circumstances. Because attitudes are also a product of affective and behavioral input, low correlations between attitudes and beliefs may be diagnostic of the noncognitive determination of these attitudes. Attitude-belief correlations may thus vary in magnitude,

233

depending on the extent to which they are based on cognitive or noncognitive input (see also Breckler & Wiggins, 1989a, and Chapter 3's discussion of evaluative-cognitive consistency).

The Adequacy of Expectancy-Value Products for Modeling Beliefs. Aside from the issue of whether causation flows from beliefs to attitudes or vice versa, there remains considerable concern about the correctness of the details of the expectancy-value equation—in particular, about the adequacy of the assumption that the evaluative content of beliefs is appropriately described by multiplying the expectancy and evaluation aspects of beliefs and summing these products across the beliefs. As we note in our discussion of information integration theory in this chapter, combinatorial models that are systematically in error can nonetheless generate relatively high attitude-belief correlations.

One of the methodological issues surrounding the implementation of the expectancy-value equation concerns the scaling of the beliefs and evaluations that are multiplied to form expectancy-value products. Usually respondents make their ratings on 7-point scales for both beliefs (e.g., likely vs. unlikely) and evaluation (e.g., good vs. bad). Consistent with the conventional assumption that evaluations can range from negative to positive, Ajzen and Fishbein (1980, p. 71) recommended bipolar scaling of evaluative ratings (from -3 to $+3$). More controversial is their recommendation that likelihood (or expectancy) ratings can be scaled on a bipolar basis (e.g., -3, very improbable, to $+3$, very probable) when respondents judge modal salient beliefs, which are not necessarily salient for each individual respondent. In contrast, they recommended unipolar scaling (0 to 1) when each respondent judges self-generated beliefs, which he or she has volunteered. The bipolar method allows respondents' ratings to express the falsity of modal beliefs and enables disbelief in negative attributes to contribute positively to the composite (i.e., -3×-3). By this method, for example, perceiving it as very unlikely (-3) that President Bush is dishonest (-3) would contribute a positive product ($+9$) to the composite score representing the evaluative content of one's beliefs about Bush. However, the unipolar method of scaling beliefs seems more reasonable given the interpretation of beliefs as subjective probabilities, which should range from 0 to 1. The unipolar method requires disbelief in negative attributes to make either no contribution (0 expectancy) or a small negative contribution (expectancy rating greater than 0) to the composite.

Whether bipolar or unipolar scoring of expectancies is implemented can affect the magnitude of correlations between attitudes and beliefs, with unipolar scoring occasionally producing higher correlations but bipolar scoring more commonly producing higher correlations (see discussion by Ajzen, 1991; Hewstone & Young, 1988; Sparks, Hedderley, & Sheperd, 1991). More generally, Schmidt (1973) showed that correlations between a criterion (i.e., direct measure of attitude) and a composite variable made by multiplying expectancies and values are highly dependent on the scales that assess expectancy and value. Only if the variables are ratio scaled and thus have a rational zero point would these correlations be unaffected by admissible scale transformations (see Chapter 2). Although theoretical arguments can be made in favor of bipolar or unipolar scorings of beliefs and evaluations, from a measurement perspective the choice is arbitrary if we assume that investigators have, at best, an interval scale (see Chapter 2). Then any linear transformation of the ratings can be made without changing the measure's scale properties; changes between unipolar and bipolar scales are linear transformations that consist of merely adding a constant.

One way to come to terms with the scaling issue is to derive optimal scalings of both beliefs and evaluations from the data. Holbrook (1977) proposed such a solution, which derives those constants that, if added to each respondent's belief and evaluation scores, maximize the correlation between Belief × Evaluation products and attitudes. Although this creative solution has been implemented by attitude researchers (e.g., Ajzen, 1991), it presents certain statistical difficulties (see Bagozzi, 1984) and does not address the more fundamental issue of whether the contribution of beliefs to attitudes can be modeled by multiplying people's ratings of their expectancies times their evaluative ratings of their beliefs.

Methodologists concerned about the adequacy of this multiplicative model have pointed out that the use of a multiplicative composite of two variables as a predictor of attitude is tantamount to assuming an interaction between the variables (e.g., Bagozzi, 1984; Evans, 1991). Such interactions are treated in a regression context by examining the separate effects of the two components of a composite and entering the cross-product of the components to represent the interaction (Cohen, 1978). Methodologists therefore have recommended that attitude researchers examine the relation between beliefs and attitudes by testing a hierarchical regression model that first enters an expectancy term and a value term and then tests for the significance of the Expectancy × Value term. Using this procedure, the multiple correlation that is produced is unaffected by linear transformations of either beliefs or values, and the adequacy of the multiplicative model is tested by the significance of the interaction term.

This suggestion is all very well and good from a statistical perspective, but unfortunately lacks theoretical import. Existing tests of the hierarchical regression procedure suggest that the interaction term is often not significant (see Bagozzi, 1984), and one is left with an "additive model" that predicts attitude from expectancies and evaluations separately. However, this model is not theoretically meaningful. Neither the probability nor the value term makes much sense as a separate predictor of attitude, particularly when investigators have estimated the expectancy and value terms from respondents' ratings of modal salient beliefs. Taken alone, the values of the attributes that respondents are presented with reflect the construction of the list and not the evaluative content of respondents' beliefs about the attitude object. The probabilities respondents attach to the list terms are also not meaningful in and of themselves; these ratings do not indicate the evaluative content of respondents' beliefs. Instead, respondents' probability ratings become interpretable in an attitudinal context only when viewed as expressions of agreement or disagreement with terms of known value given on the list.

To illustrate why it is not psychologically meaningful to treat probability or evaluation ratings as separate determinants of attitude, consider a researcher who has presented respondents with the characteristics *hostile*, *intelligent*, *incautious*, and *forceful* in a list of adjectives assessing the evaluative content of their beliefs about

Saddam Hussein. In terms of indicating this evaluative content, the probabilities respondents attach to these adjectives are meaningless without knowing the values of the adjectives. Similarly, the values respondents attach to the adjectives are meaningless without knowing the probabilities they attach to them. Respondents indicate the evaluative content of their beliefs about Hussein only when they rate the extent to which each of the listed traits validly characterizes Hussein *and* indicate the values of the traits (or the values of the traits are otherwise known and are taken into account by the researcher). Only the conjunction of expectancies and values reveals the evaluative content of respondents' beliefs.

One solution to this methodological conundrum is to avoid the modal salient belief technique and instead elicit respondents' self-reports of their own beliefs about the attitude object. Cronen and Conville (1975a) have argued that when subjects' own beliefs are elicited, the expectancy component of the model does not improve prediction. Expectancies are unnecessary when beliefs are elicited from each respondent because the probabilities of the attributes spontaneously ascribed to attitude objects are ordinarily quite high. If so, researchers can then revert to a simple model that predicts attitudes merely from the values attached to self-reported beliefs. In contrast, when respondents react to lists of modal salient beliefs, prediction is improved by taking expectancies into account. Because many of these modal beliefs may not be held by individual subjects, it is important to allow them to deny the beliefs by assigning low probabilities to them.

Expectancy-Value Model as a Theory of Persuasion

Fishbein and Ajzen have developed a number of the implications that the expectancy-value model has for persuasion (Ajzen & Fishbein, 1980; Fishbein & Ajzen, 1975, 1981). Their application of expectancy-value principles to persuasion focuses primarily on the importance of message content in producing change in beliefs, attitudes, intentions, or behavior. The approach is quite appealing as a way of thinking about persuasion and in fact has been quite popular in applied contexts (e.g., Olson & Zanna, 1987; Severy, Houlden, & Wilmoth, 1981). This popularity stems at least in part from the model's implication that, to induce people to change their attitudes in a desired direction, they need only be exposed to messages that cause them to change their underlying beliefs. The model might be seen as adopting an educational approach to persuasion in the sense that it implies that practitioners of persuasion should present appropriate beliefs to recipients in order to produce changed attitudes.

According to the model, to change an attitude in a favorable direction, the summed expectancy-value products of the beliefs that underlie the attitude must become more positive than the summed products prior to the influence attempt. Similarly, change in an unfavorable direction is produced by negative change in these summed products. In other words, to change an attitude, the beliefs underlying the attitude (the so-called *primary beliefs*) must be changed correspondingly. According to the model, these changes in beliefs can occur in either the subjective probabilities of the attributes (b_i) or the evaluations of these attributes (e_i) or both terms.

236

In comparison with the correlational studies discussed in the prior section, experiments presenting subjects with persuasive communications can provide somewhat stronger evidence for the model's assumption that beliefs determine attitudes. Persuasion experiments can be more convincing because they feature interventions designed to change recipients' beliefs. In fact, persuasive communications have been shown to change message recipients' beliefs about the attitude objects they discuss and to have corresponding effects on recipients' overall attitudes (e.g., Brubaker & Fowler, 1990; Carlson, 1953, 1956; Fishbein, Ajzen, & McArdle, 1980; McArdle, 1973). For example, in one of the conditions of McArdle's experiment, patients at a V.A. hospital who had been diagnosed as alcoholic received messages extolling the positive consequences of signing up for an alcoholic treatment program. This message successfully changed these patients' beliefs about the consequences of signing up for the program, produced positive change in their attitudes toward signing up, and increased the frequency with which these patients actually did enroll in the alcohol treatment program.

Other applications of the expectancy-value model to attitude change have demonstrated that exposure to advertisements brings about changes in beliefs about products and product use and corresponding changes in attitudes toward using or purchasing products (e.g., Lutz, 1975, 1977; A. A. Mitchell & Olson, 1981; Pomazal, 1983). Less research has addressed changing attitudes through the second route designated by the model, that is, by changing people's evaluations of the attributes that are associated with attitude objects. Further, those few messages that have been designed explicitly to change attribute evaluations have had relatively little effect on these evaluations and little corresponding effect on overall attitudes toward the attitude object (Lutz, 1975), perhaps because evaluations of attributes are often well anchored in extensive prior learning. For example, the perception that it is good that a laptop computer is *light* in weight and bad that it is *expensive* would seem to be difficult to alter. Better than trying to convince potential buyers that lightness is bad or high cost is good would be an advertising campaign suggesting that the featured laptop is relatively light and inexpensive, compared with other comparable products.

Even persuasion experiments do not provide entirely clear-cut evidence of the validity of the expectancy-value model because it is possible that a persuasive message designed to change beliefs actually had its influence on attitudes by a route other than its influence on beliefs. For example, recipients could respond affectively to such messages, and these affective reactions (e.g., joy) could influence their expressed attitudes (see discussions of affect in Chapters 1, 3, and 9). Recipients might then infer corresponding beliefs from their changed attitudes.

Strategies for Constructing Persuasive Messages. Fishbein and Ajzen (1975) have emphasized that an individual's attitude is a function of the beliefs that are accessible (or, in Fishbein and Ajzen's terminology, "salient") at the point in time when the attitude is measured. Therefore, change in an attitude could be produced by changing the beliefs that were already accessible for message recipients or by making more accessible beliefs that were not previously accessible. In view of these considerations, Ajzen and Fishbein (1980) recommended that persuasion researchers use pretesting to determine, in relation to the attitude slated for persuasive efforts, the beliefs that are commonly accessible among people in the population of potential message recipients. Although such pretesting does not solve the problem of whether communicators should attempt to change already accessible beliefs or introduce new beliefs in hope that these will be accepted, pretesting would help practitioners identify beliefs that might be targeted for change (see Marin, Marin, Perez-Stable, Otero-Sabogal, & Sabogal, 1990). If argumentation were tailored to the underlying beliefs of the members of the target audience, communications designed to change attitudes no doubt could be written more efficiently and should have greater potential persuasive power. Nevertheless, according to the assumptions of the expectancy-value model, change in beliefs underlying an attitude (i.e., in summed expectancy-value products) has taken place if a communication designed with or without the benefits of such pretesting is effective in changing this attitude.

Ajzen and Fishbein have also pointed out that the arguments contained in a message are likely to be persuasive only if they are constructed differently, depending on whether the persuader's goal is changing a belief, attitude, or behavior (Ajzen & Fishbein, 1980; Fishbein & Ajzen, 1981). Because other theories of persuasion do not make an important distinction between attitude, belief, and behavior, they do not have implications for tailoring communications dependent on the persuader's goal. These theorists assume that if a persuasive message is to be effective, its content must influence *primary beliefs*, which are those beliefs that underlie the variable that the persuader desires to change—in other words, that underlie the belief, attitude, or behavior that the message has presumably been designed to influence.

For Fishbein and Ajzen, arguments play a key role in determining persuasion and so must be selected with care. In their view, these arguments must pertain to the primary beliefs for the variable the influencer wants to change (e.g., attitude) or must represent beliefs that influence those primary beliefs. For example, if a persuader's goal is changing a general attitude (e.g., toward welfare reform), the expectancy-value principle implies that the communication should address the attributes of this attitude object because these would likely be the primary beliefs underlying the attitude. If the goal is changing a behavior, the behavior itself must be considered the relevant attitude object, and the communication should address the consequences of the behavior in an effort to change the attitude toward this behavior and the behavioral intention that presumably controls the behavior (see Chapter 4). Of course, consistent with the process theories we discuss in Chapters 6, 7, and 8, messages containing appropriately tailored arguments may nevertheless be ineffective in producing desired changes because persuasion cues such as low communicator credibility and negative audience reactions decrease susceptibility to persuasion (or because message recipients fail to attend to or comprehend the content of the communication).

The Acceptance-Yielding-Impact Model of Persuasion. Fishbein and Ajzen's (1981; Ajzen & Fishbein, 1980) acceptance-yielding-impact analysis of persuasion builds upon the general expectancy-value model by postulating three key cognitive processes that mediate the persuasiveness of messages: acceptance, yielding, and impact. Whereas the first two processes refer to the *direct* effects of a persuasive message, the last process refers to a message's *indirect* effects. That is, a message can exert direct effects by producing acceptance of and yielding to the arguments (i.e., primary beliefs) it contains, but it can also exert indirect effects by its impact on primary beliefs that are not explicitly mentioned in the message.

In this model, the terms acceptance and yielding are given precise quantitative definitions. Consider an antismoking message containing the argument "smoking is hazardous to health." The extent to which a recipient *accepts* this argument is defined in terms of belief strength (i.e., b_i), which is operationalized as the subjective probability of the argument. If the subjective probability that smoking is hazardous to health is higher for recipient A than for recipient B (e.g., .80 vs. .60), then recipient A accepts (i.e., believes) this argument more than recipient B. However, recipient A has not necessarily *yielded* to this argument more than has recipient B; after all, recipient A may have believed this argument just as strongly prior to receipt of the message. As this reasoning suggests, yielding refers to the *change* in acceptance of an argument that results from exposure to the message. For example, if the pre-message subjective probability associated with this argument was .70 for recipient A and .30 for recipient B, then recipient A has actually yielded less to this argument (.10 points on the probability scale to produce the post-message probability of .80) than recipient B (.30 points to produce the post-message probability of .60).

Impact effects occur to the extent that persuasive arguments influence recipients' acceptance of and yielding to primary beliefs that are not directly addressed by the message. Moreover, such impact effects may sometimes undermine the persuasiveness of a message. Consider an advertisement for Detergent X that contains the argument "Detergent X is strong." As Fishbein and Ajzen (1981) pointed out, this argument might lead recipients to infer that "Detergent X is harmful to clothes." If so, the persuasive effect of the advertisement on recipients' attitude toward Detergent X or toward the behavior of purchasing the product might be reduced. Consider in addition the portrayal of a car as luxurious in an advertisement. This depiction might cause potential purchasers to regard the car as expensive, a belief that would make attitude toward the behavior of purchasing the car more negative for many of them. The possibility of impact effects deserves careful evaluation when researchers and practitioners design persuasive messages.

By aggregating acceptance and yielding scores across all primary beliefs that are directly or indirectly addressed by the message's arguments, the degree to which recipients accept and yield to the message's recommended belief, attitude, or behavior can be predicted. The crux of the acceptance-yielding-impact analysis, then, is that these three cognitive processes mediate message persuasiveness.

Evaluation of Expectancy-Value Model as a Theory of Persuasion

The significance of Fishbein and Ajzen's views about persuasion resides primarily in the level of analysis that they provide. Although other theories of persuasion often agree that message content is an important determinant of persuasion, none provides the molecular analysis that Fishbein and Ajzen have stressed. Moreover, alternative theories do not accord any differential importance to the fact that a persuasive message

239

may be designed to alter beliefs, attitudes, intentions, or behavior. For Fishbein and Ajzen and, we suspect, also for practitioners of persuasion, such distinctions are crucial.

Even though the expectancy-value approach has very important implications for choosing arguments to include in persuasive messages, the framework has narrow scope as a theory of persuasion. One limitation of the approach is that in a formal sense the expectancy-value model pertains only to the change of attitudes (i.e., evaluations of attitude objects) and behavioral intentions. Although, as we have already noted, Fishbein and Ajzen acknowledged that persuasive messages are sometimes targeted to change specific beliefs, their expectancy-value approach does not provide a model of belief change. Yet the acceptance-yielding-impact amplification of their views does consider relations between beliefs—for example, Fishbein and Ajzen have warned designers of persuasive messages to be aware that recipients of persuasive messages may infer beliefs other than those actually stated in the persuasive arguments. However, the model provides no formal guidance for choosing arguments to include in messages designed to influence a specific belief. Fishbein and Ajzen have recommended that the McGuire-Wyer probabilogical approach and other formal probability models be applied to understand change of beliefs, yet have also agreed with our position that such models describe only some of the possible types of inferences that may account for belief change (see Ajzen & Fishbein, 1980; Fishbein & Ajzen, 1981).

The other principal limitation of the model is that it, like the probabilogical model, provides no mechanism for predicting the effects of persuasion variables other than those message-content variables that can be directly coordinated to the terms of the expectancy-value equation (i.e., subjective probabilities of attributes of the attitude object and the evaluations of these attributes). Not only does the model have no explicit way to predict the effects of source, recipient, and contextual variables, but also it has few implications for predicting the effects of molar message-content variables such as order of presentation. Fishbein and Ajzen (1981) have suggested that such variables be treated as *external* to the terms of the expectancy-value equation and the acceptance-yielding-impact model. They have argued that source, recipient, and other external variables have impact on the target attitude or intention only to the extent that they change the expectancies or values associated with the primary beliefs underlying the attitude or intention. Although this general idea is not without merit, it has not been developed sufficiently to enable the model to generate the kinds of specific persuasion hypotheses that are the hallmark and greatest strength of many other theories of persuasion. Moreover, the proposition that the effects of external persuasion variables are mediated by the terms of Fishbein and Ajzen's model has yet to be tested extensively by structural equation and other regression procedures that allow an examination of the causal ordering of variables (but see A. A. Mitchell & Olson, 1981).[3] Further, it is consistent with the process theories we review in Chapters 7 and 8 (e.g., heuristic-systematic model, attributional approaches) to expect that some persuasion variables have a direct impact on target attitudes or intentions without mediation by processing of argumentation or retrieval of the attributes that the individual associates with the attitude object.

Even in the case of variables whose impact is mediated by their effects on underlying beliefs, Fishbein and Ajzen's external variable perspective merely allows investigators to *track* the effects of such cues but does not suggest novel predictions about them. Linkages to other theories or to known persuasion findings are required to predict the effects of persuasion cues that affect attitudes and intentions through impact on the beliefs that are the terms of the expectancy-value equation.[4]

Information Integration Theory

As we explained in Chapter 3, the Expectancy × Value equation can be viewed as just one instance of a larger set of algebraic equations that might describe the process by which beliefs are combined to form and change attitudes. Algebraic models have been developed as a more general approach to understanding attitudes primarily by Norman Anderson, whose framework is known as *information integration theory* (e.g., 1971, 1981a, 1981b, 1991). This theory presumes that attitudes and beliefs are formed and modified as people receive and interpret new information and integrate it with their prior attitudes and beliefs.

Valuation and *integration* are the two basic operations of information integration. Valuation is represented in terms of the determination of two aspects of information: its *scale value* and its *weight*. The scale value of information is its location on the relevant dimension of judgment, and its weight is its importance or psychological impact in relation to the individual's judgment. For example, the scale value of a communication on the topic of the Bush administration's Gulf War policy is its perceived location on a pro-vs.-con scale of favorability toward the policy. The weight of the communication is its importance as a determinant of the individual's attitude toward the policy.

Integration, which is the process of combining items of information, is described by simple algebraic models in the information integration approach. For example, if a person receives n items of information, and the scale value of stimulus i is represented by s_i and its weight by w_i, the response to the total set could be described by a model that adds these items of information:

$$R = w_o s_o + w_1 s_1 + w_2 s_2 + \ldots + w_n s_n \qquad (5.10)$$

In this equation w_o and s_o are the weight and scale value of the person's initial attitude. This model becomes an averaging model if the additional requirement is made that the weights are positive and sum to one. Yet the averaging model most often appears in a form that makes its averaging principle immediately apparent:

$$R = (w_o s_o + \sum_{i=1}^{n} w_i s_i)/(w_o + \sum_{i=1}^{n} w_i) \qquad (5.11)$$

For this version of the averaging equation the sum of the weights appears in the denominator of the expression on the right-hand side of the equation, and no

241

assumption is made that the weights sum to one. Equations 5.10 and 5.11 are the same model and differ only in the form of their algebraic expression.

As we indicated in Chapter 3, the information integration approach has considered a variety of specific integration rules as plausible combinatorial models. Although the averaging model has been most widely researched and apparently has widest applicability, especially to problems of attitude formation and change, numerous other rules have been suggested by investigators for specific problems of stimulus combination (see N. H. Anderson, 1981a).

Applications of Information Integration Theory to Attitude Change

In empirical applications of information integration theory, weights and scale values are coordinated with various aspects of the stimulus information and the judgment task. As already noted, the scale value of a persuasive message is the position the communicator is perceived to advocate on the issue, and the weight or importance of the message would be identified with other parameters of the persuasion situation such as the credibility of the communicator or the strength of the message's arguments. The recipient's initial attitude can also be represented in terms of its scale value and weight. The scale value of the initial attitude is its location on the scale of favorability toward the attitude object, and the weight of the initial attitude would typically be identified with recipient factors such as degree of involvement with the issue or amount of previous knowledge.

Functional Measurement and Parallelism Prediction. Applications of information integration theory to persuasion have a number of special characteristics. These experiments generally feature designs that vary the position advocated in messages or other persuasion parameters such as communicator credibility. Such experiments are designed to enable investigators to evaluate one or more stimulus combination models as descriptions of persuasion and to test various hypotheses about weights and scale values.

Anderson's approach also has interesting implications for attitude measurement because experiments in this tradition may allow researchers to obtain an interval scaling of weights and scale values of items of information. These scaling procedures, which Anderson (e.g., 1970, 1976, 1981a) has termed *functional measurement*, are best explained through presenting a relatively simple experiment that functionally measured the scale values of communications.

Before explaining the functional measurement aspects of this experiment (Anderson, 1973), we must present its method and design. Subjects read communications about the lives and deeds of several well-known presidents (e.g., John Adams, Theodore Roosevelt, Woodrow Wilson). These paragraph-length communications were based on biographical material, and each was several sentences long. After reading the communications on a president, subjects rated him on a scale of statesmanship and accomplishment that ranged from 0 (low) to 10 (high).

TABLE 5.2

Theoretical Response to Combinations of Two Communications Constructed from a 2 × 3 Factorial Design

	Column communications		
Row communications	P (negative)	Q (neutral)	R (positive)
A (positive)	$w_1 s_A + w_2 s_P$	$w_1 s_A + w_2 s_Q$	$w_1 s_A + w_2 s_R$
B (negative)	$w_1 s_B + w_2 s_P$	$w_1 s_B + w_2 s_Q$	$w_1 s_B + w_2 s_R$
Row difference	$w_1(s_A - s_B)$	$w_1(s_A - s_B)$	$w_1(s_A - s_B)$
Column means	$c + w_2 s_P$	$c + w_2 s_Q$	$c + w_2 s_R$

Note. The row communications (A and B) are assumed to have equal weight (w_1); the column communications (P, Q, and R) are assumed to have equal weight (w_2); the weight of the initial attitude is assumed to be zero for simplicity. Scale values are denoted by s with appropriate subscripts. The constant (c) has the value $w_1(s_A + s_B)/2$.

Source: This table was adapted from one presented by N. H. Anderson (1973, Table 1, p. 3).

The sets of communications presented to subjects varied according to the 2 × 3 design represented in Table 5.2. The first factor of the design, shown by the two rows of the table, represents whether one communication was positive (A) or negative (B). The second factor, shown by the three columns of the table, represents whether a second communication was positive (P), neutral (Q), or negative (R). For each president, subjects received a communication representing one of the two levels of the row factor and a second communication representing one of the three levels of the column factor.[5] Consistent with the averaging model given by Equations 5.10 and 5.11, Anderson assumed that subjects judged statesmanship by averaging or making a composite of the information in the communications that they had read. For example, a subject who received a positive and a neutral communication about President Wilson should have a moderately positive attitude, an attitude less favorable than that of subjects who read only positive communications about President Wilson. The data shown in Figure 5.1 are consistent with this averaging prediction. This experiment thus illustrates the model's prediction that the attitude of an individual who is exposed to messages advocating divergent viewpoints is an "average" of the various messages (see also Youngblood & Himmelfarb, 1972).

A fairly stringent test of the adequacy of the averaging model to account for the data consists of examining whether the two curves shown in Figure 5.1 are parallel. In general, if data exhibit parallelism, an averaging or adding model is adequate to describe the findings.[6] Because it may not be obvious to some readers that the averaging model predicts parallelism, we show the details of this derivation in Table 5.2. Consistent with the design already noted, this table shows that each subject receives communications representing a row and a column of the design—one row

FIGURE 5.1. Mean judgment of general statesmanship for presidents. Higher numbers indicate more favorable attitudes. This figure was adapted from one presented by N. H. Anderson (1973, Figure 1, p. 5).

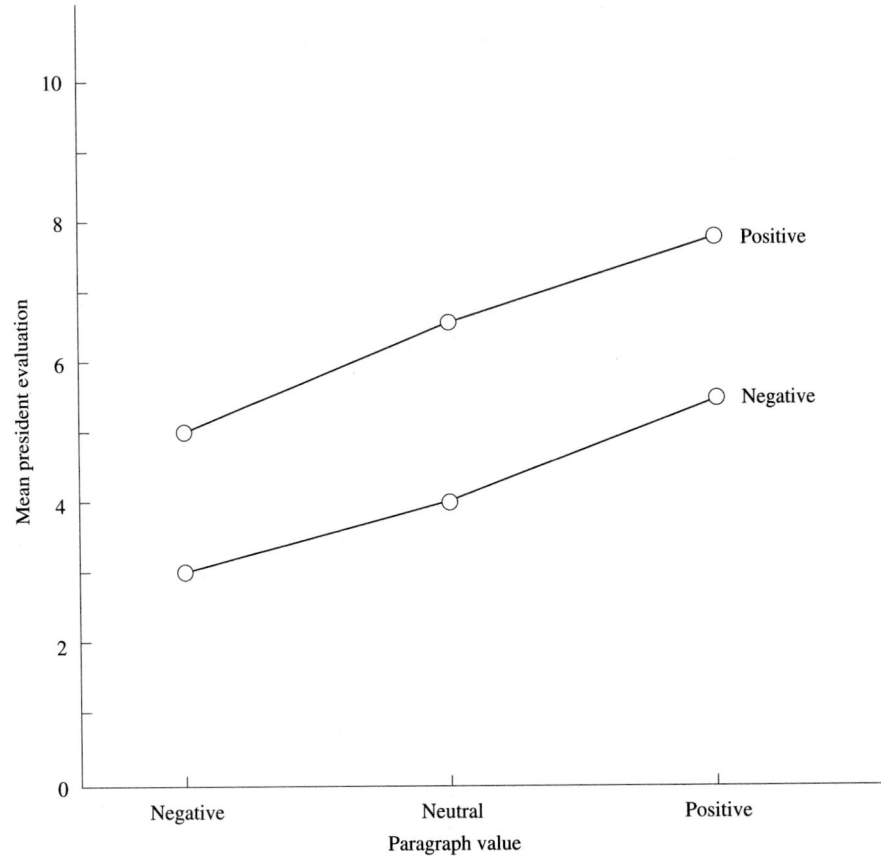

communication (A or B) and one column communication (P, Q, or R). The entries in the cells of the table represent the predicted response according to the averaging model (Equation 5.10). The row differences illustrate the parallelism prediction: Parallelism is indicated by the identity of these quantities across the columns. In other words, because the model predicts that the *difference* in attitude between those who read the A and the B communications is the *same* regardless of whether they read the P, Q, or R communication, the two curves in Figure 5.1 should be equidistant at points P, Q, and R. Stated more simply, the two curves should be parallel. The statistical test of parallelism is the nonsignificance of the interaction between the row and column factors when the data are subjected to an analysis of variance. Consistent with the averaging model, this interaction was non-significant in Anderson's (1973) presidents experiment.

The functional measurement property of the information integration approach is illustrated by the column means of Table 5.2, which are a linear function of the scale values (s_P, s_Q, and s_R) of the column communications, P, Q, and R. To understand how the column means are a linear function of the scale values of the column communications, note that the first column mean, expressed as $c + w_2s_P$ in Table 5.2, is in the form of a linear equation (i.e., $b + ax$ in its generic form). Note also that the other two column means are in the identical form. Expressing this linear equation feature in words, we can state that the column marginal means of such a table are a linear function of the scale values of the column communications. The marginal means thus serve as proxy values for the true scale values of the P, Q, and R communications. This derivation thus supports Anderson's claim that he has *scaled* the column stimuli without resorting to having judges estimate their scale values. This scaling can be assumed to be correct only to the extent that the model on which it is based (i.e., weighted averaging) is correct. Anderson regarded the model as correct for the presidents experiment because parallelism was obtained (see prior paragraph). In other words, the analysis of variance and the absence of interaction that it produced provide the *consistency check* for this form of measurement (see Chapter 2).[7]

Set-Size Effect. There are numerous specific attitude change predictions inherent in the averaging model, which is the stimulus combination rule that has been most commonly used to predict attitudes in applications of information integration theory. In addition to the prediction that people average communications located at different positions on a dimension of judgment, the model makes an exact prediction concerning the consequences of exposure to multiple messages advocating the *same* position. This prediction is based on the inclusion of the individual's prior attitude position in the averaging equation. Implemented with the prior attitude, the averaging equation makes the prediction that the attitude will become more extreme as recipients are exposed to more messages. This prediction is consistent with the well-known *set-size effect*, which indicates that adding items of information creates a more extreme judgment, even when the scale values of the items are held constant (i.e., even when all items have the same scale value). This set-size effect decelerates in the sense that the increase in judgmental extremity becomes smaller as the number of items becomes greater. In other words, the increase in the extremity of the attitude is less as an item is added to a larger number of preexisting items.

Following Anderson (1981b), a demonstration of the ability of the averaging model to predict a set-size effect is readily accomplished if we assume that the initial attitude has a scale value of 50 (the neutral point) on a 0 to 100 scale and a weight of 1. If every piece of information has a scale value of 100 and a weight of 1, the response to a set of k pieces of information is the following, according to Equation 5.11:

$$R = (50 + 100\ k)/(1 + k) \tag{5.12}$$

It can easily be calculated that R takes on the values 50, 75, 83.3, 87.5, ..., for 0, 1, 2, 3, ... items of information and approaches 100 as an asymptote. This theoretical

FIGURE 5.2.
Theoretical set-size
effect, assuming
that every piece of
information has a
scale value of 100
on a 0 to 100 scale
and a weight of 1
and that the initial
attitude has a scale
value of 50 and a
weight of 1.

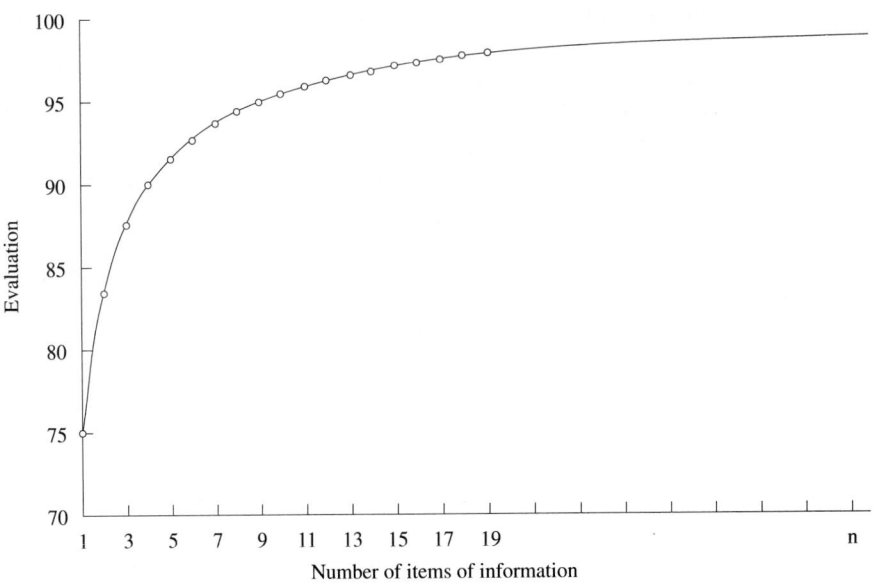

function is given in Figure 5.2. Empirical tests are in accord with this weighted averaging explanation for the set-size effect (e.g., Anderson, 1965a, 1967; Himmelfarb, 1973; Sloan & Ostrom, 1974), although alternative models can also account for these effects (see Yamagishi & Hill, 1983).

The original impetus for adding the initial attitude (or initial impression) term to the averaging model apparently was that it would enable the model to account for the set-size effect (Anderson, 1965a). An averaging model that omits the initial attitude cannot predict the polarization that occurs when information of equal value is cumulated. For example, the model without the initial attitude term would predict that the average value of two items of equal value is the same as the value of each item (e.g., the average of +2 and +2 is +2). Yet the concept of initial attitude has utility beyond its ability to allow the averaging model to account for the set-size effect. Subsequent research by M. F. Kaplan (e.g., 1971a, 1971b, 1973) has systematically explored the concept of initial attitude and documented several of its implications for information integration. For example, Kaplan demonstrated that, consistent with the averaging model, initial attitudes have less impact on final attitudes as the amount of information from external sources increases.

Interactions Between Recipient Variables and Source or Message Variables. Other interesting predictions of the weighted averaging equation are inherent in the averaging property of the model. This property is expressed in Equation 5.10 by the assumption

246

that the weights sum to one and in Equation 5.11 by the fact that the weights entered into the numerator of the right-hand side of the equation must also be entered into the denominator. One simple illustration of the implications of this averaging property can be given for a hypothetical situation in which a recipient of a message integrates the message with her prior attitude. In this situation, the weight of the message could be coordinated with source credibility, with larger weights indicating higher credibility. In addition, the weight of the initial attitude could be coordinated with the recipient's involvement in the topic of the communication, with larger weights indicating greater involvement. Because of the averaging property of the model, the lower weight given to the recipient's initial attitude when she is relatively uninvolved would imply a higher weight for the message and hence a more pronounced source credibility effect. The predicted finding that source credibility has more impact under low than high involvement is common in persuasion research (e.g., Chaiken, 1980; H. H. Johnson & Scileppi, 1969; Petty, Cacioppo, & Goldman, 1981; see Chapter 7). Numerous other predictions of interactions between variables that can be coordinated to weights on differing items of information would also follow from the weighted averaging model. In general, the model predicts interactions between recipient variables and communicator or message variables because the recipient's prior attitude and the message are represented as two weighted items of information that are integrated.

Communicator Credibility Effects. The effects of communicator characteristics on the persuasiveness of messages have been of special interest within the information integration framework. At one level, the predictions of information integration theory for source effects are quite simple. Communicators with evaluatively positive attributes are assumed to be more persuasive than communicators with less positive attributes, and communicator variables are usually assumed to affect persuasion through their effect on the weight parameter. Consequently, source variables (e.g., communicator credibility), treated as weights, would multiply the scale value of the message. This assumption that source variables typically influence the weight parameter has specific quantitative implications within designs in which communicators of differing credibility advocate differing positions.

Illustrating the implications of these assumptions for source credibility effects is research by M. H. Birnbaum, Wong, and Wong (1976). In one of their studies, hypothetical persons were described by an acquaintance who contributed a trait description conveying high, medium or low likableness (e.g., loyal, blunt, or phony, respectively). Communicator credibility was manipulated by specifying how long the acquaintance had known the person: three years (high credibility), three months (medium credibility), or one meeting (low credibility). A 3 × 3 design resulted: One factor was the three levels of likability, and the second factor was the three levels of communicator credibility. Thus, a sample description, illustrating the low credibility, medium likability cell of the design, was a person "described by an *acquaintance of one meeting* as *blunt*" (Birnbaum et al., 1976, p. 333). After reading such a description, subjects gave their attitudes by rating the stimulus person on a scale that ranged from 1 (dislike very much) to 19 (like very much).

FIGURE 5.3. Mean rating of likableness for source-adjective combinations, plotted as a function of adjective value (low, medium, high value) with a separate curve for each level of source credibility (the source has known the target person for either one meeting, 3 months, or 3 years). Higher numbers indicate greater likableness. This figure was presented by Birnbaum, Wong, and Wong (1976, Figure 3, left panel, p. 334).

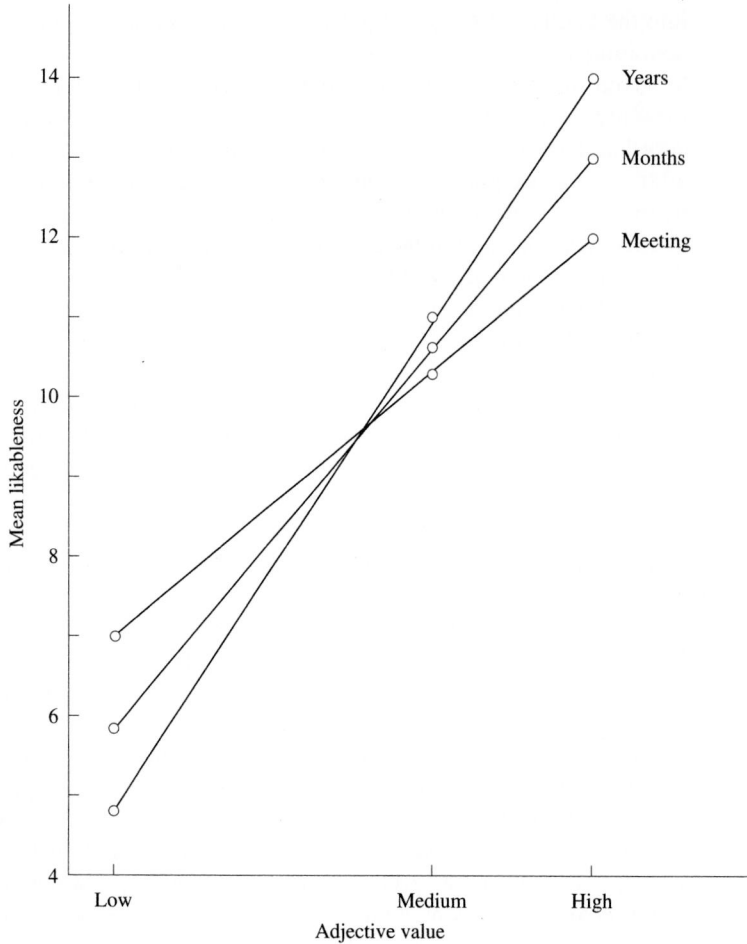

Predicting subjects' attitudes in this 3×3 design requires that we take into account the information integration assumptions that (a) source credibility affects the weight of the message and (b) weights and scale values are multiplied. It follows that factorial combinations of the position taken in the message (i.e., its scale value) and source credibility (i.e., its weight) plot as a linear fan, that is, more extreme judgments should be obtained for information provided by more credible sources. For the Birnbaum et al. (1976) experiment, this Weight $\times$ Scale Value assumption of the model would predict that the position of the message, operationalized as the likability that the trait conveyed, would be multiplied by the credibility of the source, operationalized as the length of time the source had been acquainted with the stimulus person. As shown in Figure 5.3, this linear fan prediction was substantiated by the data of this experiment, which thus supported the multiplying rule (i.e., Weight × Scale Value) that is a component of the averaging model.

Although the research by Birnbaum and collaborators (1976) showed that the credibility of more and less expert sources can be represented in algebraic models as weights attached to messages, this one idea does not exhaust the topic of communicator credibility effects. Message recipients' inferences about credibility may stem from their analysis, not only of the communicator's attributes, but also of other features of the communication situation. For example, some communicators, although expert, may seem biased because they are known to have a vested interest in inducing message recipients to favor a certain position on an issue (see discussion of attribution theories of persuasion in Chapter 8). To discern the presence of bias, message recipients need to attend to the biasing aspects of the communicator's background or situation as well as to the position the communicator advocates. If recipients in some sense discount a communicator who advocates a position in which he has a vested interest, this lessened persuasiveness might be represented by the weight variable in the manner that Birnbaum and colleagues represented communicator expertise. However, an additional possibility is that recipients adjust the scale value of the communicator's message to remove, in effect, the impact of the communicator's vested interest.

To capture more of this complexity, Birnbaum and Stegner (1979) designed a more elaborate application of information integration principles to the prediction of source effects. In this experiment, respondents estimated the monetary value of each of a number of used cars, given the value estimated by a communicator and each car's "blue book" value (i.e., a standard "fair" price for cars of that year, make, model, etc.). The communicator's expertise was manipulated by ascribing either a high, medium, or low level of automotive expertise to him. For example, the high expertise communicator was described as an "expert mechanic whose hobby is the repair and modification of sports cars" (Birnbaum & Stegner, 1979, p. 53). The communicator's bias (i.e., vested interest) was manipulated by describing him as either a friend of the buyer, a friend of the seller, or an independent individual with no relation to the buyer or seller. In addition, subjects were instructed to adopt the point of view of either the buyer, the seller, or an independent person. Thus, this experiment examined the simultaneous effects of three variables: communicator expertise, communicator bias, and the respondent's point of view (i.e., as a buyer or seller).

Although the individual effects of these variables are understandable in terms of prior research and other theories, *a priori* prediction of the simultaneous effects of such variables is extremely difficult. Thus, classic persuasion research (e.g., Hovland, Janis, & Kelley, 1953) established that persuasiveness generally increases with communicator expertise, yet it is not clear how expertise might interact with the other two independent variables. Similarly, communicator bias has been examined within an attribution framework (e.g., Eagly, Chaiken, & Wood, 1981; see Chapter 8), but it is not clear how this variable would interact with the other two variables. Even though the algebraic model approach does not provide *a priori* predictions of the effects of combining such cues, it does provide a technology suitable for evaluating various combinatorial models that might describe how such cues simultaneously affect respondents' judgments (see N. H. Anderson, 1982).

Birnbaum and Stegner (1979) examined the fit of several models to their data. In general, the averaging model was adequate, and the effects of bias, expertise, and the respondent's point of view were accounted for by effects on both weight and scale value of the communicator's message. Paralleling the Birnbaum et al. (1976) experiment we already described, expertise affected weighting. In contrast, the communicator bias manipulation had its primary effect on scale value: Scale values were adjusted up or down by roughly $30 depending on whether the communicator was a buyer's friend or a seller's friend. For example, when the communicator indicated that the car was worth $500, subjects' judgments of the car's value suggested that they had interpreted this message as indicating (a) $500 when the communicator was a person with no relation to the buyer or seller, (b) $530 when the communicator was a friend of the buyer, and (c) $470 when the communicator was a friend of the seller. Finally, the respondent's point of view affected the scale value of the messages and produced a complex configural weighting effect (by which the sign of the configural weight of the messages changed across points of view). In a later experiment, Birnbaum and Mellers (1983) also manipulated sources' expertise and bias and obtained similar effects of expertise on the weight of these sources' messages and of bias on the scale value of the messages.

Relation of Information Integration Theory to Process Theories of Persuasion

The process theories of persuasion that we consider in Chapters 6, 7, and 8 can be related to information integration theory in terms of Anderson's valuation processes—the determination of the weight and scale value of information. In other words, the processes postulated by other theories could be seen to affect attitude change through their impact on the weight or the scale value of the information. As the Birnbaum and Stegner (1979) experiment showed, shifts in scale value may occur in some persuasion settings. In related research on forming impressions of other people, many psychologists have attempted to demonstrate that the meaning (i.e., scale value) of the personal attributes ascribed to others changes, depending on the context (e.g., Hamilton & Zanna, 1974; Schümer, 1973; Wyer, 1974a; Wyer & Watson, 1969; Zanna & Hamilton, 1977). Nonetheless, Anderson has assumed that the scale value of information is ordinarily constant. Therefore, if the impact of an item of information varies from one situation to another, it is usually assumed to occur through changes in the weight of the information (see Himmelfarb, 1975).

Although information integration theory does not include a formal theory of weighting, Anderson (1981a) suggested that there are four main determinants of the weight parameter: (a) *relevance*, defined as the implicational relation between the stimulus information and the dimension of judgment, (b) *salience*, defined in terms of attentional factors, (c) *reliability*, defined as the probability that the information is valid, and (d) *quantity*, defined as amount of information.[8] Empirical work by Anderson and his colleagues, most notably research on order effects in persuasion (Anderson & Farkas, 1973) and impression formation (e.g., Anderson, 1965b, 1968a; Hendrick & Costantini, 1970) lends credibility to some of these proposed determinants of weights. For example, primacy effects may reflect attentional decrements over a series of stimuli, which cause later items in a series of stimuli to be weighted less heavily (see Anderson, 1981a). In addition, attentional factors may contribute to the well-known tendency in impression formation research for negative information to be weighted more heavily than positive information (Fiske, 1980; Hamilton & Zanna, 1972; Hodges, 1974; Kanouse & Hanson, 1972; Wyer, 1973a, 1974b).[9]

The process theories of persuasion that we discuss in the next three chapters can provide additional insights into the determinants of weighting. For example, the reception processes emphasized by McGuire could be interpreted as instances of the salience determinant of weighting (see Chapter 6). The attribution and the heuristic analyses of persuasion provide a theory of the inferences underlying the reliability aspect of weights (see Chapters 7 and 8). The cognitive elaboration emphasized in the cognitive response and elaboration likelihood frameworks could be interpreted as one process underlying the quantity aspect of weights (see Chapters 6 and 7). As our subsequent chapters will indicate, there are numerous possibilities for joining information integration theory to process theories of persuasion. The advantages of such linkages are twofold: (a) from the perspective of information integration theory, additional ability is gained to identify the determinants of weights; and (b) from the perspective of the process theories, a mathematical description is gained of the impact of process-relevant cues, including the simultaneous impact of several such cues.

The use of information integration techniques to test the predictions of process models and to provide a systematic description of the effects of processes is illustrated by Himmelfarb's attributional research (Himmelfarb, 1972; Himmelfarb & Anderson, 1975). Himmelfarb (1972) examined the persuasiveness of trait descriptions made by single or multiple sources, who had observed a person behave in one situation, several similar situations, or several dissimilar situations. For example, the following description was made by a single source: "Person 8520 was observed behaving in several highly similar situations. He was described by judge 1065 as honest, dependable, and intelligent" (Himmelfarb, 1972, p. 311). In the multiple-source condition, the traits in this description were ascribed to three different judges.

Attribution predictions for this experiment (see Chapter 8) were based on the consensus principle (greater persuasiveness for multiple versus single sources) and the consistency principle (greater persuasiveness for information gathered in multiple versus single situations, especially if these situations are dissimilar). These predictions were upheld, and the data proved to be consistent with the information integration assumption that multiple sources and multiple situations both produced increased weighting of the target trait descriptions.

In Himmelfarb and Anderson's (1975) research, subjects inferred the true attitudes of writers who had made statements under varying degrees of constraint. Relevant to this study is attribution research showing that statements a person made under constraint are less informative about his or her true attitudes or beliefs than statements made

251

without constraint (e.g., H. J. Fleming & Darley, 1989; E. E. Jones & Harris, 1967; E. E. Jones, Worchel, Goethals, & Grumet, 1971; see Chapter 1). However, attribution researchers have not dealt with the more complex issue of attitude inferences based on observations of multiple statements made on multiple occasions under varying constraints. To understand this complex type of multiple-cue prediction, the methods of information integration theory are a decided asset. In the Himmelfarb and Anderson (1975) experiments, several predictions of the averaging model were confirmed, including the attribution-influenced predictions that (a) the freedom of choice ascribed to a writer affects the weights attached to statements used to infer the writer's attitude and (b) such weights reflect both the discounting and augmentation principles (see Chapter 8).

Evaluation of Information Integration Theory

In general, the potential contribution of information integration techniques within persuasion research is considerable. As we have shown, certain predictions are inherent in particular combinatorial models—for example, the parallelism prediction, the set-size effect, and Credibility × Involvement and other interactions follow from the averaging model. More importantly, as illustrated by Birnbaum and Stegner's (1979) research, the approach provides a means to assess the relative contribution or influence of various parameters of the persuasion situation.

One of the advantages of the information integration approach is that it provides fairly rigorous methods of distinguishing between numerous combinatorial models. In other tests of such models, such as those undertaken in the expectancy-value tradition we reviewed earlier in this chapter (e.g., Jaccard & Fishbein, 1975), investigators have relied on correlations between observed attitudes and those predicted by various equations, or they merely examined scatterplots of predicted versus obtained values. As numerous investigators have shown (e.g., N. H. Anderson, 1971, 1982; M. H. Birnbaum, 1973; Slovic & Lichtenstein, 1971), models systematically in error can yield very high correlations between predicted and obtained values as well as scatterplots in which the points fall close to the diagonal line of perfect fit. Anderson (e.g., 1962, 1965a) pioneered the use of more exact analysis-of-variance tests of such models. The parallelism prediction, for example, is tested by analysis of variance: As we already indicated, the absence of a statistically significant interaction in an appropriate design indicates parallelism.

The fact that investigators can apply the information integration model at differing levels of analysis lends it considerable flexibility. As we indicated in Chapter 3, algebraic models can be applied to understand how people integrate different types of information about attitude objects (e.g., beliefs, affective reactions, behavioral input). Moreover, the units of information that are integrated may be relatively molar (e.g., entire paragraphs) or relatively molecular (e.g., single words). In a persuasion paradigm, the units that are integrated in forming a new attitude might be most usefully defined as entire communications or arguments within communications. Although the theory provides no explicit guidance concerning the most appropriate level of analysis for persuasion (or other) settings, the units that are integrated are assumed to be defined at a level that is meaningful in relation to the judgment being made (e.g., statesmanship) and the type of stimuli that are presented (e.g., descriptive paragraphs). The very general terms in which integration theory is formulated allow it to be applied very flexibly in areas of psychology ranging from psychophysics to clinical judgment, impression formation, group dynamics, and persuasion (Anderson, 1981a, 1982).

The limitations of the theory for predicting persuasion stem from the absence of a general theory of weighting as well as the absence of a theory of the conditions under which one rather than another stimulus combination rule is utilized. Yet, with links to frameworks such as attribution theory that can be regarded as dealing systematically with the determinants of weights, predictions can be made with respect to the effects of various persuasion variables. The technology associated with information integration theory provides powerful methods of testing these predictions and of determining the integration model underlying the effects that are obtained.

Evaluation of Combinatorial Theories

Although the three combinatorial models we have discussed are considerably broader than their applications to persuasion, explaining how persuasive communications change attitudes and beliefs is a central problem to which all of these approaches have been applied. Despite this common focus on persuasion, the scope of the three models varies considerably. The McGuire-Wyer probabilogical model has been directed to the problem of predicting change in target beliefs induced by changing or making salient other probabilistically related beliefs. As we have noted, this model is less appropriate for predicting change in molar attitudes. In contrast, the expectancy-value model is directed specifically to predicting change in molar attitudes as well as change in behavioral intentions.

In contrast to the more limited emphases of the probabilogical and expectancy-value models, information integration theory claims as its domain all classes of judgments or inferences. The generality of the approach is both a strength and a weakness. One strength (and the primary reason for the breadth of the approach) is that it encompasses a wide range of algebraic integration rules. Further, the weights and scale values utilized in these equations can be coordinated to various aspects of incoming stimuli and preexisting cognitions of perceivers. Given that each of the integration rules can be applied at both molar and molecular levels to aspects of persuasion settings, it seems that most persuasion phenomena could potentially be described by some form of "cognitive algebra." Yet this extreme generality is also a weakness in the absence of explicit theory concerning which stimulus combination rule is appropriate under what conditions or which aspects of the persuasion situation should be coordinated to weights and scale values. As illustrated by Birnbaum and Stegner's (1979) research on source characteristics, investigators studying persuasion within the algebraic model framework must select, from among numerous possibilities, an appropriate combinatorial rule to accommodate the effects they obtain for variables such as communicator credibility.

253

It is possible to consider the expectancy-value model as one member of the family of stimulus combination rules inherent in information integration theory. In information integration terms, the expectancy-value model is an adding rule; the weights of the equation are the expectancies or subjective probabilities attached to attributes of the attitude object, and the scale values are simply the evaluations attached to the attributes.[10] It is less clear that the conditional inference model of McGuire and Wyer can be encompassed within the information integration framework. Consistent with McGuire and McGuire's (1991) separate prediction of likelihood and evaluative judgments, probabilistic models focus on a different problem than the algebraic models of Anderson and of Fishbein and Ajzen. With the probabilistic approaches, beliefs are represented in terms of their likelihoods and not in terms of their scale values on dimensions of meaning that would represent their content (e.g., evaluation). Beliefs influence judgments, not through an aggregation of their semantic content (i.e., weighted scale values), but through their conditional relation to other beliefs, as specified by the mathematical laws of probability (e.g., Equation 5.1).

The combinatorial models share the problem of providing no explicit account of the effects of distal persuasion variables (e.g., source, context, recipient) on belief and attitude change. Such variables would presumably have their impact on attitudes and beliefs through effects on the terms of each model: (a) in the probabilogical model, through the subjective probabilities that determine belief change, (b) in the expectancy-value model, through the expectancies and evaluations associated with attributes, and (c) in information integration theory, through the weights (and occasionally the scale values) of the terms of the particular combinatorial rule utilized. Yet, as we have explained in relation to each theory, this assumption of mediation by the terms of each model yields relatively few *a priori* predictions about the effects of most persuasion variables. Nevertheless, the models can be used descriptively to track the effects of many persuasion variables. Along these lines, Fishbein and Ajzen, as we noted earlier in this chapter, claimed that variables external to the terms of the expectancy-value equation affect persuasion *only* through their impact on these terms (i.e., through effects on primary beliefs; see Ajzen & Fishbein, 1980; Fishbein & Ajzen, 1981). Yet for the purpose of providing *post hoc* descriptions of the impact of persuasion variables, information integration theory, with its variety of specific models and its methodology based on functional measurement and analysis-of-variance tests of these models, provides a considerably more powerful technology for generating a mathematical description of the effects of persuasion variables.

Despite the several advantages of combinatorial models for predicting persuasion, the general approach has in recent years lost much of the limited popularity it had gained among attitude researchers during the 1970s. Despite some attention to models of this type in reviews of attitude theory and research (Eagly & Chaiken, 1984; Hunter, Danes, & Cohen, 1984), relatively few new applications of information integration theory and related models to problems of attitude change have appeared in the research literature (but see M. H. Birnbaum & Mellers, 1983; Jaccard & Becker, 1985; Kaplowitz, Fink, Armstrong, & Bauer, 1986). The failure of the approach to gain adherents may at one level reflect most researchers' lack of familiarity with mathematical modeling. Yet the decline in interest may also reflect the fact that at least the most obvious implications of combinatorial models for attitudes have been explored, and more applications of the weighted averaging equation, for example, may strike many investigators as mere repetitions of the same principles. Attention has instead turned toward obtaining clearer understanding of the cognitive processes underlying persuasion (see Chapters 6, 7, and 8) and away from applying quantitative models that allow predictions about attitudes but do not elaborate mediating processes (e.g., counterarguing; heuristic and attributional reasoning).

Although shifts of interest of this sort are to be expected in scientific fields, psychologists should understand that the mission of combinatorial models is fundamentally different from that of process theories. That combinatorial models explicate process only to a minimal extent does not provide a justification for rejecting them. Instead, this criticism merely recognizes the unique role of these models, which is to describe only the combinatorial process *per se*, that is, to explicate how beliefs are combined to affect other beliefs and to affect attitudes. In contrast, the process theories of persuasion that we discuss in Chapters 6, 7, and 8 do not provide any but the most rudimentary accounts of combinatorial processes. Any general theory of persuasion must in the long run incorporate both elements of combinatorial models and elements of process theories.

Notes

1. Readers may well question how realistic this simplifying assumption is when applied to persuasive messages in natural settings. Particularly in relatively technical areas, communicators would attempt to modify message recipients' conditional beliefs. According to the probabilogical model, belief in a conclusion can be modified through changing the perceived relation between the premise and the conclusion (i.e., the conditional beliefs) as well as by changing belief in the premise itself.

2. We will present one of the probabilogical model's other applications to persuasion in Chapter 6, where we introduce Wyer's reformulation of McGuire's (1972) reception-yielding framework in probabilogical terms.

3. Here we refer specifically to the status of persuasion variables (e.g., communicator credibility) as variables external to Fishbein and Ajzen's model. As Chapter 4 indicated, structural equation analysis has been used extensively to test the external variable claims made by these researchers in relation to the attitude-behavior relation.

4. The expectancy-value principle has also been used to understand the persuasion induced by fear-provoking messages. We discuss these approaches in Chapter 10.

5. In addition, some subjects received two communications representing a level of the row factor and two communications representing a level of the column factor, but, for simplicity of exposition, our illustrations pertain to the subjects who received just one communication of each type.

6. However, nonparallelism does not necessarily invalidate such models because under certain conditions (e.g., unequal weighting of the stimuli within each factor of the design) averaging or adding models could predict nonparallelism (see Anderson, 1981a, p. 112; Himmelfarb & Anderson, 1975). Also, even if nonparallelism were obtained, transformations of the data might allow parallelism to be achieved (see Krantz, Luce, Suppes, & Tversky, 1971, pp. 445–447).

7. Functional measurement, which we have illustrated here and noted in Chapter 2, can be regarded as a general method of scaling attitudinal stimuli (see Dawes, 1972, pp. 86–89; Dawes & Smith, 1985). However, applications of the technique for attitude scaling have so far been limited to studies such as the Anderson (1973) experiment that we describe in detail.

8. Although the information integration approach suggests that weights would best be assessed through functional measurement, other researchers have explored various methods of directly assessing the weights attached to the attributes of attitude objects (e.g., by ratings of the importance of attributes; see Jaccard, Brinberg, & Ackerman, 1986; Jaccard & Sheng, 1984).

9. Contemporary theorizing suggests that a critical factor accounting for the negativity bias is that negative cues (i.e., behaviors such as *stealing money*) more often allow people to distinguish between alternative trait categories (i.e., they are more diagnostic than positive cues), given people's implicit theories about the relations between cues and categories (Skowronski & Carlston, 1987, 1989; see also Coovert & Reeder, 1990; Reeder & Brewer, 1979).

10. In head-to-head competition between the expectancy-value rule and the weighted averaging model typically used in information integration contexts, the weighted averaging model has generally proven superior (see Anderson 1981a; Himmelfarb, 1973; see also Chapter 3).

6

Process Theories of
Attitude Formation and Change:
Reception and Cognitive Responding

L ike the combinatorial models discussed in Chapter 5, the process theories we consider in this chapter and in Chapters 7 and 8 assume that attitudes are formed and modified as people gain information about attitude objects. Yet, the two types of theories are distinctive in other respects. For the most part, the process theories we will discuss were explicitly developed as models of persuasion. These theories provide accounts of how beliefs and attitudes form and change when people receive relatively complex verbal messages. Such messages consist of an overall position that is advocated and one or more arguments designed to support that position. In contrast, the combinatorial models' focus on how information is integrated to affect beliefs and attitudes renders them applicable not only to persuasion settings, but also to virtually any other situation in which people gain new information about attitude objects or ruminate about information they already possess. For example, people may form attitudes through direct behavioral experience (see Chapter 4), and thinking about one's attitude may increase its extremity (see Chapter 12). Some process theories of persuasion do possess explanatory power in relation to some of these other attitudinal phenomena. Nevertheless, their emphasis on persuasion renders them somewhat narrower accounts of attitude formation and change than the combinatorial models.

The greater domain specificity of process theories should not necessarily be considered a liability. Indeed when evaluated in terms of the breadth of variables whose persuasive impact has been addressed, process theories outrank combinatorial models. Although combinatorial models can predict how certain types of message content variables (e.g., arguments) affect people's acceptance of the conclusions advocated in persuasive messages, they provide no explicit *a priori* account of how most distal persuasion variables such as source factors influence attitude change (see Chapter 5). In contrast, persuasion theorists have traditionally been oriented toward illuminating the categories of independent variables highlighted in Lasswell's (1948, p. 37) classic question, "*Who* says *what* in which *channel* to *whom* [italics added] with what effect?" Thus, in terms of the range of persuasion variables addressed and the ability to provide predictive (vs. postdictive) accounts of how these variables influence persuasion (the "what effect" part of Lasswell's question), it is not surprising that the process theories of persuasion are able to claim some superiority over the combinatorial models.

Process theories and combinatorial models can also be contrasted in terms of their mathematical sophistication. As we have seen, combinatorial models provide highly specific quantitative descriptions of how people combine items of information with one another and with their prior cognitions to form new or changed beliefs and attitudes. Although not all process theories are devoid of mathematical language (e.g., McGuire, 1972), they provide primarily *qualitative* descriptions of the cognitive processes involved in people's acceptance of persuasive communications. Moreover, each process theory that we review in depth emphasizes a distinctive cognitive mechanism: (a) comprehending persuasive argumentation (McGuire, 1968a, 1972), (b) cognitive elaboration of persuasive argumentation (A. G. Greenwald, 1968; Petty & Cacioppo, 1986a), (c) heuristic-based inferences about message validity or the quality of an attitude object (Chaiken, 1980), (d) causal reasoning about the validity of persuasive messages (Eagly & Chaiken, 1975; H. H. Kelley, 1972a), and (e) biases in the perception of communicators' positions on issues (C. W. Sherif & Sherif, 1967).

This list of cognitive mechanisms emphasized by process theories of persuasion reveals an additional distinction between them and the combinatorial models. These cognitive processes typically occur *prior* to the information integration stage focused upon by the combinatorial models. The process theories attempt to explain the mechanisms that influence people's tendencies to *accept* information to which they are exposed, but are relatively silent with respect to how people integrate newly accepted information with their prior attitudes and beliefs. In contrast, the combinatorial models do an excellent job of describing how people *integrate* information they have accepted, but are relatively vague about the psychological processes underlying acceptance itself.[1] Although terms that could be interpreted as representing information acceptance are present in both the expectancy-value model (subjective probabilities) and information integration theory (weight of information), neither theory features a formal description of the determinants of information acceptance. As we discussed in Chapter 5, Fishbein and Ajzen (1981) regarded variables that influence subjective probabilities as external to their theoretical model. Similarly, such variables are external to N. H. Anderson's (e.g., 1981a) information integration theory insofar as it possesses no formal theory of weighting. Nevertheless, Anderson has suggested that there are four general determinants of information weight—the relevance, salience, reliability, and quantity of information (see Chapter 5). Process theories of persuasion could be used to illuminate the psychological mechanisms by which these factors influence information acceptance. In addition, the process theories' greater attention to distal persuasion variables can potentially provide information about the relation between these variables and the four general determinants of informational impact identified by Anderson. When possible, we will identify the bridges that can be built between process theories and combinatorial models of attitude formation and change.

It is primarily for convenience that we have used the terms "combinatorial models" and "process theories" to distinguish the theories we discussed in Chapter 5 from the theories we turn to now. Indeed, because all of these theories concern some stage of information processing, they might be more parsimoniously labeled "information-processing" models of attitude formation and change. Yet, aside from the practical difficulty of considering all of these theories in a single chapter, the distinctions we have drawn between combinatorial and process models lend some justification to the separate treatment we give them in this book.

Process theories have dominated research on attitude change for some time. Due to the volume of research these theories have generated, their continuing popularity among researchers, and our desire to examine their similarities and differences thoroughly, our coverage of them spans three chapters. In this chapter we focus our attention on a set of process theories that—along with the combinatorial models reviewed in Chapter 5—have been dubbed *systematic* approaches by Chaiken (e.g., 1980) and *central route* perspectives by Petty and Cacioppo (e.g., 1981a). These theories emphasize the importance of message recipients' detailed processing of persuasive message content in producing new or changed attitudes. This class of theories is epitomized by William McGuire's (1972) information-processing paradigm and Anthony Greenwald's (1968) cognitive response model, the two theories that we consider in most detail. In Chapters 7 and 8, we turn our attention to theoretical perspectives that either feature or incorporate mechanisms of attitude formation and change that do not implicate message recipients' comprehension or elaboration of persuasive message content. In Chapter 7 we consider two dual-process models of persuasion, the elaboration likelihood model (Petty & Cacioppo, 1981a, 1986a) and the heuristic-systematic model (Chaiken, 1980, 1987). Finally, in Chapter 8 we consider several attribution models of persuasion (Eagly, Chaiken, & Wood, 1981; Kelley, 1972a) as well as social judgment theory (M. Sherif & Hovland, 1961; C. W. Sherif & Sherif, 1967). In an Epilogue to this three-chapter sequence, we will evaluate the major process theories of attitudes, paying special attention to factors that may influence the occurrence of the different *modes* of information processing that the various theories focus upon.

McGuire's Information-Processing Paradigm

The first explicit information-processing interpretation of persuasion was proposed by William McGuire (1968a, 1968b, 1969, 1972). His analysis stemmed directly from Hovland, Janis, and Kelley's (1953) suggestion that the impact of persuasive communications could be understood in terms of three information-processing phases: (a) attention to the message, (b) comprehension of its content, and (c) acceptance of its conclusions. This "chain of responses" theme, along with the reinforcement theme that persuasion depends on providing people with incentives for adopting messages' conclusions, guided much of the experimental research on attitude change conducted by Hovland and his Yale University colleagues after World War II (Hovland, 1957; Hovland & Janis, 1959; Hovland et al., 1953). According to the Yale approach, independent variables that influence persuasion act not only *directly* on people's tendencies to accept messages' conclusions, but also *indirectly* through their impact on two causally prior processes, attention and comprehension. For example, expert communicators might induce greater persuasion than nonexpert sources because of the greater incentive value attached to accepting their recommendations. Less directly, however, experts might also engender greater influence by stimulating greater attention to and comprehension of the content of their persuasive messages. To examine attention and comprehension empirically, Hovland and his colleagues often assessed subjects' memory for the content of persuasive messages as well as their acceptance of these messages' conclusions (e.g., Hovland & Weiss, 1951; Janis & Feshbach, 1953). Although pointing to the importance of cognitive processes in persuasion, the "chain of responses" theme of the Yale program remained at a rudimentary level. Indeed, the theme that dominated this seminal research program concerned the role of incentives and drive reduction in producing attitude change. This key reinforcement perspective of the Yale approach and the empirical research it inspired are discussed in detail in Chapter 10.

The role that cognitive processes play in persuasion was developed more systematically in the late 1960s by McGuire (1968a). He proposed that the persuasive impact of messages could be viewed as the multiplicative product of six information-processing steps: (a) presentation, (b) attention, (c) comprehension, (d) yielding, (e) retention, and (f) behavior. According to this *information-processing paradigm*, the message recipient must first be presented with the persuasive message. Given that exposure occurs, the recipient must pay attention to the message in order for it to produce attitude change. If the message attracts the recipient's attention, the overall position it advocates and the arguments provided to support this position must be comprehended. It is also necessary that the recipient yield to, or agree with, the message content he has comprehended if any attitude change is to be detectable. And, if this change is to persist over a period of time, the message recipient must retain, or store in memory, his changed attitude. Finally, the recipient must behave on the basis of his changed attitude.

McGuire argued that the failure of any of these information-processing steps to occur causes the sequence of processes to be broken, with the consequence that subsequent steps do not occur. McGuire (1972) further elaborated these ideas by formulating his causal chain of processing steps as a stochastic model—a chain of responses with uncertainty at every link. Because of the assumption that subsequent steps depend on current ones, the model dictates that the probability of any step occurring is proportional to the joint probability that all previous steps occur. Given that each information-processing step occurs with a probability that rarely approaches unity (e.g., perfect comprehension is unlikely), the McGuire paradigm implies what practitioners of persuasion have long known—it is difficult to change people's attitudes and behaviors through exposing them to a message. Consider a television advertisement designed to inform the public about the risks of high blood pressure and to encourage people to have their blood pressure checked. Even if presentation (P), attention (A), comprehension (C), yielding (Y), and retention (R) all had probabilities of .8 (and assuming that these steps are independent events), the upper limit of the probability that a change in attitude would occur is $.8^4$ or .41, that is, $p(P) \times p(A) \times p(C) \times p(Y)$. Even more dismally, the upper limit of the probability that a change in behavior would occur (i.e., having one's blood pressure checked) is $.8^5$ or .33, that is, $p(P) \times p(A) \times p(C) \times p(Y) \times p(R)$.

In his numerous discussions of the information-processing paradigm, McGuire has sometimes applied slightly different labels to the six processing steps he originally outlined—for example, "exposure" rather than presentation, and "agreement" or "acceptance" rather than yielding (see McGuire, 1968a, 1968b, 1969, 1972, 1976, 1978, 1980, 1985). But more importantly, McGuire has explored both longer and shorter information-processing chains (e.g., 12 steps in McGuire, 1985; 2 steps in McGuire, 1968b). These explorations give due recognition to the multiplicity of cognitive processes that are relevant to persuasion, as well as the empirical difficulty of distinguishing processes such as attention and comprehension from one another (see Higgins & Bargh, 1987; S. E. Taylor & Fiske, 1981). For the most part, the longer chains include stages of information processing that have been featured in more recent cognitive theories of attitudes. For example, congruent with theory and research on the predictability of behavior from attitudes (see Chapter 4), McGuire (1976, 1985) proposed two additional steps that occur between retention of a changed (or new) attitude and actual behavior: retrieving the stored attitude from memory (Fazio, 1986), and integrating this attitude with other relevant information to form a behavioral intention (Fishbein & Ajzen, 1975). And, reflecting the distinctive focus of the cognitive response model, which we discuss later in this chapter (A. G. Greenwald, 1968; Petty, Ostrom, & Brock, 1981), McGuire (1985) most recently proposed that a step in which people "generate and retrieve related cognitions" intervenes between the comprehension and yielding steps of the original six-step model.

The Reception-Yielding Model. Although all of the information-processing stages enumerated by McGuire are important in effecting persisting attitude change that influences behavior, only a small portion are relevant to the typical laboratory persuasion experiment, which assesses subjects' attitudes immediately after message exposure and whose design guarantees that all subjects are exposed to the persuasive message (hence, $p(P) = 1$). Indeed, the variant of the McGuire model that is most familiar to researchers is the two-step simplification most often used to illustrate the theory (e.g., McGuire, 1968b, 1972) and to test its ability to predict the effects of distal independent variables on persuasion (e.g., Chaiken & Eagly, 1976; Eagly & Warren, 1976; Millman, 1968). Noting the empirical difficulties of obtaining separate measures of attention and comprehension in typical persuasion experiments, McGuire (1968b, 1969, 1972) combined these two processes into a single step of *reception*, and proposed that (immediate) attitude change is the multiplicative product of reception and *yielding to what one has received, or comprehended*.[2] This two-step model is given by the equation,

$$p(I) = p(R) \times p(Y) \qquad (6.1)$$

where $p(I)$ is the probability of being influenced by the persuasive message, $p(R)$ is the probability of adequately receiving the message, and $p(Y)$ is the probability of yielding to what has been received.

According to this multiplicative two-step model, if a given independent variable (e.g., source expertise) is positively related to both reception and yielding, its relation to persuasion, that is, $p(I)$, should also be positive. Similarly, if the variable were negatively related to both mediators, its relation to persuasion should be negative. The more interesting aspect of this model, however, is its implications for persuasion variables that may exert *opposing* effects on reception and yielding. For example, the fear-arousing properties of a message might negatively affect reception but positively affect yielding (McGuire, 1972), whereas a message recipient's intelligence might positively affect reception but negatively affect yielding (Eagly & Warren, 1976). The multiplicative function specified by the reception-yielding model predicts that continuous variables such as fear arousal and recipient intelligence should bear a curvilinear relation to persuasion. Figure 6.1 illustrates this prediction for the variable of intelligence. On average, recipients of moderate intelligence should be more persuaded than recipients at either lower or higher intelligence levels, and messages that induce moderate levels of fear may be more persuasive than messages that induce either lower or higher levels. The two-step model can also be applied to qualitative persuasion variables such as communication modality. For example, if written messages tended to foster greater reception than videotaped messages, whereas videotaped messages fostered greater yielding than written ones, the model predicts that there should be *no*

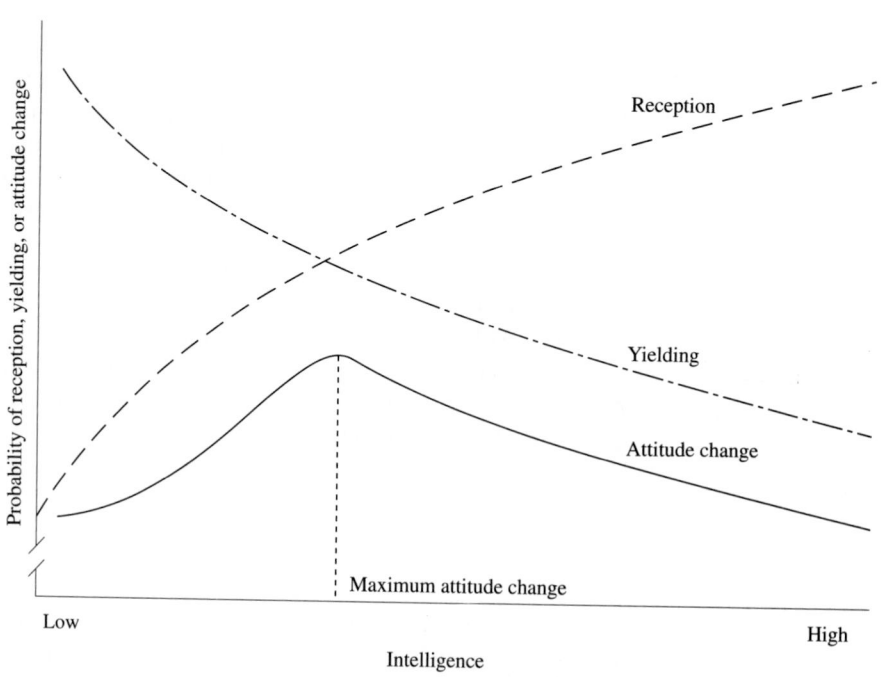

FIGURE 6.1. Probability of reception, yielding, and attitude change as a function of message recipients' level of intelligence. This figure was presented by McGuire (1972, Figure 5.2, p. 124).

overall relation between communication modality and persuasion. Thus, on average, written messages and videotaped messages might be equally persuasive (Chaiken & Eagly, 1976).

McGuire (1968b, 1969) enhanced the power of his two-step model to account for persuasion by including a postulate he called the *situational weighting* principle. According to this postulate, the relative importance of reception and yielding varies with the nature of persuasion contexts. For example, reception was assumed by McGuire to be a more important mediator of persuasion for complex, well-argued messages, whereas yielding was assumed to be more important than reception for simple, poorly argued messages. By taking the relative importance of reception and yielding into account as well as an independent variable's presumed relation to each mediator, more refined predictions can be derived. For example, in situations in which complex, well-argued messages make reception the principal mediator, the model predicts that (a) written messages will be more persuasive than videotaped messages (if written messages facilitate reception), (b) more intelligent recipients will be more persuaded than less intelligent recipients (if intelligence relates positively to reception), and (c) messages that arouse greater levels of fear will be less persuasive than messages arousing minimal levels (if fear relates negatively to reception; see Chapter 10).

The distinctive contribution of the McGuire reception-yielding model as a theory of persuasion is its focus on reception processes. Specifically, the model's key assumption is that distal persuasion variables such as recipient intelligence, fear arousal, and communication modality can influence attitude change through their effect on the reception of message content as well as on yielding, or message acceptance. Although not obvious, the reception processes featured in the McGuire model—attention and comprehension—could be linked to information integration theory's weight parameter, which indexes informational impact or acceptance. N. H. Anderson (1981a) defined the *salience* determinant of weight in terms of attentional factors (see Chapter 5; see also Fiske & Taylor, 1991): All else equal, information that receives greater attention is weighted more heavily. Within information integration theory, then, message reception can be viewed as influencing attitude judgments by its impact on information weight: All else equal, message content that receives greater attention and is better comprehended should be weighted more heavily.

Like Anderson's weight parameter, the expectancy term of Fishbein and Ajzen's (e.g., 1975) expectancy-value model can be regarded as an index of information acceptance insofar as it represents people's subjective probability judgments that attitude object X is associated with attribute i. In the context of this combinatorial model, message reception could be viewed as influencing attitude judgments through its impact on expectancies—if, following Anderson, salience is defined in terms of attentional factors and salience is regarded as a determinant of information acceptance. Despite the plausibility of considering reception as an antecedent process that influences acceptance, Fishbein and Ajzen did not attempt to incorporate reception into their model. Moreover, this neglect reflects their general viewpoint that reception of message content is neither a sufficient nor a necessary mediator of persuasion (Fishbein & Ajzen, 1975, 1981).

**Empirical Evidence That
Reception Mediates Persuasion**

To investigate the hypothesis that reception mediates persuasion, researchers have manipulated or measured independent variables that might influence persuasion by their impact on reception and have included measures of retention of message content to assess reception (see reviews by T. D. Cook & Flay, 1978; McGuire, 1966, 1969, 1985). In such studies, researchers have then examined whether independent variables exerted *parallel* effects on attitude change and retention—for example, whether high credibility sources increased retention as well as attitude change (e.g., Hovland & Weiss, 1951), or whether both retention and attitude change decreased as the amount of time since message exposure increased (e.g., Watts & McGuire, 1964). A second, more widely used, strategy has been to determine the *correlation* between measures of attitude change and measures of retention; if good reception of message content facilitates persuasion, these two classes of measures should be positively correlated (see T. D. Cook & Flay, 1978; A. G. Greenwald, 1968). Interestingly, the most direct strategy for evaluating the importance of reception—manipulating reception and examining the impact of this manipulation on persuasion—has only rarely been attempted (e.g., Eagly, 1974).

   A considerable number of studies that have used either the parallel effects or correlational strategy (or both) have yielded findings congenial to the reception-as-mediator hypothesis (e.g., Chaiken & Eagly, 1976; Chattopadhyay & Alba, 1988; Eagly, 1974; Eagly & Warren, 1976; Haaland & Venkatesan, 1968; Janis & Rife, 1959; Mackie, 1987; McGuire, 1957; Romer, 1979a; W. Wilson & Miller, 1968). Yet many other studies have not produced statistically significant evidence for a positive relation between retention of message content and attitude change (e.g., Cacioppo & Petty, 1979b; Harkins & Petty, 1981; Hovland & Weiss, 1951; Millman, 1968; Osterhouse & Brock, 1970; Papageorgis, 1963; Petty, Cacioppo, & Heesacker, 1981; Thistlethwaite, de Haan, & Kamenetzky, 1955; Zimbardo & Ebbesen, 1970). The lack of consistent covariation between measures of retention and persuasion has been widely interpreted as indicating that reception is not an important mediator of message-based persuasion (e.g., Brock & Shavitt, 1983; Fishbein & Ajzen, 1972, 1981; Gibson, 1983; A. G. Greenwald, 1968). In a subsequent section we will discuss why we believe that this conclusion is unwarranted. As a prelude to that discussion, we will first review three relatively early attempts to explore the idea that reception mediates persuasion. These three experiments illustrate the range of phenomena to which the reception-as-mediator hypothesis has been applied, the parallel effects and correlational strategies that researchers have most often used to address this hypothesis, and the mixed evidence that such studies have yielded regarding the reception-persuasion relationship.

Illustrative Research. McGuire (1957) applied the reception-mediates-persuasion hypothesis to the following question: Given that one has both good and bad news to transmit, should the good news go first and the bad last, or should one save the good news for last? According to McGuire, the good-bad sequence should be more persuasive than the bad-good sequence because the former should enhance attention to the *entire* message. With bad information placed first, McGuire reasoned that people would react negatively by decreasing their attention and that this "conditioned" selective inattention would continue even when the second, more desirable, portion of the message was communicated. McGuire's results confirmed his predictions regarding both persuasion and the mediating role of reception. Subjects who read two desirable statements and then two undesirable statements subsequently showed greater agreement with (all) the statements and greater recognition memory for them than subjects who received the same statements in reverse order. The correlation between retention and belief change in this study was also substantial ($r = .53$).[3]

Miller and Campbell (1959) applied the reception-persuasion hypothesis to a different order-of-presentation issue, one relevant to debate and courtroom contexts in which an audience (e.g., jurors) receives two messages that advocate opposing viewpoints. After receiving both messages, will recipients' attitudes be more aligned with the first message's position, a *primacy effect*, or more aligned with the second message, a *recency effect*? The earliest persuasion studies on this issue reported primacy effects (Knower, 1936; Lund, 1925), as did several subsequent (and seminal) studies of impression formation (Asch, 1946; Kelley, 1950; Luchins, 1942, 1945, 1957). Primacy effects in persuasion can be explained by a variety of mechanisms: (a) proactive inhibition, the idea that learning of the first message interferes with learning the second message (Hovland, 1951; see also N. H. Anderson, 1965a; N. H. Anderson & Hubert, 1963; Underwood & Freund, 1968), (b) decreased attention to the second message due to declining interest in the message topic (Hovland et al., 1953; see also N. H. Anderson, 1965b), (c) greater criticality toward the second message due to acceptance of the first or commitment to its position (Hovland, Campbell, & Brock, 1957; Hovland et al., 1953; Lund, 1925), and (d) meaning change, the idea that perception of the second message is distorted toward the first message (Asch, 1946; Luchins, 1942; M. Sherif, 1935; see also Helson, 1964).[4]

Unfortunately, theoretical reasons to expect recency effects were also available. For example, exposure to the first communication might make the second message more meaningful and hence more comprehensible (Hovland et al., 1953; see also N. H. Anderson & Hovland, 1957). Moreover, a subsequent wave of persuasion studies sometimes yielded primacy effects, sometimes recency effects, and sometimes neither (Bateman & Remmers, 1941; Cromwell, 1950; Hovland et al., 1957; Hovland & Mandell, 1957). These results led Hovland and Mandell (1957) to reject the universality of either primacy or recency effects and to suggest that whether one or the other obtained was dependent upon a variety of persuasion factors.

Miller and Campbell's (1959) contribution to this literature was their demonstration of the importance of temporal factors. Using Ebbinghaus's (1913) classic negatively accelerating forgetting curve, these researchers attempted to show that both primacy and recency in persuasion could be accounted for by one mechanism—the forgetting of message content. Miller and Campbell's three-session experiment manipulated both the time interval between exposure to two opposing messages (immediate vs. one week) and the time interval between exposure to the second message and the assessment of subjects' attitudes (immediate vs. one week). The two opposing messages used in this research represented the plaintiff's and defendant's case in a hypothetical lawsuit and were presented to subjects by audiotape. Presentation order was counter-balanced so that for some subjects *message one* represented the plaintiff's case and *message two* represented the defendant's case, whereas for other subjects message one represented the defendant's case and message two represented the plaintiff's case.

The four conditions created by the two time interval manipulations are shown in Figure 6.2, along with the hypothetical forgetting curves associated with the two messages that subjects received. Whereas the solid line (A) represents the decay function for message one, the dashed lines represent the decay function for message two when it is presented immediately (B) or one week (B′) after message one. The vertical distance between curve A and curves B and B′ at any point in time represents the net outcome of exposure to the two messages: Whereas recency is indicated by curve A being lower than curve B or B′, primacy is indicated by curve A being higher.

Two aspects of Figure 6.2 are noteworthy. First, the ordinate's generic label, "strength of association," refers to both memory for message content and agreement with the message. According to Miller and Campbell, because memory decays in the negatively accelerating manner described by Ebbinghaus, so should agreement. Never-theless, a second aspect of the figure reveals Miller and Campbell's one departure

FIGURE 6.2.
Hypothetical forgetting curves for two opposing persuasive communications presented successively within one experimental session (Curves A and B) or one week apart (Curves A and B′), with an added prior entry effect for the first communication (Curve A). The four vertical slicings represent the timing of attitude assessment (immediately after second communication, Conditions 1 and 3; one week after second communication, Conditions 2 and 4). This figure was presented by N. Miller and Campbell (1959, Figure 2, p. 2).

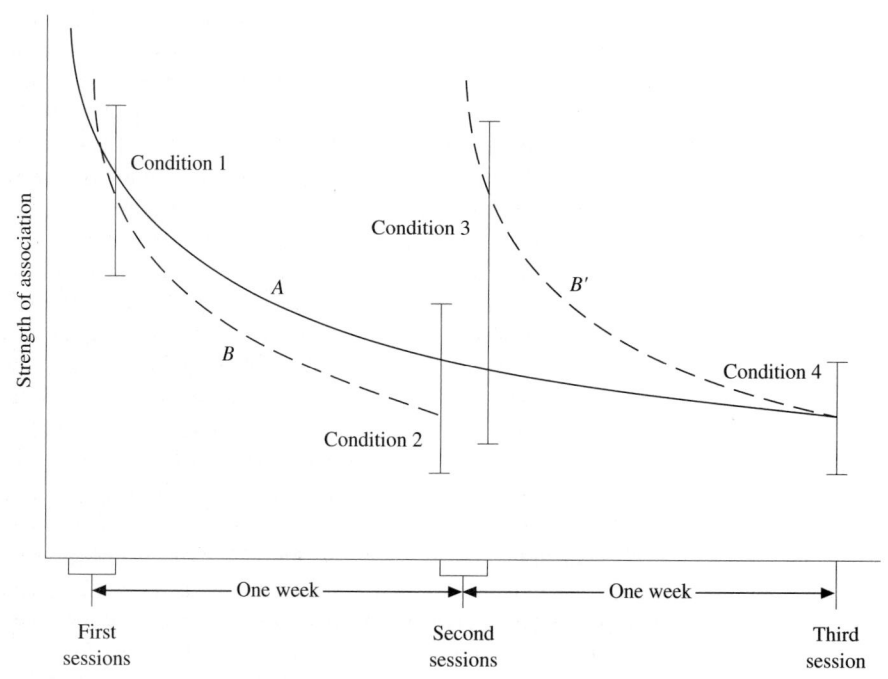

from this strict forgetting hypothesis—the decay curve for message one (A) is displaced upward from the curves associated with message two (B and B′) so that its initial "strength of association" and final asymptote are higher. Miller and Campbell drew the curves in this manner so that they could account for the primacy effects that some previous studies had found. Without this empirical adjustment, which they called the *prior entry effect*, Miller and Campbell's forgetting hypothesis would have enabled them to predict only the relative magnitude of recency effects.

As Figure 6.2 illustrates, if agreement obeys the same temporal law as memory (and if we grant the validity of the prior entry effect), recency should be greatest with a long time interval between exposure to the two messages and a short time interval between exposure to the second message and the assessment (Condition 3). In contrast, primacy should be most evident with a short exposure interval and a long assessment interval (Condition 2). Miller and Campbell's attitude data conformed to these predictions. A reliable recency effect was obtained in Condition 3 and a reliable primacy effect in Condition 2 (Conditions 1 and 4 yielded nonsignificant trends toward recency and primacy, respectively). The only fly in the ointment was the study's memory data. Although retention of message content roughly paralleled the persuasion data, the average correlation between retention and persuasion across the experiment's four conditions was neither significant nor positive ($r = -.10$).[5]

Watts and McGuire (1964) explored the hypothesis that reception mediates persuasion in a study of attitudinal persistence, a topic we discuss more fully in Chapter 12. Although supportive of the importance of reception, Watts and McGuire's findings argue against a simple one-to-one correspondence between retention and persuasion. In their study, subjects read four messages on different topics (e.g., treatment of juvenile delinquents, statehood for Puerto Rico). The messages were ascribed to high or low credibility sources and were presented to subjects over a 6-week period. Immediately after exposure to the last message, subjects' attitudes on all four message topics were assessed, as was their retention of four different aspects of the messages: the *topics* they concerned, the *positions* they advocated, the identity of their *sources*, and the *persuasive arguments* they contained. These attitude and retention measures occurred immediately, 1 week, 2 weeks, or 6 weeks after subjects' exposure to a message, depending on when they had been exposed to it in the prior 6 weeks.

The temporal decay curves observed by Watts and McGuire are shown in Figure 6.3. Although each of the four memory measures exhibits the classic negatively accelerating forgetting curve, the decay function for attitude change proved to be distinctly (and significantly) linear. The different shapes of these functions suggested to Watts and McGuire that the persistence of attitude change was only partly dependent on retention.

This interpretation was bolstered by analyses that examined the relation between retention and attitude change at the various delay intervals. Recall of the message's topic was positively related to attitudes after 1 week but negatively related after 6 weeks, and recall of the message's source was positively related to attitudes at all time points in the case of high credibility communicators but unrelated (at all time points) in the case of low credibility communicators. Clearer evidence for a simple functional dependence of attitude change on retention was found with respect to subjects' recall of the message's position and of its persuasive arguments. For both measures, the dissipation of attitude change over time was directly related to decrements in retention. Yet, arguing for a certain degree of functional independence, the retention-persuasion relation tended to be smaller at the 6-week assessment than at the 1-week assessment.

The Covariation Paradox. The three experiments we have reviewed serve as graphic illustrations of the fact that correlational evidence bearing on the reception-as-mediator hypothesis has failed to substantiate a *consistently* positive relation between retention of message content and persuasion. Whereas McGuire (1957) reported a substantial positive correlation between retention and attitude change, Miller and Campbell (1959) found a nonsignificant negative correlation. And, although Watts and

FIGURE 6.3. Temporal decay of induced attitude change and of recall for each of four aspects of the persuasive message. Assessments were made immediately, one week, two weeks, or six weeks after message exposure, and the recall data represent the percentage of subjects correctly recalling the message topic, its position, all of its arguments, and its source. Points representing percent retained attitude change were derived by calculating mean attitude change (difference from no-message control group on a 15-point agreement scale) at each of the four measurement intervals, and dividing these numbers by the mean amount of immediate attitude change. These data are collapsed across the study's two credibility conditions and across its four message topics. This figure was presented by Watts and McGuire (1964, Figure 1, p. 237).

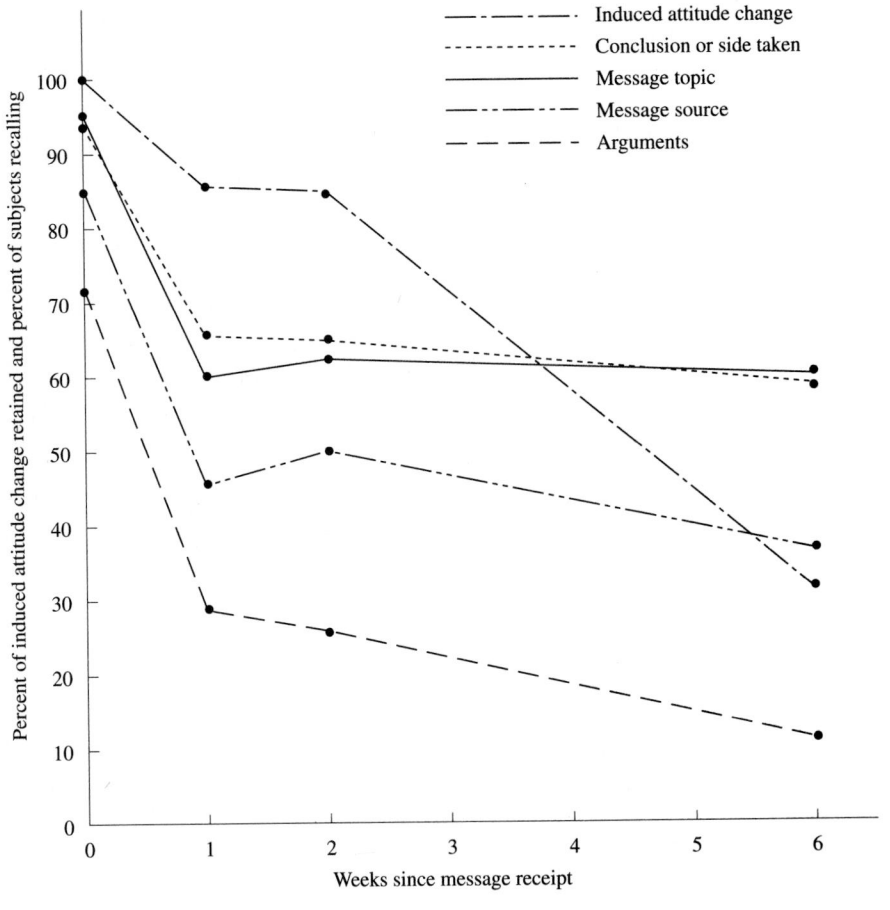

McGuire (1964) obtained some evidence for a positive relation between memory for persuasive arguments and attitude change, their time-of-assessment factor exerted nonparallel effects on the two variables (see Figure 6.3).

As noted earlier, many investigators have interpreted the absence of consistent covariation between retention and persuasion measures as proof that reception is unimportant in accounting for attitude change (e.g., Fishbein & Ajzen, 1972, 1981; A. G. Greenwald, 1968). However, there are a number of reasons why this pessimistic conclusion is not warranted (see Chaiken & Stangor, 1987; Eagly & Chaiken, 1984). Most importantly, reception was never believed to be a general, all-purpose mediator of persuasion. The Yale researchers stressed the role of incentives in producing message acceptance even more than they stressed the role of attention and comprehension (Hovland et al., 1953; see Chapter 10). Even more explicitly, McGuire's reception-yielding model specifies that persuasion should correlate highly with the *product* of reception and yielding, not reception alone (see Rhodes & Wood, 1992). Moreover, this model's *situational weighting principle* articulated McGuire's (1968b) proviso that reception is an important mediator of persuasion under some circumstances but not others (e.g., for messages that are inherently complex but not for simple messages).

In addition to ignoring factors that may moderate the importance of reception as a mediator of persuasion, most researchers have failed to appreciate that the reception-as-mediator hypothesis does not necessarily imply that the retention-persuasion relation should be invariably *positive*. The expectation of a positive relation assumes that messages contain high quality arguments. If low quality arguments characterize a message, evidence favoring the reception hypothesis should come in the form of a *negative* relation (see Chattopadhyay & Alba, 1988; Jepson & Chaiken, 1990). Although this point may strike contemporary readers as obvious, it has been ignored by most researchers. This fact, along with the failure to consider possible moderator variables, seriously compromises the evidential status of the correlational literature because the vast majority of retention-persuasion correlations that have been reported have been computed without regard for aspects of the experimental situation that may affect either the *size* or the *sign* of the retention-persuasion relation (e.g., message difficulty, message repetition, involvement, argument quality). A dissertation by one of our students illustrates this point (Shechter, 1987). In the relevant portions of this study, low self-monitoring subjects (see M. Snyder, 1974) read a message containing four strong or four weak persuasive arguments. The average within-cell correlation between post-message attitudes and argument recall was virtually zero ($r = .005$). However, when the two argument quality conditions were treated separately, the retention-persuasion correlation proved to be positive given strong arguments ($r = +.22$) and negative given weak arguments ($r = -.21$). Although modest in size, these correlations (unlike the average within-cell correlation) are favorable to the reception-as-mediator hypothesis.

The interpretation of empirical tests of the reception-persuasion relation is further clouded by reliability and validity issues that surround the use of recognition and recall measures to assess reception. In the attitudes literature, measures of recognition memory typically consist of a small number of true-false or multiple-choice items (e.g.,

Hendrick & Shaffer, 1970; Watts & McGuire, 1964). Such measures are likely to have low reliability due to the small number of items they contain (see Chapter 2); they are usually not difficult so that they often yield low variance and apparent ceiling effects (S. E. Taylor & Fiske, 1981). Moreover, they may even be misinterpreted by subjects as measures of their beliefs (Fishbein & Ajzen, 1972, 1975). The major alternative to recognition measures are free recall tasks in which subjects are asked to list the persuasive arguments given in the message (e.g., Chaiken & Eagly, 1983; Petty, Cacioppo, & Goldman, 1981). Given that most messages used in research consist of relatively few arguments, such recall measures may also lack adequate reliability. But more important, these measures are inherently poor indexes of reception. Reception refers to the encoding of message content *prior* to its integration with the recipient's initial attitude. Yet free recall measures of retention reflect not only the encoding of message content, but also the storage of message content in memory and its subsequent retrieval. Unfortunately, most investigators have obscured the important distinction between reception of message content and its retention in memory by treating the relation between message *learning* and attitude change as the critical theoretical issue (e.g., Brock & Shavitt, 1983; Fishbein & Ajzen, 1972, 1975, 1981; Gibson, 1983; A. G. Greenwald, 1968; Petty & Cacioppo, 1981a). Learning generally refers to the encoding of information, the storage of this information in memory, and its retrieval. Within McGuire's information-processing paradigm, however, it is the encoding of message content, not its storage and retrieval, that is at issue at the reception stage.[6]

In addition to these reliability and validity issues, it is likely that the effect of message reception on persuasion may be severely attenuated in the typical laboratory persuasion experiment because of methodological factors that tend to ensure a high and relatively invariant level of reception: (a) Persuasive messages are usually too simple to be miscomprehended, (b) subjects are usually college students who possess relatively high verbal skills, and (c) laboratory settings and instructions often constrain subjects to pay close attention to messages (Chaiken & Stangor, 1987; Sears, 1986). Thus, the within-cell correlations that are most often used to evaluate the reception-as-mediator hypothesis may often be attenuated due to a restricted range on message retention measures (e.g., Insko, Lind, & LaTour, 1976). In contrast, comprehension of information presented in nonlaboratory settings appears to be quite variable and, in general, not very accurate. For example, J. Jacoby and his colleagues exposed a large sample of adult respondents to brief television messages in a shopping mall testing situation and asked them to answer simple questions about these messages. They found that 30 to 40 percent of the information was miscomprehended and that comprehension was highly variable across subjects (Jacoby & Hoyer, 1982; Jacoby, Hoyer, & Sheluga, 1980; see also Schmittlein & Morrison, 1983). More recently, Jacoby and Hoyer (1987) reported lower, but still substantial, miscomprehension rates (15 to 23%) among a larger sample of adults who were tested for their comprehension of printed magazine advertisements and articles.

A final and more theoretically significant reason why low retention-persuasion correlations are ambiguous regarding the importance of reception is that details of message content may be forgotten after they are encoded or, alternatively, stored separately from the recipient's overall attitude judgment in long-term memory (N. H. Anderson, 1981a; N. H. Anderson & Hubert, 1963; Lingle & Ostrom, 1981; see also Hastie & Park, 1986). In either case, there would be no necessary reason to expect a high correlation between memory for message content and attitude change *even if* the original encoding (i.e., reception) of message content did exert a causal influence on persuasion.

In this regard, it is instructive to consider how contemporary social cognition researchers have dealt with a conceptually similar correlational paradox, the fact that subjects' overall impressions of hypothetical target persons do not consistently covary with their memory for information that experimenters provide about the targets' personalities (i.e., trait adjectives or behavioral descriptions; e.g., Dreben, Fiske, & Hastie, 1979). As Chaiken and Stangor (1987) pointed out, social cognition researchers have not concluded that the encoding of and subsequent memory for this type of information is "unimportant" in accounting for impression formation. Rather, they have treated the recall-judgment link as an important theoretical issue (e.g., Bargh & Thein, 1985; Belmore & Hubbard, 1987; Carlston & Skowronski, 1986; Hastie & Park, 1986). Research on this issue indicates that a strong memory-judgment correlation may obtain primarily when subjects do not or can not form spontaneous impressions of target persons during information acquisition (e.g., Bargh & Thein, 1985; Hastie & Park, 1986). Because subjects' impressions in these situations are presumably not formed until subsequent prompting by the experimenter, they may be heavily influenced by what subjects can recall having read or heard about the target. As a result, recall should correlate highly with impressions in such *memory-based* situations. When people form spontaneous impressions during exposure to relevant information, however, this information may be forgotten as it is encoded, or stored separately from the overall impression in long-term memory. In these *on-line* situations, then, strong correlations between memory and judgment will not necessarily obtain. This research further suggests that whether judgments will be memory-based or made on-line depends on people's *processing objectives* as well as on individual and situational differences in people's *capacity* to make on-line judgments. On-line impression formation is most likely to occur when people have the attentional resources to perform this task and the explicit goal of forming an impression about a target person (Bargh & Thein, 1985; Hastie & Park, 1986; Lichtenstein & Srull, 1987; S. J. Sherman, Zehner, Johnson, & Hirt, 1983; Srull & Wyer, 1986).

Extrapolating from these impression formation findings, Chaiken and Stangor (1987) hypothesized that the correlation between post-message attitudes and retention of message content may be relatively low in certain circumstances: (a) The setting does not constrain subjects' capacities for making on-line attitude judgments (e.g., few distractions, no time pressure), and (b) the goal of expressing an attitude on the persuasive message topic is activated due to instructional sets (e.g., "We are interested in your attitudes") or individual differences (e.g., strong prior attitudes, personal relevance of message topic). In contrast, retention-attitude correlations should prove higher in settings that (a) constrain subjects' capacity for making on-line judgments, or (b) do not make the goal of expressing an attitude particularly salient. The focus on expressing an attitude might be reduced through, for example, using unfamiliar, uninvolving topics or providing subjects with processing objectives unrelated to the attitude judgment (e.g., "We are interested in your proofreading abilities").

Findings consistent with aspects of this logic were recently reported by Mackie and Asuncion (1990, Experiment 2). Subjects whose capacity for on-line attitude judgment was constrained by having them engage in distracting cognitive tasks during message presentation (e.g., checking the message for spelling and grammatical errors) evidenced memory-based attitude change: They took a relatively long time to respond to a post-message attitude inquiry, and the amount of attitude change they exhibited correlated reliably with their recall of message content. In contrast, "on-line" subjects in this experiment, who were actively encouraged to consider their attitudes during message exposure, responded relatively quickly to the post-message attitude inquiry, and the amount of attitude change they exhibited was uncorrelated with their recall of arguments. An additional suggestive finding of this research concerned the role of *cognitive elaboration* of message content (i.e., additions and qualifications to presented arguments; see subsequent discussion of cognitive response model). In most of Mackie and Asuncion's on-line conditions, subjects exhibited considerable elaboration. In these conditions, attitude change was correlated with a valenced index of elaboration but, as just noted, not with argument recall. In a subset of one experiment's on-line conditions, however, subjects exhibited little cognitive elaboration of message content (Experiment 1, expert and nonexpert source conditions). In these low elaboration on-line conditions, attitude change *was* reliably correlated with argument recall. These findings led Mackie and Asuncion to suggest that attitude-recall correlations may be high even in settings that encourage on-line judgments and that the main determinant of their magnitude is not whether on-line judgment does or does not occur, but rather, whether cognitive elaboration of message content does or does not occur (see also Chattopadhyay & Alba, 1988; Tesser & Shaffer, 1990).

Manipulating Reception and Amount of Argumentation. Because of the ambiguity of most correlational tests of the reception-persuasion relation, Eagly (1974) manipulated message comprehensibility in order to influence reception directly. In three different experiments, subjects heard (Experiments 1 and 2) or read (Experiment 3) a message containing six high quality arguments supporting the recommendation that people should sleep fewer hours per night. In all three studies, lowering message comprehensibility reliably lowered subjects' retention of persuasive arguments and, more important, significantly lessened their agreement with the message's recommendation. This effect appeared robust because it was obtained for two different comprehensibility manipulations (poor vs. high quality audiotape recordings; randomly vs. well-ordered sentences) and did not interact with any of three additional experimental manipulations (message discrepancy, communicator credibility, instructions to counterargue message content). Compatible with these findings, McCroskey and Mehrley (1969) observed greater persuasion for an audiotaped message that was both well organized and delivered without nonfluencies relative to either a well organized message with nonfluencies or a disorganized message (randomly ordered sentences) with or without nonfluencies. Unlike Eagly's research, however, these persuasion differences cannot be attributed unequivocally to differences in the quality of subjects' reception of message content, because McCroskey and Mehrley's study included no independent indexes of reception (e.g., argument recall; see also N. Miller, Maruyama, Beaber, & Valone, 1976; Regan & Cheng, 1973).

Because lowering message comprehensibility presumably decreases the persuasiveness of (high quality) messages by lessening the amount of supportive argumentation received, it is also important to consider research that has varied the *number* of arguments that a message contains (e.g., Calder, Insko, & Yandell, 1974; Chaiken, 1980; Cook, 1969; Eagly & Warren, 1976; Insko, Lind, & LaTour, 1976; Maddux & Rogers, 1980; Norman, 1976; Petty & Cacioppo, 1984a). Much of this research has documented a reliable tendency for persuasion to decrease when fewer arguments are presented. For example, in several experiments by Insko and his colleagues, subjects were presented with varying numbers of arguments supporting the guilt or innocence of a fictitious defendant (Calder et al., 1974; Insko et al., 1976). Across the various studies, increasing the number of guilty arguments significantly increased subjects' tendencies to render guilty verdicts, whereas increasing the number of not guilty arguments increased subjects' tendencies to judge the defendant innocent. Nevertheless, correlational analyses indicated that the relation between persuasion and argument recall was not strong, although it was positive. This research, along with Eagly's (1974) comprehensibility experiments, suggests that *substantial* differences in the amount of argumentation received by subjects can exert detectable effects on their agreement with persuasive messages. Importantly, however, increasing the quantity of persuasive argumentation does not invariably enhance persuasion. Whereas increasing the number of high quality arguments can increase persuasion, increasing the number of low quality arguments can reduce it (Petty & Cacioppo, 1984a).

Research on message comprehensibility and argument quantity has also shown that the persuasive impact of these variables may not be mediated exclusively by their impact on the amount of supportive information received—the mechanism implied by McGuire's theorizing. Eagly's research showed that in addition to this informational mechanism, the decreased persuasiveness of low comprehensibility messages was also due to the negative affect that subjects experienced as they tried to comprehend these communications (Chaiken & Eagly, 1976; Eagly, 1974; also see Chapter 9). And, as we discuss in the next chapter, argument quantity may sometimes affect message acceptance directly, by influencing subjects' global judgments of message validity (Chaiken, 1987; Petty & Cacioppo, 1984a). Finally, as we will also discuss in subsequent portions of this book, variables such as message comprehensibility, argument quality, and argument quantity may exert an impact on persuasion primarily when recipients are more concerned with maximizing the validity of their attitudes than with achieving other, more interpersonal goals (Chaiken, Liberman, & Eagly, 1989; Norman, 1976; see Chapters 7 and 8).

Distal Persuasion Variables and Reception. Although Eagly's (1974) comprehensibility studies established that impaired reception of (high quality) argumentation *can* lessen persuasion, they shed little light on the question of whether the types of distal persuasion cues of most interest to investigators influence reception of message content to an extent sufficient to produce detectable effects on attitude change. Eagly's comprehensibility manipulations exerted a very strong impact on her subjects' understanding of message content. Yet these reception effects were no doubt much stronger than those that might commonly occur due to the influence of other sorts of message variables, such as McGuire's (1957) and Miller and Campbell's (1959) order-of-presentation manipulations, or most source, channel, and recipient variables. Nonetheless, there are certain classes of such distal persuasion variables that may exert a strong enough impact on reception to have a significant effect on attitude change. For example, there is good evidence that strong distractions interfere with message reception, and this lessened reception of message content appears to be one of the mechanisms by which distraction affects persuasion (e.g., Haaland & Venkatesan, 1968; Romer, 1979a; Zimbardo, Snyder, Thomas, Gold, & Gurwitz, 1970; see reviews by R. S. Baron, Baron, & Miller, 1973; Buller, 1986; McGuire, 1985).

Chaiken and Eagly (1976) found that communication modality had a strong enough impact on the reception of inherently complex messages that persuasion was affected. In their experiment, subjects were exposed to either an easy- or difficult-to-comprehend message that was presented in written, audiotaped, or videotaped form. The easy version of the message, which concerned a dispute between a company and its union employees, featured relatively short sentences and simple vocabulary, whereas the difficult version featured relatively complex sentences and sophisticated vocabulary. The results showed that with the difficult message both attitude change and retention of persuasive arguments were greater when the message was presented in written form,

TABLE 6.1

Attitude Change and Retention of Message Content as a Function of Communication Modality and Message Difficulty in the Chaiken and Eagly (1976) Experiment

	Easy Message			Difficult Message		
	Written	Audio	Video	Written	Audio	Video
Attitude change	2.94	3.75	4.78	4.73	2.32	3.02
Number of persuasive arguments recalled	2.45	2.21	2.17	2.29	1.74	1.67
Number of short-answer items correct	4.57	3.93	4.45	4.21	3.71	3.36
Perceived message difficulty	4.76	4.21	4.83	5.31	7.50	7.43

Note. Higher numbers indicate greater attitude change (15-point scale), message comprehension (from 3 arguments or 6 short-answer items), and perceived message difficulty (15-point scale).

Source: This table was adapted from one presented by Chaiken and Eagly (1976, Table 1, p. 609).

compared with when it was presented in audiotaped or videotaped form (see Table 6.1). Moreover, correlational analyses indicated that the decreased persuasion observed in the two broadcast modalities was due to the lesser amount of message content that subjects in these conditions received (and to the greater negative affect they experienced). With the easy-to-comprehend message, a different pattern emerged. As expected, comprehension of the easy message was equivalent—and high—regardless of modality. Yet attitude change was greatest when this message was videotaped, moderate when it was audiotaped, and least when it was written (see Table 6.1). The experimental results thus patterned in accord with McGuire's situational weighting principle: Reception was the important mediator of modality effects on persuasion when a difficult message was communicated, whereas yielding was presumably the more important mediator when an easy message was communicated.

Because *impaired* reception can lessen persuasion for high quality messages—and, presumably, increase persuasion when argument quality is poor—it is reasonable to ask whether distal persuasion variables that might function to *enhance* reception would produce parallel effects on persuasion. Most relevant to this question is research on the persuasive effects of message repetition. Do repeated exposures to persuasive messages lead to increased persuasion for messages that contain strong arguments and to decreased persuasion for messages that contain weak arguments; and, if so, can these effects be attributed to enhanced reception of message content? A definitive answer to this question is not possible, because, to our knowledge, only one message repetition study has manipulated argument quality (Cacioppo & Petty, 1985). Nevertheless, because most other studies in the repetition literature presumably used moderate-to-high quality messages—standard practice in most persuasion research—the question can be tentatively addressed.

Cacioppo and Petty (1985) constructed a high quality and a low quality message by assembling sets of strong and weak arguments supporting the proposal that seniors pass a comprehensive examination prior to graduation (for example arguments, see Chapter 7, Table 7.2). In the experiment proper, some subjects listened once to either the high or low quality version of the message whereas others listened to one or the other version three times in succession. The results showed that agreement with the high quality message increased from one to three exposures, whereas agreement with the low quality message decreased as exposure rate increased. Moreover, regardless of argument quality, subjects recalled more persuasive arguments after three exposures to the message than after only one exposure. The results obtained for the high quality message in this study are compatible with the findings of earlier repetition studies that used comparable exposure rates and (we assume) moderate-to-high quality persuasive messages (e.g., Cacioppo & Petty, 1979b, 1 and 3 exposure conditions; H. H. Johnson & Watkins, 1971; W. Wilson & Miller, 1968). Although Cacioppo and Petty favored a cognitive response interpretation for their persuasion data—and such an interpretation is plausible (see section on cognitive responding)—the results are also consistent with the hypothesis that repetition influenced persuasion by enhancing subjects' reception of message content.

Nonetheless, because other studies indicate that exposure frequencies greater than three often lead to decreased persuasion, whereas argument recall appears to reach an asymptote at around this number of exposures, reception enhancement alone cannot provide a full account of the persuasive effects of message repetition (Appel, 1971; Belch, 1982; Cacioppo & Petty, 1979b, 5 exposure condition; Calder & Sternthal, 1980; Gorn & Goldberg, 1980). In fact, the findings in this literature are fairly complex and indicate that the persuasive impact of message repetition may be (a) contingent on a variety of other persuasion factors (e.g., message complexity, source trustworthiness) and (b) mediated by a number of psychological processes, including cognitive ones such as reception enhancement and enhanced message-relevant thinking, and affective or motivational mechanisms such as classical conditioning and psychological reactance (see McGuire, 1985; Sawyer, 1981; see also subsequent section on cognitive response model and discussion of mere exposure in Chapter 9).

Individual Differences in Persuasibility. In the search for distal persuasion variables whose persuasive impact may be mediated by message reception, it is especially important to examine recipient characteristics because McGuire (1968a, 1968b, 1972) articulated the implications of his information-processing paradigm most completely in relation to the personality-persuasibility problem. McGuire argued that individual difference variables often exert opposing effects on reception and yielding. For example, he claimed that self-esteem and intelligence should relate positively to reception but negatively to yielding, because persons higher on these dimensions should be better able to attend to and comprehend information (reception) and also better able to defend their initial attitudes and be critical of new information (yielding). Because of this opposing-effects logic—which McGuire (1968b) labeled the *compensation principle* —the reception-yielding model predicts that the *overall* relation between such individual difference variables and persuasion should be curvilinear. Thus, persons with midscale positions on dimensions such as self-esteem, intelligence, and anxiety were predicted to be more easily influenced than those positioned either higher or lower on the dimension. Figure 6.1, which we introduced earlier in this chapter, illustrates McGuire's assumptions and the predicted non-monotonic relationship for the case of intelligence. As depicted in that figure, because intelligence relates positively to reception and negatively to yielding, recipients of moderate intelligence should, averaged across all influence contexts, be more influenced by persuasive messages than recipients of lower or higher intelligence.[7]

As we noted earlier, however, McGuire's model gained additional predictive power by virtue of its situational weighting principle, the idea that the relative importance of reception and yielding varies with the nature of persuasion contexts. Hence, the shape of the relation between attitude change and distal persuasion variables such as self-esteem depends upon whether reception or yielding (or both processes) function as important mediators in a given social influence context. In the case of recipient intelligence, for example, if reception is more important than yielding (e.g., the message is complex but well argued), intelligence should relate positively to attitude change, whereas if yielding is the more important mediator (e.g., the message is simple but poorly argued), intelligence should relate negatively to attitude change.

McGuire's predictions regarding the persuasive effects of personality variables have fared only moderately well in empirical tests (e.g., Brockner & Elkind, 1985; Eagly & Warren, 1976; H. H. Johnson & Izzett, 1969; H. H. Johnson & Stanicek, 1969; H. H. Johnson, Torcivia, & Poprick, 1968; Lehmann, 1970; Millman, 1968; Nisbett & Gordon, 1967; Romer, 1981; Zellner, 1970). These experiments concerned anxiety, authoritarianism, intelligence, and self-esteem. Although positive findings were obtained for some predictions of the McGuire model, most of these were relatively weak in magnitude. Also, only a small subset of these experiments have provided direct evidence concerning the mediational role of reception (e.g., Eagly & Warren, 1976; Johnson et al., 1968; Millman, 1968; Zellner, 1970). Nonetheless, Rhodes and Wood's (1992) meta-analysis of the literature on self-esteem and persuasion yielded findings consistent with the model. First, the relation between self-esteem and retention of message content did prove to be reliably positive in the small proportion of studies that assessed retention. Second, consistent with this finding and the presumed negative relation between self-esteem and yielding, the overall relation between self-esteem and persuasion did prove to be reliably curvilinear in persuasion studies capable of detecting such trends (i.e., studies assessing three levels of self-esteem): Recipients of moderate self-esteem were more influenced than recipients of high or low self-esteem. Rhodes and Wood's analysis of *conformity* experiments, in which subjects receive information about other people's attitudes but no supportive arguments, proved less consistent with the McGuire model. McGuire's (e.g., 1972) assumption that conformity settings minimize the importance of reception and maximize the importance of yielding implies that self-esteem should be negatively (and linearly) related to conformity. However, Rhodes and Wood found that the relation between self-esteem and conformity was reliably curvilinear; as in persuasion studies, subjects at moderate levels of self-esteem conformed more than subjects high or low in self-esteem. As the authors noted, these data can be said to fit the McGuire model if one assumes (contrary to McGuire's original logic) that reception is an important mediator of influenceability in conformity settings.

Although Rhodes and Wood also examined research on the intelligence-persuasion relationship, the fact that only one experiment in their sample investigated three levels of intelligence disallowed a meta-analytic test of McGuire's prediction that intelligence should also be curvilinearly related to persuasion. Yet they were able to document that recipients of higher intelligence were reliably less persuaded than those of lower intelligence, a finding that fits the McGuire model if one makes the not unreasonable assumption that yielding is typically more important than reception in most laboratory studies of persuasion. Eagly and Warren (1976) provided a more exact test of McGuire's predictions by manipulating the importance of reception. For subjects who received a message that lacked supportive argumentation, those high in intelligence were less persuaded than those low in intelligence. However, for subjects who received a message that included complex argumentation, both persuasion and retention of message content was greater for subjects high in intelligence. Although consistent with

McGuire's predictions, the positive relation between intelligence and persuasion in the complex arguments condition was statistically quite weak. In addition, although this study also included subjects at medium levels of intelligence, their data proved somewhat inconsistent across measures and thus difficult to interpret in terms of the McGuire model. Finally, it is noteworthy that this research concerned the effects of verbal intelligence—the dimension of individual differences that should have the most dramatic effect on comprehension of verbal materials. Because other personality traits should have a weaker impact on comprehension, it is perhaps not surprising that most experiments in this literature have failed to generate definitive evidence that individual differences in message reception can account for personality-persuasibility relationships.

Summary. In terms of its ability to account for the effects of distal variables on persuasion, the reception-as-mediator model has been shown to have predictive utility in laboratory contexts only with respect to certain independent variables. These variables all have a notably strong impact on message reception—for example, very strong distractions, recipients' verbal intelligence, and communication modality when a very difficult-to-comprehend message is presented. Although there is currently little support for the view that reception functions as a mediator of persuasion for a broad range of independent variables that have been manipulated in laboratory persuasion experiments, reception may be a considerably more important mediator of persuasion in many natural settings.

New Directions in Investigating Reception

An important limitation of existing research on reception that we have not yet mentioned is that researchers have not seriously examined the mediational role of *attention* in persuasion. Although lumping attention with comprehension and labeling the composite reception may have been a reasonable first step in examining the mediational role of these processes, numerous issues concerning the role of attention *per se* have been ignored (see McGuire, 1976). Because attention is the assignment of processing capacity to stimuli, whereas comprehension is the encoding, or interpretation, of stimuli to which processing capacity has been assigned, these two cognitive processes may have somewhat different effects in relation to persuasion.

A testimony to the importance of attention is the fact that advertisers and media workers devote considerable time and effort to designing attention-getting appeals. Psychologists investigating consumer behavior from an information-processing perspective claim that the attentional step in message processing controls a substantial portion of the variability in consumer decisions (e.g., Bettman, 1979). It is unlikely that this emphasis is misplaced. Attention has been explored extensively by cognitive psychologists (see Eysenck, 1982; Kahneman, 1973), and if broadly defined to include the phenomena of selective exposure and selective perception, it is clear that there is a great deal of relevant social psychological research on these topics (see Fiske & Taylor, 1991). In Chapter 12 we will discuss the implications for persuasion of research on attitudinal selectivity at different stages of information processing (e.g., selective exposure, perception, memory).

Although attentional processes merit careful consideration in persuasion, the laboratory experiment is probably a limited setting for examining such processes because of its implicit and explicit demands for subjects to be extremely attentive to information (see Chaiken & Stangor, 1987; Sears, 1986). Yet it is possible that greater variability in attention could be obtained in laboratory contexts by presenting messages as incidental stimuli—for example, in a "waiting room" situation such as Ickes has used in his research on social interaction (see Ickes, Bissonnette, Garcia, & Stinson, 1990). In addition, there is an obvious need for investigators to make greater use of field settings, in which there is very often considerable variability in attention to mass media messages (e.g., D. R. Anderson, 1985; J. Jacoby & Hoyer, 1987; H. L. Ross, 1982).

Theorizing and research on *vividness* signals a certain degree of interest in how attentional processes affect persuasion. Vivid information is information that presumably attracts and holds people's attention because it is concrete, imagery-provoking, or proximal in a sensory, temporal, or spatial way (see Nisbett & Ross, 1980, p. 45). As suggested by this broad definition, researchers have operationalized vividness in a variety of ways—for example, by presenting pictorially illustrated versus non-pictorially illustrated messages; videotaped versus written messages; and concrete, "colorful," or easily imageable arguments versus abstract, pallid, or "statistical" arguments (see S. E. Taylor & Thompson, 1982).

Although vividly presented information has been hypothesized to exert a greater judgmental impact than non-vivid information (Nisbett & Ross, 1980), Taylor and Thompson's (1982) review of relevant literature concluded that empirical support for this intuitively appealing hypothesis was equivocal. Moreover, subsequent research by these researchers suggested that vividness effects, when they obtain, are primarily illusory insofar as people may perceive vivid messages as relatively persuasive without actually changing their own attitudes (Collins, Taylor, Wood, & Thompson, 1988). Yet, a number of studies have confirmed that vividness manipulations can exert genuine judgmental effects, at least under certain conditions (e.g., Reyes, Thompson, & Bower, 1980; Shedler & Manis, 1986; Simpson & Borgida, 1991). And vividness logic has been applied with some success to issues such as the persuasive impact of pictorial information (Kisielius & Sternthal, 1984), communication modality (Chaiken & Eagly, 1983), eyewitness testimony (Bell & Loftus, 1989), and health and fear appeals (Meyerowitz & Chaiken, 1987; Robberson & Rogers, 1987; Rook, 1987; Sherer & Rogers, 1984; see also Chapter 10).

Any broad conclusions about the persuasive effects of vividly presented information should be viewed with caution until experimental vividness manipulations are more carefully examined to determine what information they make vivid. It is not necessarily persuasive message content that is made more vivid by typical vividness manipulations. Certain manipulations may make message content more vivid (e.g., concrete vs. abstract information), whereas other manipulations may, for example, make communicator-related information more vivid (e.g., videotaped vs. written material). As Chaiken and Eagly (1983) showed, increasing the vividness of communicator-related information enhances the persuasive impact of communicator variables and, as a consequence, increases persuasion if source attributes are positive (e.g., likable, trustworthy) but decreases persuasion if these attributes are negative (e.g., unlikable, untrustworthy; see also Andreoli & Worchel, 1978; Bell & Loftus, 1989).

Circumstances under which *pallid* information is more persuasive than vivid information have been discovered by K. Frey and Eagly (1992). These investigators presented vivid or pallid persuasive messages to subjects either in a normal way, as the focus of subjects' attention, or as an incidental part of the laboratory situation. Although vivid and pallid messages were equally persuasive when subjects were constrained to pay attention to them, pallid messages were more persuasive than the vivid ones when incidentally presented. With incidental presentation of the messages, the vivid images reduced subjects' reception of the message arguments. These findings and others we have presented call for further research to specify the conditions under which vivid or pallid information is more persuasive (see Collins et al., 1988; Fiske & Taylor, 1991; McArthur, 1980; Shedler & Manis, 1986).

To profit from social psychologists' increased understanding of attentional processes (see Lichtenstein & Srull, 1987; Uleman & Bargh, 1989), more refined theorizing is needed concerning how various aspects of attention and comprehension may relate to persuasion (e.g., Collins et al., 1988). In developing such theories, investigators would be well advised to consider more carefully how the reception of and subsequent memory for various components of persuasive messages may affect attitude change and its persistence. As noted above, heightened attention to communicator-related information may relate differently to persuasion than heightened attention to message content. Also, as suggested by social judgment theory (see Chapter 8), perceiving or comprehending a message's overall position may have different effects on attitude change than comprehending persuasive arguments. Moreover, misperceiving communicators' positions on issues may influence attention to their persuasive arguments. And finally, remembering the details of persuasive argumentation may relate differently to persistence than does remembering just the message's overall position, or remembering only that this position can be supported (T. D. Cook & Flay, 1978; Watts & McGuire, 1964; see Chapter 12).

The traditional hypothesis that good reception of argumentation enhances persuasion rests not only on the obvious assumption that the message's arguments are of high quality, but also on the assumption that recipients' acceptance of the message's overall conclusion is based on their understanding and acceptance of arguments rather than on other factors. According to the process theories we discuss in the next chapter and the functional theories we discuss in Chapter 10, this second assumption is not always warranted.

Cognitive Response Model

The cognitive response approach shares with the Hovland, Janis, and Kelley (1953) and McGuire (e.g., 1972) frameworks the assumption that some kind of learning plays a role in determining attitude change and its temporal persistence. However, whereas the Hovland group and, especially, McGuire emphasized the mediational role of reception processes, the cognitive response approach emphasizes the mediating role of the idiosyncratic thoughts or "cognitive responses" that recipients generate—and, thus, rehearse and learn—as they receive and reflect upon persuasive communications (A. G. Greenwald, 1968; Petty, Ostrom, & Brock, 1981). Indeed, the impetus for Anthony Greenwald's (1968) suggestion that "the learning of cognitive response content" may be "more fundamental to persuasion" than "the learning of communication content" (p. 149) was his desire to "salvage an associative learning interpretation of persuasion" (Greenwald, 1981, p. 127) in light of research showing low and typically nonsignificant correlations between retention of message content and persuasion (see, however, earlier discussion of the correlational literature).

The idea that recipients' idiosyncratic thoughts play at least some role in persuasion had precedent in prior research. For example, findings obtained by the Yale researchers concerning the efficacy of active versus passive participation in producing attitude change were interpreted partly in terms of recipient-generated cognitions as were findings on the persuasiveness of one-sided versus two-sided communications. As we discuss more fully in Chapters 10 and 11, the superiority of active improvisation of persuasive arguments relative to passive exposure to messages was attributed to active participants' greater tendencies to add to and elaborate upon message content (Hovland et al., 1953; Janis & King, 1954; B. T. King & Janis, 1956). And results showing that "two-sided" messages, which mention but refute opposing arguments, were more persuasive than one-sided messages were viewed as compatible with the idea that two-sided messages reduce recipients' motivation to counterargue (Hovland et al., 1953; Hovland, Lumsdaine, & Sheffield, 1949; Lumsdaine & Janis, 1953). Subsequent related research by McGuire (1964) on "inoculating" people against persuasion also implicated covert counterarguing. As we explain in Chapter 12, McGuire argued that exposing subjects to weak counterattitudinal arguments and refutations of these arguments facilitated resistance to subsequent, strong counterattitudinal arguments at least in part because such an inoculation procedure gave subjects practice refuting opposing arguments and the chance to generate supporting cognitions.

Although the ideas that people are active information processors and that their own cognitive reactions affect persuasion were therefore not foreign to researchers, Greenwald (1968) was the first to offer an explicit cognitive response account of persuasion. Moreover, although some previous attempts had been made to tap the thoughts of subjects as they listened to persuasive messages (e.g., Hovland et al., 1949; Janis & Terwilliger, 1962), Greenwald (1968) and Timothy Brock (1967) introduced and popularized the *thought-listing* task as a means of assessing cognitive responses. In this task, subjects are asked to list their thoughts or ideas relevant to the message topic. Subsequently, these listed thoughts are coded by judges into various categories. Although a variety of coding schemes have been either proposed or used in research, the vast majority of research guided by cognitive response logic has classified subjects' thoughts into two major categories, those that are favorable to the message's overall position and those that are unfavorable (i.e., counterarguments and blanket rejections; see subsequent section on "Assessing cognitive responses").

According to the cognitive response model, people actively relate information contained in persuasive messages to their existing feelings and beliefs about the message topic. Cognitive responses represent the content of this internal communication on the part of message recipients and are assumed to reflect recipient-generated thoughts that are not merely repetitions of message content. Most importantly, the model assumes that cognitive responses *mediate* the effect of persuasive messages on attitude change. Messages that evoke predominantly favorable recipient-generated thoughts should be persuasive, whereas those that evoke mostly unfavorable thoughts should be unpersuasive (and may even result in attitudes that are less favorable to the advocacy than recipients' prior attitudes). Moreover, because cognitive responding is assumed to vary in magnitude, persuasion should be a function of the *amount* of cognitive responding that occurs as well as its *favorability*. For messages that elicit mostly favorable thinking, enhanced thought should increase persuasion, whereas for messages that elicit mostly unfavorable thinking, enhanced thought should decrease persuasion. In essence, then, the cognitive response model asserts that the cognitions generated in response to persuasive messages determine both the direction and magnitude of attitude change (Greenwald, 1968; Petty, Ostrom, & Brock, 1981).

Relation to Combinatorial Models. Although the cognitive response model does not specify how recipients' cognitive responses are integrated with one another and with prior beliefs to influence post-message attitudes, either expectancy-value or information integration theory could be used to model this combinatorial process. Within the expectancy-value model, cognitive responses can be viewed as beliefs about the message topic having both an expectancy and a value component, and post-message attitudes would be predicted from the summed product of the expectancies and values associated with these beliefs. Although continuous measures of the subjective probabilities and valences associated with subjects' listed thoughts could easily be obtained (see Fishbein & Ajzen, 1975), in practice these cognitive responses are not coded for degree of belief, and they are assigned only a dichotomous or trichotomous value (i.e., favorable, unfavorable, and sometimes neutral). However, assuming expectancies of 1.0 and values of 1, -1, or 0, an approximate prediction of post-message attitude would only require summing subjects' valenced thoughts. In fact, cognitive response researchers have often obtained impressively high correlations between such summed thought indexes and post-message attitudes (e.g., Petty & Cacioppo, 1979b; see also Chapter 2).[8]

Cognitive responses can also be represented within N. H. Anderson's (e.g., 1981b) information integration theory. Similar to the reasoning above, each listed thought could be assigned equal weight and, depending on its valence, a scale value of 1, -1, or 0. Alternatively, subjects' prior attitudes and the message could be assigned scale values to represent their favorability toward the message topic, and a weight to reflect their relative importance as determinants of post-message attitude. Whereas the weight for prior attitude might be determined by recipient variables such as involvement (see Chapter 5), the weight for the persuasive message could be identified with subjects' cognitive responses, with higher weights accorded the messages evoking larger numbers of favorable thoughts.

Relation to Reception. To the extent that at least minimal levels of message comprehension are required for message-relevant thinking to occur (Ratneshwar & Chaiken,

282

1991), McGuire's (1985) insertion of a cognitive responding step between comprehension and agreement in one of his later renditions of the information-processing paradigm makes good sense. Of course, one could easily quibble with this ordering and argue that in some instances cognitive responding may occur concurrently with message reception and, in other instances, prior to actually receiving a communication (as in anticipatory attitude change experiments; see Cialdini & Petty, 1981). Yet, the important point in our view is that from a broader information-processing perspective, the elaborative thinking emphasized in the cognitive response model should be viewed as a stage of processing that complements, rather than supplants, the reception processes emphasized in McGuire's two-step model. We have also stressed in this chapter that the reception of message content is not synonymous with the retention of persuasive arguments; retention measures are imperfect operationalizations of reception (see earlier section on "The covariation paradox"). Thus, we believe it is time to discard the earlier idea that cognitive responses are somehow more "fundamental" determinants of persuasion than the comprehension of persuasive arguments (e.g., Brock & Shavitt, 1983; Greenwald, 1968; Petty & Cacioppo, 1981a). To the extent that cognitive responding most often occurs after or during message reception, a more useful viewpoint is to regard cognitive responding as the more *proximal* determinant of persuasion (Chaiken & Stangor, 1987; Mackie & Asuncion, 1990; Ratneshwar & Chaiken, 1991).

Empirical Evidence Supporting Cognitive Response Model

Distraction was the first major persuasion variable to be investigated from the cognitive response perspective. In an experiment that predated the cognitive response model, Festinger and Maccoby (1964) found that distracting subjects from attending carefully to a persuasive message enhanced attitude change. These investigators suggested that this effect may have occurred because distraction disrupted subjects' abilities to effectively counterargue message content. Subsequent research by Osterhouse and Brock (1970) replicated Festinger and Maccoby's persuasion findings and also provided more direct evidence for the mediational role of counterarguing. In two experiments, subjects listened to a six-minute-long message that advocated a tuition increase at the subjects' university. The message contained seven low quality persuasive arguments, in order to elicit counterarguing. Whereas some subjects were not distracted from this listening task, others had to (vocally) monitor a series of flashing lights during message exposure. By varying the rate at which these lights flashed, the researchers were able to create three levels of distraction in Experiment 1 and four levels in Experiment 2. After message exposure, subjects' agreement with the message's position, the number of counterarguments they generated (on a thought-listing task), and their retention of persuasive arguments were assessed. Figure 6.4 displays the results obtained in Experiment 2, which were virtually identical to those observed in Experiment 1. As distraction increased over the four levels studied, tests for linear trends indicated that subjects' agreement with the message's overall position increased significantly, whereas both the number of counterarguments that they generated and their recognition memory for persuasive arguments decreased significantly.

283

FIGURE 6.4. The effect of distraction on persuasion, counterarguing, and recognition memory for persuasive arguments. Persuasion scores represent the average of two 70-point agreement scales, with higher numbers indicating greater persuasion. Counterarguing scores represent the number of counterarguments subjects listed on a post-message thought-listing task and the memory scores represent the number of correct answers on a 10-item multiple-choice test. In the low, medium, and high distraction conditions, subjects monitored a series of lights that flashed 10, 20, or 30 times per minute. This figure depicts data reported by Osterhouse and Brock (1970, Experiment 2, Tables 1, 2, and text, pp. 351–353).

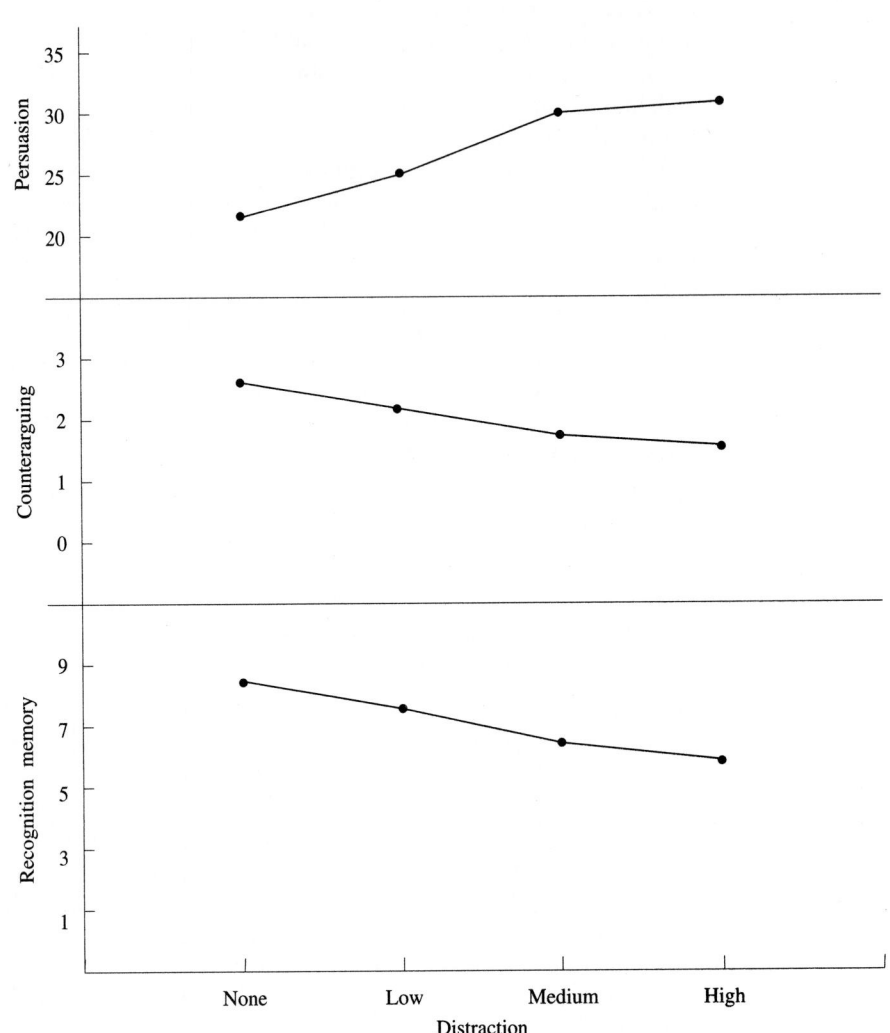

Additional analyses revealed that whereas the correlation between agreement and retention of arguments was non-significant, the agreement-counterarguing correlation was significantly negative ($r = -.53$). Furthermore, statistically controlling for counter-argument production in an analysis of covariance greatly attenuated distraction's effect on agreement. In interpreting their findings, Osterhouse and Brock suggested that extreme levels of distraction might interfere sufficiently with message reception to produce a *decrement* in persuasion (see Haaland & Venkatesan, 1968; Romer, 1979a; Vohs & Garrett, 1968; Zimbardo et al., 1970). However, on the basis of their correlational findings and the fact that increased distraction *enhanced* persuasion, Osterhouse and Brock concluded that the persuasive impact of distraction in their research was mediated by distraction's negative impact on counterarguing, rather than by its negative impact on message reception.[9]

Petty, Wells, and Brock (1976) addressed the distraction-persuasion relation more generally by arguing that distraction *inhibits* recipients' *dominant* cognitive responses to message content. For messages that elicit primarily unfavorable thoughts—as Oster-house and Brock's message presumably did—distraction should work to enhance persuasion. However, for messages that elicit primarily favorable thoughts, distraction should work to inhibit persuasion. These predictions were generally confirmed in two experiments that manipulated both distraction and persuasive argument quality and that featured either a counterattitudinal message (tuition should be increased, Experiment 1) or a proattitudinal message (tuition should be decreased, Experiment 2).[10] Among subjects who listened to messages with weak arguments, Osterhouse and Brock's (1970) findings were replicated: As distraction increased, agreement with the message's position increased significantly (for proattitudinal and counterattitudinal messages), and subjects' tendencies to generate unfavorable thoughts about the message decreased significantly (for proattitudinal messages) or marginally (for coun-terattitudinal messages). Among subjects who listened to messages containing strong persuasive arguments, the results were weaker but still compatible with predictions: As distraction increased, agreement with the message's position decreased significantly (for counterattitudinal messages) or marginally (for proattitudinal messages), and the production of favorable thoughts about the message decreased nonsignificantly (for counterattitudinal messages) or significantly (for proattitudinal messages).[11]

Petty and colleagues' (1976) distraction research set the tone for many subsequent cognitive response experiments. Analogous to their design, the strategy underlying many subsequent studies has been (a) to identify variables that, like distraction, influence the *amount* of cognitive responding that subjects engage in, (b) to identify variables that influence the *favorability* of cognitive responding (most typically argument quality), and (c) to explore the simultaneous effects of these variables on both cognitive responding and persuasion. Numerous experiments using this strategy, many of them conducted by Richard Petty, John Cacioppo, and their colleagues, have provided an impressive amount of support for the cognitive response framework (for reviews, see Petty & Cacioppo, 1981a, 1986b; Petty, Ostrom, & Brock, 1981). As the following review illustrates, this research has helped illuminate how a number of important distal persuasion variables affect attitude change.

Message Repetition. Earlier in this chapter we considered the effects of repeated exposure to persuasive communications in the context of the reception-as-mediator hypothesis. However, the persuasive effects of message repetition have also been investigated from the cognitive response perspective. Reasoning that repetition might enhance recipients' abilities to engage in cognitive responding, Cacioppo and Petty (1979b) investigated whether repeated exposure to a high quality persuasive message would increase both attitude change and the favorability of subjects' thoughts about the message. In two different experiments, subjects listened once, three times, or five times in succession to a proattitudinal or counterattitudinal message containing eight relatively strong persuasive arguments. Although both messages advocated increasing university expenditures, the proattitudinal version stated that the increased revenue could come from a tax on campus visitors, and the counterattitudinal version stated that the revenue would have to come from a tuition increase. After message exposure, subjects indicated their agreement with the message's position, responded to an argument-recall task, and (in Experiment 2 only) listed their thoughts about the message. Regardless of the direction of the message's advocacy (proattitudinal vs. counterattitudinal), the findings of the two studies were essentially the same. As repetition increased from one to three exposures, message agreement increased as did subjects' tendencies to generate favorable thoughts about the message. However, as repetition increased from three to five exposures, both persuasion and the tendency to generate favorable message thoughts decreased. Finally, subjects' recall of persuasive arguments increased linearly over the three exposure conditions in Experiment 1, whereas these scores increased between one and three exposures but showed no further increase in Experiment 2.

Cacioppo and Petty interpreted their curvilinear persuasion and thought data as reflecting a two-phase cognitive elaboration-then-tedium process. In the first phase, repeated message exposure should increase recipients' opportunities to cognitively elaborate the message's arguments; therefore repeated exposure should increase persuasion for high quality messages (such as those used in Cacioppo and Petty's two studies) but should decrease persuasion for low quality messages. When repetition reaches a "tedious" level, however, a second level is initiated in which feelings of boredom or psychological reactance (J. W. Brehm, 1972) are presumably experienced. During this tedium phase, recipients become motivated to reject the message regardless of the inherent quality of its arguments. Although Cacioppo and Petty's two-phase explanation for exposure effects in the persuasion domain has not been tested directly, we should note that it is compatible with two-factor accounts that have been proposed in related research that has examined the attitudinal impact of repeated "mere" exposure to attitude objects (see Chapter 9).

The results for the one- and three-exposure conditions of Cacioppo and Petty's (1979b) experiments were compatible with the first (or cognitive response) phase of their two-phase explanation. However, these experiments used only high-quality messages. To provide further evidence for the first phase of their explanation, Cacioppo and Petty (1985) conducted an additional study in which subjects were exposed either one or three times to a message that contained either strong or weak persuasive arguments.

As noted earlier in this chapter, their results indicated that agreement with the high-quality message increased from one to three exposures, whereas agreement with the low-quality message decreased. Also, consistent with their earlier research (Cacioppo & Petty, 1979b), subjects recalled significantly more persuasive arguments in the three (vs. one) exposure condition (cognitive response data were not reported).

Cacioppo and Petty (1985) interpreted their persuasion findings in terms of the cognitive response model. They also discounted the idea that their effects might have been due in part to repetition's enhancing effects on message reception (see also Cacioppo & Petty, 1979b), presumably because they assumed that increased reception of arguments should lead to increased persuasion, regardless of message quality. As we stressed earlier in this chapter, however, whether enhanced (or impaired) reception of message content translates into increased or decreased persuasion should depend on the quality of persuasive argumentation—just as enhanced (or impaired) ability to engage in cognitive responding does. Thus, although neither reception enhancement nor cognitive elaboration can provide a full account of the attitudinal effects of repeated exposures to persuasive messages, it is likely that *both* processes are important in understanding the sorts of repetition effects that have been obtained at low-to-moderate exposure levels (see discussion of repetition effects earlier in this chapter and discussion of mere exposure effects in Chapter 9). As we have already indicated, a similar view can be offered for the persuasive effects of distraction. In a later section we discuss more fully the value of viewing reception and cognitive responding as complementary stages of information processing.

Issue Involvement. Petty and Cacioppo have successfully applied cognitive response logic to a type of involvement known as *issue involvement* or *personal relevance*, the extent to which recipients perceive that a message topic is personally important or relevant (see B. T. Johnson & Eagly, 1989; Petty & Cacioppo, 1979b, 1986a, 1990). This construct has typically been manipulated using a technique introduced by Apsler and Sears (1968). Their subjects read a message that advocated replacing professors with supervised teaching assistants in some undergraduate classes. Low issue involvement subjects learned that the target date for implementing this proposal was ten years in the future, whereas high issue involvement subjects learned that this proposal would be used on a trial basis during the very next academic year. Borrowing this technique, Petty and Cacioppo (e.g., 1979a, 1979b) and numerous subsequent investigators have manipulated issue involvement by varying the *year* in which a proposed policy might take effect. For example, in numerous studies, subjects have received a message indicating that mandatory comprehensive examinations for seniors are being contemplated by their university and that, if adopted, the exam policy would be implemented "next year" (high issue involvement) or "in 10 years" (low issue involvement; see Petty & Cacioppo, 1986a). In a variant on this procedure, issue involvement has been manipulated by varying the *place* where a proposal will be implemented, such as the subjects' own university or state versus a distant university or state (e.g., Axsom, Yates, & Chaiken, 1987; Petty & Cacioppo, 1979a; see also Liberman, Chaiken, & Hazlewood, 1992).

287

Petty and Cacioppo (1979a, 1979b) reasoned that heightened issue involvement increases people's motivation to engage in message- and issue-relevant thinking (see also Chaiken, 1980, and Chapter 7). Consequently, they hypothesized that increased issue involvement should decrease persuasion for messages eliciting primarily unfavorable thoughts from recipients, but ought to increase persuasion for messages eliciting predominantly favorable thoughts. Findings consistent with this hypothesis were obtained in a study that presented subjects with a message on the topic of senior comprehensive exams and manipulated both issue involvement and argument quality (Petty & Cacioppo, 1979b, Experiment 2). When subjects received messages that contained weak persuasive arguments, heightened issue involvement increased their generation of unfavorable thoughts and inhibited persuasion. But when subjects received messages that contained strong arguments, heightened involvement increased their generation of favorable thoughts and enhanced persuasion.

Subsequent experiments by Leippe and Elkin (1987) and by Petty and Cacioppo (1981b, 1984a; Petty, Cacioppo, & Goldman, 1981; Petty, Cacioppo, & Schumann, 1983) have also supported the cognitive response hypothesis that increased issue involvement enhances persuasion with strong messages but inhibits persuasion with weak messages. Yet other studies using highly similar manipulations of argument quality and issue involvement have supported this hypothesis mainly in relation to messages that contain strong persuasive arguments (e.g., Axsom et al., 1987; Burnkrant & Howard, 1984, statements conditions; Sorrentino, Bobocel, Gitta, Olson, & Hewitt, 1988, Experiment 2). Issue involvement typically had no reliable effect on the persuasiveness of weak messages in these studies. Consistent with this mixed pattern of findings, B. T. Johnson and Eagly's (1989) meta-analysis of the impact of involvement on persuasion concluded that the tendency for issue involvement to facilitate persuasion for strong messages is well supported by existing research, but that the tendency for issue involvement to reduce persuasion for weak messages is more tenuous and cannot be considered an established empirical fact at this point in time.

More generally, Johnson and Eagly's review of the literature emphasized that "involvement" has been conceptualized and operationalized differently by different theorists and researchers and, as a consequence, has been shown to exert variable effects on persuasion. For example, in contrast to the above research showing that greater issue involvement *enhances* persuasion for strong messages, earlier theorizing and research on "ego-involving" attitudes—attitudes that are tied to people's enduring values—predicted and found that greater involvement generally *decreased* persuasion for (presumably strong) counter-attitudinal messages (e.g., Eagly & Telaak, 1972; N. Miller, 1965; Ostrom & Brock, 1968; Rhine & Severence, 1970; C. W. Sherif, Kelly, Rodgers, Sarup, & Tittler, 1973; see Chapters 8 and 12). In fact, Johnson and Eagly's meta-analysis of research on *value-relevant* involvement (their term for ego-involvement) showed that this type of involvement tended to reduce persuasion, *regardless* of argument quality. On empirical and conceptual grounds, these authors thus argued that value-relevant involvement and *outcome-relevant* involvement (their term for issue involvement) should be viewed as two distinctive types of involvement.[12]

288

Johnson and Eagly also examined studies that they identified as dealing with *impression-relevant* involvement, people's desires to express attitudes that are socially acceptable to potential evaluators (also called response involvement; see Leippe & Elkin, 1987; Zimbardo, 1960). Although the small number of such studies in their meta-analysis disallowed any strong conclusions regarding the persuasive impact of this type of involvement, they tentatively concluded that impression-relevant involvement was a third type of involvement not well captured by either value- or outcome-relevant involvement. Other writers too, have proposed that involvement is not one but several constructs and have implied that differing types of involvement may exert differing effects on information processing, attitude change, and its persistence (e.g., Chaiken & Stangor, 1987; A. G. Greenwald, 1982; see also Andrews & Durvasula, 1991; A. G. Greenwald & Leavitt, 1984). Moreover, as Johnson and Eagly (1989) noted, the various senses in which involvement has been used by attitude researchers can be related to the needs and motives postulated by functional theories of attitude change. We will consider the important and multifaceted involvement construct again in subsequent portions of this book (see Chapters 7, 8, 10, and 12).

Other Distal Variables. In additional experiments by Petty, Cacioppo, and their colleagues, other distal persuasion variables assumed to affect either *motivation* or *ability* for message-relevant cognitive processing have been examined in conjunction with argument quality, a variable assumed to control the *favorability* of subjects' cognitive responses (for reviews, see Petty & Cacioppo, 1986a, 1986b). For the most part, these studies have yielded findings similar to those we have described in relation to the distal persuasion variables of distraction, message repetition, and issue involvement.

Harkins and Petty (1981), for example, reasoned that relative to the standard persuasion situation in which one communicator presents multiple arguments supporting a point of view, *multiple* sources who present in succession (the same) multiple arguments should enhance recipients' motivation to think about the presented arguments. Consistent with this reasoning, these authors found that subjects who received strong arguments from multiple sources generated more favorable message-relevant thoughts and were more persuaded by the message (which concerned comprehensive exams) than subjects who received the same strong arguments from only one communicator. Conversely, subjects who received weak arguments from multiple sources generated more unfavorable thoughts and were less persuaded than subjects who received weak arguments from one communicator (see also Harkins & Petty, 1983, 1987).

Petty, Harkins, and Williams (1980) used similar logic to illustrate the relevance to persuasion of diffusion of responsibility, a social psychological construct originally proposed to explain why bystanders often fail to intervene in emergency helping situations (Darley & Latané, 1968). They reasoned that the presence of other persons who share the task of evaluating a persuasive message decreases any one person's perceived responsibility for this task and, hence, that person's motivation to engage in message-relevant cognitive responding. Consistent with this logic, when strong messages were received, subjects generated fewer favorable thoughts and were less persuaded when they shared responsibility for message evaluation than when they alone shouldered this responsibility. When weak messages were received, however, subjects who shared responsibility generated fewer unfavorable thoughts and were more persuaded than were subjects who were individually responsible for message evaluation (see also Brickner, Harkins, & Ostrom, 1986).

Petty, Cacioppo, and Heesacker (1981) used a similar though more complex logic to analyze the relative persuasive impact of arguments framed as rhetorical questions versus declarative statements—for example, "Wouldn't instituting comprehensive exams be an aid to those who seek admission to graduate and professional schools?" versus "Thus, instituting comprehensive exams would be an aid to those who seek admission to graduate and professional schools." They reasoned that the use of rhetoricals (vs. statements) would enhance recipients' *motivation* to engage in message-relevant thinking, but only when message topics are low in personal relevance. When messages concern topics of high personal relevance, motivation for message-relevant thinking should already be high, as discussed above. The researchers argued that with such messages, arguments framed as rhetoricals would be distracting to recipients and would thus reduce their *ability* to engage in message-relevant thinking. On the basis of these assumptions, Petty and colleagues predicted and found that under conditions of low issue involvement, framing arguments in rhetorical form increased persuasion for messages containing strong arguments but decreased persuasion for messages consisting of weak arguments. Conversely, under conditions of high issue involvement, the use of rhetoricals decreased persuasion for strong messages but increased persuasion for weak messages. Moreover, the patterning of favorable and unfavorable thoughts generated by subjects in this research generally paralleled the persuasion data.

Subsequent research, however, has not found that the persuasive impact of rhetoricals depends upon level of issue involvement (Burnkrant & Howard, 1984; Swasy & Munch, 1985; see also Howard, 1990). In these studies, framing arguments as rhetorical questions rather than declarative statements enhanced message-relevant thinking regardless of the message topic's personal relevance. For example, in both the high and low issue involvement conditions of Burnkrant and Howard's (1984) experiment, rhetoricals increased favorable thinking and persuasion for strong messages, but increased unfavorable thinking and decreased persuasion for weak messages. Although somewhat discrepant with Petty, Cacioppo, and Heesacker's (1981) data, these more recent studies do substantiate the value of the cognitive response model in relation to understanding the persuasive effects of rhetoricals, a stylistic variable that had received only sporadic empirical attention previously (e.g., Newcombe & Arnkoff, 1979; Zillmann, 1972).

Finally, we note that the cognitive response model has proven applicable to understanding the persistence of attitude change and the operation of distal variables that influence susceptibility and resistance to persuasion attempts (e.g., warning treatments; see Cialdini & Petty, 1981). These applications of the model are discussed in Chapter 12.

Evaluation of Cognitive Response Model and Research

The greatest strength of the cognitive response model is the many important insights it has provided about distal persuasion variables such as distraction and message repetition that seem clearly related to recipients' abilities or motivation to engage in message-relevant thinking. Indeed, the interaction effects on persuasion that the model predicts when these *extent of processing* variables are crossed with a factor—usually argument quality—that affects the *valence* of message-relevant thought often have a subtle, nonobvious quality. Many of these variables first entered the empirical literature on attitude change because of their relevance to alternate theoretical perspectives—for example, both social judgment theory and dissonance theory launched research on involvement (see Chapters 8, 10, 11, and 12). Nonetheless, with few exceptions it is doubtful that these alternate perspectives could have or would have inspired the *Extent of Processing × Valence of Thought* predictions specified by the cognitive response model. The most notable exception, of course, is the reception-as-mediator hypothesis associated with McGuire (e.g., 1968a) and Hovland et al. (1953), and its ability to predict the same interaction effects for distraction and message repetition that the cognitive response model predicts. However, had the latter model not sensitized attitude researchers to the importance of taking argument quality into account, it is doubtful that the reception-as-mediator hypothesis would have, in fact, spawned the specific predictions that distraction should *increase* persuasion or that repeated exposure should *decrease* persuasion when messages contain weak or spurious persuasive arguments.

In addition to generating fairly unique predictions concerning previously researched variables such as distraction, repetition, and issue involvement, the cognitive response model has inspired research on distal variables that prior persuasion research had largely ignored (e.g., rhetoricals, multiple sources). The model has also stimulated research demonstrating the relevance to persuasion of constructs popularized in other areas of social psychology (e.g., diffusion of responsibility). Like the reception-as-mediator perspective reviewed earlier, then, the cognitive response perspective has been of great heuristic value to researchers.

One limitation to existing cognitive response research concerns the lack of demonstrated generality of the various Extent of Processing × Valence of Thought effects that have been observed on cognitive responding and persuasion. The vast majority of this research has crossed a variety of factors that affect extent of processing with only one factor that affects the valence of message-relevant thought—the quality of persuasive argumentation.[13] There are, however, other variables that research or intuition suggests ought to influence the valence of cognitive responding—for example, message discrepancy, warning of persuasive intent, and whether messages espouse proattitudinal or counterattitudinal positions (see Bochner & Insko, 1966; Freedman & Sears, 1965b, Mackie, 1987). Unfortunately, research testing the persuasive impact of these variables in conjunction with extent-of-processing variables has been rare. Although warning studies by Petty and Cacioppo (1979a) and Watts and Holt (1979) yielded findings congenial to cognitive response logic, only the Petty and Cacioppo experiment included measures of cognitive responding. Moreover, findings obtained in several relevant studies featuring proattitudinal versus counterattitudinal messages have not consistently supported cognitive response predictions (see Cacioppo & Petty, 1979b; Petty & Cacioppo, 1979b, Experiment 1; see also Petty et al., 1976; Worth & Mackie, 1987). Thus, confidence in the generality of the model's prediction that variables such as distraction and message repetition that increase extent of processing can increase or decrease persuasion depending upon the *valence of dominant cognitive responses* elicited by persuasive messages awaits further research using a broader range of valence-of-thought manipulations.

Beyond the class of variables for which predictions of Extent of Processing × Valence of Thought interactions can easily be generated, the predictive utility of the cognitive response model is somewhat limited. This limitation stems from the fact that the model lacks clear *a priori* implications regarding the persuasive impact of variables that are *not obviously* related to recipients' abilities or motivation to engage in message-relevant thinking. For example, source variables such as communicator expertise might increase message-relevant thinking (e.g., Hass, 1981) or decrease such thinking (e.g., T. D. Cook, 1969; Sternthal, Dholakia, & Leavitt, 1978). Alternatively, instead of having its major impact on amount of processing, a variable such as expertise might (like argument quality) influence the favorability of message-relevant thought (e.g., T. D. Cook, 1969; Gillig & Greenwald, 1974). Most existing research demonstrating that communicator credibility manipulations influence cognitive responding cannot differentiate clearly among these possible effects. For example, studies showing that higher credibility is associated with fewer unfavorable thoughts may indicate that heightened credibility decreases message-relevant thinking, leads to favorable thinking, or both (e.g., R. S. Baron & Miller, 1969; T. D. Cook, 1969; Gillig & Greenwald, 1974; Sternthal, Dholakia, & Leavitt, 1978). Similarly, demonstrations that higher credibility is associated with greater numbers of unfavorable thoughts could signify that heightened credibility increases thinking, leads to unfavorable thinking, or both (e.g., Hass, 1981).[14]

Because a variable such as communicator expertise might have a range of possible effects on cognitive responding, the most reasonable strategy open to investigators is to search for conditions under which the variable is most likely to enhance or inhibit message-relevant thinking. Then under these conditions, one could test for the interaction effects on persuasion and cognitive responses of the sort predicted for variables like distraction that *are* more directly related to extent of processing. For example, variables that might affect whether high (vs. low) credibility sources enhance or diminish recipients' tendencies to engage in message-relevant thought include message discrepancy (Sternthal, Dholakia, & Leavitt, 1978), commitment to prior attitudes (Hass, 1981), and issue involvement (Heesacker, Petty, & Cacioppo, 1983).[15] Yet the rationale for why such variables should control the impact of source credibility on extensiveness of thinking does not stem directly from the cognitive response model. Nor, for that matter, are assumptions about why extent-of-processing variables affect amount of processing inherent in this model. Rather, such assumptions require the importation of extra-theoretical postulates or concepts. For example, Darley and Latané's (1968) diffusion of responsibility construct underlies the assumption that the presence of multiple recipients decreases any one recipient's motivation for message-relevant thinking (Petty et al., 1980). And the largely intuitive notion that recipients "gear up" for a communicator's arguments underlies the assumption that motivation for message processing should be greater when recipients are exposed to multiple sources rather than to only a single communicator (Harkins & Petty, 1981).

Assessing Cognitive Responses. Because of the crucial mediational role that the cognitive response model ascribes to recipient-generated thoughts, it is important to assess the adequacy of the thought-listing task (Brock, 1967; A. G. Greenwald, 1968). In the vast majority of cognitive response experiments, this task is administered to subjects after they have read or listened to a persuasive message and immediately after they have indicated their post-message attitudes. The traditional criticism of the technique has been to question whether the thoughts that subjects list validly reflect the content and amount of covert cognitive responses they generated during exposure to the persuasive message (or while anticipating the message; see Cialdini & Petty, 1981). As Norman Miller argued, to the extent that subjects view the thought-listing procedure as an opportunity to justify or explain their post-message attitudes, the favorable and unfavorable thoughts that they list on this task should be regarded as the result, rather than the cause, of attitude change (N. Miller & Baron, 1973; N. Miller & Colman, 1981). More generally, demonstrations that cognitive responses covary with post-message attitudes or that a given independent variable exerts parallel effects on cognitive responses and post-message attitudes are vulnerable to the criticism that cognitive responses represent an alternate dependent measure of persuasion rather than a mediating process that is both conceptually distinct from and antecedent to persuasion. In fact, the vast majority of cognitive response experiments consist of just such demonstrations, and valenced cognitive response indexes such as the number of unfavorable message thoughts generated often do correlate highly with the subjects' responses to more formal multi-item attitude questionnaires (e.g., Thurstone and Likert attitude scales; see Breckler & Wiggins, 1991; Cacioppo, Harkins, & Petty, 1981; N. Miller & Colman, 1981; Ostrom, 1989). Indeed, such thought indexes were mentioned as possible measures of attitude in Chapter 2. In sum, this criticism represents a potentially severe indictment of the model's core assumption that cognitive responses mediate the effects of distal independent variables on persuasion.

To test the cognitive response model's core assumption, some researchers have used analysis of covariance to examine whether the impact of a given independent variable on attitudes is attenuated when the hypothesized mediator, cognitive responding, is statistically controlled (e.g., Cacioppo & Petty, 1979b; Harkins & Petty, 1987; Insko, Turnbull, & Yandell, 1974; Osterhouse & Brock, 1970). Although these tests have generally supported the mediational role of cognitive responses, as Greenwald (1981) himself has noted, such procedures do not provide definitive evidence of causation (see also Heise, 1975; Kenny, 1985). Consider, for example, Osterhouse and Brock's (1970) finding that the effect of distraction on post-message attitude was rendered nonsignificant when counterarguing was statistically controlled in an analysis of covariance (see our earlier discussion of this research). Although this result is consistent with the view that counterarguing mediated distraction's effect on persuasion, the same finding could have been obtained spuriously if Osterhouse and Brock's measure of counterarguing was more reliable than their measure of post-message attitude. These authors reported the reliability of their counterarguing measure but they did not report on the reliability of their attitude measure. Thus, this possibility cannot be evaluated for their experiments. Moreover, this possibility cannot be evaluated in relation to most other relevant studies because cognitive response researchers—like most persuasion investigators—typically do not report reliabilities for *any* of their dependent measures. Because so much persuasion research has relied upon single-item agreement or favorability ratings to assess attitudes, whereas cognitive response measures represent multiple-item aggregate indexes, the possibility that cognitive response measures are generally more reliable than attitude measures should not be dismissed lightly (see discussion of measurement reliability in Chapter 2).

Even if attitude and cognitive response measures were equally reliable, it is important to realize that an analysis of covariance result such as Osterhouse and Brock's could be obtained if cognitive responses are, indeed, merely alternate measures of persuasion. That is, covarying on a valenced cognitive response index such as counterarguing ("persuasion measure B") to see if an independent variable's impact on attitude ("persuasion measure A") becomes attenuated is tantamount to covarying out the baby with the bathwater. To reduce the plausibility of this alternate interpretation, researchers should follow Insko, Turnbull, and Yandell's (1974) strategy of showing not only that (a) covarying on cognitive responses reduces the impact of a particular independent variable on post-message attitude, but also that (b) covarying on attitude scores *does not* reduce the impact of the independent variable on cognitive responses (see Judd & McClelland, 1989). Wider use of this strategy and other regression techniques for testing causal hypotheses (see R. M. Baron & Kenny, 1986) should enable somewhat stronger inferences about the mediating role of cognitive responses than existing research has provided.

As Greenwald (1981) has noted, unequivocal evidence favoring the mediational role of cognitive responses necessitates the development of direct and nonreactive assessments of ongoing cognitive responding. John Cacioppo's research on potential physiological correlates of cognitive responding suggests that such assessments can, in fact, be developed (e.g., Cacioppo, 1979; Cacioppo & Petty, 1979a, 1981b; Cacioppo, Petty, Losch, & Kim, 1986; Cacioppo, Sandman, & Walker, 1978; for reviews, see Cacioppo & Petty, 1987; Cacioppo, Petty, & Geen, 1989). This research program has shown that physiological responses such as accelerated heart rate and oral electromyographic (EMG) activity are associated with more extensive cognitive processing, as indexed by subjects' thought listings. For example, Cacioppo (1979) studied a group of young adult, pacemaker patients who were visiting their cardiologist for a routine checkup. By placing a capped versus uncapped magnet over a reed in each subject's pacemaker, Cacioppo was able to vary heart rate (72 vs. 88 beats per minute) without changing other bodily processes and without subjects' awareness that a heart rate change had occurred. Using this manipulation, Cacioppo found that increased heart rate was associated with an increased tendency for subjects to generate counter-arguments in response to messages designed to elicit unfavorable cognitive responding (e.g., one message argued that the drinking and voting age in Ohio should be lowered to 13). Other studies in this research program have shown that the *valence* of individuals' thoughts can be detected through the *patterning* of facial EMG activity (e.g., Cacioppo & Petty, 1979a, 1981b; Cacioppo, Petty, Losch, & Kim, 1986; see also Schwartz, Fair, Salt, Mandel, & Klerman, 1976). For example, Cacioppo and Petty (1979a) presented subjects with a counterattitudinal message designed to elicit primarily unfavorable thinking and a proattitudinal message designed to elicit favorable thinking. The results showed that exposure to the counterattitudinal message elicited greater EMG activity in subjects' corrugator (frowning) muscles and lesser EMG activity in their zygomatic (smiling) muscles than did exposure to the proattitudinal message (see Chapter 2). Although physiological recording may prove difficult in many laboratory studies of persuasion, due to the instrumentation required and the potential intrusiveness of such techniques, this research on physiological correlates of cognitive responding does support the assumption that thought listings do provide valid assessments of both the amount and valence of cognitive responding.

The post-message thought-listing technique has the potential to illuminate a wide variety of cognitive reactions that people have as they process persuasive messages. As various investigators have shown, content analyses of subjects' thought protocols can be used to identify qualitatively distinctive categories of cognitive response such as counterarguments versus supportive arguments, source derogations versus acclamations, recipient-originated versus message-originated thoughts, and self-relevant versus non-self-relevant elaborations (e.g., Axsom et al., 1987; Cacioppo et al., 1981; Chaiken, 1980; Chaiken & Eagly, 1983; Chattopadhyay & Alba, 1988; Mackie, 1987; Shavitt & Brock, 1986; Wood & Kallgren, 1988). Yet, as evidenced by our review of the literature, the vast majority of cognitive response research has investigated just two categories of thoughts: favorable and unfavorable message-relevant cognitions. Even within this simple coding scheme, little attempt has been made to distinguish specific thoughts about the message or message topic (e.g., counterarguments) from more global thoughts (e.g., simple rejections of the message). Moreover, much cognitive response research has probably unnecessarily restricted its attention to message- and issue-related thinking by using thought-listing instructions that place implicit or explicit demands on subjects to list mostly these kinds of thoughts (e.g., we are interested in your thoughts about senior comprehensive exams; Harkins & Petty, 1981).

Because of its restricted focus on message-related thinking, existing cognitive response research tends to foster too narrow a view of the cognitive response model. After all, this model's core assumption that cognitive responses mediate the persuasive impact of distal independent variables is, theoretically, somewhat broader than the assumption that the extent and valence of *message*-related thinking mediates persuasion. The latter interpretation of the cognitive response model's key thesis has been heavily influenced by Petty and Cacioppo's many empirical tests of cognitive response logic and, in fact, is also central to these authors' elaboration likelihood model of persuasion (Petty & Cacioppo, 1986a, 1986b). Although similar to the cognitive response model in many respects, the elaboration likelihood model incorporates the notion that persuasion may sometimes *not* be dependent on recipients' processing of persuasive message content. For this reason we discuss the elaboration likelihood model in Chapter 7, along with Chaiken's (1980, 1987) heuristic-systematic model.

Message Reception and Cognitive Elaboration. Many researchers have tended to regard the reception of message content and the cognitive appraisal and elaboration of this information as competing explanations for the effects of particular independent variables on persuasion. This competing theory orientation is best illustrated by research on the persuasive effects of distraction and message repetition (e.g., Cacioppo & Petty, 1979b, 1985; Osterhouse & Brock, 1970; Petty et al., 1976). As our review of this research indicated, investigators have often pitted cognitive response explanations for observed distraction and repeated exposure effects against "message learning" hypotheses (e.g., more distraction leads to less learning, which should confer less persuasion; Osterhouse & Brock, 1970). Not surprisingly, most investigators have concluded that the "mere" learning of a message's arguments cannot account for the persuasive effects of variables such as distraction and message repetition. Yet in this chapter we have tried to make clear that the reception of message content is not synonymous with the learning of persuasive arguments. Moreover, the "argument quality logic" that researchers have used to fashion cognitive response hypotheses for the persuasive impact of distraction and repetition applies equally well to the issue of message reception (or, for the historical record, "message learning"): Impaired abilities to *comprehend* message content *or cognitively respond to* message content should function to increase persuasion for weakly argued messages but decrease persuasion for strongly argued messages. Enhanced abilities of either type should have the opposite impact, that is, decrease persuasion for weak messages but increase it for strong messages.

The value of viewing comprehension and cognitive responding as complementary cognitive processes rather than as competing theoretical viewpoints is that a broader understanding of their *interactive* effect on persuasion can be gained. Because cognitive responding is no doubt the more proximal determinant of attitude change—regardless of whether such responding occurs after a comprehension stage or on-line during information acquisition—appropriate questions for research include how variations in the comprehensibility of persuasive messages influence the amount and nature of recipients' cognitive responses (see Mackie & Asuncion, 1990; Ratneshwar & Chaiken, 1991). Indeed, to the extent that distraction and message repetition manipulations are viewed more generally as manipulations of message comprehensibility, cognitive response research on these variables supports the idea that impaired comprehension of message content reduces recipients' tendencies to cognitively elaborate on this content, whereas enhanced comprehension enhances cognitive appraisal and elaboration. Although this research indicates that comprehension can influence the *amount* of message-relevant cognitive responding that people engage in, it may also be the case that comprehension may influence the *valence* of cognitive responding. For example, Eagly's (1974) finding that extreme deficits in comprehension can arouse negative affect suggests that impaired comprehension might sometimes negatively bias recipients' message-relevant thoughts (see discussion earlier in this chapter). And Ratneshwar and Chaiken (1991) have provided some evidence that incomprehensible messages may, in some circumstances, lower persuasion by causing recipients to generate negative thoughts about the sources of such messages.

In sum, future research on the role of recipient-generated cognitive responses in persuasion ought to consider more seriously how message reception processes—attention as well as comprehension—impact on these responses. When studying reception and cognitive responding as sequential (or concurrent) stages of information processing, subsequent researchers may also benefit by applying causal modeling techniques such as structural equation analyses to data sets featuring indexes of both processes (see R. M. Baron & Kenny, 1986; Judd & McClelland, 1989; Kenny, 1985). Had such techniques been used in past research, investigators studying the effects of distraction and message repetition (and, perhaps, other extent-of-processing variables) might have discovered that *both* message reception and cognitive responding mediate the persuasive impact of these variables.

Summary. Research guided by the cognitive response model has contributed and should continue to contribute to our knowledge of the cognitive mediation of attitude change. As we have seen, however, the predictive utility of the framework is somewhat limited insofar as clear-cut predictions can be generated mainly in relation to distal persuasion variables that exert an obvious influence on extent of processing when these variables are crossed with argument quality (and, potentially, other variables that influence the valence of cognitive responding). As cognitive response researchers have themselves noted, the model is perhaps best viewed not as a theory of attitudes but as a "conceptual orientation" (Ostrom, 1981, p. 287) that emphasizes the role that recipient-generated thought plays in attitude formation and change (see also A. G. Greenwald, 1981; Petty & Cacioppo, 1981a). Its ultimate success in explaining attitude formation and change thus is somewhat dependent on the bridges that can be built between this conceptual orientation and insights provided by other theoretical perspectives.

Postscript: *Wyer's Process-Theory Extension of the Probabilogical Model*

In Chapter 5 (and 3) we reviewed the McGuire-Wyer probabilogical model of cognitive organization and change. This model provides a molecular analysis of recipients' conditional inferences about the premises (i.e., arguments) and conclusions of persuasive messages and of the processes by which these inferences combine to affect beliefs and belief change (e.g., McGuire, 1960a, 1981; Wyer, 1970; Wyer & Hartwick, 1980). Stimulated by McGuire's reception-yielding model, Wyer (1974b) developed a molar application of the probabilogical model for persuasion situations. In essence, Wyer's probabilogical model of persuasion recasts reception and yielding in terms of *conditional* probabilities. We briefly summarize the model here, as it assigns importance both to reception processes and to cognitive responding.

According to Wyer's (1974b) model, the probability that a recipient is influenced by a persuasive message, $p(I)$, is given by the equation,

$$p(I) = p(R)p(I/R) + p(R')p(I/R') \qquad (6.2)$$

where $p(R)$ and $p(R')$ are the probabilities of receiving (i.e., comprehending) and not receiving the message's arguments, respectively; and $p(I/R)$ and $p(I/R')$ are the conditional probabilities of being influenced, given that one has and has not received the message's arguments, respectively. Consistent with McGuire's definition of yielding, Wyer assumed that $p(I/R) = p(Y)$, where $p(Y)$ is the probability of yielding to the message given that it is received. By substitution, Equation 6.2 becomes:

$$p(I) = p(R)p(Y) + p(R')p(I/R') \qquad (6.3)$$

Wyer further assumed that $p(Y)$ could be estimated by the equation:

$$p(Y) = p(CA)p(Y/CA) + p(CA')p(Y/CA') \qquad (6.4)$$

where $p(CA)$ and $p(CA')$ are the probabilities that persuasive argumentation is and is not refuted through counterarguing, and $p(Y/CA)$ and $p(Y/CA')$ are the probabilities of yielding, given that the arguments are and are not refuted, respectively. By substituting the above expression for $p(Y)$ in Equation 6.3, the final mathematical statement of Wyer's probabilogical model of reception and yielding becomes:

$$p(I) = p(R) \left[p(CA)p(Y/CA) + p(CA')p(Y/CA') \right] + p(R')p(I/R') \qquad (6.5)$$

Although this equation appears complex, in reality the Wyer model represents a straightforward extension of McGuire's earlier theorizing. This can be seen most clearly by reexamining Equation 6.3. The first term of this equation is simply the McGuire model, that is, $p(R)p(Y)$. What Wyer's formulation adds is conveyed by the equation's second term—the possibility that recipients' acceptance of a persuasive communication's conclusion may *not* depend upon their comprehension of message content, that is, $p(R')p(I/R')$.[16] The other main difference between these theories lies in their treatment of yielding. Although both regard yielding as *yielding to what has been received*,[17] Equation 6.4 reveals that the Wyer model differentiates yielding on the basis of counterarguing from yielding on the basis of other factors such as compliance pressures, that is, $p(Y/CA)$ vs. $p(Y/CA')$. In contrast, although McGuire (e.g., 1968b, 1972) alluded to a number of processes under the rubric of yielding—most notably, counterarguing and source derogation—his model treats this mediator as a molar construct. By decomposing yielding into counterarguing versus other (albeit largely unspecified) processes, the Wyer formulation explicitly incorporates the possibility that recipients may often accept a message (that they have comprehended) even though they have not attempted to assess the validity of its persuasive arguments. In essence, Wyer's extension of the McGuire model views persuasion in terms of three factors:

comprehension of persuasive arguments, refutation of arguments by counterarguing, and (largely unspecified) factors that affect acceptance of messages' conclusions for reasons unrelated to either comprehension or counterarguing.

Although Wyer (1974b) provided a provocative discussion of the relevance of his probabilogical model of reception and yielding to previous findings in persuasion (e.g., the effects of distraction, anticipatory attitude change), its worth as a theory of persuasion has not been validated empirically. Nevertheless, on a conceptual level, the model possesses several virtues. First, because it explicitly links yielding to counter-arguing, the model provides an important bridge between the McGuire model's emphasis on reception and the cognitive response model's emphasis on message- and issue-relevant thinking. By emphasizing both reception and cognitive responding, the Wyer formulation is compatible with our position that comprehension and cognitive elaboration of message content should be viewed as sequential (or concurrent) cognitive processes rather than as competing mediational explanations for persuasion findings (see also McGuire, 1985). Second, because Wyer's model incorporates the idea that recipients may accept persuasive messages' conclusions without thinking much about their content, that is, $p(I/R')$ and $p(Y/CA')$, it is amenable to attitude theories that do not ascribe mediational importance to message recipients' processing of persuasive argumentation. Theories of this type are considered in the next several chapters.

————— **Notes** —————

1. It might seem that the probabilogical model (McGuire, 1960a; Wyer, 1970) is immune to this criticism because of its focus on how belief in a conclusion (e.g., "marijuana will be legalized") is influenced when beliefs associated with a probabilistically related premise (e.g., "marijuana is harmless") undergo revision. Nevertheless, the probabilogical model is silent with respect to the psychological processes underlying people's acceptance of such premises.

2. In retrospect, a three-factor reception-cognitive responding-yielding model might be regarded as a more precise simplification of the McGuire paradigm for most laboratory persuasion experiments. It must be remembered, however, that theorizing about the role of cognitive responses in persuasion was only beginning to be systematized at the time McGuire articulated his simplified two-step model (A. G. Greenwald, 1968; see discussion in text), and that McGuire's suggestion that a cognitive responding step be added to the model came only years later.

3. Although McGuire did not assess subjects' affective reactions to the information they received, his theoretical reasoning clearly suggests the importance of negative affect in giving rise to his results. Presumably, initial exposure to undesirable information aroused negative affect which, in turn, caused subjects to avoid attending to the message. The impact of affective states on information processing is discussed in Chapter 10.

4. Although meaning change is often mentioned as an explanation for primacy effects in the persuasion literature (e.g., Insko, 1967; McGuire, 1969, 1985), we believe that it provides a more compelling account of primacy and other context effects in the impression formation literature. In relevant research (e.g., Hamilton & Zanna, 1974), subjects rate a target person described by two or more "context" traits (e.g., happy, intelligent vs. boring, rude) and one "critical" trait (e.g., proud). According to the meaning change hypothesis, subjects' perception of the critical trait is assimilated to the meaning provided by the context traits (i.e., "proud" is perceived as more positive in meaning in the "happy, intelligent" vs. "boring, rude" context). Important features of these studies are that subjects' attention is not explicitly drawn to the critical trait and, moreover, this trait is ambiguous enough in connotative meaning so that it rarely stands in stark contrast to the context traits. Yet, these design features are absent in the typical study of two opposing persuasive messages. In persuasion studies, the contrast between the first and second message is usually quite clear to subjects, as is (we submit) the diametrically opposed "meaning" of each message. For this reason, we tend to discount meaning change as a viable explanation for primacy effects in this literature. Indeed, when perceptual or judgmental distortions do occur, we suspect that a more likely outcome is that the meaning of the second message would be *contrasted*, or perceived as even more discrepant with the first (see M. Sherif & Hovland, 1961). Assimilation and contrast effects in attitude judgment are discussed more fully in Chapter 8 (see also Chapters 2 and 12).

5. In subsequent replications, Miller and Campbell's (1959) predictions have received only modest confirmation (Insko, 1964; Schultz, 1963; E. J. Thomas, Webb, & Tweedie, 1961; W. Wilson & Miller, 1968). In addition to the temporal factors featured in these replications, researchers have also investigated the impact of numerous other variables on primacy-recency effects in the two-opposing-messages paradigm (e.g., prior familiarity with the message topic, Lana, 1961; communication modality, Lana, 1963). Reviews of this literature have generally echoed Hovland and Mandell's (1957) conclusion that primacy-recency effects are complexly determined (Insko, 1967; McGuire, 1966, 1969, 1985). Given the complexity of the two-opposing-messages paradigm, and the numerous variables and processes that have been shown to influence persuasion in the standard one-message paradigm, a firm understanding of order effects in persuasion seems unlikely in the near future.

6. Although unfortunate, the tendency of most researchers to equate message reception with message learning is understandable. Hovland, Janis, and Kelley (1953), themselves, obscured the distinction between comprehension and learning. Although McGuire's formal descriptions of his information-processing paradigm did not confuse reception with learning on a conceptual level, he did suggest that reception could be operationalized in terms of message retention (McGuire, 1968a, 1968b). Also, in his subsequent writings, McGuire (e.g., 1972) sometimes used the terms reception, comprehension, and learning as if they were interchangeable constructs, a tendency that no doubt exacerbated researchers' misinterpretation of the reception processes he initially emphasized.

7. It is worth noting that McGuire felt that the compensation principle applied to a large set of individual difference dimensions, not only to the few variables he used to illustrate his logic and predictions (e.g., self-esteem, intelligence, anxiety). In large part, this belief was based on another, that complete susceptibility or non-susceptibility to influence attempts was less adaptive for human organisms than being susceptible in some situations and non-susceptible in others. Taken together, the compensation and situational weighting principles of the McGuire paradigm (see text) allowed him to model this viewpoint; for example, rather than being ubiquitously persuasible, people with low self-esteem were predicted to be sometimes more persuasible than people with moderate (or high) self-esteem and sometimes less persuasible.

8. Fishbein and Ajzen (1981) suggested that recipient-generated cognitive responses could be viewed as impact effects within their acceptance-yielding-impact analysis of persuasion, that is, as beliefs that are not directly addressed by the message's persuasive arguments but nonetheless are influenced by exposure to those arguments (see Chapter 5). Notwithstanding this suggestion, these authors were no more hospitable to the idea that cognitive responses are an important mediator of persuasion than they were to the idea that reception mediates persuasion (see Fishbein & Ajzen, 1981). In their view, the epistemological status of

cognitive responses has not been resolved and, in any event, these responses are likely to represent beliefs that are not the primary determinants of the attitude (or intention, etc.) that the persuasive message is designed to influence (see Chapter 5 and subsequent section on "Assessing cognitive responses").

9. Like many other investigators, Osterhouse and Brock (1970) viewed the reception issue in terms of message learning and discounted a "message learning" explanation for their data because they apparently considered it capable of predicting only decrements in persuasion due to increased distraction. Importantly, however, Osterhouse and Brock's message was purposely constructed to contain easy-to-counterargue arguments, and Petty, Wells, and Brock's (1976) follow-up study (see text) explicitly characterized the Osterhouse and Brock message as containing low quality persuasive arguments. If so, it is worth noting that the reception-as-mediator hypothesis actually makes the same prediction as does the counterargument-disruption hypothesis for the Osterhouse and Brock study—increased persuasion as an increasing function of distraction (see subsequent section on "Message reception and cognitive elaboration").

10. For the counterattitudinal message, one of the strong arguments stated that increasing tuition would improve the library, whereas one of the weak arguments stated that increasing tuition would enable more trees to be planted on campus. For the proattitudinal message, one of the strong arguments stated that tuition could be reduced because of a $22 million surplus in the state budget, whereas one of the weak arguments stated that tuition could be reduced by replacing high-prestige faculty with lower-prestige, lower-paid faculty.

11. Additional findings indicated that Experiment 1 subjects recalled significantly fewer persuasive arguments as distraction increased. The failure to replicate this effect in Experiment 2 may be due to the fact that it did not instantiate an extreme level of distraction. That is, although Experiment 1 featured low, medium, and high distraction levels

comparable to those used by Osterhouse and Brock (1970), Experiment 2 used only low and medium levels.

12. Johnson and Eagly (1989) preferred the term outcome-relevant involvement over issue involvement or personal relevance because they believed it to be a more precise description of the motivational state induced in most research using the "date" or "place" manipulations described in the text; in the vast majority of these experiments, subjects read or hear about a policy proposal that may influence their personal outcomes (e.g., subjects' abilities to obtain their bachelors' degrees). The term *personal relevance*, in particular, is quite general insofar as it could also refer to a variety of manipulations that induce differential interest in or attention to message content—for example, making subjects feel accountable for their attitude judgments (e.g., Chaiken, 1980; Tetlock & Kim, 1987), increasing personal responsibility for message evaluation (Petty, Harkins, & Williams, 1980; see text), enhancing the importance or consequentiality of subjects' processing task (e.g., Maheswaran & Chaiken, 1991), framing arguments in personal (vs. impersonal) language (Burnkrant & Unnava, 1989), and matching message content to subjects' functional predispositions (e.g., Cacioppo, Petty, & Sidera, 1982; DeBono, 1987). Manipulations such as these are discussed more fully in Chapter 7 because of their relevance to the elaboration likelihood and heuristic-systematic models.

13. Conceptual and empirical issues regarding the construct of argument quality are discussed in Chapter 7 in the context of the elaboration likelihood model.

14. There is also some ambiguity regarding whether certain extent-of-processing variables typically influence the *amount* of message-relevant thinking. For example, whereas several studies indicate that increased issue involvement increases the *total number* of message-relevant thoughts (regardless of valence) that subjects generate (e.g., Axsom, Yates, & Chaiken, 1987), this manipulation sometimes affects only the *valence* of message-

relevant thought (e.g., Burnkrant & Howard, 1984). Similar findings have been obtained with respect to rhetoricals and multiple sources (e.g., Burnkrant & Howard, 1984; Harkins & Petty, 1981, 1987; Petty, Cacioppo, & Heesacker, 1981). More generally, whereas a number of experiments have shown that extent-of-processing variables influence face-valid measures of amount of processing such as *total* message-relevant thoughts generated and argument recall (e.g., Chaiken, 1980; Maheswaran & Chaiken, 1991; Wood, Kallgren, & Preisler, 1985; Worth & Mackie, 1987), many other studies have either not found or not tested for such effects (e.g., Harkins & Petty, 1981; Petty & Cacioppo, 1984a; Petty, Cacioppo, & Goldman, 1981). In discussing this issue, Petty and Cacioppo have argued that enhanced message-relevant thinking should not necessarily influence the total number of message-relevant thoughts that subjects generate on thought-listing tasks, but should influence the *evaluative profile* of these thoughts. For example, given a strong message, higher issue involvement may not increase the total number of message thoughts listed (collapsed across valence), but should be associated with a greater number of favorable thoughts and a lesser number of unfavorable thoughts (see Petty & Cacioppo, 1981a, 1986a; also see Harkins & Petty, 1987, p. 263). In our judgment, when studies show that variables postulated to affect extensiveness of processing influence only the evaluative profile (and not the total amount) of message-relevant thinking, unequivocal evidence has not been provided that these variables enhance message-relevant thinking.

15. Heesacker, Petty, and Cacioppo (1983) hypothesized that credibility increases message-relevant thinking, given issues of high personal relevance. In partial support of this hypothesis, these researchers found (for field-dependent subjects only) that higher credibility decreased the persuasiveness of weak messages but negligibly increased the persuasiveness of strong messages. However, because this interaction between credibility and argument quality was not obtained on measures of the valence or amount of message-relevant thinking, this study does not provide unambiguous evidence that source credibility may increase extent of processing.

16. Whether the $p(R')p(I/R')$ term of Wyer's model truly extends McGuire's two-mediator analysis of persuasion is probably a matter of semantics. Whereas Wyer (1974b) explicitly defined reception in terms of comprehending persuasive arguments, McGuire defined reception more broadly as comprehending "the conclusions being urged and, to some extent, the arguments" (McGuire, 1972, p. 119). Although most researchers and writers (including McGuire himself) have subsequently viewed the reception step of McGuire's paradigm as referring primarily to the comprehension of persuasive arguments, McGuire's broad definition of comprehension clearly leaves open the same possibility that Wyer explicitly built into his model —that persuasion is not necessarily contingent upon comprehending a message's arguments.

17. Defining yielding in this way mitigates to some degree the major theoretical criticism of the McGuire model—that "yielding," a presumed mediator of influence (i.e., persuasion or attitude change), is conceptually indistinguishable from influence itself (e.g., Fishbein & Ajzen, 1972, 1975). Although McGuire's and Wyer's conceptual definition of yielding appears to sidestep this conceptual quagmire, distinguishing "yielding to what has been received" from persuasion at an empirical level has proven difficult (see Fishbein & Ajzen, 1975; McGuire, 1968b, 1972). In this regard, suggestions that valenced measures of message- and issue-relevant thinking could be used to index yielding (e.g., Wyer, 1974b) have some merit because, according to cognitive response theory, such measures index a stage of information processing that is causally prior to attitude change.

7

Process Theories of
Attitude Formation and Change:
The Elaboration Likelihood and
Heuristic-Systematic Models

The *systematic* process theories we considered in the last chapter emphasize the role of people's reception and cognitive elaboration of persuasive argumentation in producing new or changed attitudes. The process theories we turn to in this chapter and in Chapter 8 either incorporate or feature the idea that people may adopt attitudes on bases *other* than their understanding and evaluation of persuasive argumentation. The elaboration likelihood model (Petty & Cacioppo, 1981a, 1986a) incorporates this viewpoint by positing a *peripheral route* to persuasion—persuasion that occurs in the absence of argument scrutiny. The three remaining perspectives that we discuss in these chapters feature particular cognitive mechanisms that do not implicate argument-based processing. The heuristic-systematic model contrasts *systematic* processing with a *heuristic* mode in which simple decision rules mediate persuasion (Chaiken, 1980, 1987). Attribution approaches emphasize people's causal reasoning about the validity of persuasive messages (e.g., Eagly, Chaiken, & Wood, 1981; H.H. Kelley, 1967). Finally, social judgment theory focuses on how people's prior attitudes distort their perceptions of messages' positions, and how such perceptions mediate persuasion (e.g., C.W. Sherif & Sherif, 1967).

Like other *dual-process* models of social judgment (e.g., Fiske & Neuberg, 1990; Tetlock, 1985), the elaboration likelihood and heuristic-systematic models have become increasingly popular with researchers over the past decade (E.R. Smith, in press). In this chapter we present these two models and discuss their similarities and differences. These models also provide an interesting context for considering attribution approaches and social judgment theory, which we discuss in Chapter 8.

Elaboration Likelihood Model

In Chapter 6 we summarized numerous experiments by Richard Petty, John Cacioppo, and their colleagues that crossed argument quality, a variable presumed to control the valence of message-relevant thought, with an assortment of variables presumed to influence the extent of such thought (e.g., distraction, personal relevance). This research was instrumental in shaping researchers' conception of the key thesis of the cognitive response model, that persuasion is mediated by the valence and amount of message-related cognitive responding. As an outgrowth of this research, Petty and Cacioppo developed a new theory of persuasion, the *elaboration likelihood model* (ELM) (Petty & Cacioppo, 1981a, 1986a, 1986b).

Although similar to the cognitive response model in many respects, the elaboration likelihood model offers an extended view of persuasion insofar as it (a) specifies the conditions under which persuasion should be mediated by message-related thinking, and (b) postulates that alternative *peripheral* mechanisms account for persuasion when these conditions are not met. The model also represents an attempt to place existing persuasion theory and research under one conceptual umbrella (Petty & Cacioppo, 1981a, 1986a, 1986b). Regarding theory, Petty and Cacioppo specify two qualitatively different *routes* to persuasion and assert that most attitude theories can be viewed as exemplifying one or the other. Theories emphasizing the mediational importance of argument-based thinking—theories we term *systematic* in this book—are labeled *central route* perspectives. In contrast, theories that specify psychological mechanisms that do not implicate argument processing are labeled *peripheral* perspectives. Regarding research, Petty and Cacioppo suggest that most source, message, and other variables that have been investigated can be viewed as having influenced persuasion in one or more of three ways specified by their theory (see below).

Petty and Cacioppo (1986a, 1986b) articulate their model in terms of the seven postulates shown in Table 7.1. They assume that people desire to attain correct attitudes (Postulate I), but that the extent and nature of their processing of persuasive arguments depends upon motivation and ability (Postulate II). The term *elaboration* in the model refers to the extent to which people think about issue-relevant arguments contained in persuasive messages. When situational and individual difference variables ensure high motivation and ability for issue-relevant thinking, the *elaboration likelihood* is said to be high. As a consequence, the probability that recipients follow the *central route* is high. Consistent with Petty and Cacioppo's (e.g., 1986b) labeling of theories we reviewed in Chapter 5 and 6 as central route perspectives, any mechanism that implicates argument-based processing (e.g., comprehending argumentation) could potentially mediate central route persuasion. In line with their previous cognitive response research, however, Petty and Cacioppo have most frequently identified *message-relevant thinking* as the prime mediator of this type of persuasion (e.g., Cacioppo, Petty, Kao, & Rodriguez, 1986; Petty & Cacioppo, 1984a). Attitudes formed or changed via the central route are hypothesized to be relatively persistent, predictive of behavior, and resistant to change until challenged by convincing counterarguments (Postulate VII).

What happens when motivation or ability for elaboration is low? According to the model, attitudes are still formed and changed under such conditions—but not via the central route. Instead, when the elaboration likelihood is low, the probability is high that recipients will follow the *peripheral route* to persuasion. This type of persuasion is regarded as more ephemeral than central route persuasion (Postulate VII) and is conceptualized as the product of any of a variety of mechanisms that cause persuasion

TABLE 7.1

Postulates of the Elaboration Likelihood Model of Persuasion

I.	People are motivated to hold correct attitudes.
II.	Although people want to hold correct attitudes, the amount and nature of issue-relevant elaboration in which people are willing or able to engage to evaluate a message vary with individual and situational factors.
III.	Variables can affect the amount and direction of attitude change by: (A) serving as persuasive arguments, (B) serving as peripheral cues, and/or (C) affecting the extent or direction of issue and argument elaboration.
IV.	Variables affecting motivation and/or ability to process a message in a relatively objective manner can do so by either enhancing or reducing argument scrutiny.
V.	As motivation and/or ability to process arguments is decreased, peripheral cues become relatively more important determinants of persuasion. Conversely, as argument scrutiny is increased, peripheral cues become relatively less important determinants of persuasion.
VI.	Variables affecting message processing in a relatively biased manner can produce either a positive (favorable) or negative (unfavorable) motivational and/or ability bias to the issue-relevant thoughts attempted.
VII.	Attitude changes that result mostly from processing issue-relevant arguments (central route) will show greater temporal persistence, greater prediction of behavior, and greater resistance to counterpersuasion than attitude changes that result mostly from peripheral cues.

Source: These postulates were presented in Petty and Cacioppo (1986b).

in the absence of argument scrutiny (Cacioppo & Petty, 1984; Petty & Cacioppo, 1981a, 1986a, 1986b). These peripheral mechanisms include cognitive ones such as heuristic processing and attributional reasoning (see Chapter 8); affective mechanisms such as classical and operant conditioning (see Chapter 9); and social role mechanisms such as maintaining social relationships and favorable self-identities (see Chapters 10 and 13). Like the central route, then, the peripheral route refers to a family of attitude theories. Because the distinction between the two families is that central route perspectives emphasize argument-based processing whereas peripheral route perspectives do not, the model's two routes are complements of one another. Together, they exhaust the universe of mediating processes that persuasion theorists have discussed.

The term *peripheral cue* refers to any variable capable of affecting persuasion without affecting argument scrutiny (Petty & Cacioppo, 1986b, p. 134). In practice, variables are so labeled because of their presumed relevance to one or more peripheral

**FIGURE 7.1.
Antecedents and
consequences of the
elaboration
likelihood model's
central and
peripheral routes to
persuasion, which
anchor the extreme
endpoints of the
elaboration
likelihood
continuum. This
figure was presented
by Petty and
Cacioppo (1986b,
Figure 1, p. 126).**

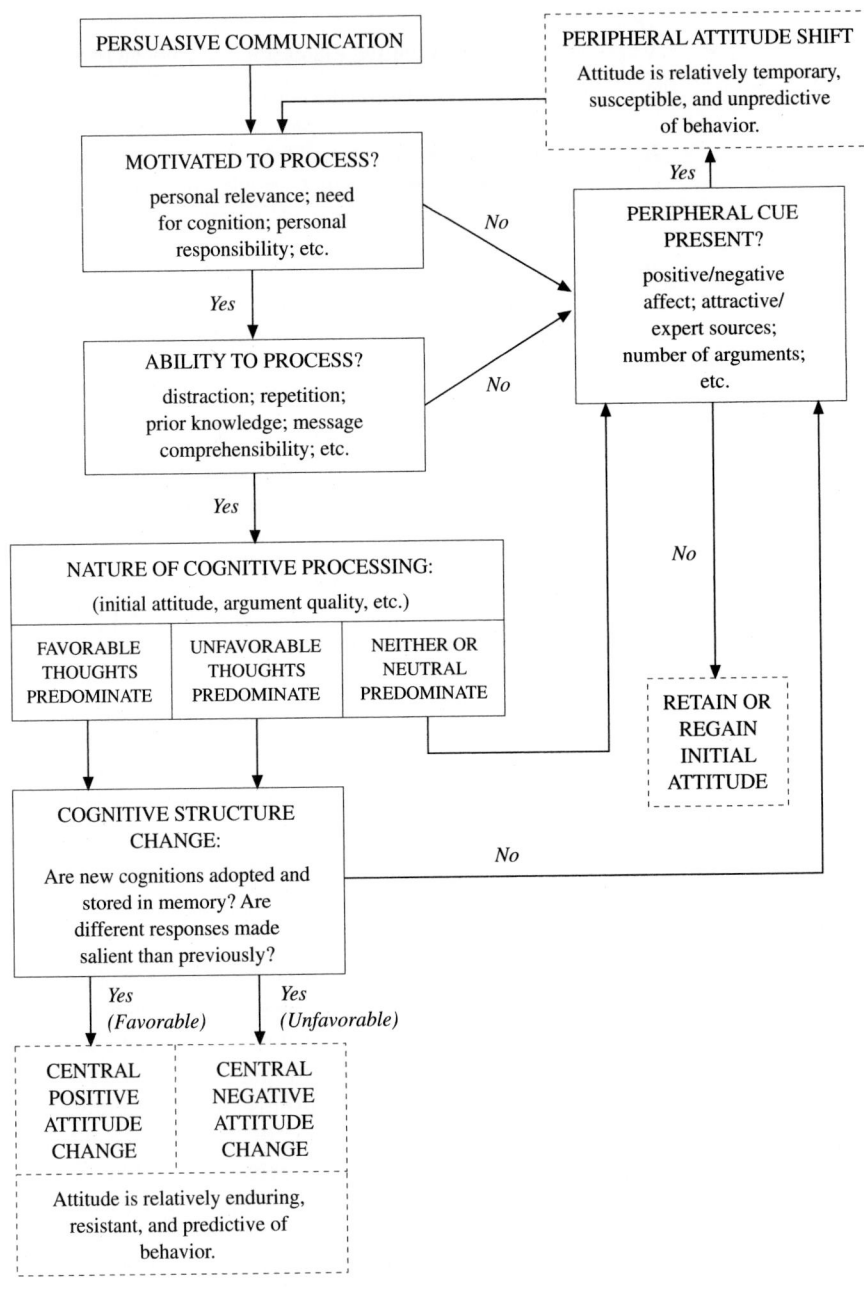

mechanisms. For example, several studies testing the model (e.g., Petty & Cacioppo, 1980; Petty, Cacioppo, & Schumann, 1983) have examined source attractiveness, a variable relevant to identification-based attitude change (Kelman, 1961; see Chapter 13), heuristic processing, and both classical and operant conditioning. Unlike the central route, the peripheral route is not operationalized in terms of any particular mechanism. Instead, Petty and Cacioppo adopt a set of empirical criteria for concluding that (some type of) peripheral route persuasion has occurred (see below).

The model's key hypothesis is that the elaboration likelihood moderates the route to persuasion. When motivation and ability for argument elaboration are high, recipients follow the central route. When motivation and ability are low, however, they follow the peripheral route. Petty and Cacioppo's (1981a, 1986a, 1986b) schematic depiction of the antecedents and consequences of the two routes to persuasion is shown in Figure 7.1. Included in this figure are examples of peripheral cues and variables postulated to influence either motivation or ability for elaboration.

Three Ways to Influence Attitudes

Postulate III states that variables affect persuasion in three distinct ways (see Table 7.1): First they can serve as persuasive arguments—"bits of information contained in a communication that are relevant to a person's subjective determination of the true merits of an advocated position" (Petty & Cacioppo, 1986b, p. 133). Second, they can serve as peripheral cues, thereby affecting persuasion via one or another peripheral mechanism. Finally, they can affect either motivation or ability for elaboration, thereby moderating the route to persuasion. For example, when people receive a personally relevant message under non-distracting conditions (establishing high motivation and high ability), the model predicts that central route persuasion will occur. However, when this same message is received under highly distracting conditions, or when a personally irrelevant message is received, the model predicts that peripheral route persuasion will occur. Importantly, Petty and Cacioppo also propose that variables influencing the elaboration likelihood may lead to either *objective* message processing (Postulate IV) or *biased* message processing (Postulate VI):

> In relatively *objective* processing, some treatment variable either motivates or enables subjects to see the strengths of cogent arguments and the flaws in specious ones, or inhibits them from doing so. In relatively *biased* processing some treatment variable either motivates or enables subjects to generate a particular kind of thought in response to a message, or inhibits a particular kind of thought (Petty & Cacioppo, 1986b, p. 136).

Argument Quality

Central to the elaboration likelihood model is a construct that Petty and Cacioppo (e.g., 1986b) have labeled *argument quality*. The model defines this variable in empirical terms and also features a method for generating high and low quality messages. Argument quality refers to a recipient's perception that a message's arguments

TABLE 7.2

Arguments Supporting the Adoption of Senior Comprehensive Exams

Strong arguments:
1. Prestigious universities have comprehensive exams to maintain academic excellence.
2. Institution of the exams has led to a reversal in the declining scores on standardized achievement tests at other universities.
3. Graduate and professional schools show a preference for undergraduates who have passed a comprehensive exam.
4. Average starting salaries are higher for graduates of schools with the exams.
5. Schools with the exams attract larger and more well-known corporations to recruit students for jobs.
6. The quality of undergraduate teaching has improved at schools with the exams.
7. University alumni would increase financial support if the exams were instituted, allowing a tuition increase to be avoided.
8. The "National Accrediting Board of Higher Education" would give the University its highest rating if the exams were instituted.

Weak arguments:
1. Adopting the exams would allow the university to be at the forefront of a national trend.
2. Graduate students have complained that since they have to take comprehensives, undergraduates should take them also.
3. By not administering the exams, a tradition dating back to the ancient Greeks is being violated.
4. Parents had written to administrators in support of the plan.
5. The exams would increase student fear and anxiety enough to promote more studying.
6. The exams would help cut costs by eliminating the necessity for other tests that varied with instructor.
7. The exams would allow students to compare their performance with that of students at other schools.
8. Job prospects might be improved.

Very weak arguments:
1. Most of the (source's) friends supported the proposal.
2. The (source's) major advisor took a comprehensive exam and now had a prestigious academic position.
3. Whatever the benefit the exams had for graduate students would also accrue to undergraduates.
4. Requiring graduate students but not undergraduates to take the exams is analogous to racial discrimination.
5. The risk of failing the exam is a challenge most students would welcome.
6. The difficulty of the exam would prepare one for later competitions in life.
7. The Educational Testing Service would not market the exams unless they had great educational value.
8. If the exams were instituted, the (subjects') university would become the American Oxford.

Source: These arguments were presented in Petty, Harkins, and Williams (1980, p. 87).

are strong and cogent as opposed to weak and specious. To construct such messages, Petty and Cacioppo (e.g., 1986b, p. 133) recommend first developing a pool of intuitively strong and weak arguments on a particular topic (e.g., raising college tuition). Pilot subjects then rate these arguments for their persuasiveness. Next, messages containing arguments rated high or low in persuasiveness are constructed. Finally, these messages are presented to other pilot subjects who are asked to evaluate them critically and to complete a thought-listing task (see Chapter 6). Using this procedure, *strong messages* are operationalized as those that elicit predominantly favorable thoughts about the message's advocated position. In parallel fashion, *weak messages* are defined as those that elicit primarily unfavorable thoughts. As this description should make clear, argument quality is thus the same construct that figured prominently in Petty and Cacioppo's earlier research on the cognitive response model (see subsequent discussion in this chapter).

Petty, Harkins, and Williams (1980) applied these procedures in developing "strong," "weak," and "very weak" messages advocating the adoption of comprehensive exams for college seniors. The arguments that formed the basis for these messages are summarized in Table 7.2. A number of additional experiments by Petty, Cacioppo, and their colleagues have featured strong messages based on the "strong" arguments shown in this table and weak messages based either on the table's "weak" arguments (e.g., Heesacker, Petty, & Cacioppo, 1983; Petty & Cacioppo, 1979b) or "very weak" arguments (e.g., Petty & Cacioppo, 1984a; Petty, Cacioppo, & Goldman, 1981).

Role of Argument Quality in Tests of the Model

Argument quality plays a critical role in tests of the elaboration likelihood model. Specifically, the persuasive impact of argument quality represents Petty and Cacioppo's primary method of identifying (a) the extent to which a treatment variable (e.g., distraction) has influenced message processing and whether this processing is objective or biased, and (b) whether central route or peripheral route persuasion has occurred. Because of its importance to the model, we will describe their empirical logic in some detail.

Panel I of Figure 7.2 displays Petty and Cacioppo's empirical criteria for concluding that a treatment variable has influenced message processing in an objective manner. The case of a variable that enhances objective processing is shown in the left half of the panel. In this case, a manipulation of argument quality should exert a stronger persuasive impact in the high elaboration treatment condition (e.g., message topic is personally relevant) than in the low elaboration control condition (e.g., topic is personally irrelevant). Moreover, the resultant Argument Quality × Treatment interaction should be symmetric. In other words, (a) subjects discriminate more between strong and weak messages in the high elaboration treatment condition (implying greater message processing), and (b) exposure to this treatment increases the persuasiveness of strong messages and decreases the persuasiveness of weak messages to a similar extent (implying objective processing). The case of a treatment variable that reduces objective processing, shown in the right half of the panel, is analogous.

311

FIGURE 7.2.
Impact of treatment variables on persuasion according to the elaboration likelihood model. Under conditions of moderate elaboration likelihood, variables may enhance or reduce message processing in an objective manner (Panel I) or in a relatively biased manner (Panel II). Under conditions of low elaboration likelihood, attitudes are affected mostly by peripheral cues (Panel III). Under conditions of high elaboration likelihood, attitudes are affected mostly by argument quality (Panel IV). This figure was adapted from one presented by Petty and Cacioppo (1986b, Figure 2, p. 135).

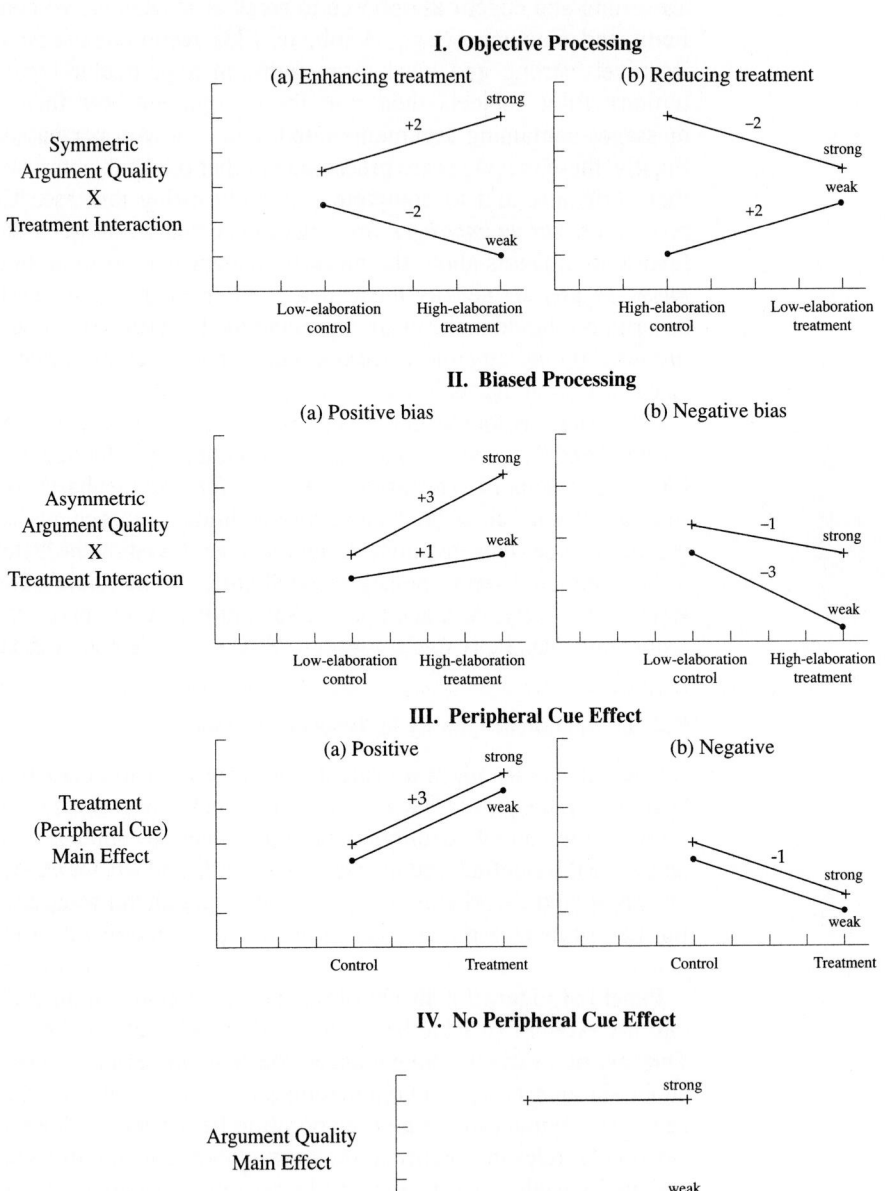

Subjects' attitudes should reflect less discrimination between strong and weak arguments in the low elaboration treatment condition (e.g., high distraction) than in the high elaboration control condition (e.g., no distraction), and the interaction should again be symmetric.

Panel II of Figure 7.2 displays the model's empirical criteria for concluding that a variable (e.g., prior knowledge) has biased message processing in a positive or negative manner (left and right halves of panel, respectively). Regardless of the direction of bias, the data should indicate that the treatment variable has influenced the elaboration likelihood. That is, subjects should discriminate more between strong and weak arguments in the high elaboration treatment condition (e.g., knowledgeable subjects) than in the low elaboration control condition (e.g., unknowledgeable subjects). However, in contrast to the case of objective processing, the resultant Argument Quality × Treatment interaction should be asymmetric. When processing is positively biased, the model assumes that recipients are more highly motivated or better able to generate favorable rather than unfavorable thoughts about the advocacy (Postulate VI), and that exposure to weak arguments constrains but does not eliminate this bias (Petty & Cacioppo, 1986b, p. 163). Similarly, when negative bias occurs, thoughts are predominantly unfavorable, and exposure to strong arguments merely lessens this bias. The asymmetric interactions shown in Panel II reflect these assumptions. In the case of positive bias, greater elaboration enhances message persuasiveness, albeit to a lesser extent for weak messages. In the case of negative bias, greater elaboration reduces message persuasiveness, albeit to a lesser extent for strong messages.

The remaining panels of Figure 7.2 illustrate how argument quality is also used to assess whether peripheral route persuasion has occurred. The left half of Panel III depicts Petty and Cacioppo's empirical criteria for concluding that a treatment variable (e.g., source expertise) has positively affected persuasion by some peripheral mechanism. First, persuasion is greater in the treatment condition (e.g., high expertise) than in the control condition (e.g., no expertise information provided). Second, the absence of a significant Argument Quality × Treatment interaction implies that the treatment variable has *not* affected message processing. Thus it is assumed that the treatment did not influence either motivation or ability for elaboration. Finally, the absence of a main effect due to argument quality implies that the elaboration likelihood is low. Thus it is assumed that the treatment variable probably did *not* function as a persuasive argument (because persuasive arguments presumably do not affect attitudes when the elaboration likelihood is low; see Petty & Cacioppo, 1980, 1986b). The right half of this panel is identical but depicts a peripheral cue treatment that exerts a negative impact on persuasion (e.g., low source expertise vs. no expertise information).

Panel IV, in contrast, depicts *no* peripheral cue effect. The only reliable effect on persuasion here is a main effect for argument quality. On this basis, the model assumes that the elaboration likelihood is high and that only central route persuasion has occurred. Finally, taken together, Panel III and IV illustrate Postulate V of the model: Peripheral cues are important determinants of persuasion under low elaboration likelihood conditions (Panel III), but are less important determinants under high elaboration likelihood conditions (Panel IV).

313

As illustrated in the following section, Petty and Cacioppo have relied extensively on the data patterns shown in Figure 7.2 in interpreting their own experiments and those of other investigators. Specifically, the pattern of observed persuasion means from such experiments is compared to the ideal data patterns of Figure 7.2 in order to diagnose whether peripheral route or central route persuasion has occurred and, in the latter case, whether elaboration has been biased or objective. Measures tracking the valence and occasionally other aspects of subjects' cognitive processing are also often included in relevant experiments (i.e., thought-listing and sometimes argument recall). However, Petty and Cacioppo typically accord such measures a secondary role in data interpretation. Instead, it is the match between observed persuasion data and the ideal ELM patterns in Figure 7.2 that Petty and Cacioppo (1986a, 1986b, 1990) have emphasized in testing the viability of their model.

Empirical Findings

The premise that central route persuasion requires motivation and ability (Postulate II) has been addressed in numerous studies, many of which we reviewed in the context of presenting the cognitive response model. As detailed in Chapter 6, these experiments crossed argument quality with a range of treatment variables presumed to influence motivation or ability for argument elaboration. In general, these studies and subsequent ones have confirmed the cognitive response/ELM prediction that the quality of persuasive argumentation influences attitude judgments more when recipients are highly motivated and/or highly able to engage in elaborative processing.[1] For example, Cacioppo, Petty, Kao, and Rodriguez (1986, Experiment 1) reasoned that people who are higher in their need for cognition (Cacioppo & Petty, 1982; Cohen, 1957) are typically more motivated to engage in issue-relevant thinking than people lower on this individual difference dimension (see also Cacioppo, Petty, & Morris, 1983). Consistent with this reasoning, the researchers' manipulation of argument quality (8 strong or 8 weak arguments advocating a tuition increase) interacted with subjects' need for cognition status in the manner depicted in the left half of Panel I, Figure 7.2. Given a strong message, high need for cognition subjects expressed more positive attitudes and listed fewer unfavorable thoughts than low need for cognition subjects. Given a weak message, however, they expressed more negative attitudes and listed more unfavorable thoughts than low need for cognition subjects.

The list of situational and individual difference variables that either motivate or enable central route (or systematic) processing is now quite extensive (for reviews, see Chaiken & Stangor, 1987; Petty & Cacioppo, 1986b; Tesser & Shaffer, 1990). In addition to need for cognition and several variables discussed in Chapter 6 (e.g., personal relevance, rhetoricals), other variables that research has implicated as motivators of elaborative thinking in attitude contexts include task importance (Maheswaran & Chaiken, 1991), accountability for one's attitude judgments (e.g., Chaiken, 1980; Tetlock, 1983a), matching message content to recipients' functional predispositions (e.g., DeBono & Harnish, 1988; see Chapter 10), and exposure to unexpected message content (Maheswaran & Chaiken, 1991). And, in addition to distraction and message repetition (reviewed in Chapter 6), variables that appear to influence ability for argument processing include time pressure (D. L. Moore, Hausknecht, & Thamodaran, 1986; Ratneshwar & Chaiken, 1991), communication modality (Chaiken & Eagly, 1983), knowledge and expertise (e.g., Alba & Marmorstein, 1987; Wood, 1982), direct experience with attitude objects (Wu & Shaffer, 1987), positive mood (Mackie & Worth, 1989), and anxiety (Jepson & Chaiken, 1990; see also Chapter 10's discussion of fear and mood effects on persuasion).

Objective versus Biased Processing. Most experiments that have manipulated argument quality in conjunction with motivational or ability variables have produced interactions more in accord with the symmetric pattern shown in Panel I of Figure 7.2 than with the asymmetric pattern shown in Panel II. By the ELM's pattern matching criteria, then, the majority of motivational and ability variables that have been examined to date would appear to foster relatively objective, rather than biased, message processing. One variable that may be an exception to this generalization is recipients' knowledgeability or expertise about the attitude object discussed in the message. In a series of studies on the attitudinal effects of prior knowledge, Wendy Wood (e.g., 1982) has measured this variable by asking subjects, usually in pre-experimental sessions, to list their beliefs and behaviors relevant to some issue. The number of beliefs and behaviors listed serves as an index of prior knowledge (i.e., access to attitude-relevant information in memory; see Wood, 1982).

Wood, Kallgren, and Priesler (1985) presented a strong or weak counterattitudinal message to subjects who differed in their knowledgeability on the topic of environmental conservation. On an overall basis, high knowledge subjects generated more negative thoughts about these messages and were less persuaded by them than low knowledge subjects. In addition, however, the finding that argument quality had a significantly stronger impact on high knowledge subjects' attitudes suggested that they had processed message content more extensively than low knowledge subjects had. Moreover, as Petty and Cacioppo (1986b) have argued, the pattern of this interaction conformed more to the ELM's criteria for biased (negative) message processing than to its objective processing criteria. That is, similar to the ideal pattern shown in the right half of Panel II, Figure 7.2, subjects who possessed a great deal of knowledge about the message topic were less persuaded than those who possessed little knowledge, and this difference was more pronounced for the weak message ($Ms =$ 2.85 vs. 5.07, $p < .001$) than for the strong message ($Ms = 3.98$ vs. 4.20, ns).[2]

Although this interaction pattern fits the ELM logic that prior knowledge biases processing negatively for counterattitudinal messages and that strong arguments merely lessen this bias (see Petty & Cacioppo, 1986b, pp. 168–169), Wood and her colleagues did not obtain a similar interaction on the evaluative profile of subjects' thoughts, as this logic also implies. Hence, the data they observed may indicate, not biased processing by high knowledge subjects, but (as Wood et al. argued) simply their greater ability to critically evaluate even strongly argued messages. Presenting pro-attitudinal messages to high and low knowledge recipients could distinguish these two interpretations (see Chaiken, Liberman, & Eagly, 1989). If greater knowledge led to greater processing and less persuasion in response to attitudinally congruent messages, the heightened criticality interpretation would be supported. If, however, greater knowledge led to more positive message-related thinking and greater persuasion, the biased processing interpretation would be favored. Indeed, two experiments conducted by Biek, Wood, Chaiken, and Nations (1992) provided just this test, and the results supported the heightened criticality hypothesis rather than the biased processing hypothesis. Yet consistent with Petty and Cacioppo's (1986b) interpretation of the Wood, Kallgren, and Priesler data, there probably are circumstances, heretofore unexplored, that would foster a more partisan form of processing on the part of highly knowledgeable message recipients (see Biek et al., 1992; Chaiken et al., 1989).

Another variable whose impact on message processing may not be uniformly objective is the extent to which the message issue is personally relevant to recipients. As we saw in Chapter 6, virtually identical personal relevance, or "issue involvement," manipulations sometimes interact with argument quality in a manner that approximates the symmetric interaction pattern prescribed by the ELM's objective processing hypothesis (e.g., Leippe & Elkin, 1987; Petty & Cacioppo, 1979b, 1981b, 1984a; Petty, Cacioppo, & Goldman, 1981), and other times in a manner that more closely resembles the asymmetric pattern prescribed by the model's biased processing hypothesis (e.g., Axsom, Yates, & Chaiken, 1987; Burnkrant & Howard, 1984, statements condition; Liberman & Chaiken, 1989).[3] The reasons for this disparity in findings are presently unclear (see Chapter 6). Relevant to this issue is Petty and Cacioppo's (1986b) argument that as involvement increases from low to relatively high, objective message processing increases, but that at very high levels of involvement, processing either terminates "in the interest of self-protection" or becomes biased "in the service of one's own ego" (p. 148). More recently, however, they have asserted that increased involvement exerts a uniformly linear effect on the extensiveness of *objective* message processing. In the context of this revised formulation, they argue that findings suggesting that involvement sometimes *biases* message processing can be ascribed to methodological confounds such as prior attitudes and knowledge (Petty & Cacioppo, 1990). In contrast to this unitary view, B. T. Johnson and Eagly (1989, 1990) advocate a distinction between outcome-relevant involvement—their term for personal relevance or issue involvement—and value-relevant involvement, a motivational state induced by an association between an activated attitude and one's enduring values. As discussed in Chapter 6, these authors argue that outcome-relevant involvement fosters a relatively open-minded form of processing whereas value-relevant involvement fosters a closed-minded form of processing (see also Chaiken et al., 1989; Chaiken & Stangor, 1987). In designing further research, then, investigators might consider measuring or manipulating value-relevant involvement along with outcome-relevant involvement (i.e., personal relevance). Because value-relevant involvement may be affected by researchers' choice of attitude issues and other idiosyncratic features of their experimental designs, it is possible that at least some of the disparity across past personal relevance studies might be traced to unassessed differences in value-relevant involvement (see further discussion of involvement in Chapter 8).

In addition to prior knowledge, Petty and Cacioppo (1986b) have speculated that other variables such as message discrepancy, warnings,[4] and audience "heckling" may at times also bias message processing (Petty & Brock, 1976; Petty & Cacioppo, 1977, 1979a; Wells & Petty, 1980). However, because these treatments have not been researched in conjunction with argument quality, the extent to which they would interact with this variable in the prescribed asymmetric manner depicted in Figure 7.2, Panel II is currently unknown.

Peripheral Cue Effects. Experiments showing that argument quality determines persuasion when motivation and ability for message processing are high address only half of Petty and Cacioppo's key hypothesis that the elaboration likelihood moderates the route to persuasion. The other half states that peripheral cues determine persuasion when motivation and ability for processing are low. Moreover, Postulate V adds that such cues are relatively unimportant determinants when motivation and ability are high. Several experiments by Petty, Cacioppo, and their colleagues and studies by other investigators support these ELM (and heuristic-systematic model) predictions (see Chaiken, 1987; Chaiken & Stangor, 1987; Petty & Cacioppo, 1986b; Tesser & Shaffer, 1990).

In a study that featured source expertise as its peripheral cue, Petty, Cacioppo, and Goldman (1981) had subjects listen to a message advocating senior comprehensive exams, a policy the university was ostensibly considering for the following year (high personal relevance) or the following decade (low personal relevance). Subjects were exposed to either eight strong or eight very weak arguments favoring this recommendation (see Table 7.2), and the tape was said to be based on a report prepared by either a local high school class or the "Carnegie Commission on Higher Education." The results showed that in the low relevance conditions of the study, only source expertise influenced subjects' post-message attitudes, presumably through some peripheral mechanism such as heuristic processing (e.g., "Experts' statements can be trusted," see next section of chapter). In the high relevance conditions, however, source expertise had no impact on attitudes. Here, as in much previous work, only argument quality influenced persuasion. Other studies that have manipulated motivation for processing in conjunction with other source variables (e.g., communicator likability, attractiveness) have yielded virtually identical findings (e.g., Chaiken, 1980; Petty et al., 1983; see, however, Chaiken & Maheswaran, 1992). Moreover, analogous results have been obtained in experiments that have featured variables presumed to influence ability for processing—for example, time pressure, message comprehensibility, prior knowledge, and recipient mood. Whereas source variables exert little persuasive impact under high ability conditions, their effect on persuasion is typically substantial when recipients lack ability for extensive processing (e.g., Mackie & Worth, 1989; Ratneshwar & Chaiken, 1991; Wood & Kallgren, 1988; Wood et al., 1985; Worth & Mackie, 1987; Wu & Shaffer, 1987).

In further support of the ELM (and heuristic-systematic model), other studies have demonstrated that variables such as message length, number of persuasive arguments, overheard audience reactions, and consensus information also exert a greater persuasive

FIGURE 7.3. Mean post-communication attitude as a function of argument quality and number of arguments for low and high personal relevance subjects. This figure was presented by Petty and Cacioppo (1984a, Figure 2, p. 77).

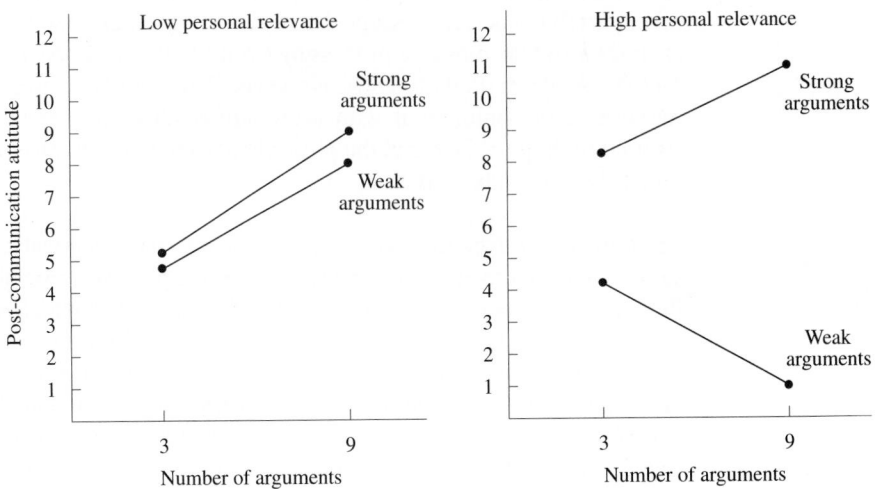

impact when ability or motivation for argument processing is low (e.g., Alba & Marmorstein, 1987; Axsom et al., 1987; Maheswaran & Chaiken, 1991; D. L. Moore et al., 1986; Petty & Cacioppo, 1984a; Wood et al., 1985). For example, Petty and Cacioppo (1984a) presented subjects with nine or three strong or nine or three weak arguments advocating senior comprehensive exams and found the pattern of results depicted in Figure 7.3. When personal relevance was low, the nine-argument message induced greater persuasion than the three-argument message, regardless of argument quality. When personal relevance was high, however, subjects agreed significantly more with strong than with weak messages. In addition, an interaction between quality and quantity of argumentation in this condition showed that argument quality exerted a more pronounced effect on attitudes when nine rather than three arguments were received (see further discussion of this result below).

Consequences of Elaboration. Postulate VII states that central route persuasion produces attitudes that are more persistent, predictive of behavior, and more resistant to counterpropaganda than attitudes formed or changed via peripheral mechanisms. The heuristic-systematic model (see next section) similarly hypothesizes that systematic processing fosters more durable attitudes. Although less research has addressed this durability proposition, several experiments that have featured delayed as well as immediate attitude posttests have yielded data consistent with the persistence hypothesis (Chaiken, 1980; Chaiken & Eagly, 1983, Experiment 2; Mackie, 1987; Petty, Cacioppo, & Heesacker, unpublished research cited in Petty & Cacioppo, 1986b; see also Chapter 12). Several demonstrations that attitudes correlate more highly with behavioral intentions among subjects induced to process messages more extensively support the attitude-behavior hypothesis but do not provide definitive evidence for it because attitudes and intentions were assessed contemporaneously in these studies (Leippe & Elkin, 1987; Pallak, Murroni, & Koch, 1983; Petty et al., 1983). Somewhat better evidence was obtained by Cacioppo, Petty, Kao, and Rodriguez (1986, Experiment 2), who found that preelection candidate preferences were better predictors of subsequent voting behavior for subjects who were higher in their need for cognition. This study suggests that central route processing can confer greater attitude-behavior consistency because, consistent with the model's criterion for determining whether central route processing has occurred, persons higher in need for cognition have been shown to discriminate more between strong and weak persuasive messages (see above). Finally, although there are findings suggesting that central route processing may foster resistance to counterpropaganda (e.g., Wu & Shaffer, 1987), this hypothesis has yet to be tested stringently.

Variables That Serve Multiple Roles. Although the elaboration likelihood model asserts that variables influence persuasion in just three distinct ways, it does not hold that any one variable must exert its influence in only one way. In fact, Petty and Cacioppo (1986a, 1986b; Petty, Cacioppo, & Kasmer, 1988) have discussed a number of variables that they believe serve multiple roles in persuasion settings (e.g., source variables, mood, warnings, number of sources, rhetoricals). For example, based on the Petty and Cacioppo (1984a) results shown in Figure 7.3, Petty and Cacioppo (1986b) have argued that the sheer number of arguments presented serves as a peripheral cue when the elaboration likelihood is low, but as an enhancer of objective message processing when the elaboration likelihood is high. This conclusion rests on the similarity (a) between the low personal relevance data observed in the 1984 experiment (left half of Figure 7.3) and the ideal peripheral cue effect pattern shown in Figure 7.2's Panel III (left half), and (b) between the 1984 study's high personal relevance data (right half of Figure 7.3) and the ideal enhancement-of-objective-processing pattern shown in Figure 7.2's Panel I (left half).

Another application of the multiple roles idea is Petty and Cacioppo's analysis of source variables (Petty & Cacioppo, 1984b; Petty, Kasmer, Haugtvedt, & Cacioppo, 1987). Their analysis proposes that this class of communication variables affects persuasion in different ways as the elaboration likelihood changes from low to moderate to high. When motivation and ability for processing are low, source variables are hypothesized to act as "simple acceptance or rejection" cues (i.e., peripheral cues; Petty & Cacioppo, 1984b, p. 669). The cue should thus affect persuasion in the manner depicted in Figure 7.2, Panel III and observed in the low personal relevance conditions of several studies (Petty, Cacioppo, & Goldman, 1981; Petty et al., 1983). However, given high motivation and ability, people are presumed to be less influenced by peripheral cues (Postulate V). Hence, as depicted in Panel IV, Figure 7.2 and observed in the high personal relevance conditions of the above studies, source variables are hypothesized to exert little persuasive impact when the elaboration likelihood is high— with one exception. In some high elaboration circumstances, Petty and Cacioppo argue, source variables might still affect persuasion to the extent that they function as *persuasive arguments*. This aspect of their analysis is based on the results of an earlier study (Petty & Cacioppo, 1980) in which they presented subjects with a strong or weak advertisement for a shampoo and also manipulated both personal relevance and the physical attractiveness of the shampoo's endorsers. Consistent with that study's hypotheses, argument quality had a greater persuasive impact when personal relevance was high than when it was low. Contrary to predictions, however, more attractive endorsers were more persuasive than less attractive ones, regardless of personal relevance. This finding led Petty and Cacioppo (1984b) to conclude that in the Petty and Cacioppo (1980) experiment, endorser attractiveness had functioned as a peripheral cue when personal relevance was low, but as a persuasive argument when personal relevance was high (see also Haugtvedt, Petty, Cacioppo, & Steidley, 1988). In the latter condition, Petty and Cacioppo (1984b) argued, attractiveness provided "persuasive visual testimony as to the effectiveness of a beauty product" (p. 671; see further discussion of this interpretation below).

What happens when motivation and ability for argument processing are at some moderate level? According to Petty and Cacioppo's analysis, source cues function to enhance (or to reduce) argument processing in such situations, in the manner depicted in Panel I of Figure 7.2, that is, such cues are used by recipients "to determine how much thinking they should do about the message." Thus, "a source factor that enhances thinking will increase persuasion if the arguments are strong, but will decrease persuasion if the arguments are weak" (Petty & Cacioppo, 1984b, p. 671). The rationale for this hypothesis derives from two studies that exposed subjects to strong or weak messages advocating senior comprehensive exams but did not manipulate personal relevance (Heesacker et al., 1983; Puckett, Petty, Cacioppo, & Fisher, 1983). In both studies, subjects learned that the University was contemplating the exam policy but no time frame for its adoption was specified. Under these conditions, both studies yielded a Panel I-type interaction between the source manipulation and argument quality. Subjects exposed to an expert source (Heesacker et al., 1983) or an attractive source (Puckett et al., 1983) were more influenced by argument quality than were subjects exposed to an inexpert or unattractive source, respectively.[5] By assuming that the elaboration likelihood was moderate (rather than either low or high) in these experiments, Petty and Cacioppo (1984b) concluded that source factors function as enhancers or reducers of message processing under moderate elaboration likelihood conditions (see also, Petty, Kasmer, Haugtvedt, & Cacioppo, 1987). Yet neither study included data relevant to verifying the important assumption that the elaboration likelihood was indeed moderate among participating subjects.[6]

Evaluation of the Elaboration Likelihood Model

The elaboration likelihood model offers a more comprehensive account of persuasion than its progenitor, the cognitive response model. The proposition that message-related thinking mediates persuasion is an unbounded one in the original model. The elaboration likelihood model delineates when this proposition should be true. Central route persuasion, wherein message-related thinking does mediate attitude change, is theorized to occur only when people possess sufficient motivation and ability for message processing. As we have seen, empirical support for this claim is abundant. Moreover, because numerous variables have been identified as motivators or enablers of message processing, researchers now possess considerable knowledge of the specific conditions under which the cognitive response model's description of persuasion should be most applicable. More generally (and for the same reasons), research guided by the elaboration likelihood model (and heuristic-systematic model) has fostered a greater understanding of the conditions under which other central route (or systematic) theories should be most predictive of persuasion. For example, the proposition that message comprehension mediates persuasion (Chapter 6) and the expectancy-value logic that persuasion entails changing existing beliefs about attitude objects or inducing new beliefs (Chapter 5; Fishbein & Ajzen, 1981) should prove most applicable when recipients possess adequate motivation for elaborative processing.

Petty and Cacioppo (e.g., 1986b, p. 192) have written that the greatest strength of their model is its specification of just three ways in which variables can affect persuasion. We agree. The postulate that variables can serve as arguments, peripheral cues, or influence elaboration in an objective or biased manner, and the model's criteria for inferring when these possibilities have occurred (see Figure 7.2) provide a powerful empirical framework for studying a diverse list of source, message, recipient, and contextual variables. As we have seen, the model can be used to test a variety of assumptions, hypotheses, or intuitions regarding how certain variables will affect persuasion. Perhaps more importantly, the fit between unpredicted findings and the model's ideal data patterns can be used to generate new hypotheses for future research. For example, the correspondence between Figure 7.2's Panel I and the unpredicted Argument Quality × Source Cue interactions observed by Heesacker and colleagues (1983) and Puckett and colleagues (1983) influenced Petty and Cacioppo's (1984b) subsequent analysis of how source factors influence persuasion. As we have seen, these findings led Petty and Cacioppo to argue that elaboration likelihood was at some moderate level in those studies, and to conclude that source variables function to enhance (or reduce) message processing under such conditions. Although this interpretation has not been tested explicitly, it nicely illustrates the generative value of the elaboration likelihood model.

Petty and Cacioppo's framework has contributed to a resurgence of interest in persuasion processes among social psychologists, and the breadth of persuasion variables that can be interpreted from their perspective should maintain its popularity with researchers for some time. Nonetheless, the elaboration likelihood model constitutes primarily a descriptive, rather than explanatory, theory of persuasion. As Petty and Cacioppo have themselves cautioned, their model does not indicate "why certain arguments are strong or weak, why certain variables serve as (peripheral) cues, or why certain variables affect information processing" (Petty & Cacioppo, 1986b, p. 192). We have seen, for example, how the fit between observed persuasion data and the model's ideal data patterns has been used to infer that the sheer number of arguments provided can enhance objective message processing when the elaboration likelihood is high, that prior knowledge enhances biased message processing, and that source variables enhance (or reduce) objective message processing when the elaboration likelihood is moderate. These inferences are descriptive ones, however, because the model does not specify on an *a priori* basis why exposure to many (vs. few) arguments ought to motivate or enable objective processing, why prior knowledge ought to motivate or enable biased processing, or why source variables ought to motivate objective processing when the elaboration likelihood is moderate.

Underlying Psychological Mechanisms. In a related vein, whereas the match between observed persuasion data and the model's criterial patterns can generate useful inferences, such matches do not, in and of themselves, provide unequivocal support for the psychological mechanisms assumed to underlie these patterns. Consider, for example, Petty and Cacioppo's (1980) finding that source attractiveness affected persuasion regardless of personal relevance. As discussed earlier, the pattern-matching technique led Petty and Cacioppo (1984b) to conclude that in that study source attractiveness influenced persuasion via some peripheral mechanism when personal relevance was low, but affected persuasion by serving as a persuasive argument when personal relevance was high. Although intriguing, no direct evidence for such differential mediation was provided in that study. Moreover, alternative interpretations exist for these data. One could argue, for example, that source attractiveness influenced persuasion via some peripheral mechanism in *both* personal relevance conditions (e.g., heuristic processing, identification-based persuasion; see Chapter 13). If so, the fact that attractiveness *and* argument quality affected persuasion under high relevance could be interpreted as evidence that peripheral mechanisms and central route processing can exert *additive* effects on persuasion (see section on heuristic-systematic model and note 9). Alternatively, attractiveness may have functioned as an easy-to-process argument in both personal relevance conditions. If so, both attractiveness and argument quality would exert a persuasive impact on subjects who were willing to engage in effortful thinking (i.e., high relevance subjects), whereas only attractiveness would impact on subjects who were less willing (i.e., low relevance subjects).[7]

As a second illustration of the potential fallibility of the pattern-matching strategy, consider Wood and colleagues' (1985) attitude data, which patterned in accord with the ELM's biased processing criteria. As discussed earlier, although these data are compatible with Petty and Cacioppo's (1986b) interpretation that prior knowledge negatively biases recipients' processing of counterattitudinal messages, they can also be interpreted in terms of heightened criticality on the part of more knowledgeable subjects (see Biek et al., 1992; Chaiken et al., 1989).[8]

Another ambiguity of the elaboration likelihood model is that it provides no conceptual rationale for its premise that peripheral cues should be relatively unimportant determinants of persuasion when the elaboration likelihood is high (Postulate V; see note 7). Do people knowingly ignore peripheral cues such as source attractiveness, pleasant music, and consensus information in such circumstances? Or, if they do not ignore them, do they somehow "resist" being influenced by peripheral mechanisms such as identification (Cacioppo & Petty, 1984, p. 135), classical conditioning, and heuristic processing in these situations? Or, if recipients do not actively resist such peripheral influence mechanisms, does central route processing somehow obscure or attenuate their persuasive impact?

322

Petty and Cacioppo's (1981a, 1986a, 1986b) schematic depiction of the elaboration likelihood model (see Figure 7.1) and their discussions of its predictions emphasize that *either* message content or peripheral cues have the primary impact on persuasion, depending on motivational and ability variables that affect the elaboration likelihood. The hydraulic flavor of these presentations, as well as the absence of hypotheses implying that the model's two routes might sometimes *both* affect judgment (or interact) would appear to support Stiff's (1986; Stiff & Boster, 1987) contention that the elaboration likelihood model posits two mutually exclusive routes to persuasion.[9]

More generally, the model's peripheral route label lacks theoretical depth because the theories that are assumed to comprise this family differ widely in their assumptions regarding recipient motives in persuasion situations, and in the processes they highlight as mediators of persuasion. Thus, these theories are a heterogeneous lot that share little in common aside from the fact that they do not emphasize the mediational role of people's processing of persuasive arguments. Because the elaboration likelihood model specifies *when* peripheral route persuasion should and has occurred, but not *which* peripheral mechanism has operated (or *why*), it leaves numerous mediational issues unaddressed. For example, are all peripheral mechanisms equally powerful determinants of persuasion when the elaboration likelihood is low, and equally ineffective in conferring attitudinal persistence? Do the motives postulated by some peripheral mechanisms (e.g., maintaining role relationships in the case of identification; see Chapter 13) also serve recipients' motivation to hold correct attitudes (Postulate I), or somehow replace this motive under low elaboration likelihood conditions?

The elaboration likelihood model represents a powerful and integrative empirical framework for studying persuasion processes. Yet, for the reasons outlined above, we are less sanguine about the model's utility as an integrative theoretical framework. Its basic assertions are that central route theories predict persuasion best when the elaboration likelihood is high, that peripheral route theories predict persuasion best when the elaboration likelihood is low, and that central route theories are more predictive of attitudinal persistence, resistance, and attitude-behavior consistency. These ideas are valuable and deserve continued exploration by researchers. However, it is not clear what other theoretical insights follow from the model's bifurcation of attitude theories. In this regard we should point out that despite their reliance on this taxonomy, Petty and Cacioppo (e.g., 1986b) have suggested that different attitudinal processes can, in actuality, be placed *along* the elaboration likelihood continuum. To the extent this is so, their model may be capable of more differentiated predictions than we have indicated. For example, if classical conditioning operated at a lower point on the elaboration likelihood continuum than, say, identification-based attitude change, the model might enable the prediction that, in the lower region of the continuum, increasing motivation and/or ability for elaboration would enhance the persuasive impact of source attractiveness (if this cue were mediated by identification) but reduce the persuasive impact of pleasant context (if this cue were mediated by classical conditioning). Nevertheless, the assertion that attitudinal processes can be ordered along the elaboration likelihood continuum is more problematic for peripheral route mechanisms than for central route mechanisms. Petty and Cacioppo (e.g., 1986b)

323

define peripheral route mechanisms as those that cause persuasion *in the absence of argument scrutiny*, but define the elaboration likelihood continuum as ranging from *none* to complete *elaboration of issue-relevant arguments*. Given these definitions, it is difficult to discern how peripheral mechanisms such as identification and classical conditioning could be located anywhere *but* the extreme low end of this continuum.

Interpretation of Argument Quality. Finally, an issue that warrants special conceptual and empirical attention in subsequent research concerns "argument quality." As we have seen, this construct has played a critical role in tests of the elaboration likelihood model. Moreover, this variable has also been featured in related research guided by the heuristic-systematic model (e.g., Axsom et al., 1987; Wood et al., 1985; Worth & Mackie, 1987). Yet the latent factor it represents is unclear. Petty and Cacioppo's labeling of this variable as argument *quality* and their descriptions of strong and weak messages that have been featured in their research imply that the latent variable is the inherent strength, plausibility, or believability of a message's arguments. For example, Petty, Cacioppo, and Goldman (1981, p. 850) characterized their strong comprehensive exam message as containing "persuasive evidence (statistics, data, etc.)," and their weak message as containing "quotations, personal opinion, and examples." Yet, Areni and Lutz (1988) have observed that strong and weak messages in most relevant research differ not only in terms of the evidence used to bolster the message's core arguments (e.g., statistics vs. personal opinion), but also in terms of the core arguments themselves. For example, the "strong" and "very weak" arguments shown in Table 7.2 formed the basis for Petty, Cacioppo, and Goldman's strong and weak messages, respectively. Areni and Lutz also observed that Petty and Cacioppo's strong arguments typically associate the attitude object (e.g., comprehensive exams) with very positive attributes (e.g., higher starting salaries), whereas their weak arguments typically associate the attitude object with less positive attributes (e.g., exams enjoy parental support) and, sometimes, with negative attributes (e.g., exams will increase fear and, therefore, studying; see Table 7.2).

Fishbein and Ajzen (1981) have pointed out that a persuasive argument can be conceptualized as a belief statement that links the attitude object to some attribute (or consequence; see Chapter 5). As we have seen, these expectancy-value theorists distinguished two aspects of beliefs, the subjective probability that an object is associated with some attribute (b_i) and the evaluation of that attribute (e_i). Using the subjective probability (or likelihood) component of beliefs to conceptualize argument *strength* and the evaluative (or desirability) component to conceptualize argument *valence*, Areni and Lutz (1988) proposed that most experiments that have varied "argument quality" have manipulated argument valence rather than argument strength or, at the least, have confounded the two dimensions (see also Petty & Wegener, 1991).[10] To explore their hypothesis, Areni and Lutz presented subjects with Petty, Cacioppo, and Goldman's (1981) strong or weak message on comprehensive exams or with Petty and associates' (1983) strong or weak advertisement for a consumer product. Afterward, subjects rated each argument's strength and valence. Strength was assessed by having subjects rate how likely it was that the attitude object (e.g., exams) was associated with the attribute mentioned in the particular argument (e.g., increased university prestige), and valence was assessed by having them rate how good (vs. bad) each attribute was.

The results of the experiment showed that the set of "strong" arguments ascribed more desirable attributes to the attitude object than the set of "weak" arguments. However, the two sets of arguments did not differ in their perceived strength (i.e., likelihoods). These findings support the notion that argument valence, not argument strength, was manipulated in the relevant studies. Although the Areni and Lutz research cannot be considered an exhaustive analysis of messages that have been used in experiments featuring argument quality manipulations, their results do suggest that the term *argument quality* may be a misnomer insofar as it connotes the strength or plausibility of persuasive argumentation.

Relabeling the argument quality construct with the arguably more appropriate term *argument valence* does not necessarily reduce the internal validity of research presently supportive of the elaboration likelihood model (and heuristic-systematic model). Evidence currently supportive of the model's key hypothesis that the elaboration likelihood moderates the route to persuasion would remain supportive even if relevant experiments have manipulated argument valence rather than argument strength (or, perhaps, some combination of the two).[11] In fact, the argument valence label would be more consistent with Petty and Cacioppo's earlier research on the cognitive response model, because the theoretical role of argument quality in that research was to control the valence of subjects' message-related cognitive responding (see Chapter 6). Indeed, relabeling this construct would also be more consistent with the main criteria that Petty and Cacioppo have used and recommended that others use in developing argument quality manipulations, that is, weakly argued messages should lead pilot subjects to list primarily unfavorable cognitions in a thought-listing task and strongly argued messages should lead them to list primarily favorable thoughts (see earlier discussion in this chapter).

Still, to the extent that researchers ought to be concerned about the persuasive impact of *strong* versus *weak* argumentation (and we believe they should), they will need to develop argument quality manipulations that possess greater validity than current ones.[12] Moreover, it will be important to investigate the extent to which these truer manipulations of strength of argumentation produce findings similar to those that current researchers have obtained with argument valence manipulations. In this regard, Areni and Lutz (1988) have speculated that sensitivity to argument valence may occur at a lower point on the elaboration likelihood than sensitivity to argument strength. In other words, higher levels of motivation and, especially, ability for message processing may be required to discern and evaluate the plausibility and logical coherence of argumentation than to discern and evaluate the positivity of attributes that arguments ascribe to attitude objects. If so, the current consensus that argument *quality* determines persuasion (and that peripheral cues do not) under the conditions that have been specified by the model may necessitate some revision.

_____ **Heuristic-Systematic Model**

Like the elaboration likelihood model, the heuristic-systematic model postulates two mediational paths to persuasion (Chaiken, 1980, 1982, 1987; Chaiken & Eagly, 1983; Chaiken et al., 1989). Although there are similarities between the two theories, there are also important differences. Their resemblance stems from similar conceptions of central route persuasion and systematic processing, and similar views on the antecedents and consequences of this processing mode. Differences include distinctive conceptions of peripheral route persuasion and heuristic processing, propositions that are unique to one or the other theory, and the level of detail each provides about mediational issues. We will compare the two frameworks as we present and discuss the heuristic-systematic model.

The heuristic-systematic model was developed to apply to "validity seeking" persuasion settings in which people's primary motivational concern is to attain accurate attitudes that square with relevant facts (Chaiken, 1980, 1987). In these settings, Chaiken assumes that the primary processing goal of accuracy-motivated recipients is to assess the validity of persuasive messages, and that both heuristic and systematic processing can serve this objective.

The elaboration likelihood model also assumes that people are motivated to hold correct attitudes (see Table 7.1). Yet attitude theory and research suggest that other motives also operate in social influence (e.g., maintaining relationships). Hence, the applicability of both models beyond the validity-seeking persuasion context is questionable. Recognizing this limitation of the heuristic-systematic model, Chaiken and colleagues (1989) proposed an expanded model that posits two additional motives that heuristic and systematic processing can serve—*defense-motivation*, the desire to form or defend particular attitudinal positions, and *impression-motivation*, the desire to form or hold socially acceptable attitudinal positions. Because it addresses a broader range of social influence settings than the original model, the multiple-motive heuristic-systematic model also features a more general vocabulary. Our treatment of the heuristic-systematic model is designed to acquaint readers with the expanded model, especially its basic propositions regarding defense-motivated and impression-motivated processing. Because these propositions have not yet received much empirical testing, however, our presentation focuses on the model's original domain of application, the validity-seeking persuasion context.

Two Concurrent Modes of Judging Message Validity

Chaiken and her colleagues (1989) conceptualize *systematic processing* as a comprehensive, analytic orientation to information processing in which perceivers access and scrutinize a great deal of information for its relevance to their judgment task. For the validity-seeking persuasion context, systematic processing is defined with greater specificity (see Chaiken et al., 1989). In such settings, systematic information processors are viewed as judging the validity of a message's advocated position by scrutinizing persuasive argumentation and by thinking about this information in relation to other information they may possess about the object or issue discussed in the message (Chaiken, 1980, 1987). Like Petty and Cacioppo's (1986a) central route, systematic processing implies that persuasion has been mediated by recipients' understanding and cognitive elaboration of persuasive argumentation. Also similar to the elaboration likelihood model, the heuristic-systematic model assumes that capacity and motivation are important determinants of systematic processing, and that this mode of processing may sometimes be biased (see further discussion below).

Heuristic processing is conceptualized as a more limited mode of information processing that requires less cognitive effort and fewer cognitive resources than systematic processing (Chaiken, 1980, 1987; Chaiken et al., 1989). When processing heuristically, people are viewed as focusing on that subset of available information that enables them to use simple decision rules or cognitive heuristics to formulate their judgments and decisions (see also Tversky & Kahneman, 1974). As with systematic processing, heuristic processing in the validity-seeking persuasion context is defined more specifically. In such settings, heuristic information processors are said to use simple decision rules such as "experts' statements can be trusted" and "consensus implies correctness" to judge the validity of messages. As a consequence, they may agree more with expert communicators, with messages that most other persons appear to endorse, and so on, without having fully absorbed the semantic content of persuasive argumentation. For this reason, the heuristic-systematic model (like the ELM) includes the hypothesis that attitudes formed or changed on the basis of heuristic processing alone will tend to be less stable, less resistant to counterpropaganda, and less predictive of subsequent behavior than those formed or changed on the basis of systematic processing (Chaiken, 1980, 1987; Chaiken & Eagly, 1983).

The model uses the term *heuristic cue* to refer to any variable whose judgmental impact is hypothesized to be mediated by a simple decision rule. In the validity-seeking persuasion context, these rules or "persuasion heuristics" associate particular levels of the heuristic cue (e.g., high consensus) with a high probability that the position advocated in the message is valid, and other levels (e.g., low consensus) with a low probability that the message's position is valid (the nature of defense-motivated and impression-motivated heuristic processing is discussed in a subsequent section). According to the model, such heuristics are learned on the basis of people's past experiences and observations and are represented in memory like other sorts of knowledge structures (see Higgins, 1989a; E. R. Smith, 1984; see also Chapter 3).

The key aspect of heuristic processing is the idea that relatively simple rules, schemata, or heuristics can mediate people's attitude judgments. This conceptualization is narrower than Petty and Cacioppo's (1986a, 1986b) description of peripheral route persuasion. As we have seen, the latter refers to any of a variety of affective and cognitive mechanisms that are presumed to produce persuasion in the absence of argument scrutiny. Because the heuristic-systematic model makes no explanatory claims in relation to mechanisms such as classical or operant conditioning, the elaboration likelihood model might be construed as the more general theory. Yet, because the latter model provides only the most rudimentary sketch of how peripheral mechanisms operate, the benefits bestowed by its broader conception are unclear.

327

Although narrower, Chaiken and her colleagues' conception of heuristic processing yields several unique hypotheses regarding the persuasive impact of heuristic cues (see below).

Neither of the model's two processing modes is assumed to be ubiquitous. Systematic processing in more than negligible amounts requires both ability and motivation, and heuristic processing depends, at a minimum, on the presence of heuristic cues and on the cognitive availability of their associated heuristics (see below). However, in situations conducive to both modes, both are assumed to occur (Chaiken, 1980, 1987; Chaiken et al., 1989). This *concurrent processing* assumption is important because it enables the model to postulate that heuristic and systematic processing can exert both independent (i.e., additive) and interdependent (i.e., interactive) effects on judgment (see below). The elaboration likelihood model lacks an explicit statement regarding whether its two processing modes can or cannot co-occur. As discussed in the previous section, however, Petty and Cacioppo's (e.g., 1986b) descriptions of their model and the absence of hypotheses implying either additive or interactive effects appear to reflect an implicit assumption that central and peripheral processing represent two nonconcurrent, mutually exclusive routes to persuasion.

Cognitive Determinants of Processing Mode. Underlying the model's *ability* hypothesis is the assumption that systematic processing both demands and consumes cognitive capacity, whereas heuristic processing makes few capacity demands. According to this hypothesis, systematic processing should be more constrained or disrupted than heuristic processing by situational and individual difference factors that reduce people's abilities for detailed information processing. For example, time pressure should constrain the amount of systematic processing that people can engage in, whereas prior knowledge about the message topic should facilitate such processing. Neither variable, however, should impact on people's capacities for heuristic processing.

Heuristic processing, then, should occur even when situational and individual difference factors conspire to constrain people's abilities for systematic processing. For this reason, the model predicts (like the ELM) that heuristic cues should exert a sizable impact on judgment when ability—or motivation (see below)—for systematic processing is low. What about settings that do promote systematic processing? The elaboration likelihood model postulates that peripheral mechanisms are unimportant determinants of persuasion in these settings, although it is silent with respect to why this should be so. As noted above, Chaiken and her colleagues assume that heuristic and systematic processing can co-occur. However, they also assume that systematic processing typically provides people with more judgment-relevant information than heuristic processing and, in some instances, with information that may contradict heuristic-based judgments of message validity (e.g., very weak arguments appear in an expert's message; Petty, Cacioppo, & Goldman, 1981). For this reason, they hypothesize that systematic processing will often *attenuate* the judgmental impact of heuristic processing. And it is because of this hypothesized attenuation effect that they predict (like the ELM) that heuristic cues may often fail to exert a detectable judgmental impact in settings that promote substantial amounts of systematic processing (see Chaiken, 1987;

Chaiken et al., 1989). As Chaiken et al. (1989) point out, however, systematic processing need not invariably quash the judgmental impact of heuristic processing, and when it does not, they assume that the two modes can exert additive effects on judgment. Thus, even in settings that foster systematic processing, the heuristic-systematic model (unlike the ELM) allows for the possibility that heuristic processing can exert a significant—and independent—influence on persuasion (see Maheswaran & Chaiken, 1991).

The view that systematic processing demands and consumes cognitive capacity coheres with Petty and Cacioppo's (e.g., 1986a) assumption that ability is a prerequisite for argument elaboration. Also similar to Petty and Cacioppo, Chaiken and her colleagues assume that cognitive factors may sometimes bias systematic processing.[13] Both models emphasize that prior knowledge about attitude objects may bias (as well as enhance) systematic processing if that knowledge is evaluatively skewed: When the evaluative implications of people's prior beliefs match their prior attitudes their capacity to rebut counterattitudinal arguments and to generate or bolster proattitudinal arguments should be enhanced (see Chaiken et al., 1989 for further discussion). In addition, Chaiken and her colleagues assume that systematic processing may, at times, be biased by heuristic processing. Unique to the heuristic systematic model, this *bias* hypothesis reflects the model's assumption that its two modes can exert interdependent effects on judgment. According to the hypothesis, recipients' processing of heuristic cues establishes expectancies about message validity which, in turn, influence their perception and evaluation of persuasive arguments. For example, if a message is delivered by an expert, its arguments may be viewed more positively than if the message is delivered by a nonexpert. Importantly, the bias hypothesis is presumed to apply only to situations in which persuasive argumentation is ambiguous, or amenable to differential interpretation (Chaiken et al., 1989; Chaiken & Maheswaran, 1992).

Aside from its postulate that peripheral route persuasion occurs when ability for elaboration is low, the elaboration likelihood model does not address potential cognitive antecedents of this route. By contrast, the heuristic-systematic model's conception of heuristics as learned procedural knowledge structures (E. R. Smith, 1984) implicates several cognitive principles that govern heuristic processing and, hence, the judgmental impact of heuristic cues. First, the model assumes that heuristics can impact on people's attitude judgments only if they are cognitively *available* (i.e., stored in memory for potential use; Higgins, King, & Mavin, 1982). A cue such as message length or number of arguments can be processed heuristically only by recipients for whom the "length implies strength" heuristic is represented in memory.

Even if available in memory, the model assumes that heuristics will not influence judgment unless they are *accessible* (i.e., activated or accessed from memory). One obvious determinant of accessibility is the presence in the persuasion setting of cues that can be processed heuristically. A more important determinant, according to the model, is the perceiver's processing goal. The goal of assessing message validity is presumed to activate heuristics relevant to performing this task, and accessibility can be further enhanced by factors that increase the salience or importance of this goal (see also Bruner, 1957; Higgins, 1989a). More generally, then, the model posits that situational and individual difference factors that affect the accessibility of heuristics should exert a corresponding effect on the judgmental impact of heuristic cues.

Finally, the model also assumes that cognitive heuristics vary in their strength or perceived *reliability*, and that the judgmental impact of heuristic cues increases with the perceived reliability of their associated heuristics. For example, people who believe that "experts can *always* be trusted" should be more willing to agree with expert sources than people who believe that "experts can *generally* be trusted." Accordingly, the model posits that individual difference and situational factors that affect the perceived reliability of heuristics should exert a corresponding effect on the judgmental impact of heuristic cues (see Chaiken et al., 1989).

Motivational Determinants of Processing Mode. Chaiken and her colleagues assume that people are "economy-minded souls" who wish to satisfy their goal-related needs in the most efficient ways possible (Chaiken, 1980, 1987; Chaiken et al., 1989). Their model's *least effort* and *sufficiency* principles reflect this motivational assumption. The least effort principle asserts that people prefer less effortful to more effortful modes of information processing. Heuristic and systematic processing are both presumed to serve the accuracy-motivated goal of assessing message validity (or other goals; see subsequent discussion). But the least effort principle holds that people often shun systematic processing in favor of the less effortful heuristic mode.[14]

The least effort principle, however, ignores perceivers' motivational concerns, such as the desire to hold accurate attitudes. The heuristic-systematic model's sufficiency principle embodies the idea that efficient information processors must strike a balance between satisfying motivational concerns and minimizing their processing efforts (Chaiken, 1987; Chaiken et al., 1989; see also Simon, 1976). In general, it asserts that people will exert whatever effort is required to attain a "sufficient" degree of confidence that they have satisfactorily accomplished their processing goals. In validity-seeking persuasion settings in particular, it holds that recipients will invest whatever amount of effort is required to attain a sufficiently confident assessment of message validity.

Chaiken et al. (1989) define the *sufficiency threshold* in terms of desired judgmental confidence—the degree of confidence a person aspires to attain in a given judgment setting. As shown in the first panel of Figure 7.4, the sufficiency threshold (ST) is conceptualized as a point located somewhere along a judgmental confidence continuum. Actual levels of confidence that fall below the ST will be regarded as insufficient (AC_1) whereas those that exceed the ST will be regarded as more than sufficient (AC_2). The second panel illustrates the model's assumption that both sufficiency thresholds and actual levels of confidence vary as a function of individual differences and situational factors. For example, a person may desire greater judgmental confidence in some situations than in others ($ST_{p1s2} > ST_{p1s1}$), and given the same situation, one person may desire greater confidence than another ($ST_{p1s1} > ST_{p2s1}$).

In the context of Figure 7.4, the sufficiency principle holds that processing effort should cease when actual confidence equals or exceeds the sufficiency threshold, but should continue (if possible) when actual confidence falls below the sufficiency threshold. Moreover, in the latter circumstances, processing effort is assumed to be a function of the discrepancy that exists between actual and desired levels of confidence. Panel C illustrates this assumption for the case in which two people engaged in the same processing task have attained similar levels of actual confidence but differ in their levels of desired confidence. In this case, the model predicts greater processing effort for the person whose sufficiency threshold is higher. Finally, Panel D illustrates the same assumption for the case in which two people with similar sufficiency thresholds have in the course of processing the same information achieved disparate levels of actual confidence. In this case, greater processing is predicted for the person with the lower level of actual confidence.

In combination with the least effort principle, the sufficiency principle implies that people engage in greater amounts of systematic processing when the less effortful heuristic mode yields insufficient judgmental confidence or, more obviously, when heuristic processing cannot occur (e.g., the setting does not contain heuristic cues). More generally, the sufficiency principle equips the heuristic-systematic model with an integrative logic for understanding motivation for systematic processing because it implies that any factor that increases processing effort has done so either by increasing

FIGURE 7.4. Sketch of the heuristic-systematic model's assumptions about perceivers' sufficiency thresholds (desired levels of judgmental confidence) and actual levels of confidence. Panel A depicts the sufficiency threshold (ST) and two levels of actual confidence, one that is perceived as insufficient (AC_1) and one that is perceived as more than sufficient (AC_2). Panel B depicts the ST and AC for two persons in one situation (p1s1, p2s1) and for one person in two situations (p1s1, p1s2) and illustrates the model's assumption that STs and ACs vary as a function of individual differences and situational factors. The remaining panels illustrate the model's assumption that two persons can manifest differing levels of processing effort either because they have different STs (Panel C) or because they have different ACs (Panel D).

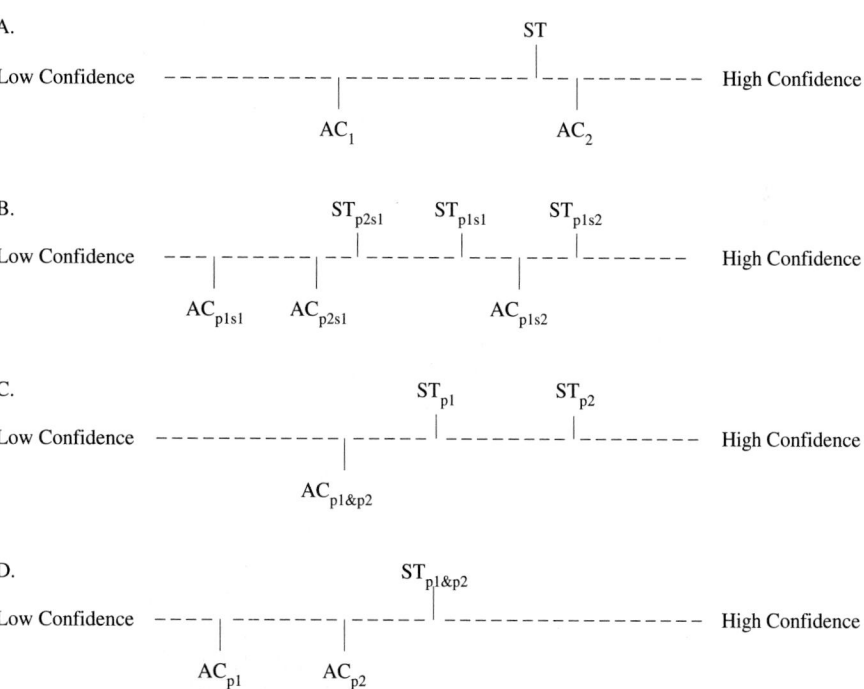

people's desired levels of confidence (i.e., sufficiency thresholds), by undermining actual confidence, or by both mechanisms. In the previous section, for example, we reviewed research showing that a range of variables appear to motivate systematic (or central route) processing—variables such as personal relevance, task importance, responsibility for message evaluation, accountability, and need for cognition. The elaboration likelihood model labels these variables motivational determinants of elaboration, but does not address *why* they enhance processing. In contrast, Chaiken and colleagues (1989) speculate that the motivational impact of these variables is mediated by their effect on people's sufficiency thresholds. That is, these variables presumably increase processing effort and, hence, systematic processing, because they increase people's desired levels of judgmental confidence. For example, recipients who receive a personally relevant message presumably desire greater confidence in their assessment of message validity than recipients who encounter a less relevant message. As such, their sufficiency thresholds should be higher (as depicted in Panel C, Figure 7.4). Yet the higher one's sufficiency threshold, the less likely it is that sufficient confidence can be attained on the basis of heuristic processing alone or only minimal levels of systematic processing (or both). Thus, to attain their higher sufficiency thresholds, high relevance recipients would typically need to engage in greater amounts of systematic processing than low relevance recipients. The same logic is presumed to explain the motivational impact of the other variables listed above. For example, people who are higher in need for cognition and people who are made to feel more accountable for their judgments are assumed to have higher sufficiency thresholds and, as a consequence, are predicted to exhibit greater amounts of systematic processing (see Maheswaran & Chaiken, 1991).

Other individual difference and situational variables, according to the model, may motivate systematic processing by reducing or undermining actual confidence (as depicted in Panel D, Figure 7.4). Although few such factors have been identified, Maheswaran and Chaiken (1991) found that expectancy disconfirmation enhances the extensiveness of information processing by undermining perceivers' confidence in their initial, heuristic-based judgments (see subsequent discussion). In addition, there are suggestive findings (largely outside the persuasion literature) indicating that mildly depressed persons and persons low in self-esteem process information more extensively, and that this effect may reflect these individuals' chronically low levels of perceived judgmental confidence (e.g., J. D. Campbell, 1986; Gleicher & Weary, 1991; Hildebrand-Saints & Weary, 1989; see also Rhodes & Wood, 1992).

The heuristic-systematic model's proposition that insufficient levels of judgmental confidence motivate systematic processing is presumed to be contingent on two factors—people must have the ability to process systematically and must believe that this mode can increase their judgmental confidence (Chaiken et al., 1989). What happens when motivational factors lead people to have high sufficiency thresholds, but their ability for systematic processing is constrained or they doubt its efficacy? Obviously, a less-than-desired degree of judgmental confidence might have to suffice in such circumstances. Less obviously, Chaiken et al. (1989) propose that in such instances perceivers might more carefully scrutinize the setting for judgment-relevant heuristic cues. In addition, they point out that motivational variables that raise people's sufficiency thresholds (e.g., personal relevance) should, according to their model, also enhance the accessibility of goal-relevant heuristics (see earlier discussion). For both these reasons, Chaiken et al. hypothesize that when actual (or perceived) ability for systematic processing is low, the judgmental impact of heuristic cues will often be greater when people's sufficiency thresholds are located at higher points of the confidence continuum. This *enhancement* hypothesis is important because it implies that variables such as personal relevance and task importance do not function solely as motivators of systematic or central route processing. According to the heuristic-systematic model, these variables can also motivate heuristic processing.

Empirical Findings

To provide a coherent review of the literature, we discussed experiments testing propositions common to the Chaiken and the Petty and Cacioppo frameworks in our section on the elaboration likelihood model. As detailed there, the assumption that systematic or central route processing requires motivation and ability has been documented in many studies, using a variety of motivational and ability variables: Persuasive argumentation is a more important determinant of persuasion when recipients are motivated and able to process attitude-relevant information than when they are not. There is also substantial empirical support for the hypothesis of these models that heuristic or peripheral cues exert a sizable persuasive impact when motivation or ability for argument processing is low, but little impact when motivation and ability are high (see below). Finally, there is some, though weaker, support for the shared hypothesis that attitudes formed on the basis of systematic or central route processing tend to be more durable than those formed on the basis of heuristic processing or other peripheral mechanisms. We turn now to research that has addressed other, more novel, aspects of the heuristic-systematic model.

Accessibility and Reliability of Heuristics. Several experiments have yielded data consistent with the model's proposition that heuristic cues affect persuasion more when their associated heuristics are highly accessible to message recipients. In two experiments featuring different attitude issues, Chaiken and Eagly (1983) presented subjects with an audiotaped, videotaped, or written persuasive message on a campus issue (e.g., increasing tuition) and attributed this message to a likable or unlikable communicator. The likability manipulation was accomplished prior to message exposure by having subjects read an interview in which the communicator either praised or ridiculed students at the subjects' university (see Chaiken, 1980). The demeanor of the male actor who subsequently delivered the message in the two broadcast modalities was held constant. Nonetheless, Chaiken and Eagly reasoned that the nonverbal visual and vocal cues available to subjects in these conditions but not available to subjects in the written modality would enhance the salience of the communicator and his likability, and hence increase the temporary accessibility of the liking-agreement heuristic, "people generally agree with people they like." On this basis, they predicted that their heuristic cue (likability) would exert a greater persuasive impact in the high accessibility, broadcast modality conditions than in the low accessibility, written modality condition.

As expected, subjects who received videotaped or audiotaped messages agreed more when the communicator was likable than when he was unlikable, whereas subjects who received written messages were uninfluenced by the study's likability manipulation. Also consistent with the authors' reasoning, thought-listing data showed that subjects generated more cognitions that pertained to the communicator (vs. message content) in the two broadcast modalities; moreover, correlational analyses showed that these cognitions (as well as ratings of source likability) were better predictors of these subjects' post-message attitudes than of written subjects' attitudes. Pallak (1983) obtained conceptually similar results in a study that manipulated argument quality and the vividness of a communicator's physical attractiveness. Vividness was manipulated by showing subjects either a color photograph of an attractive male or a degraded, xerox copy of this photograph. In the study's nonvivid (i.e., xerox) conditions, subjects engaged in systematic processing: They agreed more with the strongly than weakly argued message, and their post-message attitudes correlated highly with the valence of the message-related cognitions they had listed on a thought-listing task. In the vivid (i.e., color photo) conditions, however, subjects manifested heuristic processing and less systematic processing: Their post-message attitudes were unaffected by argument quality and were more highly correlated with their perceptions of the communicator than with their message-related cognitions. Presumably, these results occurred because the vividness manipulation enhanced the accessibility of the liking-agreement heuristic, the rule assumed to underlie the persuasive impact of attractiveness in this study.

Roskos-Ewoldsen and Fazio (1992) manipulated the accessibility of subjects' attitudes toward a liked communicator, Jacques Cousteau, by having them indicate their liking repeatedly or only once (see Chapter 4). Then subjects read a short proenvironmental message attributed to this source and indicated their agreement with it. Consistent with the idea that enhancing the accessibility of subjects' attitudes toward the liked source would, in turn, enhance the accessibility of the liking-agreement rule, subjects in the repeated expression condition of this research were more persuaded by Cousteau's proenvironmental message than were control subjects.

To provide more direct evidence for the importance of accessibility and to explore its chronic as well as temporary sources, Chaiken, Axsom, Liberman, and Wilson (1992) set up a study that crossed these two factors. In a preliminary phase of the study, chronic users and nonusers of the length-strength heuristic were identified by whether they agreed or disagreed with the statement "The more reasons a person has for some point of view the more likely he/she is correct." Subsequently, these subjects were recruited to participate in a laboratory session portrayed as consisting of multiple experiments. One study, ostensibly on proverbs, was in reality a priming task. Whereas experimental subjects read phrases designed to enhance the temporary accessibility of the length-strength heuristic (e.g., the more the merrier, the bigger the boat the farther it floats), control subjects read irrelevant phrases (e.g., absence makes the heart grow fonder). After a short break, a supposedly unrelated study about impression formation was introduced. In this phase subjects listened to a short audiotape in which a male speaker endorsed comprehensive exams for seniors and claimed to have either 10 reasons or 2 reasons for his opinion. In fact, the message that all subjects heard contained six basic arguments.

The results of this study supported the model's assumptions about accessibility and the judgmental impact of heuristic cues. Chronic users of the length-strength rule agreed more with the message that ostensibly contained 10 (vs. 2) arguments, and this result was more pronounced among subjects for whom this rule had been primed. In contrast, chronic nonusers of the rule were no more persuaded by the long message than by the short one, regardless of the priming manipulation.

Support for the model's assumption that the perceived reliability of heuristics can affect judgment has also been obtained. In a study reported by Chaiken (1987), subjects first read sentences designed to manipulate the reliability of the liking-agreement rule and then participated in a supposedly unrelated study in which they were exposed to a likable or unlikable communicator's recommendation that people should reduce their sleep time. During phase one, high reliability subjects read sentences that reinforced the liking-agreement heuristic (e.g., "When people want good advice they go to their friends"), low reliability subjects read sentences that undermined this rule (e.g., "Best friends do not necessarily make the best advisors"), and control subjects read unrelated sentences. Although high need for cognition subjects in this study were unaffected by the experimental manipulations, the data obtained among low need for cognition subjects patterned as expected. Those in the high-reliability and the control conditions agreed more with the likable than unlikable communicator, but this effect was larger in the high reliability condition as hypothesized. Also consistent with expectations, low need for cognition subjects in the low reliability condition agreed slightly *less* with the likable communicator.

Evidence that motivational manipulations can enhance people's sensitivity to the reliability of heuristics has also been obtained. Hazlewood and Chaiken (1990) told subjects that their university was considering the implementation of comprehensive exams for either the following year (high relevance) or following decade (low relevance). Subjects then learned that an informal poll conducted earlier in the term had shown that 80 percent of a sample of 10 students (vs. 1000 students) had indicated strong agreement (vs. disagreement) with the exam proposal. Analysis of the attitude data from this study yielded an interaction between personal relevance, consensus opinion, and sample size. As expected, low relevance subjects agreed more with the exam proposal when consensus opinion favored (vs. opposed) the proposal, regardless of the size of the sample on which this information was based. Thus, these subjects apparently used the "consensus implies correctness" heuristic without regard to its reliability in this situation. In contrast, high relevance subjects did take reliability into account. When consensus information was based on a small sample, it had no impact on the attitudes expressed by high relevance subjects. When consensus information was based on a large sample, however, these subjects' attitudes were more favorable toward the exam proposal in the positive consensus condition. Consistent with Chaiken and colleagues' (1989) speculation that personal relevance manipulations affect people's sufficiency thresholds, this study also found that high relevance subjects reported desiring a higher level of attitudinal confidence than low relevance subjects. In summary, several experiments have supported the heuristic-systematic model's assumption that the judgmental impact of heuristic cues depends upon both the accessibility and perceived reliability of the heuristics that are associated with these cues.

Interaction and Additivity Effects. The model's bias hypothesis asserts that heuristic processing can influence the nature of systematic processing when persuasive argumentation is ambiguous. Chaiken and Maheswaran (1992) tested this interaction hypothesis in a study that manipulated source credibility, argument ambiguity and strength, and task importance (assumed to affect accuracy motivation). In the context of a consumer survey, subjects learned about a new product, the "XT-100" telephone answering machine. High task importance subjects believed that the XT-100's manufacturer was considering marketing the product in their locale and that they were part of a small group of consumers whose judgments would weigh heavily in this decision. Low importance subjects, in contrast, believed that the XT-100 might be marketed in a distant locale and that their individual judgments would be aggregated with those of many other consumers. Source credibility was varied by telling subjects that the product description they were to read had appeared either in *Consumer Reports*, a magazine specializing in scientific product testing, or in a promotional pamphlet prepared by Kmart, a discount department store chain. Subjects then read one of three messages (i.e., product descriptions) that compared the XT-100 to competing brands on a mixture of important and unimportant attributes and asserted that the XT-100 was the superior product. The unambiguous strong message portrayed the XT-100 as superior to the other brands on four important attributes (e.g., cassette flexibility) and inferior on two unimportant ones (e.g., number of available colors). Conversely, the unambiguous weak message portrayed the XT-100 as superior on four unimportant attributes and inferior on two important ones. Finally, two renditions of an ambiguous message were created, both of which portrayed the XT-100 as superior on a mixture of important and unimportant attributes and inferior on a mixture of important and unimportant attributes.

The post-message attitude data obtained in this study are shown in Figure 7.5. The results obtained in the two unambiguous message conditions replicated past research. When task importance was low, source credibility influenced subjects' attitudes but argument quality did not. In contrast, when task importance was high, only argument quality influenced attitudes. Other findings corroborated the idea that these effects were the product of greater systematic processing on the part of high task importance subjects and its attenuating effect on the judgmental impact of heuristic processing. For example, high (vs. low) importance subjects generated more attribute-related cognitions on a thought-listing task, and the valence of these cognitions correlated highly with their post-message attitudes (whereas their perceptions of source credibility did not). By contrast, only perceived source credibility predicted the attitudes of low task importance subjects.

More important, however, were the results Chaiken and Maheswaran observed for subjects who received an ambiguous persuasive message. As the figure shows, source

FIGURE 7.5. Post-message attitudes as a function of task importance (high vs. low), source credibility (high vs. low), and argument ambiguity and strength (unambiguous strong vs. unambiguous weak vs. ambiguous). This figure was adapted from data presented by Chaiken and Maheswaran (1992).

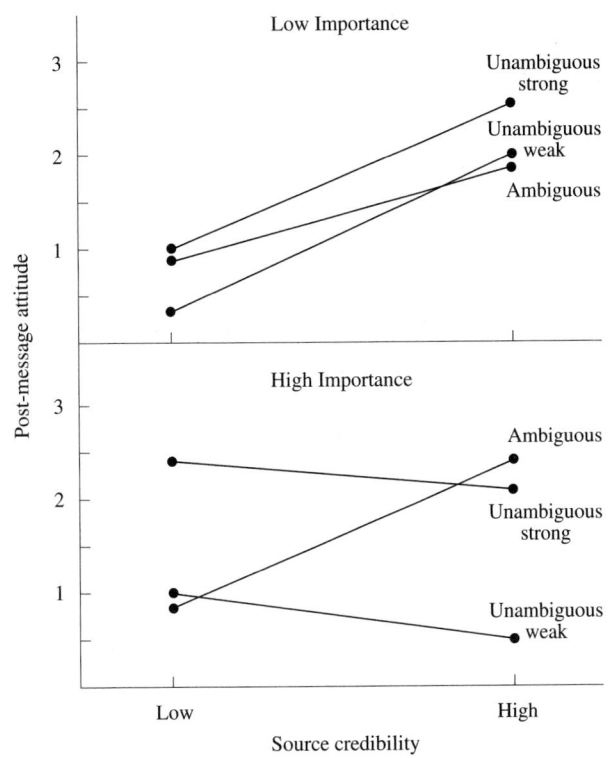

credibility exerted a strong persuasive impact on these subjects' attitudes *regardless of task importance* (the two renditions of the ambiguous message yielded identical results). Under low task importance, the ambiguous message condition mirrored the unambiguous message conditions and, like those conditions, merely replicated previous demonstrations that heuristic processing predominates when motivation for systematic processing is low. However, under high importance, the ambiguous message condition yielded a pattern of data different from the pattern obtained in the unambiguous message conditions; moreover, the pattern is exactly what the model's bias hypothesis predicts. That is, subjects' heuristic processing of the credibility cue presumably led them to form expectancies about message validity which, in turn, biased their systematic processing of ambiguous message content in a positive or negative manner, depending upon whether the source was high or low in credibility. Indeed, additional findings provided further support for the bias hypothesis. Most notably, path analyses confirmed that in this condition—and no other conditions of the study—the effect of source credibility on attitudes was partially mediated by its effect on the valence of subjects' attribute-related thinking. Consistent with the model's assumption that heuristic and systematic processing can exert additive effects on judgment, the direct path between source credibility and attitudes (indicative of heuristic processing) was also significant in this condition.[15]

As noted earlier, the sufficiency principle implies that people will engage in greater amounts of systematic processing when the less effortful heuristic mode—alone or in combination with minimal systematic processing—yields insufficient judgmental confidence. To address this issue, Maheswaran and Chaiken (1991) manipulated task importance and the congruency of consensus information and message content. After exposure to the Chaiken and Maheswaran (1992) task importance manipulation, subjects learned either that a majority or minority of consumers liked the XT-100, and then read a message asserting that the XT-100 was either better or worse than several competing brands. Thus, message content and consensus information were either evaluatively congruent (e.g., both positive) or evaluatively incongruent (e.g., positive/negative). The two messages discussed the same six important attributes (e.g., cassette flexibility, call screening). However, the positive message portrayed the XT-100 as superior on four attributes whereas the negative message portrayed it as inferior on four attributes.

Maheswaran and Chaiken hypothesized that incongruency would enhance systematic processing among subjects not otherwise motivated to engage in this mode, that is, low task importance subjects. These subjects' heuristic processing of the consensus cue should produce positive or negative evaluations of the XT-100, depending upon the valence of the consensus cue. However, the message was designed so that even the barest attention to it would reveal its congruency or incongruency with the consensus cue. In the congruent conditions, the authors reasoned that low importance subjects' minimal systematic processing would simply confirm the validity of the consensus heuristic. Because these subjects' judgmental confidence should be reasonably high—and their motivation for systematic processing low—there would be little reason for them to engage in further systematic processing. In the incongruent conditions, however, low importance subjects' marginal systematic processing should function to undermine confidence in their heuristic-based product evaluations. To attain sufficient confidence, the authors reasoned, these subjects should step up their systematic processing efforts.

The study's processing measures supported these speculations. Regardless of congruency, high task importance subjects manifested a great deal of systematic processing, as indexed by the large number of attribute-related cognitions they generated on a thought-listing task and their high recall of persuasive arguments. Low importance subjects who received congruent information exhibited significantly less systematic processing than high importance subjects. In contrast, when message valence was incongruent with consensus information, low importance subjects exhibited just as much systematic processing as their high importance counterparts. Maheswaran and Chaiken argued that these data support the idea that variables may motivate systematic processing either by affecting desired confidence or actual confidence. Specifically, task importance presumably increased processing by raising the sufficiency threshold, that is, high importance subjects desired greater judgmental confidence than low importance subjects and hence processed message content more thoroughly (see Figure 7.4, Panel

C). In contrast, the authors argued that incongruency enhanced systematic processing among low importance subjects because it reduced their confidence in their heuristic-based judgments. As a consequence, the discrepancy between low importance subjects' sufficiency thresholds and actual confidence was presumably greater for those who received incongruent (vs. congruent) information, and it is this greater discrepancy that motivated their greater levels of systematic processing (see Figure 7.4, Panel D). Consistent with the authors' reasoning, low importance subjects who received in-congruent information indicated less actual confidence than those who received congruent information.

Finally, the attitude data observed in this research paralleled the observed processing differences and, more generally, confirmed several other assumptions of the heuristic-systematic model. To index the persuasive impact of heuristic and systematic process-ing, Maheswaran and Chaiken conducted a series of analyses in which subjects' post-message attitudes were regressed on their perceptions of consensus opinion (an index of heuristic processing), the valence of their attribute-related thoughts (an index of systematic processing), and two interaction terms which tested whether the persuasive impact of heuristic processing and systematic processing differed as a function of the congruency of consensus information and message valence. Not surprisingly, the results confirmed that persuasion was mediated by systematic processing in the study's high importance conditions, regardless of congruency. However, consistent with the model's assumption that heuristic and systematic processing *can* exert additive effects on judgment, perceived consensus also proved to be a significant predictor of high importance subjects' attitudes *when* consensus information and message content were congruent. The fact that perceived consensus was not a reliable predictor of attitudes in the high importance/incongruent conditions supports the model's attenuation hypothe-sis and Chaiken et al.'s (1989) claim that attenuation effects occur primarily when message content blatantly contradicts the validity of heuristic cues. As also expected, perceived consensus proved to be the only reliable predictor of attitudes in the low importance/congruent conditions of the study, supporting the assumption that these subjects had engaged primarily in heuristic processing.

In summary, these studies support several subtleties that follow from the model's conception of heuristic processing and its assumption that heuristic and systematic processing can operate concurrently: Heuristic cues can bias the nature of systematic processing when argumentation is ambiguous; the judgmental impact of heuristic cues will often be attenuated by systematic processing; but heuristic processing can exert an independent effect on judgment when systematic processing does not furnish informa-tion that contradicts the validity of simple persuasion heuristics.

Multiple-Motive Heuristic-Systematic Model

The *accuracy-motivated* perceiver assesses the validity of attitude-relevant information in the interest of achieving valid attitudes that square with relevant facts. As we have seen, the heuristic-systematic model assumes that this task can be accomplished by heuristic processing, systematic processing, or both. As also discussed, the model assumes that accuracy-motivated systematic processing may sometimes be biased by *cognitive* factors such as prior knowledge and validity expectancies established by heuristic processing. Nonetheless, because of its motivational basis, Chaiken and her colleagues regard accuracy-motivated systematic (and heuristic) processing as open-minded (Chaiken et al., 1989).

The expanded model they proposed posits two additional motives that heuristic and systematic processing presumably serve. The first of these is intended to represent the role played in social influence by variables such as ego-involvement (or value-relevant involvement; B. T. Johnson & Eagly, 1989, 1990; M. Sherif & Cantril, 1947), attitudinal commitment (Kiesler, 1971), and vested interests and personal wishes, hopes and desires (e.g., Eagly & Whitehead, 1972; McGuire, 1957, 1969, 1981, 1990). Chaiken and her colleagues interpret previous research on these variables as indicating that they motivate a selective, closed-minded form of processing (see also Chapter 8). Accordingly, they propose that these variables arouse *defense motivation*, the desire to form or to defend particular attitudinal positions. The processing goal of defense-motivated perceivers, then, is to confirm the validity of preferred attitude positions and disconfirm the validity of non-preferred positions.

Like accuracy-motivated processing, defense-motivated processing can be either heuristic or systematic in nature. Chaiken et al. (1989) propose that defense-motivated perceivers use the *same* heuristics that accuracy-motivated perceivers do, but they use them *selectively*. Thus, heuristics such as "experts' statements can be trusted" and "consensus implies correctness" should be invoked only to the extent that they enable the defense-motivated perceiver to validate preferred attitude positions or invalidate non-preferred positions. Defense-motivated systematic processing is likewise assumed to be selective. Attitude-relevant information that supports favored positions or opposes non-favored ones should receive more attention and be more positively interpreted and elaborated upon than information that opposes favored positions or supports non-favored ones.

The second additional motive posited by Chaiken et al. (1989) reflects their attempt to accord interpersonal processes a role in their model. Similar to Johnson and Eagly's (1989) construct of impression-relevant involvement, *impression motivation* refers to the desire to express attitudes that are socially acceptable. This type of motivation is assumed to be aroused in influence settings in which the identities of significant audiences (both real and imagined) are salient, social relationships are important, or when people must communicate or justify their attitudes to others (e.g., Tetlock, 1983a). Thus, the processing goal of impression-motivated perceivers is to assess the social acceptability of alternative positions. Chaiken and colleagues regard impression-motivated processing as strategic when it reflects people's intentions to express attitudes that will please or appease potential evaluators. Research on anticipatory attitude change suggests that such attitudes often revert to prior levels when situational pressures are removed (see Cialdini & Petty, 1981, and Chapter 12). Yet, because some research indicates that attitudes expressed for strategic reasons may eventually become internalized (e.g., Higgins & McCann, 1984), the issue of whether attitudinal responses produced by impression-motivated processing are dissimulations or genuine

340

is best regarded as a theoretical and empirical issue rather than a definitional matter (see Chapters 10 and 13).

Impression-motivated heuristic processing is assumed to involve the use of simple rules to guide one's selection of socially acceptable attitude positions—for example, "moderate positions minimize disagreement" and "agreement facilitates liking." In contrast, impression-motivated systematic processing implies that the same task has been accomplished through a more extensive consideration of available information. More specific descriptions of impression-motivated heuristic and systematic processing require knowledge of particular social influence contexts, because what constitutes socially acceptable judgments should vary as a function of potential audiences, their salience, and other situational factors. For example, conformity to others' attitudes may be more acceptable in some situations than in others.

In essence, the multiple-motive heuristic-systematic model features (a) three underlying motives that give rise to three distinctive processing goals and (b) the proposition that heuristic and systematic processing can occur in the service of any of these goals. Thus the model views processing goals and processing mode as orthogonal. As noted earlier, the expanded model uses a more general vocabulary for describing heuristic and systematic processing, given the breadth of social influence situations to which it is intended to apply (see below). In all other respects, however, the multiple-motive model's assumptions and principles parallel those we have articulated in relation to the original, single-motive model. That is, regardless of which motive or processing goal is operative, the model assumes that heuristic and systematic processing can occur simultaneously; that heuristic processing depends on the availability, accessibility, and reliability of judgmental heuristics; that systematic processing is more effortful and capacity limited than heuristic processing; that heuristic processing can proceed in either a more or less self-conscious manner; and that the principles of least effort and sufficiency are crucial motivational determinants of processing mode (see Chaiken et al., 1989).

Chaiken and her colleagues claim that their expanded theory provides a general model of social influence, one that can be applied to a broad range of influence settings beyond the validity-seeking persuasion context. In particular, they believe that the model can be used to understand and predict attitudinal responding in situations in which people either *receive* attitude-relevant information from external sources or *generate* attitude-relevant information in response to direct or indirect inducements. Aside from the classic persuasion paradigm, examples of settings in which information is externally provided include a variety of group influence paradigms in which subjects receive either elaborated or unelaborated attitudinal statements from other group members (see Chapter 13), and some self-perception studies in which subjects receive information purportedly diagnostic of their own attitudes (e.g., S. E. Taylor, 1975). Examples of settings in which attitude-relevant information is generated by subjects include most renditions of the induced-compliance paradigm we discuss in Chapter 11, and Tesser's (e.g., 1978) mere thought paradigm in which people are simply asked to think about their attitudes (see Chapter 12).[16]

As discussed in Chapter 11, Stroebe and Diehl (1988) have applied the heuristic-systematic model to the induced-compliance paradigm and, as discussed in Chapter 13,

Mackie (1987) has applied the model to the domain of majority and minority group influence. In addition, Shechter (1987) explored the utility of the model's notion of impression-motivated processing for a persuasion context in which subjects high and low in self-monitoring (M. Snyder, 1974) had to discuss their judgments with another person (see also Tetlock, 1983a). Finally, Chaiken and colleagues (1989) have discussed the relevance of defense-motivated processing to influence contexts in which people's vested interests are at stake, or when unpleasant, personally threatening information is received (see also Giner-Sorolla, Hazlewood, & Chaiken, 1989; Liberman & Chaiken, in press). For the most part, however, the applicability of the heuristic-systematic model to other influence settings and the utility of its tripartite motivational system have yet to be explored.

Evaluation of the Heuristic-Systematic Model

The heuristic-systematic model's most unique contribution as a theory of attitude formation and change is its proposition that simple decision rules mediate attitudinal judgment and its assumption that such heuristics are learned knowledge structures. Although novel to persuasion theorizing, these ideas as well as other cognitive and motivational aspects of the theory harmonize with several social cognition themes that have gained force in social psychology over the past decade—the nature of information stored in memory and its impact on processing and judgment, the extent to which the effects of such stored knowledge may occur with little effort, intention, or awareness on the part of social perceivers, and the degree to which these "theory-driven" effects can be overridden by motivational factors that encourage perceivers to engage in a more "data-driven" or systematic approach to information processing (see Bargh, 1988, 1989; Fiske & Taylor, 1991; Maheswaran & Chaiken, 1991; Sherman, Judd, & Park, 1989; E. R. Smith, in press).

Although the model's conception of heuristic processing is narrower than the elaboration likelihood model's definition of peripheral route persuasion, its clearer linkage to the social cognition literature yields a more theoretically developed view of persuasion that is not based on recipients' processing of persuasive arguments. For example, the assumption that persuasion heuristics are learned knowledge structures gives rise to the model's general proposition that the judgmental impact of heuristic cues should be moderated by the availability, accessibility, and perceived reliability of their associated heuristics. This proposition is important not only because it addresses the cognitive antecedents of heuristic processing, but also because it suggests novel mechanisms by which certain distal variables (e.g., communication modality) may influence persuasion. The model's accessibility principle merits particular attention in future research because of its relevance to the general issue of salience and vividness effects in persuasion (see Chapter 6). The idea that stored knowledge impacts on judgment only to the extent that it is activated from memory is, of course, not unique to the heuristic-systematic model. It has been applied to numerous issues in social cognition (see Higgins, 1989a; E. R. Smith, in press) and, within the attitudes literature, it is the mainstay of Fazio's (e.g., 1986) model of the attitude-behavior relationship.

Yet, aside from the heuristic-systematic model, the relevance of accessibility logic to persuasion processes has not generally been recognized.

Two issues regarding heuristic processing warrant closer attention in subsequent research. First, most research stimulated by the model has produced only indirect evidence for its core assumption that simple decision rules mediate persuasion: Heuristic cues such as source expertise or consensus information do exert a greater persuasive impact when systematic processing is minimal or when the salience of these cues is increased. In addition, correlational analyses often reveal that their judgmental impact covaries with subjects' perceptions of these cues (e.g., perceived source expertise, perceived consensus) but does not covary with argument recall or message-relevant thinking as a systematic interpretation would require. Yet, these demonstrations do not provide direct evidence that subjects postulated to be processing heuristically have actually used the kinds of inferential rules specified by the model. More direct evidence has been obtained in several priming studies that have demonstrated that manipulating the accessibility of a persuasion heuristic or its perceived reliability influences the persuasive impact of relevant heuristic cues. However, these demonstrations are few in number and have not yielded particularly strong effects (see Chaiken, 1987; Chaiken et al. 1992).

The second issue that merits attention is the extent to which heuristics, like other types of stored knowledge, may influence judgment automatically, with little intention, effort, or awareness on the part of message recipients. Chaiken (1987; Chaiken et al., 1989) has argued that heuristic processing may often proceed in a relatively (if not fully) automatic manner, but that heuristics can also be applied in a highly deliberate self-conscious manner (see note 14). In particular, heuristics are most likely to be applied intentionally when people lack ability for systematic processing. Although this speculation as well as the relative automaticity view are plausible, neither has yet to be tested (for discussion of automaticity see Bargh, 1989).

Unlike the elaboration likelihood model, the heuristic-systematic model explicitly addresses the relationship between its two processing modes. As such, it clarifies why it is that heuristic or peripheral cues often exert little persuasive impact when people engage in systematic or central route processing. In contrast to the view that heuristic or peripheral processing does not occur in such instances, the theory assumes that it does but that systematic processing may attenuate its judgmental impact. More important, this assumption implies that attentuation should be most conspicuous in situations in which systematic processing yields information that contradicts the validity of persuasion heuristics. Equally important, the model's concurrent processing assumption implies that attitude judgments can be influenced by *both* heuristic and systematic processing when the two modes do not yield highly contradictory information. In these situations, heuristic and systematic processing can exert independent effects on judgment. Moreover, when message content is ambiguous, heuristic processing can, in addition, influence systematic processing by biasing people's interpretation and evaluation of persuasive arguments.

Because most experiments that have manipulated heuristic cues in settings that promote argument-based processing have used unambiguously strong or weak messages, their designs have featured blatant contradictions between levels of the heuristic cue and message content (e.g., expert source/weak arguments; lack of consensus/strong arguments). It is therefore not surprising that the vast majority of these studies have observed attenuation effects rather than the additivity and bias effects that are also postulated by the theory. Yet such explicit contradictions are no doubt much less frequent in naturalistic influence settings. Thus it is probable that existing research considerably underestimates the extent to which heuristic cues influence persuasion when recipients engage in systematic (central route) processing. By implementing experimental designs that mitigate the possibility of attenuation effects—and that are arguably more ecologically valid—subsequent investigators should be able to expand upon the preliminary demonstrations that heuristic and systematic processing can exert both independent and interdependent effects on judgment (Chaiken & Maheswaran, 1992; Maheswaran & Chaiken, 1991).

A major strength of the heuristic-systematic model is the attention it pays to motivational issues and their connection to cognitive processing. As we have seen, the proposition that people are cognitive misers (S. E. Taylor & Fiske, 1978) who must be motivated to engage in more than minimal amounts of systematic processing has been supported in numerous persuasion experiments testing the heuristic-systematic and elaboration likelihood models. The same general proposition has been addressed in a variety of other experimental paradigms in the social cognition literature (e.g., impression formation, decision making, hypothesis testing, social prediction). In these other social judgment contexts the amount or complexity of subjects' thinking has also been shown to depend upon motivational factors, some of which overlap those investigated by attitude researchers (e.g., personal relevance, task importance, accountability) and some of which do not (e.g., outcome dependency, Fiske & Neuberg, 1990; control deprivation, Pittman & D'Agostino, 1989; see Chaiken et al., 1989).

While it is now quite evident that a large number of variables act to enhance perceivers' tendencies to engage in effortful cognitive processing, most investigators—both within and outside the persuasion area—have paid little attention to the psychological mechanisms that may underlie these motivational effects. In contrast, Chaiken and her colleagues attempt to explain such effects via their sufficiency principle. This principle, which can be viewed as a formalization and extension of Simon's (e.g., 1976) notion of satisficing, implicates the discrepancy between actual and desired levels of judgmental confidence as the fundamental motivator of processing effort in social judgment settings. In this view, factors such as personal relevance, task importance, accountability, and so on exert their motivating effects on cognitive processing by influencing either perceivers' desired or actual levels of judgmental confidence. Because of its potentially broad explanatory value, the sufficiency principle warrants special attention in further research.

Like most other cognitive theories of persuasion, the heuristic-systematic model was originally developed to explain how message recipients process information in order to achieve valid attitudes that square with relevant facts. As we have seen, the expanded model that Chaiken and her colleagues have proposed posits two additional motives that heuristic and systematic processing may also serve—defense motivation and impression motivation. Although it is too early to forecast how the expanded model will fare in empirical tests, its recognition that motives other than accuracy seeking play a role in social influence and, more important, its recognition that information processing occurs in the service of defending particular attitudes and expressing socially acceptable attitudes—as well as in the service of attaining valid attitudes—represents an effort to develop a theory that accords an important role to *both* motivational and cognitive processes in social influence. B. T. Johnson and Eagly's (1989, 1990) recent tripartite analysis of involvement represents a similar attempt to link newer work on cognitive processing with earlier motivational accounts of persuasion. The idea that information processing may occur in the service of social-relational goals is also suggested by several functional theories of attitudes that we discuss in Chapters 10 and 13. These theories (e.g., D. Katz, 1960) as well as social judgment theorists' analysis of ego-involvement (see Chapter 8) and other motivational perspectives such as dissonance theory and reactance theory (see Chapters 10 and 12) also suggest that people may sometimes process attitudinal material in a defensive manner.

Summary

The two dual-process theories of persuasion we have considered complement one another in an interesting way. The elaboration likelihood model represents a highly integrative empirical framework for investigating persuasion. As we have seen, Petty and Cacioppo and others who have used their framework have shown that an impressively large number of situational and individual difference variables can be understood from the perspective of the elaboration likelihood model. The main limitation of the model is theoretical. For example, while the model predicts that peripheral cues will have little impact when the elaboration likelihood is high, it provides little insight as to why this should be the case. Moreover, although the model enables one to predict when peripheral route persuasion will occur, it does not attempt to shed light on what kind of peripheral mechanism has operated or why it has operated. In contrast, the unique strengths of the heuristic-systematic model are theoretical. Chaiken and her colleagues and others who have used the model have shown its explanatory value in relation to a fair number of distal persuasion variables. Yet its quarry of variables is less than the quarry that the elaboration likelihood model can claim. On the other hand, the heuristic-systematic model fills most of the theoretical gaps that characterize the elaboration likelihood model. For example, it explains why heuristic or peripheral cues often fail to exert a detectable persuasive impact when people engage in systematic or central route processing. Moreover, the model also goes beyond the elaboration likelihood model by suggesting ways in which heuristic and systematic processing can exert independent and interactive effects on attitude judgment, by illuminating the underlying psychological mechanisms by which motivational treatments promote systematic or central route processing, and by suggesting ways in which heuristic and systematic processing can serve motivational concerns other than the motive to achieve valid, correct attitudes.

Although the two models have often been treated as competitors or, by those less invested and less versed in their respective logics, as redundant with one another, a more productive viewpoint is to regard the two models as complementary. The empirical strengths of the elaboration likelihood model together with the theoretical strengths of the heuristic-systematic model make for a truly impressive dual-processing framework for understanding a variety of social influence phenomena. Indeed, the implications of these models for other findings and issues in the psychological literature on attitudes will become evident in subsequent chapters of our book.

——— Notes ———

1. As discussed in the following section of this chapter, the heuristic-systematic model (Chaiken, 1980, 1987) also generates this prediction. In this section, we will indicate parenthetically which ELM hypotheses are shared by the heuristic-systematic model. To facilitate a coherent review of the empirical literature, experiments relevant to the two models' shared hypotheses are discussed in this section, regardless of how they were framed by their authors. Differences between the two models are discussed in the following section of the chapter.

2. The Wood, Kallgren, and Priesler (1985) study included subjects at three levels of prior knowledge (high, medium, low). For ease of presentation, we report the mean attitude scores of only high and low knowledge subjects (W. Wood, personal communication, July 3, 1989). These means differ slightly (but not in substance) from those presented by Petty and Cacioppo (1986b, Figure 6, p. 169), who recast Wood and colleagues' data using a median-split procedure.

3. With one exception, all of these yielded data most compatible with the positive bias pattern shown in the left half of Panel II, Figure 7.2. Liberman and Chaiken's (1989) data, in contrast, suggested a negative biasing effect due to increased relevance (see right half of Panel II).

4. Warnings refer to either of two types of manipulations: warning subjects of the content or position of an upcoming persuasive message, or warning subjects that the communicator intends to persuade them. Petty and Cacioppo (1986b) have argued that such treatments may bias message processing when personal relevance is high (Petty & Cacioppo, 1977, 1979a; see also Chapter 12).

5. In the Heesacker, Petty, and Cacioppo (1983) study, only field-dependent subjects manifested this interaction pattern.

6. Petty and colleagues have recently proposed a very similar multiple-role analysis of how positive affective states influence persuasion (e.g., Petty, Cacioppo, & Kasmer, 1988). This and other theoretical analyses of the mood-persuasion relation are discussed in Chapter 10.

7. There is a certain fuzziness to the model's assertion that *if* a variable typically conceived of as a peripheral cue (e.g., source attractiveness) affects persuasion when the elaboration likelihood is high, then it must have done so by serving as a "persuasive argument." This is because at least some peripheral mechanisms (e.g., heuristic processing) presumably *do* impact on persuasion by providing recipients with "bits of information" relevant to determining the "true merits" of the message's position. We suspect that this assertion follows less from a conceptual distinction between *peripheral cues* and *persuasive arguments*, than from an attempt to achieve compatibility with the model's postulate (V) that peripheral cues are relatively unimportant determinants of persuasion under high elaboration likelihood conditions.

8. This discussion underscores the importance of collecting auxiliary data when testing hypotheses generated by the ELM and related frameworks. For example, Cacioppo, Petty, Kao, and Rodriguez's (1986) hypothesis that people high in need for cognition process information more extensively is supported not only by the Argument Quality × Need for Cognition interaction they observed on persuasion and the frequency of unfavorable thoughts generated (see earlier description of this study), but also by the fact that high (vs. low) need for cognition subjects recalled a significantly greater number of persuasive arguments. Unfortunately, recall measures and other face-valid indexes of amount of processing have only rarely been included in studies testing the elaboration likelihood and cognitive response models. The most common auxiliary data analyzed in such studies are the valence of subjects' message-relevant thoughts, and it is the *evaluative profile* of these thoughts that is used to bolster inferences that central route processing has occurred. For

example, if subjects list more favorable thoughts and fewer unfavorable thoughts in response to strong messages under high compared to low elaboration likelihood conditions, the inference is drawn that subjects processed message content more thoroughly (see Harkins & Petty, 1987; Petty & Cacioppo, 1981a, 1986a, 1986b). However, as we argued in Chapter 6, demonstrations that treatment variables influence the evaluative profile of message-relevant thinking do not provide unequivocal evidence that these variables have affected the *amount* of message-relevant thinking.

9. In response to Stiff's interpretation, Petty and Cacioppo have argued that their model does not preclude the possibility that people can process *both* arguments and cues (Petty, Cacioppo, Kasmer, & Haugtvedt, 1987; Petty, Kasmer, Haugtvedt, & Cacioppo, 1987). The focus of this debate is somewhat misplaced, however, because it seems to concern whether different types of information (i.e., arguments versus peripheral cues) can be processed (i.e., encoded, interpreted) at the same time. The important issue would seem to be whether argument-based processing and peripheral processes do or do not occur at the same time in persuasion situations and, if so, whether they exert additive effects on persuasion, interactive effects, or both (see following section on heuristic-systematic model). As presently formulated, the elaboration likelihood model appears to posit two non-concurrent routes to persuasion.

10. The distinction between likelihood and desirability judgments is accorded a great deal of theoretical importance in McGuire's (1990) analysis of thought systems, which we discuss in Chapter 5.

11. Internal validity issues aside, the ecological validity of the Argument "Quality" × Treatment interactions that much recent persuasion research has yielded deserves closer scrutiny by subsequent investigators. Specifically, the weak messages used in this research are often so blatantly poor that they might only rarely be encountered in naturalistic social influence settings and probably

not at all in the context of messages disseminated in the mass media.

12. In this regard, it is unlikely that merely varying the associative link between an attitude object and some attribute will suffice as an adequate manipulation of argument or message strength. Consider, for example, Petty, Cacioppo, and Schumann's (1983) argument that the "Edge razor floats on water." Even if subjects strongly believed this argument, it is doubtful they would consider the argument an important reason for preferring one razor over others. Areni and Lutz (1988) provide further guidance for researchers, however (see also Boller, Swasy, & Munch, 1990). For example, strong and weak versions of a message could contain the identical *core* arguments, and these core arguments would link the attitude object (e.g., exams) to positively valued attributes (e.g., higher starting salaries). What would differ across the two messages, however, would be the "quality" of supportive evidence. That is, whereas the strong message would contain good evidence supporting this core argument (e.g., studies by the *Wall Street Journal* suggest...), the weak message would contain poor supporting evidence (e.g., my cousin Alan earns a lot and he had to take the exams).

13. Within the elaboration likelihood model, biased elaboration of persuasive arguments is also postulated to stem from motivational sources (e.g., forewarnings, commitment to prior attitudes). Within the heuristic-systematic model, motivational sources of bias are not postulated in relation to accuracy-motivated processing. Instead, such factors are viewed as instigating defense-motivated and impression-motivated heuristic and systematic processing (see subsequent discussion in text).

14. Although Chaiken and her colleagues regard heuristic processing as less effortful and capacity-limited than systematic processing, they do not label it as an automatic process that occurs without *any* intention, effort, or awareness on the part of the perceiver (see Bargh, 1989). In their view, heuristic processing may sometimes proceed in a relatively spontaneous (if not fully automatic)

manner but, at other times, may represent a more highly intentional, controlled process because perceivers actively search for heuristic cues to guide their judgments (see Chaiken, 1987; Chaiken, Liberman, & Eagly, 1989).

15. In the study's low importance conditions, this direct path was the only significant determinant of attitudes, consistent with the idea that heuristic processing dominated in these conditions. Finally, consistent with the model's attenuation hypothesis, this direct path was nonsignificant in the study's high importance–unambiguous argument conditions. Instead, the path analysis confirmed that in these conditions only argument quality influenced attitudes and, moreover, did so by affecting the valence of subjects' attribute-related thinking.

16. Chaiken, Liberman, and Eagly (1989) make the further claim that their multiple-motive heuristic-systematic model provides a general cognitive-functional framework that can be applied to a variety of nonattitudinal judgment settings in which people receive or generate information about other people, themselves, or other entities, and must make some judgment or decision about these entities. These settings include causal attribution tasks, stereotyping tasks, impression formation tasks, and social prediction tasks.

8

Process Theories of Attitude Formation and Change: Attribution Approaches and Social Judgment Theory

In this chapter we conclude our three-chapter sequence on process theories of persuasion by considering attribution approaches and social judgment theory. Consistent with the theme introduced in Chapter 7, these perspectives feature mechanisms of attitude formation and change that can occur in the absence of argument-based processing. Attribution approaches emphasize how people's inferences about the causes of communicators' attitudinal statements affect their agreement with these statements. Social judgment theory emphasizes how people's prior attitudes affect their perceptions of the attitude positions that communicators express and how these perceptions, in turn, influence agreement with persuasive communications. In reviewing these frameworks, we will address ways in which they could be related to various aspects of the elaboration likelihood and heuristic-systematic models. In an epilogue to this chapter we will also summarize the various cognitive mechanisms that process theorists have discussed and suggest some general principles that may improve understanding of the conditions under which one or another may occur.

Attribution Approaches

Attribution theory approaches to understanding persuasion emphasize the mediational role of people's causal explanations for why communicators take particular positions on particular issues. In general terms, persuasion should be facilitated to the extent that people view a communicator's message as conveying the "truth" or reality about some issue and should be inhibited to the extent that the message is attributed to factors that compromise its truth value. For example, a message claiming that personal income taxes are too high would probably be judged as more valid and would therefore elicit greater agreement if it were communicated by a retired politician rather than a politician in the midst of a reelection campaign. As this example illustrates, the information that people take into account in inferring the causes of a communicator's message will often include salient contextual cues such as the communicator's personal circumstances and the audience the communicator is addressing (e.g., Is the politician merely expressing a viewpoint the audience would like to hear?). However, information relevant to performing this causal analysis may also be embedded in the content of the communicator's message. For example, the message may include statements implying that many other persons share the communicator's viewpoint (high consensus). Yet a message's persuasive arguments *per se* are not the focus of people's processing attention. Like heuristic processing, then, attributional reasoning constitutes a cognitive peripheral route mechanism within the elaboration likelihood model of persuasion. As we will see, however, the inference processes specified by attribution approaches are more complex than the simple decision rules featured in the heuristic-systematic model.

Drawing on Heider's (1958) seminal analysis of causal attributions, Harold Kelley (1967, 1972a) provided a provocative analysis of the attributional inferences that underlie persuasion. The theoretical principles suggested by Kelley and others who have examined persuasion from an attributional perspective explain how message recipients utilize principles of causation to evaluate the validity of persuasive messages. Persuasion in this approach is viewed as the direct outcome of perceivers' inferences about message validity—messages that are perceived to be valid are more persuasive than those that are perceived as less valid.[1]

According to Kelley's (1967, 1972a) analysis, the recipient of a persuasive communication faces the problem of explaining the communicator's message. In more exact terms, the recipient observes that the communicator expresses a particular attitudinal position and must decide *why* the communicator has done so. This position may be attributed to personal characteristics of the communicator (e.g., ideology, traits), to characteristics of the situation (e.g., audience or role constraints), or to the "environment" or external reality that is discussed in the message. Attribution of the message to the environment is termed a stimulus or *entity* attribution within Kelley's framework. Such an attribution increases message persuasiveness because it implies that the recipient believes that the communicator's message provides a veridical description of the external reality it purports to describe (i.e., the message is perceived to be valid).

Kelley (1967) suggested that perceivers decide whether to attribute the communicator's position to external reality by carrying out a subjective analysis of variance (ANOVA) on information arranged in a Persons × Occasions × Entities matrix. Within such a matrix, the probability of an entity attribution is assumed to be increased by a data pattern of *consensus* across persons, *consistency* across occasions (and modalities), and *distinctiveness* to the entity described. Although numerous questions have been raised concerning aspects of this ANOVA model of attribution, Kelley's assumption about the attributional impact of consensus, consistency, and distinctiveness information has proven to be generally valid (for reviews, see Kelley & Michela, 1980; M. Ross & Fletcher, 1985). With respect to persuasive messages, then, an entity attribution would be favored—and the recipient would therefore consider the message to be valid—if the communicator advocated a position that (a) was in accord with the viewpoint of other relevant information sources (consensus), (b) was stated on various occasions to various audiences (consistency), and (c) was tailored to the particular issue under discussion (distinctivenes). Consider, for example, Professor Bargh's assertion that *The Psychology of Attitudes* is a great book. You will probably regard this statement as a valid description of the book's quality (entity attribution) and be persuaded by it to the extent that other faculty and students have also praised this book (high consensus), Professor Bargh has praised the book at various class meetings and cited it in his own writings (high consistency), and Professor Bargh has been critical of other recently published psychology books and articles (high distinctiveness).

Fulfillment of Consensus, Consistency, and Distinctiveness Criteria

Multiple Observations. The relevance of Kelley's (1967) ANOVA analysis to persuasion is clearest when message recipients have multiple observations of communicators and messages, because such observations furnish the consensus, consistency, and distinctiveness information needed to perform a complete causal analysis of a particular communicator's advocated position. The causal analysis described above, for example, assumes that you have had multiple exposures to Professor Bargh's views about our book, exposure to his views about other books and articles, and exposure to other people's views about our book. Most persuasion research has not provided subjects with such multiple observations. However, there are some experiments in which subjects have been exposed to the views of *multiple sources* who advocate a similar position, or to *multiple messages* that advocate a similar position.

Multiple sources have been shown to be more persuasive than single sources, at least when messages contain reasonably strong arguments (e.g., Harkins & Petty, 1981, 1987; Himmelfarb, 1972). As we discussed in Chapter 6, one interpretation for this effect is that multiple sources enhance recipients' tendencies to engage in message-relevant thinking. An attribution interpretation is also plausible, however. That is, multiple sources might enhance persuasion by increasing the *consensus* associated with any particular communicator's position. As we have also seen, the finding that multiple messages advocating a similar viewpoint are, within limits, more persuasive than messages delivered only once (e.g., Cacioppo & Petty, 1985) can also be interpreted from the perspective of the cognitive response model (and reception-as-mediator hypothesis; see Chapter 6). Again, however, an attribution interpretation is also plausible. That is, multiple messages could be viewed as enhancing persuasion by increasing the perceived *consistency* of a communicator's position. In accord with this consistency principle, Moscovici and Nemeth (1974; Moscovici, 1976) have argued that persistent repetition of the same position by group members holding a minority position enhances their influence with other group members. Moscovici labeled this repetitive style *behavioral consistency* and proposed that its effect on the attitudes of majority group members is mediated by their causal inferences about the minority and why it holds the position that it does (see Chapter 13).

Single Observations. In natural settings the potential of Kelley's ANOVA model to account for perceivers' reactions to persuasive messages is enormous because people very often have extensive experience with multiple communicators who state their positions on related issues on multiple occasions. Examples include repeated observations of politicians' stands on social and legislative issues as well as repeated observations of friends', colleagues', and family members' views on a host of social, political, work, and personal issues. However, most laboratory persuasion experiments present subjects with a single message in which a communicator takes a position on a single issue. Because information available in such settings is rarely adequate for constructing a complete Persons × Occasions × Entities matrix, it may seem that the ANOVA model of attribution has little relevance to the typical persuasion experiment. Yet various cues in such experimental settings may nevertheless enable perceivers to make reasonable assumptions about how such a data matrix might be completed if more detailed information were available. Some relevant cues may be placed into the message itself. For example, communicators may argue that their positions are consensual with other persons, consistent across occasions, and distinctive to the issue discussed (e.g., "Other members of congress also believe..."; "I've felt this way for many years and have argued my position in congress, at town meetings, on television ..."; "I am not a financial conservative but on this issue ..."). In addition, communicator and other contextual cues can provide information relevant to the ANOVA data matrix. For example, nonexpert communicators, who are usually less persuasive than experts (see McGuire, 1985), may be regarded as lacking sufficient knowledge to make statements distinctive to the issue under discussion. And cues regarding other persons' attitudes or reactions to communicators' messages may influence persuasion by affecting recipients' perceptions of the extent to which communicators' positions are consensual with those of other information sources (see Axsom, Yates, & Chaiken, 1987; Mackie, 1987; Maheswaran & Chaiken, 1991).[2]

Although it is plausible that recipients' inferences about consensus, consistency, and distinctiveness may underlie the impact of a number of persuasion variables, few have been studied from this perspective. One exception is Goethals' research on communicator-recipient *similarity* (Goethals, 1976; Goethals & Nelson, 1973). Relevant to the attributional principle that consensus information enhances perceivers' confidence in the validity of their own judgments, this research found that agreement from a dissimilar other increased subjects' judgmental confidence to a greater extent than agreement from a similar other. When agreeing others are similar to the perceiver, they and the perceiver might share biases that lead them to hold similar but inaccurate judgments. When agreeing others are dissimilar, however, they are unlikely to share the same biases as the perceiver. Their agreement, then, should reduce the likelihood of person-based explanations for the perceiver's (or other's) judgment, and increase the plausibility that this judgment reflects the true nature of the entity being judged.[3] In a conceptually similar vein, Himmelfarb (1972) varied the consistency of multiple communicators' descriptions of a target person and whether they had observed the target in similar versus dissimilar situations. The results showed that consistency enhanced the persuasiveness of these descriptions to a greater extent when consistency was based on observations of the target person in dissimilar situations (see Chapter 5 for relevance of this study to information integration theory). Consistency across dissimilar situations is especially likely to reduce the likelihood of situation-based explanations for communicators' stated positions, thereby increasing the likelihood of entity attributions.

Multiple Plausible Causes and Message Persuasiveness

Kelley (1972a) proposed a simpler analysis of causation based not on the ANOVA cube, but on the *plausibility* of possible causes for behaviors such as communicators' expressed attitudes. According to this analysis, perceivers scan available information for potential causes of a given behavior and take into account whether there are multiple plausible causes and whether these causes are facilitative or inhibitory in relation to the observed behavior. In other words, for any given behavior, perceivers may generate one or more causes that may have functioned to encourage the behavior and also one or more causes that might have functioned to suppress it. For example, suppose you learn that President Bush has endorsed the Republican candidate for senator in your state. You would probably entertain the possibility that the president's endorsement is mere protocol—after all, one of his "jobs" is to support Republicans, regardless of their qualifications. You might also entertain the idea that the endorsement is genuine but nevertheless merely reflects the president's conservative ideological bias. Yet you also consider the possibility that the president's endorsement reflects the fact that the Republican candidate *is* better qualified than the Democratic candidate. You tend to discount this possibility, though, because of the other facilitative causes you generated. On the other hand, you remember that the candidate and the president have disagreed publicly on health and welfare issues. The fact that the president endorsed the candidate in spite of their differences makes you wonder whether the candidate might not, after all, be the right person for the Senate.

The implications of Kelley's multiple plausible causes analysis for persuasion were developed by Eagly and her colleagues and tested in experiments that presented subjects with single observations of communicators' messages (see Eagly, Chaiken, & Wood, 1981). According to their *multiple plausible causes framework*, cues that lead message recipients to infer potential causes for a communicator's position include information about the communicator's personal attributes (e.g., prior attitudes, ideology, personality traits) and information about constraints or pressures in the communicator's situation (e.g., the attitudes of an audience). These cues are often available to recipients prior to their actual exposure to the communicator's message; hence, they may often initiate their causal analysis before listening to or reading the message. Of course, such cues can also be embedded in the message (e.g., information about the communicator's ideology) or presented simultaneously with the message (e.g., audience reactions).

The framework assumes that recipients construct a mini-theory of the communicator's behavior on the basis of the above sorts of causally relevant cues. For example, knowing that Ted Koppel will be interviewing President Bush's secretary of Treasury on "Nightline," you might reason that the secretary will support a reduction in the capital gains tax because of his ideological similarity to the president (who favors a reduction), or pressures in his situation (member of an administration that favors a reduction), or both. This causal analysis, then, creates an *expectancy* about what position a communicator will take on an issue (i.e., you expect the secretary to endorse a tax reduction). This expectancy is then either confirmed or disconfirmed by the position the communicator *actually* expresses in his message. In our example, Bush's Treasury secretary will confirm your expectancy if he indeed argues for a reduced capital gains tax but will disconfirm your expectancy if he argues against reducing this tax.

Eagly and her colleagues assert that, ordinarily, expectancy *confirmation* leads to causal attributions that reduce message persuasiveness. More specifically, when recipients' expectancies are confirmed, they tend to attribute the communicator's expressed viewpoint to the personal or situational factors that generated their expectancy. Thus, the secretary's pro-reduction message might be attributed to his own conservative ideology, to situational pressures to parrot his administration's "no-tax" tax policies, or to both factors. Such causal inferences account for the communicator's message in terms of a personal or situational factor rather than in terms of the external reality that the message purports to describe—for example, that reducing the capital gains tax will spur economic growth. This weakening of an entity attribution is consistent with Kelley's (1972a) *discounting* principle. This principle implies that a viable person- or situation-based cause lessens the plausibility of external reality as a cause of the observed behavior. According to the Eagly and colleagues model, attribution of the communicator's message to a personal or situational cause leads recipients to infer that the communicator is biased. This inference, in turn, leads them to discredit the message's validity. As a consequence, recipients should be persuaded relatively little by messages that confirm their expectancies.

When a communicator *disconfirms* an expectancy by not taking the expected attitudinal position—for example, the Treasury secretary argues against reducing taxes on capital gains—recipients have a bit of a problem insofar as they must generate a new "theory" to explain the communicator's message. Usually, the most likely alternative theory is that especially compelling evidence led the communicator to overcome the bias or biases that recipients initially assumed would prejudice his or her communicative behavior. This strengthening of an entity attribution is consistent with Kelley's (1972a) *augmentation* principle. According to this attributional principle, when an expectancy based on a personal or situational cause is disconfirmed, this cause is assumed to have functioned in an inhibitory manner, that is, as a cause that ought to have impeded the observed behavior. As a consequence, the perceived strength of a facilitative cause such as external reality is considerably enhanced (e.g., "the arguments against reducing taxes on capital gains must be especially strong for the secretary to risk alienating President Bush"). When expectancies are disconfirmed, and the strength of the external reality cause is thereby strengthened, communicators will be regarded as especially unbiased, and their messages will be viewed as valid. In essence, because of the attributional impact of the discounting principle when messages confirm expectancies and the impact of the augmentation principle when messages disconfirm expectancies, messages that are unexpected in view of communicators' personal attributes and situations should be more persuasive than messages that are expected.

In developing their multiple plausible causes framework, Eagly, Wood, and Chaiken (1978) distinguished between two types of communicator bias that can underlie recipients' causal explanations for communicators' stated attitudinal positions. *Knowledge bias* refers to the perceiver's belief that a communicator's knowledge of issue-relevant information is nonveridical. For example, if the Treasury secretary supports reduced capital gains taxes, recipients might believe that his conservative ideology biased his sampling or interpretation of issue-relevant information. A knowledge-biased communicator has a distorted view of the evidence but does not willfully mislead message recipients. In contrast, *reporting bias* refers to the perceiver's belief that a communicator's willingness to convey an accurate version of issue-relevant information is compromised. For example, recipients might believe that the Treasury secretary's pro-tax reduction position was "ordered" by President Bush. A reporting-biased communicator, then, willfully misleads his or her audience.

In one experiment testing this attribution framework, Eagly and her colleagues (1978) told subjects that they would read a campaign speech given by a candidate for mayor in a western U.S. city. The communicator's (i.e., candidate's) background was varied by describing him as a lawyer who had worked for either environmental or business interests in the past, and the identity of the audience who heard his campaign speech was varied by describing them as either "citizens for the environment" or "citizens for industrial growth." Some subjects in this study received information detailing only the communicator's background (establishing a knowledge bias expectancy), some received information describing only the audience (establishing a reporting bias expectancy), and others received information of both types. Subjects then read a speech in which the communicator discussed the waste disposal methods used by the city's major industries and in which he advocated a pro-environment policy on this issue. Thus, subjects' pre-message expectancies were either confirmed or disconfirmed.

The results of this experiment, shown in Table 8.1, demonstrated that subjects' causal explanations for the communicator's message reflected whether the message confirmed or disconfirmed their pre-message expectancies. They attributed the communicator's viewpoint more strongly to the relevant biasing cue—the communicator's background in the knowledge bias conditions and the audience's beliefs in the reporting bias conditions—when their expectancy was confirmed rather than disconfirmed. Also, the communicator was perceived as more biased when his viewpoint confirmed (vs. disconfirmed) subjects' expectancies. And, consistent with the model's distinction between knowledge bias and reporting bias, the communicator was regarded as insincere only when reporting bias expectancies were confirmed. Regardless of the type of bias that subjects expected, however, they were more persuaded by the communicator's message when their expectancies were disconfirmed.

A subsequent experiment by Wood and Eagly (1981), which examined knowledge bias expectancies, replicated the Eagly et al. (1978) findings using a different message topic. Knowledge bias was manipulated in this study by varying the match between the communicator's attitude toward freedom of speech (favorable vs. unfavorable) and the position he advocated on the topic of restricting pornography (pro vs. anti). Consistent

TABLE 8.1

Major Results of the Eagly, Wood, and Chaiken (1978) Attribution Study

Variable	Expectancy confirmed			Expectancy disconfirmed		
	Knowledge bias	Reporting bias	Knowledge bias and reporting bias	Knowledge bias	Reporting bias	Knowledge bias and reporting bias
Likelihood of advocated position	10.00	8.75	8.93	5.13	4.08	3.71
Attribution of message to communicator's background	12.52	8.03	11.07	7.97	8.14	8.75
Attribution of message to audience's opinion	9.90	12.10	10.82	11.09	5.62	7.57
Perception of communicator as biased	0.39	0.69	0.76	–0.38	–0.67	–0.62
Perception of communicator as sincere	0.01	–0.66	–0.48	–0.22	1.08	0.65
Attitude change	2.87	2.60	2.71	3.44	4.55	3.86

Note: Higher numbers indicate higher likelihood (1–15 scale); stronger attribution of message to each causal factor (1–15 scales); perception of communicator as more biased and more sincere (factor scores derived from ratings on 9 evaluative scales); and greater attitude change (difference between pre-message and post-message attitude, each given on 15-point scale).

Source: All data are from persuasion subjects, with the exception of the likelihood ratings, which were provided by *expectancy-only* control subjects. This table was adapted from Eagly, Wood, and Chaiken (1978, Tables 2 and 3, pp. 429 and 431).

FIGURE 8.1.
Results of a structural analysis on the Wood and Eagly (1981) data. All path coefficients are significant beyond the $p = .05$ level. The correlation between the model's two exogenous variables is appended to the path with double arrows. This figure was adapted from one presented by Eagly, Chaiken, and Wood (1981, Figure 2.1, p. 51).

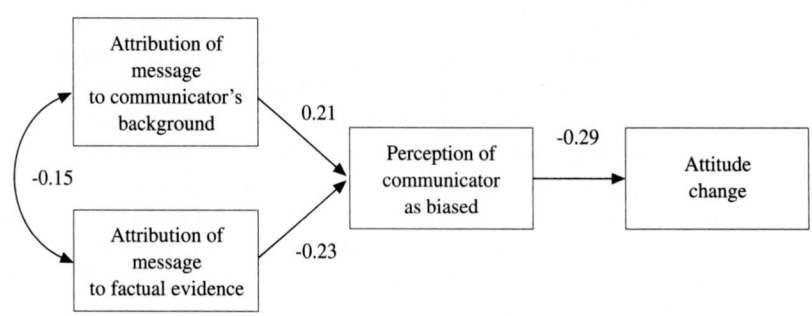

with the earlier research, subjects attributed the communicator's pornography message more to personal background factors and less to factual evidence, viewed him as more biased, and were less persuaded when his position on pornography matched his free speech viewpoint. Wood and Eagly further showed that these findings occurred regardless of whether the persuasive message advocated a position that was highly discrepant versus only moderately discrepant with subjects' initial, pre-message attitudes. More important, a path analysis that explored the sequential aspects of subjects' information processing further documented the framework's assumptions regarding the mediation of persuasion. The causal model that represents these assumptions is shown in Figure 8.1. The arrows between variables in the model indicate that a significant relationship was obtained in the analysis, and the numbers appended to the arrows are beta-weights or *path coefficients* that reveal the magnitude and direction of each relationship. As Figure 8.1 illustrates, subjects' belief that the communicator's stated position on the topic of restricting pornography (pro or anti) was influenced by his background (attitude toward freedom of speech) led to the perception of him as biased, and the belief that he was influenced by factual evidence led to the perception of him as unbiased. Then, to the extent that subjects judged the communicator as unbiased, they changed their beliefs about restricting pornography toward the position he advocated.

A secondary finding of the Wood and Eagly (1981) study was that subjects recalled more persuasive arguments when the communicator's message confirmed their expectancies. A more recent study testing the attribution framework produced conceptually similar results for subjects who were low in need for cognition (Petty & Priester, 1991). When the communicator's message confirmed (vs. disconfirmed) these subjects' expectancies, they processed message content more thoroughly, as indexed by their greater sensitivity to the quality of the communicator's arguments (but see Hunt, Smith, & Kernan, 1989).[4]

Attribution models of persuasion do not explicitly address how recipients' causal analyses of communicators' messages influence their processing of *persuasive argumentation*. However, Eagly and colleagues (1981) suggested that the increased message processing associated with expectancy confirmation may reflect recipients' response to attributional ambiguity. When messages disconfirm recipients' expectancies, they can usually be quite confident that the communicator is unbiased and that the message corresponds to external reality. Such might be your reaction to finding out that President Bush's Treasury secretary opposes reducing the capital gains tax. Given this certainty about the communicator's lack of bias, recipients of disconfirming messages may feel that they can dispense with a careful analysis of message content.[5] However, when messages confirm recipients' expectancies, external reality cannot be entirely eliminated as a *possible* cause of the communicator's message, even though recipients are likely to believe that the most *plausible* cause is the person-based or situation-based factor that originally generated their expectancy. Given this ambiguity concerning the validity of the communicator's position, recipients of confirming messages may be more likely to scrutinize what the communicator actually said in order to resolve questions concerning message validity. Such might be your response to the attributional ambiguity caused by finding out that the Treasury secretary favors reducing the capital gains tax. This explanation is consistent with the heuristic-systematic model's sufficiency principle, which implies that systematic processing will be more likely when recipients cannot attain reasonable judgmental confidence on the basis of less effortful modes of processing (see Chapter 7).

The main assertion of the multiple plausible causes framework, that unexpected messages are more persuasive than expected ones, has been substantiated in several additional experiments by Eagly and her colleagues and other investigators (Eagly & Chaiken, 1975, 1976; Hunt & Kernan, 1984; Hunt et al., 1989; Petty & Priester, 1991; Wachtler & Counselman, 1981). This framework also provides an interpretation for the findings of a number of earlier persuasion experiments that had been formulated in terms of various aspects of communicator trustworthiness. For example, consistent with the framework's proposition that messages that confirm reporting bias expectancies are unpersuasive, Walster, Aronson, and Abrahams (1966) demonstrated that, regardless of overall prestige, a communicator was more persuasive when arguing against rather than in accord with his self-interest. As a second example, research on "overheard" communications has shown that such messages are more persuasive than regular ones when the message topic is important to recipients and the message advocates a position that they would prefer to be true (Brock & Becker, 1965; Walster & Festinger, 1962). Presumably, the reduced persuasiveness of non-overheard messages in this research reflects recipients' tendencies to account for such messages in terms of a reporting bias: Communicators who knowingly advocate desirable positions on important topics may be perceived as ingratiators or, alternatively, as "nice" persons expressing viewpoints that others would like to hear. In these and other relevant experiments, communicators have proven to be more persuasive when they advocated positions that were unexpected in terms of their personal attributes or situational demands (e.g., Birnbaum & Stegner, 1979; Koeske & Crano, 1968; Mills & Jellison, 1967). Although it is parsimonious to interpret the persuasion findings of these experiments as the product of subjects' causal inferences, definitive evidence for an attribution interpretation would require direct assessments of subjects' causal explanations such as those obtained in Eagly's studies (see Eagly et al., 1981 for more detailed discussion).

Theory of Correspondent Inferences

Edward E. Jones and Keith Davis (1965) proposed a theory of attribution that concerns perceivers' inferences that other people's behaviors are caused by their traits, attitudes, and other dispositional tendencies. For example, the theory addresses the factors that might lead observers to infer that a person who performs a helpful behavior is a kind person. This theory has some relevance to persuasion because message recipients often must infer communicators' attitudes and personality traits on the basis of other information they possess about the communicator (e.g., group membership), the communicator's behavior, and the context in which the behavior occurs (see also Jones & McGillis, 1976).

Jones and Davis suggested that the less a behavior is expected, given the *actor's* (i.e., person's) situation, the stronger is the perceiver's inference that the actor's dispositions correspond to the actor's behavior. For example, perceivers' inferences that an actor is aggressive should be stronger when the actor behaves aggressively toward a friendly rather than hostile person (Ajzen, 1971b; Lay, Burron, & Jackson, 1973). When applied to persuasion, this *principle of correspondent inference* predicts that the less a communicator's position is expected, given pressures in her situation, the stronger is the recipient's inference that the communicator's private attitude corresponds to the position she has publicly expressed. In our Treasury secretary example, your inference that the secretary's private attitude corresponds to his capital gains tax message should be much stronger when his message counters White House pressure (i.e., opposes reducing these taxes) than when it goes along with this pressure (i.e., supports reducing these taxes).

Eagly and her colleagues (1978) found support for this proposition of correspondent inference theory when situational pressures stemmed from the beliefs of an ostensibly present audience. That is, subjects rated the communicator's true attitude as more closely approximating his advocated position when this position countered rather than conformed to the views of the audience he addressed. More generally, this principle has been confirmed in experiments in which subjects have been asked to make inferences about actors' private attitudes on the basis of exposure to these actors' (ostensible) attitude statements and information about the context in which these statements were made (e.g., Jones & Harris, 1967; see Chapter 1).

Despite the relevance of the Jones and Davis (1965) analysis for predicting perceivers' inferences about communicators' private attitudes, we find it less useful for predicting persuasion than Kelley's (1967, 1972a) analyses, which concern causal attributions about the communication itself. When recipients contemplate the position that a communicator advocates on some issue, their central task is the explanation of this position. Of course, they may *also* perform a causal analysis to infer the communicator's dispositional characteristics. Yet, to decide whether the communicator's message is a valid description of external reality, they must determine whether these dispositions, along with situational pressures, can or cannot be ruled out as causes of the communicator's stated position. When dispositional biases and situational pressures are ruled out, messages are perceived to be more valid.

Intuitively, it may seem that perceivers' inferences about communicators' private attitudes and other dispositions should have direct implications for the persuasiveness of their advocacies (see, for example, Maass & Clark, 1984; Moscovici, 1976; Moscovici & Nemeth, 1974). Yet it is doubtful that this is so. On the one hand, it is true that the inference that communicators' private attitudes do not correspond to the positions they take in their messages covaries with the perception that communicators are untrustworthy and with reduced persuasion (e.g., Eagly et al., 1978). Nevertheless, these inferences of attitude-message noncorrespondence and communicator untrustworthiness stem from the congruence of the communicator's stated position with external pressures that are perceived to be acting upon him. And it is the causal prominence of these pressures and the consequent discounting of external reality as a viable cause for the communicator's advocated position that are the critical determinants of decreased message persuasiveness. Thus, attributions about the communicator's attitude bear only an indirect relation to persuasion (see also Chapter 13).

Evaluation of Attribution Perspective

Sufficient research has been conducted from the attributional perspective to warrant the conclusion that message recipients' causal attributions concerning communicators' stated positions are an important determinant of persuasion. Messages are persuasive when recipients believe that they accurately transmit the facts about the objects, issues, or persons they concern. The complexity in applying attributional principles to persuasion stems from the fact that many different types of information available to message recipients can be used in their search for causal explanations for communicators' messages. Notwithstanding this complexity, existing theory and research suggest that recipients make causal inferences about message validity on the basis of (a) consensus, consistency, and distinctiveness information gained from multiple observations of communicators and messages; (b) cues available in single persuasion situations that permit reasonable guesses about consensus, consistency, and distinctiveness; and (c) causally relevant communicator attributes and situational factors observed in single persuasion situations.

The general importance of attribution principles for understanding persuasion and other types of social influence such as majority and minority group influence has been widely recognized (e.g., Gottlieb & Ickes, 1978; Moscovici & Nemeth, 1974; L. Ross, Bierbrauer, & Hoffman, 1976; Sternthal, Phillips, & Dholakia, 1978; see Chapters 11 and 13). Yet attribution theory has not been developed to the fullest extent possible as a theory of attitude change.[6] Although Kelley's (1972a) analysis of multiple plausible causes has been developed as an explicit theory of persuasion by Eagly and her colleagues and successfully tested in a number of experiments, his ANOVA model of consensus, consistency, and distinctiveness (Kelley, 1967) has received only sporadic empirical attention by influence researchers (e.g., Himmelfarb, 1972; Maass & Clark, 1984). Still other aspects of attribution theory—for example, Kelley's (1972b) analysis of causal schemata—have not been explored at all in relation to social influence.

Because the existing literature on causal attributions and persuasion is relatively small, little is currently known regarding the conditions under which persuasion is most likely to be mediated by recipients' causal inferences. As Eagly and her colleagues (1981) themselves noted, because the attribution framework assumes that message recipients' prime motivation is to obtain valid attitudes, its utility in relation to predicting social influence when other motivational goals predominate may be limited. When, for example, a recipient's main goal is to gain rapport with a communicator, agreement may follow regardless of whether the recipient thinks the communicator's knowledge about the message topic is biased (see Eagly et al., 1981, for discussion). Moreover, within validity-seeking persuasion situations, the conditions under which recipients utilize the principles of causation stressed by the attribution framework in conjunction with or instead of other processing modes such as heuristic processing or argument-based processing are largely unexplored. According to the elaboration likelihood model, causal inferences—like other peripheral mechanisms—may be most likely to mediate persuasion under low elaboration likelihood conditions. This straightforward hypothesis could be tested by research that manipulated causally relevant persuasion cues in conjunction with argument quality and variables that have been implicated as motivators or enablers of argument processing (e.g., see Petty & Priester, 1991).

More complex, contingent predictions would follow from the perspective of the heuristic-systematic model because attributional reasoning is presumably more effortful and capacity limited than heuristic processing, yet less effortful and less capacity demanding than scrutinizing persuasive argumentation itself. Extrapolating from the basic tenets of the heuristic-systematic model, whether heuristic cues, causally relevant persuasion cues, or message content manipulations (indicative of argument processing) differ in their relative persuasive impact should depend upon a number of mutable factors: (a) situational and individual differences in people's abilities to engage in argument-based processing; (b) the cognitive availability, accessibility, and reliability of heuristics and, similarly, the availability, accessibility, and reliability of knowledge structures relevant to attributional reasoning; and (c) situational and individual differences in motivation to engage in effortful information processing (i.e., factors that may affect people's desired as well as actual levels of judgmental confidence). Moreover, in situations conducive to all three processing modes, the extent to which information furnished by the three modes contradicted one another would also need to be taken into account. For example, if argument-based processing contradicted the validity of an attributionally based inference about message validity, causally relevant contextual cues might exert little judgmental impact (i.e., an attenuation effect). Of course, to the extent that such information was not contradictory, additive effects might be predicted (see Chapter 7).

Despite the considerable (and largely unrealized) potential of attributional principles for understanding persuasion and other forms of social influence, it is important to point out that such principles can provide only a partial theory of attitude formation and change. This is because only some cues in social influence settings have causal relevance. Although this set of cues may be larger than those that have been investigated to date, there are clearly many other variables whose effects on attitude formation and change are mediated by nonattributional inferences and mechanisms.

Social Judgment Theory

Social judgment theory focuses on how people's prior attitudes distort their perceptions of the positions advocated in persuasive messages, and how such perceptions mediate persuasion. In general terms, the theory assumes that a recipient's own attitudinal position serves as a judgmental standard or *anchor* that influences where along an evaluative continuum a communicator's advocated position is perceived to lie. When the recipient *assimilates* this position toward her own attitude, persuasion is assumed to be facilitated. When, however, the recipient *contrasts* this position away from her own attitude, persuasion is assumed to be inhibited.

The theory grew out of Muzafer Sherif's and Carl Hovland's collaborative efforts to apply principles of psychophysical judgment to the domain of attitudes (Hovland & Sherif, 1952; M. Sherif & Hovland, 1953). They presented the theory in a monograph published just after Hovland's death (M. Sherif & Hovland, 1961), and Sherif developed it further in collaboration with Carolyn Wood Sherif (C. W. Sherif, Sherif, & Nebergall, 1965; M. Sherif & Sherif, 1967). The theory has also been called assimilation-contrast theory (e.g., Insko, 1967) and the social judgment–involvement approach (e.g., C. W. Sherif et al., 1965), alternate names that help distinguish it from other judgment models that have been applied to attitudinal responding (e.g., Eiser & Stroebe, 1972; Helson, 1964; Ostrom & Upshaw, 1968). These names also highlight the theory's key constructs: (a) assimilation and contrast effects in perception, and (b) ego-involvement, the extent to which an attitude is part of one's self-concept and thus "intimately felt and cherished" (C. W. Sherif et al., 1965, p. vi; M. Sherif & Cantril, 1947).

Because the perceptual phenomena of assimilation and contrast occur prior to the argument-based processing that epitomizes central route persuasion, Petty and Cacioppo (1981a, 1986b) classify social judgment theory as a peripheral theory of attitude change. As we have explained, peripheral theories for these authors include models that emphasize cognitive mechanisms (e.g., attribution approaches), models that emphasize affective mechanisms (e.g., classical conditioning), and models that emphasize motivational mechanisms (e.g., identification, psychological reactance; see Chapters 12 and 13). Social judgment theory accords motivation *and* cognition a role in persuasion. It recognizes the influence of motivation by its ego-involvement construct and the influence of cognition by its perceptual mechanisms of assimilation and contrast. Nonetheless, because the theory assumes that perceptual processes mediate the persuasive effects of ego-involvement and other distal variables, we chose to present the theory in this chapter.

It is important for readers to appreciate that social judgment theory is not only a theory of persuasion. In fact, this aspect of the theory is an application of its basic principles, which concern the impact of people's prior attitudes on the encoding of attitude-relevant information. The theory has thus been applied to the issue of whether judges' own attitudes influence the scale values assigned to belief statements in Thurstone scaling (see Chapter 2) and, more generally, to the issue of whether people's attitudes exert selective effects on their perception and evaluation of, and memory for attitude-relevant information. These empirical phenomena are discussed in Chapter 12 because of their centrality to the resistance-to-influence theme we emphasize there. Social judgment theorists' assumption that attitude is best conceptualized as a range of acceptable attitudinal positions rather than as a single point along an evaluative continuum also provides a model of intra-attitude structure. As discussed in Chapter 3, the theory posits a tripartite division of the evaluative continuum. Whereas the *latitude of acceptance* refers to that region of the continuum that contains beliefs about the attitude object that the individual considers acceptable—and within which his attitude lies—the *latitude of rejection* contains beliefs that are viewed as unacceptable, and the *latitude of noncommitment* contains beliefs that are considered neither acceptable nor unacceptable. As also explained in Chapter 3, latitude width is assumed to vary as a function of ego-involvement. Specifically, heightened involvement is assumed to produce wider latitudes of rejection and smaller latitudes of noncommitment. These structural assumptions figure prominently in the theory's analysis of persuasion.

FIGURE 8.2.
Distribution of
weight judgments
for a series of
stimulus weights
without a
judgmental anchor
(top panel) and with
"heavy" anchors
located at increasing
distances above the
stimulus series
(remaining panels).
The arrow to the
right of each series
represents the
position of the
anchor. These data
were reported by M.
Sherif, Taub, and
Hovland (1958), and
the figure was
presented by M.
Sherif and Hovland
(1961, Figure 4, p.
53).

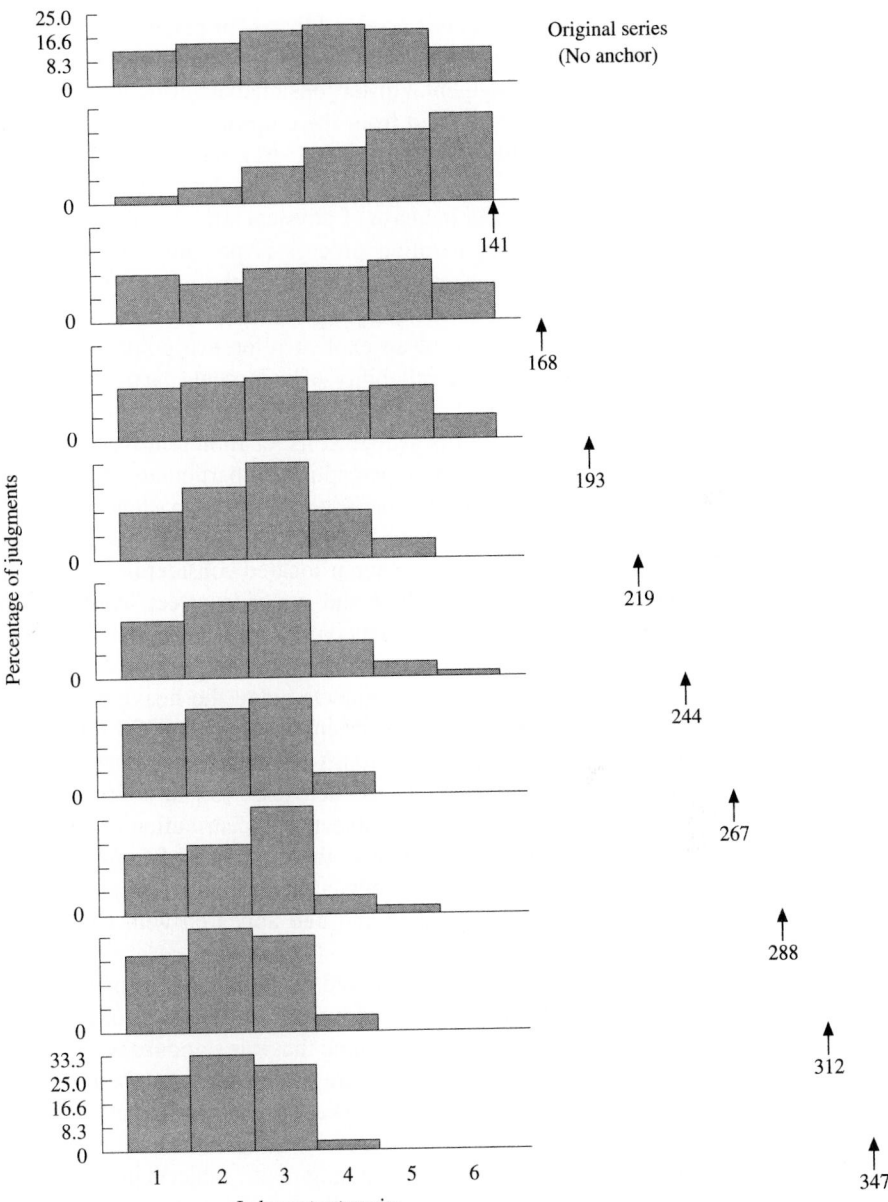

365

Assimilation and Contrast

Social judgment theory's essential thesis for persuasion is that people's prior attitudes produce systematic distortions in the way they perceive persuasive communications and that these judgmental distortions mediate attitude change. The first (and key) part of this thesis was derived from the empirical literature on psychophysical judgment. According to Sherif and Hovland (1961), the perception of social as well as physical stimuli involves categorizing these stimuli along meaningful psychological dimensions such as heaviness in the case of physical stimuli and favorability in the case of social stimuli. This categorization process is presumed to occur spontaneously, without people necessarily being aware of either the process or their judgments (M. Sherif & Hovland, 1961). The ensuing judgments, of course, are neither invariant nor perfectly reliable. The absence of an explicit reference point or standard, typically called an *anchor*, decreases the reliability of judgment, particularly for stimuli located in the middle range of psychological dimensions. More important for social judgment theory, even when an anchor is available, its location relative to the stimuli being judged can exert a distorting effect on perception. In particular, an anchor located at either end of the to-be-judged stimuli (or just beyond them) tends to produce *assimilation*—the judged stimuli are perceived to be closer or more similar to the anchor than they actually are. However, an anchor located considerably beyond the range of stimuli to be judged tends to produce the opposite effect, *contrast*—the judged stimuli are perceived to be more discrepant or more dissimilar to the anchor than they actually are.

Both of these judgmental effects were demonstrated by M. Sherif, Taub, and Hovland (1958), who had subjects judge the heaviness of a set of six weights that ranged between 55 and 141 grams. On each of 300 randomized trials (50 trials per weight), subjects were asked to lift a weight and assign it to one of six categories which ranged from "lightest" (1) to "heaviest" (6). In a first session, in which no explicit anchor was provided to the subjects, the distribution of their weight judgments proved nearly rectangular, as shown in the top panel of Figure 8.2. The pattern indicates a reasonable amount of accuracy, as the stimulus weights were evenly distributed over the weight range examined and had appeared with equal frequency across the 300 judgment trials.

The non-anchored series served as a comparison condition for subsequent judgment sessions in which a comparison weight of 141 grams or greater was introduced and the same subjects were told to assume that this standard was "heaviest" (i.e., 6). As shown in the remaining panels of Figure 8.2, the distance between this standard weight and the stimulus weights had a marked impact on judgment. Assimilation was observed when the anchor was equivalent to the heaviest stimulus weight (i.e., 141 grams): Relative to their non-anchored judgments, subjects judged a greater number of stimuli to be relatively heavy, and a smaller number to be relatively light. Little distortion was observed when a 168-gram anchor was introduced. However, starting with the 193-gram anchor, a contrast effect emerged. Moreover, increasing the discrepancy between the stimulus weights and the anchor weight in subsequent sessions generally increased the magnitude of this effect: Relative to the non-anchored series, subjects manifested an increasing tendency to judge most of the stimulus weights as relatively light and to judge fewer and fewer of them as relatively heavy. Similar effects were obtained in two replications of this experiment, one of which also used "heavy" anchors and one of which used "light" anchors (i.e., anchors located at increasingly discrepant points below the range of stimulus weights).

Social judgment theory assumes that similar anchoring effects characterize the perception of social stimuli, in particular attitudinal stimuli. Indeed, Sherif and Hovland (1961) believed that the judgmental distortions they and others had found with physical stimuli should be exacerbated with social stimuli due to their inherently greater complexity and ambiguity, stimulus factors known to decrease judgmental accuracy in the physical domain. In fact, a major caveat of social judgment theory is that stimulus ambiguity moderates the judgmental impact of anchors: Judgmental distortions should be minimal in the case of clear-cut, unambiguous attitudinal stimuli but sizable in the case of ambiguous stimuli (see M. Sherif & Hovland, 1961).

Attitudes As Judgmental Anchors

M. Sherif and colleagues' (1958) weights study investigated the impact of external physical anchors on the judgment of physical stimuli. Adopting a broader perspective, Sherif and Hovland (1961) asserted that social factors also serve as important judgmental standards in physical and social perception and that social anchors can be either external or internal to the perceiver. Indeed, Sherif's (1936) earlier work on social norms had already established that subjects' judgments of physical stimuli (a point of light that appeared to move) could be influenced by other people's judgments when subjects lacked access to spatial cues. In the absence of the internal anchors that such cues provide, Sherif argued, judgment is unstable and people depend more on external social standards in making their judgments (see Chapter 13). In contrast to this earlier focus on external social anchors or "frames of reference," Sherif and Hovland argued that a person's own attitude serves as a powerful *internal* reference point in the judgment of attitude-relevant information.

This key assertion was couched in terms of the theory's assumption that attitude statements can be ordered along an evaluative continuum that is structured in terms of three latitudes. Specifically, the widths of people's latitudes and the location of their preferred attitude position within the latitude of acceptance determine how they judge attitude statements. When a single statement or position advocated in a message falls within the latitude of acceptance or nearby in the latitude of noncommitment (M. Sherif & Sherif, 1967), assimilation occurs—the stimulus statement or position is seen as closer to the person's own attitude "anchor" than it truly is. Within this assimilation range true discrepancy is underestimated, and the magnitude of underestimation grows larger as true discrepancy increases. When an attitude statement or advocated position falls within the latitude of rejection or just outside this range in the latitude of noncommitment, contrast occurs—the statement or position is perceived to be farther from the person's own attitude than it truly is. Within this contrast range true discrepancy is overestimated, and the magnitude of overestimation grows larger as true discrepancy increases.

Explaining Attitude Change

We have so far explained the first part of social judgment theory's thesis for persuasion—people's existing attitudes distort their perception of the positions advocated in communicators' messages. The second part of this thesis is that these perceptual displacements mediate persuasion. How? Social judgment theorists' answer to this question was, unfortunately, a bit vague (M. Sherif & Hovland, 1961; M. Sherif & Sherif, 1967). Assimilating a message's advocated position toward one's own attitude leads the recipient to regard the message as "fair," "unbiased," and "factual," whereas contrasting a position away from one's own leads the recipient to regard the message as "unfair," "biased," "propagandistic," and "false" (M. Sherif & Sherif, 1967, p. 130). These evaluative responses to the message—which the theory describes only globally—apparently then determine persuasion.[7] When a communication falls within the latitude of acceptance, then, its position is assimilated, its content is positively evaluated, and attitude change occurs. Moreover, in this latitude (or nearby), greater levels of true discrepancy between the message's position and the recipient's own attitude lead to increasing degrees of assimilation and positive evaluation and, thus, to greater amounts of attitude change.[8] In parallel fashion, when a message falls within the latitude of rejection, its position is contrasted, its content is negatively evaluated, and attitude change is inhibited. In this latitude, higher levels of true discrepancy lead to increasing degrees of contrast and negative evaluation and, thus, to increasingly lesser amounts of attitude change. In fact, social judgment theorists further suggested that for recipients who were highly ego-involved in their attitudes, extreme levels of discrepancy might sometimes result in negative or *boomerang* attitude change, wherein recipients shift their attitudes in a direction opposite to that advocated in the message (see further discussion below).

In general, then, social judgment theory posits an inverted ∪-shaped relation between message discrepancy and attitude change. As discrepancy increases from minuscule to moderate, increasing amounts of attitude change should be observed since the message is likely to fall within the recipient's latitude of acceptance or just beyond it in the latitude of noncommitment. After this point, however, further increases in discrepancy should produce decreasing amounts of attitude change because the message is increasingly likely to fall within the latitude of rejection. Importantly, though, the location of the point along the discrepancy continuum where attitude change ceases to increase and starts to decline depends primarily on latitude width. This inflection point should occur at lower levels of true discrepancy for recipients whose latitudes of rejection are wider rather than narrower and, similarly, for recipients whose latitudes of acceptance are narrower rather than wider.

According to the theory, then, any factor that influences latitude widths should exert a corresponding influence on the shape of the relation between message discrepancy and persuasion. Heightened source credibility, for example, might function to extend recipients' latitudes of acceptance (M. Sherif & Sherif, 1967). As a consequence, the inflection point in the discrepancy-persuasion relation should occur at a lower level of discrepancy when the message source is lower in status, expertise, or trustworthiness. To cite another example, Sherif and Hovland (1961) suggested that recipients who lack established (i.e., strong) attitudes should have very broad latitudes of acceptance. If so, the discrepancy-persuasion relationship ought to prove predominantly positive for such persons, even at relatively high discrepancy levels. Although other width-affecting factors might be postulated, social judgment theory accords a special role to one, the recipient's degree of ego-involvement in her attitude.

Role of Ego-Involvement

We have so far described a cognitive theory of persuasion. The motivational side of social judgment theory resides in its construct of ego-involvement. In a book that predated the theory, M. Sherif and Cantril (1947) defined ego-involved attitudes as those that are part of the person's self-concept or "ego," attitudes that "have the characteristic of belonging to *me*, as being part of *me*" (p. 93). They thus viewed such attitudes as inextricably linked to other aspects of the self; in particular, to important group memberships and identifications, and to related social and personal values (see also Chapters 3 and 10). Because of this link to the self, Sherif and Cantril (1947) viewed ego-involvement as having important motivational and affective consequences:

> This degree of ego-involvement, this intensity of attitudes, will determine in large part which attitudes he will cling to, how annoyed or frustrated he will feel when his attitudes are opposed, what action (within the range of his individual temperament and ability) he will take to further his point of view (p. 131).

In developing social judgment theory, M. Sherif and his collaborators retained the Sherif-Cantril definition of involvement. As a consequence, they most often operationalized this construct in terms of subjects' memberships in or identification with groups that were known to actively support particular positions on various social or political issues. Hovland, Harvey, and Sherif's (1957) study of prohibition attitudes exemplifies this strategy. Conducted in the (then) "dry" state of Oklahoma where a referendum to repeal prohibition had recently failed by a small vote margin, the researchers compared two groups of involved subjects and one group of uninvolved subjects in terms of their responses to communications on the prohibition issue. Ego-involved "dry" subjects were drawn from several sources: Women's Christian Temperance Union groups, Salvation Army workers, and students who were either preparing for the ministry or were enrolled in strict denominational colleges. Reflecting their difficulty in finding intact groups from which to recruit ego-involved "wet" subjects, the research team ultimately secured a much smaller sample of such subjects from among their own acquaintances! Finally, students enrolled in college courses such as education, chemistry, and speech were recruited because of the presumption that they were "uninvolved" in the prohibition issue. We shall discuss the results of this well-known (and much criticized) experiment in the following section.

Social judgment theory assumes that exposure to discrepant attitude positions creates little "tension" or "incongruity" for the uninvolved person, but a great deal of psychological discomfort for the ego-involved person (M. Sherif & Sherif, 1967, p. 130). The ego-involved person "perceives his stands as parts of what *he* is and what he claims to be.... His personal identity and the stability of his conception of himself depend in no small part on the stability and perpetuation of his stands" (M. Sherif & Hovland, 1961, p. 206). Because of this need to maintain and protect the self-concept, the ego-involved person is presumed by the theory to become highly engaged in attitude-relevant tasks and to encode attitudinal information in a highly personalized, self-protective manner. By contrast, the uninvolved person is presumed to be less personally engaged in such tasks and to encode attitudinal information in a relatively detached, objective, factual manner (M. Sherif & Hovland, 1961).

These motivational assumptions are integrated with cognitive aspects of the theory in two main ways. First, ego-involvement is assumed to strengthen the anchoring effects of prior attitudes—the more involved the individual is, the more likely it is that his or her attitude will serve as an internal reference point in judging attitudinal stimuli. This anchor-strengthening assumption is central to the theory because it leads directly to its proposition that the *magnitude* of assimilation-contrast tendencies in attitudinal perception should be a positive function of ego-involvement (M. Sherif & Hovland, 1961; M. Sherif & Sherif, 1967). In other words, the tendency to assimilate a message that falls within the latitude of acceptance should be greater for the highly involved recipient than for the uninvolved recipient; similarly, the involved person should manifest a greater tendency to contrast a message that falls within the latitude of rejection.

The second way in which motivation enters the theory is via its proposition that involvement affects latitude width. Although the terms latitude of acceptance and rejection may connote "cool" cognitive concepts to some readers, M. Sherif and Hovland (1961) conceptualized these regions in motivational terms and assumed that ego-involvement would exert a marked influence on people's tolerance for beliefs different from their own. Initially, they hypothesized that ego-involved attitudes would be characterized by broader latitudes of rejection *and* narrower latitudes of acceptance. In most studies designed to test this hypothesis, subjects who were assumed to vary in involvement with respect to some issue (e.g., legalized abortion) indicated which of a set of evaluatively ordered attitude statements they considered acceptable and which they considered objectionable (e.g., Hovland et al., 1957; Larsen, 1971; C. W. Sherif, 1980; C. W. Sherif et al., 1965). These selected statements operationalized subjects' latitudes of acceptance and rejection, respectively. Nonselected statements operationalized subjects' latitudes of noncommitment (see Chapter 3).

The results of these studies and related ones in which latitude width was inferred from sorting tasks only partially supported this hypothesis (e.g., Hovland & Sherif, 1952; M. Sherif & Hovland, 1953; see C. W. Sherif, 1980, for a review). Heightened ego-involvement was typically associated with broader latitudes of rejection *and* small-to-nonexistent latitudes of noncommitment. But involvement bore little relation to the width of subjects' latitudes of acceptance. For this reason, later statements of the theory emphasized the putatively more defensible proposition that involvement primarily affects the relative sizes of the latitudes of rejection and noncommitment: Whereas high involvement attitudes are assumed to be characterized by a broad latitude of rejection and little, if any, latitude of noncommitment, low involvement attitudes are assumed to be characterized by a broad latitude of noncommitment and a small latitude of rejection (C. W. Sherif, 1980; C. W. Sherif et al., 1965; M. Sherif & Sherif, 1967).[9]

We should mention one other apparent consequence of ego-involvement. As noted earlier, social judgment theorists suggested that ego-involved recipients might exhibit boomerang attitude change in response to extremely discrepant messages. Indeed, some writers have treated this hypothesis as an integral part of social judgment theory (e.g., Eiser, 1980; Kiesler, Collins, & Miller, 1969). The hypothesis seems to have been put forth in more of a speculative vein, however (see M. Sherif & Hovland, 1961, p. 174; M. Sherif & Sherif, 1967, p. 134). Moreover, it does not follow readily from the theory's core propositions (summarized below). As such, we believe that this hypothesis is best construed as an extra-theoretical statement that reflects social judgment theorists' beliefs about the motivational significance of ego-involvement.

Empirical Predictions and Illustrative Findings

Social judgment theory's core propositions can be summarized as follows:

1. A person's own attitude serves as a judgmental anchor in encoding attitudinal stimuli.
2. Latitude widths determine whether a message's advocated position will be assimilated or contrasted. Positions falling within the latitude of acceptance (or nearby in the latitude of noncommitment) will be assimilated toward the recipient's own attitude. Positions falling within the latitude of rejection (or nearby in the latitude of noncommitment) will be contrasted away from the recipient's own attitude.
3. Ego-involvement broadens the latitude of rejection and narrows the latitude of noncommitment.
4. Both assimilation and contrast effects increase as a positive function of message discrepancy (the distance between the message's position and the recipient's own attitude).
5. Ego-involvement increases the anchoring property of initial attitudes, so that both assimilation and contrast effects are amplified for ego-involved recipients.
6. Greater assimilation produces more positive evaluations of message content which, in turn, produce greater amounts of attitude change (but see note 8). Conversely, greater contrast produces more negative evaluations of message content which, in turn, produce lesser amounts of attitude change.
7. Stimulus ambiguity enhances the likelihood of judgmental distortions. Therefore propositions 4–6 should be more apparent when recipients are exposed to persuasive messages whose positions (or, perhaps, content) are ambiguous.

Figure 8.3 portrays social judgment theory's predictions regarding the persuasive impact of message discrepancy and ego-involvement. To better understand the figure, assume that our messages deal with the issue of abortion and advocate positions

FIGURE 8.3. Sketch of social judgment theory's predictions regarding the persuasive impact of message discrepancy and ego-involvement. Width of the latitudes of acceptance (LA), noncommitment (LNC), and rejection (LR) are shown at the top of the figure for an involved recipient and at the bottom of the figure for an uninvolved recipient; the two recipients possess the same prior attitude (X), which reflects a relatively extreme pro-life position on abortion. The persuasion curves for the involved and uninvolved recipient are denoted by solid and broken lines, respectively.

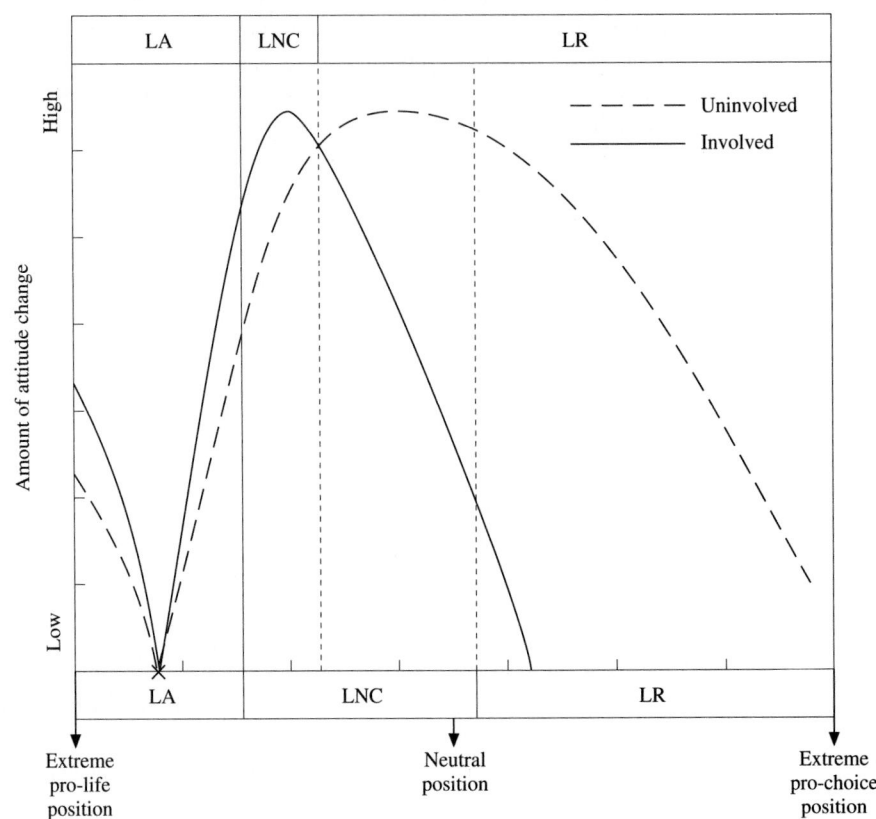

ranging from extreme pro-life to extreme pro-choice (left and right anchors on the abscissa). The figure portrays the discrepancy-persuasion relationship for two hypothetical recipients. Both hold a relatively extreme pro-life position (denoted by X on the abscissa), but differ in their level of ego-involvement. The widths of their latitudes therefore differ as shown at the top (involved recipient) and bottom (uninvolved recipient) of the figure (Proposition 3). Messages whose positions fall to the left of the recipients' position advocate more extreme pro-life positions, thus earning the label *proattitudinal* (or "consonant"). Messages whose positions lie between the recipients' position and the abscissa's midpoint advocate less extreme pro-life positions and can therefore also be labeled proattitudinal (though they are not always labeled so in the literature). Finally, messages whose positions lie to the right of the midpoint advocate increasingly extreme pro-choice positions. Such positions are truly *counterattitudinal* for our pro-life recipients, and have been labeled this way by most investigators.[10]

Effects of Message Discrepancy. The figure illustrates (for both recipients) social judgment theory's prediction of an inverted ∪-shaped relationship between message discrepancy and persuasion: When messages are assimilated (LA and approximately half of LNC), increased discrepancy increases persuasion; however, when messages are contrasted (remaining part of the LNC and the LR), increased discrepancy decreases persuasion (Propositions 1, 2, 4, 6). Data approximating this pattern have indeed been observed in some experiments (e.g., Aronson, Turner, & Carlsmith, 1963; Bochner & Insko, 1966; Freedman, 1964; Insko, Murashima, & Saiyadain, 1966; H. H. Johnson, 1966; P. D. Peterson & Koulack, 1969; White, 1975, Experiment 3). Yet such curvilinear trends have not always proven statistically reliable, primarily because decrements in persuasion typically occur only at the very highest discrepancy levels examined and, moreover, are often negligible in magnitude. Also, some studies have failed to detect any turndown even at extreme levels of discrepancy (e.g., White, 1975, Experiments 1, 2, and 4). Over most discrepancy levels that investigators have explored, persuasion tends to be a positive, negatively accelerated function of discrepancy (McGuire, 1985).[11]

More interesting theoretically are interactions between discrepancy and other variables. As we have explained, social judgment theory predicts that the point of maximum attitude change in the discrepancy-persuasion relationship depends upon latitude width (Proposition 2). Thus, variations in respondents' latitudes should interact with discrepancy, as should any other independent variable that affects latitude width. Figure 8.3 illustrates this interaction prediction in relation to ego-involvement: Maximum persuasion occurs at a lower discrepancy level for the involved recipient than for the uninvolved recipient. Importantly, studies exploring such interactions have typically featured no more than three levels of discrepancy. Thus, with few exceptions (e.g., Bochner & Insko, 1966), they have been designed to discover gross differences in the shape of the discrepancy-persuasion relationship rather than the fine differences illustrated in Figure 8.3.

Rhine and Severance (1970) found that persuasion increased linearly across three levels of message discrepancy for low involvement subjects. In contrast, high involvement subjects indicated lower levels of persuasion, regardless of message discrepancy (see also Freedman, 1964). Although these data are roughly consistent with social judgment theory, other results have been less congenial (e.g., Eagly, 1967; Rule & Renner, 1968). In particular, Eagly (1967; counterattitudinal message condition) found less overall persuasion for high than low involvement subjects. However, the discrepancy-persuasion relation was virtually identical for the two subject groups—persuasion increased as discrepancy changed from low to moderate, but then leveled off as discrepancy changed from moderate to high (see further discussion of these experiments below).

If it is assumed that heightened source credibility increases the width of the latitude of acceptance or, alternately, narrows the latitude of rejection (M. Sherif & Sherif, 1967), the theory predicts that maximum persuasion should occur at a lower level of message discrepancy when communicators lack credibility. Aronson and colleagues (1963) produced data consistent with this prediction. Persuasion generally increased across three levels of discrepancy in the case of messages attributed to a high credibility source (the poet T. S. Eliot). In contrast, persuasion first increased and then substantially decreased in the case of messages attributed to a low credibility source ("Agnes Stearns, a student at a southern college"; see also Bergin, 1962; McGinnies, 1973). Bochner and Insko (1966) examined a broader range of discrepancies by exposing subjects to high or low credibility sources whose messages advocated sleeping 8, 7, 6, 5, 4, 3, 2, 1, or 0 hours per night. Consistent with Aronson and colleagues' data, maximum persuasion occurred at a lower level of discrepancy in the low credibility conditions (3-hour message) than in the high credibility conditions (1-hour message). On the other hand, subjects tended to agree *less* with the high compared to low credibility source at moderate levels of discrepancy (i.e., 6-, 5-, 4-, and 3-hour messages). This finding is less consistent with social judgment theory because of the theory's assumption that heightened credibility increases the latitude of acceptance (or decreases the latitude of rejection). Although latitudes were not assessed by Bochner and Insko, if this assumption were valid, their subjects ought to have agreed more with the high (vs. low) credibility source at these moderate levels of discrepancy.[12]

Finally, studies that have measured subjects' latitude widths and assessed the effects of this variable in conjunction with discrepancy have also proven somewhat problematic for social judgment theory (e.g., Atkins, Deaux, & Bieri, 1967; Eagly & Telaak, 1972). Eagly and Telaak's (1972) study provided a particularly stringent test of social judgment theory by assessing not only attitude change but also subjects' perceptions of the position advocated in the message they received and their evaluation of message content (e.g., perceived fairness, unbiasedness). In the study, pro-contraception subjects with small, medium, or wide (measured) latitudes of acceptance received an anti-contraception message that was either slightly, moderately, or highly discrepant with their own attitudes. The slightly discrepant message fell within all subjects' latitudes of acceptance, and the highly discrepant message fell within almost all subjects' latitudes of rejection. Thus, only the moderately discrepant message had a variable location in relation to subjects' latitudes—it fell within the latitude of rejection for *small* latitude-of-acceptance subjects, but within the latitude of acceptance for increasing proportions of *medium-* and *wide*-latitude-of-acceptance subjects. Thus, social judgment theory predicts that the three subject groups should differ in persuasion—as well as in message perception and message evaluation—primarily in response to the study's moderately discrepant message.

The results of the study showed that subjects with wide latitudes of acceptance were more persuaded than subjects with either medium or small latitudes of acceptance (who did not differ from one another). In contrast to social judgment theory, however, this effect did not interact with message discrepancy. Subjects' message perception and message evaluation ratings also failed to yield this interaction. More troubling for the theory, neither of the latter measures were influenced by latitude width. Thus, consistent with the theory, persuasion proved greater for subjects with wider rather than narrower latitudes of acceptance. However, this effect was apparently not mediated by either differences in subjects' perceptions of the positions advocated in the experimental messages or differences in their global evaluations of these messages. These and other findings of the study led Eagly and Telaak to conclude that the width of the latitude of acceptance is an issue-specific index of influenceability, not because it spawns the biased perception and message evaluation processes specified by social judgment theory, but because it reflects people's certainty about their own attitudinal positions. Specifically, wide latitudes may be associated with low certainty and confidence, and narrow latitudes may be associated with high certainty and confidence (see also Chapter 3). This "attitude strength" conceptualization of latitude width has been widely accepted by researchers (see Chapters 4 and 12).

Ego-Involvement. In most tests of social judgment theory, ego-involvement (not discrepancy) has been the featured independent variable. Like most persuasion research, the vast majority of these studies have utilized counterattitudinal messages. In the context of Figure 8.3, for example, our hypothetical pro-life recipients might be exposed to a moderate-to-high discrepant message that advocates a pro-choice position on the abortion issue. Given such counterattitudinal messages, social judgment theory predicts less persuasion for ego-involved recipients (Propositions 2, 3, 6). The right half of Figure 8.3 illustrates this basic hypothesis as well as the more subtle one that involvement differences in persuasibility increase in magnitude as counterattitudinal messages become more extreme (Proposition 5). Because relevant studies have typically examined only two or three levels of message discrepancy, this more subtle hypothesis has remained untested.

As the left half of Figure 8.3 indicates, it is possible that our hypothetical recipients might encounter communications advocating pro-life positions either more extreme or less extreme than their own pro-life position. When such proattitudinal messages fall within the latitude of acceptance or nearby in the latitude of noncommitment, persuasion should increase as discrepancy increases; outside this assimilation band, of course, persuasion should decrease as discrepancy increases (Propositions 2, 4, 6). Given this situation, how does ego-involvement affect susceptibility to proattitudinal persuasive messages? As depicted in the figure, our involved recipient will clearly be less influenced than our uninvolved recipient by proattitudinal messages that lie outside the involved recipient's latitude of noncommitment (see area between end of involved recipient's LNC and midpoint of figure's abscissa; Propositions 2, 3, 4, 6). More important, however, the figure also reveals that our involved recipient should be *more* influenced than our uninvolved recipient by proattitudinal messages that lie within *both* recipients' bands of assimilation (Proposition 5; see area between left end of abscissa and end of involved recipient's LNC). In summary, then, social judgment theory predicts that heightened ego-involvement should *reduce* susceptibility to counterattitudinal messages and proattitudinal messages that fall beyond involved recipients' latitudes of noncommitment. However, it also predicts that higher ego-involvement should *enhance* susceptibility to proattitudinal messages that would be assimilated by both involved and uninvolved persons.[13]

The first explicit test of ego-involvement's effects on persuasion was conducted by Hovland, Harvey, and Sherif (1957). As we noted earlier, these researchers operationalized ego-involvement in terms of their subjects' known or presumed investment in the

TABLE 8.2

Design of the Hovland, Harvey, and Sherif (1957) Prohibition Study

	Message type		
Subject group	*Extreme wet*	*Moderate wet*	*Extreme dry*
Wet–involved	—	X	X
Moderate–uninvolved	X	X	X
Dry–involved	X	X	—

Note: The two dashes indicate the missing cells of this non-factorial experimental design.

topic of prohibition. Three subject groups were recruited: "dry" ego-involved subjects (e.g., members of Women's Christian Temperance Union groups), "wet" ego-involved subjects (acquaintances of the researchers known for their anti-prohibition stance), and "moderate" uninvolved subjects (unselected college students). In the main phase of the study, subjects listened to either an extreme "dry" message, an extreme "wet" message, or a "moderately wet" message, and then indicated their attitudes and other responses. Unlike most persuasion researchers, Hovland and colleagues did not implement a full factorial design. As shown in Table 8.2, the moderately wet message was heard by dry, wet, and moderate subjects. However, the wet message was heard only by dry and moderate subjects, and the dry message was heard only by wet and moderate subjects. Involvement's effect on responses to truly proattitudinal messages was therefore not examined in this study.

The main dependent measures investigated in this study were subjects' perceptions of the position advocated in the experimental messages, their global evaluations of the messages, and their post-message attitudes. The message perception data, which were collected only in relation to the study's moderately wet message, proved consistent with social judgment theory predictions. Whereas subjects with moderate positions perceived this message accurately, involved subjects contrasted it: Wet subjects judged it to be drier than it truly was, and dry subjects judged it to be wetter. Subjects' evaluations of the messages also conformed to predictions. For example, the dry message was evaluated most positively by dry subjects and least positively by wet subjects, and the moderately wet message was evaluated most positively by moderate subjects, and least positively by dry subjects. Finally, although the attitude change data were somewhat weak, they too proved consistent with theoretical expectations: Dry involved subjects were less persuaded by the extreme wet message than moderate subjects, and wet involved subjects were less persuaded by the extreme dry message than moderate subjects. Unfortunately, group comparisons for the moderately wet message were not reported by the authors.

Although the Hovland et al. (1957) data appear to offer relatively strong support for social judgment theory, the study elicited a litany of methodological criticisms (e.g., Kiesler et al., 1969; N. Miller, 1965). Most notable among these, Hovland and colleagues had confounded ego-involvement with the extremity of their subjects' prior attitudes. Moreover, their procedures for selecting subjects left open the further possibility that "dry," "wet," and "moderate" subjects differed on a host of other individual difference dimensions (e.g., age, intelligence; for an exhaustive discussion of the study's deficiencies, see Kiesler et al., 1969). Because these methodological inadequacies stemmed almost entirely from Hovland and colleagues' group membership approach to operationalizing involvement, subsequent investigators sought out other ways of operationalizing this construct. Some maintained an individual difference approach by identifying high and low involvement groups on the basis of the relative widths of subjects' latitudes or self-report measures of involvement (e.g., L. Powell, 1977; Sereno, 1968). For the most part, however, researchers developed experimental manipulations of involvement. For example, some presented subjects with messages on topics known (or assumed) to be involving or with messages on uninvolving topics (Rhine & Severance, 1970; C. W. Sherif, Kelly, Rodgers, Sarup, & Tittler, 1973). Such studies eliminate the possibility (inherent in individual difference studies) that involvement will be confounded with extraneous subject characteristics, but create the possibility that this variable will be confounded with idiosyncratic differences in message content. Nonetheless, these studies and most individual difference studies yielded data indicating less persuasion for high (vs. low) involvement subjects exposed to counterattitudinal messages.

To avoid confounds such as these, other investigators devised alternate, and often quite complex, procedures for manipulating ego-involvement. For example, Eagly (1967) had pairs of male subjects consider their probable behavior in various conflict situations and then rate either themselves or their partners in terms of assertiveness. Subsequently, subjects who had rated themselves received a message concerning their own assertiveness (high involvement), whereas subjects who had rated their partners received a message concerning their partner's assertiveness (low involvement). When this message stated that the subject/partner was less assertive than his initial rating, high involvement subjects were less persuaded than low involvement subjects (regardless of discrepancy; see earlier description of this study). However, when the message stated that the subject/partner was more assertive, high involvement subjects were more persuaded than low involvement subjects (discrepancy was not manipulated in this message condition). In line with social judgment theory, then, involvement reduced persuasion when the message was counterattitudinal (i.e., the "less assertive" message) but enhanced persuasion when the message was proattitudinal (i.e., the "more assertive" message). According to the theory, these effects presumably stemmed from high (vs. low) involvement subjects' greater tendencies to assimilate the proattitudinal message and to contrast the counterattitudinal message. However, subjects' perceptions of the position advocated in these messages failed to substantiate this expectation (i.e., the involvement effect proved non-significant for both types of messages).

Norman Miller (1965) used a combination of procedures to heighten some subjects' involvement in their initial attitudes toward fluoridation prior to presenting them with a counterattitudinal message on this topic. Specifically, "high involvement" subjects were told that this issue was important and that others felt the same way as they did;

moreover, they were then asked to list reasons that supported their attitudes and, lastly, were induced to commit themselves to distributing attitudinally congruent literature at a later date. "Low involvement" subjects were subjected to the same procedures with respect to an irrelevant topic (math and science) before being exposed to the fluoridation message. Although Miller's attitude change data showed that high involvement subjects were less persuaded by the study's counterattitudinal message, his latitude data failed to support the theory's assumption that heightened involvement increases the latitude of rejection.[14]

Although numerous other manipulations have been labeled "involvement" in the literature, most have questionable relevance to the issue of how *ego-involvement* impacts on persuasion (e.g., "issue involvement" or "personal relevance": Apsler & Sears, 1968; Petty & Cacioppo, 1979b, 1984b; "response involvement": Zimbardo, 1960; see also Freedman, 1964; Halverson & Pallak, 1978; Pallak, Mueller, Dollar, & Pallak, 1972, Experiment 1). In an attempt to clarify existing literature, B. T. Johnson and Eagly (1989) suggested that the term *value-relevant* involvement replace the term ego-involvement because true manipulations of this construct, in their view, make salient for subjects the relevance of their attitudes to important, self-defining values, or the values of important reference groups. Certain other manipulations, they argue, are better labeled *impression-relevant* involvement because they make salient for subjects the self-presentational consequences of their (to-be-expressed) post-message attitudes (e.g., Leippe & Elkin, 1987, response involvement conditions; Zimbardo, 1960). They also reject the idea (Petty & Cacioppo, 1981a, 1986b) that personal relevance (or issue involvement) manipulations are valid operationalizations of ego-involvement (i.e., value-relevant involvement). In Johnson and Eagly's view, these currently popular involvement manipulations make salient to subjects the relevance of an issue to their current goals or outcomes and should be labeled *outcome-relevant* involvement. Although this second distinction has engendered some debate (Johnson & Eagly, 1990; Petty & Cacioppo, 1990), the results of Johnson and Eagly's (1989) meta-analysis of involvement research support their conceptual distinctions insofar as the three types of involvement do appear to exert different effects on response to persuasive communications.

As noted earlier in this book, meta-analysis applies descriptive and inferential statistics to samples of experimental results (see Hedges & Olkin, 1985). Johnson and Eagly (1989) meta-analyzed a large sample of involvement studies in order to explore the effects of value-relevant, outcome-relevant, and impression-relevant involvement on the persuasiveness of counterattitudinal messages.[15] As predicted, heightened value-relevant involvement inhibited persuasion for both strongly argued and weakly argued persuasive messages. This result is consistent with social judgment theory's predictions and the research we have reviewed in this section. In contrast, heightened outcome-relevant involvement was found to enhance persuasion for strongly argued messages but to reduce persuasion for weakly argued ones. This result is consistent with the hypothesis of the elaboration likelihood and heuristic-systematic models that this type of involvement increases recipients' motivation for systematic processing, and squares with our own review of research that has manipulated this construct (see Chapters 6 and 7). In contrast to the view that the effects of outcome-relevant involvement are problematic for social judgment theory (Petty & Cacioppo, 1979b, 1981a), we conclude (in harmony with Johnson and Eagly) that these effects are irrelevant indicators of this theory's worth, because it claims explanatory power only in relation to the effects of value-relevant involvement (i.e., ego-involvement). Finally, the meta-analysis revealed that impression-relevant involvement tended to reduce persuasion slightly, regardless of argument quality. Johnson and Eagly viewed this finding as supportive of their hypothesis that impression-relevant involvement leads recipients to adopt neutral, socially defensible positions, but warned that their small sample of studies of this type disallowed strong conclusions. Nonetheless, we conclude (primarily on conceptual grounds) that the persuasive effects of impression-relevant involvement are also irrelevant to social judgment theory.

Evaluation of Social Judgment Theory

After inspiring a relatively large amount of persuasion research during the 1960s and early 1970s, social judgment theory declined in popularity. To some extent, this decline can be attributed simply to the emergence of new theories that interested researchers more. In particular, William McGuire's (e.g., 1968a) reception-yielding framework and Anthony Greenwald's (1968) cognitive response model attracted attention. Unlike dissonance theory (see note 12), these models seldom entered into predictive contention with social judgment theory.[16] Nonetheless, as they gained popularity with persuasion researchers, social judgment theory waned.

Of course, reasons other than mere fashion also played a role in social judgment theory's decline. As discussed in Chapter 6, the reception-yielding and cognitive response models stimulated research on a broad range of distal persuasion variables. Social judgment theory's quarry, by contrast, remained small. Its clearest predictions concern message discrepancy and ego-involvement. Although the theory can also predict the persuasive impact of other independent variables if these variables can be assumed to influence latitude widths, few variables other than source credibility have been researched or even identified (see M. Sherif & Hovland, 1961; M. Sherif & Sherif, 1967). Moreover, the strategy of searching for variables that influence latitude width is reasonable only if latitude width operates in the manner prescribed by the theory—by determining whether a message is assimilated or contrasted. Unfortunately, this and other mediational assumptions have fared less well in empirical tests than the theory's overall attitude change predictions, an outcome that no doubt further reduced the theory's appeal among investigators.

Consider the theory's key variable, ego-involvement. The prediction that heightened ego-involvement inhibits persuasion when messages are counterattitudinal has been supported in numerous studies. Although few studies have used proattitudinal messages, their results have also confirmed the theory's prediction that involvement can enhance persuasion when such messages advocate positions more extreme than recipients' prior attitudes. In contrast to the theory, however, it is not clear that ego-involvement has a reliable impact on latitude width (N. Miller, 1965) or, more importantly, that ego-involvement has a reliable impact on message perception (i.e., assimilation-contrast; Eagly, 1967). As a second example, consider the width of the latitude of acceptance. Although this variable has been shown to relate positively to persuasion, research casts doubt on whether this relation is mediated by the perceptual processes of assimilation-contrast (Eagly & Telaak, 1972). Finally, although source credibility has been shown to moderate the persuasive impact of message discrepancy as the theory predicts, existing data cast doubt on whether source credibility affects latitude width and, as a consequence, alters message perception (Bochner & Insko, 1966).

In summary, although social judgment theory's attitude change predictions have often been borne out, existing research provides little, if any, convincing evidence that the perceptual processes of assimilation and contrast covary with attitude change, let alone *precede* attitude change as the theory maintains. In fact, some researchers have suggested that such perceptual displacements may represent responses that *substitute* for shifts in recipients' attitudes. In other words, recipients might change their attitudes or, alternatively, view the communicator's position as little different from their own (obviating the need for attitude change; see notes 8 and 13) or displace the communicator's position away from their own (again obviating the need for attitude change; see Eagly & Telaak, 1972; Lammers & Becker, 1980; Ostrom, Steele, & Smilansky, 1974). Finally, other researchers have questioned whether assimilation and contrast effects represent true distortions in the way people *perceive* objects and issues (e.g., Eiser, 1980; Eiser & Stroebe, 1972; Ostrom & Upshaw, 1968; Upshaw, 1969, 1978). Upshaw's (e.g., 1969) variable perspective model, for example, assumes that differences in people's judgments of stimuli stem from changes and differences in the underlying reference scales that they use in describing stimuli. And Eiser and Stroebe's (1972) accentuation theory suggests that apparent shifts in judgment can sometimes be attributed to differences in the evaluative connotations of the particular words that researchers use to anchor the extreme ends of response scales. Although both models have received empirical support, more recent discussions of this issue suggest that assimilation and contrast effects can be regarded as genuine perceptual effects in at least some attitudinal contexts (e.g., Judd, Kenny, & Krosnick, 1983; Romer, 1983; see Chapter 12).

Because existing research has largely failed to document the idea that the perceptual processes of assimilation and contrast play an important role in persuasion, it might seem that social judgment theory has little to offer contemporary investigators. Such a view would be unwarranted, however, because the theory provides insights about the persuasion process that are valuable even if its assumption that the perceptual phenomena of assimilation and contrast mediate persuasion is ignored.[17] Most important among these insights is the idea that ego-involved recipients evaluate persuasive messages in a biased manner, that is, by judging counterattitudinal messages to be unfair and propagandistic and proattitudinal messages to be fair and objective. This selective evaluation mechanism provides a plausible explanation for findings indicating that ego-involvement inhibits persuasion in the case of counterattitudinal messages but can enhance persuasion in the case of proattitudinal messages that advocate positions more extreme than recipients' own attitudes.

As noted earlier, social judgment theorists described recipients' evaluative responses to persuasive messages only globally (e.g., M. Sherif & Hovland, 1961; M. Sherif & Sherif, 1967). Thus, it is unclear whether they viewed these cognitive responses as superficial evaluations of message content or more specific reactions to persuasive argumentation (see also note 7). The few experiments that have assessed message evaluation are uninformative on this point because the self-report measures they used cannot distinguish between these two levels of processing (e.g., Eagly & Telaak, 1972; Hovland et al., 1957). From the perspective of the heuristic-systematic and elaboration likelihood models, both interpretations are plausible. For example, using their prior attitudes as a standard, ego-involved recipients may reject counterattitudinal messages outright because they doubt that such messages contain valid information. Similarly, they may accept proattitudinal messages outright because they assume that such messages are valid. Of course, uninvolved recipients might also invoke such a "prior attitude" heuristic (Chaiken, Liberman, & Eagly, 1989; Liberman, De La Hoz, & Chaiken, 1988). Thus, to account for involvement differences in persuasion, one would have to assume that prior attitudes are more accessible for ego-involved recipients, perhaps because they hold their attitudes with greater certainty and confidence (see Chapters 3 and 4).

Alternatively (or in addition), ego-involvement might bias recipients' processing of persuasive argumentation. In the context of the elaboration likelihood model, ego-involvement would thus be regarded as a variable that motivates biased message processing or, assuming that it covaries with the accessibility of prior attitudes and knowledge, a variable that enables biased message processing. In the context of the heuristic-systematic model, the accessibility logic would imply that ego-involvement is a cognitive factor that can bias accuracy-motivated systematic processing. Alternatively, ego-involvement can be represented motivationally by assuming that it instigates a defense-motivated processing strategy in which recipients attempt to confirm the validity of attitudinally congruent messages and disconfirm the validity of incongruent ones. As we explained in Chapter 7, such a processing goal should foster not only selective systematic processing but also selective heuristic processing. Thus, to the extent that a defense-motivated processing strategy characterizes the ego-involved (vs. uninvolved) recipient, she should be more prone to attend to and positively elaborate proattitudinal argumentation *and also* more likely to invoke heuristics that would confirm rather than disconfirm the validity of proattitudinal messages.

Finally, we note that social judgment theory is unique in that it accords people's prior attitudes an important causal role in persuasion. Most other cognitive theories of persuasion have dealt with this variable only tangentially. Moreover, although most researchers would surely agree that prior attitudes play some role in persuasion, this variable has been neglected empirically. Many contemporary persuasion experiments do not even assess prior attitudes. In these "after-only" designs, subjects' preexperimental attitudes are typically assumed to be opposed to the message's advocacy. However, when prior attitudes are assessed, they are rarely represented in the study's analytic design. In some cases, they are "dismissed" because, consistent with random assignment of subjects to conditions, preliminary analysis reveals that they do not vary across experimental conditions. In other cases, they are used (with post-message attitudes) to create attitude change scores, but are still not represented as an independent variable in the study's design (see Mackie, 1987, for an exception). Finally, prior attitudes sometimes enter the design as a covariate, or control variable (e.g., Wood, 1982). Although the covariate strategy can yield information regarding the overall (i.e., "main") effect of prior attitudes on post-message attitudes and other responses, it ignores possible interactions between prior attitudes and other independent variables in the study (e.g., source manipulations, argument quality manipulations).

In this and the previous chapter, we have seen how the construct of prior attitude has entered into recent theoretical discussions and debates about "involvement's" impact on persuasion, the determinants of objective as opposed to biased message processing, and the role that prior knowledge plays in persuasion (e.g., Biek, Wood, Chaiken, & Nations, 1992; Chaiken et al., 1989; B.T. Johnson & Eagly, 1989, 1990; Petty & Cacioppo, 1986b, 1990; Zanna, 1990). These discussions will no doubt stimulate greater empirical attention to prior attitudes among persuasion researchers. The literature we discussed in Chapter 4 on accessibility and other cognitive processes that underlie attitude-behavior relations has clear relevance to persuasion and should serve as an additional catalyst for research (e.g., Fazio, 1986; Houston & Fazio, 1989; M. Snyder & Kendzierski, 1982). Extrapolating from that literature, prior attitudes should impact on persuasion to the extent that situational and individual difference factors facilitate their activation from memory and their perceived relevance to recipients' (to-be-expressed) post-message attitudes. Finally, as subsequent investigators explore whether, when, and how prior attitudes influence people's reactions to persuasive messages, they will need to supplement their traditional analysis of variance approach to data analysis with more sophisticated techniques that are more suitable for representing continuous independent variables (e.g., multiple regression analysis) and that allow researchers to model the temporal relations that exist between and among distal independent variables, mediating variables, and dependent variables (e.g., path analysis, structural equation modeling).

Epilogue

The process theories we have discussed in this chapter and in the previous two chapters all describe particular cognitive mechanisms that are presumed to underlie people's tendencies to agree with persuasive messages. A major distinction among these theories is that they specify differing *modes* of information processing. The heuristic-systematic model, attribution approaches, and social judgment theory provide molecular descriptions of yielding to a message's overall position. Social judgment theory suggests that such yielding is the product of distortions in the way people perceive or comprehend messages' positions. The heuristic-systematic model views such yielding as the product of simple decision rules that people apply to cues available in the message or the persuasion context. And attribution approaches view such yielding as the product of particular causal inferences that people make on the basis of such cues.

By contrast, the systematic theories of persuasion we considered in Chapter 6, and which are incorporated into both the heuristic-systematic and elaboration likelihood models, emphasize yielding to the content of persuasive messages. Whereas the reception-yielding framework stresses the idea that recipients' comprehension of persuasive argumentation must be taken into account in predicting persuasion, the cognitive response model focuses on recipients' thinking about or cognitive elaboration of message content.

With researchers' increased awareness that multiple modes of processing may operate in attitudinal settings has come an increased understanding of the conditions under which people employ one mode or another. Although much remains to be learned about the determinants of processing modes and their probable interdependent nature, some general principles that govern their usage can be derived from current research.

Prior learning is clearly an important determinant of whether people engage in a number of the processing modes that theorists have posited. As Chaiken and her colleagues (1989) have argued, for heuristic processing to occur, people must have learned and stored in memory relevant persuasion heuristics. Moreover, the persuasive impact of heuristics is assumed to depend on their strength or reliability. For example, a person whose past experiences with likable persons has yielded few exceptions to the liking-agreement rule should perceive a strong association between the concepts of liking and interpersonal agreement. This person should thus be more likely to agree with likable sources than a person whose past experience has yielded many exceptions to the liking-agreement rule. Similarly, it seems reasonable to assert that the causal reasoning processes specified by attribution approaches are also dependent on prior learning and stored knowledge. For example, to attribute a senator's statement on Social Security reform to her political ideology, people must perceive a general relation between political ideology and stands on the Social Security issue (or on related issues) and must recognize the relevance of this general relation to interpreting the senator's verbal behavior. As suggested by the heuristic-systematic model, recipients' confidence in such an attributional judgment should be a function of the strength of the general relation or schema that forms the basis for their particular causal inference.

Prior learning also affects people's abilities to comprehend and to cognitively elaborate persuasive argumentation. As Wood (e.g., 1982) has shown, comprehension and message-related thinking are both dependent upon recipients possessing at least marginal amounts of prior knowledge about persuasion issues (see also D. F. Schmidt & Sherman, 1984). Finally, the likelihood of misperceiving messages' positions in the manner assumed by social judgment theory depends on prior learning of a different sort. Specifically, the assimilation-contrast effects stressed by this theory are due to the anchoring effects of prior attitudes. Thus, perceptual distortions of communicator's positions should occur only to the extent that people have already formed an attitude and stored this evaluation in memory.

For heuristic processing and attributional reasoning to occur, relevant knowledge structures must not only be available in memory, they must also be activated upon presentation of the persuasion cues that are associated with them. Presumably, factors such as cue salience, the frequency and recency of prior activation, and processing goals influence the *accessibility* of these structures and hence their judgmental impact (see Chaiken et al., 1989; Ginossar & Trope, 1987; Higgins, 1989a). The relevance of accessibility principles to understanding the conditions under which prior attitudes and prior knowledge impact on cognitive processing should also be clear. Only when activated can prior attitudes be expected to influence either people's perception of messages' positions or their elaboration of persuasive argumentation, and only that subset of prior knowledge that is accessible to recipients has the potential to facilitate (and, perhaps, bias) their understanding and reactions to persuasive argumentation.

The extent to which differing modes of processing require *effortful thinking* is also an important consideration in predicting which modes are likely to occur in particular persuasion settings. As Chaiken (e.g., 1980) and Petty and Cacioppo (e.g., 1981a) have argued, people may prefer less effortful modes of processing unless they are especially motivated to engage in a more effortful process. In validity-seeking persuasion settings, moderate-to-high levels of accuracy motivation—induced by factors such as personal relevance, task importance, and accountability—seem necessary to motivate recipients to attend to, comprehend, and cognitively elaborate upon persuasive argumentation. Because causal reasoning is presumably less effortful than systematic processing, it may be a preferred mode when situational and individual difference factors induce somewhat lower levels of accuracy motivation. Because of its least effortful nature, heuristic processing may predominate in persuasion settings characterized by very low levels of accuracy motivation.[18] Importantly, this analysis does not imply that at particular levels of accuracy motivation *only one* mode of processing occurs. Rather, heuristic processing may predominate in low accuracy motivation settings. As motivation increases to some moderate level, both heuristic processing and causal reasoning may occur and predominate over systematic processing. As accuracy motivation increases beyond this point, recipients may be likely to engage in all three of these processing modes. In the spirit of the heuristic-systematic model's concurrent processing assumption, then, it is likely that the three modes could exert both independent and interactive effects on judgment in high motivation settings. As discussed earlier, factors such as argument ambiguity and the extent to which the three modes furnish complementary versus contradictory information may need to be taken into account in assessing the likelihood of these possibilities (see Chapter 7 and earlier discussion in this chapter).

As suggested by the heuristic-systematic model's sufficiency principle, the extent to which people utilize one processing mode rather than another may depend in part on the extent to which it confers *sufficient judgmental confidence*. As noted earlier in this chapter, Wood and Eagly (1981) found that when subjects could not unambiguously determine message validity on the basis of their causal reasoning, they scrutinized message content more carefully, presumably in order to clarify whether the message was indeed a valid portrayal of external reality (see also Petty & Priester, 1991). Similarly, Maheswaran and Chaiken (1991) found that subjects who were not particularly motivated to engage in systematic processing nevertheless did so when the validity of their heuristic-based judgments was undermined.[19] Together, these findings suggest that when a less effortful processing mode does not confer sufficient judgmental confidence, recipients may be more likely to turn to a more effortful mode of processing. It is possible, however, that the reverse sequence might sometimes obtain. As Chaiken (1987) has speculated, highly motivated message recipients who attempt systematic processing may nevertheless also turn to simple decision rules when the former (and more effortful) mode fails to confer sufficient judgmental confidence.

In harmony with earlier functional theories of attitudes (see Chapter 10), an emerging theme in persuasion research and related areas of social cognition is that information processing occurs in the service of motivational goals. When people are not concerned about achieving valid attitudes, it is unlikely that knowledge structures relevant to judging message validity would be either activated or utilized. Nor would people be likely to devote much effort to comprehending, counterarguing, or bolstering persuasive arguments, at least not for the purpose of assessing message validity. Nonetheless, current distinctions between modes of processing as well as principles such as sufficiency and effortfulness, formulated in the context of validity-seeking persuasion settings, may eventually prove applicable to settings in which other motivational goals predominate. For example, in a context which presumably aroused impression-management concerns, Tetlock (1983a) found that knowledge of a discussion partner's attitudes had a strong impact on how much subjects thought about an attitudinal issue. When the discussion partner's views were known, subjects seemed to use a simple "acceptability" heuristic (see Tetlock, 1985) and expressed an attitude that closely matched their partners' viewpoints. However, when the partner's views were unknown, subjects engaged in more extensive, "integratively complex" thinking (see Chapter 3), albeit still in the service of expressing an interpersonally acceptable attitude.

The multiple-motive heuristic-systematic model (see Chapter 7) and B. T. Johnson and Eagly's (1989, 1990) tripartite analysis of involvement both call attention to the fact that multiple motives may operate in social influence settings. The emergence of these newer perspectives has been accompanied by a renewed interest in functional approaches to understanding attitude change (e.g., Chaiken et al., 1989; DeBono, 1987; Leippe & Elkin, 1987; Mackie, 1987; Pratkanis, Breckler, & Greenwald, 1989; see Chapter 10). These theoretical and empirical trends suggest that cognitively oriented persuasion researchers' twenty-year-old preoccupation with the validity-seeking message recipient is subsiding in favor of a more multifaceted—and complex—view of the motives that guide people's cognitive processing in persuasion and other social influence settings. We will address both older and emerging perspectives on how motives other than accuracy seeking impinge on cognitive processing and attitude judgment in subsequent chapters.

——— Notes ———

1. Within information integration theory, perceivers' causal inferences about message validity can be viewed as determining the *weight* of information, with higher weights given to messages that are perceived as more valid. Moreover, in terms of the four determinants of weighting that N. H. Anderson (1981a) proposed, attribution approaches can be viewed as providing a theory of the inferences underlying the *reliability* aspect of weights (see Chapter 5).

2. The heuristic-systematic model's assumption that the persuasive impact of consensus-related cues is mediated by the simple rule "consensus implies correctness" is, for all intents and purposes, identical to this attribution interpretation. Of course, the heuristic-systematic model also features other heuristics such as the liking-agreement rule and the length-strength rule that have little to do with attributional reasoning. Moreover, the causal reasoning described by attribution theories of persuasion is more extensive and effortful than heuristic processing (unless applied in truncated form as in the consensus-cues-only example in the text). For example, in the ANOVA model recipients attempt to discern the consensual nature of the communicator's advocated position *and also* the consistency and distinctiveness of this position.

3. Within standard persuasion paradigms, the communicator's position typically disagrees, rather than agrees, with subjects' attitudes, and the primary dependent variable of interest is subjects' post-message attitude judgments rather than attitudinal confidence. Research on communicator-recipient similarity conducted within the standard paradigm has typically found greater persuasion when recipients receive messages from similar communicators (e.g., Berscheid, 1966; Brock, 1965b; Stoneman & Brody, 1981; see McGuire, 1985; Simons, Berkowitz, & Moyer, 1970).

4. High need for cognition subjects in this study indicated greater agreement with messages that contained strong (vs. weak) arguments, regardless of whether the message confirmed or disconfirmed their pre-message expectancies (see Chapter 7).

5. This prediction assumes that the message recipient is not motivated to engage in systematic processing for other reasons. For the recipient whose personal interests would be served by *reduced* capital gains, in particular, extensive—and biased—processing of the Treasury secretary's message would be likely (see the discussion of defense-motivated processing in Chapter 7).

6. Some readers will have by now noticed that we have not discussed Bem's (e.g., 1972) self-perception theory in this section. This omission occurs because self-perception theory has only sporadically been applied to the issue of understanding how beliefs and attitudes form or change in response to persuasive communications from external sources (e.g., Giesen & Hendrick, 1974; Hendrick & Giesen, 1976; Mintz & Mills, 1971; see Chapter 10's discussion of fear arousal and persuasion). Because Bem's theory has primarily been developed as a framework for understanding the attitudinal effects of counterattitudinal and proattitudinal proselytizing, we review it in Chapter 11.

7. It is somewhat unclear whether social judgment theorists believed in a three-step or a two-step process of attitude change. According to the three-step process alluded to in the text, attitude-engendered perceptual displacements influence recipients' global evaluations of the message which, in turn, lead them to accept or reject the message. According to a two-step process, recipients' global evaluations of the message co-occur with message acceptance (or rejection), that is, message evaluation does not play any special mediational role. Our interpretation of M. Sherif and Hovland's (1961) description of the theory is that they were positing a three-step process. Yet, their exposition is sufficiently unclear that we wished to caution readers on this point.

8. As far as we can decipher, social judgment theorists never confronted a highly plausible alternative to their hypothesis that assimilating a message should produce change toward that message. Instead, it might be argued that misperceiving

a communicator's position as closer to one's own *reduces* pressure to change one's attitude. As a result, greater assimilation might function to dampen attitude change rather than to enhance it (see subsequent discussion in text and note 13).

9. For the possibility that ego-involvement may sometimes influence the width of the latitude of acceptance, see Eagly and Telaak (1972).

10. Two arbitrary, but conventional, aspects of our figure should be noted. First, we have represented our hypothetical recipients' own attitude position as the midpoint of their latitude of acceptance (see M. Sherif & Sherif, 1967). Second, we have depicted the inflection point for each discrepancy-persuasion curve as lying just beyond the midpoint of the latitude of noncommitment (see also Fishbein & Ajzen, 1975; Kiesler, Collins, & Miller, 1969). We should also note that the decision to equate the height of the two curves' inflection points represents our best interpretation of social judgment theorists' writings. As on other key aspects of their theory, they were not particularly precise on this matter.

11. Message discrepancy was a popular independent variable among researchers in the 1960s and early 1970s. Afterwards, however, interest declined, perhaps because social judgment theory (and dissonance theory, see note 12) declined in popularity with persuasion researchers, but perhaps also because of challenging methodological issues. In particular, it has proven difficult for researchers to implement discrepancy manipulations that are orthogonal to other variables such as recipients' own attitudes and whether messages advocate proattitudinal or counterattitudinal positions (for discussion, see Insko, 1967; Kiesler, Collins, & Miller, 1969). Of course, discrepancy has continued to receive some theoretical and empirical attention (e.g., Fishbein & Ajzen, 1975; Lange & Fishbein, 1983; Laroche, 1977; Nemeth & Endicott, 1976; see McGuire, 1985). Of particular note is Lange and Fishbein's (1983) argument that the effects of discrepancy vary as a function of whether messages are proattitudinal or counterattitudinal.

12. In these studies as well as others on message discrepancy, social judgment theory had a theoretical competitor, dissonance theory (see Chapters 10 and 11). At first glance, dissonance theory would appear to predict only a positive relation between discrepancy and persuasion, because of the presumed positive relation between discrepancy and dissonance. However, assumptions that the magnitude of dissonance might differ as a function of attitudinal importance or commitment and that source disparagement (vs. attitude change) might serve to reduce dissonance at high discrepancy levels rendered dissonance theory capable of generating some of the same predictions as social judgment theory (albeit for different reasons). Although the two theories were thus often pitted against one another, neither ultimately emerged as the superior explanation for the persuasive effects of message discrepancy (for discussion, see Himmelfarb & Eagly, 1974; Insko, 1967; Kiesler, Collins, & Miller, 1969). Moreover, as noted in Chapter 11, research establishing the conditions apparently necessary for dissonance arousal (e.g., choice) further reduced the viability of dissonance theory in relation to message-induced persuasion.

13. This latter hypothesis has not been recognized by most researchers (e.g., Fishbein & Ajzen, 1975; Kiesler, Collins, & Miller, 1969; Petty & Cacioppo, 1981a). In fact, Kiesler, Collins, and Miller (1969, p. 260) mischaracterized the theory when they wrote "For communications within (or close to) the latitude of acceptance, the involved respondent will assimilate the communicator's position toward his own much more than the uninvolved recipient *and as a consequence will perceive the communicator as advocating less change. Being thus subject to less pressure toward change, his original position will remain less influenced than that of the uninvolved recipient* [italics added]" (p. 260). The error in this derivation is that social judgment theory posits a *positive* relation between assimilation and persuasion (Proposition 6), not the negative relation that Kiesler, Collins, and Miller assumed. Thus, however tenable the idea that assimilation should *dampen* attitude change (see note 8), the internal logic of the theory specifies a positive relation between involvement

and persuasion for proattitudinal messages that are assimilated. In this regard, we should also comment on the apparent contradiction between this prediction and M. Sherif and Sherif's (1967, p. 133) statement that involvement uniformly reduces persuasion. Although they did not qualify this statement explicitly, we surmise that they were discussing counterattitudinal, not proattitudinal, messages. In fact, social judgment theorists' general inattention to proattitudinal messages is understandable when one considers that they developed their theory in a research context that focused on counterattitudinal messages. It was not until the late 1960s and early 1970s that research interest in proattitudinal communications emerged (e.g., Eagly, 1967; Kiesler, 1971; Nisbett & Valins, 1972), and most of this interest concerned the effects of proattitudinal proselytizing (see Chapter 11).

14. As we discuss in Chapter 12, instructing subjects to merely think about their attitudes or to explain their attitudes in writing often produces polarization; compared with preexperimental attitudes, postexperimental attitudes tend to be more extreme (e.g., Chaiken & Yates, 1985; Tesser, 1978). By having high involvement subjects list reasons supporting their stands on fluoridation and low involvement subjects list reasons supporting their stands on an unrelated issue, Miller may have unwittingly confounded his involvement manipulation with the extremity of subjects' premessage fluoridation attitudes.

15. Experiments or portions of experiments that used proattitudinal messages were not included in B. T. Johnson and Eagly's (1989) meta-analysis.

16. In two studies concerning the persuasive impact of personal relevance (or issue involvement), Petty and Cacioppo (1979b) argued that social judgment theory and the cognitive response model made competing predictions. As we have pointed out, however, social judgment theory claims no predictive power in relation to this type of involvement.

17. In evaluating existing research it is important to remember that the perceptual distortions postulated by social judgment theory are assumed to occur primarily when attitudinal stimuli are *ambiguous* (see Proposition 7 in text). Because we judge that most persuasion studies testing the theory have utilized messages whose positions and arguments have been relatively unambiguous in meaning, it may be premature to discount entirely the role that assimilation-contrast effects may play in more naturalistic settings where ambiguity may be more common.

18. We omit discussion of assimilation-contrast effects here because of unresolved issues regarding how such perceptual distortions affect persuasion. That is, it is presently unclear whether such distortions impact directly on persuasion or whether they impact indirectly on persuasion through their influence on recipients' cognitive responses to message content (see earlier discussion in text).

19. The value of the sufficiency principle in relation to these findings is that it provides a parsimonious explanation for results that, on the surface, appear contradictory. In particular, Wood and Eagly (1981) and Petty and Priester (1991) found that systematic processing was enhanced by expectancy *confirmation*, whereas Maheswaran and Chaiken (1991) found that systematic processing was enhanced by expectancy *disconfirmation*. The expectancy manipulations were, of course, somewhat different across the two sets of studies. Nonetheless, when viewed solely at the manifest or *phenotypic* level of the processing effects of expectancy confirmation/disconfirmation, the results are paradoxical. However, when viewed at the underlying, *genotypic* level of judgmental confidence, the results fit together quite well: When recipients lack sufficient confidence in their assessments of message validity, they will tend to engage in more effortful modes of processing designed to attain greater confidence.

9

Affective Processes in
Attitude Formation and Change:
Conditioning and
Mere Exposure Research

Introduction: *The Cognitive Revolution and Affect in Social Psychology*

Beginning in the late 1960s, research on attitude formation and change became increasingly dominated by the cognitive perspectives we examined in the preceding four chapters. This emphasis on cognition is by no means unique. Whether one looks to other areas within the attitudes literature (e.g., attitude-behavior relations; see Chapter 4), to other literatures within social psychology, or to the discipline of psychology more generally, the ascendancy of cognitive theorizing over the past two decades has been striking.

The increased focus on cognition stemmed, in part, from experimental psychology's "cognitive revolution" (see J.R. Anderson, 1985; E.E. Jones, 1985; Zajonc, 1980a). This revolution, whose manifesto is usually attributed to Neisser (1967), transformed experimental psychology from a field that was predominantly behaviorist in orientation to the contemporary field of cognitive psychology. Drawing inspiration from a variety of sources, including the research on human factors conducted during World War II (see R.C. Atkinson & Shiffrin, 1968; Broadbent, 1958) and the person-as-computer metaphor provided by the novel field of artificial intelligence (e.g., Newell & Simon, 1972), the information-processing approach of cognitive psychology assumes that the stimulus-response link is mediated by a sequence of mental operations or cognitive processes (e.g., encoding, interpretation, storage, retrieval).

Strict behaviorist doctrine had banned not only "thought" as a proper domain of research, but also other "subjective" constructs such as "desire" and "emotion" (Watson, 1930, p. 5). Although the cognitive revolution resurrected thought as a proper topic for inquiry, emotional phenomena were disregarded, presumably because of their incompatibility with the computer analogy. For similar reasons, constructs such as drive, incentive motivation, and goal-orientation—motivational concepts used by all but the most radical of behaviorists (e.g., Skinner, 1953) to explain the mechanism of reinforcement—were also denied importance by the distinctly non-motivational information-processing approach (see J.R. Anderson, 1985).

Zajonc (1980a) and others (e.g., Fiske & Taylor, 1991; E. E. Jones, 1985; Manis, 1977) have pointed out that social psychology was cognitive long before experimental psychology's cognitive revolution. Social psychologists have traditionally placed more emphasis on people's subjective perceptions of environmental stimuli than on the objectively definable characteristics of such stimuli (e.g., Allport, 1935; Asch, 1946; Festinger, 1954, 1957; Heider, 1946, 1958; Hovland, Janis, & Kelley, 1953; Lewin, 1938, 1951; M. Sherif, 1935). However, affective and motivational processes have also been a traditional concern of social psychology. For most social psychologists between the 1930s and late 1960s, constructs such as goals, incentives, social reinforcers, social motives, needs, values, the self, emotions, arousal, *and* attitudes were viewed as exerting both an activating and directive influence on cognition and behavior.

Although traditionally concerned with both cognition and motivation, the emphasis of social psychological theory and research during the 1950s and 1960s was tilted more toward motivational dynamics (e.g., Bruner, 1957; Festinger, 1957; Hovland et al., 1953; M. B. Smith, Bruner, & White, 1956). For social psychology, the effect of the new information-processing approach was that theoretical and empirical interests shifted away from the forces that presumably energized and directed cognition toward explicating and documenting the elements and processes of social cognition itself. Intensifying the field's tilt toward cognition, many researchers adopted not only the methods and sequential processing notions of cognitive psychology, but also its belief that motivational concepts were unnecessary for understanding the processes and outputs of cognition (J. R. Anderson, 1985).

So it was that much of social psychology turned during the 1970s and early 1980s to the study of "cold" cognition. As testimony to the dominance of cognition, this period witnessed numerous attempts to reinterpret in nonmotivational information-processing terms phenomena that a previous generation of social psychologists had attributed to motivational mechanisms (see D. T. Miller & M. Ross, 1975; Nisbett & L. Ross, 1980, and the discussion of dissonance vs. self-perception theory in Chapter 11). At best, motivation was acknowledged as the catalyst of cognition and behavior—but it was cognition, not motivation (or behavior) that was the focus of empirical scrutiny. For example, in attribution research of this period the need to predict and control one's world was offered (Heider, 1958; H. H. Kelley, 1967)—but seldom studied—as the reason why people bothered to process information and make causal attributions (see Pittman & Heller, 1987).

As a counterpoint to the cognitive perspectives we emphasized in the preceding chapters, our emphasis in this chapter and in Chapter 10 will be the potential role that affective and motivational processes play in the formation and change of attitudes. In these chapters we will sometimes use the terms affect and affective processes to refer loosely to the variety of emotional and motivational constructs and mechanisms that have been contrasted with cognitive processes, that is, concepts such as emotion, mood, affect, arousal, incentives, needs, motives, conditioning, reinforcement, and the like. Of course, the term affect has often been assigned more restrictive meaning in the psychological literature (e.g., Izard, 1977; Tomkins, 1981). For example, Zajonc (1980b) considers affect to encompass concepts such as preferences and feelings, but not emotions such as surprise, anger, and guilt. In addition, we have discussed the tendency of earlier investigators to use the term affect as a synonym for evaluation, a practice we do not follow in this book (e.g., Fishbein & Ajzen, 1975; see Chapter 1). As a general label for the variety of emotional and motivational constructs that have been neglected by cognitively oriented researchers, the terms affect and affective processes have some utility. However, in the course of our discussions we will avoid these generic terms whenever more specific terminology is warranted.

Many of the theoretical perspectives and phenomena we will review predated social psychologists' intensive study of social cognition and concomitant neglect of affect. As a consequence, the links between affective and cognitive approaches to understanding attitude formation and change have not been well explored. In this chapter and Chapter 10 we purposefully adopt an advocacy stance with respect to the importance of affective processes. Moreover, we will try to speculate about possible connections that could be built between cognitive and affective approaches to attitudes. Such a stance toward our subject matter seems particularly warranted at this juncture in social psychology, for after little more than a decade of intense interest in cognitive processes, a revivalist attitude toward the importance of affect now pervades the field. Beginning with Zajonc's (1980b) provocative arguments for the primacy of affect, numerous calls for greater attention to motivational and affective issues and their relation to cognitive processes have appeared throughout the social psychological literature (e.g., Eagly & Chaiken, 1984; Fiske & Taylor, 1991; Higgins, Kuiper, & Olson, 1981; Pittman & Heller, 1987; Sorrentino & Higgins, 1986). Although it is too early to forecast the empirical and theoretical outcomes of this proselytizing, it is clear that social psychology's ice age is coming to a close and that the 1990s (at least) will be characterized by a more integrative approach to the study of the affective and cognitive mechanisms that underlie social judgment and behavior.

In Chapter 10 we will consider several theoretical perspectives that feature explicit assumptions regarding the motivational underpinnings of attitude formation and change: the incentive and drive-reduction views of Hovland and colleagues (1953), theories of cognitive consistency (e.g., Festinger, 1957; Heider, 1958), and theories of attitude functions (e.g., D. Katz, 1960). In the current chapter, we focus our attention on the question of whether simple mechanisms, traditionally viewed as largely affective in nature, can underlie attitude formation.[1] This question has been raised and debated primarily within three research paradigms. In the typical *operant conditioning* study (e.g., Insko, 1965), subjects are queried about their attitudes toward some issue, and the interviewer reinforces positive or negative attitude statements through verbal or nonverbal reactions to the subjects' responses. In this paradigm, subjects' subsequent responses have been shown to become more positive or more negative, depending upon whether the interviewer's earlier reactions reinforced positive or negative attitudinal responding. In most *classical conditioning* studies (e.g., A. W. Staats & Staats, 1958), initially neutral stimuli are paired repeatedly with other objects or events that reliably elicit positive or negative responses from subjects. In this research paradigm, subjects' attitudes toward the initially neutral stimuli have been shown to become more positive after repeated positive pairings and more negative after repeated negative pairings.

Finally, in the typical *mere exposure* study (e.g., Zajonc, 1968a), the frequency with which novel stimulus objects are presented to subjects is varied across a series of trials so that subjects are exposed to some objects more frequently than others. In this simple paradigm, subjects' subsequent ratings of the test stimuli generally reveal more positive attitudes toward those objects that have been presented more frequently.

These three results have been the focus of considerable controversy. As is often the case in research, some investigators have pursued issues of generalizability and have tried to identify conditions under which these results do not obtain (e.g., Brickman, Redfield, Harrison, & Crandall, 1972; Dabbs & Janis, 1965; Insko & Butzine, 1967). However, the most controversial issue that has traditionally been raised about these findings, and the issue we focus upon here, concerns a core question regarding their mediation: Can the attitude effects typically found in these experiments be attributed solely to simple affective mechanisms, as some investigators have claimed (e.g., A. W. Staats & Staats, 1958; Zajonc, 1980b), or are these effects more appropriately interpreted as the product of cognitive mechanisms, as most investigators have argued (e.g., Fishbein & Ajzen, 1972; P. C. Gordon & Holyoak, 1983; M. M. Page, 1970, 1974)?[2] After reviewing the evidence and arguments that have been brought to bear on this question, we will discuss the more fundamental issues of whether affective and cognitive processes are separate or interdependent systems. We will also consider the related issue of whether affective judgments can, as Zajonc (1980b, 1984) has argued, temporally precede the kinds of cognitive operations that most contemporary investigators have assumed to be the informational basis of affective judgments (e.g., Lazarus, 1982, 1984).

Operant and Classical Conditioning Studies of Attitude Formation

In Chapter 1 we stressed that the definition of attitude should not preclude the possibility that some attitudes may arise from genetic or biological sources and may therefore be "unlearned" (see McGuire, 1985). Nevertheless, most definitions have assumed that attitudes are learned predispositions (e.g., Allport, 1935; D. T. Campbell, 1963; Doob, 1947). Consensus on this point has been so widespread that very little empirical attention has been paid to the possible genetic or biological basis of some attitudes (but see Waller, Kojetin, Bouchard, Lykken, & Tellegen, 1990). Although agreeing that attitudes are learned, investigators have debated whether the same principles assumed to govern much animal learning can also be said to underlie the acquisition of people's attitudes.

Classic theories of learning describe the processes by which particular responses become associated with, or conditioned to, particular stimuli (Hull, 1943, 1951; K. W. Spence, 1956; Thorndike, 1932; Tolman, 1932). Two basic learning paradigms, operant conditioning and classical conditioning, have dominated the experimental study of learning, and both have been applied to the study of attitude formation. The *operant* or *instrumental conditioning* paradigm embodies Thorndike's (1898) famous dictum "Pleasure stamps in; pain stamps out." In this paradigm, the frequency with which a specific response occurs increases because it is followed by positive consequences and decreases because it is followed by negative consequences (Skinner, 1953; Thorndike, 1932). The to-be-conditioned or operant response must be part of the organism's behavioral repertoire if learning is to occur. The rat placed in a Skinner box, for example, must be capable of making a bar-pressing response, and this response (or one that resembles it) must occur at least once for it to be rewarded or punished. In the operant paradigm, when the frequency with which the to-be-conditioned response is emitted increases to a point that is higher than its pre-reinforcement frequency, operant conditioning or learning is said to have occurred.

The second paradigm of associative learning derives from Pavlov's work on salivary conditioning in dogs and is called *classical* or *respondent conditioning*. The top panel of Figure 9.1 illustrates this paradigm in relation to one of Pavlov's well-known experiments. Food powder, the unconditioned stimulus (US), is given to the dog who reflexively emits an unconditioned response (UR), salivation. Just prior to each presentation of the US, the dog hears a metronome beat. The metronome beat is the conditioned or to-be-conditioned stimulus (CS). This CS is neutral in the sense that, prior to being paired with the US, the dog does not salivate in its presence (although the CS may elicit other types of responses). However, after repeated pairings of the CS and US, the CS does come to elicit a response that resembles (or anticipates) the UR. This response is called the conditioned response (CR) and, in our example, would be some degree of salivation in response to the metronome beat.[3] When the CS acquires this ability to elicit the CR—a response originally elicited only by the US—classical conditioning or learning is said to have occurred.

FIGURE 9.1.
(a) Classical conditioning paradigm illustrating the classical conditioning of salivation to a metronome beat.
(b) Classical conditioning paradigm illustrating the classical conditioning of a negative evaluative response (attitude) to a minority group name. This figure was presented by Himmelfarb and Eagly (1974, Figure 2, p. 25).

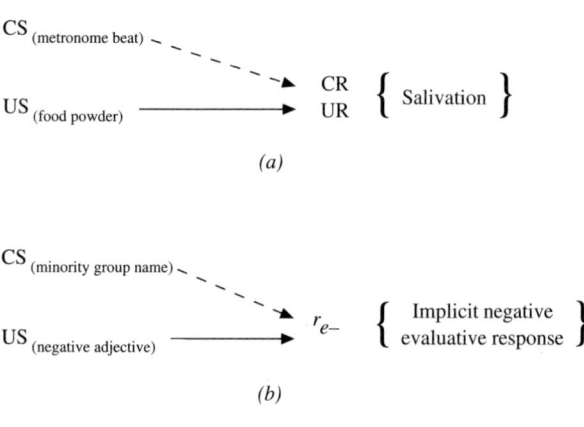

The rat's bar press and the dog's salivation in our example operant conditioning and classical conditioning situations are *overt* responses. However, the same conditioning principles that apply to these overt behaviors are also assumed to govern the learning of more covert responses (e.g., Doob, 1947; Hull, 1951; Osgood, Suci, & Tannenbaum, 1957). This assumption has been fundamental to most applications of learning theory to the problem of attitude formation. Following Doob's (1947) definition of attitude as a learned, implicit anticipatory response (see Chapter 1), most researchers who have studied attitude formation from a learning theory perspective have assumed that overt reactions to stimuli are the manifest expressions of an attitude. The attitude itself is an implicit, evaluative response that mediates these overt responses (e.g., Fishbein, 1967b; Hovland et al., 1953; A. J. Lott & Lott, 1968; Rhine, 1958; A. W. Staats & Staats, 1958).

Learning psychologists have long debated the precise nature of the learning processes that underlie operant and classical conditioning (see Hearst, 1988; Hill, 1985; Kimble, 1961; Papini & Bitterman, 1990). For example, some classic theories assume that reinforcement is necessary for learning to occur, whereas others assume that mere contiguity between stimuli and responses is sufficient. More recent models have tended to ignore the reinforcement issue and, moreover, have emphasized that what *animals and humans* learn in conditioning experiments are not responses *per se*, but rather mental representations of the relations that exist between classes of stimuli (e.g., between CS and US) or between responses and stimuli (e.g., that behavior x leads to consequence y).[4] Because some theories of conditioning have emphasized affective constructs (e.g., reinforcement) and others cognitive constructs (i.e., mental representations), it is somewhat misleading to refer to operant and classical conditioning as "affective" mechanisms. For the most part, however, social psychological research on attitude conditioning was inspired more by theories in which reinforcement and responses were emphasized. It is also important to realize that most theories of conditioning developed in the context of animal learning (although they have been widely applied to human conditioning). Thus, regardless of the exact mechanisms these theories invoke to explain conditioning, social psychologists who have applied them to attitude formation have traditionally viewed conditioning as occurring "automatically," that is, without the organism's *conscious awareness* and without mediation by *deliberative cognitive processes*. Whether operant and classical conditioning truly occurs automatically in human organisms is a complex question whose answer no doubt depends upon the kind of response that is being conditioned and the context in which conditioning takes place. Although many psychologists would have little trouble accepting the idea that a response as subtle as an eye blink probably could be conditioned automatically in human learners, far fewer have been willing to believe that awareness and deliberative cognitive processes also need not be involved in the "conditioning" of human verbal responding (see Brewer, 1974; Estes, 1988; Hearst, 1988; Hill, 1985). Indeed, it is this issue that has been the focus of traditional debate in the operant and classical conditioning literatures we consider below.

Operant Conditioning of Attitudes

Consistent with Skinner's (1957) assertion that human verbal behavior is subject to the same operant conditioning principles that govern much animal learning, numerous studies during the late 1950s and 1960s investigated the effects of social reinforcement on the conditioning of attitude statements and many other types of verbal behavior. In typical studies, subjects might be asked to construct sentences, converse informally with the experimenter, or answer specific questions that the experimenter would pose. During this task, the experimenter would reinforce a predetermined class of verbal responses (e.g., plural nouns) by responding with "good," "mm-hmmm," or an approving head nod whenever the subject emitted the to-be-conditioned response (e.g., a plural noun) and by not reacting or reacting negatively with "bad," "humph," or a disapproving head movement whenever the subject emitted an incorrect response (e.g., a singular noun). This research showed that operant techniques were successful in modifying the frequency with which experimental subjects emitted reinforced classes of verbal behavior (e.g., Greenspoon, 1955; Krasner, 1958, 1962; Levin, 1961; Levy, 1967; Oakes, 1967; Taffel, 1955).

Attitude studies of this genre typically used a question-and-answer format in which the experimenter queries subjects about their attitudes toward some issue. In one of the earlier of these experiments, Hildum and Brown's (1956) subjects were telephoned and asked a series of questions about their university's educational policies. The phone caller reinforced some subjects whenever their responses to these questions implied a favorable attitude toward university policy and reinforced others whenever their responses implied an unfavorable attitude. In addition, the verbal reinforcement used for half the subjects was the word "good," and for the other half it was the utterance "mm-hmm." The results indicated that "good" (but not "mm-hmm") was successful in increasing subjects' emission of the to-be-conditioned response. For example, the frequency of unfavorable attitude statements increased among subjects who had heard the interviewer say "good" to such statements. In an important replication of this work, Chester Insko (1965) also used a telephone interview format and also found that "good" successfully modified subjects' attitude statements. In addition, Insko's study featured a delayed measure of attitude that was administered one week after the conditioning procedure in an unrelated context (subjects' classrooms). Responses to this anonymous paper-and-pencil measure replicated the telephone data: Subjects conditioned to emit favorable attitude statements during the telephone interview indicated more favorable attitudes on this delayed measure than did subjects who had been conditioned to emit unfavorable attitude statements.

Other studies using similar methods have replicated Hildum and Brown's and Insko's conditioning results (e.g., Ekman, 1958; Insko & Butzine, 1967; Insko & Melson, 1969; Krasner, Knowles, & Ullman, 1965; Singer, 1961; Verplanck, 1955). Also, some findings demonstrating the efficacy of nonverbal reinforcers (e.g., nods of approval, smiling) have been reported (e.g., Ekman, 1958; Krasner et al., 1965). These studies, as well as others that have used somewhat different experimental procedures (e.g., Bostrom, Vlandis, & Rosenbaum, 1961; Elms & Janis, 1965; W. A. Scott, 1957), suggest that people's attitudinal responding can indeed be modified by operant techniques (see also discussion of incentives and attitude change in Chapters 10 and 11).

Mediational Issues. Although the results of numerous studies have shown that evaluative responses and other verbal behaviors can be modified by social reinforcement, the mediational issue of *why* these results occur has never been satisfactorily resolved. In the main, one affective mechanism has been pitted against the more general assertion that verbal conditioning effects are the product of higher-order cognitive processes. According to the affective interpretation, verbal conditioning effects are the direct, automatic, and unconscious consequence of reinforcement. Receipt of the verbal reinforcer "good," like the receipt of food, is inherently pleasurable and can act *directly*—independently and in the absence of deliberative cognitive processing—to strengthen any response that it follows. Although this explanation has the virtue of providing a parsimonious account of operant conditioning in both animal and human subjects, it has won few adherents (e.g., Oakes, 1967; Verplanck, 1962). Instead, it has seemed to play the role of "null hypothesis" in conditioning research—an idea that can be rejected confidently if the data suggest other interpretations, but one that in the absence of other interpretations can never be truly accepted.

Higher-order cognitive interpretations of verbal conditioning effects gained credibility primarily on the basis of correlational data. In numerous studies the amount of conditioning observed was found to covary with subjects' postexperimental reports of having been aware of the contingency between their responses and the receipt of reinforcement. In other words, subjects in much of this research were aware of the fact that their use of a plural noun or their favorable or unfavorable statement about some issue was usually followed by the experimenter saying "good" (e.g., DeNike, 1964; DeNike & Leibovitz, 1969; Dulany, 1962; Insko & Butzine, 1967; Levin, 1961; Spielberger & Levin, 1962; Uleman, 1971; M. M. Page, 1970, 1972). Conditioning effects were routinely found for subjects who were aware of this contingency, but those who were unaware often failed to be conditioned in verbal conditioning studies—though not always (Insko & Cialdini, 1969). Despite the fundamental ambiguity of correlational data and the uncertain epistemological status of postexperimental self-reports, many investigators interpreted these findings as indicating that (a) response-reinforcement contingency awareness was necessary for verbal conditioning effects to occur, and therefore that (b) verbal conditioning effects were the product of higher-order cognitive processes (e.g., Dulany, 1962, 1968; Fishbein & Ajzen, 1975; Kiesler, Collins, & Miller, 1969; M. M. Page, 1970; Spielberger, 1962; Spielberger & DeNike, 1966).

The idea that contingency awareness was a necessary mediator of verbal conditioning suggested that this type of "learning" represented a cognitively mediated process of social influence. Becoming aware that certain responses met with the experimenter's approval whereas others did not, subjects might infer that the former were "correct" in the experimenter's judgment and that the latter were not. If we assume that subjects typically desire to perform "correctly" on experimental tasks or to hold "correct" attitudes (Festinger, 1954), the effects of reinforcement on attitudes and other verbal responses could be viewed as a form of *informational* social influence (see Chapter 13). Consistent with this possibility, Farley and Hokanson (1966) found greater conditioning in a sentence completion task among subjects who were told that the word "good" signaled a correct response 90 percent of the time (vs. only 50% of the time).[5]

Other investigators explored the idea that verbal conditioning effects might reflect more of a *normative* social influence process (see Chapter 13). Like proponents of the informational social influence explanation, Insko and Cialdini (1969) assumed that the reinforcer "good" provides information about the experimenter's attitude (i.e., that the experimenter considers the subject's response to be correct). However, these authors further argued that "good" establishes rapport between the subject and experimenter and that subjects' positive feelings toward the experimenter motivated them to emit the reinforced attitude response more frequently. Support for this normative interpretation has been obtained in several experiments (Cialdini & Insko, 1969; Insko & Butzine, 1967; Insko & Cialdini, 1969; Sapolsky, 1960). For example, Insko and Butzine's (1967) subjects were telephoned and reinforced (with "good") for expressing either a positive or negative attitude toward "pay television." In addition, rapport was manipulated by having the experimenter either flatter or insult subjects during the initial moments of the phone call. Consistent with a normative influence perspective, significantly greater attitude conditioning was found for subjects in the positive rapport conditions.[6]

Interpretations of attitude conditioning studies in terms of informational and normative social influence assume that subjects' publicly expressed attitudes are also privately held (see Chapter 13). In contrast, a third, *compliance* interpretation follows from Dulany's (1962, 1968) analysis of verbal conditioning research. Dulany argued that verbal conditioning effects were dependent not only on contingency awareness, but also on (a) subjects becoming aware of the experimenter's hypothesis, and (b) their intentions to comply with this hypothesis. Abetted by the contemporaneous publication of Orne's (1962) paper on the *demand characteristics* of laboratory experimentation, Dulany's analysis suggested that verbal conditioning effects might be artifactual (see also Orne, 1973). In social influence terms, this demand characteristics logic implies that the results of attitude conditioning studies reflected mere compliance by subjects rather than a genuine attitudinal effect.

Although demand characteristics might well explain the results of some verbal conditioning studies, those that have dealt explicitly with the conditioning of attitude statements have weathered this criticism reasonably well (for a different point of view see M. M. Page, 1970, 1972; Patty & Page, 1973). The idea that conditioning effects are laboratory artifacts suggests that they should be less evident or nonsignificant in non-laboratory contexts. However, quite a few studies of attitude conditioning have been conducted with subjects contacted by telephone who were presumably unaware of their status as experimental subjects (e.g., Hildum & Brown, 1956; Insko, 1965; Insko & Butzine, 1967; Insko & Cialdini, 1969). In addition, Insko and Melson (1969) found no appreciable difference in the amount of conditioning obtained in a laboratory compared with a telephone setting. Of course, such demonstrations do not prove that the attitudes expressed by subjects in conditioning studies are privately held—pressures and desires to feign agreement with other persons do not operate solely in laboratory contexts (see Chapter 13). Better evidence that conditioning can exert a genuine influence on attitudes was provided by Insko (1965). As noted earlier, he showed that the attitudes subjects were conditioned to express during a telephone interview were still evident one week later on a measure administered in an unrelated context.

Summary and Conclusions. Because of the frequent correlation between conditioning and contingency awareness, many investigators concluded that such awareness is a necessary mediator of verbal conditioning. By this awareness criterion, they further concluded that verbal conditioning is a form of cognitively mediated social influence and *not* the direct, automatic, and unconscious consequence of reinforcement (e.g., Fishbein & Ajzen, 1975; Kiesler et al., 1969). Interpretations of verbal conditioning in terms of informational and normative social influence seem plausible, given existing theory (see Chapter 13) and some, albeit not extensive data. And notwithstanding Insko's (1965) data, it is also probably the case that apparently conditioned attitude statements are sometimes merely strategic responses designed to please or appease the human agent of reinforcement (i.e., experimenter or communicator; see Chapter 13). Despite the plausibility of each of these social influence interpretations, the possibility that verbal conditioning procedures might *sometimes* influence attitudes without mediation by higher-order cognitive processes has not been refuted directly.

Consider, for example, the Insko and Butzine (1967) study. Consistent with the authors' normative influence perspective, the attitude conditioning effect in this study did prove to be greater for subjects who were initially flattered (vs. insulted) by the experimenter. Nevertheless, subjects in the negative rapport conditions did exhibit reliable levels of conditioning. Thus, rapport facilitated conditioning, but it was not a necessary factor. More important, the assumption that verbal conditioning effects are mediated by deliberative cognitive processes is predicated on the assumption that such effects occur only when subjects are fully cognizant of the relation that exists between their responses and experimenters' responses (i.e., reinforcement). Yet this second assumption rests almost entirely on correlational data. Although response-reinforcement contingency awareness and conditioning covaried in many experiments, this relation was often small in magnitude and can explain only a small portion of variance in conditioning scores in these studies (e.g., Insko & Butzine, 1967; Insko & Cialdini, 1969; Insko & Melson, 1969). Moreover, as Insko and Cialdini observed, most of the data suggesting that conditioning effects are obtainable *only* among contingency aware subjects derive from the simplest and perhaps most transparent of verbal conditioning paradigms, Taffel's (1955) sentence construction task. In addition, the few experiments that have attempted to manipulate contingency awareness have yielded ambiguous findings (e.g., Dixon & Oakes, 1965; Levy, 1967; Oakes, 1967; see also Konečni & Slamecka, 1972). Thus, the possibility remains that attitudes can be shaped by response-reinforcement contingencies that people are largely unaware of.

Classical Conditioning of Attitudes

Arthur Staats was not the first to recognize the relevance of classical conditioning principles to the attitudes domain (see B. E. Lott, 1955; Razran, 1938, 1940). However, his work was seminal in stimulating a great deal of research on the classical conditioning of attitudes and considerable debate about how the results of this research should be interpreted (e.g., Allen & Madden, 1985; Bierley, McSweeney, & Vannieuwkerk, 1985; Krosnick, Betz, Jussim, & Lynn, 1992; Lohr & Staats, 1973; M. M. Page, 1969, 1974; Riordan & Tedeschi, 1983; A. W. Staats, 1968, 1969, 1975, 1983; A. W. Staats, Gross, Guay, & Carlson, 1973; A. W. Staats & Staats, 1958; A. W. Staats & Warren, 1974; Zanna, Kiesler, & Pilkonis, 1970).

In recalling his initial "experiment" on attitude formation, Staats (1983) noted that he pronounced the word "no" each time he punished his new cat for not using its litter box. On the applied level, Staats was no doubt banking on the universality of operant conditioning principles, hoping that punishment would decrease the cat's toiletry indiscretions and, along with reinforcement, facilitate regular use of the litter box. Theoretically, however, he was interested in a related but conceptually distinctive learning phenomenon. Specifically, given that physical punishment elicited a reflexive negative emotional response in the cat, could the word "no," if administered contiguously and repeatedly with punishment, come to elicit a similar response? If so, the cat would have developed a classically conditioned negative emotional response or, in Staats' terminology, a negative attitude to the verbal stimulus "no."[7]

Staats argued that people may acquire attitudes in a manner analogous to how his cat presumably learned a negative emotional response to the word "no" and how Pavlov's dog learned to salivate in response to a metronome beat (see top panel of Figure 9.1). For example, the child experiences positive and negative affect and thus learns the evaluative meaning of the words "good" and "bad" because these conditioned stimuli are repeatedly paired with unconditioned stimuli such as food and physical punishment. Due to their inherent qualities, these unconditioned stimuli regularly evoke positive and negative emotional reactions in the child. In the terminology of classical conditioning, the child's conditioned emotional response to the words "good" and "bad" would be viewed as an instance of primary (or first-order) conditioning.

After an attitude has been established to words such as "good" and "bad," they can be used as unconditioned stimuli to establish attitudes toward other stimuli. Indeed, most research on the classical conditioning of attitudes has used a *higher-order* (or second-order) conditioning paradigm in which words or other to-be-conditioned stimuli (e.g., photographs) are repeatedly paired with other words that are distinctively positive or negative (e.g., "good," "happy"; "bad," "failure"). Because of people's prior conditioning experiences, the latter, unconditioned stimuli have presumably already attained the power to elicit positive and negative emotional responses in subjects. The bottom panel of Figure 9.1 illustrates how a child might acquire a negative attitude toward some minority group on the basis of this higher-order conditioning principle. Imagine that the child hears a number of negative adjectives (e.g., bad, dirty, stupid) paired with the name of a particular minority group (e.g., blacks, Jews). In this application, the minority group name is the CS, and the negative adjectives are the US's. The US's are assumed to regularly evoke UR's—in this case, implicit negative evaluative responses (r_{e-}). With repeated pairings of the CS and the various US's, the minority group name comes to elicit a CR. In this case, the CR is an implicit negative evaluative response, or negative attitude toward the minority group.

Primary Conditioning Studies. Staats, Staats, and Crawford (1962) used a primary conditioning paradigm to test the classical conditioning of attitudes hypothesis. In this study, meaningful words (e.g., large) were repeatedly paired with aversive unconditioned stimuli (shocks or harsh noises). Afterwards, the CS words were presented alone and subjects were instructed to rate each word on a 7-point pleasantness scale. During this time, physiological arousal was measured by monitoring subjects' galvanic skin response (see Chapter 2). Consistent with predictions, subjects exhibited increased arousal in response to the CS words (compared to control words) and rated these CS words more negatively than did control subjects who had not undergone the conditioning procedure. In addition, CS words that elicited more extreme negative evaluations from subjects also elicited greater arousal.

Zanna, Kiesler, and Pilkonis (1970) replicated and extended these results. In their study, both negative and positive attitudes were successfully conditioned to meaningful CS words (light, dark) by repeatedly pairing these words with either the onset of shock (negative US) or the offset of shock (positive US). The predicted effects of this conditioning procedure on subjects' evaluative ratings of the CS words occurred only among subjects who showed independent physiological evidence of conditioning (indexed by galvanic skin response). Further, the conditioning procedure also influenced these subjects' evaluations of words that were synonyms of the CS words (e.g., white, black). Yet the most important feature of this study was that its questionnaire measure of attitudes was administered to subjects by a second experimenter in the context of an unrelated study.

Both of the above experiments conditioned attitudes to familiar English words. However, the same primary conditioning effects obtain with other types of CS objects. In fact, Cacioppo, Marshall-Goodell, Tassinary, and Petty (1992) found stronger conditioning effects when electric shock was repeatedly paired with unfamiliar, nonwords (e.g., "tasmer," "primet") as opposed to meaningful words (e.g., "finger," "bridge"). That is, subjects' postconditioning evaluations of the nonwords were more negative than their evaluations of the words, even though preexperimental evaluations of these stimuli were equivalent (and relatively neutral). Consistent with their elaboration likelihood model, the authors interpreted these results as indicating that classical conditioning—like other peripheral mechanisms of persuasion—is a more important determinant of attitude change when people possess little knowledge (i.e., familiarity) about the attitude object.

Higher-Order Conditioning Studies. As noted above, most research on the classical conditioning of attitudes has used a higher-order conditioning paradigm. In the best known study of this sort, Staats and Staats (1958; Experiment 1) told subjects that their task was to learn two lists of words, one to be presented visually and one orally. The visually presented list consisted of six national names, two of which served as the CS words (Dutch and Swedish). The orally presented list consisted of 18 positive words (e.g., gift, happy), 18 negative words (e.g., bitter, failure), and 72 evaluatively neutral words (e.g., chair, twelve). On each of the study's 18 conditioning trials, each national name appeared on a screen and, after one second, the experimenter pronounced a positive, negative, or neutral word (US) from the second list and had the subjects repeat this word aloud. Whereas the four control (i.e., non-CS) national names were always paired with neutral words, the two CS names were paired with either all positive or all negative words. For some subjects, "Swedish" was always paired with positive words and "Dutch" with negative words, whereas for other subjects the reverse scheme was used.

After the conditioning procedure had ended, subjects were asked to rate each national name on a 7-point scale anchored by pleasant and unpleasant. Consistent with predictions, "Swedish" and "Dutch" were rated more positively if they had previously been paired with positive, rather than negative, US words. In a second experiment, Staats and Staats used identical procedures but substituted six proper names (e.g., Harry) for the six national names featured in the first study. The results of this second experiment were essentially the same: Subjects expressed significantly more positive attitudes toward the two CS names (Tom and Bill) when these names had been paired with positive, rather than negative, US words.

Other studies using this higher-order conditioning paradigm have shown that attitudes can be conditioned not only to names and meaningful English words but also to other stimuli such as nonsense syllables (e.g., Insko & Oakes, 1966; C. K. Staats & Staats, 1957), geometric figures (Sachs & Byrne, 1970), photographs of people (Byrne & Clore, 1970), and pictures of inanimate objects (Gorn, 1982). In addition, some studies have obtained these conditioning effects using different types of positive and negative unconditioned stimuli—for example, liked and disliked food names (Staats, Minke, Martin, & Higa, 1972), liked and disliked music (Gorn, 1982), and agreeable and disagreeable attitude statements (Byrne & Clore, 1970; Sachs & Byrne, 1970). And, on the dependent variable side, some investigators have demonstrated conditioning effects using measures much less obtrusive than the semantic differential scales featured in most studies (e.g., Berkowitz & Knurek, 1969; Early, 1968; Gorn, 1982).

In a particularly innovative experiment using unobtrusive measures, Berkowitz and Knurek (1969) followed Staats and Staats' (1958, Experiment 2) procedures in order to condition half of their male subjects to dislike the name "George" and the other half to dislike the name "Ed." After completing this task, subjects reported to a different room for a study on "small group interaction." In this ostensibly unrelated experiment, each subject engaged in a brief discussion with two confederates named "Ed Foster" and "George Fuller." Afterwards, subjects rated each confederate's personality, and the confederates (blind to the experimental hypotheses) rated the subject's friendliness. The results of subjects' personality ratings showed that (the confederate) Ed was rated more negatively than (the confederate) George by subjects who had been conditioned to dislike the name Ed; similarly, George was rated more negatively than Ed by subjects who had been conditioned to dislike the name George. The confederates' ratings patterned similarly: Subjects were perceived as behaving in a less friendly manner with the confederate when his ostensible name matched the name subjects had been conditioned to dislike.[8]

Applications of Conditioning Logic. The results of Staats and Staats' (1958) experiment on the names of nationalities clearly suggest the relevance of classical conditioning to the issue of how prejudice develops. Interpersonal attraction is another domain in which this principle has proven heuristically useful (see Berscheid, 1985; Clore & Byrne, 1974; B. E. Lott & Lott, 1985). For example, classical conditioning provides one interpretation for why we seem prone to develop an immediate liking for physically attractive persons (see Berscheid & Walster, 1974). According to this interpretation, just as exposure to Michelangelo's David might elicit a positive emotional response in observers, so too does exposure to a physically attractive individual. And, because of the inevitable pairing of the "person" (the CS) with his or her physical attributes (the US), a positive evaluative response becomes conditioned to the person who is physically attractive.

Practitioners and investigators of social influence have used an extension of the above logic—that the positive emotional response elicited by physically attractive persons (and the presumably negative response elicited by unattractive persons) can be conditioned to stimuli that are paired with these persons. Indeed, much commercial advertising reflects this (and related) conditioning logic. Familiar to all of us are advertisements that link beautiful women with stimulus objects ranging from automobiles to laundry detergents (and other advertisements that pair "unconditioned" stimuli such as extraordinary vistas and pleasant music with consumer products of all stripes). The same logic has been used by academicians who study social influence. For example, classical conditioning represents one interpretation for the finding that physically attractive communicators are often more persuasive than their less attractive counterparts (e.g., Chaiken, 1979; M. Snyder & Rothbart, 1971; for a review of attractiveness and social influence, see Chaiken, 1986). According to this interpretation, the positive emotional response that physically attractive communicators elicit in message recipients becomes conditioned to these communicators' attitudinal statements, thus enhancing recipients' agreement with their messages.

Byrne and his colleagues have argued that classical conditioning principles also underlie the well replicated similarity-attraction effect, that is, our tendency to like people who possess attitudes and traits that are similar to our own and to dislike people with dissimilar attitudes and traits (e.g., Byrne, 1971; Byrne & Clore, 1970; Clore & Byrne, 1974). According to their formulation, the expression of attitude or trait similarity is inherently reinforcing because it provides consensual validation for our attitudes and traits (see Festinger, 1954; see also discussion of the strain-toward-symmetry model in Chapter 10). Thus, attitude or trait similarity is assumed to represent an unconditioned stimulus that evokes an implicit positive affective response. By the same logic, dissimilarity is assumed to be inherently punishing and hence evokes a negative affective response. And inevitably, the person (CS) is paired with his or her expression of attitude or trait similarity (+US) or dissimilarity (–US). As a consequence, positive affect becomes conditioned to the person whose attitudes or traits are similar to our own, and negative affect becomes conditioned to the person whose attitudes or traits are dissimilar.[9] Congruent with this interpretation, Byrne has shown using the Staats and Staats (1958) paradigm that conditioned stimuli such as photographs of persons (Byrne & Clore, 1970) and geometric figures (Sachs & Byrne, 1970) do come to be evaluated positively or negatively, depending upon whether they are repeatedly paired with similar or dissimilar attitude statements.

More general than this application, classical conditioning principles suggest that we may grow to like others simply because they happen to be present when we experience positive or rewarding events (Clore & Byrne, 1974; B. E. Lott & Lott, 1985). In a clever test of this hypothesis, groups of three children played a game in which some members were rewarded and others were not. As indexed by a sociometric measure of liking administered outside of this laboratory context, subjects who had been rewarded indicated significantly greater liking for their fellow group members than did un-rewarded subjects (B. E. Lott & Lott, 1960).

Mediational Issues. Numerous studies leave little doubt that the attitudes subjects express toward "conditioned stimulus" objects can be influenced by pairing these objects repeatedly with other "unconditioned stimulus" objects that routinely elicit positive or negative evaluations. Yet, paralleling discussions of the attitudinal effects of verbal reinforcement, the issue of *why* attitudes are influenced by classical conditioning procedures has been a matter of some debate. And, again one "affective" mechanism has traditionally been pitted against the more general assertion that classical conditioning effects are the product of deliberative cognitive processes. The affective mechanism holds that positive or negative evaluative (often emotional) responses are automatically elicited by exposure to the unconditioned stimulus and these responses become conditioned to any stimulus that is contiguously and repeatedly paired with the unconditioned stimulus. Contemporary associative network models of memory (see Chapter 3) provide an alternate language for describing essentially the same conditioning mechanism. In this approach, the US object or event and the evaluative response (UR) elicited by (or associated with) the US would be represented in memory as a concept node (US) and an evaluation node (UR) that are linked by an associative bond. In other words, attitude toward the US is represented as an object-evaluation association in memory (see Chapter 1). The CS object is also represented as a concept node in memory. Prior to the conditioning trials, the CS is *not* associated in memory with either the US or the UR (although a meaningful CS may have linkages to other nodes). When the CS and US are repeatedly presented in close temporal contiguity, however, a CS-US association *is* established. Moreover, because of the assumption that activating one node (e.g., US) in a network causes linked nodes (e.g., UR) to become active, repeated CS-US pairings *also* establish an association in memory between the CS and the evaluative response originally associated only with the US. In other words, an attitude toward the CS is formed. Regardless of which theoretical language one prefers, the implications are pretty much the same: Classical conditioning procedures *can* lead people to form attitudes toward objects without any conscious deliberation about those objects' attributes.

As was the case in the operant conditioning literature, the claim that the attitudinal effects of classical conditioning procedures are mediated by more deliberate cognitive processes has been based primarily on the criterion of awareness. That is, investigators have assumed that if subjects are aware of the systematic contingency between the CS and US, the effect of their repeated pairing on subjects' attitudes represents the outcome of some higher-order cognitive process (e.g., Fishbein & Ajzen, 1975; Insko & Oakes, 1966; Kiesler et al., 1969; M. M. Page, 1969). Consistent with the argument that awareness is a necessary mediator of classical conditioning effects, a number of studies have obtained significant conditioning effects only among subjects whose postexperimental reports indicated that they were aware of the CS-US contingency (e.g., B. H. Cohen, 1964; Insko & Oakes, 1966; M. M. Page, 1969). Also, several studies have found that manipulations designed to increase contingency awareness reliably increase both the magnitude of classical conditioning effects and subjects' self-reports of contingency awareness (e.g., Insko & Oakes, 1966; M. M. Page, 1969).

Page (1969) interpreted these awareness findings as supportive of a demand characteristics explanation of classical conditioning effects. Similar to the demand account of operant conditioning, Page's argument was that the major consequence of contingency awareness is "demand awareness." That is, becoming aware of the CS-US contingency leads subjects also to become aware of the hypothesis that the CS-US pairings are designed to influence their attitudes toward the CS. Assuming that subjects desire to cooperate with the experimenter (Weber & Cook, 1972), this explanation holds that it is demand awareness that causes subjects to express attitudes that are in line with the experimenter's classical conditioning hypothesis. Like the demand interpretation of operant conditioning, this interpretation views conditioning effects as artifactual or, in social influence terms, as reflecting compliance-based attitude change.

Using postexperimental awareness probes such as the one shown in Table 9.1 and, occasionally, manipulations of demand awareness, Page obtained support for the demand interpretation in several higher-order conditioning studies (Page, 1969, 1974; Page & Kahle, 1976). However, conceptually similar research by Insko and Oakes (1966) suggested that while contingency awareness was necessary for conditioning to occur, demand awareness was not. Experiments showing that conditioning effects can be found using unobtrusive attitude measures assessed in contexts unrelated to the conditioning situation also weaken the case for the demand characteristics explanation (Berkowitz & Knurek, 1969; Early, 1968; Gorn, 1982; Zanna et al., 1970). In addition, the viability of the demand interpretation has not been demonstrated in relation to studies that have featured conditioning procedures and predictions far more complex than those used in Page's research or the well-known Staats and Staats (1958) national names experiment (e.g., Das & Nanda, 1963; Maltzman, 1968; Yavuz & Bousfield, 1959).

Fishbein and Ajzen (1975; Ajzen, 1974) proposed a different cognitive interpretation of classical conditioning effects, one that views subjects' expressed attitudes as genuinely held, rather than strategic in nature. According to these authors, the major

TABLE 9.1

M. M. Page's (1969) Postexperimental Awareness Questionnaire

1. What was the purpose of this experiment and what were you supposed to do?
2. During the experiment did you ever have the idea that its purpose might be something other than what I was telling you? What?
3. Thinking back to the experiment, did you notice at the time any relationship between certain syllables on the screen and the words that were spoken? What?
4. If you noticed any relationship between the lists, is this something you were actually aware of during the experiment or is it something you thought of while filling out these questions?
5. Do you remember approximately when it was that you noticed this? (1) right away, (2) first 1/3 of learning, (3) second 1/3, (4) last 1/3, (5) while taking the first learning test, (6) while taking the second learning test.
6. What did you think was the purpose of the rating scales at the time you were filling them out, if anything?
7. How did you go about deciding what rating to give the various nonsense syllables?
8. Did you think that the experimenter might have expected that you would rate certain of the nonsense syllables in any certain way? Explain.
9. Was your answer to Question 8 something you were actually aware of before or during the marking of the rating scales, or something that you thought of afterwards?
10. What syllable was always or usually paired with travel words?
    a. How certain are you of this or are you guessing?
       Guessing __ : __ : __ : __ : __ : __ : __ Certain
    b. Is this something you were aware of during the experiment or something you thought of since? Please explain if necessary.
11. What syllable was always or usually paired with words of pleasant meaning?
    a. How certain are you of this or are you guessing?
       Guessing __ : __ : __ : __ : __ : __ : __ Certain
    b. Is this something you were aware of during the experiment or something you thought of since? Please explain if necessary.
12. What syllable was always or usually paired with words of unpleasant meaning?
    a. How certain are you of this or are you guessing?
       Guessing __ : __ : __ : __ : __ : __ : __ Certain
    b. Is this something you were aware of during the experiment or something you thought of since? Please explain if necessary.
13. Were you ever aware during the experiment that yof [wuh for the other group] was always paired with words of pleasant meaning or connotation and that wuh [yof] was always paired with words of unpleasant meaning? And, if so, were you aware of any effect this might have had on you as you marked the rating scales? Explain.
14. Assuming that you knew the pleasant and unpleasant words and what was expected on the marking of the rating scales, rate your attitude while marking the rating scales.
       Resist the influence __ : __ : __ : __ : __ : __ : __ Mark the right answers
15. Please make any other comments that you feel might help us understand your reaction to this experiment.
16. Have you had any previous courses in psychology such as in high school?
17. Do you know the meaning of the term conditioning? If so, did you think about it during this experiment?

Source: This table was presented by Page (1969, Table 1, p. 181).

consequence of contingency awareness is that subjects form beliefs about the conditioned stimulus object on the basis of information provided to them by the unconditioned stimulus or stimuli. Some subjects in Staats and Staats' (1958) study, for example may have come to believe that "Swedish" is associated with positive attributes such as "happy" while "Dutch" is associated with negative attributes such as "ugly." Subjects might even go beyond the information given and infer that the CS possesses other evaluatively consistent attributes (see Fishbein & Ajzen, 1975; Tesser, 1978; S. Rosenberg & Sedlak, 1972). For example, if "Swedish" is believed to be associated with "happy," subjects might also come to believe that "Swedish" is associated with related attributes such as "pleasant." As discussed in Chapters 3 and 5, both Fishbein and Ajzen's expectancy-value model and N. H. Anderson's information integration theory regard people's attitudes as a function of the information they possess about attitude objects. Consistent with these models, if the CS-US pairings of the typical classical conditioning study lead subjects to form beliefs that link the CS with positive attributes, they would be expected to form a positive attitude toward the CS object; similarly, if these pairings lead subjects to believe that the CS possesses negative attributes, negative attitudes should ensue.

Ajzen (1974) proposed that the same informational mechanism could also explain the similarity-attraction relationship (see also M. F. Kaplan & Anderson, 1973a). In contrast to Byrne's classical conditioning explanation, Ajzen argued that we like similar others because we form beliefs that they possess positively valued attributes. For example, learning that a person believes in God should produce the inference that the person is religious. If the subject is himself religious, religiosity should be positively valued because people evaluate self-descriptive traits positively (e.g., Stalling, 1970). If, however, the subject is not religious, this attribute should be less positively evaluated. According to Ajzen's arguments, the impact of similarity on liking is mediated by perceivers' beliefs that the similar other possesses positive attributes, and that the dissimilar other possesses negative attributes. Data consistent with this hypothesis have been obtained in a number of experiments (e.g., Ajzen, 1974; Lydon, Jamieson, & Zanna, 1988; McLaughlin, 1971; Tesser, 1969; see also Byrne, Clore, Griffit, Lamberth, & Mitchell, 1973a, 1973b; Kaplan & Anderson, 1973a, 1973b).

The belief formation hypothesis has not been directly evaluated in relation to the typical classical conditioning study, although several studies do indicate that conditioning procedures can influence subjects' beliefs about conditioned stimuli as well as their attitudes toward these stimuli. For example, Kuykendall and Keating (1990) paired the names of various countries with positive or negative US words (e.g., happy, ugly). For any one subject, one country (e.g., Turkey) was always paired with positive words, and another country (e.g., Brazil) was always paired with negative words. After the conditioning procedure, subjects completed a questionnaire concerning the economic conditions of each country and then listed their thoughts about each country. The results indicated that subjects formed more unfavorable beliefs about a country's economic conditions (e.g., indicating that Turkey had a high inflation rate) and listed more unfavorable thoughts about that country when it had previously been paired with negative, rather than positive, words.

According to the belief formation hypothesis, contingency awareness leads subjects to form beliefs about the CS, and these beliefs, in turn, shape subjects' attitudes toward the CS. Although the Kuykendall and Keating (1990) study did not assess subjects' attitudes, their belief findings are consistent with aspects of this logic. Nonetheless, the fact that beliefs were more favorable in the positive (vs. negative) conditioning cells of the study does *not* eliminate a simple conditioning explanation for these data. To the extent that attitudes were classically conditioned in this study, these evaluative tendencies should be evident on *any* measure that reflects evaluation, regardless of whether the measure assesses responses that are primarily affective, cognitive, or behavioral in nature (see Chapter 1). Alternatively, attitudes could have been formed via classical conditioning, and these (unassessed) attitudes may have then *shaped* subjects' cognitions. Moreover, this attitude-to-belief path could be explained in terms of either cognitive or motivational mechanisms (or some mix). For example, associative network models suggest that attitudes may prime (i.e., activate) concepts of similar valence. Thus, for subjects conditioned to have positive attitudes toward Turkey, instructions to list beliefs about this country may have activated their attitudes which, in turn, rendered positive beliefs about this country more accessible than negative beliefs. In contrast, consistency motivation could have operated. Assuming that Kuykendall and Keating's subjects held prior beliefs about Turkey (or Brazil), a potential consequence of the conditioning procedure is that at least some of these beliefs would be inconsistent with subjects' newly acquired positive or negative attitudes. In order to reduce the unpleasant affect associated with evaluative-cognitive inconsistencies, subjects may have modified their beliefs about Turkey (M.J. Rosenberg, 1960a; see Chapter 10).

To provide unequivocal evidence that deliberative cognitive processing is not a necessary mediator of classical conditioning effects, Krosnick, Betz, Jussim, and Lynn (1992) attempted to demonstrate that attitudes can be classically conditioned even in the absence of subjects' awareness of *unconditioned stimuli*. If subjects are unaware of having been exposed to such stimuli, they would obviously also be unaware of the CS-US contingency. In two studies, Krosnick and colleagues systematically paired US photographs designed to elicit positive or negative affect (e.g., a bridal couple vs. a bucket of snakes) with CS photographs which portrayed the same female target engaged in various evaluatively ambiguous behaviors (e.g., getting into a car, washing dishes). For half the subjects, the CS was preceded by a negative US on each of nine conditioning trials, whereas for the remaining subjects, the CS was always preceded by a positive US. On each trial, the US was projected onto a screen for a duration assumed to be too brief to be consciously recognized by subjects (see below). Immediately after exposure to the US, one of the nine CS photographs was projected for a duration of 2 seconds. After the conditioning trials, subjects indicated their attitudes toward the target person (e.g., liking ratings) and also rated her personality on various trait adjective scales (e.g., honest, considerate).

The results of Experiment 1, which presented the US photographs for 13 milliseconds, yielded reliable conditioning effects. Specifically, subjects who had been exposed to positive US photographs expressed significantly more favorable attitudes toward the target (CS) and described the target's personality in significantly more favorable terms than subjects who had been exposed to the negative US photographs. In addition, postexperimental questioning of subjects revealed that none reported any awareness that stimuli *other* than the CS photographs had been presented. Yet data provided by an auxiliary group of subjects suggested that the 13-millisecond exposure time may not have reduced awareness of the US to chance levels. These subjects' guesses as to whether the US photographs were "photographs" or "words" were better than would be expected by chance. On the other hand, and more consistent with the authors' assumptions, these subjects performed no better than chance in guessing the valence (positive vs. negative) of these stimuli. To provide stronger evidence for their hypothesis, the authors conducted a second experiment featuring a shorter US exposure time (9 milliseconds) and also included a postexperimental task similar to the auxiliary study in order to assess the extent to which their US presentations had been truly subliminal. Analyses of these data suggested that the researchers had accomplished their goal of reducing subjects' awareness of the unconditioned stimuli to chance levels. More important, the conditioning results observed in this second study, although statistically weaker than those obtained in Experiment 1, again revealed more positive attitudes and beliefs among subjects who had been exposed subliminally to the positive US photographs.

These findings are consistent with the idea that classical conditioning procedures can influence attitudes in the absence of conscious awareness of either the CS-US contingency or the US. However, two aspects of the design of the Krosnick et al. (1992) experiments raise the possibility that mechanisms other than conditioning may have produced the results these authors observed. Most attitude-conditioning studies have modeled the procedures and design of the Staats and Staats (1958) national names experiment. As in Pavlov's original work, these studies used a *forward pairing* procedure: On each conditioning trial, exposure to the *CS* precedes exposure to the US. In contrast, Krosnick and colleagues used *backward pairing*: On each conditioning trial, subjects were first exposed to the US and then to the CS. A second distinctive feature of the Krosnick and colleagues research stems from the fact that a *single* CS (female target person) was always paired with either a positive or negative US (photograph). Thus, across conditioning trials, some subjects were exposed only to positive US objects and others were exposed only to negative US objects. Although all positive versus all negative CS-US pairings also characterize most other studies of attitude conditioning, like the Staats and Staats (1958) research, these experiments typically examine *multiple* CS objects in the context of a within-subjects experimental design. Thus, across conditioning trials subjects are typically exposed to *both* positive and negative US objects (e.g., Dutch-good, Swedish-sour, Dutch-beautiful, Swedish-ugly, etc.).

Although the backward pairing procedure (i.e., US-then-CS) that Krosnick and colleagues used does not rule out conditioning as an explanation for their attitude and personality rating data, this procedure has generally been shown to produce much weaker conditioning effects than forward pairing in the standard (i.e., nonattitudinal) literature on classical conditioning (Rescorla, 1988). Moreover, the backward pairing procedure raises the possibility that these data were instead the product of *affective* (or evaluative) *priming* (see Niedenthal, 1990). According to this idea, subliminal exposure to the positive and negative US photographs in this research (e.g., bucket of snakes) may have primed concepts of like valence in memory (e.g., ugly, slimy), and these activated concepts may have then biased subjects' perceptions of the ambiguous CS photographs. That is, subjects may have "seen" the CS target person (or the behaviors she displayed) in a more positive light in the positive (vs. negative) US photograph conditions.[10] As a result, attitudes and personality ratings would be more positive in these conditions. Various *mood* interpretations for these data are also plausible, since it is possible that subliminal exposure to the positive US photographs induced a positive mood in subjects and exposure to the negative US photographs a negative mood (e.g., Robles, Smith, Carver, & Wellens, 1987). If so, subjects in the positive (vs. negative) US photograph conditions may have formed more positive impressions of the CS target due to one or more mechanisms by which mood has been posited to affect judgment. For example, people in good moods may be motivated to view people and events positively (Shaller & Cialdini, 1990), or (not unlike the evaluative priming idea) positive mood may prime positive material in memory which, in turn, biases the processing of subsequently encountered stimuli in a mood-congruent manner (Isen, 1987; see also Bower, 1981; Clark & Isen, 1982; Forgas & Bower, 1987; Isen, 1987; Niedenthal & Cantor, 1986; Schwarz, 1990; see also Chapter 10).[11]

These alternative explanations for the Krosnick et al. (1992) results are not necessarily *more* compelling than the authors' subliminal conditioning explanation. Nonetheless, this conditioning-without-awareness hypothesis clearly requires testing in an experimental context that eliminates priming and mood effects as plausible explanations; such a context is, in fact, provided by the forward pairing, within-subjects design of the traditional classical conditioning-of-attitudes paradigm. Yet regardless of how the findings observed by Krosnick and his colleagues are best interpreted, they do make a significant general point about affective processes in attitude formation—they are important. Emotionally evocative stimuli that subjects were unaware of influenced their attitudes toward a subsequently encountered object—either directly, through a simple conditioning process, or indirectly, through one or more of the alternative mechanisms discussed above.

Summary and Conclusions. Numerous studies designed to assess the attitudinal effects of classical conditioning procedures confirm that these procedures can reliably influence attitudinal responding. Yet for the most part, existing research has shed little light on mediational issues. Notwithstanding the lack of direct evidence for specific cognitive mechanisms, the traditional assumption in this literature that contingency awareness was a necessary mediator of conditioning effects fostered the conclusion during the late 1960s and 1970s that these effects were the product of deliberative cognitive processes. In particular, these effects were viewed by many investigators as experimental artifacts produced by subjects' awareness of the experimental hypothesis and their desires to perform as they believed the experimenter wished them to (see Fishbein & Ajzen, 1975; Kiesler et al., 1969; M. M. Page, 1974). At best, attitudes influenced by conditioning procedures were viewed as the genuine product of some (often unspecified) form of cogitation on the part of experimental subjects. For example, after summarizing the evidence on contingency awareness, Fishbein and Ajzen (1975) stated:

> We can thus conclude that there is little support for the notion that classical conditioning provides a noninformational basis for attitude formation. Instead, the findings of classical conditioning studies can readily be interpreted within an information processing framework. Although attitudes may be formed in a classical conditioning situation, they do not seem to be the result of automatic conditioning processes; rather they appear to be determined by beliefs that are formed about the attitude object. (p. 280)

Our conclusions differ. At this point in time, we see little firm basis for rejecting the hypothesis that attitudes can be classically conditioned in the automatic manner implied by the basic conditioning paradigm. Aside from the dearth of direct evidence for cognitive interpretations, there are several other reasons for our conclusions.

As was the case in the operant literature, information-based explanations of the effects of classical conditioning procedures on attitudes were based primarily on the assumption that awareness of the CS-US contingency was *necessary* for conditioning effects to occur. Yet evidence for the necessity of contingency awareness rests primarily on correlational data (but see note 12). Although the association between conditioning scores and measures of contingency awareness found in many studies could indicate that awareness mediates conditioning, several other interpretations are possible. For example, conditioning procedures might exert a parallel effect on attitudes and subjects' awareness of the CS-US contingency. By this third variable account, contingency awareness would be a concomitant response to the conditioning procedure but would play no causal role in determining subjects' attitudes. Illustrating this viewpoint, Arthur Staats (1969) argued that conditioning and awareness might correlate simply because awareness measures discriminate subjects who pay attention to the experimental materials, and are thus likely to be conditioned, from subjects who do not pay attention and are thus less likely to be conditioned.[12,13]

Alternatively, contingency awareness could be a *consequence* of conditioning. Once conditioned, subjects might become aware of the CS-US contingency to the extent that they sense, if only vaguely, that they feel positively or negatively toward certain stimuli (see Buck, 1985; Tucker, 1981). In other words, contingency awareness would be the product of a deliberative cognitive process, that is, subjects' attempts to analyze why they feel the way they do toward certain objects. In this regard, Buck (1985) has argued that the tendency to analyze and recognize such vaguely sensed feeling states has adaptive value because it enhances the human organism's capacity for self-regulation. This interpretation is compatible with the synergistic view of affect and cognition we discuss at the end of the chapter.

A final interpretation of the correlation between conditioning and contingency awareness turns the demand characteristics account of conditioning on its head. Staats (1969) and others (Insko, 1967; Levin, 1961) have cautioned that postexperimental questionnaires used to detect awareness may, themselves, possess demand qualities (see Table 9.1 and Dulany, 1962; M. M. Page, 1970, 1974; Spielberger & Levin, 1962).

410

This interpretation asserts that the increasingly pointed questions posed in Page's and others' awareness questionnaires suggest to subjects the nature of the CS-US contingency (and often the experimental hypothesis). If so, subjects' levels of awareness would be overestimated, and contingency (as well as demand) awareness might be more a consequence of reactive postexperimental measures than of the initial conditioning procedure (for counterarguments, see Page, 1971, 1973).

Because of these multiple interpretations of the association between contingency awareness and conditioning as well as the inherent validity limitations of self-report data (e.g., Nisbett & Wilson, 1977), the claim that contingency awareness is a necessary mediator of classical conditioning (and verbal conditioning) effects lacks empirical depth (see also Coleman & Gormezano, 1979; Dawson & Furedy, 1976; Erdelyi, 1974; Gormezano & Kehoe, 1975). Because deliberative cognitive accounts of classical conditioning rest primarily on this claim, these accounts, too, lack empirical depth. Moreover, recent mere exposure research (see next section) has called into question the utility of awareness for distinguishing between cognitive and affective mechanisms.

Importantly, the rule of parsimony does tend to favor an automatic conditioning explanation of classical conditioning effects. Whereas this mechanism can account for most results in the literature, neither of the two main cognitive mechanisms that have been proposed to date appear to have such broad applicability. As already noted, the demand characteristics explanation, unless tortuously applied, cannot account for the results of conditioning experiments that have featured delayed, disguised, or unobtrusive measures of attitudes. This interpretation also seems a strained account of studies that have featured complex conditioning procedures. Although the beliefs-mediate-attitudes hypothesis advanced by Fishbein and Ajzen (1975) would seem to have wider applicability, its relevance to experiments whose stimuli differ considerably from those used in the well-known Staats and Staats (1958) experiments is uncertain. Is it realistic to posit that subjects' attitudes toward nonsense syllables and geometric figures, for example, are based on their beliefs that these CS objects possess certain attributes? Similarly, how realistic is it to posit that unconditioned stimuli that are *not* meaningful adjectives (e.g., shock, noise) provide the informational basis for such beliefs? Our discussion of the research by Krosnick and colleagues (1992) suggested several other potential interpretations of conditioning effects such as evaluative priming and mood-congruent processing and judgment. These hybrid (i.e., part-affective, part-cognitive) explanations provide as reasonable an account of Krosnick and colleagues' experiments as conditioning and are relevant to other studies whose designs have also deviated from the traditional classical conditioning paradigm (e.g., Gorn, 1982; Riordan & Tedeschi, 1983). Their applicability to the core literature on the classical conditioning of attitudes, however, is arguable.

Thus, we conclude that an automatic conditioning process remains a viable explanation for the results of many primary and higher-order classical conditioning experiments. Subsequent research may be able to document this process with greater precision than has past research and also begin to explore its boundary conditions (e.g., Cacioppo et al., 1992). In addition, further research addressing the hypothesis that

411

attitudes can be conditioned even in the absence of people's awareness of the conditioning stimuli seems warranted given Krosnick and colleagues' (1992) preliminary findings and demonstrations that processing and judgments can be affected by stimuli and covariations among stimulus events that people cannot report having seen or heard (e.g., Bargh, 1989; Kihlstrom, 1987; Kitayama, 1990; Kunst-Wilson & Zajonc, 1980; Lewicki, 1986; see further discussion in next section).

Mere Exposure and Attitude Formation

The attitudinal effects of repeated exposure to attitude objects or to information about them has been examined in a number of contexts. In the persuasion and consumer behavior areas investigators have explored whether multiple exposures to a persuasive message enhance or inhibit persuasion. As discussed in Chapters 6 and 7, the results of these message repetition experiments have proven complex. Within the one-to-three exposure range, increased exposure appears to increase persuasion for messages containing high quality arguments and to decrease persuasion for messages containing low quality arguments. However, exposure frequencies beyond three often lead to decreased persuasion, even for well-argued messages (e.g., Cacioppo & Petty, 1979b, 1985). Exposure effects have also been the focus of some interpersonal attraction and intergroup prejudice research. Whereas attraction researchers have explored whether frequent social interaction enhances liking (e.g., Festinger, 1951; Newcomb, 1963, 1978; see Berscheid, 1985), prejudice researchers have examined whether prolonged social contact with minority group members can reduce prejudice and discrimination (e.g., S. W. Cook, 1978; Deutsch & Collins, 1951; N. Miller & Brewer, 1984; McGuire, 1985). Finally, a number of early studies of music and art appreciation investigated the effects of repeated exposure to musical selections and paintings on subjects' aesthetic preferences (e.g., Downey & Knapp, 1927; Maslow, 1937; Meyer, 1903).

In a now classic monograph, Robert Zajonc (1968a) hypothesized that mere repeated exposure to a stimulus causes increased liking of that stimulus:

> ... mere repeated exposure of the individual to a stimulus is a sufficient condition for the enhancement of his attitude toward it. By "mere exposure" is meant a condition which just makes the given stimulus accessible to the individual's perception (p. 1).

Unlike persuasion studies on message repetition, which focus on the effects of repeated exposure to *information* about attitude objects, Zajonc was concerned primarily with the effects of repeated exposure to attitude objects themselves. Zajonc also believed that previous attraction and prejudice research did not clearly address the attitudinal effects of repeated *mere* exposure because this research usually confounded mere exposure with other attitudinally relevant variables (e.g., social interaction, group interdependence). In addition, although several music and art appreciation studies had found a positive relation between exposure and aesthetic preference, their internal validity was compromised by numerous methodological shortcomings (see Zajonc, 1968a, p. 18).

**FIGURE 9.2.
Relation between
frequency of mere
exposure to Turkish
nonsense words,
Chinese-like
characters, and
photographs of men
and attitude toward
these stimuli.
Attitude was
measured on a scale
from 0 to 6 with
higher numbers
signifying a more
favorable attitude.
This figure was
adapted from those
presented by Zajonc
(1968a, Figures 2
and 5, pp. 14 and
18).**

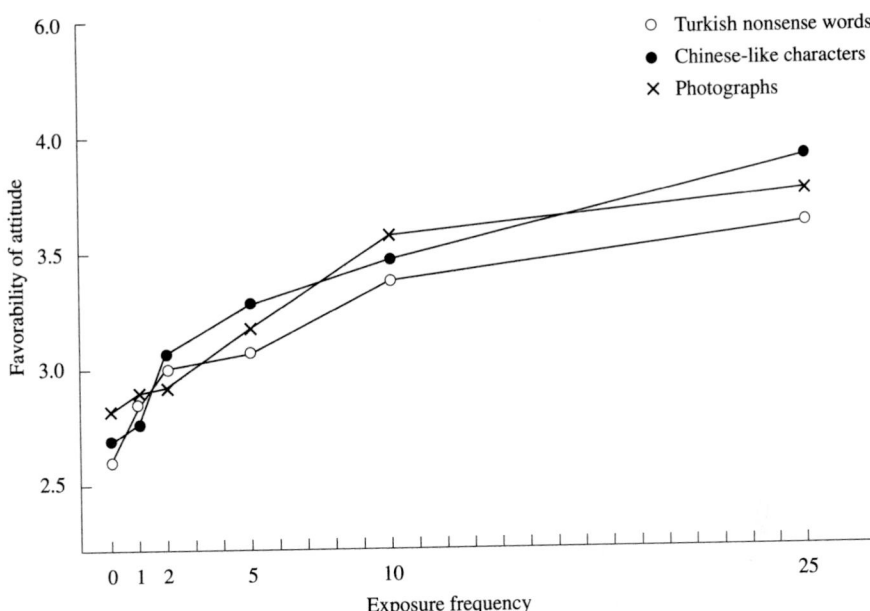

To obtain clearer evidence for his mere exposure hypotheis, Zajonc (1968a) conducted three experiments in which subjects were exposed to a set of stimuli presented at varying frequencies and then indicated their attitudes toward these stimuli. Each study used 12 stimulus objects, each of which was presented to subjects for a 2-second duration either 25 times, 10 times, 5 times, twice, once, or not at all during the exposure phase. The stimuli for the three studies were "Turkish" (actually nonsense) words (e.g., "Biwejni," "Saricik"), Chinese-like characters, and yearbook photographs, and subjects were told that the research concerned "pronouncing foreign words," "learning a foreign language," and "visual memory," respectively. Subjects' attitudes were assessed by having them rate how "good" they believed the meaning of each "Turkish" word or "Chinese" character to be, and how much they liked the man pictured in each photograph. The results of the three experiments are shown in Figure 9.2.

As Figure 9.2 shows, the three studies yielded virtually identical findings. Subjects' attitudes toward particular Turkish words, Chinese characters, and photographs became more positive as the frequency of their exposure to these stimuli increased. As the figure also indicates, however, this effect was less pronounced at higher exposure frequencies. These monotonically increasing exposure-attitude functions are completely consistent with Zajonc's basic hypothesis that repeated mere exposure is a sufficient condition for attitude enhancement. However, the apparent tendency for the slope of these functions to become flatter at higher exposure frequencies suggested to Zajonc that increased stimulus familiarity (due to repeated exposure) attenuates the mere exposure effect.[14]

413

Zajonc's (1968a) mere exposure findings have been replicated with a variety of stimuli (e.g., nonsense syllables, meaningful words, polygons, people, foods) under a wide range of conditions—for example, in laboratory and non-laboratory settings, at very high exposure frequencies, with initially disliked stimuli, and in contexts designed to promote negative feelings among subjects (e.g., Saegert, Swap, & Zajonc, 1973; Zajonc, Crandall, Kail, & Swap, 1974; Zajonc, Markus, & Wilson, 1974). In addition, exposure effects have been obtained not only with human subjects, but also with animal subjects such as precocial birds and crickets (e.g., Harrison & Fiscaro, 1974; Rajecki, 1973; Zajonc, Reimer, & Hausser, 1973). Indeed, Bornstein's (1989a) meta-analysis of over 200 experiments (with human subjects) revealed that the mere exposure effect is a highly replicable, robust phenomenon of moderate magnitude.

Limitations on the generality of the mere exposure effect and factors that affect its magnitude have, of course, been identified. In fact, the main purpose of Bornstein's (1989a) meta-analytic review of this literature was to identify such boundary conditions and moderating factors (see also Harrison, 1977; W. F. Hill, 1978). Consistent with the shape of the exposure-attitude relationships shown in Figure 9.2, this meta-analysis confirmed that attitude enhancement due to repeated mere exposure to stimuli does tend to level off after 10-to-20 stimulus presentations. Although some experiments have found downturns in subjects' evaluative ratings of stimuli at relatively high exposure frequencies (e.g., Zajonc, Crandall, Kail, & Swap, 1974), Bornstein concluded that the relationship between exposure frequency and attitude is generally positive. This review also documented that the mere exposure effect is larger (a) with complex (vs. simple) stimuli, (b) with brief (vs. long) stimulus-exposure durations (e.g., 1 second vs. 5 or more seconds), (c) with longer (vs. shorter) delays between stimulus exposures and attitude ratings, and (d) when exposure stimuli are presented in a heterogeneous sequence (i.e., with many other stimuli) rather than in a homogeneous sequence (i.e., with few or no other stimuli interspersed; see Harrison & Crandall, 1972).[15] Of perhaps greatest interest, the Bornstein meta-analysis documented that the mere exposure effect is reliable even when stimuli are presented for durations too brief to be consciously recognized by subjects. In fact, his review documented a tendency for the mere exposure effect to be *larger* when stimuli are presented in this subliminal manner than in the supraliminal manner that characterized the first decade of mere exposure research (see further discussion below).

Stimulus Recognition and Mere Exposure

As we explain in a subsequent section, traditional theoretical interpretations of mere exposure assume (implicitly or explicitly) that stimulus recognition is a necessary mediator of the effect of mere repeated exposure to stimuli on attitudes toward these stimuli. Historical precedent for this assumption can be found in Titchener's (1910) analysis of familiarity and preference. According to Titchener, recognition of a stimulus produces "a glow of warmth," and lack of recognition evokes "an uneasy restlessness" (pp. 408–409).

The assumption that stimulus recognition is necessary for mere exposure effects to occur was, for the most part, not seriously challenged during the first decade of mere exposure research. In a 1977 paper, however, Moreland and Zajonc concluded that previous findings relevant to this assumption were equivocal (e.g., Matlin, 1971; Stang, 1975; Zajonc, Shaver, Tavris, & VanKreveld, 1972). Moreover, they reported two experiments that they viewed as calling this assumption into question. In these studies, Moreland and Zajonc exposed subjects to Japanese idiographs either zero, one, three, nine, or 27 times. After this exposure period, they asked subjects to respond to one (Experiment 1) or both (Experiment 2) of the following scales: The extent to which they liked each stimulus object and the extent to which they believed that each object had or had not been previously shown. In both studies, repeated mere exposure to the Japanese ideographs enhanced both attitudes (first scale) and subjective recognition (second scale). In addition, multiple regression analyses indicated that (a) greater subjective recognition was associated with more positive attitudes when objective exposure frequency was held constant, and more important, (b) increased objective frequency was associated with more positive attitudes when subjective recognition was held constant. On the basis of these analyses as well as a subsequent reanalysis using causal modeling techniques, Moreland and Zajonc (1977, 1979; Zajonc, 1980b) concluded that stimulus recognition was a *sufficient* but not *necessary* condition for mere exposure effects to occur. More provocatively, they argued that mere exposure could influence attitudes via two independent routes: a "cold" cognitive route mediated by subjective recognition and a "hot" noncognitive route mediated by an affective mechanism they labeled "subjective affect" (see subsequent discussion).

Although intriguing, Moreland and Zajonc's (1977, 1979) data were correlational and amenable to alternate interpretations (e.g., Birnbaum & Mellers, 1979a, 1979b). To obtain more direct evidence regarding the necessity of stimulus recognition, W. R. Wilson (1979, Experiment 2) used a dichotic listening procedure in order to reduce subjects' awareness of the exposure stimuli to chance levels. Subjects were instructed to listen to a prose passage and to repeat each word aloud immediately upon hearing it. This passage was played to the subject's right ear, the "attended" channel. About 30 seconds after beginning the tracking task, a random sequence of melodic tones was played to the subject's left ear, the "unattended" channel. In all, three different melodies were presented five times each in a randomly determined sequence. Subsequent to this exposure phase, subjects completed a recognition memory test in which the three actually presented melodies and three new ones were played to them without interference. In addition to indicating whether each melody had been played during presentation of the prose passage, subjects also rated their liking for each melody.

Consistent with his assumption that the dichotic listening procedure would eliminate subjects' awareness of the exposure stimuli, Wilson found that the accuracy with which subjects discriminated the three actually presented "old" melodies from the three "new" melodies did not differ from what would be expected by chance. Nevertheless, subjects indicated significantly greater liking for the three "old" melodies than for the three "new" ones. Thus, even in the absence of stimulus recognition, repeated exposure

TABLE 9.2

**Number of Subjects Agreeing with Confederate 1 Versus Confederate 2
in Discussion Task as a Function of Subliminal Priming
in the Bornstein, Leone, and Galley (1987) Experiment**

Subliminal exposure content	Confederate 1	Confederate 2
Confederate 1	15	6
Confederate 2	7	13
Blank slide	10	11

Source: This table was adapted from one presented by Bornstein, Leone, and Galley (1987, Table 1, p. 1075).

led to more positive attitudes. Using visual stimuli (irregular polygons) presented too briefly to produce above-chance recognition, Kunst-Wilson and Zajonc (1980) conceptually replicated Wilson's (1979) mere exposure-liking results. Additional studies featuring visual stimuli highly similar to Kunst-Wilson and Zajonc's have confirmed their findings (Bonnano & Stillings, 1986; Bornstein, Leone, & Galley, 1987; Experiment 1; Seamon, Brody, & Kauf, 1983a, 1983b; Seamon, Marsh, & Brody, 1984; but see Mandler, Nakamura, & Van Zandt, 1987; Mandler & Sheebo, 1983).

Finally, Bornstein, Leone, and Galley (1987, Experiments 2 and 3) extended the above findings to social stimuli. Subjects in two experiments were subliminally exposed to photographs of people. One of these experiments conceptually replicated the Kunst-Wilson and Zajonc study: Although subjects could not discriminate between "old" (i.e., exposed) photographs and "new" (i.e., nonexposed) photographs at better than chance levels, they liked the persons portrayed in the old photographs more. The second experiment yielded more interesting results. Before participating in a discussion task with two confederates, some subjects were exposed subliminally to a photograph of one of the confederates, others to a photograph of the second confederate, and others to a blank slide. During the subsequent task, which required the subject and two confederates to consider 10 poems and reach agreement regarding the gender of their authors, the confederates disagreed with one another seven times. Thus, the subject was placed in the role of tiebreaker. The number of times the subject agreed with one confederate over the other provided an unobtrusive behavioral index of attitude in this experiment. As Table 9.2 shows, the results confirmed the authors' hypothesis that subjects would indicate more overall agreement with the confederate who, through subliminal mere exposure to his photograph, they had come to like.

Theoretical Accounts of Mere Exposure Effects

There has been no shortage of explanations for the attitude-enhancing effect of mere exposure (see Bornstein, 1989a; Grush, 1979; Harrison, 1977; W. F. Hill, 1978; Vanbeselaere, 1983). Most theoretical accounts of mere exposure effects predated the 1980s research showing that these effects can occur without subjects' awareness of having been previously exposed to experimental stimuli. After summarizing several of these explanations, none of which can account easily for subliminal exposure effects, we will return to the Moreland and Zajonc (1977, 1979) argument that mere exposure effects are not necessarily mediated by cognitive processes.

Pre-1980s Interpretations of Exposure Effects. For historical reasons alone we would be remiss not to mention that demand characteristics surfaced as an explanation for (supraliminal) mere exposure effects during the 1970s (e.g., Sawyer, 1975; Stang, 1974a; Suedfeld, Epstein, Buchanan, & Landon, 1971). This development was no doubt fueled by this explanation's earlier and rather successful debut in the operant and classical conditioning literatures (see earlier sections of this chapter). According to the demand account of mere exposure, the simplicity of the (then) typical experiment—in which exposure frequency is manipulated on a within-subjects basis (e.g., Zajonc, 1968a)—leads subjects to become aware of the contingency between stimuli and their frequency of occurrence. As a result, subjects also become aware of the experimenter's hypothesis that high frequency stimuli are to be more favorably evaluated than low frequency stimuli and, given the assumption that subjects wish to cooperate with the experimenter, they indicate more positive attitudes toward high frequency stimuli.

Stang (1974a) obtained support for this demand interpretation in several experiments. However, unlike the typical mere exposure study, Stang provided his subjects with explicit information about differences in exposure frequencies. More important, other research argues against the general viability of the demand explanation. Mere exposure effects have been obtained in experiments that have manipulated exposure frequency on a between-subjects basis, in field as well as laboratory settings, and in studies explicitly designed to mitigate demand characteristics (e.g., Grush, 1976; Moreland & Zajonc, 1976; Rajecki & Wolfson, 1973; Saegert et al., 1973; Zajonc & Rajecki, 1969). Saegart et al. (1973), for example, had subjects move from cubicle to cubicle in order to taste various liquids (e.g., vinegar) in a "taste perception" study. By this procedure, the researchers were able to arrange for each subject to encounter four other subjects either once, twice, five times, or ten times during the tasting session. Measures of interpersonal liking, assessed in a disguised postexperimental questionnaire, showed that liking was a positive function of exposure frequency.

As discussed in Chapter 6, Cacioppo and Petty (e.g., 1985) proposed a cognitive response analysis of the persuasive effects of message repetition: Multiple exposures to a message enhance cognitive responding so that repetition should increase or decrease persuasion depending upon whether one's cognitive responses are mostly favorable or mostly unfavorable to the advocacy.[16] Similar to this analysis and their own belief formation account of classical conditioning studies of attitude formation, Fishbein and Ajzen (1975) argued that repeated exposure to attitudinal stimuli fosters the development of beliefs about these stimuli. If these beliefs link the attitude object to positive attributes, more positive attitudes should result from repeated exposure; if these beliefs link the object to negative attributes, more negative attitudes should ensue. Some support for this hypothesis was obtained by Grush (1976), who found that subjects generated more associations to meaningful English words (e.g., acrobat) as an increasing function of exposure frequency. Although belief formation or cognitive responding provide a plausible account for mere exposure effects obtained with meaningful stimuli (e.g., Perlman & Oskamp, 1971), as we pointed out in relation to classical conditioning research, the relevance of these perspectives to situations in which *nonmeaningful* stimuli such as nonsense words and geometric figures are encountered is arguable.

In a dissertation sponsored by Zajonc, Harrison (1968) proposed that *response competition* mediated mere exposure effects. Harrison argued that a novel stimulus evokes a variety of response tendencies that often conflict with one another (see Berlyne, 1954), and that this response competition creates a state of tension or negative affect. However, repeated exposure to the stimulus acts to strengthen some response tendencies and weaken others, thus reducing response competition. Consequently, repeated exposure leads to a reduction in tension, which is reflected in more positive evaluations of the stimulus. Some support for this hypothesis and several extended formulations have been obtained in a number of experiments (e.g., Harrison, 1968; Harrison & Zajonc, 1970; Matlin, 1970; Saegart & Jellison, 1970; Zajonc, Markus, & Wilson, 1974; Zajonc, Shaver, Tavris, & VanKreveld, 1972; see Harrison, 1977). However, as Harrison (1977) pointed out, response competition logic predicts a reduction in negative affect with increased exposure rather than the development of positive affect. Notwithstanding the fact that most exposure experiments have featured relatively neutral stimuli (Bornstein, 1989a), this explanation seems a poor fit with the data of most exposure studies, in which attitude ratings tend to range from neutral-to-mildly positive at low exposure frequencies to moderately positive at higher frequencies.

Berlyne's (1970) two-factor account of exposure effects derives from his more general optimum arousal theory (e.g., 1967, 1971, 1974) and views *positive habituation* (uncertainty or conflict reduction) and *boredom* (or tedium) as two sequential processes that underlie exposure effects (for a similar perspective, see Stang, 1975). Because positive habituation predominates during the early phases of exposure, exposure should first lead to increased liking. Later, however, boredom predominates so that further exposures should begin to produce decrements in liking. The inflection point in the inverted ∪-shaped curve predicted by this theory is dependent on stimulus properties such as novelty, complexity, and surprisingness. Berlyne labeled these properties "collative" because "to decide how novel, surprising, complex and so on a pattern is, one must compute or collate information from two or more sources" (1971, p. 69). Collative properties determine the inflection point of the liking curve because they affect the relative strength of positive habituation and boredom. For example, because positive habituation will predominate over boredom to a greater extent if stimuli are novel, complex, and presented in a heterogeneous sequence, the point at which increased exposure begins to decrease rather than increase liking will be much higher in these situations than in situations in which stimuli are familiar, simple, and presented in a homogeneous sequence. The two-factor model is supported by the results of a number of experiments (e.g., Berlyne, 1970; Bornstein, Kale, & Cornell, 1990; Munsinger & Kessen, 1964; G. R. Smith & Dorfman, 1975). Moreover, this model has enjoyed wider acceptance than the other explanations we have discussed in this section, primarily because it is able to account for most—but not all (see below)—variables that have been found to moderate the attitudinal effect of mere exposure (e.g., stimulus complexity, exposure duration, presentation sequence, number of stimulus exposures; see Bornstein, 1989a for discussion).

Is Mere Exposure an Affective or Cognitive Phenomenon? The common limitation of all the pre-1980 explanations of mere exposure is that they cannot easily explain the phenomenon of subliminal mere exposure which, at the least, indicates that stimulus recognition is not a necessary mediator of exposure effects. The demand characteristics and cognitive response-belief formation interpretations implicitly presume that stimulus recognition is necessary insofar as they view mere exposure effects as the result of deliberative cognitive processing. The response competition and two-factor theories do accord a mediational role to affective processes by asserting that the enhancing effect of exposure on liking for attitude objects is a positive function of tension reduction (response competition model) or positive habituation (two-factor model). Yet, like the other perspectives, these models also view attitude judgments as dependent upon a prior cognitive process insofar as the processes of tension reduction and positive habituation are, themselves, presumably dependent upon the individual's ability to recognize or identify the attitude object over its successive presentations (see Berlyne, 1970; Harrison, 1977; Moreland & Zajonc, 1977; Zajonc, 1980b).

As we have seen, Moreland and Zajonc's (1977, 1979) contention that stimulus recognition is not a necessary mediator of mere exposure effects has been supported in multiple investigations featuring defensible subliminal presentation procedures. Indeed, as we have also noted, Bornstein's (1989a) meta-analysis confirmed that the mean exposure effect in these experiments was reliably positive and also somewhat greater than the mean exposure effect obtained for the larger sample of traditional experiments featuring supraliminal stimulus presentation. In fact, Bornstein showed that the mean size of the exposure effect was also larger for the subliminal studies than for that subset of studies whose stimuli could be consciously recognized even though they were only briefly presented (e.g., for 1 second). On this basis, Bornstein tentatively concluded that stimulus recognition may actually *attenuate* the mere exposure effect.

Moreland and Zajonc's (1977, 1979) conclusions went beyond the empirical statement that stimulus recognition is unnecessary for mere exposure effects to occur. Specifically they concluded that the attitudinal effects of mere exposure may sometimes occur via a "hot" affective mechanism that involves *no* prior cognitive process. In subsequent papers Zajonc (e.g., 1980b, 1984; Zajonc & Markus, 1984) argued that the Moreland and Zajonc conclusion was justified since exposure effects can occur *in the absence of awareness*:

> These experiments establish, I believe, that affective reactions to a stimulus may be acquired by virtue of experience with that stimulus even if not accompanied by such an elementary cold cognitive process as conscious recognition (Zajonc, 1980b, p. 163).

Other investigators, however, have argued that Zajonc's conclusion is, at best premature (e.g., P. C. Gordon & Holyoak, 1983; Holyoak & Gordon, 1984; Mandler et al., 1987; Seamon et al., 1983a, 1983b). Central to these investigators' resistance to

Zajonc's view is the now sizable literature indicating that perceptual and cognitive processes such as the encoding of frequency information, lexical decision making, the learning of grammatical structure and covariation between stimuli, and the categorization of social behaviors can all proceed automatically in the absence of awareness (see Bargh, Bond, Lombardi, & Tota, 1986; Bargh & Pietromonaco, 1982; Bornstein, 1989b; Fowler, Wolford, Slade, & Tasinary, 1981; Hasher & Zacks, 1984; Kihlstrom, 1987; Lewicki, 1986; Marcel, 1983; Reber & Lewis, 1977; Srull & Wyer, 1980). The importance of these findings on automatic, unconscious perceptual and cognitive processes is that they totally undermine the value of using awareness as a criterion for determining whether the attitudinal effects of mere exposure—or any other phenomenon—are the product of "cognitive" as opposed to "affective" processes. For this reason, the fact that mere exposure effects do not depend upon subjects' conscious recognition of exposure stimuli should not be interpreted as demonstrating that these effects are *not* mediated by cognitive mechanisms.

One can conclude, however, that mere exposure effects are not necessarily the product of *deliberative* or *conscious* cognitive processes. The Zajonc and Moreland view that exposure effects may be mediated by a "hot" affective mechanism is, at present, not inconsistent with the data. Yet, verification of this hypothesis as well as the competing one that preconscious cognitive processes are responsible will necessitate further research and no doubt greater precision regarding the nature of each of these postulated mediators.

New Directions in Theorizing about Mere Exposure. At this point in time, then, the mechanisms by which repeated mere exposure to stimuli results in enhanced liking for those stimuli remain unclear. Because Berlyne's (1970) two-factor model is able to explain much of the empirical literature, Bornstein (1989a) has suggested modifying this theory to incorporate implicit, unconscious learning about a stimulus in addition to deliberative, conscious learning. In addition he and several other investigators have suggested that *perceptual fluency* (L. L. Jacoby, Kelley, Brown, & Jasechko, 1989) may be the cause of subliminal mere exposure effects (Bornstein & D'Agostino, 1992; Mandler et al., 1987). Perceptual fluency, which does not require attention to or deliberative processing of a stimulus object (Jacoby et al., 1989), refers to the facilitating effect of having previously been exposed to stimuli on subsequent encoding of these stimuli, that is, previously encountered stimuli are easier to perceive and process than stimuli that have not been encountered before. When asked to report on the experience of perceptual fluency, subjects have been found to attribute easier processing to a variety of stimulus properties (e.g., Jacoby et al., 1989; Jacoby & Whitehouse, 1989). Hence, according to this explanation, the perceptual fluency that results from previous subliminal exposure to stimuli may be attributed to liking for these stimuli.

To account for the apparent fact that the mere exposure effect is smaller when stimulus exposure occurs on a supraliminal basis, Bornstein (1989a; Bornstein & D'Agostino, 1992) has argued that the deliberative processing of stimuli that ensues when people have the opportunity to ponder these stimuli will often attenuate the attitudinal impact of the lower-level perceptual fluency mechanism. This hypothesis is similar to Kihlstrom's (1987) more general proposition that deliberative scrutinization and analysis of stimuli may constrain or counteract implicit (i.e., nonconsciously induced) affective reactions to these stimuli, and is also conceptually similar to the heuristic-systematic model's assumption that systematic processing of attitude-relevant information will often attenuate the attitudinal impact of heuristic processing. Although this emerging dual-process view of mere exposure effects will require testing and refinement, it represents a promising new direction for subsequent research.

Conclusions

The question of whether attitudes are formed by affective or cognitive mechanisms has been raised and debated in each of the three literatures we reviewed in this chapter. Yet a satisfactory answer to it has remained elusive. A major impediment to progress has been the lack of clear criteria for distinguishing between affective and cognitive explanations. Throughout the 1960s and 1970s the concept of contingency awareness (and sometimes demand awareness) served as the main criterion for adjudicating between the two types of explanations in research investigating the attitudinal effects of operant and classical conditioning procedures. Although investigators have debated the efficacy of this criterion for years (e.g., Adams, 1957; Erdelyi, 1974; Ericksen, 1960; Gormezano & Kehoe, 1975; Krasner, 1958; Thorndike & Rock, 1934), the burgeoning literature on cognitive processes that may occur in the absence of awareness amplifies prior assertions that contingency and other forms of "awareness" are invalid markers of cognitive processing and should not be used as the primary basis for deciding between affective and cognitive explanations.

Our review of operant and classical conditioning research led us to conclude that, despite considerable prejudice in favor of cognitive mechanisms, the simple affective mechanisms of conditioning remain viable explanations for the attitude formation effects demonstrated in many conditioning studies. However, the previous decade of mere exposure research makes clear that the affective-cognitive issue in these older literatures involved a choice only between these affective mechanisms and several *higher-order* cognitive processes (e.g., belief formation, demand characteristics). Since exposure effects can occur without subjects' awareness of exposure stimuli, perhaps classical and operant conditioning effects can as well (see Corteen & Wood, 1972; Dawson & Schell, 1982; Krosnick et al., 1992; Konečni & Slamecka, 1972). To investigate these possibilities, researchers might use dichotic listening and other subliminal techniques to reduce subjects' awareness of relevant conditioning stimuli (e.g., CS objects, US objects; see Krosnick et al., 1992). If conditioning procedures could be shown to influence subjects' attitudes in the absence of their awareness of relevant stimuli, then the conclusion that these effects too do not necessarily depend on cognitive processes that are conscious and deliberative would be warranted. Yet like exposure effects in the absence of awareness, such effects could be plausibly explained either by affective mechanisms or by cognitive mechanisms that can proceed without conscious awareness. Regardless, mere exposure research suggests novel ways of approaching these older questions of whether attitudes can be modified "automatically" and "nonconsciously" via classical and operant conditioning procedures and may help to revitalize research in these areas.

The reigning view in psychology has been that cognition always precedes affect, that we feel because we know. Based largely on the subliminal mere exposure studies we have reviewed, Zajonc has argued for a separate systems view that affective and cognitive processes may proceed independently from one another and that, at least sometimes, affective reactions may precede and influence cognition (Zajonc, 1980b, 1981, 1984; Zajonc & Markus, 1984; Zajonc, Murphy, & Inglehart, 1989; Zajonc, Pietromonaco, & Bargh, 1982). According to Zajonc, although both affect and cognition reflect some transformation of sensory information, "energy" transformations are involved in affect whereas "informational" transformations characterize cognition. In the affective system, sensory input gets transformed immediately into autonomic or motor output (i.e., affective responding), perhaps via relatively fixed biologically determined codes (Zajonc, 1980b, 1984). In contrast, cognition requires "mental work" and "may consist of operations on sensory input that transform that input into a form that may become subjectively available, or it may consist of the activation of items from memory" (Zajonc, 1984, p. 118). In addition, Zajonc has speculated that the affective and cognitive systems respond to different features of environmental stimuli. Cognition responds to "discriminanda," the analytic features of stimuli that enable us to discriminate, recognize, and categorize objects and events. In contrast, affect responds to "preferanda," stimulus features that may be "quite gross, vague, and global" and that facilitate affective reactions though they may be "insufficient as a basis for most cognitive judgments" (Zajonc, 1980b, p. 159).

Zajonc's (1980b, 1984) claims for the primacy of affect and for the independence of affective and cognitive systems have proven controversial (e.g., Birnbaum, 1981; Epstein, 1984; Gordon & Holyoak, 1983; Lazarus, 1982, 1984; Mellers, 1981; Zajonc, 1981). To some extent this controversy revolves around definitional issues. Holyoak and Gordon (1984), for example, interpreted Zajonc's definition of cognition as referring only to "slow, effortful, conscious and rational" processes (p. 62). Consequently, they claimed that his view of affect does not distinguish it from cognitive mechanisms that can proceed automatically without awareness. Yet other aspects of the controversy reflect true disagreements. In particular, Lazarus (1984) has argued that cognition includes not only "highly differentiated symbolic" processes but also "primitive evaluative perception" (p. 124). Yet Zajonc (1984) presumably considers the latter to be affect, given his criticism that "Lazarus has broadened the definition of cognitive appraisal to include even the most primitive forms of sensory excitation" (p. 117). With respect to this disagreement, Buck (1985) suggested that Tucker's (1981) distinction between *syncretic* and *analytic* cognition resembles Zajonc's distinctions between affect and cognition and thus might satisfy both Zajonc and Lazarus. Like Zajonc's notion of affect, syncretic cognition is holistic and often vague, involves directly perceived "analog" information, and is viewed as a right hemisphere function. In contrast, analytic cognition is more differentiated, involves informational transformations of sensory data, and is identified with the left hemisphere (see Buck, 1985; Tucker, 1981).

Empirical examination of Zajonc's proposals that affect can be a direct noncognitively mediated reaction to sensory input and that such reactions can precede cognition will necessitate greater conceptual clarification regarding what constitutes both affect and cognition. Even if definitional issues were resolved and affect and cognition—or syncretic and analytic cognition—were shown to be separate, distinguishable systems, the extent to which they are functionally independent is debatable. Although Zajonc's viewpoint acknowledges that affect and cognition influence each other, it may exaggerate their autonomy. An alternate *synergistic* viewpoint suggests that affect and cognition (or Tucker's two types of cognition) most often operate jointly to produce effects that are more attributable to their combination than to either one alone (e.g., Buck, 1985; Kihlstrom, 1987; Sorrentino & Higgins, 1986; Tomkins, 1981; Tucker, 1981).

The synergistic perspective fits well with our conceptualization of attitudes as evaluations whose antecedents and observable manifestations may be affective, cognitive, or behavioral in nature (see Chapter 1). It is also consistent with the structural and dynamic relations that exist between these three classes of experience and responding (see Chapters 3, 4, 10, and 11). In addition, the synergistic perspective has interesting researchable implications. For example, Buck (1985; see also Tucker, 1981) has argued that higher-order analytic cognitive processes enable the human organism to comprehend vague feeling states that are the products of affective mechanisms (or syncretic cognition), and that this function is adaptive because it enhances the capacity for self-regulation. If attitudes can be formed purely by affective mechanisms and if such attitudes are phenomenologically perceived as vague feeling states, their impact on behavior may be highly contingent on how individuals comprehend or cognize these attitudes and the situations they are in. Emerging dual-process views of mere exposure also fit the synergistic perspective and suggest that whether subliminally induced attitude changes endure will depend upon what other sources of information are available in the exposure situation and how people's processing of this information affects their interpretations of their internal states. More generally, a synergistic perspective implies that even if attitudes can be formed purely by affective mechanisms (or purely cognitive ones), it is unlikely that they would remain purely affective (or purely cognitive) for long (see Chapter 1). Suppose, for example, that an attitude was formed in the absence of a prior cognitive process. This affectively based attitude would no doubt influence subsequent cognitions and behavior, and these cognitions and behavior, in turn, could influence affective reactions to the attitude object. The result would be an attitude based on all three classes of experience even though the impetus for its initial formation may have been affective.

These examples may help answer a question posed by one of our (brightest) graduate students. After reading Zajonc's (1980b) essay for a seminar class, the student asked skeptically, "Does all of this imply that dogs have attitudes?" Given our definition of attitude and the possibility that attitudes can be formed purely by affective mechanisms—or by "cognitive" mechanisms that govern animal as well as human behavior

(Brewer, 1974; Buck, 1985)—one is forced to admit that dogs probably do have attitudes. Yet dogs and other animals are presumably less endowed with the capacity for deliberative analytic cognition. Thus, the "attitudes" they possess can be only of the most rudimentary sort. It is the capacity for deliberative thought that gives depth and complexity to people's attitudes and to their behavior.

———— Notes ————

1. Theoretically, the principles we review in this chapter (e.g., classical conditioning) could be applied to understanding how attitudes are changed, not only how they are initially acquired. However, at the empirical level, most of the research we cite has dealt with novel stimuli as attitude objects. For this reason, we use the term attitude formation rather than attitude change throughout most of this chapter.

2. As we subsequently point out, the "affective-cognitive" debate in the operant and classical conditioning literatures on attitude formation in fact concerned the issue of whether the attitudes formed in conditioning studies should be viewed as the product of "automatic" conditioning mechanisms or deliberative cognitive mechanisms.

3. Conditioned responses, although related to unconditioned responses, are not necessarily identical to them. Often these responses appear as fractional components of the UR (e.g., the CS produces somewhat less salivation than the US). However, they may also be alternate responses that covary with the UR and that anticipate the US (e.g., orienting response, barking; see Kimble, 1961).

4. Although this cognitive view of conditioning gained ascendance in the learning area primarily during the past two decades, it was first espoused many years earlier (see Tolman, 1932). In general, the cognitive perspective views learning in animals and humans as occurring by contiguity and views reinforcement as affecting the *performance* of what has been learned (see Hearst, 1988; Hill, 1985).

5. In related studies of *concept formation*, investigators attempted to shape subjects' attitudes toward fictitious social groups by giving them feedback about the ostensible correctness of their guesses regarding group members' personality traits (e.g., Kerpelman & Himmelfarb, 1971; Rhine, 1958; see also Fishbein, 1967b). For example, to establish a positive attitude, the ex-

perimenter might say "characteristic" to guesses linking the group to positive traits and "uncharacteristic" to guesses linking the group to negative traits. In this research, the words "characteristic" and "uncharacteristic" were viewed as positive and negative verbal reinforcers, respectively, and the attitude results were explained in terms of a blend of classical and operant conditioning logic. According to this logic, when stimuli (e.g., trait adjectives) elicit a common evaluative response, this response becomes conditioned to concepts (e.g., an unknown social group) that are repeatedly paired with these stimuli. Attitudes represent these learned associations between concepts and evaluative responses and can be strengthened or weakened by varying the frequency and consistency of reinforcement.

6. Alternatively, it could be argued that a pleasant experimenter's "good" is inherently more reinforcing than an unpleasant experimenter's "good" (see also discussion in Chapter 10 of Hovland, Janis, and Kelley's, 1953, incentive interpretation of source effects in persuasion).

7. Staats (1983) did not comment on the results of his "experiment" and so leaves it to readers to intuit what they might have been. Given the robustness of conditioning, it is very probable that the word "no" could indeed have come to elicit a negative emotional response in Staats' cat. The overt appearance of this response might be labeled, at least by cat owners, as cowering or cringing.

8. Berkowitz and Knurek (1969) also examined the hypothesis that subjects' conditioned negative attitudes toward the confederates' names would impact more strongly on subjects' ratings and behavior when they had been frustrated in an earlier task. Thus, prior to leaving the "first experiment," subjects were told that their performance had been either "very poor" or "reasonably good." Although subjects' personality ratings of the confederate did prove to be stronger in the study's frustration conditions, confederates'

ratings of the subjects' behavior were unaffected by this manipulation.

9. For a critique of the Byrne model and associated research, see Rosenbaum (1986).

10. Whether the mere *valence* of automatically activated constructs can bias interpretation of ambiguous stimuli, regardless of the *semantic* content of these constructs and their applicability or relevance to to-be-judged stimuli is unclear at this point in time (see Bargh, Bond, Lombardi, & Tota, 1986; Bargh & Pietromonaco, 1982; Higgins, 1989a; Erdley & D'Agostino, 1988; Niedenthal & Cantor, 1986).

11. Krosnick, Betz, Jussim, and Lynn (1992) discounted a mood interpretation for their data because assessments of Study 2 subjects' moods yielded no effects. This null effect is difficult to interpret, however, because the conditioning effects in this experiment were statistically weak and assessments of mood states often prove insensitive to even highly explicit mood inductions (see Isen, 1984).

12. For similar reasons, Staats (1969) criticized experiments by M.M. Page (1969) and Insko and Oakes (1966), both of which found that contingency awareness and conditioning were lower when subjects' presumed abilities to decipher the CS-US contingency were interfered with. This interference was accomplished by increasing the number of irrelevant nonsense syllables in the conditioning task in the Page study and by requiring subjects to perform an intertrial color-naming task in the Insko and Oakes study. Whereas these authors concluded that the results demonstrated the necessity of contingency awareness, Staats argued that their awareness manipulations actually interfered with conditioning by adversely affecting the amount of attention subjects paid to the experimental materials.

13. This argument may seem surprising to readers given that Staats championed the idea that attitude formation *could* be the result of an automatic conditioning process. However, his argument does not contradict this viewpoint or imply that contingency awareness is necessary for conditioning effects to occur. Rather it reveals that Staats believed that conditioning effects should be stronger—and, perhaps, only evident—when conditioned stimuli are consciously *attended* to by subjects. In fact, Staats did not advance the strong form of the conditioning hypothesis that Krosnick, Betz, Jussim, Lynn, and Stephens (1992) attempted to test—that attitudes can be classically conditioned in the absence of people's awareness of conditioning stimuli.

14. This assumption led Zajonc to propose that attitude enhancement should be a positive *linear* function of the *logarithm* of frequency. Consistent with this proposal, when the data of Figure 9.2 are plotted on a logarithmic scale, the resulting three attitude-exposure frequency functions do appear linear in form (see Zajonc, 1968a, pp. 14 and 18).

15. These last two moderating factors may help clarify why persuasion studies of message repetition sometimes fail to find that repeated exposures enhance persuasion. In most of these studies, subjects have been repeatedly exposed to only a single persuasive message (i.e., homogeneous presentation) and have also indicated their attitudes immediately after their final exposure to the message. Consistent with the idea that these study attributes may minimize positive exposure effects on persuasion, W. Wilson and Miller (1968) and H. H. Johnson and Watkins (1971) found stronger evidence for the attitude enhancing effect of message repetition on delayed (vs. immediate) measures of persuasion. In addition, in a study in which the same basic message was repeated but variations in phrasing and argument order were effected, McCullough and Ostrom (1974) did find an immediate enhancement of attitudes due to message repetition.

16. Similar to two-factor accounts of mere exposure is Cacioppo and Petty's (1979b) two-phase cognitive elaboration-then-tedium explanation of message repetition effects in persuasion. At lower levels of repetition the cognitive response process noted in the text predominates. However after a certain point, a tedium process is initiated in which boredom or feelings of reactance predominate and reduce persuasion.

426

10

Motivational Processes
in Attitude Formation
and Change

I n our introduction to Chapter 9 we noted that affect has been used as a generic term for a variety of motivational and emotional constructs and mechanisms that do not fall clearly within the domain of cognition. Occasionally, distinctions between affective processes and cognitive ones can be blurry, as illustrated by the primacy of affect versus cognition debate engendered by mere exposure research (see Chapter 9). Despite such occasional vagueness, the parsing of psychological space into its affective, cognitive—and behavioral—dimensions has been a longstanding and theoretically valuable tradition in the attitudes field, and, indeed, throughout all of social psychology (see Chapter 1).

In this chapter we continue our consideration of the role that affective processes play in the formation and modification of attitudes. As detailed in Chapter 9, research on classical and operant conditioning and, subsequently, research on mere exposure focused largely on the (still unresolved) issue of whether the attitude effects routinely yielded by these paradigms are best interpreted as the product of simple affective mechanisms as opposed to more complex, deliberative cognitive processes. Given this dialectic, much of the literature we reviewed can be characterized as endorsing a view of affect and cognition as autonomous, noninteracting systems. In contrast to this separatist view, the material we address in this chapter resonates more with a synergistic view that affect and cognition are interdependent, interacting systems.

Conventional psychological wisdom has been that people's cognitive processing of external or internal stimuli influences affective responding to these stimuli (e.g., emotional reactions). Yet affect ought to influence cognition as well as vice versa if the two systems are truly synergistic. Within the psychology of attitudes, the idea that emotional and motivational forces impinge upon the cognitive system has been central to three broad theoretical traditions: the reinforcement perspective of the Yale Communication and Attitude Change Program (e.g., Hovland, Janis, & Kelley, 1953); the cognitive consistency perspective of Heider (1946, 1958), Festinger (1957, 1964b), and others (e.g., M. J. Rosenberg & Abelson, 1960); and the functional perspective of D. Katz (1960) and M. B. Smith, Bruner, and White (1956). These three traditions and the issues of attitude formation and change they spawned are the subject of this chapter.

Yale Reinforcement Perspective

Communication and Persuasion, by Carl Hovland, Irving Janis, and Harold Kelley (1953) was the first of a series of monographs that described the empirical findings of a broad program of research conducted by Hovland and his Yale University colleagues after World War II (see also Hovland, 1957; Hovland & Janis, 1959; Hovland, Lumsdaine, & Sheffield, 1949; Hovland & Rosenberg, 1960; M. Sherif & Hovland, 1961; see also Chapter 6). In their introductory chapter, Hovland, Janis, and Kelley disavowed any attempt to present a "systematic theory" of attitude change (p. 6). Instead, they emphasized their commitment to controlled laboratory experimentation and cited a variety of theoretical perspectives as sources of conceptual inspiration (e.g., learning theory, psychoanalytic theory, field theory, reference group theory). Attesting to the strong empiricist bent of the Yale approach, the organization of *Communication and Persuasion* was built around the empirical issues of attitude change raised by the question, "Who says what to whom with what effect?" (Lasswell, 1948, p. 37; see also B. L. Smith, Lasswell, & Casey, 1946).

Empiricism and theoretical eclecticism are apt descriptors of the Yale research program, especially when viewed in its entirety. Nonetheless, in their introduction to *Communication and Persuasion*, Hovland and his coauthors articulated a set of "working assumptions" that were most heavily influenced by the learning theories of Hull (1943), N. E. Miller and Dollard (1941), and others (e.g., Doob, 1947; Mowrer, 1950). These working assumptions functioned as a general conceptual framework for the Yale research on attitude change and embody its distinctive reinforcement perspective. The key idea of this perspective is that people's beliefs and attitudes become habitual because their overt or covert expression is followed by the receipt or anticipation of positive reinforcement (see Doob, 1947).

Hovland and colleagues' (1953) conceptualization of persuasion illustrates their reinforcement perspective. They viewed persuasive communications as stimuli that raise questions about entities (e.g., political issues, persons). A message about AIDS, for example, might implicitly or explicitly raise the question of whether there is a relation between sexual promiscuity and becoming infected with the AIDS virus. The message recipient's "answer" to this question constitutes his or her initial belief on this particular AIDS issue. In addition to evoking existing beliefs and attitudes, persuasive communications facilitate the learning of new beliefs and attitudes because of their recommendations and arguments. Specifically, Hovland and his colleagues assumed that as people process persuasive message content, they rehearse the message's recommended attitudinal response (as well as their initial attitude). Such practice was thought to strengthen the associative bond between this "new" attitudinal response and the stimuli conveyed in the message. Yet, associative learning alone was not regarded as a sufficient explanation of how persuasive messages induce *change* in people's beliefs and attitudes. For change to occur, the newly recommended attitudinal response must supplant the old one in the person's habit hierarchy. The Yale researchers emphasized the role of *incentives* and the *drive-reducing* aspects of persuasive message content as mechanisms for reinforcing, and thereby creating acceptance of, new beliefs and attitudes.

A subsidiary theme of the Yale program was that persuasion entailed three phases: attention to the message, comprehension of its content, and acceptance of its recommendations. As we explained in Chapter 6, this "chain of responses" theme inspired McGuire's (e.g., 1968a) subsequent information-processing model of persuasion which, in turn, facilitated the development of other cognitive persuasion theories (see Chapters 5, 6, 7, and 8). Notwithstanding the Yale program's attention to cognitive processes, the dominant theme of this approach was its focus on incentives and drive reduction as mechanisms for enhancing attention and comprehension and, most important, acceptance of the beliefs and attitudes advocated in persuasive communications.

Role of Incentives

Hovland and his colleagues often used the term incentive rather than reinforcement because of their focus on the consequences that people could *anticipate* receiving if they adopted a persuasive message's recommendation. They also took a broad view of incentives. Incentives for adopting a message's recommendation could take the form of direct financial or physical benefits (e.g., money, improved health). However, they could also take on more abstract forms such as the information value of persuasive arguments, social approval and acceptance from respected individuals or important reference groups, and self-approval stemming from the feeling that one's beliefs and attitudes were correct, "rational," or congruent with important values. As we discuss later in this chapter, a number of the psychological needs and motives that the Hovland group conceptualized under the rubric of incentives (e.g., social approval, self-approval) play a key role in functional theories of attitude formation and change.

Incentives and Communicator Variables. Incentives played an important explanatory role in Hovland and associates' (1953) analysis of communicator variables in persuasion. Their prediction that expert sources should confer greater persuasion than nonexpert sources was based on the logic that experts' statements are usually regarded as veridical (whereas nonexperts' statements are not), and that holding veridical beliefs and attitudes is inherently reinforcing. Thus, attending to and comprehending expert communicators' arguments, or accepting their recommendations, was assumed to have greater incentive value than learning the arguments or accepting the recommendations presented by nonexperts. The predictions that personally admired or prestigious communicators should induce greater persuasion than disliked or low status communicators followed from similar logic. Learning the arguments or accepting the recommendations of liked or high status sources was presumed to have greater incentive value because (a) message recipients could anticipate earning communicators' social approval by adopting their recommendations and (b) social approval is more rewarding when it is received from liked or high status persons.

The research on communicator variables that Hovland and his colleagues conducted in the 1950s generally supported their persuasion predictions (Hovland & Weiss, 1951; Kelman & Hovland, 1953; but see Hovland & Mandell, 1957). In these studies, and in many subsequent experiments by other researchers, subjects typically exhibited greater agreement with the beliefs and attitudes recommended in persuasive messages when the sources of these messages were portrayed as higher in expertise, trustworthiness, status, likability, or attractiveness (for reviews, see Chaiken, 1986; McGuire, 1969, 1985).

Hovland and his colleagues considered two information-processing explanations for their persuasion findings. Both explanations harmonized with their incentives perspective on source effects, but they differed with respect to the information-processing locus of these effects. One explanation held that positive source cues such as high expertise increased recipients' motivation to *attend to and comprehend* persuasive message content. The other held that such cues increased recipients' motivation to *accept* communicators' recommendations. Because measures of subjects' factual recall of message content were typically unaffected by the source manipulations featured in these studies, Hovland and his colleagues concluded that the persuasive impact of communicator variables was mediated most typically by differential acceptance of messages' recommendations rather than by differential attention to and comprehension of persuasive message content (see Chapter 6). Importantly though, the Hovland group never directly tested their underlying presumption that differences in acceptance (or, for that matter, differences in attention/comprehension) reflected differences between the *incentives* that positive and negative communicators represented (or could provide). Given the abstractness of the incentives the Yale researchers postulated in relation to source cues, it is not surprising that subsequent research also has not provided any explicit test of this presumption.

Incentives and Counterattitudinal Advocacy. The idea that attitude change is controlled by incentives figured even more prominently in the Hovland group's analysis of counterattitudinal proselytizing. As we discuss in Chapter 11, their initial studies on this topic documented that having *role-player* subjects improvise and deliver counterattitudinal messages typically induced greater persuasion than having *passive exposure* subjects read or listen to messages of substantially similar content (Janis & King, 1954; B. T. King & Janis, 1956). Because measures of message retention showed no effects of the manipulations featured in this research, Hovland et al. (1953) discounted enhanced comprehension as a mediator of role-playing effects. A more plausible cognitive mediator, they believed, was a process that Janis labeled *biased scanning* (Janis, 1959; Janis & Gilmore, 1965).

The biased scanning interpretation of role-playing is that the task of improvising and communicating a counterattitudinal position motivates subjects to think about the arguments that support this position and to suppress thinking about opposing arguments (because such thoughts are irrelevant to their assigned task). In other words, the incentives in the role-playing situation encourage subjects to focus on role-supportive persuasive arguments. Such incentives were assumed to be absent in passive exposure situations; hence, passive recipients of counterattitudinal messages were presumed to think about message content in a more objective, if not antagonistic, manner. This incentive-produced difference in the favorability of cognitive responding on the part of role-players as opposed to passive recipients, then, was assumed to mediate the heightened persuasiveness of counterattitudinal proselytizing.[1]

In harmony with the ideas outlined in *Communication and Persuasion*, Janis (1959, 1968) subsequently developed a more general interpretation of counterattitudinal role-playing that he called *incentive theory*. Conceptualizing attitude change as a process involving a trade-off between positive and negative incentives, Janis argued that inducing subjects to improvise and advocate counterattitudinal messages would not necessarily lead to substantial attitude change if the role-playing situation contained negative incentives that conflicted with the positive incentive value of improvising supportive arguments. As summarized in Chapter 11, several studies by Janis and his colleagues provided support for this analysis (e.g., Janis & Gilmore, 1965; Elms & Janis, 1965).

The Yale thesis that positive incentives promote attitude change proved noncontroversial among researchers studying the effects of passive exposure to persuasive communications. Janis's application of this thesis to the domain of counterattitudinal advocacy, however, met greater resistance. In particular, his incentive theory analysis and experimental findings were diametrically opposed to dissonance theory logic that counterattitudinal role-playing ought to induce greater attitude change to the extent that role-players anticipate *smaller* rewards (Festinger & Carlsmith, 1959; see subsequent discussion in this chapter). The empirical research generated by this and other theoretical controversies that arose regarding the effects of counterattitudinal proselytizing on attitude change are discussed in Chapter 11 of this book.

Emotion and Persuasion

Persuasive communications can arouse strong emotional reactions. In some instances, the nature of the communication topic and aspects of its content may elicit such reactions even though the message may not have been constructed with this purpose in mind. Health messages, in particular, may elicit fear and anxiety simply by virtue of their sometimes personally threatening topics. In fact, it may be difficult to construct messages concerning topics such as the health consequences of cigarette smoking, alcohol consumption, or poor nutrition during pregnancy *without* inducing emotional tension in at least some recipients. In other instances, communications may be constructed with the specific aim of eliciting particular emotions, the presumption being that "emotional" appeals are more persuasive than less emotional, "rational" communications (Hartmann, 1936). For example, messages about smoking may include vivid portrayals of lung cancer patients in the final stages of their disease, and messages advocating increased defense spending or protectionist trade policies may intentionally play upon people's fear of foreigners.

The efficacy of emotional appeals had received some attention by earlier investigators (e.g., Hartmann, 1936; Knower, 1935), but Hovland and his colleagues (1953) were the first to present a systematic, theoretical analysis of this subject. Although they recognized the worth of studying communications designed to arouse positive emotions such as "sympathy" and "elation," they nevertheless confined their analysis to negative emotional appeals. Moreover, within this class, the specific model they featured in *Communication and Persuasion* focused on the effects of fear-arousing communications.

Drive-Reduction Model of Fear Appeals. The core presumption of Hovland and colleagues' (1953) *drive-reduction* model is that fear or emotional tension has the functional properties of a drive (see also Dollard & Miller, 1950). According to this reasoning, fear (like other drive states) motivates instrumental responding, and a reduction in fear (like reduction in other drive states) is inherently reinforcing. As a consequence, any cognitive or behavioral response that reduces emotional tension or accompanies its reduction will be reinforced. Applying this principle to persuasion, Hovland and colleagues (1953, p. 62) postulated that fear appeals could enhance the likelihood of recipients accepting a communicator's recommendation under the following conditions: (a) if information depicting some threat (e.g., AIDS, lung cancer) were to arouse a level of fear "sufficiently intense to constitute a drive state" and (b) if the recipient's "silent rehearsal" of the communicator's "reassuring recommendation" were accompanied by a reduction in emotional tension.

The drive-reduction model is subtly complex. On the one hand, it suggests that the relation between fear arousal and persuasion can be positive because the reinforcement value of fear reduction should be a positive function of the amount of emotional tension induced. On the other hand, it implies that high levels of fear may fail to engender a gain in persuasion and may even undermine a communication's persuasiveness. In fact, the weight of the Yale analysis stressed the negative potential of messages that arouse high levels of fear. Most obviously, the model implies that such messages may fail to effect attitudinal and behavioral change because their presumably reassuring recommendations fail to reduce emotional tension. Restating a basic principle of reinforcement, Hovland and his colleagues stressed the importance of constructing fear appeals so that their recommendations appear immediately after their fear-arousing content. More interesting in light of subsequent theoretical developments, they argued that emotional tension would remain high to the extent that recipients perceived the message's recommendation(s) to be (a) ineffective in averting the depicted threat or (b) impossible to carry out. As discussed below, contemporary researchers have labeled these two factors *response efficacy* and *self-efficacy*, respectively.

Additional reasons why highly fear-inducing appeals may fail to persuade follow from the model's presumption that fear-motivated instrumental responding is spontaneous and relatively unselective. That is, people respond to fear-arousing content cues in a variety of self-protective ways, not solely by thinking about and rehearsing the message's recommended attitude or behavior. To the extent that recipients respond to such cues by discounting a threat's importance or likelihood of occurrence, or by denying its personal relevance, it is these responses rather than rehearsal of the message's recommendation that are likely to reduce emotional tension and hence be reinforced. Hovland and colleagues (1953) believed that such "minimizing" responses were common immediate defensive reactions to threatening material. Again presaging subsequent theorizing, they suggested that in order to succeed in changing attitudes and behavior a fear appeal should include "supplementary elaborations" of its depicted threat that function to counteract recipients' tendencies to deny or minimize its severity and their own vulnerability.

Three other types of fear-motivated defensive behaviors were also discussed by Hovland et al. (1953). Given especially high levels of fear, these persuasion-inhibiting responses were assumed to predominate over the persuasion-facilitating response of rehearsing a message's reassuring recommendation. *Inattention* to message content was assumed to reflect recipients' motivated efforts to avoid thinking about anxiety-provoking stimuli; alternatively, Hovland and his colleagues acknowledged that attentional deficits could also result from the debilitating effect of emotional tension on recipients' powers of concentration. The Yale researchers also speculated that fear might sometimes motivate *aggression* toward the communicator. Source derogation as well as blanket rejections of the message's recommendation were assumed to indicate this more active mode of defense. Finally, situations in which neither the message's recommendation nor recipients' self-generated responses were successful in reducing emotional tension were postulated to produce *defensive avoidance*. Recipients manifesting this *delayed* form of defensive behavior were presumed to actively avoid subsequent "thinking about and hearing about" the (original) message's depicted threat. Indicators of defensive avoidance were presumed to include forgetting of message content and delayed minimizing responses.

The Dental Hygiene Experiment. Irving Janis and Seymour Feshbach's (1953) study of high school students' responses to dental hygiene communications greatly influenced the development of the drive-reduction model, particularly its emphasis on the potential for fear arousal to undermine persuasion. In the main phase of this seminal experiment, control subjects listened to a message about the human eye, while experimental subjects listened to one of three versions of a message that discussed the causes of tooth decay, enumerated the negative consequences of poor oral hygiene (see Table 10.1), and contained five specific recommendations for effective tooth care (e.g., "the teeth should be brushed gently," "one should spend about 3 minutes on each brushing"). The three dental hygiene messages were designed to induce a *low*, *medium*, or *high* level of fear, and varied in four ways. As shown in Table 10.1, the messages differed both in terms of the number of negative consequences they cited and the proportion of these consequences that were relatively severe (on both dimensions, high > medium > low). Also, whereas the medium and low fear appeals described the consequences of ineffective tooth care using relatively impersonal language, the high fear appeal featured "personalized" language designed to enhance subjects' perceptions of vulnerability (e.g., "this can happen to you"). Finally, while the high fear appeal was accompanied by vivid photographic illustrations of tooth decay and mouth infections, the medium appeal was accompanied by milder photographic examples of oral pathology, and the low fear appeal by X-ray pictures, diagrams of cavities, and photographs of healthy teeth.

Conformity to the experimental messages' recommended toothbrushing practices was assessed by having subjects report on their toothbrushing behavior both one week prior to the experiment and one week after message exposure. Analyses on the net percentage of subjects in each condition who modified their behavior in the direction

TABLE 10.1

Frequency of References to Negative Consequences of Improper Toothbrushing in High, Medium, and Low Fear Message Conditions of the Janis and Feshbach (1953) Experiment

Type of reference	High fear	Medium fear	Low fear
1. Pain from toothaches	11	1	0
2. Cancer, paralysis, blindness or other secondary diseases	6	0	0
3. Having teeth pulled, cavities drilled, or other painful dental work	9	1	0
4. Having cavities filled or having to go to the dentist	0	5	1
5. Mouth infections: sore, swollen, inflamed gums	18	16	2
6. Ugly or discolored teeth	4	2	0
7. "Decayed" teeth	14	12	6
8. "Cavities"	9	12	9
Total references to negative consequences	71	49	18
Percentage "severe" consequences referenced	37%	14%	6%

Note: "Severe" consequences refer to items 1-4.

Source: This table was adapted from one presented by Janis and Feshbach (1953, Table 1, p. 80).

advocated by the messages yielded the negative relation between fear arousal and persuasion shown in Figure 10.1, Panel A. In fact, only the low fear appeal produced a significant gain in conformity relative to the control condition; the medium appeal engendered a marginally reliable increase, whereas the high fear appeal proved totally ineffective in increasing conformity.

At the one week follow-up, subjects' susceptibility to counterpropaganda was assessed by having them read and indicate their agreement with a brief statement that contradicted one of the original messages' recommendations—that recipients should use a particular type of toothbrush (i.e., one with "medium hard bristles"). The statement was attributed to a "well-known" dentist and asserted that despite the claims of "so-called experts," any "ordinary" toothbrush was effective in preventing tooth decay. Using subjects' preexperimental agreement with the latter viewpoint as a baseline, the net percentage in each condition who shifted toward greater agreement after the counterpropaganda induction was calculated. As Panel B of Figure 10.1 shows, only control subjects were persuaded by this induction; the negative susceptibility scores for the three fear appeal conditions indicate that each conferred resistance to the counterpropaganda induction. Yet paralleling the conformity data, resistance proved greatest among subjects who had received the low fear appeal and least among those who had received the high fear appeal.

A measure of argument comprehension administered immediately after subjects' exposure to the fear appeals yielded no group differences, suggesting that inattention

FIGURE 10.1. Panel A depicts the net percentage of subjects in each condition of the Janis and Feshbach (1953) study who exhibited greater conformity with the toothbrushing recommendations proffered in the three fear appeal messages. Panel B depicts the net percentage of subjects in each condition who shifted toward greater agreement with the counter-propagandistic statement that any toothbrush is effective if used regularly. These data were presented by Janis and Feshbach (1953, Tables 6 and 7, pp. 84 and 86).

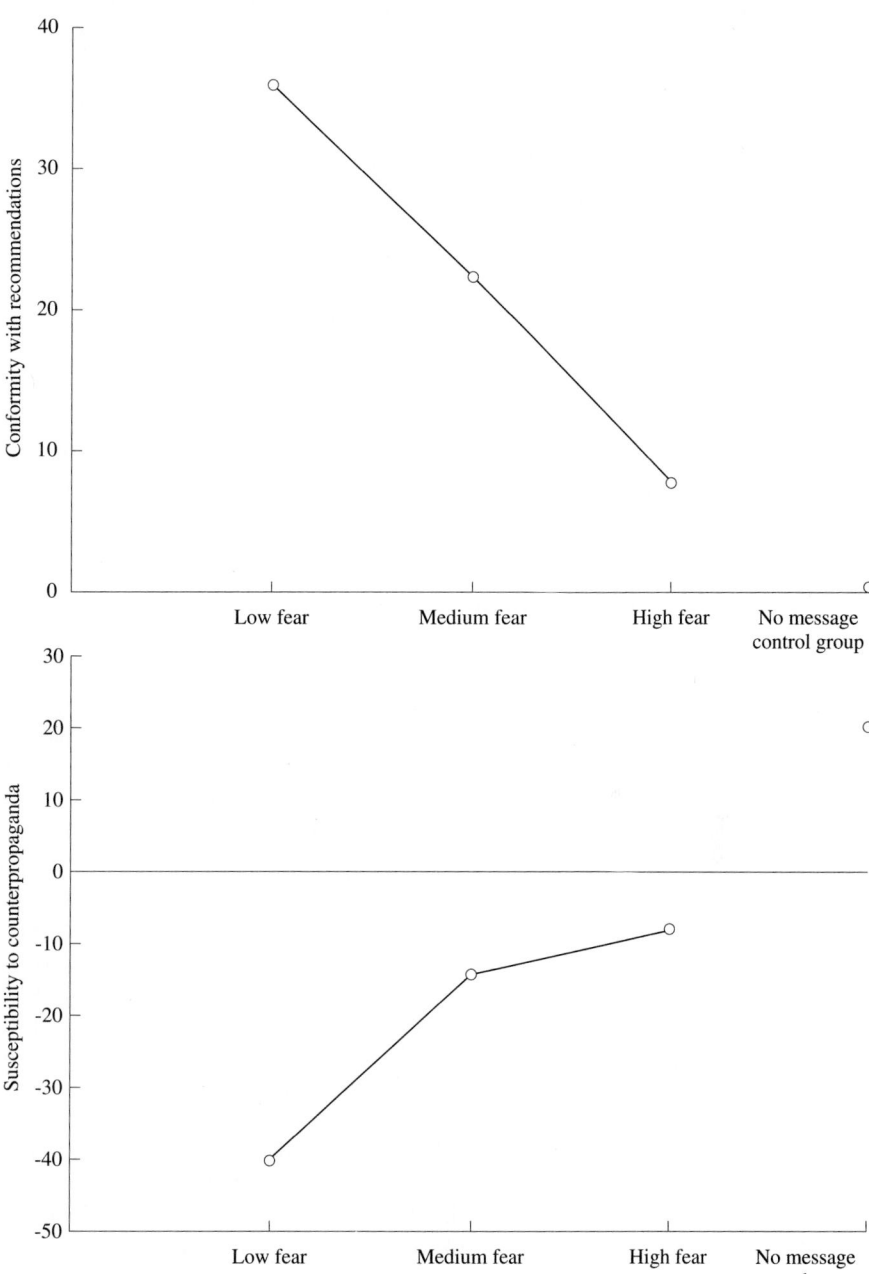

was not responsible for the ineffectiveness of the high fear appeal. Similarly, fear-motivated aggression was discounted as a mediator because of mixed findings on relevant measures.[2] Although evidence implicating defensive avoidance was meager, Janis and Feshbach (1953; Hovland et al., 1953) nonetheless concluded that their high fear appeal had failed because of this mechanism. Defensive avoidance, they argued, was indicated by two findings: high fear subjects' greater susceptibility to counterpropaganda (assumed to reflect their desire to minimize or deny the danger of the depicted health threat) and the absence of references to the original appeal in their open-ended responses to the counterpropaganda induction (assumed to reflect motivation to avoid recalling threatening material).

Extensions of the Drive-Reduction Model. Notwithstanding the negative relation between fear and persuasion observed by Janis and Feshbach (1953), the drive-reduction model implies that low to moderate levels of fear are likely to enhance persuasion, whereas further increases in emotional tension are likely to stimulate defensive behaviors and therefore reduce persuasion (see Hovland et al., 1953, pp. 83–84). This curvilinear hypothesis was elaborated in two subsequent theoretical analyses of fear appeals developed by Janis (1967) and McGuire (1968b, 1969).

McGuire's analysis represents an application of his reception-yielding model that we presented in Chapter 6. As readers will recall, this model views persuasion as the product of two mediating processes, reception (i.e., attention and comprehension) and yielding (i.e., accepting what one has comprehended). When distal persuasion variables are positively related to both mediators, the relation between those variables and persuasion should be positive; similarly, when variables relate negatively to both mediators, their relation to persuasion should be negative. For variables that bear opposite relations to reception and yielding, however, the model predicts that their relation to persuasion will be nonmonotonic, with intermediate levels of these variables producing maximum persuasion.[3] According to McGuire (1968b, 1969), fear arousal (which he treated as equivalent to anxiety) represented the kind of variable that exerts opposing effects on reception and yielding. Fear's directive or "cue" properties, he argued, should evoke habitual responses whose purpose is to escape from or avoid threatening material. Such responses should be distracting and, as such, should interfere with message reception. On the other hand, the dynamic or "drive" properties of fear should function to energize existing behavioral inclinations. McGuire's implicit assumption that fearful (or anxious) recipients would be inclined to comply led him to posit that increased fear arousal should enhance yielding to message content.

According to the McGuire analysis, then, the inverted ∪-shaped relation between fear and persuasion implied by the drive model stems from fear's negative impact on reception and positive impact on yielding. Moreover, the reception-yielding model's situational weighting principle (see Chapter 6) implies further that the point on the fear arousal continuum at which maximum persuasion occurs should vary with situational or individual difference factors that influence the relative importance of reception and yielding as determinants of persuasion. This point should be higher on the fear continuum when yielding dominates over reception (e.g., easily comprehended messages) and lower when reception eclipses yielding in importance (e.g., complex but cogently argued messages).[4]

The idea that yielding and reception processes mediate the fear-persuasion relation is also central to the *family-of-curves* model that Janis (1967) proposed. Whereas McGuire assumed only a positive relation between fear and yielding (but see note 4), Janis also assumed a negative relation. More specifically, Janis argued that fear-motivated instrumental responding was of two types: responses that *facilitate* the probability of accepting a fear appeal's recommendation and those that reduce or *interfere* with this probability. Janis assumed that facilitative responses—for example, paying attention to threatening information and thinking about means of coping—increase in frequency with increases in fear. The monotonic positive relation between emotional arousal and probability of acceptance shown in Panel A of Figure 10.2 illustrates this assumption. The changing slope of this function reflects Janis's additional assumption that facilitation effects increase more rapidly with initial increments in fear arousal than with subsequent increments. More important, Janis assumed that the *strength* of facilitation effects should vary as a function of situational and individual difference factors. For example, Janis hypothesized that facilitation—as indexed by the height and steepness of the facilitation function—would be greater given a highly credible communicator, clear and easily implemented recommendations, or an obedient (recipient) personality style.

Interfering responses is a catchall term Janis used to refer to a variety of fear-motivated cognitive defenses: minimizing the severity of a threat or one's vulnerability to it, derogating the source, being hypercritical with respect to evaluating message content, selectively attending to message content, and defensive avoidance (as originally defined by Hovland et al., 1953). Interfering responses were also presumed to increase in frequency with increases in fear arousal; hence, the monotonic negative function between emotional arousal and acceptance shown in Panel B of Figure 10.2. The changing slope of this function reflects Janis's additional assumption that interference effects increase less rapidly in the low and upper regions of the fear continuum than in its middle region. The strength of interference effects was also postulated to vary with situational and individual difference factors; the interference function's descent might be more pronounced, for example, given a low trustworthy communicator, vague or complex recommendations, relatively weak supportive argumentation, or a resistant (recipient) personality style.

Finally, Janis also posited a mediational role for reception (though he ascribed greater importance to facilitative and interfering yielding responses). Consistent with McGuire's and with Hovland and colleagues' analyses, Janis assumed that fear could reduce message acceptance by disrupting recipients' abilities to attend to and comprehend message content. Unlike McGuire, however, Janis assumed that (a) only extreme emotional tension would disrupt reception and (b) small doses of fear would exert a salutary effect on reception. The nonmonotonic function shown in Panel C of Figure 10.2 depicts these assumptions.

Simultaneous consideration of fear's facilitating, interfering, and reception effects produces an inverted ∪-shaped relation between fear and persuasion similar to the one McGuire proposed. According to the Janis model, the point on this curve at which persuasion begins to drop off as fear increases occurs when the strength of interference

FIGURE 10.2.
Panels A through C
depict the functional
relationship between
emotional arousal
and probability of
message acceptance
that Janis (1967)
posited in relation to
fear's facilitating
effects, interfering
effects, and
reception effects,
respectively. Panel D
depicts the family of
inverted ∪-shaped
curves relating fear
and persuasion that
result from this
three-mediator
model of fear
appeals. This figure
was adapted from
those presented by
Janis (1967, Figures
3 and 4, pp. 178 and
182).

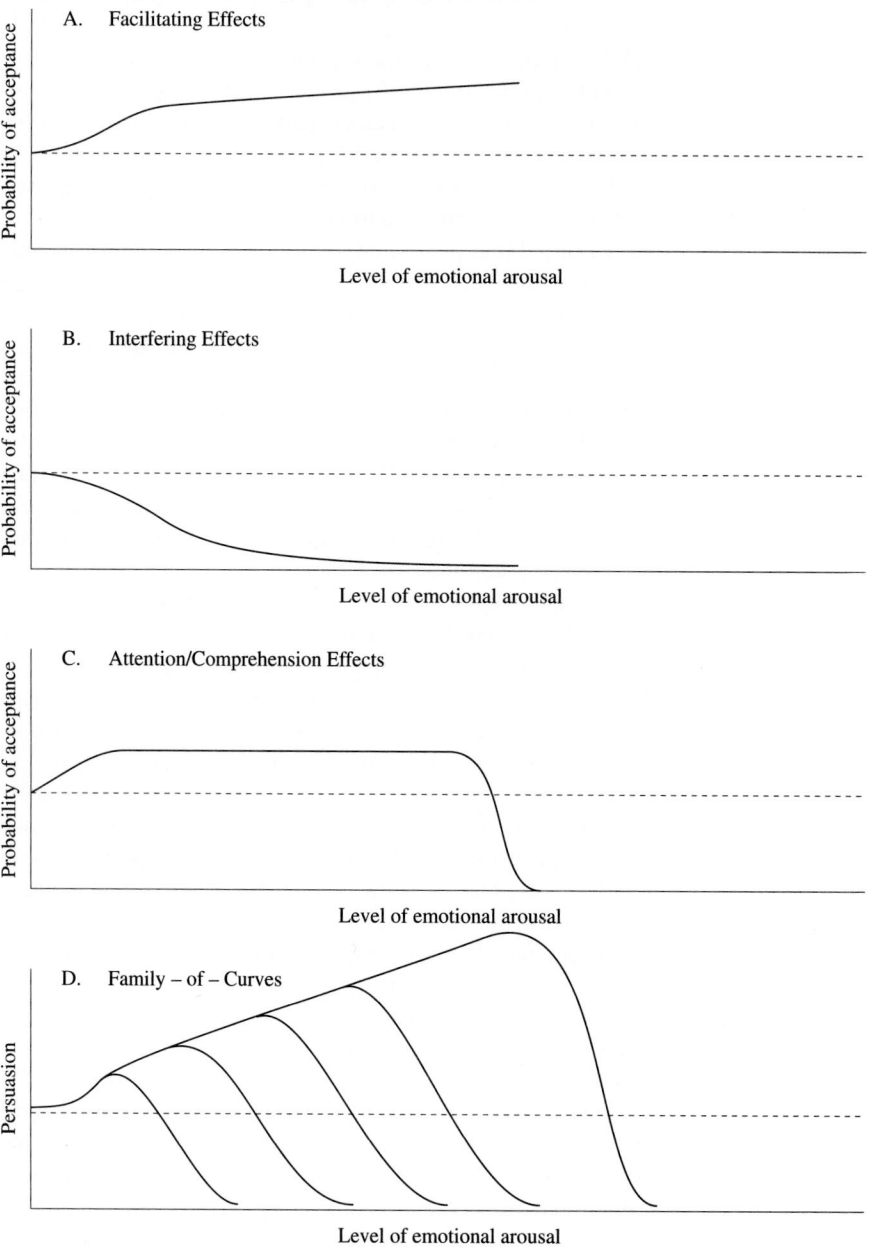

effects exceeds the strength of facilitation effects. Moreover, the theory's assumption that situational and individual difference factors influence the relative strength of facilitation and interference effects yields a prediction analogous to McGuire's situational weighting principle. Specifically, the level of "optimal fear arousal" (i.e., point of maximum persuasion) should be (a) higher on the fear continuum when situational and individual difference variables enhance the strength of facilitative responses (and/or weaken interfering responses), and (b) lower when such factors enhance the strength of interfering responses (and/or weaken facilitative responses). The family of inverted ∪-shaped curves shown in Panel D of Figure 10.2 is a consequence of this prediction. Moving from left to right, the curves illustrate circumstances in which facilitation effects become progressively stronger than interference effects.[5]

The nonmonotonic models proposed by Janis (1967) and McGuire (1968b, 1969) can be viewed as extensions of Hovland and colleagues' (1953) drive-reduction model. All three models specify a curvilinear relation between fear and persuasion when the entire fear continuum is taken into account. Given a more restricted range, it should be clear to readers that the three models can also account for monotonic positive or negative relations. In general, a positive relation should obtain when investigators' fear manipulations sample the low-to-moderate range of fear arousal, and a negative relation should obtain when the moderate-to-high end of the fear continuum is sampled. Moreover, according to the Janis (or McGuire) formulation, a positive relation should be especially evident in the lower regions of the continuum when facilitation effects dominate interference effects (or yielding dominates reception), and a negative relation should be especially evident in the continuum's upper regions when interference dominates facilitation (or reception dominates yielding).

At a deeper conceptual level, the Janis and McGuire models can be regarded as preserving two core elements of the drive-reduction model and ignoring a third. Both retain the earlier model's key presumption that fear has drive properties; that is, fear motivates instrumental responding. Both models also preserve Hovland and associates' (1953) view that this instrumental responding, which is largely cognitive in nature, mediates the effects of fear arousal on persuasion. In the McGuire model, fear's impact on persuasion is mediated by its negative impact on message reception and its positive impact on yielding. In the more elaborate model proposed by Janis, the fear-persuasion relationship is mediated by fear's positive and negative motivational effects on various cognitive processes (e.g., motivated attention and recall, source-related cognitions, message-related cognitions) and, to a lesser extent, by fear's impact on recipients' abilities to attend to and comprehend message content. The one aspect of the drive model that is not preserved in its extensions is its premise that reinforcement is the primary mechanism by which fear arousal—or, more precisely, the reduction of fear arousal—can both foster and inhibit message acceptance. The terms fear reduction and reinforcement are absent in the McGuire model. Fear reduction is accorded implicit importance by Janis insofar as facilitative and interfering responding are presumed to alleviate fear. Yet, in proposing that these fear-instigated cognitive processes mediate persuasion, Janis made no reference to their reinforcement value.

The Parallel Response Model and the Demise of Fear in Theories of Fear Appeals.
Despite their differences, the drive model and its extensions share a fundamental
assumption about the role of emotional arousal in accounting for the persuasive effects
of fear appeals: Exposure to threatening information in a message arouses fear, and
fear instigates all of the responses that determine whether the appeal succeeds or fails
in persuading recipients to adopt its recommendations (i.e., facilitative yielding responses, interfering yielding responses, attention and comprehension). In a widely cited
review paper published in 1970, Howard Leventhal highlighted several experiments
that he believed challenged the causal significance that these models ascribed to fear
arousal (e.g., Leventhal & Singer, 1966), and proposed what he regarded as a
fundamentally different model of fear appeals.

According to Leventhal's (1970) *parallel response model*, the threat cues contained in
fear appeals instigate two separate processes, *danger control* and *fear control*. Danger
control, a cognitive, "problem-solving" activity, is motivated, not by fear arousal, but
by recipients' desires to "avert danger." It involves appraising both the nature of the
threat (e.g., its severity) and potential coping behaviors (e.g., their effectiveness). Fear
control, by contrast, *is* motivated by fear arousal and involves the selection and
performance of responses that ameliorate unpleasant affect; examples include avoiding
threat cues, minimizing the threat, and engaging in behaviors such as "eating and
drinking" that "dull awareness of external dangers" (Leventhal, 1970, p. 126).
Leventhal acknowledged that the cognitive responding he associated with the danger
control process might sometimes also alleviate fear, and that the emotional responding
he associated with the fear control process might sometimes also affect danger control.
Nonetheless, his main theoretical point was that the two processes *can* proceed
independently of one another. For this reason, danger control, which leads to adaptive
action, was presumed to occur regardless of whether recipients feel frightened. Thus,
Leventhal rejected the reigning view that fear arousal instigates the cognitive processes
that mediate acceptance of fear appeals' recommendations.[6]

As Leventhal (1970) acknowledged, the parallel response model does not represent a
detailed theory of fear appeals; for example, it only broadly characterizes the danger
control process and offers few explicit hypotheses regarding the circumstances under
which its two processes interact with one another. Instead, the model can be regarded
as making the general statement that cognitive processes (i.e., danger control) sometimes matter more than affective processes (i.e., fear arousal and fear control) in
understanding and predicting people's attitudinal and behavioral reactions to fear-
arousing persuasive messages. Abetted by the growing cognitive zeitgeist in other areas
of social psychology, Leventhal's cognitive mandate exerted a pronounced influence on
the course of subsequent theorizing and research. Rogers (1975, 1983), Beck and
Frankel (1981), and Sutton (1982; S. R. Sutton & Eiser, 1984) all proposed substantially similar models of fear appeals that elaborated Leventhal's notions of danger
control but accorded fear arousal even less importance than he had. All were guided by
the general expectancy-value principle that behavior is a function of its expected
consequences and their perceived value (see Chapter 5).

The most comprehensive of these formulations is Rogers' (1975, 1983) *protection motivation theory*. Rogers (1975) proposed that danger control involves three specific appraisal "processes": (a) judging the *severity* of the depicted threat (e.g., injuries due to car accidents), (b) judging one's *vulnerability* or susceptibility to the threat, and (c) judging the *efficacy* of the message's recommended coping response (e.g., wearing seat belts). In expectancy-value language perceived vulnerability and response efficacy are expectancies and perceived severity is a value (with negative utility). As Rogers observed, most fear appeals contain information about each of these factors (see also Hovland et al., 1953). For this reason he assumed that exposure to such messages would initiate the above three cognitive processes. According to the model, recipients' perceptions of severity, vulnerability, and response efficacy arouse "protection motivation" which, in turn, fosters acceptance of the message's recommendation. In most studies relevant to this model, messages have featured behavioral recommendations (e.g., wearing seat belts), and the primary persuasion measure (assumed to reflect protection motivation) has been subjects' intentions to comply with these recommendations. Although Rogers (1975) originally postulated that severity, vulnerability, and response efficacy should combine multiplicatively to influence intentions, uncongenial empirical findings (e.g., Rogers & Mewborn, 1976; see below) led him to discard this three-way interaction prediction.[7]

The essence of Rogers' (1975) model, that severity, vulnerability, and response efficacy are important determinants of adaptive coping behavior, had substantial precedent in earlier work. Hovland and colleagues (1953), Janis (1967), and Leventhal (1970) had all ascribed importance to these variables. They were also core constructs of the *health belief model*, a variable-centered framework developed during the 1950s by a group of U.S. Public Health Service researchers (see Janz & Becker, 1984). Developed to understand phenomena such as the widespread tendency of people to fail to engage in preventive health care behaviors (e.g., obtaining vaccinations and early-detection screenings), this framework also emphasized a fourth predictor of adaptive health care behaviors: *Perceived barriers* referred to the costs of engaging in such behaviors (e.g., their inconvenience, expense, unpleasantness).

Beck and Frankel's (1981) primary contribution to the fear appeals literature was to distinguish response efficacy (as Rogers defined it) from *personal efficacy*. The latter construct refers to a person's belief that she has the ability to perform a message's recommended coping behavior(s), and is virtually identical to Bandura's (1977) notion of self-efficacy.[8] Rogers (1983; Maddux & Rogers, 1983) subsequently revised protection motivation theory to take self-efficacy (his preferred label) into account. The revision also assimilated the health belief model's perceived barriers construct (labeled "response costs") and added a related one, the rewards associated with "maladaptive" responses (e.g., continuing to smoke, not wearing seat belts). At present, then, Rogers' model asserts that protection motivation (as indexed by behavioral intentions) is a positive function of perceived severity, vulnerability, response efficacy, and self-efficacy; and a negative function of the perceived costs of adaptive responses and the perceived rewards of maladaptive ones. More specifically, Rogers divides these six

441

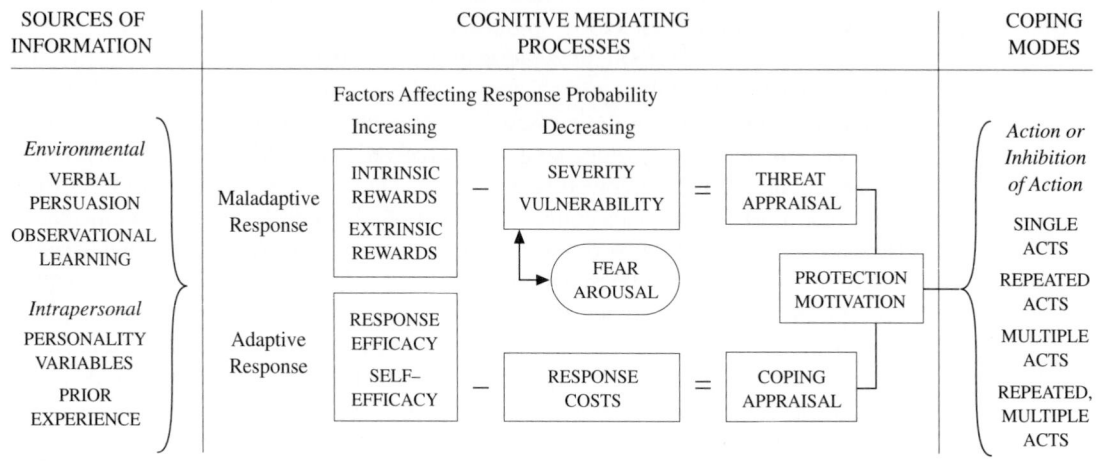

SOURCES OF INFORMATION	COGNITIVE MEDIATING PROCESSES		COPING MODES

FIGURE 10.3.
A schematic
depiction of
protection
motivation theory.
Action or inhibition
of action (far right)
refers to intentions.
This figure was
presented by
Rippetoe and Rogers
(1987, Figure 1,
p. 597).

variables into two classes, *threat appraisal* and *coping appraisal*. As shown in Figure 10.3, each of these classes is further divided into two components (e.g., response efficacy/self-efficacy and response costs in the case of coping appraisal). Rogers postulates that components (and variables) *within* each of these two classes should exert additive effects on intentions. Across the threat appraisal and coping appraisal classes, however, interaction effects are postulated. For example, Rogers assumes that if response efficacy (or self-efficacy) is high, severity (and/or vulnerability) will enhance intentions. However, if efficacy is low, severity (and/or vulnerability) is predicted to exert no impact (or negative impact) on intentions (see Rogers, 1983, pp. 169–170).[9]

What about fear arousal? This construct is assigned only minor importance in protection motivation theory and no importance in Beck and Frankel's (1981) and Sutton's (1982; Sutton & Eiser, 1984) analyses. Rogers (like the others) does not discount the assumption of the drive model and its extensions that *manipulations* of severity and vulnerability arouse fearful reactions in message recipients. However, as shown in Figure 10.3, his model gives fear no causal role other than its potential to exacerbate recipients' *perceptions* of severity and vulnerability (see Rogers, 1983, pp. 168–169).

State of the Empirical Literature. Several surveys of the empirical literature on fear appeals are available, the most recent being Boster and Mongeau's (1984) meta-analytic review (for earlier reviews, see Beck & Frankel, 1981; Higbee, 1969; Leventhal, 1970; Sutton, 1982; Zanna, Detweiler, & Olson, 1984). Our commentary emphasizes major results and issues, and their implications for the theories we have presented.

The hallmark manipulation of fear appeal experiments has been labeled "fear" or "threat," depending upon researchers' theoretical bent. Regardless, most such manipulations have followed Janis and Feshbach's (1953) procedures insofar as they include both a severity and vulnerability component, with vivid pictorial information often added to the high fear (or threat) condition. Although this procedure confounds severity and vulnerability, Rogers' attempts to manipulate these conceptually distinguishable factors independently have not been particularly successful (e.g., Rogers & Mewborn, 1976); his most recent work has manipulated threat in the Janis and Feshbach tradition (Rippetoe & Rogers, 1987). Not surprisingly, these manipulations induce differing levels of perceived threat, as indexed by subjects' ratings of severity and vulnerability. Consistent with their alternate label, these manipulations also exert reliable effects on self-report measures of fear arousal (e.g., "frightened," "anxious") and, although rarely assessed, on physiological measures as well (e.g., heart rate, Mewborn & Rogers, 1979). Interestingly, some studies that have manipulated response efficacy or self-efficacy have, in addition, yielded findings consistent with Hovland and collaborators' (1953) view that emotional tension remains high in the face of ineffective reassurances (e.g., Mewborn & Rogers, 1979; Rippetoe & Rogers, 1987).

What is the effect of fear or threat on persuasion? Health scientists concur that death and disability could be considerably reduced by increasing people's compliance with recommended preventive and diagnostic behaviors (e.g., getting exercise, practicing safer sex, performing breast self-examination; see Fisher, 1988; Stachnick, 1980). For the applied health professional, then, the most important question about public health communications is whether scare tactics enhance or inhibit their efficacy. On this bottom line issue, the research findings are fairly clear: The vast majority of experiments have found that higher levels of threat lead to greater persuasion than lower levels. Despite its notoriety, the negative relation observed by Janis and Feshbach (1953) is a rarity in the literature, as is the curvilinear relation implied by the drive model and its extensions. Reviewers have typically issued two caveats about these findings. First, as the attitude-behavior literature would suggest (see Chapter 4), the persuasive impact of fear tends to be stronger on attitudes (toward behavior) and intentions than on behavior itself (see Sutton, 1982). Second and more important, the preponderance of fear appeal experiments have induced only low to moderate levels of threat/fear. The persuasive impact of extreme fear is thus largely unknown.

On the theoretical front, things are murkier. In fact, the data have not been especially kind to any of the theories we have summarized. Consider first Rogers' (1975, 1983) protection motivation theory. On the one hand, the variables emphasized by this theory (and related formulations) do seem to influence recipients' acceptance of fear appeals. Intentions to comply with a message's recommended behavior are generally greater to the extent that any of the following conditions are met: the threat is portrayed as severe, recipients feel vulnerable to it, the recommended behavior is perceived as effective, and recipients believe they can perform this behavior. Experimental manipulations of these variables, particularly response efficacy and self-efficacy, often produce main effects on intentions (e.g., Maddux & Rogers, 1983; Mewborn & Rogers, 1979; Shelton &

443

Rogers, 1981; Rippetoe & Rogers, 1987; but see Mulilis & Lippa, 1990). Correlational findings generally tell a similar story (e.g., Beck & Lund, 1981; Meyerowitz & Chaiken, 1987; Rippetoe & Rogers, 1987; for more complex correlational findings, see Hill, Gardner, & Rassaby, 1985; Ronis & Kaiser, 1989; Steffen, 1990).[10]

Despite the predictive importance of these cognitive variables, relevant experiments rarely have found that they combine in the manner specified by protection motivation theory. As noted earlier, Rogers' (1975) original assertion that severity, vulnerability, and response efficacy combine multiplicatively to influence intentions has not been confirmed in empirical tests. More important, the "Threat" × Efficacy interactions specified by the revised model have typically also not been substantiated (e.g., Mulilis & Lippa, 1990; Rogers & Mewborn, 1976; Maddux & Rogers, 1983; Rippetoe & Rogers, 1987). There is little evidence, then, to support the theory's assumption that the effect of threat on intentions will be positive when response efficacy or self-efficacy is high, but negligible (or negative) when response efficacy or self-efficacy is low.[11] Finally, the theory's assumption that fear arousal impacts on intentions *only* insofar as it exacerbates recipients' perceptions of threat (i.e., perceived severity and vulnerability) is in doubt. Correlational data consistent with this logic were reported by Rogers and Mewborn (1976, p. 59). Yet in subsequent correlational analyses reported by Rogers and his colleagues, this indirect path (i.e., high fear → high threat → heightened intentions) has either not been evaluated or has not obtained (e.g., Maddux & Rogers, 1983; Rippetoe & Rogers, 1987). Moreover, Rippetoe and Rogers' (1987) path analysis yielded other plausible causal paths involving fear arousal, including one highly compatible with Janis's (e.g., 1967) ideas about defensive avoidance (i.e., low self-efficacy → high fear → avoidant thinking → reduced intentions).

Notwithstanding our last sentence, past reviewers have concluded (usually with high confidence) that the drive-reduction model and the extensions proposed by Janis (1967) and McGuire (1968b, 1969) are untenable in light of empirical findings (e.g., Beck & Frankel, 1981; Boster & Mongeau, 1984; Higbee, 1969; Rogers, 1983). The scarcity of negative or curvilinear threat-persuasion effects in the literature is one reason for reviewers' rejection of these theories. Yet, this fact is insufficient basis for dismissing their validity, since existing research has not sampled the high range of the threat/fear continuum, no doubt because inducing such levels in laboratory settings is both technically and ethically problematic. Therefore, the positive threat-persuasion relation found in most studies is compatible with all existing theories of fear appeals.

Research relevant to the above models' interaction hypotheses is better cause for skepticism. Because the drive model presumes that persuasion depends on the amount of emotional tension aroused and on the ability of the message's recommendations to reduce this tension, it implies that variables such as response efficacy, self-efficacy, and the positioning of this "reassuring" information should interact with fear manipulations: Fear is most likely to enhance persuasion when efficacy is high (vs. low) and when this information immediately follows fear-arousing message content. None of these variables, however, interact with fear/threat manipulations on a reliable basis (e.g., Chu, 1966; Leventhal & Singer, 1966; Leventhal, Singer, & Jones, 1965; Rippetoe & Rogers, 1987; Rogers & Mewborn, 1976; Rogers & Thistlethwaite, 1970; see Sutton, 1982, for a review). The absence of reliable "Fear" × Efficacy interactions is also problematic for the Janis and McGuire models, since efficacy should function to enhance the strength of facilitative responding and yielding, respectively.[12] Research investigating other variables that should interact with fear/threat according to these models has typically also yielded negative findings (e.g., message comprehensibility, source credibility, self-esteem, chronic anxiety; see reviews by Sutton, 1982, and Boster & Mongeau, 1984).

In contrast to some researchers' assertions, neither the drive model nor its extensions propose a *direct* relation between fear arousal and persuasion. Thus, correlations between measured fear arousal and persuasion are irrelevant indicants of the validity of these theories.[13] However, the drive model does accord mediational importance to fear *reduction*. Several studies have explored the role of this variable by monitoring changes in subjects' self-reported or physiological arousal (e.g., Mewborn & Rogers, 1979) or by giving subjects false physiological feedback indicative of increased and decreased arousal (e.g., Hendrick, Giesen, & Borden, 1975). With one exception (Harris & Jellison, 1971), the results of these studies have been uncongenial to the drive model.

The important mediators of persuasion from the standpoint of the McGuire and Janis models are the cognitive processes that fear arousal is presumed to influence. A handful of studies conducted during the 1950s and 1960s addressed fear's impact on reception. Although the retention measures used in this research were poor by today's standards, their results nonetheless yielded little support for the idea that fear arousal disrupts (or facilitates) recipients' abilities to attend to and comprehend persuasive messages (e.g., Berkowitz & Cottingham, 1960; Janis & Feshbach, 1953; Janis & Milholland, 1954; Janis & Terwilliger, 1962; Millman, 1968). Fewer studies during this period investigated fear's possible impact on recipients' cognitive responses to communications and their sources. As noted earlier, Janis and Feshbach (1953) obtained suggestive evidence that high levels of fear may stimulate defensive avoidance. Stronger evidence regarding resistance mechanisms was provided by Janis and Terwilliger (1962), who had subjects "think aloud" as they read a high fear or low fear version of an antismoking pamphlet. Content analysis of these responses revealed that subjects generated more unfavorable comments and fewer favorable comments about the pamphlet's content in the high fear condition. Consistent with these cognitive response data, the high fear pamphlet induced (marginally) less persuasion than the low fear pamphlet.

Despite Janis and Terwilliger's promising data, interest in the information-processing effects of fear effectively terminated by the end of the 1960s. Indeed, cognitive response and argument recall measures have been virtually absent in fear appeal studies conducted over the past two decades (e.g., Rogers & Mewborn, 1976; Maddux & Rogers, 1983; C. Struckman-Johnson, Gilliland, Struckman-Johnson, & North, 1990). This omission is striking given that such measures gained prominence in persuasion theorizing and research during this period (see Chapters 6 and 7). This empirical state of affairs was no doubt fueled by early reviewers' (e.g., Higbee, 1969; Leventhal, 1970) dismissal of the drive model and Janis's (1967) and McGuire's (1968b, 1969) extensions, the complexity of the latter models' persuasion predictions, and Leventhal's (1970) influential edict that research ought to focus on specific belief determinants of adaptive coping.[14] In addition, the increasing number of studies documenting positive effects of fear/threat manipulations on persuasion were widely interpreted as refuting the idea of fear-motivated defensive processing.

Back to the Future. Although none of the theories we have reviewed have emerged unscathed in empirical tests, they offer distinctive insights about fear appeals that deserve continued exploration in future research. Rogers' (1975, 1983) protection motivation theory (and related formulations) can be viewed as illuminating the proximal determinants of adaptive coping behavior. To encourage such behavior, it is clear that communications must contain information that convinces recipients that a depicted threat like AIDS is indeed severe, that they are personally vulnerable to this threat, that there exist highly effective strategies for coping with this threat, and that recipients possess the necessary skills to implement these strategies. Yet neither this theory nor related ones (e.g., Leventhal, 1970; Sutton, 1982) provide insights about the factors that influence *acceptance* of each of these proximal beliefs or the possible *relations* among these beliefs. For example, does the perception of threat influence recipients' attention to and acceptance of information about response efficacy and self-efficacy? From the perspective of the heuristic-systematic and elaboration likelihood models (see Chapter 7), heightened threat (much like heightened personal relevance) might be expected to increase people's motivation to scrutinize response efficacy and self-efficacy information. These models also recognize the possibility that threat information might *bias* cognitive processing (see Liberman & Chaiken, in press). Such information could conceivably lead people to engage in wishful thinking, thus enhancing their acceptance of implausible coping strategies (e.g., waiting for a "miracle cure"; see Rippetoe & Rogers, 1987).

The most important legacy of the drive model and its extensions is their proposition that the fear-persuasion relation can best be understood by examining how fear arousal impacts on the cognitive processes that presumably mediate acceptance of persuasive messages' recommendations. The elaboration likelihood and heuristic-systematic models provide particularly promising frameworks for readdressing this general proposition (see Gleicher & Petty, 1992; Jepson & Chaiken, 1990; Liberman & Chaiken, in press). For example, does fear arousal influence motivation for systematic processing? Does the information value of fear ever operate as a simple heuristic (see Schwarz, 1990; Schwarz, Servay, & Kumpf, 1985)? Is fear predictive of the likelihood that recipients will be influenced by heuristic cues such as source expertise or consensus opinion (see Chaiken, 1987)? Moreover, if processing effects such as these do occur, do they reflect recipients' open-minded consideration of information or a self-protective, defense-motivated form of processing (Chaiken, Liberman, & Eagly, 1989; see Chapter 7)? Like the drive model and its extensions, these newer dual-process frameworks also suggest the importance of examining whether emotional tension disrupts people's *capacity* for systematic processing. Notwithstanding the null comprehension results of early studies (see prior discussion), this hypothesis deserves renewed attention in light of recent demonstrations that high levels of stress *do* impair performance on *complex* cognitive tasks (e.g., Darke, 1988; Keinan, 1987; see also Janis, 1982). Indeed, Jepson and Chaiken (1990) recently demonstrated this effect in a persuasion experiment. College-aged subjects who manifested varying levels of chronic fear about cancer read a lengthy message advocating regular cancer check-ups that contained a number of reasoning errors. Subjects' responses to an on-line thought-listing task revealed that high fear subjects detected fewer logical errors and listed fewer message-related cognitions in general than did low fear subjects. High fear subjects also recalled fewer persuasive arguments. Importantly, this study also showed that high fear subjects were more persuaded by the message than low fear subjects. Although this result seems to contradict McGuire's (e.g., 1969) logic that poor reception *reduces* persuasion, that logic assumed that messages contain compelling arguments (see Chapter 6). As research guided by the heuristic-systematic and elaboration likelihood models has shown, reduced systematic processing should *enhance* persuasion when messages contain flawed arguments (see Chapter 7). The viability of these models for understanding the fear-persuasion relation is also suggested by recent research on how mood affects cognitive processing and persuasion.

Positive Affect and Persuasion

As we noted in introducing the drive model, Hovland and his colleagues (1953) suggested that their framework was relevant to emotions other than fear. In addition, Janis (1967) maintained that his model could be used to explore the persuasive effects of arousing guilt in recipients. Despite these suggestions, persuasion researchers have paid little attention to affective states other than fear arousal (and, as noted above, too little attention to fear's impact on information processing). The notable exception concerns the persuasive effects of the transitory affective states that most psychologists term *moods*.[15] In fact, symptomatic of social psychology's renewed interest in affective issues, research exploring the relation between recipient mood and persuasion is in a renaissance phase (see Mackie & Worth, 1991; Schwarz, Bless, & Bohner, 1991).

In one of the earliest studies relevant to this topic, Razran (1940) presented political slogans to college-aged subjects as they ate a free lunch or as noxious odors infiltrated the experimental room. He found that agreement with the slogans was greater among subjects who had viewed them in the presumably mood-enhancing free lunch context. Razran maintained that this result was due to classical conditioning: The positive affect engendered by the enjoyable food and the negative effect engendered by the noxious odors came to be associated with the contiguously presented political slogans (see Chapter 9). Similar findings, also interpreted in classical conditioning terms, were reported in subsequent studies that paired a range of stimuli assumed to elicit positive or negative affect (e.g., harsh sounds, happy vs. depressing films) with words, statements, persons, or objects toward which subjects' attitudes were then assessed (e.g., Gouaux, 1971; Griffitt, 1970; A. W. Staats, Staats, & Crawford, 1962; Zanna, Kiesler, & Pilkonis, 1970; see Chapter 9).

The prototypic persuasion experiment is more complex than the above studies because subjects receive fairly detailed messages comprised of an overall position and supportive argumentation. Intermittent demonstrations that agreement with this more complex type of "unconditioned stimulus" could be enhanced by exposure to positive

447

mood inductions—though not necessarily reduced by negative ones (Janis, Kaye, & Kirschner, 1965)—were reported during the 1960s, 1970s, and early 1980s. Examples of the types of mood inductions researchers examined include snack food (Janis et al., 1965), pleasant music (Galizio & Hendrick, 1972), having subjects study "happy" sentences (Dribben & Brabender, 1979), and depicting the message source in a pleasant context (Biggers & Pryor, 1982). These experiments were also typically interpreted in terms of classical conditioning. Yet it is not difficult to fashion alternative, cognitive explanations for their findings based on several of the process theories of persuasion that we discussed in Chapters 6 and 7. For example, mood might influence recipients' attention to message content or the valence of their cognitive responding. Unfortunately, mediational possibilities such as these were not addressed in these early mood and persuasion studies.

Mood and Magnitude of Systematic Processing. Infusing new theoretical life into the study of mood and persuasion, Worth and Mackie (1987) demonstrated that positive mood is associated with reduced levels of systematic processing and a greater tendency to be influenced by heuristic cues. Positive mood subjects in their experiment received an unexpected prize in the context of a study on lotteries. After this induction, these subjects as well as "neutral" mood control subjects (who had simply answered questions about lotteries) participated in an ostensibly unrelated study in which they read a persuasive message on the topic of acid rain. This message was attributed to either an expert or nonexpert source and contained either nine strong or nine weak persuasive arguments. Supporting the hypothesis that positive mood reduces systematic processing, positive mood subjects recalled fewer persuasive arguments than neutral mood subjects, and their attitude judgments revealed much less discrimination between strong and weak argumentation. In fact, as shown in the top panel of Figure 10.4, subjects who were in a good mood were unaffected by argument quality. In contrast, those in the control condition indicated greater agreement with the message comprised of strong arguments. As the second panel of the figure shows, positive mood subjects but not neutral mood subjects were influenced by the study's heuristic cue, agreeing more with the message when it purportedly stemmed from an expert source.

Attesting to the robustness of the negative relation between positive mood and systematic processing, the Mood × Argument Quality interaction shown in Figure 10.4 has been replicated in several additional experiments that have featured different mood manipulations and different message topics (for reviews, see Mackie & Worth, 1991; Schwarz, Bless, & Bohner, 1991). For example, Bless, Bohner, Schwarz, and Strack (1990, Experiment 1) found that subjects who had recently written about a "happy" life event were no more persuaded by a strong message advocating increased student fees than by a weak version of this message; in contrast, subjects who had written about a "sad" life event agreed more with the strongly argued message.[16] Moreover, this interaction obtained regardless of whether subjects were told that the researchers were interested in studying "language comprehension" (the "moderate" elaboration condition) or subjects' evaluation of arguments (the "high" elaboration condition; see further discussion below).

FIGURE 10.4.
Attitude change
exhibited by Worth
and Mackie's (1987)
positive and neutral
mood subjects as a
function of
argument quality
(top panel) and
source expertise
(bottom panel). This
figure was adapted
from one presented
by Mackie and
Worth (1991).

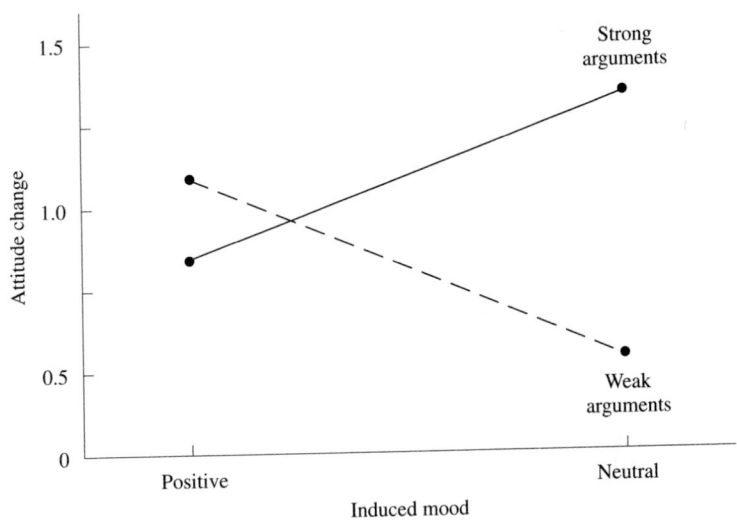

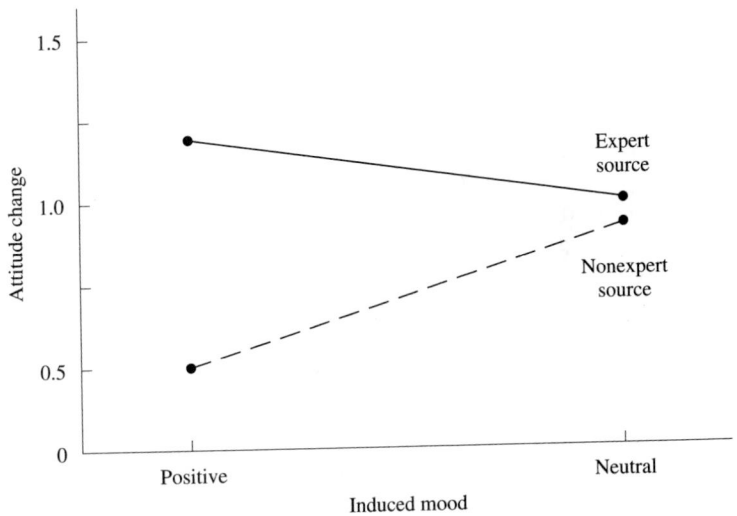

The Mood × Expertise interaction shown in Figure 10.4 was replicated in a subsequent study by Mackie and Worth (1989, Experiment 2, limited exposure conditions; see further discussion below). Also consistent with the idea that positive mood fosters heuristic processing, Bodenhausen (in press) has shown that group stereotypes (e.g., "Hispanics are aggressive") exert a greater impact on judgments about individuals who are members of such groups when subjects are placed in good (vs.

449

sad or neutral) moods (for relevance of the heuristic-systematic model to stereotyping, see Chaiken et al., 1989). Yet Bohner, Crow, and Erb (unpublished study reported by Schwarz et al., 1991) found no greater tendency on the part of elated (vs. depressed) subjects to be influenced by consensus information, another variable whose judgmental impact has been ascribed to heuristic processing (see Chapter 7). Additional research will therefore be required to gauge the extent to which (and, no doubt, the conditions under which) positive mood enhances people's susceptibility to influence by heuristic cues. In addition, the reasons for such heuristic cue effects deserve further investigation. The obvious explanation would seem to be that people in good (vs. neutral) moods are more likely to engage in heuristic processing (see Schwarz et al., 1991). Yet, it is also reasonable to assume that such effects are merely a consequence of greater systematic processing among neutral mood subjects (see Worth & Mackie, 1987). As discussed in Chapter 7, the heuristic-systematic model suggests that systematic processing may attenuate the judgmental impact of heuristic processing, especially when message content contradicts the validity of persuasion heuristics (see also Maheswaran & Chaiken, 1991; Schwarz et al., 1991). Nonetheless, the notion that positive mood does enhance the likelihood of heuristic processing is reasonable in light of related research on the impact of positive mood states on problem solving and decision making (e.g., Isen & Means, 1983; Isen, Means, Patrick, & Nowicki, 1982; Sinclair & Mark, 1991). For example, in experiments by Isen and her colleagues, subjects exposed to positive (vs. neutral) mood inductions have been observed to make their decisions relatively quickly, to base their decisions on relatively little information, and to prefer intuitive, heuristic problem-solving strategies to more effortful, detailed algorithms (see Isen, 1987).

Capacity and Motivational Interpretations of Mood Effects. According to the heuristic-systematic and elaboration likelihood models, there are two reasons why positive mood might be negatively related to systematic processing: People in good moods may lack *motivation* for systematic processing or they may lack *capacity* for this effortful, comprehensive mode of information processing. There is sound basis for both of these possibilities. Since being in a good mood is intrinsically pleasurable, people may be motivated to engage in cognitive and behavioral activities that maintain or enhance this state and to avoid activities that would negate it (see Isen, 1987). As Worth and Mackie (1987) argued, because systematic processing is effortful, minimal levels of such processing along with satisficing decision rules presumably allow people to maintain their good moods. The alternative, diminished capacity idea stems from research suggesting that positive mood states consume cognitive capacity because they activate positively valenced material in memory, which is appreciable (see Bower, 1981; Isen, 1987; Isen, Shalker, Clark, & Karp, 1978). Because cognitive capacity is limited, people in good moods might therefore have less capacity for other processing tasks such as attending to, comprehending, elaborating upon, and integrating attitude-relevant information (Isen, 1984, 1987; Mackie & Worth, 1989; Worth & Mackie 1987).[17]

Whether lack of motivation or diminished capacity underlies the negative relation between positive mood and systematic processing is a matter of current debate (Mackie

& Worth, 1991; Schwarz et al., 1991; see also Isen, 1987). Although Mackie and her colleagues do not discount the idea that motivational factors can account for this relation, the results of several experiments in which they attempted to test between the two interpretations have led them to favor the diminished capacity explanation (Mackie & Worth, 1989; Worth, Mackie, & Asuncion, reported by Mackie & Worth, 1991). For example, Mackie and Worth (1989, Experiment 2) provided half of their subjects an ample but nonetheless limited amount of time to read a strong versus weak message from an expert or nonexpert source. The attitude data from these conditions replicated Worth and Mackie's (1987) earlier findings: Compared to subjects in a neutral mood, positive mood subjects were less influenced by the strength of the message's arguments and more influenced by the expertise of its source. The remaining subjects in this experiment were given as much time as they wished to read and consider the persuasive message. If positive mood subjects lack motivation for systematic processing, the authors reasoned, they should spend less time with the message than neutral mood subjects, and the attitude data from these unlimited time conditions ought to replicate that observed in the limited time exposure conditions. However, if positive mood consumes cognitive capacity, subjects in good moods could presumably overcome this limitation by allotting themselves more time to read and think about the message. The data from the unlimited time conditions supported the capacity interpretation. Positive mood subjects spent *more* time reading the message than neutral mood subjects, and they manifested an equivalent amount of systematic processing, as indexed by the fact that argument quality exerted an equally strong impact and source expertise an equally weak (i.e, nonsignificant) impact on the attitude judgments of neutral *and* positive mood subjects.

Some evidence for the motivational interpretation of positive mood's impact on processing has also been obtained (Bless et al., 1990; see also Forgas, 1989; Innes & Ahrens, 1991; Smith & Shaffer, 1990). For example, Bless et al. (1990, Exp. 1) observed a somewhat greater tendency for positive mood subjects to discriminate between strongly argued and weakly argued messages in a condition in which they were told explicitly to evaluate message content. Moreover, Schwarz et al. (1991) have argued that Mackie and Worth's (1989) unlimited time exposure results can be explained in motivational terms; specifically, these authors believe that the instructions subjects received in these conditions may have provided them with an incentive for scrutinizing message content. Despite this argument and our own intuition that both motivational and capacity factors play a role in accounting for the processing effects of positive mood, Worth, Mackie, and Asuncion (reported in Mackie & Worth, 1991) recently documented a reliable decrement in systematic processing due to positive mood even when subjects were told that it was important to be thorough and accurate in evaluating the message and that they would receive a monetary reward commensurate with the quality of their performance on this processing task.

Additional Mechanisms by which Mood May Affect Persuasion. Notwithstanding the motivation–cognitive capacity issue, existing studies have provided strong and consistent support for Worth and Mackie's (1987) original proposition that the relation

451

between positive mood and persuasion can be understood in terms of the effects of positive mood on the magnitude of systematic processing.[18] There are, of course, other mechanisms by which positive (and negative) mood could conceivably influence persuasion. For example, positive mood might function to bias the valence of systematic processing in a positive direction, either because positive cognitions are primed by this mood state (see earlier discussion) or because people in good moods are motivated to view things in a positive light (see Shaller & Cialdini, 1990). Alternately, mood could be conceptualized as a "peripheral cue," that is, a variable that influences persuasion in the absence of argument scrutiny (see discussion of elaboration likelihood model in Chapter 7). As Schwarz et al. (1991) have noted, the peripheral mechanisms that might underlie mood's persuasive impact include classical conditioning and heuristic processing. The former mechanism should be clear to readers from our earlier discussion (see also Chapter 9). The heuristic processing mechanism Schwarz proposes assumes that people misinterpret their (induced) mood states as diagnostic of their affective reactions to the persuasive message and/or its source. As a consequence of this misattribution, they may rely on a "How-do-I-feel-about-it" heuristic in forming their attitude judgments (Schwarz, 1990; Schwarz et al., 1991; Schwarz & Clore, 1983). Both the biased processing hypothesis and the peripheral cue hypothesis predict a main effect for mood on subjects' attitude judgments; the former hypothesis also predicts a mood main effect on the valence of subjects' message-related thinking. Neither finding has been observed in the studies that Mackie and her colleagues and Schwarz and his colleagues have conducted, however.

It is possible, of course, that the biased processing hypothesis and the peripheral cue hypothesis hold under circumscribed conditions. Indeed, this is the thrust of Petty and Cacioppo's recent *multiple-role* analysis of affect (Petty, Cacioppo, & Kasmer, 1988; Petty, Cacioppo, Sedikides, & Strathman, 1988; Petty, Gleicher, & Baker, 1991). Similar to their elaboration likelihood analysis of the role of source variables (see Chapter 7), Petty and his colleagues hypothesize that mood and other affective states (including fear arousal) influence persuasion in different ways depending upon a host of factors (e.g., personal relevance, distraction) that raise or lower the elaboration likelihood, that is, the probability that recipients scrutinize persuasive argumentation. When the elaboration likelihood is low (e.g., low personal relevance), mood is postulated to function as a peripheral cue. Under such circumstances, mood would presumably influence persuasion via either or both of the peripheral mechanisms identified by Schwarz et al. (1991). However, when the elaboration likelihood is moderate (e.g., uncertain personal relevance), mood is postulated to influence the extensiveness of argument processing. Under such circumstances, positive mood presumably reduces the extensiveness of argument processing, as both Mackie and Schwarz have demonstrated (and for either motivational or capacity reasons; see Petty et al., 1991). Finally, when the elaboration likelihood is high (e.g., high personal relevance), mood is postulated to influence persuasion in one of two ways, depending upon whether it is "relevant" or "irrelevant" to determining the "central merits of an attitude object" (Petty, Cacioppo, & Kasmer, 1988, p. 137). When relevant, mood is assumed to serve as a persuasive argument. For example, you might reason that the film you just saw is very good because you find yourself feeling happy coming out of the theater. When irrelevant to judging an attitude object, however, mood is assumed to bias the valence of systematic processing. For example, the positive mood induced by seeing a good film may positively bias your reactions to a newspaper editorial (on an unrelated topic) you read later that night.

Two recent experiments by Petty, Schumann, Richman, and Strathman (in press) provide preliminary support for two aspects of the above analysis, that "irrelevant" positive affect functions as a peripheral cue when the elaboration likelihood is low but biases systematic processing in a positive direction when the elaboration likelihood is high. In Experiment 1 positive mood subjects wrote about a positive life event, whereas neutral mood subjects listened to classical music; in Experiment 2 positive mood subjects viewed an episode from a popular television situation comedy program ("The Cosby Show"), whereas neutral mood subjects viewed a segment from an information program designed to appeal to medical practitioners ("Cardiology Update"). The mood state induced by these manipulations was labeled "irrelevant" affect by the authors because of its presumed irrelevance to the messages used in the two studies (requirements for foster care parents and a commercial ad for a pen, respectively). In Experiment 1 individual differences in need for cognition (Cacioppo & Petty, 1982) served to operationalize the elaboration likelihood, whereas in Experiment 2 a task involvement manipulation operationalized this variable. Specifically, the authors assumed that the elaboration likelihood was "high" for Study 1 subjects whose need for cognition scores were above the sample median and for Study 2 subjects who received the high task involvement induction; they assumed also that the elaboration likelihood was "low" for Study 1 subjects whose need for cognition scores were below the median and for Study 2 subjects who received the low involvement induction. Argument quality was also manipulated in each study by presenting subjects with messages comprised of either strong or weak persuasive arguments.

The experiments yielded identical results. The decrement in systematic processing evidenced by positive mood subjects in Mackie's and Schwarz's experiments was not observed in this research (i.e., neither study yielded the Mood × Argument Quality interaction shown in Figure 10.4). Instead, elated subjects agreed more with the experimental messages than neutral mood subjects regardless of argument quality and regardless of presumed elaboration likelihood level. As noted earlier, this mood main effect is predicted both by the peripheral cue hypothesis and the biased processing hypothesis. To distinguish between these two explanations, the authors examined the proportion of positive cognitions that subjects generated on a thought-listing task. In both experiments, exposure to the positive mood induction enhanced positive message-related thinking in the high but not low elaboration likelihood conditions. Moreover, the results of path analyses suggested that the mood-persuasion relation was mediated by positive message-related thinking in the high elaboration conditions but not in the low elaboration conditions; in the latter conditions, mood exerted a direct impact on persuasion. These results thus support the authors' contention that positive mood functions as a peripheral cue when the elaboration likelihood is low but biases the valence of systematic processing when the elaboration likelihood is high (and mood is irrelevant to judging message validity; see note 19).

Although these findings fit the multiple-role analysis presented by Petty and his colleagues, other findings are more difficult to interpret within this framework. For example, Bless et al. (1990, Exp. 1) assumed that the focus-on-arguments condition of their study established a "high" elaboration likelihood. In contrast to the biased processing prediction that the multiple-role framework makes under these conditions, mood exerted no main effect on these subjects' attitudes or on the valence of their cognitive responses (see also Batra & Stayman, 1990). In a second experiment Bless and colleagues created a "low" elaboration likelihood condition by distracting subjects from paying attention to message content. According to the multiple-role framework, mood should have functioned as a peripheral cue in this situation. The mood main effect on attitudes predicted by this logic was not observed, however. Finally, Mackie's and Schwarz's demonstrations that positive (vs. neutral or sad) mood states reduce systematic processing can be said to fit the multiple-role analysis to the extent that such demonstrations have been conducted in settings that establish a "moderate" elaboration likelihood. Although this assumption is plausible for some studies (e.g., Worth & Mackie, 1987) it is less plausible for others (e.g., Worth, Mackie, & Asuncion's high incentive conditions; see earlier discussion of this experiment).

These ambiguities underscore the need to develop *a priori* criteria for determining whether an experiment or experimental condition has induced a low, moderate, or high elaboration likelihood (see Chapter 7). Although Petty and his colleagues (e.g., Petty & Cacioppo, 1984b; Petty et al., 1991) have discussed these three levels in general terms, they have not yet provided explicit guidelines for how these levels could be assessed independent of the attitude effects that they are postulated to produce. Without such criteria, rigorous tests of the multiple-role analysis are not possible.[19]

Summary and Conclusions. The next few years will no doubt witness additional empirical attempts to document alternative mechanisms by which mood influences persuasion. Further efforts to distinguish between motivational and cognitive capacity accounts of the processing effects of positive (and negative) mood inductions are also likely. It is probable that both of these accounts will receive empirical support, especially since capacity limitations may sometimes spill over to influence motivation for processing (see Chaiken, 1987; Chaiken et al., 1989). Additional research concerning the impact of positive mood on people's propensities to engage in heuristic processing is also called for given the limited nature of existing findings and some lack of clarity as to how they should be interpreted. And to the extent that multiple peripheral mechanisms can account for direct effects of mood on persuasion (see Petty et al., 1991), research designed to discriminate between such mechanisms will be important. Finally, it will also be important for future investigators to examine more thoroughly the processing and attitudinal consequences of truly negative affect. Findings from a number of studies indicate that subjects who have received mildly negative mood inductions and subjects who are (mildly) depressed on a chronic basis tend to engage in more extensive systematic processing than subjects who receive either neutral or positive mood inductions and subjects who are not depressed (e.g., Bless et al., 1990; Bodenhausen, in press; Gleicher & Weary, 1991, but see Sullivan &

Conway, 1989). Yet the generalization that negative mood enhances systematic processing should be regarded with some caution pending the results of research that examines more extreme levels of induced or measured negative affect than have been investigated to date.

Despite its limitations, the recent research on mood and persuasion represents an important new direction in attitude change research with obvious implications for other judgment phenomena as well (e.g., stereotyping; Bodenhausen, in press). The dual-process model approach that Mackie, Schwarz, and others have adopted has already yielded important insights regarding the attitudinal and processing consequences of positive mood, and has the potential to yield important insights about negative affective states, including fear arousal, as well. In the larger research context, this recent work has also contributed to social psychology's renewed interest in exploring the interplay of affective and cognitive processes. Although the effects that mood and other emotional states exert on cognitive processing and judgment are no doubt complex, the sophistication of contemporary attitude theories and contemporary research suggests to us that a true cumulation of knowledge in this area is in the offing.

Theories of Cognitive Consistency

As we explained in Chapter 3, a variety of structural properties have been ascribed to attitudinal responding. Yet one principle in particular has dominated psychologists' descriptions of the relations that exist between and among people's mental representations of their beliefs, attitudes (and values), and attitudinally significant behaviors, decisions, and commitments. In its most generic form, this principle of *cognitive consistency* holds that these various elements of the "attitudinal cognitorium" (as M. J. Rosenberg, 1968b, dubbed it) are mutually interdependent parts of a system that tends toward a state of harmony, balance, or consonance. The principle is a dynamic one: When the state of the cognitorium is disharmonious, imbalanced, or dissonant, a tendency will arise for its elements to be transmuted in ways that promote or restore equilibrium. The origins of this principle derive from the Gestalt tenets that certain configurations of the perceptual field are preferred because of their simplicity and coherence, and that perceptual processes operate to make the state of the field as "good" as possible (Koffka, 1935; Köhler, 1929). Like the Gestalt psychologists' view of perception, then, theories of cognitive consistency emphasize that *motivation* for directed cognitive change can stem from structural considerations.

Theories of cognitive consistency became popular in the late 1950s and retained their popularity with attitude researchers throughout the 1960s and much of the 1970s. Earliest among these was Fritz Heider's (1946, 1958) balance theory. Several other members of this theoretical family can be viewed (and often were viewed by their creators) as extensions, variations, or specific applications of Heider's seminal ideas. The theories share the common principle that inconsistency among attitudinal elements creates "tension," and that this tension represents a motivational force for cognitive change.[20] They also differ in a variety of ways—for example, in their particular definitions of consistency and their descriptions of the "tension" created by inconsistency as well as in the types of attitudinal elements and therefore the forms of inconsistency they concern.

Consistency theories are models of attitude structure as well as models of attitude change. Those that offer particularly important insights about structure were discussed in Chapter 3. In this chapter we emphasize members of the consistency family that have provided particularly important insights about the motivating effects of inconsistency on attitude and belief change. We will first review balance theory and several closely related formulations. Afterwards, we will review what many social psychologists view as the jewel in the consistency family crown, Festinger's (1957, 1964b) theory of cognitive dissonance.

Balance Theory and Related Formulations

As explained in Chapter 3, Heider's (1946, 1958) balance theory deals with a person's perceptions of the liking and unit relations that exist between himself (p) and (usually) two additional elements. These other elements are typically another person (o) and an impersonal entity (x; e.g., a social issue, a value, a physical object), but they can also be two other persons (o, q) or two impersonal entities (x, y). The liking relation corresponds to attitude, albeit one that can assume only two values, positive or negative. The unit relation corresponds to any nonattitudinal bond between elements (e.g., causality, proximity, membership). It too may assume only a positive versus negative value (e.g., p shares an office with o, p does not belong to x, o caused x, o is not responsible for x).[21]

Triadic structures are *balanced* when (a) all three relations among elements are positive (e.g., p likes o, o likes x, p likes x) or (b) two relations are negative and one is positive (e.g., p likes o, o dislikes x, p dislikes x). *Imbalance* exists when these conditions are not met; that is, (a) all three relations are negative (e.g., p dislikes o, o dislikes x, p dislikes x) or (b) two relations are positive and one is negative (e.g., p likes o, o likes x, p dislikes x). In the context of p-o-x triads, then, balance exists when we agree with people we like and disagree with people we dislike. In contrast, imbalance exists when we disagree with people we like and agree with people we dislike. Heider (1958) assumed that people "prefer" balanced to imbalanced states, and that imbalanced states produce "tension" or "unpleasantness" (for relevant research, see Chapter 3). Notwithstanding these allusions to the arousal properties of inconsistency, Heider's fundamental proposition that imbalanced structures gravitate toward balanced ones was based more on the Gestalt notion that perceptions tend toward simple "good figures" than on the drive-reduction notion that cognitive change occurs in the service of reducing negative affect (e.g., Festinger, 1957).

Heider (1958) described three distinct ways in which imbalanced triads can be converted to balanced ones. To illustrate, consider the case of disagreement with a liked other shown in the top panel of Figure 10.5: Eva (p) likes Doug (o) and endorses legalized abortion (x) but sees Doug as opposing abortion. *Attitude change* is one means for resolving imbalance. As shown in the second panel, Eva could adopt a negative

FIGURE 10.5 An imbalanced *p-o-x* triad illustrating disagreement between friends and three modes of restoring balance: attitude change, denial, and cognitive differentiation. An unbroken arrow signifies a positive attitude, and a broken arrow signifies a negative attitude. This figure was adapted from one presented by Heider (1958, p. 208).

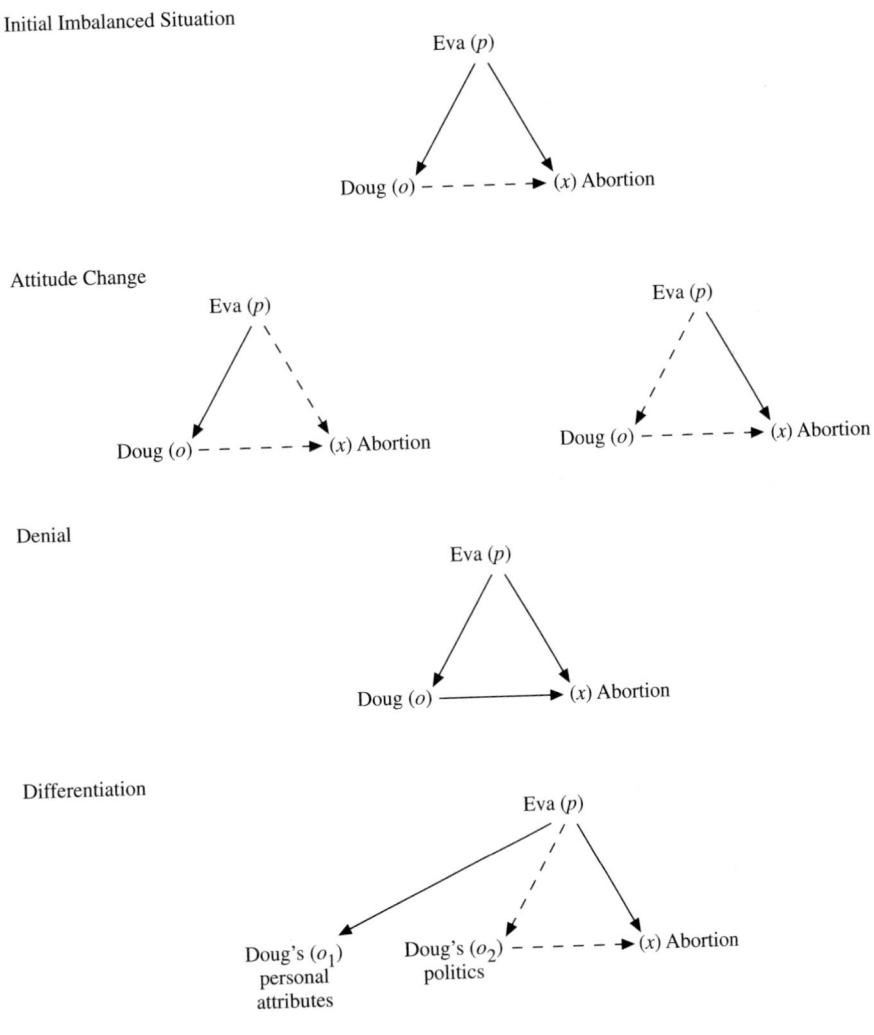

attitude toward abortion or, alternatively, begin to dislike Doug. A second way that balance can be restored is by changing the *o-x* relation; Eva might convince herself that Doug actually favors rather than opposes abortion (third panel). This second mode of inconsistency reduction can be labeled *belief change* or, more dynamically, distortion or *denial* (see Abelson, 1959). The idea that people distort others' opinion statements to be more congruent (or less congruent) with their own is also fundamental to social judgment theory (see Chapters 8 and 12), and both theories have been examined in studies on citizens' perceptions of liked and disliked candidates' stands on political issues (e.g., Brent & Granberg, 1982; Granberg & Brent, 1974; Kinder, 1978; Krosnick,

FIGURE 10.6.
A series of *p-o-x*
triads that are
equally imbalanced
according to
Heiderian logic, but
not according to
Newcomb's or
Osgood and
Tannenbaum's
formulations. In
Panel 1, the left
("adore") triad is
assumed to induce
greater levels of
inconsistency or
"incongruity"
because *p*'s attitudes
are more extreme.
Congruity theory's
specification of the
amount of incon-
gruity induced by
these triads and the
amount of attitude
change toward *x* and
o that should ensue
are also shown.
Panel 2 displays the
same congruity the-
ory calculations for
two triads in which
p's attitudes toward
x and *o* are not
equally polarized,
and illustrates the
theory's prediction
that strong attitudes
change less than
weaker ones. The
theory's attitude
change formulae for
these triads, which
involve dissociative
assertions, appear at
the bottom of the
figure. See note 25
for definition of the
terms in these for-
mulae and the mod-
el's formulae for
predicting change in
the case of associa-
tive assertions.

1990a; Ottati, Fishbein, & Middlestadt, 1988). Finally, as a third mode of balance restoration, Eva could also engage in *cognitive differentiation*. Perceivers exhibiting this integrative mode of thinking identify a component of the "whole" *o* (or *x*) toward which they hold an attitude that would balance the triad. For example, as shown in the fourth panel of the figure, Eva might distinguish Doug's politics, which she admits to disliking, from his personal attributes, which she truly does like. To the extent Eva focuses her attention on the former component, balance can be restored, for she favors abortion and dislikes the "political Doug" who opposes it.[22]

Even seminal theories have their flaws. For balance theory, these were mostly sins of simplification and omission—for example, its failure to consider larger than three-element structures and its lack of predictions concerning when each of the above modes of inconsistency resolution might be most likely to occur. With varying degrees of precision and success, subsequent formulations addressed these sorts of limitations.

A notable limitation of the balance model is that it ignores attitude extremity, a variable often thought to index the importance of involvingness of attitudes. By treating attitude (i.e., liking) as a dichotomous variable, Heider gave no weight to these (or other) properties that have been ascribed to "strong" attitudes (see Chapters 3, 4, 12). Yet

1. Incongruous triads where $p - o$ and $p - x$ are equally polarized

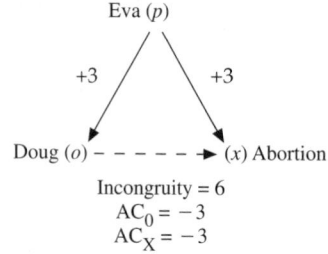
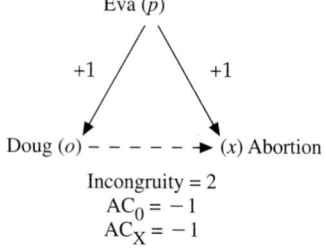

2. Incongruous triads where $p - o$ and $p - x$ are not equally polarized

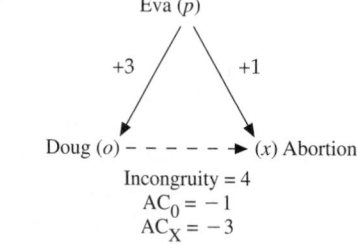
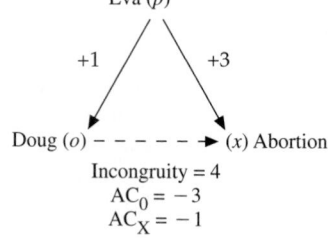

$AC_O = [abs\ X\ /\ (abs\ O + abs\ X)]\ \ (-X - O)$

$AC_X = [abs\ O\ /\ (abs\ O + abs\ X)]\ \ (-O - X)$

intuition suggests that inconsistency in one's cognitorium ought to create greater tension when important, strongly held attitudes are in conflict. In our disagreement-between-friends scenario, for example, it seems likely that Eva would experience her psychological situation as more disturbing if she *adores* Doug and is *ardently* pro-choice than if she merely *likes* Doug and is only *mildly* pro-choice. These two possibilities are shown in the top panel of Figure 10.6, where we have used a scale running from −3 to 0 to +3 to operationalize the intensity (as well as sign) of Eva's attitudes. Although the two triads are equally imbalanced according to Heider's theory, several other balance models satisfy our intuitions by proposing that the triad on the left produces greater tension and thus greater motivation for cognitive resolution than the triad on the right.

Strain-Toward-Symmetry Model. The idea that imbalanced *p-o-x* triads are problematic for perceivers primarily when important attitudinal elements are involved is an explicit assumption of Newcomb's (1953, 1959, 1968) *strain-toward-symmetry* model. Equating importance with intensity, Newcomb thus hypothesized that the tension induced by inconsistency and, therefore, motivation for cognitive resolution increase with increases in the extremity of *p*'s attitudes toward *o* and *x*, and *o*'s attitude toward *x*. The implication of this hypothesis for our disagreement-between-friends example is clear: Pressure for Eva to change her attitudes, misperceive Doug's attitude, or to engage in cognitive differentiation should be greater when she adores (vs. likes) Doug and is ardently (vs. mildly) pro-choice. Like balance theory, however, Newcomb's model offers no clear predictions regarding the conditions under which each of these modes of resolution is most likely to occur.[23]

Newcomb's assumption that inconsistency induces greater tension when strong attitudes are at stake has received support in several studies in which subjects rate hypothetical *p-o-x* triads for pleasantness (see Newcomb, 1968, for a summary; see also Chapter 3). This research has also yielded findings compatible with another assumption of his model, that inconsistency is most disturbing to perceivers when the *p-o* relation is positive. Newcomb and Heider both believed that disagreement with friends creates psychological tension. Yet agreement with disliked others—an equally imbalanced structure for Heider—was considered "nonbalanced" by Newcomb. He argued that such structures "invite neither modification nor acceptance"; in short, they fail to engage perceivers' attention (Newcomb, 1968, p. 31). More generally, Newcomb believed that cognitive inconsistency is psychologically meaningful only in the context of ongoing interpersonal relationships. Newcomb (1953) also diverged from Heider by proposing a reinforcement interpretation of perceivers' preference for balanced structures, that is, situations in which *p* and a *liked o* agree in their attitudes toward *x*. Such structures acquire secondary reinforcement value, Newcomb argued, because *o*'s attitudinal similarity to *p* enhances both *p*'s belief that *o*'s behavior is predictable and *p*'s confidence in the validity of his own attitudes (see also Festinger, 1954). For Newcomb, then, the tension aroused by imbalanced structures and the consequent pressure to restore balance stems, not from relatively benign Gestalt forces, but from the fact that such structures thwart these epistemic needs.

Congruity Theory. Like Newcomb's model, Osgood and Tannenbaum's (1955) *congruity theory* views inconsistency and pressure for cognitive change to be a positive function of the intensity of perceivers' attitudes. Yet, compatible with Heider's Gestalt perspective, Osgood and Tannenbaum assumed that a desire for structural simplicity underlies perceivers' tendencies to transmute "incongruous" *p-o-x* structures into "congruous" ones. Pertinent to situations in which a perceiver is exposed to a communicator's views on some issue,[24] congruity theory represents *p*'s attitude toward both the source (*o*) and the issue (*x*) along the bipolar evaluative scale we introduced earlier. The *o-x* relation is called an *assertion* in the theory, as it refers to the source's expressed attitude toward *x*. This attitude could also be defined as a continuous variable. However, Osgood and Tannenbaum (like Heider) treated it as having only two values: *associative* when the source's attitude is favorable toward the issue and *disassociative* when this attitude is unfavorable. In congruity theory terms, the triads shown in Figure 10.6 concern disassociative assertions. In all of them, Doug (the source) has expressed a negative attitude toward abortion.

In the case of associative assertions, congruity—a perfect state of equilibrium— exists when *p*'s attitude toward *o* and *p*'s attitude toward *x* are *equally polarized* and have the *same valence*. In the case of disassociative assertions, congruity exists when these two attitudes are equally polarized but have the *opposite valence*. Any deviation from congruity represents some degree of incongruity. The total amount of incongruity present in the *p-o-x* system is operationalized with the aid of the theory's bipolar evaluative scale. Specifically, if one holds constant *p*'s attitude toward one element (e.g., *x*), degree of incongruity is defined as the distance that *p*'s attitude toward the other element (e.g., *o*) would have to traverse along this scale in order for congruity to be restored. Given this operationalization, it should be clear that incongruity is much greater in the case in which Eva adores Doug and is ardently pro-choice than in the case in which she merely likes Doug and is mildly pro-choice (top panel of Figure 10.6). In the first case, incongruity equals 6: Eva's attitude toward Doug would have to shift 6 units (from +3 to −3) for congruity to be restored (the same calculation obtains when "abortion" is treated as the traveling element). In the second case, incongruity equals 2: Eva's attitude toward Doug would have to shift only 2 units (from +1 to −1) for congruity to be restored (again, the same result obtains if "abortion" is the traveling element). As magnitude of incongruity can range between 0 and 6, it is at its maximum level in the "adore" triad and at a low-to-moderate level in the "like" triad.

Osgood and Tannenbaum (1955) acknowledged that perceivers might react to very high levels of incongruity by misperceiving or denying the source's assertion (i.e., by changing the *o-x* relation). However, the focus of their model was on attitude change as a mode of incongruity resolution. Faced with imbalance, the Heiderian perceiver can change his attitude toward *o* or his attitude toward *x*, or perhaps both (Heider was not explicit on this point). According to congruity theory, *both* of these attitudes undergo change when incongruity exists. Moreover, the theory features attitude change formulas that yield precise quantitative predictions regarding the amount of change that perceivers should manifest. These formulas differ slightly as a function of whether associative or disassociative assertions are at issue; those for disassociative assertions appear in Figure 10.6.[25] Applying these to the "adore" triad in the top panel of the figure yields the prediction that Eva's attitude toward Doug *and* her attitude toward abortion will shift from strongly positive (+3) to neutral (0). Similarly, for the "like" triad, Eva's attitude toward Doug and her attitude toward abortion are predicted to shift from mildly positive (+1) to neutral (0).

The triads shown in the second panel of Figure 10.6 reveal something more interesting about congruity theory because they represent situations in which the perceiver's attitude toward the source and attitude toward the issue are *not* equally polarized. In the left triad, Eva holds a more extreme attitude toward Doug than she does toward abortion; in the triad on the right, her attitude toward abortion is more extreme. The two triads are equally incongruous according to the theory, as in each Eva's attitude toward one element (e.g., Doug) would have to traverse 4 scale units in order for perfect congruity to exist. Thus the *total* amount of attitude change predicted should be the same for each triad. However, close examination of the model's change equations reveals Osgood and Tannenbaum's assumption that highly polarized attitudes are more resistant to change. For the triad on the left, Eva's attitude toward Doug is predicted to change less than her attitude toward abortion. More specifically, the change formulae dictate that Eva's attitude toward Doug should shift from +3 to +2 and her attitude toward abortion should shift from +1 to −2. Thus, whereas total attitude change is 4 scale units, the less polarized element (abortion) changes 3 units while the more polarized element (Doug) changes only 1 unit. For the triad on the right, the reverse should obtain. That is, Eva's attitude toward Doug, the less polarized element, should change more than her attitude toward abortion.

When evaluated in terms of the accuracy of its attitude change predictions, congruity theory has not fared particularly well (see Kerrick, 1958; Osgood & Tannenbaum, 1955; Rokeach & Rothman, 1965; Tannenbaum, 1967, 1968). Most notably, accuracy declines precipitously with increases in incongruity. Indeed, subjects' most common reaction to experimental materials suggesting that a well liked source has endorsed a much disliked attitude object is not attitude change at all; rather, it is disbelief that the source really made the assertion claimed by the researcher (see also Eagly & Chaiken, 1976). Osgood and Tannenbaum dubbed this denial of a unit relation the "incredulity reaction." In addition, the theory more accurately predicts changes in subjects' attitudes toward communication sources than toward the issues that are the objects of these communications; in particular, attitude change toward issues is underestimated by the theory's equations.[26]

Despite these quantitative shortcomings, congruity theory's more general aspects have received empirical support (e.g., Osgood & Tannenbaum, 1955; Tannenbaum, 1966, 1967; Tannenbaum & Gengel, 1966). For example, its premise that stronger (i.e., more extreme) attitudes change less than weaker ones is consistent both with focused tests of the model and the larger empirical literature on resistance to persuasion that we cover in Chapter 12. As the resistance literature is what led Osgood and Tannenbaum (1955) to build this premise into their change equations, however, its empirical verification can hardly be considered a coup for their theory. More provocative is the theory's proposition, verified in empirical tests, that exposure to persuasive communications leads recipients to change their attitudes not only toward the issue discussed in the communication, but also toward the communication source. Although this proposition is derivable from other balance formulations, it is explicit only in congruity theory. Moreover, the implications of this aspect of the model have generally been underappreciated by persuasion researchers, few of whom test for the possibility that their experimental messages—or other, manipulated variables for that matter—may impact on subjects' attitudes toward communicators (for an exception, see Ratneshwar & Chaiken, 1991).

Tannenbaum (1966) provided a particularly compelling demonstration that this type of attitude change matters. In phase one of his experiment, subjects learned about a fictitious and evaluatively neutral source's views on two evaluatively neutral issues. Four treatments were formed by crossing the valence of the source's assertion about issue 1 (teaching machines) with the valence of his assertion about issue 2 (Spence learning theory). Some subjects, for example, learned that the source favored issue 1 but opposed issue 2. In phase two of the study, subjects read a "news article" about issue 1. This message either favored or opposed the issue but made *no* reference to the phase one source. Not surprisingly, the results of this study showed that subjects who had read the positive (vs. negative) news article rated issue 1 more favorably. More important, subjects' attitudes toward the source *and* issue 2 changed in accord with congruity theory predictions. For example, subjects who now liked teaching machines and had learned in phase one that the source favored teaching machines but disliked Spence learning theory exhibited an increase in their liking for the source, and a decrease in their liking for Spence learning theory.

In essence, Tannenbaum's research demonstrates that people's attitudes on a particular issue can influence both their attitudes toward communicators who express positions on that issue and their attitudes toward other (unrelated) issues on which those communicators take stands. Although these and other implications of congruity theory have been underexplored by persuasion researchers, it seems safe to say that practitioners of persuasion have an intuitive understanding of this theory's principles. The behavior of American politicians, for example, appears to reflect their belief that the way to enhance their image with voters is to (a) associate themselves with popular, often symbolic causes (e.g., "education," "housing"), (b) disassociate themselves from unpopular policies (e.g., cutting Social Security benefits, raising taxes), and of course (c) remain mute on issues about which voter opinion is divided (e.g., abortion)!

Evaluative-Cognitive Consistency Theory. We introduced Milton J. Rosenberg's (1956, 1960a, 1960c, 1968b) *evaluative-cognitive consistency theory* in Chapter 3, focusing our attention on its implications for attitude structure. Here we emphasize its motivational aspects. As readers will recall, the theory posits a tendency for people's attitudes to be consistent with their beliefs, which Rosenberg defined in terms of expectancy-value products (see Chapter 3).[27] For example, given a positive attitude toward protecting the environment, consistent beliefs would be those asserting a positive link between environmental protection and positively-valued attributes (goals, consequences, etc.) or those asserting a negative link between this attitude object and negatively-valued attributes. Inconsistent beliefs, in contrast, would be those asserting that environmental protection is either positively associated with negative attributes or negatively associated with positive ones.

Like other consistency theorists, Rosenberg assumed that attitude-belief inconsistency motivates perceivers to engage in one or more cognitive strategies that allow them to restore consistency to their cognitoriums. His views on the causes of consistency motivation were detailed in a collaborative paper with Hovland. In accord with the Gestalt perspective underlying balance theory and congruity theory, Hovland and Rosenberg (1960) acknowledged that consistency motivation might reflect perceivers' general striving for simplicity in cognitive structure. They also suggested that consistency motivation might also stem from external, social forces. In this view, perceivers seek to maximize consistency in their attitudinal responding because cultural standards, or norms, demand (and reinforce) such responding. This view implies that whereas inconsistency may cause little internal disturbance for perceivers, it is disturbing to others, perhaps because of their own needs for predictability. Hovland and Rosenberg did not entirely dismiss either of these possibilities. In fact, Rosenberg (e.g., 1960a) argued that pressures to account for one's attitudes and beliefs publicly should intensify perceivers' "intolerance for inconsistency." Nonetheless, Hovland and Rosenberg preferred a third, "ambivalence" interpretation of consistency motivation (see also Abelson, 1968; Rosenberg & Abelson, 1960). Informed by earlier analyses of psychological conflict (Lewin, 1935; N. E. Miller, 1944), this view holds that inconsistency is unpleasant, even painful, to perceivers because it embodies an approach-avoidance conflict. That is, whereas one or more elements of the cognitorium imply positive action tendencies (e.g., p likes o implies approach o), one or more other elements imply negative action tendencies (e.g., o dislikes an x that p likes implies avoid o). Because cognitive changes that restore consistency presumably reduce the negative tension associated with such conflict, Hovland and Rosenberg assumed that consistent attitudinal responding would, over time, gain the status of a learned incentive (see earlier discussion of the Yale reinforcement perspective).

In developing his theory, Rosenberg focused most of his attention on the consistency between people's attitudes toward social and political policies such as "allowing members of the Communist party to address the public," and their beliefs about the instrumental relation between such policies and values such as freedom and equality. In balance theory terms, the theory thus focuses on a perceiver's (p) evaluation of an impersonal attitude object (x), her evaluation of one or more values (y_1, y_2, etc.), and her perception of the (positive or negative) relation between the attitude object and each such value. The case in which x is linked to only one value in p's mind can be represented, then, as a simple p-x-y triad. Rosenberg (1960a; Rosenberg & Abelson, 1960) called such triads "bands." When x is linked to multiple values, a more complex structure composed of multiple p-x-y_i bands results. Several examples of these multiple value evaluative-cognitive structures are illustrated in Figure 10.7.

Using Heider's (1958) definition of balanced and imbalanced triads, Rosenberg (1960a) considered an evaluative-cognitive structure to be consistent when "all or most" of its p-x-y_i bands are balanced. Two such (fully) consistent attitudinal structures

FIGURE 10.7.
A balance theory representation of Rosenberg's evaluative-cognitive consistency theory using unbroken arrows to signify positive relations and broken arrows to signify negative relations. The top panel presents two consistent evaluative-cognitive structures. In the first, *p* holds a positive attitude toward an issue (*x*) that is perceived to facilitate the attainment of positively evaluated values (*y*₁, etc.); in the second structure, *p* holds a negative attitude toward an issue that is perceived to inhibit the attainment of these (same) values. The bottom panel presents two

1. Two consistent evaluative–cognitive structures

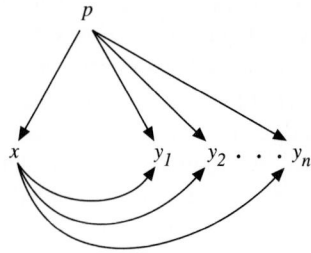
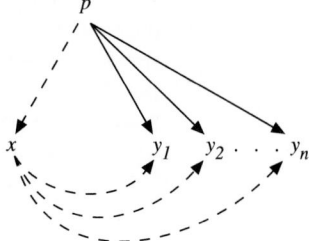

2. Two inconsistent evaluative–cognitive structures

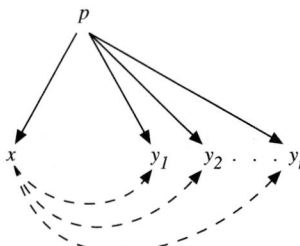
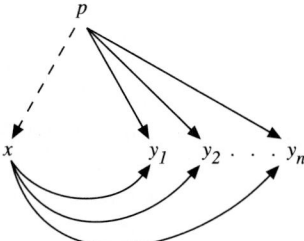

inconsistent structures. In the first, a positively evaluated issue is seen as blocking positive values, and, in the second, a negatively evaluated issue is seen as facilitating these values. To envision the remaining four structures dictated by this theory, readers need only change the sign of the *p-y*ᵢ relations that are shown, from positive to negative. This accomplished, the top panel of the figure would depict two additional *inconsistent* structures, and the bottom panel would depict two additional *consistent* structures.

are shown in the top panel of Figure 10.7. In the first one, for example, p holds a positive attitude toward x and believes that x is positively related to (i.e., facilitates) values $y_1 \ldots y_n$, all of which p evaluates positively. In parallel fashion, Rosenberg considered an evaluative-cognitive structure to be inconsistent when all or most of its p-x-y_i bands are imbalanced. The bottom panel of the figure illustrates two such (fully) inconsistent attitude structures. The second one, for example, refers to a situation in which p holds a negative attitude toward x but nonetheless believes that x facilitates positively evaluated values.[28]

Because Rosenberg (e.g., 1968b) assumed that a frequent cause of attitude-belief inconsistency was exposure to counterattitudinal communications, he proposed that "blanket rejection" of such messages' assertions (i.e., x-y linkages) represented one means of restoring consistency. In the spirit of psychoanalytic theorizing about defense mechanisms (see Chapter 12), he also speculated that perceivers might respond to "irreconcilable" inconsistencies by ceasing to think about the incompatibility between their attitudes and beliefs, in effect pushing the inconsistency "beyond the range of active awareness" (Rosenberg, 1960a, p. 22). Notwithstanding these first two possibilities, Rosenberg assumed that perceivers' most common response to attitude-belief inconsistency entailed changing either their attitudes or their beliefs.

The typical persuasive communication attempts to change recipients' attitudes by altering their beliefs (see Chapters 3, 5, 6, 7). Content that the persuasion literature provided ample evidence that people reduce *belief*-engendered attitude-belief inconsistency by changing their attitudes, Rosenberg (1960a, 1960b, 1960c; Rosenberg & Gardner, 1958) conducted several experiments designed to test the reverse proposition, that *attitude*-engendered attitude-belief inconsistency is typically resolved by belief change.

In these well-known experiments, Rosenberg first assessed hypnotizable subjects' attitudes and beliefs, then used posthypnotic suggestion to induce attitude change, and finally reassessed their attitudes and beliefs. For example, in one study subjects indicated in an initial session their overall evaluation of the proposal that "the United States abandon its policy of economic aid to foreign nations," the extent to which they perceived that this proposal would help (vs. block) the attainment of each of 32 values, and the extent to which they considered each value to be a source of satisfaction (vs. dissatisfaction). The summed cross-products of these instrumentality and value ratings provided an evaluative index of subjects' beliefs, which were generally pro-foreign aid. Three days later, experimental subjects met a different experimenter who hypnotized them and gave the following posthypnotic suggestion:

> After you awake, and continuing until our next meeting, you will feel very strongly opposed to the United States policy of giving economic aid to foreign nations. The mere idea of the United States giving economic aid to foreign nations will make you feel very displeased and disgusted. Until your next meeting with me you will continue to feel very strong and thorough opposition to the United States policy of economic aid to foreign nations (Rosenberg, 1960a, p. 38).

After awakening, as well as two days later and four days later, subjects' attitudes and beliefs were reassessed by the original experimenter. Confirming the success of the posthypnotic induction, reliably greater attitude change in the anti-foreign policy direction was observed among hypnotized subjects than among non-hypnotized control subjects at each of the three posttests. Of greater importance, belief change in the anti-foreign policy direction was also reliably greater among hypnotized subjects at each of the three posttests. Thus, hypnotized subjects apparently resolved inconsistency between their "new" anti-foreign aid attitudes and their prior pro-foreign aid beliefs by changing these "old" beliefs.

As the structures in Figure 10.7 suggest, Rosenberg's theory implies that his hypnotized subjects may have changed their beliefs either by modifying their view of the instrumental relation between foreign aid and the 32 values they were asked to consider (i.e., changing the sign or intensity of x-y_i linkages), by modifying their evaluation of these values (i.e., changing the sign or intensity of p-y_i linkages), or both.[29] Although changes of both sorts occurred, Rosenberg (1960a) observed that instrumentality change was far more common. He interpreted this result in terms of the greater "psychological cost" of value change. More specifically, on the assumption that evaluative-cognitive structures pertinent to different attitude objects (e.g., x_1 and x_2) are likely to feature many of the same values (i.e., y_1 etc.), he argued that value change was more likely than instrumentality change to upset the consistency of additional evaluative-cognitive structures, and thus less likely to be selected as a mode of consistency restoration. The related assumption that values are highly resistant to change because of the number and strength of their linkages to other cognitive entities, including the self, is a common one in attitude theory and research (e.g., Liberman & Chaiken, 1991; Rokeach, 1968, 1973; see Chapter 12).[30]

As explained earlier, both Newcomb (1953) and Osgood and Tannenbaum (1955) assumed that inconsistency and pressure for cognitive change is a positive function of the importance or intensity of perceivers' attitudes. Similarly, Rosenberg (1968b, p. 97) assumed that holding extreme attitudes or attitudes that are important to one's self-concept or "significant group loyalties" should increase perceivers' "intolerance for inconsistency." In other words, he believed that attitude-belief inconsistency produced greater tension and thus greater motivation for consistency restoration when strong, ego-involved attitudes were at stake. Rosenberg (1960a, 1965a, 1968b) also discussed other variables and experimental treatments that he believed would increase the tension associated with inconsistency and, hence, increase consistency-driven cognitive change. Of particular interest to contemporary investigators, he hypothesized that tension and change would be greater when people are forced to think "closely" about cognitive inconsistencies, when such inconsistencies involve personally relevant cognitive elements, and when people believe that they are publicly accountable for their attitudes and beliefs (see also Hovland & Rosenberg, 1960). Cacioppo and Petty's (1981a) demonstration that subjects given ample (vs. limited) time to ponder p-o-x triads and subjects told to consider x personally important (vs. unimportant) rate imbalanced triads as more unpleasant is consistent with the first two of these hypotheses (see also Rosenberg, 1965a). The third, accountability hypothesis has not been tested directly. However, it is possible to interpret some of Tetlock's work on integrative complexity (see Chapter 3) as consistent with the view that accountability pressures heighten perceivers' tendencies to engage in consistency-driven thought (e.g., Tetlock, 1986; Tetlock, Skitka, & Boettger, 1989).

The Microprocesses of Inconsistency Reduction

Although the consistency principle has been applied to numerous phenomena in social psychology (see Abelson, 1983), theories of cognitive consistency were developed primarily as models of attitude structure and attitude change. It is therefore not surprising that they emphasize attitude and belief change as a prime means by which perceivers resolve inconsistencies in their cognitoriums. As we have seen, however, the theories also recognize other modes of resolving inconsistency. The cessation of thinking mode of coping suggested by Rosenberg (1960a) represents a passive and somewhat autistic means of dealing with inconsistency. In contrast, other modes that theorists have discussed represent somewhat more active coping strategies.

Perceivers who engage in *denial* reject or dismiss attitudinally inconsistent information. Heider (1958) conceptualized this mode in terms of rejecting unit relations (see earlier discussion and Figure 10.5, Panel 3). Osgood and Tannenbaum's (1955) "incredulity reaction," whereby recipients restore congruity by disbelieving an alleged source-issue linkage, and Rosenberg's (e.g., 1968b) "blanket rejection" mode are largely synonymous with Heider's conceptualization. In several papers that explicitly addressed the microprocesses of inconsistency reduction, Robert Abelson (1959, 1963, 1968) introduced the term denial and gave it broader meaning. In his view denial referred to a perceiver's "direct attack" upon information that, if accepted, would cause inconsistency. Moreover, he viewed denial as encompassing more than simple, un-elaborated rejections of such information ("Does U.S. military policy discourage Communist expansion? Ridiculous!"). Specifically, he felt that denial often reflected perceivers' deliberate efforts to counterargue inconsistency-provoking information ("Does U.S. military policy discourage Communist expansion? No, on the contrary, it encourages such expansion by creating sympathy for the underdog"; see Abelson, 1968, p. 119). For this reason, Abelson (1968) regarded this second type of denial as a relatively effortful cognitive *process* in which perceivers search for and retrieve relevant stored knowledge that can support their denial attempts. This conceptualization of denial fits well with the assumption of dual-process models of persuasion that counterarguing, a type of systematic processing, requires cognitive effort. Moreover, these models also lead to the conclusion that denial requires ability insofar as it is a process that depends upon stored knowledge and its retrieval from memory (see Chapters 7 and 8).

Abelson (1959, 1968) also proposed *bolstering* as a mode of inconsistency reduction. Perceivers who engage in bolstering add consistent elements to an existing, inconsistent structure. Although bolstering does not entirely remove inconsistency from the resultant (larger) structure, it does dilute its magnitude (see discussion of dissonance theory in next section). For example, the tension you experience in relation to knowing that you and your best friend hold opposite views about an issue important to you both (e.g., abortion) can be alleviated to a certain extent by remembering that the two of

467

you do see eye-to-eye on a host of other important issues. Abelson assumed that bolstering also required perceivers to search for and retrieve relevant stored knowledge. Like denial, then, bolstering, that is, generating supportive cognitions, requires both effort and capacity. Yet because bolstering merely lessens inconsistency, Abelson (1959, 1968) viewed it as a less efficacious mode of resolution than denial.

As we have discussed, perceivers who engage in *cognitive differentiation* redefine inconsistent elements so that, in redefined form, they are consistent with other elements of an attitudinal structure (see earlier discussion and Figure 10.5, bottom panel). Abelson conceptualized this mode in terms similar to Heider's. Yet he also recognized that, like denial and bolstering, differentiation was also a deliberative cognitive process, one that entailed search and retrieval of stored information and elaboration of this information. Indeed, he assumed that differentiation was a more effortful cognitive process than either denial or bolstering, because it involved more sophisticated cognitive operations. He also believed that it was more capacity constrained insofar as it demanded greater intellectual ability and flexibility.[31]

Consideration of the microprocesses involved in the various modes of inconsistency reduction suggested to Abelson (1959, 1968) an answer to a question that other theorists had skirted: Given that perceivers can resolve inconsistencies in a variety of ways, which way or ways are preferred? Abelson's answer was based upon his assumptions about the relative *effortfulness* and *efficacy* of the different modes. More specifically, he proposed that perceivers' attempts to resolve inconsistency would generally proceed in the following order: denial, bolstering, a second denial attempt, and differentiation. The first denial attempt in this list refers to its less effortful, outright rejection form, whereas the second denial attempt refers to its more effortful, counter-arguing form (see Abelson, 1959, p. 347). Abelson presumed that the option of last resort was attitude change, the mode of resolution emphasized by most consistency theories. That is, if the above sequence of strategies failed to resolve inconsistency, perceivers would, by default, change their attitudes (see Abelson, 1968, p. 124).[32]

Rosenberg and Abelson (1960) provided suggestive evidence that perceivers do prefer low effort solutions to inconsistency in several studies in which they operationalized effort in terms of the number of relations between elements that would need to change in order to restore consistency to four-element attitude structures (i.e., the perceiver and three additional entities). Yet this research did not investigate denial, bolstering, or differentiation processes, and so did not speak to the issue of whether perceivers' resolution attempts progress in the hierarchical ordering that Abelson (1959) proposed. To our knowledge, no subsequent research has explored this issue either.

This inattention is unfortunate because Abelson's (1959, 1968) analysis represents a unique attempt to understand the resolution of inconsistency as a *cognitive process*, or sequence of processes, by which perceivers attempt to defend their attitudes when confronted with information that is inconsistent with those attitudes. Other analyses of cognitive consistency tend to foster a view of denial, bolstering, and differentiation as *alternatives* to attitude change. In contrast, Abelson's analysis regards these modes of resolution as cognitive processes and, as such, implies that they may often *mediate* attitude change. For example, successful denial (i.e., counterarguing) should reduce the likelihood of attitude change, whereas unsuccessful denial (or bolstering, differentiation) should enhance its likelihood. In fact, Abelson (1959) hypothesized that effective bolstering should have a polarizing effect on perceiver's (prior) attitudes (cf. C. G. Lord, 1989, p. 514). Research showing that thought often polarizes attitudes by promoting evaluatively consistent beliefs is consistent with this hypothesis (e.g., Chaiken & Yates, 1985; Tesser, 1978; see Chapter 12). More generally, Abelson's analysis portrays the consistency-seeking individual as being somewhat more rational and thoughtful than the image that is often conveyed in textbook presentations of consistency theory. Although inconsistency is disturbing to Abelson's perceivers, and they do attempt to preserve the attitudinal status quo, they do not twist reality beyond recognition. Instead, inconsistency-provoking information alerts perceivers that all is not well in their cognitoriums, and sets in motion active attempts to examine new information and to reexamine existing attitudes and beliefs (see also Abelson, 1983; Kelman & Baron, 1968b).

Finally, of greater significance than Abelson's (1959) proposition about how preferences for modes of resolution are ordered are his underlying assumptions about how these modes vary in terms of the effort and ability they require of perceivers. That effort and ability *are* important determinants of whether perceivers engage in cognitive processes such as denial, bolstering, and differentiation may seem obvious to contemporary investigators who are familiar with the basic tenets of dual-process models of persuasion (see Chapter 7). Indeed, the insights that these models have provided about how motivation and capacity impinge on cognitive processing and persuasion suggest that the time may be ripe for investigators to reconsider and extend the interesting ideas Abelson introduced over thirty years ago.

Dissonance Theory

In 1957 Leon Festinger published a book in which he presented his *theory of cognitive dissonance* and discussed its relevance to a variety of attitudinal phenomena. As most readers probably know, the theory was a major success. Although its many vaguenesses engendered a great deal of criticism from scholars who studied the theory and its implications, the volume, diversity, and value of the research it inspired stands even today as a remarkable testimony to the theory's—and Festinger's—contribution to social psychology.[33]

In introducing the consistency principle we noted that in its most generic form it refers to the idea that people's mental representations of their beliefs, attitudes, and attitudinally significant behaviors, decisions, and commitments tend to exist in harmony with one another, and that disharmony motivates cognitive changes designed to restore harmony. Dissonance theory more closely approximates this generic principle than the other theories we have considered. Evaluative-cognitive consistency concerns attitude-belief inconsistencies, and congruity theory and the strain-toward-symmetry model concern attitude-attitude inconsistencies. Although the generality of balance theory renders it applicable to both of these forms of inconsistency (and others), it too was developed mainly in relation to the attitude-attitude inconsistency issue. In contrast, Festinger formulated dissonance theory at a level that allowed him to apply it to virtually any form of inconsistency implied by the above list of cognitive elements. Although the primary reason that the theory captivated researchers was its relevance to inconsistencies between people's attitudes and their *behaviors* and *behavioral decisions and commitments*, its broad scope was clearly a contributing factor.

Essence of the Theory. The breadth of dissonance theory stems from its broad conceptualization of what constitutes a "cognitive element." For Festinger, anything that the perceiver cognizes or "knows" is a cognitive element. Such elements or "bits of knowledge" refer to "the things a person knows about himself, about his behavior, and about his surroundings" (Festinger, 1957, p. 9). The cognitive elements of dissonance theory are not the molecular entities found in other consistency theories (e.g., p, o, x). Indeed, they are molar and sentence-like in form—for example, "I smoke cigarettes," "I said the experimental task was fun," "I chose to buy the Toyota over the Honda," "My friend Doug opposes abortion," and "I voted for George Bush."

The relation between any two cognitive elements may be *dissonant*, *consonant*, or *irrelevant*. Two elements stand in a dissonant relation when, in the perceiver's mind, they imply the opposite of one another or, in any other way, do not seem to "fit" together. More formally, Festinger (1957, p. 13) stated that two elements, x and y, are dissonant if not-x "follows" from y. For most people, for example, the knowledge that "smoking is a health threat" would be dissonant with the knowledge that "I smoke cigarettes," because the former element would seem to imply the opposite of the latter element (i.e., "I do *not* smoke cigarettes"). The first column of Table 10.2 presents the rest of our example cognitive elements, and the second column presents examples of elements that might be considered dissonant with them. These examples illustrate that dissonance does not refer (although it can) to *logical* inconsistency (as for example, McGuire's probabilogical model does; see Chapter 3). According to Festinger (1957,

TABLE 10.2

Examples of Dissonant and Consonant Pairs of Cognitive Elements

Focal element	Dissonant element	Consonant element
1. I smoke cigarettes	Smoking is a health hazard	Smoking keeps my weight down
2. I said the experimental task was fun	I found the task dull	I got $20 for saying the task was fun
3. I chose to buy the Toyota over the Honda	Hondas get better mileage than Toyotas	Toyota has a better repair record than Honda
4. My friend Doug opposes abortion	I favor abortion	Doug is Catholic and can't go against the Church
5. I voted for George Bush	I'm a registered Democrat	Bush has increased American prestige abroad

p. 13), dissonance might exist "because of what the person has learned to come to expect, because of what is considered appropriate or usual, or for any of a number of other reasons." This reasoning, of course, also implies that what one person considers dissonant may not be considered dissonant by another. Fortunately, researchers have been relatively clever in circumventing this somewhat idiosyncratic definition of dissonance (see Chapter 11).

When either one of two cognitive elements *does follow* from the other, the relation between the two is consonant. Cognitive elements that would be consonant with our examples are shown in column three of Table 10.2. For example, knowledge that "My friend Doug opposes abortion" does seem to follow from the knowledge that "Doug is Catholic and can't go against the Church." Finally, when one cognitive element implies nothing at all about the other, the two are irrelevant. For example, the elements "I voted for George Bush" and "I chose to buy the Toyota over the Honda" would seem to have little to do with one another. Irrelevant relations play little role in the theory. It is *relevant* relations of the dissonant and consonant kind that concerned Festinger.

Consistent with congruity theory and other models that view inconsistency as a continuous variable, Festinger assumed that dissonance varies in *magnitude*. In particular, he assumed that the amount of dissonance associated with any two dissonant cognitive elements would be positively related to the *importance* of these elements to the perceiver. Although Festinger (1957, p. 16) did not give a conceptual definition of this construct, his discussion implied two meanings. First, important elements are those that are more highly "valued" by the perceiver. This sense of importance and its impact on magnitude of dissonance is similar to Newcomb's (1953) and Osgood and Tannenbaum's (1955) assumption that inconsistency increases with increases in the intensity or extremity with which attitudes are held. Thus, the magnitude of dissonance associated with the first two elements in Table 10.2's row 4 should be greater to the extent that the perceiver ("I") holds an extreme pro-choice attitude, and still greater to the extent that the perceiver values Doug's friendship immensely and views Doug as holding an extreme pro-life attitude.[34] Second, important elements are those that are more central to the perceiver's self-concept. This sense of importance and its impact on dissonance is similar to M. J. Rosenberg's (1968b) assumption that self-defining or ego-involving attitudes create greater evaluative-cognitive inconsistency. Thus, the magnitude of dissonance associated with the cognitions "I voted for George Bush" and "I'm a registered Democrat" (row 5, Table 10.2) should be greater to the extent that being a Democrat is an important self-defining attribute for the perceiver. Likewise, the first two elements shown in row 1 of Table 10.2 may cause greater dissonance for the male who views smoking as central to his self-concept (e.g., men who were influenced by the "Marlboro Man" advertisements of a previous era) than for the female who views smoking as irrelevant or even a bit at odds with her self-concept (e.g., women who smoked before the "you've come a long way" Virginia Slims advertisements tried to convince them that smoking was consistent with femininity and feminism).

To understand the second determinant of magnitude of dissonance it must be appreciated that focusing only on the relation between *two* cognitive elements oversimplifies perceivers' cognitoriums. As each row of Table 10.2 illustrates, any one

471

element (e.g., "I chose to buy the Toyota over the Honda") may be relevant to *more than one* other element. Moreover, whereas some of these other elements may be dissonant with the focal element (e.g., "Hondas get better mileage than Toyotas"), others may be consonant with it (e.g., "Toyota has a better repair record than Honda"). Indeed, the three-element rows of our table considerably underestimate the *total* number of elements that may be dissonant or consonant with some focal element in some perceiver's mind. To the focal element in row 3, for example, we could probably add several more dissonant elements (e.g., "Toyotas have limited trunk space") and several more consonant ones (e.g., "Honda doesn't allow Americans to fill its top management positions"). Intuitively, the more dissonant elements that exist in the perceiver's mind, the more dissonance he should experience.

Consistent with this intuition, Festinger posited that the second factor that determines the magnitude of dissonance is the *proportion* of relevant elements in a structure that are *dissonant* with a focal element relative to the proportion that are consonant with this element. For the person who has chosen to buy the Toyota rather than the Honda, then, dissonance should be an increasing function of the proportion of other cognitions that are dissonant (vs. consonant) with this decision. Combining the two factors that determine magnitude of dissonance, Festinger offered the general conclusion that the amount of dissonance characterizing any *n*-element set of cognitive elements should be a positive function of the proportion of elements that are dissonant with one another relative to the total number of consonant and dissonant elements, with each element in the set weighted for its importance to the perceiver.[35]

Like the other theories we have reviewed, at the heart of Festinger's theory is the assumption that the presence of dissonance gives rise to pressures to eliminate or at least reduce it. Moreover, the strength of this pressure increases as the magnitude of dissonance increases. For Festinger, the motivational force of dissonance was more dramatic than the Gestalt pressures toward good form emphasized in balance theory and congruity theory. He considered dissonance to be a drive state analogous to hunger. Just as hunger is aversive and leads to activity designed to reduce it, so too is dissonance aversive and so too does dissonance lead to activity designed to reduce it (Festinger, 1957, p. 3). The theory thus features the drive-reduction notion that dissonance constitutes a state of negative arousal whose reduction is intrinsically gratifying or reinforcing (see earlier section on the Yale perspective and its drive-reduction view of fear arousal).[36]

How then is dissonance eliminated or reduced? Eliminating dissonance requires the perceiver to *change* one or more cognitive elements. The person who favors abortion and whose friend opposes abortion might change her attitude (or convince her friend to change his; Festinger, 1957, p. 182). The person who smokes cigarettes and "knows" that smoking is a health threat might stop smoking (i.e., behavior change) or, alternatively, might decide that smoking is *not* a health threat. And the registered Democrat who has voted for George Bush might change her party affiliation.

An important caveat of dissonance theory is that cognitive elements are responsive to "reality" and thus sometimes difficult to change. Thus, it is unlikely that our registered Democrat could eliminate dissonance by denying that she voted for Bush, and the publicity surrounding smoking makes it unlikely that today's smoker could decide that smoking isn't a health threat. Indeed, in experimental tests of the theory researchers enhance their abilities to predict which of two dissonant cognitive elements will undergo change by subjecting one to reality constraints. For example, inducing subjects to tell a confederate that the task they found boring was actually quite fun effectively rules out the possibility of changing the behavioral element, while increasing the probability that the attitudinal element will change (Festinger & Carlsmith, 1959; see Chapter 11).

Because of reality constraints, it may often be the case that perceivers cannot eliminate dissonance by changing cognitive elements. Luckily, Festinger granted them another option, *adding consonant elements*. Consistent with Abelson's (1959) discussion of bolstering, adding consonant elements does not eliminate dissonance but can go a long way toward *reducing* its magnitude. For example, the smoker who cannot deny the health risks of smoking and who cannot (or won't) quit smoking can reduce dissonance by adding consonant elements such as "Smoking keeps my weight down," "I only smoke one pack a day," and "More people die from car accidents than lung cancer." As this example and the others shown in Table 10.2 illustrate, dissonance is reduced by adding consonant elements because their addition functions to reduce the proportion of dissonant relations among the perceiver's (accessible) cognitions. Yet close inspection of the three consonant cognitions adduced by our hypothetical smoker reveals that certain of them reduce dissonance in another way as well. Specifically, the added elements "I only smoke one pack a day" and "More people die from car accidents than lung cancer" could conceivably *reduce the importance* of the dissonant cognition "Smoking is a health threat." Similarly, the consonant element shown in row 3 of Table 10.2 could conceivably reduce our car buyer's dissonance not only by lowering the dissonance ratio from 1.0 to 0.5, but also by reducing the importance of the dissonant element. Because adding consonant elements often (though not always) functions to reduce the importance of elements, dissonance theory has sometimes been interpreted as positing *three* modes of dissonance resolution: changing elements, adding consonant elements, and reducing the importance of dissonant elements (e.g., Fishbein & Ajzen, 1975; Petty & Cacioppo, 1981a). Yet as we have seen, the last of these modes is ordinarily a consequence of the second.

In summary, Festinger (1957) proposed that dissonance, a negative affective state, motivates perceivers to reduce dissonance by changing cognitive elements or by adding consonant elements. To this main hypothesis he added one other. Given that dissonance is present, perceivers do not seek only to *reduce* it. They also attempt to *avoid* information that might result in further increments in its magnitude.

Involuntary Exposure to Attitude-Discrepant Information. Exposure to beliefs and attitudes different from one's own is an inescapable feature of everyday life. Friends, acquaintances, and coworkers sometimes express opinions that do not cohere with our own, and we may sometimes be forced or cajoled into listening to or reading persuasive messages that advocate disagreeable positions. Festinger (1957) maintained that such "involuntary" exposure to attitude-discrepant information was a frequent source of dissonance arousal. Thus, like other consistency theorists, he assumed that interpersonal disagreement and exposure to counterattitudinal messages would instigate cognitive activity designed to restore consonance to perceivers' cognitoriums. The main modes of dissonance reduction he discussed in this context represent instances of changing elements or adding consonant elements and, for the most part, parallel those posited by other consistency theorists: changing one's attitude toward the issue or toward the communication source, blanket rejection of communications' positions and counterarguing of their content (i.e., denial), and generating cognitions that support one's own attitude, disparage the communicator's trustworthiness or expertise, or in other ways dilute the magnitude of dissonance (i.e., bolstering). Like Newcomb (1953; see note 23) Festinger assumed that in the case of interpersonal disagreement dissonance might also be reduced by convincing others to change their attitudes. In the case of exposure to counterattitudinal persuasive messages, Festinger proposed a number of additional defensive processes: biased perception or miscomprehension of information, inattention to information, and forgetting of information. These processes, which are not easily categorized under the rubric of adding or changing cognitive elements, were characterized by Festinger (1957, p. 137) as functioning to "prevent the new cognition from ever becoming firmly established."

The prime weakness in Festinger's (1957) analysis of interpersonal disagreement and message-based persuasion is one that most consistency theories share—little direction regarding when one or another mode of dissonance reduction should occur. When applied to persuasion, a second, also nonunique, weakness is that the theory provides a mechanism of attitude change (dissonance reduction) but few insights about how distal communicator, recipient, message, and contextual variables influence this mechanism. As we noted in Chapter 6, the dominance of process theories in the persuasion area is largely due to the emphasis they give to distal persuasion cues. Dissonance theory has inspired some persuasion research, most notably a handful of experiments on message discrepancy (e.g., Aronson, Turner, & Carlsmith, 1963; see Chapter 8), involvement (e.g., Zimbardo, 1960), and communicator characteristics (e.g., R. A. Jones & Brehm, 1967). Like other consistency theories, however, it never flourished as a theory of message-based persuasion (see also J. Cooper & Fazio, 1989). The theory has been more influential in a related area of research, understanding the mechanisms that underlie *resistance* to attitude change. In particular, the defensive processes outlined by Festinger (1957) have been implicated as mechanisms by which attitudes exert selective effects at virtually all stages of information processing (see Chapter 12).

Had Festinger (1957) restricted his attention to involuntary exposure settings, it is doubtful that dissonance theory would have attracted the great attention it did. Festinger's provocative and novel dissonance analyses of several other important attitudinal phenomena were the primary reasons for the theory's impact.

Effects of Counterattitudinal Advocacy. As noted earlier in this chapter, the persuasive impact of counterattitudinal role-playing was studied by the Yale researchers (Hovland et al., 1953). In their view, the efficacy of role-playing procedures stemmed from the positive incentives they provided role-players for selectively thinking about arguments supportive of their counterattitudinal advocacies (i.e., biased scanning; Janis, 1959). Festinger (1957) proposed a very different interpretation. He regarded role-players as confronted with two dissonant cognitive elements—knowledge of their private attitudes (e.g., "I favor gun control") and knowledge of their publicly expressed attitudes (e.g., "I argued against gun control"). The dissonance presumably aroused by this attitude-behavior discrepancy was, for Festinger, the cause of the attitude change that Janis and others had observed in their role-playing experiments (e.g., Janis & King, 1954; Kelman, 1953): Changing their private attitudes to conform to their overt (and therefore difficult to recant) behaviors allowed role-players to reduce cognitive dissonance.

This novel interpretation gained force with the publication of Festinger and Carlsmith's (1959) demonstration of an *inverse* relation between incentive magnitude and attitude change. Subjects in this study were induced to advocate a counterattitudinal position for either $1 or $20. This attitude-discrepant behavior was assumed to arouse dissonance for all subjects. However, the researchers reasoned that $20 subjects would not need to change their attitudes because they could reduce dissonance by adducing the consonant cognition that their high payment was *sufficient justification* for their counterattitudinal behavior. Because this option was not viable for subjects who had been paid only $1, they were expected to reduce dissonance by shifting their attitudes in the direction of their advocacies. The results of the study confirmed these expectations.

Although incentive-oriented researchers criticized this experiment and garnered additional evidence supporting their viewpoint (e.g., Elms & Janis, 1965), dissonance theory nevertheless emerged from this initial controversy as the more widely accepted interpretation of counterattitudinal advocacy effects. Indeed, the theory and the *induced-compliance* paradigm that Festinger and Carlsmith created provided a framework that generated an extensive amount of subsequent research on the attitudinal effects of engaging in counterattitudinal behavior *and* additional theoretical controversies regarding interpretation of these effects. This interesting and important literature is reviewed in detail in Chapter 11. Here it suffices to note that this research played a crucial role in clarifying and reshaping investigators' understanding of dissonance theory. Most notably the theory was gradually modified to take account of findings showing that a number of conditions had to be in place in order to verify Festinger's (1957) prediction of an inverse relation between justification for attitude-discrepant behavior and attitude change. Specifically, this dissonance effect occurs when subjects *freely choose* to engage in counterattitudinal behavior, they feel *committed* to this behavior, the behavior leads to *unwanted consequences*, and subjects feel *personally responsible* for those consequences. Although modern dissonance theory (J. Cooper & Fazio, 1984) continues to provide a plausible account of attitude change in the induced-compliance paradigm, as we explain in Chapter 11, it represents a considerably different theory of attitude change than the theory Festinger (1957) presented. Indeed, according to the newer formulation, it is not inconsistency between attitude and behavior that causes dissonance and attitude change in induced-compliance settings, but rather taking responsibility for bringing about an undesirable consequence

(J. Cooper & Fazio, 1984). Still other investigators assume that dissonance and attitude change in these settings are due to engaging in behavior that is inconsistent with the self-concept (e.g., Aronson, 1969; Schlenker, 1982).

Cognitive and Attitudinal Consequences of Decision Making. The psychology of decision making was a major theme of Festinger's (1957) first book on dissonance theory and the exclusive focus of a subsequent volume (Festinger, 1964b). Festinger characterized the pre-decisional process as an open-minded, conscientious search for and scrutiny of information that facilitates people's (presumed) desires to make good (i.e., correct) decisions. For example, in deciding which of several cars to buy or which of several job offers to accept, the decision maker seeks out and thinks about the pros and cons of each available option and, in line with expectancy-value principles (see Chapters 3 and 5) chooses the one option that she evaluates most highly (Festinger, 1964b). Yet once the decision is made, Festinger argued, such impartial or unbiased systematic processing (see Chapter 7) gives way to pressures to defend or justify the decision. The source of this pressure is dissonance. Specifically, Festinger postulated that making a decision often creates dissonance because it will frequently be the case that there exist some features or consequences of the chosen alternative and also some features of choices foregone that are incompatible with the person's decision. For example, although you may have purchased the Toyota rather than the Honda because your balance sheet of pros and cons pointed rationally to that decision, your decision does not "follow from" the several negative aspects of Toyotas and several positive aspects of Hondas that you no doubt encountered during your deliberations.

Dissonance is a matter of degree, of course, and so not all decisions create appreciable amounts of dissonance. Festinger (1957, 1964b) assumed that post-decisional dissonance would be strong enough to motivate cognitive resolutions when important decisions are made, when the decision alternatives are distinctive but close in overall value or attractiveness, and when the person cannot change or revoke the decision (i.e., commitment is high; see Brehm & Cohen, 1962, and Chapter 11). Under these circumstances Festinger (1957, 1964b) argued that the decision makers reduce dissonance through post-decision processing tendencies that selectively favor decision-congruent information. In the immediate aftermath of a decision, selectivity biases were assumed to occur primarily with respect to the decision maker's existing information base (vs. new information; see below). Moreover, bias exists both with respect to what decision-relevant cognitive elements are *retrieved* from memory and how this information is *elaborated*. More specifically, the person may retrieve mostly decision-congruent information and will tend to elaborate this information in a way that bolsters the decision. Moreover, if decision-incongruent information is retrieved, it will be reexamined with a hypercritical eye. Thus, the Toyota purchaser may focus most of his attention on positive facts about Toyotas and negative facts about Hondas and in ruminating about this information may generate additional decision-congruent cognitive elements (e.g., "With the economy floundering, it's more important than ever to buy a car with a good repair record"). And if he does consider a dissonant element such as "Hondas get better mileage," he will be prone to minimize its importance (e.g., "The mileage differential is pretty small, and I don't go on many long trips anyway").

To the extent that such post-decisional selectivity biases operate, Festinger (1957, 1964b) argued, the decision maker's evaluations of his chosen and unchosen alternatives will be more divergent at some point after the decision than at the point the decision was made (or just prior to it). As noted above, Festinger assumed that people initially *do* choose the alternative they evaluate most highly: You decided to buy the Toyota over the Honda because your scrutiny of both cars' attributes led you to form a more favorable attitude toward Toyotas. However, assuming (as the theory does in this application) that you regarded both cars as reasonably attractive choices to begin with, the Toyota's initial attitudinal advantage might be relatively small. Yet because the cognitions you retrieved and elaborated during the post-decisional recapitulation phase favor the Toyota and disfavor the Honda to a much greater extent than the mix of cognitions that guided the original decision, the Toyota's post-decisional attitudinal advantage should be appreciably enhanced. This attitudinal effect has been called the *spreading apart of choice alternatives.*

This prediction was first tested in an experiment by Jack Brehm (1956), and most subsequent experiments have used procedures similar to his. In the typical "free-choice" study, subjects first evaluate a number of alternatives like magazines, job candidates, or political candidates. Next they are asked to choose which of two similarly rated alternatives they most prefer—for example, which magazine they would like as a gift, job candidate they would hire, or political candidate they would vote for. After making their decisions, subjects are asked to reevaluate both the chosen and unchosen alternative. The extent to which the value of the chosen alternative relative to the unchosen one increases from before to after the decision gauges the spreading apart of choice alternatives. Brehm's (1956) results showed both an increase in subjects' attitudes toward the chosen alternative and a decrease in their attitudes toward the unchosen alternative.

Although subsequent studies have not consistently yielded this symmetrical pattern of pre- and post-decision attitude means (e.g., J. Converse & Cooper, 1979), the more general hypothesis that the evaluative advantage of the chosen alternative is larger after subjects' decisions than before has generally been confirmed, both in laboratory investigations (e.g., Brehm & Cohen, 1959; Cottrell, Rajecki, & Smith, 1974; M. H. Davis, 1979; Gerard & White, 1983; see also Festinger, 1964b) and field settings (e.g., Knox & Inkster, 1968; Lawler, Kuleck, Rhode, & Sorensen, 1975; Younger, Walker & Arrowood, 1977). Moreover, with one exception, decision-congruent attitude change does tend to occur primarily under the high dissonance conditions specified by Festinger (1957, 1964b). Consistent with induced compliance research, subjects must feel that they have made their decisions freely and must feel relatively committed to their decisions. The exception concerns decision importance. Studies that have manipulated this variable have shown that increased decision importance does not necessarily increase decision-congruent attitude change (although it can; Deutsch, Krauss, & Rosenau, 1962). Indeed, importance sometimes reduces such change (J. Converse & Cooper, 1979; H. J. Greenwald, 1969). The reasons for the latter findings are unclear, although it is conceivable that importance increases the vigilance of pre-decisional processing and thus reduces the likelihood of post-decisional dissonance (see Cialdini, Petty, & Cacioppo, 1981; J. Converse & Cooper, 1979).

477

A significant limitation of this decision-making literature is that the selective retrieval and elaboration processes presumed to mediate decision-congruent attitude change have rarely been addressed (for an exception, see Beckmann & Gollwitzer, 1987). This limitation was recognized by Festinger (1964b, pp. 61–62), who at the time he wrote lamented the absence of valid and reliable methods for tracking the subtleties of ongoing cognitive processes. Inattention to cognitive processes is, in fact, understandable in relation to the late 1950s and 1960s research on post-decisional attitude change, although even this research could have benefited by adopting the memory and thought-listing measures that were being developed by persuasion researchers during this period (see Chapter 6 and earlier discussion in this chapter of the Yale research program). Unfortunately, as social psychologists' interest and success in documenting cognitive processes flowered during the 1970s and 1980s, the study of post-decisional attitude change remained inattentive to cognitive processes and, moreover, ceased to be the lively area it was during dissonance theory's first decade. With the methods and measures available to contemporary investigators, a renewed examination of Festinger's (1957, 1964b) still interesting hypotheses about the nature of pre-decisional and post-decisional information processing and their attitudinal consequences seems to us to be a fertile pursuit. In addition to Beckmann and Gollwitzer's (1987) work, which used recall measures to assess the partiality of cognitive processing, interested investigators might also consult the literature on thought-induced attitude polarization (see Chapter 12). Consistent with aspects of Festinger's analysis, this research has shown that attitudes become more extreme when people are given some opportunity to think about their attitudes (Tesser, 1978), that the tendency to generate attitude-congruent cognitions during thought mediates this polarization effect (Chaiken & Yates, 1985), and that this effect is exacerbated when people feel committed to their initial attitudes (Millar & Tesser, 1986b; see also Liberman & Chaiken, 1991).

Selective Exposure. An important aspect of Festinger's (1957) analysis of decision making concerned selective exposure to *new* information. That is, in addition to positing that decision makers engage in the selective retrieval and elaboration processes outlined above, Festinger hypothesized that post-decisional dissonance would also lead them to selectively *seek out* decision-congruent information and *avoid* exposure to decision-incongruent information. Although Festinger's (1957, 1964b) discussions of the *selective exposure* hypothesis emphasized decision-making contexts, he did not restrict the hypothesis to such settings. The more general form of the selective exposure hypothesis follows readily from the theory's assumption that dissonance arousal motivates both attempts to reduce dissonance and attempts to avoid further increases in its magnitude (see above): When dissonance is present, people will exhibit both a tendency to seek out consonant information and a tendency to avoid dissonant information.

Consistent with the narrower version of the selective exposure hypothesis, some research has examined subjects' propensities to approach or avoid information pertinent to a recent decision (e.g., Sears, 1965). Consistent with the broader version, other research has examined information approach and avoidance tendencies after subjects have been exposed to other types of dissonance inductions (e.g., exposure to counterattitudinal messages, J. S. Adams, 1961; inducing attitude-discrepant behavior, D. Frey &

Wicklund, 1978). However, other researchers have examined information seeking and avoidance simply as a function of subjects' initial attitudes, without attempting to induce dissonance (e.g., Sweeney & Gruber, 1984). The hypothesis of such studies, that people approach attitude-congruent information and avoid incongruent information, is meaningfully labeled "selective exposure" (e.g., Klapper, 1960). Yet this version of the hypothesis does not technically obey Festinger's (1957) logic, which specified that dissonance had to be present for selective exposure to occur. Despite this logical blemish, studies of this sort have traditionally been viewed as reasonable tests of dissonance theory (e.g., Freedman & Sears, 1965a; D. Frey, 1986). We review the very interesting history of research on selective exposure, including Festinger's (1964b) revised analysis, in Chapter 12.

Functional Approach to Attitudes and Their Change

A fundamental question about attitudes concerns their purpose, that is, what psychological functions do attitudes serve? Rather than viewing attitudes as motivationally vacuous, most investigators have assumed that attitudes serve and therefore reflect important personal and social needs and goals. Assumptions about attitude function can be discerned in most attitude theories. For example, implicit in most cognitive persuasion theories (and explicit in some) is the assumption that people are motivated to attain valid attitudes that correspond to external reality (see Chapters 5, 6, 7, 8). Hovland, Janis, and Kelley's (1953) discussion of incentives implicated this motivational basis of attitude change and several others, including the desire to gain approval from respected persons and reference groups (see earlier discussion in this chapter). Indeed, the idea that attitudes serve both *informational* and *normative* needs has been an enduring theme of social influence research, a literature we consider in detail in Chapter 13. Although allusions to the functions that attitudes serve are not uncommon in attitude theory, they are usually just that. Most theories offer accounts of *how* attitudes are structured, formed, or changed, not *why* they are held or *what* psychological purposes they serve. Fortunately, there have been some attempts to explicate the core psychological functions of attitudes. Indeed, interest in this topic has increased dramatically in recent years, after a long period of inactivity. At the heart of functional perspectives is the idea that people hold and express attitudes for different reasons and that knowledge of the motivational basis for an attitude is key to understanding how it can be changed.

Classic Conceptions of Attitude Functions

Functional theories of attitude entered the literature during the 1950s when two independent groups of investigators developed the idea that attitudes serve various psychological needs and thus have variable motivational bases.[37] Common and central to both groups' efforts was a listing of specific personality functions that attitudes serve for the individual. M. Brewster Smith and his colleagues derived their three-function taxonomy inductively, through detailed clinical interviews that probed the personality styles and attitudes (toward Russia) of 10 adult males (Smith et al., 1956; Smith, 1947). In a more deductive manner, Daniel Katz and his collaborators derived their four-function taxonomy by drawing upon their own research on ego-defense as a source of prejudice (e.g., Sarnoff & Katz, 1954) and, more generally, by scrutinizing existing psychological theory for insights about essential motivational processes (Katz, 1960; Katz & Stotland, 1959). For the most part, the two groups proposed similar core functions and advanced the same key hypothesis, that successful persuasion entails implementing change procedures that match the functional basis of the attitude one is trying to change. Our coverage emphasizes the Katz (1960) formulation, as it was the more detailed of the two.

In Chapter 1, we introduced Katz's (1960) proposal that any given attitude held by any given individual serves one or more of four distinct personality functions: a utilitarian function, a knowledge function, an ego-defensive function, and a value-expressive function. The *utilitarian* function, which Katz also called the "instrumental" or "adjustive function," acknowledges the behaviorist principle that people are motivated to gain rewards and avoid punishments from their environment. Utilitarian attitudes are instrumental in securing positive outcomes or preventing negative ones. A parent's opposition to school busing would be an example if this attitude reflected the parent's belief that busing would yield negative outcomes for her child. More generally, attitudes based on self-interest exemplify utilitarian attitudes (e.g., Green & Gerken, 1989). Katz's discussion also implied that utilitarian attitudes might reflect conditioned affective associations to stimuli. For example, you might acquire a positive feeling toward the month of June merely because it coincides with the end of the interminably long school year.

Consistent with Gestalt principles and consistency theories, the *knowledge* function presumes a basic need to attain a meaningful, stable, and organized view of the world. Attitudes serve this function because they supply a standard or "frame of reference" for organizing and simplifying people's perceptions of an often complex or ambiguous informational environment (Katz, 1960, p. 175). Katz's description of the knowledge function thus corresponds to the schematic conception of attitudes we discussed in Chapter 1. This conception is an old one in attitudinal theorizing (see Allport, 1935, p. 806) and has been particularly influential in research exploring how attitudes bias information processing (see Chapter 12).

Smith and associates (1956) proposed a function that has traditionally been interpreted as a combination of Katz's knowledge and utilitarian functions (e.g., Herek, 1986; Kiesler, Collins, & Miller, 1969; Tesser & Shaffer, 1990). Attitudes serving this *object-appraisal* function provide guidelines for "sizing up" objects and events in terms of a person's "major interests and going concerns." Such attitudes spare the person from the "sometimes painful" process of "figuring out *de novo*" how to relate to objects and events in their environment (Smith et al., 1956, p. 41).

Katz's *ego-defensive* function and the very similar *externalization* function proposed by the Smith group emphasize the psychoanalytic principle that people use defense mechanisms such as denial, repression, and projection to protect their self-concepts against internal and external threats. Attitudes serving the ego-defensive function enable people to cope with emotional conflicts and, more generally, defend their self-images. Katz and his collaborators elaborated this function primarily in relation to prejudice, suggesting that people may unconsciously project their own feelings of inferiority onto convenient racial, religious, and ethnic minority groups. By doing so, the prejudiced person bolsters his own ego by feeling superior to members of the out-group (Katz, 1960; Sarnoff, 1960; Sarnoff & Katz, 1954). Such attitudes are thus not grounded in realistic perceptions of the attitude object, and the individual is assumed to be largely unaware of their ego-defensive function. This conception largely parallels earlier psychoanalytic accounts of prejudice (e.g., Adorno, Frenkel-Brunswik, Levinson, & Sanford, 1950; see Chapter 12), and is also consistent with analyses that have stressed the personality roots of political intolerance and other political attitudes (e.g., Lane, 1962; Sniderman, 1975; Sullivan, Marcus, Feldman, & Piereson, 1981). While emphasizing prejudice, Katz (1960) did not restrict ego-defensive attitudes to this domain. For example, in line with the Yale research on fear appeals, he suggested that attitudes implying apathy or indifference toward threatening health and political issues (e.g., AIDS, nuclear warfare) might reflect avoidance and denial mechanisms.

Katz's *value-expressive* function acknowledges the importance of psychological perspectives that emphasize needs for self-expression and self-actualization (see McGuire, 1983). According to this fourth function, attitudes are a means for expressing personal values and other core aspects of the self-concept. Expressing such attitudes is inherently gratifying because it satisfies people's needs to clarify and affirm their self-concepts. A person who draws self-esteem from being a liberal and an environmentalist, or who wishes to attain these identities, should be motivated to hold attitudinal positions that appropriately reflect these prized ideologies and their component values.

Attitudes expressing the values of the person's important reference groups were also considered by Katz to be value-expressive in nature. However, he did not explicitly consider how attitudes mediate a person's relations with others. Smith and associates' (1956) *social adjustment* function fills this void. Attitudes serving this function facilitate, maintain, and at times, disrupt social relationships (see also M. B. Smith, 1973). In other words, expressing attitudes that are agreeable to others or that square with group norms and values can facilitate entry into desired relationships and help maintain them, whereas expressing unacceptable attitudes threatens such relationships (or facilitates one's desire to exit the relationship).[38] This description emphasizes the strategic nature of attitude expression and, as such, resembles Kelman's (1958) *compliance* mode of influence, wherein people express—but do not internalize—attitudes in order to gain tangible rewards or avoid tangible punishments from communication sources. Yet Smith and colleagues' discussion also implied that adopting the attitudes of reference groups can affirm that aspect of self-identity that stems from one's group memberships. This group identification interpretation therefore resembles aspects of Katz's value-expressive function. In addition, it resembles Kelman's (1958) *identification* mode of influence, wherein people genuinely adopt the attitudes of admired communication sources.[39]

As noted at the outset of this section, the key thesis of functional theories is that changing an attitude requires understanding its motivational basis. More specifically, knowing what function an attitude serves dictates the form persuasion attempts should take (Katz, 1960). For example, if we know that Archie Bunker opposes school busing because he feels it will harm his child (utilitarian function), our persuasive overtures must address and negate this concern and also stress the positive outcomes that busing might achieve. If, however, we suspect that Archie's busing attitude is a manifestation of racial prejudice and that the latter has an ego-defensive basis, our persuasion overtures must take on more subtle, therapeutic forms, perhaps one in which we provide Archie with nonthreatening information about the maladaptive aspects of prejudice and insight into his likely defense mechanisms (Katz, 1960; Katz, McClintock, & Sarnoff, 1957).

Identifying the core functions of attitudes, as the Katz and Smith groups tried to do, is obviously step one in testing this key functional thesis. However, a crucial second step entails *assessing* what functions particular attitudes serve for particular persons (in particular situations; see below). This step proved to be the major stumbling block in testing the functional perspective. Katz (1960) and Smith et al. (1956) proposed idealized types of functions that are unlikely to appear in a pure form in reality; in most cases attitudes probably serve several functions. Although Katz (1960), in particular, discussed the measurement issue, he provided few guidelines for researchers. Moreover, the initial 1950s attempts to test the functional approach concerned ego-defensive attitudes, arguably one of the more difficult functions to assess. This research, which we review in Chapter 12, relied on broad personality measures such as the F scale and the MMPI to infer the ego-defensive basis of racial attitudes. Although aspects of Katz's (1960) formulation implied that there should be variation in attitude functions across persons, attitude domains, and situations, the personality strategy of this work fostered a narrower, trait-based conception of the functional approach. Neither trait approaches nor the psychodynamic flavor of the initial work on functions held much interest for 1960s and 1970s social psychologists. These factors, and the lack of clear methods for operationalizing attitude functions, resulted in little empirical or theoretical develop- ment during these decades (see Eagly & Himmelfarb, 1974, 1978; Herek, 1986).

Contemporary Conceptions and Research

Attesting to social psychologists' return to motivational themes, there has been a recent resurgence of interest in the functional approach to attitudes. We first consider modern conceptions of attitude functions.

Conceptions. Although contemporary investigators have not added any new functions to those originally described by Katz (1960) and Smith and colleagues (1956; Smith, 1973), they have proposed a number of clarifying elaborations and integrations. One such clarification concerns the overlapping nature of attitude functions. It has long been assumed that any given attitude may serve multiple functions for the individual. In addition, however, current consensus favors the idea that one function in particular is primary. Specifically, newer discussions have stressed that most attitudes serve the *schematic* function Katz termed "knowledge" and Smith termed "object appraisal" (e.g., Fazio, 1989; A. G. Greenwald, 1989; Jamieson & Zanna, 1989; Shavitt, 1990). Thus, regardless of what other functions attitudes serve, they are also presumed to provide a frame of reference for comprehending and categorizing objects, persons, and events in one's environment. The main caveat to the assumption that all or most attitudes possess "schema power" derives from Fazio's (e.g., 1986, 1989) research on attitude accessibility. This research suggests that the schematic function may be restricted to strong, well established attitudes, those that in Fazio's view correspond to the strong object-evaluation associations in memory but which may also correspond to other structural properties (see Chapters 3, 4, and 12).

Contemporary analyses have also helped clarify the utilitarian function of attitudes. Since attitudes serving a schematic function facilitate people's transactions with environmental stimuli, they are *instrumental* in this sense. More generally, earlier reviews of functional theories suggested that the utilitarian function provided an interpretation of all other functions insofar as holding attitudes for the reasons these other functions imply (e.g., affirming core values, defending self-image) yields rewarding outcomes for the individual (e.g., Himmelfarb & Eagly, 1974; Kiesler, Collins, & Miller, 1969). Perhaps for this reason, some contemporary lists of functions omit the seemingly ubiquitous utilitarian function (e.g., A. G. Greenwald, 1989; M. Snyder & DeBono, 1989). Yet this function has been retained in other recent taxonomies, in a form that clarifies its singular qualities (e.g., Abelson & Prentice, 1989; Herek, 1986; Shavitt, 1989, 1990).

Herek's (1986) analysis is informative. Its starting point is the recognition that, according to the functional perspective, all attitudes are instrumental insofar as they provide psychological benefits to their possessors. Herek divides attitude functions into two categories, each emphasizing a different *source* of psychological benefit: the *attitude object* itself or the *expression* of the attitude. In this scheme, the utilitarian function emerges as the *evaluative* function of attitudes. For attitudes in this category, the primary source of benefit is the rewards and punishments that are associated with the attitude object: "Positive attitudes toward an object tend to result when it is perceived as a source of benefit, reward, or pleasure; negative attitudes result from past or anticipated detrimental, unpleasant, or punishing experiences with it" (Herek, 1986, p. 105). This conceptualization, which is consistent with the tenor of Katz's (1960) discussion, helps delimit the utilitarian (or evaluative) function. Consider a cigarette smoker's negative attitude toward banning smoking in public areas. It is conceivable that the smoker opposes such restrictions because he sees them as an infringement of individual rights, and expressing his opposition is rewarding because it enables him to affirm an important personal value. Although this attitude serves a value-expressive function, it would not also be considered a utilitarian attitude since the attitude object itself (banning smoking in public areas) is not the prime source of psychological benefit. If, however, the smoker opposes smoking restrictions because he believes that restrictions will cause him personal discomfort, the attitude would be appropriately labeled utilitarian.[40]

The first, value-expressive attitude in this example would be placed in Herek's (1986) second category of attitude functions, wherein the primary source of psychological benefit lies not in the attitude object but in the expression of the attitude. The other "sub-functions" in this symbolic or *expressive* category are social adjustment and ego-defense. According to Herek, the psychological benefits of the three expressive functions are affirming core values and aligning oneself with important reference groups (value-expressive function), obtaining social acceptance from others in one's immediate social environment (social adjustment or "social-expressive" function), and reducing anxiety caused by intrapsychic conflicts (ego-defensive function).

The distinction between utilitarian/instrumental versus symbolic/expressive attitudes has also been made by Abelson and Prentice (1989; Prentice, 1987b), and both these authors and Herek (1986) point out its relevance to "symbolic politics" research. Much of this research has tried to determine whether people's attitudes toward political and social policies such as affirmative action and school busing are better predicted by self-interest or by *symbolic beliefs*, where the latter construct refers, among other things, to the influence of internalized societal values such as fairness and equality (e.g., Kinder & Sears, 1981; Sears, Lau, Tyler, & Allen, 1980). Although the bulk of this now sizable literature suggests that self-interest exerts little apparent influence on political attitudes while symbolic beliefs exert a strong impact, findings supporting the importance of self-interest have also obtained (e.g., D. P. Green & Gerken, 1989; Sears & Lau, 1983; Sears et al., 1980; Young, Borgida, Sullivan, & Aldrich, 1987; for reviews see Kinder & Sears, 1985; Sears & Funk, 1991). In functional terms, the self-interest versus symbolic belief debate is about determining the motivational bases of people's political attitudes. Whereas it is fairly clear that self-interest-based attitudes serve a utilitarian function, the functional status of symbolic beliefs is murkier because of the vagueness with which this construct has been defined (see Chapter 3). Such beliefs can presumably be regarded as serving a value-expressive function. Whether they also serve other expressive functions, as some discussions have implied (e.g., Abelson, 1982; Herek, 1986), deserves scrutiny in subsequent research.

The value-expressive, social adjustment, and ego-defensive functions have also been the focus of elaboration. Shavitt (1989, 1990), for example, suggests viewing the value-expressive and social adjustment functions as two *social identity* sub-functions insofar as value-expression emphasizes private identity concerns and social adjustment (in its strategic sense) emphasizes public identity concerns. In addition, she proposes a *self-esteem maintenance* function. Attitudes serving this function include classic ego-defensive attitudes, but also attitudes that protect and bolster self-esteem in other ways—for example, by distancing the self from disliked or threatening objects and by associating the self with liked, positively regarded objects. We welcome this more expansive view of the ego-defensive function (a view implied but not elaborated upon by D. Katz, 1960). Yet, as Anthony Greenwald (1989) has noted, the value-expressive and social adjustment functions can also be interpreted in terms of self-esteem maintenance.

A unique feature of Greenwald's (1989) analysis is its distinction between the *strategic* and *group identification* interpretations of the social adjustment function we noted earlier. Although political scientists have discussed group identification as a basis of political attitudes (see Kinder & Sears, 1985), most social psychologists have either not distinguished the two conflated aspects of the social adjustment function (e.g., Shavitt, 1990; M. Snyder & DeBono, 1989) or have emphasized its strategic form (e.g., Herek, 1986; B. T. Johnson & Eagly, 1989). Greenwald relates both interpretations and the value-expressive function to three aspects of the self-concept and three associated strategies of self-esteem maintenance (see Greenwald & Breckler, 1985). Specifically, he associates the value-expressive function with the *private* self, which achieves self-worth by striving to meet internalized standards; the strategic form of the social adjustment function with the *public* self, which tries to achieve self-worth by securing positive evaluations from significant others; and the group identification form of the social adjustment function with the *collective* self, which tries to achieve self-worth by striving to meet the goals of important reference groups. Greenwald (1989) also points out the resemblance between his scheme and Kelman's (1958) ideas about *compliance*, *identification*, and *internalization*. As noted earlier, the strategic form of the social adjustment function resembles compliance-based attitudes, and the group identification form resembles identification-based attitudes. As Greenwald further points out, the value-expressive function resembles Kelman's internalization mode of influence, wherein people genuinely adopt the attitudes advocated by communication sources because these attitudes are perceived to be congruent with the individual's own values (see note 39 and Chapter 13).

The linkages Greenwald (1989) draws between the different facets of the self and different attitude functions also resemble the linkages that he and others have drawn between aspects of the self-concept and different types of involvement (Greenwald, 1982; B. T. Johnson & Eagly, 1989; M. Sherif & Cantril, 1947). As such, these analyses call attention to the relation between theorizing about involvement and theorizing about attitude functions, both of which aim to elucidate the motivational bases of attitude formation, expression, and change. Indeed, Johnson and Eagly (1989) point out that the motivational concerns reflected in their constructs of outcome-relevant involvement, value-relevant involvement, and impression-relevant involvement parallel the motivational concerns highlighted by the utilitarian function, the value-expressive function, and the social adjustment function (strategic form), respectively (see discussions of involvement in Chapters 6, 7, and 8).

Research. As we have noted, although Katz's (1960) analysis implied that there should be variation in attitude functions across persons, attitude domains, and situations, initial empirical work nonetheless emphasized individual differences. While modern researchers have continued this tradition (e.g., M. Snyder & DeBono, 1989), they have also paid attention to the idea that different attitude objects may engage different functions and that different functions may be aroused in different settings (e.g., Abelson & Prentice, 1989; Herek, 1986; Shavitt, 1989, 1990).

The assumption of Katz and his colleagues that personality measures can serve as indirect indicators of attitude functions remains strong among contemporary investigators. But although a number of personality variables have been proposed for this role (e.g., Herek, 1986; M. Snyder & DeBono, 1987), only Mark Snyder's (1974) self-monitoring construct has been explored systematically. Indeed, an impressive number of findings are consistent with Snyder and DeBono's (1985) claim that the attitudes of high self-monitoring individuals are more likely to serve a social adjustive than value-expressive function, while the attitudes of low self-monitors are more likely to serve a value-expressive than social adjustive function (e.g., DeBono, 1987; DeBono & Edmonds, 1989; DeBono & Harnish, 1988; Jamieson & Zanna, 1989; Kristiansen & Zanna, 1988; Snyder & DeBono, 1985, 1987, 1989). Much of this work has tested and confirmed the classic functional hypothesis that persuasive messages will be most effective in changing attitudes when their content is tailored to the functional under-pinnings of the target attitude. In a particularly compelling demonstration, DeBono (1987) presented subjects who favored deinstitutionalization of the mentally ill with one of two messages that opposed deinstitutionalization. Although the two messages were similar in most respects, the *social adjustive* version included additional informa-tion indicating that most of the subjects' peer group (i.e., other college students) opposed deinstitutionalization, whereas only a minority favored it. In contrast, the *value-expressive* version included additional information indicating that opposition to deinstitutionalization was associated with holding values that subjects considered important (e.g., responsibility), whereas favoring deinstitutionalization was associated with holding values that subjects considered relatively unimportant (e.g., imaginative-ness). Consistent with the matching hypothesis, high self-monitor subjects in this research expressed attitudes that were more opposed to deinstitutionalization when they heard the social adjustive message than when they heard the value-expressive message. Low self-monitors, on the other hand, expressed more negative attitudes toward deinstitutionalization after hearing the value-expressive message. An additional finding of this research was that subjects who received functionally relevant messages scrutinized persuasive arguments more thoroughly than subjects who received func-tionally irrelevant messages. This finding goes beyond the simple matching hypothesis by suggesting that the greater persuasiveness of functionally congruent messages may be mediated, at least partially, by systematic processing (see also DeBono & Harnish, 1988; Snyder & DeBono, 1989).

In a subsequent study, DeBono and Edmonds (1989, Exp. 2) induced high and low self-monitors to write counterattitudinal essays. Some subjects were led to believe that the position to be espoused in these essays opposed the attitudes of the majority of their peers (social adjustive condition), while others were led to believe that the essay position was contrary to their personal values (value-expressive condition). On the assumption that social adjustment should be more central than value-expression to the self-concepts of high self-monitors, they were expected to modify their attitudes in the direction of their essays more in the social adjustive condition than in the value-expressive condition. Conversely, since value-expression should be more central to the self-concepts of low self-monitors, they were expected to modify their attitudes more in the value-expressive condition. The results supported these predictions. As such, this experiment demonstrates the value of the functional perspective beyond its traditional, persuasion domain, and also supports self-concept interpretations of dissonance effects in the induced-compliance paradigm (see Chapter 11).[41]

486

Other researchers have addressed variation in functions across persons using more specific individual difference measures. For example, Fazio (1989) has argued that the most functional attitudes are those that are highly accessible to the person. Although Fazio does not restrict this claim to the schematic function of attitudes, he regards this function as primary, and his empirical work has addressed phenomena most relevant to it. Among other findings, this research suggests that highly accessible attitudes are more likely than inaccessible attitudes to bias judgments about attitude-relevant information (Houston & Fazio, 1989), to predict attitude-congruent behavior (Fazio & Williams, 1986), and to alleviate the perceived stressfulness of decision-making tasks (Fazio & Driscoll in Fazio, 1989, pp. 173–174). Because accessibility correlates with other indicators of attitude strength, it remains to be seen whether the schematic effects shown in this research program are uniquely attributable to accessibility (see Chapters 4 and 12). Nonetheless, the research does support the more general intuition that strong attitudes are more likely than weak ones to serve a schematic function.

In a very different approach to individual differences, Prentice (1987b) used multidimensional scaling procedures to assess the extent to which people tend to view their "favorite" material possessions (e.g., stereos, wallets, photographs) in utilitarian versus symbolic terms. Subjects identified by this method as either "instrumental possessors" or "symbolic possessors" subsequently received six messages, each of which described a different issue (e.g., education for disabled children), proposed a course of action, and supported it with four arguments. For each issue, a utilitarian message (stressing costs and benefits) and a symbolic message (stressing values) was constructed, so that of the six messages each subject received, three were utilitarian and three were symbolic. After reading each message, subjects indicated their favorability toward its proposal. The results proved consistent with Prentice's assumption that a person's functional orientation toward material objects can be used to infer his or her functional orientation toward attitudinal issues. That is, in line with functional theory's basic matching hypothesis, the symbolic messages were more favorably received by symbolic (vs. utilitarian) subjects, and the utilitarian messages were (slightly) more favorably received by utilitarian (vs. symbolic) subjects. Although Prentice's individual difference approach holds promise, greater attention to the nature of the symbolic functional orientation tapped in this research would be desirable (for discussion, see Abelson & Prentice, 1989).

Given the success of self-monitoring research and other individual difference studies of attitude function, subsequent research testing functional hypotheses should pursue additional individual difference indicators of attitude functions. Nevertheless, because this strategy tends to ignore variation in function across attitude objects and situations, other measurement strategies are necessary. To address this need, several researchers have explored the utility of open-ended techniques to assess attitude functions more directly. For example, Herek (1987) had subjects write essays about their attitudes toward homosexuality and then content-analyzed these essays for their functional themes. And Shavitt (1990) used a more traditional thought-listing task in order to determine the functional basis of subjects' attitudes toward a number of consumer products that had been preselected for their potential to engage particular functions (e.g., utilitarian vs. social identity). The results of both endeavors indicate that such measures have the potential to yield valid and reliable direct assessments of function. Moreover, Shavitt's (1990) work, and also Prentice's (1987b), supports the idea that different attitude objects do activate different functional concerns and, in addition, that attitude objects differ in their functional complexity. That is, whereas some objects engage primarily one function (e.g., coffee and air conditioners serve utilitarian needs), other objects—indeed most objects (Shavitt, 1989)—may engage multiple functions (e.g., automobiles may serve utilitarian, social adjustment, and value-expressive needs; Ennis & Zanna, 1991).

The obvious disadvantage of free response assessments of attitude function is that they are time-consuming to score and vulnerable to scorer biases. For this reason Herek (1987) attempted to develop a more objective direct measure of attitude functions (see also Lutz, 1981). The Attitude Functions Inventory (AFI) is designed to assess the functional bases of respondents' attitudes toward stigmatized groups (e.g., homosexuals, the mentally ill), although it could presumably be modified to apply to a larger range of attitude objects (Herek, 1987; Tesser & Shaffer, 1990). It contains 10 items, subsets of which pertain to particular functions (utilitarian, value-expressive, defensive, and social adjustment). For example, one of the value-expressive items reads "My opinions about _____ mainly are based on my moral beliefs about how things should be." And reminiscent of Fishbein and Ajzen's (e.g., 1975) concept of normative beliefs (see Chapter 4), one of the social adjustment items on this scale reads "My opinions about _____ mainly are based on my perceptions of how the people I care about have responded to _____ as a group." Although Herek (1987) presented preliminary evidence for the AFI's validity, to our knowledge it has not yet been evaluated in the context of testing specific functional hypotheses. Given the absence of such data and the lack of viable alternatives to the AFI, the direct assessment of attitude functions remains more a goal than an accomplishment of recent functional research.

As earlier paragraphs have revealed, investigators have gotten round the direct measurement issue by emphasizing individual differences in attitude functions. The recognition that attitude objects vary in the functions they engage and that situations may arouse different functions has also enabled researchers to circumvent this issue. For example, the hypothesis that functionally relevant messages enhance persuasion, confirmed in several individual difference studies (see above), has also been confirmed using an attitude object approach. Specifically, Shavitt (1990) selected single-function consumer products based on pretesting and presented subjects with advertisements whose content either matched or mismatched the products' functions. Consistent with the matching hypothesis, subjects indicated more favorable attitudes toward the products when exposed to the functionally congruent versus incongruent advertisement.

Several additional experiments illustrate the utility of the situational approach. Jamieson and Zanna (1989) reasoned that circumstances which heighten people's need for cognitive clarity or structure (see Kruglanski, 1990) should enhance the schematic effects of attitudes. Consistent with this reasoning, they showed that subjects' attitudes toward affirmative action correlated more highly with their verdicts about a specific discrimination case when they were given only three minutes (vs. unlimited time) to study the case, presumably because need for structure was aroused in the time pressure condition.[42] In a very different type of study, Young, Thomsen, Borgida, Sullivan, and Aldrich (1991) showed that the typically stronger impact of value-laden beliefs as opposed to self-interest beliefs on political attitudes can be reduced by increasing the accessibility of the latter. Specifically, subjects for whom self-interest had been primed (i.e., activated) in a first experimental task subsequently manifested a greater tendency than non-primed control subjects to express policy preferences (e.g., on environmental pollution) that reflected their self-interest. Similarly, Sears and Lau (1983) found a greater correspondence between self-interest and policy preferences when question-naire items dealing explicitly with self-interest immediately preceded those that tapped respondents' policy preferences, presumably because exposure to the former items primed self-interest (see also discussion of context effects in Chapter 2). In other studies, priming manipulations have been used to test the classic hypothesis that functionally congruent messages enhance persuasion (Prentice, 1987a), and the more novel hypothesis that attitude-behavior correspondence will be greater when the function salient at the time attitudes are assessed matches the function salient at the time behaviors are performed (Shavitt & Fazio, 1991; see also Millar & Tesser, 1986a, 1989; Tesser & Shaffer, 1990).

Because it is likely that most attitude objects engage multiple functions, additional research varying the importance, salience, or accessibility of function-relevant concerns should be a high priority for researchers testing the functional perspective. Such research will also reveal commonalities between contemporary thinking about attitude functions and contemporary thinking about involvement and modes of processing (e.g., Chaiken et al., 1989; B. T. Johnson & Eagly, 1989; Petty & Cacioppo, 1990; see also Chapters 7 and 8). For example, increasing the personal relevance of an attitude issue can be viewed either as a means of arousing utilitarian concerns or of arousing outcome-relevant involvement. And making public audiences salient for subjects can be viewed as a means of arousing social adjustive concerns or of arousing impression-relevant involvement or of instigating impression-motivated processing. Linking the two traditions more explicitly should enrich both. The functional perspective can benefit because theorizing and research on involvement and modes of processing tries to link motivational factors to the cognitive processes that mediate persuasion. And the involvement-processing tradition can benefit by drawing more heavily on the functional perspective's distinctive motivational insights.

Because the functional perspective emphasizes that attitudes vary in their motivational origins, this approach suggests that attitudes serving different functions may vary in their structural properties (see Chapter 3). In particular, it is possible that attitudes serving some functions (e.g., ego-defense) have a stronger affective than cognitive basis, whereas attitudes serving other functions (e.g., utilitarian) have a stronger cognitive basis. Recent research on attitude structure has, in fact, explored hypotheses that resemble the classic matching hypothesis of the functional approach (K. Edwards, 1990; Millar & Millar, 1990; Millar & Tesser, 1989). For example, Edwards (1990) found that an affectively oriented appeal was more persuasive than a cognitively oriented appeal among subjects with affect-based attitudes, whereas the reverse effect obtained among subjects with cognition-based attitudes. In addition, she found that affect-based attitudes were expressed with greater confidence by subjects than cognition-based attitudes. Although Edwards did not link affect-based and cognition-based attitudes to specific functions, she did endorse the general point that knowing the functional basis of an attitude should provide clues as to its affective and cognitive foundations or correlates.

In conclusion we note that skeptics of the functional perspective might argue that the perspective boils down to Fishbein and Ajzen's (1972, 1975) point that to be persuasive, a message must address a person's salient beliefs (see Chapter 5). The task of operationalizing functions, in other words, could be viewed as an attempt to discover the salient utilitarian, value-expressive, social adjustive (and so on) beliefs that underlie people's attitudes toward various objects in various situations. Yet the emphasis of the Fishbein-Ajzen approach on the manifest content of beliefs is quite limiting in relation to the issues raised by functional theories. The unique value of the functional approach is its effort to reveal the more latent, motivational significance of people's attitudes and associated beliefs, and these meanings would not necessarily be revealed in their manifest content. Although belief elicitation procedures such as those that Fishbein and Ajzen have used can be helpful in exploring these issues, we think it likely that the same salient beliefs could have multiple functional meanings (e.g., "BMWs are overpriced"). The functional perspective's explicit focus on the motivational underpinnings of attitude formation, expression, and change has the potential to enrich numerous domains of attitudinal research.

Conclusion

The three theoretical traditions we have considered in this chapter were all developed during the 1950s and early 1960s. Their breadth and focus on motivational issues contributed to the perception of this era as one of grand theorizing and intense interest in motivational dynamics among social psychologists. Although the popularity of these perspectives declined during the 1970s as somewhat narrower and definitely more cognitively oriented theories of attitude change flourished (see Chapters 6, 7, and 8), they have each had a pronounced and relatively enduring intellectual impact on the field (see Chapter 14). The Yale researchers' incentive and drive-reduction constructs are not part of the vocabulary of most modern investigators. Yet these constructs led the Yale researchers to address basic issues about how motivational states influence information processing and persuasion, particularly in their work on fear appeals. This work stimulated a number of subsequent theories of fear appeals (e.g., Janis, 1967; Leventhal, 1970; Rogers, 1975, 1983). Although our review indicated that no one of these newer perspectives provides a complete integration of the relatively large empirical literature on fear appeals, each offers worthwhile insights about the persuasiveness of threat-provoking persuasive communications. Moreover, recent research on mood and persuasion (e.g., Mackie & Worth, 1991; Schwarz, Bless, & Bohner, 1991) as well as several recent studies of fear appeals (e.g., Gleicher & Petty, 1992; Jepson & Chaiken, 1990) can be seen as continuing the Yale legacy insofar as this newer research reasserts the importance of examining how emotional states impinge on the cognitive processes that mediate persuasion. Much of this recent work has been directed by newer theories of persuasion that emphasize multiple modes of processing information (e.g., Chaiken, 1980, 1987; Petty & Cacioppo, 1986a, 1986b), theories that evolved in part from the Yale tradition (see Chapters 6, 7, and 14). As our review suggested, the newer research on mood and fear provides an excellent foundation for advancing our understanding of the interplay between affective and cognitive processes in persuasion settings and related judgment contexts (e.g., decision making, stereotyping).

The core principle of cognitive consistency theories, that people seek to maintain and reestablish consistency among cognitive elements, has also been of enduring value. As we have seen, this principle has been applied to numerous attitudinal phenomena, most notably attitudinal structure (see Chapter 3), perception of candidates' stands on political issues, message-based persuasion, attitudinal resistance, attitudinal selectivity in information processing (see Chapter 12), the evaluative consequences of decision making, and counterattitudinal advocacy (see Chapter 11). During the 1980s the issue of whether consistency theory might be dead, dying, or hiding under new labels was raised (e.g., Abelson, 1983; Aronson, 1989; Berkowitz & Devine, 1989). However, there is little doubt that the basic principle remains an important one, both within the attitudes field (e.g., Brent & Granberg, 1982; Judd & Krosnick, 1989; Kinder, 1978; Ottati, Fishbein, & Middlestadt, 1988), and within other areas of social personality psychology (e.g., Higgins, 1989b; Jussim, 1986; Swann, 1990). Although in the case of dissonance theory and the induced-compliance setting, Festinger's (1957) original assumption that dissonance follows from attitude-behavior inconsistency has been challenged, the alternative causes of dissonance arousal that have been proposed for this setting (and others; e.g., Aronson, 1969; J. Cooper & Fazio, 1989; D. Frey, 1986) are still fundamentally concerned with psychological discrepancies (e.g., behavior that violates the self-concept; see Chapter 11).

Although the basic consistency principle has persevered, modern investigators would do well to reexamine several consistency theorists' ideas about modes of inconsistency restoration. In particular, Festinger's (1957, 1964b) discussions of post-decisional dissonance and involuntary exposure settings alluded to a number of defensive cognitive processes by which people defend their decisions and prior attitudes, and which presumably *mediate* the effects that decision making and receiving attitude-discrepant information have on attitude change. These mediational processes have been largely ignored in mainstream dissonance research (see Chapter 11), although they have been addressed to a certain extent in research on attitudinal selectivity (see Chapter 12). In addition, we noted that Abelson's (1959, 1968) ideas about the microprocesses of inconsistency reduction deserve renewed attention by modern investigators. These ideas represented an important early effort to understand consistency restoration as a sequence of cognitive processes and included still reasonable assumptions about perceivers' preferences for the various modes of resolution highlighted by various consistency theories (e.g., bolstering, denial, attitude change). The thrust of Abelson's analysis was also a mediational one insofar as he implied that attitude change (and also attitude polarization) was often an outcome of other modes of inconsistency resolution, rather than an alternative mechanism of resolution. Moreover, compatible with the dual-process models of persuasion, Abelson's analysis suggested that issues such as motivation and ability for cognitive processing must be taken into account in order to understand whether and by what means perceivers resolve inconsistency in their cognitoriums.

The classic functional theories of attitudes that Katz (1960) and Smith, Bruner, and White (1956) proposed were more purely motivational than either the Yale perspective or the cognitive consistency perspective. These theories also inspired considerably less empirical work than the other perspectives, due to the difficulty early researchers had in operationalizing the various attitude functions that the theories specified. Nonetheless, the functional theories remained conceptually intriguing to investigators in the decades following their development, because of their breadth and unique focus on the motivational bases of attitudes and their expression (see Eagly & Himmelfarb, 1974; Herek, 1986). Moreover, as our review indicated, the last several years have been a growth period for functional theorizing and research. Although no new functions have been proposed, there have been significant clarifications and elaborations of the functional approach and promising empirical attempts to test and extend functional hypotheses. Moreover, some of this research has also begun to forge links between the functional approach and cognitive themes of more recent attitudinal theorizing (e.g., accessibility, modes of processing). As well, recent persuasion theorizing has begun to redress that area's longtime focus on the "validity-seeking" message recipient by postulating alternative motives and different forms of involvement that reflect in part the influence of the functional perspective. These developments, along with recent advances in research on mood and persuasion and continued interest in the cognitive consistency perspective, suggest that theorizing and research about attitudes are entering a new era of greater balance between motivational and cognitive themes.

Notes

1. Hovland, Janis, and Kelley (1953) used the term "implicit responses" to refer to the thoughts presumably generated by active role-players in their experiments. Although this emphasis on the mediational role of thinking anticipated the central thesis of the cognitive response model (A. G. Greenwald, 1968), the Yale studies did not progress very far in developing measures designed to document their ideas about biased scanning (see discussion in Chapter 11).

2. For example, high fear subjects listed more complaints about the message (e.g., "I did not care for the gory illustrations"), but rated it more favorably on several dimensions (e.g., interest value).

3. Readers may wish to review Figure 6.1, which illustrates this curvilinear prediction for the case of recipient intelligence, a variable that McGuire argued is positively related to reception but negatively related to yielding.

4. It is worth noting that McGuire (1972) subsequently presented a revised, somewhat speculative, and considerably more complex analysis of fear appeals. Taking only the cue aspects of fear into account, McGuire reasoned that fear should relate *negatively* to reception (for the reasons noted in the text) but *positively* to yielding (assuming that subservience represents a characteristic response to anxiety). Next, taking only its drive aspects into account, McGuire reasoned that fear should relate (a) *positively* to reception (assuming that most persons would be inclined to pay some attention to the message), and either (b) positively to yielding assuming some initial inclination to be compliant or (c) *negatively* to yielding assuming some initial inclination to be resistant. The cue analysis implies a nonmonotonic fear-persuasion relation, whereas the drive analysis implies either a positive monotonic relation (with option "b" for yielding) or a nonmonotonic one (with option "c" for yielding). Finally, simultaneous consideration of fear's cue and drive aspects produces a functional relation between fear and persuasion that is best described in McGuire's (1972, p. 131) own words: "a nonmonotonic effect of even more complex, multimodal form, perhaps an M-shaped one." Readers disposed to dismiss this theory for being overly complex may be placated by an additional McGuire quotation, also about the nature of the fear-persuasion relationship: "if we are seeking to describe a pretzel-shaped reality we must be allowed to use pretzel-shaped hypotheses" (McGuire, 1969, p. 205).

5. The contribution of the reception mediator to the shape of these curves is relatively minor—a slight boost in persuasion at the low end of the fear continuum (due to the additive effects of facilitation and reception), and a more pronounced drop-off in persuasion at the very high end of the continuum relative to all other regions (due to the additive effects of interference and reception). Lest readers infer from Panel D's multiple curves that Janis's nonmonotonic model is considerably more complex than McGuire's, we note that a similar "family of curves" could be drawn for the latter. In such a rendering, the various curves would represent the fear-persuasion function that should obtain as the relative importance of reception versus yielding shifted. Moving from left to right on the fear continuum, the curves would represent circumstances in which the yielding mediator becomes progressively more important than the reception mediator.

6. Leventhal (1970) characterized the drive model and Janis's (1967) extension as dealing only with his model's fear control process. Yet as we have seen, the fear-motivated processes discussed by these models are broader than this. In fact, Leventhal's descriptions of danger control and fear control resemble Janis's descriptions of facilitative and interfering responding, respectively (although interfering responses are more broadly defined than fear control). Thus, the main difference between the models seems to us to reduce to a debate concerning whether fear arousal is (Janis) or isn't (Leventhal) a necessary antecedent of danger control/facilitative responding. Finally,

it is also worth noting that danger control and fear control also resemble the distinction that Lazarus and his colleagues have made in their research on stress and coping between "problem-focussed" and "emotion-focussed" coping (e.g., Folkman & Lazarus, 1985; Lazarus, 1966).

7. Rogers' (1975) original combinatorial postulate reflected his reasoning that expectancy-value logic dictated multiplying his model's (two) expectancy and (one) value terms (i.e., *Intentions = Expectancy*vulnerability × *Value*severity × *Expectancy*efficacy). As Sutton (1982) has noted, however, whereas multiplying severity by vulnerability does follow from expectancy-value logic, multiplying the resultant product by response efficacy does not. This and other reservations about Rogers' (1975) model led Sutton (1982) to propose his own *subjective expected utility* model of fear appeals. Although highly similar to Rogers' (1975) model in substance, Sutton's model represents a more exact translation of expectancy-value principles. It should also be noted that Sutton (like Rogers, see text) subsequently expanded his model to take self-efficacy into account (e.g., Sutton & Eiser, 1984).

8. Self-efficacy is the major construct in Bandura's (1977) social learning theory of behavioral change, which holds that the processes of psychological change are mediated by changes in self-efficacy beliefs. As discussed in Chapter 4, self-efficacy, under the label of *perceived behavioral control*, is featured in Ajzen's (e.g., 1987) theory of planned behavior.

9. With few exceptions (e.g., Ronis & Kaiser, 1989), response costs and maladaptive response rewards have not yet been examined in conjunction with other components of protection motivation theory.

10. Leventhal's earlier research on "specific action instructions" also supports the importance of self-efficacy beliefs in determining recipients' acceptance of fear appeals' recommendations (e.g., Leventhal, Singer, & Jones, 1965; Leventhal, Watts, & Pagano, 1967).

11. Two-way interactions in accord with the theory have been obtained in several studies (e.g., Rogers & Mewborn, 1976; Self & Rogers, 1990). However, these interactions have not proven stable across the health issues investigated.

12. It should be apparent to readers that the "Threat" × Efficacy interactions specified by protection motivation theory are identical to the "Fear" × Efficacy interactions implied by the drive model and its extensions (albeit for different theoretical reasons).

13. Another reason why fear arousal measures and their correlation with persuasion are ambiguous is that they are assessed only once in the typical experiment, immediately after message exposure. As Sutton (1982) has noted, such measures could reflect initial arousal, residual arousal, or some intermediate level of partly reduced arousal.

14. In fact, fear appeal researchers' embrace of expectancy-value theorizing and their focus on predicting behavioral intentions (e.g., Rogers, 1983; Sutton, 1982) bears closer resemblance to research on attitude-behavior relations (see Chapter 4) than to other contemporary research in persuasion (see Chapter 7).

15. As we noted in Chapter 3, Schwarz and Clore (1988) have provided a useful distinction between moods and emotions. Whereas moods represent general positive or negative feelings that are not typically held with respect to any particular object or event (e.g., another person), emotions (e.g., anger, fear) are more distinctive in tone and typically do have an identifiable cause (e.g., a particular event). Most of the research we review in this section has concerned positive mood states. To a large extent this research emphasis, which holds across subareas of mood research, reflects the greater difficulty investigators have had in ordering existing findings on negative mood states (see Isen, 1987).

16. In this and other studies by Schwarz and his colleagues (see Schwarz, Bless, & Bohner, 1991), the mean self-reported mood of "sad" life event subjects has hovered around the scale midpoint.

On Bless, Bohner, Schwarz, and Strack's (1990) mood scale, which ran from "very bad" (1) to "very good" (9), for example, this mean was above the scale midpoint (6.1 in Experiment 1 and 5.4 in Experiment 2). For this reason, we suggest caution in interpreting the results observed for such subjects as diagnostic of the processing effects of *negative mood* (cf. Schwarz, Bless, & Bohner, 1991).

17. Mackie and Worth (1991) have cautioned that the interfering effects of positive affect on cognitive performance may be restricted to capacity-intensive tasks that require detailed, analytic thinking. Indeed, there is some evidence that the cognitive attributes of positive mood states (diffuse attention, accessibility of diverse types of stored information) can enhance the likelihood of achieving creative solutions in some problem-solving tasks (see Isen, 1987).

18. The temporal duration of induced moods is unclear, leaving open the possibility that the processing effects of mood occur at the time of *judgment* as well as (or instead of) at the time of initial encoding and elaboration of information. To address this issue, Bless, Mackie, and Schwarz (in press) manipulated mood before or after message exposure. Data from the *before* conditions replicated earlier experiments' demonstrations that positive mood reduces systematic processing, indicating that mood does influence encoding/elaboration. Demonstrating that mood also impacts on judgment processes, the *after* conditions data showed that all subjects were influenced by argument quality but that positive mood subjects' attitude judgments were more extreme. The latter findings, which were replicated and extended in a second study, were interpreted as showing that at judgment (as well as at encoding) subjects in good moods adopt simplifying processing strategies. Nonetheless, no direct evidence for heuristic processing by good mood subjects was provided in this research.

19. Several other distinctions made by this analysis also deserve clarification in subsequent work. In particular, it will be important to develop *a priori* criteria for distinguishing "irrelevant" from "relevant" affect, and a means (independent of the presumed elaboration likelihood level) of detecting when mood has functioned as a *peripheral cue* versus a *persuasive argument*. At present, for example, it is not clear how the persuasive argument function of mood differs from Schwarz's (e.g., Schwarz, Bless, & Bohner, 1991) description of the "How-do-I-feel-about-it" heuristic, even though Petty and his colleagues consider the latter to be one of several mechanisms by which mood *as a peripheral cue* influences persuasion.

20. Whether the relations among attitudinal elements obey the laws of formal logic is not the focus of these theories. Rather, they deal with *psycho*-logical consistency, the extent to which elements fit together or cohere in the mind of the perceiver. Among consistency theories, McGuire's (e.g., 1960c) probabilogical model, discussed in Chapters 3 and 5, deviates most from this characterization.

21. Consistent with most applications of balance theory, the remainder of our discussion emphasizes the liking relations that characterize three-element structures. For more detailed description of the theory (e.g., its two-element structures), several of its graph theory extensions, and relevant empirical research, see Chapter 3. Readers may also wish to review Figure 3.5 at this time, as it illustrates the eight possible configurations of positive and negative relations in the three-element structure composed of p, o, and x.

22. When the larger system of p's cognitions is considered, whether differentiation fully restores balance should depend on whether the two components of the differentiated element are themselves linked in the perceiver's mind. In our example, Eva may well perceive a positive unit relation between o_1 and o_2 (because both components belong to the same person; see Heider, 1958, p. 209). If so, imbalance remains in her cognitorium: Although the p-o_2-x triad is balanced, the p-o_1-o_2 triad is not. Yet, to the extent that o's constituent parts are not linked in Eva's mind (or are linked by a negative unit relation), the larger system can be viewed as balanced. Although

495

Heider's discussion of differentiation recognizes the existence of structures composed of greater than three elements, his theory does not deal with such structures on a formal basis. Several extensions that do are presented in Chapter 3 (e.g., Cartwright & Harary, 1956; Insko, 1984).

23. In addition to Heider's three modes of restoring balance, Newcomb granted his perceivers the option of trying to change o's attitude toward x. Indeed, the distinctive contribution of Newcomb's theory is its focus on communicative acts between p and o as a means of restoring equilibrium to p-o-x triads (or, in Newcomb's terminology, to A-B-X systems).

24. For other applications of the theory, see Tannenbaum (1968).

25. In the case of associative assertions, the change formulae are as follows:

$$AC_O = [\text{abs } X / (\text{abs } O + \text{abs } X)] (X - O)$$

$$AC_X = [\text{abs } O / (\text{abs } O + \text{abs } X)] (O - X)$$

In these equations, AC is the amount of attitude change; O and abs O are the perceiver's evaluation of O (the source) and absolute value of this evaluation, respectively; and X and abs X are the perceiver's evaluation of X (the issue) and the absolute value of this evaluation, respectively.

26. To address the model's inaccuracies, Osgood and Tannenbaum (1955) suggested adding two corrections to their attitude change equations. The *correction for incredulity* involves subtracting from predicted change a number whose value increases as incongruity increases. The *assertion constant* involves adding a constant value to the equation predicting attitude change toward the *object*. Both corrections were empirically derived; that is, both were formulated on the basis of comparing observed attitude change means with predicted means. That these corrections improve the model's accuracy should not be surprising, given that they have been applied primarily to the same data sets that shaped their formulation.

27. As noted in Chapter 3, Rosenberg equated "affect" with "evaluation" and, in contrast to our terminology, used the term *affective-cognitive* consistency to refer to the consistency between attitudes and beliefs.

28. Figure 10.7 does not depict relations *between* values because such relations were not posited by Rosenberg. Several other aspects of Rosenberg's theory should also be noted. First, although its definition of consistency suggests that the ratio of imbalanced to balanced bands in an evaluative-cognitive structure could serve as an index of degree of inconsistency, Rosenberg did not offer such a quantitative definition. Second, although the theory does not formally represent the intensity with which attitudes and beliefs are held, Rosenberg's empirical research employed continuous measures of both, and his theoretical discussions clearly recognized that attitude and belief "change" referred not simply to sign changes but to extremity changes as well.

29. In light of Heider's (1958) discussion of cognitive differentiation (see text), it is worth noting that Rosenberg (1960a) reported a tendency on the part of some hypnotized subjects to redefine the attitude object in a manner that facilitated the anti-foreign aid belief changes they manifested (e.g., one subject focused on the "bad" *financial* aspects of foreign aid).

30. As readers will recall, we define values as *attitudes* toward relatively abstract goals and end states of human existence (see Chapters 1 and 3). Given this definition, Rosenberg's evaluative-cognitive consistency theory can be construed as a theory of *inter*-attitudinal structure and balancing. Yet, because people may often derive their attitudes by considering their values, as Rosenberg (e.g., 1960a) and other theorists (e.g., Rokeach, 1968) have argued, the theory can also be construed as dealing with *intra*-attitudinal structure and balancing. Indeed, Rosenberg (e.g., 1968b) described his theory in the latter terms, and we discuss the theory in Chapter 3 in the context of other perspectives on intra-attitudinal structure.

31. Two other modes of inconsistency reduction were also discussed by Abelson. *Transcendence*, which he viewed as the most effortful of the modes he discussed, involved combining elements into larger, superordinate units that form a consistent structure. To illustrate this mode, Abelson (1959) asked readers to consider the imbalance that exists for the person who likes God, dislikes evil, yet believes that God created evil. A transcendent resolution to this imbalance could be obtained by combining good and evil into the superordinate unit "free will," by reasoning that God created both good and evil in order to give people free will. As a consequence, balance can be restored, for the person likes God, likes free will, and believes that God created free will. We do not discuss transcendence in the text since, to our knowledge, its existence has not been empirically documented. Finally, Abelson (1968) also discussed a mode of resolution that he termed *rationalization*. We ignore this mode in the text because we see it as largely synonymous with bolstering. For example, in discussing this mode, Abelson (1968) considered the generic imbalanced case of a liked actor who performs a bad action. To reduce imbalance, perceivers might reason that the bad action nevertheless produced (or could produce) a good outcome, yielding a positive link between the liked actor and the good final outcome. Constructing a good outcome, rationalization, can also be seen as bolstering. Finally, the main distinction between bolstering (or rationalization) and denial (in either its direct attack or counterarguing form) is that bolstering *adds* a cognitive bond between elements (e.g., the bad deed nonetheless yielded a good outcome) whereas denial *weakens* such bonds (e.g., the actor didn't do anything bad).

32. Although we emphasize Abelson's (1959, 1968) views on the selection of modes issue, we note that Kelman and Baron (1968a) also provided an interesting and still useful discussion.

33. Like previous interpreters of dissonance theory, we are forced at times to impose our own interpretation on certain of its constructs and mechanisms (e.g., importance of cognitive elements, modes of dissonance reduction). We do not devote a great deal of space to analyzing the theory's ambiguities and weakness, however, as this task has been accomplished ably by many others (e.g., R. Brown, 1965; Fishbein & Ajzen, 1975; Insko, 1967; Kiesler, Collins, & Miller, 1969; see also Abelson, Aronson, McGuire, Newcomb, Rosenberg, & Tannenbaum, 1968).

34. This example of a dissonant pair of elements was expressly chosen to illustrate the fact that Festinger's two-element relations can often be translated into balance theory terms. The dissonant relation in question depicts exactly the same "imbalanced" triad shown in the top panel of Figure 10.5. The other examples of dissonant pairs shown in Table 10.2 can also be given a three-element balance theory representation. In these cases, however, one of the three relations must be inferred. For example, regarding the first two elements of row 5 one must infer a negative unit relation between being a Democrat and voting for Bush. The perceiver (p or "I") is therefore positively linked to two entities (Democrat and Bush) that are themselves negatively linked, a state of imbalance. That such inferences are required to translate between the dissonance and balance perspectives by no means undermines the value of balance theory. On the contrary, it makes *explicit* what is only *implicit* in dissonance theory. That is, the dissonance theorist's assertion that voting for Bush and being a registered Democrat creates dissonance *rests on* the assumption that the latter element implies the opposite of the former element (or vice versa). The point that implied or "suppressed premises" (R. Brown, 1965) are the stuff that makes dissonance theory's cognitive elements dissonant with one another has been discussed by numerous commentators (e.g., R. Brown, 1965; Insko, 1967; Kiesler, Collins, & Miller, 1969).

35. Although this postulate suggests that Festinger aspired to develop a precise, quantitative assessment of magnitude of dissonance in the manner that Osgood and Tannenbaum (1955) quantified

497

incongruity, the bulk of his theorizing and associated research has treated this variable primarily in qualitative (i.e., more vs. less) terms.

36. As noted earlier, Hovland and Rosenberg's (1960) "ambivalence" interpretation of consistency motivation also views inconsistency as an unpleasant drive state. Unlike these authors, however, Festinger (1957) did not articulate his views on the etiology of dissonance motivation. It would be consistent with his earlier views on social comparison processes (Festinger, 1954), however, to assume that he believed that consistency motivation was a manifestation of perceivers' more basic needs to hold stable, accurate appraisals of their opinions and abilities.

37. As a general perspective or school of psychology, functionalism emerged around the turn of the century and represented a shift away from structuralism. Whereas structuralists (e.g., Wundt, Tichener) emphasized the description and classification of mental events, functionalists (e.g., Dewey, James) stressed the purposive and adaptive nature of human thought and behavior (see Boring, 1950; Hilgard, 1987).

38. The underlying assumption of this formulation, that expressing attitudinal similarity breeds liking, follows readily from consistency theory, particularly Newcomb's (1953) balance model (see earlier discussion in this chapter; see also Chapter 9 for a classical conditioning interpretation of the attitude similarity-liking relationship).

39. Kelman's analysis of compliance, identification, and internalization processes in social influence can be interpreted as a third classic theory of attitude function (see Himmelfarb & Eagly, 1974; Insko, 1967; A. G. Greenwald, 1989). Because of this model's centrality to the social influence literature, we discuss Kelman's ideas in most detail in Chapter 13.

40. Herek (1986) posits three evaluative (or utilitarian) sub-functions: *experiential-specific*, *experiential-schematic*, and *anticipatory*. For example, experiential-specific attitudes are based on direct experience with a particular attitude object. Because Herek has not yet developed the theoretical implications of these sub-functions, we do not elaborate upon them here.

41. As others have noted, it is likely that the social adjustive versus value-expressive dichotomy oversimplifies the functional bases of high and low self-monitors' attitudes; in particular, the attitudes of low self-monitors may be more functionally complex than this scheme suggests (see Shavitt, 1989; Tesser & Shaffer, 1990).

42. These results (and also those of a second replication) held predominantly for subjects low in self-monitoring status. We also note that an alternative interpretation for Jamieson and Zanna's (1989) results views the time pressure variable as a manipulation of capacity for systematic processing (see Ratneshwar & Chaiken, 1991). According to this interpretation, the judgmental impact of subjects' attitudes was detectable when opportunity for systematic processing was constrained (time pressure condition) but attenuated when specific case-relevant information could also be brought to bear on judgment (no time pressure condition).

11

The Impact of Behavior on Attitude Formation and Change

The attitudes and beliefs that people communicate to others do not always reflect their private convictions; self-presentational concerns, social norms, and the requirements and constraints inherent in social roles often lead people to say things they do not genuinely believe. A professor, when among her colleagues, may find herself contributing to their unfavorable comments about the abilities of undergraduate students, despite her positive attitude toward undergraduates. Of what consequence are such dissimulations? The professor who disparages undergraduates may become more negative toward them as a product of the self-persuasion induced by her own statements as well as the persuasion induced by her colleagues' comments. As Chapters 6, 7, and 8 have detailed, persuasion by others' messages can be more or less effective, depending on various features of the message source, the message itself, the recipient, and, as contemporary research has highlighted, the cognitive and motivational context in which the message is received. Similarly, people's self-generated messages can have more or less impact on their attitudes, depending on their own personal attributes, their messages, and the context in which their advocacies occur.

As we explain in this chapter, self-persuasion can occur through endorsing a position inconsistent with one's attitude, an act known as *counterattitudinal advocacy*, or less obviously, through advocating a position consistent with one's attitude, an act known as *proattitudinal advocacy*. Attitudes can be changed, not only by advocating attitudinal positions, but also by engaging in a variety of other attitude-relevant behaviors. Such methods, however, do not have a ubiquitous power to change attitudes, and understanding the conditions under which they are effective has received theoretical and empirical attention from social psychologists for approximately four decades. In fact, predicting how and why people are persuaded by their own communications proved to be the crucible of cognitive dissonance theory and a ground from which newer theories emphasizing self-identity and self-presentation have emerged. The influence of behaviors on attitudes has thus been of considerable importance for the development of attitude theory.

The general idea that behavior can change attitudes, especially when the behavior is counterattitudinal, follows from the tripartite analysis we presented in Chapter 1. People express their attitudes through their beliefs, behaviors, and affective responses. Given the synergistic relation between these classes of responses and between these classes and overall evaluation, we can expect that substantial alteration in any type of attitudinal responding may well act back on the attitude and influence other classes of attitudinal responding as well. As we discussed in Chapters 5, 6, and 7, message-based persuasion relies on the capacity of the message to make certain beliefs salient and plausible for recipients, and these beliefs then impact on the attitude and on various attitude-relevant responses. Inducing a person to engage in attitudinally relevant behavior could similarly change an attitude, as could inducing certain emotional reactions to the attitude object.

In examining the effects of behavior on attitudes, social psychologists have tried to develop an understanding of the cognitive and motivational processes that mediate this type of attitude change. To some extent, these developments resemble those which we reviewed in discussing the impact of persuasive messages. To understand message-induced persuasion, investigators have formulated theories that emphasize one or more mediating processes. Similarly, to understand the attitudinal impact of behavior, psychologists have formulated theories that presume one or more mediating processes. However, in contrast to the main trends in research on persuasion, much of the emphasis in theories about the effects of behavior has been on motivational rather than cognitive processes. We initiated discussion of these motivational themes in Chapter 10, and in this chapter we apply many of these motivational principles, especially those introduced in Festinger's (1957) dissonance theory, to counterattitudinal and proattitudinal advocacy.

As we point out in this chapter, researchers adopted an unusually confrontational stance in their study of the effects of behavior. Rather than proceeding from the assumption that all theories just might have a corner on some portion of the psychology of behavior–attitude relations (see McGuire, 1983), investigators often behaved as if one theory was right and the others wrong. This combative atmosphere surely attracted attention and inspired research. Nonetheless, proceeding in a largely competitive mode, researchers have devoted too little effort to discerning the *conditions* under which various theories are valid. Consistent with our belief that the time has come for researchers to pose "when" questions more frequently in this research area, we will make a number of suggestions about the conditions under which various theories apply. We attempt to show that, to some extent, the competing theories of the behavior-attitude relation illuminate different modes of processing the information that attitude-relevant behavior furnishes to perceivers.

Role-Playing and Attitude Change

In Chapter 10 we noted that research on the effects of advocating attitudinal positions began in the 1950s, when some of Carl Hovland's collaborators at Yale began research on the process that they termed *role-playing*. At the time this research was initiated, social scientists were already interested in the effects that role-playing experiences have on people's attitudes and beliefs. Role-playing procedures had been developed for use in areas such as leadership and management training, employee counseling, and psychotherapy (e.g., Bavelas, 1947; Lippitt, 1943; Zander & Lippitt, 1944), and some writers argued that the effects of role-playing on attitudes could ameliorate social conflict and other human relations problems (e.g., Maier, 1952). Another source of the Yale researchers' interest in role-playing was the research that Kurt Lewin and his colleagues had carried out on the beneficial effects of active participation in group decisions (e.g., Coch & French, 1948; Lewin, 1947). In view of the considerable importance already accorded to role-playing and related phenomena, determining by means of controlled experimentation whether role-playing and other forms of attitudinal proselytizing could influence attitudes seemed a worthy goal for research psychologists (see J. H. Mann, 1956).

Social scientists had generally thought about role-playing in a dramaturgic sense that implies that role-players, like actors, temporarily take on a complex persona. In the Yale experiments, however, subjects merely gave an informal talk in which they advocated a particular viewpoint to an audience of other subjects. In one of the first experiments of this type, Janis and King (1954) compared male college students' responses to a message that they themselves had delivered with their responses to messages delivered by other students. In groups of three, subjects took part in a study ostensibly designed to investigate their aptitude for public speaking. Each subject delivered a communication on one topic and listened to communications delivered by the other two subjects on two additional topics. When delivering the communication (advocating, for example, that a completely effective cure for the common cold would soon be discovered), each subject gave the other subjects an informal talk based on a prepared outline that he had been given. Subjects presumably followed the experimenter's instruction to deliver the talk as a sincere advocate of the point of view represented in the outline. Demonstrating the self-persuasive power that this sort of role-playing can have, subjects' responses to questionnaire items administered at the end of the experimental session showed that, on two of the three topics, they changed their beliefs more toward the position advocated in the persuasive messages when they had delivered the communication themselves rather than merely listened to another subject deliver a communication. This comparison between ordinary message-based persuasion and self-persuasion thus favored self-persuasion as the more effective method for changing attitudes.

Consistent with the emerging interest of the Yale researchers in constructive cognitive processes (see Chapter 6), Janis and King (1954) speculated that an active improvisational process was critical to obtaining the self-persuasion effect. This speculation stemmed from their informal observation that subjects in their study who talked on the two issues that yielded the role-playing effect engaged in more improvisation than the subjects who spoke on the remaining issue. To be effective, they reasoned, the advocacy task had to stimulate the role-player to think up various arguments that would support his position. The supportive arguments, although somewhat convincing to members of the audience, were evidently especially convincing to the role-player himself, presumably because of the active process by which he had produced them. Janis and his colleagues' concern with active improvisation thus presaged persuasion researchers' interest in cognitive responses and message elaboration (see Chapters 6 and 7).

To examine this hypothesized improvisational process more closely, King and Janis (1956) varied the extent to which subjects had to improvise persuasive arguments.

All subjects first silently read a completely prepared script arguing that most male college students would be drafted soon after graduation (i.e., to participate in the Korean War) and be required to serve three or more years in the military. While being audiotaped, role-playing subjects then gave a talk in which they advocated the view taken by the script. In giving this talk, non-improvisational role-players merely read aloud from the script, whereas improvisational role-players had no further access to the script and therefore talked extemporaneously. As King and Janis expected, the subjects who improvised their talks showed considerably more belief change in the direction advocated by the talk compared with the subjects who read their talks from the script, and these non-improvisational role-players did not differ from the control subjects who had only read the script silently.[1]

Subsequent studies in the Janis and King tradition have confirmed that role-playing subjects generally change their attitudes and beliefs toward the positions they advocate and that role-playing typically produces greater change than passive exposure to comparable information (e.g., Culbertson, 1957; Elms, 1966; A. G. Greenwald & Albert, 1968; but see Stanley & Klausmeier, 1957). In a particularly vivid study of this genre, Janis and Mann (1965) had female subjects who were heavy smokers role-play a cancer patient who was told by a physician that she had a severe case of lung cancer and must have an operation even though there is little chance for full recovery.[2] The role-playing sessions were elaborately staged with the experimenter playing the role of a physician. In order to provide control subjects with the identical information as the role-playing subjects, control subjects each listened to an audiotape of one of the role-playing sessions. Measures of attitudes about smoking and intention to stop smoking showed that role-playing was more persuasive than passive exposure to the same information. In addition, a measure of self-reported smoking administered over the telephone two weeks later showed a greater reduction in smoking among role-playing than passive exposure subjects. More impressively, subsequent telephone surveys by an interviewer ostensibly unrelated to the study indicated that this difference between the two groups was maintained over an 18-month period (L. Mann & Janis, 1968).

Although these studies on role-playing demonstrated the general efficacy of the procedure for changing attitudes, they did not progress very far in explicating the psychological processes that might underlie role-playing effects, despite the insightfulness of Janis and King's (1954) speculations about mediation. King and Janis's (1956) demonstration that improvisation is important represented one advance, but the more general issue of the cognitive and motivational processes by which improvisational behavior acts to change attitudes remained unresolved. Janis in addition introduced his *biased scanning* interpretation of role-playing at a fairly early point but developed it only gradually, in concert with the Yale researchers' more general incentive-theory interpretation of attitude change, which we presented in Chapter 10 (see Elms & Janis, 1965; Hovland, Janis, & Kelley, 1953; Janis, 1959, 1968; Janis & Gilmore, 1965).

According to Janis's biased scanning hypothesis, an individual who improvises arguments that favor one side of an issue is temporarily motivated to think of arguments favoring that viewpoint. The incentives in the situation thus encourage the role-player to focus his thoughts on role-supportive arguments. He also suppresses thoughts that would be critical of the viewpoint because such thoughts are irrelevant to the assigned task. This *biased scanning* thus increases the accessibility of arguments that favor the position advocated by the role-player. However, consistent with the reinforcement perspective of the Yale researchers, mere accessibility was not thought to be sufficient to induce substantial attitude change. An additional feature had to be present—positive incentives in the form of anticipated positive consequences of the advocated position. The arguments themselves might produce these positive incentives, provided that the role-player "appraises the recalled or improvised arguments with a psychological set that fosters open-minded cognitive exploration of their positive incentive value, rather than a negativistic set of the type engendered by the arousal of hostility, resentment, or suspicion" (Janis, 1968, p. 811). Attitude change should thus be enhanced, not only by the presence of positive incentives associated with the advocated position, but also by the absence of negative incentives in the form of unfavorable expectations about the consequences of adopting the recommended position. Such unfavorable expectations could stem from the role-players' doubts or reservations about the prestige or motives of the person who induced the role-playing.[3]

Janis and his colleagues carried out two experiments designed to test the efficacy of this theoretical framework (Elms & Janis, 1965; Janis & Gilmore, 1965). Both of these experiments manipulated the incentives for writing a counterattitudinal essay by varying the sponsor who requested that subjects engage in the role-playing task. For example, in the Elms and Janis study, the experimenter asked students to advocate the position that American students should be allowed to attend college in the Soviet Union. In the positive sponsorship conditions, subjects learned that the experimenter represented a private attitude research firm that the U.S. State Department had contracted to survey American students' attitudes toward this exchange student program; subjects' arguments would be used to design questions for this survey. In the negative sponsorship conditions, subjects learned instead that the attitude research firm had been hired by the Soviet Union to prepare a pamphlet to distribute on all U.S. college campuses; subjects' arguments would be included in the booklet to convince American students of the merits of the program. In the manner of the cognitive dissonance experiments that we consider in the next section of this chapter, Janis and his colleagues also varied the monetary incentive offered to students for writing the essay.

These experiments showed that role-playing by writing out the requested arguments induced more attitude change with positive sponsorship than with negative sponsorship, although in the Elms and Janis (1965) experiment this effect was significant only with the larger monetary incentive. These experiments thus provided some support for the view that the self-persuasiveness of role-playing is controlled at least in part by the positive and negative incentives available as role-players engage in the biased scanning that allows them to accomplish their advocacy task. Still, these experiments did not progress very far in obtaining process measures that might directly document that biased scanning served as a mediator of attitude change. Yet as a step in this direction, Janis and his colleagues obtained judges' blind ratings of the role-players' essays and argued that open-minded exploration of role-supportive information would produce plausible, relatively high quality arguments. However, these ratings of the quality of subjects' essays did not consistently covary with attitude change in this research program.

Janis's ideas about biased scanning have much in common with the views developed somewhat later by cognitive response researchers, who argued that the thoughts generated by recipients of persuasive messages are critical in mediating attitude change (A. G. Greenwald, 1968; Petty, Ostrom, & Brock, 1981). As we showed in Chapter 6, these researchers were successful in designing measures that documented this mediational process. With the benefit of these methodological developments, it would be useful to return to Janis's ideas about biased scanning to explore in more detail the function of role-players' constructive thinking and perceptions of the incentives associated with the position they advocate.

In subsequent research consistent with Janis's ideas about biased scanning, A. G. Greenwald (1969, 1970) argued that an underlying factor accounting for the tendency of improvisational role-players to change toward the positions they advocate is that they are especially receptive to information supporting their roles. Given that the role-player is motivated to do a good job of carrying out the fairly challenging task of improvising convincing arguments that favor a particular attitudinal position, information that supports that role is quite useful. In other words, role-supportive information has some positive incentive value merely because it allows the role-player to perform the advocacy task competently. To substantiate this view, Greenwald (1969) had subjects merely *expect* to play a role that took the form of writing an essay; they were randomly assigned to advocate the virtues of a general liberal arts education or a specialized career preparatory education. While expecting to play the assigned role, subjects were presented with arguments favoring and opposing their assigned position and rated these statements for their validity. Subjects rated statements favoring their assigned position as more valid than statements that opposed it. Moreover, their attitudes on the education issue were influenced in the direction of their assigned position.

The research literature on role-playing thus established that contemplation of an attitudinal position either during a role-playing performance or in anticipation of that performance can change attitudes and can be more effective than the passive reception of information that is typical of the persuasion experiments we considered in Chapters 6, 7, and 8. However, role-playing is not universally persuasive and is more likely to be convincing when role-players must improvise their arguments and are exposed to positive incentives for adopting their advocated positions. These findings should be viewed in the context of the experimental settings in which improvisational role-playing has been studied—a context that probably encouraged role-players to give thorough consideration to the persuasive arguments they generated and delivered. Such scrutiny of information resembles the type of processing that we have labeled *systematic* in this book (see Chapter 7). Consistent with the interpretation that improvisation induces systematic processing, improvisational role-playing can have particularly enduring persuasive effects (L. Mann & Janis, 1968; Watts, 1967) and is especially impactful for people who are relatively high in verbal intelligence (Watts, 1973, 1977) and fantasy ability (Elms, 1966).

The practical value of improvisation as a persuasive technique is considerable. At least an an implicit level, this value has not gone unrecognized. Advertisers who sponsor contests that require consumers to submit advertising slogans capitalize on improvisational role-playing. Similarly, many religions feature improvisation as part of their ceremonies and other activities—for example, silent praying, recounting one's personal religious experiences to members of the congregation, and engaging in proselytizing to recruit new members into the group. When unconvinced or doubting members of religious groups engage in these behaviors, they are likely to alter their own religious attitudes in the direction of greater faith. Self-help groups committed to behavior change, such as Weight Watchers and Alcoholics Anonymous, also make extensive use of personal testimony in their programs. Moreover, role-playing is an important component of many programs designed to reduce prejudice (e.g., Byrnes & Kiger, 1990). Finally, many educators believe that students gain more from active participation—in class discussions, for instance—than from mere passive exposure to information in a lecture format.

Cognitive Dissonance and Counterattitudinal Advocacy

Classic Period of Dissonance Research

Challenging the incentive theory viewpoint of Janis and his colleagues, Leon Festinger developed an interpretation of counterattitudinal role-playing based on his theory of cognitive dissonance (see Chapter 10). In Festinger's highly streamlined interpretation of role-playing, subtleties such as biased scanning and improvisational versus non-improvisational role-playing were ignored. The role-player who advocates a position different from his or her private attitude was regarded simply as possessing two cognitions that were dissonant with one another. One of these cognitions, or cognitive elements, corresponds to the role-player's private attitude, and the other to the position advocated in the role-playing behavior. Festinger (1957) viewed these elements as dissonant because "the overt expression or behavior would certainly not follow from the private opinion considered alone" (p. 89). The resulting state of arousal that Festinger termed *dissonance* was assumed to cause the type of attitude change that Janis and King (1954) and other researchers had observed in their role-playing experiments. In other words, such attitude change occurs in the service of dissonance reduction.

In Festinger's (1957) initial statement of cognitive dissonance theory, he proposed that the self-persuasive effects of counterattitudinal advocacy depended on the incentive used to induce the individual to advocate a counterattitudinal position. As implied by the term *forced compliance* that Festinger applied to counterattitudinal role-playing situations, some inducement is required to motivate people to advocate a view that violates their own attitudes; in the absence of at least some threat of punishment or offer of reward, people would not ordinarily take attitude-inconsistent positions. In the experimental situations in which counterattitudinal advocacy was typically studied, subjects were thus to some degree *forced* to *comply* with an experimenter's request to advocate a particular view. However, because the word *force* implies a higher level of pressure than the mild pressures actually used in dissonance experiments, forced compliance is something of a misnomer, and the term *induced compliance* came to be preferred by many psychologists (e.g., J. Cooper & Fazio, 1984).

The strength of the inducement used to influence people to advocate a counterattitudinal position was a decisive variable for Festinger. Building his argument on an earlier experiment by Kelman (1953) that had manipulated the incentive that role-players were offered for counterattitudinal advocacy, Festinger maintained that the *strength of the justification* or inducement used to produce the role-playing is the critical feature controlling the amount of attitude change. The rationale for this prediction was that the inducement provides the role-player with cognitions consonant with the counterattitudinal behavior; a strong inducement can thoroughly justify taking a position in violation of one's own attitudes. From a dissonance theory perspective, justification is important because the magnitude of dissonance reflects the proportion of cognitive elements that are in dissonant relation with one another (see Chapter 10). Because justification adds one or more elements consonant with the element representing the counterattitudinal behavior, the total amount of dissonance in this multi-element situation is less than it would be if this justification were more minimal and the role-player therefore had only two dissonant elements in mind (i.e., the behavioral element and the element corresponding to the attitude). Festinger thus maintained that attitude change would be maximal when the reward or punishment offered for compliance with the request to take the attitude-discrepant position is just sufficient to elicit compliance. Having only two highly dissonant cognitions in mind with just-sufficient justification, the role-player is highly motivated to reduce the unpleasant arousal that results, and changing her attitude toward the counterattitudinal behavior reduces the dissonance. Attitude change makes the role-player more favorable toward what she said, and she is then faced with less inconsistency between her attitude and her behavior.

Dissonance theory posed an obvious challenge to the incentive ideas developed by Janis and his colleagues (e.g., Hovland et al., 1953; Janis, 1959; Janis & King, 1954) because the dissonance principle about the effects of justification led to the prediction that attitude change would be greater with *smaller* than larger rewards. According to Janis's incentive theory ideas, the counterattitudinal role-player should be especially persuaded to the extent that the position he or she advocates is associated with positive incentives (i.e., reward) and an absence of negative incentives (i.e., avoidance of a threatened punishment). More generally, Festinger's justification prediction violated the then-popular secondary reinforcement idea that reinforcing a behavior should stamp in associated cognitions more thoroughly with a large than a small reward. Because of this apparent conflict with incentive and reinforcement notions as well as a presumed violation of people's intuition about the effects of rewards or justification, dissonance predictions about induced compliance were widely regarded as counter-intuitive and nonobvious.[4]

The Festinger and Carlsmith (1959) Experiment. To test dissonance theory logic, Festinger and Carlsmith conducted an experiment that turned out to be one of the most controversial ever conducted in social psychology and, when all was said and done, one of the most influential. Serving as subjects in an experiment that ostensibly had to do with "measures of performance," male undergraduates spent an hour performing two tasks that had been designed to be very boring: putting spools onto a tray and turning pegs on a board. Afterwards, the experimenter disclosed that the study concerned the effect that a prior expectation has on task performance and explained that subjects in another experimental group were being given a favorable expectation about the task. According to the experimenter, this expectation was usually conveyed by an assistant who, pretending to be a subject who had just finished the experiment, told a waiting subject that the experiment had been enjoyable and intriguing. Claiming that the assistant who was supposed to perform this chore had failed to show up, the experimenter then asked the subject to fill in for the absent assistant by conveying this expectation to the next participant. The experimenter promised the subject money for this service and for being on call in the future if help was needed again. He also told the subject that the decision to help out with the experiment was up to him. The fact that only 3 out of the 51 subjects who served in the role-playing conditions refused to be hired suggests that the students who participated in the experiment were fairly willing to deliver this little white lie.

Festinger and Carlsmith (1959) introduced the critical incentive manipulation at the point the money was mentioned by offering half of their experimental subjects $1 and half $20 for engaging in the counterattitudinal behavior. Because the inducement to comply with the experimenter's request was much greater with the larger amount of money, the counterattitudinal behavior should have been perceived by subjects as thoroughly justified in this condition, and little dissonance and, therefore, little attitude change toward the counterattitudinal statements should have occurred. The $1 reward was designed to provide just enough pressure to induce subjects to comply but an insufficient rationale for them to believe that their behavior was justified by the money. The result was predicted to be maximum dissonance and considerable attitude change.

In the $1 and $20 experiment, the subject then engaged in what was evidently a very brief rendition of improvisational role-playing by praising the experiment to a con-federate who pretended to be waiting to participate. This confederate appeared to be convinced by the subject's statements. Next the subject was referred to an interviewer, who was supposedly conducting a survey associated with the introductory psychology course. This interviewer asked, among other questions, how interesting and enjoyable the experimental tasks involving the spools and pegs had been. As shown in Table 11.1, subjects who had been offered $1 for praising the experiment evaluated the tasks significantly more favorably than did subjects who had been offered $20. The subjects offered $20 did not differ from the control subjects, who participated in the dull tasks but not the part of the experiment that involved making insincere statements to the confederate. Although three other items did not produce significant findings (see Table 11.1), these other questions were less relevant to the subject's counterattitudinal advocacy than the question about how interesting and enjoyable the tasks were. The

TABLE 11.1

Mean Attitudes Toward Dull Task in the Festinger and Carlsmith (1959) Experiment

Question in interview	No-advocacy control	Twenty dollar incentive	One dollar incentive
How enjoyable and interesting tasks were (rated from –5 to +5)	–0.45	–0.05	1.35
How much subjects learned (rated from 0 to 10)	3.08	3.15	2.80
Scientific importance (rated from 0 to 10)	5.60	5.18	6.45
Participate in similar experiment (rated from –5 to +5)	–0.62	–0.25	1.20

Note: On the first question, the one dollar condition differed significantly from the twenty dollar condition and from the no-advocacy control condition, $ps < .05$. Comparisons on the other items were not significant.

Source: This table was adapted from one presented by Festinger and Carlsmith (1959, Table 1, p. 207).

results of this experiment thus confirmed Festinger's prediction that increased justification for role-playing would reduce attitude change toward the advocated view.

Several other early experiments that varied justification for taking a counterattitudinal position also obtained evidence that self-persuasion was greater with smaller incentives, although these studies were somewhat less convincing than the Festinger and Carlsmith (1959) experiment on account of the complexity of their justification manipulations as well as other procedural details (e.g., Brock & Blackwood, 1962; A. R. Cohen, Brehm, & Fleming, 1958; Rabbie, Brehm, & Cohen, 1959). Two of Festinger's associates, Jack Brehm and Arthur Cohen, summarized the then-existing evidence from the dissonance studies of counterattitudinal role-playing in their 1962 book *Explorations in Cognitive Dissonance* and included a brief report of a previously unreported counterattitudinal advocacy study by Cohen (pp. 73–78). In this experiment, four levels of rewards, varying from $0.50 to $10.00, were offered to induce Yale undergraduates to write an essay in favor of the New Haven police, who had been recently accused of brutality toward students in an incident of student rioting. Consistent with Festinger's prediction, the attitude change detected after this essay-writing task was greater to the extent that a smaller monetary inducement had been used. This inverse relation between incentive (i.e., justification) and attitude change came to be known as the *dissonance effect*.[5]

Criticisms of the Induced Compliance Paradigm. To write that the Festinger and Carlsmith (1959) experiment attracted attention would be an understatement. Debates over the merits of this experiment raged among social psychologists in many universities. Some considered the experiment quite convincing (A. R. Cohen, 1964; Zajonc, 1960a). Others regarded it as an excellent illustration of all that was wrong, not only with dissonance research, but with much of experimental social psychology—the web of deceit woven in the experimental procedure, the casual elimination of subjects who did not accept the experimental situation at face value, and the tenuousness of interpretations generated in the absence of converging evidence from multiple dependent variables (see Chapanis & Chapanis, 1964; Elms, 1967). Still other commentators took a middling view that recognized the ambiguities of the Festinger and Carlsmith study but accepted its basic claims (R. Brown, 1965).

Specific criticisms were proposed by researchers who suggested that the inverse relation between incentive and attitude change was the product of a particular artifact. For example, the large reward used in the high incentive condition of the Festinger and Carlsmith (1959) experiment might have produced shock, surprise, and suspicion in subjects and thereby lowered attitude change because the ostensibly positive incentive provided by the money actually functioned as a negative incentive (Chapanis & Chapanis, 1964; Elms, 1967; Janis & Gilmore, 1965). Similarly, the high reward might have caused subjects to suffer from *evaluation apprehension*, a belief that their mental health or honesty was being evaluated (M. J. Rosenberg, 1965b). Although the critics who argued in these terms offered experiments showing that such artifacts could indeed be produced in counterattitudinal advocacy studies, suffice it to say that these critiques did not prove compelling in the long run. Festinger and Carlsmith's offer of the $20 had been very carefully staged so that subjects believed the reward was for the single counterattitudinal advocacy *and* for being on call the rest of the semester to perform the same role on what might turn out to be a number of additional occasions. In addition, to provide some protection against artifacts such as evaluation apprehension and demand characteristics, the attitudinal dependent variable had been separated from the other experimental procedures by having a supposedly independent interviewer administer the attitudinal measures. Although critics proposed that the dissonance experiments on counterattitudinal advocacy had a number of other flaws as well (e.g., inappropriate rejection of subjects from some conditions, faulty statistical analyses; see Chapanis & Chapanis, 1964), later experimentation that was much freer from such methodological flaws satisfactorily established the replicability of the dissonance effect under conditions similar to those of the Festinger and Carlsmith experiment.

The Dissonance Effect in Alternative Paradigms. Another reason that the dissonance experiments survived the first round of methodological criticisms with their claims intact is that the dissonance effect was repeatedly obtained in experiments involving quite different types of counterattitudinal behavior than the improvisational role-playing featured in the Festinger and Carlsmith (1959) paradigm.[6] Given Festinger's uncomplicated interpretation of induced compliance in terms of an inconsistency between two cognitive elements—one corresponding to an attitude and the other to an attitude-discrepant behavior, there should be many ways of creating this type of dissonance. Simple behavioral acts that violate one's attitudes should have the same impact as more complex improvisational speeches. In experiments inducing such behaviors, subjects either (a) engaged in a behavior that they negatively evaluated or (b) refrained from engaging in a behavior that they positively evaluated. The justification that subjects were promised in return for their counterattitudinal behavior took several forms as well.[7]

Experiments in which subjects engaged in a behavior that they negatively evaluated include the grasshopper experiments loved by writers of social psychology textbooks. Following the precedent set in the original grasshopper experiment (E. E. Smith, 1961), Zimbardo, Weisenberg, Firestone, and Levy (1965) contributed the best-known of these studies. In this experiment, justification was manipulated by varying the attractiveness of an experimenter who attempted to induce subjects to eat grasshoppers: He was either friendly and affable or unfriendly and cold. Presumably the attractiveness of the experimenter provided a reasonably good justification for engaging in the counter-attitudinal act of eating grasshoppers, whereas justification was minimal with the unattractive experimenter. Therefore, more dissonance should have been induced when grasshoppers were eaten at the behest of the unattractive communicator. Among the subjects who actually ate one or more grasshoppers (approximately 50%), the findings were consistent with dissonance theory: The subjects who complied with the unattractive experimenter reported themselves more in favor of grasshoppers as food than the subjects who complied with the attractive experimenter (see also Powell, 1965; Schlenker, 1975). Other dissonance experiments invoking this same logic have induced subjects to engage in several other disagreeable behaviors for high or low justification—for example, eating a disliked vegetable (J. W. Brehm, 1960), writing down numbers or plus and minus symbols in the small squares on a piece of graph paper (Freedman, 1963), administering electric shock to another subject (Brock & Buss, 1962), and reading to another subject an extremely negative evaluation of his personality (K. F. Davis & Jones, 1960).[8]

Experiments in which subjects were enjoined from engaging in a favorably evaluated behavior include the *forbidden toy* studies. In this research, children were told that they should not play with a certain toy, and the justification for staying away from the toy was varied. In the first of these experiments, Aronson and Carlsmith (1963) allowed each of the preschool children who participated in the experiment to play with five toys and then had each child indicate his or her preferences for these toys. The experimenter then placed the second-ranked toy on a table and forbade the child to play with it. In the severe threat condition, which provided a strong justification for compliance, the child was told that playing with this toy would result in the experimenter being very angry, taking all of the toys away, and thinking that the child was "just a baby" (Aronson & Carlsmith, 1963, p. 585). In the mild threat condition, which provided only a weak justification for compliance, the experimenter merely said that he would be annoyed if the child disobeyed.

After the experimenter left the room, none of the children played with the forbidden toy. Upon returning, the experimenter allowed the child to play with all of the toys and then obtained the child's rankings of the five toys once again. This situation produced counterattitudinal behavior in the sense that the behavior of *not playing* with the toy was inconsistent with the child's positive attitude toward the toy. Yet, viewed from the dissonance perspective, the severe threat condition did not create much dissonance because it provided the child with a good justification for his compliant behavior. Dissonance should have been greater in the mild threat condition, and, consistent with this interpretation, the children in this condition valued the toy less highly on the second ranking than the children in the severe threat condition did.

This relation between threat and children's attitudes proved replicable within the forbidden toy paradigm (e.g., Lepper, 1973; Pepitone, McCauley, & Hammond, 1967; Turner & Wright, 1965; Zanna, Lepper, & Abelson, 1973). In one of these replications (Freedman, 1965b), fourth grade boys were restricted from playing with a very attractive robot toy and then were brought back to the experimental room to participate in an apparently unrelated study approximately forty days later. Even though the children were told that they could play with any of the toys, only 33 percent of the children who had been in the mild threat condition at the first session but 71 percent who had been in the severe threat condition played with the robot. These behavioral differences presumably reflected the more negative attitudes that the children in the mild threat condition held toward the robot. Given the 40-day period between the two sessions of the experiment, this finding suggests that dissonance effects represent more than just ephemeral shifts in attitudes (see discussion of impression management interpretation later in this chapter).

Evolution of Dissonance Theory

As the question of the sheer replicability of the dissonance effect eroded, the important issue that researchers faced was understanding in a more abstract way what the conditions are for obtaining the inverse relation between justification for an attitude-discrepant behavior and attitude change. Subsequent experimentation established that these conditions are quite specialized. Although Festinger and his colleagues no doubt had an intuitive understanding of how to tailor experimental settings to produce the findings predicted by dissonance theory, they did not identify these specialized conditions in their early formulations of the theory. Instead, the experimentation was guided by many implicit understandings, as suggested by Aronson's (1968) statement that, "Although investigators who have had experience working with the theory seem to have little difficulty intuiting its boundary conditions, they have had considerable difficulty communicating this to other people; indeed, a situation has evolved which can best be described by the statement: 'If you want to be sure, ask Leon.'" (p. 8). These intuitive understandings became explicit only very gradually as researchers varied aspects of the induced compliance situation and found that they could make the dissonance effect appear and disappear. In response to these experimental findings, the researchers active in dissonance experimentation, a dwindling cohort, gradually modified the theory to accommodate the implications of this new knowledge. The expanded theory lacks the elegant simplicity of Festinger's original statement and therefore has failed to remain at center stage in social psychology. Modern dissonance theory is a more elaborate structure capable of predicting attitude change in a much narrower range of situations than Festinger had originally envisioned.

Freedom of Choice. We do not review in detail the individual experiments by which dissonance theory evolved but refer the reader to several books and chapters that provide such reviews (J. W. Brehm & Cohen, 1962; J. Cooper & Fazio, 1984; Wicklund & Brehm, 1976). To initiate a brief summary of the major limiting conditions for producing the inverse relation between incentive and attitude change, we note that a number of studies have shown that this effect is obtained only when subjects believe that they have *freedom of choice* to engage in the counterattitudinal act (Holmes & Strickland, 1970; Linder, Cooper, & Jones, 1967; S.J. Sherman, 1970). In typical manipulations of choice the experimenter stressed to high choice subjects that the decision to engage in the counterattitudinal advocacy was up to them, whereas the experimenter made no such statements to low choice subjects and merely acted as if they would be willing to comply with his request. Of course, choice was somewhat illusory in dissonance experiments because subjects rarely refused the experimenter's request to advocate the counterattitudinal position.[9] Nonetheless, because coercion in the form of an absence of free choice provided a justification for subjects to behave contrary to their attitudes, the effect of perceived choice is understandable in terms of the justification idea that Festinger had originally emphasized. Indeed, early experiments in which choice but not inducement to comply was manipulated showed that attitude change toward the attitude-discrepant behavior was greater when the experimenter offered subjects a choice about engaging in the behavior (e.g., Brock, 1962; Brock & Buss, 1962; Cohen & Latané in J.W. Brehm & Cohen, 1962, pp. 88–91).

Commitment. The importance of another variable, *commitment to the counterattitudinal behavior*, is somewhat less obvious in terms of the original statement of dissonance theory and proved quite consequential in the evolution of the theory. The commitment variable was introduced by J.W. Brehm and Cohen (1962), who realized that the version of dissonance theory that Festinger had presented in *A Theory of Cognitive Dissonance* (1957) did not allow for clear predictions about whether attitude change or some other dissonance-reducing response would follow from attitude-discrepant behavior. Why couldn't counterattitudinal role-players merely change their behavior (or their memory of their behavior) or seek out cognitive elements consonant with their behavior—dissonance-reducing reactions that would be consistent with Festinger's statement of his theory? In the logic of the typical dissonance study, such as the Festinger and Carlsmith experiment (1959), these alternative modes of reducing dissonance were presumably closed off or unavailable, and attitude change remained as the only viable method for reducing dissonance. Understanding why certain modes of reducing dissonance might be unavailable was initially somewhat vague, although Festinger had maintained that cognitive elements, especially those corresponding to one's behavior, are *resistant to change* when they are firmly anchored in an unalterable reality (e.g., of having recently engaged in a behavior in a clear-cut way). Somewhat later Brehm and Cohen provided a more definite statement of this logic when they argued that *commitment* to a dissonant cognitive element makes it resistant to change and thus displaces dissonance pressures onto one or more other elements.

For Brehm and Cohen, commitment occurs "when a person engages in an activity or when he decides on one thing rather than another" (Brehm & Cohen, 1962, p. 8).[10] Advocating an attitudinal position is thus an instance of engaging in an activity. Presumably such an act makes the corresponding cognitive element (e.g., I said X) difficult to change or cognitively distort. In the prototypical dissonance experiment, commitment was established by having subjects publicly engage in the insincere behavior of advocating a position with which they disagreed. No chance was provided for subjects to undo this behavior or renege on their advocacy, and the recency and clarity of the behavior made it difficult for subjects to distort its meaning or to believe that they had actually not engaged in the behavior. According to this reasoning, attitude change remained the only viable way to reduce the inconsistency between attitude and behavior.

Without the addition of the commitment variable, dissonance theory had no clear prediction about how people would respond to inconsistent cognitive elements, and therefore Brehm and Cohen (1962) essentially restricted the theory to situations in which commitment is present.[11] By taking this step, these theorists greatly limited the scope of dissonance theory, but enabled it to become a predictive theory in a more formal sense than it possessed when the theory appeared to be simple but the tests of its propositions were actually guided by a set of intuitive and extratheoretical understandings.

Consistent with Brehm and Cohen's (1962) insights about commitment, dissonance researchers attempted to show that the dissonance effect (i.e., greater attitude change with less justification for counterattitudinal behavior) occurs only when the behavior is carried out in a manner that *commits* subjects to their positions. In research by Carlsmith, Collins, and Helmreich (1966) and Helmreich and Collins (1968), high commitment was induced by publicly identifying subjects with their counterattitudinal statements in such a manner that they could not recant their statements. In contrast, commitment was assumed to be low when subjects merely wrote an anonymous essay, audiotaped their views without disclosing their names, or videotaped their views while anticipating an opportunity to recant these statements (see also K. F. Davis & Jones, 1960). Although the findings of these and other experiments suggested that commitment to the counterattitudinal position is critical to obtaining the dissonance effect, some research failed to produce the expected effects of commitment (e.g., Melson, Calder, & Insko, 1969). At best, the exact determinants of commitment remained poorly understood. For example, the Carlsmith and colleagues' (1966) experiment suggested that public advocacy was critical and that dissonance would not be produced by private, anonymous essay writing, yet many experiments that produced the dissonance effect involved relatively anonymous essay-writing tasks (e.g., Brock, 1962; Cohen in Brehm & Cohen, 1962, pp. 73–78). As Kiesler (1971) subsequently argued, there are probably many different conditions that can commit people to their advocacy of an attitudinal position—for example, (a) the irrevocability of the advocacy and (b) the explicitness of the advocacy in terms of its public nature and the clarity of its meaning to the role-player.

Dissonance researchers also established that *mere commitment* to a counterattitudinal behavior (i.e., agreeing to engage in the behavior) is sufficient to produce attitudinal adjustments; actually engaging in an attitude-discrepant behavior is not a necessary condition for self-persuasion. For example, subjects merely agreed to spend three hours copying random numbers in an experiment by Brehm that obtained data supportive of dissonance predictions; the subjects did not actually copy the numbers (Brehm, reported in Brehm & Cohen, 1962, pp. 84–88). And, in an experiment by Waterman (1969), findings congenial to dissonance theory were obtained among subjects who only committed themselves to writing a counterattitudinal essay as well as among subjects who actually wrote such an essay. Moreover, Wilhelmy (1974) showed that *releasing* subjects from their commitment to perform a dissonance-arousing behavior (tasting bitter liquids) in the future reversed the attitude change that had been produced by committing them to this behavior for low justification.

Aversive Consequences. Based initially on experiments by Nel, Helmreich, and Aronson (1969) and J. Cooper and Worchel (1970), dissonance theorists (e.g., Collins, 1969) have argued that counterattitudinal behavior must lead to an unwanted or aversive consequence in order to produce the effects predicted by dissonance theory. An aversive consequence can be defined as one that "blocks one's self-interest or serves to bring about a situation that one would rather have not occur" (Goethals & Cooper, 1972, p. 300). In many of the empirical studies that have supported this generalization, aversive consequences consisted of having the target of one's counterattitudinal advocacy appear to be convinced by it. The rationale was that no harm has been done from the role-player's view if the target remains unconvinced; the dissonance that drives the attitudinal adjustments is presumably considerably less.

Cooper and Worchel's (1970) study, which was modeled closely on the Festinger and Carlsmith (1959) experiment, provided a clear demonstration of the effects of unwanted consequences. Subjects engaged in a dull peg-turning task and then told a waiting confederate that the task was interesting. Perceived choice to engage in this insincere behavior was maintained at a high level by asking subjects if they would be willing to fill in for an absent research assistant. To induce the behavior, subjects were offered either a high incentive of one full hour of additional experimental credit or a low incentive of one-half hour of credit. In addition to this conventional set of arrangements, Cooper and Worchel manipulated the aversiveness of the consequences of subjects' advocacy by having the waiting confederate either appear convinced by the subject's statements (undesirable consequence) or appear not convinced (desirable consequence). The dissonance effect of greater attitude change with the smaller incentive was obtained only for the subjects who apparently convinced the confederate. In fact, the only subjects who changed their attitudes, compared with the baseline provided by control (no advocacy) subjects, were those who convinced the confederate for the low inducement.

In a study that further refined understanding of unwanted consequences, Cooper, Zanna, and Goethals (1974) led subjects either to like or dislike the confederate to whom they delivered a counterattitudinal speech. To manipulate liking, subjects were shown a videotape of the confederate in which he behaved in either a polite, sincere, and generally nice way or an impolite, cynical, and generally unpleasant manner. This confederate appeared to be either convinced or not convinced by the subject's speech. Subjects changed their attitudes in the direction of their insincere advocacy only in the experimental condition in which the liked confederate appeared to be successfully convinced. Misleading another person apparently is not an aversive consequence if one has a negative attitude toward that person (see also Verhaeghe, 1976).

Although aversive consequences were first manipulated by having the confederate appear to be either convinced or not convinced, the variable has been operationalized in other ways, with similar results. For example, B. E. Collins and Hoyt (1972) had students write essays opposed to a popular "open visitation" dormitory policy and established aversive consequences by telling these subjects that university administrators would use the essay in deciding whether to make this policy permanent (vs. telling them that the essay would *not* be used by administrators). Although these experiments on unwanted consequences lack internal evidence that the consequences that researchers have labeled aversive were truly aversive to subjects, we judge that knowing that one's insincere statements are impactful or consequential at the very least makes the counterattitudinal role-player uncomfortable.

Personal Responsibility. Dissonance researchers have added the additional contingency that, for dissonance to occur, the person who engages in attitude-discrepant behavior must take personal responsibility for the consequences of the behavior. One type of evidence establishing the importance of a sense of personal responsibility for one's actions is that, as we have already explained, experimental conditions that confirm dissonance predictions give subjects at least the illusion that they have freedom of choice about engaging in counterattitudinal advocacy. Without choice, people would be unlikely to regard themselves as personally responsible for what they have done (see also Heider, 1958).

As understanding of responsibility was further honed in dissonance research, it became apparent that personal responsibility for one's actions could be established in more than one way. In an experiment that explored personal responsibility through a direct manipulation of this variable, Collins and Hoyt (1972) merely told subjects in one condition that they were responsible for the effects of their advocacy and in the other condition that they were not responsible for these effects. Zanna and Sande (1987) found that personal responsibility for counterattitudinal behavior can be reduced by having subjects engage in counterattitudinal behavior as a group action and therefore diffuse responsibility for the action to other group members. Other researchers have argued that the *foreseeability* of the aversive consequences of one's actions influences whether one feels personally responsible for these consequences. When people do things that turn out badly, they evidently do not feel responsible for the unfortunate consequences unless they foresaw that the action could have such consequences (see also Heider, 1958). This general point about the foreseeability of aversive consequences was established experimentally in research by Cooper (1971) and Hoyt, Henley, and Collins (1972). In addition, Goethals, Cooper, and Naficy (1979) displayed some of the subtleties of foreseeability by showing that the attitude change predicted by dissonance theory is produced if the unwanted consequence is merely retrospectively foreseeable when that consequence is finally made known. Thus, attitude change toward a counterattitudinal behavior is considerable if subjects merely think that they *should* have foreseen the aversive consequence of their behavior even though they did not in fact foresee it.

Conjunction of Conditions that Produce the Dissonance Effect. As experimental findings on induced compliance accumulated in the late 1960s and early 1970s, it was

515

initially somewhat difficult to discern whether one or several variables were necessary to produce the attitudinal effects predicted by dissonance theory. Was *choice* the critical condition, or *commitment*, or perhaps *unwanted consequences*? As our review has noted, not all experiments on commitment, for example, indicated that this variable had the power to make dissonance effects appear and disappear. Because of these and other apparent inconsistencies in findings on induced compliance (e.g., Collins, Ashmore, Hornbeck, & Whitney, 1970; Nuttin, 1966, 1975), some observers of research programs on dissonance regarded these attitudinal effects as quite unstable and the evidence supporting dissonance theory as mixed (e.g., Elms, 1967; M.J. Rosenberg, 1968a). To a great extent, this unfavorable judgment was countered when it became clear that *all* of the various conditions are necessary to confirm dissonance predictions. Thus, neither choice, nor commitment, nor consequences, nor personal responsibility proved to be the critical condition. Rather, all of these conditions must be simultaneously present.

Among the early demonstrations of the multiple determination of dissonance effects are experiments by Calder, Ross, and Insko (1973) and Collins and Hoyt (1972). In the Calder and collaborators experiment, which was modeled after Festinger and Carlsmith's (1959) study, subjects were offered either two hours or one-half hour of experimental credit to tell a waiting confederate that a dull experimental task was interesting. Subjects were either given or not given a choice about engaging in this insincere behavior, and the confederate appeared to be either convinced (undesirable consequence) or unconvinced (desirable consequence) by this advocacy. As shown in Table 11.2, the effect predicted by dissonance theory (i.e., greater attitude change with lower incentive) was produced only in the presence of high choice and the undesirable consequence. Thus, both choice about engaging in a behavior and a negative outcome of this behavior were necessary for the dissonance prediction to be confirmed. The

TABLE 11.2

**Mean Attitudes Toward the Dull Task
in the Calder, Ross, and Insko (1973) Experiment**

Consequences and incentive	High choice	Low choice
Undesirable consequences		
Low incentive	21.33	9.60
High incentive	14.80	16.20
Desirable consequences		
Low incentive	13.20	12.33
High incentive	16.40	9.40

Note: Control group mean = 13.20. Means are on a scale ranging from 1 to 36, with higher numbers indicating greater enjoyment of the task.

Source: This table was adapted from one presented by Calder, Ross, and Insko (1973, Table 1, p. 91).

516

other conditions we have mentioned as critical to obtaining dissonance effects—commitment to the counterattitudinal behavior and personal responsibility for it—were present as well in this study, although they were not manipulated. Commitment followed from subjects' active advocacy in a situation that did not allow them to renege on their behavior. Moreover, at least in the high choice condition, subjects would have found it difficult to avoid taking personal responsibility for their behavior because its consequences were foreseen or at least clearly foreseeable.

In the conceptually similar Collins and Hoyt (1972) experiment, the subjects engaged in a counterattitudinal essay-writing task. As noted above, the consequences manipulation consisted of having the essay be used (vs. not used) by the administration; the personal responsibility manipulation consisted of telling the subjects that they were responsible (vs. not responsible) for the effects of their essay. Incentive was manipulated by offering $0.50 or $2.50 for writing the essay. In this experiment, attitude change was substantial only in the low incentive, undesirable consequences, high responsibility condition, which differed significantly from the other conditions in the design.

In recognition of the growing evidence that a conjunction of several conditions is necessary to produce the sort of attitude change studied by dissonance researchers, several investigators have argued that dissonance is produced by the belief that one is personally responsible for aversive consequences (e.g., Collins & Hoyt, 1972; Cooper & Fazio, 1984; A. G. Greenwald & Ronis, 1978). In the most detailed statement of this viewpoint, Joel Cooper and Russell Fazio (1984) maintained that processes leading to dissonance arousal begin when people notice that their actions have resulted in an aversive consequence that cannot be easily rectified. This perception then activates a search for responsibility for this consequence. Given freedom of choice and foreseeability of the consequence, people conclude that they are personally responsible, and dissonance is aroused (see Figure 11.1). Provided that this arousal is not misattributed to some external source (see subsequent discussion in this chapter), the behavior itself is regarded as the source of the discomfort, and people become motivated to reduce the dissonance. People can then reduce dissonance by changing their perception of the aversiveness of the outcome they produced. In the induced compliance paradigm, attitude change in the form of greater approval of the advocated position allows people to view the consequence of their insincere behavior as more benign—there is no problem in persuading someone to believe that a task is interesting if the task really is fairly interesting.

FIGURE 11.1. The sequence of events leading to dissonance arousal. The symbols are ⟶ dissonance path and ⟶ alternative possibilities. This figure was adapted from one presented by Cooper and Fazio (1984, Figure 1, p. 242).

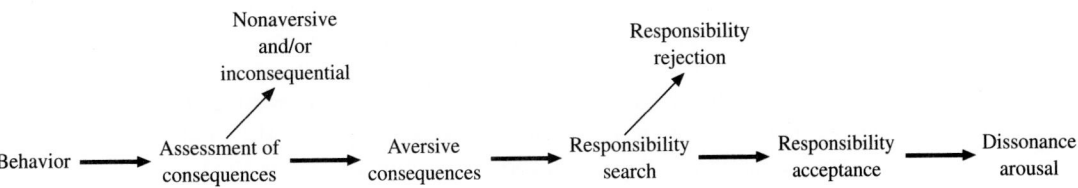

This interpretation delineates the cognitive inconsistency that produces dissonance in the induced compliance paradigm. It is not inconsistency between an attitude and a behavior that produces cognitive dissonance but, rather, responsibility for bringing about an unwanted consequence. This interpretation implies that an attitude-behavior inconsistency—engaging in counterattitudinal behavior or committing oneself to engage in such behavior—is not necessary to produce the attitudinal reorientations typical of dissonance experiments. To demonstrate this point, Scher and Cooper (1989) had subjects write an essay on student fees that was either proattitudinal (in support of a fee increase) or counterattitudinal (in opposition to a fee increase). All subjects were given the choice of declining to write this essay. They were also told that the essays would be given to the Dean's Committee on Policy, which was studying the matter of a fee increase. In addition, they learned that the first couple of essays a committee reads generally have a boomerang effect (i.e., "the opposite effect of the way they were written"; Scher & Cooper, 1989, p. 900), whereas the last couple of essays are convincing in the ordinary, straightforward way. In the boomerang condition, subjects learned that their essay would be the second one read by the Dean's Committee, and in the no boomerang condition, subjects learned that their essay would be the next to the last one read by the committee. Although subjects learned whether their essay would be read early or late only after they had written it, the experimenter had carefully explained the relation between the sequence of the essays and their persuasive direction at the outset of the experiment so that subjects would view the effect of their essays as foreseeable, regardless of whether they subsequently believed that their essay would produce straightforward persuasion or boomerang change.

If dissonance is produced by inconsistency between one's attitude and an attitude-relevant behavior, the boomerang manipulation should have had no impact, and all subjects who wrote counterattitudinal essays should have changed their attitudes in the direction of the position they advocated. In contrast, if dissonance is produced by the perception of responsibility for aversive consequences, attitude change in the form of increased approval of a student fee increase should have been greatest in the two experimental conditions in which subjects' essays were expected to influence the committee to increase student fees—among (a) subjects who wrote a counterattitudinal essay (i.e., favoring the fee increase) that they believed would have a straightforward persuasive impact and (b) subjects who wrote a proattitudinal essay (i.e., countering the fee increase) that they believed would have a boomerang impact. As shown in Figure 11.2, these predictions from the responsibility-for-aversive-consequences hypothesis were confirmed: Regardless of whether subjects wrote a proattitudinal or counterattitudinal essay, those who believed that their essays would have the unfortunate effect of causing the committee to favor raising student fees changed their attitudes more than subjects in the other conditions, including low choice control conditions in which subjects were not given a choice about writing their essay. This experiment thus established quite decisively that the attitudinal adjustments typically observed in induced compliance experiments are produced by responsibility for aversive consequences, not by attitude-behavior inconsistency *per se* (i.e., not by inconsistency between one's attitudinal position and the position one advocates).

518

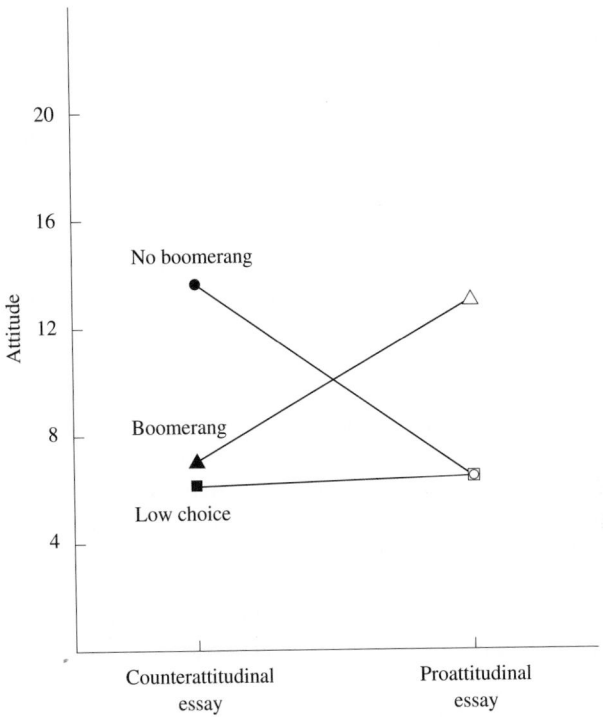

FIGURE 11.2. Mean attitudes toward increasing student fees on a 31-point scale on which higher numbers indicate more positive attitudes. This figure was presented by Scher and Cooper (1989, Figure 2, p. 904).

Although Cooper and his colleagues maintained that their responsibility-for-aversive-consequences interpretation and the results of the Scher and Cooper (1989) experiment require a fairly radical reorientation of dissonance theory away from its consistency theory heritage, we regard this provocative work as having more ambiguous implications. It provides one important piece of the puzzle that attitude researchers have been trying to assemble in this area: The results show that attitude-behavior discrepancy is not critical to producing attitude change. But what, then, is critical? Scher and Cooper suggested that responsibility for aversive consequences is distressing because of the disjunction between one's own wish for a certain outcome (i.e., for fees not to increase) and the tendency of one's behavior to thwart this outcome and instead to bring about a different, unwanted outcome (i.e., to increase the likelihood that a fee increase will take place).

Equally plausible as Cooper and colleagues' claim that the critical inconsistency is between one's wish and the impact of one's behavior is a "good person–bad deed" form of inconsistency. In fact, this alternative portrayal is consistent with an earlier balance theory interpretation by Insko, Worchel, Folger, and Kutkus (1975) (see Chapter 3). In accounting for induced compliance findings showing the importance of responsibility for aversive consequences, these authors maintained that the typical induced compliance experiment establishes an association between the subject's self, which is ordinarily positively evaluated, and his insincere advocacy, which is negatively evaluated because of its aversive consequences. This association between the self and these bad consequences is based on the perception of personal responsibility for the outcome, a link that balance theorists would interpret as a unit relation. The resulting unbalanced triad consists of (a) the subject and his self-concept (positive sentiment relation), (b) the subject and his behavior (negative sentiment relation), and (c) the subject's self-concept and his behavior (positive unit relation). This balance interpretation also does not regard attitude-behavior discrepancy as critical; rather, the conjunction between a good self and a bad deed produces the conditions that underlie attitudinal realignments.

Attitude Change without Responsibility for Aversive Consequences. As our presentation has shown, the attention of dissonance researchers became focused quite narrowly on delineating the conditions that produce the theory-relevant inverse relation between incentive for compliance and attitude change. As a result, the broader issue of understanding the various conditions under which role-playing and other behaviors change attitudes no longer attracted much attention. In an evolution that began with Brehm and Cohen (1962) and other dissonance researchers and proceeded to Cooper and Fazio's (1984) statement, the *dissonance theory of counterattitudinal behavior* was transformed from the quite general theory that Festinger (1957) had envisioned into a mini-theory that delineates a particular set of circumstances that produce a particular type of attitudinal adjustment within the induced compliance paradigm.

If we were to argue that responsibility for aversive consequences *must* be present for people's own behavior to change their attitudes, such change would occur only under a very limited set of circumstances. Although the issue of the ecological validity of experimental findings is difficult to address in any but the most speculative way, we can well wonder how common it is in daily life that people engage in attitude-discrepant behavior under conditions of free choice, high commitment, the production of aversive consequences, and personal responsibility for these consequences. Most attitude-relevant behavior may occur under conditions that fall short of meeting all of these requirements. Can such behavior affect attitudes when one or more of these requirements are *not* met?

The answer to this question is undeniably affirmative. Behavior does produce effects on attitudes in the absence of responsibility for aversive consequences, although the processes that mediate these effects are probably different from those illuminated by dissonance research. Negative consequences were unlikely to have been present, for example, in the early role-playing experiments conducted by Janis and King (e.g., 1954). That unwanted consequences are not necessarily critical has been shown even within experiments intended to demonstrate principles of cognitive dissonance. Not only do significant (albeit typically not large) amounts of attitude change sometimes occur in the absence of responsibility for aversive consequences, but also the patterning of change across experimental conditions sometimes approximates the predictions of Janis's incentive theory views (Janis, 1968; see prior discussion). Thus, when experiments include both a high incentive and a low incentive condition, a fairly common finding is that in the absence of one of the critical determinants of the dissonance effect, the relation between incentive and attitude change is positive, as predicted by incentive theory (e.g., Linder et al., 1967; Holmes & Strickland, 1970; S. J. Sherman, 1970). In predicting this positive relation, Janis had argued that role-players, who are engaged in biased scanning when producing their advocacy, should be more persuaded to the extent that genuinely positive incentives are present for role-playing (see prior discussion).

Some prototypical findings showing both a positive and a negative relation between incentive and attitude change were obtained by Calder and colleagues (1973) in the experiment varying choice and consequences that we have already described. As shown in Table 11.2, the negative relation between incentive (hours of experimental credit promised) and attitude (reported enjoyableness of the dull task) emerged in the condition providing both undesirable consequences and high choice. In contrast, in the condition with high consequences but low choice, the difference in the attitudes of the high and low incentive subjects was equally large, but the relation between incentive and attitude change was positive. In the two desirable consequences conditions the effect of incentive was relatively small (and nonsignificant). As these findings illustrate, incentives sometimes did relate positively to attitudes in dissonance experiments, but not within the responsibility-for-aversive-consequences conditions of these experiments. These positive relations were given little attention theoretically within the dissonance camp, but were frequently labeled *incentive effects*, to imply that some logic such as that proposed earlier by Janis (e.g., 1968) might account for them. Yet the conditions for obtaining such effects have not been well delineated, and the possibility that these effects might be due to reduced attitude change in low incentive conditions as well as increased change in high incentive conditions has not been sufficiently explored. In any event, the early view that "where little or no dissonance exists, an incentive effect emerges" (Aronson, 1969, p. 21) is insufficient to account for the available empirical findings, as can be seen by inspecting the outcome of the Calder et al. (1973) experiment in Table 11.2.

It is also typical in studies of counterattitudinal advocacy that attitude change is greatest in the cell of the design in which subjects experience the prototypical dissonance-producing conditions—in the Calder et al. (1973) study the high choice, undesirable consequences, low incentive cell. In fact, in this particular experiment only in this condition were subjects' attitudes significantly different from those of the control subjects, who did not engage in counterattitudinal advocacy. Thus, attitude change does appear to be especially great under the circumstances isolated by dissonance experimentation and succinctly stated by Cooper and Fazio (1984) in terms of personal responsibility for bringing about an unwanted consequence.

Self-Identity and Self-Presentation Interpretations of the Effects of Induced Compliance

Notwithstanding the accuracy of Cooper and Fazio's (1984) generalization about responsibility for aversive consequences as a statement of the conditions under which maximum attitude change occurs in induced-compliance experiments, this generalization does not sufficiently delineate the underlying conditions that create the motivational state known as cognitive dissonance. Indeed, we already made this point by describing Insko and colleagues' (1975) good person–bad deed interpretation, which illustrates the critical role that can be given to the self-concept in interpreting the findings of induced-compliance research. In this section, we discuss several other theorists' attempts to place the results of dissonance experimentation in a broader framework that explains *why* taking personal responsibility for unwanted events causes people to adjust their attitudes to rid themselves of this perception.

Before introducing these more recent theoretical efforts, we note that Festinger's own conception of induced compliance is no longer viable because he emphasized inconsistency between attitudes and behaviors, which now appears not to be critical. To provide a theoretical context that more adequately encompasses the now-large empirical literature on induced compliance, numerous theorists in addition to Insko and colleagues (1975) have invoked the self-concept and thus have argued that the attitude change manifested by counterattitudinal role-players allows them either to preserve a favorable view of themselves or to save face with others.

Self-Concept Interpretations

In the earliest self interpretation, Eliot Aronson (1968, 1969) suggested that subjects in dissonance experiments are trying to preserve a positive self-concept in the face of some threat to the self. Aronson argued that, across a range of dissonance paradigms (e.g., induced compliance, decision making; see Chapter 10), the dissonant cognitions are a positive self-concept and cognitions about some behavior. More specifically, Aronson maintained that the cognitions that created dissonance in the Festinger and Carlsmith (1959) and similar induced-compliance experiments are the following: " 'I am a decent truthful human being' and 'I have misled a person; I have conned him into believing something which just isn't true; he thinks that I really believe it and I cannot set him straight because I probably won't see him again'" (Aronson, 1968, p. 24). Although Aronson did not firmly restrict dissonance theory to self-relevant discrepancies, he regarded it as making its clearest predictions when some aspect of one's positive self-regard is at stake.

Aronson's (1968, 1969) self-concept interpretation seems quite plausible, especially in view of the emphasis on unwanted consequences that began to develop among dissonance researchers at about the same time (e.g., B. E. Collins, 1969; J. Cooper & Worchel, 1970), and it is even more plausible in terms of the experimentation that is now available. Accepting personal responsibility for consequences that impact adversely on other people, in the manner of the typical induced-compliance experiment, would seem to threaten one's self-concept as a decent and moral person. Yet this self-concept perspective remained to be developed into a comprehensive explanation of the effects obtained in dissonance experiments. In view of the many facets that the self-concept may have (e.g., public self, private self; see James, 1890/1952; Markus & Nurius, 1986), more detailed theorizing was required, along with systematic experimentation, before a self interpretation of dissonance could be regarded as more than an intriguing possibility.

Moral and Hedonic Dissonance. Emphasizing that at least two different aspects of the self-concept could be placed in jeopardy in typical induced-compliance experiments, Herbert Kelman and Reuben Baron (1968b, 1974) outlined a distinction between *moral dissonance* and *hedonic dissonance*. Kelman and Baron argued that moral dissonance arises from violations of important moral principles or values and that the arousal that is produced (see Chapter 10) would take on the coloration of guilt. In prototypical dissonance experiments raising issues of morality, subjects engaged in insincere behavior (Festinger & Carlsmith, 1959), cheated in a contest (Mills, 1958), shocked a helpless subject (e.g., Brock & Buss, 1962), or wrote an essay on personal reasons for becoming a Roman Catholic, despite the fact that they were non-Catholics (Brock, 1962).

Yet moral integrity was not the issue in all of the induced-compliance experiments. For example, in experiments by Wilhelmy (1974; Wilhelmy & Duncan, 1974), subjects merely agreed to taste bitter liquids. Although this commitment was presumably inconsistent with subjects' negative attitude toward this unpleasant behavior, the unwanted consequence was aversive merely to the subjects themselves and was unlikely to have compromised subjects' values or personal morality. Kelman and Baron (1968b, 1974) suggested that the term hedonic dissonance be applied to dissonance inductions of this type. Hedonic dissonance arises from violations of one's own standards of equity or reciprocity, which occurs when one receives insufficient reward for engaging in tasks that have little intrinsic value and that therefore are boring or unpleasant. The arousal produced in these situations would take on the coloration of feeling gullible, foolish, or inequitably treated rather than guilty. In prototypical dissonance experiments raising hedonic issues, subjects ate grasshoppers (Zimbardo et al., 1965) or disliked vegetables (J. W. Brehm, 1960) or wrote down numbers or symbols in the squares on a piece of graph paper (Freedman, 1963). Kelman and Baron reasoned that both types of violations of the self-concept would produce attitudinal adjustments (if opportunities for other sorts of resolutions were unavailable) but that variables such as the magnitude of incentives for counterattitudinal behavior would have different impact with moral and hedonic dissonance.[12]

The distinction between the two types of dissonance raises an important question in view of the fact that most of the research on induced compliance, modeled fairly closely after the Festinger and Carlsmith (1959) experiment, has pertained to the type of dissonance that Kelman and Baron labeled *moral*. Merely because of the relative lack of attention to hedonic dissonance, it is not clear whether some of the generalizations that dissonance research has yielded about the conditions that produce maximal attitude change would be valid for dissonance of the purely hedonic type. It would be consistent with Kelman and Baron's (1968b, 1974) theorizing to think that many of these generalizations would in fact *not* hold for hedonic dissonance.

Self-Presentation Interpretations

Impression Management View. In a reinterpretation of cognitive dissonance that featured self-presentation rather than self-identity, James Tedeschi, Barry Schlenker, and Thomas Bonoma (1971) maintained that a concern to appear consistent to other people underlies the attitudinal adjustments observed in induced-compliance experiments. According to this viewpoint, attitude change is more apparent than real in induced-compliance experiments because it is a strategic self-presentation that occurs at the level of subjects' public displays of their attitudes rather than their private, internalized attitudes. Change in subjects' attitudes is substantial with low inducement, high choice, and a lack of other compelling justifications for engaging in the counterattitudinal behavior because in these circumstances observers would probably make an internal attribution about the behavior, that is, they would ascribe the advocacy behavior to the role-player's own attitude (see discussions of self-perception theory later in this chapter and of attitudinal attribution in Chapters 1 and 8). In the presence of observers who are likely to make such an attribution, the role-player is motivated to feign consistency between her behavior and subsequent expressions of her attitude. If observers are likely to make a situational attribution instead, the role-player does not have to worry about appearing consistent because the observers would not draw conclusions about her real attitudes and intentions. In short, Tedeschi and his colleagues argued that the dissonance effects observed within the induced compliance paradigm reflect subjects' efforts to manage an impression of attitude-behavior consistency.

In a later statement of this impression management view of induced compliance findings, Tedeschi and Rosenfeld (1981) also took into account the importance of aversive consequences in dissonance experiments by arguing that subjects are concerned with managing an impression of moral integrity as well as of attitude-behavior consistency. In such experiments, subjects are induced to carry out actions with unfavorable impact on another person and appear to have carried out the action freely. Even though the experimenter has asked these subjects to behave in this way, they are likely to feel anxious and somewhat at risk for receiving a negative evaluation from him. This anxiety is presumably based on prior learning that causing others harm often brings social disapproval.

According to impression-management theory, in situations in which people engage in a disapproved action, they ordinarily provide (a) an *excuse*, which minimizes their intentionality or responsibility, or (b) a *justification*, which denies the negative meaning that the observer might otherwise give to their actions. The responsibility-denying device of giving an excuse is relatively unavailable in dissonance experiments because the perception of relatively free choice is carefully maintained. Subjects therefore take the justification route to saving face: Moderating their attitudes (e.g., toward the dull task) allows them a justification because it communicates to the experimenter that they did not advocate a position that they thought was truly wrong.

This provocative explanation of the findings of induced compliance experiments has generated quite a few empirical tests. Several of these studies used the *bogus pipeline* device for assessing attitudes (E. E. Jones & Sigall, 1971; see Chapter 2). This method is designed to motivate subjects to report their true attitudes by making them think that feigned responses will be revealed as duplicity by a lie detector apparatus. Supporting the impression management interpretation, some experiments using the bogus pipeline to measure attitudes following counterattitudinal advocacy have eliminated or greatly reduced the attitude change typically displayed by subjects in dissonance experiments (e.g., Gaes, Kalle, & Tedeschi, 1978; Paulhus, 1982; Riess, Kalle, & Tedeschi, 1981), but other experiments using the bogus pipeline and similar procedures have not shown these effects (J. Cooper, 1971; Guild, Strickland, & Barefoot, 1977; Jamieson & Zanna, 1982). Moreover, various reservations have been expressed about the adequacy of the bogus pipeline demonstrations that have favored the impression management view. In particular, the suggestion has been made that subjects might have misattributed their dissonance-produced arousal to their anticipation of having their attitudes assessed with the aid of a device strongly resembling a lie detector (see Riess et al., 1981; Stults, Messé, & Kerr, 1984; see subsequent discussion of misattribution). Although experimental efforts to compare the impression management and misattribution interpretations have had varying outcomes, the latest study (Tedeschi, Rivera, Dixit, Taylor, & Nesler, 1988) favors impression management and appears to have accounted for prior data that seemed to favor the misattribution critique (Stults et al., 1984). However, other alternative explanations exist for bogus pipeline effects.[13] Given the controversy that surrounds the adequacy of bogus pipeline procedures to circumvent demand characteristics and other self-presentational pressures (see Chapter 2), such demonstrations provide only suggestive evidence favoring the impression-management interpretation.

Another variation of induced-compliance experiments that is relevant to impression management entails making the counterattitudinal advocacy completely private. If the attitude change observed in induced-compliance experiments functions merely to rescue the impression that the subject has made on the experimenter, there is no rationale for such change provided that no one, not even the experimenter, knows about the subject's behavior. However, compromising the capacity of privacy manipulations to provide a critical test of dissonance as opposed to impression management is the fact that dissonance theorists have argued that public advocacy produces a stronger commitment to the counterattitudinal position and, hence, produces greater dissonance and attitude change (see discussion of commitment in prior section). In addition, as Gaes et al. (1978) argued, it may be difficult to convince subjects that their behavior is truly anonymous because they would ordinarily believe that their behavior is accessible to the experimenter, if not to a wider audience. Although elaborate procedures intended to establish true anonymity have reduced the attitude change typically obtained to a level not different from that shown by control subjects (e.g., Gaes et al., 1978; Malkis, Kalle, & Tedeschi, 1982), these findings do not present a strong challenge to dissonance theory.

Given the reliance of Tedeschi and his colleagues on the bogus pipeline methodology and on predictions about the impact of public versus private advocacy, the evidence remains ambiguous that the attitude change displayed in dissonance experiments is merely an uninternalized, feigned response intended to rescue a spoiled identity. We suspect that, even if self-presentational concerns are paramount in the situations created by induced-compliance studies, the subjects' attitudinal response may often not be discrepant enough from their private attitudes to be recognized by them as lies or distortions. More generally, whether attitudinal responses under the control of situational constraints (such as saving face with the experimenter) reflect attitude change that is in some sense *genuine* is an issue that is difficult to resolve. Attitudinal expressions dictated by impression management concerns do not necessarily entail a self-conscious attempt to manipulate an audience but instead may proceed without conscious attention to providing a response acceptable to an audience. Under such circumstances, the subject in an induced-compliance experiment may express a particular attitude to save face yet fully believe in this changed attitude when he expresses it. Thus, the expressed attitude may not be feigned in the sense that it is either consciously intended to deceive an audience or recognized as false by the subject (for discussion of related issues, see Leary & Kowalski, 1990; E. E. Jones & Pittman, 1982; Tetlock & Manstead, 1985).

Although an attitude expression that is under the control of situational pressures may often be ephemeral (see Chapter 13), it could induce attitude change that becomes internalized. In fact, various findings suggest that internalized change can follow from dissonance-producing situations. For example, Collins and Hoyt (1972) reported that changed attitudes were manifested on a survey that was administered two weeks after their induced-compliance experiment and portrayed to subjects as independent of the experiment. As noted earlier, Freedman (1965b) found behavioral evidence for the attitudinal effects predicted by dissonance theory forty days after the event that had induced the dissonance; Lepper (1973) found evidence nineteen days after the event. And, in a field study with delayed attitudinal and behavioral measures, Staw (1974) investigated students who had joined the Reserve Officer Training Corps (ROTC) shortly before the institution of the draft lottery system in 1969 during the Vietnam War. The low dissonance condition consisted of ROTC students who received low lottery numbers, making it likely they would be drafted and thereby creating high justification for ROTC participation. The high dissonance condition consisted of ROTC students who received high lottery numbers, making it unlikely they would be drafted and creating low justification for ROTC participation. Over a year later students who had received high lottery numbers and presumably had experienced cognitive dissonance indicated that they were more satisfied with ROTC than were students who had received low lottery numbers. Moreover, students with the high numbers performed better and received higher grades in their military sciences courses two semesters later. Although the relevance of this powerful, naturalistic manipulation of dissonance to the manipulations used in laboratory experiments remains uncertain, surely the effects obtained by Staw reflect private, internalized attitude change.

If we broaden our view of impression management to encompass attitude change that is under the control of situational pressures but is not necessarily feigned or limited to the public expression of the attitude, a number of experiments carried out by investigators other than Tedeschi and his colleagues become relevant to substantiating a self-presentational interpretation of induced-compliance experiments. The most convincing evidence in favor of this modified impression management interpretation of dissonance findings can be found in a series of experiments by Scheier and Carver (1980). Crucial to this research is the concept of self-attention, which is defined as the directing of one's attention inward toward the self. Yet attention can be directed mainly toward the private self, creating private self-attention, or toward the public self, creating public self-attention (see Buss, 1980; Fenigstein, Scheier, & Buss, 1975; Scheier & Carver, 1981). Private self-attention entails increased awareness of the private self, that is, of one's personal thoughts, values, attitudes, and the like; public self-attention entails increased awareness of the public self, that is, of the aspects of the self that are displayed to others. People are assumed to differ in their chronic tendency to be privately or publicly self-attentive, and this tendency has been assessed by a self-report instrument known as the Self-Consciousness Scale (Fenigstein et al., 1975). Also, situations can induce private or public self-attention, and experimental manipulations have been developed that heighten one or the other form of self-attention. In particular, placing subjects before a mirror is assumed to produce private self-attention, whereas placing subjects before a camera, videotaping equipment, or an audience is assumed to produce public self-attention.

In Scheier and Carver's (1980) studies, subjects were given high or low choice to write a counterattitudinal essay arguing that students should have little or no control over the university curriculum. In one experiment, the type of self-attention a situation induced was experimentally manipulated by having subjects complete the attitude questionnaires either in front of a mirror (to create private self-attention) or with a TV camera focused on them (to create public self-attention). In another experiment, self-attention was varied by selecting subjects who were high in private or public self-consciousness according to their responses on the Self-Consciousness Scale.

In these two experiments, attitude change toward the counterattitudinal essays was greater when subjects had greater choice about writing the essay. Yet this attitude change manifested by high choice subjects was much more pronounced if they were publicly self-attentive, either on a situational basis (as induced by the camera compared with the mirror) or on a chronic basis (as defined by a high compared with a low score on the Self-Consciousness Scale). Subjects who were privately self-attentive on either basis reacted differently: They did not show much attitude change toward their essays but instead reinterpreted their essay-writing behavior by rating their essays as less opposed to student control than did other subjects. This perception of the essays appeared to be biased because it was not discerned by independent judges who rated the essays. These interesting findings are shown in Table 11.3, for the Scheier and Carver experiment that used the situational manipulation of self-attention. This research thus demonstrates that both the privately and publicly self-attentive subjects realigned their cognitions in this induced-compliance situation, but did so in different

TABLE 11.3

**Mean Attitudes Toward Student Control of Curriculum and Perceptions of
Counterattitudinal Behavior in the Scheier and Carver (1980) Experiment 2**

Dependent measure	No choice control	Choice control	Choice with mirror (Private self-attention)	Choice with camera (Public self-attention)
Attitude	29.44	35.15	33.06	40.68
Perception of behavior	10.56	14.77	20.48	9.16

Note: Means are on 61-point scales on which higher numbers indicate more favorable attitudes toward the position taken in counterattitudinal essay or perceptions of behavior as taking a weaker position.

Source: This table was adapted from one presented by Scheier and Carver (1980, Table 2, p. 397).

ways: The privately self-attentive subjects reinterpreted their behavior and thereby avoided any substantial change in their private attitudes, whereas the publicly self-attentive subjects changed their attitudes and thereby maintained an apparently objective interpretation of their behavior.

In addition to suggesting that dissonance can be reduced by alternative mechanisms, Scheier and Carver's (1980) findings can be viewed as providing support for a self-presentational interpretation of dissonance processes. This interpretation follows from the finding that attitude change, the response predicted by dissonance theory, was most pronounced when subjects were focused on the public aspects of their self-identity. If making subjects aware of others' reactions induces attitude change in induced compliance situations (and making them aware of their private attitudes reduces or eliminates this attitude change), the attitude change typical of these experiments may indeed arise from a desire to preserve a positive public identity, as Tedeschi and his colleagues have argued.

Using an innovative *template-matching* methodology, Bem and Funder (1978) also produced findings congenial to a self-presentational perspective. Reasoning that people are more likely to behave in a particular way if their personality matches the template that describes the type of person who would typically engage in that behavior, these investigators had expert judges create templates that described the kinds of people who would change their attitudes in induced-compliance experiments according to the predictions of dissonance theory, self-presentation theory, and self-perception theory (see later discussion in this chapter). By this template procedure, the ideal attitude changer according to dissonance theory was alert to inconsistencies and found inconsistencies aversive. The ideal attitude changer according to self-presentation theory was a helpful, cooperative, "good" subject who would likely conform to social norms—a somewhat different type than Tedeschi's more manipulative subject who feigns an attitudinal response. Subjects were each rated by two acquaintances on descriptive (Q-sort) items that typified the three theories; each subject thus received a score on each template. The attitude change that these subjects manifested after writing counterattitudinal essays under high choice conditions in a classic induced-compliance experiment was then correlated with scores on each of the templates. This correlation was highest for the impression management template ($r = .53$); it was intermediate for the self-perception template ($r = .32$; see subsequent discussion), and negative for the dissonance template ($r = -.25$). Yet these findings were not fully replicated in further research by Funder (1982), and it is difficult to weigh the implications of this rather complex methodology, which relies on the ability of expert judges to translate theoretical propositions into personality types.

Finally, in research by Paulhus (1982) exploring individual differences in induced-compliance situations, the attitude change that occurred in a prototypical dissonance-producing condition and in a control condition was assessed by regular paper-and-pencil measures and the bogus pipeline and related to measures of the tendency to be concerned with making a favorable impression (Need for Social Approval Scale, Crowne & Marlowe, 1964; Other Deception Questionnaire, Gur & Sackeim, 1979). Consistent with the impression management perspective, subjects concerned (vs. less concerned) with self-presentation showed greater attitude change only in the dissonance-producing condition and with the paper-and-pencil measure. The fact that this relation of attitude change to self-presentational concern was weaker in the control condition and near zero with bogus pipeline measurement is highly congenial to a self-presentational perspective. However, some other efforts to relate personality variables to attitude change have produced findings less congenial to the impression-management view (e.g., Chris & Zanna, 1981; McCann, Zanna, & Higgins, 1980).

Identity-Analytic View. Barry Schlenker, one of the authors of the Tedeschi and collaborators (1971) article that introduced the impression management interpretation of dissonance, has developed a broader identity-analytic interpretation of induced-compliance phenomena (Schlenker, 1980, 1982). In this later work, he has concurred with Tedeschi's view that the essential problem faced by counterattitudinal role-players is providing an acceptable explanation of their conduct. Integrating thinking about self-identity and self-presentation, Schlenker argued that the explanations people construct need to be acceptable both to themselves and to other people—both the public and the private self need to be defended in situations that appear to violate standards of appropriate conduct. Schlenker (1980, 1982) aptly characterized such situations as *predicaments*: "Predicaments are situations in which events have undesirable implications for the identity-relevant images actors have claimed or desire to claim in front of real or imagined audiences" (Schlenker, 1980, p. 125). Predicaments are more serious to the extent that these undesirable implications are very disagreeable and the actor is personally responsible for the event that has these implications. Serious predicaments threaten the actor's self-identity and may expose him or her to punitive responses from others. Schlenker argued that predicaments elicit *accounts*, which are explanations that maximize the desirability (and minimize the undesirability) of identity-threatening events. Paralleling Tedeschi and Rosenfeld's (1981) treatment is Schlenker's division of accounts into two classes: *excuses*, which minimize responsibility for an event, and *justifications*, which minimize the undesirable meaning of an event. Schlenker also maintained that the attitude change produced by counterattitudinal behavior that has undesired consequences should be classified as a justification because it minimizes the negative implications of the behavior. Yet, other reactions could also provide justifications [e.g., the behavioral reinterpretation typical of Scheier and Carver's (1980) privately self-attentive subjects].

Schlenker's (1982) viewpoint encompasses the responsibility-for-aversive-consequences interpretation evolved by Cooper and his colleagues (e.g., Cooper & Fazio, 1984). Undesirable consequences place subjects in a predicament, that is, in a situation in which they have violated standards for conduct and threatened their identities. Because of the high level of choice they perceive and the other constraints of the situation (e.g., no opportunity to explain themselves to the confederate), responsibility-denying excuses are difficult to manage, and instead, a justification is in order—attitude change that makes the counterattitudinal behavior seem more acceptable to themselves and to the experimenter.

Schlenker's views can be distinguished from those of Tedeschi and his colleagues by his broader focus on self-identity as well as self-presentation. Consistent with this focus, Schlenker has maintained that the attitude change displayed by subjects in dissonance experiments is not necessarily feigned. Moreover, he has placed research on counterattitudinal advocacy in a broader theoretical context that considers the possibility that people are as motivated to take credit for events that meet commendable standards as they are to avoid responsibility for events that violate standards (see, for example, Mori, Chaiken, & Pliner, 1987). Events that meet commendable standards and those that fail to meet them both elicit motivated information processing, and attitude change is one of the possible outcomes of this motivated processing. The self-serving explanations that people generate to indicate why they have met or exceeded important standards are termed *acclamations* by Schlenker. Acclamations can take the form of *entitlements*, which maximize personal responsibility for an event, or *enhancements*, which affirm the beneficial qualities of the event.

The relevance of this analysis of acclamations to attitude change was displayed in research by Schlenker and Schlenker (1975) in which subjects engaged in a counterattitudinal behavior that produced positive consequences. Thus, subjects were given high or low choice to deliver undeserved praise to a rather ordinary and dull-seeming confederate who appeared to be another research participant. The consequences of this act were positive because the evaluation should have made this individual feel very good. The importance of obtaining credit for the evaluation was manipulated by telling subjects that they either would or would not meet with this individual at a later point. The subjects who expected to meet the other participant knew that this other participant would learn that (a) the evaluation was merely a standard statement prepared for the research project, and (b) the subject had (vs. had not) been given a choice between delivering a positive or a negative evaluation. After delivering the insincere evaluation, subjects indicated their actual attitude toward the other participant on a questionnaire.

In contrast to findings typical of counterattitudinal advocacy studies, significant attitude change, in this case toward a more favorable evaluation of the other participant, occurred among the subjects who had *low choice* about delivering the evaluation and expected to meet the individual they had evaluated. This interesting result presumably occurred because subjects who would meet the other participant were in a position to take credit for their evaluation and thus experience some personal gain from their good deed yet those lacking freedom of choice were restricted from claiming responsibility. To characterize their act in the most beneficial manner, they came to believe in their positive evaluation. If these subjects truly evaluated the other person favorably, their actions were a reasonable manifestation of their private attitudes, and they could obtain some credit for their good act, despite their lack of choice in the experimental situation. Schlenker and Schlenker's interpretation thus suggests that garnering credit for positive consequences can motivate internalized attitude change, just as avoiding responsibility for negative consequences can. More generally, this experiment thus illustrates another variety of attitude change produced by counter-attitudinal behavior and displays some of the advantages of the broader context provided by the identity-analytic view.

Evaluation of Self-Presentation Views. In our opinion, the self-presentational interpretation of the attitudinal effects of induced compliance developed in the work of Tedeschi, Schlenker, and other investigators deserves serious attention.[14] The well-known association of the impression-management perspective with the controversial bogus pipeline methodology as well as with the idea that attitudinal responses are merely strategic or feigned may have distracted many social psychologists from appreciating the theoretical importance of self-presentational interpretations of induced compliance.

The significance of this work follows in part from self-presentation theorists' stronger emphasis on the social context within which attitude change occurs. The idea that attitudes evolve as people engage in social interaction, although essential in theories of social influence (see Chapter 13), has not been important in most theories of attitude change. Yet the social context is likely to be especially consequential for understanding the role of behavior in producing attitude change because behavior is a form of attitudinal expression that is readily observable by others. One's attitude-relevant behaviors are thus inevitably shaped to some extent by others' reactions, and these behaviors then act back on one's internalized attitudes.

Admittedly, a few investigators other than those we have noted as associated with self-presentational views have given at least some recognition to the importance of other interpersonal considerations in dissonance-producing situations (e.g., Pepitone, 1966; Stroebe & Diehl, 1981; Zanna & Sande, 1987; Zimbardo, 1969). However, the best-known analyses of induced compliance, that is, dissonance theory and its close relatives, have emphasized individualistic concerns. Although the notion of responsibility for aversive consequences advanced by Cooper and Fazio (1984) surely has interpersonal implications, these have not been developed in much detail in their work or in the dissonance theory tradition more generally. Because of the emphasis of self-presentational theory on an audience of other people, it offers more potential for understanding how attitude change is affected by the role relationships that link the holder of an attitude to various audiences for his or her attitude-relevant behaviors.

Yet, even in the hands of self-presentation theorists, these interpersonal implications have not been analyzed in much detail. They have not considered, for example, the implications of various types of role relationships, an issue that has been considered in some depth by theorists of social influence (e.g., Kelman, 1961; see Chapter 13).

Effects of Self-Affirmation

In another self-concept interpretation of induced-compliance experiments, Claude Steele proposed that attitude change observed in the dissonance-producing conditions of induced-compliance experiments serves to reaffirm the general integrity of the self (Steele, 1988; Steele & Liu, 1983). He further reasoned that *any reaction* that achieves this self-affirmation can reduce the dissonance produced by induced compliance as long as the reaction casts the self in a positive light. According to Steele, an effective dissonance-reducing reaction need not resolve the particular dilemma that threatened the self because "people respond more fluidly to self-threat than is typically recognized" (Steele, 1988, p. 267). In contrast, other self theorists consider the specific aspects of the dilemma produced by induced compliance and regard people as rescuing their public and private images of themselves as protagonists in that particular situation. What if, instead, the self is more like a reservoir filled with self-esteem that is drawn down when one accepts personal responsibility for unwanted consequences? The reservoir needs to be brought back to its usual, safe level. Self-justifying attitude change can perform this function, but so can other self-affirming thoughts, even thoughts that have no obvious relevance to the problem that produced the deficit of self-esteem. A person whose self is threatened because he has engaged in consequential insincere behavior might reduce dissonance by, for example, being especially kind to another person, going to a religious service, visiting an art museum, or engaging in whatever form of behavior might affirm his or her particular values. Consistent with this reasoning, altruistic behavior (e.g., helping the victim of a minor accident) has been shown to be enhanced by the dissonance produced by counterattitudinal role-playing (Dietrich & Berkowitz, 1989; Kidd & Berkowitz, 1976). If self-affirming reactions that are apparently unrelated to the situation that produced a responsibility-for-aversive consequences dilemma still reduce dissonance, the self must be a system that is organized to maintain its general integrity rather than to resolve particular troubling situations.

According to Steele, the fluidity of self-protective reactions has not been readily discerned in dissonance experiments because investigators have constructed these situations to make available only one particular reaction—the consistency-restoring attitude change that made sense in terms of Festinger's (1957) original formulation of cognitive dissonance theory. If other self-affirming reactions had been possible in these situations, people might have responded in these other ways and might have foregone attitude change or any attempt to resolve the specifics of the dilemma that created the dissonance.

To probe this self-affirmation theory of dissonance processes, Steele and Liu (1983) allowed subjects to reaffirm their self-worth in an induced-compliance situation in a

532

manner that was unrelated to the dilemma produced by the induced compliance. This self-affirmation was predicted to eliminate the attitude change ordinarily observed in dissonance experiments. In the experiment, students known to be opposed to a tuition increase at their university were given considerable choice (vs. no choice) about writing an essay supporting a substantial increase in tuition. Half of these students had been selected to have a particularly strong economic-political value orientation, and half had been selected to be particularly weak in this respect. The high choice subjects then completed a set of items assessing their economic-political orientation (e.g., "If you were a university professor and had the necessary ability, would you prefer to teach: (a) poetry, (b) economics?" (Steele & Liu, 1983, p. 7). Completion of these items should have allowed subjects with a strong economic-political orientation to affirm a valued aspect of their self-concepts, whereas this activity would not be self-affirming for subjects low in economic-political orientation. Subjects then completed the attitude measure. In other conditions of the experiment subjects merely completed the attitude measure without having responded to the economic-political items.

If self-affirmation restores integrity and therefore reduces dissonance, dissonance-reducing attitude change should have been eliminated among high choice subjects who held the economic-political value and were allowed the opportunity to affirm their values. Consistent with this prediction, self-affirmation by endorsing personal values reduced attitude change among the high choice subjects to the level shown by the low choice subjects, whereas responding to the value items had no such impact on the subjects for whom this task was not value affirming. In other experiments in this series, Steele and Liu (1983) successfully countered various alternative explanations for their self-affirmation effect and conceptually replicated their experiment by having subjects write a counterattitudinal essay on a different topic (funding of research on chronic diseases and handicaps) and affirm a different value (aesthetic).

Steele's position is thus consistent with Cooper's (Cooper & Fazio, 1984; Scher & Cooper, 1989) view that inconsistency between one's attitude and a cognition of one's behavior is not the motivating feature of cognitive dissonance. However, in contrast to Cooper's position that responsibility for aversive consequences is the issue and that one is therefore likely to ameliorate the aversiveness of these consequences to reduce dissonance, Steele's perspective provides the broader principle that threats to integrity are the issue and that *any response* useful in restoring integrity reduces dissonance. Therefore, attitude change has no special priority according to self-affirmation theory. Nor, for that matter, does responsibility for aversive consequences have any special priority as a cause of self-threats. According to Steele, dissonance theorists have merely focused on one of the many types of events that instigate effort to restore integrity because they threaten the self-concept.

Missing from self-affirmation theory, however, is any specification of the conditions under which attitude change is a likely response to threats to the integrity of the self. Surely there are circumstances, like those in dissonance experiments, in which the situation that precipitated the self-threat remains highly salient. In daily life, one's close associates may continue to draw this situation to one's attention, or the implications of the disturbing event may be difficult to ignore. An individual whose careless behavior injures a family member, for example, may be constantly reminded of the unwanted consequences of this behavior. Restoring integrity through a response unrelated to the precipitating event may be a short-term palliative because frequent reminders of the consequences of the careless behavior repeatedly threaten self-integrity. Under these circumstances, atttitude change *may* occur, and so may other excuses and justifications.

Steele's (1988) interesting work reintroduces the *multiple-mode* problem that initially plagued dissonance theory, that is, the problem of which of many possible resolutions of dissonance would occur. As we explained earlier in this chapter, Brehm and Cohen's (1962) initial solution of this issue was in terms of *committing* subjects to their counter-attitudinal advocacy. Steele's experiments quite forcefully make the point that commitment constrains subjects to reduce dissonance through attitude change only in the quite restricted situation created in the classic experimental paradigm used in research on induced compliance. Not only is it difficult for subjects to deny responsibility in this situation and impossible for them to renege on their behavior, but other means of restoring self-integrity are unavailable. In contrast, natural settings ordinarily present a rich array of possibilities. To discover the implications that the induced-compliance paradigm has for natural settings, social psychologists need to investigate how modes of restoring self-integrity are shaped by the broader social context as well as psychological factors.

In provocative illustrations of the use of dissonance ideas to make predictions for behavior in natural settings, researchers have made study participants aware that their chronic behavior has undesirable consequences. For example, Kantola, Syme, and Campbell (1984) informed a group of Australian citizens that they were high consumers of electricity and reminded them that on an earlier survey they had indicated that citizens have a duty to save electricity. Thibodeau, Aronson, Dickerson, and Miller (1990) made a group of California college students aware of their positive attitudes toward water conservation and the wastefulness of their showering behavior (and in addition publicly committed them to taking shorter showers). In comparison to appropriate control treatments, these treatments induced greater conservation of energy and water. We think it plausible that these treatments were motivating because of the threats to self-integrity that they produced. Why did participants change their behavior to resolve this dissonance? The probable strength of their attitudes on these conservation issues no doubt made attitude change unlikely, and denying responsibility for their personal energy or water use seems an implausible resolution in relation to this type of volitional behavior. Changing behavior provided a socially sanctioned and effective mode of restoring integrity in this situation. These studies illustrate some of the possibilities for designing natural setting applications of the dissonance analysis of induced compliance. Such applications should help psychologists map the conditions under which people restore self-integrity by one or the other mode of response.

Evaluation of Dissonance and Self Theories

We comment on dissonance theory and the self reinterpretations of dissonance theory together because to some extent, these theories represent a common evolution of a single theory. Dissonance theory enjoyed unparalleled attention from social psychologists for more than a decade following its introduction by Festinger (1957; see

534

Möntmann & Irle, 1978). Then Aronson's (1968, 1969) initial suggestion that dissonance processes implicate the self was followed by a chorus of related suggestions. These newer ideas have come in several variants, as we have shown. Some theorists, like Aronson, emphasized the self-concept (Kelman and Baron; Steele), others emphasized self-presentation (Tedeschi), and still others considered both the public and the private aspects of the self (Schlenker). Among these self theories, Schlenker's views are especially appealing because of the greater breadth inherent in considering both the public and the private self as well as the positive and the negative consequences of behaviors. Steele's theory adds another sort of breadth in regarding attitude change as only one of many responses that may preserve the integrity of the self.[15]

Interestingly, self-related processes have not been embraced by those theorists most closely associated with the cognitive dissonance tradition. In fact, Greenwald and Ronis's (1978) claim that cognitive dissonance theory had already evolved into a self theory by the late 1970s appears, from a contemporary perspective, to have been an oversimplification of the intellectual currents in social psychology. In particular, the mid-1970s integration of dissonance research provided by Wicklund and Brehm (1976) was not sympathetic to the self interpretations that were available at that time. And, in the mid-1980s, Cooper and Fazio (1984) remained similarly unreceptive to self interpretations of dissonance processes. Among Cooper and Fazio's criticisms of the self perspective is their statement that the more evolved self theories (e.g., Tedeschi & Rosenfeld, 1981) bear a close resemblance to dissonance theory. Their perception of similarity has some validity: Resemblance is not surprising given that the self theorists all accept the basic findings of dissonance-inspired studies of induced compliance and thus have not challenged the fundamental generalization that responsibility for aversive consequences does produce attitude change in appropriate settings. Yet the various self theories all yield important predictions that go beyond those of dissonance theory—for example, impression management theory predicts effects of bogus pipeline assessments and certain individual differences variables; identity-analytic theory predicts reactions to behavior that has desirable consequences; and self-affirmation theory predicts effects of restoring integrity by means unrelated to the original dissonance-producing situation. The dissonance theory of induced compliance, even in its most elaborated form (Cooper & Fazio, 1984) is silent with respect to these additional predictions. As we have already stated, the major advantage of the self theories is the broader theoretical context they provide for understanding why people sometimes change their attitudes in induced compliance situations.

In attempting to understand the processes that mediate the effects of behavior on attitudes, researchers have emphasized motivational processes much more than cognitive processes. Festinger (1957) treated dissonance as a motivational construct (see Chapter 10), and in the contemporary dissonance interpretation of induced compliance (Cooper & Fazio, 1984), responsibility for aversive consequences serves to motivate attitude change. In the various self theories, discrepancies from the self-concept, compromised self-presentations, or threats to self-integrity serve to motivate attitudinal adjustments. Yet the cognitive processes that are invoked to enable motivated people to change their attitudes remain poorly understood.

Because of the broader context provided by the theories of induced compliance formulated in terms of the self-concept, possibilities exist for exploring cognitive processes by linking such theories to general theories of the self. Interest in the self has increased greatly among social psychologists in recent years (see A. G. Greenwald & Pratkanis, 1984; Markus & Wurf, 1987). Some association with this work might aid investigators in understanding the cognitive processes that underlie the attitude change produced by induced compliance. Particularly significant is the focus of self research on understanding the cognitive properties of the self and the impact of the self on information processing (see Higgins & Bargh, 1987; Kihlstrom et al., 1988). Yet most of this work has a quite general focus and has not dealt with the details of how self-relevance affects reactions in the specific types of situations studied in induced compliance research. Nonetheless, some of the principles pursued in this research as well as aspects of the methodology deserve closer scrutiny by attitude researchers.

In a welcome exception to the general neglect of the cognitive mediation of attitude change within the induced-compliance paradigm,[16] Stroebe and Diehl (1988) developed predictions about attitudinal realignments from explicit assumptions about how role-players process the information that they have available. According to this analysis, under conditions that maximize cognitive dissonance, people are motivated to put forth considerable cognitive effort in order to justify their behavior. In the Stroebe and Diehl experiment, female students at a German university freely chose to write (and subsequently be audio-recorded while reading) a counterattitudinal essay favoring compulsory national service for women that would parallel men's military service. They anticipated that this advocacy either would or would not have the undesirable consequence of being used to persuade another student. The critical manipulations of this study involved giving the subjects cues that they could use to interpret their behavior. Specifically, after the subjects complied with the experimenter's request, they heard a confederate subject who was attitudinally similar or dissimilar to them on a range of other issues either refuse the experimenter's request or comply with it.

In the undesirable consequences conditions of this experiment, designed to arouse dissonance, subjects showed relatively little attitude change toward compulsory national service when a similar confederate had complied with the experimenter's request or a dissimilar confederate had refused. According to Stroebe and Diehl, the attitude change that subjects would usually have manifested under such conditions was reduced because subjects had managed to use the information in the confederate's behavior to justify their own compliance. With the similar, complying confederate, subjects presumably reasoned that what they had done was not so bad, given that a very similar woman did it too; with the dissimilar, noncomplying confederate, subjects presumably reasoned that what they had done was actually fairly reasonable, given that an unreasonable woman, whose attitudes were quite unacceptable to them, did not comply. These somewhat complex resolutions presumably took considerable cognitive effort. Only in the absence of these opportunities for self-justification (i.e., when the similar confederate had refused or the dissimilar confederate had complied) did subjects justify their behavior through attitude change.

In contrast, in the absence of aversive consequences, when subjects lacked motivation for such thorough information processing, they used the more obvious and less effortful liking-agreement heuristic ("people I like usually have correct opinions on issues"; see discussion of heuristic-systematic model in Chapter 7). These subjects changed their attitudes *away* from the position they had agreed to advocate if a similar confederate had refused the experimenter's request or a dissimilar confederate had complied.

In general, given a sufficient level of motivation, cues such as the social support cue that Stroebe and Diehl (1988) manipulated can justify behavior and thereby be used in the service of dissonance reduction. This idea that dissonance reduction is somewhat demanding cognitively is also consistent with earlier demonstrations that forced attention to dissonant cognitions increases dissonance reduction (Zanna et al. 1973), whereas distraction from dissonant cognitions decreases dissonance reduction (Zanna & Aziza, 1976). When dissonance is absent or considerably less severe, people are much less motivated to engage in the detailed processing that would enable them to use these cues to justify their behavior. Instead, cues available in the situation are more likely to be processed heuristically, as Stroebe and Diehl's findings suggest. More generally, we believe that the heuristic-systematic model and other information-processing theories developed in the context of persuasion research have potentially important implications for understanding the cognitive mediation of reactions to induced compliance.

Finally, another concern that we have in relation to the contemporary developments of dissonance and self theories is that the generalizability of their key propositions (e.g., that responsibility for undesirable consequences is the critical determinant of dissonance) has not been demonstrated in relation to the other experimental paradigms that earlier dissonance researchers introduced and once regarded as providing evidence for dissonance theory. For example, we know little about the extent to which freely choosing to engage in a behavior such as grasshopper eating (Zimbardo et al., 1965) that is unpleasant merely to oneself produces attitudinal reactions via the same mechanisms articulated in the induced compliance tradition that followed from Festinger and Carlsmith's (1959) counterattitudinal advocacy experiment. In fact, as we have noted, Kelman and Baron (1968b, 1974) suggested that the dynamics of such hedonic-dissonance situations are quite different. Moreover, the range of variables shown to be important in counterattitudinal advocacy experiments has not been investigated in the forbidden toy paradigm, in which subjects merely refrain from engaging in a valued activity (e.g., Aronson & Carlsmith, 1963), or in Festinger's (1957, 1964b) post-decision paradigm (see Chapter 10), in which subjects presumably perceive a mix of favorable and unfavorable consequences after making a decision. If the modern dissonance and self interpretations could be shown to apply to these other paradigms as Cooper and Fazio (1989) suggest they should, these theories would map a substantially larger domain than they now do, yet provide a considerably more detailed mapping than the generalities of Festinger's own presentation of dissonance theory. Indeed, some of the breadth and scope that dissonance theory once seemed to possess might be recovered once again.

Self-Perception Theory

Although the various self-concept interpretations of the findings produced by dissonance experiments have mounted a continuous challenge to dissonance theory from the late 1960s onward, a more radical challenge came from a different front at an even earlier point. This challenge came initially from Daryl Bem, who proposed an innovative account of dissonance effects in terms of a viewpoint that he labeled *self-perception theory* (Bem, 1965, 1967). This theory was a much greater departure from dissonance theory than the various self reinterpretations were because it contested dissonance theory's fundamental motivational assumptions. In a prescient manner that anticipated the shift to information-processing themes that took place in social psychology in the late 1960s, Bem proposed a purely cognitive interpretation of the attitudinal adjustments that dissonance theorists had explained as accommodations to an aversive state of arousal. Yet Bem's analysis was initially framed, not in information-processing terms, but in terms of radical behavioral concepts imported from Skinner's (1953, 1957) analysis of verbal behavior. Only in his later presentations of self-perception theory did Bem (e.g., 1972) invoke vocabulary more compatible with the cognitive approaches that became increasingly dominant in social psychology as the 1960s progressed. As we explain in this section, Bem's analysis was especially compatible with the attribution theory concepts that were first popularized in social psychology in the mid-1960s through seminal papers by E. E. Jones and Davis (1965) and Kelley (1967). In fact, Kelley was the first to subsume Bem's analysis in a more general attributional analysis (see Kelley, 1967).

Although Bem had no quarrel with the findings produced by dissonance researchers, he challenged their interpretation by denying their assumption that actions discrepant from attitudes produce a state of arousal that motivates attitude change. Bem reasoned that subjects in dissonance experiments act as observers of their own behavior and merely infer their attitudes from their actions. The attitudes of these subjects change because they use their recent behavior, which differs from their earlier attitudes, to infer their current attitudes.

Bem (1965) argued that people rely on their own behavior to inform them what their attitudes are because agents of socialization have had to rely on observable stimuli and responses to interpret younger children's inner states. For example, in order to determine whether a child is hungry, a parent might observe the child's behavior, looking for behaviors such as restlessness or temporary bad humor, and take cues external to the child into account as well (e.g., time since last meal). Teaching a child to describe his or her own internal states (e.g., hunger or thirst) is especially difficult for parents and other socializers because they lack access to the internal stimuli impinging directly on the child. Just as these socializing agents had to resort to interpreting behavior to estimate what children's inner states might be, they in turn teach children to use their own behavior as a guide to interpreting their inner states, including their attitudes. This method of training results in learners achieving relatively poor discrimination in labeling internal states and maintaining a dependence on the very same external cues for the control of their self-descriptive responses as those used by socializing agents. For example, a child may learn to describe herself as hungry when certain stimuli are present (e.g., she is restless and it is 12 o'clock) because she was often told by her parents that she must be hungry because it is 12 o'clock and she is restless. In short, Bem's argument was that, particularly if internal cues that might signal an inner state are weak, ambiguous, or uninterpretable, people must rely on their own behavior as a guide to interpreting their inner states.

To the extent that people use their own behavior to ascertain their attitudes, they are functionally in the same position as an outside observer who has access to their behavior. When observers try to determine what someone's attitude is, they take into account, not only the individual's behavior, but also the conditions under which it occurs (see discussions of attitude attribution in Chapters 1 and 8). In some situations, these circumstances may cause observers to locate the cause for another person's behavior in some external circumstance rather than a characteristic of that person. In analyzing why people sometimes ascribe behavior to situations and sometimes to persons, Bem (1965) invoked the Skinnerian concepts of *tact*, which is a verbal response under the discriminative control of some portion of the environment, and *mand*, which is a verbal response under the control of a specific reinforcing contingency. He reasoned that people infer an attitude from observing a behavior that seems congruent with such an attitude to the extent that they judge the behavior to be a tact and not a mand. If, in contrast, a behavior appears to be emitted merely to achieve an immediate specific reinforcement (i.e., the individual seems to be manding), this behavior is not taken as indicative of an underlying attitude, either by an outside observer or by the actor himself. For example, if a student of less than outstanding ability goes out of his way (immediately before grades are determined) to tell a professor that her course has been wonderful, she might judge that the student's praise is intended merely to achieve the specific reinforcement of a higher grade and does not provide evidence of an underlying positive attitude toward the course.

This analysis is highly compatible with attribution theory (see Chapter 8) and was largely supplanted by that theory. As Bem (1972) himself acknowledged, "The Skinnerian parentage of the theory has become increasingly muted in successive translations" (p. 44). Thus, Bem's idea that mands do not inform people about underlying tendencies and dispositions is consistent with the *discounting principle* of attribution theory (Kelley, 1972a). According to the discounting principle, to the extent that observers perceive some external circumstance as a possible cause for another person's behavior, they are uncertain whether the behavior follows from the individual's inner dispositions (e.g., attitude) or is merely a response to the external events. In contrast, if external causes seem to be lacking, observers are likely to interpret the behavior as a product of the individual's personal characteristics. Thus, behavior that seemingly is not under the control of external circumstances would be especially revealing of one's attitudes as well as other dispositions and tendencies.

Consider the Festinger and Carlsmith (1959) experiment from the viewpoint of observers who see a subject in the experiment carry out a dull task, hear this subject praise the experience to someone else, and know that the subject was paid only $1 to do so. If the observers desire to infer the subject's attitude toward the seemingly dull task, they can examine the subject's behavior—the favorable statements he made about the task. In judging these statements, observers can disregard the possibility of financial motivation because compensation was only $1. The lack of financial inducement suggests that the subject's attitude is responsible for his statements, and observers would likely judge the subject's attitude to be consistent with his behavior. If the observers knew that the subject had been offered $20, their conclusion would be quite different. They would likely conclude that the external circumstances (namely, the financial incentive) probably explain the behavior; they would be unlikely to account for the behavior in terms of the subject's attitude.

Bem suggested that people regard their own behavior much as outside observers would. For example, in the $1 condition of the Festinger and Carlsmith (1959) experiment, a subject would have surmised that because there is no obvious external pressure causing his behavior, his actions must reflect his true attitude toward the task. His act of praising the experiment would imply that he has a positive attitude toward the experiment. From this perspective, the attitude change obtained in induced compliance experiments reflects subjects' inference from their behavior to their attitude. In short, Bem's argument is that participants in dissonance experiments changed their attitudes, not as a means of reducing an unpleasant state of arousal, but as a by-product of inferring their attitudes from their behavior and the circumstances under which the behavior occurred. Examined from this new viewpoint that empha-sized perceivers' interpretations of behavior, the predictions of cognitive dissonance theory lost much of their nonobvious quality, and another theory, namely Bem's self-perception theory, appeared equally able to make the predictions that were once the exclusive domain of dissonance theory.

Interpersonal Simulations of Dissonance Experiments

To support his claim that the individual who estimates her own attitude is functionally in the same position as an outside observer, Bem carried out experiments that came to be known as *interpersonal simulations* (or *replications*) (e.g., Bem, 1965, 1967). According to the requirements of this innovative methodology, subjects served as observers of the behavior of participants in dissonance experiments: Bem's subjects were given a description of a generic subject's behavior in one of the conditions of a dissonance experiment and then were asked to estimate this subject's attitude. If people are functionally in the same position as outside observers when they estimate their own attitudes, observer-subjects should give approximately the same estimate of the attitudes of the induced compliance subjects as these subjects had given when they estimated their own attitudes.

For example, in a replication of the Festinger and Carlsmith (1959) study, the observer-subjects heard a tape recording of a college sophomore, Bob Downing, stating that he had participated in an experiment involving two motor tasks, which were described to these observers (Bem, 1967). Control observers estimated Bob's attitude after hearing only this part of the experiment. The observer-subjects in the experi-mental conditions were told that Bob had accepted an offer of either $1 or $20 to tell the next subject that the tasks had been fun and interesting. After the observer-subjects heard Bob telling a young woman in the waiting room that the tasks had been fun and enjoyable, they estimated Bob's attitude toward the tasks. Observers' estimates were nearly identical to the evaluations of the tasks that Festinger and Carlsmith's subjects had given, that is, the observers estimated that subjects who complied for only $1 had more favorable attitudes toward the task than subjects who complied for $20 or control subjects (who were not given the opportunity to engage in insincere behavior). Also, in an earlier interpersonal replication that presented observer-subjects with a written description of an induced compliance experiment, Bem's (1965) observer-subjects reproduced the findings of Cohen's (J. W. Brehm & Cohen, 1962, pp. 73–78) essay-writing study in which Yale students wrote essays in favor of the New Haven police (see earlier section of this chapter).

Bem's interpersonal simulations attracted considerable attention and quickly became controversial. The debate concerned the information that the observer-subjects should be given from the dissonance study that they observed. Specifically, critics claimed that Bem failed to reproduce the phenomenology of the subjects in dissonance experiments because he did not give his observers one salient piece of information that the dissonance subjects presumably had—those subjects' own attitudes prior to the experiment (R. A. Jones, Linder, Kiesler, Zanna, & Brehm, 1968; Mills, 1967). The critics' argument was that Bem's observer-subjects perceived that the *initial attitudes* of subjects in dissonance experiments differed between the experimental conditions. Specifically, the observers would presume that the subjects who engaged in insincere behavior for a small inducement must have had more favorable initial attitudes. The final attitudes inferred by the observers then reflected this selection bias.

The critics thus argued that Bem's failure to give observer-subjects access to the dissonance subjects' initial attitudes caused his interpersonal simulations to yield artifactual results. This artifact allowed Bem to reproduce the results of dissonance experiments, albeit by an inference of subject self-selection on the basis of their initial attitudes—a judgmental process quite different from the process that he had postulated. In other words, Bem's simulation worked, but for the wrong reasons. Consistent with this argument, several experiments demonstrated that giving observer-subjects information that prevented them from ascribing initial attitudinal differences to subjects in various incentive conditions destroyed these observers' ability to reproduce the true attitudes of subjects of dissonance experiments (see R. A. Jones et al., 1968; Piliavin, Piliavin, Loewenton, McCauley, & Hammond, 1969).

Bem (1968) turned this criticism around by arguing that his critics' experimental procedures made the initial attitudes of the dissonance subjects salient to the observers, a condition that he claimed did not exist for the subjects in the dissonance experiments. The issue thus became whether Bem or his critics' simulations more adequately represented the phenomenology of the subjects in induced compliance experiments. To determine whether subjects in dissonance experiments were knowledgeable about their initial attitudes, Bem and McConnell (1970) carried out a two-session experiment in which students indicated their attitudes on a number of campus issues in the first session and were given high or low choice to write a counterattitudinal essay in a second session. Subsequent to this insincere advocacy, half of the subjects merely gave their final attitudes and the other half were asked to recall their initial attitudes (and then to give their final attitudes). Bem and McConnell found that subjects' recall of their initial attitudes was distorted in the direction of their changed attitudes and that there was a very high correlation between subjects' final attitudes and recalled initial attitudes. These findings thus supported Bem's argument that the initial attitudes of subjects in dissonance experiments are not salient to them at the point that they give their final attitudes and that subjects may infer their attitudes from their recent behavior in the manner proposed by self-perception theory.

Still, the demonstration that initial attitudes are forgotten could be seen as consistent with dissonance theory as well because, as Bem and McConnell (1970) themselves pointed out, "forgetting an earlier conflicting attitude is itself a mode of dissonance reduction" (p. 30). Their experiment thus did not resolve the controversy between self-perception and dissonance theories, although it did provide support for Bem's interpersonal simulation methodology (but see Shaffer, 1975). Some researchers remained interested in the role of initial attitudes in induced-compliance experiments and manipulated the salience of subjects' initial attitudes prior to inducing them to engage in counterattitudinal behavior (e.g., M. Ross & Shulman, 1973; Scheier & Carver, 1980; M. Snyder & Ebbesen, 1972). The additional research also failed to resolve the controversy between the two theories because, as Greenwald (1975b) pointed out in a review of many of these studies, the theories are not precise enough to produce distinctive predictions about how the salience of initial attitudes affects attitude change.

Finally, further questioning of the evidence from interpersonal simulations stemmed from research on the differences between actors' and observers' attributions of causality. Specifically, E. E. Jones and Nisbett (1972) argued that actors tend to attribute causality for their behavior to situational influences whereas observers tend to attribute causality to actors' stable dispositions. Moreover, according to the concept of the *fundamental attribution error*, perceivers insufficiently weight situational constraints and overestimate the importance of personal tendencies and dispositions (see L. Ross, 1977). Consistent with such analyses, researchers have demonstrated differences between actors' and observers' causal attributions (e.g., Nisbett, Caputo, Legant, & Maracek, 1973; Semin & Fiedler, 1989; see M. Ross & Fletcher, 1985). The differences found in actors' and observers' interpretations of behavior raised questions about the extent to which Bem was correct in his assumption that actors are functionally in the same position as an outside observer of their behavior.

Other Evidence Favoring Self-Perception Theory

The Truth Light—Lie Light Experiments. Another demonstration that Bem (1965) initially offered in support of his self-perception theory was an experiment demonstrating that stimuli can be conditioned to serve as cues for the truthfulness of certain belief statements. This demonstration is relevant to Bem's interpretation of dissonance experiments because he argued that subjects in these experiments used external cues—the magnitude of the incentive offered to engage in insincere advocacy—to determine whether their behavior was a valid indicator of their own attitudes. Subjects presumably inferred that their behavior was not indicative of an underlying attitude if they had been offered a large incentive to engage in this behavior.

In Bem's (1965) experiment subjects were trained to regard lights of differing color as cues for truthfulness or insincerity by following the experimenter's instructions to give a truthful response (about how funny a cartoon was) in the presence of a light of one color (the truth light) and to give a false response in the presence of a light of another color (the lie light). In the next phase of the experiment, subjects were required to give judgments deviant from their true beliefs about the funniness of each of a set of cartoons. Just before subjects gave each of these judgments, one of the lights turned on, and after this false judgment, the light turned off. (Subjects had been told that the lights were merely incidental at this point and went on and off because they were linked to the apparatus that recorded their judgments.) Then subjects indicated how they genuinely felt about the cartoon. Bem predicted that subjects' attitudes would be more influenced by their insincere statements when they were given in the presence of the truth light rather than the lie light. The experiment produced these findings and thus substantiated Bem's view that people use their behavior to infer their attitudes but moderate this inference by taking into account the circumstances under which their behavior has occurred (for related research, see Bandler, Madaras, & Bem, 1968; Bem, 1966).

Overjustification Effects and Proattitudinal Behavior. Self-perception theory inspired Nisbett and Valins (1972) to argue that overly sufficient justification for engaging in a behavior would cause people to infer that the behavior does not reflect their true attitudes, even when that behavior is consistent with their attitudes. These investigators thus suggested applying self-perception theory in new territory, that is, in situations in which behavior is justified both by one's attitude and by the external circumstances. Because dissonance theory predicts that cognitive realignments ensue only from dissonant cognitions, it could not be similarly applied to understand reactions to proattitudinal or consonant behaviors.

Experiments on oversufficient justification for consonant behavior give people rewards for doing what they would otherwise do spontaneously. An example of oversufficient justification is offering a child a reward for playing with an attractive new toy. A reward is thoroughly unnecessary to induce this proattitudinal behavior. If we consider overjustification from the viewpoint of self-perception theory, it follows that individuals offered such rewards may tend to view their actions as caused by the rewards, not by their own positive attitudes. In the toy situation, the child would reason, "I must be playing with this toy because I'll get a reward for doing it." The child would not infer that his liking for the toy accounted for playing with it (or the child would discount this explanation). It follows from self-perception theory, therefore, that overly sufficient rewards should undermine intrinsic interest in activities or "turn play into work." This prediction was confirmed in experiments that examined preschool children's activities and were framed in terms of self-perception theory (Lepper & Greene,

1975; Lepper, Green, & Nisbett, 1973). The self-perception prediction was consistent with Deci's experiments on intrinsic motivation as well (e.g., Deci, 1971, 1972, 1975).[17]

Overjustification effects have also been examined by having subjects advocate a position with which they already agree. Tangible rewards, such as large monetary incentives, should undermine one's positive attitude and cause individuals given such rewards to have less favorable attitudes on the issue than subjects who advocated the same position for little or no incentive. Indeed, such findings have been obtained. For example, in an experiment by Kiesler and Sakamura (1966), subjects were paid $1 or $5 to be audio-recorded while reading a proattitudinal communication in favor of lowering the voting age to 18 years. Some of these subjects then heard a counterattitudinal persuasive communication arguing against this position: They were more persuaded by this second communication if they had been paid $5 rather than $1 for their prior advocacy, presumably because this larger reward had undermined their attitudes and made them vulnerable to counter-persuasion. More direct evidence that incentives for attitude-consistent behavior can undermine attitudes came from an experiment by Benware and Deci (1975) in which subjects read a proattitudinal statement arguing for student control of course offerings. These subjects read this statement through a microphone to a (fictitious) audience of other students who were in another room. Showing that monetary incentives can undermine attitudes, the findings indicated less favorable attitudes toward student control among subjects paid $7.50 for reading the statement compared with subjects who were not paid.[18]

Although self-perception theory once provided a popular framework for interpreting the effects of oversufficient justification on proattitudinal advocacy, newer research suggests that the approach is not sufficient to handle the range of findings that have been produced. Crano and Sivacek (1984; see also Crano, Gorenflo, & Shackelford, 1988) proposed an alternative model suggesting that extrinsic rewards for proattitudinal behavior produce an ambivalent reaction toward the behavior because the incentive is unnecessary and unexpected. People engaging in such behavior feel overcompensated and therefore, as Crano and Sivacek's findings suggested, somewhat uneasy about the legitimacy of the induced behavior.[19] This ambivalence creates a certain readiness to modify the attitude underlying the induced behavior; however, this attitude change occurs only in circumstances that confirm one's apprehensions about the behavior. In Crano and Sivacek's experiment subjects favorable to the decriminalization of marijuana were either given no payment or paid $5 for advocating this position. The $5 undermined the attitude only if subjects were exposed to a countercommunication that stressed the health hazards of marijuana use and other negative consequences of decriminalization. This research thus suggests that more detailed and specific principles than those provided by self-perception theory will have to be taken into account to understand fully the impact that proattitudinal behavior has on attitudes.

Conditions under which Self-Perception Effects Occur

The model of information processing underlying Bem's self-perception theory assumes that people's attitudes are merely inferred from recent behavior and therefore are not grounded in an attitudinal knowledge structure that is accessed when people attempt to ascertain their attitudes. According to Bem, people often lack internal cues about their own attitudes. Therefore, to find out what their attitudes are, they turn to their own recent behavior. However, Bem did not maintain that people *necessarily* look to their own behavior when deciding what their attitudes are; rather, people do so when the internal cues that might signal the attitude are weak, ambiguous, or uninterpretable. This suggestion about the conditions that limit self-perception processes has been amplified and tested empirically in several important studies.

This research has shown that attitudes that are *strong* or in certain senses *important* to those who hold them are relatively unaffected by recent behavior. In the first demonstration of this point, Shelley E. Taylor (1975) manipulated whether attitudes had important future consequences (see discussion of *outcome-relevant involvement* in Chapter 7). The attitudes investigated in this experiment were female subjects' evaluations of men whose pictures they viewed. In the condition in which these attitudes had consequences for future events, each subject was told that she would have an informal meeting with the man whom she evaluated most favorably. In the condition lacking future consequences, subjects did not expect to meet any of the men but merely expected the typical sort of experiment in which questionnaire measures would be taken. In order to provide subjects with feedback about their behavior, each subject was hooked up to a physiological recording apparatus while viewing the pictures, ostensibly to help the experimenter's colleague obtain some GSR readings. The subject then overheard this colleague say that, based on the physiological data, she had reacted very strongly and positively to the picture of one of the men. If subjects had processed this representation of their behavior in the manner suggested by self-perception theory, they would merely have adjusted their attitudes to be consistent with this recent behavior and therefore have rated the relevant photo very favorably. Attitudinal realignments of this type occurred only among the subjects whose attitudes toward the men had no future consequences. Not only were the subjects who believed their attitudes to be consequential relatively unaffected by the feedback, but also they spent more time looking at the pictures in a later phase of the experiment and thus engaged in a more time-consuming and complete evaluation of information relevant to their attitudes.

In further research on variables that limit the impact of behavior on attitudes, both Chaiken and Baldwin (1981) and W. Wood (1982) examined aspects of attitude structure. In the Chaiken and Baldwin (1981) experiment, the *evaluative-cognitive consistency* of subjects' attitudes toward being an environmentalist was assessed (see Chapter 3). Subjects then completed a questionnaire containing items worded to make salient either their past pro-ecology behaviors (e.g., picking up other persons' garbage and taking it to the trash can) or their past anti-ecology behaviors (e.g., leaving on lights in rooms that were not in use). Self-perception theory suggests that people's attitudes would be congruent with whichever set of behaviors—pro-ecology or anti-ecology—was made salient (see Salancik & Conway, 1975). Yet this result was obtained only for subjects who were low in evaluative-cognitive consistency and whose attitudes therefore were not supported by a set of beliefs consistent with their attitudes.

The aspect of attitude structure examined in Wood's research (1982) was subjects' *ability to retrieve information* relative to their attitudes (i.e., toward preservation of the environment). Subjects were given a reward (vs. no reward) for their decision to proselytize for the environmentalist cause (a proattitudinal act). Consistent with self-perception theory, the reward for this proattitudinal behavior should have undermined the attitude (see discussion of overjustification effects above). Wood's finding that this undermining effect occurred only for subjects who retrieved relatively little attitude-relevant information suggests that self-perception effects are more pronounced when people do not have an extensive knowledge structure underlying their attitudes.

A different sort of limiting condition, *the extent to which an attitude is anchored in immediate sensory data*, was proposed by Tybout and Scott (1983). Anchoring of an attitude in sensory data was achieved by having subjects taste a product described as a new diet soft drink; subjects lacking sensory data merely overheard a research assistant tell the experimenter how other people evaluated the diet drink. Subjects then agreed to try the soft drink for an incentive consisting of a coupon worth 50 cents at a fast-food restaurant, or no incentive was given. Because trying the drink was a proattitudinal behavior, the incentive should have undermined the positive attitude from Bem's perspective. Yet this result was obtained only for subjects who had not tasted the soft drink and therefore lacked sensory data, which Tybout and Scott argued provides people with well-defined internal knowledge about an attitude object.

In general, self-perception theory maintains that people function as relatively superficial information processors who merely generalize their attitudes from currently available external cues. By this account, people look to see what their recent behavior has been and assume that their attitudes are congruent with this behavior. In contrast, a view of attitudes as relatively enduring tendencies suggests instead that people generalize their attitudes from internal data; they have stored their attitudes in memory and retrieve them from this internal source when called upon to make an attitudinal judgment. If people have access to their prior attitudes, they are unlikely to be overly impressed by their most recent behavior. Consistent with the research we have reviewed on moderators of self-perception effects, people function in the superficial manner suggested by self-perception theory when their attitudes are in some sense inconsequential or are not well anchored in an internal structure of beliefs or in sensory experience.[20] Although these studies are consistent with Bem's (1972) own suggestions about the limits of self-perception theory, they amplify his position by introducing a set of specific variables that moderate the impact of behavior on attitudes.

Finally, research has also shown that failures to take advantage of an opportunity to behave, which Fazio (1987) has called *nonbehaviors*, are less likely to be taken as indicators of one's attitude than behaviors are. This tendency may mirror the more general *feature-positive effect* whereby people have difficulty in using nonoccurrences of events as positive cues for making judgments (e.g., Newman, Wolff, & Hearst,

1980). In a demonstration of this effect in a self-perception context, Fazio, Sherman, and Herr (1982) had subjects judge the funniness of cartoons, as Bem (1965) had done in his truth light/lie light experiments. Subjects were given cartoons that they had rated as neutral in an earlier session and were asked to judge whether each cartoon was "very funny" or "very unfunny." These subjects were required to indicate one of these reactions by making an active response (e.g., pressing a button or blowing a whistle) and to indicate the other reaction by the absence of this response. Subjects' final ratings of the funniness of the cartoons (given on a rating scale) were more influenced by their active behavioral responses than by their nonresponses, even though logically the behaviors and nonbehaviors were equally informative. Perhaps, as Fazio (1987) suggested, behavioral information is more salient than nonbehavioral information and thus is more likely to be used as a basis for judgment.

Role of Arousal in Self-Perception
and Dissonance Theories

In offering a cool, cognitive alternative to the hot, motivational theory proposed by Festinger (1957), Bem (1965) challenged the assumptions that dissonance theorists had made about arousal (see Chapter 10). If people merely infer their attitudes from their behavior, they proceed as processors of the behavioral information that happens to be salient; they are not driven to reduce an uncomfortable state of arousal. As research relevant to the arousal issue became available over the years, Bem's challenge to the motivational assumptions of dissonance theory fared quite poorly. There is ample evidence that traditional dissonance experiments—most especially those conducted within the induced compliance paradigm—produce a state of arousal.

Several types of research have supported the proposition that the experimental manipulations popular in dissonance research create a state of psychological tension, and several informative summaries of this research are available (Cooper & Fazio, 1984; Fazio & Cooper, 1983; Kiesler & Pallak, 1976). To indicate very briefly the main research paradigms that have been used to test this proposition about arousal, we note that some studies have attempted to show that the psychological state produced by dissonance manipulations energizes dominant responses, just as other arousal states do (e.g., Cottrell & Wack, 1967; Gaes, Melburg, & Tedeschi, 1986; M.S. Pallak & Pittman, 1972; Waterman, 1969; Waterman & Katkin, 1967). In addition, other investigators have attempted to measure dissonance arousal directly by assessing indicators presumed to reflect physiological arousal. Although many of these studies had somewhat inconclusive results, Croyle and Cooper's (1983) induced-compliance experiment produced more impressive evidence of arousal. In this experiment, male undergraduates were given high or low choice about writing a counterattitudinal essay arguing that alcohol use by students should be completely banned on campus (and other subjects were given high choice about writing a proattitudinal essay on the alcohol topic). Only in the high dissonance condition, in which subjects were given high choice concerning the counterattitudinal essay, was an elevation of subject's non-specific skin conductance responses (an index of autonomic arousal) detected during the rest period following the essay writing. In view of confirmation from an independent sample of subjects that this high dissonance condition also produced greater attitude change than the other two conditions, Croyle and Cooper's findings suggest that the typical high dissonance situations in induced-compliance experiments do produce physiological arousal. Moreover, other researchers subsequently replicated the finding that electrodermal activity is elevated following attitude-discrepant behavior under high choice conditions (Elkin & Leippe, 1986; Losch & Cacioppo, 1990).

The best-known evidence that dissonance manipulations are arousing was produced within an experimental paradigm known as *misattribution of arousal*. Research of this type was inspired by Schachter and Singer's (1962) demonstration that states of arousal can be cognitively labeled in accordance with cues available in the situation, with the consequence that people experience emotional states that are congruent with situational cues. Consistent with this logic, the arousal induced by a dissonance manipulation might be misattributed to some external source, if the situation offered cues compatible with such an interpretation. If people no longer believed that their arousal was due to the negative implications of their counterattitudinal behavior, they would have no need to change their attitudes.

This misattribution logic yielded a notable experiment by Mark Zanna and Joel Cooper (1974) in which subjects were given an opportunity to ascribe to a pill the arousal that was actually produced by their own behavior. In this study subjects wrote a counterattitudinal essay (arguing that inflammatory speakers should be banned from college campuses) under conditions of high or low choice. Prior to writing the essay, subjects had participated in an ostensibly unrelated experiment in which they were given a placebo pill and told that the pill would make them either tense or relaxed or would have no side effects. As shown in Table 11.4, under the no side-effects instruction, the typical dissonance results were obtained whereby subjects changed their attitudes significantly more with high than low choice. Consistent with the

TABLE 11.4

Mean Attitudes Toward Banning Speakers on Campus in the Zanna and Cooper (1974) Experiment

Choice	Potential side effects of the pill		
	Arousal	None	Relaxation
High	3.40$_a$	9.10$_b$	13.40$_c$
Low	3.50$_a$	4.50$_a$	4.70$_a$

Note: Control group mean = 2.30$_a$. Means are on a 31-point scale on which higher numbers indicate more favorable attitudes toward position taken in counterattitudinal essay. Means not sharing a common subscript differ at the .01 level by the Newman-Keuls procedure; cells showing a common subscript do not differ at the .05 level.

Source: This table was adapted from one presented by Zanna and Cooper (1974, Table 2, p. 706).

misattribution logic, in the condition in which subjects were told that the pill would make them feel tense, the subjects in the high choice condition changed their attitudes no more than the subjects in the low choice condition. Presumably these high choice subjects misattributed to the pill the state of arousal that had actually been produced by writing a counterattitudinal essay; no longer seeing their arousal as caused by their act, these subjects did not face discomfort that could be resolved by changing their attitudes. Moreover, in the condition in which subjects thought that the pill was supposed to relax them, the tendency for high choice subjects to change their attitudes more than low choice subjects was greater than it was in the no-side-effects condition. Presumably the arousal that these high choice subjects experienced from writing the counterattitudinal essay seemed more extreme because they believed that they were under the influence of a sedative; consequently they experienced more dissonance. Because the only interpretation that subjects had available for this arousal was their counterattitudinal essay, their attitude change was especially pronounced.

The attenuation of attitude change that Zanna and Cooper produced by influencing subjects to misattribute their dissonance-produced arousal to an external source has proven to be replicable (e.g., Fazio, Zanna, & Cooper, 1979; Pittman, 1975; Zanna, Higgins, & Taves, 1976). In addition, Cooper, Zanna, and Taves (1978) demonstrated that administering a tranquilizer (phenobarbital) to subjects inhibited the usual attitude change that is produced by induced compliance, and Steele, Southwick, and Critchlow (1981) showed that alcohol consumption has the same impact. Finally, other research has shown that the misattribution of externally produced arousal (e.g., from ingestion of amphetamines) to one's own attitude-discrepant behavior can enhance dissonance and thereby exaggerate the usual attitudinal realignments (Cooper et al., 1978; Fazio & Cooper, 1983; Worchel & Arnold, 1974).

Other investigators have concentrated on the related issue of whether the attitude change that is commonly elicited in dissonance-producing situations occurs in the service of reducing negative affect or reducing arousal more generally, regardless of whether it is positive or negative. As we noted in Chapter 10, Festinger (1957) maintained that dissonance is a state, not merely of arousal, but of negative or unpleasant arousal. It would be consistent with Festinger's reasoning to find that attitude change occurs only in the presence of arousal that people experience as unpleasant. In general, studies using Zanna and Cooper's (1974) misattribution paradigm have supported Festinger's reasoning (Higgins, Rhodewalt, & Zanna, 1979; Losch & Cacioppo, 1990; Zanna et al., 1976). This research has shown that the presentation of a cue, such as a pill, to which arousal could potentially be misattributed, in fact dampens attitude change in induced-compliance situations only if subjects believe that this cue has affectively negative implications (e.g., creates a feeling of unpleasant tension). These findings suggest that subjects can misattribute their arousal to the cue that the experimenter introduced only when the presumed effects of this cue and subjects' negative affective state have the same valence. These misattribution findings thus suggest that subjects' affective state in high dissonance conditions of induced compliance experiments is in fact negative and that attitude change has the function of reducing this negative affect.

In sum, converging evidence from several lines of research indicates that taking responsibility for aversive consequences in the typical induced-compliance paradigm produces an unpleasant state of arousal. The effort of self-perception theory to explain dissonance-produced attitude change solely in terms of a simple inference from a behavioral cue to an attitude, without recourse to assumptions about arousal, thus failed to survive the vigorous empirical challenge from the dissonance camp. Despite this conclusion that dissonance theory's arousal-reduction model is correct under the circumstances established in classic induced-compliance experiments, there may well be circumstances under which self-perception theory's simple inference model is correct as well.

An interesting experiment by Fazio, Zanna, and Cooper (1977) using the misattribution of arousal paradigm delineated one of the circumstances determining whether the dissonance model or the self-perception model is more valid. These researchers reasoned that (a) arousal is ordinarily produced by advocacy of a counterattitudinal position, which they defined as within one's latitude of rejection (see Chapter 3), and (b) arousal is *not* ordinarily produced by advocacy of a proattitudinal position, which they defined as within one's latitude of acceptance. If this logic is correct, only the attitude change produced by counterattitudinal advocacy would be explicable by dissonance mechanisms, whereas the attitude change produced by proattitudinal advocacy would be explicable by self-perception mechanisms. The findings of this experiment, which showed that misattribution of arousal to an external cue lessened attitude change only for subjects who engaged in counterattitudinal advocacy, were supportive of these investigators' reasoning.

Although this experiment is widely cited in textbooks and elsewhere (e.g., Abelson, 1983) as providing a resolution of the contest between dissonance and self-perception theory, we point out that these researchers proposed the distinction between proattitudinal and counterattitudinal advocacy, not as a general resolution, but merely as one variable relevant to dissonance versus self-perception processes. The importance of this point is now more obvious in view of Scher and Cooper's (1989) demonstration that, to produce dissonance, one's advocacy need not be counterattitudinal at all. Rather, it is the aversive consequences of one's behavior that are critical, and such consequences can occur, regardless of whether the advocacy itself is proattitudinal or counterattitudinal. Consistent with Fazio, Zanna, and Cooper's reasoning, it just happens that the implications of people's counterattitudinal behavior *ordinarily* turn out to be more unwelcome than those of their proattitudinal behavior. Therefore, the location of role-players' advocacies in relation to their own attitude may be consequential only because it is correlated with a more fundamental determinant of dissonance—the aversiveness of the consequences of the advocacy.

Finally, we note once more the general weakness in social psychologists' understanding of the cognitive processes that mediate dissonance effects. As we have shown, the motivational ground of these effects is better understood, given the converging evidence for the importance of arousal. Perhaps, as Stroebe and Diehl (1988) suggested, substantial cognitive work is required to achieve self-justifying attitude change in induced-compliance situations, and this cognitive work is motivated by the desire to reduce an unpleasant state of arousal. If so, the less effortful and more superficial cognitive process described by self-perception theory—a simple inference from a behavioral cue to one's attitude—may indeed be more prevalent in the absence of the arousal that would motivate more thorough consideration of behavioral information. Yet the presence or absence of dissonance arousal is no doubt only one determinant of the extent to which people engage in the more demanding cognitive work that may underlie dissonance effects. Indeed, persuasion theorists have confronted similar issues in attempting to specify the conditions under which people process persuasive messages more simply (i.e., via heuristic or attributional inferences) or more complexly (i.e., by scrutinizing the semantic content of persuasive arguments; see Chapters 7 and 8).

Evaluation of Self-Perception Theory

Self-perception theory provided a vigorous challenge to dissonance theory within a few years after Festinger (1957) proposed the theory. The boldness of Bem's (1965) challenge can only incite admiration. However, even if Bem had not proposed self-perception theory, similar ideas probably would have been proposed a few years later under the influence of attribution theory. Thus, the timing of Bem's challenge attests, not merely to his own creativity, but to the benefits that sometimes accrue from atypical intellectual background—in Bem's case a blending of Skinnerian behavior theory and more traditional social psychology.

Bem's theory has fared moderately well over the years: It continues to provide a useful perspective that directs researchers toward a number of new insights (see Fazio, 1987). Nonetheless, as our discussion has shown, Bem was wrong in his central claim that dissonance effects do not implicate arousal. Yet his views on the arousal issue stimulated researchers in the dissonance camp to obtain evidence that negative arousal is produced in induced-compliance situations presumed to be dissonance arousing.

Because Bem never claimed that simple inferences from behaviors to attitudes provide the only mechanism by which people ascertain their attitudes, the various demonstrations that self-perception effects occur under limited circumstances (e.g., Taylor, 1975) do not contradict his initial theory. This later research merely details his idea that people infer their attitudes from their behavior when internal cues are weak or ambiguous. Although Bem's descriptions of the simple inferences from behavior to attitudes that occur under such circumstances can make attitudes seem like trivial afterthoughts that trail along after behaviors, Fazio (1987) has made the important point that self-perception theory is thus more useful as a theory of attitude formation than attitude change. People who lack an attitude (or possess a nonattitude; see Chapter 3) may first determine their attitude at least in part by examining their own behavior; if they already have a well formed attitude, they do not find recent behaviors all that consequential for telling them what their attitudes are. Perhaps behavior affects relatively well formed attitudes only if it has unwanted consequences or is otherwise arousing; this arousal may be necessary to motivate the more thorough information processing that is required to change a genuine attitude.

As Fazio (1987) has also argued, inferring an attitude from one's behavior strengthens the attitude. Research suggests that inferring one's attitude from freely chosen behaviors makes the attitude more accessible from memory (Fazio, Herr, & Olney, 1984) and more likely to guide later behaviors (e.g., Zanna, Olson, & Fazio, 1981). Thus, if self-perception processes strengthen attitudes, these attitudes are subsequently less likely to be influenced by the attitudinal implications of one's recent behavior. Viewed from this broader perspective, the attitude-relevant information that people produce on the basis of their own behavior makes them more confident of their attitudinal positions and less vulnerable to the impact of simple inferences from this behavior.

The Effects of Behavior on Attitudes: *A Reprise*

We have told a very long story in this chapter—a story of substantial scientific progress. From initial and rather general ideas about role-playing influencing attitudes, research has progressed to testing a large number of specific principles about the conditions under which information produced by one's own behavior influences one's attitudes. This set of principles is a substantial achievement. The route by which these principles were derived is noteworthy because, unlike other areas of attitude research, the study of behavior-attitude relations engendered numerous debates that brought distinct theories into contention. For quite a few years, the controversy between dissonance theory, self-perception theory, and other viewpoints fueled interest in attitude research and in experimental social psychology more generally. These debates would not have occurred had Leon Festinger not proposed his disarmingly simple theory of the effects of counterattitudinal behavior and had Festinger himself not been a charismatic intellectual leader in social psychology. Without Festinger's contribution, knowledge concerning the impact of behavior on attitudes surely would have cumulated in a different mode. Despite the simplicity of Festinger's description of the attitudinal effects of counterattitudinal advocacy, a more complex and contingent understanding of this phenomenon eventually emerged by the long, evolutionary route we have described.

In large part because of the events chronicled in this chapter, interest in dissonance theory waned considerably in social psychology (see Bagby, Parker, & Bury, 1990).[21] The necessity of continually modifying dissonance theory and the absence of a clear winner in the theoretical debates between dissonance and other theories caused dissonance theory in general and research on counterattitudinal advocacy more specifically to lose their glamour status in social psychology. Some psychologists have mourned this loss of interest in the classic version of dissonance theory (e.g., Aronson, 1989, 1990; Berkowitz & Devine, 1989). We are of two minds about the contemporary inattention to dissonance theory. On the one hand, the loss of interest reflects the growth of understanding about the conditions and processes responsible for the phenomena that Festinger investigated. Because scientific progress is not something to be mourned, we instead take pride in the fact that psychologists are now working within alternative theoretical paradigms that more adequately encompass the research findings that have been produced. On the other hand, we recognize that the endeavor of the original theory of cognitive dissonance was far broader than the task of delineating the conditions that produce attitude change with laboratory-induced compliance experiments. We give this broader scope due recognition elsewhere in this book (Chapters 10 and 12) and argue that contemporary researchers can gain useful insights from the ideas that Festinger put forth in several areas. However provocative some of these ideas are, most of them seem somewhat vague and underdeveloped from a contemporary perspective. In contrast, in the area of induced compliance that we reviewed in this chapter, Festinger's ideas received careful clarification and empirical testing, and because of this attention eventually had to be reformulated. That at least some of one's ideas stimulate considerable research and are therefore replaced in due course by a more precise set of understandings is about the best fate that one can hope for in a scientific career.

The growth of knowledge about behavior's impact on attitudes is genuine and may be somewhat underappreciated by many contemporary observers. We believe that this research area now poses unique challenges that should inspire vigorous theoretical development once again. Such development should favor a more general theory of behavior-attitude relations that encompasses earlier theories. Indeed, there are signs of more integrative theorizing in the assimilation of dissonance theory into broader theories that emphasize self-identity.

In our opinion, the missing link in contemporary theories—the link that must be in place before more general theories will be developed—is an understanding of the cognitive processing underlying the attitudinal effects of counterattitudinal and pro-attitudinal advocacy. In this chapter, we have set forth our speculations about the modes of information processing underlying the impact of behavior on attitudes. Thus, we suggested that the early role-playing experiments placed implicit if not explicit demands on their role-playing subjects to process the information in their counterattitudinal advocacy relatively thoroughly and systematically. We also suggested that the self-threat inherent in classic dissonance experiments on induced compliance also produced relatively thorough processing of information. In this case, however, the information that role-players scrutinized presumably was not the argumentation in their advocacy but the negative consequences that ensued from this advocacy and their own responsibility in producing these consequences. In contrast, self-perception theory described a type of superficial processing of the information in one's behavior—a simple inference that if one engaged in a behavior, one must have an attitude congruent with the behavior. As we have explained, this simple inference can be subverted quite readily by other attitude-relevant information (i.e., by stored knowledge about the attitude object; by clear-cut sensory input). Yet this simple inference may often be an important input when people initially form their attitudes.

Greatly needed are experiments that assess indicators of the cognitive mechanisms that may underlie the attitude change produced by one's own behavior. Once the cognitive processing that mediates self-persuasion is better understood, this knowledge can be integrated with the more extensive understanding that psychologists already possess of the motivational mechanisms underlying self-persuasion. The special challenge in this area is to develop theory that takes into account both motivational and informational processes. We expect that the more general and complete theory that should result will share many principles with the theories of message-based persuasion we presented in Chapters 6, 7, and 8.

——— Notes ———

1. The fact that the subjects in the non-improvisation condition reported more satisfaction with their performance than the subjects who had the more demanding improvisational task suggested to King and Janis (1956) that the self-persuasive effect of role-playing was not produced by the reinforcement that follows from assurance of having done a good job as a role-player. However, contrary to this conclusion, several subsequent experiments found that role-players who received approval for their performance were more persuaded than role-players who received disapproval or neutral feedback (e.g., Bostrom, Vlandis, & Rosenbaum, 1961; W. A. Scott, 1957; Wallace, 1966; see Elms, 1967).

2. Janis and Mann (1965) referred to this type of personally threatening improvisation as *emotional role-playing*. The fear-provoking elements of this procedure may well have contributed to its effectiveness (see L. Mann, 1967).

3. Although we use the term *incentive theory* to refer to Janis's general perspective on the attitudinal effects of role-playing, he sometimes referred to his interpretation as a *conflict model* (Janis, 1959, 1968; see also Janis & Mann, 1977). In this more general theory of conflict, Janis treated decisional conflicts in terms of a personal balance sheet containing positive and negative values that correspond to the potential gains (positive incentives) and losses (negative incentives) anticipated by a decision maker when he or she evaluates each available alternative. In the application of this balance sheet notion to the attitudinal effects of role-playing, the alternatives available to role-players were treated as (a) maintenance of their private attitudinal position and (b) adoption of the position they advocated in their message.

4. For example, commenting on the Festinger and Carlsmith (1959) study (see below), Roger Brown (1965) wrote, "The outcome of the Festinger and Carlsmith experiment is not an obvious one, in terms either of psychological theory or of common sense. The non-obviousness of their predictions is

a characteristic in which dissonance theorists take pride" (p. 588).

5. Yet we are sympathetic to B. E. Collins and Hoyt's (1972) suggestion that the term "dissonance-predicted effect" is more accurate, given that other theories can predict this inverse relation between incentive and attitude change (e.g., self-perception theory; see subsequent discussion).

6. Additional demonstrations of the dissonance effect within the counterattitudinal advocacy paradigm accumulated as well (e.g., J. Cooper & Duncan, 1971; Greenbaum & Zemach, 1972).

7. The post-decisional dissonance studies in which subjects evaluated alternatives after they had chosen between them (e.g., J. W. Brehm, 1956) provided another, somewhat more complex paradigm. In this research, which is considered in Chapter 10, one's choice was assumed to be dissonant with the negative features of the chosen alternative and the positive features of the nonchosen alternative.

8. In a clever variant of the paradigm in which subjects engage in a negatively evaluated behavior, Aronson and Mills (1959) had college women undergo a screening test before they could join a discussion group on the psychology of sex. In a severe initiation condition, this screening test was quite embarrassing because subjects had to read aloud obscene words and graphic descriptions of sexual activity. In a mild initiation condition, subjects read sexual words commonly used in polite discourse (e.g., prostitute, virgin). After the discussion, they listened to one of the group's discussions. This discussion was extremely dull and incoherent. Aronson and Mills regarded the effort of undergoing the severe initiation as dissonant with the disappointing outcome. To reduce this dissonance, subjects could evaluate the discussion and its participants more positively. Indeed, subjects exposed to the severe initiation showed more positive evaluations than subjects exposed to the mild initiation or control subjects,

who did not undergo an initiation. Replications of this experiment have shown that the effect is robust (e.g., Schopler & Bateson, 1962) and have ruled out various alternative explanations (Gerard & Mathewson, 1966). The general principle illustrated by the Aronson and Mills study—that people love what they suffer for—is known as *effort justification* and has seen numerous applications in dissonance research (e.g., Aronson, 1961; Arrowood & Ross, 1966; Axsom, 1989; Axsom & Cooper, 1985; Lawrence & Festinger, 1962; Wicklund, Cooper, & Linder, 1967; Yaryan & Festinger, 1961).

9. Having all or virtually all subjects comply with the experimenter's request is a necessary condition for an unambiguous demonstration of dissonance effects. Experiments in which only a portion of the subjects complied (e.g., Zimbardo, Weisenberg, Firestone, & Levy, 1965) are vulnerable to the criticism that dissonance effects occur only for self-selected samples of people. Also, whatever self-selection factors caused only some subjects to comply could be confounded with comparisons between high and low justification conditions and between these conditions and a control condition not subjected to the experimenter's request.

10. This definition as well as others given by Brehm and Cohen (1962) leave the conceptual meaning of commitment somewhat vague. In a more abstract vein, Festinger (1964b) subsequently wrote that "a decision carries commitment with it if the decision unequivocally affects subsequent behavior. This is not intended to mean that the decision is irrevocable, but rather that the decision has clear implications for the subsequent unrolling of events as long as the person stays with that decision" (p. 156). More simply, Kiesler (1971) defined commitment as the "pledging or binding of the individual to behavioral acts" (p. 30).

11. We note that Brehm and Cohen's (1962) restriction led them to argue that message-based persuasion should be removed from the domain of dissonance theory, even though Festinger (1957)

had included it (see Chapter 10). However, Brehm and Cohen believed that dissonance theory predicted reactions to persuasive communications when message recipients in some way committed themselves to the communicator's position or freely chose to expose themselves to a message (e.g., Eagly & Whitehead, 1972; Himmelfarb & Arazi, 1974; R. A. Jones & Brehm, 1967).

12. The empirical status of predictions about moral and hedonic dissonance is difficult to evaluate because only partial reports have been published of the several studies that explored these predictions (see Kelman, 1980; Kelman & Baron, 1974). The concepts might fruitfully be explored in relation to Higgins' (1987, 1989b) self-discrepancy theory, which argues that violating different aspects of the self produces different sorts of affect.

13. In particular, Scheier and Carver (1980) suggested that the bogus pipeline redirects subjects' attention to their initial attitudes (see discussion of public and private self-attention in subsequent paragraphs).

14. See also Alexander and Knight (1971) for a *situated identity* perspective that is closely related to the impression management viewpoint of Tedeschi and his colleagues. The situated identity approach has seen only limited empirical development in relation to induced-compliance research.

15. The general emphasis on dissonance as a defensive process may remind readers of our discussion of *defense motivation*, one of three motivational bases we proposed as relevant to persuasion settings (Chaiken, Liberman, & Eagly, 1989; see Chapter 7). Defense motivation, viewed as the desire to defend particular attitudinal positions, could encompass the state we judge is relevant to induced compliance, that is, the desire to defend one's positive attitude toward one's self.

16. See Beckmann and Gollwitzer (1987) for an information-processing analysis of post-decisional dissonance (see Chapter 10).

17. A substantial research literature has grown up on the undermining of positive attitudes by providing tangible rewards for engaging in a behavior (see reviews by Deci & Ryan, 1985; Lepper & Greene, 1978; Pittman & Heller, 1987). This research suggests that straightforward applications of self-perception theory and attribution theory no longer provide totally adequate accounts of the diverse findings in this area (e.g., the apparent inability of young children to use the discounting principle is awkward from the perspective of attribution theory).

18. In the absence of tangible rewards, engaging in highly committing behaviors such as proselytizing for a proattitudinal cause (or merely agreeing to proselytize) has been shown to make people's attitudes more extreme, at least under some circumstances (Kiesler, Nisbett, & Zanna, 1969; M. S. Pallak & Kleinhesselink, 1976; Zanna & Kiesler, 1971).

19. This point is reminiscent of the argument by some of the early critics of the Festinger and Carlsmith (1959) experiment that the $20 reward lessened attitude change because it was implausibly high and thus produced interfering reactions (e.g., Janis & Gilmore, 1965; M. J. Rosenberg, 1965b). In addition, Freedman, Cunningham, and Krismer (1992) have argued that high incentives allow people to infer that an activity is difficult or unpleasant.

20. Readers might note some striking parallels between these self-perception findings and some of the persuasion findings that we reviewed when discussing the heuristic-systematic and the elaboration likelihood models in Chapter 7. For example, message recipients often base their attitudes on heuristic cues (e.g., communicator characteristics) when message positions are relatively inconsequential (e.g., Chaiken, 1980; Petty, Cacioppo, & Goldman, 1981). In addition, recipients process messages heuristically when they are able to retrieve relatively little knowledge about the message topic (e.g., W. Wood & Kallgren, 1988).

21. Despite this decline of interest within social psychology, we have observed that the concept of cognitive dissonance has survived to some extent in the general culture, where it is sometimes invoked by people who have little or no knowledge of theory or research related to the concept in social psychology. Cognitive dissonance has even enjoyed a certain vogue among historians, who have invoked it to help explain why the leaders of the Confederacy persevered so long in the U.S. Civil War. These historians argued that, given the South's commitment and sacrifices for the war, admitting the necessity of surrender or negotiation with the North threatened to create an intolerable amount of dissonance (e.g., Beringer, Hattaway, Jones, & Still, 1986).

557

12

Resistance and Persistence Processes
in Attitude Change

We have devoted the prior six chapters of this book to the examination of attitude change. Although our focus on change might be thought to imply that attitudes are fairly easily altered, any such conclusion would be wrong. On the contrary, the study of attitude change fascinates and challenges psychologists in part because of the apparent difficulty of creating substantial change in natural settings. In fact, the observation that change is not easily accomplished is frequent in social scientists' discussions of attitudes—for example, in discussions of the impact of the mass media.[1] Explicating the psychology of attitude change may thus help solve what is widely acknowledged to be a perplexing problem.

However informative the principles of attitude change may be, understanding change does not necessarily give us much insight into the question of why resistance to change is often so pervasive and effective. The insight that persuasion theories provide concerning why attitudes can be unchanging is merely that persuasion attempts are badly designed or inappropriate, according to the dictates of one or more theories. For example, an attractive or famous person hired to endorse a product in an advertising campaign might prove ineffective if most consumers believe that this source praised the product merely because he was paid to do so. The attribution model of attitude change would explain why such a communicator might have limited effectiveness (see Chapter 8). Yet the more profound reason why attitudes can be difficult to change is not well illuminated by most theories of attitude change: People have available to them psychological processes that facilitate resistance to persuasion and that can hamper even well designed persuasive efforts. Such processes are the focus of this chapter.

Even a superficial analysis of attitudes suggests that researchers should give systematic attention to resistance to change. The idea that people ordinarily would be willing to change their attitudes is not plausible when analyzed with care. Complete and continuous openness to new influences would leave the individual with a constantly shifting view of reality. The adaptive difficulties that extreme open-mindedness would create have already been implied in our discussion of attitudes' knowledge function (see Chapter 10), by which attitudes provide guidelines for judging the environment. Adults possess large numbers of attitudes that have been formed in interaction with the environment and that often reflect a very long history of direct and indirect experience with the objects of these attitudes. These attitudes allow people to anticipate events and to cope easily and effectively with events that occur repeatedly. Although attitudes reflecting substantial past experience may be maladaptive in a changing environment, they ordinarily serve people quite well. Such attitudes are not easily discarded in response to a small amount of new information that is inconsistent with the prior viewpoint. Existing attitudes may thus produce rigidity that is not acknowledged by theories of persuasion. Because established attitudes are themselves a major source of resistance to change, this chapter features research in which attitude serves as an independent variable in studies that display its sometimes powerful efforts on information processing.

In the attitudinal arena, pressures toward stability are countered by pressures toward change. A mind that is completely closed to new input would not serve humans' adaptive requirements, nor would a mind that is completely flexible and open to change at any point. E. E. Jones and Gerard (1967) referred to this conflict as the "*basic antinomy* between openness to change and the desire to preserve a pre-existing view or conviction" (p. 227). In recognition of this antinomy, psychologists need to specify the differing conditions under which resistance to change or openness to change is likely to predominate. The research we review in this chapter has in fact shed some light on these conditions.

Despite the obvious importance of studying mechanisms of resistance, few formal theories of attitudinal resistance have flourished in social psychology. McGuire's (1964) inoculation theory is an exception to this generalization as it was specifically developed to explain resistance to persuasion. Most other insights that investigators have gained about resistance have stemmed from somewhat broader theories of attitudes (e.g., social judgment theory) or of psychological functioning (e.g., reactance theory; psychoanalytic theory). Although such theories are not tailored specifically to understanding attitudinal resistance, some of their theoretical principles do have straightforward implications for resistance processes.

In addition to the contributions that a number of theories have made to understanding resistance to attitude change, a substantial amount of the knowledge that psychologists have gained on this topic has flowed from attitude researchers' empirical work on several phenomena. Attitudinal selectivity in information processing (e.g., attention, perception, judgment, memory) is one such phenomenon. As we show in this chapter, attitudinal selectivity at various stages of information processing has been widely studied by social psychologists from a very early point in the history of attitude research. Not surprisingly, psychologists have generally postulated tendencies for selectivity to favor individuals' prior attitudes. Common reasoning is that once attitudes have been established, they set up a certain force toward maintaining themselves. Such a force should operate in favor of attitudinally congenial information and against uncongenial information and thereby produce attitudes that are resistant to change. Similarly, the tendency for attitudes to polarize when people think about them (Tesser, 1978) should enhance resistance to change. Thus, research on selectivity and polarization, which we review in this chapter, has yielded important insights into the psychological processes by which people resist changing their attitudes.

In this chapter we also give some attention to the temporal persistence of attitudes. This often neglected topic bears some relation to the topic of resistance to change because attitudes that are change resistant endure over time. Although there are no

560

theories devoted exclusively to the persistence of attitudes, certain more general theories have implications for persistence (e.g., associationist models; the heuristic-systematic model). Also, certain research paradigms have drawn researchers' attention to attitudinal persistence—most notably, research on the *sleeper effect* (e.g., Cook, Gruder, Hennigan, & Flay, 1979). This paradigm and others have yielded insights into the psychological processes by which attitudes persist over time.

Inoculation Theory

The grandparent theory of resistance to attitude change is William McGuire's (1964) inoculation theory, a framework that sets forth both motivational and cognitive principles that may underlie resistance. The initial insight underlying this theory emerged in the Yale persuasion researchers' early work on one-sided and two-sided communications (Hovland, Janis, & Kelley, 1953). In their principal experiment on the sidedness of communications (Lumsdaine & Janis, 1953), high school students received a communication in the form of a radio program arguing that the Soviet Union would not be able to produce large numbers of atomic bombs for at least five years. Some students received a one-sided version of this communication, which contained only arguments supporting this conclusion, whereas others received a two-sided version, which contained the supportive arguments but also presented opposing arguments (of which some were refuted and others were not). Although the initial persuasive impact of these two messages was equivalent, subjects who had received the two-sided message were considerably more resistant to a later counter-communication arguing that the Soviet Union would be producing large numbers of atomic bombs within two years.[2] In language that was prophetic of later theoretical developments, Lumsdaine and Janis (1953) speculated about the mechanisms underlying the greater resistance to persuasion conferred by two-sided messages:

> [The listener] is not only familiar with the opposing point of view, but has been led to the positive conclusion in a context in which the negative arguments were in evidence. In effect, he has been given an advance basis for ignoring or discounting the opposing communication, and thus "inoculated," he will tend to retain the positive conclusion (p. 318).

McGuire (1964) elaborated this insight by developing *inoculation theory*. The name of this theory stems from the biological analogy that provides its guiding logic. Specifically, immunization against viruses can be achieved by administering a weakened dose of a virus. Such inoculation protects people against disease because the weakened dose stimulates the body to develop antibodies that defend it against the effects of a subsequent full-scale exposure to the virus. When an inoculation is effective, it confers complete protection against the viral attack. By analogy, McGuire reasoned that attitudes and beliefs are vulnerable to persuasive attack by opposing arguments and that protection against such attacks may be achieved by exposing people to weakened forms of the attacking message. A relatively weak attack should encourage people to develop defenses against such attacks while not changing their attitudes or beliefs—in other words, confer immunity without causing them to fall ill.

Pursuing this biological analogy, McGuire argued that the attitudes and beliefs that people have seldom heard attacked should be most vulnerable to attack, just as people brought up with little exposure to viruses should be most vulnerable to viral illnesses. Therefore, McGuire's research dealt with a class of beliefs that he termed *cultural truisms*—ideas that are widely shared in a culture and rarely attacked or questioned. Truisms used in this research, all of which pertained to health issues, included "It's a good idea to brush your teeth after every meal if at all possible" and "Mental illness is not contagious" (McGuire, 1964, p. 201).

Inoculation Research Paradigm. In the prototypical inoculation experiment, a first session provides subjects with defenses against persuasive attacks on several cultural truisms. The attacks, which occur in a second session, each consist of a three-paragraph essay arguing against one of the truisms. On one of the issues, subjects have been inoculated against attack during the first session. This inoculation takes the form of a treatment that McGuire named *refutational defense* and that consists of a presentation of the cultural truism followed by two arguments opposing it. Depending on whether the refutational defense takes an active or passive form, subjects are asked either to generate their own refutation of each attacking argument or to read statements that refute each argument.[3]

Also in the first session but on another issue, subjects receive a different treatment, termed *supportive defense*, which consists of a presentation of two arguments defending the truism. Subjects are asked either to generate their own support for these arguments or to read statements that support the arguments. Again building on the biological analogy, McGuire (1964) likened this treatment to supportive therapy that might provide adequate rest, an excellent diet, and sufficient exercise. People who have this healthful life-style might be generally somewhat more resistant to disease than people who have a less healthful life-style but would nonetheless be quite vulnerable to attack by a virus such as measles, provided that they have not been immunized against it. McGuire thus reasoned that supportive defenses would provide relatively little protection against ideological attack.

In the typical inoculation experiment, beliefs are assessed at the end of the second session, in which the attacks occur. To provide a baseline against which the efficacy of the refutational and supportive defenses can be judged, an *attack only* condition displays the impact of attack in the absence of any defensive material. In this control condition, an attack occurs in the second session, without prior exposure to either defense. Comparison of the defense conditions with this condition allows an estimate of the protective value of the two types of defenses. To provide a prior belief baseline, some beliefs are not attacked nor are defenses provided. This *neither defense nor attack* condition estimates subjects' preexisting beliefs. Because many inoculation experiments have within-subjects designs, each subject may appear in both defense conditions (i.e., refutational defense plus attack; supportive defense plus attack) as well

TABLE 12.1

Mean Belief Levels in the McGuire and Papageorgis (1961) Inoculation Experiment

Treatment	Mean belief level
Refutational defense plus attack	10.33
Supportive defense plus attack	7.39
Attack only	6.64
Neither defense nor attack	12.62

Note. 15.00 indicates complete adherence to truism; 1.00 indicates complete disagreement.

Source: This table was adapted from one presented by McGuire (1964, Table 1, p. 207).

as in both control conditions (attack only; neither defense nor attack). The issues are rotated around these conditions so that each issue appears equally often in each condition.

Findings from McGuire and Papageorgis's (1961) inoculation experiment appear in Table 12.1. Clearly, attacks not preceded by defense pretreatments severely weakened subjects' beliefs. Refutational defenses conferred considerable resistance to attack, as shown by the significant difference between subjects' beliefs in the refutational defense and the attack only conditions. Refutational defenses conferred significantly more resistance than supportive defenses. In fact, because the supportive defenses produced beliefs that did not differ significantly from those in the attack only condition, this experiment did not produce evidence that supportive defenses conferred any protection from the persuasive effect.

Interestingly, supportive defenses proved marginally *more* effective than refutational defenses in strengthening *pre-attack* beliefs, as demonstrated in this experiment by an assessment of subjects' beliefs at the end of the *first* session, before they were exposed to the attacking message. However, this ability of supportive defenses to strengthen beliefs does not indicate that such defenses confer resistance to later counterattack. As McGuire and Papageorgis wrote, "Some treatments (e.g., the refutational defenses) that appear to leave the beliefs relatively weak actually confer on them hidden reserves of resistance, while other treatments (e.g., the supportive defenses) that seem to have much strengthened the beliefs have actually left them 'paper tigers'" (p. 332).

Cognitive and Motivational Bases of Resistance. Although the practical value of inoculation treatments is suggested by these data, more detailed theory and additional research were needed to shed light on the psychological processes that underlie the effectiveness of refutational defenses. Moving beyond his biological analogy into the realm of psychological theory, McGuire suggested two principles underlying the vulnerability of cultural truisms to attack. One of these principles emphasized cognition, and the other emphasized motivation. The cognitive principle is that people

563

have little or no practice in defending truisms. They have not engaged in defense and often lack informational resources that could enable them to mount a defense. The motivational principle is that people have not been goaded to undertake the necessary practice because their beliefs have never been threatened and therefore seem unassailable. McGuire reasoned that these cognitive and motivational deficits must be reversed to protect people from persuasion. The lack of practice and skill can be reversed by providing people with guided practice in defending their beliefs. The lack of motivation can be reversed by threatening people's beliefs so that they become aware of the vulnerability of their beliefs to attack. As we noted in Chapter 6, McGuire's descriptions of these cognitive and motivational aspects of defending oneself against attack could be construed as implicating an underlying process of covert counterarguing. Yet McGuire did not conceptualize such a process with the detail that the subsequent cognitive response theorists did (e.g., A. G. Greenwald, 1968), nor did he focus empirical efforts on directly assessing this underlying defensive process through thought listing or other devices.

In an experiment containing a manipulation that shed some light on underlying processes, Papageorgis and McGuire (1961) compared two types of refutational defenses with the two control conditions used in their earlier research (attack only and neither defense nor attack). The message labeled *refutational-same* presented and refuted weak versions of the same attacking arguments used in the later full-scale attack, as in the experiment by McGuire and Papageorgis (1961). The message labeled *refutational-different* presented and refuted weak versions of attacking arguments that were different from those used in the later attack. If refutational defenses gain their effectiveness only because of a narrowly defined informational gain (i.e., only because they provide people with specific rebuttals of the particular arguments contained in the subsequent attack), the refutational-same message should confer greater resistance than the refutational-different message. However, the effectiveness of refutational defenses may depend on other factors—namely, conveying more general knowledge about how to defend one's own position and motivating defense of this position. If so, the refutational-different treatment should be as effective as the refutational-same one.

Papageorgis and McGuire's (1961) findings showed that the same and different renditions of the refutational defenses were equally effective and that both instilled considerable resistance to persuasion, compared with the attack-only control condition. This experiment (and others, e.g., Pfau & Burgoon, 1988; Szybillo & Heslin, 1973) thus suggested that refutational defenses do not aid resistance merely because they communicate the specific information that is useful in counterarguing a later attack. Nonetheless, in view of Tannenbaum's (1967) contrary finding that refutational-same defenses induced significantly more resistance to attack than refutational-different defenses, it is worth noting that in several studies by McGuire and his colleagues (see also Szybillo & Heslin, 1973), there was a nonsignificant tendency for refutational-same defenses to confer greater resistance. This evidence, which is consistent with at least a slight superiority of refutational-same defenses, suggests that the effectiveness of refutational defenses may stem in part from the specific information that they convey and its usefulness for countering a later attack.

564

In subsequent experimentation, McGuire and his colleagues elaborated various aspects of inoculation theory and provided additional demonstrations of the theory's principles (McGuire, 1961a, 1961b, 1962; McGuire & Papageorgis, 1962; see McGuire, 1964). For example, this research established that (a) supportive defenses gain effectiveness when combined with refutational defenses (McGuire, 1961a) and (b) both supportive and refutational defenses, especially the supportive, gain effectiveness when preceded by a warning of the upcoming persuasive attack (McGuire & Papageorgis, 1962).[4] In general, these experiments confirmed the view that the efficacy of inoculations stems from both motivational and cognitive sources. Moreover, the specific circumstances under which refutational and supportive defenses are effective were shown to depend on whether the processes that mediate their impact are mainly motivational, mainly cognitive, or a more even mix of these types of processes. For example, McGuire reasoned that to the extent that a defense depends on the specific information it conveys, its effectiveness should decay over time in conformity with an ordinary forgetting curve (see Chapter 6). In contrast, a defense grounded more strongly in motivation should have a somewhat delayed effect because the passage of time allows a threatened individual to accumulate and organize material appropriate to fending off the subsequent attack. In a study of the persistence of the resistance to attack conferred by various defenses, McGuire's (1962) reasoning received support. Specifically, the resistance imparted by the supportive and the refutational-same defenses, which is presumably mediated primarily by cognitive mechanisms, decayed over time. In contrast, the refutational-different defense, whose effects are presumably grounded in motivation, was *more* effective when the attack occurred after a moderate interval of two days rather than immediately after the inoculation.

Evaluation of Inoculation Theory. The theory underlying McGuire's more detailed predictions is, as Insko (1967) observed, an unusual mix of biological analogy, established psychological principles, and intuitions about the interaction of these factors. In contrast to the strong empirical support for the predictions based directly on the analogy to biological immunization, it is much more difficult to judge the extent to which McGuire's psychological theory about cognitive and motivational processes should be regarded as supported by research. Our presentation has emphasized supportive findings, but other aspects of this research program fared less well (e.g., research on the sequencing of attacks and defenses; see Insko, 1967).

One barrier to evaluating inoculation theory is a relative absence of measures intended to assess directly the processes assumed to mediate resistance to change. However, such measures were occasionally included in this research. For example, Papageorgis and McGuire (1961) had subjects rate the attacking arguments on evaluative scales. This measure was intended to assess the extent to which prior exposure to refutations of attacking arguments reduced the credibility of subsequent attacks. Indeed, their findings suggested that refutational defenses did reduce attack credibility. Such efforts foreshadowed the more explicit attention to underlying processes typical of persuasion research of the 1970s and 1980s (see Chapters 6, 7, and 8).

If we assess McGuire's theory by the amount of research it has inspired, it has fared well. Researchers have conducted numerous extensions and replications of inoculation experiments (e.g., Suedfeld & Borrie, 1978), often using beliefs other than cultural truisms (W. C. Adams & Beatty, 1977; Burgoon, Cohen, Miller, & Montgomery, 1978; Cronen & LaFleur, 1977; Hunt, 1973; B. Pryor & Steinfatt, 1978). For example, Szybillo and Heslin (1973) examined a somewhat controversial belief not held as strongly as the truisms McGuire had presented—specifically, "Inflatable air bags should be installed as passive safety devices in all new cars" (p. 398). These researchers replicated typical inoculation findings concerning refutational and supportive defenses. Although findings have not been as favorable to inoculation predictions in some other replications and extensions (e.g., B. Pryor & Steinfatt, 1978), the fact that McGuire's findings have replicated in at least some independent tests using materials other than truisms has alleviated the anxiety, expressed by McGuire (1964) himself, that the theory might apply only to one special type of belief—cultural truisms. However, successful extensions of inoculation theory to more controversial issues raise questions about the boundary conditions of the theory. Perhaps beliefs do not have to be formed and maintained in a "germ-free" environment in order to be vulnerable to attacks yet protected from attacks by inoculations.

In recent years, inoculation theory has been used in the design of health education programs that focus on prevention (see reviews by Alcalay, 1983; Chassin, Presson, & Sherman, 1990; Flay, 1985; Killen, 1985; Moscowitz, 1983). For example, intervention programs designed to discourage smoking or prevent alcohol abuse have included refutational defense treatments (e.g., Duryea, 1983; Flay et al., 1985). In such field experiments, teenagers are exposed to various arguments, for example, in favor of drinking and driving. These arguments constitute the weak attack on what are presumed to be these teenagers' disapproving attitudes about drinking and driving. They then role-play resistant responses to pro-alcohol social pressures and may be given feedback instructing them how to refute pro-alcohol arguments more effectively (see discussion of role-playing in Chapter 11). Teenagers exposed to such interventions have proved to be somewhat less favorable to drinking and less likely to engage in risky alcohol-related behavior compared with teenagers not exposed to such interventions. In addition, Pfau and Burgoon (1988) examined the use of refutational defense messages in political campaigns, where such messages have sometimes been designed to inoculate supporters of candidates against opposing candidates' attacking messages. Among attitude theories, McGuire's inoculation theory is thus notable for the amount of practical application it has seen.[5]

Other Treatments that Produce Resistance to Persuasion. Research related to inoculation theory was conducted by Tannenbaum and his associates within the conceptual framework of congruity theory, one of the variants of balance theory that we discussed in Chapter 10 (Tannenbaum, 1967). Consistent with congruity and balance theory, incongruity (or imbalance) results when a favorably evaluated source, o, rejects (i.e., attacks) a favorably evaluated concept, x. In this triad, both the p-o and the p-x relations are positive, but the o-x relation is negative. To reduce the resulting imbalance, the perceiver, p, may well decrease his or her liking of the concept, x. In other words, the source's attack on concept x may prove to be persuasive.

From a balance (or congruity) perspective, refutational defenses confer resistance to attack by fostering counterarguing that weakens the o-x relation in the imbalanced triad established by a liked source's attack on a liked concept. In contrast, supportive defenses bolster p's attitude toward the concept, x, with the result that imbalance tends to be reduced through resolutions other than p changing his attitude toward x. In addition, the congruity perspective suggests other treatments that may confer some resistance to change. One of these, labeled *denial*, consists of severing the link between the source, o, and the concept, x, by instructing subjects, for example, that an institutional source (the United States Public Health Service) did not make the statements that were ascribed to it. A second proposed mechanism, labeled *source attack*, consists of derogating the source, o, by instructing subjects, for example, that a source who was a professor had been recommended for dismissal from his university because of "unethical and unprofessional behavior," including "unjustified statements to the public" (Tannenbaum, 1967, p. 280).

In studies comparing denial and source attack with treatments modeled after the refutational and supportive defenses used in inoculation research, the refutational treatment proved particularly effective in inducing resistance to change, but the supportive treatment conferred some resistance as well (Tannenbaum, 1967; Tannenbaum, Macaulay, & Norris, 1966). Although the source attack was effective in inducing resistance under some circumstances, the denial treatment proved ineffective.[6] Yet the amount of resistance conferred would no doubt depend on many specific features of Tannenbaum and his colleagues' instantiations of these four types of treatments. Thus, the importance of this additional work lies, not primarily in the details of the findings, but in the demonstration that there are other treatments that may make message recipients resistant to persuasion. These investigations suggest as well that an alternative theoretical perspective, that of balance theory, can be applied to understand resistance to persuasion.

Reflections on Inoculation Theory. Although research in the inoculation tradition has stressed brief experimental treatments that confer resistance to subsequent persuasive messages, the importance of this approach extends beyond such contexts. In fact, ideological immunizations may be commonly experienced in natural settings. Even though people may tend to expose themselves selectively to attitudinally supportive information (see subsequent discussion), on certain issues they are probably exposed to attacking arguments with some regularity—for example, during a political campaign or while a controversial issue is widely discussed. Some exposure to attacking arguments may indeed be threatening enough to motivate people to have "answers" to such attacks if they encounter them again. Individuals who have been attacked may therefore work very hard to develop adequate counterarguments to attacking arguments. In fact, activists on certain issues may receive explicit training in the refutation of opposing arguments, as suggested by the material we presented in Chapter 3 on pro-choice advocates' efforts to educate their supporters about pro-life arguments and to provide counterarguments to these arguments (see Table 3.3). Thus inoculated, activists may have attitudes that are extremely difficult to change.

Inoculation theory has not seen much development for many years. Although McGuire's biological analogy is admittedly clever and vivid, many of the questions it raised about psychological processes remain unresolved. In view of the apparent effectiveness of refutational defenses, these issues deserve renewed study in the context of contemporary theory and methodology.

Two Motivational Theories of Resistance

In assuming that refutational defenses threaten people's beliefs and therefore induce them to seek supportive information, McGuire (1964) introduced motivational language into his theory of resistance to persuasion. Given that he developed this theory in the early 1960s, it is not surprising that he relied to some extent on motivational constructs. As we have pointed out in our prior two chapters, such concepts were more popular among research psychologists active at that time, compared with psychologists active in later decades. Psychology's cognitive revolution directed attention to cognitive processing and away from study of the motives that may drive such processes.

To locate other theories that address resistance to persuasion from a motivational perspective, one need only read attitude theory and research of the 1950s and 1960s. Given the zeitgeist of that period, it would be surprising if attitudinal resistance were not understood primarily in motivational terms. The guiding idea of strictly motivational theories of resistance is that information discrepant from one's existing attitudes and beliefs will fail to be persuasive because such information threatens certain general motives or needs. Most commonly, psychologists argued that attitudinally challenging information can threaten the freedom to do or believe what one desires (J. W. Brehm, 1966) or threaten the self or ego (D. Katz, 1960; Sarnoff, 1960).

Resistance to Preserve Freedom

Jack Brehm's theory of psychological reactance provides what is probably the best-known motivational theory of resistance to persuasion (J. W. Brehm, 1966, 1968, 1972; S. S. Brehm & Brehm, 1981). This theory asserts that when individuals perceive their freedom to engage or not engage in some behavior as threatened or eliminated, they experience *reactance*, a state of motivational arousal that leads them to attempt to restore their threatened or lost freedom. With respect to persuasion, the theory assumes that people want to feel free to adopt particular positions on issues or not to adopt any position at all. Under some conditions, persuasive messages that attempt to influence recipients to adopt particular positions may threaten this attitudinal freedom. Moreover, the more important the attitudinal freedom that is threatened and the greater the coercive pressure exerted on the individual to adopt a particular position, the greater will be the magnitude of reactance experienced. Thus, the theory predicts that when people receive persuasive messages that they construe to be threats to their attitudinal freedom, they attempt to reassert their freedom by maintaining their initial opinions or, more provocatively, by changing their opinions in a direction opposite to the position advocated in the message, a shift often termed a *boomerang effect*. Such reactance-induced attitudes should be maintained over time, unless the threats to attitudinal freedom are removed (see S. S. Brehm & Brehm, 1981). If such threats are eliminated, people may be more favorable to a message's position after a delay than they were immediately after receiving the message (i.e., a sleeper effect would be obtained; see subsequent discussion).

Research on overt, obvious attempts to force subjects to take attitudinal positions advocated in communications has generally supported the predictions of reactance theory. For example, in several experiments that Brehm (1966) conducted with his associates and reported in his initial book on reactance theory, subjects first completed a questionnaire in which they gave their attitudes on various issues. In a second session, subjects received a message that challenged one or more of these attitudes. In the high threat condition of these experiments, designed to produce reactance, a very coercive statement accompanied the communicator's views (e.g., "You, as college students, must inevitably draw the same conclusion," Brehm, 1966, p. 110). This additional instruction was omitted in the low threat condition. After receiving either a high threat or low threat message, subjects gave their own attitudes once again. Although the findings of these experiments displayed some complexity (e.g., occasional interactions when reactance was crossed with other independent variables), in general subjects exposed to a high threat communication were less persuaded than were subjects exposed to a low threat communication. Similar demonstrations that high pressure tactics reduce or eliminate the attitude change that would occur without such tactics have been reported in subsequent experiments (e.g., Heller, Pallak, & Picek, 1973; Sensenig & Brehm, 1968; M. Snyder & Wicklund, 1976; Wicklund & Brehm, 1968; Worchel & Brehm, 1970).

Despite the general confirmation of the principle that reactance induced by obvious, high-pressure persuasive tactics fosters resistance to persuasion, the reactance theory hypothesis that counterattitudinal messages cause greater reactance and thus greater *negative* (or boomerang) attitude change than proattitudinal messages (because of the greater discrepancy of counterattitudinal messages) has not received support (e.g., M. Snyder & Wicklund, 1976; Worchel & Brehm, 1970). For example, Worchel and Brehm (1970) presented subjects with a message advocating that the Communist party should be treated like any other political party in the United States. For some subjects, this position was proattitudinal, and for others it was counterattitudinal. For the subjects in the high threat condition, the message contained extra statements of the sort "you cannot believe otherwise" or "you have no choice but to believe this" (Worchel & Brehm, 1970, p. 19). For the subjects in the low threat condition, these statements were omitted. Contrary to their expectation, Worchel and Brehm found that the negative persuasive impact of the message was greater in the high threat than the low threat condition only for subjects who received a proattitudinal message.

The support of reactance predictions regarding boomerang attitude change primarily for proattitudinal messages has been interpreted in terms of *prior exercise of freedom*

(M. Snyder & Wicklund, 1976; Wicklund, 1974; Wright, 1986). According to this interpretation, recipients of counterattitudinal messages have already asserted their freedom by expressing initial attitudes that oppose those advocated by the message. They can thus preserve their attitudinal freedom merely by maintaining their initial attitudes. In contrast, in order to restore their attitudinal freedom, recipients of proattitudinal messages must change their attitudes *away* from the position advocated in the message (see S. S. Brehm & Brehm, 1981).

Brehm (1968) also suggested that more *subtle* pressures to adopt an attitudinal position, such as a communicator's stated intention or desire to influence recipients, can arouse reactance, albeit to a lesser extent than more overt pressures. Subtle pressures could thus inhibit persuasion or even produce boomerang change. To test this hypothesis, Heller et al. (1973) had subjects encounter an experimental confederate who expressed a desire to persuade as many people as possible on the topic of building nuclear power plants near populated areas (or who expressed little interest in the topic). Although the confederate did not disclose his position on the issue, opposition to building plants was probably expected because over 90 percent of the students held such an unfavorable attitude on this issue. In a condition that examined the impact of subtle pressures to adopt an attitudinal position, subjects then freely chose to write an essay on either side of this issue. Before writing the essay, subjects exposed to the confederate who desired to persuade changed their attitudes away from their initial positions (and therefore away from the confederate's presumed antinuclear attitude). Also, in their essays, they generated more arguments against their initial positions. These reactions presumably restored the freedom threatened by the subtle persuasive pressure from the confederate.

Also consistent with Brehm's reasoning about subtle pressures are studies showing that at least under some conditions, warning recipients of a communicator's expressed intent to influence them inhibits persuasion (e.g., Freedman & Sears, 1965b; Hass & Grady, 1975; Kiesler & Kiesler, 1964; Petty & Cacioppo, 1979a). Nevertheless, other research indicates that warnings of a communicator's persuasive intent may have no impact on attitude change (Allyn & Festinger, 1961; McGuire & Millman, 1965; McGuire & Papageorgis, 1962) and under some conditions may even enhance persuasion (e.g., Mills, 1966; Mills & Aronson, 1965; see note 4). Thus, if relatively subtle pressures, such as those inherent in warnings about a communicator's intent to persuade, do lead people to resist influence in the interest of maintaining or restoring freedom, the conditions under which such pressures are likely to instill reactance have yet to be delineated.

Because reactance is relevant only to that subset of persuasion settings in which messages threaten recipients' freedom to hold particular attitudinal positions, Brehm's (1968) theory does not provide a general model of resistance to persuasion. Nonetheless, as our discussion of warning has shown, reactance theory has proven useful for interpreting the effects of certain persuasion variables. Also included in these interpretations is an explanation of why likable sources sometimes engender less persuasion than less likable sources—because the pressure recipients experience to agree with liked sources can threaten their freedom (Brehm & Mann, 1975; Dickenberger & Grabitz-Gniech,

1972). Reactance also explains why direct communications can be less persuasive than communications that are inadvertently overheard—because the intent to influence ascribed to communicators of direct messages can threaten recipients' freedom (e.g., Brock & Becker, 1965; Walster & Festinger, 1962). In a more applied vein, the theory has generated predictions regarding the impact of censorship on people's reactions to censored materials (Worchel & Arnold, 1973; Worchel, Arnold, & Baker, 1975). Specifically, people who believe that they have the freedom to hear or read a persuasive communication may experience reactance if this freedom is thwarted by censorship. If people are then unable to receive the message, they may attempt to restore their freedom by changing their attitudes toward the position that they believe they would have heard or read had they been allowed to receive the message.

The issue of how reactance, the negative emotional state that ensues when freedom is threatened or eliminated, influences the processing of information remains largely unexplored. Researchers who have used reactance theory to generate predictions or to explain obtained persuasion findings have rarely included measures that may provide evidence of subjects' cognitive processing (e.g., thought-listing, recall). This omission is not surprising given that most research on reactance predated attitude researchers' contemporary preoccupation with underlying cognitive processes. Moreover, reactance researchers have not attempted to assess subjects' motivation directly. As a consequence, many persuasion findings that have been interpreted in terms of reactance theory are vulnerable to alternative interpretations within theoretical frameworks that assume different motives or specific modes of information processing not considered by reactance theory. For example, an alternative to Brehm's (1968) reactance interpretation of the lesser persuasive impact of direct than overheard communications is provided by attribution theory (see Chapter 8).

Impression Management Interpretation of Reactance Effects. Impression management theory (see Chapter 11; Leary & Kowalski, 1990; Tetlock & Manstead, 1985) has provided the most widely discussed alternative interpretation for attitudinal phenomena that have been considered manifestations of reactance. From the impression management perspective, the attitudes that subjects express in the high threat conditions of reactance studies may represent, not genuine changes in attitudes, but strategic and therefore more temporary shifts designed to manage an impression of being free or independent. If the attitudes expressed by subjects presumed to be experiencing reactance could be shown to be strategic shifts, the motivational state induced in reactance experiments would be more accurately described as a desire to project an image of autonomy to others rather than a desire to preserve one's freedom. Such an interpretation of reactance effects was first stated by Heilman and Toffler (1976), who argued that inductions of reactance commonly used in experiments create a desire "to project to the other an image of oneself as an autonomous being, thereby maintaining the previous status in the relationship, a status which has been implicitly challenged by attempts at freedom-reduction" (p. 20).

In an excellent test of this impression management interpretation of reactance effects, Baer, Hinkle, Smith, and Fenton (1980) had subjects read a proattitudinal communication on the issue of student participation in university administrative decisions, ostensibly written by their partner in the experiment. The high threat version of this communication threatened subjects' attitudinal freedom, whereas the low threat version did not. The threat consisted of high-pressure statements of the type typically used in reactance experiments featuring overt, obvious pressures (e.g., "You really have no choice but to believe," Baer et al., 1980, p. 419). In addition, some subjects had been given a prior opportunity to write an essay giving their views on the issue (i.e., prior exercise of attitudinal freedom). Among the subjects who wrote the essay, some believed the essay would be communicated to their partner (i.e., public exercise of freedom condition), and others believed it would be kept private (i.e., private exercise of freedom condition). After reading their partner's views, subjects responded to an attitude measure on the student participation issue, while expecting that this expression of their attitude would either be given to the partner (i.e., public attitude condition) or be kept confidential (i.e., private attitude condition).

Results of this study are shown in Figure 12.1. As predicted by impression management theory, subjects whose responses were confidential expressed attitudes that did not differ from the attitude responses they had given before reading their partner's statement. Among subjects whose attitudes were to be shown to their partner and were therefore public, the boomerang attitude change predicted by reactance theory occurred if they had received the high threat message (although not if they had been given the earlier opportunity to exercise attitudinal freedom by stating their views to their partner). The absence of reactance effects on privately expressed attitudes supports the claim that the attitudinal shifts obtained in reactance experiments may be superficial,

FIGURE 12.1. Mean attitude change for each experimental condition in Baer, Hinkle, Smith, and Fenton's (1980) experiment. This figure was presented by Baer et al. (1980, Figure 1, p. 420).

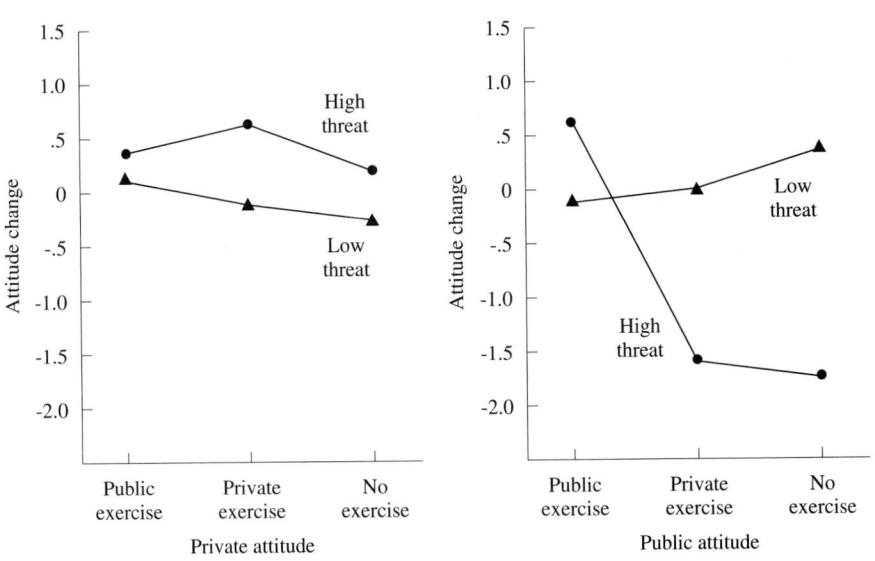

strategic changes that have the function of preserving the outward appearance that one is free to advocate whatever attitudinal position one desires.

Wright and S. S. Brehm (1982) provided an assertive rejoinder to the impression management interpretation proposed by Heilman and Toffler (1976) and Baer et al. (1980). In addition to criticizing some of the details of impression management experiments, Wright and Brehm pointed out that reactance effects have been obtained in quite a few studies in which subjects expressed their attitudes under relatively anonymous conditions in which the influencing agent was not particularly salient and had no surveillance over subjects' expressions of their attitudes (see also Wright, 1986). Nonetheless, Wright and Brehm adopted an integrative view that encompassed aspects of the impression management critique. Specifically, they argued that attacks on attitudinal freedom from an individual with whom one anticipates interaction may threaten attitudinal freedom more strongly than a relatively more anonymous communication from an individual with whom one does not expect to interact. Similarly, they acknowledged that public attitudinal statements may be more effective in restoring freedom because they may be perceived as safeguarding one against future threats from the influencing agent. In this manner, Wright and Brehm elaborated reactance theory to take into account certain interpersonal contingencies that may determine the amount of reactance people experience and the effectiveness of various modes of reducing reactance.

Reflections on Reactance Theory. It is very plausible that people sometimes resist persuasion because it threatens their freedom to believe what they want to believe. When threatened, they may be unreceptive to potentially persuasive arguments. Yet the fact that experimental demonstrations of resistance have been most reliably successful when communications included quite heavy-handed threats raises more general questions about the effectiveness of coercive appeals. Indeed, high-pressure social influence techniques may be counterproductive in many contexts. In commercial settings, for example, the hard sell may often be less effective than the soft sell. Nonetheless, psychologists have long been interested in the apparent effectiveness of psychologically coercive influence techniques—those that are sometimes popularly labeled *brainwashing*. Well known instances of persuasion that many psychologists have considered coercive include the ideological indoctrination of American prisoners during the Korean War (e.g., Lifton, 1961; Schein, Schneier, & Barker, 1961; see also Cialdini, 1988) and the conversion of young adults into religious cults, particularly during the 1970s (Conway & Siegelman, 1978). In addition, remarkable case histories are available of successful persuasion that apparently involved highly coercive elements. Examples include the case of Patricia Hearst, who presumably underwent an ideological conversion induced by members of a radical group known as the Symbionese Liberation Army (Hearst & Moscow, 1982), as well as the case of Peter Reilly, who was wrongfully persuaded by police that he had murdered his mother (Barthel, 1977). Successful coercive persuasion may occur only under specialized circumstances involving both extreme stress (Sargant, 1957) and a powerful social relationship with one or more agents of influence (Schein et al., 1961). Under more ordinary circumstances, highly coercive efforts to persuade are less likely to be successful, perhaps because of the reactance that such efforts induce. Admittedly, however, the conditions under which coercive persuasion is effective or produces resistance remain poorly understood.

Personality Bases of Resistance

Psychoanalytic theory, a general theory of personality and psychopathology developed by Freud, also has important implications for attitudinal resistance. This approach provides not only a theory of resistance to some classes of persuasive appeals, but also an explanation of why some people hold prejudiced attitudes toward racial and ethnic minorities. The key assumption of this perspective is Freud's (1920/1953) idea that people are motivated to protect themselves from unacceptable impulses emanating from within and threatening forces situated in the external environment. Freud labeled as *ego* the executive portion of the personality that mediates between the demands of instinctual drives and external reality (and the superego, or conscience). The ego can be threatened from within or without. Impulses having to do with sex and aggression, for example, might be experienced as threatening by people who were subjected to harsh child-rearing practices involving punishment for expression of such impulses. Because external stimuli can arouse forbidden impulses, events in daily life can also be threatening to the ego. Erotic films or magazines, for example, might arouse unacceptable sexual impulses and therefore would be experienced as threatening.

According to psychoanalytic theory, people use *defense mechanisms* (e.g., denial, projection, repression, reaction formation) to protect themselves against internal and external threats. As we noted in Chapters 1 and 10, this idea was featured in Daniel Katz's concept of the *ego-defensive* function of attitudes (D. Katz, 1960; see also D. Katz & Stotland, 1959). The approach was elaborated by Irving Sarnoff (1960, 1968), one of Katz's collaborators. Katz and Sarnoff maintained that people sometimes hold particular attitudes because these attitudes protect them from their own unacceptable impulses as well as from external threats. Attitudes are thus at the service of mechanisms of defense. For example, as Katz (1960) stated, "When we cannot admit to ourselves that we have deep feelings of inferiority we may project those feelings onto some convenient minority group and bolster our egos by attitudes of superiority toward this underprivileged group" (p. 172).[7] This ego-defensive function that attitudes can serve is presumably hidden from one's own view in the sense that one does not realize that an attitude protects the ego and is therefore not grounded in realistic perceptions of the external environment.

Authoritarian Personality Study. Critical aspects of Sarnoff's and Katz's analyses invoked the theory and empirical findings associated with research on the authoritarian personality, a project on the origins of prejudice (Adorno, Frenkel-Brunswik, Levinson, & Sanford, 1950). The authors of the authoritarian personality study also emphasized the psychoanalytic principle that people use defense mechanisms to protect themselves from unacceptable impulses. People may, for example, project their unacceptable aggressive impulses onto others by believing that these others are hostile. In a cultural context that provides many negative stereotypes about minority groups, the unacceptable motives existing inside oneself may very often be projected onto such groups (e.g., whites may believe that blacks are violent and sexually unrestrained). People may also express their unacceptable impulses more directly, but render them less threatening by displacing them onto weaker individuals and groups. For example, one might express hostility by aggressing against members of a minority group but not against one's parents or one's boss. In fact, the projection of unacceptable impulses onto minority groups would transform these groups into suitable targets for attack.

Evidence that the authoritarian personality study provided for this explanation of racial and ethnic prejudice is indirect, at best. Consistent with their individual differences perspective, these researchers assumed that some individuals, more than others, have had experiences that lead them to develop ego-defensive attitudes. The dimension of personality that presumably reflects these defensive tendencies was labeled *authoritarianism* by Adorno and his colleagues. To examine the origins of authoritarianism, some of the research of Adorno and his colleagues related respondents' accounts of their childhood to the personality variable of authoritarianism, which they assessed by a questionnaire measure known as the *F Scale* (i.e., Fascism Scale, so named because authoritarianism presumably made people vulnerable to the appeal of fascist ideology). Indeed, retrospective reports of childhood experiences obtained from people who scored high in authoritarianism did differ in the expected ways from the reports of those who scored lower in authoritarianism. For example, authoritarian people indicated that they had been subjected to harsher and more rigid discipline that was often experienced as threatening or traumatic.

As shown in Table 12.2, the F Scale included items designed to represent the types of defensive processes that presumably underlie prejudice (Adorno et al., 1950; see also Altemeyer, 1988; Robinson & Shaver, 1973). Whether endorsement of items representing projectivity, for example, indicates defensive projection or a more realistic perception is of course impossible to determine. Yet the items on the F Scale, which were written to reflect the researchers' psychoanalytic logic, did show acceptable internal consistency.

The claim that prejudice derives from ego-defensive processes, at least for people high in authoritarianism, was based primarily on the positive correlations obtained between the F Scale and various direct measures of prejudice toward minority groups (e.g., the E or Ethnocentrism Scale). However, these positive correlations between authoritarianism and prejudice remain causally ambiguous, in view of multiple alternative explanations for this relation (e.g., response sets; see Hyman & Sheatsley, 1954, and Chapter 2). In fact, soon after the research on the authoritarian personality was published, it was subjected to a barrage of criticism, primarily on methodological grounds (see Bass, 1955; Christie & Jahoda, 1954; Kirscht & Dillehay, 1967). Because the methods of the authoritarian personality study have been widely acknowledged to be less than rigorous, its empirical findings provide only limited support for Adorno and colleagues' claims about the ego-defensive nature of prejudice. Yet some of the findings of the early authoritarianism research, such as the relation between authoritarianism and prejudice, have been replicated by researchers whose methods are less vulnerable to methodological criticisms (see Altemeyer, 1988).

TABLE 12.2

Selected Items From the F Scale

Aspect of authoritarianism assessed	Items
Projectivity: Tendency to project one's unacceptable impulses onto others	Nowadays when so many different kinds of people move around and mix together so much, a person has to protect himself especially carefully against catching an infection or disease from them.
	The wild sex life of the old Greeks and Romans was tame compared to some of the goings-on in this country, even in places where people might least expect it.
Authoritarian aggression: Rejection of people who violate conventional values	An insult to our honor should always be punished.
	Most of our social problems would be solved if we could somehow get rid of the immoral, crooked, and feebleminded people.
Conventionalism: Rigid adherence to conventional, middle-class values	Obedience and respect for authority are the most important virtues children should learn.
	A person who has bad manners, habits, and breeding can hardly expect to get along with decent people.

Source: These items were presented by Adorno, Frenkel-Brunswik, Levinson, and Sanford (1950, Table 7, pp. 255–257).

Ego Defense and Resistance. Attitudes that have the function of defending the ego are thought to be impervious to ordinary persuasive appeals. To the extent that attitudes toward minority groups, for example, are grounded in one's own inner conflicts, they are rooted in one's efforts to resolve the powerful conflicts of early childhood. Such attitudes should not be susceptible to rational appeals or to contemporaneous rewards and punishments. By definition, ego-defensive attitudes would be difficult to change.

Despite the general pessimism that Freudian theory engenders about changing defensively motivated attitudes through brief persuasive appeals, Katz (1960) produced an analysis of how to change such attitudes via message-based persuasion. This analysis is part of Katz's more general functional theory of attitudes that we reviewed in Chapter 10. In implementing the general idea that persuasive appeals should match the functional basis of an attitude, Katz advocated changing ego-defensive attitudes through an approach that we might label therapeutic because it is designed to give people insight into their own mechanisms of defense. For example, if prejudiced individuals could be made to understand that their negative attitudes toward minorities

576

are grounded in fears about their own hostility or inferiority, they might be willing to forego these defensive attitudes and to adopt attitudes based on veridical perceptions of minority groups. According to Katz (1960), "Not all defensive behavior, then, is so deep rooted in the personality as to be inaccessible to awareness and insight. Therefore, procedures for arousing self-insight can be utilized to change behavior, even in mass communication" (p. 184). Consistent with this reasoning, Katz's research program on reducing racial prejudice examined the effectiveness of persuasive appeals that encouraged message recipients to interpret their own prejudiced attitudes in defensive terms.

Katz and his colleagues carried out three experiments in which white subjects were exposed to a written communication explaining that prejudice toward blacks can be defensive (D. Katz, Sarnoff, & McClintock, 1956; Katz, McClintock, & Sarnoff, 1957; Stotland, Katz, & Patchen, 1959). This communication contained some general information about how defensive processes relate to anti-minority attitudes and presented a case study of a college student whose ethnic prejudice appeared to be rooted in ego-defense. Subjects responded to a measure of antiblack prejudice, both immediately after reading the communication and several weeks later.[8]

Consistent with the individual differences orientation of research on authoritarianism, the major hypothesis of Katz and his colleagues was that communications explaining the ego-defensive nature of prejudice would be effective only for people intermediate in defensiveness. Highly defensive individuals would not be influenced because their attitudes are too deeply implicated in their very serious needs for ego defense, and nondefensive individuals would not be influenced because defensive processes would be irrelevant to their attitudes. To test this hypothesis, these investigators classified subjects by their level of defensiveness, as assessed by various personality measures such as the F Scale. Consistent with our main point that ego-defensive attitudes are resistant to change, highly defensive subjects were relatively invulnerable to the appeal in all three studies. However, less supportive of Katz's perspective were the inconsistent findings that the subjects who were relatively more influenced were either (a) low or medium in defensiveness (Katz et al., 1956), (b) medium in defensiveness (Katz et al., 1957), or (c) low in defensiveness (Stotland et al., 1959).

However bold the effort to unravel ego-defensive attitudes via a brief persuasive message, we have considerable doubt about a paradigm in which demand characteristics would be as strong as they probably were in these studies by Katz and his associates (see S. R. Sherman, 1967). After a communication exposed prejudice as psychologically unhealthy, could there have been much doubt in most subjects' minds about the sorts of responses that would be "correct" on the attitude questionnaire? The inclusion of disguised measures of attitudes (see Chapter 2) or conventional measures that appear unrelated to the main study (e.g., Festinger & Carlsmith, 1959; Zanna, Kiesler, & Pilkonis, 1970) would have lent credibility to the findings of these experiments.

Despite the emphasis of this research on changing ego-defensive attitudes, the perspective that attitudes can express defensive processes qualifies better as a theory of resistance to change than a theory of persuasion. Ordinarily psychoanalysts do not believe that defensive tendencies are cured, so to speak, by a brief explanation of the dynamics of the behavior, let alone by a relatively impersonal, written communication. If such changes were so easily accomplished, short persuasive communications could readily substitute for longer-term psychotherapy, at least for the less serious forms of psychological distress. However, the very limited amount of research devoted to the psychoanalytic theory of attitudes does not provide us with an empirical basis for drawing conclusions either about the changeability of ego-defensive attitudes or about the validity of the more general assumption that prejudice toward minority groups often serves ego-defensive needs.

Other Personality Variables and Resistance. A personality variable developed by Milton Rokeach (1954, 1956, 1960) and termed *dogmatism* has also been thought to have implications for resistance to change. Although this variable is conceptually related to authoritarianism, one of the principal reasons why Rokeach developed an alternative measure was that authoritarianism scales expressed the ideology of the political right (Christie, 1954; Shils, 1954; see also Altemeyer, 1981, 1988). As Rokeach showed, dogmatism is much freer from confounding with right-wing ideology than authoritarianism (although dogmatism still shows some relation to political conservatism; see Palmer & Kalin, 1991). In addition, Rokeach's formulation was framed in terms that were more cognitive and less psychoanalytic than the work on the authoritarian personality. To understand the tenacity with which some people hold their beliefs, Rokeach thus proposed that dogmatic people tend to have a cognitive structure with certain characteristics: (a) clear distinctions between beliefs and dis-beliefs (i.e., propositions that are rejected), with little differentiation between disbeliefs; (b) pessimism, fearfulness, and concern with power and status; and (c) trust in authority and intolerance of disagreement. Dogmatic people were characterized as *closed-minded*, in contrast to more *open-minded*, nondogmatic people.

Rokeach (1956) developed a *Dogmatism Scale*, which contains items designed to measure these various aspects of this construct (see also Robinson & Shaver, 1973). Illustrative items appear in Table 12.3. Although the Dogmatism and F Scales may be factorially distinguishable (see Kerlinger & Rokeach, 1966), they are nevertheless quite highly correlated.

A principal tenet of Rokeach's formulation is that dogmatic people are resistant to influence. Suggesting that dogmatic people are intolerant of disagreement, Palmer and Kalin (1985) found that subjects' dogmatism scores related positively to their tendency to reject a stranger who disagreed with them on seven relatively important issues (e.g., penalties for the use of illicit drugs). In addition, Israeli students for whom a govern-ment report on the Beirut massacre was counterattitudinal were less influenced by this report to the extent that they were high in dogmatism (Temkin, 1987). Notwithstanding this general tendency for dogmatic people to be closed-minded, the theory allows for a somewhat more subtle set of predictions than simple resistance to influence (see G. R. Miller & Rokeach, 1968). For example, dogmatic people may be especially vulnerable to influence from high status sources, consistent with the trust that they are presumed to place in authority. Indeed, Vidulich and Kaiman (1961) reported such a finding in a

TABLE 12.3

Selected Items from the Dogmatism Scale

Aspect of dogmatism assessed	Items
Accentuation of differences between beliefs and disbeliefs	The United States and Russia have just about nothing in common.
Lack of differentiation between disbeliefs	There are certain "isms" which are really the same even though those who believe in these "isms" try to tell you they are different.
Intolerance of disagreement	There are two kinds of people in this world: those who are for the truth and those who are against the truth.
Compulsive repetition of ideas and arguments	In a discussion I often find it necessary to repeat myself several times to make sure I am being understood.
Concern with power and status	The main thing in life is for a person to want to do something important.
Paranoid outlook on life	People say insulting and vulgar things about me.

Source: These items were presented by Rokeach (1956, pp. 7–10).

conformity experiment in which subjects judged the movement of a point of light in a classic autokinetic effect paradigm (M. Sherif, 1935; see Chapter 13): Dogmatic subjects were especially influenced by the judgments of a high status source (a professor experienced in psychological research) and shifted their judgments slightly *away* from those of a low status source (a high school student). Dogmatism also related positively to attitude change toward a counterattitudinal communication (opposing disarmament) that subjects expected to write, presumably because of the greater dissonance that such counterattitudinal advocacy would create in dogmatic people (M. F. Hunt & Miller, 1968; see Chapter 11).

Conceptually related to dogmatism is a personality variable that Sorrentino and his colleagues call *uncertainty-orientation* (Sorrentino & Hancock, 1987; Sorrentino & Short, 1986). This variable is assessed via two component measures: a need for uncertainty measure developed by the Sorrentino research group and a measure of authoritarianism. The uncertainty-oriented person, who resembles Rokeach's open-minded type, is presumed to seek new information to attain clarity about the self and the environment. In contrast, the certainty-oriented person, who resembles Rokeach's closed-minded type, prefers to maintain clarity by sticking to tried-and-true prior beliefs. Moreover, under some circumstances, certainty-oriented subjects have been found to resemble dogmatic subjects by showing more vulnerability to influence from high than low status sources (Sorrentino, Bobocel, Gitta, Olson, & Hewitt, 1988). Finally, another

579

personality variable with possible implications for resistance, *repression-sensitization*, assesses the extent to which people avoid or approach threatening or anxiety-provoking stimuli (e.g., Byrne, 1964; Olson & Zanna, 1982). The relation of these variables to one another and to authoritarianism and dogmatism needs to be understood more thoroughly before their implications for resistance to persuasion can be adequately evaluated. Nonetheless, it is clear that some individuals are more open to new influences than others are and that these individual differences have often been conceptualized by psychologists in terms of the family of personality variables that derives from the early work on authoritarianism.

Attitude Strength and Resistance

Consistent with our discussions of involvement, accessibility, and related variables in Chapters 3, 4, 7, and 8, numerous variables thought to index the strength of attitudes have been regarded as causing people to resist changing their attitudes. The general assumption in this work is that strong attitudes are difficult to change. Despite the simplicity of this basic hypothesis, the specifics of theorizing about attitude strength and resistance to change are worthy of close scrutiny in terms of both the cognitive and the motivational issues that are raised. Some strength variables have thus been defined primarily in motivational terms, and others have been defined primarily in cognitive terms. In this section, we consider these two traditions for thinking about attitude strength and subsequently evaluate whether it is reasonable to consider all of these variables as variants of a single underlying construct.

Attitude Strength as a Motivational Determinant of Resistance

At an early point, M. Sherif and Cantril (1947) defined ego-involvement primarily in motivational and affective terms and regarded this variable as indexing the intensity of attitudes. They assumed that people who are highly ego-involved in a topic experience tension and discomfort when they encounter information that challenges their attitudes on the topic. The reason for this discomfort was presumably that change in ego-involving attitudes would be threatening to their personal identity. The threat was thus more generally described than it was in the psychoanalytic tradition that we have already considered in this chapter. Under such circumstances of threat to personal identity, people are presumed to react in a manner that preserves their prior attitudes and thus their identities.

Although variables representing attitude strength took on a cognitive coloration in the 1960s and 1970s, motivational interpretations have again become popular in contemporary discussions. For example, Krosnick (1990b) defined attitude *importance* as "the degree to which a person is passionately concerned about and personally invested in an attitude" (p. 60) and indicated that important attitudes are those that people "care deeply about" (Krosnick, 1989, p. 297). Abelson (1988) suggested that people have *conviction* about such attitudes and maintained that one key aspect of conviction is *emotional commitment*. Abelson thus described questionnaire items that assessed emotional commitment as "primarily noncognitive" and as having "the phenomenological flavor that seems to capture the raw stuff of emotional conviction" (e.g., "I think my view is absolutely correct," p. 273). In a similar vein, Abelson and Prentice (1989) wrote about the *emotional force* of attitudes and beliefs, which they defined as "the power of the belief to evoke strong feelings in the individual" (p. 376). Also, definitions of symbolic attitudes generally include explicit references to affect. For example, the term "antiblack affect" is generally included in definitions of whites' "symbolic racism" (Kinder & Sears, 1981, p. 416; see Chapter 3).

In a program of research on attitudinal importance, Krosnick (1988a) showed that Americans' attitudes toward governmental policies (e.g., social welfare programs) during the 1980 and 1984 presidential election campaigns were more stable to the extent that they reported their attitudes as important. This research carefully ruled out interpretations of this finding in terms of methodological artifacts such as a tendency for people to respond to measuring instruments less reliably for unimportant attitudes. Similarly, on the basis of a telephone survey of Chicago respondents, Abelson (1988) reported greater stability of attitudes on each of four social issues (e.g., aid to the contras in Nicaragua) over a one-month period to the extent that these respondents were higher in self-reported conviction on the issue. Although positive correlations between the strength and stability of attitudes are consistent with the proposition that attitude strength facilitates active resistance to persuasive attempts, such findings are of course subject to many alternative interpretations. For example, people might engage in a more passive form of resistance by avoiding exposure to information discrepant from their stronger attitudes (see subsequent discussion of selective exposure).

Laboratory research has provided additional data suggesting that the importance of attitudes increases their resistance to change. In some experiments, researchers have presented persuasive messages to subjects on issues selected to be important and unimportant and found greater persuasion on the relatively unimportant issues (e.g., Aiello, 1967; C. W. Sherif, Kelly, Rodgers, Sarup, & Tittler, 1973, Study 4). In one experiment of this type, Rhine and Severance (1970) presented messages on two topics to their undergraduate respondents: college tuition increases and increases in the size of parks in a distant city. The tuition issue was unusually important at the time of this study because "tuition was being actively discussed by the regents of the university, the Governor of the state, the press, the faculty, and the students. A student march on the State Capital had been held to protest suggestions for increased tuition" (p. 177). Not surprisingly, subjects' ratings of the issues confirmed the greater importance of the tuition issue, and they were less persuaded on this issue. In addition, numerous laboratory studies have found negative correlations between the attitude change induced by persuasive communications and subjects' ratings of their interest in or the importance of the persuasive issues (e.g., Ewing, 1942; Fine, 1957). Of course, laboratory persuasion studies operationalizing importance by presenting important and unimportant issues or by obtaining subjects' ratings of issues' importance have correlational designs that are particularly vulnerable to alternative interpretations (see

Chapter 8). Moreover, none of these investigators operationalized importance in a manner that rules out cognitive interpretations of the impact of the variable (e.g., more important attitudes might be linked to a greater number of other cognitions). Nonetheless, the interpretations these researchers have given to their findings have often had a motivational flavor.

Latitude of Rejection. Because Muzafer Sherif and his associates (e.g., C. W. Sherif, Sherif, & Nebergall, 1965; M. Sherif & Cantril, 1947) defined ego-involvement largely in motivational terms, their version of the involvement concept should be considered along with other attitude-strength variables that researchers have proposed as motivational determinants of resistance. Yet given their stress on linkages between attitudes and aspects of self-identity, their treatment can be given a cognitive interpretation as well (see subsequent discussion). Moreover, their principal method of assessing ego-involvement, the width of the latitude of rejection, relies on a cognitive classification of positions along attitudinal continua and thus received emphasis in our consideration of attitude structure in Chapter 3. As we explained there and in Chapter 8, ego-involvement is assumed to broaden the latitude of rejection and narrow the latitude of noncommitment. According to the theory, communications located in the latitude of rejection produce judgmental contrast, negative evaluations of message content, and resistance to attitude change. The critical determinant of resistance is thus a message's placement in the latitude of rejection. This approach thus draws researchers' attention, not merely to attitude strength as represented in ego-involvement, but also to the discrepancy between one's own attitude and the position advocated in the message (see Zanna, in press).

Commitment. Another motivational variable with implications for resistance is *commitment*, a construct that we considered in Chapter 11 in relation to counterattitudinal advocacy. As we explained at that point, commitment was introduced into dissonance theory by Brehm and Cohen (1962) and defined in terms of the individual committing herself to a cognition by engaging in a behavior or deciding to engage in a behavior that supports or endorses the cognition. As dissonance theorists argued, behavioral commitment to a dissonant cognitive element makes this element resistant to change. For example, in the counterattitudinal advocacy paradigm, subjects commit themselves to a cognition discrepant from their prior attitude by publicly advocating the dissonant position; as a consequence, the cognitive representation of the dissonant behavior becomes fixed, and their own attitudes become vulnerable to change. Thus, essential to dissonance predictions about the effects of attitude-discrepant behavior are the ideas that commitment to a cognition makes it resistant to change and renders linked, inconsistent cognitions vulnerable to change.

Charles Kiesler (1971) provided a broader analysis of commitment that is nonetheless consistent with the treatment of the variable in the dissonance tradition. Kiesler's conceptual definition of commitment as "the pledging or binding of the individual to behavioral acts" (p. 30) was thus compatible with Brehm and Cohen's (1962) discussion. Yet Kiesler and his colleagues examined the impact of this variable beyond the counterattitudinal advocacy paradigm and argued that commitment to an attitude creates a general resistance to attitude change. To explain why commitment would have this effect, Kiesler invoked the reasoning inherent in his definition of the construct by maintaining that commitment binds a cognition to the self. To the extent that a cognition is an important part of the self-concept, he reasoned, other attitudes and beliefs must be changed if this cognition comes into conflict with them.

Especially germane to our present discussion is Kiesler's claim that committing an individual to one of his existing attitudes would make him resistant to attacks on the attitude. In relevant studies, commitment took the form of an individual publicly advocating a position or engaging in some other behavior that would be seen as linking him to his attitude. To create maximum commitment (and maximum resistance to subsequent attack), the behavior should be very explicit and unambiguous, important to the subject, irrevocable, repeated, and freely chosen.

Kiesler and his colleagues carried out a number of experiments designed to demonstrate that commitment to an attitude does indeed render it resistant to counter-persuasion. For example, Kiesler and Sakamura (1966) had subjects audiotape a speech in which they supported their attitudes on lowering the voting age (then 21 years) to 18 years. Subjects were paid for making the speech: Those who made the speech for a $5 reward presumably lacked freedom of choice (they were coerced by the money), whereas those who made the speech for $1 were less coerced and therefore more committed by their behavioral act. Supposedly as part of a different experiment, subjects then read a counter-communication and indicated their agreement with it. As predicted, subjects in the $1 (high commitment) condition were less persuaded by this message than those in the $5 (low commitment) condition. Although this manipulation of commitment seems vulnerable to alternative interpretations in terms of justification and incentive, other operational definitions were more distinctive to the commitment concept. For example, in other experiments that demonstrated commitment's dampening effect on attitude change, high commitment subjects believed that their speech or essay would be made public to an audience, whereas low commitment subjects had no such expectation (e.g., Halverson & Pallak, 1978; Kiesler, Pallak, & Kanouse, 1968; M. S. Pallak, Mueller, Dollar, & Pallak, 1972).

Because Kiesler and dissonance theorists reasoned that commitment increases the strength of attitudes, this variable belongs to our larger family of strength and importance variables. The difference in emphasis between commitment and these other variables is that commitment pertains specifically to *behavioral* methods of strengthening attitudes. Attitudes become stronger and therefore resistant to change to the extent that people engage in some sort of behavior that links them to their existing attitudinal position. Because this behavior is generally public in commitment experiments, impression management becomes important, and the commitment construct may take on the characteristics of impression-relevant involvement (B. T. Johnson & Eagly, 1989; see Chapters 6, 7, and 8). Yet, consistent with Kiesler's ideas, linking an attitude to a behavior may induce resistance in and of itself, aside from concerns about the potential audience for the behavior. Indeed, in a cognitive rendition of a commitment manipulation, M. Ross, McFarland, Conway, and Zanna (1983) had subjects merely recall their attitudinally relevant behaviors and still demonstrated increased resistance to attack on the attitude.

Finally, the treatment of commitment by Kiesler and dissonance theorists shares features with other discussions of commitment by social psychologists. In particular, Brickman (1987) and his colleagues placed attitudinal research on commitment in a wider context of other research in social psychology. Interesting in terms of the relation between commitment and resistance to attitude change is Brickman's definition of commitment as "a force that stabilizes individual behavior under circumstances where the individual would otherwise be tempted to change that behavior" (p. 2). For Brickman, resistance to change is the defining property of commitment.

Attitude Strength as a Cognitive Determinant of Resistance

Many discussions of resistance framed in cognitive terms have been predicated on the idea that the embedding of an attitude in a cognitive structure creates resistance to change because the other aspects of the molar structure would have to change if the attitude changed. As we explained in Chapter 3, these attitudinal structures are *intra-attitudinal* when we consider the internal structure of beliefs, affects, and behaviors that underlies attitudes. These structures are *inter-attitudinal* when we consider the other attitudes to which an attitude is linked. In our own conversations about the effects of these two types of structure on resistance to attitude change, we have often invoked a casual foreign policy metaphor by labeling this resistance hypothesis the *domino theory* of resistance to change. According to the domino principle, some attitudes are resistant to change because of the extensiveness of the knowledge structures within which these attitudes are situated: Change in such an attitude would be disruptive because it would tend to induce a chain reaction of interrelated changes in associated cognitions. Change is thus resisted because of the cognitive disruption it would produce. In this section, we articulate in more detail the rationale for this prediction that structural connections or linkages would produce resistance to change. In addition, we review the relevant empirical evidence.

A good starting point for our analysis is William A. Scott's (1968) general definition of attitudinal embeddedness as the degree of connectedness as opposed to isolation of an attitude in relation to "other cognitive elements (for example, beliefs, values, other attitudes)" (p. 207). More specific definitions of the structural embeddedness of attitudes have implicated linkages of attitudes to self structures, which include representations of reference groups and individuals (C. W. Sherif et al., 1965). Other definitions have emphasized linkages to values, which we have treated as attitudes toward relatively abstract goals or end states of human existence (M. Sherif & Cantril, 1947; Ostrom & Brock, 1968; see Chapter 1). The idea that attitudes can be linked to values was also featured in B. T. Johnson and Eagly's (1989) concept of *value-relevant involvement*. As we indicated in Chapters 6, 7, and 8, this construct refers to the linkage of an activated attitude to one's enduring values. Finally, among the several attitudinal concepts that Abelson and Prentice (1989; Abelson, 1986) discussed was the *value-*

centrality of attitudes and beliefs, a property that they defined as "the degree to which a given belief expresses deeper, more fundamental beliefs" (p. 375).

At a theoretical level, the implications that the cognitive embeddedness of attitudes has for resistance can be understood in terms of the anchoring of attitudes to other cognitions. Once an attitude is linked to another attitude or to some other cognition, change in the target attitude is more difficult, presumably because this change would necessitate changes in the linked elements. The assumption that change in one attitude requires changes in cognitions linked to it derives from cognitive consistency theories, especially of the balance theory variety (see Chapters 3 and 10). Indeed, a considerable amount of research has supported the proposition that change reverberates through cognitive structures that are composed of linked elements (e.g., Ball-Rokeach, Rokeach, & Grube, 1984; Hendrick & Seyfried, 1974; McGuire, 1960c, 1981; Tannenbaum, 1966, 1967; Tannenbaum & Gengel, 1966). Moreover, in a more detailed development of this idea of remote impact, McGuire and McGuire (1991; McGuire, 1990) have demonstrated that manipulations of the desirability or likelihood of anticipated events have remote effects on perceived antecedents and consequences of these events. To the extent that an attitude is extensively linked to other cognitions, people may resist changing it because the reverberating change that would follow could destabilize a large number of cognitions (see also McGuire, 1981).

As already noted, involvement (i.e., ego-involvement, value-relevant involvement) and related attitude-strength variables have generally been viewed as motivational constructs. Yet the cognitive interpretation of these variables in terms of embeddedness in larger structures has been examined in several studies of resistance to change. In a few experiments, researchers have operationalized this cognitive embeddedness idea directly by creating links between a target attitude and other cognitions and have demonstrated that such a treatment reduced subsequent attitude change in response to a persuasive message. For example, Ostrom and Brock (1968) first presented subjects with a message advocating that Greenland should not be given membership in the Pan-American Bank. This communication was intended to produce a relatively uniform initial position opposed to Greenland's participation. Subjects then carried out a *value-bonding* task that required them to indicate the extent to which various general values were reflected in one-sentence excerpts from this message. In one condition, these values were ones that subjects had previously judged as personally important (e.g., "keeping promises to others"; "having a steady income," p. 380); in a second condition, these values were ones that subjects had previously judged as relatively unimportant (e.g., "people honoring their ancestors"; "people paying inheritance taxes," p. 381). Subsequent to this value-bonding task, subjects received a second message, which contradicted the first message by arguing that Greenland *should* participate in the Bank either partially (i.e., low discrepancy message) or fully (i.e., high discrepancy message). Subjects in the important-value condition were significantly less influenced by this message than those in the unimportant-value condition, although only with the high discrepancy message. Thus, linking one's attitude to values that were in some sense important created resistance to a counterattitudinal message (see also Nelson, 1968). Finally, in other studies, subjects' values were assessed but value linkages were not established experimentally. In such research, subjects proved more resistant to social influence that was highly related to their personal values than to influence that was unrelated to their values, presumably because change on value-relevant topics would require extensive cognitive change (A. F. Snyder, Mischel, & Lott, 1960; Vaughan & Mangan, 1963).[9]

Also consistent with the Sherifs' treatment of ego-involvement (e.g., C. W. Sherif et al., 1965; M. Sherif & Cantril, 1947) is the idea that links between message recipients' attitudes and their valued reference groups also underlie resistance to changing these attitudes. For example, in a classic experiment by Kelley and Volkart (1952), Boy Scouts who highly valued their membership in their Scout troop were less persuaded by a message that was critical of some of the traditional values of scouting than were Scouts who valued their membership less highly. More speculatively, Shils and Janowitz (1948) argued that German soldiers' resistance to Allied propaganda in World War II, despite their hopeless situation toward the end of the war, was rooted in their loyalty to their own unit.

In another effort to show that embeddedness in larger structures produces resistance to change, Rokeach (1968) argued that beliefs vary in *centrality*: "The more a given belief is functionally connected or in communication with other beliefs, the more implications and consequences it has for other beliefs, and therefore, the more central the belief" (p. 5). On an *a priori* basis, Rokeach classified beliefs into five categories that ranged from extremely central *primitive beliefs* such as beliefs about person constancy and self constancy to extremely peripheral *inconsequential beliefs* about "more or less arbitrary matters of taste" (Rokeach, 1968, pp. 6–11).

While subjects were in a hypnotic state, Rokeach and his collaborators induced change in each of the five classes of more central and more peripheral beliefs. They found that this hypnotic induction had less impact on the target beliefs to the extent that these beliefs were more central. Moreover, consistent with the domino principle, Rokeach argued that any changes induced in central beliefs would produce greater change in connected beliefs than would changes induced in more peripheral beliefs. Indeed, in the hypnosis experiment, the changes induced in more central beliefs, despite their smaller magnitude compared with the changes induced in peripheral beliefs, produced proportionally larger changes in other beliefs.

This centrality theme was also important in Rokeach's (1964) remarkable *Three Christs of Ypsilanti* study, in which he brought together for a two-year period three chronic paranoid schizophrenic patients, each of whom believed he was the reincarnation of Jesus Christ. For these patients, living in close quarters (in adjacent beds in the same ward) with men who laid claim to the same identity surely threatened a central aspect of their attitudes and beliefs. Although the reactions of the three men differed, in general little fundamental change in their identities ensued, especially in the two older men. Rokeach interpreted this general resistance to change in terms of the centrality of these men's Christ identities within their overarching knowledge structures. This qualitative study thus supports the view that attitudes and beliefs are difficult to modify to the extent that they are closely linked to a relatively large number of other cognitions. Also in a qualitative vein, Batson and Ventis (1982) maintained that the religious beliefs held by devout people are highly resistant to change and, moreover, often become even more intense in the face of disconfirming or challenging information. Consistent with Batson and Ventis's analysis, the centrality of religious beliefs in the personal identities of devout people may account for the change-resistant character of these beliefs. Similarly, Lydon and Zanna (1990) have shown that people become committed to endeavors that they perceive as linked to their important values and often become even more committed in the face of adversity or challenge.

Finally, another useful way of thinking about the embeddedness of attitudes in a structure of other cognitions is represented in W. Wood's (e.g., 1982) research on the retrieval of attitude-relevant information from memory (see also Chapters 3, 4, and 7). Subjects who were able to retrieve many behaviors (as well as beliefs) on the topic of environmental preservation proved more resistant to a counterattitudinal message arguing that preservation would have negative consequences. Although message recipients' ability to retrieve beliefs and past experiences also appeared to affect their processing strategy (see Chapter 7), the typical impact of this variable is resistance to persuasion (Wood & Kallgren, 1988; Wood, Kallgren, & Preisler, 1985).[10] Explicitly connecting her information retrieval measure to the traditional family of attitude-strength variables, Wood reported that subjects' self-reported involvement in the preservation issue related positively to their ability to retrieve more past experiences from memory. In general, Wood's research on working knowledge and persuasion is consistent with our view that linkages of an attitude object to other cognitions—in this case, to beliefs and prior experiences—are a source of resistance to attitude change.

Evaluative-Cognitive Consistency. Another cognitive structural variable with implications for resistance to change is *evaluative-cognitive consistency*, the extent to which the evaluative implications of one's beliefs about an attitude object are consistent with one's overall evaluation of it (see Chapters 3 and 10, and M.J. Rosenberg, 1956, 1960a, 1968b). As we indicated in Chapter 3, evaluative-cognitive inconsistency could stem from several sources, including (a) a relative lack of beliefs about the attitude object (Rosenberg's notion of vacuous attitudes), (b) the organization of beliefs by some principle other than evaluation, or (c) a grounding of evaluation in affective or behavioral input rather than cognitive. Whatever the determinants of evaluative-cognitive consistency, there is considerable evidence that people who are consistent in this sense are less receptive to persuasive efforts than those who are inconsistent. First, Rosenberg (1968b) reported that male undergraduates' attitudes on two issues (the United States expressing support of French policy in Algeria; Yale University becoming coeducational) were more stable over a two-week period to the extent that their attitudes were high in evaluative-cognitive consistency (see also Norman, 1975). Second, Rosenberg (1968b) also reported that subjects were more resistant to a persuasive communication to the extent that their attitudes on the issue were consistent. Third, Chaiken and her colleagues also reported positive relations between consistency and attitudinal resistance (see Chaiken, Pomerantz, & Giner-Sorolla, in press). One of these studies found more resistance to a persuasive communication and greater counterarguing of its content among consistent subjects (Chaiken, 1982, described in

Chaiken & Yates, 1985). Also, in a self-perception paradigm, Chaiken and Baldwin (1981) found that consistent subjects' attitudinal judgments were less influenced by the salience of their past behaviors than were inconsistent subjects' judgments (see Chapter 11). Converging evidence thus suggests that evaluative-cognitive consistency, a variable that could well be placed within the larger family of attitude-strength variables, provides one index of the extent to which people are likely to resist changing their attitudes.

Multifaceted Nature of Attitude Strength. In this chapter we have shown that resistance has often been thought to stem from a family of variables that we have classified as assessing attitude strength: ego-involvement, importance, centrality, conviction, and so on. An important question about these attitudinal properties, a question that we also raised in Chapters 3 and 4, is whether they can be reduced to a single variable that we might call *attitude strength*. This very treatment has in fact been proposed in the context of the associative networks approach (see Chapters 3 and 4), within which strength has been variously defined as the strength of the association between an attitude object and an evaluation (e.g., Fazio, 1986, 1989) and the strength of the attitude object node (Judd & Krosnick, 1989). By a process of spreading activation with a network, a node is activated when other, linked nodes are activated. Because node strength is assumed to derive from past activation of the node, ascribing a high level of strength to an attitude object node implies that it is strongly linked to other nodes. It also follows that strong attitudes are ones that people think about often. And Fazio (1986, 1989) has argued that strong attitudes are more accessible from memory and therefore are more likely to be activated when people perceive cues related to the attitude object.

Despite the appeal of parsimony, we think that it is premature to assume that the various strength variables we have discussed can be reduced to a single, unitary construct, even though psychologists who proposed motivational interpretations of attitude strength and those who proposed cognitive interpretations have made the same prediction with respect to resistance to persuasion. Available empirical studies do not support the idea of a single, underlying strength variable. Raden's (1985) examination of a large number of strength variables showed that correlations between these variables are often quite modest. On this basis, Raden argued that attitude strength would best be considered multidimensional (see also Krosnick, Boninger, Chuang, & Carnot, 1991). In addition, Abelson (1988) developed a set of questionnaire items assessing conviction, another strength variable. From factor analyses, he isolated at least three clusters of items: those expressing *emotional commitment* (e.g., "My beliefs about X express the real me"), *ego preoccupation* (e.g., "I think about X often"), and *cognitive elaboration* (e.g., "Several other issues could come up in a conversation about it," p. 273). Items assessing emotional commitment and ego preoccupation were substantially correlated, whereas the correlations between cognitive elaboration and these two clusters of items were relatively low. The emotional commitment and ego preoccupation items are generally compatible with abstract definitions of strength associated with motivational interpretations, and the cognitive elaboration items are compatible with the abstract definitions associated with cognitive interpretations. Thus, Abelson's partition between emotional commitment and ego preoccupation on the one hand and cognitive elaboration on the other hand is supportive of at least a partial separability of the motivational and cognitive aspects of attitude strength.

Processes by which People Protect Strong Attitudes. Although researchers generally agree that a closed-minded reaction to challenging information is associated with strong attitudes, relatively little attention has been given to understanding the processes by which such resistance occurs. As discussed in Chapter 10, several theorists posited inconsistency-reducing, or defensive, cognitive processes by which people resist changing their attitudes (e.g., Abelson, 1959; Festinger, 1957; see also subsequent section of this chapter). In addition, a contemporary perspective that addresses this issue is the heuristic-systematic model, which we considered in Chapter 7 (see also Petty & Cacioppo's, 1986a, 1986b, consideration of biased processing). Relevant to attitudinal resistance is the heuristic-systematic model's concept of *defense motivation*, the desire to form or to defend particular attitudinal positions (Chaiken, Liberman, & Eagly, 1989). If we assume that strength increases defense motivation, the heuristic-systematic model suggests that defense of one's attitudes can proceed through the *selective* application of both heuristic and systematic processing. Moreover, message recipients may engage in other modes of processing (e.g., attributional reasoning) on a selective basis as well.

With respect to defense-motivated heuristic processing, the selectivity principle assumes that people whose attitudes are challenged attend to those heuristic cues that are linked to decision rules that allow them to defend their initial attitudes. Heuristic cues that allow recipients to invalidate a message (e.g., the communicator's lack of expertise or likability) would thus be attended to when messages threaten important attitudes, whereas heuristic cues that allow recipients to strengthen message validity (e.g., the communicator's expertise or likability) would be attended to when messages support important attitudes. Systematic processing would also be invoked on a selective basis. Persuasive argumentation favorable to recipients' initial attitudes would be systematically processed to lend support to their attitudes, whereas argumentation unfavorable to their attitudes would not be. The end result of this selective application of systematic processing would be cognitive elaboration of one's own attitudinal position. Even if the attitude strength that impels defense motivation initially arose from motivational sources more than cognitive linkages, this biased systematic processing would tend to produce an elaborated network of cognitions surrounding one's preexisting attitude.

Impact of Attitudes on Information Processing

In this chapter we have reviewed a formidable array of evidence suggesting that strong attitudes are resistant to change. In fact, we believe that few researchers would disagree with the idea that people's prior attitudes represent an important source of their resistance to attitude change. Furthermore, we have suggested that this resistance operates through a biased and selective application of the processes by which people judge the validity of persuasive messages (e.g., heuristic processing, attributional reasoning, systematic processing). Therefore, it might seem that prior attitudes would be a very important component of theories of attitude change. Paradoxically, however, investigators working within classic attitude change paradigms have largely ignored message recipients' prior attitudes. As we noted in Chapter 8, persuasion experiments rarely represent subjects' prior attitudes as an independent variable, and with the exception of social judgment theory (e.g., M. Sherif & Hovland, 1961), prior attitudes have rarely been emphasized in cognitive theories of persuasion. Likewise, attention to prior attitudes, at least on the empirical level, has been the exception rather than the rule in the counterattitudinal advocacy research that we reviewed in Chapter 11 and the research on group influence phenomena that we discuss in Chapter 13.

Fortunately, there do exist two identifiable literatures that have furnished important information about the information processing that underlies the resistance-conferring effects of prior attitudes. The first of these is a relatively large and varied literature on attitudinal selectivity, a body of research that has accumulated over a period of some 50 years. Researchers who have conducted such research have explored the general question of whether attitudes exert selective effects on people's cognitive processing of attitude-relevant information. The second literature, which is both more recent and more homogeneous than the first, has examined the effects of mere thought on attitude change. The general idea upon which research on both selectivity and mere thought has been based is that attitude is a structure in memory that affects information processing (see Chapter 1). Moreover, the typical assumption of this research is that people's attitudes bias cognitive processing in a manner that favors attitudinally congruent, or congenial, information. Resistance to attitude change efforts, of course, should be a consequence of such selectivity in processing.

Attitudinal Selectivity

One of the earliest and most enduring principles in social psychological theorizing is that perception and cognition are influenced not only by the intrinsic or structural characteristics of stimuli, but also by psychological factors such as the perceiver's expectancies, motives, goals, moods, attitudes, and values (e.g., Asch, 1946; Bruner & Goodman, 1947; R. Levine, Chein, & Murphy, 1942; Lewin, 1935; Murray, 1933; M. Sherif, 1935). The idea that attitudes exert selective effects at all stages of information processing is derived from this basic doctrine, which Bruner (1957) dubbed the "new look in perception." As such, it is one of the oldest assumptions in attitude theory (see Allport, 1935; Asch, 1952). Indeed, as we noted in Chapter 10, one of the major functions that attitudes have been thought to serve is that of organizing and structuring an ambiguous informational environment. As Allport (1935, p. 806) put it, "Attitudes determine for each individual what he will see and hear, what he will think and what he will do. To borrow a phrase from William James, they 'engender meaning upon the world'; they draw lines about and segregate an otherwise chaotic environment; they are our methods for finding our way about in an ambiguous universe."

The empirical literature on attitudinal selectivity can be divided into three general categories: studies that have examined *selective exposure* or *selective attention*, those that have examined *selective perception* or *selective judgment*, and those that have examined *selective memory*. As noted above, selectivity researchers have assumed that people's attitudes bias information processing in favor of attitudinally congruent material. Such congeniality effects have been attributed primarily to motivational sources in research on selective exposure and attention, whereas both motivational and cognitive sources have been implicated in research on selective perception, judgment, and memory. Of course, the particular mechanisms that researchers have invoked in this literature vary somewhat depending upon which stage of processing is examined.

The intellectual history of research on attitudinal selectivity bears a certain resemblance to the story we told in Chapter 4 about the attitude-behavior relation. Neatly summarized, the story is the not uncommon sequence of "first they believed in it, then they didn't, and now they do again (at least to some extent)." Thus, there was an early and perhaps somewhat naive belief in a strong and robust selectivity phenomenon. This state prevailed through the first half of the 1960s, when the president's Science Advisory Committee recognized attitudinal selectivity as one of the most basic principles established by behavioral research (Behavioral Science Subpanel, 1962).[11] Once a substantial amount of empirical evidence had accumulated, support for selectivity phenomena appeared weak, at least to certain prominent attitude researchers, and selectivity came to be regarded as another one of those reasonable-seeming principles that just aren't true. However, the verdict against selectivity effects has been gradually modified, as social psychologists developed a more complex and contingent view of the conditions under which selectivity operates. The road to scientific progress seems often to be a winding one.

Selective Exposure and Attention. The idea that people tend to approach and attend to information that upholds their attitudes and beliefs but avoid or pay little attention to conflicting information can be traced to William James (1890/1952), and before him, to Francis Bacon (1620/1960). Among social psychologists, this idea is largely synonymous with the name of Leon Festinger and his theory of cognitive dissonance (Festinger, 1957, 1964b). In fact, this theory can be credited with stimulating most of the selective exposure and attention research that has been conducted. As discussed in Chapter 10, the theory predicts that in the interest of reducing dissonance and ensuring consonance, people seek out information that supports their attitudes (or decisions) and avoid information that challenges their attitudes (or decisions).

Consistent with McGuire's (1985, p. 259) treatment of "tuning in that produces exposure to the communication" and "attending to it" as separable steps in some versions of his information-processing theory of persuasion (see Chapter 6), it might be possible to examine selective exposure and selective attention separately. Thus, the tuning in or exposure step is an active attentional process that involves seeking out information. This process is followed by what might be considered a more passive attentional process as people attend to the information that they have sought out (or, in some laboratory studies, have been unable to avoid). To some extent, empirical researchers have operationalized their dependent variables in ways that would allow them to separate exposure and attention. Typical dependent variables in experimental research on selective exposure have consisted of (a) subjects' self-reported preferences for exposing themselves to supportive or nonsupportive attitude-relevant materials (e.g., Brock, 1965a; Freedman, 1965c; D. Frey, 1982), (b) the time subjects spend engaging in exposure behaviors such as reading (e.g., Jecker, reported in Festinger, 1964b; Sears & Freedman, 1965), and (c) subjects' behavioral acts that indicate attention to the material (Olson & Zanna, 1979) or screening out interfering stimuli (Brock & Balloun, 1967; Kleinhesselink & Edwards, 1975). Although preference measures tap exposure, the other types of measures are more heavily weighted toward attention. Yet systematic efforts to distinguish between exposure and attention have not yet appeared in attitude research, and there is little evidence that findings differ for the two processes. Therefore, we consider them together but believe that the distinction between selective exposure and attention warrants further examination.

Selective exposure was a major theme of Festinger's (1957) first book on dissonance theory. In that volume, he maintained that exposure to information is relatively unbiased prior to the time when people have committed themselves to a decision (see prior discussion of commitment in this chapter and Chapter 11). Following commitment to a decision, Festinger maintained, people seek out information supportive of their decision and avoid information contrary to it. For example, when an individual is trying to decide what graduate program to enroll in, she would seek out relevant information in an unbiased fashion, taking into account favorable and unfavorable information about each of the programs that she is considering. However, once she has made her decision, she would *selectively seek out* information favorable to the program she has chosen as well as information unfavorable to the programs she has rejected. In addition, she would *selectively avoid* information unfavorable to her chosen program or favorable to the rejected programs.[12]

In view of Festinger's emphasis on post-decisional selectivity, the main point of his discussion of selective exposure was somewhat narrower than the general proposition that people tune in and attend to attitudinally congenial information. Yet the boundary conditions of dissonance theory were not clear in the 1957 book. Festinger and his colleagues (e.g., Brehm & Cohen, 1962) had not yet confined dissonance to situations involving commitment, choice, aversive consequences, and the other conditions we discussed in Chapter 11. Therefore, the broader proposition that people favor information that agrees with their attitudes and avoid information that disagrees with their attitudes, regardless of commitment, should be regarded as consistent with the general tenor of Festinger's initial consideration of selective exposure (and of dissonance more generally) and certainly with other early discussions of selective exposure (e.g., Klapper, 1960).

Both the general proposition that people favor attitudinally congenial information and the narrower proposition that people favor information that increases consonance and reduces dissonance were widely accepted by social psychologists, based on Festinger's (1957) discussion and other early treatments. This belief in selective exposure was shattered by the publication of Freedman and Sears' (1965a) review of research on the topic. These authors made an important distinction between (a) *de facto* selectivity in exposure and (b) selectivity produced by preference for supportive information and avoidance of nonsupportive information. *De facto* selectivity means that people are exposed to more attitudinally congenial than uncongenial information, regardless of whether this selectivity is caused by their preference for supportive information and avoidance of nonsupportive information. Because many variables affect the type of information to which people are exposed, the fact that they are exposed to more congenial than uncongenial information need not be a product of psychological tendencies to seek out congenial information or to avoid uncongenial information. Instead, *de facto* selectivity *may* be a by-product of other psychological tendencies, such as preferences for information that can be easily obtained or that is useful in relation to attaining goals. The obtainable or useful information may just happen to be attitudinally congenial. In addition, environmental factors such as the extent to which congenial or uncongenial information is available in one's environment can also contribute to *de facto* selectivity. If, for example, an individual lives in a city in which all newspapers are conservative, his greater exposure to conservative than liberal editorials would reflect an environmental factor.

Freedman and Sears (1965a) affirmed that *de facto* selectivity is widespread in natural settings. However, they concluded that there was no evidence for selective exposure and attention in laboratory experiments, where non-attitudinal causes of *de facto* selectivity were presumably controlled (but in actuality may *not* have been well controlled; see Cotton's, 1985, critique). Although the narrative methods used in Freedman and Sears' review as well as their lack of attention to interacting conditions and possible methodological problems of the research would surely give pause to a modern audience, social psychologists of the day found the review convincing (e.g., McGuire, 1969), and many accepted the claim that people neither prefer congenial information nor avoid uncongenial information. In fact, the review was so convincing that most researchers heeded Freedman and Sears' call to "turn away from questions dealing primarily with the selective exposure hypotheses" (1965a, p. 94).

This decline in the volume of research carried out on selective exposure occurred, despite the fact that Freedman and Sears' (1965a) review was published nearly contemporaneously with Festinger's (1964b) second book on dissonance, in which he clarified and developed his predictions for selective exposure and reported a promising pattern of empirical support for them. For example, he maintained that people would not avoid dissonant information (and perhaps would prefer it) if they anticipated that it would be easy to refute because of the weakness of the information, the low credibility of its source, or the strength of their own position. He also emphasized that dissonant information may sometimes be useful in relation to future decisions and therefore not avoided (and perhaps preferred; see also note 12). Yet Festinger's additional work on selective exposure did not attract much attention, and there was only limited acknowledgment of his advocacy of a more complex and contingent set of predictions. The Freedman and Sears review took its toll, just as the Wicker (1969) review of research on the attitude-behavior relation took its toll in that area of research just a few years later (see Chapter 4). Indeed, the period from the mid-1960s to the mid-1970s was generally a pessimistic one in attitude research.

Recovery of interest in selective exposure has been gradual. Yet a modest number of additional studies appeared subsequent to the Freedman and Sears (1965a) review. An informative narrative review of this literature has been provided by Dieter Frey (1986), who has been an active contributor to this research area (see also Cotton's, 1985, review). According to Frey's integration of this research, Festinger's (1957, 1964b) view that selective exposure would be stronger under dissonance-producing circumstances has indeed received support. In particular, some of the conditions necessary for producing dissonance effects on attitudes in the counterattitudinal behavior paradigm (see Chapter 11) have also proven to be determinants of selectivity effects. For example, when people have *freely chosen* to perform an attitude-relevant behavior or have made a decision in favor of an alternative, they are more likely to seek out supportive information (e.g., Cotton & Hieser, 1980; Frey & Wicklund, 1978). *Commitment* has been shown to have a similar impact (Frey & Stahlberg, reported in Frey, 1986; Schwarz, Frey, & Kumpf, 1980). Also, selective exposure appears to be confined to situations in which one's decision or behavior is irreversible; with reversibility, there may even be a weak tendency to expose oneself to nonsupportive information (Frey, 1981b; Frey & Rosch, 1984). Consistent with Festinger's predictions, nonsupportive information is at least as acceptable as supportive information if both types of information are weak in the sense that they are implausible or derive from a low credibility source; when information is strong, supportive information is preferred over nonsupportive (Frey, 1981a; Lowin, 1967, 1969; Kleinhesselink & Edwards, 1975). Finally, consistent with Olson and Zanna's (1979) demonstration that repressors showed more selective exposure than sensitizers (see prior discussion of repression-sensitization), individual differences may also moderate the tendency to prefer supportive information.

These findings on selective exposure need to be qualified somewhat in relation to information avoidance. Despite some studies suggesting that people avoid receiving uncongenial information, reviewers have judged that evidence for selective avoidance of non-supportive information is in general weaker than for selective approach of supportive information (see Frey, 1986; Wicklund & Brehm, 1976). In particular, the variables that moderate selective exposure (e.g., choice, commitment, decision reversibility) have shown stronger and more consistent effects on information seeking than information avoidance, perhaps because only information seeking can actually *reduce* dissonance (whereas information avoidance can only prevent new dissonance from arising). Finally, there is abundant evidence that a number of tendencies other than attitudinal selectivity also govern exposure to information. Especially important in relation to attitude-relevant information is the tendency, also noted by Festinger (1957, 1964b), to prefer information that has high utility in relation to goal attainment or future decisions (e.g., Freedman, 1965a; Lowe & Steiner, 1968) as well as the tendency to prefer unfamiliar information (Brock, Albert, & Becker, 1970; Ray, 1968; Sears, 1965).

In contemporary research and theorizing, selective exposure in favor of one's attitudes and behavioral commitments is once more regarded as a genuine phenomenon, albeit one of considerably more complexity than originally believed. Yet it is important to note that, like the early research, most of the contemporary research responsible for instilling this contingent view of selective exposure has been conducted in experimental laboratories under conditions that may tend to dampen selectivity effects. In particular, the attitudes and behavioral commitments that are examined in laboratory research are often relatively unimportant. It would be consistent with the findings we presented on attitude strength and resistance to persuasion to argue that selective exposure should be more pronounced in relation to strong attitudes (see Clarke & James, 1967). The laboratory may provide a poor context for studying selective exposure for other reasons as well: (a) the presentation of supportive and nonsupportive information has a certain artificiality when it occurs during an experimental session, and (b) self-presentational concerns may cause subjects to appear less biased in favor of their attitudes and commitments than they would if their informational preferences were not under scrutiny.[13]

In a refreshing departure from the conditions that have prevailed in experimental laboratories, Sweeney and Gruber (1984) examined interest in and attention to the Watergate scandal on the part of three groups of voters: Nixon supporters, McGovern supporters, and undecided citizens. This survey-research study was conducted in 1973 in three waves: before the Watergate hearings, midway through the hearings, and near their end. Confirming the selective approach hypothesis, McGovern supporters reported more interest in and attention to the Watergate hearings than undecided citizens (or the Nixon supporters). Confirming the selective avoidance hypothesis, Nixon supporters reported less interest and attention than undecided citizens. Moreover, suggesting that selective avoidance affected knowledgeability, Nixon supporters appeared to know less about Watergate than the McGovern supporters or undecided citizens. This study thus suggests that when attitudes are strong and are challenged or supported by highly credible, real-world events, selectivity effects may be more clearly discernible.

Selective Perception and Judgment. We introduced the idea that attitudes may distort the perception and judgment of attitudinal stimuli when we discussed social judgment theory in Chapter 8. As detailed there, M. Sherif and Hovland (1961) argued that people's own attitudes serve as judgmental anchors and that, as a consequence, statements that are relatively close to one's own attitude are assimilated, whereas statements that are relatively distant from one's attitude are contrasted. Moreover, these perceptual distortions were assumed to influence judgment such that statements that are assimilated are evaluated relatively positively (e.g., as fair and unbiased), whereas those that are contrasted are evaluated relatively negatively (e.g., as unfair and biased). Thus, by means of the perceptual mechanism of assimilation-contrast, people's attitudes should exert a congeniality bias in both perception and judgment, that is, attitudinally congruent information should be perceived and evaluated more positively than attitudinally incongruent information. Of course, motivational factors such as the need to maintain cognitive consistency may also be responsible for selectivity in judgment and thereby cause people to be more critical of information that counters rather than confirms their prior attitudes. As we noted in Chapter 10, Festinger (1957) emphasized that forced exposure to attitudinally uncongenial information would be countered by biased perception and evaluation of the information, responses that he characterized as "quick defensive processes which prevent the new cognition from ever becoming firmly established" (p. 137).

Just as it is possible to distinguish between exposure and attention, we could distinguish between perception and judgment of attitude-relevant stimuli. *Perception* concerns the encoding of information, a constructive process that encompasses the assignment of meaning to stimuli. The term *judgment* pertains to the drawing of conclusions about the evaluative meaning of information or its relevance to one's goals. Thus, one might *perceive* that a senator's speech on foreign trade policy makes certain points and takes a certain position on the issue and then *judge* that this position is dangerous to U.S. interests. Although some studies, such as those examining the assimilation-contrast of messages' positions, have in these terms assessed perception, others, such as those examining the fairness of messages, have assessed judgment. Yet, because judgment (or evaluation) of messages is assumed to reflect a prior perceptual process, the distinction has not usually been made in attitude research, and we thus consider these processes together.

Early studies of the impact of attitudes on perception and judgment examined subjects' reactions to ambiguous information (e.g., Proshansky, 1943; Seeleman, 1940). In the best known of these studies, Hastorf and Cantril (1954) had Princeton and Dartmouth students watch a film of a controversial football game in which several players had been injured, including Princeton's star player (whose picture had just appeared on the cover of *Time* magazine). While watching the film, students noted any infractions of the rules that they saw. Whereas Princeton and Dartmouth students ascribed equal numbers of infractions to the Princeton team, Princeton students ascribed many more infractions to the Dartmouth team than the Dartmouth students did. Furthermore, in a more general sample of students (only some of whom had actually seen the game), Princeton students viewed the game as "dirtier" and much less fair than Dartmouth students did. Subsequent studies in this tradition have also shown selective perception of complex stimulus materials (e.g., Vidmar & Rokeach, 1974).

Other early studies concerned the influence of judges' own attitudes on the placement of items on pro-con attitudinal scales (see Chapters 2 and 8). Research has shown that judges with more extreme attitudes *contrasted* attitude statements away from their own position, that is, they viewed statements that were relatively distant from their own position as more extreme than did judges whose attitudes were more neutral (e.g., Dawes, Singer, & Lemons, 1972; Hovland & Sherif, 1952; Manis, 1960, 1961a, 1961b). Somewhat less reliably, this research has also suggested that statements relatively close to judges' own positions may be *assimilated*, that is, judges with extreme attitudes may view such statements as closer to their own end of the scale than judges with more neutral attitudes do. In other words, people exaggerate the dissimilarity of statements that differ from their own position and (at least sometimes) minimize the dissimilarity of statements that are close to their own position.

596

Various theoretical interpretations and methodological critiques have been offered in relation to demonstrations of attitudes' impact on perception and judgment. In particular, the status of assimilation and contrast as perceptual effects has been called into question by the criticism that they merely reflect the impact of subjects' own attitudes on their use of the response scale that they have available for rating attitudinal statements. The view was thus offered that findings interpreted as evidence for assimilation and contrast did not represent true differences between subjects in how they perceived stimuli (Upshaw, 1969). These debates have been complex, and we do not review them in detail here (see Petty & Cacioppo's, 1981a, review). Suffice it to say that more recent discussions that take a variety of methodological issues into account suggest that assimilation and contrast are at least to some extent genuine perceptual phenomena in attitudinal contexts (Dawes et al., 1972; Judd, Kenny, & Krosnick, 1983; Romer, 1983; see also Chapters 2 and 8). However, even when assimilation and contrast are considered perceptual effects, their proper interpretation remains at issue. Sherif and Hovland's (1971) ascription of these effects to the judges' use of their own attitude as an anchor is certainly not the only possibility (see Eiser & Stroebe, 1972; Judd & Harackiewicz, 1980; Krosnick, 1988b; Upshaw & Ostrom, 1984).

In the theoretical tradition of social judgment theory, contrast has generally been viewed as a motivated effort to reduce the persuasive impact of information that is discrepant from one's own attitudes (see also Manis, 1961a, 1961b). Thus, people who contrast information discrepant from their own attitudes are passing a value judgment on this information by viewing it as too extreme to be given serious consideration. Indeed, as Sherif and Hovland (1961) demonstrated, information that is contrasted is also evaluated as propagandistic and unfair, and both contrast and these negative evaluative reactions are more pronounced to the extent that message recipients are highly ego-involved in the topic of the communication. An important claim of social judgment theorists is that these perceptual and judgmental responses underlie message recipients' resistance to persuasive communications that are highly divergent from their own attitudes (see Chapter 8).

The idea that message recipients evaluate discrepant communications negatively has received support in other contexts. Specifically, persuasion studies using thought-listing methodology have shown that subjects list more counterarguments for counterattitudinal than proattitudinal messages (Cacioppo & Petty, 1979b; Petty & Cacioppo, 1979b). In addition, television viewers have been shown to evaluate presidential debates selectively; their judgments of who won the debate were biased in favor of the candidate they preferred prior to the debate (e.g., Bothwell & Brigham, 1983). Moreover, in a particularly interesting demonstration of biased evaluation, C. G. Lord, Ross, and Lepper (1979) had subjects who supported capital punishment and subjects who opposed it read reports portrayed as empirical studies on capital punishment, along with some criticisms of the studies and rebuttals of these criticisms. One of these studies confirmed subjects' attitude on capital punishment, and one disconfirmed it. Both the proponents and opponents of capital punishment rated the report that confirmed their own views as more convincing and better conducted than the one that disconfirmed their views.[14] In addition, subjects reported that their attitudes were more extreme after reading these materials (see subsequent discussion of attitude polarization). Also, in an extension of this experiment, Houston and Fazio (1989) showed that these biased evaluations of research reports were more pronounced to the extent that subjects had either (a) responded more quickly to an attitudinal inquiry on capital punishment or (b) repeatedly expressed their attitude. In other words, evaluations were more biased to the extent that subjects' attitudes were strong and therefore more accessible (see Chapter 4). Finally, analogous bias in evaluations of research reports has also been found among research scientists, whose evaluations of such reports were shown to depend, not on studies' methodology, but on the match between studies' findings and scientists' own theoretical orientation (Mahoney, 1977).

The tendency to reject materials that contradict one's own attitudes and preconceptions was also vividly demonstrated in Vallone, Ross, and Lepper's (1985) study of pro-Israel, pro-Arab, and neutral students' reactions to videotapes they were shown of the major networks' television news coverage of the Beirut massacre. Rather than assimilate these presentations toward their own attitudes, the partisan students viewed them as biased against their own side. Thus, the pro-Israel students thought that television news was biased against Israel, and the pro-Arab students thought that the news was biased against the Arabs; the perceptions of the neutral students fell in between those of the two groups of partisans. This "hostile media" phenomenon probably occurred because these materials were sufficiently challenging to the attitudes of both partisan groups that they fell outside of the range of possible assimilation to their own views (i.e., they were located in their latitude of rejection, in social judgment terms). Partisans thus viewed the materials as biased, propagandistic, unfair—in a word, hostile to their own interests. Similar findings were obtained by Zanna, Klosson, and Darley (1976), who examined the reactions of pro-student and pro-police subjects to a television newscast in which either students or police were blamed for initiating a violent confrontation. Such findings are thus consistent with the contrast effects and negative evaluations that other researchers have produced in relation to materials that challenge subjects' attitudes. Being perceived as hostile and extreme by both parties to a dispute is no doubt a familiar experience to people who are caught in the middle of disputes—for example, labor arbitrators, referees of basketball games, family counselors, and mediators of all types.

Finally, assimilation and contrast have been of considerable interest in relation to voters' perceptions of political candidates' stands on issues. In general, voters believe that disliked candidates disagree with their own policy preferences and that liked candidates agree with their preferences (see Krosnick, 1988b, 1990a). Investigators have often assumed that such findings show that voters contrast the positions taken by disliked candidates, a phenomenon Krosnick labeled *negative projection*, and assimilate the positions taken by liked candidates, a phenomenon he labeled *positive projection*. This interpretation suggests that one's evaluation of the *sources* of attitudinal statements is a critical determinant of contrast and assimilation. Reflecting on the potential of attitudes toward sources to moderate perceptual displacements, readers may find it hard to resist drawing a balance theory diagram representing a voter's attitude toward the source, her attitude toward the issue, and the source's attitude toward the issue as three relations of a *p-o-x* triad. The balance interpretation that would follow from this diagram would certainly be consistent with the view that voters may perceptually distort candidates' positions on issues (i.e., modify the *o-x* relation) in order to produce balanced triads in which liked candidates agree with their own positions and disliked candidates disagree. However, consistent with our discussions of balance theory in Chapters 3 and 10, balance can be achieved in such a triad in various other ways. Most obviously, people may change the *p-o* relation by coming to like candidates whom they accurately perceive as taking agreeable positions and to dislike candidates whom they perceive as taking disagreeable positions. Moreover, people may change the *p-x* relation by changing their attitudes toward liked candidates' positions (and changing their attitudes away from disliked candidates' positions).

Compatible with this balance analysis is Krosnick's (1990a) attempt to determine the extent to which assimilation and contrast account for the balanced relations observed between voters' attitudes toward Reagan and Mondale and their perceptions of these candidates' positions on issues during the 1984 presidential campaign. He found that voters were, on the whole, quite accurate in perceiving candidates' positions and that relatively little of the relation between voters' attitudes and their perceptions of candidates' positions could be ascribed to voters' distortions of these positions. The conditions under which assimilation and contrast may be important in people's perceptions of the political domain thus remain to be delineated.

Selective Memory. Consistent with attitudes' presumed impact on exposure, perception, and judgment, they have also been thought to affect memory. Most researchers who have investigated the relation between attitude and memory have done so by presenting subjects with information that is evaluatively congruent or incongruent with their prior attitudes and then testing subjects' abilities to recall or recognize this information. Nearly all such experiments have sought to demonstrate that attitudinally congruent information is more memorable.

This focus on verifying a congeniality bias in memory is not surprising given the variety of psychological mechanisms that could produce such an effect. To the extent that people *do* selectively attend to attitudinally congruent information, greater memory for such information should ensue. Holding attention constant, attitude-incongruent information might nonetheless be more difficult to remember. In line with Freud's (1946) views on repression, such information might be suppressed from consciousness due to its inherent unpleasantness. Alternatively, people may forget and, perhaps, cognitively distort attitude-discrepant information over time as a means of reducing the dissonance that exposure to such information presumably arouses (Festinger, 1957). Discrepant information may be less memorable for purely cognitive reasons as well. Attitude-incongruent information may be more difficult to retrieve from memory because it conforms less well, or is less strongly linked, to previously stored knowledge about the attitude object (see Chapters 1 and 3). In addition, reconstructive views of memory (e.g., F. C. Bartlett, 1932) suggest that when people are asked to remember attitudinally relevant information, their attitudes—like other stored knowledge—may be used to reconstruct what they might have seen, heard, or done. In other words, attitudes may bias memory by serving as retrieval cues. As a consequence of this reconstructive influence, attitude-congruent information should over time become increasingly more likely to be recalled or recognized than attitude-incongruent information.

Early studies generally yielded support for an attitude congeniality bias in memory (e.g., Edwards, 1941; J. M. Levine & Murphy, 1943; Postman & Murphy, 1943; Watson & Hartmann, 1939). Levine and Murphy's (1943) widely cited study provided a particularly striking demonstration of this effect. Five times over a five-week period five pro-communist and five anti-communist college-aged subjects read and then recalled a pro-communist message and an anti-communist message. Both within and across trials, the results showed that pro-communist subjects recalled more of the pro-communist message than anti-communist subjects did, whereas anti-communist subjects retained more of the anti-communist message than pro-communist subjects did. On five subsequent occasions, subjects returned to the laboratory and, without benefit of re-exposure, again tried to recall both experimental passages. These data also revealed greater memory for attitude-congruent information. Moreover, the observed recall differences tended to increase somewhat over time (although this trend was not evaluated statistically).

Several conceptual replications of the attitude congeniality effect were reported during the 1950s, although the findings were often weak and not wholly consistent within studies (e.g., Alper & Korchin, 1952; Doob, 1953; Garber, 1955; Gilkinson, Paulson, & Sekkink, 1953; Taft, 1954). Most notable among this second wave of experiments were Edward E. Jones's demonstrations that the congeniality effect could be reversed in certain circumstances. Thus, Jones and Aneshansel (1956) found that attitude-*incongruent* information was better remembered among subjects who believed that such information would be useful to them in a subsequent counterarguing task. Among subjects who did not anticipate this second task, attitude-congruent information was better remembered, though not significantly so. In a subsequent study, Jones and Kohler (1958) reasoned that implausible (i.e., weak, incredible) arguments that support one's attitude are not really congenial, whereas implausible arguments that oppose one's position are. In accord with this reasoning, their recall data yielded the "standard" congeniality effect only in relation to plausible (i.e., strong) material. Given implausible information, subjects recalled more opposing than supportive arguments.[15]

A spate of studies published during the 1960s failed to reveal *any* reliable effect of attitude on memory (e.g., Brigham & Cook, 1969; Fitzgerald & Ausubel, 1963; A. G. Greenwald & Sakumura, 1967; Waly & Cook, 1966). These null results were accompanied by the perception that many earlier studies had produced fragile effects at best and by the expression of doubts about the methodological rigor of the early attitude memory literature (see A. G. Greenwald, 1975a; A. G. Greenwald & Sakumura, 1967). Several other data sets proved to be ambiguous (e.g., Malpass, 1969; S. S. Smith & Jamieson, 1972). These events proved sufficient to convince most 1970s investigators and textbook writers that people's attitudes exert little, if any, impact on their memory for attitude-relevant information (e.g., Fishbein & Ajzen, 1972; Freedman, Carlsmith, & Sears, 1978; D. J. Schneider, 1976). For example, Anthony Greenwald (1975a;

Greenwald & Sakumura, 1967) described the accumulated literature as comprised of a few methodologically suspect confirmations of the attitude congeniality effect and a larger number of methodologically rigorous failures to replicate the phenomenon.[16]

Although critiques such as Greenwald's dampened research interest in the relation between attitude and memory, a modest number of additional experiments have accumulated over the past two decades.[17] In addition, J. V. Roberts (1985) conducted a meta-analytic review of the literature. The congeniality effect Roberts observed was small in magnitude but significant. Thus, he concluded that it was a reliable, though not particularly strong, phenomenon. Secondary analyses led Roberts to conclude further that selective attention was relatively unimportant in accounting for congeniality effects, whereas retrieval and reconstructive processes were important. If selective attention was important, Roberts reasoned, the size of the congeniality effect (a) ought to be just as large in contexts in which immediate memory tests are administered as in contexts in which delayed tests are administered, but (b) ought to be much smaller in *intentional learning* contexts in which subjects are warned that their memory will be tested than in *incidental learning* contexts in which subjects are not so explicitly warned. Contrary to this reasoning, however, the size of the congeniality effect proved significantly larger in delayed (vs. immediate) memory contexts and was no smaller in intentional (vs. incidental) learning contexts.

Although Roberts' (1985) meta-analysis provides a needed corrective to earlier, overly pessimistic conclusions about the attitude-memory relation, its value is somewhat limited (see also B. T. Johnson, 1991). First, his conclusion that selective attention plays little role in accounting for attitude memory effects is, at best, premature. Although we agree that the positive relation Roberts observed between the size of the congeniality effect and the length of the interval between exposure and assessment provides suggestive evidence that retrieval and reconstructive mechanisms play a role in producing memory effects, this finding does not rule out a role for selective attention. Simply put, any memory effect that results from attentional differences should increase over time, not remain the same as Roberts reasoned. In addition, Roberts' contrast between incidental and intentional learning contexts is diagnostic of the role played by selective attention only to the extent that incidental contexts truly did not constrain subjects' attention to attitudinal information. Yet many supposedly incidental learning contexts in the attitude memory literature do not satisfy this conceptual criterion; in some studies, subjects have been told to pay close attention to stimulus materials and, in others, to make judgments that would necessitate careful attention (see Chaiken, 1984, and Chapter 6).

The second, more critical limitation of Roberts' (1985) meta-analysis is that it was not designed to explore complexities in the attitude memory literature. Most notably, it did not investigate variables other than "learning context" and measurement delay that might affect the magnitude and, more important, the *direction* (i.e., positive vs. negative) of attitude memory effects.[18] In fact, a sizable number of studies in the literature have yielded incongruency effects, occasionally on an overall basis (e.g., Cacioppo & Petty, 1979b), but more typically under certain circumstances or for certain types of subjects (e.g., E. E. Jones & Aneshansel, 1956; J. T. Johnson & Judd,

1983; Kleck & Wheaton, 1967; Malpass, 1969; Zanna & Olson, 1982; Spiro & Sherif, 1975). For example, whereas *closed-minded* subjects and *repressor* subjects manifested better recall for attitudinally congruent information, *open-minded* and *sensitizer* subjects exhibited better recall for incongruent information (Kleck & Wheaton, 1967; Zanna & Olson, 1982; see earlier discussion of dogmatism and repression sensitization). In a more recent demonstration that individual differences matter in this literature, Chaiken and colleagues obtained an incongruency effect among subjects whose attitudes toward capital punishment were high in evaluative-cognitive consistency, and a congruency effect among subjects whose attitudes were low in evaluative-cognitive consistency (see Chaiken et al., in press).

Differential attention and elaborative processing provide a plausible interpretation for these individual difference findings. Consistent with traditional selective attention logic, some people may deal with attitude-discrepant information by ignoring it; because attitude-congruent information would therefore receive more attention, it should be more memorable. Other people, however, may deal with discrepant information more actively, by attending to it and trying to refute it; because attitude-congruent information would therefore receive less attention, it should be less memorable. Such a defense-motivated processing style may be prompted by other individual difference factors (e.g., ego-involvement, commitment; George, 1979; Spiro & Sherif, 1975) as well as certain situational variables (e.g., threats to attitudinal freedom). It is likely, for example, that defensive processing produced the incongruency effect that Cacioppo and Petty (1979b) observed. Their subjects were exposed to a set of persuasive arguments in the context of a message that was described as proattitudinal or counterattitudinal. Although all subjects were thus exposed to the identical arguments, argument recall and the frequency of counterarguing were significantly higher among subjects exposed to the message labeled as counterattitudinal.

Defense-motivated processing and its consequence, heightened attention to and elaboration of incongruent information, have not been emphasized in past attitude memory research. Because such processing should function either to minimize the likelihood of observing the classic attitude congeniality bias in memory or to reverse this bias, exploration of the variables that foster this kind of processing should be given high priority in subsequent research. Greater attention to attitudinally incongruent information need not always reflect a desire to defend one's attitudes, of course. As suggested by selective exposure research, people may sometimes attend more to incongruent information because such material has greater information value or utility than congruent information. E. E. Jones and Aneschansel's (1956) demonstration that an incongruency effect obtained among subjects who stood to benefit from studying attitude-discrepant belief statements is easily understood in these terms. The role of informational utility, and perhaps other factors that influence attention, also deserves closer scrutiny in subsequent research.

Although encoding mechanisms clearly play a role in producing attitude memory effects, so do retrieval and reconstructive mechanisms. The theoretical importance of the latter processes has long been recognized, but few studies have paid them much empirical attention (e.g., George, 1979; Pratkanis, 1989; Read & Rosson, 1982).

Among the studies showing that attitudes exert a congeniality bias on the retrieval of information from memory is a series of experiments by Michael Ross and his colleagues (e.g., Conway & Ross, 1984; Lydon, Zanna, & Ross, 1988; M. Ross, McFarland, & Fletcher, 1981; see M. Ross, 1989). In this research, subjects were exposed to some treatment (e.g., a persuasive message) designed to change their attitudes and, afterwards, were asked to list past behaviors or beliefs about the attitude object. Consistent with the researchers' selective retrieval hypothesis, the attitude-relevant information subjects listed was more congruent with their changed attitudes than with their prior attitudes. The implications of this research for the relation between attitude and memory are straightforward: Although both congruent and incongruent information may be stored in memory, congruent information is more likely to be retrieved, particularly when memory is assessed after a temporal delay. The work of Ross and his colleagues further suggests that at least some portion of information "retrieved" from memory was, in actuality, never really stored. Rather, it has been constructed by subjects on the basis of their attitudes and their implicit theories that beliefs and behaviors are typically congruent with people's attitudes (see M. Ross, 1989). Yet most research on attitude memory has been poorly designed to detect the operation of reconstructive processes, because the vast majority of studies have relied exclusively on memory measures that tap only the quantity of subjects' accurate recall of previously presented information (for exceptions, see George, 1979; Read & Rosson, 1982). An important additional agenda for future research on this topic is the development and use of measures that can detect distortions and intrusions in memory.

Attitude memory effects are also dependent on the nature of people's preexisting knowledge about attitude objects. To the extent that this knowledge tends to be unipolar in nature, that is, evaluatively congruent with people's attitudes (see Feather, 1969), congruency effects are relatively likely to be observed, particularly as veridical memory for presented information erodes (see Pratkanis, 1989). Yet to the extent that both supportive and opposing attitudinal viewpoints are represented in memory (that is, a bipolar attitude schema), neither congruent nor incongruent information may have a memorial advantage. Instead, as several studies have suggested, attitudinally extreme information may be better recalled than attitudinally moderate information, regardless of its congruency (e.g., Judd & Kulik, 1980; Postman & Murphy, 1943; Pratkanis, 1989). Thus, to predict whether congruent, incongruent, or extreme information will be better remembered, it will also be important for future research to address more systematically the nature of stored attitude-relevant knowledge. The idea that attitudes toward controversial issues and attitudes held by activists are likely to be associated with bipolar rather than unipolar knowledge representations (see Chapter 3) implies that attitude extremity effects are most likely to be obtained for such issues and such persons.

Finally, the magnitude of the relation between attitude and memory is no doubt also influenced by the accessibility of people's prior attitudes and knowledge. That is, only when activated can such structures be expected to influence cognitive processing, and, therefore, memory. As suggested by Houston and Fazio's (1989) selective judgment findings, the effects of attitudes on memory ought to prove larger for people who possess strong, accessible attitudes. Likewise, situational factors that influence activation should also influence the magnitude of attitude-memory effects. Consistent with this expectation, Chaiken et al. (in press) reported significant effects of attitude on memory when subjects were instructed to rate their agreement with a set of belief statements, but not when subjects were instructed to rate their familiarity with these statements. Presumably, the agreement task served to activate subjects' prior attitudes. These results suggest that future researchers should give at least as much attention to the "pretext" they use to expose subjects to attitudinal stimuli as to other aspects of their experimental designs.

Some Final Comments on Attitudinal Selectivity. We hope that our discussion of research on attitudinal selectivity will help restore interest in one of the fundamental issues of attitude theory—the impact of attitudes at various stages of information processing. If attitude is an important structure in memory—a structure that is often accessible—it should indeed influence exposure and attention, perception and judgment, and memory. However, the fact that research findings have not shown simple and invariant congeniality trends requires that psychologists become more sophisticated about what research findings should reveal, given various theoretical expectations. It is especially important for attitude researchers to consider psychological tendencies other than attitudes—for example, a tendency to prefer useful information and to process it carefully and systematically. And it is equally important to consider the demands and limitations of typical laboratory research methods. Once these and other factors are taken into account, it should be possible to partial out attitudinal influences on information processing.

Thought and the Polarization of Attitudes

Merely thinking about one's attitude often makes it more extreme. This important finding was first produced in research by Abraham Tesser (1978). In his initial experiment on the impact of mere thought, male subjects were exposed to an experimental partner (in actuality, an audiotaped simulation of a partner) who described himself in a manner that made him seem likable or unlikable (Sadler & Tesser, 1973). Before rating their partner on evaluative scales, subjects were instructed either to think about him or to work on an irrelevant task intended to distract them from thinking about him. Compared with subjects who were distracted, subjects who had thought about their partner gave him more favorable ratings if he was likable but less favorable ratings if he was unlikable.

This polarization effect was replicated by Tesser and his colleagues in a series of subsequent experiments. For example, Tesser and Conlee (1975) presented their subjects with a heterogeneous set of attitudinal issues such as the legalization of prostitution and the value of pass-fail grading in college courses. In their first experiment, subjects gave their attitude on each issue on an agree-disagree scale and then thought about the issue until the experimenter told them to stop. They then gave their attitude again. The duration of thought was manipulated to range from 30 to 180

TABLE 12.4

Number of Subjects Whose Attitude Became More Polarized in the Tesser and Conlee (1975) Experiment

	Thought condition		
Attitude change	No thought condition	Short duration (28 sec.)	Long duration (90 sec.)
Polarized	1	7	14
Not polarized	21	37	30

Source: This table was adapted from one presented by Tesser and Conlee (1975, Experiment 3, Table 1, p. 268).

seconds. Subjects' evaluations polarized on a higher proportion of issues to the extent that they spent more time thinking about the attitude object. Findings from a second experiment replicated this effect on issues that were chosen so that subjects' initial attitudes ranged from moderately positive to moderately negative across the issues. A third experiment replicated the polarization effect with stimuli in the form of slides of news photos. Findings from this experiment appear in Table 12.4. Tesser's (1978) early review of his own and other investigators' research on thought-induced attitude change showed that the great majority of relevant studies had supported the hypothesis that thinking about attitude objects polarizes attitudes.

Tesser reasoned that this polarization effect was mediated by cognitive changes that occur during thought. When people think about attitude objects, they tend to produce beliefs that are evaluatively consistent with their prior attitudes. This assumption of pressure toward evaluative consistency follows from cognitive consistency theories such as balance theory, which maintain that people prefer that associated cognitions be evaluatively consistent (see Chapters 3 and 10). Therefore, people would tend to produce new beliefs consistent with their attitude and suppress or refute inconsistent beliefs. This tendency for beliefs to become progressively more consistent with one's overall evaluation should lead to a more polarized attitude.

This theorizing about the cognitive processes that may account for polarization led Tesser to reason that holding a relatively large amount of knowledge about an attitude object should facilitate the production of consistent thoughts about it as well as the refutation of inconsistent thoughts. Polarization should thus be more pronounced when people are knowledgeable concerning the attitude objects they think about. Substantiating this reasoning, Tesser and Leone (1977) found that men's evaluations of football plays (i.e., tackles) and women's evaluations of women's fashions polarized more as a product of thought than did women's evaluations of football plays and men's evaluations of fashions. Presumably women typically have relatively elaborated knowledge structures for women's fashions, as men do for football. Also, in an experiment in which subjects were shown four trait adjectives that characterized either an individual or a group of people, Tesser and Leone showed that thought caused attitudes toward individuals to polarize more often than attitudes toward groups. Consistent with the assumption that this polarization effect was due to the better developed knowledge structures that people possess about the personalities of individuals compared with the characteristics of groups, subjects reported that it was easier to think about the individuals.

Tesser's emphasis on constructive thought processes that mediate polarization effects is of course quite in harmony with the cognitive-response view of message-based persuasion (see Chapter 6). Therefore, thought-listing measures and related methodologies should be informative about the details of the processes that mediate polarization. Indeed, Tesser and others have attempted to generate such evidence for mediating processes (see Tesser, 1978; see also Chaiken & Yates, 1985; Liberman & Chaiken, 1991).

Tesser's reasoning about the causes of attitudinal polarization suggests that the phenomenon would occur only for some people and only under some circumstances. Special attention should be given to understanding these limiting conditions in view of Tesser's (1978) evidence that many attitudes do not polarize as a consequence of thought. In fact, less than 50 percent of attitudes became more polarized even in experimental conditions producing maximal polarization; the remaining attitudes either stayed the same or depolarized (see sample findings in Table 12.4). Yet the percentage of attitudes polarizing was much smaller in no-thought or distraction conditions. Thought thus does produce an overall trend toward polarization, but the phenomenon is far from uniform across attitudes and subjects.

In a contribution to understanding the limits that attitude structure places on thought-induced polarization, Chaiken and Yates (1985) found greater polarization on the social issues of capital punishment and censorship to the extent that subjects were high in evaluative-cognitive consistency, one of the attitude-strength variables that we implicated in relation to attitudinal resistance. Not surprisingly, bringing to mind beliefs that are evaluatively consistent with one's attitude polarizes the attitude, but inconsistent beliefs do not have this effect. In addition, Liberman and Chaiken (1991) showed that subjects did not polarize on a public policy issue when their values relevant to the issue were conflicting (see discussion of attitudinal ambivalence in Chapter 3). For example, on the issue of whether the CIA should have the authority to open citizens' mail, value conflict was indexed by the extent to which subjects judged as equally important two values with conflicting implications for the issue: national security and individual freedom. Only the subjects low in value conflict polarized. Moreover, analyses of subjects' thought listings confirmed the authors' reasoning that the thoughts of high value-conflict subjects failed to polarize their attitudes because these thoughts were evaluatively inconsistent.

Complementing the proposition that attitude structure places constraints on polarization, situational constraints can motivate or dampen polarization. For example, Millar and Tesser (1986b) reasoned that commitment to one's initial attitude would favor polarization because it would lead to attempts to justify the attitude (see prior discussion of commitment). Indeed, polarization was increased by committing subjects to their attitudes by instructing them that their attitudes were under scrutiny and would be compared with their subsequent attitudes. Additional findings suggested that this relation was mediated by a tendency for commitment to cause beliefs to become more intercorrelated and therefore more evaluatively redundant. Yet commitment does not appear to be a necessary condition for polarization, and it is entirely possible that other situationally induced constraints would dampen polarization or even cause moderation.

In a related literature also investigating situationally induced constraints, researchers have examined the attitudinal effects of expecting to be exposed to a person whose beliefs differ from one's own. In this context, both moderation and polarization have been observed (see Cialdini & Petty, 1981). Although researchers have suggested that these shifts are typically strategic maneuvers that achieve self-presentational goals and therefore are ephemeral, such changes have been shown to become more enduring to the extent that they have been accompanied by a rehearsal of thoughts supporting the changed attitude (e.g., Cialdini, Levy, Herman, Kozlowski, & Petty, 1976; Fitzpatrick & Eagly, 1981). Similarly, Tetlock (1983a) has shown that having subjects expect to justify their attitudes to an audience can create moderation or polarization, depending on the attitudinal position that the audience is expected to have. More generally, instead of polarizing as a product of thought about one's own attitudes, people may instead moderate their attitudes, presumably because they anticipate a situation in which a relatively neutral attitude might be advantageous. Under such circumstances, they probably rehearse thoughts less extreme than their own attitude. Directed thinking can thereby cause attitude depolarization, even though "mere thought" generally produces polarization.

In general, attitude polarization appears to occur if people are allowed to think about an attitude object in a relatively unconstrained way, provided that their attitudes toward the object are accompanied by a structure of beliefs that is at least moderately elaborated and consistent with their overall evaluation. In persuasion settings, this effect would seem to favor resistance to persuasion because it would cause people's attitudes to become more distant from alternative positions on issues, a condition that social judgment theory suggests would increase the likelihood that these positions would fall in the latitude of rejection. Therefore, if opponents on an issue both engage in thinking about it, their subsequent encounter may be more contentious than it would otherwise have been. Yet before generalizing about thought polarization in natural settings, it is wise to keep in mind the point we have already made about the likely sensitivity of people's thought to a variety of situational pressures. After all, people generally do not engage in "mere thought" in the manner that they do in polarization experiments. Instead, they think for a purpose, and this purpose may often constrain their thoughts.

Reflections on Attitudinal Selectivity and Polarization. Research on both attitudinal selectivity and polarization have helped illuminate the impact of attitudes on information processing. There is ample support for the claim that, if attitudes are relatively strong, people tend to be biased in favor of their attitudes. By means of a variety of specific processes, people often screen out challenging information and shore up their strongly held attitudes, unless situational constraints impel them to do otherwise. Although some of these effects have been less robust than psychologists once believed, congeniality trends appear to be genuine but of course only part of a larger picture wherein information processing is influenced by a variety of other pressures as well (e.g., tendencies to favor useful information, and, more generally, to place one's thinking in the service of goal attainment). Finally, this area of investigation would profit from increased effort to carry out research in naturalistic settings that weaken self-presentational pressures to appear fair and unbiased. We suspect that people often favor their attitudes in an unashamedly biased manner when they are alone or among ideologically compatible friends.

Theories of the Persistence of Changed Attitudes

Ordinarily the attitude change induced by persuasive messages and other stimuli decays over time, as attitudes gravitate toward the positions held before the change was induced (T. D. Cook & Flay, 1978). Yet even this broad and plausible generalization about persistence has only a weak empirical basis because the inclusion of delayed measures has been a rare event in almost all traditions of research on attitude change. Even when research pertains directly to theories that include predictions about temporal persistence, the delayed measures that would allow these predictions to be tested are usually omitted. There are two research literatures, however, in which persistence has been explored systematically. These two literatures concern *associative interference* and *the sleeper effect*.

Research on both associative interference and the sleeper effect invokes ideas about cognitive linkages in order to explain persistence. Although the idea that attitudes are cognitively embedded in larger structures has also been important in understanding resistance, different ideas about cognitive linkages have been seen as relevant to the temporal persistence of changed attitudes. In research on associative interference, the key notion is that people's memories for certain attitudes may interfere with or become confused with their memories for other attitudes. In research on the sleeper effect, the central idea is that positive or negative cues attached to memories of message content can become dissociated from them over time. These two themes, interference in memory and dissociation of persuasive cues, have not yet come under scrutiny in this book.

Associative Interference

The concept of *associative interference*, which concerns the ease with which cognitions are confused in memory, has been applied by Anthony Greenwald and his colleagues to understand the persistence of changed attitudes (e.g., Baumgardner, Leippe, Ronis, & Greenwald, 1983; Leippe, Greenwald, & Baumgardner, 1982). To comprehend this theory of attitudinal persistence, readers should recall that in the 1950s and 1960s investigators associated with the field then known as *verbal learning* formulated theories of forgetting that invoked the idea that forgetting can be explained by assuming various interference effects (e.g., Postman, Stark, & Fraser, 1968; Underwood, 1957). Rather than thinking about forgetting as explained by the decay or deterioration of memory traces, these psychologists typically viewed memories as stored permanently. From their perspective, the reason that memories can be difficult to retrieve was assumed to be interference from other memories.

Experiments in this tradition focused on the phenomena known as *proactive* and *retroactive interference* (see W. C. Gordon, 1989, for review). Proactive interference refers to the disruption of memories formed at one point in time by memories that were formed earlier. In contrast, retroactive interference refers to the disruption of memories formed earlier by memories formed at a later point in time. Experiments on these varieties of interference generally used *paired associates* methods whereby subjects learned a list of paired nonsense syllables or words (e.g., book-dog; pencil-house; car-sky). A second list, often containing the same stimulus words (e.g., book, pencil, car), would present other pairs (e.g., book-light; pencil-cup; car-shoe). Presentation of a second list, either before or after the learning of a target list, generally resulted in poorer recall of the target list. If the interfering list preceded the target list, the poor recall was ascribed to proactive interference; if the interfering list followed the target list, the poor recall was ascribed to retroactive interference. However, under specialized conditions, the presentation of a second list was shown to improve memory for the first list—specifically, if the response words in the second list were quite similar to those in the first list and presumably cued the first-list words (e.g., first list was book-dog, pencil-house, and car-sky; second list was book-canine, pencil-home, and car-cloud). Such enhancement effects were sometimes termed *positive transfer* (e.g., Ellis, 1969).

To the extent that learning and memory mediate attitudes (see Chapter 6), the verbal learning paradigm, with its paired associates experiments and emphasis on concepts such as interference and transfer, could well have implications for the persistence of attitudes over time. Although the influence of this approach on attitude research has not been strong, it did see application in research by Greenwald and his associates that examined attitudinal persistence within a single experimental session (e.g., Baumgardner et al., 1983; Leippe et al., 1982). These investigators framed their hypotheses in terms of an *associative learning model* by which a persuasive message is assumed to establish an association between an attitude object and an evaluation, much as a paired associate item was assumed to establish an association between a stimulus word and a response word.[19]

In the major set of experiments framed in terms of this associative learning model, Baumgardner et al. (1983) presented subjects with persuasive messages on consumer products (e.g., automobiles, televisions, cereals). Each message linked a fictitious brand (e.g., Wilson automobiles; Miller television sets) with two persuasive arguments that were either (a) favorable to the product (e.g., "Wilson automobiles have excellent brakes with short stopping distances and high reliability," p. 526), (b) unfavorable to it (e.g., "Miller television sets have poor interlace and seriously distorted or blurred vertical detail," p. 526), or (c) mixed (i.e., one favorable argument and one unfavorable argument). Each subject received messages concerning as many as 54 brands from as many as 12 product categories. These messages were presented on a video monitor via a computer-controlled procedure (see Ronis, Baumgardner, Leippe, Cacioppo, & Greenwald, 1977), and subjects proceeded through them at their own pace. Subjects rated each brand on an evaluative scale immediately after the message and after various delays. In this experimental setting, which these investigators dubbed a *message-dense environment*, there were of course many opportunities to examine interference and transfer effects.

The major hypothesis of this research was that persuasion should decay rapidly when highly similar attitude objects (i.e., brands *within* a product category) are associated with differing evaluations and decay more slowly when dissimilar stimuli (i.e., brands from *different* product categories) are associated with differing evaluations. In other words, associative interference should be greater to the extent that attitude objects are similar and therefore quite easily confused. This more rapid decay was obtained with the similar stimuli, although only on the first block of trials. In contrast, according to the transfer effect logic, when highly similar stimuli are associated with *the same* evaluation, this evaluative response should generalize or produce a positive transfer effect whereby persuasion should be more persistent over time. Indeed, decay of persuasion was attenuated when similar stimuli were associated with the same evaluation. The role of memory as a mediator of these phenomena was suggested by the substantial relation obtained between subjects' attitudes and their memory for the evaluative content of the messages.

Another study by Greenwald and his colleagues demonstrated a *context confusion effect*, also presumed to be a product of associative interference (Leippe et al., 1982). In this experiment, subjects received messages about various fictitious consumer product brands such as "Tucker electronic calculators." Some brands were described by neutral messages, which portrayed the brand as "average." These neutral messages appeared in a context of a larger number of messages about other brands in the same product class. These other messages were either predominantly positive or predominantly negative. With delayed ratings of the brands, subjects' evaluations of the neutral brands shifted progressively toward the positive or negative context provided by the other messages. In contrast, subjects' evaluations of the brands described by the context-consistent positive and negative messages showed some decay toward the midpoint of the scale. These findings are shown in Figure 12.2. Thus, the associations between the other brands and their consistently positive or consistently negative evaluations interfered with the association between the target brand and its neutral evaluation.

In general, the associative interference effects produced by the Greenwald research group provide convincing demonstrations that the rate at which persuasion decays depends on the context in which messages are presented. The particular aspects of context explored in this research are the similarity of the positions that messages advocate and the similarity of the content domain of the messages. However, the term *associative interference* provides primarily a description of a class of phenomena rather than a detailed psychological theory about the processes that underlie these effects. For example, as Leippe et al. (1982) acknowledged, their context confusion findings do

**FIGURE 12.2.
Mean brand
evaluation as a
function of positive,
neutral, or negative
content of message
and positive (+) or
negative (−)
surrounding
message context in
Leippe, Greenwald,
and Baumgardner's
experiment (1982).
This figure was
presented by Leippe
and colleagues
(1982, Figure 1,
p. 648).**

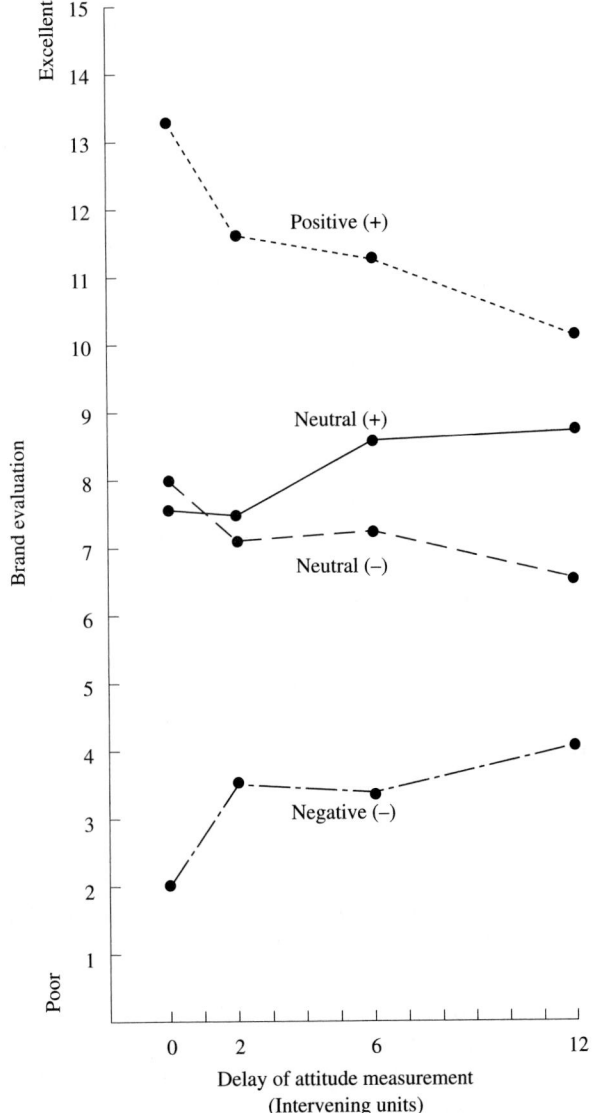

not indicate the exact nature of the interference process implicated (e.g., failures of stimulus discrimination or associative learning; competition between different response sets). In fact, the analogous paired-associate phenomena, which were studied extensively by verbal learning researchers, generated considerable debate about correct theoretical explanations (see W. C. Gordon, 1989). However important these theoretical developments were in earlier decades, interest in them declined in the 1970s and

611

1980s. Although the idea of associative interference has not been discarded in contemporary thinking, it has come to be regarded primarily as a general label for one class of complexly determined difficulties that people experience in the retrieval of memories. If encoding and retrieval processes have considerable complexity even for simple words and nonsense syllables, understanding these processes for relatively more complicated persuasive messages is surely a much more formidable task. Therefore, the research we have cited on associative interference and the persistence of persuasion stands as a set of provocative demonstrations that persistence depends on the context in which a persuasive message was initially received. Detailed theoretical understanding of these phenomena awaits more developed theory.

Discounting Cues and Research on the Sleeper Effect

One of the better-known empirical phenomena in persuasion research is a delayed increase in the amount of attitude change induced by a message, a finding dubbed the *sleeper effect* by Hovland, Lumsdaine, and Sheffield (1949). When a sleeper effect occurs, the change measured immediately after a message is *smaller* than the change measured at some later point, as if the message had lain dormant for some time in people's minds, until its full impact was unleashed. Sleeper effects are thus the opposite of the more typical tendency for persuasion to decay over time.

Early sightings of the sleeper effect include Peterson and Thurstone's (1933/1970) demonstration that the attitude change that certain films induced in children and adolescents was greater several months subsequently than immediately after viewing them. Better known is Hovland and colleagues' (1949) demonstration that the impact on American soldiers of a World War II propaganda film was greater 9 weeks (as opposed to 5 days) after the film. Yet both demonstrations were exceedingly modest. Peterson and Thurstone obtained the more typical decay of persuasion for most of the films they investigated. Moreover, Hovland and associates obtained a sleeper effect on only a subset of the items that assessed the impact of the film. The other items showed a decline in persuasion, and the sleeper effect was not significant when the entire set of items was taken into account.

Although the sleeper effect has attracted attention primarily as an intriguing and somewhat counterintuitive empirical phenomenon, a particular theoretical principle has commonly been invoked to explain it. This principle reflects the same associationist tradition that underlies the work that we have just reviewed on associative interference. However, the principle invoked to explain the sleeper effect is *dissociation* of memory traces rather than associative interference between them: An unfavorably evaluated persuasion cue (e.g., a negative source) that was initially associated with the message presumably becomes dissociated from it over time (see Hovland et al., 1953). This negative cue, generally known as a *discounting cue*, is defined as a feature of the persuasive situation that recipients associate with the message and that causes them to discount it, that is, to perceive the message as less valid than it would otherwise be perceived. A dissociation between the message and this discounting cue (i.e., a forgetting of the link) is assumed to allow the message's inherent persuasiveness to emerge. The resulting tendency for message impact to increase over time contrasts with the considerably more common tendency for the persuasiveness of messages to dissipate over time (see T. D. Cook & Flay, 1978).

In the Hovland and colleagues (1949) experiment, for example, the discounting cue may well have been the source of the film. This source was the army, which the soldiers evidently viewed as a biased and untrustworthy source of information about the war. As time passed, this source cue might have become dissociated from the film itself in the soldiers' minds. If so, the change-inhibiting impact of the army source would have lessened, and the soldiers' attitudes would have risen to the level of persuasion induced by the film alone.

This explanation gained support in subsequent studies carried out by the Yale persuasion researchers (see Hovland et al., 1953). In an experiment in which the message source served as a discounting cue, Hovland and Weiss (1951) found the usual decay of persuasion with high credibility sources and a sleeper effect with low credibility sources. Consequently the two types of sources appeared equally persuasive at the time of the delayed measurement (four weeks after the presentation), even though the high credibility sources had been more persuasive than the low credibility sources immediately after the presentation. Because evidence was slight that recipients had truly forgotten the source of the communication, the findings of this experiment did not support the particular version of the discounting cue explanation that had been suggested by Hovland et al. (1949)—that the source of the message was more quickly forgotten than message content. Consequently, Hovland and Weiss (1951) modified the original dissociation interpretation by arguing that recipients became less likely "to associate spontaneously" (p. 648) the source with the message. Rather than a simple forgetting explanation, this idea pertained to the likelihood that the source would come to mind along with the message when subjects responded to message-relevant attitudinal questions. In modern parlance, the idea that the message had been delivered by a particular source was not very accessible to the subjects at the time of the delayed measure.

In a study designed to substantiate this version of the dissociation principle, Kelman and Hovland (1953) extended the Hovland and Weiss (1951) design by adding a condition that reinstated a positive, neutral, or negative communicator at the time of the delayed measurement. This reinstatement, which was intended to reverse the dissociation that might otherwise occur, consisted of replaying at the delayed session the introduction to the audiotaped communication, that is, the part of the message that had established the communicator's identity in the first session. The first session data showed the usual tendency for credibility to relate positively to persuasion. Although this credibility effect had dissipated three weeks later among subjects for whom the communicator had not been reinstated, the effect was restored among subjects for whom the communicator had been reinstated. These findings appear in Figure 12.3. On this basis, Kelman and Hovland argued that, without reinstatement, the change-inhibiting negative source cue became dissociated from the message, and so did the change-promoting positive source cue.

FIGURE 12.3. Immediate and delayed persuasive effects of communication content (C, C′) and communicator prestige (+P, +P′, –P, –P′) with and without reinstatement of the communicator. Values are shown relative to C + P, which is given the arbitrary value of 50. Distances between circled points are based on empirical data from Kelman and Hovland (1953). Other values are hypothetical. This figure was presented by Hovland, Janis, and Kelley (1953, Figure 17, p. 258).

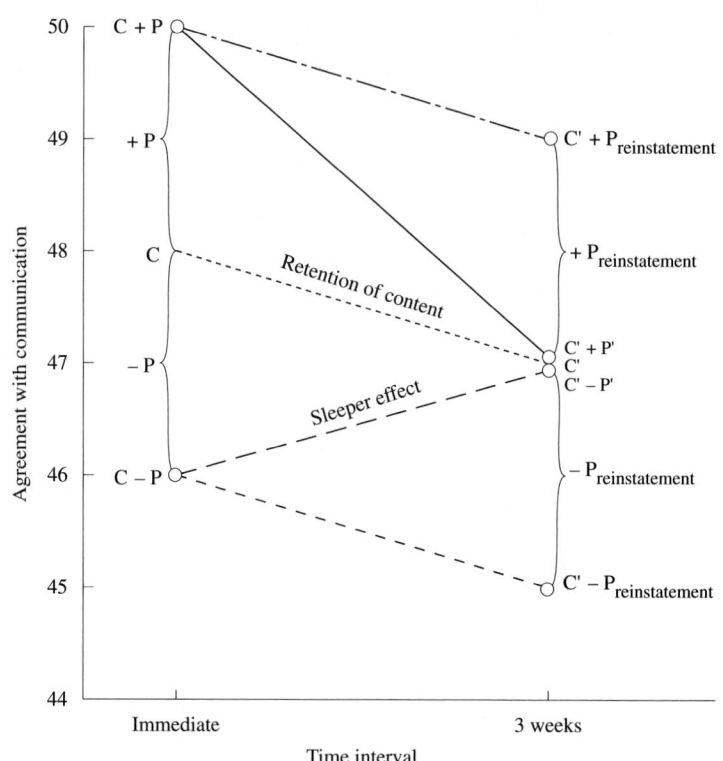

Subsequent to these experiments a number of investigators carried out persuasion studies that included immediate and delayed measures and the presentation of a discounting cue, which usually was a low credibility communicator (see T. D. Cook et al.'s, 1979 review). Although some of these investigators maintained that they had produced a sleeper effect, the criterion for this claim was often quite weak, that is, the presence of a statistically significant interaction between the time of testing (immediate vs. delayed) and the discounting cue (present vs. absent). Such an interaction would indicate that the discounting cue had a different effect at the two points of time. However, the specific pattern that produces the interaction need not include a genuine sleeper effect—a statistically significant increase in persuasion between the immediate and delayed sessions.[20] This increase in persuasion has been called the *absolute sleeper effect*, in contrast to a *relative sleeper effect*, which has been defined by the weaker criterion of less decay of persuasion in the group receiving the discounting cue than the group not receiving it (Cook & Flay, 1978; Cook et al., 1979). An absolute and a relative sleeper effect are shown in Figure 12.4. Consistent with the relative sleeper effect shown in this figure, attitude change might decay sharply without the discounting

FIGURE 12.4. Illustrations of hypothetical absolute and relative sleeper effects. This figure was presented by T. D. Cook, Gruder, Hennigan, and Flay (1979, Figure 1, p. 666).

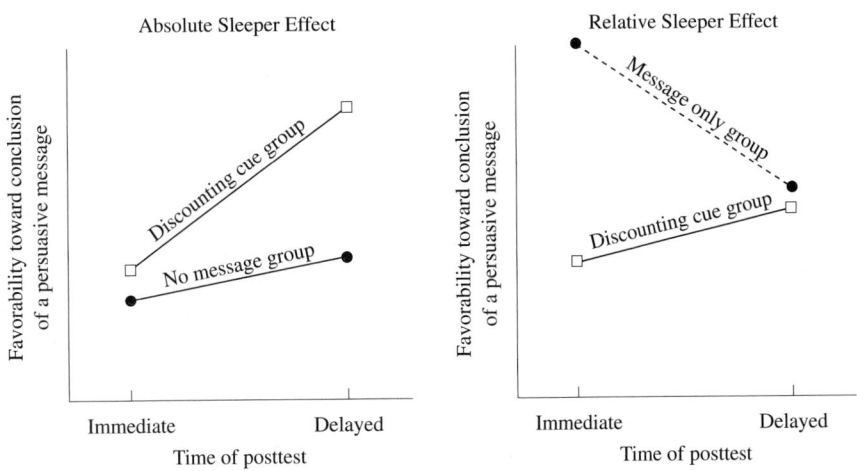

cue (message only group) and increase only slightly with this cue. Alternatively, attitude change with the discounting cue might decline, but less sharply than without the cue; the Time of Testing × Discounting Cue interaction could nonetheless be significant.

Despite the widespread acceptance of the sleeper effect by textbook authors and reviewers from the 1950s to the mid-1970s, a careful evaluation of the empirical status of the effect would have led to a considerably less confident generalization, as Gillig and Greenwald (1974) pointed out during the decade when widely accepted attitudinal findings were questioned. Even those researchers who had obtained a temporal increase in message persuasiveness had often failed to test the statistical significance of this shift. This omission left unanswered the question of whether an absolute sleeper effect had been obtained. Initially unaware of this lack of strong empirical support for the effect, Gillig and Greenwald attempted to produce an absolute sleeper effect in a series of laboratory investigations, but were unable to do so in seven attempts. However, their conclusion that it is "time to lay the sleeper effect to rest" (p. 132) was subsequently challenged by Cook, Gruder, and their associates, who argued that Gillig and Greenwald had not set up the conditions theoretically necessary to obtaining the sleeper effect (Cook et al., 1979; Gruder, Cook, Hennigan, Flay, Alessis, & Halamaj, 1978).

Cook, Gruder, and colleagues argued that the discounting cue hypothesis implied that certain conditions are necessary to produce a sleeper effect. First of all, the message itself must be persuasive, that is, have a significant impact on attitudes. Without this condition being met, there is no possibility for the discounting cue to dampen message impact and for subsequent dissociation to produce a recovery of impact. Second, the discounting cue must have a strong enough immediate impact to inhibit the attitude change that the message would otherwise have produced. Third, enough time must elapse before the delayed posttest that the discounting cue and the message have become dissociated. Fourth, the impact of the message itself must not have decayed so much by the time of the delayed posttest that the restoration of message impact in the discounting cue condition would reveal little gain over the inhibited change shown immediately after the message. This fourth condition recognizes that the usual temporal course of message-induced persuasion is decline. Therefore, the dissociation of the cue and message must occur quickly enough that the message itself still has some residual impact after the dissociation has occurred. Moreover, the delayed posttest must occur at the precise time when enough dissociation but not too much decay of message impact has occurred. Given the complexity (and the manifest reasonableness) of these requirements for obtaining a sleeper effect, the difficulty of obtaining a reliable effect is understandable. As Cook, Gruder, and their associates pointed out, Gillig and Greenwald had not attempted to meet these requirements for obtaining a strong test of the sleeper effect, and it was impossible to assess after the fact whether they had met them.

Gruder et al. (1978) set out to produce a sleeper effect by meeting the requirements that they deemed theoretically necessary to produce it. The messages that they presented to subjects argued against either a 4-day work week or permitting right turns when traffic lights are red. Their discounting cues, which were placed at the end of their written messages, instructed the subjects that the message was inaccurate and wrong and that its conclusion was false. Also, in some conditions, reactance-inducing cues of the "you must inevitably conclude" (p. 1068) type were added to the conclusion of the message (see earlier discussion of reactance). The immediate measures were administered during the session in which the messages were presented, and the delayed measures were administered 5 or 6 weeks later in a context that made it unlikely that subjects connected the attitude assessment with the first session of the experiment.

In those experimental conditions of their two studies for which the Gruder-Cook group demonstrated that they satisfied the requirements for producing a strong test of the sleeper effect, they did indeed obtain a statistically significant increase in persuasion from the immediate to the delayed measure. In those conditions that did *not* meet all of these requirements, they did not obtain a sleeper effect. This impressive pair of experiments demonstrated, not merely that it was possible to obtain a statistically significant sleeper effect, but that such an effect is reliably obtained under theoretically relevant conditions.

As Gruder et al. (1978) noted, because all of their discounting cues were administered at the end of their persuasive messages, the sleeper effect might be reliably obtained only if the discounting cue followed the message. Subsequent experiments by Pratkanis, Greenwald, Leippe, and Baumgardner (1988) examined this possibility. Pursuing the sleeper effect in a series of 16 experiments, these researchers presented subjects with relatively short messages on sociopolitical topics (e.g., statehood for Puerto Rico) or consumer products (e.g., Miller television sets). The discounting cues attacked the credibility of the source of the messages. This research was conducted in a message-dense environment using the same computer-controlled procedure that Greenwald and his colleagues implemented when studying associative interference

616

(see prior discussion). In contrast to most other research on the sleeper effect, both the immediate and delayed measures were administered in the same session, with subjects reading additional messages between these two measures. In general, these studies supported the generalization that the sleeper effect requires that the discounting cue be introduced *after* the message.

Pratkanis et al. (1988) conducted a final experiment with procedures, discounting cues, and messages modeled closely after the Gruder et al. (1978) research. Their manipulation of the placement of the discounting cue (i.e., before or after the message) confirmed that having the cue follow the message is indeed critical to obtaining the sleeper effect. Based on computation of effect sizes for the entire series of experiments, the magnitude of the sleeper effect obtained with post-message presentation of the discounting cue appeared to be somewhat larger in this final experiment than the effect typically obtained in their earlier experiments using the computer-controlled procedure. Yet even their largest effect sizes suggest that the sleeper effect is at best a somewhat modest phenomenon.

Armed with these findings, Pratkanis and his associates proposed a *differential decay* explanation of the sleeper effect. In this explanation, the message itself and the discounting cue are regarded as two communications, albeit with opposite impact. Although the influence of these communications might be about equal immediately after the presentation, the message is assumed to be relatively more influential than the discounting cue at a later point because the impact of the second communication (i.e., the discounting cue) decays somewhat more rapidly than the impact of the first communication (i.e., the message itself). This idea of more rapid decay of a second communication derives from N. Miller and Campbell's (1959) suggestion of a *prior entry effect* by which the impact of the first message was assumed to decay somewhat more slowly than the impact of a second message (see Chapter 6). Pratkanis and colleagues further argued that differential decay would be relevant only to the situation in which the discounting cue follows the message and therefore is not well integrated with it in memory. When the cue precedes the message, the cue is likely to affect message processing by causing the recipients to counterargue, and the discounting cue and the message become a single unit in memory. Alternatively, we suggest that a discounting cue might cause recipients to lose interest in a subsequent message and therefore to process it minimally (see Chaiken, 1980).

The differential decay theory of the sleeper effect, which is based on principles of forgetting, needs more substantiation before it can be regarded as having strong support. As we explained in Chapter 6 (see especially note 5), forgetting theories of message impact have not been very successful in providing fully adequate theories of order effects in persuasion. Just as there are many competing theories of primacy and recency effects, there are many competing theories of the effects of discounting cues (see McGuire, 1985). For example, as we noted earlier, an attempt to influence may produce reactance, which dissipates once the overt pressure to comply is removed (J. W. Brehm & Mann, 1975; S. S. Brehm & Brehm, 1981). Or, as L. L. Jacoby, Kelley, Brown, and Jesechko (1989) have argued, the increased familiarity of an attitudinal position due to its prior presentation may make it seem more plausible, despite the absence of any conscious recollection of the prior presentation or of the source of the message. However, the status of these other theories remains uncertain because they have received even less testing than the dissociation and differential decay theories. Moreover, as Pratkanis et al. (1988) acknowledged, the dissociation hypothesis favored by Cook and Gruder could readily be modified to account for the impact of the timing of the discounting cue. The dissociation hypothesis need only include the assumption that dissociation is less likely to occur if the message and discounting cue are initially strongly linked, as they would be if the cue preceded the message and therefore affected encoding of the message. Dissociation would occur more readily when the cue followed the message and therefore was less strongly linked to it. Whether such a modified dissociation interpretation can be distinguished from a differential decay explanation is a matter that only additional research can solve. Both theories are based on forgetting, with the dissociation theory emphasizing decay of the source-message association and the differential decay theory emphasizing different rates of decay for the evaluative impact of the source and the message.

What do we know based on the now-large body of research on the sleeper effect? This extensive experimentation suggests that an absolute sleeper effect is *not* a reliable phenomenon when the discounting cue precedes the message, even though the early research was based on this pre-message timing of the cue. However, when the cue follows the message, the sleeper effect *is* moderately reliable under the specialized conditions which the Gruder-Cook group set forth. Therefore, the early, widely cited demonstrations of the sleeper effect (Hovland et al., 1949; Hovland & Weiss, 1951; Kelman & Hovland, 1953), none of which may have been significant absolute sleeper effects, now appear anomalous in their implication that a negatively evaluated source presented *before* a persuasive message is likely to produce a sleeper effect.

The history of the sleeper effect and of psychologists' shifts in their belief in it tell an interesting story about progress in science. As Greenwald, Pratkanis, Leippe, and Baumgardner (1986) reconstruct this history, the theory based on dissociation of discounting cues impeded progress in understanding the sleeper effect and the conditions under which it occurs. This theory and a bias in favor of confirming it ostensibly deterred investigators from understanding the conditions under which the effect obtains and retarded the discovery of a better theory—the differential decay theory. We are skeptical of this reasoning. We believe that the sleeper effect lived primarily as an interesting finding that attracted attention because of its counter-intuitive quality. From the time of the Kelman and Hovland (1953) experiment to the mid-1970s, there was little systematic attention given to the effect. The amount of research was not large, and only about half of this research appeared in the key journals where it was likely to be noticed by reviewers or persuasion researchers. Consequently, there was not a great deal of null evidence readily available, and the statistical weakness of the original demonstrations of the sleeper effect was understandably not fixed upon, given that standards of reporting findings in the 1950s were considerably more lenient than they were by the mid-1970s.

We believe that the tendency for reviewers and textbook writers to ignore null findings and to fail to scrutinize the quality of empirical evidence has more to do with faulty scholarship than it does with the dampening influence of theory. Lacking

618

systematic methods of research integration, reviewers cumulated research findings according to their rough impressions of the nature of these findings (see Chapter 14). As we have shown in this chapter and elsewhere in this book, sometimes these impressions have been overly pessimistic but, especially prior to the mid-1960s, these impressions were often quite optimistic. An additional problem is the tendency for textbook writers to base their generalizations on early, well-known findings, such as those reported in the Hovland et al. (1953) volume. This tendency was common in the past and has to some extent prevailed well into the present era.

Contemporary persuasion researchers quite properly have taken an interest in developing a better understanding of the sleeper effect as well as a more accurate reading of the empirical status of the effect. Far from clouding researchers' views, the dissociation hypothesis proved extremely helpful in allowing the Cook-Gruder research group to delineate many of the requirements for obtaining the effect. The Greenwald research group's less theory-driven and more "result-centered" approach isolated an additional condition (timing of the cue)—a condition that the Cook-Gruder group had suspected might be important. This finding opened up new theoretical possibilities in terms of differential decay. Ascertaining the validity of this theory in competition with other theories would require new empirical work.

Other Determinants of Attitudinal Persistence

Delayed Impact of Attitude Change on Related Cognitions. As we noted earlier in this chapter in discussing cognitive interpretations of why strong attitudes are change resistant, change often reverberates through linked elements of a structure (Ball-Rokeach et al., 1984; Hendrick & Seyfried, 1974; McGuire, 1981; Tannenbaum, 1966, 1967; Tannenbaum & Gengel, 1966). Thus, a change in an attitude or belief may impact on logically or psychologically related attitudes and beliefs, so that compatible changes occur (see also Chapter 5). Indeed, the concept of synergism that we introduced in Chapter 1 implies that change induced by any one type of input to attitudes (i.e., cognitive, affective, or behavioral) is likely to spill over to other classes of responses and to general evaluation. If the temporal course of change is to be fully understood, the rate at which changes travel through attitude structures must be evaluated.

In addressing this issue, McGuire (1960c, 1981, 1990; McGuire & McGuire, 1991) postulated that attitudinal structures respond somewhat slowly to change. It requires time for change to reverberate through a structure because its elements are somewhat "loosely linked" (see McGuire, 1990, p. 505). For remote effects to occur, people must think about the implications of changes in their attitudes and beliefs, and sometimes this thinking process requires considerable time. As a consequence, the remote impact of induced change may be somewhat delayed. Although this idea predicts that remote changes would increase over time, such delayed action effects (i.e., remote sleeper effects) are relatively rare, although they have been observed (McGuire, 1960c; Watts & Holt, 1970). More common are relative effects whereby change in the attitude targeted by a persuasive message decays more rapidly than change in more remote elements of a structure (e.g., Dillehay, Insko, & Smith, 1966). Yet, changes in remote

619

elements of a structure may be difficult to detect because of another manifestation of the loose linkage between elements—McGuire's *spatial attenuation* postulate. According to this principle, change induced at one point in the structure has a somewhat decreasing impact on remote elements of the structure. Therefore, remote effects can be quite small.

Persistence Induced by Systematic Processing. As we indicated in Chapter 7, the heuristic-systematic and elaboration likelihood models predict that persuasion induced by systematic processing or the central route is more persistent than persuasion induced by heuristic processing or the peripheral route. Only a few of the studies relevant to these models have supplemented the usual immediate measures of attitude change with delayed measures that would allow this prediction to be tested. Yet these studies have yielded generally confirming findings (Chaiken, 1980; Chaiken & Eagly, 1983, Experiment 2; Mackie, 1987; Petty, Cacioppo, & Heesacker, reported in Petty & Cacioppo, 1986b). Also consistent with this reasoning about the relatively enduring effects of systematic processing is Moscovici's (1980) thinking about the effects of minority influence. Specifically, the more thorough processing of persuasive information that Moscovici maintained that minority influence instigates may produce more enduring change than the more superficial processing that majority influence instigates (Moscovici, Mugny, & Papastamou, 1981; See Chapter 13).

The general rationale for such persistence predictions is that heuristic processing (and other mechanisms such as attributional reasoning that are not based on scrutiny of persuasive arguments) fails to provide message recipients with a set of beliefs that support their newly adopted or revised attitudes. In contrast, attitudes adopted or changed after careful scrutiny of persuasive argumentation should be supported by those issue-relevant cognitions that the message has conveyed or elicited from recipients. The resulting attitudes should therefore be more enduring. Yet we caution that the persistence issue has more nuances than this relatively simple rationale would suggest. Heuristic cues could remain strongly associated with one's attitude (e.g., I might persistently recall that my broker recommended a particular mutual fund), despite the argument in the sleeper effect literature that such cues tend to become dissociated from messages. With a persisting association, the persuasion such cues induce could be quite enduring. Nonetheless, such an attitude would be vulnerable to counterpropaganda because it lacks elaborated cognitive supports (e.g., beyond my broker's preference, I would have no rationale for choosing one mutual fund over another).

Other Considerations. The theme of attitudinal persistence appears in several other places in this book. For example, earlier in this chapter we noted that stronger attitudes have been shown to be more stable than weaker attitudes (Abelson, 1988; Krosnick, 1988a; M. J. Rosenberg, 1968b). Consistent with this general principle, Lydon, Zanna, and Ross (1988) found that having subjects recall their attitude-relevant behaviors after persuasion produced greater persistence of the attitude change that was induced, presumably because this recall bolstered the attitude. Moreover, Zanna, Fazio, and Ross (1990) showed that more accessible attitudes are more persistent.

In this chapter, we also noted the implications that inoculation theory and Katz's (1960) ego-defensive model have for persistence. Kelman's (1961) theory of three processes of social influence, which we examine in Chapter 13, also has important implications. Change induced by Kelman's internalization process is assumed to be most enduring because it is produced by scrutiny of a communication in relation to one's values. Change induced by the two other processes—compliance and identification—is persistent only under limited conditions.

Most other theories of attitude change have remained under-elaborated with respect to the temporal persistence of changed attitudes. Yet the issue of persistence has surfaced in research on the effects of counterattitudinal behavior, as our discussion in Chapter 11 indicated. Indeed, some studies in this tradition demonstrated considerable persistence of changed attitudes and behaviors (B. E. Collins & Hoyt, 1972; Freedman, 1965b; Lepper, 1973; L. Mann & Janis, 1968; Staw, 1974). In recognition of such studies, Cook and Flay (1978) maintained that the attitude change induced by persuasive messages is less likely to persist than the change induced by other persuasive techniques such as counterattitudinal advocacy or some types of role-playing. We prefer to reserve judgment about this issue because of its weak empirical base, given the paucity of evidence on attitudinal persistence. Yet we agree that self-persuasion can be enduring. As we indicated in Chapter 11, certain types of behavioral inductions such as role-playing and counterattitudinal advocacy under high dissonance circumstances probably do motivate considerable attitude-relevant thought. It is most likely this effortful thinking that favors attitudinal persistence, and such thinking can be induced by persuasive messages as well as by one's own behavior.

Conclusion

Our discussion has indicated that resistance to attitude change has differing causes. Broadly described, these causes can be classified into motivational and cognitive classes. Thus, the motivational perspective suggests that people resist influence because change brings various threats—threats to the ego, self, or personal freedom or merely to the stability of important attitudes. The cognitive perspective suggests that people resist influence when their attitudes are linked to many other cognitions in larger structures, which would be destabilized by changes in any central elements. Moreover, linkages of attitudes to other cognitions give people cognitive resources that allow them to scrutinize and ward off attacks on their attitudes. McGuire's inoculation theory was prophetic in its consideration of these two classes of determinants of resistance, and other theories have emphasized either the motivational or the cognitive determination of resistance.

In view of the research we have reviewed in this chapter, the most important generalization that we offer about attitudinal resistance is that attitudes are difficult to alter to the extent that they are strong or important. Strong attitudes create biases in information processing—biases that tend to maintain and even to polarize existing attitudes. If closed-mindedness is the rule, precisely on those issues that people care most about, theories of attitude change would do well to devote more study to strong attitudes, in order to fathom how they might be changed. Most contemporary experiments on message-based persuasion have been conducted on attitudes that have the character of nonattitudes in the sense that message recipients possess little knowledge about the issue and may not have formed a prior attitude at all. In an exception to this trend, social judgment theory considered change in ego-involving attitudes (M. Sherif & Hovland, 1961), and the psychoanalytic approach we reviewed in this chapter considered methods of changing attitudes that may serve deeply rooted ego-defensive needs (D. Katz, 1960).

Systematic study of the temporal persistence of attitudes has been rare, with the exception of the research programs we reviewed on associative interference and the sleeper effect. As we have shown, theorizing and research on persistence has followed from a cognitive perspective, with little attention to the motivational themes that have been important in discussions of resistance to change. Greater consideration of motivation in relation to persistence could well prove fruitful. More generally, a better integration of persistence issues into theories of attitude change is sorely needed, along with the inclusion of delayed measures in research.

—— Notes ——

1. Although mass media were once thought to have powerful and pervasive impact, beginning in the 1960s the opposite view tended to prevail—that mass communication has quite limited effects (e.g., Klapper, 1960). Consistent with this view, empirical studies of the impact of television and other media have tended to show null or quite small effects (see McGuire, 1985, 1986a). Yet in recent years communication scholars have evolved more detailed theories emphasizing that media may have sizable impact under limited conditions (see D. F. Roberts & Maccoby, 1985).

2. For additional research on one-sided and two-sided messages, see Hovland, Lumsdaine, and Sheffield (1949), Thistlethwaite and Kamenetzky (1955), Insko (1962), Chu (1967), McCroskey, Young, and Scott (1972), and Sorrentino, Bobocel, Gitta, Olson, and Hewitt (1988).

3. Both active defenses (i.e., generate own refutation) and passive defenses (i.e., read refutation) were thought to have advantages. In terms of the cognitive and motivational determinants of resistance that McGuire proposed (see subsequent discussion), active defenses were thought to confer greater motivational advantages by threatening people with their inability to defend their beliefs, whereas passive defenses were thought to confer greater cognitive advantages by giving people explicit practice in using bolstering material to defend their beliefs. For discussion of various manipulations of active and passive defenses and the findings that were produced, see McGuire (1964) and Insko (1967).

4. Research on inoculation bears some relation to research on warning people of persuasive attacks. However, warnings used in persuasion research have come in several variants—for example, (a) warning people of the topic and direction of an impending persuasive message and (b) merely warning people that the impending message is intended to persuade. The effects of warnings on acceptance of subsequent persuasive messages vary widely, depending on specific features of warnings (see reviews by Cialdini & Petty, 1981; Papageorgis, 1968).

5. Inoculation theory is certainly not unique in having stimulated practical applications. The accolade for having inspired the most application would surely go to Fishbein and Ajzen's (1975) theory of reasoned action (see Chapter 4).

6. The ineffectiveness of denial in Tannenbaum's (1967) research, whether occurring in a denial-then-attack order or an attack-then-denial order, resembles the perseverance effect that has been demonstrated within an experimental debriefing paradigm (C. A. Anderson, Lepper, & Ross, 1980; L. Ross, Lepper, & Hubbard, 1975). In these debriefing studies, subjects received false information (for example, false feedback about their success or failure on a discrimination task) and were subsequently debriefed quite thoroughly concerning the fraudulent nature of this information. Nonetheless, the beliefs instilled by the false information showed considerable perseverance.

7. This viewpoint is echoed in contemporary research on *downward comparison*, by which threatened individuals compare themselves to those who are inferior or less fortunate, in order to raise their self-esteem (e.g., S. E. Taylor & Lobel, 1989; J. V. Wood, Taylor, & Lichtman, 1985).

8. Only in the Katz, Sarnoff, and McClintock (1956) experiment was this self-insight communication compared with a more conventional communication containing information about blacks designed to lessen anti-black prejudice. Although the impact of the two communications did not differ at the immediate measurement, the self-insight communication was significantly more persuasive than the conventional one at the delayed measurement. Katz and his colleagues had hypothesized that self-insight communications would have a delayed impact, but the empirical status of their prediction remains

ambiguous because of the omission of appropriate control groups and statistical tests comparing immediate and delayed change.

9. More generally, B. T. Johnson and Eagly (1989) established in their meta-analysis that value-relevant involvement reduces the amount of attitude change that messages induce, presumably because of the defense-motivated processing that linkage to values produces. Although we have interpreted value-relevant involvement in terms of linkages to values, the majority of researchers' operationalizations of value-relevant involvement were not based directly on the cognitive linkages idea we are discussing in this section but were more indirect (e.g., widths of latitudes of acceptance and rejection).

10. This resistance could reflect (a) the inertia that follows from knowledgeable subjects' more extensive linkages of their attitudes to other cognitions or (b) the enhanced criticality that follows from knowledgeable subjects' greater cognitive resources (see Chapter 7 and Biek, Wood, Chaiken, & Nations, 1992).

11. Their statement is quite interesting: "Individuals engage in selective exposure and selective perception. Those least predisposed to change are least likely to allow themselves to be exposed to a persuasive communication, and if they are exposed, are most likely to engage in misperception, a kind of motivated missing-the-point. If a new piece of information would weaken the existing structure of their ideas and emotions, it will be shunned, rejected, or quickly forgotten; if it reinforces the structure, it will be sought out, quickly accepted, and remembered" (Behavioral Sciences Subpanel, 1962, p. 277). It is worth noting that Leon Festinger was a member of the panel.

12. As Festinger acknowledged, selective exposure might not prevail under conditions of extremely high dissonance. With very high dissonance (e.g., an extraordinarily upsetting first week in the chosen graduate program), consonant information would presumably be insufficient to reduce much

dissonance. Therefore, an individual might seek out dissonant information, which would likely cause some radical realignment of cognitions in the interest of restoring consonance (e.g., she might drop out of her chosen program).

13. To the extent that self-presentational concerns influence behavior, unobtrusive measures may produce more evidence of attitudinal selectivity than more typical measures that require subjects to indicate their informational preferences. See Olson and Zanna's (1979) use of eye gaze monitored from videotapes of subjects' behavior.

14. Lord, Lepper, and Preston (1984) subsequently showed that such biases in evaluations can be considerably reduced by inducing subjects to "consider the opposite"—specifically, by explaining to them the process by which such biased evaluations presumably occur and recommending that they consider how they would have evaluated the evidence had the same study produced the opposite results.

15. Conceptually, Jones and Kohler's (1958) data are best interpreted in terms of Feather's (1969, 1970) *balance* definition of attitudinal consistency. According to this definition, belief statements that lie on the same side of an attitude dimension as the subject's prior attitude will be perceived as attitudinally consistent only if the subject *agrees* with those statements; *disagreeable* statements of this sort should be perceived as attitudinally inconsistent. Similarly, opposing-side belief statements that are disagreeable are presumably perceived as attitudinally consistent, whereas those that are agreeable are perceived as inconsistent. In addition to Jones and Kohler, a small number of other studies have used this balance definition (e.g., Spiro & Sherif, 1975; Waly & Cook, 1966; Zanna & Olson, 1982). In contrast, the vast majority of attitude-memory studies have relied exclusively on a *sidedness* definition of attitude congruency. A final subset of studies has used an *agreeability* definition only (e.g., Garber, 1955; A. G. Greenwald & Sakumura, 1967; Judd & Kulik, 1980). Although it is possible that differences in definition may affect

the nature of attitude memory results obtained, casual inspection of this literature does not reveal pronounced differences among these three classes of experiments (see Chaiken, 1984).

16. The criticisms Greenwald and others (e.g., Waly & Cook, 1966) expressed about the early literature on attitude memory focused primarily on the Levine and Murphy (1943) experiment. The repetitive nature of the learning (and then forgetting) trials in that study and the fact that subjects had been selected on the basis of their "reputations" (i.e., as pro- or anti-communists) raised the distinct possibility that demand characteristics might have contributed to the memory effects observed. More generally, the critics proposed a *differential familiarity* interpretation of the attitude congeniality effect. According to this explanation, the memory results obtained by Levine and Murphy and others were due to subjects' greater familiarity with attitude congruent (vs. incongruent) information. Although plausible, several tests of this familiarity interpretation have failed to support it (e.g., Greenwald & Sakumura, 1967; Waly & Cook, 1966; see also Chaiken, Pomerantz, & Giner-Sorolla, in press; Weldon & Malpass, 1981).

17. These studies include the following: Bothwell & Brigham, 1983; Chaiken, Pomerantz, & Giner-Sorolla, in press; Eiser & Monk, 1978; Furnham & Proctor, 1989; George, 1979; Hymes, 1986; Judd & Kulik, 1980; McGraw & Pinney, 1990; Pratkanis, 1989; Read & Rosson, 1982; J. V. Roberts, 1984; Spiro & Sherif, 1975; Weldon & Malpass, 1981; Zanna & Olson, 1982.

18. Because Roberts ignored such variables, his results probably underestimate the true extent to which people's attitudes influence memory, at least under some circumstances. The Jones and Aneschansel (1956) experiment illustrates this point. Since the study yielded a *congruency* effect in its low utility conditions and an *incongruency* effect in its high utility conditions, separate effect size calculations would have yielded a positive and negative number, respectively. Moreover, averaging their absolute values to achieve an overall (albeit nondirectional) estimate of the impact of attitude on memory would clearly have yielded a more-than-negligible number. Yet, because the one effect size Roberts computed for this study ignored this interaction finding, the study was represented in the meta-analysis as demonstrating *exactly no* memory effect (i.e., the effect size was 0.00; see J. V. Roberts, 1985, p. 230).

19. Note that this associationist terminology is the same as that used by Fazio (e.g., 1986, 1989) and others (e.g., Judd & Krosnick, 1989) who have discussed attitudes in terms of associative network models. However, the specific hypotheses pursued in this associative-interference research reflect the earlier verbal-learning phase of associationist models rather than their contemporary manifestations in network models (e.g., J. R. Anderson, 1983, 1985).

20. Note that this increase should be greater than any increase that might have occurred in a no message control group (see Figure 12.4).

13

The Social Context of
Attitude Formation and Change

The psychology of attitudes is a component of a larger topic that can be called the psychology of social influence. Whereas the study of attitudes is based primarily on analysis of the psychological processes and structures of individuals, the study of social influence considers in addition the social context within which attitudes are formed and changed. That attitude formation and change involve social processes is an obvious point—after all, the stimulus input that shapes attitudes often consists of actions and statements of other people. Even when this input is feedback from one's own behavior (see Chapter 11), other people have often induced this behavior and provided an audience for its performance. Because attitudes are thus formed and changed as a by-product of social interaction, it seems eminently sensible to design theories to take into account the social relationships that link the sources and targets of influence.

Many considerations remain the same as we change our focus from attitudes to social influence. The dependent variables of interest to researchers remain attitudes and beliefs as well as behaviors presumed to reflect attitudes. Also remaining intact is an emphasis on internal mediating processes (e.g., causal attributions) that underlie changes in attitudes and beliefs. What is added by theories of social influence is an explicit recognition of the interpersonal aspects of the processes by which individuals' attitudes are changed. Thus, the role relationships that link the recipient and the source of influence are incorporated into theoretical analyses, and social processes are considered along with individual processes.

If we take the perspective that both social and psychological processes affect attitudes, it becomes clear that fully adequate theories of attitudes must recognize some of the processes and structures that are traditionally considered by sociologists. The field of sociology deals with social processes and the structure of the social environment, that is, its organization into norms, roles, groups, organizations, and larger political structures such as nations. In contrast, following the division of labor between academic disciplines, the field of psychology ordinarily deals with individual processes and structures, without much systematic consideration of social context. Because social and individual processes impinge on one another, it is not surprising that the interdisciplinary field of social psychology grew up on the interface between psychology and sociology. The existence of this interdisciplinary field should allow attitudes to be examined in terms of frameworks that take both individual and social processes into account.

Despite this interdisciplinary possibility, the study of attitudes, for better or worse, has been carried on primarily by psychologically oriented social psychologists who apparently have little familiarity with sociology. In fact, psychologists' paradigms for studying attitudes have become decreasingly attentive to social context over the years. This shift is no doubt due in part to the disciplinary constraints of academic departments and is probably also a product of social psychology's embrace of cognition (see Chapters 1 and 9). Moreover, this increasingly psychological focus is not unusual in social psychology, as most research problems that are seemingly within the domain of the interdisciplinary field of social psychology have taken on a psychological or a sociological emphasis, depending on whether they have been studied primarily by social psychologists housed in psychology or sociology departments. This fact is problematic when psychologists attempt to apply their theories in natural settings, where social norms and other social structural factors affect psychological processes. Effective applications and interventions cannot be achieved within the restrictions of wholly psychological frameworks. Fortunately, a portion of the theory and research on the change of attitudes and beliefs has transcended these disciplinary limitations to some extent. The social influence label has been applied to most of this work, and it is to this material that we turn in this chapter.

Normative and Informational Influence

Extremely important in instigating the systematic study of social influence was the classic research that Muzafer Sherif (1935) and Solomon Asch (1951, 1956) carried out on conformity. In Sherif's "autokinetic" experiment, subjects seated in a dark laboratory room observed a stationary pinpoint of light. Under such conditions, a perceptual illusion occurs such that the light appears to move, and this apparent motion suggested the term autokinetic or self-moving. Sherif's subjects were required to make repeated estimates of the distance the light moved. Working in groups, subjects announced their judgments out loud. Although group members' estimates initially differed considerably, after a number of trials the great majority of their judgments converged within a relatively restricted range. The particular range in which these estimates converged differed between the groups, but within each group considerable uniformity developed.

In contrast to Sherif, Asch (1951, 1955, 1956) designed an experimental situation that would seem less conducive to social influence because his subjects judged stimuli that were exceedingly unambiguous. These stimuli were presented to the subjects on two cards. One card displayed a single line, called the standard, and the other displayed three lines, one the same length as the standard and the other two discriminably different from the standard. One each trial, subjects indicated which of the three lines was the same length as the standard line. Control subjects who were alone when they performed this task very rarely made an error. Experimental subjects each performed the task as a member of a group in which all of the other participants were confederates who had been coached to give the wrong answer on certain trials. On these trials, 36.8 percent of the subjects' responses agreed with those of the confederates and thus were

FIGURE 13.1. The percent of the subjects who made correct estimates of length of lines in Asch's (1955, 1956) research. The experimental subjects judged lines in the presence of six to eight confederates. The control subjects judged the lines in the absence of confederates. This figure was adapted from one presented by Asch (1955, upper left panel, p. 35).

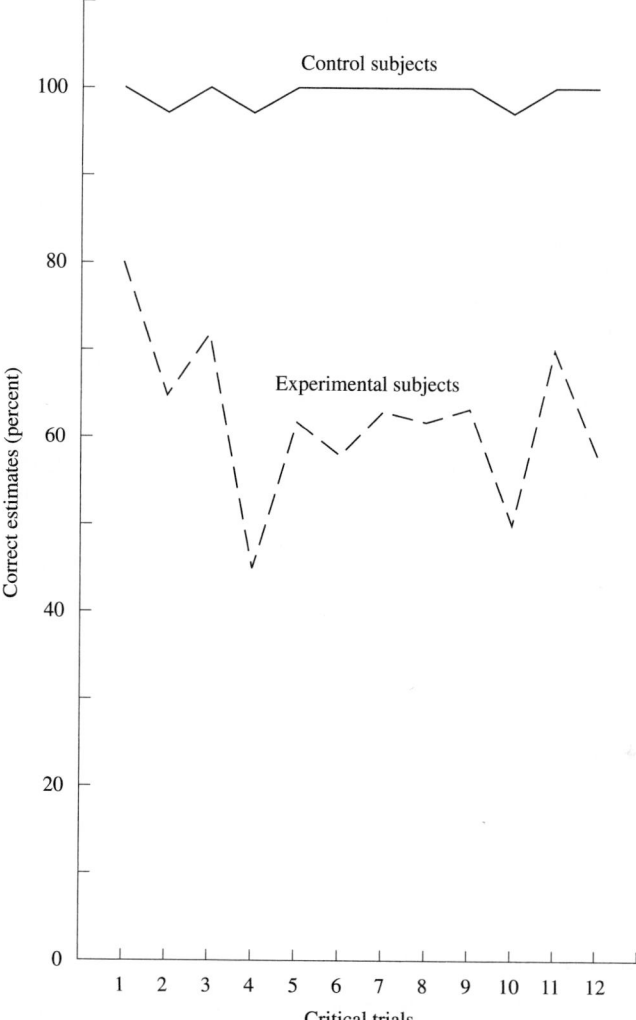

erroneous. Figure 13.1 shows the percentage of correct responses given by subjects in the experimental and control groups on the critical trials in Asch's classic experiment.[1]

Although Sherif's and Asch's research mainly served to demonstrate the impact that group members can have on each other's responses, it also inspired thoughtful analyses of *how* people are influenced in social situations. Central in these early analyses was a distinction between *normative influence* and *informational influence*. Although related concepts were also proposed in the 1950s, the terms normative and informational influence, which were contributed by Deutsch and Gerard (1955), have proven especially useful and enduring. Thus, Deutsch and Gerard defined normative influence as "influence to conform with the positive expectations of another" and informational influence as "influence to accept information obtained from another as *evidence* about reality" (p. 629). This distinction concerns the extent to which people communicate to one another (a) expectations about appropriate conduct or (b) evidence about the nature of reality. For example, on a hot day a person sending a normative message to a target individual might indicate what sort of clothing should be worn in such weather, whereas a person sending an informational message might provide an estimate of the day's likely maximum temperature.

A very similar distinction had been articulated somewhat earlier by H. H. Kelley (1952), who suggested that reference groups have both a *normative* and a *comparison* function. Kelley defined the normative function as the setting of standards for appropriate attitudes, beliefs, and behaviors and the delivery of rewards and punishments in accordance with people's conformity to or deviation from these standards. He defined the comparison function as the setting of standards or comparison points against which people can evaluate themselves and others. Following Kelley's analysis, reference groups thus influence people through both normative and comparative processes. More generally, according to both Kelley's and Deutsch and Gerard's analyses, one reason why people are influenced by others is that they desire to gain positive outcomes from these others, including social approval and liking, and to avoid negative outcomes, including social rejection and personal embarrassment. A second reason why people are influenced is that they rely on others' actions and attitudes as a potentially valid source of information about the nature of reality. The motivational basis of these two forms of influence therefore differs: The motivation presumed to underlie normative influence is a desire to gain the rewards and avoid the punishments that others provide, whereas the motivation presumed to underlie informational influence is a desire to form attitudes and beliefs that validly represent reality.

Importance of Social Norms

The concepts of normative and informational influence could not have emerged in the 1950s without having been preceded in earlier decades by analyses of social norms. Central to these early discussions of norms was Sherif's (1935) portrayal of his conformity experiment as illustrating the development of a norm. He thus interpreted the tendency for group members' estimates of the movement of the point of light to converge on a common estimate as demonstrating norm formation. When group members judged the movement of the light and were influenced by each other's judgments, they developed a shared expectation about the distance the light moved. This expectation functioned like a rule about the nature of this reality and influenced subjects' judgments even when they later gave estimates in the absence of the other group members.

The idea that people in groups develop common standards or rules suggested to various social psychologists that *norm* should be defined as a standard or rule that is accepted by the members of the group. In an analysis of dyadic interaction, Thibaut and Kelley (1959) defined norm as "a behavioral rule that is accepted, at least to some degree, by both members of the dyad" (p. 129). Similarly, Newcomb, Turner, and Converse (1965; see also Newcomb, 1950) wrote that a group norm "exists insofar as a set of group members share favorable attitudes toward...a regularity [in behavior]—insofar, that is, as they agree and are aware that they agree that the regularity should be regarded as a *rule* that properly applies to the specified persons in the specified situations" (p. 229). This understanding of norm implies that each participant in a social interaction not only has a favorable attitude toward a particular regularity in behavior but also perceives that most other participants hold this same attitude.

Social psychologists' insight that social norms originate in both normative and informational processes owed much to the Asch (1956) and Sherif (1935) experiments. The fact that Asch's subjects were influenced by other group members fostered understanding especially of the normative sources of social influence.[2] Because physical reality was unambiguous in this paradigm, subjects did not need to rely on the other group members to confirm their sense impressions of the lengths of the lines. Were social influence essentially an informational process, little influence should have occurred. Therefore, interpretations of the Asch experiment tended to take into account other factors, such as a desire to avoid appearing deviant, which came to be labeled normative.

In contrast, the idea that norms can arise through informational processes provided a coherent interpretation of the Sherif (1935) autokinetic experiment, because of the extreme ambiguity of the stimuli that the subjects encountered. Their own perceptions of the point of light no doubt left them with considerable uncertainty, and they understandably turned to one another for additional information about the true nature of reality.

Another source of the idea that social norms can have informational roots was Festinger's (1950, 1954) theorizing about social comparison processes. Festinger developed his ideas about social comparison when analyzing how people validate their beliefs that are not supported by clear-cut physical reality. He reasoned that people turn to *social reality* to evaluate these beliefs: "where the dependence on physical reality is low, the dependence upon social reality is correspondingly high. An opinion, a belief, an attitude is 'correct,' 'valid,' and 'proper' to the extent that it is anchored in a group of people with similar beliefs, opinions, and attitudes" (Festinger, 1950, p. 272). In a later statement, Festinger (1954) made the much stronger claim that people have a basic need or drive to evaluate their beliefs and abilities and must therefore use one another to perform such evaluations when physical reality is too ambiguous to provide much guidance. Whatever the merits of invoking drives or needs in this context, Festinger's papers on social comparison were widely read and cited and thus drew the informational aspects of social influence to social psychologists' attention.

Continued Importance of Concepts of
Normative and Informational Influence

Given the importance of normative and informational concepts in the thinking of so many of the major theorists of social psychology in the 1950s, it is not surprising that analyses formulated in terms of these two types of processes continued to appear. For example, these concepts provided guiding principles for E. E. Jones and Gerard (1967) in their widely admired social psychology textbook. In their version of the normative versus informational distinction, Jones and Gerard maintained that the dependence of human beings on others takes the form of *effect dependence* and *information dependence*. Effect dependence is the reliance of one person on another for direct satisfaction of needs, which leads people to be concerned about how others evaluate them. Information dependence is the reliance of one person on another for "information about the environment, its meaning, and the possibilities for action in it" (Jones & Gerard, 1967, p. 714). Application of these concepts gave Jones and Gerard a means of organizing large amounts of the social psychological research that was available to them when they wrote their text.

Fishbein and Ajzen's (1975) theory of reasoned action provides yet another illustration of the normative-informational dichotomy (see Chapter 4). They divided the determinants of behavior into two classes—attitude toward the behavior and subjective norm. Attitude toward the behavior, because it reflects the information one possesses about the consequences of one's behavior, can be seen as an informational determinant of action, whereas subjective norm, because it reflects others' wishes about what one should do, can be seen as a normative determinant of action. Finally, the continued usefulness of the normative-informational distinction is confirmed by its reactivation in contemporary accounts of how group members influence one another (see subsequent sections of this chapter).

Public Compliance and
Private Acceptance

The concepts of normative and informational influence drew attention to the distinction between public compliance with others' views versus private acceptance (or internalization) of these views. In a situation such as the Asch (1956) experiment in which influence probably arises largely from normative sources, subjects' public agreement with the other group members would not necessarily indicate that they truly believed the views they stated. After all, subjects' statements about the length of the lines were objectively wrong. While privately maintaining their belief in the objectively correct response, subjects may have agreed with the other group members merely to avoid the embarrassment of deviating from their judgments. In this manner, people may publicly conform while not changing their private attitudes. Particularly when influence has primarily normative origins, social pressure may often produce public agreement with the other group members, accompanied by little or no private acceptance. To the extent that influence has informational origins, however, public compliance is likely to be accompanied by private acceptance because others' views are interpreted as valid evidence about the nature of reality.

The distinction between public and private agreement implies that social scientists face distinct tasks in predicting social influence. The first of these is predicting the overt behavior of agreeing with others, and the second is predicting genuine change in attitudes and beliefs. This distinction has not arisen in most research on attitude change because the attitudinal responses obtained in the typical study are presumed to represent subjects' attitudes validly. Despite the availability of a few assessment methods such as the bogus pipeline and randomized response technique that are designed to discourage people from expressing attitudes that deviate from those they privately hold (see Chapter 2), investigators of attitude change have less often acknowledged that their subjects' responses to direct attitudinal inquiries may be systematically displaced from their private attitudes. In contrast, investigators of social influence have assumed that publicly stated and privately held attitudes often differ. In the group settings of social influence research, public agreement allows people to garner short-term rewards such as approval from other group members and to avoid short-term costs such as embarrassment and social rejection, whereas private agreement is irrelevant to these extrinsic rewards and costs. Thus, public and private attitudes may be under the control of a somewhat different set of variables.

Theorists of social influence have proposed a variety of terms to label various combinations of public and private agreement. Nail's (1986) discussion of these terms is integrative of distinctions made earlier by several other conformity researchers (e.g., V. L. Allen, 1965; Crutchfield, 1962, 1963; Krech, Crutchfield, & Ballachey, 1962; Willis, 1963, 1965). Nail suggested that in the typical situation of conformity experiments in which subjects initially disagree with other group members, these subjects may conform publicly *and* privately, a response Nail termed *conversion*. Subjects may conform publicly but not privately, a response termed *compliance*, or conform privately but not publicly, a response termed *anti-compliance*. The absence of conformity at both public and private levels is termed *independence*. Although we have followed tradition in this chapter by using the term *conformity* to refer to public agreement, Nail's and other theorists' distinctions reveal the ambiguity of the term. A more elaborate vocabulary has merit because it takes both public and private responding into account.

Public Compliance and Private Acceptance in Attitude Change Research. Outside of the social influence tradition, some research programs on attitude change have also addressed the distinction between public and private agreement. Most notably, the research and theory concerning the impact of behavior on attitudes have considered the effect of public compliance on private acceptance (see Chapter 11). In studies of counterattitudinal advocacy, for example, research participants publicly endorse an attitudinal position that is discrepant with their private attitudes. As a consequence, these attitudes may change toward their advocacy.

Impression management interpretations of attitude change experiments have also distinguished between public and private attitudes. We reviewed such interpretations in

633

Chapter 11 in relation to induced compliance experiments (Tedeschi, Schlenker, & Bonoma, 1971) and in Chapter 12 in relation to reactance experiments (Baer, Hinkle, Smith, & Fenton, 1980). In both areas, the impression management view is that research participants are motivated to present themselves favorably on a measure of ostensibly private attitudes and therefore express attitudes that they do not privately endorse.

The possibility that public responding may not reveal one's attitudes has also been considered in persuasion experiments on *warning* subjects about impending persuasive messages (see also Chapter 12). Although shifts of attitudes have been shown to occur as a product of warnings, these shifts apparently often take place at the level of mere public agreement with the anticipated message (see Cialdini & Petty, 1981). Suggesting that private attitudes may not change in such situations are demonstrations that canceling an anticipated message or discussion by telling subjects that they would not be exposed to it after all caused them to "snap back" to their original positions (e.g., Cialdini, Levy, Herman, & Evenbeck, 1973; Cialdini, Levy, Herman, Kozlowski, & Petty, 1976; Hass, 1975; Hass & Mann, 1976).

Attitude change research on several topics has thus sensitized researchers to the possibility that apparent attitude change may sometimes be confined to a superficial level of public responding and may not reflect change in the underlying evaluative tendency that constitutes the attitude. Nonetheless, distinguishing between public compliance and private acceptance is relatively rare in attitude change research. In contrast, understanding the conditions under which public compliance reflects private acceptance is a continuing theme of research on social influence.

Social Influence in Dyadic Relationships

Subsequent to the seminal conformity experiments of Sherif (1935) and Asch (1951, 1956), research and theory on social influence developed in two major directions. Some social psychologists analyzed influence as a dyadic process that transpires between a source of influence (often called an *influencing agent*) and a recipient of influence (often called a *target*). Other investigators, following the lead of the early conformity research, analyzed social influence as a group process that occurs when a number of people interact. We turn first to influence in dyadic relationships.

French and Raven's Typology of Types of Power

In early analyses of influence in dyadic relationships, investigators developed typologies based on qualitative distinctions between various types of power that influencing agents can hold over others. Among the best known of these schemes is John French and Bertram Raven's delineation of six bases of social power: reward, coercive, legitimate, referent, expert, and informational power (French, 1956; French & Raven, 1959; Raven, 1965). These concepts represent different types of social relationships between the targets and agents of influence as well as differing conditions under which influence will be maintained.

Reward power is based on the influencing agent's ability to deliver rewards contingent on the target complying with the agent's wishes, and *coercive power* is based on the agent's ability to deliver punishments. Successful use of reward and coercive power depends on the ability of the agent to monitor whether the target complies with her wishes. In contrast, *legitimate power* is based on the target's perception that the agent has a legitimate right to prescribe behavior for him. Legitimacy derives from broader group or societal norms that endow the agent with certain privileges and responsibilities. For example, citizens may comply with a law enforcement officer's instructions for vehicle parking even when the officer has left the vicinity, because they accept the officer's right to prescribe behavior in this realm. Thus, because authority is based on common standards accepted by the target and agent, exercise of legitimate power does not require direct surveillance by the agent.

Referent power is based on the agent's attractiveness to the target in the sense that the target has a "feeling of oneness" (French & Raven, 1959, p. 161) with the agent or a desire for such an identity. *Expert power* is based on the target's perception that the influencing agent possesses some superior knowledge or expertise. Thus, a teenager's tendency to dress like an admired film star might be based on the star's referent power, whereas his tendency to solve math problems in the way his teacher has taught would probably follow from the teacher's expert power. Neither referent nor expert power is contingent on the ability of the source to monitor the target's compliance.[3]

French and Raven (1959; Raven, 1965) compared influence stemming from these five bases of the source's power (reward, coercive, legitimate, referent, and expert) with influence deriving from *informational power*. The latter type of influence is independent of the target's perception of the source because it derives solely from the information communicated by the source, that is, from characteristics of the source's message such as the logic of the argumentation. This type of influence, termed *informational influence*, parallels Deutsch and Gerard's (1955) identically labeled concept.

The relation between French and Raven's other types of influence and the normative-informational dichotomy is for the most part clear-cut. Reward, coercive, and legitimate power provide the best examples of normative influence, because sources exercising power of these types communicate expectations about how recipients should think or behave. Although sources with referent and expert power may also communicate such expectations, expert power (and referent power to some extent) operate through inducing the communicator's message to be taken as evidence about the nature of reality. Thus, these types of power might be considered to induce informational influence.

French and Raven's distinction between expert and informational power is quite interesting in terms of modern theories of the cognitive processes underlying persuasion (see Chapter 7). In particular, Chaiken's (e.g., 1987) heuristic-systematic model, in agreement with the distinction between expert and informational influence, suggests that perception of a source's expertise can provide a simple decision rule for evaluating the validity of a message. Heuristic processing of this sort, which could mediate the effects of French and Raven's expert power, should be distinguished from systematic processing of the semantic content of messages, which could underlie informational influence in their framework.

More generally, each power base, with the exception of informational power, specifies a particular variety of social relationship. The power that the agent has to influence the target within this relationship stems from the agent's possession of a resource that is valued or recognized by the target—specifically, (a) the ability to deliver rewards, (b) the ability to withhold punishments, (c) legitimate authority, (d) attractiveness as an object of identification, or (e) expertise. Research implementing this framework has examined the determinants of the agent's use of available power bases and the consequences of using one or another base (see reviews by Raven & Kruglanski, 1970, and Schopler, 1965). Other applications of the paradigm include research on differences in the power bases of women and men (P. Johnson, 1976) as well as numerous studies of the types of power held by supervisors and managers in various organizations (e.g., Frost & Stahelski, 1988; Stahelski, Frost, & Patch, 1989; see Podsakoff & Schriesheim, 1985).

Milgram's Obedience Paradigm. The role relationship that French and Raven described as based on legitimate authority was examined in a very well known series of experiments by Stanley Milgram (1963, 1974). In these experiments, male subjects were placed in the role of a teacher who was supposed to monitor the correctness of responses given by a subject who took the role of a pupil in a paired-associate learning task. This pupil, who actually was a confederate of the experimenter, made many errors, and, in response to each mistake, the teacher was supposed to deliver electric shock to the pupil. Although no shock was actually delivered, the experiment was staged so that the subjects believed they were delivering shock. The experimenter, who presumably possessed legitimate power in this situation, ordered the teacher-subject to deliver more severe shock every time the pupil made an error. As the shock increased, the pupil was heard to pound on the wall of the room in which he had been placed, and as the shock increased further, the pupil finally discontinued responding and fell silent. If the subject did not refuse to continue shocking the pupil, he eventually delivered shock at levels that were identified by extreme labels on the shock generator ("Danger: Severe shock" and "XXX"). Despite these extraordinary conditions, 65 percent of the subjects obeyed the experimenter's commands fully and thus administered the highest level of shock (Milgram, 1963). In later experiments, Milgram (1964a, 1965a, 1965b, 1974) manipulated the proximity of the victim, the presence of voice feedback from the victim, and other aspects of the situation. Although amount of obedience varied, in all renditions of the experimental paradigm the overall level of obedience was surprisingly high.

Milgram's obedience research attracted an unprecedented amount of attention, largely because of the possible link, emphasized by Milgram himself, between the cruel behavior of his subjects and the inhumane actions sometimes observed in natural settings in which authorities order subordinates to carry out destructive actions. Parallels to the Holocaust, the My Lai massacre, and other crimes of obedience readily come to mind. Milgram's research also elicited severe ethical criticisms, mainly on the basis of the unexpected stress that the subjects experienced in what they had thought was a simple learning experiment and the unanticipated self-knowledge they gained concerning their potential for inhumane behavior (Baumrind, 1964; Milgram, 1964b). A. G. Miller (1986) provided an excellent review of these and other reactions to Milgram's experiment. In addition, Blass (1991) has reviewed empirical research on personality and situational correlates of obedience.

Of greater interest in terms of the themes of this book is Milgram's theoretical analysis of obedience, which was developed most fully in his 1974 book. This analysis emphasized the potential for obedience inherent in hierarchical role relationships. In such relationships, individuals higher in the hierarchy are given the right to exert influence by virtue of their position, and individuals lower in the hierarchy have the obligation to comply with the superior's demands. Milgram reasoned that, in such conditions, people of lower status may cede control to those of higher status and cease to view themselves as responsible for their actions. Having given authority to someone else, people place themselves in a psychological state that Milgram labeled a *state of agency*. Thus, Milgram (1974) wrote, "From a subjective standpoint, a person is in a state of agency when he defines himself in a social situation in a manner that renders him open to regulation by a person of higher status. In this condition the individual no longer views himself as responsible for his own actions but defines himself as an instrument for carrying out the wishes of others" (p. 134).

In contrast to Milgram's view that subordinates merely cede control to superiors, political theorists have emphasized that authority must be exercised within certain limits to be perceived as rightful. These limits follow from the fact that authority exists within a social structure where it is regulated by the very norms that lend it legitimacy (Locke, 1690/1960; Weber, 1947). From this perspective, subordinates evaluate authorities' demands in a normative context that is wider than the particular role relationship that links the subordinate and the authority. Yet research such as Milgram's (see also Orne & Evans, 1965) shows that subordinates often agree to a very wide range of requests made by persons who possess legitimate authority. It thus appears relatively easy to exert influence from at least some authoritative roles, even when the authority's requests violate the preferences of the individuals who must carry them out. Nonetheless, some people do defy authority at least under some circumstances. How people weigh a superior's authority in terms of personal conscience and broader ethical standards is indeed an important issue, which was not addressed in much detail by Milgram.

Kelman and Hamilton's (1989; Kelman & Lawrence [Hamilton], 1972) subsequent research on how Americans perceived Lt. William Calley's responsibility for the events of the My Lai massacre examined people's interpretations of a well-known and widely discussed incident of destructive obedience. Using survey research methods, Kelman and Hamilton found that some Americans viewed the My Lai situation in terms of a soldier's obligation to obey a legitimate authority and therefore to follow orders. In contrast, other Americans viewed the situation in terms of a soldier personally causing the negative outcomes of killing unarmed women, men, and children. Thus, people

evidently differ in whether they assign responsibility to the authority or the subordinate in a situation of potential obedience. The knowledge structures underlying these contrasting interpretations may be relevant, not only to perceptions of these situations, but also to people's decisions to be obedient or defiant when they are ordered by superiors to carry out destructive actions. Kelman and Hamilton provided an insightful analysis of this and other issues related to obedience to authority.

Kelman's Typology of Types of Social Influence

Another theory of influence within dyadic relationships was developed by Herbert Kelman (1958, 1961, 1974b), who distinguished three processes of influence mainly on the basis of the motivational significance of the individual's relationship to the influencing agent (see also Chapter 10). These processes, termed compliance, identification, and internalization, also differ in whether influence occurs at a superficial level of public response or at the deeper level of private agreement, involving more durable attitude change integrated with a person's significant role relationships or values. Although this theory is similar in some respects to French and Raven's social power typology, it includes only three types of power and features a more detailed description of how changes in attitudes and beliefs link to people's cognitions related to the influence situation. In terms of Deutsch and Gerard's (1955) normative-informational distinction, Kelman's compliance should be considered normative and internalization should be considered informational. In contrast, identification incorporates elements of both normative and informational influence.

Compliance, which takes place at the surface level of public agreement with the influence source, occurs when a recipient changes his or her attitudinal response in order to gain a favorable reaction or forestall an unfavorable reaction from this source. A person who elicits compliance from another individual possesses the quality that Kelman termed *means control*, that is, the power to give or withhold the means that the individual requires to reach his or her goals. The influence of superiors over subordinates in organizations may thus often take the form of compliance.

With compliance, the recipient's changed responses are integrated into a knowledge structure that specifies routes to social rewards. Kelman's idea that the cognitive structure relevant to compliance is a *means-ends framework* is compatible with the expectancy-value models considered in Chapters 3, 4, and 5. Because compliance is a change in behavior (i.e., the behavior of advocating a position), the compliance model's underscoring of means and ends coordinates well with the theory of reasoned action (Fishbein & Ajzen, 1975). Thus, the reasoned action perspective suggests that a communicator's means control contributes to a favorable attitude toward the behavior of publicly agreeing with his or her position because some of the consequences of this behavior are believed to be under the communicator's control.

The means control possessed by communicators who induce compliance encompasses French and Raven's reward and coercive power. As French and Raven argued with respect to reward and coercive influence, compliance can be quite temporary and superficial because people comply only to obtain a particular effect from a source.

Kelman, like French and Raven, also reasoned that compliance occurs only when the target's behavior is directly under the surveillance of the influencing agent.

Identification, which resembles French and Raven's referent influence, occurs when a recipient adopts the position recommended by the communicator because this change helps establish or maintain a positive self-defining relationship with the communicator. Kelman regarded an individual who elicits identification as possessing *attractiveness*, which consists of those attributes that make a continued relationship with this individual desirable. This relationship may take the form of classical identification, with the target desiring to adopt the role of the influencing agent, or it may take the form of a reciprocal role relationship in which the target desires to participate vis-à-vis the agent. The influence of mentors over their pupils and friends over one another may often take the form of identification.

Influence that occurs through identification is accepted privately as well as publicly, although it is maintained only in the context of the role relationship that underlies the identification. Such influence is therefore dependent on the continuing salience of the relationship with the agent of influence, but it is not dependent on the source's direct surveillance of the target's behavior, as is compliance. The changed attitudes and beliefs are not thoroughly reconciled with the recipient's abstract knowledge structures relevant to the topic of the influence induction. Instead, the knowledge structures that are assumed to regulate identification are those that represent the recipient's role relationship with the source: Identification is, by definition, one aspect of a self-defining role relationship with the source.

Internalization occurs when a recipient adopts the position recommended by the communicator because the position is congruent with what Kelman termed one's overall *values*. Although Kelman emphasized the integration of message content with the recipient's values, we believe that the term values can be interpreted quite generally in this context. Thus, the message is evaluated in terms of the abstract knowledge structures (i.e., beliefs, attitudes, and values) that are relevant to the issue of the persuasive message.

Because the person who is influenced through Kelman's internalization evaluates the content of the source's recommendation against his or her issue-relevant knowledge structures and deems that the recommendation is sensible in these terms, internalization encompasses French and Raven's concept of informational influence. Internalization also resembles French and Raven's expert influence because an influence source who elicits internalization possesses the quality that Kelman termed *credibility*, that is, the ability to make statements that are perceived as credible and valid. Influence by internalization is accepted privately as well as publicly and, in contrast to identification, is maintained even when the relationship with the source is no longer salient. The influence that technical experts have over those who seek their advice probably often takes the form of internalization.

One of the advantages of Kelman's typology is his distinction between identification and internalization, both of which represent genuine change at the level of private attitudes. Yet these two forms of influence differ in the range of conditions under which changed attitudes and beliefs are maintained, with identification persisting only as long as the role relationship with the influence source remains salient and internalization persisting as long as the changed attitudes and beliefs continue to be perceived as the best path for maximizing one's values.

Predictions derived from Kelman's distinction between identification and internalization are supported by empirical tests (e.g., Kelman, 1958; Kelman & Eagly, 1965; Romer, 1979b). Especially interesting from an information processing standpoint are several findings consistent with the idea that a communicator's credibility or expertise affects persuasion through its impact on issue-relevant thinking, whereas a communicator's attractiveness affects persuasion without issue-related mediation and presumably through the mediation of beliefs about one's relationship to the communicator (Mills & Aronson, 1965; Mills & Harvey, 1972; Norman, 1976; but see Maddux & Rogers, 1980). Kelman's ideas about identification and communicator attractiveness are unique and warrant elaboration and empirical testing.

TABLE 13.1

Summary of the Distinctions Between the Three Processes

	Compliance	*Identification*	*Internalization*
Antecedents:			
1. Basis for the *importance of the induction*	Concern with social effect of behavior	Concern with social anchorage of behavior	Concern with value congruence of behavior
2. Source of power *of the influencing agent*	Means control	Attractiveness	Credibility
3. Manner of achieving *prepotency of the induced response*	Limitation of choice behavior	Delineation of role requirements	Reorganization of means-ends frameworks
Consequents:			
1. Conditions of performance of induced response	Surveillance by influencing agent	Salience of relationship to agent	Relevance of values to issue
2. Conditions of change and extinction of induced response	Changed perception of conditions for social rewards	Changed perception of conditions for satisfying self-defining relationships	Changed perception of conditions for value maximization
3. Type of behavior system in which induced response is embedded	External demands of a specific setting	Expectations defining a specific role	Person's value system

Source: This table was presented by Kelman (1961, p. 67).

In general, typological theories of power and influence have proven somewhat difficult to test, in part because of the complex way that the types are distinguished from one another. The qualitative nature of these distinctions is shown for Kelman's theory by the fact that the antecedents and consequents of the types are not defined along the same dimensions. For example, as shown in Table 13.1, one of the antecedents of influence in Kelman's scheme is the source of the power of the influencing agent: Power is based on means control to induce compliance, attractiveness to induce identification, and credibility to induce internalization. Means control, attractiveness, and credibility are three *different* aspects of communicator characteristics—not three locations on a single dimension.

In a test of the three-process theory, Kelman (1958) created three communicators: one high in means control, a second high in attractiveness, and a third high in credibility. Kelman then examined the impact of the communicator's power (means control, attractiveness, or credibility) on the conditions under which the changed attitudes were expressed. Although this experiment obtained generally supportive results, the unconventional nature of this experimental design illustrates the typological nature of the theory. A conventional design for an experiment examining Kelman's distinction between different types of communicator power might cross means control (high vs. low) with attractiveness (high vs. low) and credibility (high vs. low). Yet a design of this sort would not provide a clear test of the implications of Kelman's typology, by which a high level of only one of the communicator characteristics is an antecedent of each of the three forms of influence, and the two other characteristics remain unspecified. The challenge of testing typological theories is further compounded by the fact that each type is defined by a conflux of variables, in the manner that Kelman's theory takes into account the source of the communicator's power, the nature of the motivation induced in the target of influence, the conditions under which the influence is manifested, and several other factors (see Table 13.1).

Because of the complexities we have noted, it is probably fair to say that typological theories of social influence have been more useful conceptually than empirically—as idealized types of influence processes that are seldom represented in pure form in reality. Illustrative of the conceptual fruitfulness of Kelman's model are applications to psychotherapy (Kelman, 1963), international educational exchange (Bailyn & Kelman, 1962), the integration of individuals into the national system (Kelman, 1969), and, in the work we have already noted, destructive obedience (Kelman & Hamilton, 1989).

Other Typologies of Power and Influence

Numerous other social scientists have also proposed typologies of power and influence (e.g., Cartwright, 1965; Kipnis, 1976; Schank & Abelson, 1977; Tedeschi, Schlenker, & Bonoma, 1973; Thibaut & Kelley, 1959; K. Thomas, 1976). Although these and other schemes feature distinctions that are important within certain contexts, our review of the French and Raven and the Kelman typologies should be sufficient to give readers a general idea of this type of theorizing about social influence. Also, more than competing schemes, the frameworks we have described link to the issues of attitude change and information processing that are emphasized in this book. Kelman's typology is especially interesting in relation to these issues and warrants further exploration.

Other investigators have examined types of influence inductively by asking respondents to report how they or others exercise influence (e.g., Cialdini, 1987, 1988; R. A. Clark, 1979; Cody, McLaughlin, & Jordan, 1980; Falbo, 1977; Kipnis, Schmidt, & Wilkinson, 1980; Rule & Bisanz, 1987). The influence methods reported for oneself or others may then be rated by experts or by other subjects. These ratings are typically subjected to a multivariate analysis (e.g., multidimensional scaling, factor analysis) to determine their underlying dimensionality (e.g., Falbo, 1977). Alternatively, experts may classify subjects' reports into the categories of a deductive typology of influence (e.g., Rule & Bisanz, 1987). Although such research is very valuable for developing an understanding of the schemas that people use to plan and interpret social influence, review of this material is beyond the scope of this book.

Social Influence in Groups

Further Research on Conformity

Because the conformity experiments of Sherif (1935) and Asch (1951, 1956) were conducted in groups, understanding how social influence is integrated with group processes was an important theme from the beginning of systematic analysis of social influence. Research on conformity through group pressure became exceedingly popular in the 1950s and 1960s, especially after Crutchfield (1955) invented a method for efficiently conducting conformity experiments with a high degree of experimental control. In Crutchfield's paradigm, subjects were seated in individual booths so that they could not see one another. Each booth had a panel containing switches that the subject used to signal his or her judgments on items that were generally presented on slides projected on a screen or wall in front of the group. Although these items, as in the Asch experiment, often consisted of physical stimuli, researchers, including Crutchfield, frequently substituted attitudinal items. Each panel in the subject's booth also had signal lights that indicated the judgments that each of the other members of the group gave to each item. Each subject usually learned that all members of the group would give their judgments in a sequence in which he or she would be last. In fact, false judgments were substituted for the other subjects' real judgments, and these false judgments were displayed on the panel of lights. For physical stimuli, the false judgments, like those in Asch's experiment, generally violated physical reality, whereas for attitudinal items, these false judgments violated a known consensus in the subject population. Because all subjects believed they were the last person in the group to give their judgments, they actually received the exact same sequence of (falsified) judgments from the other group members. Also, in a similarly streamlined but less widely used method for simulating group pressure, other members' responses were presented as tape-recorded voices (Blake & Brehm, 1954). These paradigms thus eliminated the need for confederates and greatly increased experimental control over the stimuli. However, mundane realism (see Aronson, Brewer, & Carlsmith, 1985) was sacrificed as subjects retreated into cubicles and did not engage in the face-to-face interaction that is typical of the group meetings that occur in daily life.[4]

Additional Evidence for the Normative and Informational Origins of Conformity. As we have already explained in this chapter, the concepts of normative and informational influence were important in developing an understanding of why conformity occurs in groups. The addition of the Crutchfield paradigm to the existing Asch and Sherif paradigms allowed researchers to amass relatively quickly a body of findings supporting the claim that conformity serves both normative and informational motivations. For example, experiments on the effects of task difficulty and ambiguity were consistent with the *informational interpretation* of conformity. Thus, to the extent that the task that group members face is difficult or ambiguous, they should be more conforming for informational reasons, that is, because they turn to the other members to develop an interpretation of the stimuli (e.g., Asch, 1956; Deutsch & Gerard, 1955; H. H. Kelley & Lamb, 1957). In an illustrative experiment by J. F. Coleman, Blake, and Mouton (1958), task difficulty was indexed by the percentage of control subjects (i.e., subjects responding individually) who gave incorrect answers on items about current events, geography, government, literature, language, and science. Subjects' conformity when confronted by group pressure was greater the more difficult the items.

Also pertinent to informational interpretations of conformity are the effects of people's perception of their own competence relative to that of other group members. To the extent that people consider themselves relatively incompetent, they should be influenced by other group members. In Hochbaum's (1954) experiment demonstrating this principle, subjects received individual feedback concerning their success in making judgments of case histories during a series of practice trials. When later placed in a group pressure situation, subjects who believed they had performed poorly on the practice trials conformed more than subjects who believed they had performed well. Other experiments obtained complementary effects of the competence of the other group members (e.g., Mausner, 1954). To the extent that other members' success on the group's task had been demonstrated, their views elicited greater conformity.

Research also supported the *normative interpretation* of conformity. Particularly relevant to the idea that conformity originates in normative processes are demonstrations that the attractiveness or cohesiveness of groups affects conformity. To the extent that other group members are attractive and desirable, being liked by them and winning their approval should be more rewarding and serve as more effective incentives for conformity by means of normative processes. In an experiment by Festinger, Gerard, Hymovitch, Kelley, and Raven (1952), attraction to the other group members was manipulated by telling subjects either that they would like each other and get along well or that they might not like each other or get along. Greater conformity to an apparent group consensus was obtained in the high attraction groups compared with the low attraction groups.

Also consistent with the normative interpretation of conformity are the demonstrated effects that group members' surveillance has on conformity. Only when a person's responses are under other members' surveillance can these others selectively deliver outcomes such as social approval that are presumed to underlie normative influence. As several studies of public versus private responding have shown, when subjects' judgments were accessible to others and identified with each subject as an individual (as in face-to-face interaction), conformity was greater than it was when subjects' judgments were anonymous or completely inaccessible to the other group members (e.g., Argyle, 1957; Asch, 1956; Deutsch & Gerard, 1955; Mouton, Blake, & Olmstead, 1956).

Additional research confirming the normative origins of conformity examined the impact of group goals on conformity. To the extent that group members have a common goal that is important to them, they are dependent on one another to reach this positive outcome. For example, members of an athletic team generally have a group goal of winning games. The resulting dependence on one another for rewards should make group members particularly vulnerable to one another's influence, primarily by normative processes. Among the studies supporting this prediction is an experiment by Deutsch and Gerard (1955), which was modeled after the Asch experiment. Subjects in one condition of this experiment were told that each member of the group that made the fewest errors would receive a pair of tickets to a play. Other subjects received no such instruction. Presumably the possibility of winning this prize induced a group goal, and, as predicted, subjects yielded more to one another's judgments in the condition in which the goal had been introduced. Of course, in natural settings groups very often pursue an extremely important common goal such as winning a game or maximizing profits for a company, and these goals often induce powerful motivations in group members. Although the conformity pressures in these situations have been decried (see Janis's, 1972, analysis of "groupthink"), some degree of conformity is no doubt required in order that group members have sufficient unity to pursue a goal in an organized and effective manner.

Cognitive Mediation of Conformity. Consistent with the growing emphasis of social psychologists on information processing, subsequent research on conformity explored some of the cognitive processes that underlie the tendency to agree with other group members. This work follows a tradition begun by Asch (1956), who attempted to understand the phenomenology of the subjects in his conformity experiment. Asch interviewed his subjects to obtain their interpretation of their behavior and reported lengthy interview protocols (see also Tuddenham & McBride, 1959). Although certainly not devoid of interest, data of this sort presume that subjects actually have insight into their internal psychological processes, an assumption that has been questioned (e.g., Nisbett & Wilson, 1977). Moreover, given the potential for embarrassment from having conformed in the Asch paradigm, such data are no doubt quite vulnerable to subjects' tendencies to justify their behavior in order to save face with the experimenter.

Later investigators attempted to understand the cognitive mediation of conformity by designing studies that tested explicit mediational hypotheses. For example, L. Ross, Bierbrauer, and Hoffman (1976) argued that subjects faced a perplexing attributional dilemma in the Asch (1956) experiment. Consistent with the assumptions of attribution theory (see Chapter 8), Asch's subjects desired to explain why the other subjects gave apparently erroneous judgments concerning the lines. Because these judgments could not be readily explained in terms of external pressures on the other group members or in terms of their internal dispositions, subjects could not discount the other subjects' responses by ascribing them to a biasing cause (see Eagly, Chaiken, & Wood, 1981, and Chapter 8). Consequently, these apparently erroneous responses tended to be given serious consideration as descriptions of reality.[5]

In a conceptual replication of the Asch experiment, Ross and his colleagues supplemented Asch's design by adding some experimental conditions that *did* provide possible explanations for the other group members' behavior. For example, in one such condition, the other members were apparently working under a different matrix of payoffs for right and wrong answers. Presumably subjects used this difference in payoffs to explain the other members' behavior. Accounting for this behavior by an external pressure operating on the other group members, subjects found these otherwise puzzling responses less valid as descriptions of the judged stimuli and therefore conformed to them less. Although subjects' attributional inferences were not assessed in this experiment, the conformity findings obtained in the various experimental conditions lend plausibility to an attributional interpretation of conformity in the Asch paradigm.

Consistent with another aspect of the attributional mediation of conformity, Wilder (1977; see also Wilder, 1978) hypothesized and found that conformity increased to the extent that the people who presented their views (on a legal case) to the subjects were perceived as independent sources of information, that is, as an aggregate of independent individuals rather than as members of a group. People who share the same environment as members of a group are largely redundant as sources of information because they likely share the same biases, and their views therefore fail to provide the potent consensus information that independent sources of information provide. Wilder's findings are reminiscent of Goethals's (1976; Goethals & Nelson, 1973) demonstration that agreement from a dissimilar other increased judgmental confidence on matters of fact more than agreement from a similar other—a finding that we interpreted in Chapter 8 in terms of the consensus dimension of Kelley's (1967) ANOVA model. Because the same interpretation is appropriate for Wilder's findings, his research, as well as Ross and collaborators' (1976) research, suggests that causal attributions may mediate the informational influence that occurs in many conformity paradigms.

In an experiment investigating a different aspect of the cognitive mediation of conformity, V. L. Allen and Wilder (1980) pursued Asch's (e.g., 1940, 1948) idea that agreement with others' statements can be facilitated by perceivers' modification of the meaning of the statements. Thus, Asch maintained that apparent attitude change often does not truly reflect change in the evaluation of the attitude object but change in the meaning of the attitude object, that is, change in the characteristics ascribed to the attitude object that is evaluated.[6] Although Asch proposed this hypothesis as an interpretation of so-called *prestige suggestion* experiments, in which subjects rated statements ascribed to well-known individuals, modification of the meaning of the stimuli may also occur in at least some types of conformity experiments. According to this account of the processes underlying conformity, the subject assimilates the other group members' views to his or her existing knowledge structures (see Chapters 8 and 12), particularly in conformity experiments involving attitudes concerning various issues. After having been reinterpreted in this way, the other members' views would be less discrepant from the subject's attitudes than the original stimuli were.

In Allen and Wilder's (1980) experiment, subjects were presented with the judgments of other group members on statements such as the following: "I would never go out of my way to help another person if it meant giving up some personal pleasure" (p. 1118). Because most people disagree with this statement, to induce group pressure the experiment was arranged so that the other group members agreed with it. When asked to interpret such a statement, subjects who received this dissent from the other group members interpreted the statement differently from subjects who did not receive dissent. For the sample statement, they interpreted "go out of my way" as having potentially serious consequences (e.g., "risk my life"), whereas the more typical interpretation of "go out of my way" approximates "be inconvenienced." Shifting their understanding of the statement in this uncommon direction, subjects found it more agreeable. Thus, uncommon interpretations of the statements provided subjects with a sensible framework for understanding the other members' otherwise puzzling responses. In fact, in a variation of this experiment, Allen and Wilder (1980) showed that direct exposure to such interpretations increased conformity. As these investigators acknowledged, such alterations of meaning are probably less likely in experiments such as Asch's (1956) in which physical reality is unambiguous. Yet much social interaction is grounded in a relatively more ambiguous social reality, as Festinger (1950, 1954) argued. These more ambiguous conditions probably favor the sort of meaning change demonstrated by Allen and Wilder.

Minority Influence

The emphasis on conformity in the social influence research of the 1950s and early 1960s fostered a view of people as vulnerable to group pressure and hesitant to depart from a group consensus. The power of the group seemed quite formidable to social psychologists who contemplated Sherif's (1935) subjects' ready acceptance of each other's judgments on a matter as trivial as the amount of movement of a point of light or Asch's (1956) subjects' agreement with one another even when such agreement violated the clear-cut evidence presented to their own eyes. Research showing that people who deviate from a group consensus are rejected by other group members further reinforced the view that people are submissive to the force of majority attitudes (Emerson, 1954; Schachter, 1951; see J. M. Levine's, 1980, review).

In reaction to what was no doubt an overemphasis on the power of a group consensus, Serge Moscovici and his colleagues (see Moscovici, 1976) argued that conformity research failed to recognize that minorities frequently influence majorities and in fact are often agents of social change and innovation. In an initial demonstration of this point, Moscovici, Lage, and Naffrechoux (1969) carried out an experiment that can be considered a mirror image rendition of the Asch experiment. Groups of four subjects and two confederates judged stimuli that, like Asch's (1956) stimuli, were unambiguous enough that subjects in a control group not exposed to discrepant judgments rarely made an error. These stimuli were slides that were blue and varied only in luminance. In a consistent minority condition, the confederates claimed to see green on each of 36 trials, and in an inconsistent condition the confederates indicated they saw green on 24 trials and blue on 12. Although the subjects were much less influenced by the minority than Asch's subjects were by the majority, responses complying with the minority's view were given 8.42 percent of the time by subjects exposed to the consistent minority, 1.25 percent of the time by subjects exposed to the inconsistent minority, and only 0.25 percent of the time by control subjects whose judgments were made in the absence of confederates. Thus, a minority—albeit only a consistent one—indeed exerted some influence. Subsequent to this initial experiment on color perception, consistent minorities have been shown to exert influence in groups carrying out a diverse array of experimental tasks, including jury decisions (Nemeth & Wachtler, 1974) and discussions of social issues such as military budgets (Mugny, 1975), feminism (Paicheler, 1976), the death penalty (Maass, Clark, & Haberkorn, 1982), and abortion policy (Clark & Maass, 1990).

On the basis of findings in this minority influence paradigm, Moscovici (1976) argued that minorities—whether they are individuals or subgroups within groups—should not be viewed only as recipients of influence or as deviates from the majority. They should in addition be viewed as "potential influence emitters and norm originators" (Moscovici, 1976, p. 67). This view of minorities and majorities as reciprocally influencing one another has much to recommend it. Not only in small groups, but in the society at large, social change often flows from minorities to the majority. Social movements such as the civil rights movement and the women's movement represent efforts of what was initially a small minority to convince the majority that existing social arrangements are inequitable or otherwise insufficient.

Mediation by Attributional Processes. The rationale that Moscovici and his collaborators initially proposed for the impact of minorities is that a minority induces a conflict with the majority by challenging the majority norm. The minority can successfully exert influence only if it provides a stable alternative norm. Such an alternative norm emerges to the extent that the minority advocates its position in a behavioral style that suggests certainty and commitment. Although several aspects of behavioral style may be relevant (see Moscovici, 1976), the minority's *behavioral consistency* in advocating its position has received the most attention. Indeed, consistency has been repeatedly shown to be a necessary condition for producing minority influence (e.g., Bray, Johnson, & Chilstrom, 1982; Moscovici & Personnaz, 1980; Mugny, 1982; Nemeth, Swedlund, & Kanki, 1974), although under some conditions consistency does not have the typical effect (see J. M. Levine & Russo, 1987).

The minority's consistent advocacy of its position presumably leads the majority to regard the minority as certain and confident (see Moscovici & Faucheux, 1972; Moscovici & Nemeth, 1974). Research on the ascription of traits to group members has shown that the minority, compared with the majority, is perceived as more confident (e.g., Maass et al., 1982; Moscovici & Lage, 1976; Moscovici et al., 1969; Nemeth & Wachtler, 1974, 1983) and sometimes as more competent (Moscovici et al., 1969; Moscovici & Néve, 1973). This "dispositional" attribution of confidence and competence is regarded as the proximal determinant of conformity to the minority's position.

Although this attributional account of the effects of the minority's consistency has been widely accepted, it has also been criticized (Chaiken & Stangor, 1987; Maass & Clark, 1984). Thus, despite evidence that minorities are perceived as more certain and confident when they are consistent, the mediational role of this perception in relation to the minority's influence has not been rigorously tested using appropriate experimental designs or causal modeling procedures, in the manner that attributional hypotheses have been tested in persuasion research (see Chapter 8). Furthermore, as Maass and Clark (1984) argued, a minority's consistent advocacy of a deviant position could lead the members of the majority to ascribe quite different dispositional qualities to the minority—in particular, negative attributes such as dogmatism and self-interest.

The ascription of other, less positive qualities to consistent minorities is consonant with demonstrations that a consistent minority manifesting a behaviorally *rigid* style, consisting of simple repetition of one's position in exactly the same form, is ineffective in inducing influence (e.g., Mugny, 1975; Mugny & Papastamou, 1980; Nemeth et al., 1974). Also relevant are studies of influence by *double minorities*, defined as subgroups who represent both a natural minority in the society (e.g., blacks, Jews, Hispanics) and a numerical minority in the experimental group (defined by their deviation from the majority's position). Research has found that stronger self-interest was ascribed to double than single (i.e., numerical) minorities and that, in addition, double minorities exerted less influence (e.g., Maass & Clark, 1982; Maass et al., 1982).

Although Maass and Clark (1984) have proposed a more complex attributional model that applies both Kelley's cube model and his augmentation and discounting principles to understanding the dispositional qualities ascribed to minorities, another attributional perspective may be more useful, that is, a framework that focuses, not on perceptions of the minority's underlying dispositions, but on explanations of the minority's position. As the discussion of attribution models of persuasion in Chapter 8 indicated, an emphasis on underlying dispositions of the sources of messages has more in common with correspondent inference theory (E. E. Jones & Davis, 1965) than with the Kelley (1967, 1972a) model, even though the Kelley model is more often invoked in discussions of minority influence. In Kelley's attributional analyses, the perceiver's central task when facing challenging information does not consist of inferring the communicator's dispositions, but instead consists of inferring the causes of the communicator's position. In his ANOVA account of persuasion, Kelley used the terms *entity* or *stimulus* attribution to refer to the attribution of the communicator's message to the environment under discussion. This attribution, which Kelley argued is maximized by a pattern of high consensus, consistency, and distinctiveness, increases persuasiveness because it implies that the communicator's message provides a truthful description of external reality. By this account, the link between the minority's consistency and its influence is mediated by the perceiver's explanations of the minority's *message*.

Also, in Kelley's (1972a) subsequent multiple plausible causes framework, which featured the augmentation and discounting principles, perceivers were viewed as scanning available information for possible causes of the communicator's message and taking into account whether there were one or more plausible causes and whether these causes would be facilitative or inhibitory in relation to the position stated in the message. In this framework, the double minority's membership in a societal minority group is perceived as a plausible facilitative cause of their deviant position, leading perceivers to discount external reality as the cause. Although such causal explanations of the minority's position may also affect the traits that are ascribed to them, these inferred traits are, at best, only indirectly related to the persuasiveness of the minority's position (see Eagly & Chaiken, 1984, and Chapter 8).

Researchers have much to gain by exploring the utility of attribution theory for explaining minority influence. Yet current attributional analyses would have to be expanded in order to capture the complexities of the minority influence paradigm where group members face the task of simultaneously inferring the causes of the minority's and the majority's position. Even with additions, however, attribution theory is unlikely to provide a sufficient framework for understanding minority influence. Because attributional approaches assume that perceivers are oriented to maximizing the validity of their attitudes (see Chapter 8), these approaches prescribe an informational model of social influence by which perceivers judge the extent to which the minority's position veridically represents external reality. Unless informed by conceptions of influence as a normative process, the attributional perspective is incomplete, especially in group settings in which motives such as winning social approval are important.

Dual-Process Views of Mediation. Building on his earlier theorizing, Moscovici (1980, 1985) subsequently proposed that minority and majority influence induce qualitatively different modes of processing persuasive information. Majorities instigate a *comparison* process by which a group member's attention focuses on "what the others say, so as to fit in with their opinions or judgments" (Moscovici, 1980, p. 214). In contrast, minorities, if consistent, induce a *validation* process by which a group member's attention focuses on trying to "see what the minority saw, to understand what it understood" (Moscovici, 1980, p. 214). Comparison thus presumes fairly superficial information processing focusing on the position that is advocated, and validation presumes more active information processing focusing on the more complex matter of how this position was derived from an external reality. Moscovici's proposal thus resembles to some extent the heuristic-systematic and peripheral-central distinctions considered in Chapter 7. Consistent with this interpretation, Moscovici argued that minority influence is deeper and more enduring than majority influence. Thus, differences in information processing are presumed to cause majorities to produce ephemeral change at a surface level of public compliance and to cause minorities to produce longer-term change at the deeper level of private acceptance. Along with these processing differences, motivational forces, based on group members' desire to gain the majority's approval, conspire to encourage public agreement with the majority. Desires to avoid appearing deviant and viewing oneself as an outgroup member might also discourage public agreement with the minority (Moscovici & Personnaz, 1980; Mugny, 1982).

Moscovici also introduced the terms *compliance* and *conversion* in his dual process interpretation of minority influence. He argued that majorities induce compliance, by which change is publicly expressed but tends to remain only at a manifest, direct level, whereas minorities induce conversion, by which change occurs at a latent, indirect level.[7] The distinction between compliance and conversion thus embraces the distinction between public and private acceptance of others' views that emerged in the earlier conformity literature. In addition, the terms compliance and conversion incorporate a distinction between *direct* and *indirect* influence. According to this distinction, influence defined as direct affects (a) judgments of the physical properties of the stimuli that were presented or (b) beliefs directly related to the issue under discussion. In contrast, influence defined as indirect affects judgments or beliefs that bear a more remote relation to the stimuli or issues. The compliance-conversion distinction also presumes a difference in the persistence of influence, with compliance being ephemeral and conversion more enduring. Taking these several aspects of compliance and conversion into account, Moscovici reasoned that compliance should be detectable immediately after the influence induction and mainly on public measures that relate directly to the experimental stimuli or issue. In contrast, conversion should be detectable for a longer period of time and mainly on private measures, especially those that relate somewhat indirectly to the experimental stimuli or issue.[8]

The major strategy for investigating this dual process model has consisted of comparing the impact of majority and minority sources to see if they produce different amounts of public versus private influence or direct versus indirect influence, or different degrees of persistence. Consistent with Chaiken and Stangor's (1987) review of such studies, majority influence is generally greater than minority influence on public measures (see also Maass & Clark, 1984; Maass, West, & Cialdini, 1987). And, although majority influence often occurs publicly, it is not restricted entirely to the public level since effects of majority influence are sometimes found on private, direct measures and occasionally on private, indirect measures. Minority influence, in contrast, is rarely manifested publicly but is often observed on private, direct measures as well as on private, indirect measures. Findings are less consistent concerning the relative persistence of influence by minority versus majority sources.

Also relevant to these issues are studies that attempt to track the cognitive processes that underlie majority versus minority influence. Studies comparing subjects exposed to minority and majority sources have examined (a) their attention to the judged stimuli (Tesser, Campbell, & Mickler, 1983), (b) their recall of others' judgments (Moscovici, Mugny, & Papastamou, reported in Moscovici, 1980), and (c) their cognitive responses (thought listings; e.g., Maass & Clark, 1983; Mackie, 1987).

Among the studies that assessed subjects' cognitive processes, Mackie's (1987) experiments provided a particularly useful bridge to persuasion research that has distinguished between systematic and heuristic processing of persuasive material (Chapter 7). Mackie found considerable evidence that persuasive messages ascribed to majority sources were processed systematically and therefore produced private acceptance of the advocated position, long-term maintenance of the change, and generalization to a related issue. Furthermore, the influence produced by majorities correlated with message-oriented processing of their messages, as indexed by cognitive responses and recall of the message content. In contrast, messages ascribed to minority sources produced considerably less influence, although some indirect influence occurred for subjects initially uncommitted on the issue. However, this influence did not appear to be accompanied by the issue- or message-oriented cognitive responding implied by Moscovici's concept of conversion. However, because Mackie's research merely exposed subjects to recorded messages in which communicators took positions described as endorsed by a majority or minority of other students, the generalizability of her findings to the sorts of face-to-face groups typically studied by investigators of majority and minority influence remains to be determined. The knowledge that one's own position is being evaluated by other group members may induce processes quite different from those induced in the persuasion paradigm employed by Mackie.

Divergent Thinking. Research by Charlan Nemeth (1985, 1986, 1987) also bears on the dual-process perspective. Like Moscovici, Nemeth maintained that in majority influence settings, attention and thought focus on the majority's position. Whereas Moscovici elaborated little on this comparison process, Nemeth contended that the stressfulness of such situations (e.g., Nemeth, 1976) and perhaps other factors lead to relatively superficial processing by which group members' attention and thought converge on the majority's stated position but do not extend to a full consideration of the issue. In contrast, minority sources are postulated to stimulate a greater amount of thinking, and this thinking tends to be more *divergent*, where the term divergent refers to thinking that branches out from the information that is given and focuses on new information and possible alternative positions. For Nemeth, the divergent quality of the thinking inspired by minorities is critical. She argued that a unique contribution of minorities is that they stimulate the sort of thinking that leads to creative, high quality decisions and judgments.

Support for Nemeth's views comes from a series of studies on group problem solving (Nemeth & Kwan, 1985, 1987; Nemeth & Wachtler, 1983). For example, Nemeth and Wachtler (1983) asked subjects to detect "standard" figures that were embedded in one or more of six "comparison" figures. On each trial, the standard was easily seen in one comparison but not in the remaining five. Subjects made their judgments in six-member groups in which either two confederates (i.e., a minority) or four confederates (i.e., a majority) claimed to see the standard in both the easy comparison figure (a correct response) and in one other figure. The choice of this other figure was correct or incorrect, depending on the experimental condition. Consistent with other research, majorities exerted greater influence, regardless of their correctness. More important, however, is the finding that subjects exposed to minority sources were more likely to find novel, correct solutions than subjects exposed to majority sources.

Other research has also supported Nemeth's description of the cognitive processes that underlie minority influence. In an experimental paradigm in which high school students evaluated a proposal to modify their graduation examination, Volpato, Maass,

Mucchi-Faina, and Vitti (1990) found that influence from a minority within the subjects' own group stimulated them to propose alternatives to the proposal they were given. In an experiment in which Italian university students evaluated proposals to promote the international image of the city of Perugia, original and creative proposals were inspired by the presentation of an original (but not a conventional) proposal from the minority, but not by an original proposal from the majority (Mucchi-Faina, Maass, & Volpato, 1991). Moreover, minorities, compared with majorities, have been shown to produce superior recall of information related to their influence attempt (Nemeth, Mayseless, Sherman, & Brown, 1990). Various findings thus support Nemeth's claims that minority influence stimulates issue-relevant thinking that is more divergent, creative, original, and thorough than the thinking stimulated by majority influence.

Relation of Moscovici's Viewpoint to Other Dual-Process Theories. In terms of the normative-informational dichotomy that we have emphasized in this chapter (Deutsch & Gerard, 1955), Moscovici's dual-process perspective presumes primarily normative motivation for majority influence and informational motivation for minority influence. The normative processes mediating majority influence flow from group members' desire to fit in with the majority to gain their approval, to avoid appearing deviant, and so on. The informational processes mediating minority influence flow from group members' attributional analysis of the minority's position as well as their efforts to understand the details of the minority's thinking. Yet, as L. Ross et al.'s (1976) analysis of the Asch paradigm contended, attributional mechanisms are relevant to majority influence as well, thus underscoring that majority influence engages informational as well as normative motivation.

We have already noted some of the implications of Moscovici's dual-process interpretation for the modes of information processing that we emphasized in Chapter 7. In general, heuristic processing is implicated by majority influence, whereas systematic processing is implicated by minority influence. However, as Chaiken and Stangor (1987) suggested, there are a number of complexities cautioning against a simple equation between majority influence and heuristic processing and between minority influence and systematic processing. For example, although the presumably deeper change implied by Moscovici's conversion construct suggests that minority influence is more enduring than majority influence, research in persuasion paradigms, such as the Mackie (1987) study that we have already noted, suggests that this view is too limited. Moreover, other research suggests that systematic processing would be a particularly likely mediator of majority influence under some circumstances. For example, because outcome-relevant involvement (see B. T. Johnson & Eagly, 1989) often facilitates systematic processing, group members confronted with a majority advocating a position that is likely to affect their ability to reach their goals may engage in the kind of message- and issue-relevant thinking that confers greater persistence. Similarly, individuals high in need for cognition (Cacioppo, Petty, & Morris, 1983) may process messages systematically, regardless of whether they emanate from minority or majority sources. Also, public compliance with majorities may ultimately result in internalized attitude change because of motivational forces such as dissonance reduction (see Chapter 10) or because of the delayed cognitive consequences that such goal-directed social communications may have for communicators' own attitudes (Higgins & McCann, 1984). Further, as suggested by Kelman's identification process, genuine, albeit somewhat shallow, attitude change might result from individuals' desire to identify with an attractive majority group, and such change could persist if the group continues to be a source of social identity for these individuals as time passes (see J. M. Levine & Moreland, 1985).

Demonstrating the common roots that research on minority influence and on persuasion have in contemporary social psychological theory, the same three processing modes that have emerged as especially important in modern persuasion research also have become pivotal in research on majority and minority influence: heuristic processing, attributional reasoning, and message- and issue-relevant thinking (see Chapters 6, 7, and 8). Nemeth (1987) has added another mode, divergent thinking, to this list. Although researchers still have only incomplete understanding of how these modes operate and impact on one another, it is probably safe to assume at this point that multiple cognitive processes underlie both majority and minority influence, just as multiple cognitive processes underlie persuasion. Indeed, Maass et al. (1987) have proposed a theoretical integration of findings on majority and minority influence that takes these (and other) aspects of cognitive processing into account. This integration focuses on minorities' greater distinctiveness, lower credibility, and greater tendency to be a target of social pressures from the majority. These three factors are held to foster conversion and impede compliance, through the mediation of several cognitive processes and motivational states (e.g., stress).

Single-Process Interpretations of Majority and Minority Influence. Two mathematically formulated influence models have posed an apparent challenge to the dual-process perspective. Social impact theory (Latané, 1981; Latané & Wolf, 1981) and Tanford and Penrod's (1984) social influence model treat majority and minority influence within a common theoretical framework and view both forms of influence as part of a single process. Social impact theory asserts that the degree to which people are influenced is a multiplicative function of the number of sources, their strength (e.g., expertise), and their immediacy (e.g., proximity). The strength and immediacy terms are the theory's vehicle for representing several important distal determinants of influence such as behavioral style and group cohesiveness (see Mullen, 1985; Jackson, 1986). Nevertheless, most tests of the theory's predictive power in majority and minority situations have focused on group size, that is, the number of sources who advocate a position. Social impact theory assumes that a negatively accelerating positive power function relates group size to observed influence. By such a function, the first source exerts the greatest impact, and each additional source has a progressively smaller impact. Latané and Wolf (1981) fit power functions to some conformity and minority influence studies in which the number of influence sources had been manipulated and found that their model accounted for a substantial portion of the variance in the influence that sources exerted in both domains.

Tanford and Penrod (1984) have developed a more elaborate social influence model (SIM), which differs from social impact theory (SIT) in some respects yet still focuses primarily on the size of minorities and majorities. The most important difference between the models is that, in contrast to SIT's group size function, the SIM posits an S-shaped "Gompertz" growth function. By this function, the second and third influence sources are expected to exert a greater impact than the first, and after this (inflection) point, each additional source exerts a progressively smaller impact. Another notable difference is the fact that SIM's parameters include features of the experimental context (e.g., type of group, type of task, and consistency of the source) and individual differences in persuasibility, whereas SIT either does not address these parameters or represents them by its strength and immediacy variables (see Tanford & Penrod, 1984; Wolf, 1987). On the basis of a meta-analysis of a selected sample of studies on conformity, minority influence, and deviate rejection, Tanford and Penrod found that the SIM provided a somewhat better fit to existing data than did SIT. More important, however, are findings from regression analyses indicating that the amount of influence observed in these studies was largely a function of the number of influence sources and targets. Yet it should be noted that the issue of whether group size interacts with variables such as source consistency was not addressed by Tanford and Penrod, who included no relevant interaction terms in their regression analyses.

On the basis of these results, Tanford and Penrod (1984) concluded that majority and minority influence are part of a single process, a view shared by Latané and Wolf (e.g., Wolf & Latané, 1985), who claimed further that the differences between majority and minority influence are merely "quantitative." On the surface, such claims seem odd since both of these models are silent with respect to underlying psychological mechanisms.[9] It appears, however, that single-process and dual-process theorists have been using the same term differently. Specifically, Latané and Wolf's and Tanford and Penrod's use of process seems to refer to the predictive power of their models and to their models' functional principles (e.g., SIT's multiplicative function). In contrast, dual-process theorists seem to use this term in its more usual sense to refer to psychological processes such as attributional reasoning or issue-relevant thinking. Even though multiple processes (more than two, we contend) may be needed to account for influence in the second, more usual sense of the term process, it may well be the case, as the single-process theorists contend, that the impact of both majorities and minorities can be predicted with some accuracy by the equations of social impact theory and the social influence model.

A related issue concerns whether differences between majority and minority influence are of a qualitative nature, as dual-process theorists see it (e.g., Moscovici, 1980; Nemeth, 1986), or are merely quantitative, as single-process theorists have argued (e.g., Wolf & Latané, 1985). Here again it seems that both positions bear some truth and that the apparent controversy can be resolved by disentangling discrepancies in terminology. If the term qualitatively different is reserved for attitude change processes that reflect different motivational goals (e.g., seeking social approval vs. valid attitudes), there is merit to the view that some processes that probably occur in majority settings (e.g., compliance, identification) are qualitatively different from those that may occur in minority settings (e.g., causal reasoning about message validity). Yet, to the extent that similar motivational goals (e.g., seeking veridical attitudes and beliefs) underlie both forms of influence, the qualitative-quantitative distinction loses meaning. For example, even investigators who maintain that systematic processing occurs primarily with minority influence would probably agree with our position that systematic processing occurs in majority settings for certain people (e.g., those high in need for cognition) or under certain circumstances (e.g., involving issues). Similarly, although attributional reasoning has often been discussed in the context of minority influence, this mode of processing is no doubt important in majority influence settings as well (see prior discussion of conformity). Whether such modes occur to a greater or lesser degree in majority versus minority settings would seem to be primarily a quantitative issue.

In summary, differences between majority and minority influence may sometimes be qualitative (when different motives and processes operate) and other times quantitative (when similar motives and processes operate). Group influence researchers, like persuasion researchers (see Chapters 6, 7, and 8), need to attain a better understanding of which motives or goals are aroused in influence settings, how these goals impact on modes of processing, and how different modes of processing may interact. In addition, researchers should not lose sight of important motivational issues by focusing excessively on cognition or by utilizing paradigms that are impoverished in terms of their motivational aspects. Limiting the extent to which experiments engage strong motives, much research on minority and majority influence has studied "minimal" groups with no history and no future, sometimes with majority and minority sources that were not physically present in the influence setting (e.g., Maass & Clark, 1983; Mackie, 1987; Volpato et al., 1990). To understand more fully the societal issues of social control and innovation to which minority influence researchers wish to generalize, investigators should also examine real groups that have real histories and futures and whose members interact over a length of time.

Group Polarization

Another important phenomenon observed in groups is that the decisions and attitudes that groups produce are more extreme than those produced by their individual members acting alone. This effect, which has come to be known as *group polarization*, was originally discovered by Stoner (1961). In this initial experiment, small groups, usually consisting of five members, first responded individually to a series of vignettes, which were *choice-dilemma* items developed by Kogan and Wallach (1964). Each dilemma described a fictional character who faced a choice between an attractive, risky alternative and a less attractive, safer alternative. The subject's task was to advise the character how much risk he should take. For example, in one vignette the main character was an engineer who had to choose between continuing in his adequate job that offered little possibility for substantially increased income or changing to a more highly paid job with a new company that, if successful, could offer greatly increasing income and opportunity. Subjects' task was advising the protagonist how much risk he should take. Thus, for the engineer vignette, subjects indicated the lowest probability of the company's proving financially sound that would be acceptable to make it worthwhile to change to the new job.

After making their choices individually, the subjects met in groups and discussed each item until they reached a consensus. Stoner (1961) found that the choices made by groups were riskier than the average of the decisions that these same subjects had made individually. Although this phenomenon was initially labeled the *risky shift*, this term quickly lost favor as subsequent researchers discovered that on some items group decisions were more cautious than decisions by their individual members (e.g., Rabow, Fowler, Bradford, Hofeller, & Shibuya, 1966; Stoner, 1968). Moreover, systematic shifts occurred on issues having nothing to do with the amount of risk that people are willing to accept (Doise, 1969; Moscovici & Zavalloni, 1969). Described in general terms, the effect found in this research is that the initial tendency of individual group members in a pro or con direction on an issue is more extreme following group discussion. If group members acting individually have a moderate tendency toward one side or the other of some psychological midpoint, group discussion tends to change their views so that they gain a more extreme tendency in the same direction. Moscovici and Zavalloni (1969) proposed the term group-induced attitude polarization or group polarization for this phenomenon.[10]

A large research literature has accumulated on group polarization, and several excellent reviews of this research are available (e.g., Cartwright, 1971, 1973; Isenberg, 1986; Lamm & Myers, 1978; Myers, 1982; Myers & Lamm, 1976). Part of the excitement generated by this research stemmed from the potentially serious implications that polarization might have for the wisdom and effectiveness of decisions that groups produce in natural settings. Yet, at least for experimental social psychologists, a large part of the excitement of polarization effects stemmed from the opportunity to test the sizable number of explanatory mechanisms that initially seemed to provide plausible accounts of the findings. Although at least eleven explanatory mechanisms were proposed (see Pruitt, 1971a, 1971b), rapidly accumulating studies gradually eliminated all but two major possibilities, one emphasizing normative processes and the other emphasizing informational processes.

Normative Processes. Normative explanations of group polarization focus on interpersonal comparison processes and assume that group members are motivated to perceive themselves favorably and to present themselves to others in a socially desirable manner. To achieve a relatively positive self-concept and self-presentation in a group situation, a group member must take into account other members' self-presentations and adjust his or her own self-presentation accordingly. Because the information that group members have about one another in this situation consists mainly of others' positions on a number of issues, each member presumably considers these positions and then tries to adopt a desirable position. To attain a favorable presentation, a member must adopt at least as adequate a position on each issue as those already adopted by the other group members, and, if possible, adopt a somewhat more desirable position.

Various assumptions are required to explain why self-presentational pressures produce attitudes that are more extreme than those held at the outset of a group meeting. One of the most popular explanations is a pluralistic ignorance explanation that has appeared in several forms (see Isenberg, 1980; Levinger & Schneider, 1969; Pruitt, 1971a; Schroeder, 1973). The term *pluralistic ignorance* refers to a situation in which all group members tend to hold one attitude but believe that the other members hold a different attitude (Schanck, 1932). According to this idea, group members are "ignorant" in the sense that they misperceive other members' positions prior to the group discussion. Pluralistic ignorance implies, for example, that subjects thought that the other subjects would not be as risky as they turned out to be on the choice-dilemma items used by Stoner (1961). The subjects wanted to appropriate a desirable position for themselves by advocating that the protagonists of the vignettes take risks for attractive outcomes; at the same time the subjects did not want to be very far from the others in their group. When the subjects found out that the other group members were riskier than they thought, they were motivated to move toward the risky end of the scale in order to adopt a position that was desirable in their own and others' perceptions yet not too deviant from others' positions. The pluralistic ignorance theory thus maintains that in a variety of domains in addition to discussions of risky decisions, group members perceive somewhat extreme positions as desirable and initially underestimate the extremity of others' positions. The initial misperception is changed by the communication that subsequently occurs in the group.

Slightly different assumptions were made in another version of this pluralistic ignorance explanation. Departing from the assumption that people avoid deviating from others' positions, investigators postulated that people desire to be *different* from other group members in a valued direction in order to be perceived more favorably than these others (R. Brown, 1974; Myers, 1978; Myers, Bruggink, Kersting, & Schlosser, 1980; Myers, Wojcicki, & Aardema, 1977). When group members find out others' attitudes, they then engage in a sort of one-upmanship by shifting their positions in the direction that seems to be most valued.

More recent elaborations of the idea that normative processes mediate group polarization incorporate ideas from social identity theory (e.g., Tajfel & Turner, 1979; J. C. Turner, 1987). According to this view, group membership is essential to group polarization. To produce polarization, the people who are sources of information must be perceived not merely as members of a group but as members of one's own *in-group*, as was probably typical of experiments on group polarization. When information comes from members of a distinct social group, it is perceived as more extreme than it would otherwise be, a phenomenon labeled *extremitization*. Subjects then conform to this perceived group norm only if they regard the group as their own in-group, presumably because they are motivated to be similar to other group members only if they are an in-group. As Mackie (1986) has explained, social identity theory amplifies the normative theory of polarization by identifying three processes that underlie the phenomenon: an initial social categorization of influence sources as group members, an extremitization of their positions on an issue, and conformity to the resulting group norm, provided that the group is perceived as an in-group.

Informational Processes. This alternative explanation of group polarization focuses on the cognitive learning that results from exposure to group members' arguments during the discussion. This type of theory has much in common with the cognitive response and dual-process approaches considered in Chapters 6 and 7 and could even be considered an application of these frameworks. Thus, this explanation of polarization effects maintains that the discussion predominantly generates arguments supporting the alternative initially favored in the group as a whole and that for the typical member at least some of these arguments are not already familiar. Hearing some novel and reasonable arguments, mainly in support of the initially favored alternative, the typical group member shifts his or her attitude in that direction, producing an overall shift in this direction.

This informational explanation of group polarization has been investigated most thoroughly by Burnstein, Vinokur, and their colleagues, who labeled it the *persuasive arguments theory* (Burnstein & Vinokur, 1975, 1977; Burnstein, Vinokur, & Trope, 1973; Vinokur & Burnstein, 1974, 1978a), although very similar ideas have been pursued in other frameworks, including information integration theory (N. H. Anderson & Graesser, 1976). According to the specifics of the persuasive arguments theory, a group member's position is a function of the number and persuasiveness of pro and con arguments recalled from memory when he or she formulates this position. Group members shift their positions in a given direction to the extent that they are exposed to arguments favoring that direction and not exposed to arguments opposing that direction. In addition, these arguments were assumed to be persuasive to the extent that they are perceived to be *valid* and to the extent that they are *novel* and thus have not already been taken into account in group members' formulation of their initial positions. From the informational perspective, the number of pro and con arguments, along with their validity and novelty, determine change in group members' attitudes.

Evidence for Normative and Informational Processes. Both the normative and informational views of the polarization phenomenon have been pursued energetically, and detailed review of this now-large empirical literature is beyond the scope of this book. In concert with other reviewers (e.g., Isenberg, 1986; Myers, 1982), we believe that both interpretations have ample experimental support and that therefore both normative and informational processes contribute to polarization, although to differing degrees, depending on the context. Support for normative mechanisms has centered on demonstrations that mere knowledge of other group members' positions (without exposure to discussion, which would acquaint the members with arguments) can produce polarization (e.g., Blascovich, Ginsburg, & Veach, 1975; Myers, 1978). Also, polarization produced by listening to a group discussion has been shown to depend on subjects believing that they are members of the group (Mackie & Cooper, 1984). When subjects believed instead that the overheard group would compete with their own group, polarization was not obtained. Other studies supporting the social identity variant of the normative interpretation of polarization have manipulated whether influence emanates from group members or unrelated individuals and whether the group members belong to an in-group or out-group (Mackie, 1986; J. C. Turner, 1987).

658

Findings show that polarization does indeed require that subjects perceive influence coming from members of an in-group.

A variety of other findings have supported the persuasive arguments theory. For example, polarization correlates with the preponderance of pro and con arguments available to group members (e.g., Ebbesen & Bowers, 1974; Madsen, 1978) and can be produced by manipulations of the preponderance of pro and con arguments (e.g., Ebbesen & Bowers, 1974). Moreover, exploration of the validity and novelty of the arguments has generated evidence that polarization increases to the extent that the arguments members hear are valid and novel (e.g., M. F. Kaplan & Miller, 1977; Vinokur & Burnstein, 1978b).

Much more controversial are the stronger claims by the advocates of the persuasive arguments theory that their theory is sufficient to account for polarization effects and that the alternative normative theory is unnecessary. Expert reviewers have remained unconvinced that the persuasive arguments theory is the only valid theory of group polarization and tend to favor the dualist position that a combination of normative and informational processes ordinarily produces group polarization. Particularly informative is Isenberg's (1986) meta-analysis, which summarized 33 independent effect sizes. Isenberg found that, although the effects predicted by the persuasive arguments theory were larger than those predicted by the alternative normative viewpoint, the average effect size was substantial for both types of study and departed significantly from the zero effect size predicted by the null hypothesis.

Although Isenberg's (1986) conclusion was supported by the details of his quantitative summary of the research literature, many important issues remain unresolved in polarization experiments, as Isenberg pointed out. For example, the conditions under which normative or informational processes are more important are not well understood. Impression-relevant involvement (see B. T. Johnson & Eagly, 1989) may be one such condition because it engages the motive presumed to be important by the normative theories—group members' desire to achieve a favorable self-presentation on the issue they discuss. In contrast, value-relevant involvement may weaken informational mediation because people may already have been exposed to most of the available arguments on issues relevant to their values, thus decreasing the likelihood that other group members' arguments are novel. Although such interacting conditions have not yet been explored, it is significant that in this research literature, as in others we have considered in this chapter, normative and informational processes have both generated viable theories supported by ample evidence.

Conclusion

In terms of volume of research and certainly in terms of interest generated, the study of social influence is one of the richest areas of social psychology. The area is also notable for a continuity of theoretical orientations, as the early formulation of the concepts of normative and informational influence provided a general framework for theorizing over the years. As M. F. Kaplan (1987, 1989) has shown, the importance of these concepts for understanding group and interpersonal processes is difficult to under-estimate. They have provided overall guidance as investigators searched for more detailed explanations of newly discovered phenomena such as group polarization and minority influence.[11]

Despite the many virtues of social psychological research on social influence, the tradition is somewhat limited in some respects. Most important is the remarkable fact that very little of the research we have reviewed has been conducted in field settings, despite the applicability and potential importance of social influence phenomena for social interaction in natural settings.[12] From this perspective, it is somewhat discour-aging to observe that in contemporary research on both minority influence and group polarization, investigators have increasingly retreated even from the complexities of laboratory face-to-face groups and have substituted simulated group members with whom subjects do not interact. This trend recalls the fondness that an earlier generation of conformity researchers developed for the efficiencies of the Crutchfield (1955) apparatus, which allowed them to run conformity studies in the absence of actual groups. Reliance on simulated groups only exacerbates problems of generalizability. Nonetheless, many social psychologists believe that conformity pressures are strong in ongoing groups, that minority influence is a source of innovation and social change in natural settings, and that polarization is a common pitfall of natural groups. However, unless the phenomena of social influence are investigated from time to time in natural settings, such claims remain unsubstantiated. Although disentangling the specifics of competing theoretical explanations of social influence effects is indeed important and readily engages the intellects and creativity of experimental social psychologists, this endeavor has been pursued to the neglect of issues of generalizability and external validity. Perhaps in coming decades, now that certain phenomena have been firmly established in laboratory research, social influence will be probed more thoroughly in natural settings.

The research on social influence that we have reviewed in this chapter is also limited by its concentration on the psychological processes that mediate influence, to the exclusion of systematic analysis of social processes. Given the focus of this book on the psychology of attitudes, we have deliberately chosen theories of influence that are primarily psychological and that therefore link to the general themes of this book. Yet psychological social psychologists would benefit from incorporating at least some aspects of social process into their theories. For example, a more sociological focus would consider cultural factors that may establish a context that fosters or constrains conformity to majorities (see Paicheler, 1988; Perrin & Spencer, 1981). Such a focus would also provide an interpretation of the effects of the characteristics that group members bring to social situations as members of identifiable societal subgroups that differ in power, privilege, and status. Thus, individuals possess group membership characteristics based on sex, race, national origin, religion, social class, and other factors. The importance of such attributes for social influence has been considered by sociologists working within the *theory of expectation states* (Berger, Rosenholtz, & Zelditch, 1980; Berger & Zelditch, 1985). According to this theory, attributes such as sex and race function as status cues or *diffuse status characteristics*. People utilize such attributes as status cues because of their extensive prior experience in natural settings where they observed that these attributes were correlated with power and prestige.

According to the theory of expectation states, people tend to infer others' general competence and value from diffuse status characteristics, and the competence and value ascribed to group members then affects the extent to which they are able to influence others. People who have less valued status characteristics (e.g., women, members of racial minorities) therefore have less power and are more readily influenced by others. Although these ideas have been applied to the sex differences observed in various social influence settings (e.g., Eagly, 1983a, 1987; Lockheed & Hall, 1976; Meeker & Weitzel-O'Neill, 1977), and other applications are available as well (see Berger et al., 1980), this perspective has not had much impact within the traditions developed by psychological social psychologists for studying social influence. Little of the research within the minority influence paradigm has given more than cursory consideration to the implications of membership in societal subgroups.[13] Yet in a pluralistic society in which people commonly interact across lines of gender, race, religion, and national origin, these factors should not continue to be neglected.

661

——— Notes ———

1. As Friend, Rafferty, and Bramel (1990) pointed out, Asch (1952, 1956) interpreted this experiment as establishing a conflict between independence and conformity and gave considerable emphasis to the fact that two-thirds of subjects' judgments were independent. Nonetheless, in social psychology, the experiment took on importance as a demonstration of conformity rather than independence. This interpretation is understandable given Asch's stimulus situation in which conformity required that subjects deny the evidence of their own eyes. Moreover, 75.6 percent of the subjects conformed on at least one trial.

2. However, Asch's (1956) own interpretation of his experiment had primarily an informational emphasis. He thus maintained that the severity of the conflict his subjects experienced stemmed from the disagreement they encountered between two sources of information (their own senses and others' judgments) that would ordinarily be trustworthy in a situation such as that of the experiment (see also Deutsch & Krauss, 1965, pp. 27–28).

3. In French and Raven's scheme, the influencing agent's expectations about the target's behavior are not necessarily communicated explicitly. For example, a film star's ideas about how to dress would not be communicated in the form of explicit advice about what his fans should wear.

4. Yet, exact replications of Asch's (1956) original experiments are not uncommon. See Larsen (1990) for an example.

5. This interesting explanation of the processes that mediate conformity in the Asch experiment is informational rather than normative in character and is therefore quite in harmony with Asch's own interpretation of his experiment.

6. Asch's well-known statement is that attitude change is due to *"a change in the object of judgment rather than in the judgment of the object"* (Asch, 1940, p. 458, italics in the original). Readers should note that Asch's statement can be

viewed as consistent with our treatment of attitudes in Chapter 1. Thus, because cognitive input is one source of attitudes, a change in the attributes ascribed to an attitude object ordinarily changes the attitude.

7. Note that this usage of the term *conversion* differs from Nail's (1986), which refers to changing publicly and privately in a majority influence paradigm (see earlier discussion).

8. Although minorities have been held to produce *latent influence*, and majorities to produce *manifest influence* (e.g., Moscovici, 1980), the latent-manifest distinction remains somewhat less clear than the other distinctions we discuss. Characteristics of latent influence implicit in Moscovici's writings are that such influence is quite indirect and that people are unaware that they have been so influenced. Yet Wolf (1987) suggested that latent influence consists of greater private than public agreement, and the term might well also imply greater indirect than direct influence. Within Moscovici's color perception paradigm, operational definitions of latent influence have included chromatic afterimages (Moscovici & Personnaz, 1980, 1991; Personnaz, 1981) and shifts in the categorizing of ambiguous colors (Moscovici, Lage, & Naffrechoux, 1969). Consistent with the idea that latent influence is beyond awareness and not subject to self-control, measures of latent influence are quite unobtrusive.

9. Mullen's (1983) model of group size did attempt a more process-oriented account of the effects of group size. In brief, Mullen argued that in groups with two or more subgroups, members' levels of self-attention increase as the relative size of their subgroup decreases and that increased self-attention heightens subjects' motivation to match their behavior to salient standards (i.e., norms; see also Carver & Scheier, 1981). Thus, for conformity experiments, in which the majority's position is assumed to be the standard, Mullen argued and provided evidence that self-attention and conformity covary and that both increase with majority size.

10. Although the term polarization may connote increasing disagreement among group members, such an interpretation of its meaning is wrong in this application. Polarization instead means that, on average, members' attitudes become more extreme.

11. See also Witte's (1987) attempt to apply the concepts of normative and informational influence within an information integration framework (N. H. Anderson, 1981a; see Chapters 3 and 5).

12. Although relatively little of the research within the traditions we have reviewed in this chapter has been conducted in field settings, there is a broader tradition of field studies that concern the shaping of attitudes and behavior by social norms. Excellent examples include studies of rental tenants' attitudes toward a tenant organization (Festinger, Schachter, & Back, 1950), college students' liberal versus conservative attitudes on political issues (Newcomb, 1943), and sorority members' binge eating (Crandall, 1988).

13. Exceptions include the research we noted earlier on double minorities as well as research on whether the source of influence is a minority within a societal ingroup or outgroup (Volpato, Maass, Mucchi-Gaina, & Vitti, 1990). Within the group polarization paradigm, some consideration has also been given to the status of group members (van Knippenberg, de Vries, & van Knippenberg, 1990).

14

Future Directions
in the Study
of Attitudes

The current renaissance in the field of attitudes has been in development for over a decade and a half. In the early years of this period, only practitioners of attitude research may have sensed a renaissance. When Eagly and Himmelfarb (1978) wrote their enthusiastic *Annual Review* chapter in which they noted some important advances in research on the attitude-behavior relation and on persuasion, psychologists outside the attitudes area (who read the chapter) may well have believed that these authors were an overly optimistic duo trying to persuade readers that something interesting was happening in the then-moribund field of attitude research. As explained at several points in this book, attitude research suffered greatly during social psychology's decade of crisis, roughly 1965–1975 (Elms, 1975). As the leading area of social psychology during the 1950s and 1960s, attitude research was the natural and leading target of many criticisms that, on a deeper level, represented the crisis generation's critical self-reflection on the nature of method and theory in social psychology. The late 1970s was therefore the time when social psychologists' attitudes toward attitude research were most negative. Given the cycles of interest that afflict intellectual fields, in hindsight this negativism was probably an excellent sign that something important had begun or was about to.

Given many social psychologists' low regard for attitude research, the renaissance of interest was inevitably somewhat tentative at first. However, that cautiousness has been replaced by an increasing appreciation of a common body of concepts and methods. As in most other fields of psychology, theory consists of a multiplicity of theories and models that can readily be grouped into various families. Some theories, like balance theory, are relatively old and enduring, but most are much newer. Yet the newer theories are for the most part built on the foundations of the older ones, as our presentation in this book has emphasized. Research findings on many issues are moderately cumulative and sensible in terms of the theories that have been proposed. To substantiate our view that progress in many subareas of attitude research is impressive, we begin this chapter with a brief review of the major topics for which there is some consensus about concepts and phenomena and some growth of theory. In the second half of the chapter, we undertake the tougher task of discussing significant omissions in theory and research and of diagnosing some of the difficulties that beset this large literature.

Overview of Systematic Knowledge About Attitudes

Definition and Measurement

There is growing recognition that the concept of attitude is interpreted with precision in terms of a psychological tendency that is expressed by evaluating a particular entity with some degree of favor or disfavor. Evaluation is the core of the attitude concept, when evaluation is understood in a general and abstract sense. Attitude is thus an abstract construct in people's knowledge structures and should not be equated with its less abstract manifestations in terms of particular beliefs, affects, or behaviors. Critical to this definition of attitude is the differentiation that has occurred between the terms *affect* and *evaluation*. Affect refers to the feelings or emotions that people experience in relation to attitude objects and is not synonymous with evaluation. Affect can be positive or negative, but provides only one source of the experience from which attitudes are formed. Beliefs about attitude objects can be positive or negative too and provide another type of experience (i.e., cognitive) from which attitudes develop. Similarly, behaviors that people engage in can be positive or negative and provide a third experiential basis of attitudes. Although affective experience *can* underlie evaluations (see Chapter 9), it has no special or general priority and should not be equated with the concept of attitude.

The idea that attitudes can or should be viewed in terms of three components—understood as affective, cognitive, and behavioral—has generated a certain amount of confusion among social psychologists and more than its share of fruitless debate. Particularly with the aid of the excellent conceptual analysis provided by Zanna and Rempel (1984, 1988), the issues surrounding components have come into better focus. The so-called components are merely three types of evaluative responses that may underlie attitudes. In all three cases, it is the evaluative meaning of the responses that is relevant to attitudes. There is no sense in which proponents of a three-component approach have advanced a model based on non-evaluative as well as evaluative meaning. Rather, the critical issue in thinking about components is whether there is some discriminant validity achieved by dividing evaluative responses into three classes. In essence, this discriminant validity would be shown by higher correlations between responses within a class than between responses in different classes. As our review in Chapter 1 showed, the answer to the question of whether such discriminant validity has been demonstrated is "only sometimes," and therefore in this book we have advocated treating the terms cognitive, affective, and behavioral merely as convenient labels for three classes of evaluative responses that would not necessarily sort out into three components on an empirical basis. In this book, the terms merely provide a heuristically convenient language for discussing various issues relevant to attitudes.

The expectation that cognitive, affective, and behavioral components would be routinely separable on an empirical basis is quite implausible from the synergistic viewpoint that we have advocated in this book. Synergism implies that the different classes of evaluative responses impinge on one another and exist in an interactive, cooperative relation. For example, people reflect on the emotional experiences induced by an attitude object and thereby form beliefs about it, and they may act on their beliefs and emotions. Experience in any one of these domains—cognitive, affective, or behavioral—tends to elicit responses in the other domains, and the total set of responses can determine the more abstract evaluation that is formed. It is therefore likely that most attitudes are probably based on interdependent and correlated cognitive, affective, and behavioral responses. Some attitudes, of course, may be heavily weighted toward one or two classes of responses. For example, without direct experience with an attitude object, little behavioral responding is likely to occur, and perhaps little emotional responding as well. Such an attitude would be based mainly on beliefs.

The technology of attitude measurement anticipated the conceptualization of attitudes in terms of evaluation and from an early point assessed attitudes by scaling individuals on a continuum of favorable versus unfavorable evaluation of attitude objects (e.g., Likert, 1932; Thurstone, 1928). The best-known techniques for measuring attitudes are the scaling methods that were featured in Chapter 2—in particular, the Likert, Thurstone, Guttman, and semantic differential methods. The first three of these methods are general purpose in the sense that they can be applied to any class of attitudinal responses. Thus, researchers can scale items that reflect people's beliefs, affects, or behaviors. In an abstract sense, the goal of each scaling method, placing people on an evaluative continuum in relation to the attitude object, is the same, regardless of the domain of responding used in the particular application of the scaling method. In contrast, the semantic differential method requires that respondents rate an attitude object on general attributes such as good-bad and nice-awful that are presumably synonymous with evaluation itself.

The challenges of attitude measurement have resided in the issues of reliability and validity that surround all techniques of psychological measurement. Of special concern in attitude measurement are the inherent limitations of self-report instruments, which provide the usual method of attitude assessment. These limitations follow from respondents' awareness that their attitudes are being assessed and their attendant desire to present themselves positively to others (often to a researcher or an experimenter). These self-presentational concerns are acute when the attitudes that are the focus of research are those for which normative pressures are strong (e.g., prejudice toward minority groups; attitudes related to sexual and moral issues). Researchers have shown considerable creativity in designing measurement techniques that circumvent the strong demands and self-presentational pressures that may operate in many of the settings in which sensitive attitudes are assessed. These methods include the bogus pipeline and the randomized response techniques considered in Chapter 2. In addition, psychophysiological measures have been explored, especially in recent years. These measures appear to be particularly useful as indexes of the processing of attitude-relevant information (see Cacioppo, Petty, & Geen, 1989). Finally, contemporary research has shown that unreliability in attitude measurement can stem, not only from self-presentational pressures, but also from contextual features of measurement settings (e.g., placement of items in relation to other items; see Schwarz & Strack, 1991; Tourangeau & Rasinski, 1988).

Attitude Structure

Although social scientists typically assess attitudes by placing people's evaluative responses on a bipolar evaluative continuum that represents favorable versus unfavorable evaluation of an attitude object, people do not necessarily represent their own attitudes as a point on a dimension. The knowledge structures by which people represent their attitudes as well as their associated beliefs, affects, and behaviors could take on forms other than the continuum used by psychologists to measure people's attitudes.

Consistent with the measurement approach, social judgment theorists assumed that attitudes take the form of bipolar schemas in people's cognitions (e.g., C. W. Sherif, Sherif, & Nebergall, 1965), and so has an occasional contemporary researcher (e.g., Judd & Kulik, 1980). However, the research we reviewed in Chapter 3 has shown that people on opposing sides of attitudinal issues may base their attitudes on quite different sets of beliefs. Moreover, proponents of a position on one side of an issue are often relatively unfamiliar with and indifferent to the views of people who hold an opposite attitudinal position. When only a person's own evaluation and the cognitions that support it are stored in long-term memory, a dimension locating this position at a particular point does not appropriately portray the person's psychological structure. More sensible is some form of propositional representation such as advocated by Fishbein and Ajzen (1975) as well as by theorists who have drawn upon the associative network tradition of cognitive psychology (e.g., Fazio, 1986; Ostrom, 1987, 1988). Yet with social activism and increasing expertise on an issue, people no doubt do represent opposing views along with their own views, and, under such circumstances, dimensional representations of attitudes are quite plausible. In the heat of an election campaign, for example, politically knowledgeable Democrats and Republicans do become aware of opposing positions on critical issues debated in the campaign and thus probably represent each other's stands as well as their own.

Most research on attitude structure has pertained to the structure of the beliefs that accompany attitudes. Substantial bodies of research have demonstrated the importance of certain structural features of these beliefs. For example, the beliefs held in relation to an attitude object can be relatively simple or relatively complex when complexity is defined in terms of the dimensionality of beliefs (e.g., Linville, 1982). Beliefs attached to an attitude object can also vary in the relatively more complicated property of integrative complexity, which has been defined in terms of both dimensionality and integrative bonds between beliefs (e.g., Tetlock, 1989). Another well-known structural variable assesses the evaluative consistency between people's overall attitudes and the beliefs associated with their attitudes (e.g., M. J. Rosenberg, 1956). Also of interest as a structural property of beliefs is their ambivalence, typically defined in this context as the extent to which people hold both favorable and unfavorable beliefs about an attitude object (e.g., Katz & Hass, 1988).

As demonstrated by research reviewed in Chapter 3 and elsewhere in this book, these and other structural properties of the beliefs associated with attitudes have important implications for the functioning of attitudes—in particular, for their relation to behavior and their resistance to change. To understand these implications more thoroughly, it is critical to evolve more detailed analyses of the circumstances under which attitudes are represented in bipolar schemas, unipolar schemas, or possibly other forms. Moreover, as we have shown especially in Chapter 12, attitude structure affects the processing of attitudinally relevant information. Knowledge of how attitudes are represented should foster more exact understanding of the selective effects that attitudes have at various stages of information processing.

In terms of the structural variables we considered, the construct of *cognitive consistency* takes on new and more interesting meaning. Consistency and inconsistency can exist in many aspects of attitude structure—for example, between evaluation and beliefs, between evaluation and affect, and between evaluation and behaviors. In addition, responses within or between any of these classes can be consistent or inconsistent with one another (i.e., ambivalent when some responses are positive and some are negative). Sorting out the implications of various types of consistency and inconsistency will no doubt continue to occupy attitude researchers and should renew interest in the cognitive consistency themes that dominated attitude research in the 1950s and 1960s (see Abelson, Aronson, McGuire, Newcomb, Rosenberg, & Tannenbaum, 1968).

One very general structural property that has come under repeated consideration in this book is the strength of attitudes. Although in contemporary work this property has sometimes been treated as the strength of the associative link between an attitude object node and an evaluation node (e.g., Fazio, 1989), at various points in this book we have indicated that strength can be coordinated to a variety of attitudinal variables. Indeed, researchers have advanced some strength variables that coordinate to various types of cognitive structural arrangements (e.g., evaluative-cognitive consistency, cognitive embeddedness, value centrality) and other strength variables that coordinate to various motivational states (e.g., ego-involvement, importance, personal relevance, commitment). Although from some perspectives it may be possible to place all these variables under a single rubric, we believe that this family of variables needs to be scrutinized more carefully, both theoretically and empirically, before such a conclusion can be drawn with confidence. Disentangling the various meanings of attitude strength is a prerequisite for obtaining a more comprehensive theory of the effects that attitude-strength variables have been shown to have on attitudinal selectivity, change and resistance to change, and behavior. Investigating convergences and divergences between various attitudinal properties that have been interpreted in terms of strength is a critical task for contemporary research.

The broader structural issues addressed in this book pertain to relations between attitudes, which we have named *inter-attitudinal structure*. Balance theory, which has often been applied to represent perceivers' links between attitudes toward people and attitudes toward nonperson entities, provides the most enduring perspective for systematically examining this aspect of structure. Of course, balance theory has been applied as a model of intra-attitudinal structure as well—for example, as a model of the relations between beliefs associated with a single attitude object. In general, balance research has been thoughtful and cumulative, and the commonality between the representational language of balance theory and the associative network ideas borrowed from cognitive psychology has begun to be recognized.

669

Much of the interest in inter-attitudinal structure is focused on the idea that people often place their attitudes within broader ideologies, which are general principles or themes that provide overarching organization for sets of attitudes. Citizens of the United States, for example, may have ideologies about politics, about race, and about the workings of their country's stratification system. They may derive their attitudes toward specific policies from the more general principles of their ideologies. Values, interpreted as attitudes toward general and quite abstract goals or end states of human existence, appear to be among the principles or themes that provide this broader organization for sets of attitudes. Values and other ideological themes may underlie the attitudes that social scientists have labeled symbolic and contrasted with attitudes presumably based on self-interest. Discerning the extent to which attitudes have broad, thematic organization based on values and ideology and delineating the specific themes that govern this organization are prerequisites for understanding the implications that attitudes have for political phenomena.

Attitude-Behavior Relation

Exploring the attitude-behavior relation and delineating the circumstances under which attitudes exert a causal impact on behavior has been a principal focus of attitude research in the modern period. Indeed, one of the major accusations during social psychology's crisis period was the claim that attitudes do not even predict behavior, let alone cause behavior. In response to this accusation, Fishbein and Ajzen's (1974; Ajzen & Fishbein, 1977) compatibility (or correspondence) analysis was an important contribution. Most social scientists now understand at least the most simple and obvious implication of this analysis—that one way to produce relatively high correlations between a general attitude and behavior is to design a multiple-act criterion that aggregates acts over an appropriate sample of behaviors, contexts, and occasions.

That attitudes cause behavior is one possible reason why attitudes are often correlated with behaviors. Theories with causal pretensions place attitude in a sequence of psychological processes that determine behavior; Fishbein and Ajzen's (1975) theory of reasoned action provides the best-known model of this type. Although this much-discussed and much-criticized theory can no longer be regarded as a fully adequate model of attitude-behavior relations, its seminal role in developing a formal model of attitudes' causal relation to behavior must be acknowledged. Moreover, the special features of this model, such as the importance it accords to intentions and to behavioral beliefs, drew psychologists' attention to many of the complexities inherent in predicting behavior from attitudes. Much contemporay theorizing about the attitude-behavior relation has built upon and modified the theory of reasoned action. In developing these newer theories, researchers are beginning to shoulder the burden of predicting, not only simple and relatively easily executed behaviors that are under one's own control, but also more complex behaviors and behavioral outcomes that require planning, arranging for resources, and obtaining the cooperation of other people. With guidance from theories that consider planning and goal-oriented behavior, investigators should no longer have to confine themselves to examining the relatively simple, easily executed, and controllable behaviors that have predominated in attitude-behavior research (e.g., voting, attending class, giving blood, purchasing inexpensive consumer products, engaging in laboratory tasks).

Also needed in work on the attitude-behavior relation is a fuller understanding of a causal sequence that takes into account both attitudes toward behaviors and attitudes toward the entities or targets toward which behaviors are directed. Although attitudes toward targets may often come to mind automatically in the presence of attitude-relevant stimuli (Fazio, 1986), such an attitude does not, in and of itself, prescribe any particular behavior. For example, one's attitude toward the politicians who tried to protect insolvent savings and loan institutions may come to mind in the presence of a TV news spot on the savings and loan crisis, but this attitude does not prescribe any particular behavior, such as writing to one's congressional representative to urge vigorous prosecution of these politicians. To decide on any particular course of action, a positive attitude must form toward this act. Moreover, attitudes toward targets and attitudes toward behaviors must be coordinated with other psychological tendencies that regulate behavior (e.g., habits, self-identity, norms). In Chapter 4 we sketched a model that takes these various determinants of behavior into account. Once broader models of this type have been more fully examined and tested, social psychologists will have made a fundamental contribution to the essential endeavor of all psychologists—understanding the causes of behavior.

Attitude Change

To anyone familiar with attitude research, it is hardly surprising that we have devoted much of this book to attitude formation and change. Both theorists and researchers of attitudes have devoted the greatest amount of their collective efforts over the years to studying the dynamic processes by which attitudes change and are initially formed. Therefore, theories of change come in many variants.

The prior chapters of this book contain extensive discussion of four families of attitude-change theory: theories about (a) relatively simple affective processes, (b) persuasion, (c) the impact of one's own behavior, and (d) social influence. Each set of theories is associated with a distinctive experimental paradigm: (a) the presentation of simple stimuli over trials, (b) the presentation of a message containing complex arguments favoring a moderately counterattitudinal position, (c) the induction of counterattitudinal behavior, and (d) influence from simple messages presented by other people who are present in a small group setting. Reflecting on the initial findings produced within these experimental paradigms, social psychologists began to develop theories of attitude change several decades ago.

Although each family of theories has grown across the generations (some prospering more than others), they have led strikingly separate lives, as if each lived in a somewhat isolated village and was not bound with the others in a larger community. Both researchers and theorists have for the most part focused on somewhat limited phenomena, and, as a consequence, theories of attitude change have not developed a common body of integrative theory. Despite this relative separateness of these four traditions of attitude-change theory, common themes pertaining to mediational processes have surfaced repeatedly in these diverse literatures, perhaps because of the more general intellectual context shared by the approaches. We have often drawn these shared themes to readers' attention and have noted the parallel issues that developed across these four traditions. We now comment on each of these traditions.

Simple Affective Processes. Although research on attitude formation and change has been dominated by cognitive theory in the contemporary period, an important earlier tradition considered several relatively simple processes that may underlie the formation and change of attitudes. These mechanisms, which were considered to be largely affective in nature, have been investigated primarily within three research paradigms: operant conditioning, classical conditioning, and mere exposure. In operant conditioning experiments, subjects are asked questions about their attitudes by an interviewer who "reinforces" favorable or unfavorable attitudinal responses by his or her verbal or nonverbal reactions to the subjects' responses (e.g., Insko, 1965). In this paradigm, subjects' attitudinal responses have been shown to become more positive or more negative, depending on whether the interviewer's behavior reinforces favorable or unfavorable attitudinal responding. In classical conditioning experiments, initially neutral stimuli are paired repeatedly with other objects or events that reliably elicit positive or negative responses from subjects (A. W. Staats & Staats, 1958). In such experiments, subjects' attitudes toward the initially neutral stimuli typically become more positive after repeated positive pairings and more negative after repeated negative pairings. In mere exposure experiments, subjects are exposed to novel stimuli, and the frequency with which these stimuli are presented varies so that some stimuli are presented much more often than others (Zajonc, 1968a). Subjects' subsequent attitudes toward the stimuli are typically more positive to the extent that the stimuli have been frequently presented.

Within each of these paradigms, the basic phenomenon is thoroughly replicable: If one of the seminal experiments in the paradigm is replicated exactly, similar results are obtained. Nonetheless, the generality of each of these phenomena has been probed, and research has identified conditions under which the basic effect is and is not obtained. Despite these demonstrations, each paradigm seems to have sufficient generality that identification of moderating conditions ceased to be a central research issue. Instead, the critical issue that evolved in each of these paradigms concerned the psychological mediation of these effects. The mediational issue has taken the form of an affective versus cognitive debate, that is, whether the phenomena demonstrated in these experiments should be attributed to simple affective mechanisms, regarded as relatively automatic and nonconscious by their proponents, or to more complex, deliberative cognitive processes. In our view, the higher-order cognitive reinterpretations of what were originally proposed in each case as essentially affective mechanisms have not been entirely persuasive, although they seemed at one point to have gained considerable credence among psychologists. We thus maintained in Chapter 9 that relatively simple processes that are largely affective can provide plausible explanations for the phenomena of conditioning and mere exposure.

The lively debates surrounding these mediational issues have been instructive and in recent years have raised basic concerns about the meaning of the terms cognitive and affective. To the extent that these terms have not allowed researchers to make precise distinctions between cognitive and affective phenomena, the arguments between advocates of affective and cognitive views have been misplaced. Most notably, this controversy becomes murky when we take into account the fact that cognitive mechanisms can be relatively simple and nonconscious and at this level are difficult to distinguish from mechanisms that some psychologists would prefer to label as affective (see Bargh, 1989). Moreover, consistent with the synergistic view of attitudes we have advocated in this book, affect and cognition interact and have joint impact on people's evaluations of stimuli. From this perspective, an affectively based attitude would quickly influence cognition, and it would therefore be difficult to rule out cognitive involvement from what might originally have been an affective phenomenon.

Persuasion. Following the lead of the early Yale research group (Hovland, Janis, & Kelley, 1953), the process theories of attitude change that we considered at length in Chapters 6, 7, and 8 are the perspectives that have been regarded as more or less synonymous with attitude-change research in social psychology. Most of these theories were explicitly developed as models of persuasion and were applied to situations in which experimental subjects receive a relatively complex verbal message, which is typically moderately counterattitudinal and presented by a communicator, generally in a laboratory setting.

Some of these theories considered what we have termed *systematic processing*. In the persuasion context, such theories have emphasized the importance of message recipients' detailed processing of message content. In this category we considered McGuire's (e.g., 1972) information-processing paradigm, with its heritage in Hovland et al.'s (1953) suggestion that the impact of persuasive communications can be understood in terms of a sequence of processes—attention to the message, comprehension of its content, and acceptance of its conclusions. From this perspective, reception of message content should facilitate persuasion, at least under the ordinary circumstances in which the message contains cogent persuasive arguments. Yet empirical findings on the relation between message reception and persuasion have been mixed. Unfortunately, this mix of findings led many persuasion researchers to reject McGuire's reception-yielding theory prematurely, without either careful analysis of the theory's predictions or thoughtful consideration of the methodological barriers to testing the theory adequately in typical laboratory settings. Consequently numerous neglected research possibilities exist in this area.

We also considered the cognitive response model initially proposed by Greenwald (1968) and developed by several social psychologists (see Petty, Ostrom, & Brock, 1981). This perspective reflects the general proposition that people's attitudes are a function of the cognitions that they generate about the objects of their attitudes. This idea is very basic to attitude theory (see Chapter 1) and has received expression in other attitude research—for example, in Janis's (1968) work on biased scanning as a mediator of role-playing effects (see Chapter 11) and Tesser's (1978) research on the

673

self-generated origins of the attitude polarization often produced by mere thought about an attitude object (see Chapter 12). Yet the best-known manifestation of the proposition that people construct their attitudes from the thoughts that come to mind is the cognitive-response model of the impact of persuasive messages. This approach thus emphasizes the mediating role of the idiosyncratic thoughts or "cognitive responses" that recipients generate as they receive and reflect upon persuasive communications. Messages that evoke predominantly favorable thoughts should be persuasive, whereas messages that evoke predominantly unfavorable thoughts should be unpersuasive.

The cognitive-response perspective produced numerous persuasion experiments, each of which manipulated a variable that impacted on extent of message processing (e.g., distraction, message repetition, issue involvement) and crossed this variable with a single other variable—argument quality, which reliably affects the valence of message-relevant thoughts. The general pattern of findings in these cognitive-response experiments is well known: Valence of recipients' thoughts (as controlled by argument quality) determines persuasion only to the extent that recipients process the message relatively thoroughly and therefore react to the quality of the arguments. Although quite a few persuasion variables have been investigated within this framework, the theory nonetheless appears to be relevant mainly to those variables that are clearly related to message recipients' abilities or motivation to engage in message-relevant thinking. Yet this general analysis could be applied beyond the persuasion context—for example, to examine impression formation and other judgmental phenomena.

In the 1980s, persuasion theories have taken on a broader mission than the systematic processing theories did. Whereas the systematic theories had emphasized message reception and cognitive elaboration of persuasive argumentation, the newer theories consider in addition the idea that people adopt attitudes on bases other than their understanding and evaluation of the semantic content of persuasive argumentation. We thus featured the elaboration likelihood model (Petty & Cacioppo, 1986a, 1986b), which incorporates a peripheral route to persuasion, and the heuristic-systematic model (Chaiken, 1980, 1987), which considers simple decision rules or heuristics that mediate persuasion. These theories emphasize modes of processing and trade at least in part on the depth-of-processing idea borrowed from cognitive psychology. Also important to these theories is the *cognitive miser* theme (see Fiske & Taylor, 1991) that developed at about the same time in social cognition research on impression formation, decision making, hypothesis testing, and social prediction. Following the general notion that people process information superficially and minimally unless they are motivated to do otherwise, these attitude theories thus stress that people must have sufficient motivation to turn to more effortful, systematic forms of processing. They must also have the capacity to engage in this more deliberative form of processing, which in a persuasion context entails careful evaluation of the argumentation contained in messages.

Unfortunately ideas about heuristic and systematic processing have often been oversimplified, especially in textbook presentations, with the result that modes of processing are reduced to two alternatives, one "easy" and the other "effortful," which exist in a simple, trade-off relation. Discussions of modes of processing need to

674

acknowledge the multiplicity of modes available to message recipients and to recognize that these modes can coexist and interact with one another. For example, attribution theory advances a mode of processing persuasive messages that is neither extremely easy nor extremely effortful and that can coexist and interact with the systematic processing of message content and no doubt with the use of heuristic decision rules as well. Indeed, heuristic and systematic processing can coexist and interact, and such possibilities have been made explicit in the heuristic-systematic model (e.g., Chaiken, Liberman, & Eagly, 1989).

Finally, social judgment theory provides yet another perspective on some of the processes that may underlie persuasion (e.g., C. W. Sherif et al., 1965). Unique among persuasion theories, it draws attention to the message recipient's prior attitude and the relation of this attitude to the attitudinal position advocated in the message. If the distance between the prior attitude and the message's position is considerable, recipients may contrast the message by viewing it as more distant from their own position, judge that the message is propagandistic and unfair, and therefore not be influenced by it. Social judgment theorists also emphasized the construct of ego-involvement. This variable, which is quite different from the subsequently popular concept of issue involvement (or personal relevance), was construed as a motivational variable that produces resistance to attitude change. The role of ego-involvement and recipients' prior attitudes (and the discrepancy between the message and these attitudes) has been neglected in contemporary persuasion research, but these variables deserve more careful examination with modern methods that allow relatively detailed evaluation of the processes that underlie change and resistance to change.

In persuasion research, motivational processes have also been proposed as possible mediators of persuasion, but have never received as much emphasis as cognitive processes. In relation to motivation, the incentive and drive-reduction views of Hovland and his associates (1953) are historically important. Particularly in the early work on fear appeals carried out by these researchers, basic issues were raised about how motivational states influence information processing and persuasion. From this provocative beginning, several theories of the impact of fear on message persuasiveness evolved (Janis, 1967; Leventhal, 1970; Rogers, 1975, 1983; S. R. Sutton, 1982). Although no one of these theories provides a convincing integration of the now-large empirical literature on fear appeals, they delineate several possible forms of psychological mediation, and each offers worthwhile insights about the persuasiveness of threat-provoking appeals. Research on fear appeals as well as on mood and persuasion (Mackie & Worth, 1991; Schwarz, Bless, & Bohner, 1991), provides an excellent opportunity for developing a better understanding of the interplay between motivational and cognitive processes in persuasion settings. Moreover, much of this work has proven compatible with the newer theories of persuasion that emphasize multiple modes of processing information (e.g., Chaiken et al., 1989; Petty & Cacioppo, 1986a, 1986b).

Although most theories of persuasion provide verbal descriptions of particular mechanisms or processes involved in changing attitudes, we also reviewed theories that provide a mathematical description of how people combine or integrate the various cues that are available to them. These combinatorial theories have the capacity to provide precise descriptions of the rules that people use in integrating items of information to form attitudes. As we indicated in Chapters 3 and 5, these theories have many applications. They provide models of attitude structure because they specify a relation between attitudes toward an attitude object and the evaluative beliefs that may contribute to these attitudes. Yet one of their most common uses in attitude research is as models of persuasion. Thus, combinatorial theories detail possible relations between new information, prior attitudes, and changed attitudes. In contrast to most of the other theories that have been applied to persuasion, they do not elaborate the cognitive processes that underlie attitude change. Nor do they provide an explicit account of the impact that distal attitude-change variables (e.g., source, context, recipient variables) have on attitude change.

The generality of combinatorial models makes it difficult to know *a priori* how they might apply to specific problems of attitude change. For example, the models might imply a systematic approach to processing information in a persuasion setting, with message recipients averaging the various informational items in a persuasive message. However, there is no barrier to representing recipients' use of heuristic cues via combinatorial models. The difficulty is that the models give us no guidance concerning the information that recipients are likely to use under given conditions in informationally complex situations. Combinatorial theories thus provide only a partial description of attitude change and need to be coordinated to other types of theories that consider processes in a more explicit way and consequently provide wider-ranging predictions about attitude change. Because of some of these problems, combinatorial theories have attracted somewhat less interest in the last decade. Nonetheless, they have played an important role in describing how beliefs and other constituents of attitudes may be combined to affect overall evaluations.

Impact of Behavior on Attitude Formation and Change. The fact that an attitude may be changed by engaging in a behavior that has implications for the attitude attracted a great deal of research attention in the 1950s and 1960s, and there has been a moderate amount of continuing research in this area. Most studies have concerned counter-attitudinal advocacy, the endorsing of a position inconsistent with one's attitude, although proattitudinal advocacy, the endorsing of a position consistent with one's attitude, has received some attention as well. In the early phase of this research, Hovland et al. (1953) studied the effects that role-playing experiences have on people's attitudes and beliefs. In the well-known Janis and King (1954) experiment, for example, students' responses to a message that they themselves had delivered (or role-played) were compared with their responses to messages delivered by other students. These subjects were more persuaded when they had delivered a message themselves rather than merely listened to another subject deliver a message. This and other early demonstrations of the power of self-persuasion convinced social psychologists that such techniques could be quite effective in changing attitudes. Over the years, little controversy has surrounded the basic idea that one's own behavior can have considerable impact on one's attitude. Rather, controversy concerns the correct description of the psychological processes by which behavior impacts on attitudes.

Festinger's (1957) dissonance theory and Janis's (1968; Hovland et al., 1953) incentive theory were the early contenders for explaining the attitudinal effects of counterattitudinal advocacy. Dissonance theory quickly became the better-known of these theories, no doubt because of its greater simplicity and generality. With Festinger's charismatic leadership and the energies of talented associates, dissonance theory provided a framework within which extensive research was carried out on counterattitudinal advocacy, beginning with the early Festinger and Carlsmith (1959) experiment and continuing to the present. The dissonance interpretation of the psychology underlying the effects of counterattitudinal advocacy evolved over a period of years in response to the accumulating research findings. Although the state of arousal known as cognitive dissonance and the attitude change that was thought to result from this state of arousal were originally viewed as consequences of an inconsistency between an attitude and a behavior, the most viable interpretation now appears to be that dissonance and attitude change follow from taking responsibility for bringing about an unwanted consequence (J. Cooper & Fazio, 1984). This empirical generalization encompasses the great majority of the complex and contingent attitude-change findings produced by experiments on counterattitudinal advocacy.

The unwanted consequences principle is congenial to theories of behavior-attitude relations that emphasize self-identify and self-concept (Aronson, 1969; Kelman & Baron, 1974; Schlenker, 1982; Tedeschi & Rosenfeld, 1981). Self interpretations of the impact of one's own behavior move beyond the empirical generalization about taking responsibility for undesirable consequences. Self theories help delineate the types of consequences that are ordinarily unwanted and the reasons that these unwanted consequences are motivating. The various perspectives differ in their emphasis on the public and private aspects of the self, and we agree with Schlenker's (1982) view that dissonance has sources in both public self-presentation and private self-awareness. In the coming era, research on dissonance and attitude change could gain theoretical and empirical breadth by becoming better integrated with other work on the self (e.g., Higgins & Bargh, 1987; Markus & Wurf, 1987). It is also important to cast attitude change as one of many inconsistency-reducing responses that can help preserve the integrity of the self. Although this insight was, at least in retrospect, evident to some degree in Festinger's (1957, 1964b) writing, it has been reintroduced by Steele (1988), who has shown that integrity-restoring responses may be quite unrelated to the event that threatened self-esteem.

Another instructive component of the debates on why behavior impacts on attitudes was Bem's (1972) self-perception theory, which proposed that changes of attitude reflect, not the motivationally driven process described by Festinger (1957), but a cool interpretive process of explaining why one has engaged in a behavior. According to Bem, when counterattitudinal behavior occurs in the presence of a strong inducing force, no attitude change occurs because the actor infers that the behavior reflects the inducing force, not his underlying attitude. When counterattitudinal behavior occurs in the absence of such a force, attitude change reflects the actor's inference that his behavior must follow from an underlying attitude that is congruent with the behavior. This self-perception interpretation of the effects of counterattitudinal advocacy does not now appear viable, in part because dissonance researchers established that arousal is a prerequisite for obtaining attitude change in the Festinger and Carlsmith (1959) paradigm. However, the self-perception process that Bem described may account for people's attitudes under more limited circumstances, that is, when they form their initial attitudes or when their prior attitudes are weak. Then, superficial as such an inference may seem, people evidently do draw the conclusion that their attitudes are consistent with the attitudinal implications of their recent behavior.

Missing from the various theories of the impact of behavior on attitudes is any more than a rudimentary consideration of the cognitive processes that mediate the attitudinal effects documented in research on counterattitudinal advocacy. In contrast to the strongly cognitive flavor of most recent work on persuasion, the tradition in research on the behavior-attitude relation gives considerably more attention to motivation than cognition, despite Janis's (1968) early emphasis on cognitive mediation via biased scanning and despite the importance of cognitive themes in much of the seminal work on cognitive consistency (e.g., Abelson, 1959; Heider, 1958; M.J. Rosenberg & Abelson, 1960). Surely the efforts to develop relatively direct indicators of cognitive processing within persuasion and social cognition research provide important guidelines for future work on the effects of behavior on attitudes. In the light of these methodological advances, it would be worth taking a renewed look at Festinger's (1957, 1964b) brief descriptions of the cognitive mechanisms that he believed mediated the impact of cognitive dissonance on attitudes in other contexts (see Chapter 10).

Social Influence. Attitudes have sometimes been studied in a social context, particularly as ingredients of dyadic and small group social interaction. This tradition is a long and famous one in social psychology and stems from the well-known conformity studies of Muzafer Sherif (1935) and Solomon Asch (1951, 1956). Early in discussions of this conformity research, the conceptual distinction between normative and informational influence emerged as important. As defined by Deutsch and Gerard (1955), the critical distinction is between changing attitudes or behaviors to conform to other's expectations and changing them to conform to the evidence that others provide about the nature of reality. This distinction has been elaborated in various ways in theories of social influence and has proven very enduring as a conceptual rule for classifying the social psychological processes that account for the influence that people have on one another in group settings. The normative-informational partition has also been given voice in functional theory distinctions between attitudes' social-adjustive function and their object-appraisal or knowledge function (see Chapter 10).

One tradition that grew from the early conformity work consists of typologies based on qualitative distinctions between types of power or types of role relationships within which influence occurs. These typologies allow finer distinctions than the broad normative-informational dichotomy. Among frameworks of this genre, French and Raven's (1959) and Kelman's (1961) models have been particularly influential.

A second tradition of social psychological thinking about social influence has stemmed from group research. Consistent with the origins of social influence research in conformity experiments, a good deal of this research has been framed in terms of conformity (e.g., V.L. Allen & Wilder, 1980). In the contemporary period, conformity studies carried out in the group-pressure tradition of Asch and Sherif have focused on the cognitive mediation of conformity. In contrast to this conformity research, which typically has examined the effect of the majority on the individual subject, research on minority influence has examined the effect of numerical minorities on the majority of other group members (Moscovici, 1976). Although minorities have less influence than majorities, particularly on more overt or public measures of influence, their persuasive power is discernible. Given these findings, considerable debate has surrounded the cognitive mediation of both minority and majority influence as well as the claim that different processes underlie these two types of influence. Some of the interpretations popular in this domain (e.g., Moscovici, 1980, 1985) share important features with the dual-process models of persuasion that we considered in Chapter 7.

Other research has investigated group polarization, the tendency for the decisions and attitudinal positions that groups produce to be more extreme than those produced by their members acting alone. Once again, the debates among researchers in this area for the most part have not concerned the basic phenomenon but its psychological mediation, by predominantly normative or predominantly informational processes or some mix of these two types of processes.

Research on social influence, existing as it does within the interactional and group-oriented tradition of social psychology, has been relatively isolated from other research on attitudes during most of its history. Yet there is reason to predict that this isolation may lessen considerably. Especially relevant to the modern work on social influence is research on persuasion, which has a well developed cognitive tradition. In contrast, the theoretical tradition within social influence is richly developed in a motivational direction: People are influenced *in order to* make sense out of their world or to meet others' expectations, as suggested by the concepts of informational and normative influence. These and other concepts that elaborate the goal-oriented nature of thought could well inform persuasion theory and attitude theory more generally. Yet the motivational themes of social-influence theory are beginning to be seen more often in contemporary discussions of persuasion processes (e.g., Chaiken et al., 1989; B.T. Johnson & Eagly, 1989). Moreover, earlier theorizing about attitude change (e.g., Hovland et al., 1953) took into account motivational themes similar to those important in work on social influence.

Resistance and Persistence Processes

Relatively few attitude theories have resistance to attitude change as their primary focus, and systematic analysis of the persistence of changed attitudes over time is even rarer. Nonetheless, McGuire's (1964) inoculation model was explicitly formulated to predict resistance to persuasion, and several more general theories (e.g., reactance theory, functional theories, consistency theories) have important implications for attitudinal resistance and persistence. These theories have provided a variety of insights into the motivational and cognitive origins of resistance to change. From a motivational

679

standpoint, people resist influence because change is threatening to the self or to one's personal freedom or merely to the stability of important, self-defining attitudes. From a cognitive standpoint, people resist influence when an attitude is linked to other attitudes and beliefs, and change in the attitude would therefore destabilize a larger cognitive structure. In addition, the linkages of attitudes to other cognitions give people intellectual resources that allow them to scrutinize and ward off attacks on their attitudes. More generally, attitudes that are motivationally significant and that are linked to many other attitudes and beliefs can be considered *strong*. In both contemporary and more traditional theorizing about resistance to change, psychologists have argued that strong attitudes are difficult to change. Indeed, explaining why people are often so effective at resisting efforts to change their strong attitudes remains one of the core issues of attitude theory.

Highly relevant to understanding resistance processes is the large body of research on the impact of attitudes on information processing. Individuals resist influence through multiple cognitive processes that are biased in favor of their initial attitudes. By means of a variety of specific processes, people often screen out challenging information and shore up their strongly held attitudes. Such congeniality effects have different loci in cognitive processing and thus can take the form of selective exposure or attention, selective perception or judgment, or selective memory. Careful reading of the several research literatures on attitudinal selectivity suggests that congeniality trends are genuine, but part of a larger picture whereby information processing is selective in response to numerous other factors such as a preference for useful information and (sometimes) an advantage for attitudinally polarized information. Because of these competing effects, attitudinal selectivity should not be a uniformly strong tendency in research findings, and investigators should not expect such trends to emerge uncontaminated by other psychological tendencies.

The study of the persistence of changed attitudes has been elaborated primarily in two limited areas: in research on associative interference (e.g., Baumgardner, Leippe, Ronis, & Greenwald, 1983) and on the sleeper effect (e.g., Gruder et al., 1978). These two experimental paradigms have been built around specific cognitive hypotheses concerning interference effects in memory and the dissociation of various cues (e.g., the identity of the communicator) from memories of message content. Although numerous attitude theories that we have considered in this book have fairly clear implications for persistence, these implications remain untested or tested in only an occasional empirical study. This paucity of empirical work can be understood in large part because of the practical difficulties of extending studies beyond a single session and the consequent reluctance of researchers to complicate their research efforts by including delayed attitudinal measures. Due to this relative lack of an empirical base, attitude researchers can offer little in the way of firm generalizations about attitudinal persistence. Nonetheless, given the established importance of certain attitudinal variables (particularly attitude strength) and the knowledge of cognitive mechanisms already developed in the persuasion literature and elsewhere, progress in understanding attitudinal persistence should be forthcoming.

General Issues: *Some More Troubling than Others*

Serious Omissions and Limitations

Lack of Attention to the Developmental Issue of How Attitudes Are Formed and Become Strong. Implicit in our discussions of attitude strength (see Chapters 3, 4, and 12) is the idea that strength develops over time. Yet we have relatively little knowledge about the processes by which attitudes become strong. After attitudes are initially formed, they evidently go through some transition in terms of their structure in order to develop the characteristics ordinarily associated with strong attitudes. For example, they are more likely to be supported by beliefs and to elicit emotional responses. Weaker or newly formed attitudes are generally relatively unstable and open to change; their effect on information processing can be difficult to discern, and their relation to behavior is slight. In contrast, older attitudes, if they have become strong, are more stable and closed to change; they have a more pronounced effect on information processing and a stronger relation to behavior. These and other consequences of attitude strength have been well documented in research, but the antecedents of strong attitudes and the processes by which strength develops are less certain. Surely, as Fazio (1986) has argued, repeated attitudinal responding strengthens an attitude. However, such responding does not occur in a vacuum in natural settings, and the context in which people respond would be critical. For example, in social interactions in which people state their attitudes, they often receive new information, including approval and disapproval from significant others.

The weakness of our knowledge about how attitudes become strong is at least in part a manifestation of the limitations of laboratory experimentation. The sort of emotion-arousing, value-linked, behavior-impelling attitudes that are extremely important in natural settings cannot be grown in the laboratory in a single experimental session. The attitudes that drive social movements and incite riots and wars can be measured among committed partisans and other citizens, but this type of survey research does not ordinarily allow scrutiny of the processes by which attitudes have become strong. Yet survey research offers some unique opportunities for studying attitude strength. For example, comparisons of the attitudes of younger and older respondents are informative to the extent that age serves as an inexact proxy for the strength of many social attitudes (see Krosnick & Alwin, 1989; Sears, 1981, 1986).

Naturalistic studies carried out in settings in which people develop strong attitudes are badly needed to understand how attitudes crystallize and become strong. The precedent of Newcomb's well-known (1943) Bennington study is highly instructive. During their four-year stay at Bennington College, most of the students who took part in this research became more committed to the liberal political attitudes that were prevalent at this institution. In addition, sociologists have used participant-observer techniques to examine the development of religious attitudes and beliefs (e.g., Lofland, 1977), and psychologists and other social scientists have examined the formation of political attitudes in children (Easton & Dennis, 1969; Hess & Torney, 1967). Although much of this sociological and developmental work is embedded in theoretical traditions quite different from those considered in this book, the methods these researchers have used are instructive. By examining the development of attitudes over time in natural settings, investigators could evolve a natural history of attitude development that would allow the antecedents of strong attitudes to be recognized.

Insufficient Consideration of the Social Context of Attitudes. Given that most work on attitudes has been accomplished by social psychologists and that other researchers contributing to this area are social scientists in allied fields (e.g., communications, sociology, political science, marketing), an outside observer not acquainted with this field of study would probably expect that one aspect of attitudes that would be carefully conceptualized is the social context within which attitudes exist. People form and change their attitudes as they interact, both directly and indirectly, with other people. To live up to their name as *social* psychologists and *social* scientists, surely researchers would stress this social aspect of attitudes in their theories and probe it in empirical studies. Yet in reading theory and research on attitudes, our mythical outside observer would be surprised to find little emphasis on the structure of the social environment relative to the considerable emphasis on psychological structure and processes, especially of the cognitive variety. It would thus be evident that this work was carried out primarily by psychologists, but not by ones that seem to have made their primary investment in analyzing the interplay between social and psychological factors.

Of course there are exceptions to the tendency for attitude researchers to neglect the social environment. For example, we have repeatedly acknowledged the concept of normative influence. Fishbein and Ajzen (1975) included a normative term, representing others' expectations, in their influential theory of reasoned action. Others' expectations are also critical to impression management models, which have as their guiding principle a motive to maintain a favorable public image vis-à-vis the audience for one's attitudes. Impression management theorizing has been important in research on both resistance to change (Baer, Hinkle, Smith, & Fenton, 1980) and the effects of counterattitudinal advocacy (Tedeschi & Rosenfeld, 1981). This theme has once more been invoked in the concept of impression-relevant involvement, a motivational state induced when people expect that their attitudes will be made known to an evaluative audience (B. T. Johnson & Eagly, 1989; Leippe & Elkin, 1987). Similar are the concepts of impression motivation (Chaiken et al., 1989) and social-adjustive function (M. B. Smith, Bruner, & White, 1956).

What is missing from these efforts to take attitudes' social context into account? However useful the ideas we have just named, they rely on a distinctively psychological conception of the social environment. Thus, the social context is rendered as a set of stimuli (i.e., social pressures, others' expectations) or as a motive that guides individual psychology (e.g., a desire to project a positive self-image). Little attention is given to conceptualizing the structure of the social environment in terms of norms and roles that govern interaction. To understand the particular rules and norms that are relevant to various settings, psychologists would have to move beyond treating the social environment merely as stimuli and represent variation in the rules that govern social interaction. As these rules change, so do the psychological principles that govern attitude formation and change.

For developing attitudinal analyses that take the structure of social settings into account, research on social influence, which we reviewed in Chapter 13, provides some useful models. Noteworthy are the typologies of social influence, which delineated forms of social power or of role relationships that bind influencing agents and targets together. In particular, Kelman's (1958, 1961) typology of three processes of influence provides a paradigm worthy of close scrutiny. A central postulate of this theory is that the type of psychological processes that mediate influence depend on the role relationship within which influence occurs. Kelman argued, for example, that in the credibility-salient relationship described in his *internalization* model, communicator characteristics affect persuasion through their impact on issue-relevant thinking. In the attractiveness-salient relationship described in his *identification* model, communicator characteristics affect persuasion without issue-related mediation and through the mediation of beliefs about one's relationship to the communicator. These hypotheses would not have been formulated had Kelman conceptualized communicator characteristics merely as *stimuli* or *cues* rather than as features embedded in certain types of role relationships linking a communicator and a recipient of influence. Whatever the merit of Kelman's particular suggestions, the general point of this approach, that the dynamics of role relationships constrain psychological process, is a lesson that warrants pondering.

Other researchers have described particular types of role relationships and proposed forms of processing that occur within these relationships. Milgram's (1974) obedience model specified a type of hierarchical role relationship in which an individual assigns responsibility for his acts to the person who is "in charge" in the situation. Although Milgram did not provide much elaboration of the thought processes that occur in such a situation, we suggest that his obedient subjects did not evaluate the consequences of their actions in what might be considered the ordinary, rational fashion. Also relevant is Higgins' (1981) "communication game" analysis, which advanced the view that certain rules govern interaction in which people communicate their views to one another. Examples of these rules are that "communicators should take the audience's or recipient's characteristics into account," "communicators should convey the truth as they see it," and "recipients should try to understand the message." According to Higgins, violations of these and other rules of the communication game can damage the persuasiveness of messages (e.g., Ratneshwar & Chaiken, 1991). For example, if a communicator is thought not to convey the truth as she sees it, her credibility is seriously compromised. Moreover, communicators and recipients who operate successfully within the rules of the communication game are motivated to establish or maintain a social bond and to establish a consensus about the nature of social reality. Such goals lead recipients and communicators to modify their attitudes to establish greater agreement. Also relevant are the efforts of scholars in the communication field to delineate many of the rules and regularities of communicative behavior (Donohue, Cushman, & Nofsinger, 1980; Pearce et al., 1980; M.J. Smith, 1984). In social psychological and communication analyses based on rules and roles, attitude formation

683

and change are assumed to proceed differently, depending on the rules that govern communicative exchanges, the role relationship within which communication occurs, and the ability and willingness of role occupants to interact within the rules that govern that relationship.

The fact that attitudes are often formed and changed within larger groups as well as within dyadic relationships raises the multifaceted issue of how group processes are best conceptualized and attitudinal processes taken into account within such an analysis. Despite the considerable progress within the three group research paradigms we reviewed in Chapter 13 (conformity, minority influence, group polarization), this research seems only to have scratched the surface of understanding the powerful pressures on people's attitudes and behaviors within interacting groups. Practitioners interested in changing behaviors in natural settings do acknowledge the critical importance of reference groups and identification within the primary groups where people spend much of their time. For example, AIDS researchers have found that the social structure of primary risk groups of gay men and intravenous drug users is a feature that can prevent or facilitate behavior change (see O'Keeffe, Nesselhof-Kendall, & Baum, 1990). To induce people in at-risk populations to adopt AIDS-preventive behaviors, these behaviors must be perceived as consistent with the norms of these individuals' most influential reference groups. Although this general theme is a very old one in social psychology (e.g., Brodbeck, 1956; Festinger, 1950), it has not received much attention in the contemporary period.

Also of potential importance is the subgrouping that occurs within social groups. Despite the widespread interest in social identity and intergroup relations (Tajfel, 1981; van Knippenberg & Ellemers, 1990) as well as in the impact of societal status on group processes (e.g., Berger, Rosenholtz, & Zelditch, 1980; Berger & Zelditch, 1985), this work has yet to be fully integrated with the themes of attitude theory.

Constraints Inherent in Laboratory Experimentation. The relative lack of concentration on the social context of attitudes stems at least in part from the overreliance of researchers on a single social setting, the psychological laboratory. Over 30 years ago, Carl Hovland (1959) provided a substantial discussion of the relative advantages of laboratory and field methods for attitude research. Despite his sage advice about the benefits to be gained from a balance between field and laboratory research, laboratory methods have continued to be the overwhelmingly popular choice for research on the psychology of attitudes. The reasons for this preference are too obvious to warrant lengthy discussion. The practical advantages of the laboratory are many, including low-cost subjects who are ordinarily adept and willing research participants. In addition, laboratory settings offer possibilities for relatively precise control of stimulus conditions as well as multiple possibilities for the efficient administration of measuring instruments. With the brass instruments era of psychological experimentation having long ago given way to the electronic age, a wide range of attitude-relevant responses can be closely monitored in the laboratory via computerized equipment (see Blascovich & Kelsey, 1990; Fazio, 1990b).

Laboratory settings, however, pose numerous issues of ecological validity. For example, it is difficult to assign subjects to the various role relationships where social interaction most commonly transpires in daily life. Although attitudinal processes are generally embedded in long-term work and family relationships, they are embedded in fleeting relationships with strangers in the laboratory. The presentation of these strangers by written documents, audio recordings, and video displays only increases the remoteness of these relationships in such experiments. Moreover, subjects' responses, which were traditionally given on questionnaires, are now frequently given by typing them on a computer keyboard. These remote and highly structured interactions that subjects have with standardized stimuli in electronic environments may have little to do with the stuff of everyday life. Can we be surprised that the social context rarely finds its way into attitude theory if this larger context is highly impoverished and artificially invariant in the great majority of our research settings?

The typical laboratory setting also makes it difficult to study certain types of psychological processes that are probably very important in natural settings. For example, in Chapter 6, we noted attitude researchers' failure to acknowledge and investigate the attentional processes that constrain persuasion in natural settings. Whereas advertisers seem to work hard merely to capture consumers' attention for their products, most contemporary theories of persuasion give relatively little emphasis to reception as a determinant of the impact of persuasion cues on attitude change. Surely overreliance on the laboratory is once more part of the problem. Most often laboratory subjects are constrained by an implicit demand that they "do their job" by paying attention to the materials that they are given and dutifully processing them on a relatively systematic basis. By fulfilling this obligation, laboratory subjects ensure that attentional and reception processes operate at a relatively constant, high level. The importance of these processes is consequently underestimated, and the importance of effortful, elaborative processing of message content is overestimated.

Another limiting feature of laboratory settings is that they tend to constrain subjects' motivation to the validity- and accuracy-seeking motives that have implicitly been assumed in most attitude theories, especially in theories of persuasion (see Chapters 6, 7, and 8). In a typical attitude-change or attitude-formation experiment, for example, subjects receive certain types of information or engage in certain behaviors and are then asked to indicate their attitudes. In this respect the experimental laboratory, especially with students serving as subjects, is not unlike a classroom setting (in fact, the locale for many questionnaire studies is a university classroom). Under surveillance in a laboratory, subjects are no doubt motivated to come up with the best, most valid attitude, in view of the information that they have in hand.

Motives other than validity-seeking would be less important in the artificial social setting of the laboratory. For example, impression motivation would become important only to the extent that subjects have a meaningful audience for their attitudes. Sometimes the experimenter, a confederate, or other subjects can provide this audience, but often the audience is only the somewhat vaguely defined research team who views the responses at some later date, presumably after the removal of all information that

685

would identify the subject as an individual. It is unlikely that subjects become very concerned about making a good impression if they view themselves only as constituents of group means that will be computed at some later point. Nor would they be as concerned with defending their prior attitudes as they would be in long-term relationships in which yielding may reduce their power vis-à-vis a role partner. Thus, defense motivation may also be somewhat difficult to engage in laboratory settings (Chaiken et al., 1989).

Sears (1986) has analyzed many of these same issues in terms of the difficulties that stem from studying "college sophomores" in laboratory settings. Sears surveyed the 1980 volumes of three major journals in which research on the psychology of attitudes is published (*Journal of Personality and Social Psychology*, *Journal of Experimental Social Psychology*, *Personality and Social Psychology Bulletin*) and determined that 75 percent of their articles used only undergraduate subjects, almost exclusively from the United States. His analysis highlighted some of the specific characteristics of college students that may constrain research findings. These subjects are of course younger than the average person, and their relatively high level of academic skills may favor psychological processes in the cognitive family (especially those that might be deemed rational) over processes that are more affective. According to Sears, students, given their developmental stage, also have a weaker self-definition than the average person, a stronger tendency to comply with authority, and a weaker tendency to be empathic and sympathetic. Their social and political attitudes may ordinarily be uncrystallized and unintegrated, and they may be less motivated by material self-interest than older adults are. Quite aside from the constraints inherent in laboratory settings, these and other characteristics of students may favor some but not other psychological processes. Consistent with Sears' analysis, we recommend that attitude researchers make use of not only a wider variety of research settings but also a greater diversity of subjects.

To provide some additional directives to attitude researchers, we suggest, first of all, more extensive use of survey research. Although survey research is common in the social sciences, it has been used mainly to describe public opinion rather than to address the psychological issues that constitute our domain in this book. Yet exceptions abound, and these exceptions provide very instructive models. For example, we have noted Lusk and Judd's (1988) research on attitude structure, Krosnick's (1988a) work on attitude importance, Kelman and Hamilton's (1989) investigations of destructive obedience (Chapter 13), and several researchers' work on context effects in questionnaire responding (Schwarz & Strack, 1991; Tourangeau & Rasinski, 1988). Such investigations show that important psychological issues can be addressed with survey methods.

It is also possible to increase the ecological validity of laboratory settings. Some counterattitudinal advocacy experiments provided such a model by establishing a seemingly spontaneous interaction between the experimental subject and a confederate who provided the audience for the subject's attitudinal advocacy (e.g., Festinger & Carlsmith, 1959; see Chapter 11). Another laboratory experimental model is provided by Ickes and his colleagues' creation of an unstructured social setting that appears inconsequential and unmonitored to subjects (Ickes & Barnes, 1977; Ickes, Bissonnette, Garcia, & Stinson, 1990).

Field studies and experiments are severely underutilized in the modern era, despite the precedent established by early research on attitudes and social influence. The classic examples of such field research include Newcomb's (1943) study of change in Bennington students' attitudes; Festinger, Schachter, and Back's (1950) examination of social pressures among residents of a university's off-campus housing units; Festinger, Riecken, and Schachter's (1956) study of cult members' behavioral commitment to their ideology in the face of disconfirming evidence; Newcomb's (1961) research on balance processes among a group of students living together in an off-campus house; and Rokeach's (1964) study of the ideological consequences of bringing together three schizophrenic men, each of whom believed he was Jesus Christ. Unfortunately field research is considerably less common than experimental research in contemporary work on attitudes, but we have described a moderate number of more recent field studies in this book (e.g., Ajzen & Madden, 1986; Staw, 1974). Although the limitations of such field studies are known (see Newcomb, 1978), research in natural settings can demonstrate theories' generalizability and thereby considerably strengthen support for them (see also T. D. Cook & Campbell, 1979).

Lack of a Strongly Cumulative Research Tradition. In some areas of attitude research (e.g., attitude-behavior relation; persuasion), the quantity of empirical findings is now extremely large. In an ideal world of scientific activity, these studies would have built on one another's findings in clear-cut fashion, and knowledge would have increased in an orderly way. The reality falls short of this ideal, especially in some research areas, although some growth of ordered knowledge has occurred, at least in relation to certain questions. Key phenomena such as attitudinal selectivity in memory and the effects of communicator variables on persuasion were recognized at quite an early point (in the 1930s and 1940s in many instances), and researchers have continued to investigate these issues with the guidance provided by increasingly sophisticated theoretical frameworks. Despite the increase of knowledge that has occurred in many key areas such as research on persuasion and the attitude-behavior relation, findings have not been as cumulative as they might have been.

The imperfect growth of knowledge in the attitudes area can in large part be laid at the feet of researchers themselves, who have had only a rudimentary understanding of the conceptual issues that underlie the integration of research findings. Researchers and reviewers have often had the expectation that, if we are to regard a hypothesis as validated, all or nearly all tests of it must yield statistically significant findings. As many methodologists have pointed out (e.g., Meehl, 1978), the practice of judging study outcomes by their significance is problematic because it fails to take into account the statistical power of studies. For example, one study may produce a significant finding and another study a nonsignificant finding merely because of a difference in sample size. Despite an inconsistency in significance levels, the two findings may be consistent when judged by a metric that is unaffected by sample size. Thus, a set of findings may differ in statistical significance but actually be quite consistent in the magnitude of their effects. In fact, distributions of findings in which even the majority of findings are nonsignificant could yield strong support for a given hypothesis. The truth of this claim becomes apparent if one merely contemplates the fact that under the null hypothesis of no difference, a significant result would appear in only 5 percent of the available findings (i.e., 2½% in each tail of the distribution, given 2-tailed statistical tests). From this perspective, it is easy to understand that distributions of findings in which modest proportions (e.g., 30%) of the findings are significant in the predicted direction but other findings are nonsignificant generally allow the null hypothesis of no difference to be rejected. Reviewers' incorrect expectations that the majority of findings must reject a null hypothesis has often led them to conclude erroneously in favor of no difference. This conservative bias appears to be a widespread problem in interpreting research throughout psychology (H. M. Cooper & Rosenthal, 1980), and in this book, we have frequently noted reviewers' and researchers' premature discounting of phenomena on the basis of such reasoning. Recall—for example—our discussions of the attitude-behavior relation (Chapter 4), selective exposure (Chapter 12), and selective memory (Chapter 12).

More subtle problems than reliance on a statistical significance rule hamper the interpretation of attitude research. For example, much confusion surrounds the size of effects that can be deemed consequential. Although most reviewers have ignored the magnitude of the effects they discussed in favor of a simple emphasis on statistical significance, others have translated findings into variance accounted for and dismissed findings and phenomena that do not account for a relatively large amount of variability. For example, McGuire (1976) declared that "one of the many scandals of social psychology is the low correlation between attitudes and actions" (p. 312; see also Wicker, 1969). Zajonc (1980b) referred to "the dismal failure in achieving substantial attitude change through various forms of communication or persuasion" (p. 158). Such statements imply that quite large effects should be seen in attitude research. Yet because a single variable (e.g., attitude) is rarely the only cause of a particular response (e.g., a behavior), a study usually isolates only one part of a more complex causal picture (see Chapter 4). Indeed, for this and other reasons (e.g., unreliable measuring instruments), the great majority of social science findings seem small when viewed in terms of variance accounted for (Cohen, 1977). There is no evidence whatsoever that attitude research, on average, yields smaller effects than research on other topics in social psychology or psychology more generally. Moreover, effects that account for relatively small proportions of variance can still be consequential, and often are regarded as extremely important in applied areas (Abelson, 1985; Rosenthal, 1990; Rosenthal & Rubin, 1982).

Reviewers and interpreters of research findings also sometimes fail to appreciate that the outcomes of studies may be inconsistent in direction or magnitude for eminently interpretable reasons—for example, because of theoretically meaningful interactions between studies' attributes and the outcome of interest. As we pointed out in Chapter 12 when discussing research on selective exposure, reviewers have sometimes neglected to search for interacting conditions, with the result that interesting and interpretable patterns of inconsistent findings were regarded merely as support for the null hypothesis.

688

Another difficulty in many interpretations of research is that reviewers insufficiently address the issue of findings' consistency at a psychologically meaningful level. They expect a particular independent variable always to have the same impact on attitudes, regardless of the underlying process this variable elicits. For example, in examining the effects of distraction, a reviewer might look to see if distraction manipulations uniformly facilitate or uniformly inhibit persuasion. Taking this concrete approach, he would fail to define consistency in terms of the persuasive impact of the cognitive processes that are influenced by such independent variables (e.g., distraction-induced decrements in message reception and issue-relevant thinking). The empirical literature indicates that particular distal variables such as distraction are often mediated by different cognitive processes (e.g., reception vs. issue-relevant thinking), depending on other factors in persuasion situations (e.g., the strength of the distraction manipulation or the difficulty of understanding message content; see Chapter 6). Therefore, despite the inconsistency across studies of the persuasive impact of variables such as distraction, their effects on persuasion are nevertheless predictable to the extent that the processes underlying them are understood.

There is reason to hope that some of these difficulties in traditional interpretations of research will be remedied to some extent due to the availability and dissemination of the quantitative techniques of research integration known as meta-analysis (H. M. Cooper, 1989; Hedges & Olkin, 1985; Glass, McGaw, & Smith, 1981; Rosenthal, 1991). In providing explicit and statistically justified methods of drawing conclusions from the available empirical literature, these methods correct reviewers' overreliance on statistical significance in judging sets of studies. In a meta-analysis, a quantitative summary is made of the results of studies testing the same hypothesis. The magnitude of a finding is assessed for each study in terms of its effect size, represented by d, which expresses the finding in standard deviation units, or by r, the familiar correlation coefficient. The magnitude of both d and r is independent of the sample sizes of individual studies, although both statistics are of course more reliably estimated from larger samples.

Among the features of meta-analysis that allow reviewers to make good use of existing research are the tests of the consistency of research findings across studies (i.e., tests of homogeneity; Hedges & Olkin, 1985; Rosenthal, 1991). The issue of whether studies can be considered to have consistent outcomes is extremely important in reviewing. The demonstration that findings are inconsistent across studies shifts attention away from the aggregated finding itself, that is, away from the mean effect size, which displays the overall or "main effect" in the research literature. Instead, attention moves to a search for the attributes of studies that are correlated with the estimates of effect size and therefore produce interactions. For example, Bornstein (1989a), in his quantitative review of the mere exposure literature, was not interested only in the main-effect question of whether there is an overall tendency for attitudes to become more positive with a greater number of exposures to the attitude object. Instead, he gave more emphasis to a considerably more subtle set of questions about the conditions under which the effect is larger or smaller. In quantitative reviews, the relations between study attributes such as exposure duration and the effect of interest can be evaluated statistically, using a variety of meta-analytic statistical methods.

In this book, we have cited several informative meta-analyses of attitudinal effects (e.g., Bornstein, 1989a; Isenberg, 1986; B. T. Johnson & Eagly, 1989; Rhodes & Wood, 1992; Sheppard, Hartwick, & Warshaw, 1988). Also, we have noted many domains where narrative reviewing seems to have led to faulty conclusions and in which meta-analytic integrations are sorely needed. Yet it would be a very serious mistake to view meta-analysis as a surefire recipe for orderly cumulation of findings and a cure-all for misinterpretations of research. One problem is that meta-analysts, like traditional, narrative reviewers, can fail to retrieve the existing empirical literature. Unless meta-analysts use careful and systematic techniques for retrieving the research literature, they may obtain a systematically biased sample of studies. Certainly if reviewers, be they narrative or quantitative, retrieve only the studies that come to mind or that they happen to be aware of, they are very likely to be working with a biased sample of findings. In addition, a biased sample typically results from reviewers confining themselves to only the published research literature, which usually contains stronger findings than the research literature as a whole. Accessing unpublished studies, including dissertations, is an aid to overcoming this publication bias problem. Drawing conclusions from a biased sample of studies is a major failing of many narrative reviews, but unfortunately it continues to be a major failing of many quantitative reviews as well. Even though methodological discussions of meta-analysis generally emphasize the importance of obtaining a complete or a systematic sample of available studies, quantitative reviewers often undersample the empirical literature by, for example, excluding unpublished studies from their sample. Although computer-based literature searching is a definite asset, this tool is not an easy remedy for defects in locating studies. More often than not, a simple search strategy using the most obvious key words does not in fact locate the available literature on a given hypothesis.

Meta-analysts can be guilty of poor scholarship in other senses as well: They may ignore interacting conditions and thereby portray empirical findings too simply. A meta-analysis is not a helpful contribution to scholarship if it merely averages inconsistent findings to present a "main effect" conclusion in relation to a given hypothesis. Quantitative reviewing requires theoretical sophistication. Without considerable knowledge of the empirical literature and excellent theoretical skills, a quantitative reviewer is unlikely to discern the interacting conditions that would affect the finding of interest, from the perspective of relevant psychological models. Unfortunately, many published meta-analyses have shown relatively little theoretical sophistication. And, as already noted, successful meta-analyses require extraordinary patience and perseverance, not only in locating the relevant studies, but also in analyzing them thoroughly.

Because most summaries of various attitudinal phenomena have been based on traditional, narrative methods and, moreover, suffer from many of the other flaws we have noted (e.g., search for consistency at the phenotypic level of concrete variables rather than the genotypic level of underlying process), it is not surprising that pessimistic conclusions about attitude research have not been infrequent. Some of these statements are quite interesting, although, in our view, quite wrong. For example, Brown (1965) wrote that the findings of persuasion studies, particularly the findings

690

of the Yale communication and persuasion researchers (Hovland et al., 1953) "lack something of intellectual interest because the results do not fall into any general compelling pattern. They summarize as a set of elaborately contingent, and not very general, generalizations" (p. 549). Fishbein and Ajzen (1975) observed that "the literature on communication and persuasion reveals virtually no consistent findings concerning the effects of any given manipulation on 'attitude change'" (p. 478). Other psychologists have echoed these conclusions (e.g., Billig, 1987; Jaccard, 1981b; Jaspers, 1978).

Scrutiny of these psychologists' views suggests that they were and perhaps still are expecting something quite simple from attitude research—namely, uniformly large and statistically significant relations between a given independent variable (e.g., communicator credibility) and persuasion. First of all, such expectations are inconsistent with theories of attitude change, which almost always make contingent predictions. Moreover, as we have noted, the perceptions of inconsistency in findings were based on informal, implicit rules of narrative reviewing. Discerning whether findings are actually consistent or inconsistent demands considerably more sophisticated processing of empirical findings by quantitative techniques that are informed by relevant theoretical frameworks. The quick scan based on a statistical significance rule cannot yield a correct description, yet some interpreters of the attitudes literature have based their conclusions on precisely such methods.

Finally, valid interpretations of attitude research and better cumulation of findings require greater tolerance for complexity in explanations and for the patterns of findings that would substantiate these explanations. A tolerance for ambiguity is required as well because the reviewer must search sympathetically for the sometimes complex interactions that are implied by psychological theories. Among many reviewers and textbook writers, especially those who are not expert in a research area, tolerance for complexity and ambiguity seems to be in short supply. Often findings are dismissed as inconsistent or weak. Alternatively, simple frameworks that ignore complexity are sometimes embraced as the truth of the matter. Of course, parsimony is properly regarded as an asset of theories, but the desire for parsimony should not be allowed to override accurate mapping of psychological phenomena. Although it is too extreme to argue that bad theories drive out good ones, we believe that theories that simplify reality have had a decided edge in popularity over theories that represent the complexity of attitudinal phenomena. For example, the enormous popularity of dissonance theory during the 1950s and 1960s and its great success in stimulating research seemed to be based in part on its initial simplification of the issues surrounding the effects of behavior on attitudes. Compare the history of dissonance work with the lesser interest researchers took in balance theory, which rapidly developed along lines of increasing complexity (Abelson, 1959; Rosenberg & Abelson, 1960; Wiest, 1965).

Despite their initial popularity, simplifying theories are highly vulnerable, as was dissonance theory, to summary rejection by critics, once the true complexity of attitudinal phenomena asserts itself with clarity in the empirical literature. This tendency to reject simple theories after an initial burst of interest in them is only exacerbated by the further simplification of theorists' ideas that sometimes occurs in followers' applications of them and that almost always occurs in textbooks and reviews. A result is the cycles of belief in theories followed by total rejection that slows down the growth of scientific knowledge. These cycles of optimism and despair have been described at several points in this book (Chapters 4 and 12, in particular), and, indeed, it would be instructive for readers to scan currently popular theories and consider which may be vulnerable to summary rejection within the next few years.

Growth of Attitude Theories

Although this book deals with the entire domain of the psychology of attitudes, it announces no general theory of attitudes. This chapter does not contain a grand flow chart portraying the variables and causal relations that determine people's attitudes and indicate attitudes' influence on information processing, judgment, and behavior. Although we are as capable as other psychologists of drawing such general flow charts, we believe that none could be drawn at a meaningful level given the current state of knowledge about attitudes. Despite the fact that we cannot announce a single, general theory of attitudes, we believe that the last years have witnessed a substantial growth in the breadth of theorizing.

Extremely broad theories of attitudes were characteristic of earlier decades. In fact, anyone familiar with the history of attitude theory would quickly point out that the broadest theories were the theories of attitude change formulated in the 1950s and investigated empirically in the 1950s and 1960s. Cognitive consistency theories were the major focus of interest during this era, with dissonance and balance theories attracting the major share of attention. Other popular and relatively broad frameworks included functional theories, social judgment theory, and learning theory (including the Yale persuasion researchers' drive-reduction and incentive model). Each of these theories attempted to encompass a wide range of attitudinal phenomena, through the use of a relatively small set of theoretical constructs.

The popularity of these theories gradually declined, for a variety of reasons including no doubt a simple boredom with familiar ideas, which hastens shifts in zeitgeist. Yet perhaps more important in many cases was the failure of theories to encompass the detail of the empirical findings that they helped inspire (see Eagly & Himmelfarb, 1974). When relatively simple frameworks face the complexity of empirical findings, these frameworks may become discredited, as we have noted; alternatively, they may grow and change. More commonly, however, the reaction is a mix of rejection and growth. The majority of researchers lose interest and regard the framework as discredited—its popularity and glamour erode. Yet a minority of loyalists may "keep the faith," so to speak, and develop the theory to encompass the challenge of empirical findings. Dissonance theory, due to its empirical provocativeness as well as the energy and talent of its practitioners, provides the best example of a theory that refused to give up. As early as the late 1960s, the scuttlebutt around many social psychology programs was that "dissonance theory is dead." Yet a dwindling band of dissonance researchers developed the theory in response to empirical findings (see Chapter 11), and the theory is by no means dead even now.

692

In response to empirical challenges, balance theorists did not change its core proposi-tions but applied them in increasingly complex ways (see Chapter 3). The functional theories we discussed in Chapter 10 had a somewhat different history. They did not inspire empirical research programs of much scope. The very breadth of functional theories made them difficult to operationalize. At least until the recent renewal of interest in these ideas, they were more important as classificatory schemas and meta-theoretical frameworks than as theories generating hypotheses for research.

In the immediate aftermath of the critiques of 1950s theories, some theoretical growth occurred in the form of limited range theories (see Eagly & Himmelfarb, 1974). For example, theories of fear appeals (see Chapter 10), of personality and persuasibility (see Chapter 6), and attributional inferences in persuasion settings (see Chapter 8) were proposed. Although such viewpoints had roots in broader theories of social behavior (e.g., expectancy-value models, attribution theory), they encompassed only a limited range of attitudinal phenomena. These limited range theories restricted their scope at the outset, whereas earlier theories more often allowed limits to develop by default because hypothesis testing, for one reason or another, became focused on particular phenomena.

In the 1980s and 1990s theories of attitudes have achieved greater breadth once again, but these theories are still somewhat modest in scope compared to 1950s theo-ries and are linked considerably more closely to empirical findings. For example, recent persuasion theories such as the heuristic-systematic model (Chaiken et al., 1989) and the elaboration likelihood model (Petty & Cacioppo, 1986a, 1986b) consider a wide range of persuasion variables and take into account more than one mechanism by which persuasive communications change attitudes. Prototypical of contemporary atti-tude theory is McGuire and McGuire's (1991) dynamic theory of thought systems, a theory in the tradition of combinatorial models (Chapter 5). This theory predicts both likelihood judgments and desirability judgments and incorporates a variety of prin-ciples that govern these judgments. Also introducing greater breadth are the self theo-ries of behavior-attitude relations that we introduced in Chapter 11. These theories, especially Schlenker's framework (1982), place dissonance research on counteratti-tudinal advocacy in a broader context of theory about the self. Another example of increasing scope is Fazio's (1990a) MODE model, which considers more automatic and more controlled mechanisms by which attitudes may direct behavior.

Despite this movement toward theories of greater scope, much work on attitudes and social influence remains encapsulated in rather narrow models. We believe that much greater breadth of theory can be achieved, particularly if investigators will allow themselves to take inspiration from a variety of domains of research. In the narrowest of worlds, investigators regard as relevant to their own work only those studies that are conducted within the identical research paradigm. From such a per-spective, only studies of message-based persuasion are relevant to persuasion theory, only studies of mere exposure are relevant to theory about this phenomenon, only studies of group polarization are relevant to theory about this phenomenon, and so on. If one looks to only the most obviously relevant research, many potentially useful theoretical ideas are missed, and theory is drastically limited by the very real con-straints of experimental paradigms, which often allow only certain processes to be manifest. Theory encapsulated within an experimental paradigm is thus quite limited in scope.

At various points in this book, we have recommended greater cross-fertilization between research domains. We have thus suggested that process theories of attitude change be coordinated with combinatorial models, in order to produce hypotheses about how information is weighted when it is integrated to form an overall attitude. We have suggested that persuasion theory has much to offer theories of behavior-attitude relations and of social influence. Theories of social influence have enriched persuasion theory as well and should continue to contribute to an understanding of motivational issues in persuasion. Persuasion researchers have already begun to incorporate some of the lessons of earlier theorizing about attitude functions and social influence processes, and they ought to take a closer look at the literature on attitudinal selectivity that we analyzed in Chapter 12. Such movement of ideas across domains of attitude research would increase the breadth of theory. Also helpful is the input of ideas from the social cognition literature, as suggested by the attention this book has paid to associative networks theories and various cognitive structural concepts.

Another important goal for contemporary attitude theory is a better balance between cognitive and motivational themes. Of course, attitude theory has never been extremely weighted toward either cognition or motivation, and therefore few of the theories we have considered in this book are pure types of cognitive or motivational theories. In fact, the integration of these two themes is a traditional feature of attitude theory, one that makes it unique in social psychology. However, the strength of the cognitive revolution in psychology not surprisingly set attitude theory on a cognitive course in the 1970s and 1980s. Although the balance never shifted as far away from motivational issues as it did in some other areas of social psychology (notably in the "person perception" area that came to be labeled *social cognition*), more thorough reintegration of motivational issues into discussions of attitudes is desirable and would certainly increase the scope of theory. Indeed, in our own work, we have elaborated on motivational concepts in a manner that we believe increases the scope of persuasion theory (Chaiken et al., 1989; B. T. Johnson & Eagly, 1989).

One of the admirable features of attitude theory is its tendency to cumulate in the sense that newer theories have built on some of the themes of older ones and often developed some theme that remained underdeveloped in an earlier theory. Particularly instructive is an examination of the influence of the Yale communication and persuasion research group (Hovland et al., 1953). Their perspective, although fairly described as having Hullian learning theory as its major emphasis, was actually quite eclectic and certainly included important cognitive themes (see Chapters 6 and 10). In McGuire's work, some of these themes were then developed, especially in his reception-yielding or information-processing model (McGuire, 1968b, 1972). The emphasis of the Yale school on the message recipient as an active, constructive processor of information was developed by the cognitive response researchers (e.g., A. G. Greenwald, 1968), and their work in turn provided the main ground from which the heuristic-systematic and elaboration likelihood models developed (see Chapter 7). McGuire's (1969) occasionally mentioned idea about a lazy organism message recipient who is

694

unmotivated to process the content of messages systematically was then developed as an explicit theme in these models' ideas about heuristic processing and a peripheral route to persuasion. Given such a progression, the newer theories are broader and more sophisticated than the earlier theories, and a certain cumulation of ideas is readily apparent. Similar histories can be traced in other areas of investigation, such as the study of attitude-behavior (Chapter 4) and behavior-attitude relations (Chapter 11).

The potential for functional theories of attitudes to provide a considerably more general integration of attitude-change theory must be acknowledged. Functional approaches specify alternative motives that may be invoked by attitude-relevant stimuli and thereby suggest differing ways that attitudes are formed and changed. As we showed in Chapter 10, each of these functions built on existing psychological theory. Although functional theories are in this sense not original (after all, they are built from reconditioned parts), they contribute an important dimension by suggesting conditions under which one or another of several types of theory is likely to provide a useful description of the psychological processes underlying attitude change. Perhaps more integrative theories will emerge from the recent renewal of interest in functional theory.

Applications of Attitude Theories

This book has not been especially concerned with applications of attitude theory because our focus has been on theories themselves and on the evidence that seems most relevant to establishing their validity. Nonetheless, the evidence that applied studies provide was relevant to evaluating some attitude theories, and we have therefore noted many such studies. Yet applications are more important than our occasional mention of them would suggest. Because natural settings are the domain to which attitude researchers wish to generalize, making one's theory "work" in natural settings is in a sense the ultimate test of the theory.

A foray into an applied setting, be it health education, political campaigning, or marketing, can be as instructive for the attitude theorist as it is for the practitioners in these settings. Surely we have theories that are useful and informative in such settings, but the complexity of these settings is likely to reveal some of the theories' limitations and make clear that these theories must be pieced out with stretches of implicit psychology before they can be usefully mapped onto natural settings. Therefore, attitude researchers who try to apply their theories in natural settings should go forward with a healthy respect for the practitioners in these settings. These people very often possess naive theories of attitudes that, when combined with their intuitive knowledge of the many variables operative in their unique settings, may in fact have substantial predictive power. It is sometimes an open question whether the attitude theorist has more to offer than the practitioner. Because of many uncertainties that researchers face in trying to apply existing theories, exploratory research in the applied setting is generally essential to problem solving in the environment (see Lévy-Leboyer, 1988).

Applications of attitude theory are often particularly demanding because they require broader integrations of knowledge about attitudes than our theories currently offer. Practitioners in health or consumer areas, for example, desire to use communications to change behavior. They are not interested merely in having people *think* that certain health practices or products are good, but in having people engage in healthful behaviors or buy advertised products. Attitude theorists may find it problematic to bring a systematic perspective to bear on these concerns because theories of attitude change and theories of attitude-behavior relations have been quite separate traditions.

Interest in attitude theory is widespread, because of the desire of many groups to change attitudes and behaviors. At times, this interest may be overzealous and may result in loose and inappropriate applications of theories, at least some of which have little scientific validity (see Lévy-Leboyer, 1988). Health educators, political strategists, and marketers are thus quite eager to apply whatever attitude researchers have available in a useful form. We have noted successful applications in several areas, including attitude-behavior research (Chapter 4) and inoculation theory (Chapter 12).

From a broader perspective, practitioners' interest in attitude theory is testimony to the larger political and economic context provided by North American and European societies. In these largely democratic political systems and capitalistic economic systems, people are presented with many choices. Under such circumstances, citizens' decisions are not generally determined by coercive pressures, overt incentives, or large rewards and punishments. In the consumer area, for example, an extremely wide range of products is often available. Consumers are not ordinarily subjected to demands that they must buy certain products, nor are they necessarily swayed by monetary rebates offering explicit incentives for purchasing a product. Instead, they may often engage in a more complex attitudinal process whereby they determine which product is "best." This positive attitude then influences buying, in conjunction with other factors such as habit and others' expectations (see Chapter 4). In the political arena, many potential candidates campaign vigorously to win citizens' favor. By expressing their attitudinal preferences in primaries and through more complex political means, citizens then choose a favored candidate. This political process is generally absent in less democratic countries, which may offer no elections at all, elections with only one viable candidate, or coercive pressures to vote for particular candidates.

In more totalitarian societies, people's choices are typically constrained, because of both a relative lack of alternatives and the use of more coercive forms of political and economic control. Coercive control of behavior has seen some emphasis in this book—for example, in Kelman's (1961) compliance process, Milgram's (1963) obedience paradigm, and French and Raven's (1959) ideas about reward and punishment power. As these theorists have implied, totalitarian forms of control are effective only when the targets of influence are under the surveillance of the influencing agent. Therein lies one of the chief limitations of these forms of control, as shown by the reliance of totalitarian governments on informers and secret police. The body of science described in this book could only have developed in democratic societies, where attitudinal influence is the form of control that is most often relied upon. The consequent importance of attitude control means that this area of social science will enjoy more and more attention as its theories become more general and more sophisticated and therefore more useful.

References

Abelson, R. P. (1959). Modes of resolution of belief dilemmas. *Journal of Conflict Resolution*, *3*, 343–352.

Abelson, R. P. (1963). Computer simulation of "hot" cognition. In S. S. Tomkins & S. Messick (Eds.), *Computer simulation of personality* (pp. 277–298). New York: Wiley.

Abelson, R. P. (1968). Psychological implication. In R. P. Abelson, E. Aronson, W. J. McGuire, T. M. Newcomb, M. J. Rosenberg, & P. H. Tannenbaum (Eds.), *Theories of cognitive consistency: A sourcebook* (pp. 112–139). Chicago: Rand McNally.

Abelson, R. P. (1976). Script processing in attitude formation and decision making. In J. S. Carroll & J. W. Payne (Eds.), *Cognition and social behavior* (pp. 33–45). Hillsdale, NJ: Erlbaum.

Abelson, R. P. (1981). Psychological status of the script concept. *American Psychologist*, *36*, 715–729.

Abelson, R. P. (1982). Three modes of attitude-behavior consistency. In M. P. Zanna, E. T. Higgins, & C. P. Herman (Eds.), *Consistency in social behavior: The Ontario Symposium* (Vol. 2, pp. 131–146). Hillsdale, NJ: Erlbaum.

Abelson, R. P. (1983). Whatever became of consistency theory? *Personality and Social Psychology Bulletin*, *9*, 37–54.

Abelson, R. P. (1985). A variance explanation paradox: When a little is a lot. *Psychological Bulletin*, *97*, 129–133.

Abelson, R. P. (1986). Beliefs are like possessions. *Journal for the Theory of Social Behavior*, *16*, 223–250.

Abelson, R. P. (1988). Conviction. *American Psychologist*, *43*, 267–275.

Abelson, R. P. Aronson, E., McGuire, W. J., Newcomb, T. M., Rosenberg, M. J., & Tannenbaum, P. H. (Eds.). (1968). *Theories of cognitive consistency: A sourcebook*. Chicago: Rand McNally.

Abelson, R. P., Kinder, D. R., Peters, M. D., & Fiske, S. T. (1982). Affective and semantic components in political person perception. *Journal of Personality and Social Psychology*, *42*, 619–630.

Abelson, R. P., & Levi, A. (1985). Decision making and decision theory. In G. Lindzey & E. Aronson (Eds.), *Handbook of social psychology* (3rd ed., Vol. 1, pp. 231–309). New York: Random House.

Abelson, R. P., & Prentice, D. A. (1989). Beliefs as possessions: A functional perspective. In A. R. Pratkanis, S. J. Breckler, & A. G. Greenwald (Eds.), *Attitude structure and function* (pp. 361–381). Hillsdale, NJ: Erlbaum.

Abelson, R. P., & Rosenberg, M. J. (1958). Symbolic psychologic: A model of attitudinal cognition. *Behavioral Science*, *3*, 1–13.

Abul-Ela, A. L. A., Greenberg, B. G., & Horvitz, D. G. (1967). A multi-proportions randomized response model. *Journal of the American Statistical Association*, *62*, 990–1008.

Adams, J. A. (1957). Laboratory studies of behavior without awareness. *Psychological Bulletin*, *54*, 383–405.

Adams, J. S. (1961). Reduction of cognitive dissonance by seeking consonant information. *Journal of Abnormal and Social Psychology*, *62*, 74–78.

Adams, W. C., & Beatty, M. J. (1977). Dogmatism, need for social approval, and the resistance to persuasion. *Communication Monographs*, *44*, 321–325.

Adorno, T. W., Frenkel-Brunswik, E., Levinson, D. J., & Sanford, R. N. (1950). *The authoritarian personality*. New York: Harper & Row.

Aiello, T. J. (1967). Ambiguity, involvement, judgment, and persuasibility (Doctoral dissertation, Yeshiva University). *Dissertation Abstracts International*, *28*, 775A.

Ajzen, I. (1971a). Attitudinal vs. normative messages: An investigation of the differential effects of persuasive communications on behavior. *Sociometry*, *34*, 263–280.

Ajzen, I. (1971b). Attribution of dispositions to an actor: Effects of perceived decision freedom and behavioral utilities. *Journal of Personality and Social Psychology*, *18*, 144–156.

Ajzen, I. (1974). Effects of information on interpersonal attraction: Similarity versus affective value. *Journal of Personality and Social Psychology*, *29*, 374–380.

Ajzen, I. (1984). Attitudes. In R. J. Corsini (Ed.), *Wiley encyclopedia of psychology* (Vol. 1, pp. 99–100). New York: Wiley.

Ajzen, I. (1985). From intentions to actions: A theory of planned behavior. In J. Kuhl & J. Beckmann (Eds.), *Action control: From cognition to behavior* (pp. 11–39). New York: Springer-Verlag.

Ajzen, I. (1987). Attitudes, traits, and actions: Dispositional prediction of behavior in personality and social psychology. In L. Berkowitz (Ed.), *Advances in experimental social psychology* (Vol. 20, pp. 1–63). San Diego, CA: Academic Press.

Ajzen, I. (1988). *Attitudes, personality, and behavior*. Chicago: Dorsey.

Ajzen, I. (1991). The theory of planned behavior. *Organizational Behavior and Human Decision Processes*, *50*, 179–211.

Ajzen, I., & Driver, B. L. (1991). Prediction of leisure participation from behavioral, normative, and control beliefs: An application of the theory of planned behavior. *Leisure Sciences*, *13*, 185–204.

Ajzen, I., & Driver, B. L. (1992). Application of the theory of planned behavior to leisure choice. *Journal of Leisure Sciences*, *24*, 204–224.

Ajzen, I., & Fishbein, M. (1973). Attitudinal and normative variables as predictors of specific behaviors. *Journal of Personality and Social Psychology*, *27*, 41–57.

Ajzen, I., & Fishbein, M. (1977). Attitude-behavior relations: A theoretical analysis and review of empirical research. *Psychological Bulletin*, *84*, 888–918.

Ajzen, I., & Fishbein, M. (1980). *Understanding attitudes and predicting social behavior*. Englewood Cliffs, NJ: Prentice-Hall.

Ajzen, I., & Madden, T. J. (1986). Prediction of goal-directed behavior: Attitudes, intentions, and perceived behavioral control. *Journal of Experimental Social Psychology*, *22*, 453–474.

Ajzen, I., Timko, C., & White, J. B. (1982). Self-monitoring and the attitude-behavior relation. *Journal of Personality and Social Psychology*, *42*, 426–435.

Alba, J. W., & Marmorstein, H. (1987). The effects of frequency knowledge on consumer decision making. *Journal of Consumer Research*, *14*, 14–25.

Albrecht, S. L., & Carpenter, K. E. (1976). Attitudes as predictors of behavior versus behavior intentions: A convergence of research traditions. *Sociometry*, *39*, 1–10.

Alcalay, R. (1983). The impact of mass communication campaigns in the health field. *Social Science and Medicine*, *17*, 87–94.

Alexander, C. N., Jr., & Knight, G. W. (1971). Situated identities and social psychological experimentation. *Sociometry*, *34*, 65–82.

Allen, C. T., & Madden, T. J. (1985). A closer look at classical conditioning. *Journal of Consumer Research*, *12*, 301–315.

Allen, M. J., & Yen, W. M. (1979). *Introduction to measurement theory*. Monterey, CA: Brooks/Cole.

Allen, V. L. (1965). Situational factors in conformity. In L. Berkowitz (Ed.), *Advances in experimental social psychology* (Vol. 2, pp. 133–175). San Diego, CA: Academic Press.

Allen, V. L., & Wilder, D. A. (1980). Impact of group consensus and social support on stimulus meaning: Mediation of conformity by cognitive restructuring. *Journal of Personality and Social Psychology*, *39*, 1116–1124.

Allport, G. W. (1935). Attitudes. In C. Murchison (Ed.), *Handbook of social psychology* (pp. 798–844). Worcester, MA: Clark University Press.

Allyn, J., & Festinger, L. (1961). The effectiveness of unanticipated persuasive communications. *Journal of Abnormal and Social Psychology*, *62*, 35–40.

Alper, T. G., & Korchin, S. J. (1952). Memory for socially relevant material. *Journal of Abnormal and Social Psychology*, *47*, 25–37.

Altemeyer, B. (1981). *Right-wing authoritarianism*. Winnipeg: University of Manitoba Press.

Altemeyer, B. (1988). *Enemies of freedom: Understanding right-wing authoritarianism*. San Francisco: Jossey-Bass.

Alwin, D. F. (1974). Approaches to the interpretation of relationships in the multitrait–multimethod matrix. In

H. L. Costner (Ed.), *Sociological methodology: 1973–74* (pp. 79–105). San Francisco: Jossey-Bass.

Anderson, A. B., Basilevsky, A., & Hum, D. P. J. (1983). Measurement: Theory and techniques. In P. H. Rossi, J. D. Wright, & A. B. Anderson (Eds.), *Handbook of survey research* (pp. 231–287). San Diego, CA: Academic Press.

Anderson, C. A., Lepper, M. R., & Ross, L. (1980). Perseverance of social theories: The role of explanation in the persistence of discredited information. *Journal of Personality and Social Psychology*, *39*, 1037–1049.

Anderson, D. R. (1985). Online cognitive processing of television. In L. F. Alwitt & A. A. Mitchell (Eds.), *Psychological processes and advertising effects: Theory, research, and application* (pp. 177–199). Hillsdale, NJ: Erlbaum.

Anderson, J. R. (1983). *The architecture of cognition*. Cambridge, MA: Harvard University Press.

Anderson, J. R. (1985). *Cognitive psychology and its implications* (2nd ed.). San Francisco: Freeman.

Anderson, J. R., & Bower, G. H. (1973). *Human associative memory*. Washington, DC: Winston.

Anderson, J. R., & Bower, G. H. (1974). A propositional theory of recognition memory. *Memory and Cognition*, *2*, 406–412.

Anderson, N. H. (1961). Scales and statistics: Parametric and nonparametric. *Psychological Bulletin*, *58*, 305–316.

Anderson, N. H. (1962). Application of an additive model to impression formation. *Science*, *138*, 817–818.

Anderson, N. H. (1965a). Averaging versus adding as a stimulus-combination rule in impression formation. *Journal of Experimental Psychology*, *70*, 394–400.

Anderson, N. H. (1965b). Primacy effects in personality impression formation using a generalized order effect paradigm. *Journal of Personality and Social Psychology*, *2*, 1–9.

Anderson, N. H. (1967). Averaging model analysis of set-size effect in impression formation. *Journal of Experimental Psychology*, *75*, 158–165.

Anderson, N. H. (1968a). Application of a linear-serial model to a personality-impression task using serial presentation. *Journal of Personality and Social Psychology*, *10*, 354–362.

Anderson, N. H. (1968b). A simple model for information integration. In R. P. Abelson, E. Aronson, W. J. McGuire, T. M. Newcomb, M. J. Rosenberg, & P. H. Tannenbaum (Eds.), *Theories of cognitive consistency: A sourcebook* (pp. 731–743). Chicago: Rand McNally.

Anderson, N. H. (1970). Functional measurement and psychophysical judgment. *Psychological Review*, *77*, 153–170.

Anderson, N. H. (1971). Integration theory and attitude change. *Psychological Review*, *78*, 171–206.

Anderson, N. H. (1973). Information integration theory applied to attitudes about U.S. Presidents. *Journal of Educational Psychology*, *64*, 1–8.

Anderson, N. H. (1974). Cognitive algebra: Integration theory applied to social attribution. In L. Berkowitz (Ed.), *Advances in experimental social psychology* (Vol. 7, pp. 1–101). San Diego, CA: Academic Press.

Anderson, N. H. (1976). How functional measurement can yield validated interval scales of mental quantities. *Journal of Applied Psychology, 61*, 677–692.

Anderson, N. H. (1981a). *Foundations of information integration theory*. San Diego, CA: Academic Press.

Anderson, N. H. (1981b). Integration theory applied to cognitive responses and attitudes. In R. E. Petty, T. M. Ostrom, & T. C. Brock (Eds.), *Cognitive responses in persuasion* (pp. 361–397). Hillsdale, NJ: Erlbaum.

Anderson, N. H. (1982). *Methods of information integration theory*. San Diego, CA: Academic Press.

Anderson, N. H. (Ed.). (1991). *Contributions to information integration theory* (Vols. 1, 2, and 3). Hillsdale, NJ: Erlbaum.

Anderson, N. H., & Farkas, A. J. (1973). New light on order effects in attitude change. *Journal of Personality and Social Psychology, 28*, 88–93.

Anderson, N. H., & Graesser, C. C. (1976). An information integration analysis of attitude change in group discussion. *Journal of Personality and Social Psychology, 34*, 210–222.

Anderson, N. H., & Hovland, C. I. (1957). The representation of order effects in communication research (Appendix A). In C. I. Hovland (Ed.), *The order of presentation in persuasion* (pp. 158–169). New Haven, CT: Yale University Press.

Anderson, N. H., & Hubert, S. (1963). Effects of concomitant verbal recall on order effects in personality impression formation. *Journal of Verbal Learning and Verbal Behavior, 2*, 379–391.

Anderson, N. H., & Shanteau, J. C. (1970). Information integration in risky decision making. *Journal of Experimental Psychology, 84*, 441–451.

Andreoli, V., & Worchel, S. (1978). Effects of media, communicator, and message position on attitude change. *Public Opinion Quarterly, 42*, 59–70.

Andrews, J. C., & Durvasula, S. (1991). Suggestions for manipulating and measuring involvement in advertising message content. *Advances in Consumer Research, 18*, 194–201.

Andrews, K. H., & Kandel, D. B. (1979). Attitude and behavior: A specification of the contingent consistency hypothesis. *American Sociological Review, 44*, 298–310.

Appel, V. (1971). On advertising wearout. *Journal of Advertising Research, 11*(1), 11–13.

Apsler, R., & Sears, D. O. (1968). Warning, personal involvement, and attitude change. *Journal of Personality and Social Psychology, 9*, 162–166.

Areni, C. S., & Lutz, R. J. (1988). The role of argument quality in the elaboration likelihood model. *Advances in Consumer Research, 15*, 197–203.

Argyle, M. (1957). Social pressures in public and private situations. *Journal of Abnormal and Social Psychology, 54*, 172–175.

Arkin, R. M., Appelman, A. J., & Burger, J. M. (1980). Social anxiety, self-presentation, and the self-serving bias in causal attribution. *Journal of Personality and Social Psychology, 38*, 23–35.

Arkin, R. M., & Lake, E. A. (1983). Plumbing the depths of the bogus pipeline: A reprise. *Journal of Research in Personality, 17*, 81–88.

Aronson, E. (1961). The effect of effort on the attractiveness of rewarded and unrewarded stimuli. *Journal of Abnormal and Social Psychology, 63*, 375–380.

Aronson, E. (1968). Dissonance theory: Progress and problems. In R. P. Abelson, E. Aronson, W. J. McGuire, T. M. Newcomb, M. J. Rosenberg, & P. H. Tannenbaum (Eds.), *Theories of cognitive consistency: A sourcebook* (pp. 5–27). Chicago: Rand McNally.

Aronson, E. (1969). The theory of cognitive dissonance: A current perspective. In L. Berkowitz (Ed.), *Advances in experimental social psychology* (Vol. 4, pp. 1–34). San Diego, CA: Academic Press.

Aronson, E. (1989). Analysis, synthesis, and the treasuring of the old. *Personality and Social Psychology Bulletin, 15*, 508–512.

Aronson, E. (1990, December). *The return of the repressed: Dissonance theory makes a comeback*. Presidential address presented at the meeting of the Western Psychological Association, Los Angeles.

Aronson, E., Brewer, M. B., & Carlsmith, J. M. (1985). Experimentation in social psychology. In G. Lindzey & E. Aronson (Eds.), *Handbook of social psychology* (3rd ed., Vol. 1, pp. 441–486). New York: Random House.

Aronson, E., & Carlsmith, J. M. (1963). Effect of the severity of threat on the devaluation of forbidden behavior. *Journal of Abnormal and Social Psychology, 66*, 584–588.

Aronson, E., & Cope, V. (1968). My enemy's enemy is my friend. *Journal of Personality and Social Psychology, 8*, 8–12.

Aronson, E., & Mills, J. (1959). The effect of severity of initiation on liking for a group. *Journal of Abnormal and Social Psychology, 59*, 177–181.

Aronson, E., Turner, J. A., & Carlsmith, J. M. (1963). Communicator credibility and communication discrepancy as determinants of opinion change. *Journal of Abnormal and Social Psychology, 67*, 31–36.

Arrow, K. J. (1951). Alternative approaches to the theory of choice in risk-taking situations. *Econometrica, 19*, 404–437.

Arrowood, A.J., & Ross, L. (1966). Anticipated effort and subjective probability. *Journal of Personality and Social Psychology, 4,* 57-64.

Asch, S. E. (1940). Studies in the principles of judgments and attitudes: II. Determination of judgments by group and by ego standards. *Journal of Social Psychology, 12,* 433-465.

Asch, S. E. (1946). Forming impressions of personality. *Journal of Abnormal and Social Psychology, 41,* 258-290.

Asch, S. E. (1948). The doctrine of suggestion, prestige, and imitation in social psychology. *Psychological Review, 55,* 250-276.

Asch, S. E. (1951). Effects of group pressure upon the modification and distortion of judgments. In H. Guetzkow (Ed.), *Groups, leadership and men* (pp. 177-190). Pittsburgh, PA: Carnegie Press.

Asch, S. E. (1952). *Social psychology.* Englewood Cliffs, NJ: Prentice-Hall.

Asch, S. E. (1955). Opinions and social pressure. *Scientific American, 193,* 31-35.

Asch, S. E. (1956). Studies of independence and conformity: I. A minority of one against a unanimous majority. *Psychological Monographs, 70*(9, Whole No. 416).

Ashmore, R. D., & Del Boca, F. K. (1981). Conceptual approaches to stereotypes and stereotyping. In D. L. Hamilton (Ed.), *Cognitive processes in stereotyping and intergroup behavior* (pp. 1-35). Hillsdale, NJ: Erlbaum.

Atkins, A. L., Deaux, K. K., & Bieri, J. (1967). Latitude of acceptance and attitude change: Empirical evidence for a reformulation. *Journal of Personality and Social Psychology, 6,* 47-54.

Atkinson, J. W. (Ed.). (1958). *Motives in fantasy, action, and society: A method of assessment and study.* Princeton, NJ: Van Nostrand.

Atkinson, R. C., & Shiffrin, R. M. (1968). Human memory: A proposed system and its control processes. In K. W. Spence & J. T. Spence (Eds.), *The psychology of learning and motivation* (Vol. 2, pp. 89-195). San Diego, CA: Academic Press.

Attneave, F. (1949). A method of graded dichotomies for the scaling of judgments. *Psychological Review, 56,* 334-340.

Attneave, F. (1959). *Applications of information theory to psychology.* New York: Holt.

Atwood, R. W., & Howell, R. J. (1971). Pupillometric and personality test score differences of female aggressing pedophiliacs and normals. *Psychonomic Science, 22,* 115-116.

Axsom, D. (1989). Cognitive dissonance and behavior change in psychotherapy. *Journal of Experimental Social Psychology, 25,* 234-252.

Axsom, D., & Cooper, J. (1985). Cognitive dissonance and psychotherapy: The role of effort justification in inducing weight loss. *Journal of Experimental Social Psychology, 21,* 149-160.

Axsom, D., Yates, S. M., & Chaiken, S. (1987). Audience response as a heuristic cue in persuasion. *Journal of Personality and Social Psychology, 53,* 30-40.

Bacon, F. (1960). *The new organon and related writings.* New York: Liberal Arts Press. (Original work published 1620)

Baer, R., Hinkle, S., Smith, K., & Fenton, M. (1980). Reactance as a function of actual versus projected autonomy. *Journal of Personality and Social Psychology, 38,* 416-422.

Bagby, R. M., Parker, J. D. A., & Bury, A. S. (1990). A comparative citation analysis of attribution theory and the theory of cognitive dissonance. *Personality and Social Psychology Bulletin, 16,* 274-283.

Bagozzi, R. P. (1978). The construct validity of the affective, behavioral, and cognitive components of attitude by analysis of covariance structures. *Multivariate Behavior Research, 13,* 9-31.

Bagozzi, R. P. (1981). Attitudes, intentions, and behavior: A test of some key hypotheses. *Journal of Personality and Social Psychology, 41,* 607-627.

Bagozzi. R. P. (1984). Expectancy-value attitude models: An analysis of critical measurement issues. *International Journal of Marketing, 1,* 295-310.

Bagozzi, R. P. (1989). An investigation of the role of affective and moral evaluations in the purposeful behaviour model of attitude. *British Journal of Social Psychology, 28,* 97-113.

Bagozzi, R. P., Baumgartner, J., & Yi, Y. (1989). An investigation into the role of intentions as mediators of the attitude-behavior relationship. *Journal of Economic Psychology, 10,* 35-62.

Bagozzi, R. P., & Burnkrant, R. E. (1979). Attitude organization and the attitude-behavior relationship. *Journal of Personality and Social Psychology, 37,* 913-929.

Bagozzi, R. P., & Burnkrant, R. E. (1985). Attitude organization and the attitude-behavior relation: A reply to Dillon and Kumar. *Journal of Personality and Social Psychology, 49,* 47-57.

Bagozzi, R. P., & Warshaw, P. R. (1990). Trying to consume. *Journal of Consumer Research, 17,* 127-140.

Bagozzi, R. P., & Warshaw, P. R. (in press). An examination of the etiology of the attitude-behavior relation for goal-directed behaviors. *Multivariate Behavioral Research.*

Bagozzi, R. P., & Yi, Y. (1989). The degree of intention formation as a moderator of the attitude-behavior relationship. *Social Psychology Quarterly, 52,* 266-279.

Bagozzi, R. P., Yi, Y., & Baumgartner, J. (1990). The level of effort required for behaviour as a moderator of the attitude-behaviour relation. *European Journal of Social Psychology, 20,* 45-59.

Bailyn, L., & Kelman, H. C. (1962). The effects of a year's experience in America on the self-image of Scandinavians: A preliminary analysis of reactions to a new environment. *Journal of Social Issues, 18*(1), 30-40.

Ball-Rokeach, S.J., Rokeach, M., & Grube, J.W. (1984). *The great America values test: Influencing behavior and belief through television.* New York: Free Press.

Bandler, R.J., Madaras, G.R., & Bem, D.J. (1968). Self-observation as a source of pain perception. *Journal of Personality and Social Psychology, 9,* 205-209.

Bandura, A. (1977). Self-efficacy: Toward a unifying theory of behavioral change. *Psychological Review, 84,* 191-215.

Bandura, A. (1982). Self-efficacy mechanism in human agency. *American Psychologist, 37,* 122-147.

Bandura, A., Adams, N.E., & Beyer, J. (1977). Cognitive processes mediating behavioral change. *Journal of Personality and Social Psychology, 35,* 125-139.

Bandura, A., Adams, N.E., Hardy, A.B., & Howells, G.N. (1980). Tests of the generality of self-efficacy theory. *Cognitive Therapy and Research, 4,* 39-66.

Barclay, J.E., & Weaver, H.B. (1962). Comparative reliabilities and ease of construction of Thurstone and Likert attitude scales. *Journal of Social Psychology, 58,* 109-120.

Bargh, J.A. (1982). Attention and automaticity in the processing of self-relevant information. *Journal of Personality and Social Psychology, 43,* 425-436.

Bargh, J.A. (1984). Automatic and conscious processing of social information. In R.S. Wyer Jr., & T.K. Srull (Eds.), *Handbook of social cognition* (Vol. 3, pp. 1-43). Hillsdale, NJ: Erlbaum.

Bargh, J.A. (1988). Automatic information processing: Implications for communication and affect. In L. Donohew, H.E. Sypher, & E.T. Higgins (Eds.), *Communication, social cognition, and affect* (pp. 9-32). Hillsdale, NJ: Erlbaum.

Bargh, J.A. (1989). Conditional automaticity: Varieties of automatic influence in social perception and cognition. In J.S. Uleman & J.A. Bargh (Eds.), *Unintended thought* (pp. 3-51). New York: Guilford Press.

Bargh, J.A., Bond, R.N., Lombardi, W.J., & Tota, M.E. (1986). The additive nature of chronic and temporary sources of construct accessibility. *Journal of Personality and Social Psychology, 50,* 869-878.

Bargh, J.A., Chaiken, S., Govender, R., & Pratto, F. (1992). The generality of the automatic attitude activation effect. *Journal of Personality and Social Psychology, 62,* 893-912.

Bargh, J.A., & Pietromonaco, P. (1982). Automatic information processing and social perception: The influence of trait information presented outside of conscious awareness on impression formation. *Journal of Personality and Social Psychology, 43,* 437-449.

Bargh, J.A., & Thein, R.D. (1985). Individual construct accessibility, person memory, and the recall-judgment link: The case of information overload. *Journal of Personality and Social Psychology, 49,* 1129-1146.

Barlow, J.D. (1969). Pupillary size as an index of preference in political candidates. *Perceptual and Motor Skills, 28,* 587-590.

Baron, R.M., & Kenny, D.A. (1986). The moderator-mediator variable distinction in social psychological research: Conceptual, strategic, and statistical considerations. *Journal of Personality and Social Psychology, 51,* 1173-1182.

Baron, R.S., Baron, P.H., & Miller N. (1973). The relation between distraction and persuasion. *Psychological Bulletin, 80,* 310-323.

Baron, R.S., & Miller, N. (1969). Credibility, distraction, and counterargument in a forewarning situation. *Proceedings of the 77th Annual Convention of the American Psychological Association, 4,* 411-412.

Barthel, J. (1977). *A death in Canaan.* New York: Dell.

Bartlett, F.C. (1932). *Remembering: A study in experimental and social psychology.* Cambridge, England: Cambridge University Press.

Bass, B.M. (1955). Authoritarianism or acquiescence? *Journal of Abnormal and Social Psychology, 51,* 616-623.

Bateman, R.M., & Remmers, H.H. (1941). A study of the shifting attitude of high school students when subjected to favorable and unfavorable propaganda. *Journal of Social Psychology, 13,* 395-406.

Batra, R., & Stayman, D.M. (1990). The role of mood in advertising effectiveness. *Journal of Consumer Research, 17,* 203-214.

Batson, C.D., & Ventis, W.L. (1982). *The religious experience: A social-psychological perspective.* New York: Oxford University Press.

Bauman, K.E., & Dent, C.W. (1982). Influence of an objective measure on self-reports of behavior. *Journal of Applied Psychology, 67,* 623-628.

Baumeister, R.F., & Tice, D.M. (1984). Role of self-presentation and choice in cognitive dissonance under forced compliance: Necessary or sufficient causes? *Journal of Personality and Social Psychology, 46,* 5-13.

Baumgardner, M.H., Leippe, M.R., Ronis, D.L., & Greenwald, A.G. (1983). In search of reliable persuasion effects: II. Associative interference and persistence of persuasion in a message-dense environment. *Journal of Personality and Social Psychology, 45,* 524-537.

Baumrind, D. (1964). Some thoughts on ethics of research: After reading Milgram's "Behavioral study of obedience." *American Psychologist, 19,* 421-423.

Bavelas, A. (1947). Role playing and management training. *Sociatry, 1,* 183-191.

Beale, D.A., & Manstead, A.S.R. (1991). Predicting mothers' intentions to limit frequency of infants' sugar intake: Testing the theory of planned behavior. *Journal of Applied Social Psychology, 21,* 409-431.

Beck, K.H., & Frankel, A. (1981). A conceptualization of threat communications and protective health behavior. *Social Psychology Quarterly, 44,* 204-217.

Beck, K. H., & Lund, A. K. (1981). The effects of health threat seriousness and personal efficacy upon intentions and behavior. *Journal of Applied Social Psychology*, *11*, 401–415.

Beck, L., & Ajzen, I. (1991). Predicting dishonest actions using the theory of planned behavior. *Journal of Research in Personality*, *25*, 285–301.

Beckmann, J., & Gollwitzer, P. M. (1987). Deliberative versus implemental states of mind: The issue of impartiality in predecisional and postdecisional information processing. *Social Cognition*, *5*, 259–279.

Behavioral Science Subpanel of President's Science Advisory Committee. (1962). Strengthening the behavioral sciences. *Behavioral Science*, *7*, 275–288.

Belch, G. E. (1982). The effects of television commercial repetition on cognitive response and message acceptance. *Journal of Consumer Research*, *9*, 56–65.

Belk, R. W. (1985). Issues in the intention-behavior discrepancy. *Research in Consumer Behavior*, *1*, 1–34.

Bell, B. E., & Loftus, E. F. (1989). Trivial persuasion in the courtroom: The power of (a few) minor details. *Journal of Personality and Social Psychology*, *56*, 669–679.

Belmore, S. M., & Hubbard, M. L. (1987). The role of advance expectancies in person memory. *Journal of Personality and Social Psychology*, *53*, 61–70.

Bem, D. J. (1965). An experimental analysis of self-persuasion. *Journal of Experimental Social Psychology*, *1*, 199–218.

Bem, D. J. (1966). Inducing belief in false confessions. *Journal of Personality and Social Psychology*, *3*, 707–710.

Bem, D. J. (1967). Self-perception: An alternative interpretation of cognitive dissonance phenomena. *Psychological Review*, *74*, 183–200.

Bem, D. J. (1968). The epistemological status of interpersonal simulations: A reply to Jones, Linder, Kiesler, Zanna, and Brehm. *Journal of Experimental Social Psychology*, *4*, 270–274.

Bem, D. J. (1970). *Beliefs, attitudes, and human affairs*. Belmont, CA: Brooks/Cole.

Bem, D. J. (1972). Self-perception theory. In L. Berkowitz (Ed.), *Advances in experimental social psychology* (Vol. 6, pp. 1–62). San Diego, CA: Academic Press.

Bem, D. J., & Funder, D. C. (1978). Predicting more of the people more of the time: Assessing the personality of situations. *Psychological Review*, *85*, 485–501.

Bem, D. J., & McConnell, H. K. (1970). Testing the self-perception explanation of dissonance phenomena: On the salience of premanipulation attitudes. *Journal of Personality and Social Psychology*, *14*, 23–31.

Bentler, P. M. (1968a). Heterosexual behavior assessment: I. Males. *Behavior Research and Therapy*, *6*, 21–25.

Bentler, P. M. (1968b). Heterosexual behavior assessment: II. Females. *Behavior Research and Therapy*, *6*, 27–30.

Bentler, P. M. (1980). Multivariate analysis with latent variables: Causal modeling. *Annual Review of Psychology*, *30*, 419–456.

Bentler, P. M., & Speckart, G. (1979). Models of attitude-behavior relations. *Psychological Review*, *86*, 452–464.

Bentler, P. M., & Speckart, G. (1981). Attitudes "cause" behaviors: A structural equation analysis. *Journal of Personality and Social Psychology*, *40*, 226–238.

Benware, C., & Deci, E. L. (1975). Attitude change as a function of the inducement for espousing a proattitudinal communication. *Journal of Experimental Social Psychology*, *11*, 271–278.

Berger, J., Rosenholtz, S. J., & Zelditch, M., Jr. (1980). Status organizing processes. *Annual Review of Sociology*, *6*, 479–508.

Berger, J., & Zelditch, M., Jr. (1985). *Status, rewards, and influence*. San Francisco: Jossey-Bass.

Bergin, A. E. (1962). The effect of dissonant persuasive communications upon changes in a self-referring attitude. *Journal of Personality*, *30*, 423–438.

Beringer, R. E., Hattaway, H., Jones, A., & Still, W. N., Jr. (1986). *Why the South lost the Civil War*. Athens: University of Georgia Press.

Berkowitz, L., & Cottingham, D. R. (1960). The interest value and relevance of fear arousing communications. *Journal of Abnormal and Social Psychology*, *60*, 37–43.

Berkowitz, L., & Devine, P. G. (1989). Research traditions, analysis, and synthesis in social psychological theories: The case of dissonance theory. *Personality and Social Psychology Bulletin*, *15*, 493–507.

Berkowitz, L., & Knurek, D. (1969). Label-mediated hostility generalization. *Journal of Personality and Social Psychology*, *13*, 200–206.

Berlyne, D. E. (1954). A theory of human curiosity. *British Journal of Psychology*, *45*, 180–191.

Berlyne, D. E. (1967). Arousal and reinforcement. In D. Levine (Ed.), *Nebraska Symposium on Motivation* (Vol. 15, pp. 1–110). Lincoln: University of Nebraska Press.

Berlyne, D. E. (1970). Novelty, complexity, and hedonic value. *Perception & Psychophysics*, *8*, 279–286.

Berlyne, D. E. (1971). *Aesthetics and psychobiology*. New York: Appleton-Century-Crofts.

Berlyne, D. E. (1974). Novelty, complexity, and interestingness. In D. E. Berlyne (Ed.), *Studies in the new experimental aesthetics: Steps toward an objective psychology of aesthetic appreciation* (pp. 175–180). Washington, DC: Hemisphere.

Berscheid, E. (1966). Opinion change and communicator-communicatee similarity and dissimilarity. *Journal of Personality and Social Psychology*, *4*, 670–680.

Berscheid, E. (1985). Interpersonal attraction. In G. Lindzey & E. Aronson (Eds.), *Handbook of social psychology* (3rd ed., Vol. 2, pp. 413–484). New York: Random House.

Berscheid, E., & Walster, E. (1974). Physical attractiveness. In L. Berkowitz (Ed.), *Advances in experimental social*

702

psychology (Vol. 7, pp. 157-215). San Diego, CA: Academic Press.

Bettman, J.R. (1979). *An information processing theory of consumer choice*. Reading, MA: Addison-Wesley.

Bettman, J.R. (1981). A functional analysis of the role of overall evaluation of alternatives in choice processes. *Advances in Consumer Research*, *9*, 87-93.

Biddle, B.J., Bank, B.J., & Slavings, R.L. (1987). Norms, preferences, identities and retention decisions. *Social Psychology Quarterly*, *50*, 322-337.

Biek, M., Wood, W., Chaiken, S., & Nations, C. (1992). *Working knowledge, cognitive processing, and attitudes: On the inevitability of bias*. Unpublished manuscript, Texas A & M University, College Station, TX.

Bieri, J. (1966). Cognitive complexity and personality development. In O.J. Harvey (Ed.), *Experience, structure & adaptability* (pp. 13-37). New York: Springer.

Bierley, C., McSweeney, F.K., & Vannieuwkerk, R. (1985). Classical conditioning of preferences for stimuli. *Journal of Consumer Research*, *12*, 316-323.

Biggers, T., & Pryor, B. (1982). Attitude change: A function of emotion-eliciting qualities of environment. *Personality and Social Psychology Bulletin*, *8*, 94-99.

Billig, M. (1987). *Arguing and thinking: A rhetorical approach to social psychology*. Cambridge, England: Cambridge University Press.

Birnbaum, A. (1968). Some latent trait models and their use in inferring an examinee's ability. In F.M. Lord & M.R. Novick, *Statistical theories of mental test scores* (pp. 397-479). Reading, MA: Addison-Wesley.

Birnbaum, M.H. (1973). Morality judgment: Test of an averaging model with differential weights. *Journal of Experimental Psychology*, *99*, 395-399.

Birnbaum, M.H. (1981). Thinking and feeling: A skeptical review. *American Psychologist*, *36*, 99-101.

Birnbaum, M.H. (1982). Controversies in psychological measurement. In B. Wegener (Ed.), *Social attitudes and psychophysical measurement* (pp. 401-485). Hillsdale, NJ: Erlbaum.

Birnbaum, M.H., & Mellers, B.A. (1979a). One-mediator model of exposure effects is still viable. *Journal of Personality and Social Psychology*, *37*, 1090-1096.

Birnbaum, M.H., & Mellers, B.A. (1979b). Stimulus recognition may mediate exposure effects. *Journal of Personality and Social Psychology*, *37*, 391-394.

Birnbaum, M.H., & Mellers, B.A. (1983). Bayesian inference: Combining base rates with opinions of sources who vary in credibility. *Journal of Personality and Social Psychology*, *45*, 792-804.

Birnbaum, M.H., & Stegner, S.E. (1979). Source credibility in social judgment: Bias, expertise, and the judge's point of view. *Journal of Personality and Social Psychology*, *37*, 48-74.

Birnbaum, M.H., Wong, R., & Wong, L.K. (1976). Combining information from sources that vary in credibility. *Memory and Cognition*, *4*, 330-336.

Bishop, G.F. (1990). Issue involvement and response effects in public opinion surveys. *Public Opinion Quarterly*, *54*, 209-218.

Blake, R.R., & Brehm, J.W. (1954). The use of tape recording to simulate a group atmosphere. *Journal of Abnormal and Social Psychology*, *49*, 311-313.

Blascovich, J., Ginsburg, G.P., & Veach, T.L. (1975). A pluralistic explanation of choice shifts on the risk dimension. *Journal of Personality and Social Psychology*, *31*, 422-429.

Blascovich, J., & Kelsey, R.M. (1990). Using electrodermal and cardiovascular measures of arousal in social psychological research. In C. Hendrick & M.S. Clark (Eds.), *Review of personality and social psychology* (Vol. 11, pp. 45-73). Newbury Park, CA: Sage.

Blass, T. (1991). Understanding behavior in the Milgram obedience experiment: The role of personality, situations, and their interactions. *Journal of Personality and Social Psychology*, *60*, 398-413.

Bless, H., Bohner, G., Schwarz, N., & Strack, F. (1990). Mood and persuasion: A cognitive response analysis. *Personality and Social Psychology Bulletin*, *16*, 331-345.

Bless, H., Mackie, D.M., & Schwarz, N. (in press). Mood effects on encoding and judgmental processes in persuasion. *Journal of Personality and Social Psychology*.

Blumer, H. (1955). Attitudes and the social act. *Social Problems*, *3*, 59-65.

Bobo, L. (1983). Whites' opposition to busing: Symbolic racism or realistic group conflict? *Journal of Personality and Social Psychology*, *45*, 1196-1210.

Bochner, S., & Insko, C.A. (1966). Communicator discrepancy, source credibility, and opinion change. *Journal of Personality and Social Psychology*, *4*, 614-621.

Bodenhausen, G.V. (in press). Emotions, arousal, and stereotypic judgments: A heuristic model of affect and stereotyping. In D.M. Mackie & D.L. Hamilton (Eds.), *Affect, cognition, and stereotyping: Interactive processes in group perception*. San Diego, CA: Academic Press.

Bogardus, E.S. (1925). Measuring social distances. *Journal of Applied Sociology*, *9*, 299-308.

Bogardus, E.S. (1959). *Social distance*. Yellow Springs, OH: Antioch Press.

Bohrnstedt, G.W. (1983). Measurement. In P.H. Rossi, J.D. Wright, & A.B. Anderson (Eds.), *Handbook of survey research* (pp. 69-121). San Diego, CA: Academic Press.

Boller, G.W., Swasy, J.L., & Munch, J.M. (1990). Conceptualizing argument quality via argument structure. *Advances in Consumer Research*, *17*, 321-328.

Bonnano, G.A., & Stillings, N.A. (1986). Preference, familiarity and recognition after repeated brief exposures to random geometric shapes. *American Journal of Psychology*, *99*, 403-415.

Borgatta, E. F., & Bohrnstedt, G. W. (1980). Level of measurement: Once over again. *Sociological Methods and Research*, *9*, 147–160.

Borgida, E., & Campbell, B. (1982). Belief relevance and attitude-behavior consistency: The moderating role of personal experience. *Journal of Personality and Social Psychology*, *42*, 239–247.

Borgida, E., Conner, C., & Manteufel, L. (1992). Understanding living kidney donation: A behavioral decision making perspective. In S. Spacapan & S. Oskamp (Eds.), *Helping and being helped: Naturalistic studies* (pp. 183–212). Newbury Park, CA: Sage.

Boring, E. G. (1950). *A history of experimental psychology* (2nd ed.). New York: Appleton-Century-Crofts.

Bornstein, R. F. (1989a). Exposure and affect: Overview and meta-analysis of research, 1968–1987. *Psychological Bulletin*, *106*, 265–289.

Bornstein, R. F. (1989b). Subliminal techniques as propaganda tools: Review and critique. *Journal of Mind and Behavior*, *10*, 231–262.

Bornstein, R. F., & D'Agostino, P. R. (1992). *Stimulus recognition and the mere exposure effect*. Unpublished manuscript, Gettysburg College, Gettysburg, PA.

Bornstein, R. F., Kale, A. R., & Cornell, K. R. (1990). Boredom as a limiting condition on the mere exposure effect. *Journal of Personality and Social Psychology*, *58*, 791–800.

Bornstein, R. F., Leone, D. R., & Galley, D. J. (1987). The generalizability of subliminal mere exposure effects: Influence of stimuli perceived without awareness on social behavior. *Journal of Personality and Social Psychology*, *53*, 1070–1079.

Boster, F. J., & Mongeau, P. (1984). Fear-arousing persuasive messages. In R. N. Bostrom (Ed.), *Communication yearbook* (Vol. 8, pp. 330–375). Beverly Hills, CA: Sage.

Bostrom, R. N., Vlandis, J. W., & Rosenbaum, M. E. (1961). Grades as reinforcing contingencies and attitude change. *Journal of Educational Psychology*, *52*, 112–115.

Bothwell, R. K., & Brigham, J. C. (1983). Selective evaluation and recall during the 1980 Reagan-Carter debate. *Journal of Applied Social Psychology*, *13*, 427–442.

Bower, G. H. (1981). Mood and memory. *American Psychologist*, *36*, 129–148.

Bradburn, N. M. (1983). Response effects. In P. H. Rossi, J. D. Wright, & A. B. Anderson (Eds.), *Handbook of survey research* (pp. 289–328). San Diego, CA: Academic Press.

Bransford, J. D., & Johnson, M. K. (1972). Contextual prerequisites for understanding: Some investigations of comprehension and recall. *Journal of Verbal Learning and Verbal Behavior*, *11*, 717–726.

Bray, R. M., Johnson, D., & Chilstrom, J. T., Jr. (1982). Social influence by group members with minority opinions: A comparison of Hollander and Moscovici. *Journal of Personality and Social Psychology*, *43*, 78–88.

Breckler, S. J. (1984a). Empirical validation of affect, behavior, and cognition as distinct components of attitude. *Journal of Personality and Social Psychology*, *47*, 1191–1205.

Breckler, S. J. (1984b). Validation of affect, behavior, and cognition as distinct components of attitude (Doctoral dissertation, Ohio State University, 1983). *Dissertation Abstracts International*, *44*, 3569B.

Breckler, S. J., & Wiggins, E. C. (1989a). Affect versus evaluation in the structure of attitudes. *Journal of Experimental Social Psychology*, *25*, 253–271.

Breckler, S. J., & Wiggins, E. C. (1989b). Scales for the measurement of attitudes toward blood donation. *Transfusion*, *29*, 401–404.

Breckler, S. J., & Wiggins, E. C. (1991). Cognitive responses in persuasion: Affective and evaluative determinants. *Journal of Experimental Social Psychology*, *27*, 180–200.

Brehm, J. W. (1956). Postdecision changes in the desirability of alternatives. *Journal of Abnormal and Social Psychology*, *52*, 384–389.

Brehm, J. W. (1960). Attitudinal consequences of commitment to unpleasant behavior. *Journal of Abnormal and Social Psychology*, *60*, 379–383.

Brehm, J. W. (1966). *A theory of psychological reactance*. San Diego, CA: Academic Press.

Brehm, J. W. (1968). Attitude change from threat to attitudinal freedom. In A. G. Greenwald, T. C. Brock, & T. M. Ostrom (Eds.), *Psychological foundations of attitudes* (pp. 277–296). San Diego, CA: Academic Press.

Brehm, J. W. (1972). *Responses to loss of freedom: A theory of psychological reactance*. Morristown, NJ: General Learning Press.

Brehm, J. W., & Cohen, A. R. (1959). Reevaluation of choice alternatives as a function of their number and qualitative similarity. *Journal of Abnormal and Social Psychology*, *58*, 373–378.

Brehm, J. W., & Cohen, A. R. (1962). *Explorations in cognitive dissonance*. New York: Wiley.

Brehm J. W., & Mann, M. (1975). Effect of importance of freedom and attraction to group members on influence produced by group pressure. *Journal of Personality and Social Psychology*, *31*, 816–824.

Brehm, S. S., & Brehm, J. W. (1981). *Psychological reactance: A theory of freedom and control*. San Diego, CA: Academic Press.

Brent, E., & Granberg, D. (1982). Subjective agreement with the presidential candidates of 1976 and 1980. *Journal of Personality and Social Psychology*, *42*, 393–403.

Brewer, W. F. (1974). There is no convincing evidence for operant or classical conditioning in adult humans. In W. B. Weimer & D. S. Palermo (Eds.), *Cognition and the symbolic processes* (pp. 1–42). Hillsdale, NJ: Erlbaum.

704

Brickman, P. (1987). *Commitment, conflict, and caring.* Englewood Cliffs, NJ: Prentice-Hall.

Brickman, P., Redfield, J., Harrison, A. A., & Crandall, R. (1972). Drive and predisposition as factors in the attitudinal effects of mere exposure. *Journal of Experimental Social Psychology, 8,* 31-44.

Brickner, M. A., Harkins, S. G., & Ostrom, T. M. (1986). Effects of personal involvement: Thought-provoking implications for social loafing. *Journal of Personality and Social Psychology, 51,* 763-769.

Brigham, J. C., & Cook, S. W. (1969). The influence of attitude on the recall of controversial material: A failure to confirm. *Journal of Experimental Social Psychology, 5,* 240-243.

Brinberg, D. (1979). An examination of the determinants of intention and behavior: A comparison of two models. *Journal of Applied Social Psychology, 9,* 560-575.

Brinberg, D., & Cummings, V. (1983). Purchasing generic prescription drugs: An analysis using two behavioral intention models. *Advances in Consumer Research, 11,* 229-234.

Brinberg, D., & Durand, J. (1983). Eating at fast-food restaurants: An analysis using two behavioral intention models. *Journal of Applied Social Psychology, 13,* 459-472.

Broadbent, D. E. (1958). *Perception and communication.* New York: Pergamon Press.

Brock, T. C. (1962). Cognitive restructuring and attitude change. *Journal of Abnormal and Social Psychology, 64,* 264-271.

Brock, T. C. (1965a). Commitment to exposure as a determinant of information receptivity. *Journal of Personality and Social Psychology, 2,* 10-19.

Brock, T. C. (1965b). Communicator-recipient similarity and decision change. *Journal of Personality and Social Psychology, 1,* 650-654.

Brock, T. C. (1967). Communication discrepancy and intent to persuade as determinants of counterargument production. *Journal of Experimental Social Psychology, 3,* 296-309.

Brock, T. C., Albert, S. M., & Becker, L. A. (1970). Familiarity, utility, and supportiveness as determinants of information receptivity. *Journal of Personality and Social Psychology, 14,* 292-301.

Brock, T. C., & Balloun, J. L. (1967). Behavioral receptivity to dissonant information. *Journal of Personality and Social Psychology, 6,* 413-428.

Brock, T. C., & Becker, L. A. (1965). Ineffectiveness of "overheard" counterpropaganda. *Journal of Personality and Social Psychology, 2,* 654-660.

Brock, T. C., & Blackwood, J. E. (1962). Dissonance reduction, social comparison, and modification of others' opinions. *Journal of Abnormal and Social Psychology, 65,* 319-324.

Brock, T. C., & Buss, A. H. (1962). Dissonance, aggression, and evaluation of pain. *Journal of Abnormal and Social Psychology, 65,* 197-202.

Brock, T. C., & Shavitt, S. (1983). Cognitive-response analysis in advertising. In L. Percy & A. G. Woodside (Eds.), *Advertising and consumer psychology* (pp. 91-116). Lexington, MA: Lexington/Heath.

Brockner, J., & Elkind, M. (1985). Self-esteem and reactance: Further evidence of attitudinal and motivational consequences. *Journal of Experimental Social Psychology, 21,* 346-361.

Brodbeck, M. (1956). The role of small groups in mediating the effects of propaganda. *Journal of Abnormal and Social Psychology, 52,* 166-170.

Brown, G. H., & Harding, F. D. (1973). *A comparison of methods of studying illicit drug usage* (HumRRO Tech. Rep. No. 73-9). Alexandria, VA: Human Resources Research Organization.

Brown, R. (1965). *Social psychology.* New York: Free Press.

Brown, R. (1974). Further comment on the risky shift. *American Psychologist, 29,* 468-470.

Brubaker, R. G., & Fowler, C. (1990). Encouraging college males to perform testicular self-examination: Evaluation of a persuasive message based on the revised theory of reasoned action. *Journal of Applied Social Psychology, 17,* 1411-1422.

Bruner, J. S. (1957). On perceptual readiness. *Psychological Review, 64,* 123-152.

Bruner, J. S., & Goodman, C. C. (1947). Value and need as organizing factors in perception. *Journal of Abnormal and Social Psychology, 42,* 33-44.

Buck, R. (1985). Prime theory: An integrated view of motivation and emotion. *Psychological Review, 92,* 389-413.

Budd, R. J., North, D., & Spencer, C. (1984). Understanding seat-belt use: A test of Bentler and Speckart's extension of the "theory of reasoned action." *European Journal of Social Psychology, 14,* 69-78.

Buller, D. B. (1986). Distraction during persuasive communication: A meta-analytic review. *Communication Monographs, 53,* 91-114.

Burgoon, M., Cohen, M., Miller, M. D., & Montgomery, C. L. (1978). An empirical test of a model of resistance to persuasion. *Human Communication Research, 5,* 27-39.

Burnkrant, R. E., & Howard, D. J. (1984). Effects of the use of introductory rhetorical questions versus statements on information processing. *Journal of Personality and Social Psychology, 47,* 1218-1230.

Burnkrant, R. E., & Unnava, R. (1989). Self-referencing: A strategy for increasing processing of message content. *Personality and Social Psychology Bulletin, 15,* 628-638.

Burnstein, E., & Vinokur, A. (1975). What a person thinks upon learning he has chosen differently from others: Nice evidence for the persuasive-arguments explanation of choice shifts. *Journal of Experimental Social Psychology, 11*, 412-426.

Burnstein, E., & Vinokur, A. (1977). Persuasive argumentation and social comparison as determinants of attitude polarization. *Journal of Experimental Social Psychology, 13*, 315-332.

Burnstein, E., Vinokur, A., & Trope, Y. (1973). Interpersonal comparison versus persuasive argumentation: A more direct test of alternative explanations for group-induced shifts in individual choice. *Journal of Experimental Social Psychology, 9*, 236-245.

Buss, A. H. (1980). *Self-consciousness and social anxiety*. San Francisco: Freeman.

Byrne, D. E. (1964). Repression-sensitization as a dimension of personality. In B. H. Maher (Ed.), *Progress in experimental personality research* (Vol. 1, pp. 169-220). San Diego, CA: Academic Press.

Byrne, D. E. (1971). *The attraction paradigm*. San Diego, CA: Academic Press.

Byrne, D. E., & Cherry, F. (1978). A plumber's friend in need is a plumber's friend indeed. *Journal of Research in Personality, 12*, 193-196.

Byrne, D. E., & Clore, G. L. (1970). A reinforcement model of evaluative responses. *Personality: An International Journal, 1*, 103-128.

Byrne, D. E., Clore, G. L., Griffit, W., Lamberth, J., & Mitchell, H. E. (1973a). One more time. *Journal of Personality and Social Psychology, 28*, 323-324.

Byrne, D. E., Clore, G. L., Griffit, W., Lamberth, J., & Mitchell, H. E. (1973b). When research paradigms converge: Confrontation or integration? *Journal of Personality and Social Psychology, 28*, 313-320.

Byrnes, D. A., & Kiger, G. (1990). The effect of a prejudice-reduction simulation on attitude change. *Journal of Applied Social Psychology, 20*, 341-356.

Cacioppo, J. T. (1979). Effects of exogenous changes in heart rate on the facilitation of thought and resistance to persuasion. *Journal of Personality and Social Psychology, 37*, 489-498.

Cacioppo, J. T., Harkins, S. G., & Petty, R. E. (1981). The nature of attitudes and cognitive responses and their relationships to behavior. In R. E. Petty, T. M. Ostrom, & T. C. Brock (Eds.), *Cognitive responses in persuasion* (pp. 31-54). Hillsdale, NJ: Erlbaum.

Cacioppo, J. T., Marshall-Goodell, B. S., Tassinary, L. G., & Petty, R. E. (1992). Rudimentary determinants of attitudes: Classical conditioning is more effective when prior knowledge about the attitude stimulus is low than high. *Journal of Experimental Social Psychology, 28*, 207-233.

Cacioppo, J. T., & Petty, R. E. (1979a). Attitudes and cognitive response: An electrophysiological approach. *Journal of Personality and Social Psychology, 37*, 2181-2199.

Cacioppo, J. T., & Petty, R. E. (1979b). Effects of message repetition and position on cognitive response, recall, and persuasion. *Journal of Personality and Social Psychology, 37*, 97-109.

Cacioppo, J. T., & Petty, R. E. (1981a). Effects of extent of thought on the pleasantness ratings of P-O-X triads: Evidence for three judgmental tendencies in evaluating social situations. *Journal of Personality and Social Psychology, 40*, 1000-1009.

Cacioppo, J. T., & Petty, R. E. (1981b). Electromyograms as measures of extent and affectivity of information processing. *American Psychologist, 36*, 441-456.

Cacioppo, J. T., & Petty, R. E. (1982). The need for cognition. *Journal of Personality and Social Psychology, 42*, 116-131.

Cacioppo, J. T., & Petty, R. E. (1984). The need for cognition: Relationship to attitudinal processes. In R. P. McGlynn, J. E. Maddux, C. D. Stoltenberg, & J. H. Harvey (Eds.), *Social perception in clinical and counseling psychology* (pp. 113-119). Lubbock, TX: Texas Tech Press.

Cacioppo, J. T., & Petty, R. E. (1985). Central and peripheral routes to persuasion: The role of message repetition. In L. F. Alwitt & A. A. Mitchell (Eds.), *Psychological processes and advertising effects* (pp. 91-111). Hillsdale, NJ: Erlbaum.

Cacioppo, J. T., & Petty, R. E. (1987). Stalking rudimentary processes of social influence: A psychophysiological approach. In M. P. Zanna, J. M. Olson, & C. P. Herman (Eds.), *Social influence: The Ontario Symposium* (Vol. 5, pp. 41-74). Hillsdale, NJ: Erlbaum.

Cacioppo, J. T., Petty, R. E., & Geen, T. R. (1989). Attitude structure and function: From the tripartite to the homeostasis model of attitudes. In A. R. Pratkanis, S. J. Breckler, & A. G. Greenwald (Eds.), *Attitude structure and function* (pp. 275-309). Hillsdale, NJ: Erlbaum.

Cacioppo, J. T., Petty, R. E., Kao, C. F., & Rodriguez, R. (1986). Central and peripheral routes to persuasion: An individual difference perspective. *Journal of Personality and Social Psychology, 51*, 1032-1043.

Cacioppo, J. T., Petty, R. E., Losch, M. E., & Kim, H. S. (1986). Electromyographic activity over facial muscle regions can differentiate the valence and intensity of affective reactions. *Journal of Personality and Social Psychology, 50*, 260-268.

Cacioppo, J. T., Petty, R. E., & Morris, K. J. (1983). Effects of need for cognition on message evaluation, recall, and persuasion. *Journal of Personality and Social Psychology, 45*, 805-818.

Cacioppo, J. T., Petty, R. E., & Sidera, J. (1982). The effects of a salient self-schema on the evaluation of proattitudinal editorials: Top-down versus bottom-up message processing. *Journal of Experimental Social Psychology, 18*, 324-338.

Cacioppo, J. T., & Sandman, C. A. (1981). Psychophysiological functioning, cognitive responding, and attitudes. In R. E. Petty, T. M. Ostrom, & T. C. Brock (Eds.), *Cognitive responses in persuasion* (pp. 81-103). Hillsdale, NJ: Erlbaum.

Cacioppo, J. T., Sandman, C. A., & Walker, B. B. (1978). The effects of operant heart rate conditioning on cognitive elaboration and attitude change. *Psychophysiology, 15*, 330-338.

Calder, B. J., Insko, C. A., & Yandell, B. (1974). The relation of cognitive and memorial processes to persuasion in a simulated jury trial. *Journal of Applied Social Psychology, 4*, 62-93.

Calder, B. J., Ross, M., & Insko, C. A. (1973). Attitude change and attitude attribution: Effects of incentive, choice, and consequences. *Journal of Personality and Social Psychology, 25*, 84-99.

Calder, B. J., & Sternthal, B. (1980). Television commercial wear-out: An information-processing view. *Journal of Marketing Research, 17*, 173-186.

Campbell, A., Converse, P. E., Miller, W. E., & Stokes, D. E. (1960). *The American voter*. New York: Wiley.

Campbell, D. T. (1950). The indirect assessment of social attitudes. *Psychological Bulletin, 47*, 15-38.

Campbell, D. T. (1963). Social attitudes and other acquired behavioral dispositions. In S. Koch (Ed.), *Psychology: A study of a science* (Vol. 6, pp. 94-172). New York: McGraw-Hill.

Campbell, D. T., & Fiske, D. W. (1959). Convergent and discriminant validation by the multitrait-multimethod matrix. *Psychological Bulletin, 56*, 81-105.

Campbell, J. D. (1986). Similarity and uniqueness: The effects of attribute type, relevance, and individual differences in self-esteem and depression. *Journal of Personality and Social Psychology, 50*, 281-294.

Canary, D. J., & Seibold, D. R. (1984). *Attitudes and behavior: An annotated bibliography*. New York: Praeger.

Cantril, H. (1940). Experiments in the wording of questions. *Public Opinion Quarterly, 4*, 330-332.

Carlsmith, J. M., Collins, B. E., & Helmreich, R. L. (1966). Studies in forced compliance: I. The effect of pressure for compliance on attitude change produced by face-to-face role playing and anonymous essay writing. *Journal of Personality and Social Psychology, 4*, 1-13.

Carlson, E. R. (1953). Attitude change through modification of attitude structure (Doctoral dissertation, University of Michigan). *Dissertation Abstracts International, 14*, 726.

Carlson, E. R. (1956). Attitude change through modification of attitude structure. *Journal of Abnormal and Social Psychology, 52*, 256-261.

Carlston, D. E., & Skowronski, J. J. (1986). Trait memory and behavior memory: The effects of alternative pathways on impression judgment response times. *Journal of Personality and Social Psychology, 50*, 5-13.

Cartwright, D. (1965). Influence, leadership, control. In J. G. March (Ed.), *Handbook of organizations* (pp. 1-47). Chicago: Rand McNally.

Cartwright, D. (1971). Risk taking by individuals and groups: An assessment of research employing choice dilemmas. *Journal of Personality and Social Psychology, 20*, 361-378.

Cartwright, D. (1973). Determinants of scientific progress: The case of research on the risky shift. *American Psychologist, 28*, 222-231.

Cartwright, D., & Harary, F. (1956). Structural balance: A generalization of Heider's theory. *Psychological Review, 63*, 277-293.

Cartwright, D., & Harary, F. (1979). Balance and clusterability: An overview. In P. Holland & S. Leinhardt (Eds.), *Perspectives on social network research* (pp. 25-50). San Diego, CA: Academic Press.

Carver, C. S., & Scheier, M. F. (1981). *Attention and self-regulation: A control-theory approach to human behavior*. New York: Springer-Verlag.

Chaiken, S. (1979). Communicator physical attractiveness and persuasion. *Journal of Personality and Social Psychology, 37*, 1387-1397.

Chaiken, S. (1980). Heuristic versus systematic information processing and the use of source versus message cues in persuasion. *Journal of Personality and Social Psychology, 39*, 752-766.

Chaiken, S. (1982, October). *The heuristic/systematic processing distinction in persuasion*. Paper presented at the meeting of the Society of Experimental Social Psychology, Nashville, TN.

Chaiken, S. (1984, August). *Memory for attitudinally consistent versus inconsistent information*. Paper presented at the meeting of the American Psychological Association, Toronto.

Chaiken, S. (1986). Physical appearance and social influence. In C. P. Herman, M. P. Zanna, & E. T. Higgins (Eds.), *Physical appearance, stigma, and social behavior: The Ontario Symposium* (Vol. 3, pp. 143-177). Hillsdale, NJ: Erlbaum.

Chaiken, S. (1987). The heuristic model of persuasion. In M. P. Zanna, J. M. Olson, & C. P. Herman (Eds.), *Social influence: The Ontario Symposium* (Vol. 5, pp. 3-39). Hillsdale, NJ: Erlbaum.

Chaiken, S., Axsom, D., Liberman, A., & Wilson, D. (1992). *Heuristic processing of persuasive messages: Chronic and temporary sources of rule accessibility*. Unpublished manuscript, New York University, New York, NY.

Chaiken, S., & Baldwin, M. W. (1981). Affective-cognitive consistency and the effect of salient behavioral information on the self-perception of attitudes. *Journal of Personality and Social Psychology*, *41*, 1-12.

Chaiken, S., & Eagly, A. H. (1976). Communication modality as a determinant of message persuasiveness and message comprehensibility. *Journal of Personality and Social Psychology*, *34*, 605-614.

Chaiken, S., & Eagly, A. H. (1983). Communication modality as a determinant of persuasion: The role of communicator salience. *Journal of Personality and Social Psychology*, *45*, 241-256.

Chaiken, S., Liberman, A., & Eagly, A. H. (1989). Heuristic and systematic processing within and beyond the persuasion context. In J. S. Uleman & J. A. Bargh (Eds.), *Unintended thought* (pp. 212-252). New York: Guilford Press.

Chaiken, S., & Maheswaran, D. (1992). *Heuristic processing can bias systematic processing: The effect of source credibility, argument ambiguity, and task importance on attitude judgment*. Unpublished manuscript, New York University, New York, NY.

Chaiken, S., Pomerantz, E. M., & Giner-Sorolla, R. (in press). Structural consistency and attitude strength. In R. E. Petty & J. A. Krosnick (Eds.), *Attitude strength: Antecedents and consequences*. Hillsdale, NJ: Erlbaum.

Chaiken, S., & Stangor, C. (1987). Attitudes and attitude change. *Annual Review of Psychology*, *38*, 575-630.

Chaiken, S., & Yates, S. M. (1985). Affective-cognitive consistency and thought-induced attitude polarization. *Journal of Personality and Social Psychology*, *49*, 1470-1481.

Chapanis, N. P., & Chapanis, A. (1964). Cognitive dissonance: Five years later. *Psychological Bulletin*, *61*, 1-22.

Charng, H., Piliavin, J. A., & Callero, P. L. (1988). Role identity and reasoned action in the prediction of repeated behavior. *Social Psychology Quarterly*, *51*, 303-317.

Chassin, L., Presson, C. C., & Sherman, S. J. (1990). Social psychological contributions to the understanding and prevention of adolescent cigarette smoking. *Personality and Social Psychology Bulletin*, *16*, 133-151.

Chattopadhyay, A., & Alba, J. W. (1988). The situational importance of recall and inference in consumer decision making. *Journal of Consumer Research*, *15*, 1-12.

Chein, I. (1948). Behavior theory and the behavior of attitudes: Some critical comments. *Psychological Review*, *55*, 175-188.

Cherry, F., Byrne, D. E., & Mitchell, H. E. (1976). Clogs in the bogus pipeline: Demand characteristics and social desirability. *Journal of Research in Personality*, *10*, 69-75.

Chris, S. A., & Zanna, M. P. (1981, June). *Self-monitoring and anonymity in the forced-compliance situation: A test of dissonance and impression management theories*. Paper presented at the meeting of the Canadian Psychological Association, Toronto.

Christie, R. (1954). Authoritarianism re-examined. In R. Christie & M. Jahoda (Eds.), *Studies in the scope and method of "The authoritarian personality"* (pp. 123-196). Glencoe, IL: Free Press.

Christie, R., & Jahoda, M. (Eds.). (1954). *Studies in the scope and method of "The authoritarian personality."* Glencoe, IL: Free Press.

Chu, G. C. (1966). Fear arousal, efficacy and imminency. *Journal of Personality and Social Psychology*, *4*, 517-524.

Chu, G. C. (1967). Prior familiarity, perceived bias, and one-sided versus two-sided communications. *Journal of Experimental Social Psychology*, *3*, 243-254.

Cialdini, R. B. (1987). Compliance principles of compliance professionals: Psychologists of necessity. In M. P. Zanna, J. M. Olson, & C. P. Herman (Eds.), *Social influence: The Ontario Symposium* (Vol. 5, pp 165-184). Hillsdale, NJ: Erlbaum.

Cialdini, R. B. (1988). *Influence: Science and practice* (2nd ed.). Glenview, IL: Scott, Foresman.

Cialdini, R. B., & Insko, C. A. (1969). Attitudinal verbal reinforcement as a function of informational consistency: A further test of the two-factor theory. *Journal of Personality and Social Psychology*, *12*, 342-350.

Cialdini, R. B., Levy, A., Herman, C. P., & Evenbeck, S. (1973). Attitudinal politics: The strategy of moderation. *Journal of Personality and Social Psychology*, *25*, 100-108.

Cialdini, R. B., Levy, A., Herman, C. P., Kozlowski, L. T., & Petty, R. E. (1976). Elastic shifts of opinion: Determinants of direction and durability. *Journal of Personality and Social Psychology*, *34*, 663-672.

Cialdini, R. B., & Petty, R. E. (1981). Anticipatory opinion effects. In R. E. Petty, T. M. Ostrom, & T. C. Brock (Eds.), *Cognitive responses in persuasion* (pp. 217-235). Hillsdale, NJ: Erlbaum.

Cialdini, R. B., Petty, R. E., & Cacioppo, J. T. (1981). Attitude and attitude change. *Annual Review of Psychology*, *32*, 357-404.

Clark, M. S., & Isen, A. M. (1982). Feeling states and social behavior. In A. Hastorf & A. M. Isen (Eds.), *Cognitive social psychology* (pp. 73-108). New York: Elsevier/North-Holland.

Clark, R. A. (1979). The impact on selection of persuasive strategies of self-interest and desired liking. *Communication Monographs*, *46*, 257-273.

Clark, R. D., III, & Maass, A. (1990). The effects of majority size on minority influence. *European Journal of Social Psychology*, *20*, 99-117.

Clarke, P., & James, J. (1967). The effects of situation, attitude intensity and personality on information-seeking. *Sociometry*, *30*, 235-245.

Clore, G. L., & Bryne, D. E. (1974). A reinforcement-affect model of attraction. In T. L. Huston (Ed.), *Foundations of interpersonal attraction* (pp. 143-170). San Diego, CA: Academic Press.

Coch, L., & French, J. R. P., Jr. (1948). Overcoming resistance to change. *Human Relations, 1*, 512-532.

Cody, M. J., McLaughlin, M. L., & Jordan, W. J. (1980). A multidimensional scaling of three sets of compliance gaining strategies. *Communication Quarterly, 3*, 34-46.

Cohen, A. R. (1957). Need for cognition and order of communication as determinants of opinion change. In C. I. Hovland (Ed.), *The order of presentation in persuasion* (pp. 79-97). New Haven, CT: Yale University Press.

Cohen, A. R., Brehm, J. W., & Fleming, W. H. (1958). Attitude change and justification for compliance. *Journal of Abnormal and Social Psychology, 56*, 276-278.

Cohen, B. H. (1964). Role of awareness in meaning established by classical conditioning. *Journal of Experimental Psychology, 67*, 373-378.

Cohen, J. (1977). *Statistical power analysis for the behavioral sciences* (rev. ed.). San Diego, CA: Academic Press.

Cohen, J. (1978). Partialled products *are* interactions; partialled powers *are* curve components. *Psychological Bulletin, 85*, 858-866.

Coleman, J. F., Blake, R. R., & Mouton, J. S. (1958). Task difficulty and conformity pressures. *Journal of Abnormal and Social Psychology, 57*, 120-122.

Coleman, S. R., & Gormezano, I. (1979). Classical conditioning and the "law of effect": Historical and empirical assessment. *Behaviorism, 7*, 1-33.

Collins, A. M., & Quillian, M. R. (1969). Retrieval time from semantic memory. *Journal of Verbal Learning and Verbal Behavior, 8*, 240-247.

Collins, B. E. (1969). The effect of monetary inducements on the amount of attitude change produced by forced compliance. In A. C. Elms (Ed.), *Role playing, reward, and attitude change: An enduring problem in psychology* (pp. 209-223). New York: Van Nostrand Reinhold.

Collins, B. E., Ashmore, R. D., Hornbeck, F. W., & Whitney, R. (1970). Studies in forced compliance: XIII and XV. In search of a dissonance-producing forced compliance paradigm. *Representative Research in Social Psychology, 1*, 11-23.

Collins, B. E., Ellsworth, P. C., & Helmreich, R. L. (1967). Correlations between pupil size and the semantic differential: An experimental paradigm and pilot study. *Psychonomic Science, 9*, 627-628.

Collins, B. E., & Hoyt, M. F. (1972). Personal responsibility-for-consequences: An integration and extension of the "forced compliance" literature. *Journal of Experimental Social Psychology, 8*, 558-593.

Collins, R. L., Taylor, S. E., Wood, J. V., & Thompson, S. C. (1988). The vividness effect: Elusive or illusory? *Journal of Experimental Social Psychology, 24*, 1-18.

Converse, J., Jr., & Cooper, J. (1979). The importance of decisions and free-choice attitude change: A curvilinear finding. *Journal of Experimental Social Psychology, 15*, 48-61.

Converse, P. E. (1964). The nature of belief systems in mass publics. In D. E. Apter (Ed.), *Ideology and discontent* (pp. 206-261). New York: Free Press.

Converse, P. E. (1970). Attitudes and non-attitudes: Continuation of a dialogue. In E. R. Tufte (Ed.), *The quantitative analysis of social problems* (pp. 168-189). Reading, MA: Addison-Wesley.

Converse, P. E. (1975). Public opinion and voting behavior. In F. Greenstein & N. W. Polsby (Eds.), *Handbook of political science* (Vol. 4, pp. 75-169). Reading, MA: Addison-Wesley.

Conway, F., & Siegelman, J. (1978). *Snapping: America's epidemic of sudden personality change.* New York: Lippincott.

Conway, M., & Ross, M. (1984). Getting what you want by revising what you had. *Journal of Personality and Social Psychology, 47*, 738-748.

Cook, S. W. (1978). Interpersonal and attitudinal outcomes in cooperating interracial groups. *Journal of Research in Development and Education, 12*, 97-113.

Cook, S. W., & Selltiz, C. (1964). A multiple-indicator approach to attitude measurement. *Psychological Bulletin, 62*, 36-55.

Cook, T. D. (1969). Competence, counterarguing, and attitude change. *Journal of Personality, 37*, 342-358.

Cook, T. D., & Campbell, D. T. (1979). *Quasi-experimentation: Design and analysis issues for field settings.* Chicago: Rand McNally.

Cook, T. D., & Flay, B. R. (1978). The persistence of experimentally induced attitude change. In L. Berkowitz (Ed.), *Advances in experimental social psychology* (Vol. 11, pp. 1-57). San Diego, CA: Academic Press.

Cook, T. D., Gruder, C. L., Hennigan, K. M., & Flay, B. R. (1979). History of the sleeper effect: Some logical pitfalls in accepting the null hypothesis. *Psychological Bulletin, 86*, 662-679.

Coombs, C. H. (1950). Psychological scaling without a unit of measurement. *Psychological Review, 57*, 145-158.

Coombs, C. H. (1964). *A theory of data.* New York: Wiley.

Coombs, C. H., Dawes, R. M., & Tversky, A. (1970). *Mathematical psychology: An elementary introduction.* Englewood Cliffs, NJ: Prentice-Hall.

Cooper, H. M. (1989). *Integrating research: A guide for literature reviews* (2nd ed.). Newbury Park, CA: Sage.

Cooper, H. M., & Rosenthal, R. (1980). Statistical versus traditional procedures for summarizing research findings. *Psychological Bulletin, 87*, 442-449.

Cooper, J. (1971). Personal responsibility and dissonance: The role of foreseen consequences. *Journal of Personality and Social Psychology*, *18*, 354–363.

Cooper, J., & Duncan, B. L. (1971). Cognitive dissonance as a function of self-esteem and logical inconsistency. *Journal of Personality*, *39*, 289–302.

Cooper, J., & Fazio, R. H. (1984). A new look at dissonance theory. In L. Berkowitz (Ed.), *Advances in experimental social psychology* (Vol. 17, pp. 229–266). San Diego, CA: Academic Press.

Cooper, J., & Fazio, R. H. (1989). Research traditions, analysis, and synthesis: Building a faulty case around misinterpreted theory. *Personality and Social Psychology Bulletin*, *15*, 519–529.

Cooper, J., & Worchel, S. (1970). Role of undesired consequences in arousing cognitive dissonance. *Journal of Personality and Social Psychology*, *16*, 199–206.

Cooper, J., Zanna, M. P., & Goethals, G. R. (1974). Mistreatment of an esteemed other as a consequence affecting dissonance reduction. *Journal of Experimental Social Psychology*, *10*, 224–233.

Cooper, J., Zanna, M. P., & Taves, P. A. (1978). Arousal as a necessary condition for attitude change following induced compliance. *Journal of Personality and Social Psychology*, *36*, 1101–1106.

Cooper, J. B., & Pollock, D. (1959). Identification of prejudicial attitudes by the galvanic skin response. *Journal of Social Psychology*, *50*, 241–245.

Cooper, J. B., & Siegel, H. E. (1956). The galvanic skin response as a measure of emotion in prejudice. *Journal of Psychology*, *42*, 149–155.

Cooper, J. B., & Singer, D. N. (1956). The role of emotion in prejudice. *Journal of Social Psychology*, *44*, 241–247.

Coovert, M. D., & Reeder, G. D. (1990). Negativity effects in impression formation: The role of unit formation and schematic expectations. *Journal of Experimental Social Psychology*, *26*, 49–62.

Corteen, R. S., & Wood, B. (1972). Autonomic responses to shock-associated words in an unattended channel. *Journal of Experimental Psychology*, *94*, 308–313.

Cotton, J. L. (1985). Cognitive dissonance in selective exposure. In D. Zillman & J. Bryant (Eds.), *Selective exposure to communication* (pp. 11–33). Hillsdale, NJ: Erlbaum.

Cotton, J. L., & Hieser, R. A. (1980). Selective exposure to information and cognitive dissonance. *Journal of Research in Personality*, *14*, 518–527.

Cottrell, N. B. (1975). Heider's structural balance principle as a conceptual rule. *Journal of Personality and Social Psychology*, *31*, 713–720.

Cottrell, N. B., Rajecki, D. W., & Smith, D. U. (1974). The energizing effects of postdecision dissonance upon performance of an irrelevant task. *Journal of Social Psychology*, *93*, 81–92.

Cottrell, N. B., & Wack, D. L. (1967). Energizing effects of cognitive dissonance upon dominant and subordinate responses. *Journal of Personality and Social Psychology*, *6*, 132–138.

Couch, A., & Keniston, K. (1960). Yeasayers and naysayers: Agreeing response set as a personality variable. *Journal of Abnormal and Social Psychology*, *60*, 151–174.

Crandall, C. S. (1988). Social contagion of binge eating. *Journal of Personality and Social Psychology*, *55*, 588–598.

Crano, W. D., Gorenflo, D. W., & Shackelford, S. L. (1988). Overjustification, assumed consensus, and attitude change: Further investigation of the incentive-aroused ambivalence hypothesis. *Journal of Personality and Social Psychology*, *55*, 12–22.

Crano, W. D., & Sivacek, J. (1984). The influence of incentive-aroused ambivalence on overjustification effects in attitude change. *Journal of Experimental Social Psychology*, *20*, 137–158.

Crawford, T. J., & Boyer, R. (1985). Salient consequences, cultural values, and childbearing intentions. *Journal of Applied Social Psychology*, *15*, 16–30.

Crocker, L., & Algina, J. (1986). *Introduction to classical and modern test theory*. New York: Holt, Rinehart, & Winston.

Crockett, W. H. (1965). Cognitive complexity and impression formation. In B. A. Maher (Ed.), *Progress in experimental personality research* (Vol. 2, pp. 47–90). San Diego, CA: Academic Press.

Cromwell, H. (1950). The relative effect on audience attitude of the first versus second argumentative speech of a series. *Speech Monographs*, *17*, 105–122.

Cronbach, L. J. (1946). Response sets and test validity. *Educational and Psychological Measurement*, *6*, 475–494.

Cronbach, L. J. (1950). Further evidence on response sets and test design. *Educational and Psychological Measurement*, *10*, 3–31.

Cronbach, L. J. (1951). Coefficient alpha and the internal structure of tests. *Psychometrika*, *16*, 297–334.

Cronen, V. E., & Conville, R. L. (1975a). Fishbein's conception of belief strength: A theoretical, methodological, and experimental critique. *Speech Monographs*, *42*, 143–150.

Cronen, V. E., & Conville, R. L. (1975b). Summation theory and the predictive power of subjects' own salient beliefs. *Journal of Social Psychology*, *97*, 47–52.

Cronen, V. E., & LaFleur, G. (1977). Inoculation against persuasive attacks: A test of alternative explanations. *Journal of Social Psychology*, *102*, 255–265.

Crowne, D. P., & Marlowe, D. (1964). *The approval motive: Studies in evaluative dependence*. New York: Wiley.

Croyle, R., & Cooper, J. (1983). Dissonance arousal: Physiological evidence. *Journal of Personality and Social Psychology*, *45*, 782–791.

Crutchfield, R. S. (1955). Conformity and character. *American Psychologist*, *10*, 191–198.

Crutchfield, R.S. (1962). Conformity and creative thinking. In H.E. Gruber, G. Terrell, & M. Wertheimer (Eds.), *Contemporary approaches to creative thinking* (pp. 120-140). New York: Atherton.

Crutchfield, R.S. (1963). Independent thought in a conformist world. In S.M. Farber & R.H.L. Wilson (Eds.), *Man and civilization: Conflict and creativity* (Pt. 2 of Conference on Control of the Mind, pp. 208-228). New York: McGraw-Hill.

Culbertson, F.M. (1957). Modification of an emotionally held attitude through role playing. *Journal of Abnormal and Social Psychology, 54*, 230-233.

Cureton, E.E. (1957). The upper and lower twenty-seven per cent rule. *Psychometrika, 22*, 293-296.

Dabbs, M.J. Jr., & Janis, I.L. (1965). Why does eating while reading facilitate opinion change?—An experimental inquiry. *Journal of Experimental Social Psychology, 1*, 133-144.

Darke, S. (1988). Effects of anxiety on inferential reasoning task performance. *Journal of Personality and Social Psychology, 55*, 499-505.

Darley, J.M., & Latané, B. (1968). Bystander intervention in emergencies: Diffusion of responsibility. *Journal of Personality and Social Psychology, 8*, 377-383.

Darwin, C.R. (1872). *The expression of the emotions in man and animals.* London: Murray.

Das, J.P., & Nanda, P.C. (1963). Mediated transfer of attitudes. *Journal of Abnormal and Social Psychology, 66*, 12-16.

Davidson, A.R., & Jaccard, J.J. (1975). Population psychology: A new look at an old problem. *Journal of Personality and Social Psychology, 31*, 1073-1082.

Davidson, A.R., & Jaccard, J.J. (1979). Variables that moderate the attitude-behavior relation: Results of a longitudinal survey. *Journal of Personality and Social Psychology, 37*, 1364-1376.

Davidson, A.R., Jaccard, J.J., Triandis, H.C., Morales, M.L., & Diaz-Guerrero, R. (1976). Cross-cultural model testing: Toward a solution of the etic-emic dilemma. *International Journal of Psychology, 11*, 1-13.

Davidson, A.R., & Morrison, D.M. (1983). Predicting contraceptive behavior from attitudes: A comparison of within-versus-across subjects procedures. *Journal of Personality and Social Psychology, 45*, 997-1009.

Davidson, A.R., Yantis, S., Norwood, M., & Montano, D.E. (1985). Amount of information about the attitude object and attitude-behavior consistency. *Journal of Personality and Social Psychology, 49*, 1184-1198.

Davis, D., & Ostrom, T.M. (1984). Attitude measurement. In R.J. Corsini (Ed.), *Wiley encyclopedia of psychology* (Vol. 1, pp. 97-99). New York: Wiley.

Davis, K.F., & Jones, E.E. (1960). Changes in interpersonal perception as a means of reducing cognitive dissonance. *Journal of Abnormal and Social Psychology, 61*, 402-410.

Davis, M.H. (1979). Changes in evaluative beliefs as a function of behavioral commitment. *Personality and Social Psychology Bulletin, 5*, 177-181.

Davison, M.L., & Sharma, A.R. (1988). Parametric statistics and levels of measurement. *Psychological Bulletin, 104*, 137-144.

Davison, M.L., & Sharma, A.R. (1990). Parametric statistics and levels of measurement: Factorial designs and multiple regression. *Psychological Bulletin, 107*, 394-400.

Dawes, R.M. (1972). *Fundamentals of attitude measurement.* New York: Wiley.

Dawes, R.M., Singer, D., & Lemons, F. (1972). An experimental analysis of the contrast effect and its implications for intergroup communication and the indirect assessment of attitude. *Journal of Personality and Social Psychology, 21*, 281-295.

Dawes, R.M., & Smith, T.L. (1985). Attitude and opinion measurement. In G. Lindzey & E. Aronson (Eds.), *Handbook of social psychology* (3rd ed., Vol. 1, pp. 509-566). New York: Random House.

Dawson, M.E., & Furedy, J.J. (1976). The role of awareness in human differential autonomic classical conditioning: The necessary-gate hypothesis. *Psychophysiology, 13*, 50-53.

Dawson, M.E., & Schell, A.M. (1982). Electrodermal responses to attended and nonattended significant stimuli during dichotic listening. *Journal of Experimental Psychology: Human Perception and Performance, 8*, 315-324.

Dawson, W.E. (1982). On the parallel between direct ratio scaling of social opinion and of sensory magnitude. In B. Wegener (Ed.), *Social attitudes and psychophysical measurement* (pp. 151-176). Hillsdale, NJ: Erlbaum.

Dawson, W.E., & Brinker, R.P. (1971). Validation of ratio scales of opinion by multimodality matching. *Perception & Psychophysics, 9*, 413-417.

DeBono, K.G. (1987). Investigating the social-adjustive and value-expressive functions of attitudes: Implications for persuasion processes. *Journal of Personality and Social Psychology, 52*, 279-287.

DeBono, K.G., & Edmonds, A.E. (1989). Cognitive dissonance and self-monitoring: A matter of context? *Motivation and Emotion, 13*, 259-270.

DeBono, K.G., & Harnish, R.J. (1988). Source expertise, source attractiveness, and the processing of persuasive information: A functional approach. *Journal of Personality and Social Psychology, 55*, 541-546.

Deci, E.L. (1971). Effects of externally mediated rewards on intrinsic motivation. *Journal of Personality and Social Psychology, 18*, 105-115.

Deci, E.L. (1972). Intrinsic motivation, extrinsic reinforcement and inequity. *Journal of Personality and Social Psychology, 22*, 113-120.

Deci, E.L. (1975). *Intrinsic motivation.* New York: Plenum Press.

Deci, E. L., & Ryan, R. M. (1985). *Intrinsic motivation and self-determination in human behavior*. New York: Plenum Press.

DeFleur, M. L., & Westie, F. R. (1958). Verbal attitudes and overt acts: An experiment on the salience of attitudes. *American Sociological Review, 23,* 667-673.

DeFleur, M. L., & Westie, F. R. (1963). Attitude as a scientific concept. *Social Forces, 42,* 17-31.

DeNike, L. D. (1964). The temporal relationship between awareness and performance in verbal conditioning. *Journal of Experimental Psychology, 68,* 521-529.

DeNike, L. D., & Leibovitz, M. P. (1969). Accurate anticipation of reinforcement in verbal conditioning. *Journal of Personality, 37,* 158-170.

Deutsch, M., & Collins, M. E. (1951). *Interracial housing: A psychological evaluation of a social experiment*. Minneapolis: University of Minnesota Press.

Deutsch, M., & Gerard, H. B. (1955). A study of normative and informational social influences upon individual judgment. *Journal of Abnormal and Social Psychology, 51,* 629-636.

Deutsch, M., & Krauss, R. M. (1965). *Theories in social psychology*. New York: Basic Books.

Deutsch, M., Krauss, R. M., & Rosenau, N. (1962). Dissonance or defensiveness? *Journal of Personality, 30,* 16-28.

Deutscher, I. (1966). Words and deeds: Social science and social policy. *Social Problems, 13,* 235-254.

Deutscher, I. (1973). *What we say/what we do: Sentiments and acts*. Glenview, IL: Scott, Foresman.

DeVillis, B. M., Blalock, S. J., & Sandler, R. S. (1990). Predicting participation in cancer screening: The role of perceived behavioral control. *Journal of Applied Social Psychology, 20,* 639-660.

de Vries, B., & Walker, L. J. (1987). Conceptual/integrative complexity and attitudes toward capital punishment. *Personality and Social Psychology Bulletin, 13,* 448-457.

Dickenberger, D., & Grabitz-Gniech, G. (1972). Restrictive conditions for the occurrence of psychological reactance: Interpersonal attraction, need for social approval, and a delay factor. *European Journal of Social Psychology, 2,* 177-198.

Dietrich, D. M., & Berkowitz, L. (1989). *The role of the self in dissonance-motivated behavior*. Unpublished manuscript, University of Wisconsin, Madison, WI.

Dillehay, R. C., Insko, C. A., & Smith, M. B. (1966). Logical consistency and attitude change. *Journal of Personality and Social Psychology, 3,* 646-654.

Dillon, W. R., & Kumar, A. (1985). Attitude organization and the attitude-behavior relation: A critique of Bagozzi and Burnkrant's reanalysis of Fishbein and Ajzen. *Journal of Personality and Social Psychology, 49,* 33-46.

Dixon, P. W., & Oakes, W. F. (1965). Effect of intertrial activity on the relationship between awareness and verbal operant conditioning. *Journal of Experimental Psychology, 69,* 152-157.

Doise, W. (1969). Intergroup relations and polarization of individual and collective judgments. *Journal of Personality and Social Psychology, 12,* 136-143.

Doll, J., & Ajzen, I. (in press). Accessibility and stability of predictors in the theory of planned behavior. *Journal of Personality and Social Psychology*.

Dollard, J., & Miller, N. E. (1950). *Personality and psychotherapy*. New York: McGraw-Hill.

Donohue, W. A., Cushman, D. P., & Nofsinger, R. E., Jr. (1980). Creating and confronting social order: A comparison of rules perspectives. *Western Journal of Speech Communication, 44,* 5-19.

Doob, L. W. (1947). The behavior of attitudes. *Psychological Review, 54,* 135-156.

Doob, L. W. (1953). Effects of initial serial position and attitude upon recall under conditions of low motivation. *Journal of Abnormal and Social Psychology, 48,* 199-205.

Dotson, L. E., & Summers, G. F. (1970). Elaboration of Guttman scaling techniques. In G. F. Summers (Ed.), *Attitude measurement* (pp. 203-213). Chicago: Rand McNally.

Downey, J. E., & Knapp, G. E. (1927). The effect on a musical programme of familiarity and of sequence of selections. In M. Schoen (Ed.), *The effects of music* (pp. 223-243). New York: Harcourt, Brace.

Downing, J. W., Judd, C. M., & Brauer, M. (1992). Effects of repeated expressions on attitude extremity. *Journal of Personality and Social Psychology, 63,* 17-29.

Dreben, E. K., Fiske, S. T., & Hastie, R. (1979). The independence of evaluative and item information: Impression and recall order effects in behavior-based impression formation. *Journal of Personality and Social Psychology, 37,* 1758-1768.

Dribben, E., & Brabender, V. (1979). The effect of mood inducement upon audience receptiveness. *Journal of Social Psychology, 107,* 135-136.

DuBois, B., & Burns, J. A. (1975). An analysis of the meaning of the question mark response category in attitude scales. *Educational and Psychological Measurement, 35,* 869-884.

Dulany, D. E. (1961). Hypotheses and habits in verbal "operant conditioning." *Journal of Abnormal and Social Psychology, 63,* 251-263.

Dulany, D. E. (1962). The place of hypotheses and intentions: An analysis of verbal control in verbal conditioning. *Journal of Personality, 30,* 102-129.

Dulany, D. E. (1968). Awareness, rules, and propositional control: A confrontation with S-R behavior theory. In T. Dixon & D. Horton (Eds.), *Verbal behavior and general behavior theory* (pp. 340-387). Englewood Cliffs, NJ: Prentice-Hall.

Duryea, E. J. (1983). Utilizing tenets of inoculation theory to develop and evaluate a preventive alcohol education intervention. *Journal of School Health, 53,* 250-256.

712

Eagly, A. H. (1967). Involvement as a determinant of response to favorable and unfavorable information. *Journal of Personality and Social Psychology, 7* (No. 3, Whole No. 643).

Eagly, A. H. (1974). Comprehensibility of persuasive arguments as a determinant of opinion change. *Journal of Personality and Social Psychology, 29,* 758–773.

Eagly, A. H. (1983a). Gender and social influence: A social psychological analysis. *American Psychologist, 38,* 971–981.

Eagly, A. H. (1983b, April). *Who says so? The processing of communicator cues in persuasion.* Invited address presented at meeting of the Eastern Psychological Association, Philadelphia.

Eagly, A. H. (1987). *Sex differences in social behavior: A social-role interpretation.* Hillsdale, NJ: Erlbaum.

Eagly, A. H., & Chaiken, S. (1975). An attribution analysis of the effect of communicator characteristics on opinion change: The case of communicator attractiveness. *Journal of Personality and Social Psychology, 32,* 136–144.

Eagly, A. H., & Chaiken, S. (1976). Why would anyone say that? Causal attribution of statements about the Watergate scandal. *Sociometry, 39,* 236–243.

Eagly, A. H., & Chaiken, S. (1984). Cognitive theories of persuasion. In L. Berkowitz (Ed.), *Advances in experimental social psychology* (Vol. 17, pp. 267–359). San Diego, CA: Academic Press.

Eagly, A. H., Chaiken, S., & Wood, W. (1981). An attribution analysis of persuasion. In J. H. Harvey, W. J. Ickes, & R. F. Kidd (Eds.), *New directions in attribution research* (Vol. 3, pp. 37–62). Hillsdale, NJ: Erlbaum.

Eagly, A. H., & Himmelfarb, S. (1974). Current trends in attitude theory and research. In S. Himmelfarb & A. H. Eagly (Eds.), *Readings in attitude change* (pp. 594–610). New York: Wiley.

Eagly, A. H., & Himmelfarb, S. (1978). Attitudes and opinions. *Annual Review of Psychology, 29,* 517–554.

Eagly, A. H., & Mladinic, A. (1989). Gender stereotypes and attitudes toward women and men. *Personality and Social Psychology Bulletin, 15,* 543–558.

Eagly, A. H., & Telaak, K. (1972). Width of the latitude of acceptance as a determinant of attitude change. *Journal of Personality and Social Psychology, 23,* 388–397.

Eagly, A. H., & Warren, R. (1976). Intelligence, comprehension, and opinion change. *Journal of Personality, 44,* 226–242.

Eagly, A. H., & Whitehead, G. I., III. (1972). Effect of choice on receptivity to favorable and unfavorable evaluations of oneself. *Journal of Personality and Social Psychology, 22,* 223–230.

Eagly, A. H., Wood, W., & Chaiken, S. (1978). Causal inferences about communicators and their effect on opinion change. *Journal of Personality and Social Psychology, 36,* 424–435.

Early, C. J. (1968). Attitude learning in children. *Journal of Educational Psychology, 59,* 176–180.

Easton, D., & Dennis, J. (1969). *Children in the political system: Origins of political legitimacy.* New York: McGraw-Hill.

Ebbesen, E. B., & Bowers, R. J. (1974). Proportion of risky to conservative arguments in a group discussion and choice shift. *Journal of Personality and Social Psychology, 29,* 316–327.

Ebbinghaus, H. (1913). *Memory: A contribution to experimental psychology* (H. A. Roger & E. E. Bussenius, Trans.). New York: Teachers College, Columbia University. (Original work, *Über das Gedächtnis,* published 1885)

Echabe, A. E., Rovira, D. P., & Garate, J. F. V. (1988). Testing Ajzen and Fishbein's attitudes model: The prediction of voting. *European Journal of Social Psychology, 18,* 181–189.

Edgell, S. E., Himmelfarb, S., & Cira, D. J. (1986). Statistical efficiency of using two randomized response techniques to estimate correlation. *Psychological Bulletin, 100,* 251–256.

Edwards, A. L. (1941). Rationalization in recognition as a result of a political frame of reference. *Journal of Abnormal and Social Psychology, 36,* 224–235.

Edwards, A. L. (1957a). *The social desirability variable in personality assessment and research.* New York: Dryden.

Edwards, A. L. (1957b). *Techniques of attitude scale construction.* New York: Appleton-Century-Crofts.

Edwards, A. L., & Thurstone, L. L. (1952). An internal consistency check for scale values determined by the method of successive intervals. *Psychometrika, 17,* 169–180.

Edwards, K. (1990). The interplay of affect and cognition in attitude formation and change. *Journal of Personality and Social Psychology, 59,* 212–216.

Edwards, W. (1954). The theory of decision making. *Psychological Bulletin, 51,* 380–417.

Edwards, W., Lindman, H., & Savage, L. J. (1963). Bayesian statistical inference for psychological research. *Psychological Review, 70,* 193–242.

Ehrlich, H. J. (1969). Attitudes, behavior, and the intervening variables. *American Sociologist, 4,* 29–34.

Eiser, J. R. (1971). Enhancement of contrast in the absolute judgment of attitude statements. *Journal of Personality and Social Psychology, 17,* 1–10.

Eiser, J. R. (1980). *Cognitive social psychology: A guidebook to theory and research.* London: McGraw-Hill.

Eiser, J. R. (1987). *The expression of attitude.* New York: Springer-Verlag.

Eiser, J. R., & Monk, A. F. (1978). Is the recognition of attitude statements affected by one's own opinion? *European Journal of Social Psychology, 8,* 529–533.

Eiser, J. R., & Stroebe, W. (1972). *Categorization and social judgement.* London: Academic Press.

Ekman, P. (1958). *Nonverbal and verbal behavior as reinforcing stimuli of opinion responses.* Unpublished doctoral dissertation, Adelphi University.

Elkin, R. A., & Leippe, M. R. (1986). Physiological arousal, dissonance, and attitude change: Evidence for a dissonance-arousal link and a "Don't remind me" effect. *Journal of Personality and Social Psychology, 51,* 55-65.

Ellis, H. C. (1969). Transfer and retention. In M. H. Marx (Ed.), *Learning: Processes* (pp. 381-445). New York: Macmillan.

Ellsworth, P. C., & Ross, L. (1983). Public opinion and capital punishment: A close examination of the views of abolitionists and retentionists. *Crime and Delinquency, 29,* 116-169.

Elms, A. C. (1966). Influence of fantasy ability on attitude change through role playing. *Journal of Personality and Social Psychology, 4,* 36-43.

Elms, A. C. (1967). Role playing, incentive, and dissonance. *Psychological Bulletin, 68,* 132-148.

Elms, A. C. (1975). The crisis of confidence in social psychology. *American Psychologist, 30,* 967-976.

Elms, A. C., & Janis, I. L. (1965). Counter-norm attitudes induced by consonant versus dissonant conditions of role-playing. *Journal of Experimental Research in Personality, 1,* 50-60.

Emerson, R. M. (1954). Deviation and rejection: An experimental replication. *American Sociological Review, 19,* 688-694.

Ennis, R., & Zanna, M. P. (1991, June). *Psychological function and attitudes toward automobiles.* Paper presented at the meeting of the Canadian Psychological Association, Calgary, Alberta.

Epstein, S. (1979). The stability of behavior: I. On predicting most of the people much of the time. *Journal of Personality and Social Psychology, 37,* 1097-1126.

Epstein, S. (1984). Controversial issues in emotion theory. In P. Shaver (Ed.), *Review of personality and social psychology* (Vol. 5, pp. 64-88). Beverly Hills, CA: Sage.

Erdelyi, M. H. (1974). A new look at the new look: Perceptual defense and vigilance. *Psychological Review, 81,* 1-25.

Erdley, C. A., & D'Agostino, P. R. (1988). Cognitive and affective components of automatic priming effects. *Journal of Personality and Social Psychology, 54,* 741-747.

Ericksen, C. W. (1960). Discrimination and learning without awareness: A methodological survey and evaluation. *Psychological Review, 67,* 279-300.

Estes, W. K. (1988). Human learning and memory. In R. C. Atkinson, R. J. Herrnstein, G. Lindzey, & R. D. Luce (Eds.), *Steven's handbook of experimental psychology* (2nd ed., pp. 351-416). New York: Wiley.

Evans, M. G. (1991). The problem of analyzing multivariate composites: Interactions revisited. *American Psychologist, 46,* 6-15.

Evans, R. I., Hansen, W. B., & Mittelmark, M. B. (1977). Increasing the validity of self-reports of smoking behavior in children. *Journal of Applied Psychology, 62,* 521-523.

Ewing, T. N. (1942). A study of certain factors involved in changes of opinion. *Journal of Social Psychology, 16,* 63-88.

Eysenck, M. W. (1982). *Attention and arousal, cognition and performance.* New York: Springer-Verlag.

Falbo, T. (1977). Multidimensional scaling of power strategies. *Journal of Personality and Social Psychology, 35,* 537-547.

Farley, J. A., & Hokanson, J. E. (1966). The effect of informational set on acquisition in verbal conditioning. *Journal of Verbal Learning and Verbal Behavior, 5,* 14-17.

Farley, J. U., Lehmann, D. R., & Ryan, M. J. (1981). Generalizing from "imperfect" replication. *Journal of Business, 54,* 597-610.

Fazio, R. H. (1986). How do attitudes guide behavior? In R. M. Sorrentino & E. T. Higgins (Eds.), *Handbook of motivation and cognition: Foundations of social behavior* (pp. 204-243). New York: Guilford Press.

Fazio, R. H. (1987). Self-perception theory: A current perspective. In M. P. Zanna, J. M. Olson, & C. P. Herman (Eds.), *Social influence: The Ontario Symposium* (Vol. 5, pp. 129-150). Hillsdale, NJ: Erlbaum.

Fazio, R. H. (1989). On the power and functionality of attitudes: The role of attitude accessibility. In A. R. Pratkanis, S. J. Breckler, & A. G. Greenwald (Eds.), *Attitude structure and function* (pp. 153-179). Hillsdale, NJ: Erlbaum.

Fazio, R. H. (1990a). Multiple processes by which attitudes guide behavior: The MODE model as an integrative framework. In M. P. Zanna (Ed.), *Advances in experimental social psychology* (Vol. 23, pp. 75-109). San Diego, CA: Academic Press.

Fazio, R. H. (1990b). A practical guide to the use of response latency in social psychological research. In C. Hendrick & M. S. Clark (Eds.), *Review of personality and social psychology* (Vol. 11, pp. 74-97). Newbury Park, CA: Sage.

Fazio, R. H., Chen, J., McDonel, E. C., & Sherman, S. J. (1982). Attitude accessibility, attitude-behavior consistency, and the strength of the object-evaluation association. *Journal of Experimental Social Psychology, 18,* 339-357.

Fazio, R. H., & Cooper, J. (1983). Arousal in the dissonance process. In J. T. Cacioppo & R. E. Petty (Eds.), *Social psychophysiology: A sourcebook* (pp. 122-152). New York: Guilford Press.

Fazio, R. H., Herr, P. M., & Olney, T. J. (1984). Attitude accessibility following a self-perception process. *Journal of Personality and Social Psychology, 47,* 277-286.

Fazio, R. H., Powell, M. C., & Herr, P. M. (1983). Toward a process model of the attitude-behavior relation: Accessing one's attitude upon mere observation of the attitude object. *Journal of Personality and Social Psychology, 44,* 723-735.

Fazio, R. H., Powell, M. C., & Williams, C. J. (1989). The role of attitude accessibility in the attitude-to-behavior process. *Journal of Consumer Research, 16,* 280-288.

Fazio, R. H., Sanbonmatsu, D. M., Powell, M. C., & Kardes, F. R. (1986). On the automatic activation of attitudes. *Journal of Personality and Social Psychology, 50,* 229-238.

Fazio, R. H., Sherman, S. J., & Herr, P. M. (1982). The feature-positive effect in the self-perception process: Does not doing matter as much as doing? *Journal of Personality and Social Psychology, 42,* 404-411.

Fazio, R. H., & Williams, C. J. (1986). Attitude accessibility as a moderator of the attitude-perception and attitude-behavior relations: An investigation of the 1984 presidential election. *Journal of Personality and Social Psychology, 51,* 505-514.

Fazio, R. H., & Zanna, M. P. (1978a). Attitudinal qualities relating to the strength of the attitude-behavior relationship. *Journal of Experimental Social Psychology, 14,* 398-408.

Fazio, R. H., & Zanna, M. P. (1978b). On the predictive validity of attitudes: The roles of direct experience and confidence. *Journal of Personality, 46,* 228-243.

Fazio, R. H., & Zanna, M. P. (1981). Direct experience and attitude-behavior consistency. In L. Berkowitz (Ed.), *Advances in experimental social psychology* (Vol. 14, pp. 161-202). San Diego, CA: Academic Press.

Fazio, R. H., Zanna, M. P., & Cooper, J. (1977). Dissonance and self-perception: An integrative view of each theory's proper domain of application. *Journal of Experimental Social Psychology, 13,* 464-479.

Fazio, R. H., Zanna, M. P., & Cooper, J. (1979). On the relationship of data to theory: A reply to Ronis and Greenwald. *Journal of Experimental Social Psychology, 15,* 70-76.

Feather, N. T. (1969). Attitude and selective recall. *Journal of Personality and Social Psychology, 12,* 310-319.

Feather, N. T. (1970). Organization and discrepancy in cognitive structures. *Psychological Review, 78,* 355-379.

Feather, N. T. (Ed.). (1982). *Expectations and actions: Expectancy-value models in psychology.* Hillsdale, NJ: Erlbaum.

Feldman, J. M., & Lynch, J. G., Jr. (1988). Self-generated validity and other effects of measurement on belief, attitude, intention, and behavior. *Journal of Applied Psychology, 73,* 421-435.

Fenigstein, A., Scheier, M. F., & Buss, A. H. (1975). Public and private self-consciousness: Assessment and theory. *Journal of Consulting and Clinical Psychology, 43,* 522-527.

Ferguson, L. W. (1935). The influence of individual attitudes on construction of an attitude scale. *Journal of Social Psychology, 6,* 115-117.

Festinger, L. (1950). Informal social communication. *Psychological Review, 57,* 271-282.

Festinger, L. (1951). Architecture and group membership. *Journal of Social Issues, 7*(1), 152-163.

Festinger, L. (1954). A theory of social comparison processes. *Human Relations, 7,* 117-140.

Festinger, L. (1957). *A theory of cognitive dissonance.* Evanston, IL: Row, Peterson.

Festinger, L. (1964a). Behavioral support for opinion change. *Public Opinion Quarterly, 28,* 404-417.

Festinger, L. (1964b). *Conflict, decision, and dissonance.* Stanford, CA: Stanford University Press.

Festinger, L., & Carlsmith, J. M. (1959). Cognitive consequences of forced compliance. *Journal of Abnormal and Social Psychology, 58,* 203-210.

Festinger, L., Gerard, H. B., Hymovitch, B., Kelley, H. H., & Raven, B. (1952). The influence process in the presence of extreme deviants. *Human Relations, 5,* 327-346.

Festinger, L., & Maccoby, N. (1964). On resistance to persuasive communications. *Journal of Abnormal and Social Psychology, 68,* 359-366.

Festinger, L., Riecken, H. W., & Schachter, S. (1956). *When prophecy fails: A social and psychological study of a modern group that predicted the destruction of the world.* Minneapolis: University of Minnesota Press.

Festinger, L., Schachter, S., & Back, K. W. (1950). *Social pressures in informal groups.* New York: Harper.

Fine, B. J. (1957). Conclusion-drawing, communicator credibility, and anxiety as factors in opinion change. *Journal of Abnormal and Social Psychology, 54,* 369-374.

Fischhoff, B., & Beyth-Marom, R. (1983). Hypothesis evaluation from a Bayesian perspective. *Psychological Review, 90,* 239-260.

Fishbein, M. (1961). *A theoretical and empirical investigation of the interrelation between beliefs about an object and the attitude toward that object.* Unpublished doctoral dissertation, University of California at Los Angeles.

Fishbein, M. (1963). An investigation of the relationships between beliefs about an object and the attitude toward that object. *Human Relations, 16,* 233-240.

Fishbein, M. (1965). Prediction of interpersonal preference and group member satisfaction from estimated attitudes. *Journal of Personality and Social Psychology, 1,* 663-667.

Fishbein, M. (1967a). Attitude and the prediction of behavior. In M. Fishbein (Ed.), *Readings in attitude theory and measurement* (pp. 477-492). New York: Wiley.

Fishbein, M. (1967b). A behavior theory approach to the relations between beliefs about an object and the attitude toward the object. In M. Fishbein (Ed.), *Readings in attitude theory and measurement* (pp. 389-400). New York: Wiley.

Fishbein, M. (1967c). A consideration of beliefs, and their role in attitude measurement. In M. Fishbein (Ed.), *Readings in attitude theory and measurement* (pp. 257–266). New York: Wiley.

Fishbein, M. (1980). A theory of reasoned action: Some applications and implications. In H. E. Howe, Jr. & M. M. Page (Eds.), *Nebraska Symposium on Motivation, 1979* (Vol. 27, pp. 65–116). Lincoln: University of Nebraska Press.

Fishbein, M., & Ajzen, I. (1972). Attitudes and opinions. *Annual Review of Psychology, 23,* 487–544.

Fishbein, M., & Ajzen, I. (1974). Attitudes toward objects as predictors of single and multiple behavioral criteria. *Psychological Review, 81,* 59–74.

Fishbein, M., & Ajzen, I. (1975). *Belief, attitude, intention, and behavior: An introduction to theory and research.* Reading, MA: Addison-Wesley.

Fishbein, M., & Ajzen, I. (1981). Acceptance, yielding and impact: Cognitive processes in persuasion. In R. E. Petty, T. M. Ostrom, & T. C. Brock (Eds.), *Cognitive responses in persuasion* (pp. 339–359). Hillsdale, NJ: Erlbaum.

Fishbein, M., Ajzen, I., & McArdle, J. (1980). Changing the behavior of alcoholics: Effects of persuasive communication. In I. Ajzen & M. Fishbein, *Understanding attitudes and predicting social behavior* (pp. 217–242). Englewood Cliffs, NJ: Prentice-Hall.

Fishbein, M., & Coombs, F. S. (1974). Basis for decision: An attitudinal analysis of voting behavior. *Journal of Applied Social Psychology, 4,* 95–124.

Fishbein, M., Middlestadt, S. E., & Chung, J. (1986). Predicting participation and choice among first time voters in U.S. partisan elections. In S. Kraus & R. Perloff (Eds.), *Mass media and political thoughts: An information processing approach* (pp. 65–82). Beverly Hills, CA: Sage.

Fishbein, M., & Stasson, M. (1990). The role of desires, self-predictions, and perceived control in the prediction of training session attendance. *Journal of Applied Social Psychology, 20,* 173–198.

Fisher, J. D. (1988). Possible effects of reference group–based social influence on AIDS-risk behavior and AIDS prevention. *American Psychologist, 43,* 914–920.

Fiske, S. T. (1980). Attention and weight in person perception: The impact of negative and extreme behavior. *Journal of Personality and Social Psychology, 38,* 889–906.

Fiske, S. T., & Linville, P. W. (1980). What does the schema concept buy us? *Personality and Social Psychology Bulletin, 6,* 543–557.

Fiske, S. T., & Neuberg, S. L. (1990). A continuum of impression formation, from category-based to individuating processes: Influences of information and motivation on attention and interpretation. In M. P. Zanna (Ed.), *Advances in experimental social psychology* (Vol. 23, pp. 1–74). San Diego, CA: Academic Press.

Fiske, S. T., & Pavelchak, M. A. (1986). Category-based versus piecemeal-based affective responses: Developments in schema-triggered affect. In R. M. Sorrentino & E. T. Higgins (Eds.), *Handbook of motivation and cognition: Foundations of social behavior* (pp. 167–203). New York: Guilford Press.

Fiske, S. T., Pratto, F., & Pavelchak, M. A. (1983). Citizens' images of nuclear war: Content and consequences. *Journal of Social Issues, 39*(1), 41–65.

Fiske, S. T., & Taylor, S. E. (1991). *Social cognition* (2nd ed.). New York: McGraw-Hill.

Fitzgerald, D., & Ausubel, D. P. (1963). Cognitive versus affective factors in the learning and retention of controversial material. *Journal of Educational Psychology, 54,* 73–84.

Fitzpatrick, A. R., & Eagly, A. H. (1981). Anticipatory belief polarization as a function of the expertise of a discussion partner. *Personality and Social Psychology Bulletin, 7,* 636–642.

Flay, B. R. (1985). What we know about the social influences approach to smoking prevention: Review and recommendation. In C. S. Bell & R. Battjes (Eds.), *Prevention research: Deterring drug abuse among children and adolescents* (NIDA Research Monograph No. 63, pp. 67–112). Washington, DC: U.S. Government Printing Office.

Flay, B. R., Ryan, K. B., Best, J. A., Brown, K. S., Kersell, M. W., d'Avernas, J. R., & Zanna, M. P. (1985). Are social-psychological smoking prevention programs effective? The Waterloo study. *Journal of Behavioral Medicine, 8,* 37–59.

Fleishman, J. A. (1986). Types of political attitude structure: Results of a cluster analysis. *Public Opinion Quarterly, 50,* 371–386.

Fleming, D. (1967). Attitude: The history of a concept. *Perspectives in American History, 1,* 285–365.

Fleming, H. J., & Darley, J. M. (1989). Perceiving choice and constraint: The effects of contextual and behavioral cues on attitude attribution. *Journal of Personality and Social Psychology, 56,* 27–40.

Folkman, S., & Lazarus, R. S. (1985). If it changes it must be a process: Study of emotion and coping during three stages of a college examination. *Journal of Personality and Social Psychology, 48,* 150–170.

Forgas, J. P. (1989). Mood effects on decision making strategies. *Australian Journal of Psychology, 41,* 197–214.

Forgas, J. P., & Bower, G. H. (1987). Mood effects on person-perception judgments. *Journal of Personality and Social Psychology, 53,* 53–60.

Fowler, C. A., Wolford, G., Slade, R., & Tassinary, L. (1981). Lexical access with and without awareness. *Journal of Experimental Psychology: General, 110,* 341–362.

Fox, J. A., & Tracy, P. E. (1984). Measuring associations with randomized response. *Social Science Research, 13,* 188–197.

Fox, J. A., & Tracy, P. E. (1986). *Randomized response: A method for sensitive surveys.* Beverly Hills, CA: Sage.

Fredricks, A. J., & Dossett, D. L. (1983). Attitude-behavior relations: A comparison of the Fishbein-Ajzen and the Bentler-Speckart models. *Journal of Personality and Social Psychology, 45,* 501–512.

Freedman, J. L. (1963). Attitudinal effects of inadequate justification. *Journal of Personality, 31,* 371–385.

Freedman, J. L. (1964). Involvement, discrepancy, and change. *Journal of Abnormal and Social Psychology, 69,* 290–295.

Freedman, J. L. (1965a). Confidence, utility, and selective exposure: A partial replication. *Journal of Personality and Social Psychology, 2,* 778–780.

Freedman, J. L. (1965b). Long-term behavioral effects of cognitive dissonance. *Journal of Experimental Social Psychology, 1,* 145–155.

Freedman, J. L. (1965c). Preference for dissonant information. *Journal of Personality and Social Psychology, 2,* 287–289.

Freedman, J. L. (1969). Role playing: Psychology by consensus. *Journal of Personality and Social Psychology, 13,* 107–114.

Freedman, J. L., Carlsmith, J. M., & Sears, D. O. (1978). *Social psychology* (3rd ed.). New York: Prentice-Hall.

Freedman, J. L., Cunningham, J. A., & Krismer, K. (1992). Inferred values and the reverse-incentive effect in induced complaince. *Journal of Personality and Social Psychology, 61,* 357–368.

Freedman, J. L., & Sears, D. O. (1965a). Selective exposure. In L. Berkowitz (Ed.), *Advances in experimental social psychology* (Vol. 2, pp. 57–97). San Diego, CA: Academic Press.

Freedman, J. L., & Sears, D. O. (1965b). Warning, distraction and resistance to influence. *Journal of Personality and Social Psychology, 1,* 262–266.

French, J. R. P., Jr. (1956). A formal theory of social power. *Psychological Review, 63,* 181–194.

French, J. R. P., Jr., & Raven, B. (1959). The bases of social power. In D. Cartwright (Ed.), *Studies in social power* (pp. 150–167). Ann Arbor: University of Michigan.

Freud, S. (1946). *The ego and the mechanisms of defense.* New York: International Universities Press.

Freud, S. (1953). *A general introduction to psychoanalysis.* Garden City, NY: Permabooks. (Original work published 1920)

Frey, D. (1981a). Postdecisional preference for decision-relevant information as a function of the competence of its source and the degree of familiarity with this information. *Journal of Experimental Social Psychology, 17,* 51–67.

Frey, D. (1981b). Reversible and irreversible decisions: Preference for consonant information as a function of attractiveness of decision alternatives. *Personality and Social Psychology Bulletin, 7,* 621–626.

Frey, D. (1982). Different levels of cognitive dissonance, information seeking, and information avoidance. *Journal of Personality and Social Psychology, 43,* 1175–1183.

Frey, D. (1986). Recent research on selective exposure to information. In L. Berkowitz (Ed.), *Advances in experimental social psychology* (Vol. 19, pp. 41–80). San Diego, CA: Academic Press.

Frey, D., & Rosch, M. (1984). Information seeking after decisions: The roles of novelty of information and decision reversibility. *Personality and Social Psychology Bulletin, 10,* 91–98.

Frey, D., & Wicklund, R. (1978). A clarification of selective exposure: The impact of choice. *Journal of Experimental Social Psychology, 14,* 132–139.

Frey, K., & Eagly, A. H. (1992). *Vividness can undermine the persuasiveness of messages.* Unpublished manuscript, Purdue University, West Lafayette, IN.

Friend, R., Rafferty, Y., & Bramel, D. (1990). A puzzling misinterpretation of the Asch "conformity" study. *European Journal of Social Psychology, 20,* 29–44.

Frost, D. E., & Stahelski, A. J. (1988). The systematic measurement of French and Raven's bases of social power in workgroups. *Journal of Applied Social Psychology, 18,* 375–389.

Funder, D. C. (1982). On assessing social psychological theories through the study of individual differences: Template matching and forced compliance. *Journal of Personality and Social Psychology, 43,* 100–110.

Furnham, A., & Proctor, E. (1989). Memory for information about nuclear power: A test of the selective recall hypothesis. *Current Psychology: Research & Reviews, 8,* 287–297.

Gaes, G. G., Kalle, R. J., & Tedeschi, J. T. (1978). Impression management in the forced compliance situation. *Journal of Experimental Social Psychology, 14,* 493–510.

Gaes, G. G., Melberg, V. M., & Tedeschi, J. T. (1986). A study examining the arousal properties of the forced compliance situation. *Journal of Experimental Social Psychology, 22,* 136–147.

Gaes, G. G., Quigley-Fernandez, B., & Tedeschi, J. T. (1978). Unclogging the bogus pipeline: A critical reanalysis of the Cherry, Byrne, and Mitchell study. *Journal of Research in Personality, 12,* 189–192.

Gaito, J. (1980). Measurement scales and statistics: Resurgence of an old misconception. *Psychological Bulletin, 87,* 564–567.

Galizio, M., & Hendrick, C. (1972). Effect of musical accompaniment on attitude: The guitar as a prop for persuasion. *Journal of Applied Social Psychology, 2,* 350–359.

Garber, R. B. (1955). Influence of cognitive and affective factors in learning and retaining attitudinal materials. *Journal of Abnormal and Social Psychology, 51,* 384–389.

George, J. M. (1979). The influence of commitment on recall of consistent and inconsistent information. *Representative Research in Social Psychology*, *9*, 89-102.

Gerard, H. B. (1964). Physiological measurement in social psychological research. In P. H. Leiderman & D. Shapiro (Eds.), *Psychological approaches to social behavior* (pp. 43-58). Stanford, CA: Stanford University Press.

Gerard, H. B., & Mathewson, G. (1966). The effects of severity of initiation on liking for a group: A replication. *Journal of Experimental Social Psychology*, *2*, 278-287.

Gerard, H. B., & White, G. L. (1983). Post-decisional reevaluation of choice alternatives. *Personality and Social Psychology Bulletin*, *9*, 365-369.

Gergen, K. J., & Jones, E. E. (1963). Mental illness, predictability, and affective consequences as stimulus factors in person perception. *Journal of Abnormal and Social Psychology*, *67*, 95-104.

Ghiselli, E. E. (1964). *Theory of psychological measurement*. New York: McGraw-Hill.

Gibson, L. D. (1983). If the question is copy testing, the answer is..."Not recall." *Journal of Advertising Research*, *23*, 39-46.

Giesen, M., & Hendrick, C. (1974). Effects of false positive and negative arousal feedback on persuasion. *Journal of Personality and Social Psychology*, *30*, 449-457.

Gilkinson, H., Paulson, S. F., & Sekkink, D. E. (1953). Conditions affecting the communication of controversial statements in connected discourse: Forms of presentation and the political frame of reference of the listener. *Speech Monographs*, *20*, 253-260.

Gillig, P. M., & Greenwald, A. G. (1974). Is it time to lay the sleeper effect to rest? *Journal of Personality and Social Psychology*, *29*, 132-139.

Giner-Sorolla, R., Hazlewood, J. D., & Chaiken, S. (1989, June). *Effects of personal involvement on the heuristic and systematic processing of persuasive information*. Paper presented at the meeting of the American Psychological Society, Arlington, VA.

Ginossar, Z., & Trope, Y. (1987). Problem solving in judgment under uncertainty. *Journal of Personality and Social Psychology*, *52*, 464-474.

Glass, G. V., McGaw, B., & Smith, M. L. (1981). *Meta-analysis in social research*. Beverly Hills, CA: Sage.

Gleicher, F., & Petty, R. E. (1992). Expectations of reassurance influence the nature of fear-stimulated attitude change. *Journal of Experimental Social Psychology*, *28*, 86-100.

Gleicher, F., & Weary, G. (1991). The effect of depression on the quantity and quality of social inferences. *Journal of Personality and Social Psychology*, *61*, 105-114.

Goethals, G. R. (1976). An attributional analysis of some social influence phenomena. In J. H. Harvey, W. J. Ickes, & R. F. Kidd (Eds.), *New directions in attribution research* (Vol. 1, pp. 291-310). Hillsdale, NJ: Erlbaum.

Goethals, G. R., & Cooper, J. (1972). Role of intention and postbehavioral consequence in the arousal of cognitive dissonance. *Journal of Personality and Social Psychology*, *23*, 293-301.

Goethals, G. R., Cooper, J., & Naficy, A. (1979). Role of foreseen, foreseeable, and unforeseeable behavioral consequences in the arousal of cognitive dissonance. *Journal of Personality and Social Psychology*, *37*, 1179-1185.

Goethals, G. R., & Nelson, R. E. (1973). Similarity in the influence process: The belief-value distinction. *Journal of Personality and Social Psychology*, *25*, 117-122.

Gollob, H. F. (1974). The subject-verb-object approach to social cognition. *Psychological Review*, *81*, 286-321.

Gollob, H. F., & Lugg, A. M. (1973). Effects of instruction and stimulus presentation on the occurrence of averaging responses in impression formation. *Journal of Experimental Psychology*, *98*, 217-219.

Goodstadt, M. S., & Gruson, V. (1975). The randomized response technique: A test on drug use. *Journal of the American Statistical Association*, *70*, 814-818.

Gordon, P. C., & Holyoak, K. J. (1983). Implicit learning and generalization of the "mere exposure" effect. *Journal of Personality and Social Psychology*, *45*, 492-500.

Gordon, W. C. (1989). *Learning and memory*. Pacific Grove, CA: Brooks/Cole.

Gormezano, I., & Kehoe, E. J. (1975). Classical conditioning: Some methodological-conceptual issues. In W. K. Estes (Ed.), *Handbook of learning and cognitive processes* (Vol. 2, pp. 143-179). Hillsdale, NJ: Erlbaum.

Gorn, G. J. (1982). The effects of music in advertising on choice behavior: A classical conditioning approach. *Journal of Marketing*, *46*(1), 94-101.

Gorn, G. J., & Goldberg, M. E. (1980). Children's responses to repetitive television commercials. *Journal of Consumer Research*, *6*, 421-424.

Gorsuch, R. L., & Ortberg, J. (1983). Moral obligation and attitudes: Their relation to behavioral intentions. *Journal of Personality and Social Psychology*, *44*, 1025-1028.

Gottlieb, A., & Ickes, W. (1978). Attributional strategies of social influence. In J. H. Harvey, W. Ickes, & R. F. Kidd (Eds.), *New directions in attribution research* (Vol. 2, pp. 261-296). Hillsdale, NJ: Erlbaum.

Gouaux, C. (1971). Induced affective states and interpersonal attraction. *Journal of Personality and Social Psychology*, *20*, 37-43.

Granberg, D., & Brent, E. E. (1974). Dove-hawk placements in the 1968 election: Application of social judgment and balance theories. *Journal of Personality and Social Psychology*, *29*, 687-695.

Granberg, D., & Holmberg, S. (1990). The intention-behavior relationship among U.S. and Swedish voters. *Social Psychology Quarterly*, *53*, 44-54.

Green, B. F. (1954). Attitude measurement. In G. Lindzey (Ed.), *Handbook of social psychology* (1st ed., Vol. 1, pp. 335–369). Cambridge, MA: Addison-Wesley.

Green, B. F. (1956). A method of scalogram analysis using summary statistics. *Psychometrika, 21,* 79–88.

Green, D. P., & Gerken, A. E. (1989). Self-interest and public opinion toward smoking restrictions and cigarette taxes. *Public Opinion Quarterly, 53,* 1–16.

Greenbaum, C. W., & Zemach, M. (1972). Role-playing and change of attitude toward the police after a campus riot: Effects of situational demand and justification. *Human Relations, 25,* 87–99.

Greenberg, B. G., Abul-Ela, A. L. A., Simmons, W. R., & Horvitz, D. G. (1969). The unrelated question randomized response model: Theoretical framework. *Journal of the American Statistical Association, 64,* 520–539.

Greenberg, B. G., Kuebler, R. R., Jr., Abernathy, J. R., & Horvitz, D. G. (1971). Application of the randomized response technique in obtaining quantitative data. *Journal of the American Statistical Association, 66,* 243–250.

Greene, V. L., & Carmines, E. G. (1980). Assessing the reliability of linear composites. In K. Schuessler (Ed.), *Sociological methodology: 1980* (pp. 160–175). San Francisco: Jossey-Bass.

Greenspoon, J. (1955). The reinforcing effect of two spoken sounds on the frequency of two responses. *American Journal of Psychology, 68,* 409–416.

Greenwald, A. G. (1968). Cognitive learning, cognitive response to persuasion, and attitude change. In A. G. Greenwald, T. C. Brock, & T. M. Ostrom (Eds.), *Psychological foundations of attitudes* (pp. 147–170). San Diego, CA: Academic Press.

Greenwald, A. G. (1969). The open-mindedness of the counterattitudinal role player. *Journal of Experimental Social Psychology, 5,* 375–388.

Greenwald, A. G. (1970). When does role playing produce attitude change? Toward an answer. *Journal of Personality and Social Psychology, 16,* 214–219.

Greenwald, A. G. (1975a). Consequences of prejudice against the null hypothesis. *Psychological Bulletin, 82,* 1–20.

Greenwald, A. G. (1975b). On the inconclusiveness of "crucial" cognitive tests of dissonance versus self-perception theories. *Journal of Experimental Social Psychology, 11,* 490–499.

Greenwald, A. G. (1980). The totalitarian ego: Fabrication and revision of personal history. *American Psychologist, 35,* 603–618.

Greenwald, A. G. (1981). Cognitive response analysis: An appraisal. In R. E. Petty, T. M. Ostrom, & T. C. Brock (Eds.), *Cognitive responses in persuasion* (pp. 127–133). Hillsdale, NJ: Erlbaum.

Greenwald, A. G. (1982). Ego-task analysis. In A. H. Hastorf & A. M. Isen (Eds.), *Cognitive social psychology* (pp. 109–147). New York: Elsevier/North Holland.

Greenwald, A. G. (1989). Why attitudes are important: Defining attitude and attitude theory 20 years later. In A. R. Pratkanis, S. J. Breckler, & A. G. Greenwald (Eds.), *Attitude structure and function* (pp. 429–440). Hillsdale, NJ: Erlbaum.

Greenwald, A. G., & Albert, R. D. (1968). Acceptance and recall of improvised arguments. *Journal of Personality and Social Psychology, 8,* 31–34.

Greenwald, A. G., & Breckler, S. J. (1985). To whom is the self presented? In B. R. Schlenker (Ed.), *The self and social life* (pp. 126–145). New York: McGraw-Hill.

Greenwald, A. G., & Leavitt, C. (1984). Audience involvement in advertising: Four levels. *Journal of Consumer Research, 11,* 581–592.

Greenwald, A. G., & Pratkanis, A. R. (1984). The self. In R. S. Wyer, Jr. & T. K. Srull (Eds.), *Handbook of social cognition* (Vol. 3, pp. 129–178). Hillsdale, NJ: Erlbaum.

Greenwald, A. G., Pratkanis, A. R., Leippe, M. R., & Baumgardner, M. H. (1986). Under what conditions does theory obstruct research progress? *Psychological Review, 93,* 216–229.

Greenwald, A. G., & Ronis, D. L. (1978). Twenty years of cognitive dissonance: Case study of the evolution of a theory. *Psychological Review, 85,* 53–57.

Greenwald, A. G., & Sakumura, J. S. (1967). Attitude and selective learning: Where are the phenomena of yesteryear? *Journal of Personality and Social Psychology, 7,* 387–397.

Greenwald, H. J. (1969). Dissonance and relative versus absolute attractiveness of decision alternatives. *Journal of Personality and Social Psychology, 11,* 328–333.

Griffitt, W. B. (1970). Environmental effects on interpersonal affective behavior: Ambient effective temperature and attraction. *Journal of Personality and Social Psychology, 15,* 240–244.

Grube, J. W., & Morgan, M. (1990). Attitude-social support interactions: Contingent consistency effects in the prediction of adolescent smoking, drinking, and drug use. *Social Psychology Quarterly, 53,* 329–339.

Gruder, C. L., Cook, T. D., Hennigan, K. M., Flay, B. R., Alessis, C., & Halamaj, J. (1978). Empirical tests of the absolute sleeper effect predicted from the discounting cue hypothesis. *Journal of Personality and Social Psychology, 36,* 1061–1074.

Grush, J. E. (1976). Attitude formation and mere exposure phenomena: A nonartificial explanation of empirical findings. *Journal of Personality and Social Psychology, 33,* 281–290.

Grush, J. E. (1979). A summary review of mediating explanations of exposure phenomena. *Personality and Social Psychology Bulletin, 5,* 154–159.

Guerin, B., & Innes, J. M. (1989). Cognitive tuning sets: Anticipating the consequences of communication. *Current Psychology: Research & Reviews, 8,* 234–239.

Guild, P.D., Strickland, L.H., & Barefoot, J.C. (1977). Dissonance theory, self-perception and the bogus pipeline. *European Journal of Social Psychology*, *7*, 465-476.

Guilford, J.P. (1938). The computation of psychological values from judgments in absolute categories. *Journal of Experimental Psychology*, *22*, 32-42.

Guilford, J.P. (1954). *Psychometric methods* (2nd ed.). New York: McGraw-Hill.

Gulliksen, H. (1950). *Theory of mental tests.* New York: Wiley.

Gur, R.C., & Sackeim, H.A. (1979). Self-deception: A concept in search of a phenomenon. *Journal of Personality and Social Psychology*, *37*, 147-169.

Guttman, L. (1941). The quantification of a class of attributes: A theory and method of scale construction. In P. Horst, *The prediction of personal adjustment* (Bulletin No. 48, pp. 319-348). New York: Social Science Research Council.

Guttman, L. (1944). A basis for scaling qualitative data. *American Sociological Review*, *9*, 139-150.

Guttman, L. (1947a). The Cornell technique for scale and intensity analysis. *Educational and Psychological Measurement*, *7*, 247-280.

Guttman, L. (1947b). On Festinger's evaluation of scale analysis. *Psychological Bulletin*, *44*, 451-465.

Guttman, L. (1950). The basis for scalogram analysis. In S.A. Stouffer, L. Guttman, E.A. Suchman, P.F. Lazarsfeld, S.A. Star, & J.A. Clausen, *Measurement and prediction* (pp. 60-90). Princeton, NJ: Princeton University Press.

Guttman, L. (1959). A structural theory for intergroup beliefs and actions. *American Sociological Review*, *24*, 318-328.

Guttman, L. (1968). A general nonmetric technique for finding the smallest coordinate space for a configuration of points. *Psychometrika*, *33*, 469-506.

Haaland, G.A., & Venkatesan, M. (1968). Resistance to persuasive communications: An examination of the distraction hypotheses. *Journal of Personality and Social Psychology*, *9*, 167-170.

Hackman, J.R., & Anderson, L.R. (1968). The strength, relevance, and source of beliefs about an object in Fishbein's attitude theory. *Journal of Social Psychology*, *76*, 55-67.

Halverson, R.R., & Pallak, M.S. (1978). Commitment, ego-involvement, and resistance to attack. *Journal of Experimental Social Psychology*, *14*, 1-12.

Hamblin, R.L. (1974). Social attitudes: Magnitude measurement and theory. In H.M. Blalock, Jr. (Ed.), *Measurement in the social sciences* (pp. 61-120). Chicago: Aldine.

Hamilton, D.L., & Huffman, L.J. (1971). Generality of impression-formation processes for evaluative and non-evaluative judgments. *Journal of Personality and Social Psychology*, *20*, 200-207.

Hamilton, D.L., & Zanna, M.P. (1972). Differential weighting of favorable and unfavorable attributes in impressions of personality. *Journal of Experimental Research in Personality*, *6*, 204-212.

Hamilton, D.L., & Zanna, M.P. (1974). Context effects in impression formation: Changes in connotative meaning. *Journal of Personality and Social Psychology*, *29*, 649-654.

Hammond, K.R. (1948). Measuring attitudes by error choice: An indirect method. *Journal of Abnormal and Social Psychology*, *43*, 38-48.

Harary, F., Norman, R.Z., & Cartwright, D. (1965). *Structural models: An introduction to the theory of directed graphs.* New York: Wiley.

Harkins, S.G., & Petty, R.E. (1981). Effects of source magnification of cognitive effort on attitudes: An information-processing view. *Journal of Personality and Social Psychology*, *40*, 401-413.

Harkins, S.G., & Petty, R.E. (1983). Social context effects in persuasion: The effects of multiple sources and multiple targets. In P. Paulus (Ed.), *Basic group processes* (pp. 149-175). New York: Springer-Verlag.

Harkins, S.G., & Petty, R.E. (1987). Information utility and the multiple source effect. *Journal of Personality and Social Psychology*, *52*, 260-268.

Harris, V.A., & Jellison, J.M. (1971). Fear-arousing communications, false physiological feedback, and acceptance of recommendations. *Journal of Experimental Social Psychology*, *7*, 269-279.

Harrison, A.A. (1968). Response competition, frequency, exploratory behavior, and liking. *Journal of Personality and Social Psychology*, *9*, 363-368.

Harrison, A.A. (1977). Mere exposure. In L. Berkowitz (Ed.), *Advances in experimental social psychology* (Vol. 10, pp. 39-83). San Diego, CA: Academic Press.

Harrison, A.A., & Crandall, R. (1972). Heterogeneity-homogeneity of exposure sequence and the attitudinal effects of exposure. *Journal of Personality and Social Psychology*, *21*, 234-238.

Harrison, A.A., & Fiscaro, S.A. (1974). Stimulus familiarity and alley illumination as determinants of approach response latencies of house crickets. *Perceptual and Motor Skills*, *39*, 147-152.

Harrison, A.A., & Zajonc, R.B. (1970). The effects of frequency and duration of exposure on response competition and affective ratings. *Journal of Psychology*, *75*, 163-169.

Hartmann, G.W. (1936). A field experiment on the comparative effectiveness of "emotional" and "rational" political leaflets in determining election results. *Journal of Abnormal and Social Psychology*, *31*, 99-114.

Hasher, L., & Zacks, R.T. (1984). Automatic processing of fundamental information: The case of frequency of occurrence. *American Psychologist*, *39*, 1372-1388.

Hass, R.G. (1975). Persuasion or moderation? Two experiments on anticipatory belief change. *Journal of Personality and Social Psychology, 31,* 1155–1162.

Hass, R.G. (1981). Effects of source characteristics on cognitive responses and persuasion. In R.E. Petty, T.M. Ostrom, & T.C. Brock (Eds.), *Cognitive responses in persuasion* (pp. 141–172). Hillsdale, NJ: Erlbaum.

Hass, R.G., & Grady, K. (1975). Temporal delay, type of forewarning, and resistance to influence. *Journal of Experimental Social Psychology, 11,* 459–469.

Hass, R.G., Katz, I., Rizzo, N., Bailey, J., & Eisenstadt, D. (1991). Cross-racial appraisal as related to attitude ambivalence and cognitive complexity. *Personality and Social Psychology Bulletin, 17,* 83–92.

Hass, R.G., Katz, I., Rizzo, N., Bailey, J., & Moore, L. (in press). When racial ambivalence evokes negative affect: Using a disguised measure of mood. *Personality and Social Psychology Bulletin.*

Hass, R.G., & Mann, R.W. (1976). Anticipatory belief change: Persuasion or impression management? *Journal of Personality and Social Psychology, 34,* 105–111.

Hastie, R. (1991). A review from a high place: The field of judgment and decision making as revealed in its current textbooks. *Psychological Science, 2,* 135–141.

Hastie, R., & Park, B. (1986). The relationship between memory and judgment depends on whether the judgment task is memory-based or on-line. *Psychological Review, 93,* 258–268.

Hastorf, A.H., & Cantril, H. (1954). They saw a game: A case study. *Journal of Abnormal and Social Psychology, 49,* 129–134.

Haugtvedt, C., Petty, R.E., Cacioppo, J.T., & Steidley, T. (1988). Personality and ad effectiveness. *Advances in Consumer Research, 15,* 209–212.

Hays, W.L. (1963). *Statistics for psychologists.* New York: Holt, Rinehart & Winston.

Hazlewood, J.D., & Chaiken, S. (1990, August). *Personal relevance, majority influence, and the law of large numbers.* Paper presented at the meeting of the American Psychological Association, Boston, MA.

Hearst, E. (1988). Fundamentals of learning and conditioning. In R.C. Atkinson, R.J. Herrnstein, G. Lindzey, & R.D. Luce (Eds.), *Steven's handbook of experimental psychology* (2nd ed., pp. 3–110). New York: Wiley.

Hearst, P.C., & Moscow, A. (1982). *Every secret thing.* Garden City, NY: Doubleday.,

Hedges, L.V., & Olkin, I. (1985). *Statistical methods for meta-analysis.* San Diego, CA: Academic Press.

Heesacker, M., Petty, R.E., & Cacioppo, J.T. (1983). Field dependence and attitude change: Source credibility can alter persuasion by affecting message-relevant thinking. *Journal of Personality, 51,* 653–666.

Heider, F. (1946). Attitudes and cognitive organization. *Journal of Psychology, 21,* 107–112.

Heider, F. (1958). *The psychology of interpersonal relations.* New York: Wiley.

Heilman, M.D., & Toffler, B.L. (1976). Reacting to reactance: An interpersonal interpretation of the need for freedom. *Journal of Experimental Social Psychology, 12,* 519–529.

Heise, D.R. (1970). The semantic differential and attitude research. In G.F. Summers (Ed.), *Attitude measurement* (pp. 235–253). Chicago: Rand McNally.

Heise, D.R. (1975). *Causal analysis.* New York: Wiley-Interscience.

Heise, D.R. (1977). Group dynamics and attitude-behavior relations. *Sociological Methods and Research, 5,* 259–288.

Heller, J.F., Pallak, M.S., & Picek, J.M. (1973). The interactive effects of intent and threat on boomerang attitude change. *Journal of Personality and Social Psychology, 26,* 273–279.

Helmreich, R., & Collins, B.E. (1968). Studies in forced compliance: Commitment and magnitude of inducement to comply as determinants of opinion change. *Journal of Personality and Social Psychology, 10,* 75–81.

Helson, H. (1964). *Adaptation-level theory: An experimental and systematic approach to behavior.* New York: Harper & Row.

Hendrick, C. (1968). Averaging vs. summation in impression formation. *Perceptual and Motor Skills, 27,* 1295–1302.

Hendrick, C. (Ed.). (1977). Role-playing as a methodology for social research: A symposium. *Personality and Social Psychology Bulletin, 3,* 454–522.

Hendrick, C., & Costantini, A.F. (1970). Effects of varying trait inconsistency and response requirements on the primacy effects in impression formation. *Journal of Personality and Social Psychology, 15,* 158–164.

Hendrick, C., & Giesen, M. (1976). Self-attribution of attitude as a function of belief feedback. *Memory and Cognition, 4,* 150–155.

Hendrick, C., Giesen, M., & Borden, R. (1975). False physiological feedback and persuasion: Effect of fear arousal vs. fear reduction on attitude change. *Journal of Personality, 43,* 196–214.

Hendrick, C., & Seyfried, B.A. (1974). Assessing the validity of laboratory-produced attitude change. *Journal of Personality and Social Psychology, 29,* 865–870.

Hendrick, C., & Shaffer, D.R. (1970). Effects of arousal and credibility on learning and persuasion. *Psychonomic Science, 20,* 241–243.

Henninger, M., & Wyer, R.S., Jr. (1976). The recognition and elimination of inconsistencies among syllogistically related beliefs: Some new light on the "Socratic effect." *Journal of Personality and Social Psychology, 34,* 680–693.

Herek, G.M. (1986). The instrumentality of attitudes: Toward a neofunctional theory. *Journal of Social Issues, 42*(2), 99–114.

Herek, G. M. (1987). Can functions be measured? A new perspective on the functional approach to attitudes. *Social Psychology Quarterly*, *50*, 285–303.

Hess, E. H. (1965). Attitude and pupil size. *Scientific American*, *212*, 46–54.

Hess, E. H., & Polt, J. M. (1960). Pupil size as related to interest value of visual stimuli. *Science*, *132*, 349–350.

Hess, E. H., Seltzer, A. L., & Shlien, J. M. (1965). Pupil response of hetero- and homosexual males to pictures of men and women: A pilot study. *Journal of Abnormal Psychology*, *70*, 165–168.

Hess, R. D., & Torney, J. V. (1967). *The development of political attitudes in children*. Chicago: Aldine.

Hewstone, M., & Young, L. (1988). Expectancy-value models of attitude: Measurement and combination of evaluations and beliefs. *Journal of Applied Social Psychology*, *18*, 958–971.

Higbee, K. L. (1969). Fifteen years of fear arousal: Research on threat appeals: 1953–1968. *Psychological Bulletin*, *72*, 426–444.

Higgins, E. T. (1981). The "communication game": Implications for social cognition and persuasion. In E. T. Higgins, C. P. Herman, & M. P. Zanna (Eds.), *Social cognition: The Ontario Symposium* (Vol. 1, pp. 343–392). Hillsdale, NJ: Erlbaum.

Higgins, E. T. (1987). Self-discrepancy: A theory relating self and affect. *Psychological Review*, *94*, 319–340.

Higgins, E. T. (1989a). Knowledge accessibility and activation: Subjectivity and suffering from unconscious sources. In J. S. Uleman & J. A. Bargh (Eds.), *Unintended thought* (pp. 75–123). New York: Guilford Press.

Higgins, E. T. (1989b). Self-discrepancy theory: What patterns of self-beliefs cause people to suffer? In L. Berkowitz (Ed.), *Advances in experimental social psychology* (Vol. 22, pp. 93–136). San Diego, CA: Academic Press.

Higgins, E. T., & Bargh, J. A. (1987). Social cognition and social perception. *Annual Review of Psychology*, *38*, 369–425.

Higgins, E. T., & King, G. A. (1981). Accessibility of social constructs: Information processing consequences of individual and contextual variability. In N. Cantor & J. Kihlstrom (Eds.), *Personality, cognition, and social interaction* (pp. 69–122). Hillsdale, NJ: Erlbaum.

Higgins, E. T., King, G. A., & Mavin, G. H. (1982). Individual construct accessibility and subjective impressions and recall. *Journal of Personality and Social Psychology*, *43*, 35–47.

Higgins, E. T., Kuiper, N. A., & Olson, J. M. (1981). Social cognition: A need to get personal. In E. T. Higgins, C. P. Herman, & M. P. Zanna (Eds.), *Social cognition: The Ontario Symposium* (Vol. 1, pp. 395–420). Hillsdale, NJ: Erlbaum.

Higgins, E. T., & McCann, C. D. (1984). Social encoding and subsequent attitudes, impressions, and memory: "Context-driven" and motivational aspects of processing. *Journal of Personality and Social Psychology*, *47*, 26–39.

Higgins, E. T., Rhodewalt, F., & Zanna, M. P. (1979). Dissonance motivation: Its nature, persistence, and reinstatement. *Journal of Experimental Social Psychology*, *15*, 16–34.

Higgins, E. T., Rholes, W. S., & Jones, C. R. (1977). Category accessibility and impression formation. *Journal of Experimental Social Psychology*, *13*, 141–154.

Hildebrand-Saints, L., & Weary, G. (1989). Depression and social information gathering. *Personality and Social Psychology Bulletin*, *15*, 150–160.

Hildum, D. C., & Brown, R. W. (1956). Verbal reinforcement and interviewer bias. *Journal of Abnormal and Social Psychology*, *53*, 108–111.

Hilgard, E. R. (1987). *Psychology in America: A historical survey*. San Diego, CA: Harcourt Brace Jovanovich.

Hill, D., Gardner, G., & Rassaby, J. (1985). Factors predisposing women to take precautions against breast and cervix cancer. *Journal of Applied Social Psychology*, *15*, 59–79.

Hill, P. C., Henderson, A. H., Bray, J. H., & Evans, R. I. (1981). Generalizing a self-report validator of cigarette smoking to older adolescents. *Replications in Social Psychology*, *1*, 38–40.

Hill, W. F. (1978). Effects of mere exposure on preferences in nonhuman mammals. *Psychological Bulletin*, *85*, 1177–1198.

Hill, W. F. (1985). *Learning: A survey of psychological interpretations* (4th ed.). New York: Harper & Row.

Himmelfarb, S. (1972). Integration and attribution theories in personality impression formation. *Journal of Personality and Social Psychology*, *23*, 309–313.

Himmelfarb, S. (1973). General test of a differential weighted averaging model of impression formation. *Journal of Experimental Social Psychology*, *9*, 379–390.

Himmelfarb, S. (1975). On scale value and weight in the weighted averaging model of integration theory. *Personality and Social Psychology Bulletin*, *1*, 580–583.

Himmelfarb, S., & Anderson, N. H. (1975). Integration theory applied to opinion attribution. *Journal of Personality and Social Psychology*, *31*, 1064–1072.

Himmelfarb, S., & Arazi, D. (1974). Choice and source attractiveness in exposure to discrepant messages. *Journal of Experimental Social Psychology*, *10*, 516–527.

Himmelfarb, S., & Eagly, A. H. (1974). Orientations to the study of attitudes and their change. In S. Himmelfarb & A. H. Eagly (Eds.), *Readings in attitude change* (pp. 2–49). New York: Wiley.

Himmelfarb, S., & Edgell, S. E. (1980). Additive constants model: A randomized response technique for eliminating evasiveness to quantitative response questions. *Psychological Bulletin*, *87*, 525–530.

Himmelfarb, S., & Edgell, S. E. (1982). Note on "the randomized response approach": Addendum to Fox and Tracy. *Evaluation Review, 6*, 279-284.

Himmelfarb, S., & Edgell, S. E. (1988). *A bibliography of research on the randomized response technique*. Unpublished manuscript, University of Louisville, Louisville, KY.

Himmelfarb, S., & Lickteig, C. (1982). Social desirability and the randomized response technique. *Journal of Personality and Social Psychology, 43*, 710-717.

Hinckley, E. D. (1932). The influence of individual opinion on construction of an attitude scale. *Journal of Social Psychology, 3*, 283-296.

Hippler, H.-J., Schwarz, N., & Sudman, S. (Eds.). (1987). *Social information processing and survey methodology*. New York: Springer-Verlag.

Hochbaum, G. M. (1954). The relation between group members' self-confidence and their reactions to group pressure to conformity. *American Sociological Review, 19*, 678-687.

Hodges, B. H. (1974). Effect of valence on relative weighting in impression formation. *Journal of Personality and Social Psychology, 30*, 378-381.

Holbrook, M. B. (1977). Comparing multiattribute attitude models by optimal scaling. *Journal of Consumer Research, 4*, 165-171.

Holmes, J. G., & Strickland, L. H. (1970). Choice freedom and confirmation of incentive expectancy as determinants of attitude change. *Journal of Personality and Social Psychology, 14*, 39-45.

Holt, L. E. (1970). Resistance to persuasion on explicit beliefs as a function of commitment to and desirability of logically related beliefs. *Journal of Personality and Social Psychology, 16*, 583-591.

Holt, L. E., & Watts, W. A. (1969). Salience of logical relationships among beliefs as a factor in persuasion. *Journal of Personality and Social Psychology, 11*, 193-203.

Holyoak, K. J., & Gordon, P. C. (1984). Information processing and social cognition. In R. S. Wyer, Jr. & T. K. Srull (Eds.), *Handbook of social cognition* (Vol. 1, pp. 39-70). Hillsdale, NJ: Erlbaum.

Horvitz, D. G., Greenberg, B. G., & Abernathy, J. R. (1975). Recent developments in randomized response designs. In J. N. Srivastava (Ed.), *A survey of statistical design and linear models* (pp. 271-285). New York: American Elsevier.

Houston, D. A., & Fazio, R. H. (1989). Biased processing as a function of attitude accessibility: Making objective judgments subjectively. *Social Cognition, 7*, 51-66.

Hovland, C. I. (1951). Human learning and retention. In S. S. Stevens (Ed.), *Handbook of experimental psychology* (pp. 613-689). New York: Wiley.

Hovland, C. I. (Ed.). (1957). *The order of presentation in persuasion*. New Haven, CT: Yale University Press.

Hovland, C. I. (1959). Reconciling conflicting results derived from experimental and survey studies of attitude change. *American Psychologist, 14*, 8-17.

Hovland, C. I., Campbell, E. H., & Brock, T. (1957). The effects of "commitment" on opinion change following communication. In C. I. Hovland (Ed.), *The order of presentation in persuasion* (pp. 23-32). New Haven, CT: Yale University Press.

Hovland, C. I., Harvey, O. J., & Sherif, M. (1957). Assimilation and contrast effects in reactions to communication and attitude change. *Journal of Abnormal and Social Psychology, 55*, 244-252.

Hovland, C. I., & Janis, I. L. (Eds.). (1959). *Personality and persuasibility*. New Haven, CT: Yale University Press.

Hovland, C. I., Janis, I. L., & Kelley, H. H. (1953). *Communication and persuasion: Psychological studies of opinion change*. New Haven, CT: Yale University Press.

Hovland, C. I., Lumsdaine, A. A., & Sheffield, F. D. (1949). *Experiments on mass communication*. Princeton, NJ: Princeton University Press.

Hovland, C. I., & Mandell, W. (1952). An experimental comparison of conclusion-drawing by the communicator and by the audience. *Journal of Abnormal and Social Psychology, 47*, 581-588.

Hovland, C. I., & Mandell, W. (1957). Is there a "law of primacy in persuasion"? In C. I. Hovland (Ed.), *The order of presentation in persuasion* (pp. 13-22). New Haven, CT: Yale University Press.

Hovland, C. I., & Rosenberg, M. J. (1960). Summary and further theoretical issues. In C. I. Hovland, & M. J. Rosenberg (Eds.), *Attitude organization and change: An analysis of consistency among attitude components* (pp. 198-232). New Haven, CT: Yale University Press.

Hovland, C. I., & Sherif, M. (1952). Judgmental phenomena and scales of attitude measurement: Item displacement in Thurstone scales. *Journal of Abnormal and Social Psychology, 47*, 822-832.

Hovland, C. I., & Weiss, W. (1951). The influence of source credibility on communication effectiveness. *Public Opinion Quarterly, 15*, 635-650.

Howard, D. J. (1990). Rhetorical question effects on message processing and persuasion: The role of information availability and the elicitation of judgment. *Journal of Experimental Social Psychology, 26*, 217-239.

Hoyt, M. F., Henley, M. D., & Collins, B. E. (1972). Studies in forced compliance: Confluence of choice and consequence on attitude change. *Journal of Personality and Social Psychology, 23*, 205-210.

Huber, J., & Form, W. H. (1973). *Income and ideology*. New York: Free Press.

Hull, C. L. (1943). *Principles of behavior: An introduction to behavior theory*. New York: Appleton-Century-Crofts.

Hull, C. L. (1951). *Essentials of behavior*. New Haven, CT: Yale University Press.

Hummert, M. L., Crockett, W. H., & Kemper, S. (1990). Processing mechanisms underlying use of the balance schema. *Journal of Personality and Social Psychology, 58*, 5-21.

Hunt, H. K. (1973). Effects of corrective advertising. *Journal of Advertising Research, 13*, 15-22.

Hunt, J. M., & Kernan, J. B. (1984). The role of disconfirmed expectancies in the processing of advertising messages. *Journal of Social Psychology, 124*, 227-236.

Hunt, J. M., Smith, M. F., & Kernan, J. B. (1989). Processing effects of expectancy-discrepant persuasive messages. *Psychological Reports, 65*, 1359-1376.

Hunt, M. F., Jr., & Miller, G. R. (1968). Open- and closed-mindedness, belief-discrepant communication behavior, and tolerance for cognitive inconsistency. *Journal of Personality and Social Psychology, 8*, 35-37.

Hunter, J. E., Danes, J. E., & Cohen, S. H. (1984). *Mathematical models of attitude change: Change in single attitudes and cognitive structure* (Vol. 1). San Diego, CA: Academic Press.

Hyman, H. H., & Sheatsley, P. B. (1950). The current status of American public opinion. In J. C. Payne (Ed.), *The teaching of contemporary affairs* (21st yearbook, pp. 11-34). Washington, DC: National Council for the Social Studies.

Hyman, H. H., & Sheatsley, P. B. (1954). "The authoritarian personality": A methodological critique. In R. Christie & M. Jahoda (Eds.), *Studies in the scope and method of "The authoritarian personality"* (pp. 50-122). Glencoe, IL: Free Press.

Hymes, R. W. (1986). Political attitudes as social categories: A new look at selective memory. *Journal of Personality and Social Psychology, 51*, 233-241.

I-Cheng, C., Chow, L. P., & Rider, R. V. (1972). The randomized response technique as used in the Taiwan outcome of pregnancy study. *Studies in Family Planning, 3*, 265-269.

Ickes, W., & Barnes, R. D. (1977). The role of sex and self-monitoring in unstructured dyadic interactions. *Journal of Personality and Social Psychology, 5*, 315-330.

Ickes, W., Bissonnette, V., Garcia, S., & Stinson, L. L. (1990). Implementing and using the dyadic interaction paradigm. In C. Hendrick & M. S. Clark (Eds.), *Review of personality and social psychology* (Vol. 11, pp. 16-44). Newbury Park, CA: Sage.

Innes, J. M., & Ahrens, C. R. (1991). Positive mood, processing goals and the effects of information on evaluative judgment. In J. Forgas (Ed.), *Emotion and social judgment* (pp. 221-239). Oxford, England: Pergamon Press.

Insko, C. A. (1962). One-sided versus two-sided communications and countercommunications. *Journal of Abnormal and Social Psychology, 65*, 203-206.

Insko, C. A. (1964). Primacy versus recency in persuasion as a function of the timing of arguments and measures. *Journal of Abnormal and Social Psychology, 69*, 381-391.

Insko, C. A. (1965). Verbal reinforcement of attitude. *Journal of Personality and Social Psychology, 2*, 621-623.

Insko, C. A. (1967). *Theories of attitude change*. New York: Appleton-Century-Crofts.

Insko, C. A. (1981). Balance theory and phenomenology. In R. E. Petty, T. M. Ostrom, & T. C. Brock (Eds.), *Cognitive responses in persuasion* (pp. 309-338). Hillsdale, NJ: Erlbaum.

Insko, C. A. (1984). Balance theory, the Jordan paradigm, and the Wiest tetrahedron. In L. Berkowitz (Ed.), *Advances in experimental social psychology* (Vol. 18, pp. 89-140). San Diego, CA: Academic Press.

Insko, C. A., & Butzine, K. W. (1967). Rapport, awareness, and verbal reinforcement of attitude. *Journal of Personality and Social Psychology, 6*, 225-228.

Insko, C. A., & Cialdini, R. B. (1969). A test of three interpretations of attitudinal reinforcement. *Journal of Personality and Social Psychology, 12*, 333-341.

Insko, C. A., Lind, E. A., & LaTour, S. (1976). Persuasion, recall, and thoughts. *Representative Research in Social Psychology, 7*, 66-78.

Insko, C. A., & Melson, W. H. (1969). Verbal reinforcement of attitude in laboratory and nonlaboratory contexts. *Journal of Personality, 37*, 25-40.

Insko, C. A., Murashima, F., & Saiyadain, M. (1966). Communicator discrepancy, stimulus ambiguity, and influence. *Journal of Personality, 34*, 262-274.

Insko, C. A., & Oakes, W. (1966). Awareness and the "conditioning" of attitudes. *Journal of Personality and Social Psychology, 4*, 487-496.

Insko, C. A., & Schopler, J. (1967). Triadic consistency: A statement of affective-cognitive-conative consistency. *Psychological Review, 74*, 361-376.

Insko, C. A., Songer, E., & McGarvey, W. (1974). Balance, positivity, and agreement in the Jordan paradigm: A defense of balance theory. *Journal of Experimental Social Psychology, 10*, 53-83.

Insko, C. A., Turnbull, W., & Yandell, B. (1974). Facilitative and inhibiting effects of distraction on attitude change. *Sociometry, 37*, 508-528.

Insko, C. A., Worchel, S., Folger, R., & Kutkus, A. (1975). A balance theory interpretation of dissonance. *Psychological Review, 82*, 169-183.

Isen, A. M. (1984). Toward understanding the role of affect in cognition. In R. S. Wyer, Jr. & T. K. Srull (Eds.), *Handbook of social cognition* (Vol. 3, pp. 179-236). Hillsdale, NJ: Erlbaum.

Isen, A. M. (1987). Positive affect, cognitive processes, and social behavior. In L. Berkowitz (Ed.), *Advances in experimental social psychology* (Vol. 20, pp. 203-253). San Diego, CA: Academic Press.

Isen, A. M., & Means, B. (1983). The influence of positive affect on decision making strategy. *Social Cognition, 2*, 18–31.

Isen, A. M., Means, B., Patrick, R., & Nowicki, G. (1982). Some factors influencing decision-making strategy and risk taking. In M. S. Clark & S. T. Fiske (Eds.), *Affect and cognition* (pp. 243–261). Hillsdale, NJ: Erlbaum.

Isen, A. M., Shalker, T. E., Clark, M. S., & Karp, L. (1978). Affect, accessibility of material in memory, and behavior: A cognitive loop? *Journal of Personality and Social Psychology, 36*, 1–12.

Isenberg, D. J. (1980). Levels of analysis of pluralistic ignorance phenomena: The case of receptiveness to interpersonal feedback. *Journal of Applied Social Psychology, 10*, 457–467.

Isenberg, D. J. (1986). Group polarization: A critical review and meta-analysis. *Journal of Personality and Social Psychology, 50*, 1141–1151.

Izard, C. E. (1977). *Human emotions*. New York: Plenum Press.

Jaccard, J. J. (1974). Predicting social behavior from personality traits. *Journal of Research in Personality, 7*, 358–367.

Jaccard, J. J. (1981a). Attitudes and behavior: Implications of attitudes toward behavioral alternatives. *Journal of Experimental Social Psychology, 17*, 286–307.

Jaccard, J. J. (1981b). Toward theories of persuasion and belief change. *Journal of Personality and Social Psychology, 40*, 260–269.

Jaccard, J. J., & Becker, M. A. (1985). Attitudes and behavior: An information integration perspective. *Journal of Experimental Social Psychology, 21*, 440–465.

Jaccard, J. J., Brinberg, D., & Ackerman, L. J. (1986). Assessing attribute importance: A comparison of six methods. *Journal of Consumer Research, 12*, 463–468.

Jaccard, J. J., & Davidson, A. R. (1975). A comparison of two models of social behavior: Results of a survey sample. *Sociometry, 38*, 497–517.

Jaccard, J. J., & Fishbein, M. (1975). Inferential beliefs and order effects in personality impression formation. *Journal of Personality and Social Psychology, 31*, 1031–1040.

Jaccard, J. J., & Sheng, D. (1984). A comparison of six methods for assessing the importance of perceived consequences in behavioral decisions: Applications for attitude research. *Journal of Experimental Social Psychology, 20*, 1–28.

Jaccard, J., Weber, J., & Lundmark, J. (1975). A multitrait-multimethod analysis of four attitude assessment procedures. *Journal of Experimental Social Psychology, 11*, 149–154.

Jackson, J. M. (1986). In defense of social impact theory: Comment on Mullen. *Journal of Personality and Social Psychology, 50*, 511–513.

Jacoby, J., & Hoyer, W. D. (1982). Viewer miscomprehension of televised communication: Selected findings. *Journal of Marketing, 46*(4), 12–26.

Jacoby, J., & Hoyer, W. D. (1987). *The comprehension and miscomprehension of print communications: An investigation of mass media magazines*. Hillsdale, NJ: Erlbaum.

Jacoby, J., Hoyer, W. D., & Sheluga, D. A. (1980). *Miscomprehension of televised communications*. New York: American Association of Advertising Agencies.

Jacoby, J., Jaccard, J. J., Kuss, A., Troutman, T., & Mazursky, D. (1987). New directions in behavioral process research: Implications for social psychology. *Journal of Experimental Social Psychology, 23*, 146–175.

Jacoby, L. L., Kelley, C., Brown, J., & Jasechko, J. (1989). Becoming famous overnight: Limits on the ability to avoid unconscious influences of the past. *Journal of Personality and Social Psychology, 56*, 326–338.

Jacoby, L. L., & Whitehouse, K. (1989). An illusion of memory: False recognition influenced by unconscious perception. *Journal of Experimental Psychology: General, 118*, 126–135.

James, W. (1952). *The principles of psychology*. Chicago: Encyclopaedia Britannica. (Original work published 1890)

Jamieson, D. W., & Zanna, M. P. (1982, August). *Attitude change under threat of lie detection: A dissonance or impression management phenomenon?* Paper presented at the meeting of the American Psychological Association, Washington, DC.

Jamieson, D. W., & Zanna, M. P. (1983, June). *The lie detector expectation procedure: Ensuring veracious self-reports of attitudes*. Paper presented at the meeting of the Canadian Psychological Association, Winnepeg.

Jamieson, D. W., & Zanna, M. P. (1989). Need for structure in attitude formation and expression. In A. R. Pratkanis, S. J. Breckler, & A. G. Greenwald (Eds.), *Attitude structure and function* (pp. 383–406). Hillsdale, NJ: Erlbaum.

Janis, I. L. (1959). Motivational factors in the resolution of decisional conflicts. In M. R. Jones (Ed.), *Nebraska Symposium on Motivation, 1959* (Vol. 7, pp. 198–231). Lincoln: University of Nebraska Press.

Janis, I. L. (1967). Effects of fear arousal on attitude change: Recent developments in theory and experimental research. In L. Berkowitz (Ed.), *Advances in experimental social psychology* (Vol. 3, pp. 166–224). San Diego, CA: Academic Press.

Janis, I. L. (1968). Attitude change via role playing. In R. P. Abelson, E. Aronson, W. J. McGuire, T. M. Newcomb, M. J. Rosenberg, & P. H. Tannenbaum (Eds.), *Theories of cognitive consistency: A sourcebook* (pp. 810–818). Chicago: Rand McNally.

Janis, I. L. (1972). *Victims of groupthink: A psychological study of foreign-policy decisions and fiascoes*. Boston: Houghton Mifflin.

Janis, I. L. (1982). Decision-making under stress. In L. Goldberger & S. Breznitz (Eds.), *Handbook of stress: Theoretical and clinical aspects* (pp. 69–87). New York: Free Press.

Janis, I. L., & Feshbach, S. (1953). Effects of fear-arousing communications. *Journal of Abnormal and Social Psychology, 48*, 78–92.

Janis, I. L., & Gilmore, J. B. (1965). The influence of incentive conditions on the success of role-playing in modifying attitudes. *Journal of Personality and Social Psychology, 1*, 17–27.

Janis, I. L., Kaye, D., & Kirschner, P. (1965). Facilitating effects of "eating while reading" on responsiveness to persuasive communications. *Journal of Personality and Social Psychology, 1*, 181–186.

Janis, I. L., & King, B. T. (1954). The influence of role playing on opinion change. *Journal of Abnormal and Social Psychology, 49*, 211–218.

Janis, I. L., & Mann, L. (1965). Effectiveness of emotional role-playing in modifying smoking habits and attitudes. *Journal of Experimental Research in Personality, 1*, 84–90.

Janis, I. L., & Mann, L. (1977). *Decision making: A psychological analysis of conflict, choice, and commitment.* New York: Free Press.

Janis, I. L., & Milholland, W. (1954). The influence of threat appeals on selective learning of the content of a persuasive communication. *Journal of Psychology, 37*, 75–80.

Janis, I. L., & Rife, D. (1959). Persuasibility and emotional disorder. In C. I. Hovland & I. L. Janis (Eds.), *Personality and persuasibility* (pp. 121–137). New Haven, CT: Yale University Press.

Janis, I. L., & Terwilliger, R. (1962). An experimental study of psychological resistances to fear-arousing communications. *Journal of Abnormal and Social Psychology, 65*, 403–410.

Janz, N. K., & Becker, M. H. (1984). The health belief model: A decade later. *Health Education Quarterly, 11*, 1–47.

Jaspers, J. M. F. (1978). Determinants of attitudes and attitude change. In H. Tajfel & C. Fraser (Eds.), *Introducing social psychology* (pp. 277–301). Harmondsworth, Middlesex, England: Penguin.

Jepson, C., & Chaiken, S. (1990). Chronic issue-specific fear inhibits systematic processing of persuasive communications. *Journal of Social Behavior and Personality, 5*, 61–84.

Jobe, J. B., & Mingay, D. J. (1991). Cognition and survey measurement: History and overview. *Applied Cognitive Psychology, 5*, 175–192.

Johnson, B. T. (1991). Insights about attitudes: Meta-analytic perspectives. *Personality and Social Psychology Bulletin, 17*, 289–299.

Johnson, B. T., & Eagly, A. H. (1989). The effects of involvement on persuasion: A meta-analysis. *Psychological Bulletin, 106*, 290–314.

Johnson, B. T., & Eagly, A. H. (1990). Involvement and persuasion: Types, traditions, and the evidence. *Psychological Bulletin, 107*, 375–384.

Johnson, H. H. (1966). Some effects of discrepancy level on responses to negative information about one's self. *Sociometry, 29*, 52–66.

Johnson, H. H., & Izzett, R. R. (1969). Relationship between authoritarianism and attitude change as a function of source credibility and type of communication. *Journal of Personality and Social Psychology, 13*, 317–321.

Johnson, H. H., & Scileppi, J. A. (1969). Effects of ego-involvement conditions on attitude change to high and low credibility communicators. *Journal of Personality and Social Psychology, 13*, 31–36.

Johnson, H. H., & Stanicek, F. F. (1969). Relationship between authoritarianism and attitude change as a function of implicit and explicit communications. *Proceedings of the 77th Annual Convention of the American Psychological Association, 4*, 415–416.

Johnson, H. H., Torcivia, J. M., & Poprick, M. A. (1968). Effects of source credibility on the relationship between authoritarianism and attitude change. *Journal of Personality and Social Psychology, 9*, 179–183.

Johnson, H. H., & Watkins, T. A. (1971). The effects of message repetitions on immediate and delayed attitude change. *Psychonomic Science, 22*, 101–103.

Johnson, J. T., & Judd, C. M. (1983). Overlooking the incongruent: Categorization biases in the identification of political statements. *Journal of Personality and Social Psychology, 45*, 978–996.

Johnson, P. (1976). Women and power: Toward a theory of effectiveness. *Journal of Social Issues, 32*(3), 99–110.

Jones, E. E. (1979). The rocky road from acts to dispositions. *American Psychologist, 34*, 107–117.

Jones, E. E. (1985). Major developments in social psychology during the past five decades. In G. Lindzey & E. Aronson (Eds.), *Handbook of social psychology* (3rd ed., Vol. 1, pp. 47–107). New York: Random House.

Jones, E. E., & Aneshansel, J. (1956). The learning and utilization of contravaluant material. *Journal of Abnormal and Social Psychology, 53*, 27–33.

Jones, E. E., & Davis, K. E. (1965). From acts to dispositions: The attribution process in person perception. In L. Berkowitz (Ed.), *Advances in experimental social psychology* (Vol. 2, pp. 219–266). San Diego, CA: Academic Press.

Jones, E. E., & Gerard, H. B. (1967). *Foundations of social psychology.* New York: Wiley.

Jones, E. E., & Harris, V. A. (1967). The attribution of attitudes. *Journal of Experimental Social Psychology, 3*, 1–24.

Jones, E. E., & Kohler, R. (1958). The effects of plausibility on the learning of controversial statements. *Journal of Abnormal and Social Psychology, 57*, 315–320.

Jones, E. E., & McGillis, D. (1976). Correspondent inferences and the attribution cube: A comparative reappraisal. In

J. H. Harvey, W. J. Ickes, & R. F. Kidd (Eds.), *New directions in attribution research* (Vol. 1, pp. 389-420). Hillsdale, NJ: Erlbaum.

Jones, E. E., & Nisbett, R. E. (1972). The actor and the observer: Divergent perceptions of the causes of behavior. In E. E. Jones, D. E. Kanouse, H. H. Kelley, R. E. Nisbett, S. Valins, & B. Weiner (Eds.), *Attribution: Perceiving the causes of behavior* (pp. 79-94). Morristown, NJ: General Learning Press.

Jones, E. E., & Pittman, T. S. (1982). Toward a general theory of strategic self-presentation. In J. Suls (Ed.), *Psychological perspectives on the self* (Vol. 1, pp. 231-262). Hillsdale, NJ: Erlbaum.

Jones, E. E., & Sigall, H. (1971). The bogus pipeline: A new paradigm for measuring affect and attitude. *Psychological Bulletin, 76,* 349-364.

Jones, E. E., Worchel, S., Goethals, G. R., & Grumet, J. F. (1971). Prior expectancy and behavioral extremity as determinants of attitude attribution. *Journal of Experimental Social Psychology, 7,* 59-80.

Jones, R. A., & Brehm, J. W. (1967). Attitudinal effects of communicator attractiveness when one chooses to listen. *Journal of Personality and Social Psychology, 6,* 64-70.

Jones, R. A., Linder, D. E., Kiesler, C. A., Zanna, M., & Brehm, J. W. (1968). Internal states or external stimuli: Observers' attitude judgments and the dissonance-theory—self-persuasion controversy. *Journal of Experimental Social Psychology, 4,* 247-269.

Jordan, N. (1953). Behavioral forces that are a function of attitudes and of cognitive organization. *Human Relations, 6,* 273-287.

Jöreskog, K. G. (1969). A general approach to confirmatory maximum likelihood factor analysis. *Psychometrika, 34,* 183-202.

Jöreskog, K. G., & Sörbom, D. (1978). *LISREL IV: Analysis of linear structural relationships by the method of maximum likelihood.* Chicago: National Education Resources.

Judd, C. M., & Downing, J. W. (1990). Political expertise and the development of attitude consistency. *Social Cognition, 8,* 104-124.

Judd, C. M., Drake, R. A., Downing, J. W., & Krosnick, J. A. (1991). Some dynamic properties of attitude structures: Context-induced response facilitation and polarization. *Journal of Personality and Social Psychology, 60,* 193-202.

Judd, C. M., & Harackiewicz, J. M. (1980). Contrast effects in attitude judgment: An examination of the accentuation hypothesis. *Journal of Personality and Social Psychology, 38,* 390-398.

Judd, C. M., Kenny, D. A., & Krosnick, J. A. (1983). Judging the positions of political candidates: Models of assimilation and contrast. *Journal of Personality and Social Psychology, 44,* 952-963.

Judd, C. M., & Krosnick, J. A. (1982). Attitude centrality, organization, and measurement. *Journal of Personality and Social Psychology, 42,* 436-447.

Judd, C. M., & Krosnick, J. A. (1989). The structural bases of consistency among political attitudes: Effects of political expertise and attitude importance. In A. R. Pratkanis, S. J. Breckler, & A. G. Greenwald (Eds.), *Attitude structure and function* (pp. 99-128). Hillsdale, NJ: Erlbaum.

Judd, C. M., Krosnick, J. A., & Milburn, M. A. (1981). Political involvement and attitude structure in the general public. *American Sociological Review, 46,* 660-669.

Judd, C. M., & Kulik, J. A. (1980). Schematic effects of social attitudes on information processing and recall. *Journal of Personality and Social Psychology, 38,* 569-578.

Judd, C. M., & Lusk, C. M. (1984). Knowledge structures and evaluative judgments: Effects of structural variables on judgmental extremity. *Journal of Personality and Social Psychology, 46,* 1193-1207.

Judd, C. M., & McClelland, G. H. (1989). *Data analysis: A model comparison approach.* San Diego, CA: Harcourt Brace Jovanovich.

Judd, C. M., & Milburn, M. A. (1980). The structure of attitude systems in the general public: Comparisons of a structural equation model. *American Sociological Review, 45,* 627-643.

Jussim, L. (1986). Self-fulfilling prophecies: A theoretical and integrative review. *Psychological Review, 93,* 429-445.

Kahle, L. R., & Berman, J. J. (1979). Attitudes cause behavior: A cross-lagged panel analysis. *Journal of Personality and Social Psychology, 37,* 315-321.

Kahneman, D. (1973). *Attention and effort.* Englewood Cliffs, NJ: Prentice-Hall.

Kallgren, C. A., & Wood, W. (1986). Access to attitude-relevant information in memory as a determinant of attitude-behavior consistency. *Journal of Experimental Social Psychology, 22,* 328-338.

Kalton, G., Collins, M., & Brook, L. (1978). Experiments in wording opinion questions. *Journal of the Royal Statistical Society Series C, 27,* 149-161.

Kalton, G., Roberts, J., & Holt, D. (1980). The effects of offering a middle response option with opinion questions. *Statistician, 29,* 11-24.

Kanouse, D. E., & Hanson, L. R., Jr. (1972). Negativity in evaluations. In E. E. Jones, D. E. Kanouse, H. H. Kelley, R. E. Nisbett, S. Valins, & B. Weiner (Eds.), *Attribution: Perceiving the causes of behavior* (pp. 47-62). Morristown, NJ: General Learning Press.

Kantola, S. J., Syme, G. J., & Campbell, N. A. (1984). Cognitive dissonance and energy conservation. *Journal of Applied Psychology, 69,* 416-421.

Kaplan, K. J. (1972). On the ambivalence-indifference problem in attitude theory and measurement: A suggested modification of the semantic differential technique. *Psychological Bulletin, 77,* 361-372.

Kaplan, K. J., & Fishbein, M. (1969). The source of beliefs, their saliency, and prediction of attitude. *Journal of Social Psychology*, *78*, 63–74.

Kaplan, M. F. (1971a). Dispositional effects and weight of information in impression formation. *Journal of Personality and Social Psychology*, *18*, 279–284.

Kaplan, M. F. (1971b). The effect of judgmental dispositions on forming impressions of personality. *Canadian Journal of Behavioural Science*, *3*, 259–267.

Kaplan, M. F. (1973). Stimulus inconsistency and response dispositions in forming judgments of other persons. *Journal of Personality and Social Psychology*, *25*, 58–64.

Kaplan, M. F. (1981). State dispositions in social judgment. *Bulletin of the Psychonomic Society*, *18*, 27–29.

Kaplan, M. F. (1987). The influencing process in group decision making. In C. Hendrick (Ed.), *Review of personality and social psychology* (Vol. 8, pp. 189–212). Newbury Park, CA: Sage.

Kaplan, M. F. (1989). Task, situational, and personal determinants of influence processes in group decision making. In E. J. Lawler & B. Markovsky (Eds.), *Advances in group processes* (Vol. 6, pp. 87–105). Greenwich, CT: JAI Press.

Kaplan, M. F. (1991). The joint effects of cognition and affect on social judgment. In J. P. Forgas (Ed.), *Emotion and social judgments* (pp. 73–82). Oxford, England: Pergamon Press.

Kaplan, M. F., & Anderson, N. H. (1973a). Comment on "When research paradigms converge: Confrontation or integration?" *Journal of Personality and Social Psychology*, *28*, 321–322.

Kaplan, M. F., & Anderson, N. H. (1973b). Information integration theory and reinforcement theory as approaches to interpersonal attraction. *Journal of Personality and Social Psychology*, *28*, 301–312.

Kaplan, M. F., & Miller, C. E. (1977). Judgments and group discussion: Effect of presentation and memory factors on polarization. *Sociometry*, *40*, 337–343.

Kaplowitz, S. A., Fink, E. L., Armstrong, G. B., & Bauer, C. L. (1986). Message discrepancy and the persistence of attitude change: Implications of an information integration model. *Journal of Experimental Social Psychology*, *22*, 507–530.

Kardes, F. R., Sanbonmatsu, D. M., Voss, R. T., & Fazio, R. H. (1986). Self-monitoring and attitude accessibility. *Personality and Social Psychology Bulletin*, *12*, 468–474.

Katz, D. (1960). The functional approach to the study of attitudes. *Public Opinion Quarterly*, *24*, 163–204.

Katz, D., McClintock, C., & Sarnoff, I. (1957). The measurement of ego defense as related to attitude change. *Journal of Personality*, *25*, 465–474.

Katz, D., Sarnoff, D., & McClintock, C. (1956). Ego-defense and attitude change. *Human Relations*, *9*, 27–45.

Katz, D., & Stotland, E. (1959). A preliminary statement to a theory of attitude structure and change. In S. Koch (Ed.), *Psychology: A study of a science* (Vol. 3, pp. 423–475). New York: McGraw-Hill.

Katz, I. (1981). *Stigma: A social psychological analysis.* Hillsdale, NJ: Erlbaum.

Katz, I., & Glass, D. C. (1979). An ambivalence-amplification theory of behavior toward the stigmatized. In W. Austin & S. Worchel (Eds.), *The social psychology of intergroup relations* (pp. 55–84). Monterey, CA: Brooks/Cole.

Katz, I., Glass, D. C., & Cohen, S. (1973). Ambivalence, guilt, and the scapegoating of minority group victims. *Journal of Experimental Social Psychology*, *9*, 423–436.

Katz, I., & Hass, R. G. (1988). Racial ambivalence and American value conflict: Correlational and priming studies of dual cognitive structures. *Journal of Personality and Social Psychology*, *55*, 893–905.

Katz, I., Wackenhut, J., & Hass, R. G. (1986). Racial ambivalence, value duality, and behavior. In J. F. Dovidio & S. L. Gaertner (Eds.), *Prejudice, discrimination, and racism* (pp. 35–59). San Diego, CA: Academic Press.

Keinan, G. (1987). Decision making under stress: Scanning of alternatives under controllable and uncontrollable threats. *Journal of Personality and Social Psychology*, *52*, 639–644.

Kelley, H. H. (1950). The warm-cold variable in first impressions of persons. *Journal of Personality*, *18*, 431–439.

Kelley, H. H. (1952). Two functions of reference groups. In G. E. Swanson, T. M. Newcomb, & E. L. Hartley (Eds.), *Readings in social psychology* (2nd ed., pp. 410–414). New York: Holt.

Kelley, H. H. (1967). Attribution theory in social psychology. In D. Levine (Ed.), *Nebraska Symposium on Motivation* (Vol. 15, pp. 192–238). Lincoln: University of Nebraska Press.

Kelley, H. H. (1972a). Attribution in social interaction. In E. E. Jones, D. E. Kanouse, H. H. Kelley, R. E. Nisbett, S. Valins, & B. Weiner (Eds.), *Attribution: Perceiving the causes of behavior* (pp. 1–26). Morristown, NJ: General Learning Press.

Kelley, H. H. (1972b). Causal schemata and the attribution process. In E. E. Jones, D. E. Kanouse, H. H. Kelley, R. E. Nisbett, S. Valins, & B. Weiner (Eds.), *Attribution: Perceiving the causes of behavior* (pp. 151–174). Morristown, NJ: General Learning Press.

Kelley, H. H., Hovland, C. I., Schwartz, M., & Abelson, R. P. (1955). The influence of judges' attitudes in three methods of attitude scaling. *Journal of Social Psychology*, *42*, 147–158.

Kelley, H. H., & Lamb, T. W. (1957). Certainty of judgment and resistance to social influence. *Journal of Abnormal and Social Psychology*, *55*, 137–139.

Kelley, H.H., & Michela, J.L. (1980). Attribution theory and research. *Annual Review of Psychology*, *31*, 457-501.

Kelley, H.H., & Volkart, E.H. (1952). The resistance to change of group-anchored attitudes. *American Sociological Review*, *17*, 453-465.

Kelley, T.L. (1939). The selection of upper and lower groups for the validation of test items. *Journal of Educational Psychology*, *30*, 17-24.

Kelman, H.C. (1953). Attitude change as a function of response restriction. *Human Relations*, *6*, 185-214.

Kelman, H.C. (1958). Compliance, identification, and internalization: Three processes of attitude change. *Journal of Conflict Resolution*, *2*, 51-60.

Kelman, H.C. (1961). Processes of opinion change. *Public Opinion Quarterly*, *25*, 57-78.

Kelman, H.C. (1962). The induction of action and attitude change. In G. Nielson (Ed.), *Proceeding of the XIVth International Congress of Applied Psychology: Personality Research*, *2*, 81-110.

Kelman, H.C. (1963). The role of the group in the induction of therapeutic change. *International Journal of Group Psychotherapy*, *13*, 399-432.

Kelman, H.C. (1969). Patterns of personal involvement in the national system: A social-psychological analysis of political legitimacy. In J.N. Rosenau (Ed.), *International politics and foreign policy: A reader in research and theory* (2nd ed., pp. 276-288). New York: Free Press.

Kelman, H.C. (1974a). Attitudes are alive and well and gainfully employed in the sphere of action. *American Psychologist*, *29*, 310-324.

Kelman, H.C. (1974b). Further thoughts on the processes of compliance, identification, and internalization. In J.T. Tedeschi (Ed.), *Perspectives on social power* (pp. 125-171). Chicago: Aldine.

Kelman, H.C. (1980). The role of action in attitude change. In H.E. Howe, Jr. & M.M. Page (Eds.), *Nebraska Symposium on Motivation, 1979* (Vol. 27, pp. 117-194). Lincoln: University of Nebraska Press.

Kelman, H.C., & Baron, R.M. (1968a). Determinants of modes of resolving inconsistency dilemmas: A functional analysis. In R.P. Abelson, E. Aronson, W.J. McGuire, T.M. Newcomb, M.J. Rosenberg, & P.H. Tannenbaum (Eds.), *Theories of cognitive consistency: A sourcebook* (pp. 670-683). Chicago: Rand McNally.

Kelman, H.C., & Baron, R.M. (1968b). Inconsistency as a psychological signal. In R.P. Abelson, E. Aronson, W.J. McGuire, T.M. Newcomb, M.J. Rosenberg, & P.H. Tannenbaum (Eds.), *Theories of cognitive consistency: A sourcebook* (pp. 331-336). Chicago: Rand McNally.

Kelman, H.C., & Baron, R.M. (1974). Moral and hedonic dissonance: A functional analysis of the relationship between discrepant action and attitude change. In S. Himmelfarb & A.H. Eagly (Eds.), *Readings in attitude change* (pp. 558-575). New York: Wiley.

Kelman, H.C., & Eagly, A.H. (1965). Attitude toward the communicator, perception of communication content, and attitude change. *Journal of Personality and Social Psychology*, *1*, 63-78.

Kelman, H.C., & Hamilton, V.L. (1989). *Crimes of obedience: Toward a social psychology of authority and responsibility*. New Haven: Yale University Press.

Kelman, H.C., & Hovland, C.I. (1953). "Reinstatement" of the communicator in delayed measurement of opinion change. *Journal of Abnormal and Social Psychology*, *48*, 327-335.

Kelman, H.C., & Lawrence, L.H. [Hamilton, V.L.]. (1972). Assignment of responsibility in the case of Lt. Calley: Preliminary report on a national survey. *Journal of Social Issues*, *28*(1), 177-212.

Kendzierski, D. (1990). Decision making versus decision implementation: An action control approach to exercise adoption and adherence. *Journal of Applied Social Psychology*, *20*, 27-45.

Kenny, D.A. (1979). *Correlation and causality*. New York: Wiley.

Kenny, D.A. (1985). Quantitative methods for social psychology. In G. Lindzey & E. Aronson (Eds.), *Handbook of social psychology* (3rd ed., Vol. 1, pp. 487-508). New York: Random House.

Kerlinger, F.N. (1984). *Liberalism and conservatism: The nature and structure of social attitudes*. Hillsdale, NJ: Erlbaum.

Kerlinger, F.N., & Rokeach, M. (1966). The factorial nature of the F and D Scales. *Journal of Personality and Social Psychology*, *4*, 391-399.

Kerpelman, J.P., & Himmelfarb, S. (1971). Partial reinforcement effects in attitude acquisition and counterconditioning. *Journal of Personality and Social Psychology*, *19*, 301-305.

Kerrick, J. (1958). The effect of relevant and non-relevant sources on attitude change. *Journal of Social Psychology*, *47*, 15-20.

Kidd, R.F., & Berkowitz, L. (1976). Effect of dissonance arousal on helpfulness. *Journal of Personality and Social Psychology*, *33*, 613-622.

Kidder, L.H., & Campbell, D.T. (1970). The indirect testing of social attitudes. In G.F. Summers (Ed.), *Attitude measurement* (pp. 333-385). Chicago: Rand McNally.

Kiesler, C.A. (1971). *The psychology of commitment: Experiments linking behavior to belief*. San Diego, CA: Academic Press.

Kiesler, C.A., Collins, B.E., & Miller, N. (1969). *Attitude change: A critical analysis of theoretical approaches*. New York: Wiley.

Kiesler, C. A., & Kiesler, S. B. (1964). Role of forewarning in persuasive communications. *Journal of Abnormal and Social Psychology, 68,* 547-549.

Kiesler, C. A., Nisbett, R. E., & Zanna, M. P. (1969). On inferring one's beliefs from one's behavior. *Journal of Personality and Social Psychology, 11,* 321-327.

Kiesler, C. A., & Pallak, M. S. (1976). Arousal properties of dissonance manipulations. *Psychological Bulletin, 83,* 1014-1025.

Kiesler, C. A., Pallak, M. S., & Kanouse, D. E. (1968). Interactive effects of commitment and dissonance. *Journal of Personality and Social Psychology, 8,* 331-338.

Kiesler, C. A., & Sakamura, J. (1966). A test of a model for commitment. *Journal of Personality and Social Psychology, 3,* 349-353.

Kihlstrom, J. F. (1987). The cognitive unconscious. *Science, 237,* 1445-1452.

Kilhstrom, J. F., Cantor, N., Albright, J. S., Chew, B. R., Klein, S. B., & Niedenthal, P. M. (1988). Information processing and the study of the self. In L. Berkowitz (Ed.), *Advances in experimental social psychology* (Vol. 21, pp. 145-178). San Diego, CA: Academic Press.

Killen, J. D. (1985). Prevention of adolescent tobacco smoking: The social pressure resistance training approach. *Journal of Child Psychology and Psychiatry and Allied Disciplines, 26,* 7-15.

Kimble, G. A. (1961). *Hilgard & Marquis' conditioning and learning* (2nd ed.). New York: Appleton-Century-Crofts.

Kinder, D. R. (1978). Political person perception: The asymmetrical influence of sentiment and choice on perceptions of presidential candidates. *Journal of Personality and Social Psychology, 36,* 859-871.

Kinder, D. R. (1986). The continuing American dilemma: White resistance to racial change 40 years after Myrdal. *Journal of Social Issues, 42*(2), 151-171.

Kinder, D. R., & Sears, D. O. (1981). Prejudice and politics: Symbolic racism versus racial threats to the good life. *Journal of Personality and Social Psychology, 40,* 414-431.

Kinder, D. R., & Sears, D. O. (1985). Public opinion and political action. In G. Lindzey & E. Aronson (Eds.), *Handbook of social psychology* (3rd ed., Vol. 2, pp. 659-741). New York: Random House.

King, B. T., & Janis, I. L. (1956). Comparison of the effectiveness of improvised versus non-improvised role-playing in producing opinion changes. *Human Relations, 9,* 177-186.

King, G. W. (1975). An analysis of attitudinal and normative variables as predictors of intentions and behavior. *Speech Monographs, 42,* 237-244.

Kipnis, D. (1976). *The powerholders.* Chicago: University of Chicago Press.

Kipnis, D., Schmidt, S. M., & Wilkinson, I. (1980). Intraorganizational influence tactics: Explorations in getting one's way. *Journal of Applied Psychology, 65,* 440-452.

Kirscht, J. P., & Dillehay, R. C. (1967). *Dimensions of authoritarianism: A review of research and theory.* Lexington: University of Kentucky Press.

Kisielius, J., & Sternthal, B. (1984). Detecting and explaining vividness effects in attitudinal judgments. *Journal of Marketing Research, 21,* 54-64.

Kitayama, S. (1983). Majority-minority relations in a changing context. *Japanese Psychological Research, 25,* 164-169.

Kitayama, S. (1990). Interaction between affect and cognition in word perception. *Journal of Personality and Social Psychology, 58,* 209-217.

Klapper, J. T. (1960). *The effects of mass communications.* New York: Free Press.

Kleck, R. E., & Wheaton, J. (1967). Dogmatism and responses to opinion-consistent and opinion-inconsistent information. *Journal of Personality and Social Psychology, 5,* 249-252.

Kleinhesselink, R. R., & Edwards, R. E. (1975). Seeking and avoiding belief-discrepant information as a function of its perceived refutability. *Journal of Personality and Social Psychology, 31,* 787-790.

Klopfer, F. J., & Madden, T. M. (1980). The middlemost choice on attitude items: Ambivalence, neutrality, or uncertainty? *Personality and Social Psychology Bulletin, 6,* 97-101.

Kluegel, J. R., & Smith, E. R. (1986). *Beliefs about inequality: Americans' views of what is and what ought to be.* New York: Aldine de Gruyter.

Knower, F. H. (1935). Experimental studies of changes in attitudes: I. A study of the effect of oral argument on changes of attitude. *Journal of Social Psychology, 6,* 315-347.

Knower, F. H. (1936). Experimental studies of change in attitude—II: A study of the effect of printed argument on changes in attitude. *Journal of Abnormal and Social Psychology, 30,* 522-532.

Knox, R. E., & Inkster, J. A. (1968). Postdecision dissonance at post time. *Journal of Personality and Social Psychology, 8,* 319-323.

Koeske, G. F., & Crano, W. D. (1968). The effect of congruous and incongruous source-statement combinations upon the judged credibility of a communication. *Journal of Experimental Social Psychology, 4,* 384-399.

Koffka, K. (1935). *Principles of gestalt psychology.* London: Routledge & Kegan Paul.

Kogan, N., & Wallach, M. A. (1964). *Risk taking: A study in cognition and personality.* New York: Holt, Rinehart & Winston.

Köhler, W. (1929). *Gestalt psychology*. New York: Liveright.

Konečni, V. J., & Slamecka, N. J. (1972). Awareness of verbal nonoperant conditioning: An approach through dichotic listening. *Journal of Experimental Psychology*, *94*, 248-254.

Kothandapani, V. (1971). Validation of feeling, belief, and intention to act as three components of attitude and their contribution to prediction of contraceptive behavior. *Journal of Personality and Social Psychology*, *19*, 321-333.

Kraemer, H. C. (1980). Estimation and testing of bivariate association using data generated by the randomized response technique. *Psychological Bulletin*, *87*, 304-308.

Krantz, D. H., Luce, R. D., Suppes, P., & Tversky, A. (1971). *Foundations of measurement* (Vol. 1). San Diego, CA: Academic Press.

Krasner, L. (1958). Studies of the conditioning of verbal behavior. *Psychological Bulletin*, *55*, 148-170.

Krasner, L. (1962). The therapist as a social reinforcement machine. In H. H. Strupp & L. Luborsky (Eds.), *Research in psychotherapy* (Vol. 2, pp. 61-94). Washington, DC: American Psychological Association.

Krasner, L., Knowles, J. B., & Ullman, L. P. (1965). Effect of verbal conditioning of attitudes on subsequent motor performance. *Journal of Personality and Social Psychology*, *1*, 407-412.

Krech, D., & Crutchfield, R. S. (1948). *Theory and problems of social psychology*. New York: McGraw-Hill.

Krech, D., Crutchfield, R. S., & Ballachey, E. L. (1962). *Individual in society: A textbook of social psychology*. New York: McGraw-Hill.

Kristiansen, C. M., & Zanna, M. P. (1988). Justifying attitudes by appealing to values: A functional perspective. *British Journal of Social Psychology*, *27*, 247-256.

Krosnick, J. A. (1988a). Attitude importance and attitude change. *Journal of Experimental Social Psychology*, *24*, 240-255.

Krosnick, J. A. (1988b, July). *Psychological perspectives on political candidate perception: A review of research on the projection hypothesis*. Paper presented at the meeting of the Midwest Political Science Association, Chicago.

Krosnick, J. A. (1989). Attitude importance and attitude accessibility. *Personality and Social Psychology Bulletin*, *15*, 297-308.

Krosnick, J. A. (1990a). Americans' perceptions of presidential candidates: A test of the projection hypothesis. *Journal of Social Issues*, *46*(2), 159-182.

Krosnick, J. A. (1990b). Government policy and citizen passion: A study of issue publics in contemporary America. *Political Behavior*, *12*, 59-92.

Krosnick, J. A., & Alwin, D. F. (1989). Aging and susceptibility to attitude change. *Journal of Personality and Social Psychology*, *57*, 416-425.

Krosnick, J. A., Betz, A. L., Jussim, L. J., & Lynn, A. R. (1992). Subliminal conditioning of attitudes. *Personality and Social Psychology Bulletin*, *18*, 152-162.

Krosnick, J. A., Boninger, D. S., Chuang, Y. C., & Carnot, C. G. (1991). *Attitude strength: One construct or many related constructs?* Unpublished manuscript, Ohio State University, Columbus, OH.

Krosnick, J. A., & Schuman, H. (1988). Attitude intensity, importance, and certainty and susceptibility to response effects. *Journal of Personality and Social Psychology*, *54*, 940-952.

Krotki, K. J., & Fox, B. (1974). The randomized response technique, the interview, and the self-administered questionnaire: An empirical comparison of fertility reports. *Proceedings of the Social Statistics Section, American Statistical Association*, 367-371.

Kruglanski, A. W. (1990). Motivations for judging and knowing: Implications for causal attribution. In E. T. Higgins & R. M. Sorrentino (Eds.), *Handbook of motivation and cognition: Foundations of social behavior* (Vol. 2, pp. 333-368). New York: Guilford Press.

Kruskal, J. B., & Wish, M. (1978). *Multidimensional scaling*. Beverly Hills, CA: Sage.

Kuhl, J. (1986). Motivation and information processing: A new look at decision making, dynamic change, and action control. In R. M. Sorrentino & E. T. Higgins (Eds.), *Handbook of motivation and cognition: Foundations of social behavior* (pp. 404-434). New York: Guilford Press.

Kunst-Wilson, W. R., & Zajonc, R. B. (1980). Affective discrimination of stimuli that cannot be recognized. *Science*, *207*, 557-558.

Kutner, B., Wilkins, C., & Yarrow, P. R. (1952). Verbal attitudes and overt behavior involving racial prejudice. *Journal of Abnormal and Social Psychology*, *47*, 649-652.

Kuykendall, D., & Keating, J. P. (1990). Altering thoughts and judgements through repeated association. *British Journal of Social Psychology*, *29*, 79-86.

Lamm, H., & Myers, D. G. (1978). Group-induced polarization of attitudes and behavior. In L. Berkowitz (Ed.), *Advances in experimental social psychology* (Vol. 11, pp. 145-195). San Diego, CA: Academic Press.

Lammers, H. B., & Becker, L. A. (1980). Distraction: Effects on the perceived extremity of a communication and on cognitive responses. *Personality and Social Psychology Bulletin*, *6*, 261-266.

Lana, R. E. (1961). Familiarity and the order of presentation of persuasive communications. *Journal of Abnormal and Social Psychology*, *62*, 573-577.

Lana, R. E. (1963). Interest, media, and order effects in persuasive communications. *Journal of Psychology*, *56*, 9-13.

Landman, J., & Manis, M. (1983). Social cognition: Some historical and theoretical perspectives. In L. Berkowitz

(Ed.), *Advances in experimental social psychology* (Vol. 16, pp. 49-123). San Diego, CA: Academic Press.

Lane, R. E. (1962). *Political ideology: Why the American common man believes what he does*. New York: Free Press.

Lane, R. E. (1973). Patterns of political belief. In J. Knutson (Ed.), *Handbook of political psychology* (pp. 83-116). San Francisco: Jossey-Bass.

Lange, R., & Fishbein, M. (1983). Effects of category differences on belief change and agreement with the source of a persuasive communication. *Journal of Personality and Social Psychology*, *44*, 933-941.

Langer, E. J. (1975). The illusion of control. *Journal of Personality and Social Psychology*, *32*, 311-328.

Langer, E. J. (1978). Rethinking the role of thought in social interaction. In J. H. Harvey, W. Ickes, & R. F. Kidd (Eds.), *New directions in attribution research* (Vol. 2, pp. 35-58). Hillsdale, NJ: Erlbaum.

Langer, E. J. (1989a). *Mindfulness*. Reading, MA: Addison-Wesley.

Langer, E. J. (1989b). Minding matters: The consequences of mindlessness-mindfulness. In L. Berkowitz (Ed.), *Advances in experimental social psychology* (Vol. 22, pp. 137-173). San Diego, CA: Academic Press.

Langer, E. J., & Roth, J. (1975). Heads I win, tails it's chance: The illusion of control as a function of the sequence of outcomes in a purely chance task. *Journal of Personality and Social Psychology*, *32*, 951-955.

LaPiere, R. T. (1934). Attitudes vs. actions. *Social Forces*, *13*, 230-237.

Laroche, M. A. (1977). A model of attitude change in groups following a persuasive communication: An attempt at formalizing research findings. *Behavioral Science*, *22*, 246-257.

Larsen, K. S. (1971). Affectivity, cognitive style and social judgment. *Journal of Personality and Social Psychology*, *19*, 119-123.

Larsen, K. S. (1990). The Asch conformity experiment: Replication and transhistorical comparisons. *Journal of Social Behavior and Personality*, *5*, 163-168.

Lasswell, H. D. (1948). The structure and function of communication in society. In L. Bryson (Ed.), *The communication of ideas: Religion and civilization series* (pp. 37-51). New York: Harper & Row.

Latané, B. (1981). The psychology of social impact. *American Psychologist*, *36*, 343-356.

Latané, B., & Wolf, S. (1981). The social impact of majorities and minorities. *Psychological Review*, *88*, 438-453.

Lawler, E. E. III, Kuleck, W. J., Jr., Rhode, J. G., & Sorensen, J. E. (1975). Job choice and post decision dissonance. *Organizational Behavior and Human Performance*, *13*, 133-145.

Lawrence, D. H., & Festinger, L. (1962). *Deterrents and reinforcement: The psychology of insufficient reward*. Stanford, CA: Stanford University Press.

Lay, C. H., Burron, B. F., & Jackson, D. N. (1973). Base rates and informational value in impression formation. *Journal of Personality and Social Psychology*, *28*, 390-395.

Lazarsfeld, P. F. (1950). The logic and mathematical foundation of latent structure analysis. In S. A. Stouffer, L. Guttman, E. A. Suchman, P. F. Lazarsfeld, S. A. Star, & J. A. Clausen, *Measurement and prediction* (pp. 362-412). Princeton, NJ: Princeton University Press.

Lazarsfeld, P. F. (1954). A conceptual introduction to latent structure analysis. In P. F. Lazarsfeld (Ed.), *Mathematical thinking in the social sciences* (pp. 349-387). Glencoe, IL: Free Press.

Lazarsfeld, P. F., & Henry, N. W. (1968). *Latent structure analysis*. New York: Houghton Mifflin.

Lazarus, R. S. (1966). *Psychological stress and the coping process*. New York: McGraw-Hill.

Lazarus, R. S. (1982). Thoughts on the relations between emotion and cognition. *American Psychologist*, *37*, 1019-1024.

Lazarus, R. S. (1984). On the primacy of cognition. *American Psychologist*, *39*, 124-129.

Leary, M. R., & Kowalski, R. M. (1990). Impression management: A literature review and two-component model. *Psychological Bulletin*, *107*, 34-47.

Lehmann, S. (1970). Personality and compliance: A study of anxiety and self-esteem in opinion and behavior change. *Journal of Personality and Social Psychology*, *15*, 76-86.

Leippe, M. R., & Elkin, R. A. (1987). When motives clash: Issue involvement and response involvement as determinants of persuasion. *Journal of Personality and Social Psychology*, *52*, 269-278.

Leippe, M. R., Greenwald, A. G., & Baumgardner, M. H. (1982). Delayed persuasion as a consequence of associative interference: A context confusion effect. *Personality and Social Psychology Bulletin*, *8*, 644-650.

Lepper, M. R. (1973). Dissonance, self-perception, and honesty in children. *Journal of Personality and Social Psychology*, *25*, 65-74.

Lepper, M. R., & Greene, D. (1975). Turning play into work: Effects of adult surveillance and extrinsic rewards on children's intrinsic motivation. *Journal of Personality and Social Psychology*, *31*, 479-486.

Lepper, M. R., & Greene, D. (Eds.). (1978). *The hidden costs of reward: New perspectives on the psychology of human motivation*. Hillsdale, NJ: Erlbaum.

Lepper, M. R., Greene, D., & Nisbett, R. E. (1973). Undermining children's intrinsic interest with extrinsic reward: A test of the "overjustification" hypothesis. *Journal of Personality and Social Psychology*, *28*, 129-137.

Levanthal, H. (1970). Findings and theory in the study of fear communications. In L. Berkowitz (Ed.), *Advances in experimental social psychology* (Vol. 5, pp. 119–186). San Diego, CA: Academic Press.

Leventhal, H., & Singer, R.P. (1966). Affect arousal and positioning of recommendations in persuasive communications. *Journal of Personality and Social Psychology, 4,* 137–146.

Leventhal, H., Singer, R.P., & Jones, S. (1965). Effects of fear and specificity of recommendations upon attitudes and behavior. *Journal of Personality and Social Psychology, 2,* 20–29.

Leventhal, H., Watts, J.C., & Pagano, F. (1967). Effects of fear and instructions on how to cope with danger. *Journal of Personality and Social Psychology, 6,* 313–321.

Levin, S.M. (1961). The effects of awareness on verbal conditioning. *Journal of Experimental Psychology, 61,* 67–75.

Levine, J.M. (1980). Reaction to opinion deviance in small groups. In P.B. Paulus (Ed.), *Psychology of group influence* (pp. 375–429). Hillsdale, NJ: Erlbaum.

Levine, J.M., & Moreland, R.L. (1985). Innovation and socialization in small groups. In S. Moscovici, G. Mugny, & E. Van Avermaet (Eds.), *Perspectives on minority influence* (pp. 143–169). Cambridge, England: Cambridge University Press.

Levine, J.M., & Russo, E.M. (1987). Majority and minority influence. In C. Hendrick (Ed.), *Review of personality and social psychology* (Vol. 8, pp. 13–54). Newbury Park, CA: Sage.

Levine, J.M., & Murphy, G. (1943). The learning and forgetting of controversial material. *Journal of Abnormal and Social Psychology, 38,* 507–517.

Levine, R., Chein, I., & Murphy, G. (1942). The relation of the intensity of a need to the amount of perceptual distortion: A preliminary report. *Journal of Psychology, 13,* 283–293.

Levinger, G., & Schneider, D.J. (1969). Test of the "risk is a value" hypothesis. *Journal of Personality and Social Psychology, 11,* 165–169.

Levy, L.H. (1967). Awareness, learning, and the beneficent subject as expert witness. *Journal of Personality and Social Psychology, 6,* 365–370.

Lévy-Leboyer, C. (1988). Success and failure in applying psychology. *American Psychologist, 43,* 779–785.

Lewicki, P. (1986). *Nonconscious social information processing.* San Diego, CA: Academic Press.

Lewin, K. (1935). *A dynamic theory of personality.* New York: McGraw-Hill.

Lewin, K. (1936). *Principles of topological psychology.* New York: McGraw-Hill.

Lewin, K. (1938). *The conceptual representation and the measurement of psychological forces.* Durham, NC: Duke University Press.

Lewin, K. (1947). Frontiers in group dynamics. *Human Relations, 1,* 5–41.

Lewin, K. (1951). *Field theory in social science: Selected theoretical papers.* New York: Harper.

Lewin, K., Dembo, T., Festinger, L., & Sears, P.S. (1944). Level of aspiration. In J.M. Hunt (Ed.), *Personality and the behavior disorders* (pp. 333–378). New York: Ronald Press.

Liberman, A., & Chaiken, S. (1989, April). *Involvement and biased processing of persuasive messages.* Paper presented at the meeting of the Eastern Psychological Association, Boston, MA.

Liberman, A., & Chaiken, S. (1991). Value conflict and thought-induced attitude change. *Journal of Experimental Social Psychology, 27,* 203–216.

Liberman, A., & Chaiken, S. (in press). Defensive processing of personally relevant health messages. *Personality and Social Psychology Bulletin.*

Liberman, A., Chaiken, S., & Hazlewood, J.D. (1991). *The direct effect of personal relevance on attitudes.* Unpublished manuscript, New York University, New York, NY.

Liberman, A., de La Hoz, V., & Chaiken, S. (1988, April). *Prior attitudes as heuristic information.* Paper presented at the meeting of the Western Psychological Association, Burlingame, CA.

Lichtenstein, M., & Srull, T.K. (1987). Processing objectives as a determinant of the relationship between recall and judgment. *Journal of Experimental Social Psychology, 23,* 93–118.

Lifton, R.J. (1961). *Thought reform and the psychology of totalism: A study of "brainwashing" in China.* New York: Norton.

Likert, R. (1932). A technique for the measurement of attitudes. *Archives of Psychology, 140,* 5–53.

Likert, R., Roslow, S., & Murphy, G. (1934). A simple and reliable method of scoring the Thurstone attitude scales. *Journal of Social Psychology, 5,* 228–238.

Linder, D.E., Cooper, J., & Jones, E.E. (1967). Decision freedom as a determinant of the role of incentive magnitude in attitude change. *Journal of Personality and Social Psychology, 6,* 245–254.

Lingle, J.H., & Ostrom, T.M. (1981). Principles of memory and cognition in attitude formation. In R.E. Petty, T.M. Ostrom, & T.C. Brock (Eds.), *Cognitive responses in persuasion* (pp. 399–420). Hillsdale, NJ: Erlbaum.

Lingoes, J.C. (1963). Multiple scalogram analysis: A set-theoretic model for analyzing dichotomous items. *Educational and Psychological Measurement, 23,* 501–524.

Linn, L.S. (1965). Verbal attitudes and overt behavior: A study of racial discrimination. *Social Forces, 43,* 353–364.

Linville, P. W. (1982). The complexity-extremity effect and age-based stereotyping. *Journal of Personality and Social Psychology*, *42*, 193–211.

Linville, P. W., & Jones, E. E. (1980). Polarized appraisals of out-group members. *Journal of Personality and Social Psychology*, *38*, 689–703.

Linville, P. W., Salovey, P., & Fischer, G. W. (1986). Stereotyping and perceived distributions of social characteristics: An application to ingroup-outgroup perception. In J. F. Dovidio & S. L. Gaertner (Eds.), *Prejudice, discrimination, and racism* (pp. 165–208). San Diego, CA: Academic Press.

Lippitt, R. (1943). The psychodrama in leadership training. *Sociometry*, *6*, 286–292.

Liska, A. E. (1984). A critical examination of the causal structure of the Fishbein/Ajzen attitude-behavior model. *Social Psychology Quarterly*, *47*, 61–74.

Liu, P. T., & Chow, L. P. (1976). A new discrete quantitative randomized response model. *Journal of the American Statistical Association*, *71*, 72–73.

Liu, P. T., Chow, L. P., & Mosley, W. H. (1975). Use of the randomized response technique with a new randomizing device. *Journal of the American Statistical Association*, *70*, 329–332.

Locke, J. (1960). *Two treatises of government*. Cambridge, England: Cambridge University Press. (Original work published 1690)

Lockheed, M. E., & Hall, K. P. (1976). Conceptualizing sex as a status characteristic: Applications to leadership training strategies. *Journal of Social Issues*, *32*(3), 111–124.

Lodge, M. (1981). *Magnitude scaling*. Beverly Hills, CA: Sage.

Lodge, M., Cross, D. V., Tursky, B., & Tanenhaus, J. (1975). The psychophysical scaling and validation of a political support scale. *American Journal of Political Science*, *19*, 611–649.

Lodge, M., & Tursky, B. (1979). Comparisons between category and magnitude scaling of political opinion employing SRC/CPS items. *American Political Science Review*, *73*, 50–66.

Lodge, M., & Tursky, B. (1982). The social-psychophysical scaling of political opinion. In B. Wegener (Ed.), *Social attitudes and psychophysical measurement* (pp. 177–198). Hillsdale, NJ: Erlbaum.

Lofland, J. (1977). *Doomsday cult: A study of conversion, proselytization, and maintenance of faith*. New York: Irvington.

Lohr, J. M., & Staats, A. W. (1973). Attitude conditioning in Sino-Tibetian languages. *Journal of Personality and Social Psychology*, *26*, 196–200.

Lord, C. G. (1989). The "disappearance" of dissonance in an age of relativism. *Personality and Social Psychology Bulletin*, *15*, 513–518.

Lord, C. G., DesForges, D. M., Fein, S., & Lepper, M. R. (1992). *Typicality effects in attitudes toward social policies: A concept mapping approach*. Unpublished manuscript, Texas Christian University, Fort Worth, TX.

Lord, C. G., Lepper, M. R., & Mackie, D. (1984). Attitude prototypes as determinants of attitude-behavior consistency. *Journal of Personality and Social Psychology*, *46*, 1254–1266.

Lord, C. G., Lepper, M. R., & Preston, E. (1984). Considering the opposite: A corrective strategy for social judgment. *Journal of Personality and Social Psychology*, *47*, 1231–1243.

Lord, C. G., Ross, L., & Lepper, M. R. (1979). Biased assimilation and attitude polarization: The effects of prior theories on subsequently considered evidence. *Journal of Personality and Social Psychology*, *37*, 2098–2109.

Lord, F. M. (1953). On the statistical treatment of football numbers. *American Psychologist*, *8*, 750–751.

Lord, F. M., & Novick, M. R. (1968). *Statistical theories of mental test scores*. Reading, MA: Addison-Wesley.

Losch, M. E., & Cacioppo, J. T. (1990). Cognitive dissonance may enhance sympathetic tonus, but attitudes are changed to reduce negative affect rather than arousal. *Journal of Experimental Social Psychology*, *26*, 289–304.

Lott, A. J., & Lott, B. E. (1968). A learning theory approach to interpersonal attitudes. In A. G. Greenwald, T. C. Brock, & T. M. Ostrom (Eds.), *Psychological foundations of attitudes* (pp. 67–88). San Diego, CA: Academic Press.

Lott (Eisman), B. E. (1955). Attitude formation: The development of a color preference response through mediated generalization. *Journal of Abnormal and Social Psychology*, *50*, 321–326.

Lott, B. E., & Lott, A. J. (1960). The formation of positive attitudes toward group members. *Journal of Abnormal and Social Psychology*, *61*, 297–300.

Lott, B. E., & Lott, A. J. (1985). Learning theory in contemporary social psychology. In G. Lindzey & E. Aronson (Eds.), *Handbook of social psychology* (3rd ed., Vol. 1, pp. 109–136). New York: Random House.

Lowe, R. H., & Steiner, I. D. (1968). Some effects of the reversibility and consequences on postdecision information preferences. *Journal of Personality and Social Psychology*, *8*, 172–179.

Löwenstein, O. (1920). Experimentelle Beiträge zur Lehre von den katatonischen Pupillenveränderungen [Experimental contributions to the theory of catatonic pupillary responses]. *Monatsschrift für Psychiatrie und Neurologie*, *47*, 194–215.

Lowin, A. (1967). Approach and avoidance: Alternative modes of selective exposure to information. *Journal of Personality and Social Psychology*, *6*, 1–9.

Lowin, A. (1969). Further evidence for an approach-avoidance interpretation of selective exposure. *Journal of Experimental Social Psychology*, *5*, 265–271.

Luchins, A. S. (1942). Mechanization in problem solving: The effect of Einstellung. *Psychological Monographs, 54*(6, Whole No. 248).

Luchins, A. S. (1945). Social influences on perception of complex drawings. *Journal of Social Psychology, 21,* 257–273.

Luchins, A. S. (1957). Primacy-recency in impression formation. In C. I. Hovland (Ed.), *The order of presentation in persuasion* (pp. 33–61). New Haven, CT: Yale University Press.

Luker, K. (1984). *Abortion and the politics of motherhood.* Berkeley: University of California Press.

Lumsdaine, A. A., & Janis, I. L. (1953). Resistance to "counter-propaganda" produced by one-sided and two-sided "propaganda" presentations. *Public Opinion Quarterly, 17,* 311–318.

Lumsden, C. J., & Wilson, E. O. (1981). *Genes, mind, and culture: The coevolutionary process.* Cambridge, MA: Harvard University Press.

Lund, F. H. (1925). The psychology of belief: IV. The law of primacy in persuasion. *Journal of Abnormal and Social Psychology, 20,* 183–191.

Lusk, C. M., & Judd, C. M. (1988). Political expertise and the structural mediators of candidate evaluations. *Journal of Experimental Social Psychology, 24,* 105–126.

Lutz, R. J. (1975). Changing brand attitudes through modification of cognitive structure. *Journal of Consumer Research, 1*(4), 49–59.

Lutz, R. J. (1977). An experimental investigation of causal relations among cognitions, affect, and behavioral intention. *Journal of Consumer Research, 3,* 197–208.

Lutz, R. J. (1981). A reconceptualization of the functional approach to attitudes. *Research in Marketing, 5,* 165–210.

Lydon, J. E., Jamieson, D. W., & Zanna, M. P. (1988). Interpersonal similarity and the social and intellectual dimensions of first impressions. *Social Cognition, 6,* 269–286.

Lydon, J. E., & Zanna, M. P. (1990). Commitment in the face of adversity: A value-affirmation approach. *Journal of Personality and Social Psychology, 58,* 1040–1057.

Lydon, J., Zanna, M. P., & Ross, M. (1988). Bolstering attitudes by autobiographical recall: Attitude persistence and selective memory. *Personality and Social Psychology Bulletin, 14,* 78–86.

Lykken, D. T. (1982). Research with twins: The concept of emergenesis. *Psychophysiology, 19,* 361–373.

Maass, A., & Clark, R. D., III. (1982, September). *Minority influence theory: Is it applicable only to majorities?* Paper presented at the meeting of the German Psychological Association, Mainz, West Germany.

Maass, A., & Clark, R. D., III. (1983). Internalization versus compliance: Differential processes underlying minority influence and conformity. *European Journal of Social Psychology, 13,* 197–215.

Maass, A., & Clark, R. D., III. (1984). Hidden impact of minorities: Fifteen years of minority influence research. *Psychological Bulletin, 95,* 428–450.

Maass, A., Clark, R. D., III, & Haberkorn, G. (1982). The effects of differential ascribed category membership and norms on minority influence. *European Journal of Social Psychology, 12,* 89–104.

Maass, A., West, S. G., & Cialdini, R. B. (1987). Minority influence and conversion. In C. Hendrick (Ed.), *Review of personality and social psychology* (Vol. 8, pp. 55–79). Newbury Park, CA: Sage.

MacCorquodale, K., & Meehl, P. E. (1948). On a distinction between hypothetical constructs and intervening variables. *Psychological Review, 55,* 95–107.

Mackie, D. M. (1986). Social identification effects in group polarization. *Journal of Personality and Social Psychology, 50,* 720–728.

Mackie, D. M. (1987). Systematic and nonsystematic processing of majority and minority persuasive communications. *Journal of Personality and Social Psychology, 53,* 41–52.

Mackie, D. M., & Asuncion, A. G. (1990). On-line and memory-based modification of attitudes: Determinants of message recall–attitude change correspondence. *Journal of Personality and Social Psychology, 59,* 5–16.

Mackie, D. M., & Cooper, J. (1984). Attitude polarization: The effects of group membership. *Journal of Personality and Social Psychology, 46,* 575–585.

Mackie, D. M., & Worth, L. T. (1989). Cognitive deficits and the mediation of positive affect in persuasion. *Journal of Personality and Social Psychology, 57,* 27–40.

Mackie, D. M., & Worth, L. T. (1991). Feeling good, but not thinking straight: The impact of positive mood on persuasion. In J. Forgas (Ed.), *Emotion and social judgments* (pp. 201–219). Oxford, England: Pergamon Press.

Maddux, J. E., & Rogers, R. W. (1980). Effects of source expertness, physical attractiveness, and supporting arguments on persuasion: A case of brains over beauty. *Journal of Personality and Social Psychology, 39,* 235–244.

Maddux, J. E., & Rogers, R. W. (1983) Protection motivation and self-efficacy: A revised theory of fear appeals and attitude change. *Journal of Experimental Social Psychology, 19,* 469–479.

Madsen, D. B. (1978). Issue importance and choice shifts: A persuasive arguments approach. *Journal of Personality and Social Psychology, 36,* 1118–1127.

Maheswaran, D., & Chaiken, S. (1991). Promoting systematic processing in low motivation settings: Effect of incongruent information on processing and judgment. *Journal of Personality and Social Psychology, 61,* 13–25.

Mahoney, M. J. (1977). Publication prejudices: An experimental study of confirmatory bias in the peer review system. *Cognitive Therapy and Research, 1,* 161–175.

Maier, N.R.F. (1952). *Principles of human relations*. New York: Wiley.

Malkis, F., Kalle, R., & Tedeschi, J.T. (1982). Attitudinal politics in the forced compliance situation. *Journal of Social Psychology, 117*, 79–91.

Malpass, R.S. (1969). Effects of attitude on learning and memory: The influence of instruction-induced sets. *Journal of Experimental Social Psychology, 5*, 441–453.

Maltzman, I. (1968). Theoretical conceptions of semantic conditioning and generalization. In T.R. Dixon & D.L. Horton (Eds.), *Verbal behavior and general behavior theory* (pp. 291–339). Englewood Cliffs, NJ: Prentice-Hall.

Mandler, G., Nakamura, Y., & Van Zandt, B.J.S. (1987). Nonspecific effects of exposure on stimuli that cannot be recognized. *Journal of Experimental Psychology: Learning, Memory, and Cognition, 13*, 646–648.

Mandler, G., & Sheebo, B.J. (1983). Knowing and liking. *Motivation and Emotion, 7*, 125–144.

Manis, M. (1960). The interpretation of opinion statements as a function of recipient attitude. *Journal of Abnormal and Social Psychology, 60*, 340–344.

Manis, M. (1961a). The interpretation of opinion statements as a function of message ambiguity and recipient attitude. *Journal of Abnormal and Social Psychology, 63*, 76–81.

Manis, M. (1961b). The interpretation of opinion statements as a function of recipient attitude and source prestige. *Journal of Abnormal and Social Psychology, 63*, 82–86.

Manis, M. (1977). Cognitive social psychology. *Personality and Social Psychology Bulletin, 3*, 550–566.

Mann, J.H. (1956). Experimental evaluations of role playing. *Psychological Bulletin, 53*, 227–234.

Mann, L. (1967). The effects of emotional role playing on desire to modify smoking habits. *Journal of Experimental Social Psychology, 3*, 334–348.

Mann, L., & Janis, I.L. (1968). A follow-up study on the long-term effects of emotional role playing. *Journal of Personality and Social Psychology, 8*, 339–342.

Manstead, A.S.R., Proffitt, C., & Smart, J.L. (1983). Predicting and understanding mothers' infant-feeding intentions and behavior: Testing the theory of reasoned action. *Journal of Personality and Social Psychology, 44*, 657–671.

Marcel, A.J. (1983). Conscious and unconscious perception: Experiments on visual masking and word recognition. *Cognitive Psychology, 15*, 197–237.

Marin, B.V., Marin, G., Perez-Stable, E.J., Otero-Sabogal, R., & Sabogal, F. (1990). Cultural differences in attitudes toward smoking: Developing messages using the theory of reasoned action. *Journal of Applied Social Psychology, 20*, 478–493.

Markus, H., & Nurius, P. (1986). Possible selves. *American Psychologist, 41*, 954–969.

Markus, H., & Wurf, E. (1987). The dynamic self-concept: A social psychological perspective. *Annual Review of Psychology, 38*, 299–337.

Markus, H., & Zajonc, R.B. (1985). The cognitive perspective in social psychology. In G. Lindzey & E. Aronson (Eds.), *Handbook of social psychology* (3rd ed., Vol. 1, pp. 137–230). New York: Random House.

Marsh, H.W., & Hocevar, D. (1988). A new, more powerful approach to multitrait-multimethod analyses: Application of second-order confirmatory factor analysis. *Journal of Applied Psychology, 73*, 107–117.

Maslow, A.H. (1937). The influence of familiarization on preference. *Journal of Experimental Psychology, 21*, 162–180.

Matlin, M.W. (1970). Response competition as a mediating factor in the frequency-affect relationship. *Journal of Personality and Social Psychology, 16*, 536–552.

Matlin, M.W. (1971). Response competition, recognition, and affect. *Journal of Personality and Social Psychology, 19*, 295–300.

Mausner, B. (1954). The effect of one partner's success in a relevant task on the interaction of observer pairs. *Journal of Abnormal and Social Psychology, 49*, 557–560.

McArdle, J.A. (1973). Positive and negative communications and subsequent attitude and behavior change in alcoholics (Doctoral dissertation, University of Illinois, Urbana-Champaign, 1972). *Dissertation Abstracts International, 34*, 877B.

McArthur, L.Z. (1980). Illusory causation and illusory correlation: Two epistemological accounts. *Personality and Social Psychology Bulletin, 6*, 507–519.

McArthur, L.Z., Kiesler, C.A., & Cook, B.P. (1969). Acting on an attitude as a function of self-percept and inequity. *Journal of Personality and Social Psychology, 12*, 295–302.

McCann, C.D., Zanna, M.P., & Higgins, E.T. (1980, June). *Attitude change following induced compliance: An individual difference perspective*. Paper presented at the meeting of the Canadian Psychological Association, Calgary, Alberta.

McCaul, K.D., O'Neill, H.K., & Glasgow, R.E. (1988). Predicting the performance of dental hygiene behaviors: An examination of the Fishbein and Ajzen model and self-efficacy expectations. *Journal of Applied Social Psychology, 18*, 114–128.

McConahay, J.B. (1983). Modern racism and modern discrimination: The effects of race, racial attitudes, and context on simulated hiring decisions. *Personality and Social Psychology Bulletin, 9*, 551–558.

McConahay, J.B., & Hough, J.C., Jr. (1976). Symbolic racism. *Journal of Social Issues, 32*(2), 23–45.

McCroskey, J.C., & Mehrley, R.J. (1969). The effects of disorganization and nonfluency on attitude change and source credibility. *Speech Monographs, 36*, 13–21.

McCroskey, J.C., Young, T.J., & Scott, M.D. (1972). The effects of message sidedness and evidence on inoculation against counterpersuasion in small group communication. *Speech Monographs, 39*, 205-212.

McCullough, J.L., & Ostrom, T.M. (1974). Repetition of highly similar messages and attitude change. *Journal of Applied Psychology, 59*, 395-397.

McGinnies, E. (1973). Initial attitude, source credibility, and involvement as factors in persuasion. *Journal of Experimental Social Psychology, 9*, 285-296.

McGraw, K.M., & Pinney, N. (1990). The effects of general and domain-specific expertise on political memory and judgment. *Social Cognition, 8*, 9-30.

McGuire, W.J. (1957). Order of presentation as a factor in "conditioning" persuasiveness. In C.I. Hovland (Ed.), *The order of presentation in persuasion* (pp. 98-114). New Haven, CT: Yale University Press.

McGuire, W.J. (1960a). Cognitive consistency and attitude change. *Journal of Abnormal and Social Psychology, 60*, 345-353.

McGuire, W.J. (1960b). Direct and indirect persuasive effects of dissonance-producing messages. *Journal of Abnormal and Social Psychology, 60*, 354-358.

McGuire, W.J. (1960c). A syllogistic analysis of cognitive relationships. In C.I. Hovland, & M.J. Rosenberg (Eds.), *Attitude organization and change: An analysis of consistency among attitude components* (pp. 65-111). New Haven, CT: Yale University Press.

McGuire, W.J. (1961a). The effectiveness of supportive and refutational defenses in immunizing and restoring beliefs against persuasion. *Sociometry, 24*, 184-197.

McGuire, W.J. (1961b). Resistance to persuasion conferred by active and passive prior refutation of the same and alternative counterarguments. *Journal of Abnormal and Social Psychology, 63*, 326-332.

McGuire, W.J. (1962). Persistence of the resistance to persuasion induced by various types of prior belief defenses. *Journal of Abnormal and Social Psychology, 64*, 241-248.

McGuire, W.J. (1964). Inducing resistance to persuasion: Some contemporary approaches. In L. Berkowitz (Ed.), *Advances in experimental social psychology* (Vol. 1, pp. 191-229). San Diego, CA: Academic Press.

McGuire, W.J. (1966). Attitudes and opinions. *Annual Review of Psychology, 17*, 475-514.

McGuire, W.J. (1968a). Personality and attitude change: An information-processing theory. In A.G. Greenwald, T.C., Brock, & T.M. Ostrom (Eds.), *Psychological foundations of attitudes* (pp. 171-196). San Diego, CA: Academic Press.

McGuire, W.J. (1968b). Personality and susceptibility to social influence. In E.F. Borgatta & W.W. Lambert (Eds.), *Handbook of personality theory and research* (pp. 1130-1187). Chicago: Rand McNally.

McGuire, W.J. (1969). The nature of attitudes and attitude change. In G. Lindzey & E. Aronson (Eds.), *Handbook of social psychology* (2nd ed., Vol. 3, pp. 136-314). Reading, MA: Addison-Wesley.

McGuire, W.J. (1972). Attitude change: The information-processing paradigm. In C.G. McClintock (Ed.), *Experimental social psychology* (pp. 108-141). New York: Holt, Rinehart & Winston.

McGuire, W.J. (1976). Some internal psychological factors influencing consumer choice. *Journal of Consumer Research, 2*, 302-319.

McGuire, W.J. (1978). The communication/persuasion matrix. In B. Lipstein & W.J. McGuire (Eds.), *Evaluating advertising: A bibliography of the communications process* (pp. xxvii-xxxv). New York: Advertising Research Foundation.

McGuire, W.J. (1980). The communication-persuasion model and health-risk labeling. In L.A. Morris, M.B. Mazis, & I. Barofsky (Eds.), *Product labeling and health risks* (pp. 99-122). Cold Spring Harbor, NY: Cold Spring Harbor Laboratory.

McGuire, W.J. (1981). The probabilogical model of cognitive structure and attitude change. In R.E. Petty, T.M. Ostrom, & T.C. Brock (Eds.), *Cognitive responses in persuasion* (pp. 291-307). Hillsdale, NJ: Erlbaum.

McGuire, W.J. (1983). A contextualist theory of knowledge: Its implications for innovation and reform in psychological research. In L. Berkowitz (Ed.), *Advances in experimental social psychology* (Vol. 16, pp. 1-47). San Diego, CA: Academic Press.

McGuire, W.J. (1985). Attitudes and attitude change. In G. Lindzey & E. Aronson (Eds.), *Handbook of social psychology* (3rd ed., Vol. 2, pp. 233-346). New York: Random House.

McGuire, W.J. (1986a). The myth of massive media impact: Savagings and salvagings. In G. Comstock (Ed.), *Public communication and behavior* (Vol. 1, pp. 173-257). San Diego, CA: Academic Press.

McGuire, W.J. (1986b). The vicissitudes of attitudes and similar representational constructs in twentieth century psychology. *European Journal of Social Psychology, 16*, 89-130.

McGuire, W.J. (1990). Dynamic operations of thought systems. *American Psychologist, 45*, 504-512.

McGuire, W.J., & McGuire, C.V. (1991). The content, structure, and operation of thought systems. In R.S. Wyer, Jr., & T. Srull (Eds.), *Advances in social cognition* (Vol. 4, pp. 1-78). Hillsdale, NJ: Erlbaum.

McGuire, W.J., & Millman, S. (1965). Anticipatory belief lowering following forewarning of a persuasive attack. *Journal of Personality and Social Psychology, 2*, 471-479.

McGuire, W.J., & Papageorgis, D. (1961). The relative efficacy of various types of prior belief-defense in producing immunity against persuasion. *Journal of Abnormal and Social Psychology*, *62*, 327–337.

McGuire, W. J., & Papageorgis, D. (1962). Effectiveness of forewarning in developing resistance to persuasion. *Public Opinion Quarterly*, *26*, 24–34.

McIver, J. P., & Carmines, E. G. (1981). *Unidimensional scaling*. Beverly Hills, CA: Sage.

McKeachie, W. J. (1954). Individual conformity to attitudes of classroom groups. *Journal of Abnormal and Social Psychology*, *49*, 282–289.

McLaughlin, B. (1971). Effects of similarity and likableness on attraction and recall. *Journal of Personality and Social Psychology*, *20*, 65–69.

Meehl, P. E. (1978). Theoretical risks and tabular asterisks: Sir Karl, Sir Ronald, and the slow progress of soft psychology. *Journal of Consulting and Clinical Psychology*, *46*, 806–834.

Meeker, B. F., & Weitzel-O'Neill, P. A. (1977). Sex roles and interpersonal behavior in task-oriented groups. *American Sociological Review*, *42*, 91–105.

Mellers, B. A. (1981). Feeling more than thinking. *American Psychologist*, *36*, 802–803.

Melson, W. H., Calder, B. J., & Insko, C. A. (1969). The social psychological status of reward. *Psychonomic Science*, *17*, 240–242.

Mewborn, C. R., & Rogers, R. W. (1979). Effects of threatening and reassuring components of fear appeals on physiological and verbal measures of emotion and attitudes. *Journal of Experimental Social Psychology*, *15*, 242–253.

Meyer, M. (1903). Experimental studies in the psychology of music. *American Journal of Psychology*, *14*, 456–478.

Meyerowitz, B. E., & Chaiken, S. (1987). The effect of message framing on breast self-examination attitudes, intentions, and behavior. *Journal of Personality and Social Psychology*, *52*, 500–510.

Michell, J. (1986). Measurement scales and statistics: A clash of paradigms. *Psychological Bulletin*, *100*, 398–407.

Milburn, M. A. (1987). Ideological self-schemata and schematically induced attitude consistency. *Journal of Experimental Social Psychology*, *23*, 383–398.

Milgram, S. (1963). Behavioral study of obedience. *Journal of Abnormal and Social Psychology*, *67*, 371–378.

Milgram, S. (1964a). Group pressure and action against a person. *Journal of Abnormal and Social Psychology*, *69*, 137–143.

Milgram, S. (1964b). Issues in the study of obedience: A reply to Baumrind. *American Psychologist*, *19*, 848–852.

Milgram, S. (1965a). Liberating effects of group pressure. *Journal of Personality and Social Psychology*, *1*, 127–134.

Milgram, S. (1965b). Some conditions of obedience and disobedience to authority. *Human Relations*, *18*, 57–76.

Milgram, S. (1974). *Obedience to authority: An experimental view*. New York: Harper & Row.

Millar, M. G., & Millar, K. U. (1990). Attitude change as a function of attitude type and argument type. *Journal of Personality and Social Psychology*, *59*, 217–228.

Millar, M. G., & Tesser, A. (1986a). Effects of affective and cognitive focus on the attitude-behavior relation. *Journal of Personality and Social Psychology*, *51*, 270–276.

Millar, M. G., & Tesser, A. (1986b). Thought-induced attitude change: The effects of schema structure and commitment. *Journal of Personality and Social Psychology*, *51*, 259–269.

Millar, M. G., & Tesser, A. (1989). The effects of affective-cognitive consistency and thought on the attitude-behavior relation. *Journal of Experimental Social Psychology*, *25*, 189–202.

Miller, A. G. (1972). Role playing: An alternative to deception? A review of the evidence. *American Psychologist*, *27*, 623–636.

Miller, A. G. (1976). Constraint and target effects in the attribution of attitudes. *Journal of Experimental Social Psychology*, *12*, 325–339.

Miller, A. G. (1986). *The obedience experiments: A case study of controversy in social science*. New York: Praeger.

Miller, D. T., & Ross, M. (1975). Self-serving biases in the attribution of causality: Fact or fiction? *Psychological Bulletin*, *82*, 213–225.

Miller, G. A., Galanter, E., & Pribram, K. H. (1960). *Plans and the structure of behavior*. New York: Holt.

Miller, G. R., & Rokeach, M. (1968). Individual differences and tolerance for inconsistency. In R. P. Abelson, E. Aronson, W. J. McGuire, T. M. Newcomb, M. J. Rosenberg, & P. H. Tannenbaum (Eds.), *Theories of cognitive consistency: A sourcebook* (pp. 624–632). Chicago: Rand McNally.

Miller, N. (1965). Involvement and dogmatism as inhibitors of attitude change. *Journal of Experimental Social Psychology*, *1*, 121–132.

Miller, N., & Baron, R. S. (1973). On measuring counterarguing. *Journal for the Theory of Social Behaviour*, *1*, 101–118.

Miller, N., & Brewer, M. B. (Eds.). (1984). *Groups in contact: The psychology of desegregation*. San Diego, CA: Academic Press.

Miller, N., & Campbell, D. T. (1959). Recency and primacy in persuasion as a function of the timing of speeches and measurements. *Journal of Abnormal and Social Psychology*, *59*, 1–9.

Miller, N., & Colman, D. E. (1981). Methodological issues in analyzing the cognitive mediation of persuasion. In R. E. Petty, T. M. Ostrom, & T. C. Brock (Eds.), *Cognitive responses in persuasion* (pp. 105–125). Hillsdale, NJ: Erlbaum.

Miller, N., Maruyama, G., Beaber, R. J., & Valone, K. (1976). Speed of speech and persuasion. *Journal of Personality and Social Psychology, 34*, 615-624.

Miller, N. E. (1944). Experimental studies of conflict. In J. McV. Hunt (Ed.), *Personality and the behavior disorders* (Vol. 1, pp. 431-465). New York: Ronald Press.

Miller, N. E., & Dollard, J. (1941). *Social learning and imitation.* New Haven, CT: Yale University Press.

Millman, S. (1968). Anxiety, comprehension, and susceptibility to social influence. *Journal of Personality and Social Psychology, 9*, 251-256.

Mills, J. (1958). Changes in moral attitudes following temptation. *Journal of Personality, 26*, 517-531.

Mills, J. (1966). Opinion change as a function of the communicator's desire to influence and liking for the audience. *Journal of Experimental Social Psychology, 2*, 152-159.

Mills, J. (1967). Comment on Bem's "Self-perception: An alternative interpretation of cognitive dissonance phenomena." *Psychological Review, 74*, 535.

Mills, J., & Aronson, E. (1965). Opinion change as a function of the communicator's attractiveness and desire to influence. *Journal of Personality and Social Psychology, 1*, 173-177.

Mills, J., & Harvey, J. (1972). Opinion change as a function of when information about the communicator is received and whether he is attractive or expert. *Journal of Personality and Social Psychology, 21*, 52-55.

Mills, J., & Jellison, J. M. (1967). Effect on opinion change of how desirable the communication is to the audience the communicator addressed. *Journal of Personality and Social Psychology, 6*, 98-101.

Miniard, P. W., & Cohen, J. B. (1981). An examination of the Fishbein-Ajzen behavioral-intentions model's concepts and measures. *Journal of Experimental Social Psychology, 17*, 309-339.

Mintz, P. M., & Mills, J. (1971). Effects of arousal and information about its source upon attitude change. *Journal of Experimental Social Psychology, 7*, 561-570.

Mischel, W. (1968). *Personality and assessment.* New York: Wiley.

Mitchell, A. A., & Olson, J. C. (1981). Are product attribute beliefs the only mediator of advertising effects on brand attitude? *Journal of Marketing Research, 18*, 318-332.

Mitchell, T. R. (1974). Expectancy models of job satisfaction, occupational preference and effort: A theoretical, methodological, and empirical appraisal. *Psychological Bulletin, 81*, 1053-1077.

Mitchell, T. R., & Biglan, A. (1971). Instrumentality theories: Current uses in psychology. *Psychological Bulletin, 76*, 432-454.

Mittal, B. (1988). Achieving higher seat belt usage: The role of habit in bridging the attitude-behavior gap. *Journal of Applied Social Psychology, 18*, 993-1016.

Mohazab, F., & Feger, H. (1985). An extension of Heiderian balance theory for quantified data. *European Journal of Social Psychology, 15*, 147-165.

Möntmann, V., & Irle, M. (1978). Bibliographie der wichtigsten seit 1956 erschienenen Arbeiten zur Theorie der Kognitiven Dissonanz [Bibliography of the most important work appearing since 1956 on the theory of cognitive dissonance]. In L. Festinger, *Theorie der kognitiven Dissonanz* [A theory of cognitive dissonance] (M. Irle & V. Möntmann, Trans.; pp. 366-413). Bern: Huber Verlag (Original work published 1957)

Moore, D. L., Hausknecht, D., & Thamodaran, K. (1986). Time compression, response opportunity, and persuasion. *Journal of Consumer Research, 13*, 85-99.

Moore, M. (1973). Ambivalence in attitude measurement. *Educational and Psychological Measurement, 33*, 481-483.

Moore, M. (1980). Validation of the attitude toward any practice scale through the use of ambivalence as a moderator variable. *Educational and Psychological Measurement, 40*, 205-208.

Moreland, R. L., & Zajonc, R. B. (1976). A strong test of exposure effects. *Journal of Experimental Social Psychology, 12*, 170-179.

Moreland, R. L., & Zajonc, R. B. (1977). Is stimulus recognition a necessary condition for the occurrence of exposure effects? *Journal of Personality and Social Psychology, 35*, 191-199.

Moreland, R. L., & Zajonc, R. B. (1979). Exposure effects may not depend on stimulus recognition. *Journal of Personality and Social Psychology, 37*, 1085-1089.

Mori, D., Chaiken, S., & Pliner, P. (1987). "Eating lightly" and the self-presentation of femininity. *Journal of Personality and Social Psychology, 53*, 693-702.

Morrissette, J. O. (1958). An experimental study of the theory of structural balance. *Human Relations, 11*, 239-254.

Moscovici, S. (1976). *Social influence and social change.* London: Academic Press.

Moscovici, S. (1980). Toward a theory of conversion behavior. In L. Berkowitz (Ed.), *Advances in experimental social psychology* (Vol. 13, pp. 209-239). San Diego, CA: Academic Press.

Moscovici, S. (1985). Innovation and minority influence. In S. Moscovici, G. Mugny, & E. Van Avermaet (Eds.), *Perspectives on minority influence* (pp. 9-51). Cambridge, England: Cambridge University Press.

Moscovici, S., & Faucheux, C. (1972). Social influence, conformity bias, and the study of active minorities. In L. Berkowitz (Ed.), *Advances in experimental social psychology* (Vol. 6, pp. 149-202). San Diego, CA: Academic Press.

Moscovici, S., & Lage, E. (1976). Studies in social influence: III. Majority versus minority influence in a group. *European Journal of Social Psychology*, *6*, 149-174.

Moscovici, S., Lage, E., & Naffrechoux, M. (1969). Influence of a consistent minority on the responses of a majority in a color perception task. *Sociometry*, *32*, 365-380.

Moscovici, S., Mugny, G., & Papastamou, S. (1981). "Sleeper effect" et/ou effet minoritaire? Etude theorique et experimentale de l'influence sociale à retardement ["Sleeper effect" and/or minority effect? Theoretical and experimental study of delayed social influence.] *Cahiers de Psychologie Cognitive*, 1981, 199-221.

Moscovici, S., & Nemeth, C. (1974). Social influence: II. Minority influence. In C. Nemeth (Ed.), *Social psychology: Classic and contemporary integrations* (pp. 217-249). Chicago: Rand McNally.

Moscovici, S., & Néve, P. (1973). Studies in social influence: II. Instrumental and symbolic influence. *European Journal of Social Psychology*, *3*, 461-471.

Moscovici, S., & Personnaz, B. (1980). Studies in social influence: V. Minority influence and conversion behavior in a perceptual task. *Journal of Experimental Social Psychology*, *16*, 270-282.

Moscovici, S., & Personnaz, B. (1991). Studies in social influence: VI. Is Lenin orange or red? Imagery and social influence. *European Journal of Social Psychology*, *21*, 101-118.

Moscovici, S., & Zavalloni, M. (1969). The group as a polarizer of attitudes. *Journal of Personality and Social Psychology*, *12*, 125-135.

Moskowitz, J. M. (1983). Preventing adolescent substance abuse through drug education. *National Institute on Drug Abuse Research Monograph Series*, *47*, 233-249.

Mosteller, F. (1951). Remarks on the method of paired comparisons: III. A test of significance for paired comparisons when equal standard deviations and equal correlations are assumed. *Psychometrika*, *16*, 207-218.

Mouton, J. S., Blake, R. R., & Olmstead, J. A. (1956). The relationship between frequency of yielding and the disclosure of personal identity. *Journal of Personality*, *24*, 339-347.

Mowrer, O. H. (1950). *Learning theory and personality dynamics: Selected papers*. New York: Ronald Press.

Mucchi-Faina, A., Maass, A., & Volpato, C. (1991). Social influence: The role of originality. *European Journal of Social Psychology*, *21*, 183-197.

Mueller, D. J. (1970). Physiological techniques of attitude measurement. In G. F. Summers (Ed.), *Attitude measurement* (pp. 534-552). Chicago: Rand McNally.

Mueller, J. E. (1973). *War, presidents and public opinion*. New York: Wiley.

Mugny, G. (1975). Negotiations, image of the other and the process of minority influence. *European Journal of Social Psychology*, *5*, 209-228.

Mugny, G. (1982). *The power of minorities*. London: Academic Press.

Mugny, G., & Papastamou, S. (1980). When rigidity does not fail: Individualization and psychologization as resistances to the diffusion of minority innovations. *European Journal of Social Psychology*, *10*, 43-61.

Mulilis, J., & Lippa, R. (1990). Behavioral change in earthquake preparedness due to negative threat appeals: A test of protection motivation theory. *Journal of Applied Social Psychology*, *20*, 619-638.

Mullen, B. (1983). Operationalizing the effect of the group on the individual: A self-attention perspective. *Journal of Experimental Social Psychology*, *19*, 295-322.

Mullen, B. (1985). Strength and immediacy of sources: A meta-analytic evaluation of the forgotten elements of social impact theory. *Journal of Personality and Social Psychology*, *48*, 1458-1466.

Munsinger, H., & Kessen, W. (1964). Uncertainty, structure, and preference. *Psychological Monographs*, *78*(9, Whole No. 586).

Murray, H. A. (1933). The effect of fear upon estimates of the maliciousness of other personalities. *Journal of Social Psychology*, *4*, 310-329.

Myers, D. G. (1978). Polarizing effects of social comparison. *Journal of Experimental Social Psychology*, *14*, 554-563.

Myers, D. G. (1982). Polarizing effects of social interaction. In H. Brandstätter, J. H. Davis, & G. Stocher-Kreichgauer (Eds.), *Group decision making* (pp. 125-161). San Diego, CA: Academic Press.

Myers, D. G., Bruggink, J. B., Kersting, R. C., & Schlosser, B. A. (1980). Does learning others' opinions change one's opinion? *Personality and Social Psychology Bulletin*, *6*, 253-260.

Myers, D. G., & Lamm, H. (1976). The group polarization phenomenon. *Psychological Bulletin*, *83*, 602-627.

Myers, D. G., Wojcicki, S. B., & Aardema, B. S. (1977). Attitude comparison: Is there ever a bandwagon effect? *Journal of Applied Social Psychology*, *7*, 341-347.

Nail, P. R. (1986). Toward an integration of some models and theories of social response. *Psychological Bulletin*, *100*, 190-206.

Nathan, G. (1988). A bibliography on randomized response: 1965-1987. *Survey Methodology*, *14*, 331-346.

Nederhof, A. J. (1985). Methods of coping with social desirability bias: A review. *European Journal of Social Psychology*, *15*, 263-280.

Neisser, U. (1967). *Cognitive psychology*. New York: Appleton-Century-Crofts.

Nel, E., Helmreich, R., & Aronson, E. (1969). Opinion change in the advocate as a function of the persuasibility of his audience: A clarification of the meaning of dissonance. *Journal of Personality and Social Psychology*, *12*, 117-124.

Nelson, C. E. (1968). Anchoring to accepted values as a technique for immunizing beliefs against persuasion. *Journal of Personality and Social Psychology, 9,* 329–334.

Nemeth, C. J. (1976). *A comparison between conformity and minority influence.* Paper presented at the International Congress of Psychology, Paris, France.

Nemeth, C. J. (1985). Dissent, group process, and creativity: The contribution of minority influence. In E. Lawler (Ed.), *Advances in group processes* (Vol. 2, pp. 57–75). Greenwich, CT: JAI Press.

Nemeth, C. J. (1986). Differential contributions of majority and minority influence. *Psychological Review, 93,* 23–32.

Nemeth, C. J. (1987). Influence processes, problem solving and creativity. In M. P. Zanna, J. M. Olson, & C. P. Herman (Eds.), *Social influence: The Ontario Syposium* (Vol. 5, pp. 237–246). Hillsdale, NJ: Erlbaum.

Nemeth, C. J., & Endicott, J. (1976). The midpoint as an anchor: Another look at discrepancy of position and attitude change. *Sociometry, 39,* 11–18.

Nemeth, C. J., & Kwan, J. L. (1985). Originality of word associations as a function of majority vs. minority influence. *Social Psychology Quarterly, 48,* 277–282.

Nemeth, C. J., & Kwan, J. L. (1987). Minority influence, divergent thinking and detection of correct solutions. *Journal of Applied Social Psychology, 17,* 788–799.

Nemeth, C. J., Mayseless, O., Sherman, J., & Brown, Y. (1990). Exposure to dissent and recall of information. *Journal of Personality and Social Psychology, 58,* 429–437.

Nemeth, C. J., Swedlund, M., & Kanki, B. (1974). Patterning of the minority's responses and their influence on the majority. *European Journal of Social Psychology, 4,* 53–64.

Nemeth, C. J., & Wachtler, J. (1974). Creating the perceptions of consistency and confidence: A necessary condition for minority influence. *Sociometry, 37,* 529–540.

Nemeth, C. J., & Wachtler, J. (1983). Creative problem solving as a result of majority vs. minority influence. *European Journal of Social Psychology, 13,* 45–55.

Netemeyer, R. G., & Burton, S. (1990). Examining the relationships between voting behavior, intention, perceived behavioral control, and expectation. *Journal of Applied Social Psychology, 20,* 661–680.

Newcomb, T. M. (1943). *Personality & social change: Attitude formation in a student community.* New York: Holt, Rinehart & Winston.

Newcomb, T. M. (1950). *Social psychology.* New York: Dryden.

Newcomb, T. M. (1953). An approach to the study of communicative acts. *Psychological Review, 60,* 393–404.

Newcomb, T. M. (1959). Individual systems of orientation. In S. Koch (Ed.), *Psychology: A study of a science* (Vol. 3, pp. 384–422). New York: McGraw-Hill.

Newcomb, T. M. (1961). *The acquaintance process.* New York: Holt, Rinehart & Winston.

Newcomb, T. M. (1963). Stabilities underlying changes in interpersonal attraction. *Journal of Abnormal and Social Psychology, 66,* 376–386.

Newcomb, T. M. (1968). Interpersonal balance. In R. P. Abelson, E. Aronson, W. J. McGuire, T. M. Newcomb, M. J. Rosenberg, & P. H. Tannenbaum (Eds.), *Theories of cognitive consistency: A sourcebook* (pp. 28–51). Chicago: Rand McNally.

Newcomb, T. M. (1978). The acquaintance process: Looking mainly backward. *Journal of Personality and Social Psychology, 36,* 1075–1083.

Newcomb, T. M., Turner, R. H., & Converse, P. E. (1965). *Social psychology: The study of human interaction.* New York: Holt, Rinehart & Winston.

Newcombe, N., & Arnkoff, D. B. (1979). Effects of speech style and sex of speaker on person perception. *Journal of Personality and Social Psychology, 37,* 1293–1303.

Newell, A., & Simon, H. A. (1972). *Human problem solving.* Englewood Cliffs, NJ: Prentice-Hall.

Newman, J., Wolff, W. T., & Hearst, E. (1980). The feature-positive effect in adult human subjects. *Journal of Experimental Psychology: Human Learning and Memory, 6,* 630–650.

Niedenthal, P. M. (1990). Implicit perception of affective information. *Journal of Experimental Social Psychology, 26,* 505–527.

Niedenthal, P. M., & Cantor, N. (1986). Affective responses as guides to category-based influences. *Motivation & Emotion, 10,* 217–231.

Nisbett, R. E., Caputo, C., Legant, P., & Maracek, J. (1973). Behavior as seen by the actor and as seen by the observer. *Journal of Personality and Social Psychology, 27,* 154–164.

Nisbett, R. E., & Gordon, A. (1967). Self-esteem and susceptibility to social influence. *Journal of Personality and Social Psychology, 5,* 268–276.

Nisbett, R. E., & Ross, L. (1980). *Human inference: Strategies and shortcomings of social judgment.* Englewood Cliffs, NJ: Prentice-Hall.

Nisbett, R. E., & Valins, S. (1972). Perceiving the causes of one's own behavior. In E. E. Jones, D. E. Kanouse, H. H. Kelley, R. E. Nisbett, S. Valins, & B. Weiner (Eds.), *Attribution: Perceiving the causes of behavior* (pp. 63–78). New York: General Learning Press.

Nisbett, R. E., & Wilson, T. D. (1977). Telling more than we can know: Verbal report on mental processes. *Psychological Review, 84,* 231–259.

Norman, R. (1975). Affective-cognitive consistency, attitudes, conformity, and behavior. *Journal of Personality and Social Psychology, 32,* 83–91.

Norman, R. (1976). When what is said is important: A comparison of expert and attractive sources. *Journal of Experimental Social Psychology, 12,* 294–300.

Nowlis, V. (1965). Research with the Mood Adjective Check List. In S.S. Tomkins & C.E. Izard (Eds.), *Affect, cognition, and personality* (pp. 352-389). New York: Springer.

Nunnally, J.C. (1978). *Psychometric theory* (2nd ed.). New York: McGraw-Hill.

Nunnally, J.C., Knott, P.D., Duchnowski, A., & Parker, R. (1967). Pupillary response as a general measure of activation. *Perception and Psychophysics, 2*, 149-155.

Nuttin, J.M., Jr. (1966). Attitude change after rewarded dissonant and consonant "forced compliance": A critical replication of the Festinger and Carlsmith experiment. *International Journal of Psychology, 1*, 39-57.

Nuttin, J.M., Jr. (1975). *The illusion of attitude change: Towards a response contagion theory of persuasion*. London: Academic Press.

Oakes, W.F. (1967). Verbal operant conditioning, intertrial activity, and the extended interview. *Journal of Personality and Social Psychology, 6*, 198-202.

O'Keefe, D.J., & Sypher, H.E. (1981). Cognitive complexity measures and the relationship of cognitive complexity to communication. *Human Communication Research, 8*, 72-92.

O'Keeffe, M.K., Nesselhof-Kendall, S., & Baum, A. (1990). Behavior and prevention of AIDS: Bases of research and intervention. *Personality and Social Psychology Bulletin, 16*, 166-180.

Olson, J.M., & Zanna, M.P. (1979). A new look at selective exposure. *Journal of Experimental Social Psychology, 15*, 1-15.

Olson, J.M., & Zanna, M.P. (1982). Repression-sensitization differences in responses to a decision. *Journal of Personality, 50*, 46-57.

Olson, J.M., & Zanna, M.P. (1987). Understanding and promoting exercise: A social psychological perspective. *Canadian Journal of Public Health, 78*, S1-S7.

Orne, M.T. (1962). On the social psychology of the psychological experiment: With particular reference to demand characteristics and their implications. *American Psychologist, 17*, 776-783.

Orne, M.T. (1973). Communication by the total experimental situation: Why it is important, how it is evaluated, and its significance for the ecological validity of findings. In P. Pliner, L. Krames, & T. Alloway (Eds.), *Communication and affect: Language and thought* (pp. 157-191). San Diego, CA: Academic Press.

Orne, M.T., & Evans, F.J. (1965). Social control in the psychological experiment: Antisocial behavior and hypnosis. *Journal of Personality and Social Psychology, 1*, 189-200.

Osgood, C.E., Suci, G.J., & Tannenbaum, P.H. (1957). *The measurement of meaning*. Urbana: University of Illinois Press.

Osgood, C.E., & Tannenbaum, P.H. (1955). The principle of congruity in the prediction of attitude change. *Psychological Review, 62*, 42-55.

Osterhouse, R.A., & Brock, T.C. (1970). Distraction increases yielding to propaganda by inhibiting counterarguing. *Journal of Personality and Social Psychology, 15*, 344-358.

Ostrom, T.M. (1969). The relationship between the affective, behavioral and cognitive components of attitude. *Journal of Experimental Social Psychology, 5*, 12-30.

Ostrom, T.M. (1973). The bogus pipeline: A new *ignis fatuus*? *Psychological Bulletin, 79*, 252-259.

Ostrom, T.M. (1981). Theoretical perspectives in the analysis of cognitive responses. In R.E. Petty, T.M. Ostrom, & T.C. Brock (Eds.), *Cognitive responses in persuasion* (pp. 283-290). Hillsdale, NJ: Erlbaum.

Ostrom, T.M. (1987). Bipolar survey items: An information processing perspective. In H.-J. Hippler, N. Schwarz, & S. Sudman (Eds.), *Social information processing and survey methodology* (pp. 71-85). New York: Springer-Verlag.

Ostrom, T.M. (1988). Dimensional versus information processing conceptions of social judgment. *Wissenshaftliche Zeitschrift der Friedrich-Schiller-Universität, 6*, 629-638.

Ostrom, T.M. (1989). Interdependence of attitude theory and measurement. In A.R. Pratkanis, S.J. Breckler, & A.G. Greenwald (Eds.), *Attitude structure and function* (pp. 11-36). Hillsdale, NJ: Erlbaum.

Ostrom, T.M., & Brock, T.C. (1968). A cognitive model of attitudinal involvement. In R.P. Abelson, E. Aronson, W.J. McGuire, T.M. Newcomb, M.J. Rosenberg, & P.H. Tannenbaum (Eds.), *Theories of cognitive consistency: A sourcebook* (pp. 373-383). Chicago: Rand McNally.

Ostrom, T.M., Steele, C.M., & Smilansky, J. (1974). Perceived discrepancy and attitude change: An unsubstantiated relationship. *Representative Research in Social Psychology, 5*, 7-15.

Ostrom, T.M., & Upshaw, H.S. (1968). Psychological perspective and attitude change. In A.G. Greenwald, T.C. Brock, & T.M. Ostrom (Eds.), *Psychological foundations of attitudes* (pp. 217-242). San Diego, CA: Academic Press.

Ottati, V., Fishbein, M., & Middlestadt, S.E. (1988). Determinants of voters' beliefs about the candidates' stands on issues: The role of evaluative bias heuristics and the candidates' expressed message. *Journal of Personality and Social Psychology, 55*, 517-529.

Page, M.M. (1969). Social psychology of a classical conditioning of attitudes experiment. *Journal of Personality and Social Psychology, 11*, 177-186.

Page, M.M. (1970). Demand awareness, subject sophistication, and the effectiveness of a verbal "reinforcement." *Journal of Personality, 38*, 287-301.

Page, M.M. (1971). Postexperimental assessment of awareness in attitude conditioning. *Educational and Psychological Measurement, 31*, 891-906.

Page, M. M. (1972). Demand characteristics and the verbal operant conditioning experiment. *Journal of Personality and Social Psychology, 23*, 372-378.

Page, M. M. (1973). On detecting demand awareness by postexperimental questionnaire. *Journal of Personality and Social Psychology, 91*, 305-323.

Page, M. M. (1974). Demand characteristics and the classical conditioning of attitudes experiment. *Journal of Personality and Social Psychology, 30*, 468-476.

Page, M. M., & Kahle, L. R. (1976). Demand characteristics in the satiation-deprivation effect on attitude conditioning. *Journal of Personality and Social Psychology, 33*, 553-562.

Page, R. A., & Moss, M. K. (1975). Attitude similarity and attraction: The effects of the bogus pipeline. *Bulletin of the Psychonomic Society, 5*, 63-65.

Paicheler, G. (1976). Norms and attitude change I: Polarization and styles of behaviour. *European Journal of Social Psychology, 6*, 405-427.

Paicheler, G. (1988). *The psychology of social influence.* New York: Cambridge University Press.

Pallak, M. S., & Kleinhesselink, R. R. (1976). Polarization of attitudes: Belief inference from consonant behavior. *Personality and Social Psychology Bulletin, 2*, 55-58.

Pallak, M. S., Mueller, M., Dollar, K., & Pallak, J. (1972). Effect of commitment on responsiveness to an extreme consonant communication. *Journal of Personality and Social Psychology, 23*, 429-436.

Pallak, M. S., & Pittman, T. S. (1972). General motivational effects of dissonance arousal. *Journal of Personality and Social Psychology, 21*, 349-358.

Pallak, S. R. (1983). Salience of a communicator's physical attractiveness and persuasion: A heuristic versus systematic processing interpretation. *Social Cognition, 2*, 158-170.

Pallak, S. R., Murroni, E., & Koch, J. (1983). Communicator attractiveness and expertise, emotional versus rational appeals, and persuasion: A heuristic versus systematic processing interpretation. *Social Cognition, 2*, 122-141.

Palmer, D. L., & Kalin, R. (1985). Dogmatic responses to belief dissimilarity in the "bogus stranger" paradigm. *Journal of Personality and Social Psychology, 48*, 171-179.

Palmer, D. L., & Kalin, R. (1991). Predictive validity of the Dogmatic Rejection Scale. *Personality and Social Psychology Bulletin, 17*, 212-218.

Papageorgis, D. (1963). Bartlett effect and the persistence of induced opinion change. *Journal of Abnormal and Social Psychology, 67*, 61-67.

Papageorgis, D. (1968). Warning and persuasion. *Psychological Bulletin, 70*, 271-282.

Papageorgis, D., & McGuire, W. J. (1961). The generality of immunity to persuasion produced by pre-exposure to weakened counterarguments. *Journal of Abnormal and Social Psychology, 62*, 475-481.

Papini, M. R., & Bitterman, M. E. (1990). The role of contingency in classical conditioning. *Psychological Review, 97*, 396-403.

Patty, R. A., & Page, M. M. (1973). Manipulations of a verbal conditioning situation based upon demand characteristics theory. *Journal of Experimental Research in Personality, 6*, 307-313.

Paulhus, D. (1982). Individual differences, self-presentation, and cognitive dissonance: Their concurrent operation in forced compliance. *Journal of Personality and Social Psychology, 43*, 838-852.

Payne, S. L. (1951). *The art of asking questions.* Princeton: Princeton University Press.

Peak, H. (1955). Attitude and motivation. In M. R. Jones (Ed.), *Nebraska Symposium on Motivation* (Vol. 3, pp. 149-188). Lincoln: University of Nebraska Press.

Pearce, W. B., Cushman, D., Cronen, V. E., Johnson, K., Jones, G., & Raymond, R. (1980). The structure of communication rules and the form of conversation: An experimental simulation. *Western Journal of Speech Communication, 44*, 20-34.

Pepitone, A. (1966). Some conceptual and empirical problems of consistency models. In S. Feldman (Ed.), *Cognitive consistency: Motivational antecedents and behavioral consequents* (pp. 257-297). San Diego, CA: Academic Press.

Pepitone, A., McCauley, C., & Hammond, P. (1967). Change in attractiveness of forbidden toys as a function of severity of threat. *Journal of Experimental Social Psychology, 3*, 221-229.

Perlman, D., & Oskamp, S. (1971). The effects of picture content and exposure frequency on evaluations of Negroes and whites. *Journal of Experimental Social Psychology, 7*, 503-514.

Perrin, S., & Spencer, C. (1981). Independence or conformity in the Asch experiment as a reflection of cultural and situational factors. *British Journal of Social Psychology, 20*, 205-209.

Personnaz, B. (1981). Study of social influence using the spectrometer method: Dynamics of the phenomena of conversion and covertness in perceptual responses. *European Journal of Social Psychology, 11*, 431-438.

Peterson, P. D., & Koulack, D. (1969). Attitude change as a function of latitudes of acceptance and rejection. *Journal of Personality and Social Psychology, 11*, 309-311.

Peterson, R. C., & Thurstone, L. L. (1970). *Motion pictures and the social attitudes of children.* New York: Arno Press and the New York Times. (Original work published 1933)

Pettigrew, T. F. (1985). New black-white patterns: How best to conceptualize them? *Annual Review of Sociology, 11*, 329-346.

Petty, R. E., & Brock, T. C. (1976). Effects of responding or not responding to hecklers on audience agreement with a speaker. *Journal of Applied Social Psychology, 6*, 1-17.

Petty, R. E., & Cacioppo, J. T. (1977). Forewarning, cognitive responding, and resistance to persuasion. *Journal of Personality and Social Psychology, 35*, 645–655.

Petty, R. E., & Cacioppo, J. T. (1979a). Effects of forewarning of persuasive intent and involvement on cognitive responses and persuasion. *Personality and Social Psychology Bulletin, 5*, 173–176.

Petty, R. E., & Cacioppo, J. T. (1979b). Issue involvement can increase or decrease persuasion by enhancing message-relevant cognitive responses. *Journal of Personality and Social Psychology, 37*, 1915–1926.

Petty, R. E., & Cacioppo, J. T. (1980). Effects of issue involvement on attitudes in an advertising context. In G. Gorn & M. Goldberg (Eds.), *Proceedings of the Division 23 program* (pp. 75–79). Montreal: Division 23 of the American Psychological Association.

Petty, R. E., & Cacioppo, J. T. (1981a). *Attitudes and persuasion: Classic and contemporary approaches*. Dubuque, IA: Brown.

Petty, R. E., & Cacioppo, J. T. (1981b). Issue involvement as a moderator of the effects on attitude of advertising content and context. *Advances in Consumer Research, 8*, 20–24. Ann Arbor, MI: Association for Consumer Research.

Petty, R. E., & Cacioppo, T. J. (1983). The role of bodily responses in attitude measurement and change. In J. T. Cacioppo & R. E. Petty (Eds.), *Social psychophysiology: A sourcebook* (pp. 51–101). New York: Guilford Press.

Petty, R. E., & Cacioppo, J. T. (1984a). The effects of involvement on responses to argument quantity and quality: Central and peripheral routes to persuasion. *Journal of Personality and Social Psychology, 46*, 69–81.

Petty, R. E., & Cacioppo, J. T. (1984b). Source factors and the elaboration likelihood model of persuasion. *Advances in Consumer Research, 11*, 668–672.

Petty, R. E., & Cacioppo, J. T. (1986a). *Communication and persuasion: Central and peripheral routes to attitude change*. New York: Springer-Verlag.

Petty, R. E., & Cacioppo, J. T. (1986b). The elaboration likelihood model of persuasion. In L. Berkowitz (Ed.), *Advances in experimental social psychology* (Vol. 19, pp. 123–205). San Diego, CA: Academic Press.

Petty, R. E., & Cacioppo, J. T. (1990). Involvement and persuasion: Tradition versus integration. *Psychological Bulletin, 107*, 367–374.

Petty, R. E., Cacioppo, J. T., & Goldman, R. (1981). Personal involvement as a determinant of argument-based persuasion. *Journal of Personality and Social Psychology, 41*, 847–855.

Petty, R. E., Cacioppo, J. T., & Heesacker, M. (1981). Effects of rhetorical questions on persuasion: A cognitive response analysis. *Journal of Personality and Social Psychology, 40*, 432–440.

Petty, R. E., Cacioppo, J. T., & Kasmer, J. A. (1988). The role of affect in the elaboration likelihood model of persuasion. In L. Donohew, H. E. Sypher, & E. T. Higgins (Eds.), *Communication, social cognition and affect* (pp. 117–146). Hillsdale, NJ: Erlbaum.

Petty, R. E., Cacioppo, J. T., Kasmer, J. A., & Haugtvedt, C. P. (1987). A reply to Stiff and Boster. *Communication Monographs, 54*, 257–263.

Petty, R. E., Cacioppo, J. T., & Schumann, D. W. (1983). Central and peripheral routes to advertising effectiveness: The moderating role of involvement. *Journal of Consumer Research, 10*, 135–146.

Petty, R. E., Cacioppo, J. T., Sedikides, C., & Strathman, A. J. (1988). Affect and persuasion: A contemporary perspective. *American Behavioral Scientist, 31*, 355–371.

Petty, R. E., Gleicher, F., & Baker, S. M. (1991). Multiple roles for affect in persuasion. In J. Forgas (Ed.), *Emotion and social judgments* (pp. 181–200). Oxford, England: Pergamon Press.

Petty, R. E., Harkins, S. G., & Williams, K. D. (1980). The effects of group diffusion of cognitive effort on attitudes: An information processing view. *Journal of Personality and Social Psychology, 38*, 81–92.

Petty, R. E., Kasmer, J. A., Haugtvedt, C. P., & Cacioppo, J. T. (1987). Source and message factors in persuasion: A reply to Stiff's critique of the elaboration likelihood model. *Communication Monographs, 54*, 233–249.

Petty, R. E., & Krosnick, J. A. (Eds.). (in press). *Attitude strength: Antecedents and consequences*. Hillsdale, NJ: Erlbaum.

Petty, R. E., Ostrom, T. M., & Brock, T. C. (1981). Historical foundations of the cognitive response approach to attitudes and persuasion. In R. E. Petty, T. M. Ostrom, & T. C. Brock (Eds.), *Cognitive responses in persuasion* (pp. 5–29). Hillsdale, NJ: Erlbaum.

Petty, R. E., & Priester, J. R. (1991). *Expectancy disconfirmation and attitude change: A reexamination of the attributional analysis of persuasion*. Unpublished manuscript, Ohio State University, Columbus, OH.

Petty, R. E., Schumann, D. W., Richman, S. A., & Strathman, A. J. (in press). Positive mood and persuasion: Different roles for affect under high and low elaboration conditions. *Journal of Personality and Social Psychology*.

Petty, R. E., & Wegener, D. T. (1991). Thought systems, argument quality, and persuasion. In R. S. Wyer, Jr., & T. K. Srull (Eds.), *Advances in social cognition* (Vol. 4, pp. 147–161). Hillsdale, NJ: Erlbaum.

Petty, R. E., Wells, G. L., & Brock, T. C. (1976). Distraction can enhance or reduce yielding to propaganda: Thought disruption versus effort justification. *Journal of Personality and Social Psychology, 34*, 874–884.

Pfau, M., & Burgoon, M. (1988). Inoculation in political campaign communication. *Human Communication Research, 15*, 91–111.

Piliavin, J. A., Piliavin, I. M., Loewenton, E. P., McCauley, C., & Hammond, P. (1969). On observers' reproductions of dissonance effects: The right answers for the wrong reasons? *Journal of Personality and Social Psychology, 13*, 98–106.

Pintner, R., & Forlano, G. (1937). The influence of attitude upon scaling of attitude items. *Journal of Social Psychology, 8*, 39–45.

Pittman, T. S. (1975). Attribution of arousal as a mediator in dissonance reduction. *Journal of Experimental Social Psychology, 11*, 53–63.

Pittman, T. S., & D'Agostino, P. R. (1989). Motivation and cognition: Control deprivation and the nature of subsequent information processing. *Journal of Experimental Social Psychology, 25*, 465–480.

Pittman, T. S., & Heller, J. F. (1987). Social motivation. *Annual Review of Psychology, 38*, 461–489.

Podell, L., & Perkins, J. (1957). A Guttman scale for sexual experience: A methodological note. *Journal of Abnormal and Social Psychology, 54*, 420–422.

Podsakoff, P. M., & Schriesheim, C. A. (1985). Field studies of French and Raven's bases of power: Critique, reanalysis, and suggestions for future research. *Psychological Bulletin, 97*, 387–411.

Pomazal, R. J. (1983). Salient beliefs and attitude change over time: An experimental approach. *Representative Research in Social Psychology, 13*(2), 11–22.

Pomazal, R. J., & Jaccard, J. J. (1976). An informational approach to altruistic behavior. *Journal of Personality and Social Psychology, 33*, 317–326.

Poppleton, P. K., & Pilkington, G. W. (1963). A comparison of four methods of scoring an attitude scale in relation to its reliability and validity. *British Journal of Social and Clinical Psychology, 3*, 36–39.

Porier, G. W., & Lott, A. J. (1967). Galvanic skin responses and prejudice. *Journal of Personality and Social Psychology, 5*, 253–259.

Postman, L. (1976). Methodology of human learning. In W. K. Estes (Ed.), *Handbook of learning and cognitive processes* (Vol. 3: Approaches to human learning and motivation, pp. 11–69). Hillsdale, NJ: Erlbaum.

Postman, L., & Murphy, G. (1943). The factor of attitude in associative memory. *Journal of Experimental Psychology, 33*, 228–238.

Postman, L., Stark, K., & Fraser, J. (1968). Temporal changes in interference. *Journal of Verbal Learning and Verbal Behavior, 7*, 672–694.

Powell, F. A. (1965). Source credibility and behavioral compliance as determinants of attitude change. *Journal of Personality and Social Psychology, 2*, 669–676.

Powell, L. (1977). Satirical persuasion and topic salience. *Southern Speech Communication Journal, 42*, 151–162.

Powell, M. C., & Fazio, R. H. (1984). Attitude accessibility as a function of repeated attitudinal expression. *Personality and Social Psychology Bulletin, 10*, 139–148.

Powers, W. T. (1973). *Behavior: The control of perception*. Chicago: Aldine.

Pratkanis, A. R. (1984, August). *Attitude structure and selective learning*. Paper presented at the meeting of the American Psychological Association, Toronto.

Pratkanis, A. R. (1985). Attitudes and memory: The heuristic and schematic functions of attitudes (Doctoral dissertation, Ohio State University, 1984). *Dissertation Abstracts International, 45*, 3657B.

Pratkanis, A. R. (1989). The cognitive representation of attitudes. In A. R. Pratkanis, S. J. Breckler, & A. G. Greenwald (Eds.), *Attitude structure and function* (pp. 71–98). Hillsdale, NJ: Erlbaum.

Pratkanis, A. R., Breckler, S. J., & Greenwald, A. G. (Eds.). (1989). *Attitude structure and function*. Hillsdale, NJ: Erlbaum.

Pratkanis, A. R., Greenwald, A. G., Leippe, M. R., & Baumgardner, M. H. (1988). In search of reliable persuasion effects: III. The sleeper effect is dead. Long live the sleeper effect. *Journal of Personality and Social Psychology, 54*, 203–218.

Prentice, D. A. (1987a, April). *The effects of priming possessions on attitude functions*. Paper presented at the meeting of the Eastern Psychological Association, Arlington, VA.

Prentice, D. A. (1987b). Psychological correspondence of possessions, attitudes, and values. *Journal of Personality and Social Psychology, 53*, 993–1003.

Proshansky, H. M. (1943). A projective method for the study of attitudes. *Journal of Abnormal and Social Psychology, 38*, 393–395.

Pruitt, D. G. (1971a). Choice shifts in group discussion: An introductory review. *Journal of Personality and Social Psychology, 20*, 339–360.

Pruitt, D. G. (1971b). Conclusions: Toward an understanding of choice shifts in group discussion. *Journal of Personality and Social Psychology, 20*, 495–510.

Pryor, B., & Steinfatt, T. M. (1978). The effects of initial belief level on inoculation theory and its proposed mechanisms. *Human Communication Research, 4*, 217–230.

Pryor, J. B., Reeder, G. D., Vinacco, R., Jr., & Kott, T. L. (1989). The instrumental and symbolic functions of attitudes toward persons with AIDS. *Journal of Applied Social Psychology, 19*, 377–404.

Puckett, J. M., Petty, R. E., Cacioppo, J. T., & Fisher, D. L. (1983). The relative impact of age and attractiveness stereotypes on persuasion. *Journal of Gerontology, 38*, 340–343.

Quigley-Fernandez, B., & Tedeschi, J. T. (1978). The bogus pipeline as lie detector: Two validity studies. *Journal of Personality and Social Psychology, 36*, 247–256.

Rabbie, J. M., Brehm, J. W., & Cohen, A. R. (1959). Verbalization and reactions to cognitive dissonance. *Journal of Personality, 27*, 407–417.

Rabow, J., Fowler, F. J., Jr., Bradford, D. L., Hofeller, M. A., & Shibuya, Y. (1966). The role of social norms and leadership in risk taking. *Sociometry*, *29*, 16–27.

Raden, D. (1985). Strength-related attitude dimensions. *Social Psychology Quarterly*, *48*, 312–330.

Rajecki, D. W. (1973). Imprinting in precocial birds: Interpretation, evidence, and evaluation. *Psychological Bulletin*, *79*, 48–58.

Rajecki, D. W., & Wolfson, C. (1973). The rating of materials found in the mailbox. Effects of frequency of receipt. *Public Opinion Quarterly*, *37*, 110–114.

Rankin, R. E., & Campbell, D. T. (1955). Galvanic skin response to Negro and white experimenters. *Journal of Abnormal and Social Psychology*, *51*, 30–33.

Rasch, G. (1960). *Probabilistic models for some intelligence and attainment tests*. Copenhagen: Danish Institute of Educational Research.

Ratneshwar, S., & Chaiken, S. (1991). Comprehension's role in persuasion: The case of its moderating effect on the persuasive impact of source cues. *Journal of Consumer Research*, *18*, 52–62.

Raven, B. H. (1965). Social influence and power. In I. D. Steiner & M. Fishbein (Eds.), *Current studies in social psychology* (pp. 371–382). New York: Holt, Rinehart & Winston.

Raven, B. H., & Kruglanski, A. W. (1970). Conflict and power. In P. Swingle (Ed.), *The structure of conflict* (pp. 69–109). San Diego, CA: Academic Press.

Ray, M. L. (1968). Biases in selection of messages designed to induce resistance to persuasion. *Journal of Personality and Social Psychology*, *9*, 335–339.

Razran, G. H. S. (1938). Conditioning away social bias by the luncheon technique. *Psychological Bulletin*, *35*, 693.

Razran, G. H. S. (1940). Conditioned response changes in rating and appraising sociopolitical slogans. *Psychological Bulletin*, *37*, 481.

Read, S. J., & Miller, L. C. (1989). Inter-personalism: Toward a goal-based theory of persons in relationships. In L. Pervin (Ed.), *Goal concepts in personality and social psychology* (pp. 413–472). Hillsdale, NJ: Erlbaum.

Read, S. J., & Rosson, M. B. (1982). Rewriting history: The biasing effects of attitudes on memory. *Social Cognition*, *1*, 240–255.

Reaser, J. M., Hartsock, S., & Hoehn, A. J. (1975). *A test of the forced-alternative random response questionnaire technique* (HumRRO Tech. Rep. No. 75-9). Alexandria, VA: Human Resources Research Organization.

Reber, A. S., & Lewis, S. (1977). Implicit learning: An analysis of the form and structure of a body of tacit knowledge. *Cognition*, *5*, 333–361.

Reeder, G. D., & Brewer, M. B. (1979). A schematic model of dispositional attribution in interpersonal perception. *Psychological Review*, *86*, 61–79.

Regan, D. T., & Cheng, J. B. (1973). Distraction and attitude change: A resolution. *Journal of Experimental Social Psychology*, *9*, 138–147.

Regan, D. T., & Fazio, R. H. (1977). On the consistency between attitudes and behavior: Look to the method of attitude formation. *Journal of Experimental Social Psychology*, *13*, 28–45.

Reis, H. T. (1982). An introduction to the use of structural equations: Prospects and problems. In L. Wheeler (Ed.), *Review of personality and social psychology* (Vol. 3, pp. 255–287). Beverly Hills, CA: Sage.

Reiser, M. (1980). Latent trait modeling of attitude items. In G. W. Bohrnstedt & E. F. Borgatta (Eds.), *Social measurement: Current issues* (pp. 117–144). Beverly Hills, CA: Sage.

Remmers, H. H. (1934). Studies in attitudes. *Bulletin of the Purdue University Studies of Higher Education*, *26*(Whole No. 4). West Lafayette, IN: Purdue University.

Remmers, H. H., & Silance, E. B. (1934). Generalized attitude scales. *Journal of Social Psychology*, *5*, 298–312.

Rescorla, R. A. (1988). Behavioral studies of Pavlovian conditioning. *Annual Review of Neuroscience*, *11*, 329–352.

Reyes, R. M., Thompson, W. C., & Bower, G. H. (1980). Judgmental biases resulting from differing availabilities of arguments. *Journal of Personality and Social Psychology*, *39*, 2–12.

Rhine, R. J. (1958). A concept-formation approach to attitude acquisition. *Psychological Review*, *65*, 362–370.

Rhine, R. J., & Severance, L. J. (1970). Ego-involvement, discrepancy, source credibility, and attitude change. *Journal of Personality and Social Psychology*, *16*, 175–190.

Rhodes, N., & Wood, W. (1992). Self-esteem and intelligence affect influenceability: The mediating role of message reception. *Psychological Bulletin*, *111*, 156–171.

Rholes, W. S., & Bailey, S. (1983). The effects of level of moral reasoning on consistency between moral attitudes and related behaviors. *Social Cognition*, *2*, 32–48.

Riess, M., Kalle, R. J., & Tedeschi, J. T. (1981). Bogus pipeline attitude assessment, impression management, and misattribution in induced compliance settings. *Journal of Social Psychology*, *115*, 247–258.

Riordan, C. A., & Tedeschi, J. T. (1983). Attraction in aversive environments: Some evidence for classical conditioning and negative reinforcement. *Journal of Personality and Social Psychology*, *44*, 683–692.

Rippetoe, P. A., & Rogers, R. W. (1987). Effects of components of protection-motivation theory on adaptive and maladaptive coping with a health threat. *Journal of Personality and Social Psychology*, *52*, 596–604.

Robberson, M. R., & Rogers, R. W. (1988). Beyond fear appeals: Negative and positive persuasive appeals to health and self-esteem. *Journal of Applied Social Psychology*, *18*, 277–287.

Roberts, D. F., & Maccoby, N. (1985). Effects of mass communication. In G. Lindzey & E. Aronson (Eds.), *Handbook of social psychology* (3rd ed., Vol. 2, pp. 539-598). New York: Random House.

Roberts, J. V. (1984). Public opinion and capital punishment: The effects of attitudes upon memory. *Canadian Journal of Criminology, 26,* 283-291.

Roberts, J. V. (1985). The attitude-memory relationship after 40 years: A meta-analysis of the literature. *Basic and Applied Social Psychology, 6,* 221-241.

Robinson, J. P., Rusk, J. G., & Head, K. B. (1968). *Measures of political attitudes* (rev. ed.). Ann Arbor, MI: Survey Research Center, Institute for Social Research.

Robinson, J. P., & Shaver, P. R. (1973). *Measures of social psychological attitudes* (rev. ed.). Ann Arbor, MI: Survey Research Center, Institute for Social Research.

Robinson, J. P., Shaver, P. R., & Wrightsman, L. S. (Eds.). (1991). *Measures of personality and social psychological attitudes* (Vol. 1). San Diego, CA: Academic Press.

Robles, R., Smith, R., Carver, C. S., & Wellens, A. R. (1987). Influence of subliminal visual images on the experience of anxiety. *Personality and Social Psychology Bulletin, 13,* 399-410.

Rogers, R. W. (1975). A protection motivation theory of fear appeals and attitude change. *Journal of Psychology, 91,* 93-114.

Rogers, R. W. (1983). Cognitive and physiological processes in fear appeals and attitude change: A revised theory of protection motivation. In J. T. Cacioppo & R. E. Petty (Eds.), *Social psychophysiology: A sourcebook* (pp. 153-176). New York: Guilford Press.

Rogers, R. W., & Mewborn, C. R. (1976). Fear appeals and attitude change: Effects of a threat's noxiousness, probability of occurrence, and the efficacy of coping responses. *Journal of Personality and Social Psychology, 34,* 54-61.

Rogers, R. W., & Thistlethwaite, D. L. (1970). Effects of fear arousal and reassurance upon attitude change. *Journal of Personality and Social Psychology, 15,* 227-233.

Rokeach, M. (1954). The nature and meaning of dogmatism. *Psychological Review, 61,* 194-204.

Rokeach, M. (1956). Political and religious dogmatism: An alternative to the authoritarian personality. *Psychological Monographs, 70*(18, Whole No. 425).

Rokeach, M. (1960). *The open and closed mind: Investigations into the nature of belief systems and personality systems.* New York: Basic Books.

Rokeach, M. (1964). *The three Christs of Ypsilanti: A psychological study.* New York: Knopf.

Rokeach, M. (1968). *Beliefs, attitudes, and values: A theory of organization and change.* San Francisco: Jossey-Bass.

Rokeach, M. (1973). *The nature of human values.* New York: Free Press.

Rokeach, M. (1980). Some unresolved issues in theories of beliefs, attitudes, and values. In H. E. Howe, Jr., & M. M. Page (Eds.), *Nebraska Symposium on Motivation, 1979* (Vol. 27, pp. 261-304). Lincoln: University of Nebraska Press.

Rokeach, M., & Mezei, L. (1966). Race and shared belief as factors in social choice. *Science, 151,* 167-172.

Rokeach, M., & Rothman, G. (1965). The principle of belief congruence and the congruity principle as models of cognitive interaction. *Psychological Review, 72,* 128-142.

Romer, D. (1979a). Distraction, counterarguing and the internalization of attitude change. *European Journal of Social Psychology, 9,* 1-17.

Romer, D. (1979b). Internalization versus identification in the laboratory: A causal analysis of attitude change. *Journal of Personality and Social Psychology, 37,* 2171-2180.

Romer, D. (1981). A person-situation causal analysis of self-reports of attitudes. *Journal of Personality and Social Psychology, 41,* 562-576.

Romer, D. (1983). Effects of own attitude on polarization of judgment. *Journal of Personality and Social Psychology, 44,* 273-284.

Ronis, D. L., Baumgardner, M. H., Leippe, M. R., Cacioppo, J. T., & Greenwald, A. G. (1977). In search of reliable persuasion effects: I. A computer-controlled procedure for studying persuasion. *Journal of Personality and Social Psychology, 35,* 548-569.

Ronis, D. L., & Kaiser, M. K. (1989). Correlates of breast self-examination in a sample of college women: Analyses of linear structural relations. *Journal of Applied Social Psychology, 19,* 1068-1084.

Rook, K. S. (1987). Effects of case history versus abstract information on health attitudes and behaviors. *Journal of Applied Social Psychology, 17,* 533-553.

Rorer, L. (1965). The great response-style myth. *Psychological Bulletin, 63,* 129-156.

Rosander, A. C. (1937). An attitude scale based upon behavior situations. *Journal of Social Psychology, 8,* 3-15.

Rosenbaum, M. E. (1986). The repulsion hypothesis: On the nondevelopment of relationships. *Journal of Personality and Social Psychology, 51,* 1156-1166.

Rosenberg, M. (1965). *Society and the adolescent self-image.* Princeton, NJ: Princeton University Press.

Rosenberg, M. J. (1953). The experimental investigation of a value-theory of attitude structure (Doctoral dissertation, University of Michigan). *Dissertation Abstracts International, 13,* 899.

Rosenberg, M. J. (1956). Cognitive structure and attitudinal affect. *Journal of Abnormal and Social Psychology, 53,* 367-372.

Rosenberg, M. J. (1960a). An analysis of affective-cognitive consistency. In C. I. Hovland, & M. J. Rosenberg (Eds.), *Attitude organization and change: An analysis of con-*

sistency among attitude components (pp. 15-64). New Haven, CT: Yale University Press.

Rosenberg, M. J. (1960b). Cognitive reorganization in response to the hypnotic reversal of attitudinal affect. *Journal of Personality*, 28, 39-63.

Rosenberg, M. J. (1960c). A structural theory of attitude dynamics. *Public Opinion Quarterly*, 24, 319-340.

Rosenberg, M. J. (1965a). Some content determinants of intolerance for attitudinal inconsistency. In S. S. Tomkins & C. I. Izard (Eds.), *Affect, cognition and personality* (pp. 130-147). New York: Springer.

Rosenberg, M. J. (1965b). When dissonance fails: On eliminating evaluation apprehension from attitude measurement. *Journal of Personality and Social Psychology*, 1, 28-42.

Rosenberg, M. J. (1968a). Discussion: On reducing the inconsistency between consistency theories. In R. P. Abelson, E. Aronson, W. J. McGuire, T. M. Newcomb, M. J. Rosenberg, & P. H. Tannenbaum (Eds.), *Theories of cognitive consistency: A sourcebook* (pp. 827-833). Chicago: Rand McNally.

Rosenberg, M. J. (1968b). Hedonism, inauthenticity, and other goads toward expansion of a consistency theory. In R. P. Abelson, E. Aronson, W. J. McGuire, T. M. Newcomb, M. J. Rosenberg, & P. H. Tannenbaum (Eds.), *Theories of cognitive consistency: A sourcebook* (pp. 73-111). Chicago: Rand McNally.

Rosenberg, M. J., & Abelson, R. P. (1960). An analysis of cognitive balancing. In C. I. Hovland, & M. J. Rosenberg (Eds.), *Attitude organization and change: An analysis of consistency among attitude components* (pp. 112-163). New Haven, CT: Yale University Press.

Rosenberg, M. J., & Gardner, C. W. (1958). Some dynamic aspects of post-hypnotic compliance. *Journal of Abnormal and Social Psychology*, 57, 351-366.

Rosenberg, M. J., & Hovland, C. I. (1960). Cognitive, affective, and behavioral components of attitudes. In C. I. Hovland, & M. J. Rosenberg (Eds.), *Attitude organization and change: An analysis of consistency among attitude components* (pp. 1-14). New Haven, CT: Yale University Press.

Rosenberg, S., & Sedlak, A. (1972). Structural representations of implicit personality theory. In L. Berkowitz (Ed.), *Advances in experimental social psychology* (Vol. 6, pp. 235-297). San Diego, CA: Academic Press.

Rosenthal, R. (1990). How are we doing in soft psychology? *American Psychologist*, 45, 775-777.

Rosenthal, R. (1991). *Meta-analytic procedures for social research* (rev. ed.). Newbury Park, CA: Sage.

Rosenthal, R., & Rubin, D. B. (1982). A simple, general purpose display of magnitude of experimental effect. *Journal of Educational Psychology*, 74, 166-169.

Roskos-Ewoldsen, D. R., & Fazio, R. H. (1988, April). *The role of belief accessibility in the attitude-belief relation*. Paper presented at meeting of Midwestern Psychological Association, Chicago.

Roskos-Ewoldsen, D. R., & Fazio, R. H. (1992). The accessibility of source likability as a determinant of persuasion. *Personality and Social Psychology Bulletin*, 18, 19-25.

Ross, H. L., Jr. (1982). Recall versus persuasion: An answer. *Journal of Advertising Research*, 22, 13-16.

Ross, L. (1977). The intuitive psychologist and his shortcomings: Distortions in the attribution process. In L. Berkowitz (Ed.), *Advances in experimental social psychology* (Vol. 10, pp. 173-220). San Diego, CA: Academic Press.

Ross, L., Bierbrauer, G., & Hoffman, S. (1976). The role of attribution processes in conformity and dissent: Revisiting the Asch situation. *American Psychologist*, 31, 148-157.

Ross, L., Lepper, M. R., & Hubbard, M. (1975). Perseverance in self-perception and social perception: Biased attributional processes in the debriefing paradigm. *Journal of Personality and Social Psychology*, 32, 880-892.

Ross, M. (1989). Relation of implicit theories to the construction of personal histories. *Psychological Review*, 96, 341-357.

Ross, M., & Conway, M. (1986). Remembering one's own past: The construction of personal histories. In R. M. Sorrentino & E. T. Higgins (Eds.), *Handbook of motivation and cognition: Foundations of social behavior* (pp. 122-144). New York: Guilford Press.

Ross, M., & Fletcher, G. J. O. (1985). Attribution and social perception. In G. Lindzey & E. Aronson (Eds.), *Handbook of social psychology* (3rd ed., Vol. 2, pp. 73-122). New York: Random House.

Ross, M., McFarland, C., Conway, M., & Zanna, M. P. (1983). Reciprocal relation between attitudes and behavior recall: Committing people to newly formed attitudes. *Journal of Personality and Social Psychology*, 45, 257-267.

Ross, M., McFarland, C., & Fletcher, G. J. O. (1981). The effect of attitude on the recall of personal histories. *Journal of Personality and Social Psychology*, 40, 627-634.

Ross, M., & Shulman, R. F. (1973). Increasing the salience of initial attitudes: Dissonance versus self-perception theory. *Journal of Personality and Social Psychology*, 28, 138-144.

Rotter, J. B. (1954). *Social learning and clinical psychology*. New York: Prentice-Hall.

Rugg, D. (1941). Experiments in wording questions: II. *Public Opinion Quarterly*, 5, 91-92.

Rule, B. G., & Bisanz, G. L. (1987). Goals and strategies for persuasion: A cognitive schema for understanding social events. In M. P. Zanna, J. M. Olson, & C. P. Herman (Eds.), *Social influence: The Ontario Symposium* (Vol. 5, pp. 185-206). Hillsdale, NJ: Erlbaum.

Rule, B.G., & Renner, J. (1968). Involvement and group effects on opinion change. *Journal of Social Psychology*, *76*, 189-198.

Runkel, P.J., & Peizer, D.B. (1968). The two-valued orientation of current equilibrium theory. *Behavioral Science*, *13*, 56-65.

Sachs, D.H., & Byrne, D. (1970). Differential conditioning of evaluative responses to neutral stimuli through association with attitude statements. *Journal of Experimental Research in Personality*, *4*, 181-185.

Sadler, O., & Tesser, A. (1973). Some effects of salience and time upon interpersonal hostility and attraction during social isolation. *Sociometry*, *36*, 99-112.

Saegert, S.C., & Jellison, J.M. (1970). Effects of initial level of response competition and frequency of exposure on liking and exploratory behavior. *Journal of Personality and Social Psychology*, *16*, 553-558.

Saegert, S.C., Swap, W.C., & Zajonc, R.B. (1973). Exposure, context, and interpersonal attraction. *Journal of Personality and Social Psychology*, *25*, 234-242.

Saffir, M.A. (1937). A comparative study of scales constructed by three psychophysical methods. *Psychometrika*, *2*, 179-198.

Safire, W. (1990, November 25). The mood of 'tude. *New York Times Magazine*, p. 18.

Salancik, G.R. (1982). Attitude-behavior consistencies as social logics. In M.P. Zanna, E.T. Higgins, & C.P. Herman (Eds.), *Consistency in social behavior: The Ontario Symposium* (Vol. 2, pp. 51-73). Hillsdale, NJ: Erlbaum.

Salancik, G.R., & Conway, M. (1975). Attitude inferences from salient and relevant cognitive content about behavior. *Journal of Personality and Social Psychology*, *32*, 829-840.

Sanbonmatsu, D.M., & Fazio, R.H. (1990). The role of attitudes in memory-based decision making. *Journal of Personality and Social Psychology*, *59*, 614-622.

Sapolsky, A. (1960). Effect of interpersonal relationships upon verbal conditioning. *Journal of Abnormal and Social Psychology*, *60*, 241-246.

Sargant, W. (1957). *Battle for the mind: A physiology of conversion and brain-washing*. Garden City, NY: Doubleday.

Sarnoff, I. (1960). Psychoanalytic theory and social attitudes. *Public Opinion Quarterly*, *24*, 251-279.

Sarnoff, I. (1968). Psychoanalytic theory and cognitive dissonance. In R.P. Abelson, E. Aronson, W.J. McGuire, T.M. Newcomb, M.J. Rosenberg, & P.H. Tannenbaum (Eds.), *Theories of cognitive consistency: A sourcebook* (pp. 192-200). Chicago: Rand McNally.

Sarnoff, I., & Katz, D. (1954). The motivational basis of attitude change. *Journal of Abnormal and Social Psychology*, *49*, 115-124.

Sawyer, A.G. (1975). Demand artifacts in laboratory experiments in consumer research. *Journal of Consumer Research*, *1*(4), 20-30.

Sawyer, A.G. (1981). Repetition, cognitive responses, and persuasion. In R.E. Petty, T.M. Ostrom, & T.C. Brock (Eds.), *Cognitive responses in persuasion* (pp. 237-261). Hillsdale, NJ: Erlbaum.

Schachter, S. (1951). Deviation, rejection, and communication. *Journal of Abnormal and Social Psychology*, *46*, 190-207.

Schachter, S., & Singer, J. (1962). Cognitive, social, and physiological determinants of the emotional state. *Psychological Review*, *69*, 379-399.

Schanck, R.L. (1932). A study of a community and its groups and institutions conceived of as behaviors of individuals. *Psychological Monographs*, *43*(2, Whole No. 195).

Schank, R.C., & Abelson, R.P. (1977). *Scripts, plans, goals, and understanding: An inquiry into human knowledge structures*. Hillsdale, NJ: Erlbaum.

Scheier, M.F., & Carver, C.S. (1980). Private and public self-attention, resistance to change, and dissonance reduction. *Journal of Personality and Social Psychology*, *39*, 390-405.

Scheier, M.F., & Carver, C.S. (1981). Private and public aspects of self. In L. Wheeler (Ed.), *Review of personality and social psychology* (Vol. 2, pp. 189-216). Beverly Hills, CA: Sage.

Scheier, M.F., & Carver, C.S. (1988). A model of behavioral self-regulation: Translating intention into action. In L. Berkowitz (Ed.), *Advances in experimental social psychology* (Vol. 21, pp. 303-346). San Diego, CA: Academic Press.

Schein, E.H., Schneier, I., & Barker, C.H. (1961). *Coercive persuasion: A socio-psychological analysis of the "brainwashing" of American civilian prisoners by the Chinese communists*. New York: Norton.

Scher, S.J., & Cooper, J. (1989). Motivational basis of dissonance: The singular role of behavioral consequences. *Journal of Personality and Social Psychology*, *56*, 899-906.

Schiffman, S.S., Reynolds, M.L., & Young, F.W. (1981). *Introduction to multidimensional scaling: Theory, methods, and applications*. San Diego, CA: Academic Press.

Schifter, D.E., & Ajzen, I. (1985). Intention, perceived control, and weight loss: An application of the theory of planned behavior. *Journal of Personality and Social Psychology*, *49*, 843-851.

Schlegel, R.P., & DiTecco, D. (1982). Attitudinal structures and the attitude-behavior relation. In M.P. Zanna, E.T. Higgins, & C.P. Herman (Eds.), *Consistency in social behavior: The Ontario Symposium* (Vol. 2, pp. 17-49). Hillsdale, NJ: Erlbaum.

Schlenker, B.R. (1975). Liking for a group following an initiation: Impression management or dissonance reduction? *Sociometry*, *38*, 99-118.

Schlenker, B. R. (1980). *Impression management: The self-concept, social identity, and interpersonal relations*. Monterey, CA: Brooks/Cole.

Schlenker, B. R. (1982). Translating actions into attitudes: An identity-analytic approach to the explanation of social conduct. In L. Berkowitz (Ed.), *Advances in experimental social psychology* (Vol. 15, pp. 193–247). San Diego, CA: Academic Press.

Schlenker, B. R., Bonoma, T. V., Hutchinson, D., & Burns, L. (1976). The bogus pipeline and stereotypes toward blacks. *Journal of Psychology, 93*, 319–329.

Schlenker, B. R., & Schlenker, P. A. (1975). Reactions following counterattitudinal behavior which produces positive consequences. *Journal of Personality and Social Psychology, 31*, 962–971.

Schmidt, D. F., & Sherman, R. C. (1984). Memory for persuasive messages: A test of a schema-copy-plus-tag model. *Journal of Personality and Social Psychology, 47*, 17–25.

Schmidt, F. L. (1973). Implications of a measurement problem for expectancy theory research. *Organizational Behavior and Human Performance, 10*, 243–251.

Schmitt, N., & Stults, D. M. (1986). Methodology review: Analysis of multitrait-multimethod matrices. *Applied Psychological Measurement, 10*, 1–22.

Schmittlein, D. C., & Morrison, D. G. (1983). Measuring miscomprehension for televised communications using true-false questions. *Journal of Consumer Research, 10*, 147–156.

Schneider, D. J. (1976). *Social psychology*. Reading, MA: Addison-Wesley.

Schneider, D. J., Hastorf, A. H., & Ellsworth, P. C. (1979). *Person perception* (2nd ed.). Reading, MA: Addison-Wesley.

Schneider, W., & Shiffrin, R. M. (1977). Controlled and automatic human information processing: I. Detection, search, and attention. *Psychological Review, 84*, 1–66.

Schopler, J. (1965). Social power. In L. Berkowitz (Ed.), *Advances in experimental social psychology* (Vol. 2, pp. 177–218). San Diego, CA: Academic Press.

Schopler, J., & Bateson, N. (1962). A dependence interpretation of the effects of a severe initiation. *Journal of Personality, 30*, 633–649.

Schroder, H. M. (1971). Conceptual complexity and personality organization. In H. M. Schroder & P. Suedfeld (Eds.), *Personality theory and information processing* (pp. 240–273). New York: Ronald Press.

Schroder, H. M., Driver, M. J., & Streufert, S. (1967). *Human information processing: Individuals and groups functioning in complex social situations*. New York: Holt, Rinehart & Winston.

Schroeder, H. E. (1973). The risky shift as a general choice shift. *Journal of Personality and Social Psychology, 27*, 297–300.

Schultz, D. P. (1963). Time, awareness, and order of presentation in opinion change. *Journal of Applied Psychology, 47*, 280–283.

Schuman, H., & Johnson, M. P. (1976). Attitudes and behavior. *Annual Review of Sociology, 2*, 161–207.

Schuman, H., & Kalton, G. (1985). Survey methods. In G. Lindzey & E. Aronson (Eds.), *Handbook of social psychology* (3rd ed., Vol. 1, pp. 635–697). New York: Random House.

Schuman, H., & Ludwig, J. (1983). The norm of evenhandedness in surveys as in life. *American Sociological Review, 48*, 112–120.

Schuman, H., & Presser, S. (1981). *Questions and answers in attitude survey: Experiments on question form, wording, and context*. San Diego, CA: Academic Press.

Schümer, R. (1973). Context effects in impression formation as a function of the ambiguity of test traits. *European Journal of Social Psychology, 3*, 333–338.

Schwartz, G. E., Ahern, G. L., & Brown, S. L. (1979). Lateralized facial muscle response to positive and negative emotional stimuli. *Psychophysiology, 16*, 561–571.

Schwartz, G. E., Fair, P. L., Salt, P., Mandel, M. R., & Klerman, G. L. (1976). Facial muscle patterning to affective imagery in depressed and nondepressed subjects. *Science, 192*, 489–491.

Schwartz, S. H., & Tessler, R. C. (1972). A test of a model for reducing measured attitude-behavior discrepancies. *Journal of Personality and Social Psychology, 24*, 225–236.

Schwarz, N. (1990). Feelings as information: Informational and motivational functions of affective states. In E. T. Higgins & R. M. Sorrentino (Eds.), *Handbook of motivation and cognition: Foundations of social behavior* (Vol. 2, pp. 527–561). New York: Guilford Press.

Schwarz, N., Bless, H., & Bohner, G. (1991). Mood and persuasion: Affective states influence the processing of persuasive communications. In M. P. Zanna (Ed.), *Advances in experimental social psychology* (Vol. 24, pp. 161–199). San Diego, CA: Academic Press.

Schwarz, N., & Clore, G. L. (1983). Mood, misattribution, and judgments of well-being: Informative and directive functions of affective states. *Journal of Personality and Social Psychology, 45*, 513–523.

Schwarz, N., & Clore, G. L. (1988). How do I feel about it? The informative function of affective states. In K. Fiedler & J. Forgas (Eds.), *Affect, cognition, and social behavior: New evidence and integrative attempts* (pp. 44–62). Toronto: Hogrefe.

Schwarz, N., Frey, D., & Kumpf, M. (1980). Interactive effects of writing and reading a persuasive essay on attitude change and selective exposure. *Journal of Experimental Social Psychology, 16*, 1–17.

Schwarz, N., Servay, W., & Kumpf, M. (1985). Attribution of arousal as a mediator of the effectiveness of fear-arousing communications. *Journal of Applied Social Psychology*, *15*, 178-188.

Schwarz, N., & Strack, F. (1991). Context effects in attitude surveys: Applying cognitive theory to social research. In W. Stroebe & M. Hewstone (Eds.), *European review of social psychology* (Vol. 2, pp. 31-50). Chichester, England: Wiley.

Schwarz, N., Strack, F., Hippler, H.-J., & Bishop, G. F. (1991). The impact of administration mode on response effects in survey measurement. *Applied Cognitive Psychology*, *5*, 193-212.

Schwarz, N., Strack, F., & Mai, H. P. (1991). Assimilation and contrast effects in part-whole question sequences: A conversational logic analysis. *Public Opinion Quarterly*, *55*, 3-23.

Schwarz, N., & Sudman, S. (Eds.). (1992). *Context effects in social and psychological research*. New York: Springer-Verlag.

Scott, J. (1989). Conflicting beliefs about abortion: Legal approval and moral doubts. *Social Psychology Quarterly*, *52*, 319-326.

Scott, W. A. (1957). Attitude change through reward of verbal behavior. *Journal of Abnormal and Social Psychology*, *55*, 72-75.

Scott, W. A. (1962). Cognitive complexity and cognitive flexibility. *Sociometry*, *25*, 405-414.

Scott, W. A. (1963). Conceptualizing and measuring structural properties of cognition. In O. J. Harvey (Ed.), *Motivation and social interaction: Cognitive determinants* (pp. 266-288). New York: Ronald Press.

Scott, W. A. (1968). Attitude measurement. In G. Lindzey & E. Aronson (Eds.), *Handbook of social psychology* (2nd ed., Vol. 2, pp. 204-273). Reading, MA: Addison-Wesley.

Scott, W. A. (1969). Structure of natural cognitions. *Journal of Personality and Social Psychology*, *12*, 261-278.

Scott, W. A., Osgood, D. W., & Peterson, C. (1979). *Cognitive structure: Theory and measurement of individual differences*. New York: Winston.

Seamon, J. G., Brody, N., & Kauff, D. M. (1983a). Affective discrimination of stimuli that are not recognized: Effects of shadowing, masking, and cerebral laterality. *Journal of Experimental Psychology: Learning, Memory, and Cognition*, *9*, 544-555.

Seamon, J. G., Brody, N., & Kauff, D. M. (1983b). Affective discrimination of stimuli that are not recognized: II. Effect of delay between study and test. *Bulletin of the Psychonomic Society*, *21*, 187-189.

Seamon, J. G., Marsh, R. L., & Brody, N. (1984). Critical importance of exposure duration for affective discrimination of stimuli that are not recognized. *Journal of Experimental Psychology: Learning, Memory, and Cognition*, *10*, 465-469.

Sears, D. O. (1965). Biased indoctrination and selectivity of exposure to new information. *Sociometry*, *28*, 363-376.

Sears, D. O. (1981). Life stage effects on attitude change, especially among the elderly. In S. B. Kiesler, J. N. Morgan, & V. K. Oppenheimer (Eds.), *Aging: Social change* (pp. 183-204). San Diego, CA: Academic Press.

Sears, D. O. (1986). College students in the laboratory: Influences of a narrow data base on social psychology's view of human nature. *Journal of Personality and Social Psychology*, *51*, 515-530.

Sears, D. O., & Freedman, J. L. (1965). Effects of expected familiarity with arguments upon opinion change and selective exposure. *Journal of Personality and Social Psychology*, *2*, 420-426.

Sears, D. O., & Funk, C. L. (1991). The role of self-interest in social and political attitudes. In M. P. Zanna (Ed.), *Advances in experimental social psychology* (Vol. 24, pp. 2-91). San Diego, CA: Academic Press.

Sears, D. O., & Kinder, D. R. (1985). Whites' opposition to busing: On conceptualizing and operationalizing group conflict. *Journal of Personality and Social Psychology*, *48*, 1141-1147.

Sears, D. O., & Lau, R. R. (1983). Inducing apparently self-interested political preferences. *American Journal of Political Science*, *27*, 223-252.

Sears, D. O., Lau, R. R., Tyler, T. R., & Allen, H. R., Jr. (1980). Self-interest versus symbolic politics in policy attitudes and presidential voting. *American Political Science Review*, *74*, 670-684.

Sechrest, L., & Belew, J. (1983). Nonreactive measures of social attitudes. *Applied Social Psychology Annual*, *4*, 23-63.

Secord, P. F., & Backman, C. W. (1964). *Social psychology*. New York: McGraw-Hill.

Seeleman, V. (1940). The influence of attitudes upon the remembering of pictorial material. *Archives of Psychology*, No. 258.

Seiler, L. H., & Hough, R. L. (1970). Empirical comparisons of the Thurstone and Likert techniques. In G. F. Summers (Ed.), *Attitude measurement* (pp. 159-173). Chicago: Rand McNally.

Sejwacz, D., Ajzen, I., & Fishbein, M. (1980). Predicting and understanding weight loss: Intentions, behaviors, and outcomes. In I. Ajzen & M. Fishbein, *Understanding attitudes and predicting social behavior* (pp. 101-112). Englewood Cliffs, NJ: Prentice-Hall.

Self, C. A., & Rogers, R. W. (1990). Coping with threats to health: Effects of persuasive appeals on depressed, normal, and antisocial personalities. *Journal of Behavioral Medicine*, *13*, 343-357.

Selltiz, C., & Cook, S. W. (1966). Racial attitude as a determinant of judgments of plausibility. *Journal of Social Psychology*, *70*, 139-147.

Selltiz, C., Edrich, H., & Cook, S.W. (1965). Ratings of favorableness of statements about a social group as an indicator of attitude toward the group. *Journal of Personality and Social Psychology, 2,* 408–415.

Semin, G.R., & Fiedler, K. (1989). Relocating attributional phenomena within a language-cognition interface: The case of actors' and observers' perspectives. *European Journal of Social Psychology, 19,* 491–508.

Sensenig, J., & Brehm, J.W. (1968). Attitude change from an implied threat to attitudinal freedom. *Journal of Personality and Social Psychology, 8,* 324–330.

Sentis, K.P., & Burnstein, E. (1979). Remembering schema-consistent information: Effects of a balance schema on recognition memory. *Journal of Personality and Social Psychology, 37,* 2200–2211.

Sereno, K.K. (1968). Ego-involvement, high source credibility, and response to a belief-discrepant communication. *Speech Monographs, 35,* 476–481.

Severy, L.J., Houlden, P., & Wilmoth, G.H. (1981). Community acceptance of innovative programs. In L. Bickman (Ed.), *Applied social psychology annual* (Vol. 2, pp. 71–95). Beverly Hills, CA: Sage.

Shaffer, D.R. (1975). Another look at the phenomenological equivalence of pre- and postmanipulation attitudes in the forced-compliance experiment. *Personality and Social Psychology Bulletin, 1,* 497–500.

Shaller, M., & Cialdini, R.B. (1990). Happiness, sadness, and helping: A motivational integration. In E.T. Higgins & R.M. Sorrentino (Eds.), *Handbook of motivation and cognition* (Vol. 2, pp. 265–296). New York: Guilford Press.

Shanteau, J.C., & Anderson, N.H. (1969). Test of a conflict model for preference judgment. *Journal of Mathematical Psychology, 6,* 312–325.

Shapiro, D., & Crider, A. (1969). Psychophysiological approaches to social psychology. In G. Lindzey & E. Aronson (Eds.), *Handbook of social psychology* (2nd ed., Vol. 3, pp. 1–49). Reading, MA: Addison-Wesley.

Shavitt, S. (1989). Operationalizing functional theories of attitude. In A.R. Pratkanis, S.J. Breckler, & A.G. Greenwald (Eds.), *Attitude structure and function* (pp. 311–338). Hillsdale, NJ: Erlbaum.

Shavitt, S. (1990). The role of attitude objects in attitude functions. *Journal of Experimental Social Psychology, 26,* 124–148.

Shavitt, S., & Brock, T.C. (1986). Self-relevant responses in commercial persuasion: Field and experimental tests. In J. Olson & K. Sentis (Eds.), *Advertising and consumer psychology* (Vol. 3, pp. 149–171). New York: Praeger.

Shavitt, S., & Fazio, R.H. (1991). Effects of attribute salience on the consistency between attitudes and behavior predictions. *Personality and Social Psychology Bulletin, 17,* 507–516.

Shaw, M.E., & Wright, J.M. (1967). *Scales for the measurement of attitudes.* New York: McGraw-Hill.

Sheatsley, P.B. (1983). Questionnaire construction and item writing. In P.H. Rossi, J.D. Wright, & A.B. Anderson (Eds.), *Handbook of survey research* (pp. 195–230). San Diego, CA: Academic Press.

Shechter, D. (1987). *Relational and integrity involvement as determinants of persuasion: The self-monitoring of attitudes.* (Doctoral dissertation, New York University, New York) *Dissertation Abstracts International, 48,* 3451B.

Shedler, J., & Manis, M. (1986). Can the availability heuristic explain vividness effects? *Journal of Personality and Social Psychology, 51,* 26–36.

Shelton, M.L., & Rogers, R.W. (1981). Fear-arousing and empathy-arousing appeals to help: The pathos of persuasion. *Journal of Applied Social Psychology, 11,* 366–378.

Shepard, R.N., Romney, A.K., & Nerlove, S. (1972). *Multidimensional scaling and applications in behavioral science* (Vols. 1 & 2). New York: Seminar Press.

Sheppard, B.H., Hartwick, J., & Warshaw, P.R. (1988). The theory of reasoned action: A meta-analysis of past research with recommendations for modifications and future research. *Journal of Consumer Research, 15,* 325–343.

Sherer, M., & Rogers, R.W. (1984). The role of vivid information in fear appeals and attitude change. *Journal of Research in Personality, 18,* 321–334.

Sherif, C.W. (1980). Social values, attitudes, and the involvement of the self. In H.E. Howe, Jr., & M.M. Page (Eds.), *Nebraska Symposium on Motivation, 1979* (Vol. 27, pp. 1–64). Lincoln: University of Nebraska Press.

Sherif, C.W., Kelly, M., Rodgers, H.L., Jr., Sarup, G., & Tittler, B.I. (1973). Personal involvement, social judgment, and action. *Journal of Personality and Social Psychology, 27,* 311–328.

Sherif, C.W., & Sherif, M. (Eds.). (1967). *Attitude, ego-involvement, and change.* New York: Wiley.

Sherif, C.W., Sherif, M., & Nebergall, R.E. (1965). *Attitude and attitude change: The social judgment-involvement approach.* Philadelphia: Saunders.

Sherif, M. (1935). A study of some social factors in perception. *Archives of Psychology, 27,* 1–60.

Sherif, M. (1936). *The psychology of social norms.* New York: Harper and Brothers.

Sherif, M., & Cantril, H. (1947). *The psychology of ego-involvements: Social attitudes and identifications.* New York: Wiley.

Sherif, M., & Hovland, C.I. (1953). Judgmental phenomena and scales of attitude measurement: Placement of items with individual choice of number of categories. *Journal of Abnormal and Social Psychology, 48,* 135–141.

Sherif, M., & Hovland, C.I. (1961). *Social judgment: Assimilation and contrast effects in communication and attitude change.* New Haven, CT: Yale University Press.

Sherif, M., & Sherif, C.W. (1967). Attitude as the individual's own categories: The social judgment-involvement approach to attitude and attitude change. In C. W. Sherif & M. Sherif (Eds.), *Attitude, ego-involvement and change* (pp. 105-139). New York: Wiley.

Sherif, M., Taub, D., & Hovland, C. I. (1958). Assimilation and contrast effects of anchoring stimuli on judgments. *Journal of Experimental Psychology, 55*, 150-155.

Sherman, S. J. (1970). Effects of choice and incentive on attitude change in a discrepant behavior situation. *Journal of Personality and Social Psychology, 15*, 245-252.

Sherman, S. J., & Fazio, R. H. (1983). Parallels between attitudes and traits as predictors of behavior. *Journal of Personality, 51*, 308-345.

Sherman, S. J., Judd, C. M., & Park, B. (1989). Social cognition. *Annual Review of Psychology, 40*, 281-326.

Sherman, S. J., Zehner, K. S., Johnson, J., & Hirt, E. R. (1983). Social explanation: The role of timing, set, and recall on subjective likelihood estimates. *Journal of Personality and Social Psychology, 44*, 1127-1143.

Sherman, S. R. (1967). Demand characteristics in an experiment on attitude change. *Sociometry, 30*, 246-261.

Shils, E. A. (1954). Authoritarianism: Right and left. In R. Christie & M. Jahoda (Eds.), *Studies in the scope and method of "The authoritarian personality"* (pp. 24-49). Glencoe, IL: Free Press.

Shils, E. A., & Janowitz, M. (1948). Cohesion and disintegration in the Wehrmacht in World War II. *Public Opinion Quarterly, 12*, 280-315.

Short, J. F., Jr., & Meier, R. F. (1981). Criminology and the study of deviance. *American Behavioral Scientist, 24*, 462-478.

Shotland, R. L., & Yankowski, L. D. (1982). The random response method: A valid and ethical indicator of the "truth" in reactive situations. *Personality and Social Psychology Bulletin, 8*, 174-179.

Shye, S. (1978). Partial order scalogram analysis. In S. Shye (Ed.), *Theory construction and data analysis in the behavioral sciences* (pp. 265-279). San Francisco: Jossey-Bass.

Sidanius, J. (1988). Political sophistication and political deviance: A structural equation examination of context theory. *Journal of Personality and Social Psychology, 55*, 37-51.

Siegel, S. (1956). *Nonparametric statistics for the behavioral sciences.* New York: McGraw-Hill.

Sigall, H., & Page, R. (1971). Current stereotypes: A little fading, a little faking. *Journal of Personality and Social Psychology, 18*, 247-255.

Simmel, G. (1955). *[Conflict].* (K. H. Wolff trans.). Glencoe, IL: Free Press. (Originally published in 1908)

Simon, H. A. (1976). *Administrative behavior* (3rd ed.). New York: Free Press.

Simons, H. W., Berkowitz, N. N., & Moyer, R. J. (1970). Similarity, credibility and attitude change: A review and a theory. *Psychological Bulletin, 73*, 1-16.

Simpson, J. A., & Borgida, E. (1991). *The effects of vividness on persuasion: The role of personal involvement.* Unpublished manuscript, Texas A & M University, College Station, TX.

Sinclair, R. C., & Mark, M. M. (1991). Mood and the endorsement of egalitarian macrojustice versus equity-based microjustice principles. *Personality and Social Psychology Bulletin, 17*, 369-375.

Singer, R. D. (1961). Verbal conditioning and generalization of prodemocratic responses. *Journal of Abnormal and Social Psychology, 63*, 43-46.

Sirota, A. D., & Schwartz, G. E. (1982). Facial muscle patterning and lateralization during elation and depression imagery. *Journal of Abnormal Psychology, 91*, 25-34.

Sivacek, J., & Crano, W. D. (1982). Vested interest as a moderator of attitude-behavior consistency. *Journal of Personality and Social Psychology, 43*, 210-221.

Sjöberg, L. (1982). Attitude-behaviour correlation, social desirability and perceived diagnostic value. *British Journal of Social Psychology, 21*, 283-292.

Skinner, B. F. (1953). *Science and human behavior.* New York: Macmillan.

Skinner, B. F. (1957). *Verbal behavior.* New York: Appleton-Century-Crofts.

Skowronski, J. J., & Carlston, D. E. (1987). Social judgment and social memory: The role of cue diagnosticity in negativity, positivity, and extremity biases. *Journal of Personality and Social Psychology, 52*, 689-699.

Skowronski, J. J., & Carlston, D. E. (1989). Negativity and extremity biases in impression formation: A review of explanations. *Psychological Bulletin, 105*, 131-142.

Sloan, L. R., & Ostrom, T. M. (1974). Amount of information and interpersonal judgment. *Journal of Personality and Social Psychology, 29*, 23-29.

Slovic, P., & Lichtenstein, S. (1971). Comparison of Bayesian and regression approaches to the study of information processing in judgment. *Organizational Behavior and Human Performance, 6*, 649-744.

Smetana, J. G., & Adler, N. E. (1980). Fishbein's Value × Expectancy Model: An examination of some assumptions. *Personality and Social Psychology Bulletin, 6*, 89-96.

Smith, A. J., & Clark, R. D., III. (1973). The relationship between attitudes and beliefs. *Journal of Personality and Social Psychology, 26*, 321-326.

Smith, B. L., Lasswell, H. D., & Casey, R. D. (1946). *Propaganda, communication, and public opinion.* Princeton, NJ: Princeton University Press.

Smith, E. E. (1961). The power of dissonance techniques to change attitudes. *Public Opinion Quarterly, 25*, 626-639.

Smith, E. R. (1984). Model of social inference processes. *Psychological Review, 91*, 392-413.

Smith, E. R. (in press). Procedural knowledge and processing strategies in social cognition. In R. S. Wyer, Jr., & T. K.

Srull (Eds.), *Handbook of social cognition* (2nd ed.). Hillsdale, NJ: Erlbaum.

Smith, G. R., & Dorfman, D. D. (1975). The effect of stimulus uncertainty on the relationship between frequency of exposure and liking. *Journal of Personality and Social Psychology, 31*, 150–155.

Smith, M. B. (1947). The personal setting of public opinions: A study of attitudes toward Russia. *Public Opinion Quarterly, 11*, 507–523.

Smith, M. B. (1973). Political attitudes. In J. Knutson (Ed.), *Handbook of political psychology* (pp. 57–82). San Francisco: Jossey-Bass.

Smith, M. B., Bruner, J.S., & White, R. W. (1956). *Opinions and personality*. New York: Wiley.

Smith, M.J. (1984). Contingency rules theory, context, and compliance behaviors. *Human Communication Research, 10*, 489–512.

Smith, S. M., & Shaffer, D. R. (1990, August). *Good moods and the inhibition of systematic processing: The impact of issue relevance*. Paper presented at the meeting of the American Psychological Association, Boston.

Smith, S. S., & Jamieson, B. D. (1972). Effects of attitude and ego involvement on the learning and retention of controversial material. *Journal of Personality and Social Psychology, 22*, 303–310.

Smith, T. W. (1982). *Conditional order effects* (General Social Survey Technical Report No. 33). Chicago: National Opinion Research Center.

Smith, T. W. (1984). Nonattitudes: A review and evaluation. In C. F. Turner & E. Martin (Eds.), *Surveying subjective phenomena* (Vol. 2, pp. 215–255). New York: Russell Sage Foundation.

Smith, T. W. (1987). That which we call welfare by any other name would smell sweeter: An analysis of the impact of question wording on response patterns. *Public Opinion Quarterly, 51*, 75–83.

Sniderman, P. M. (1975). *Personality and democratic politics*. Berkeley: University of California Press.

Sniderman, P. M., & Tetlock, P. E. (1986a). Reflections on American racism. *Journal of Social Issues, 42*(2), 173–187.

Sniderman, P. M., & Tetlock, P. E. (1986b). Symbolic racism: Problems of motive attribution in political analysis. *Journal of Social Issues, 42*(2), 129–150.

Snyder, A. F., Mischel, W., & Lott, B. E. (1960). Value, information, and conformity behavior. *Journal of Personality, 28*, 333–341.

Snyder, M. (1974). Self-monitoring of expressive behavior. *Journal of Personality and Social Psychology, 30*, 526–537.

Snyder, M. (1982). When believing means doing: Creating links between attitudes and behavior. In M. P. Zanna, E. T. Higgins, & C. P. Herman (Eds.), *Consistency in social behavior: The Ontario Symposium* (Vol. 2, pp. 105–130). Hillsdale, NJ: Erlbaum.

Snyder, M. (1987). *Public appearances/private realities: The psychology of self-monitoring*. New York: Freeman.

Snyder, M., & DeBono, K. G. (1985). Appeals to images and claims about quality: Understanding the psychology of advertising. *Journal of Personality and Social Psychology, 49*, 586–597.

Snyder, M., & DeBono, K. G. (1987). A functional approach to attitudes and persuasion. In M. P. Zanna, J. M. Olson, & C. P. Herman (Eds.), *Social influence: The Ontario Symposium* (Vol. 5, pp. 107–125). Hillsdale, NJ: Erlbaum.

Snyder, M., & DeBono, K. G. (1989). Understanding the functions of attitudes: Lessons for personality and social behavior. In A. R. Pratkanis, S. J. Breckler, & A. G. Greenwald (Eds.), *Attitude structure and function* (pp. 339–359). Hillsdale, NJ: Erlbaum.

Snyder, M., & Ebbesen, E. B. (1972). Dissonance awareness: A test of dissonance theory versus self-perception theory. *Journal of Experimental Social Psychology, 8*, 502–517.

Snyder, M., & Ickes, W. (1985). Personality and social behavior. In G. Lindzey & E. Aronson (Eds.), *Handbook of social psychology* (3rd ed., Vol. 2, pp. 883–947). New York: Random House.

Snyder, M., & Kendzierski, D. (1982). Acting on one's attitudes: Procedures for linking attitudes and behavior. *Journal of Experimental Social Psychology, 18*, 165–183.

Snyder, M., & Rothbart, M. (1971). Communicator attractiveness and opinion change. *Canadian Journal of Behavioural Science, 3*, 377–387.

Snyder, M., & Swann, W. B., Jr. (1976). When actions reflect attitudes: The politics of impression management. *Journal of Personality and Social Psychology, 34*, 1034–1042.

Snyder, M., & Wicklund, R. A. (1976). Prior exercise of freedom and reactance. *Journal of Experimental Social Psychology, 12*, 120–130.

Sorrentino, R. M., Bobocel, D. R., Gitta, M. Z., Olson, J. M., & Hewitt, E. C. (1988). Uncertainty orientation and persuasion: Individual differences in the effects of personal relevance on social judgments. *Journal of Personality and Social Psychology, 55*, 357–371.

Sorrentino, R. M., & Hancock, R. D. (1987). Information and affective value: A case for the study of individual differences and social influence. In M. P. Zanna, J. M. Olson, & C. P. Herman (Eds.), *Social influence: The Ontario Symposium* (Vol. 5, pp. 247–268). Hillsdale, NJ: Erlbaum.

Sorrentino, R. M., & Higgins, E. T. (Eds.). (1986). *Handbook of motivation and cognition: Foundations of social behavior*. New York: Guilford Press.

Sorrentino, R. M., & Short, J. C. (1986). Uncertainty orientation, motivation, and cognition. In R. M. Sorrentino & E. T. Higgins (Eds.), *Handbook of motivation and cognition: Foundations of social behavior* (pp. 379–403). New York: Guilford Press.

Sparks, P., Hedderley, D., & Shepherd, R. (1991). Expectancy-value models of attitudes: A note on the relationship between theory and methodology. *European Journal of Social Psychology, 21,* 261–271.

Spence, K. W. (1956). *Behavior theory and conditioning.* New Haven, CT: Yale University Press.

Spence, J. T., Helmreich, R., & Stapp, J. (1973). A short version of the Attitudes toward Women Scale (AWS). *Bulletin of the Psychonomic Society, 2,* 219–220.

Spencer, H. (1862/1895). *First principles.* New York: Appleton. (Preface dated 1862)

Spielberger, C. D. (1962). The role of awareness in verbal conditioning. *Journal of Personality* (Supplement), *30,* 73–101.

Spielberger, C. D., & DeNike, L. D. (1966). Descriptive behaviorism versus cognitive theory in verbal operant conditioning. *Psychological Review, 73,* 306–326.

Spielberger, C. D., & Levin, S. M. (1962). What is learned in verbal conditioning? *Journal of Verbal Learning and Verbal Behavior, 1,* 125–132.

Spiro, R. J., & Sherif, C. W. (1975). Consistency and relativity in selective recall with differing ego-involvement. *British Journal of Social and Clinical Psychology, 14,* 351–361.

Srull, T. K., & Wyer, R. S., Jr. (1980). Category accessibility and social perception: Some implications for the study of person memory and interpersonal judgments. *Journal of Personality and Social Psychology, 38,* 841–856.

Srull, T. K., & Wyer, R. S., Jr. (1986). The role of chronic and temporary goals in social information processing. In R. M. Sorrentino & E. T. Higgins (Eds.), *Motivation and cognition: Foundations of social behavior* (pp. 503–549). New York: Guilford Press.

Staats, A. W. (1968). Social behaviorism and human motivation: Principles of the attitude-reinforcer-discriminative system. In A. G. Greenwald, T. C. Brock, & T. M. Ostrom (Eds.), *Psychological foundations of attitudes* (pp. 33–66). San Diego, CA: Academic Press.

Staats, A. W. (1969). Experimental demand characteristics and the classical conditioning of attitudes. *Journal of Personality and Social Psychology, 11,* 187–192.

Staats, A. W. (1975). *Social behaviorism.* Homewood, IL: Dorsey Press.

Staats, A. W. (1983). Paradigmatic behaviorism: Unified theory for social-personality psychology. In L. Berkowitz (Ed.), *Advances in experimental social psychology* (Vol. 16, pp. 125–179). San Diego, CA: Academic Press.

Staats, A. W., Gross, M. C., Guay, P. F., & Carlson, C. C. (1973). Personality and social systems and attitude-reinforcer-discriminative theory: Interest (attitude) formation, function, and measurement. *Journal of Personality and Social Psychology, 26,* 251–261.

Staats, A. W., Minke, K. A., Martin, C. H., & Higa, W. R. (1972). Deprivation-satiation and strength of attitude conditioning: A test of attitude-reinforcer-discriminative theory. *Journal of Personality and Social Psychology, 24,* 178–185.

Staats, A. W., & Staats, C. K. (1958). Attitudes established by classical conditioning. *Journal of Abnormal and Social Psychology, 57,* 37–40.

Staats, A. W., Staats, C. K., & Crawford, H. L. (1962). First-order conditioning of meaning and the parallel conditioning of a GSR. *Journal of General Psychology, 67,* 159–167.

Staats, A. W., & Warren, D. R. (1974). Motivation and three-function learning: Food deprivation and approach-avoidance to food words. *Journal of Experimental Psychology, 103,* 1191–1199.

Staats, C. K., & Staats, A. W. (1957). Meaning established by classical conditioning. *Journal of Experimental Psychology, 54,* 74–80.

Stachnik, T. J. (1980). Priorities for psychology in medical education and health care delivery. *American Psychologist, 35,* 8–15.

Stahelski, A. J., Frost, D. E., & Patch, M. E. (1989). Uses of socially dependent bases of power: French and Raven's theory applied to workgroup leadership. *Journal of Applied Social Psychology, 19,* 283–297.

Stalling, R. B. (1970). Personality similarity and evaluative meaning as conditioners of attraction. *Journal of Personality and Social Psychology, 14,* 77–82.

Stang, D. J. (1974a). Intuition as artifact in mere exposure studies. *Journal of Personality and Social Psychology, 30,* 647–653.

Stang, D. J. (1974b). Methodological factors in mere exposure research. *Psychological Bulletin, 81,* 1014–1025.

Stang, D. J. (1975). Effects of "mere exposure" on learning and affect. *Journal of Personality and Social Psychology, 31,* 7–12.

Stangor, C., & McMillan, D. (1992). Memory for expectancy-congruent and expectancy-incongruent social information: A review of the social and social developmental literatures. *Psychological Bulletin, 111,* 42–61.

Stanley, J. C., & Klausmeier, H. J. (1957). Opinion constancy after formal role playing. *Journal of Social Psychology, 46,* 11–18.

Staw, B. M. (1974). Attitudinal and behavioral consequences of changing a major organizational reward: A natural field experiment. *Journal of Personality and Social Psychology, 29,* 742–752.

Steele, C. M. (1988). The psychology of self-affirmation: Sustaining the integrity of the self. In L. Berkowitz (Ed.), *Advances in experimental social psychology* (Vol. 21, pp. 261–302). San Diego, CA: Academic Press.

Steele, C. M., & Liu, T. J. (1983). Dissonance processes as self-affirmation. *Journal of Personality and Social Psychology*, *45*, 5–19.

Steele, C.M., Southwick, L.L., & Critchlow, B. (1981). Dissonance and alcohol: Drinking your troubles away. *Journal of Personality and Social Psychology*, *41*, 831–846.

Steffen, V.J. (1986). The effects of direct experience on attitude, subjective norm, intention, and behavior: Performance of the testicle self exam for cancer. (Doctoral dissertation, Purdue University, 1985). *Dissertation Abstracts International*, *47*, 434B.

Steffen, V.J. (1990). Men's motivation to perform the testicle self-exam: Effects of prior knowledge and an educational brochure. *Journal of Applied Social Psychology*, *20*, 681–702.

Sternberg, L. (1990). *From velleity to specific plans: How planning affects attitude, intention, behavior relations.* Unpublished doctoral dissertation, Purdue University.

Sternthal, B., Dholakia, R., & Leavitt, C. (1978). The persuasive effect of source credibility: Tests of cognitive response. *Journal of Consumer Research*, *4*, 252–260.

Sternthal, B., Phillips, L.W., & Dholakia, R. (1978). The persuasive effect of source credibility: A situational analysis. *Public Opinion Quarterly*, *42*, 285–314.

Stevens, S.S. (1946). On the theory of scales of measurement. *Science*, *103*, 677–680.

Stevens, S.S. (1951). Mathematics, measurement, and psychophysics. In S.S. Stevens (Ed.), *Handbook of experimental psychology* (pp. 1–49). New York: Wiley.

Stevens, S.S. (1956). The direct estimation of sensory magnitudes—loudness. *American Journal of Psychology*, *69*, 1–25.

Stevens, S.S. (1966). A metric for the social consensus. *Science*, *151*, 530–541.

Stevens, S.S. (1972). *Psychophysics and social scaling.* Morristown, NJ: General Learning Press.

Stevens, S.S., & Galanter, E.H. (1957). Ratio scales and category scales for a dozen perceptual continua. *Journal of Experimental Psychology*, *54*, 377–411.

Stevenson, M.K., Busemeyer, J.R., & Naylor, J.C. (1990). Judgment and decision-making theory. In M.D. Dunnette & L.M. Hough (Eds.), *Handbook of industrial and organizational psychology* (2nd ed., Vol. 1, pp. 283–374). Palo Alto, CA: Consulting Psychologists Press.

Stiff, J.B. (1986). Cognitive processing of persuasive message cues: A meta-analytic review of the effects of supporting information on attitudes. *Communication Monographs*, *53*, 75–89.

Stiff, J.B., & Boster, F.J. (1987). Cognitive processing: Additional thoughts and a reply to Petty, Kasmer, Haugtvedt, and Cacioppo. *Communication Monographs*, *54*, 250–256.

Stoneman, Z., & Brody, G.H. (1981). Peers as mediators of television food advertisements aimed at children. *Developmental Psychology*, *17*, 853–858.

Stoner, J.A.F. (1961). *A comparison of individual and group decisions involving risk.* Unpublished master's thesis, Massachusetts Institute of Technology, Cambridge, MA.

Stoner, J.A.F. (1968). Risky and cautious shifts in group decisions: The influence of widely held values. *Journal of Experimental Social Psychology*, *4*, 442–459.

Stotland, E., Katz, D., & Patchen, M. (1959). The reduction of prejudice through the arousal of self-insight. *Journal of Personality*, *27*, 507–531.

Stouffer, S.A., Guttman, L., Suchman, E.A., Lazarsfeld, P.F., Star, S.A., & Clausen, J.A. (1950). *Measurement and prediction* (Vol. IV). Princeton, NJ: Princeton University Press.

Strack, F., & Martin, L.L. (1987). Thinking, judging, and communicating: A process account of context effects in attitude surveys. In H.-J. Hippler, N. Schwarz, & S. Sudman (Eds.), *Social information processing and survey methodology* (pp. 123–148). New York: Springer-Verlag.

Stroebe, W., & Diehl, M. (1981). Conformity and counter-attitudinal behavior: The effect of social support on attitude change. *Journal of Personality and Social Psychology*, *41*, 876–889.

Stroebe, W., & Diehl, M. (1988). When social support fails: Supporter characteristics in compliance-induced attitude change. *Personality and Social Psychology Bulletin*, *14*, 136–144.

Struckman-Johnson, C.J., Gilliland, R.C., Struckman-Johnson, D.L., & North, T.C. (1990). The effects of fear of AIDS and gender on responses to fear-arousing condom advertisements. *Journal of Applied Social Psychology*, *20*, 1396–1410.

Stults, D.M., Messé, L.A., & Kerr, N.L. (1984). Belief discrepant behavior and the bogus pipeline: Impression management or arousal attribution. *Journal of Experimental Social Psychology*, *20*, 47–54.

Suchman, E.A. (1950). The intensity component in attitude and opinion research. In S.A. Stouffer, L. Guttman, E.A. Suchman, P.F. Lazarsfeld, S.A. Star, & J.A. Clausen, *Measurement and prediction* (pp. 213–276). Princeton, NJ: Princeton University Press.

Sudman, S., & Bradburn, N.M. (1974). *Response effects in surveys: A review and synthesis.* Chicago: Aldine.

Sudman, S., & Bradburn, N.M. (1982). *Asking questions: A practical guide to questionnaire design.* San Francisco: Jossey-Bass.

Suedfeld, P., & Borrie, R.A. (1978). Sensory deprivation, attitude change, and defense against persuasion. *Canadian Journal of Behavioural Science*, *10*, 16–27.

Suedfeld, P., Epstein, Y.M., Buchanan, E., & Landon, P.B. (1971). Effect of set on the "effects of mere exposure."

Journal of Personality and Social Psychology, *17*, 121–123.

Suedfeld, P., & Ramirez, C. (1977). War, peace, and integrative complexity: UN speeches on the Middle East problem, 1947–1976. *Journal of Conflict Resolution*, *21*, 427–442.

Suedfeld, P., & Rank, A. D. (1976). Revolutionary leaders: Long-term success as a function of changes in conceptual complexity. *Journal of Personality and Social Psychology*, *34*, 169–178.

Suedfeld, P., & Tetlock, P. E. (1977). Integrative complexity of communications in international crises. *Journal of Conflict Resolution*, *21*, 169–184.

Sujan, M. (1985). Consumer knowledge: Effects on evaluation strategies mediating consumer judgments. *Journal of Consumer Research*, *12*, 31–46.

Sullivan, J. L., Marcus, G. E., Feldman, S., & Piereson, J. E. (1981). The sources of political tolerance: A multivariate analysis. *Amercian Political Science Review*, *75*, 92–106.

Sullivan, M. J. L., & Conway, M. (1989). Negative affect leads to low-effort cognition: Attributional processing for observed social behavior. *Social Cognition*, *7*, 315–337.

Suppes, P., & Zinnes, J. L. (1963). Basic measurement theory. In R. D. Luce, R. R. Bush, & E. Galanter (Eds.), *Handbook of mathematical psychology* (Vol. 1, pp. 1–76). New York: Wiley.

Sutton, S. R. (1982). Fear-arousing communications: A critical examination of theory and research. In J. R. Eiser (Ed.), *Social psychology and behavioral medicine* (pp. 303–337). Chichester, England: Wiley.

Sutton, S. R., & Eiser, J. R. (1984). The effect of fear-arousing communications on cigarette smoking: An expectancy-value approach. *Journal of Behavioral Medicine*, *7*, 13–33.

Sutton, S. R., & Hallett, R. (1989). Understanding seat-belt intentions and behavior: A decision-making approach. *Journal of Applied Social Psychology*, *19*, 1310–1325.

Sutton, S. R., Marsh, A., & Matheson, J. (1990). Microanalysis of smokers' beliefs about the consequences of quitting: Results from a large population sample. *Journal of Applied Social Psychology*, *20*, 1847–1862.

Swann, W. B., Jr. (1990). To be adored or to be known? The interplay of self-enhancement and self-verification. In E. T. Higgins & R. M. Sorrentino (Eds.), *Handbook of motivation and cognition: Foundations of social behavior* (Vol. 2, pp. 408–448). New York: Guilford Press.

Swasy, J. L., & Munch, J. M. (1985). Examining the target of receiver elaborations: Rhetorical question effects on source processing and persuasion. *Journal of Consumer Research*, *11*, 877–886.

Sweeney, P. D., & Gruber, K. L. (1984). Selective exposure: Voter information preferences and the Watergate affair. *Journal of Personality and Social Psychology*, *46*, 1208–1221.

Sypher, H. E., Witt, D. E., & Sypher, B. D. (1986). Interpersonal cognitive differentiation measures as predictors of written communication ability. *Communication Monographs*, *53*, 376–382.

Szybillo, G. J., & Heslin, R. (1973). Resistance to persuasion: Inoculation theory in a marketing context. *Journal of Marketing Research*, *10*, 396–403.

Taffel, C. (1955). Anxiety and the conditioning of verbal behavior. *Journal of Abnormal and Social Psychology*, *51*, 496–501.

Taft, R. (1954). Selective recall and memory distortion of favorable and unfavorable material. *Journal of Abnormal and Social Psychology*, *49*, 23–28.

Tajfel, H. (1981). *Human groups and social categories: Studies in social psychology*. Cambridge, England: Cambridge University Press.

Tajfel, H., & Turner, J. C. (1979). An integrative theory of intergroup conflict. In W. G. Austin & S. Worchel (Eds.), *The social psychology of intergroup relations* (pp. 33–47). Monterey, CA: Brooks/Cole.

Tanaka, J. S., Panter, A., Winborne, W. C., & Huba, G. J. (1990). Theory testing in personality and social psychology with structural equation models: A primer in 20 questions. In C. Hendrick & M. S. Clark (Eds.), *Review of personality and social psychology* (Vol. 11, pp. 217–242). Newbury Park, CA: Sage.

Tanford, S., & Penrod, S. (1984). Social influence model: A formal integration of research on majority and minority influence processes. *Psychological Bulletin*, *95*, 189–225.

Tannenbaum, P. H. (1966). Mediated generalization of attitude change via the principle of congruity. *Journal of Personality and Social Psychology*, *3*, 493–499.

Tannenbaum, P. H. (1967). The congruity principle revisited: Studies in the reduction, induction, and generalization of persuasion. In L. Berkowitz (Ed.), *Advances in experimental social psychology* (Vol. 3, pp. 271–320). San Diego, CA: Academic Press.

Tannenbaum, P. H. (1968). The congruity principle: Retrospective reflections and recent research, In R. P. Abelson, E. Aronson, W. J. McGuire, T. M. Newcomb, M. J. Rosenberg, & P. H. Tannenbaum (Eds.), *Theories of cognitive consistency: A sourcebook* (pp. 52–72). Chicago: Rand McNally.

Tannenbaum, P. H., & Gengel, R. W. (1966). Generalization of attitude change through congruity principle relationships. *Journal of Personality and Social Psychology*, *3*, 299–304.

Tannenbaum, P. H., Macaulay, J. R., & Norris, E. L. (1966). Principle of congruity and reduction of persuasion. *Journal of Personality and Social Psychology*, *3*, 233–238.

Tashakkori, A., & Insko, C. A. (1979). Interpersonal attraction and the polarity of similar attitudes: A test of three balance models. *Journal of Personality and Social Psychology*, *37*, 2262–2277.

Tashakkori, A., & Insko, C. A. (1981). Interpersonal attraction and person perception: Two tests of three balance models. *Journal of Experimental Social Psychology*, *17*, 266-285.

Taylor, I. A., (1960). Similarities in the structure of extreme social attitudes. *Psychological Monographs*, *74*(2, Whole No. 489).

Taylor, J. B. (1961). What do attitude scales measure: The problem of social desirability. *Journal of Abnormal and Social Psychology*, *62*, 386-390.

Taylor, S. E. (1975). On inferring one's attitudes from one's behavior: Some delimiting conditions. *Journal of Personality and Social Psychology*, *31*, 126-131.

Taylor, S. E., & Crocker, J. (1981). Schematic bases of social information processing. In E. T. Higgins, C. P. Herman, & M. P. Zanna (Eds.), *Social cognition: The Ontario Symposium* (Vol. 1, pp. 89-134). Hillsdale, NJ: Erlbaum.

Taylor, S. E., & Fiske, S. T. (1978). Salience, attention, and attribution: Top of the head phenomena. In L. Berkowitz (Ed.), *Advances in experimental social psychology* (Vol. 11, pp. 249-288). San Diego, CA: Academic Press.

Taylor, S. E., & Fiske, S. T. (1981). Getting inside the head: Methodologies for process analysis in attribution and social cognition. In J. H. Harvey, W. Ickes, & R. F. Kidd (Eds.), *New directions in attribution research* (Vol. 3, pp. 459-524). Hillsdale, NJ: Erlbaum.

Taylor, S. E., & Lobel, M. (1989). Social comparison activity under threat: Downward evaluation and upward contacts. *Psychological Review*, *96*, 569-575.

Taylor, S. E., & Thompson, S. C. (1982). Stalking the elusive "vividness" effect. *Psychological Review*, *89*, 155-181.

Tedeschi, J. T., Rivera, A., Dixit, N., Taylor, E., & Nesler, M. (1988). *Impression managment versus cognitive dissonance: Three studies using the bogus pipeline*. Unpublished manuscript, State University of New York at Albany.

Tedeschi, J. T., & Rosenfeld, P. (1981). Impression management theory and the forced compliance situation. In J. T. Tedeschi (Ed.), *Impression management theory and social psychological research* (pp. 147-177). San Diego, CA: Academic Press.

Tedeschi, J. T., Schlenker, B. R., & Bonoma, T. V. (1971). Cognitive dissonance: Private ratiocination or public spectacle? *American Psychologist*, *26*, 685-695.

Tedeschi, J. T., Schlenker, B. R., & Bonoma, T. V. (1973). *Conflict, power and games*. Chicago: Aldine.

Temkin, B. (1987). Attitude change, dogmatism, and ascription of responsibility: The case of the State Commission of Inquiry on the massacres at Sabra and Shatila. *Political Psychology*, *8*, 21-33.

Teske, R. H. C., Jr., & Hazlett, M. H. (1985). A scale for the measurement of attitudes toward handgun control. *Journal of Criminal Justice*, *13*, 373-379.

Tesser, A. (1969). Trait similarity and trait evaluation as correlates of attraction. *Psychonomic Science*, *15*, 319-320.

Tesser, A. (1978). Self-generated attitude change. In L. Berkowitz (Ed.), *Advances in experimental social psychology* (Vol. 11, pp. 289-338). San Diego, CA: Academic Press.

Tesser, A., Campbell, J., & Mickler, S. (1983). The role of social pressure, attention to the stimulus, and self-doubt in conformity. *European Journal of Social Psychology*, *13*, 217-233.

Tesser, A., & Conlee, M. C. (1975). Some effects of time and thought on attitude polarization. *Journal of Personality and Social Psychology*, *31*, 262-270.

Tesser, A., & Leone, C. (1977). Cognitive schemas and thought as determinants of attitude change. *Journal of Experimental Social Psychology*, *13*, 340-356.

Tesser, A., & Shaffer, D. R. (1990). Attitudes and attitude change. *Annual Review of Psychology*, *41*, 479-523.

Tetlock, P. E. (1981a). Personality and isolationism: Content analysis of senatorial speeches. *Journal of Personality and Social Psychology*, *41*, 737-743.

Tetlock, P. E. (1981b). Pre- to postelection shifts in presidential rhetoric: Impression management or cognitive adjustment? *Journal of Personality and Social Psychology*, *41*, 207-212.

Tetlock, P. E. (1983a). Accountability and complexity of thought. *Journal of Personality and Social Psychology*, *45*, 74-83.

Tetlock, P. E. (1983b). Cognitive style and political ideology. *Journal of Personality and Social Psychology*, *45*, 118-126.

Tetlock, P. E. (1984). Cognitive style and political belief systems in the British House of Commons. *Journal of Personality and Social Psychology*, *46*, 365-375.

Tetlock, P. E. (1985). Accountability: The neglected social context of judgment and choice. In L. L. Cummings & B. M. Staw (Eds.), *Research in organizational behavior* (Vol. 7, pp. 297-332). Greenwich, CT: JAI Press.

Tetlock, P. E. (1986). A value pluralism model of ideological reasoning. *Journal of Personality and Social Psychology*, *50*, 819-827.

Tetlock, P. E. (1989). Structure and function in political belief systems. In A. R. Pratkanis, S. J. Breckler, & A. G. Greenwald (Eds.), *Attitude structure and function* (pp. 129-151). Hillsdale, NJ: Erlbaum.

Tetlock, P. E., Bernzweig, J., & Gallant, J. L. (1985). Supreme Court decision making: Cognitive style as a predictor of ideological consistency of voting. *Journal of Personality and Social Psychology*, *48*, 1227-1239.

Tetlock, P. E., Hannum, K. A., & Micheletti, P. M. (1984). Stability and change in the complexity of senatorial debate: Testing the cognitive versus rhetorical style hypotheses. *Journal of Personality and Social Psychology*, *46*, 979-990.

Tetlock, P. E., & Kim, J. I. (1987). Accountability and judgment processes in a personality prediction task. *Journal of Personality and Social Psychology*, *52*, 700-709.

758

Tetlock, P. E., & Manstead, A. S. R. (1985). Impression management versus intrapsychic explanations in social psychology: A useful dichotomy? *Psychological Review*, *92*, 59-77.

Tetlock, P. E., Skitka, L., & Boettger, R. (1989). Social and cognitive strategies for coping with accountability: Conformity, complexity, and bolstering. *Journal of Personality and Social Psychology*, *57*, 632-640.

Thibaut, J. W., & Kelley, H. H. (1959). *The social psychology of groups*. New York: Wiley.

Thibodeau, R., Aronson, E., Dickerson, C., & Miller, D. (1990). *Hypocrisy & the self-concept: Arousing dissonance without aversive consequences*. Unpublished manuscript, University of California at Santa Cruz.

Thistlethwaite, D. L. (1950). Attitude and structure as factors in the distortion of reasoning. *Journal of Abnormal and Social Psychology*, *45*, 442-458.

Thistlethwaite, D. L., de Haan, H., & Kamenetzky, J. (1955). The effects of "directive" and "nondirective" communication procedures on attitudes. *Journal of Abnormal and Social Psychology*, *51*, 107-113.

Thistlethwaite, D. L., & Kamenetzky, J. (1955). Attitude change through refutation and elaboration of audience counterarguments. *Journal of Abnormal and Social Psychology*, *51*, 3-12.

Thomas, E. J., Webb, S., & Tweedie, J. (1961). Effects of familiarity with a controversial issue on acceptance of successive persuasive communications. *Journal of Abnormal and Social Psychology*, *63*, 656-659.

Thomas, K. (1975). The relationship between attitudes and beliefs: Comments on Smith and Clark's classification of belief type and predictive value. *Journal of Personality and Social Psychology*, *32*, 748-751.

Thomas, K. (1976). Conflict and conflict management. In M. D. Dunnette (Ed.), *Handbook of industrial and organizational psychology* (pp. 889-935). Chicago: Rand McNally.

Thorndike, E. L. (1898). Animal intelligence: An experimental study of the associative processes in animals. *Psychological Monographs*, *2*(4, Whole No. 8).

Thorndike, E. L. (1932). *The fundamentals of learning*. New York: Teachers College.

Thorndike, E. L., & Rock, R. T., Jr. (1934). Learning without awareness of what is being learned or intent to learn it. *Journal of Experimental Psychology*, *17*, 1-19.

Thurstone, L. L. (1927a). A law of comparative judgment. *Psychological Review*, *34*, 273-286.

Thurstone, L. L. (1927b). Psychophysical analysis. *American Journal of Psychology*, *38*, 368-389.

Thurstone, L. L. (1928). Attitudes can be measured. *American Journal of Sociology*, *33*, 529-554.

Thurstone, L. L. (1930). A scale for measuring attitude toward the movies. *Journal of Educational Research*, *22*, 89-94.

Thurstone, L. L., & Chave, E. J. (1929). *The measurement of attitude*. Chicago: University of Chicago Press.

Tiffany, S. T. (1990). A cognitive model of drug urges and drug-use behavior: The role of automatic and nonautomatic processes. *Psychological Review*, *97*, 147-168.

Titchener, E. B. (1910). *A text-book of psychology* (rev. ed.). New York: Macmillan.

Tittle, C. R., & Hill, R. J. (1967). Attitude measurement and prediction of behavior: An evaluation of conditions and measurement techniques. *Sociometry*, *30*, 199-213.

Tolman, E. C. (1932). *Purposive behavior in animals and men*. New York: Appleton-Century-Crofts.

Tolman, E. C. (1958). *Behavior and psychological man: Essays in motivation and learning*. Berkeley: University of California Press.

Tomkins, S. (1981). The quest for primary motives: Biography and autobiography of an idea. *Journal of Personality and Social Psychology*, *41*, 306-329.

Toneatto, T., & Binik, Y. (1987). The role of intentions, social norms, and attitudes in the performance of dental flossing: A test of the theory of reasoned action. *Journal of Applied Social Psychology*, *17*, 593-603.

Torgerson, W. S. (1958). *Theory and methods of scaling*. New York: Wiley.

Tourangeau, R., & Rasinski, K. A. (1988). Cognitive processes underlying context effects in attitude measurement. *Psychological Bulletin*, *103*, 299-314.

Tourangeau, R., Rasinski, K. A., & D'Andrade, R. (1991). Attitude structure and belief accessibility. *Journal of Experimental Social Psychology*, *27*, 48-75.

Townsend, J. T., & Ashby, F. G. (1984). Measurement scales and statistics: The misconception misconceived. *Psychological Bulletin*, *96*, 394-401.

Triandis, H. C. (1964). Exploratory factor analyses of the behavioral component of social attitudes. *Journal of Abnormal and Social Psychology*, *68*, 420-430.

Triandis, H. C. (1971). *Attitude and attitude change*. New York: Wiley.

Triandis, H. C. (1977). *Interpersonal behavior*. Monterey, CA: Brooks/Cole.

Triandis, H. C. (1980). Values, attitudes, and interpersonal behavior. In H. E. Howe, Jr. & M. M. Page (Eds.), *Nebraska Symposium on Motivation, 1979* (Vol. 27, pp. 195-259). Lincoln: University of Nebraska Press.

Triandis, H. C., & Triandis, L. M. (1960). Race, social class, religion, and nationality as determinants of social distance. *Journal of Abnormal and Social Psychology*, *61*, 110-118.

Triandis, H. C., & Triandis, L. M. (1965). Some studies of social distance. In I. D. Steiner & M. Fishbein (Eds.), *Current studies in social psychology* (pp. 207-217). New York: Holt, Rinehart & Winston.

Tucker, D. M. (1981). Lateral brain function, emotion, and conceptualization. *Psychological Bulletin*, *89*, 19-46.

Tuddenham, R.D., & McBride, P.D. (1959). The yielding experiment from the subject's point of view. *Journal of Personality, 27,* 259-271.

Tulving, E., & Pearlstone, Z. (1966). Availability versus accessibility of information in memory for words. *Journal of Verbal Learning and Verbal Behavior, 5,* 381-391.

Turner, C.F., & Kraus, E. (1978). Fallible indicators of the subjective state of the nation. *American Psychologist, 33,* 456-470.

Turner, E.A., & Wright, J.C. (1965). Effects of severity of threat and perceived availability on the attractiveness of objects. *Journal of Personality and Social Psychology, 2,* 128-132.

Turner, J.C. (1987). *Rediscovering the social group: A self-categorization theory.* Oxford, England: Blackwell.

Tversky, A. (1972). Elimination by aspects: A theory of choice. *Psychological Review, 79,* 281-299.

Tversky, A., & Kahneman, D. (1974). Judgment under uncertainty: Heuristics and biases. *Science, 185,* 1124-1131.

Tversky, A., & Sattath, S. (1979). Preference trees. *Psychological Review, 86,* 542-573.

Tybout, A.M., & Scott, C.A. (1983). Availability of well-defined internal knowledge and the attitude formation process: Information aggregation versus self-perception. *Journal of Personality and Social Psychology, 44,* 474-491.

Uleman, J.S. (1971). Awareness and motivation in generalized verbal conditioning. *Journal of Experimental Research in Personality, 5,* 257-267.

Uleman, J.S., & Bargh, J.A. (Eds.). (1989). *Unintended thought.* New York: Guilford Press.

Underwood, B.J. (1957). Interference and forgetting. *Psychological Review, 64,* 49-59.

Underwood, B.J., & Freund, J.S. (1968). Effect of temporal separation of two tasks on proactive inhibition. *Journal of Experimental Psychology, 78,* 50-54.

Upshaw, H.S. (1962). Own attitude as an anchor in equal-appearing intervals. *Journal of Abnormal and Social Psychology, 64,* 85-96.

Upshaw, H.S. (1965). The effects of variable perspectives on judgments of opinion statements for Thurstone scales: Equal-appearing intervals. *Journal of Personality and Social Psychology, 2,* 60-69.

Upshaw, H.S. (1969). The personal reference scale: An approach to social judgment. In L. Berkowitz (Ed.), *Advances in experimental social psychology* (Vol. 4, pp. 315-371). San Diego, CA: Academic Press.

Upshaw, H.S. (1978). Social influence on attitudes and on anchoring of congeneric attitude scales. *Journal of Experimental Social Psychology, 14,* 327-339.

Upshaw, H.S., & Ostrom, T.M. (1984). Psychological perspective in attitude research. In J.R. Eiser (Ed.), *Attitudinal judgment* (pp. 23-41). New York: Springer-Verlag.

Vallacher, R.R., & Wegner, D.M. (1985). *A theory of action identification.* Hillsdale, NJ: Erlbaum.

Vallacher, R.R., & Wegner, D.M. (1987). What do people think they're doing? Action identification and human behavior. *Psychological Review, 94,* 3-15.

Vallone, R.P., Ross, L., & Lepper, M.R. (1985). The hostile media phenomenon: Biased perception and perceptions of media bias in coverage of the Beirut massacre. *Journal of Personality and Social Psychology, 49,* 577-585.

Vanbeselaere, N. (1983). Mere exposure: A search for an explanation. In W. Doise & S. Moscovici (Eds.), *Current issues in European social psychology* (Vol. 1, pp. 239-278). Cambridge, England: Cambridge University Press.

van den Putte, B. (1991). *20 years of the theory of reasoned action of Fishbein and Ajzen: A meta-analysis.* Unpublished manuscript, University of Amsterdam, The Netherlands.

van den Putte, B., Hoogstraten, J., Meertens, R. (1991). *A comparison of behavioral alternative models in the context of the theory of reasoned action.* Unpublished manuscript, University of Amsterdam, The Netherlands.

van der Pligt, J., & Eiser, J.R. (1984). Dimensional salience, judgment, and attitudes. In J.R. Eiser (Ed.), *Attitudinal judgment* (pp. 161-177). New York: Springer-Verlag.

van Knippenberg, A., & Ellemers, N. (1990). Social identity and intergroup differentiation processes. In W. Stroebe & M. Hewstone (Eds.), *European review of social psychology* (Vol. 1, pp. 137-169). Chichester, England: Wiley.

van Knippenberg, D., de Vries, N., & van Knippenberg, A. (1990). Group status, group size and attitude polarization. *European Journal of Social Psychology, 20,* 253-257.

Vannoy, J.S. (1965). Generality of cognitive complexity-simplicity as a personality construct. *Journal of Personality and Social Psychology, 2,* 385-396.

Vaughn, G.M., & Mangan, G.L. (1963). Conformity to group pressure in relation to the value of task material. *Journal of Abnormal and Social Psychology, 66,* 179-183.

Verhaeghe, H. (1976). Mistreating other persons through simple discrepant role playing: Dissonance arousal or response contagion. *Journal of Personality and Social Psychology, 34,* 125-137.

Verplanck, W.S. (1955). The control of the content of conversation: Reinforcement of statements of opinion. *Journal of Abnormal and Social Psychology, 51,* 668-676.

Verplanck, W.S. (1962). Unaware of where's awareness: Some verbal operants—notates, monents, and notants. In C.W. Ericksen (Ed.), *Behavior and awareness: A Symposium of Research and Interpretation* (pp. 130-158). Durham, NC: Duke University Press.

Vidmar, N., & Rokeach, M. (1974). Archie Bunker's bigotry: A study in selective perception and exposure. *Journal of Communication, 24,* 36-47.

Vidulich, R.N., & Kaiman, I.P. (1961). The effects of information source status and dogmatism upon conformity behavior. *Journal of Abnormal and Social Psychology, 63,* 639-642.

Vidulich, R. N., & Krevanick, F. W. (1966). Racial attitudes and emotional response to visual representations of the Negro. *Journal of Social Psychology*, *68*, 85-93.

Vinokur, A., & Burnstein, E. (1974). Effects of partially shared persuasive arguments on group-induced shifts: A group-problem-solving approach. *Journal of Personality and Social Psychology*, *29*, 305-315.

Vinokur, A., & Burnstein, E. (1978a). Depolarization of attitudes in groups. *Journal of Personality and Social Psychology*, *36*, 872-885.

Vinokur, A., & Burnstein, E. (1978b). Novel argumentation and attitude change: The case of polarization following group discussion. *European Journal of Social Psychology*, *8*, 335-348.

Vohs, J. L., & Garrett, R. L. (1968). Resistance to persuasion: An integrative framework. *Public Opinion Quarterly*, *32*, 445-452.

Volpato, C., Maass, A., Mucchi-Faina, A., & Vitti, E. (1990). Minority influence and social categorization. *European Journal of Social Psychology*, *20*, 119-132.

Wachtler, J., & Counselman, E. (1981). When increasing liking for a communicator decreases opinion change: An attribution analysis of attractiveness. *Journal of Experimental Social Psychology*, *17*, 386-395.

Wallace, J. (1966). Role reward and dissonance reduction. *Journal of Personality and Social Psychology*, *3*, 305-312.

Waller, N. G., Kojetin, B. A., Bouchard, T. J., Jr., Lykken, D. T., & Tellegen, A. (1990). Genetic and environmental influences on religious interests, attitudes, and values: A study of twins reared apart and together. *Psychological Science*, *1*, 138-142.

Walster, E., Aronson, E., & Abrahams, D. (1966). On increasing the persuasiveness of a low prestige communicator. *Journal of Experimental Social Psychology*, *2*, 325-342.

Walster, E., & Festinger, L. (1962). The effectiveness of "overheard" persuasive communications. *Journal of Abnormal and Social Psychology*, *65*, 395-402.

Waly, P., & Cook, S. W. (1965). Effect of attitude on judgments of plausibility. *Journal of Personality and Social Psychology*, *2*, 745-749.

Waly, P., & Cook, S. W. (1966). Attitude as a determinant of learning and memory: A failure to confirm. *Journal of Personality and Social Psychology*, *4*, 280-288.

Warner, S. L. (1965). Randomized response: A survey technique for eliminating evasive answer bias. *Journal of the American Statistical Association*, *60*, 63-69.

Warshaw, P. R. (1980). A new model for predicting behavioral intentions: An alternative to Fishbein. *Journal of Marketing Research*, *17*, 153-172.

Warshaw, P. R., & Davis, F. D. (1985). Disentangling behavioral intention and behavioral expectation. *Journal of Experimental Social Psychology*, *21*, 213-228.

Warshaw, P. R., Sheppard, B. H., & Hartwick, J. (1982). *The intention and self-prediction of goals and behaviors* (Working paper No. 80-18, McGill University). Reprinted in R. P. Bagozzi (Ed.) (in press). *Advances in communication and marketing research*. Greenwich, CT: JAI Press.

Waterman, C. K. (1969). The facilitating and interfering effects of cognitive dissonance on simple and complex paired associates learning tasks. *Journal of Experimental Social Psychology*, *5*, 31-42.

Waterman, C. K., & Katkin, E. S. (1967). The energizing (dynamogenic) effect of cognitive dissonance on task performance. *Journal of Personality and Social Psychology*, *6*, 126-131.

Watson, J. B. (1930). *Behaviorism* (rev. ed.). New York: Norton.

Watson, W. S., & Hartmann, G. W. (1939). The rigidity of a basic attitudinal frame. *Journal of Abnormal and Social Psychology*, *34*, 314-335.

Watts, W. A. (1967). Relative persistence of opinion change induced by active compared to passive participation. *Journal of Personality and Social Psychology*, *5*, 4-15.

Watts, W. A. (1973). Intelligence and susceptibility to persuasion under conditions of active and passive participation. *Journal of Experimental Social Psychology*, *9*, 110-122.

Watts, W. A. (1977). Intelligence and opinion change through active participation as a function of requirements for improvisation and time of opinion measurement. *Social Behavior and Personality*, *5*, 171-176.

Watts, W. A., & Holt, L. E. (1970). Logical relationships among beliefs and timing as factors in persuasion. *Journal of Personality and Social Psychology*, *16*, 571-582.

Watts, W. A., & Holt, L. E. (1979). Persistence of opinion change induced under conditions of forewarning and distraction. *Journal of Personality and Social Psychology*, *37*, 778-789.

Watts, W. A., & McGuire, W. J. (1964). Persistence of induced opinion change and retention of the inducing message contents. *Journal of Abnormal and Social Psychology*, *68*, 233-241.

Webb, E. J., Campbell, D. T., Schwartz, R. D., & Sechrest, L. (1966). *Unobtrusive measures: Nonreactive research in the social sciences*. Chicago: Rand McNally.

Webb, E. J., Campbell, D. T., Schwartz, R. D., Sechrest, L., & Grove, J. B. (1981). *Nonreactive measures in the social sciences* (2nd ed.). Boston, MA: Houghton Mifflin.

Weber, M. (1947). *The theory of social and economic organization* (T. Parsons, Ed.; A. M. Henderson & T. Parsons, Trans.). New York: Oxford University Press.

Weber, S. J., & Cook, T. D. (1972). Subject effects in laboratory research: An examination of subject roles, demand characteristics, and valid inference. *Psychological Bulletin*, *77*, 273-295.

Wegener, B. (1982). Fitting category to magnitude scales for a dozen survey-assessed attitudes. In B. Wegener (Ed.), *Social attitudes and psychophysical measurement* (pp. 379-399). Hillsdale, NJ: Erlbaum.

Wegner, D. M., & Vallacher, R. P. (1986). Action identification. In R. M. Sorrentino & E. T. Higgins (Eds.), *Handbook of motivation and cognition: Foundations of social behavior* (pp. 550-582). New York: Guilford Press.

Weigel, R. H., & Howes, P. W. (1985). Conceptions of racial prejudice: Symbolic racism reconsidered. *Journal of Social Issues, 41*(3), 117-138.

Weigel, R. H., & Newman, L. S. (1976). Increasing attitude-behavior correspondence by broadening the scope of the behavioral measure. *Journal of Personality and Social Psychology, 33*, 793-802.

Weir, A. J. (1983). Notes for a prehistory of cognitive balance theory. *British Journal of Social Psychology, 22*, 351-362.

Weiss, D. J., & Davison, M. L. (1981). Test theory and methods. *Annual Review of Psychology, 32*, 629-658.

Weldon, D. E., & Malpass, R. S. (1981). Effects of attitudinal, cognitive, and situational variables on recall of biased communications. *Journal of Personality and Social Psychology, 40*, 39-52.

Wellens, A. R., & Thistlethwaite, D. L. (1971a). An analysis of two quantitative theories of cognitive balance. *Psychological Review, 78*, 141-150.

Wellens, A. R., & Thistlethwaite, D. L. (1971b). Comparison of three theories of cognitive balance. *Journal of Personality and Social Psychology, 20*, 82-92.

Wells, G. L., & Petty, R. E. (1980). The effects of overt head-movements on persuasion: Compatibility and incompatibility of responses. *Basic and Applied Social Psychology, 1*, 219-230.

Werner, P. D. (1978). Personality and attitude-activism correspondence. *Journal of Personality and Social Psychology, 36*, 1375-1390.

Westie, F. R., & DeFleur, M. L. (1959). Autonomic responses and their relationship to race attitudes. *Journal of Abnormal and Social Psychology, 58*, 340-347.

White, G. M. (1975). Contextual determinants of opinion judgments: Field experimental probes of judgmental relativity boundary conditions. *Journal of Personality and Social Psychology, 32*, 1047-1054.

Wicker, A. W. (1969). Attitude versus actions: The relationship of verbal and overt behavioral responses to attitude objects. *Journal of Social Issues, 25*(4), 41-78.

Wicklund, R. A. (1974). *Freedom and reactance.* Hillsdale, NJ: Erlbaum.

Wicklund, R. A. (1982). Self-focused attention and the validity of self-reports. In M. P. Zanna, E. T. Higgins, & C. P. Herman (Eds.), *Consistency in social behavior: The Ontario Symposium* (Vol. 2, pp. 149-172). Hillsdale, NJ: Erlbaum.

Wicklund, R. A., & Brehm, J. W. (1968). Attitude change as a function of felt competence and threat to attitudinal freedom. *Journal of Experimental Social Psychology, 4*, 64-75.

Wicklund, R. A., & Brehm, J. W. (1976). *Perspectives on cognitive dissonance.* Hillsdale, NJ: Erlbaum.

Wicklund, R. A., Cooper, J., & Linder, D. E. (1967). Effects of expected effort on attitude change prior to exposure. *Journal of Experimental Social Psychology, 3*, 416-428.

Widaman, K. F. (1985). Hierarchically nested covariance structure models for multitrait-multimethod data. *Applied Psychological Measurement, 9*, 1-26.

Wiest, W. M. (1965). A quantitative extension of Heider's theory of cognitive balance applied to interpersonal perception and self-esteem. *Psychological Monographs, 79* (14, Whole No. 607).

Wilder, D. A. (1977). Perception of groups, size of opposition, and social influence. *Journal of Experimental Social Psychology, 13*, 253-268.

Wilder, D. A. (1978). Perceiving persons as a group: Effects on attributions of causality and beliefs. *Social Psychology, 41*, 13-23.

Wilensky, R. (1983). *Planning and understanding: A computational approach to human reasoning.* Reading, MA: Addison-Wesley.

Wilhelmy, R. A. (1974). The role of commitment in cognitive reversibility. *Journal of Personality and Social Psychology, 30*, 695-698.

Wilhelmy, R. A., & Duncan, B. L. (1974). Cognitive reversibility in dissonance reduction. *Journal of Personality and Social Psychology, 29*, 806-811.

Willis, R. H. (1963). Two dimensions of conformity-nonconformity. *Sociometry, 26*, 499-513.

Willis, R. H. (1965). Conformity, independence, and anticonformity. *Human Relations, 18*, 373-388.

Wilson, T. D., & Dunn, D. S. (1986). Effects of introspection on attitude-behavior consistency: Analyzing reasons versus focusing on feelings. *Journal of Experimental Social Psychology, 22*, 249-263.

Wilson, T. D., Dunn, D. S., Bybee, J. A., Hyman, D. B., & Rotondo, J. A. (1984). Effects of analyzing reasons on attitude-behavior consistency. *Journal of Personality and Social Psychology, 47*, 5-16.

Wilson, T. D., Dunn, D. S., Kraft, D., & Lisle, D. J. (1989). Introspection, attitude change, and attitude-behavior consistency: The disruptive effects of explaining why we feel the way we do. In L. Berkowitz (Ed.), *Advances in experimental social psychology* (Vol. 22, pp. 287-343). San Diego, CA: Academic Press.

Wilson, T. D., Kraft, D., & Dunn, D. S. (1989). The disruptive effects of explaining attitudes: The moderating effect of knowledge about the attitude object. *Journal of Experimental Social Psychology, 25*, 379-400.

762

Wilson, W., & Miller, H. (1968). Repetition, order of presentation, and timing of arguments and measures as determinants of opinion change. *Journal of Personality and Social Psychology, 9,* 184–188.

Wilson, W. R. (1979). Feeling more than we can know: Exposure effects without learning. *Journal of Personality and Social Psychology, 37,* 811–821.

Winter, L., & Uleman, J. S. (1984). When are social judgments made? Evidence for the spontaneousness of trait inferences. *Journal of Personality and Social Psychology, 47,* 237–252.

Winter, L., Uleman, J. S., & Cunniff, C. (1985). How automatic are social judgments? *Journal of Personality and Social Psychology, 49,* 904–917.

Witte, E. H. (1987). Behaviour in group situations: An integrative model. *European Journal of Social Psychology, 17,* 403–429.

Wittenbraker, J., Gibbs, B. L., & Kahle, L. R. (1983). Seat belt attitudes, habits, and behaviors: An adaptive amendment to the Fishbein model. *Journal of Applied Social Psychology, 13,* 406–421.

Wolf, S. (1987). Majority and minority influence: A social impact analysis. In M. P. Zanna, J. M. Olson, & C. P. Herman (Eds.), *Social influence: The Ontario Symposium* (Vol. 5, pp. 207–235). Hillsdale, NJ: Erlbaum.

Wolf, S., & Latané, B. (1985). Conformity, innovation and the psychosocial law. In S. Moscovici, G. Mugny, & E. Van Avermaet (Eds.), *Perspectives on minority influence* (pp. 201–215). Cambridge, England: Cambridge University Press.

Wood, J. V., Taylor, S. E., & Lichtman, R. R. (1985). Social comparison in adjustment to breast cancer. *Journal of Personality and Social Psychology, 49,* 1169–1183.

Wood, W. (1982). Retrieval of attitude-relevant information from memory: Effects on susceptibility to persuasion and on intrinsic motivation. *Journal of Personality and Social Psychology, 42,* 798–810.

Wood, W., & Eagly, A. H. (1981). Stages in the analysis of persuasive messages: The role of causal attributions and message comprehension. *Journal of Personality and Social Psychology, 40,* 246–259.

Wood, W., & Kallgren, C. A. (1988). Communicator attributes and persuasion: Recipients' access to attitude-relevant information in memory. *Personality and Social Psychology Bulletin, 14,* 172–182.

Wood, W., Kallgren, C. A., & Preisler, R. M. (1985). Access to attitude-relevant information in memory as a determinant of persuasion: The role of message attributes. *Journal of Experimental Social Psychology, 21,* 73–85.

Woodmansee, J. J. (1970). The pupil response as a measure of social attitudes. In G. F. Summers (Ed.), *Attitude measurement* (pp. 514–533). Chicago: Rand McNally.

Worchel, S., & Arnold, S. E. (1973). The effects of censorship and attractiveness of the censor on attitude change. *Journal of Experimental Social Psychology, 9,* 365–377.

Worchel, S., & Arnold, S. E. (1974). The effect of combined arousal states on attitude change. *Journal of Experimental Social Psychology, 10,* 549–560.

Worchel, S., Arnold, S. E., & Baker, M. (1975). The effects of censorship on attitude change: The influence of censor and communication characteristics. *Journal of Applied Social Psychology, 5,* 227–239.

Worchel, S., & Brehm, J. W. (1970). Effect of threats to attitudinal freedom as a function of agreement with the communicator. *Journal of Personality and Social Psychology, 14,* 18–22.

Worth, L. T., & Mackie, D. M. (1987). Cognitive mediation of positive affect in persuasion. *Social Cognition, 5,* 76–94.

Wright, R. A. (1986). Attitude change as a function of threat to attitudinal freedom and extent of agreement with a communicator. *European Journal of Social Psychology, 16,* 43–50.

Wright, R. A., & Brehm, S. S. (1982). Reactance as impression management: A critical review. *Journal of Personality and Social Psychology, 42,* 608–618.

Wu, C., & Shaffer, D. R. (1987). Susceptibility to persuasive appeals as a function of source credibility and prior experience with the attitude object. *Journal of Personality and Social Psychology, 52,* 677–688.

Wyer, R. S., Jr. (1970). Quantitative prediction of belief and opinion change: A further test of a subjective probability model. *Journal of Personality and Social Psychology, 16,* 559–570.

Wyer, R. S., Jr. (1973a). Category ratings as "subjective expected values": Implications for attitude formation and change. *Psychological Review, 80,* 446–467.

Wyer, R. S., Jr. (1973b). Further test of a subjective probability model of social inference. *Journal of Research in Personality, 7,* 237–253.

Wyer, R. S., Jr. (1974a). Changes in meaning and halo effects in personality impression formation. *Journal of Personality and Social Psychology, 29,* 829–835.

Wyer, R. S., Jr. (1974b). *Cognitive organization and change: An information-processing approach.* Hillsdale, NJ: Erlbaum.

Wyer, R. S., Jr. (1975). Functional measurement methodology applied to a subjective probability model of cognitive functioning. *Journal of Personality and Social Psychology, 31,* 94–100.

Wyer, R. S., Jr. (1976). Effects of previously formed beliefs on syllogistic inference processes. *Journal of Personality and Social Psychology, 33,* 307–316.

Wyer, R. S., Jr., & Carlston, D. E. (1979). *Social cognition, inference, and attribution.* Hillsdale, NJ: Erlbaum.

Wyer, R. S., Jr., Carlston, D. E., & Hartwick, J. (1979). The role of syllogistic reasoning in inferences based upon new and old information. In R. S. Wyer, Jr., & D. E. Carlston, *Social cognition, inference, and attribution* (pp. 221–274). Hillsdale, NJ: Erlbaum.

763

Wyer, R. S., Jr., & Goldberg, L. (1970). A probabilistic analysis of the relationships among beliefs and attitudes. *Psychological Review*, *77*, 100–120.

Wyer, R. S., Jr., & Hartwick, J. (1980). The role of information retrieval and conditional inference processes in belief formation and change. In L. Berkowitz (Ed.), *Advances in experimental social psychology* (Vol. 13, pp. 241–284). San Diego, CA: Academic Press.

Wyer, R. S., Jr., & Hartwick, J. (1984). The recall and use of belief statements as bases for judgments: Some determinants and implications. *Journal of Experimental Social Psychology*, *20*, 65–85.

Wyer, R. S., Jr., & Srull, T. K. (1981). Category accessibility: Some theoretical and empirical issues concerning the processing of social stimulus information. In E. T. Higgins, C. P. Herman, & M. P. Zanna (Eds.), *Social cognition: The Ontario Symposium* (Vol. 1, pp. 161–197). Hillsdale, NJ: Erlbaum.

Wyer, R. S., Jr., & Watson, S. F. (1969). Context effects in impression formation. *Journal of Personality and Social Psychology*, *12*, 22–33.

Yamagishi, T., & Hill, C. T. (1983). Initial impression versus missing information as explanations of the set-size effect. *Journal of Personality and Social Psychology*, *44*, 942–951.

Yaryan, R. B., & Festinger, L. (1961). Preparatory action and belief in the probable occurrence of future events. *Journal of Abnormal and Social Psychology*, *63*, 603–606.

Yavuz, H. S., & Bousfield, W. A. (1959). Recall of connotative meaning. *Psychological Reports*, *5*, 319–320.

Young, J., Borgida, E., Sullivan, J. L., & Aldrich, J. (1987). Personal agendas and the relationship between self-interest and voting behavior. *Social Psychology Quarterly*, *50*, 64–71.

Young, J., Thomsen, C. J., Borgida, E., Sullivan, J. L., & Aldrich, J. H. (1991). When self-interest makes a difference: The role of construct accessibility in political reasoning. *Journal of Experimental Social Psychology*, *27*, 271–296.

Youngblood, J., & Himmelfarb, S. (1972). The effects of prior neutral messages on resistance to evaluative communications. *Psychonomic Science*, *29*, 349–350.

Younger, J. C., Walker, L., & Arrowood, A. J. (1977). Post-decision dissonance at the fair. *Personality and Social Psychology Bulletin*, *3*, 284–287.

Zajonc, R. B. (1960a). The concepts of balance, congruity, and dissonance. *Public Opinion Quarterly*, *24*, 280–296.

Zajonc, R. B. (1960b). The process of cognitive tuning in communication. *Journal of Abnormal and Social Psychology*, *61*, 159–167.

Zajonc, R. B. (1968a). Attitudinal effects of mere exposure. *Journal of Personality and Social Psychology*, *9*(No. 2, Pt. 2).

Zajonc, R. B. (1968b). Cognitive theories in social psychology. In G. Lindzey & E. Aronson (Eds.), *Handbook of social psychology* (2nd ed., Vol. 1, pp. 320–411). Reading, MA: Addison-Wesley.

Zajonc, R. B. (1980a). Cognition and social cognition: A historical perspective. In L. Festinger (Ed.), *Retrospections on social psychology* (pp. 180–204). New York: Oxford University Press.

Zajonc, R. B. (1980b). Feeling and thinking: Preferences need no inferences. *American Psychologist*, *35*, 151–175.

Zajonc, R. B. (1981). A one-factor mind about mind and emotion. *American Psychologist*, *36*, 102–103.

Zajonc, R. B. (1984). On the primacy of affect. *American Psychologist*, *39*, 117–123.

Zajonc, R. B., & Burnstein, E. (1965a). The learning of balanced and unbalanced social structures. *Journal of Personality*, *33*, 153–163.

Zajonc, R. B., & Burnstein, E. (1965b). Structural balance, reciprocity, and positivity as sources of cognitive bias. *Journal of Personality*, *33*, 570–583.

Zajonc, R. B., Crandall, R., Kail, R. B., & Swap, W. (1974). Effect of extreme exposure frequencies on different affective ratings of stimuli. *Perceptual and Motor Skills*, *38*, 667–678.

Zajonc, R. B., & Markus, H. (1982). Affective and cognitive factors in preferences. *Journal of Consumer Research*, *9*, 123–131.

Zajonc, R. B., & Markus, H. (1984). Affect and cognition: The hard interface. In C. E. Izard, J. Kagan, & R. B. Zajonc (Eds.), *Emotions, cognition, and behavior* (pp. 73–102). New York: Cambridge University Press.

Zajonc, R. B., Markus, H., & Wilson, W. R. (1974). Exposure effects and associative learning. *Journal of Personality and Social Psychology*, *10*, 248–263.

Zajonc, R. B., Murphy, S. T., & Inglehart, M. (1989). Feeling and facial efference: Implications of the vascular theory of emotion. *Psychological Review*, *96*, 395–416.

Zajonc, R. B., Pietromonaco, P., & Bargh, J. A. (1982). Independence and interaction of affect and cognition. In M. S. Clark & S. T. Fiske (Eds.), *Affect and cognition: The 17th Annual Carnegie Symposium on Cognition* (pp. 211–227). Hillsdale, NJ: Erlbaum.

Zajonc, R. B., & Rajecki, D. W. (1969). Exposure and affect: A field experiment. *Psychonomic Science*, *17*, 216–217.

Zajonc, R. B., Reimer, D. J., & Hausser, D. (1973). Imprinting and the development of object preference in chicks by mere repeated exposure *Journal of Comparative and Physiological Psychology*, *83*, 434–440.

Zajonc, R. B., Shaver, P., Tavris, C., & VanKreveld, D. (1972). Exposure, satiation, and stimulus discriminability. *Journal of Personality and Social Psychology*, *21*, 270–280.

Zander, A., & Lippitt, R. (1944). Reality-practice as educational method. *Sociometry*, *7*, 129–151.

Zanna, M. P. (in press). Message receptivity: A new look at the old problem of open- versus closed-mindedness. In A. A. Mitchell (Ed.), *Advertising exposure, memory and choice.* Hillsdale, NJ: Erlbaum.

Zanna, M. P., & Aziza, C. (1976). On the interaction of repression-sensitization and attention in resolving cognitive dissonance. *Journal of Personality, 44,* 577–593.

Zanna, M. P., & Cooper, J. (1974). Dissonance and the pill: An attribution approach to studying the arousal properties of dissonance. *Journal of Personality and Social Psychology, 29,* 703–709.

Zanna, M. P., Detweiler, R. A., & Olson, J. M. (1984). Physiological mediation of attitude maintenance, formation, and change. In W. M. Waid (Ed.), *Sociophysiology* (pp. 163–195). New York: Springer-Verlag.

Zanna, M. P., & Fazio, R. H. (1982). The attitude-behavior relation: Moving toward a third generation of research. In M. P. Zanna, E. T. Higgins, & C. P. Herman (Eds.), *Consistency in social behavior: The Ontario Symposium* (Vol. 2, pp. 283–301). Hillsdale, NJ: Erlbaum.

Zanna, M. P., Fazio, R. H., & Ross, M. (1990, June). *The mediation of attitudinal persistence.* Paper presented at the North American-European Conference on Social Influence, Valencia, Spain.

Zanna, M. P., & Hamilton, D. L. (1977). Further evidence for meaning change in impression formation. *Journal of Experimental Social Psychology, 13,* 224–238.

Zanna, M. P., Higgins, E. T., & Taves, P. A. (1976). Is dissonance phenomenologically aversive? *Journal of Experimental Social Psychology, 12,* 530–538.

Zanna, M. P., & Kiesler, C. A. (1971). Inferring one's beliefs from one's behavior as a function of belief relevance and consistency of behavior. *Psychonomic Science, 24,* 283–285.

Zanna, M. P., Kiesler, C. A., & Pilkonis, P. A. (1970). Positive and negative attitudinal affect established by classical conditioning. *Journal of Personality and Social Psychology, 14,* 321–328.

Zanna, M. P., Klosson, E. C., & Darley, J. M. (1976). How television news viewers deal with facts that contradict their beliefs: A consistency and attribution analysis. *Journal of Applied Social Psychology, 6,* 159–176.

Zanna, M. P., Lepper, M. R., & Abelson, R. P. (1973). Attentional mechanisms in children's devaluation of a forbidden activity in a forced-compliance situation. *Journal of Personality and Social Psychology, 28,* 355–359.

Zanna, M. P., & Olson, J. M. (1982). Individual differences in attitudinal relations. In M. P. Zanna, E. T. Higgins, & C. P. Herman (Eds.), *Consistency in social behavior: The Ontario Symposium* (Vol. 2, pp. 75–103). Hillsdale, NJ: Erlbaum.

Zanna, M. P., Olson, J. M., & Fazio, R. H. (1981). Self-perception and attitude-behavior consistency. *Personality and Social Psychology Bulletin, 7,* 252–256.

Zanna, M. P., & Rempel, J. K. (1984, June). *Attitudes: A new look at an old concept.* Paper presented at the Conference on the Social Psychology of Knowledge, Shefayim, Israel.

Zanna, M. P., & Rempel, J. K. (1988). Attitudes: A new look at an old concept. In D. Bar-Tal & A. W. Kruglanski (Eds.), *The social psychology of knowledge* (pp. 315–334). Cambridge, England: Cambridge University Press.

Zanna, M. P., & Sande, G. N. (1987). The effects of collective actions on the attitudes of individual group members: A dissonance analysis. In M. P. Zanna, J. M. Olson, & C. P. Herman (Eds.), *Social influence: The Ontario Symposium* (Vol. 5, pp. 151–163). Hillsdale, NJ: Erlbaum.

Zavalloni, M., & Cook, S. W. (1965). Influence of judges' attitudes on ratings of favorableness of statements about a social group. *Journal of Personality and Social Psychology, 1,* 43–54.

Zdep, S. M., & Rhodes, I. N. (1976). Making the randomized response technique work. *Public Opinion Quarterly, 40,* 531–537.

Zdep, S. M., Rhodes, I. N., Schwarz, R. M., & Kilkenny, M. J. (1979). The validity of the randomized response technique. *Public Opinion Quarterly, 43,* 544–549.

Zellner, M. (1970). Self-esteem, reception, and influenceability. *Journal of Personality and Social Psychology, 15,* 87–93.

Zillmann, D. (1972). Rhetorical elicitation of agreement in persuasion. *Journal of Personality and Social Psychology, 21,* 159–165.

Zimbardo, P. G. (1960). Involvement and communication discrepancy as determinants of opinion conformity. *Journal of Abnormal and Social Psychology, 60,* 86–94.

Zimbardo, P. G. (1969). *The cognitive control of motivation: The consequences of choice and dissonance.* Glenview, IL: Scott, Foresman.

Zimbardo, P. G., & Ebbesen, E. B. (1970). Experimental modification of the relationship between effort, attitude, and behavior. *Journal of Personality and Social Psychology, 16,* 207–213.

Zimbardo, P. G., Snyder, M., Thomas, J., Gold, A., & Gurwitz, S. (1970). Modifying the impact of persuasive communications with external distraction. *Journal of Personality and Social Psychology, 16,* 669–680.

Zimbardo, P. G., Weisenberg, M., Firestone, I., & Levy, B. (1965). Communicator effectiveness in producing public conformity and private attitude change. *Journal of Personality, 33,* 233–255.

Zuckerman, M., & Reis, H. (1978). Comparison of three models for predicting altruistic behavior. *Journal of Personality and Social Psychology, 36,* 498–510.

Zvulun, E. (1978). Multidimensional scalogram analysis: The method and its application. In S. Shye (Ed.), *Theory construction and data analysis in the behavioral sciences* (pp. 237–264). San Francisco: Jossey-Bass.

Acknowledgments

Sources are identified where they occur in text. Full citations appear in References.

Chapter 2
Table 2.2, p. 31, adapted by permission of Dr. Conrad Thurstone, for the Estate of Prof. Louis L. Thurstone; original work published by Macmillan Publishers, Inc. **Table 2.3**, p. 34, adapted by permission of Dr. Stephen J. Breckler. **Table 2.4**, p. 35, adapted by permission of Dr. Harry C. Triandis; original work published by the American Psychological Association. **Table 2.8**, p. 46, adapted by permission of *Sociology and Social Research: An International Journal*; original work published by the Southern California Sociological Society. **Table 2.9**, p. 49, adapted by permission of Dr. Raymond H. C. Teske, Jr. and Pergamon Press, Inc. **Table 2.10**, p. 52, adapted by permission of Dr. Janet T. Spence and the Psychonomic Society, Inc.

Chapter 3
Table 3.1, p. 92, reprinted by permission of University of Nebraska Press; copyright © 1980 by University of Nebraska Press. **Table 3.2**, p. 94, and **Figures 3.1** and **3.2**, pp. 95–96, reprinted by permission of Saunders, a subsidiary of Harcourt Brace Jovanovich, Inc. **Table 3.3**, p. 100, adapted by permission of Polly Rothstein and the Westchester Coalition for Legal Abortion, Inc.; copyright © 1983 by the Westchester Coalition for Legal Abortion, Inc. **Figure 3.3**, p. 130, adapted by permission of Dr. Robert S. Wyer, Jr.; original work published by the American Psychological Association. **Table 3.4**, p. 137, adapted by permission of the Plenum Publishing Corporation. **Figure 3.6**, p. 139, reprinted by permission of Dr. Chester A. Insko and Academic Press, Inc.

Chapter 4
Table 4.1, p. 160, adapted by permission of Dr. Martin Fishbein; original work published by the American Psychological Association. **Table 4.2**, p. 161, adapted by permission of Dr. Russell Weigel; original work published by the American Psychological Association. **Table 4.3**, p. 170, reprinted by permission of University of Nebraska Press; copyright © 1980 by University of Nebraska Press. **Figure 4.1**, p. 172, adapted by permission of Prentice-Hall, Inc.; copyright © 1980 by Prentice-Hall, Inc. **Figures 4.2** and **4.3**, p. 179, adapted by permission of Dr. Peter M. Bentler; original work published by the American Psychological Association. **Figure 4.4**, p. 187, reprinted by permission of Dr. Icek Ajzen and Academic Press, Inc. **Figure 4.5**, p. 202, reprinted by permission of Guilford Press.

Chapter 5
Table 5.2 and **Figure 5.1**, pp. 243–244, adapted by permission of Dr. Norman H. Anderson; original work published by the American Psychological Association. **Figure 5.3**, p. 248, reprinted by permission of Dr. Michael H. Birnbaum and The Psychonomic Society, Inc.

Chapter 6
Figure 6.1, p. 262, reprinted by permission of Dr. William J. McGuire and Holt, Rinehart and Winston, Inc.; copyright © 1972 by Holt, Rinehart and Winston, Inc. **Figure 6.2**, p. 266, reprinted by permission of Dr. Norman Miller; original work published by the American Psychological Association. **Figure 6.3**, p. 268, adapted by permission of Dr. William J. McGuire; original work published by the American Psychological Association. **Table 6.1**, p. 274, adapted by permission of Dr. Shelly Chaiken; original work published by the American Psychological Association. **Figure 6.4**, p. 284, adapted by permission of Dr. Timothy C. Brock; original work published by the American Psychological Association.

Chapter 7
Table 7.1 and **Figure 7.1**, pp. 307–308, reprinted by permission of Dr. Richard E. Petty and Academic Press, Inc. **Table 7.2**, p. 310, and **Figure 7.3**, p. 318, adapted by permission of Dr. Richard E. Petty; original work published by the American Psychological Association. **Figure 7.2**, p. 312, adapted by permission of Dr. Richard E. Petty and Academic Press, Inc.

Chapter 8
Table 8.1, p. 358, adapted by permission of Dr. Alice H. Eagly; original work published by the American Psychological Association. **Figure 8.1**, p. 358, reprinted by permission of Dr. Alice H. Eagly and Lawrence Erlbaum Associates, Inc. **Figure 8.2**, p. 365, reprinted by permission of the American Psychological Association.

Chapter 9
Figure 9.1, p. 393, adapted by permission of Dr. Alice H. Eagly and John Wiley & Sons, Inc.; copyright © 1974 by John Wiley & Sons, Inc. **Table 9.1**, p. 405, reprinted by permission of Dr. Monte M. Page; original work published by the American Psychological Association. **Figure 9.2**, p. 413, adapted by permission of Dr. Robert B. Zajonc; original work published by the American Psychological Association. **Table 9.2**, p. 416, adapted by permission of Dr. Robert F. Bornstein; original work published by the American Psychological Association.

Chapter 10
Table 10.1, p. 434, and **Figure 10.1**, p. 435, adapted by permission of Dr. Seymour Feshbach; original work published by the American Psychological Association. **Figure 10.2**, p. 438, adapted by permission of Mrs. Marjorie Janis, for the Estate of Prof. Irving L. Janis. **Figure 10.3**, p. 442, reprinted by permission of Dr. Ronald W. Rogers; original work

published by the American Psychological Association. **Figure 10.4**, p. 449, reprinted by permission of Dr. Diane M. Mackie and Pergamon Press, Inc. **Figure 10.5**, p. 457, adapted by permission of Prof. Grace M. Heider, for the Estate of Prof. Fritz Heider.

Chapter 11
Table 11.1, p. 508, adapted by permission of Prof. Trudy Festinger, for the Estate of Prof. Leon Festinger; original work published by the American Psychological Association. **Table 11.2**, p. 516, adapted by permission of Dr. Bobby J. Calder; original work published by the American Psychological Association. **Figure 11.1**, p. 517, adapted by permission of Dr. Joel Cooper and Academic Press, Inc. **Figure 11.2**, p. 519, reprinted by permission of Dr. Steven J. Scher; original work published by the American Psychological Association. **Table 11.3**, p. 528, adapted by permission of Dr. Michael Scheier; original work published by the American Psychological Association. **Table 11.4**, p. 548, adapted by permission of Dr. Mark P. Zanna; original work published by the American Psychological Association.

Chapter 12
Table 12.1, p. 563, adapted by permission of Dr. William J. McGuire and Academic Press, Inc. **Figure 12.1**, p. 572, reprinted by permission of Dr. Stephen W. Hinkle; original work published by the American Psychological Association. **Table 12.2**, p. 576, reprinted by permission of Harper Collins Publisher, Inc.; copyright © 1950 by the American Jewish Committee. **Table 12.3**, p. 579, adapted by permission of Prof. Sandra Ball-Rokeach, for the Estate of Prof. Milton Rokeach; original work published by the American Psychological Association. **Table 12.4**, p. 605, adapted by permission of Dr. Abraham Tesser; original work published by the American Psychological Association. **Figure 12.2**, p. 611, reprinted by permission of Sage Publications, Inc.; copyright © 1982 by Sage Publications, Inc. **Figure 12.3**, p. 614, adapted by permission of Yale University Press; copyright © 1953 Yale University Press. **Figure 12.4**, p. 615, adapted by permission of Dr. Thomas D. Cook; original work published by the American Psychological Association.

Chapter 13
Figure 13.1, p. 629, adapted by permission of *Scientific American*; copyright © 1955 by Scientific American, Inc., all rights reserved. **Table 13.1**, p. 640, reprinted by permission of Dr. Herbert C. Kelman; original work published by University of Chicago Press.

767

—— Subject Index* ——

Italic page numbers indicate items located in chapter endnotes.

Author Index